The New Illustrated Encyclopedia of

WORLD HISTORY

The New Illustrated

VOLUME I

ANCIENT, MEDIEVAL, AND MODERN HISTORY CHRONOLOGICALLY ARRANGED

COMPILED AND EDITED BY

Encyclopedia of
WORLD
HISTORY

AND ILLUSTRATED WITH MORE THAN 2000 PHOTOGRAPHS, MAPS, CHARTS AND DRAWINGS

WILLIAM L. LANGER

Coolidge Professor of History, Emeritus, Harvard University

HARRY N. ABRAMS, INC. · PUBLISHERS · NEW YORK

LIBRARY OF CONGRESS CATALOGING IN PUBLICATION DATA

Langer, William Leonard, 1896-
  The new illustrated encyclopedia of world history.

  Bibliography: p.
  Includes index.
  1.   History—Outlines, syllabi, etc.   I.   Title.
D21.I276   902'.02   74-31218
ISBN 0-8109-0117-X

Library of Congress Catalogue Card Number: 74-31218

FIRST EDITION

PUBLISHER'S FOREWORD
TO THE NEW ILLUSTRATED EDITION

Living in a visually oriented age, we have become accustomed to *seeing* momentous events. We need only recall the popularity of newsreels and of such great picture magazines as *Life* and *Look,* periodicals that developed an important new concept in news reportage— photo-journalism—which showed their readers battles, natural disasters, coronations, elections, and assassinations soon after they happened. Today, television brings the raw materials of history into our homes as it occurs. Because we have become used to seeing history happen (if not necessarily learning its lessons), it seems appropriate to publish an illustrated edition of Professor Langer's classic reference work.

Recording historical events in images is as old as civilization itself. Indeed, the walls of caves inhabited by our ancestors are decorated with painted hunting scenes, depicting what was undoubtedly the most important activity in the life of prehistoric man, since it produced the food on which he and his tribe subsisted. As villages developed into organized city-states and power was subdivided into a structured government, the images memorialized more complex events, and even emotions. One need only turn to page 52 to see how a picture lends immediacy to an event that took place thousands of years ago: the crowd of prisoners of war captured by the triumphant King Shalmaneser III of Assyria makes us realize how little the face of war has changed over the millennia.

Wherever possible, the editors of *The New Illustrated Encyclopedia of World History* have selected works contemporary with the events they depict; when this has not been possible, the most pictorially reliable and historically accurate examples from a later age have been chosen. Altogether, there are nearly 2,000 illustrations, including more than 100 in full color, enabling the reader to see the major events, the protagonists, the works of art, the cities and citadels, the palaces, temples, and cathedrals, all the materials that are woven into the fabric of history. The illustrations represent the full range of artistic mediums, including paintings, graphic works, sculpture, and of course photographs. Many of these illustrations are in themselves of historical interest: for example, reproduced on page 509 is the earliest known European depiction of American Indians, a woodcut published in Germany in 1505, only thirteen years after they were seen for the first time by Columbus.

Like illustrations in any other reference book, these in *The New Illustrated Encyclopedia of World History* are intended not as a substitute for the text but as a supplement to it. Taken together, words and pictures form a work that invites not only use as a serious reference work, but absorbing and delightful browsing through a record of humanity's actions and accomplishments, both tragic and triumphant.

CONTRIBUTORS TO
THE FOURTH AND FIFTH EDITIONS

Geoffrey Bruun

George Busalla

Carleton Coon

Frank M. Cross, Jr.

Sterling Dow

Robert H. Dyson, Jr.

Marija Gimbutas

Madeleine Gleason

Carol R. Harting

Stephen N. Hay

Halil Inalcik

Melvin Kranzberg

Dwight E. Lee

Derwood Lockard

J. A. B. Van Buitenen

CONTRIBUTORS TO EARLIER EDITIONS

*Crane Brinton

Geoffrey Bruun

*Robert S. Chamberlain

*Paul P. Cram

John K. Fairbank

*Charles S. Gardner

Hans W. Gatzke

Mason Hammond

*James B. Hedges

*Michael Karpovich

*Donald C. McKay

*Robert H. Pfeiffer

Edwin O. Reischauer

*Penfield Roberts

Robert O. Schlaifer

*William Thomson

*Lauriston Ward

* Since deceased.

PREFACE TO THE FIRST EDITION

This *Epitome of History* itself has a long and interesting history. More than seventy years ago Dr. Karl Ploetz, in his time a well-known German teacher, published an *Auszug aus der alten, mittleren und neueren Geschichte,* intended as a factual handbook for the use of students and for the convenience of the general reader. That his compilation filled a real need is attested by the fact that within a few years it went through seven editions, and by the further fact that to date more than twenty editions have appeared in Germany, revised and edited by noted scholars. The book has easily held its own despite competition of numerous similar works.

Ploetz's *Epitome* was translated into English by William H. Tillinghast and published by Houghton Mifflin Company in this country in 1883. The translator, recognizing that the original was designed particularly to meet the needs of the German student and that therefore the history of central Europe was weighted as against the history of France, England, and America, took the opportunity to enlarge a number of sections and to add others. No less a scholar than Edward Channing contributed the new sections on modern England and the United States. Furthermore, Tillinghast first added brief sections on the Middle and Far Eastern countries, which had been completely omitted from the German version. The book appeared under the title *An Epitome of Ancient, Medieval, and Modern History,* and proved so popular that no less than twenty-four printings were necessary before 1905. Occasional revisions were made and in 1915 the title was changed to *A Handbook of Universal History.*

Since historical knowledge and historical conceptions are notoriously fluid, it is not to be wondered at that even so sound and reliable a book as the old Ploetz-Tillinghast *Epitome* should ultimately have fallen behind the times.

After the First World War the publishers therefore commissioned Dr. Harry Elmer Barnes to overhaul the book and bring it up to date. The new editor, with a number of collaborators, left the kernel of the old work (the Greek and Roman history, the medieval sections, and the early modern parts) as it was, judging quite rightly that in the large it was not so badly out of line as to justify rewriting and resetting. But the sections dealing with the early Near East, of which little was known in Ploetz's day, were completely redone, and a great deal of material on the period from 1883 to 1923 was added. The *Epitome,* thus revised, was published in 1925 as *A Manual of Universal History.* Like the preceding versions it has been widely used by students and laymen alike.

But despite revisions of one kind or another, it became increasingly clear that sooner or later the original book would require drastic changes if it were to keep abreast of modern knowledge and meet contemporary requirements. It stands to reason that in seventy years our command of the facts and our views of even those subjects best treated by Ploetz and Tillinghast have changed substantially. Above all, the past fifty years have witnessed the expansion of western influence over the entire globe and, as a result, there is now a much greater need to know something of the past of non-European countries and cultures, and a much livelier interest in formerly neglected fields. To fill the new requirements no amount of revision of the old book would do, for the original author wrote as a German and treated European history primarily as it touched his own country's development. Tillinghast attempted to give the English translation a somewhat more Anglo-American slant, and Dr. Barnes did what was humanly possible to adapt the old text to a more world-wide approach. But the point had been definitely reached where adaptations and adjustments would no longer suffice. The publishers therefore invited me to undertake a complete rewriting of the entire book, securing the aid of collaborators qualified to treat of special fields where it seemed desirable. It was my great good fortune to be able to interest fifteen of my colleagues to take over particular sections and to secure from them the most whole-hearted co-operation in what, after all, was an enterprise of some magnitude. Their names, with the sections for which they made themselves responsible, are listed above.

When embarking upon this project I still had hope that considerable parts of the old book might yet be salvaged and that a thoroughgoing revision would prove adequate for the ancient, medieval, and early modern sections. But it soon became apparent to all of us engaged in the work that the whole plan and approach required rethinking and that, consequently, there was but little use in trying to adhere to the old text. Here and there a few pages (thoroughly emended) have been retained, but they are relatively so few in number as to be hardly worth mentioning. Almost nothing of the substance of the old book remains; every single section has been gone over in thorough fashion, reduced or expanded and, above all, brought into line with present-day knowledge. Many other sections, naturally, have been newly written, so that I think we can honestly say that the book is no longer a manual of European history with some perfunctory reference to other countries, but genuine world history, in which the geographical divisions are dealt with on their merits.

In the course of rewriting we have, however, stuck by Ploetz's original conception. That is, we have tried to compile a handbook of historical facts, so arranged that the dates stand out while the material itself flows in a reasonably smooth narrative. Individual judgments have been kept in the background and divergent interpretations have been adduced only where they seemed to be indispensable. The great diversity of type which had crept into the old book has been done away with and we have broken the uniformity of the print only by the use of small and capital boldface and very occasional employment of italics. The number of genealogical charts has been much increased: new tables have been added for some of the non-European dynasties and all charts have been brought up to date. Furthermore, a considerable number of maps has been included, not with the idea of supplying a complete historical atlas, but simply for the convenience of the user who, when he is checking one event or another, cannot be expected to have always at hand the necessary map material.

In the preface to the 1925 edition Dr. Barnes referred to the growing interest in non-political aspects of history

and to his attempt to expand sections dealing with economic and cultural developments. Though deeply interested in these phases of history, Dr. Barnes felt obliged to recognize that the majority of those who would use the book would come seeking information on political, military, and diplomatic history and that therefore those angles would have to be primarily considered. I subscribe entirely to this view, but I take this opportunity to point out further that cultural history does not lend itself readily to the method of treatment upon which this particular work is based. The backbone of this book is chronology which, in the case of general economic trends, religious and artistic movements, and intellectual currents, is both hard to define and of relatively less significance. For methodological reasons, if for no other, we could therefore give but slight emphasis to these aspects of history. In addition we had to consider the further difficulties presented by space limitation: obviously anything like adequate treatment of literature, art, science, and economics would have taken us so far afield that the results could not possibly have been enclosed within two covers. In some sections the reader will find brief summaries of cultural activities, in others not; but in any case we offer them only for what they may be worth, as a matter of convenience, without any thought of sufficiency, much less exhaustiveness. And these remarks apply equally to the special sections at the beginning of the nineteenth century, entitled *Social Thought and Social Movements, Scientific Thought and Progress*, and *Mechanical Inventions and Technical Achievements*.* The material we adduce in these sections appeared to us indispensable for an understanding of nineteenth-century development. It cannot be suitably included under any one country, for its application is general. We could not aim or hope for completeness; hence our only objective in these sections has been to bring together an irreducible minimum of pertinent information.

Each successive editor of this *Handbook* has come away from his task impressed with the difficulties of attaining accuracy in dealing with so vast a number of dates covering so wide a range of time and territory. I am no exception to the rule and am far from being arrogant enough to suppose that this new book is even more free from error than the old. There is some consolation, however, in the thought that we collaborators have all done what we reasonably could to guard against blunders and that, as a matter of fact, many dates are so uncertain or disputed that they will probably never be satisfactorily fixed.

*In the present edition these sections are entitled *Philosophical, Religious, and Social Thought; Science and Learning; Technological Achievements.*

The success of the *Epitome of History* over a period of more than two generations is ample proof of the need for a manual of this type. In the revised and extended form here presented, it ought to be more valuable than ever. Its use for students of history is obvious enough, but it ought to prove as helpful to many others. Students of the history of literature and of art should find a concise guide to political history a great boon and all readers of historical novels or biographies should welcome a book of reference to events of the past, to genealogical relationships, and so on. My own experience with the old book was that I used it more as I became better acquainted with it.

Nothing would please me more than to have the new edition find a secure place on the shelves of all book-lovers.

In presenting the new *Epitome* I cannot refrain from expressing my profound gratitude to all the contributors and also to Professors Walter Clark and Vincent Scramuzza, to Professor Sterling Dow, Mr. Eugene Boardman, and to Miss Katharine Irwin for the ready help they gave in reading proof. My secretaries, Mrs. Elizabeth Fox and Mrs. Rosamund Chapman, took care of countless loose ends and deserve more than a little credit for whatever merit the book may have.

PREFACE TO THE FIFTH EDITION

Less than a decade has passed since the publication of the fourth edition of the present work, which was a basic redoing of the earlier editions and incorporated a great deal of new subject matter. Such drastic changes are necessary perhaps once in a generation, but in our fast-moving world important events are constantly occurring. For that reason it has seemed to the editor and the publisher desirable to bring the fourth edition chronologically up-to-date in a fifth edition which covers developments throughout the world through the year 1970.

In recent years important advances have been made in the fields of prehistory and early civilizations, and these have required some rewriting by experts in those matters. But most importantly, account has had to be taken of the events of the past seven years. During that time numerous states, former colonies of the European powers, have attained their independence and become members of the United Nations. Furthermore, dangerous conflicts have developed that are not even yet concluded. In the Middle East there has been a third round in the duel between the Israelis and the Arabs, while in Southeast Asia the war in Vietnam has grown to the point where it not only threatens to produce a world crisis, but has shaken the domestic politics of the United States to their foundations. Communist China has been racked by the so-called Cultural Revolution, and the antagonism between the two Communist giants, Soviet Russia and Communist China, has become steadily aggravated. Japan has risen to the rank of a prime industrial power, while in the midst of general affluence almost all nations have been confronted with a revolt of youth which has culminated in student upheavals and drastic changes in the educational systems. Race conflict, too, has become a major factor in political and social development. Yet these recent years have witnessed also the rapid development of the space age, vividly symbolized by the first landings of men on the moon and the initiation of explorations that will broaden and deepen our understanding of the entire universe.

Merely to catalogue a few major changes of the past decade suffices to indicate the extensive alterations and additions required by the fifth edition of this world-renowned historical handbook. As on previous occasions, I have called upon friends and colleagues for expert help and have benefited greatly from their continued interest and knowledge. Like former editions, this one also has gained from the correspondence of readers throughout the world who have discovered inconsistencies or errors. In short, no effort has been spared to make this one of the really indispensable reference books for all the innumerable readers who continue in the hectic present to find counsel and comfort from the study of man's past.

WILLIAM L. LANGER

Contents

CONTENTS

III. THE MIDDLE AGES

CONTENTS

IV. THE EARLY MODERN PERIOD

V. THE MODERN PERIOD

CONTENTS

VI. THE FIRST WORLD WAR AND THE INTER-WAR PERIOD, 1914–1939

CONTENTS

VII. THE SECOND WORLD WAR
AND ITS AFTERMATH, 1939–1970

VIII. THE RECENT PERIOD

APPENDIX

Genealogical Tables

Maps

I. The Prehistoric Period

I. The Prehistoric Period

A. Introduction

1. *Definition, Data, and Methods*

HISTORY in its broadest sense should be a record of Man and his accomplishments from the time when he ceased being merely an animal and became a human being. The efforts to reconstruct this record may be classed under two heads: (1) **History** (in the stricter sense), which is based on written documents and covers part of the last five thousand years of Man's activities, and (2) **Prehistory,** which is based largely on archaeological evidence and covers all the long preceding period, which probably amounts to more than one million years.

The prehistoric period is important, not only by reason of its vast length, but also because during this time Man made almost all his major discoveries and adaptations to environment and group-life (except those connected with the recent machine age) and evolved physically into our living species and its races. Hence at least a brief summary of the prehistoric period is a necessary introduction to any account of the recorded history of Man.

The main body of material upon which the work of prehistoric reconstruction is based comprises: first, remains left by early peoples, largely in the form of tools, other artifacts, and animal bones found by excavation in old habitation sites or burials; secondly, other traces of their activities, such as buildings and rock-carvings or rock-paintings; and lastly, the bones of the people themselves. This material gives good evidence of the physical type of prehistoric peoples and their material culture, very slight evidence of their social, intellectual, and religious life and no evidence of their language. It can be supplemented to some extent—and with great caution—by a comparative study of the physical types, blood groups, languages, and material culture of modern peoples.

The time when prehistory ends and true history begins varies greatly in different parts of the world. Traditional history often covers the borderline between the two and can sometimes be successfully correlated with the archaeological evidence.

2. *The Origin of Man*

MAN'S PLACE AMONG THE ANIMALS. The various living and extinct species of Man are assigned by zoologists to the super-family *Hominoidea,* which belongs to the sub-order *Catarrhinae* (containing Old World monkeys, apes, and baboons), of the order Primates (containing also the *Platyrrhinae* [South American monkeys], *Tarsius,* the lemurs, and *Tupaia* [the tree shrew]), of the class **Mammalia.** His nearest living relatives are the three genera of the super-family *Pongidae* (the so-called Anthropoid Apes): the gorilla and chimpanzee of equatorial Africa and the orang-utan of southeastern Asia and the East Indies. Man is distinguished from the higher apes by the greater size of his brain (especially the forebrain), his fully erect position in walking, the better adaptation of his hands for grasping and holding, and his use of language for communication.

MAN'S ANIMAL ANCESTORS. All living men belong to the species *Homo sapiens,* in some regions 250,000 years old. Specimens of its ancestral species, *Homo erectus,* have been found in Java, China, and Africa from about 1,100,000 years onward. A third species, *Homo habilis,* has also been identified from bones found in Olduvai Gorge, Tanganyika, dated at 1,750,000 years by Argon-40 tests. A related genus, *Australopithe-*

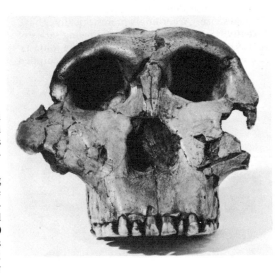

Skull of Homo habilis

cus, lived in Africa and possibly South Asia at the same time. Although related to *Homo, Australopithecus* was not our ancestor.

Proconsul, a 24,000,000-year-old Early Miocene primate from East Africa, may have been ancestral to apes, *Australopithecenes,* and Man. Three 14,000,000-year-old primates (late Miocene or Early Pliocene) have been considered as our ancestors—*Ramapithecus* from India, *Kenyapithecus* from East Africa, and (the least likely) *Oreopithecus* from Italy.

DATE OF MAN'S ORIGIN. This has not yet been definitely established. The ancestors of the great apes and the ancestor of Man probably diverged from one another as early as the Miocene period, and Man acquired certain essentially human characteristics probably in the Pliocene period. The earliest known skeletal remains that are accepted as human are believed to date from near the end of the Lower Pleistocene. For the purposes of the prehistorian, who has to rely largely on archaeological evidence, the record of Man may be said to begin at the moment when he was able to fashion the first stone tools that can be unmistakably recognized to be of human workmanship. This was late in the Lower Pleistocene, or possibly in the very late Pliocene.

PLACE OF MAN'S ORIGIN. This is still uncertain. The old theory of Central Asia as the "Cradle of Mankind" was based on false premises, which have been abandoned. From the distribution of the living and fossil great apes, Australopithecenes, and men, it is thought that Man's divergence from the general anthropoid stem probably occurred somewhere in Africa.

Proconsul

3. *Cultures and Their Dating*

a. CULTURES AND PERIODS

Archaeological investigation of the material remains of prehistoric Man has shown that a wide variety of cultures flourished in different parts of the world and at different times. For convenience these have been grouped into a series of major cultures based primarily on the nature of the principal material used for implements (whether stone or one of the metals), and sometimes on the technique used in fashioning these implements. The oldest culture in the world was characterized by the use of chipped stone for implements and has been named Paleolithic culture. Neolithic culture, on the other hand, was characterized by the use of polished stone implements; Bronze culture, by the use of bronze implements, and so forth.

In most parts of the world the discovery and use of these different materials and techniques took place in a regular sequence in time. In the absence of fixed dates, it was thus found convenient to use these cultural terms in a chronological sense. Accordingly prehistoric times have usually been divided into the following series of periods or ages (beginning with the oldest): **Paleolithic** (Old Stone), characterized by chipped

Paleolithic hand-axes

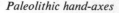

stone implements; **Mesolithic** (Intermediate Stone), a transitional period; **Neolithic** (New Stone), with polished stone implements; **Chalcolithic** (Stone and Copper), characterized by the first tentative use of copper implements; **Bronze Age,** with full development of copper and bronze implements; and **Iron Age,** with iron implements.

These names are excellent to identify cultures, but their use to designate periods of time has led to much inaccuracy and confusion, as the dates of the cultures to which they refer differ widely in different parts of the world. It is proper, for example, to speak of the Bronze Age of Hungary or some other limited area, where the beginning and end of the bronze culture can be fairly accurately dated. But it is quite impossible to speak with any meaning of the Bronze Age of the Old World, for this period began some thousand or fifteen hundred years earlier in Mesopotamia, for instance, than it did in western Europe, and it gave way to the Iron Age one or two thousand years earlier in Asia Minor than it did in some parts of Siberia; while in Japan there was no true Bronze Age and in Australia no Bronze Age at all. The names of these periods are, however, too well established to be abandoned and are often useful, if employed with caution.

DATING. As there are no written documents, a variety of other means have been employed to determine the duration and dates of prehistoric cultures.

b. RELATIVE DATING

This is established by the following methods:

(1) **Stratigraphy.** When there is accurate excavation of a site, the undisturbed remains in any given level may fairly safely be assumed to be earlier than the remains in the levels that overlie it.

(2) **Typology.** The age of a given culture may sometimes be determined approximately when most of the objects representing it appear to be identical in type with objects found elsewhere in a culture that has been dated by other means.

(3) **Geology.** The relative age of different remains can often be ascertained by finding the relative age of the geological strata in which the remains occur, as in the case of a series of sedimentary deposits, or river terraces and raised beaches, marking former shorelines or flood levels in valleys at times when the mutual relation of land and water was different from that of the present.

(4) **Paleontology.** The presence (with the human remains) of extinct or still existing species of animals (including marine and lacustrine fauna) frequently provides a fairly exact basis for dating the human remains, in terms of geological periods. **K. P. Oakley** has developed a method of comparing the fluorine content of associated human and animal bones to test their contemporaneity.

(5) **Paleobotany.** The presence of plant remains furnishes a further basis for assigning associated human remains to certain geological periods.

(6) **Climatic evidence.** When the past record of major climatic sequences in an area is known, human remains can often be dated in terms of glacial advances and retreats or pluvial and dry periods, if the remains are found in deposits characteristic of such periods. The kinds of animals and plants found in association with the human remains frequently show whether the climate of the period in question was wet or dry or warm or cold. Thanks to the great progress that has recently been made in paleobotany it is now possible to trace climatic fluctuations (as reflected by the immigration of new forest forms) through microscopic examination of pollen grains preserved intact for thousands of years in peat beds and elsewhere. Associated archaeological remains can thus often be referred with great accuracy to a given climatic phase.

There is considerable room for error in the

use of each of these methods, unless the greatest care is exercised, but they are all sound in principle and in general they may be relied upon, particularly when one confirms another. The ideal system would make use of all the methods listed above, establishing for any area the sequence of climatic changes, earth movements, and deposits, and using this as a chronological framework into which to fit the successive cultures, reconstructed on the basis of the stratigraphy of the archaeological remains. For very few regions has this been done.

c. ABSOLUTE DATING

This is more difficult, but several methods have been used.

(1) **Estimate of the time needed to produce observed changes in culture.** There is no exact basis for such estimates, and this method, though often the only one available, is extremely inaccurate and inadequate.

(2) **Estimate of the time necessary for the performance of certain geological work.** This is used to date geological horizons in which human remains occur. For example, the date of a high river terrace may be given if it is estimated that it must have taken the river at least one hundred thousand years to cut down its bed to the present level. Such estimates are almost equally uncertain and inadequate for the purposes of the prehistorian.

(3) **Geochronology;** that is, the counting of the annual layers (varves) of sediment deposited by the melt-waters of a retreating ice-sheet. This method, first devised by the Swedish scientist, Baron **G. J. de Geer,** has been applied to the Scandinavian region as the basis of an absolute system of chronology covering the last twelve thousand years. Owing to the scarcity of archaeological remains found *in situ* in dated varves, this system is of value principally in correlating and dating the different stages of the retreat of the last ice-sheet and the major fluctua-

tions in sea-level in the Baltic area. These in turn serve to date many deposits which, by pollen analysis, can be assigned to the various postglacial climatic cycles. Thus indirectly the archaeological remains found in these deposits can be tentatively dated.

(4) **Dendrochronology.** This method, devised by **Andrew E. Douglass** and applied first in the southwestern United States, is based on the fact that certain species of trees, especially in arid regions, show by the thickness of their annual rings of growth the alternation of relatively wet or dry years. By matching many specimens from trees of various ages it has been possible to construct a time scale by which to date timbers found in prehistoric ruins.

(5) **Historical evidence.** Late prehistoric cultures in backward areas can sometimes be dated in a general way by the presence of imported objects from a known historical culture in some more advanced area, where written documents already exist.

The foregoing methods of dating archaeological sites have been greatly supplemented by advances in chemistry and atomic physics. In addition to the fluorine test, Oakley has also used a nitrogen test, which gives some measure of absolute age in bones. The Carbon-14 test, invented by **Willard F. Libby,** determines the amount of C-14 remaining in charcoal, wood, and a few other organic substances, and calculates a date based on the half-life of this element of 5,760 years, with a probable error of no more than 2,000 years, depending on the size of the sample and its age. The oldest C-14 date yet obtained is $64,000 \pm 1,100$ years (GRO-1379). Thousands of such dates have been determined in many laboratories, each designated by a symbol for the laboratory (e.g. GRO = Groningen) and a number (GRO-1379). The Argon-40 test takes us much farther. It depends on the measurement of the amount of Ar-40 gas formed by the decay of Potassium-40 into Ar-40 and Calcium-40 in

Dendrochronological dating

Weathered front of a lava flow

Geological strata in Bryce Canyon

YEARS					
← B.C.			A.D. →		
	Jan. 1 to Dec. 31	Jan. 1 to Dec. 31	Jan. 1 to Dec. 31	Jan. 1 to Dec. 31	
Year 3	Year 2	Year 1	Year 1	Year 2	Year 3

CENTURIES					
← B.C.			A.D. →		
300 B.C. to 201 B.C.	200 B.C. to 101 B.C.	100 B.C. to 1 B.C.	1 A.D. to 100 A.D.	101 A.D. to 200 A.D.	201 A.D. to 300 A.D.
Third Century	Second Century	First Century	First Century	Second Century	Third Century

material which had been subjected to great heat, after it had cooled. Our most recent Ar–40 date is 230,000 years, leaving a gap of 160,000 years between it and the oldest C–14 determination.

The study of cores of sediment cut from the bottom of the ocean, which includes a whole battery of tests and observations, fills in this gap and confirms the accuracy of the Ar–40 method.

(6) **Centuries and years before and after Christ (B.C. and A.D.).** In civilizations of the past many and various schemes of designating and counting years have been used, starting from specific "era" dates. Thus the Greeks came to reckon from the year of the first Olympic Games, which they put at a year correspond-ing to our 776 B.C. The Romans settled on 753 B.C. as the year of the traditional founding of Rome, and called that 1 A.U.C. (*ab urbe condita*).

These and other schemes are reduced in modern histories to dates reckoned from the year (actually only approximate) of the birth of Christ, both backward and forward. Years of Our Lord (*Anno Domini*) are reckoned forward beginning with the year 1 A.D. Years before Christ begin with the year 1 B.C. The year before 1 B.C. was 2 B.C. and so on. But in counting days B.C., the months and days run forward: the first day of 3 B.C. was January 1, and the last day December 31, which was followed at once by January 1 of the year 2 B.C.

The same procedure applies to centuries.

The 1st Century A.D. runs from 1 A.D. through 100 A.D.; the 2nd from 101 A.D. through 200 A.D., etc. Similarly the 1st Century B.C. runs from 100 B.C. (January 1) through 1 B.C. (December 31); the 2nd Century B.C. includes the years 200 B.C.—101 B.C., etc.

Millennia (thousands of years) are reckoned in the same way. Thus the span of recorded history extends from the 3rd millennium B.C. (when the Bronze Age began) into the 2nd millennium A.D., which began in 1001 A.D. and will end in 2000 A.D.

(7) **The Julian and Gregorian Calendars.** Until the 16th century the Christian world used the **Julian Calendar,** introduced in 46 B.C. by Julius Caesar. This calendar provided for a year of 365 days plus, every fourth (leap) year, an additional day. This system is generally referred to as **Old Style** (O.S.).

In 1582 Pope Gregory XIII introduced the **Gregorian Calendar** to correct the error in the Julian Calendar, which had fallen ten days behind, astronomically. Thenceforth dates were advanced ten days and, in order to forestall future error, it was provided that only those centesimal years (such as 1600, 1700, etc.) that could be divided by 400 should be leap years. This calendar is referred to as **New Style** (N.S.). It was not adopted by Great Britain, which was Protestant, until 1752, nor by Russia and other Greek Orthodox countries until 1917. The difference in the 19th century was twelve days, and thirteen days in the 20th. By 1950 the adoption of the Gregorian Calendar was worldwide.

In this Encyclopedia all dates have been reduced to New Style unless otherwise indicated.

B. The Paleolithic Period

I. *Culture and Industries*

THE WORD *Paleolithic* is used to describe a stage of human culture, the earliest of which we have sure evidence. Although this culture persisted longer in some parts of the world than in others, we can use the term with reasonable accuracy to characterize a period of time. This period includes probably 99 per cent of Man's life on earth (at least since he became a tool-using animal), all the other periods down to the present covering the remaining 1 per cent.

Our knowledge of Paleolithic culture is based principally on implements and animal and human bones found in the gravels of old river terraces, in open camp sites, and in caves. Dis-

Paleolithic men hunting giant bear and mammoth

*Ram in a Thicket; find from the
Royal Tombs of Ur (p.31)*

Wall painting from the cave of Santamanine, Spain (p.7)

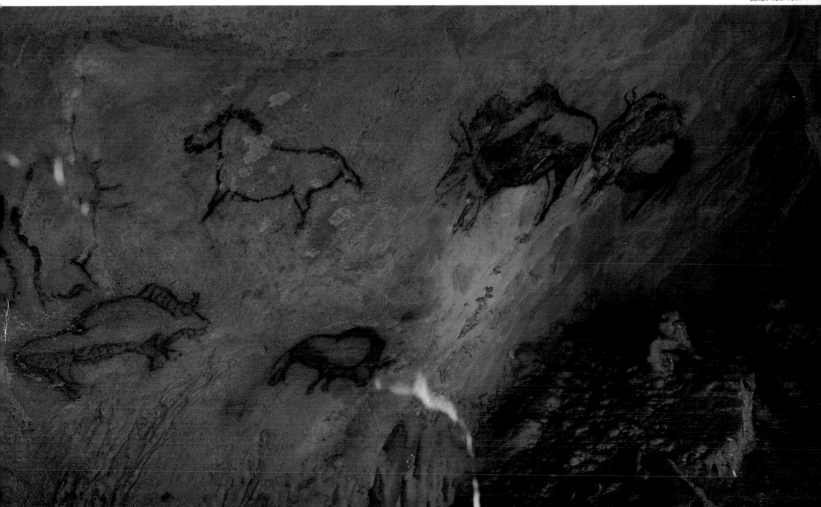

*Flabellum depicting an ostrich hunt,
from the tomb of Tut'ankhamun (p.39)*

THE EGYPTIAN MUSEUM, CAIRO, EGYPT

Cover of Tut'ankhamun's coffin (p.39)

THE EGYPTIAN MUSEUM, CAIRO, EGYPT

regarding the variations of time and place, one may say in general that Paleolithic men knew the use of fire and lived by hunting and collecting vegetable foods, as the Australian natives and the Bushmen of South Africa do today. They had no agriculture and no domestic animals, excepting possibly the dog. For shelter they probably made wind-breaks and crude huts of branches, occasionally occupying caves. Their clothing was undoubtedly of skins (no textiles). Their tools and utensils were of stone, bone, and undoubtedly also of wood and basketry (no metal and no pottery). We know almost nothing of their social organization, religion, and intellectual life, except that late cave paintings and burials indicate belief in magic (in connection with hunting) and in some kind of existence of the individual after death. It is fairly safe to assume, however, that a large part of the fundamental institutions and beliefs of modern primitive peoples and of our own early historical ancestors had their origin and first development in this period.

The **stone tools,** which are such important criteria for this period, were usually made of flint or other hard rock by a process of chipping. They are classified as **core tools,** when the basis of the implement was a piece of rock, improved by chipping, or **flake tools,** when one of the flakes knocked off from a core (which is then termed a nucleus) was used as the basis for the implement, or **blade tools,** when the core was carefully prepared for striking off long, parallel-edged blades. In the manufacture of **Levallois flakes** and of blades, the core was first made ready by creating a flat surface or striking platform. Chips were then removed by striking it, preferably through the intermediacy of a wooden or horn dowel. Sometimes the edges of a flake were improved by secondary chipping or flaking (retouching). The principal types of implements were hand-axes or *coups de poing* (large pear-shaped or almond-shaped cores, chipped on both sides); scrapers of various shapes; points; awls (borers); and, in late times, long blades with roughly parallel edges, and gravers (small tools of many shapes improved for use as chisels or gouges by striking a special blow near the point).

Cave painting from Lascaux, France

Levallois core and flake

2. *Europe*

The **Pleistocene epoch,** or Ice Age, in the last two-thirds of which Paleolithic culture developed and flourished, is divided into Lower, Middle, and Upper. According to the conventional chronology, the **Lower Pleistocene** began about 1,000,000 years ago when cold-adapted mollusks appeared in previously warm waters and modern genera of horses, cattle, elephants, and camels appeared in North America, Eurasia, and Africa. Toward the end of the Lower Pleistocene the first of four mountain glaciers arose in the Alps (Günz), and in the Himalayas, and in North America the first of four successive icecaps, the Nebraskan, was

The new dating is as follows:*

Günz (Nebraskan) glaciation	1,500,000–1,375,000 years ago
First (Aftonian) interglacial	1,375,000–1,205,000
Mindel (Kansan) glaciation	1,205,000–1,060,000
Second (Yarmouth) interglacial	1,060,000– 420,000
Riss (Illinoisan) glaciation	420,000– 340,000
Third (Sangoan) interglacial	340,000– 115,000
Early Würm glaciation	115,000– 95,000
Interstadial	95,000– 65,000
Main Würm glaciation	65,000– 11,000

*From D. Ericson and G. Wollin, *The Deep and the Past* (New York: Alfred A. Knopf, 1964).

formed. The **Middle Pleistocene** began about one half million years ago with the first continental icecap in Europe (the Elster), the second Alpine glaciation (Mindel), and the second North American icecap, the Kansan. Then followed the Second or **Great Interglacial,** succeeded by the Saal icecap and Riss mountain glaciation, and the Illinoisan icecap in North America. The **Late Pleistocene** includes the **Third Interglacial,** beginning about 150,000 years ago and the two Würm glaciations, with the Weichsel icecap. Würm I lasted from about 75,000 to 40,000 years ago, Würm II from about 30,000 to 10,000. In between was a cool period, or Interstadial.

The new chronology, based on sea-cores, Ar–40 and C–14 tests, and other methods, extends the base of the Middle Pleistocene to 1,500,000 years ago, and returns the Lower Pleistocene or Villafranchian to the Pliocene where it was before being shifted to the Pleistocene by an international geological congress in 1948.

LOWER PALEOLITHIC. This period covers the greater part of the Pleistocene. Almost our only information about the peoples and movements of this time consists of what may be inferred from the stone implements, which show, according to Abbé **Henri Breuil,** the contem-

Aurignacian scrapers, burin, and points

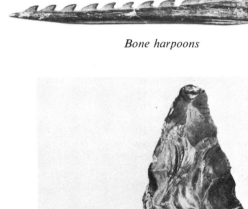

Bone harpoons

Mousterian flake tools

Acheulean hand-axe

porary but more or less independent development and mutual inter-influence in western Europe of four separate techniques of manufacture (industries): (1) **Hand-axe** industry (French *biface*), developing through Pre-Chellean (Abbevillian) to Acheulean types; (2) **Clactonian** industry, characterized by rough flakes with an unfaceted striking-platform inclined at a high angle to the main flake surface; (3) **Levalloisean** industry, characterized by large flakes struck from a previously prepared core (tortoise core) and retaining a faceted striking-platform; and (4) **Mousterian** industry, consisting of smaller flakes of various forms, usually exhibiting a characteristic technique of retouching the edges (stepped retouch). These industries are found both separate and mixed, and there are additional intermediate forms. Chronologically they have been grouped into four periods: (1) **Pre-Chellean** (Abbevillian) period, characterized by extremely crude hand-axes; (2) **Chellean** period (now usually included with Acheulean), having hand-axes somewhat less crude than the Abbevillian, as well as some Clactonian tools; (3) **Acheulean**

period, marked by more highly evolved hand-axes and, particularly in its later stages, by Levallois flakes; and (4) **Mousterian** period (sometimes designated as Middle Paleolithic), with typical flake tools (points and scrapers) and a continuation in some places of Levallois flakes. The Mousterian industry proper (which has Pre-Mousterian or Proto-Mousterian forerunners in northern and eastern Europe) is found particularly in the caves of central France, associated with bones of mammoth and reindeer and of Neanderthal Man.

UPPER PALEOLITHIC. This is a relatively short period, coinciding with the last part of the Ice Age from the **Göttweig Interstadial** to the retreat of the Scandinavian icecap. Modern European men replaced the Neanderthals and blade tools appeared, along with an extensive use of bone and ivory for spearheads and harpoons. The Upper Paleolithic Europeans left a priceless heritage of art including engraving, carving in the round, and cave paintings. Four principal cultures have been noted: (1) **Perigordian,** the earliest in France, characterized

especially by "backed" blades, blunted on one edge for holding or hafting. (2) **Aurignacian,** marked by great use of the blade and including a variety of characteristic scrapers, gravers, points (Châtelperron, Gravette, Font Robert types), and beginning of very small tools (*microliths*); also bone implements and ornaments of shell and bone. Aurignacian remains are found widely through central and western Europe and the Mediterranean region. (3) **Solutrean,** distributed from eastern and central Europe as far as France, intruding on the Aurignacian. The climate was cold. The Solutreans lived in open camps and rock shelters, were great hunters of horses, and introduced the technique of pressure flaking (willow-leaf and laurel-leaf points). (4) **Magdalenian,** the latest to develop, flourished in northern and central Europe and southern France.

The Paleolithic period in Europe ended with the great changes in climate, fauna, and flora that marked the termination of the Pleistocene or Ice Age.

3. *Africa*

The Paleolithic period of Africa is characterized by a variety of stone industries, some of which are purely local, while others are similar to or practically identical with certain of the industries of Europe. Geological investigation, which has only recently been undertaken on an adequate basis, indicates that owing to fluctuations in rainfall the Pleistocene period throughout most of Africa can perhaps be divided into a succession of pluvial and interpluvial periods, which it is hoped may eventually be correlated in some way with the glacial and interglacial periods of Europe. The succession of cultures is well established for certain areas, but not yet for the continent as a whole.

NORTHWEST AFRICA. Heavily patinated hand-axes of definitely Chellean and Acheulean types together with an early fauna have been found, usually without stratigraphy, in Tunisia, Algeria, Morocco, and to the south in the Sahara region, which was apparently once less arid than now. A so-called Mousterian industry (accompanied by a later fauna) is also represented, and excavations show an evolution from Levalloisean types, without typical Mousterian, to a special development known as the **Aterian** industry, characterized by small, tanged, leaf-shaped points, delicately trimmed all over both faces. This was succeeded by the overlapping cultures, the **Mouillian** and the **Capsian,** and the **Oranian,** which were terminal Upper Paleolithic and Mesolithic in date and marked by blades, gravers, and microlithic forms, the earliest phases of which bear a fundamental though distant relationship to the early Aurignacian of Europe and western Asia.

EGYPT. The presence of Paleolithic Man is shown by discoveries of the following succession of industries, all *in situ,* in the terraces of the Nile Valley: Chellean, a primitive Acheulean and an Egyptian form of the Clactonian, in the 100-foot terrace (no human implements were

found in the 150-foot terrace); developed Acheulean in the 50-foot terrace; Levalloisean (first reported as Early Mousterian) in the 30-foot terrace; and developed Levalloisean (reported as Egyptian Mousterian) in the 15- to 10-foot terrace. These were followed, in deposits of later age, by an Egyptian version of the Aterian and a local industry, the Sebilian.

EAST AFRICA. According to **Louis** and **Mary Leakey** and others, there is a Lower Pleistocene industry in Kenya, Uganda, and Tanganyika, which consisted of simple pebbles

and unrolled stones, roughly chipped on one side to make a cutting edge (choppers) or on both sides (chopping-tools). These constitute the **Oldowan** industry, found in stratification in Oldovai Gorge, below true hand-axe types (Chellean and Acheulean industries). In higher geological horizons are found Levalloisian implements followed by the **Stillbay**—pressure-flaked bifacial points similar to the Aterian of North Africa. The Oldowan tools are believed to have been mostly Lower Pleistocene, the Chellean and Acheulean mostly Middle and early Upper

Oldowan hand-axe and cleaver

Stillbay pressure-flaked implements

Pleistocene, and the Levalloisean and Stillbay late Upper Pleistocene. The so-called "Aurignacian" of East Africa is now known to be Capsian and post-Pleistocene.

SOUTH AFRICA. Pebble tools have been found in the late Lower Pleistocene of the Vaal Valley. The Middle Pleistocene contains Chellean and Acheulian hand-axes and cleavers and the so-called **Victoria West core-tools,** all lumped under the term *Stellenbosch.* These continued through the early Upper Pleistocene

and were gradually replaced by the **Fauresmith** culture (hand-axes and also flakes with faceted striking-platform, suggesting Levalloisian influence). The so-called Middle Stone Age, which was late Upper Pleistocene and even post-Pleistocene in date, was marked by a series of more or less contemporary flake industries (Mossel-bay, Glen Grey Falls, Howieson's Poort, Bambata Cave, Stillbay, etc.), suggesting by the shapes and technique of their implements a combination of Levalloisean and Capsian

influences, together with pressure-flaking in one case (Stillbay).

OTHER AREAS. Ethiopia and Somaliland go with East Africa, and the Rhodesias form a transition to South Africa. In the forested regions of the Congo and West Africa are found so-called **Sangoan** or **Tumbian core-tools,** crude and picklike, derived from the hand-axe tradition, and lasting until the end of the Pleistocene if not later. The sequence of West Africa outside the forest has not been fully worked out.

4. *Asia and Oceania*

WESTERN ASIA. A remarkably complete sequence of stone industries, paralleling quite closely those of Europe, has been established for the Palestine-Syria region. Surface finds of Chellean implements are supplemented (in three caves in the Wady-el-Mughara, near Mt. Carmel) by the following stratigraphic series: Tayacian, Upper Acheulean, Levalloiseo-Mousterian (with skeletons of Neanderthaloid type), Aurignacian, and Natufian (a Mesolithic industry). Occasional sites with implements of one or another of these or similar types have been reported from northern Arabia, Asia Minor, Armenia, Transcaucasia, Mesopotamia, and Iran.

INDIA. Many implements of Chellean type, as well as Acheulean hand-axes and cleavers, have been reported in northern, central, and southern India. In the Punjab, **Hellmut de Terra** found Acheulean hand-axes in a deposit contemporary with the second Himalayan glaciation or somewhat later. These were succeeded by a crude pebble industry (Soan industry) in strata contemporary with the third Himalayan glaciation. A few Upper Paleolithic types, with some suggestions of Aurignacian, have also been found in central and northwestern India, as well

as cave sites with rock paintings of uncertain age.

AFGHANISTAN. North of the Hindu Kush Mountains Levalloiseo-Mousterian implements have been found in the Haibak Valley, and an Upper Paleolithic blade culture was discovered in the cave of Kara Kamar and dated by Carbon-14 as over 34,000 years, probably during the local equivalent of the Göttweig Interstadial.

CHINA AND JAPAN. With the skeletal material found at Chou-kou-tien, southwest of Peking, were also discovered stone tools, dated at around 360,000 years, and thus of Second Glacial (Mindel-Elster) age. They include choppers and chopping-tools and bipolar flakes (struck on a stone anvil so that the blow comes, in effect, from both ends). From then on in China these tools were gradually refined until the end of the Pleistocene, and also, in northwest China, flake tools resembling Mousterian implements were made in Upper Pleistocene times. Tools similar to those of China have been found in Japan. In northern Hokkaido a number of sites have yielded large obsidian blade tools resembling the European Upper Paleolithic, but still of undetermined age.

SIBERIA AND RUSSIAN TURKESTAN.

Mousterian tools have been excavated in Turkmenistan and Uzbekistan, particularly with the Neanderthal boy of Teshik Tash, and hearth sites. Paleolithic implements and remains of extinct animals have been found in southwestern and central Siberia, especially in the basin of the Ob River and its tributaries, the valleys of the Upper Yenisei (Minusinsk region) and Angara Rivers and around Lake Baikal. Some of the implements resemble quite closely certain Mousterian, Aurignacian, and Magdalenian forms of western Europe. The deposits in which they occur and the fauna suggest that they are probably mostly, if not entirely, post-glacial.

SOUTHEASTERN ASIA AND OCEANIA. Paleolithic implements have been found in Burma, Thailand, Indo-China, Java, Borneo, and the Philippines. They are essentially similar to those of China in that they consist of choppers, chopping-tools, and flakes of varying degrees of crudity. The oldest tools from Australia are probably about 16,000 years old, or late Upper Pleistocene, and they resemble the southeast Asian and Indonesian industries. No Paleolithic implements have been found in Oceania.

5. *America*

Folsom arrowhead

During the latter part of the Würm or Wisconsian glaciation the ancestors of the **American Indians** first crossed from Asia to Alaska over a wide corridor of dry land, now submerged. The earliest Carbon-14 date so far recovered is 16,375 ± 400 B.C. (O-999), from Venezuela, where a chopper-chopping tool industry of Chou-kou-tien facies is associated with clumsy extinct animals, including mastodon, glyptodon, megatherium, and macrauchenia, which could not long have survived the presence of Man. The remains of some of these animals, with similar artifacts, have also been found at the Strait of Magellan, at 8,760 ± 300 B.C. (W-915). If it took 8,000 years for Man to get from Venezuela to the Strait of Magellan, it is reason-

able to postulate an initial entry over Bering Strait in the neighborhood of 20,000 years ago. So far the earliest date for a similar culture in North America is 9,580 ± 600 B.C. (C-609) at Danger Cave, Utah. Similar tools were made in the California Desert in modern times.

Well-made projectile points, pressure flaked on both sides, and in some sites fluted, go back to 9,330 ± 500 B.C. (M-811) at the Lehner Mammoth Site, Arizona (Clovis Points); 8,820 ± 375 B.C. (I [UW]-141) at Lindenmeier, Colorado; and about 7,000 B.C. (M-807, 808, 809, 810) at Bull Brook, Ipswich, Mass. (Folsom Points). These points, used in killing mammoths, seem not to have been made after the extinction of that animal.

THE PALEOLITHIC PERIOD

6. *Interrelationship of Paleolithic Cultures*

It should be clear from the foregoing that at present we know a great deal more about Paleolithic stone implements than we do about the Paleolithic people who made them. Our data are still too insufficient to warrant any sure account of the way in which the various elements of Paleolithic culture were developed by different groups of mankind and spread by them throughout the world. However, three fundamental facts relating to this problem may be regarded as reasonably well established:

First, some of the more highly evolved implements and groups of implements found in widely different areas are so similar in shape and technique that we are forced to infer that the cultures in which they occur bear some time-relationship to one another, i.e. the art of making the typical implements in question (such as the hand-axe, the Levallois flake and the Aurignacian blade, to name three fundamental examples) was not evolved independently at different times and in different places but was spread from some original center, either by actual migrations of people or by cultural diffusion.

Second, the geographical distribution of these various type implements, although very wide, is not haphazard, but each one of the fundamental industries has its own distinct area of major development, with outliers along natural routes of migration. For example, the industry characterized by core implements of hand-axe type is found in one continuous area, comprising southwestern Asia, eastern and northern Africa, and southern and western Europe, with outliers in South Africa and India. A less sharply definable industry, characterized by the use of flake implements in preference to cores and (in its most developed form) by the use of flake implements of Levalloisean type with a faceted striking-platform, has its home in the same area, with addition of a broad belt stretching through central and eastern Europe and northern Asia. Finally the blade industry has a distribution which is practically identical with that last described, though with a less characteristic development in South Africa and India. The southeastern part of Asia, from the North China plain to Indonesia, seems to form a separate culture province, with an almost entirely independent development throughout Paleolithic times.

Third, the three major industries just referred to had their principal development at different periods of time, as is shown by the fact that wherever there is stratigraphic evidence they occur in the same order of succession, with the hand-axe industry the earliest, succeeded in turn by the Levalloisean flake industry and that by the blade industry, the latest of all. The foregoing outline is, of course, oversimplified and disregards many problems of local development and relations, but it is based on a mass of evidence, it represents the best opinion of archaeologists today, and it may be accepted provisionally as a true interpretation of the facts.

7. *Dates of Paleolithic Cultures*

The Paleolithic period of Man's development is considered to be roughly contemporary, in some places, with most of the Pleistocene period of the earth's history and may best be dated in geological terms. The Pleistocene may be broadly divided, on the basis of faunal remains, into Lower, Middle, and Upper or (in Europe at least), on the basis of Alpine glacial deposits, into four major periods of glacial advance (Günz, Mindel, Riss, and Würm) with three corresponding interglacial periods. The dating of Paleolithic industries in terms of Alpine glacial and interglacial periods is still, however, a highly speculative affair, owing to the fact, which is not always properly appreciated, that almost no archaeological remains have yet been found in actual glacial deposits of the Alpine region. Attempts have been made to correlate glaciations in Asia and Africa with these Alpine glaciations and to correlate with both the series of implement-bearing river terraces (especially of the Thames, Somme, and Nile) and implement-bearing deposits of so-called Pluvial periods in non-glaciated regions (notably in East Africa), but only preliminary work has yet been done on this large and complicated problem. Hence statements of experts regarding the age of the earlier Paleolithic cultures differ greatly and should be regarded as opinions or theories only, which require further evidence before they can be accepted as established fact.

That tool-making man existed as early as the Lower Pleistocene period has been contended by

Clactonian yew wood point

Chellean hand-axe

a number of authorities. **Teilhard de Chardin** has dated the Sinanthropus finds at Chou-kou-tien as Lower Pleistocene, and **Breuil** considers that deposits containing his Abbevillian (Pre-Chellean) industry and the earliest Clactonian industry belong to the First (Günz-Mindel) Interglacial period. Various alleged implements of a very primitive nature (including the so-called *eoliths*) found in Europe and Africa have been ascribed to this period and **Reid Moir** claims to have found tools of primitive types in deposits that are presumably of pre-Günz age. Such early dates are not yet universally accepted by archaeologists and geologists.

When we come to the Middle Pleistocene, however, there is a more general agreement that the early phases of the hand-axe and flake industries (Chellean, Clactonian, etc.) in Europe and Africa probably existed in the Second (Mindel-Riss) Interglacial period. De Terra has found similar implements in India in deposits contemporary with the end of his Second Himalayan Glacial Advance or the following interglacial period (which may be contemporary respectively with the Second or Mindel Glaciation of Europe and the Mindel-Riss Interglacial).

Furthermore, it is thought very probable that in Europe the fully developed Acheulean and associated Levalloisean industries belong to the Third (Riss-Würm) Interglacial period, the typical Mousterian to the end of this period and the first maximum of the Fourth Glacial period (Würm I), the Perigordian and early Aurignacian to the time of the Göttweig Interstadial, while various phases of the Aurignacian, Solutrean, and Magdalenian take up the rest of the Pleistocene. African and Asiatic implements that show relationship to some of the above industries are probably roughly contemporary with them.

8. *Species and Sub-species of Fossil Man*

The remains of Pleistocene men so far discovered total about 230 individuals complete enough to enable useful study. Of these, three come possibly from the Lower or earliest Middle, 40 probably from the Middle, and the rest from the Upper Pleistocene. In the past these specimens were given many individual generic and specific names which will be used here for identification only, because modern workers assign them all to two successive species, *Homo erectus* and *Homo sapiens*. This classification does not include the so-called *Homo habilis* who was definitely from the Lower Pleistocene. While the transition between the two species was gradual, they may be distinguished by a combination of criteria, including the ratio between arcs and chords in the sagittal line of the frontal, parietal, and occipital bones, brow-ridge size, form of the tracks of the mid-meningeal blood vessels on the inside of the parietal bone, relative flatness of the base of the skull, ratios between palate size and tooth size versus brain size, the size of the seat of the pituitary

(*Sella turcica*), and, to a lesser extent, cranial capacity itself, ranging from 750 cc. to 1280 cc. in *Homo erectus* and from 1175 cc. to at least 1710 cc. in fossil *Homo sapiens*.

Specimens of both species may be divided spatially into five geographical races or sub-species: the Australoid, Mongoloid, Caucasoid, Capoid, and Congoid, evolving respectively in

Australopithecus (*Australoid line*)

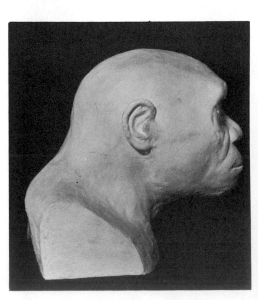

Early Java man (Australoid line)

Sinanthropus pekinensis (*Mongoloid line*)

southeast Asia and Indonesia, China, western Asia and Europe, North Africa, and Sub-Saharan Africa.

The **Australoid** line begins with four specimens from the Djetis Beds of Java, of late Lower Pleistocene Age; two lower jaws named *Meganthropus* variously called *Australopithecine* and *Homo erectus*, an adult *erectus* skull called *Pithecanthropus* No. 4, and an infant skull of the same type, *Homo modjokertensis*. From the Middle Pleistocene beds of Central Java (the Trinil Beds) come three other *Pithecanthropus* skulls, Nos. 1, 2, and 3. This line carries on through the 11 skulls of *Homo soloensis* found at Ngangdong in the Notopuro Beds of the Upper Pleistocene. All these form an evolutionary progression within *Homo erectus*. An adolescent skull from the Niah Cave, North Borneo, dated at about 40,000 years by Carbon–14, is *sapiens*, and so are two very late Pleistocene skulls from Wadjak in Java. Australoid skulls have heavy, straight browridges, steeply sloping frontal bones, keeled vaults, flattish upper faces, broad nasal openings, great alveolar prognathism, and large teeth with particularly large molars.

The **Mongoloid** line begins with 14 skulls and 12 lower jaws and a total of 147 teeth (in and out of jaws) from Chou-kou-tien, dated in the early to middle Middle Pleistocene, followed by three teeth from Ting-tsin (Shansi), a maxilla from Changyang (Hupei), a skull from Mapa (Kwangtung), all in the Middle Pleistocene. The Upper Pleistocene contains Mongoloid skulls from Tze-yang (Sze-chuan) and Lin-kiang (Kwang-si), one tooth from Sjara-Osso-Gol

Neanderthals (Caucasoid line)

Crô-Magnons (Caucasoid line)

(Ordos), and an as yet racially unidentified skull from Aichi, Honshu, Japan. Three skulls from the Upper Cave of Chou-kou-tien date from the very end of the Pleistocene.

The transition from *Homo erectus* to *Homo sapiens* in the Mongoloid line came probably at the level of Mapa or Ting-tsin, in the late Middle or early Upper Pleistocene, but all are Mongoloid. Mongoloid skulls have straight browridges, steeply rising, curved frontal bones, flat faces, protruding lower orbital rims, guttered nasal sills, alveolar prognathism, mandibular torus, and teeth noted for heavy shoveling of the incisors and canines.

The oldest **Caucasoid** specimen is the Mauer or Heidelberg mandible, from the early Middle Pleistocene. Two skulls from the Second or Great Interglacial, Steinheim and Swanscombe, bring the Middle Pleistocene roster to three. Twenty-six early Upper Pleistocene (pre-Würm) individuals are represented by specimens from France, Germany, Czechoslovakia, and Yugoslavia, and one from Israel. Würm I Caucasoids include remains of 55 individuals from western and central Europe, four from the U.S.S.R., and 39 from western Asia. All but eight from Palestine and Lebanon are considered to be Neanderthals. The Upper Paleolithic (Göttweig Interstadial and Würm II) include individuals from 161 sites in Europe and western Asia, of which 25 have been more or less adequately described.

With the possible exception of the Heidelberg jaw, which is in doubt because it has no cranium, all the Caucasoid skulls are *Homo sapiens* in the sense that they are all as fully evolved as those of living Australian aborigines, but in them an evolutionary progression may be seen, more or less, through time. Fully modern Caucasoids appear first in Würm I in Palestine and Lebanon and during the Göttweig Interstadial in Europe.

Caucasoid criteria are: a projecting nasal skeleton, laterally curved browridges, prognathism midfacial or absent, relatively narrow jaws, and relatively small teeth with little or no shoveling. The Neanderthals, who were not as aberrent as usually stated, had particularly prow-like faces, large noses, long faces, and relatively broad, low braincases. While the exact relationship between the Neanderthals and their predecessors and followers remains to be determined they were, in any case, Caucasoids, and probably cold-adapted. Although the Upper Paleolithic specimens have been assigned to several races on the basis of individual skulls (Crô-Magnon, Grimaldi, Chancelade, etc.) they were a single subspecific population no more variable than living Europeans.

The racial situation in Africa during the Pleistocene is more obscure. In North Africa a series of three mandibles and one parietal from Ternefine, Algeria, resemble those of Sinanthropus, and are of about the same age. Two Upper Pleistocene skulls from Jebel Ighoud, Morocco, three mandibles from the Moroccan Atlantic coast, and a child's maxilla from Tangier, carry this line at least into Würm I. With large, straight browridges, a curved frontal bone, flat upper facial skeleton, great prognathism, and large teeth with shoveling, this line resembles the Mongoloid in many respects and also the prehistoric skeletons of full-sized African Bushmen; Carleton Coon designates it as **Capoid.** At the end of the Pleistocene this race was displaced by an invasion of Mouillian Caucasoids.

Before the southward migration of the Bushman ancestors, Africa south of the Sahara was, apparently, Negro country **(Congoid),** although the evidence is limited to one early Middle Pleistocene skullcap from Olduvai Gorge (Chellian–3 Man) and Upper Pleistocene skulls and fragments thereof from Broken Hill (N. Rhodesia), Saldanha Bay (Cape Province), and Kanjera (Kenya). All but the last are *Homo erectus,* who seems to have lasted in South Africa until late in the Pleistocene, and all are racially Negro, as far as we can tell. The date of the Kanjera specimens is in doubt, but they may be as much as 50,000 years old. No material of any antiquity has yet been found in West Africa, the historic center of Negro differentiation.

C. The Post-Paleolithic Period

1. *Nature and Sequence of Post-Paleolithic Cultures*

IN THE absence of exact dates, archaeologists have divided the time from the end of the Paleolithic to the present into the following major periods: Mesolithic period, Neolithic period, Chalcolithic period, Bronze Age, Iron Age, and Modern Age. As has been previously pointed out, this nomenclature has many disadvantages, since the names refer really to cultural stages rather than to periods of time. The words were first employed in the description of cultures as observed in Europe and the order of succession is not always the same for other continents. Furthermore, it is impossible to assign even estimated dates to these so-called periods, for each one began and ended at a different time in different parts of the world. On the whole, however, this chronological division does represent the general progress of culture, in the Old World at least, and although it often leads to confusion, unless applied with the greatest care, still it has the advantage of convenience and almost universal usage. The dividing line between prehistory and history comes at no particular place in this series, but varies in different areas. Following is a brief definition of the different periods, after which the Post-Paleolithic cultures of the world will be described by geographical areas.

a. MESOLITHIC PERIOD

The disappearance of the last ice-sheet, which marked the end of the Pleistocene period and, with it, the end of the Paleolithic, led to the rise of a new culture, generally referred to as the Mesolithic, in which the Paleolithic economy of food-gathering, though basically unchanged, was partly modified in some parts of the world under the influence of new climatic conditions. The big animals of the Pleistocene, on which the Paleolithic hunters had largely depended for their food, disappeared everywhere except in Africa and south Asia, and their place was taken by the present-day fauna. Also with the ice retreat new regions were opened to settlement. The stone implements of the Mesolithic cultures were still produced by chipping, but a preference was shown for extremely small forms (*microliths*), often of geometric shapes. Some of these forms had a wide distribution in Asia, Africa, and Europe, showing that there were certain cultural relations and also actual movements of peoples—the latter probably connected to some extent with the drying up of the Sahara and central Asiatic regions. The Mesolithic

period is usually considered to have begun (in northern Europe at least) c. 8000 B.C., and Mesolithic cultures lasted for several thousand years until supplanted (at different dates in different areas) by the food-producing economy of the Neolithic peoples.

b. NEOLITHIC PERIOD

The next stage of development, the Neolithic, is marked by the invention and almost universal adoption of techniques for **producing food, grinding stone,** and **making pottery.** These new techniques and the results which flowed from them were revolutionary. Man ceased being a nomad, eternally following his food supply, and became a sedentary being, residing and growing his food in one spot. He now had an assured food supply to carry over lean seasons and this led to a great increase in the population in most of the formerly inhabited areas, and the opening up to settlement of new areas, such as loess lands of Asia and Europe. The altered conditions likewise made possible the accumulation of possessions, the creation and satisfaction of new needs, the leisure for invention and specu-

Neolithic pottery, c. 5000–3100 B.C.

lation, the growth of large communities and cities, the development of more complex social organization, and in fact all the progress that has taken place since that time.

The new techniques that characterized the Neolithic did not all originate in the same place at the same time. The grinding of stone began during late Mesolithic times while the first domestication of plants and animals occurred before the invention of pottery. This division has been partly formalized in the terms *Prepottery* and *Pottery Neolithic*. However, there is good reason to believe that these developments followed one another in a limited area and spread from there in successive waves to the ends of Asia, Africa, and Europe, but not in any significant sense to the New World. This original center was probably southwestern Asia, for the wild relatives of the cereals and animals that were first domesticated have their home there, and it was the region in which the higher culture or civilization which the Neolithic discoveries made possible was first developed. The earliest remains of **Prepottery Neolithic** culture which have yet been found occur in an arc from the southwest corner of Iran through northern Mesopotamia and Syria into the Jordan valley of Palestine. The earliest **Pottery Neolithic** appears to have been localized in the highlands of northern Mesopotamia, Iran, Syria and the southwestern Anatolian plateau. By about 6000 B.C. it was distributed from both Aegean shores to the western border of Iran, with a major development in the Konya Plain of the southern Anatolian plateau. The Neolithic economy is fully developed with wheat and barley in cultivation and sheep, goats, pigs, and possibly cattle as domesticated animals.

Neolithic remains of primitive character have been found in other parts of the Old World, but they are all apparently later than this in date. The first traces of the Neolithic that have been found in western Europe are not older than 5000 B.C., and Neolithic culture did not begin in many parts of Asia and Africa until much later still.

c. CHALCOLITHIC PERIOD

In a strict sense this is not a true period at all. The word *Chalcolithic* is a term conveniently but loosely used to describe a culture that is still essentially Neolithic in character, but in which the metal copper is just beginning to be used, without, however, replacing stone as the principal material for implements. It is a time during which villages began to develop into towns, and oxen and plow agriculture began largely to replace hoe cultivation. Chalcolithic cultures are thus transitional to urban civilization. People in many areas of the world did not pass through this intermediate stage, but obtained their first knowledge of copper directly from other peoples who had already fully developed the art of copper metallurgy. The dates of Chalcolithic cultures differ everywhere, depending upon the time it took for the knowledge of metal-working to spread. The earliest cultures in which copper has been found are in the Near East, and their estimated date is somewhere between 4500 and 3500 B.C. Copper did not appear in Europe much before 2500 B.C.

d. BRONZE AGE

In most regions of the Old World (but not in all of them) there was a period in which copper or bronze came into general use as a material for tools and weapons, but iron was still practically unknown. Because the ores required for the making of bronze and other alloys had a limited distribution, their increase in use led to the breakdown of the self-sufficiency of local Neolithic economies with a resultant growth of international trade and eventually the establishment of political units larger than the traditional city-state. This period is for convenience termed the **Bronze Age** (although strictly speaking the word *bronze* should refer only to true bronze, a mixed metal composed of copper alloyed with a certain percentage of tin). The date and duration of the Bronze Age in various parts of the Old World vary greatly. As already has been stated, the earliest known use of copper was in the Near East—in Mesopotamia and Egypt—in the early 4th millennium B.C. Considerable evidence points to the mountainous ore-bearing regions of Anatolia, Armenia, and Caucasia as the probable area in which copper metallurgy was first discovered and developed. Copper was in widespread use in the Near East by 3000 B.C. and this may be considered a good rough date for the beginning of the Bronze Age in southwestern Asia, although the general use of true bronze itself did not begin until five or six centuries later.

The Bronze Age in Europe did not begin until 2000 B.C. or later, and it was more retarded or entirely absent in parts of Asia, most of

Early Bronze Age dagger

Top view of handle

Massive Bronze Age axe with haft-hole

Bronze Age men at work

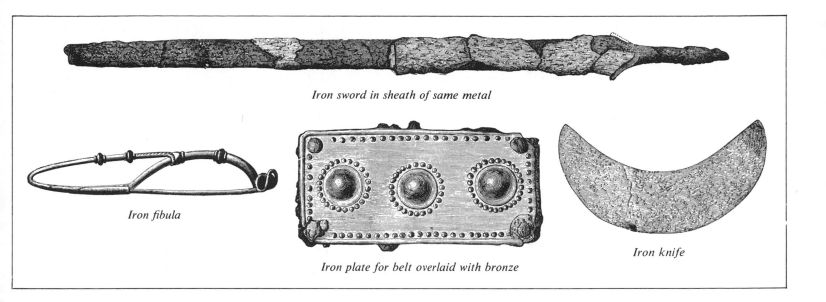

Iron sword in sheath of same metal

Iron fibula

Iron plate for belt overlaid with bronze

Iron knife

Africa, and all of Oceania. In the Near East iron began to be used extensively around 1000 B.C. The first use of iron for implements, even at considerably later dates, is considered in any area to bring the Bronze Age to a close.

e. IRON AGE

The **Iron Age** is usually considered by archaeologists to be the period of some centuries immediately following the time when iron began to replace bronze as the principal material for implements and weapons. In one sense, we are still living in the Iron Age, but the term is actually seldom used in connection with any specific culture that is later in date than the beginning of the Christian Era, except in referring to primitive peoples living in remote regions. Rare examples of early ornaments made of meteoric iron are known, and at least two cases of objects made of iron that was not meteoric (and hence may have been smelted) have been reported in Mesopotamia from levels dating before 2200 B.C. The first certain development of iron metallurgy on any scale, however, began in Asia Minor about the 14th century B.C. and in Europe in the Hallstatt region of Austria in the 11th or 10th century B.C. Iron did not penetrate to large parts of Asia and Africa until many centuries later and did not form part of any culture in the New World until introduced from Europe in the 15th and 16th centuries A.D.

2. *Modern Races of Man*

Although we know from the skeletal evidence that the five living subspecies of Man existed as far back as we can trace them in the Pleistocene, we have no evidence of soft-part morphology or pigmentation before the Upper Paleolithic cave paintings and sculptures, nor any of blood groups before modern times. But because the American Indians are as **Mongoloid** as the eastern Asiatics, we may assume that Mongoloid soft-part peculiarities go back at least to the late Upper Pleistocene.

These include straight, coarse, black head hair which grays late in life if at all, and rarely falls out; scanty beard and body hair; somewhat protuberant, relatively small eyeballs; brown iris color; a high frequency of epicanthic (inner) eye folds; skin ranging from a yellowing brunet white to a rich brown, according to latitude; and a scarcity of apocrine glands with a consequent paucity or absence of body odor. Characteristically, Mongoloids have relatively long bodies and short extremities, with small hands and feet, and little lumbar curve. Differences between the sexes in size, shape, and hair development are less than in Australoids or Caucasoids. Two face forms, one flattish nosed and the other aquiline, are found in many Mongoloid populations, with aquilinity commonest in American Indians and the Nagas of Burma and Upper Assam.

Although the **Australoids** evolved in southeastern Asia and Indonesia, at the end of the Pleistocene these lands began to be invaded by Mongoloids, leaving only dwarfed remnant populations in forested mountains and on offshore islands, and at about the same time the ancestors of the Australian aborigines, Papuans, and Melanesians moved to their previously uninhabited new homes. Other Australoids, with or without Mongoloid admixture, went to India at a time unknown. Some authorities consider it likely that the **Ainu** of northern Japan, Sakhalin Island, and the Kuriles may be the mixed, relatively depigmented descendants of an early Australoid movement up the chain of islands fringing the Pacific coast of Asia.

Australoid characteristics are skin varying from black to light brown; hair ranging from woolly to straight, and, in some areas, often blond (central Australia); full beards, body hair ranging from scant to very heavy, hair graying early in life and sometimes balding; brown eyes, large browridges, relatively flat nasal profiles, large, broad nasal tips, large teeth, and in most regions slender body build. Australoid trunk and limb proportions resemble the Caucasoid.

The **Caucasoids** invaded India postglacially on several occasions, and now they form the predominant population element in the subcontinent. They also invaded North Africa and the Sahara, siring the Berbers. Caucasoid Arabs came later. Caucasoids include Europeans and most of the western Asiatic peoples from the Mediterranean through Iran, Afghanistan, and West Pakistan to India, as well as the modern white inhabitants of the Americas, South Africa, Australia, New Zealand, and Siberia.

They resemble the Australoids most closely in body build, hair cover, graying and balding, but have a smaller frequency of curly hair. In skin color they range from virtually unpigmented to almost black, in hair color from blond to black, and in eye color from blue to brown. Their most distinctive characteristics are a relatively pointed, narrow face with little or no flattening, a narrow nose, relatively small teeth with small lateral incisors, and a reduced molar cusp formula.

The **Capoids,** represented today by the Bushmen and a few remnant tribes in Tanganyika, differ from their full-sized ancestors, whose skeletons have been found in North Africa, the Sudan, Kenya, and the Rhodesias, in being small of stature, relatively infantile in face and jaw development, and in certain aberrant features of the genitalia. They have very flat faces, often with an epicanthic fold, yellowish skin which wrinkles in mature adulthood,

tightly spiraled black hair, and brown eyes.

The **Congoids,** like the Australoids, include both full-sized and dwarfed populations, Negro and Pygmy. Negroes have relatively long forearms and lower limbs, muscles with short bellies and long tendons, narrow hips, considerable lumbar curvature, black or dark brown skins, often bulbous foreheads, large, heavily pigmented eyes, broad noses, thick, everted lips, alveolar prognathism, and large teeth. Their hair is spiral, their head hair and beards full, and their body hair usually scant. They gray relatively late. The Pygmies are short, with relatively short extremities, usually lighter in

skin color and hairier. Both have a relative abundance of apocrine glands and a body odor at the opposite extreme from the Mongoloids'.

Modern studies of blood group frequencies and fingerprints confirm the division of living man into the five subspecies listed, except that they fail to show as great a difference between Congoids and Capoids as between the others. This may perhaps be explained by the history of the Capoids, who moved from one end of Africa to the other over previously Negro territory.

3. *Regional Distribution of Post-Paleolithic Cultures*

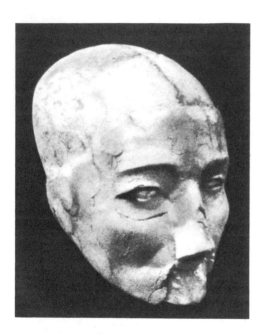

Prepottery Neolithic finds from Jericho

a. ASIA

SOUTHERN MESOPOTAMIA. Excavations at Eridu, Hajji Mohammad, Warka, Ur, Kish, Tello, Fara, Nippur, and other sites reveal the existence of a Late Neolithic or Chalcolithic culture in southern Mesopotamia during the late 5th and 4th millennia B.C. This culture has been divided into four broad periods:

c. 4500 B.C. The **Al Ubaid** period began with the appearance of painted pottery and a simple agricultural economy in the area. It is subdivided into three stylistic pottery phases: the Eridu, the Hajji Mohammad, and the Classic Ubaid. Monumental temple architecture had its inception in this period. The **Uruk** period, which followed, saw the decline of pottery painting as a craft with the first appearance of copper, cylinder seals, and writing. Monumental architecture was further developed.

c. 3000–2850 B.C. The **Jamdat Nasr** period marked the culmination of the prehistoric culture of southern Mesopotamia and led up to the **Early Dynastic** (Sumerian) period and the beginning of recorded history.

NORTHERN MESOPOTAMIA. A similar

progress can be traced in northern Mesopotamia, beginning with the Prepottery Neolithic culture of Jarmo and continuing through the later levels at sites like Matarrah, Hassuna, Nineveh, Gawra, and Arpachiyah. In many respects the northern culture differs from the southern. It is particularly marked by the appearance of the brilliant Tell Halaf pottery of about 5000 B.C. *(Cont. p. 29.)*

PALESTINE AND SYRIA. A Mesolithic culture, the **Natufian,** followed the end of the Upper Paleolithic in Palestine and lasted until about 7000 B.C. At Jericho it was succeeded by Prepottery Neolithic cultures with relationships to Syro-Cilicia and southern Anatolia. A town of unique size with stone fortification walls grew up at Jericho. The people made houses of mudbrick with polished plaster floors, and practiced a cult that made use of human skulls plastered over with clay modeled to represent human features. Around 5500 B.C. a Pottery Neolithic culture became widespread in the area.

c. 3000–2000 B.C. With the Early Bronze Age recorded history begins in this area, although our information for many centuries comes from Egyptian sources, supplemented by exca-

Painted pottery of the Al Ubaid period c. 4500 B.C.

vations at Bisan, Megiddo, Jericho, etc. An Early Bronze Age culture in Phoenicia has been revealed at Ras Shamra and Byblos, while Neolithic and Chalcolithic levels have been unearthed at Sakje-Geuzi, Carchemish, Tell Judeideh, Tabbat al-Hammam, and Chagar Bazar in northern Syria. *(Cont. p. 46.)*

ARABIA. With the exception of settlements connected with the Persian Gulf trade in the late 2nd millennium B.C. on Bahrein Island and nearby Qatar, and the historical Minaean and Sabaean kingdoms of southwestern Arabia in the 1st millennium B.C., practically nothing is known of this area.

ANATOLIA. A Pottery Neolithic culture flourished at Çatal Hüyük in the Konya Plain around 7000 B.C. Remains of textiles, clay figurines, wooden vessels, stone statuettes, shrines and private houses with beautiful wall paintings show a high level of cultural achievement. The later development of the Neolithic, Chalcolithic (3000–2600 B.C.), and Early Bronze Age (2600–1900 B.C.) is known from excavations at Haçilar, Troy, Alaça and Alishar Hüyük. The historical period begins with the founding of the first **Hittite** kingdom about 1900 B.C. *(Cont. p. 54.)*

ARMENIA AND TRANSCAUCASIA. Almost nothing is known of this region before the founding of the kingdom of **Urartu** in the 1st millennium B.C., and the beginning of history. A Chalcolithic culture has been discovered at Shamiramalti, on Lake Van, and there are dubious Neolithic and Bronze Age finds from the late 3rd and 2nd millennia B.C. south of the Caucasus. During the Early Iron Age (1000 B.C. and later) Georgia and Soviet Armenia were occupied by people who buried their dead in tumuli and who practiced an advanced metallurgy. *(Cont. p. 56.)*

IRAN AND SOVIET TURKMENISTAN. A little before 6000 B.C. Prepottery Neolithic people had begun to settle along the western edge of the Zagros Mountains at sites like Ali Kosh. By 6000 B.C. Pottery Neolithic cultures had been established in the higher valleys around Kermanshah (Tepe Sarab) and at the southern end of Lake Urmia (Hajji Firuz Tepe). By 5000 B.C. related agricultural cultures had become established along the Caspian shore (at Belt and Hotu Caves) and in Turkmenistan at Djeitun. Chalcolithic cultures characterized by fine painted pottery flourished widely in the 4th millennium B.C., notably at Anau, Namazga

Tepe, Tepe Hissar, Rayy, and Tepe Sialk in the north, at Tepe Giyan (Nihavand) in the west, and at Susa, and Persepolis in the southwest. During the 3rd millennium B.C. a Bronze Age culture using much copper, and making burnished gray pottery, spread slowly over the northern part of the country, appearing first in the east at Tepe Hissar. At the end of the 2nd and the beginning of the 1st millennia B.C. new people, who buried their dead in stone cist graves with quantities of bronze weapons, spread through the mountains of northwestern Iran. A remarkable craftsmanship in gold is also evidenced for this period in the royal tombs of Marlik Tepe near Rudbar. The ancestors of the Medes and Persians probably entered Iran at about this time. The Early Iron Age is known from excavations at Tepe Sialk and Hasanlu. *(Cont. p. 57.)*

PAKISTAN AND INDIA. Excavations and scattered finds of microlithic implements and polished stone celts attest the existence of a Mesolithic and Neolithic culture in India as early as the 4th millennium B.C., but little is known of them. At the end of the 3rd millennium B.C. a copper-using Bronze Age culture, the **Harappa culture,** flourished in the northwest at such sites as Mohenjo Daro, Chanhu Daro, Kot Diji, and Harappa. The Harappa culture occupied the Indus Valley from the Punjab to the Indian Ocean, with outposts as far west as the Iranian border (Sutkagen-dor), and as far south as Bombay (Lothal). Material remains show a civilization that rivaled that of Mesopotamia and Egypt. Toward the middle of the 2nd millennium B.C. the Harappa culture declined and was replaced in the Indus Valley by local cultures such as the **Jhukar, Jhangar,** and **Harappa Cemetery H** cultures. Traditional history begins for northern India shortly after the invasion of the Indo-Aryans toward the end of the 2nd millennium B.C., but no archaeological remains have as yet been satisfactorily identified with this event. In the 1st millennium B.C. iron was introduced, probably from Iran, and a new Iron Age civilization arose in the Ganges Valley. Many of the cities famous in later history became important during this period, which was also marked by the use of a beautiful lustrous black pottery. In central and southern India local Chalcolithic cultures persisted until the late 2nd millennium B.C. Early in the 1st millennium B.C. a southern Iron Age culture char-

Figurine from Mohenjo Daro, Harappa culture

acterized by cemeteries of megalithic tombs appeared. This culture overlapped the historic **Andhra** period and the beginning of Roman trade around the time of Christ. *(Cont. p. 60.)*

SIBERIA AND MANCHURIA. This is a marginal area, which apparently retained a Mesolithic and later a Neolithic culture longer than other parts of the continent. The Bronze Age is represented in a few places, particularly the Minusinsk region of the Upper Yenisei Valley and the region from the western slopes of the Altai Mountains to the upper courses of the Ob and Irtish Rivers. Iron was introduced late in most parts of Siberia and in the extreme north and east many of the tribes were living in a Neolithic stage of culture until the Russian explorations and colonization in the 17th century A.D.

CENTRAL ASIA. Mesolithic and Neolithic cultures existed in Mongolia, but archaeologically we know little about them and practically nothing about Chinese Turkestan and Tibet before the opening centuries of the Christian Era. Such information as we have from Chinese records does not run much before the beginning of Han times (3rd century B.C.).

CHINA. Implements of Neolithic type but of uncertain date have been found in many parts of China. The **Yang-Shao culture,** characterized by the absence of metal and the presence of painted pottery suggesting that of western Asia, existed in Honan and neighboring provinces of northern China by at least 2000

Chinese bronze ritual food vessel, 11th century B.C.

B.C. This culture partially overlapped and was succeeded by a black ware culture, the **Lungshan,** located further east in the lacustrine lowlands. Around 1400 B.C. followed the rich Bronze Age culture of the **Shang Dynasty** and the first written documents in the Far East (as found at An-yang). Numerous other remains, variously assigned to Neolithic or Bronze Ages, have been found in western Kansu, and central and south China, but are not yet well known.

JAPAN AND KOREA. The **Jomonshiki culture** (Neolithic) flourished in the northern half of the Main Island of Japan (Earliest, 4500–3700 B.C.; Early, 3700–3000 B.C.; Middle, 3000–2000 B.C.; Late, 2000–1000 B.C.; Latest 1000–250 B.C.). In the southern half of the Main Island and Kyushu there was a somewhat different Neolithic culture, represented by scattered finds dating before 250 B.C. This culture was followed by the Bronze Age **Yaiyoishiki culture** (250 B.C.–A.D. 200), with its nearest relationships with Korea, from which there were imports of bronze and, occasionally, even iron implements. Last of all was the Iron Age **Yamato,** or **Tomb, culture** (A.D. 200–A.D. 600) of the protohistoric period in central Japan, characterized by the gradual spread of iron implements and burial mounds through the whole of the Main Island.

(Cont. p. 159.)

SOUTHEASTERN ASIA. A series of prehistoric cultures has been reported from Indo-China, especially from the Hoabinhian and Bacsonian areas in Tonkin. The earliest are Mesolithic, with Paleolithic survivals (Archaic period and Intermediate period of Hoabinhian and Keo-Phay period of Bacsonian), and possibly belong to the 3rd millennium B.C. They were followed by certain Proto-Neolithic cultures (Latest period of Hoabinhian and Early and Late Bacsonian). The full Neolithic is represented by the **Somrong-Sen culture,** which spread through all parts of Indo-China in the 2nd millennium B.C. and lasted until the beginning of the Bronze Age, about 500 B.C. Cultures somewhat similar to those of Indo-China have been reported from Burma and the Malay Peninsula.

b. EUROPE

In its broad outlines the prehistory of Europe from the close of the Paleolithic Age is a record of (1) a series of profound climatic changes, producing modifications of culture and the settlement of new areas; (2) a series of cultural influences coming in from Asia and Africa; (3) a series of invasions of new peoples from Asia and Africa; and (4) the formation of new peoples and the development of new cultures as a result of the interaction of these major factors.

(1) Climatic Changes and Time-Scale

By counting and comparing the varves, or annual layers of gravel and clay laid down in post-glacial lakes in many parts of the Baltic area, archaeologists have been able tentatively to tell the year in which each layer was formed over a period covering the past 10,000 years. The thickness of the varves and an analysis of the pollen contained in them and other deposits furnish a record of the progressive climatic changes year by year and date with reasonable accuracy typical archaeological remains found in some clear relation to these deposits. This gives a basic time-scale for northern Europe,

Lung-shan pottery

which can be applied (in a general way and with modifications) to the rest of Europe, and can be checked, for the later periods, against tentative dates determined archaeologically on the basis of contacts with the historical cultures of Mesopotamia, Egypt, Greece, and Rome.

Following is the sequence of climatic periods in the Baltic region:

-8300 B.C. Sub-Arctic period. Contemporary with the Götiglacial stage of the ice retreat and end of the Paleolithic period. Very cold and characterized by *Dryas* flora, dwarf birch, willow, and tundra and steppe types of animals.

8300–7500. Pre-Boreal period. Contemporary with the Finiglacial stage of the ice retreat, the Yoldia Sea and first half of the Ancylus Lake phase of the Baltic and the beginning of the Mesolithic period. Less cold, and characterized by birch, pine, and willow trees and mixed tundra and forest types of animals.

7500–5500. Boreal period. Post-glacial and contemporary with the last half of the Ancylus Lake phase of the Baltic. Rise in sea-level. Cool, dry "continental" climate, with birch and pine dominant, but alder and oak-mixed forest coming in and animals mostly of forest and lake type.

5500–3000. Atlantic period. Contemporary with the transgression of the Litorina Sea in the Baltic. Sea-level still high. Warm and moist "oceanic" climate (the so-called *period of climatic optimum*), with alder and oak-mixed forest (oak, elm, and lime) dominant, and forest, lake, and sea types of animals.

3000–400. Sub-Boreal period. Land relatively stable with relation to the sea and the Baltic Sea largely landlocked as at present. Dry, warm climate.

400– Sub-Atlantic period. Wet, cold climate.

(2) Cultural Changes and Periods

The principal outside cultural influences that came into Europe at different times followed four main routes: (1) from western Asia through

Russia to central and western Europe; (2) from Asia Minor through the Aegean to Greece and also through Thrace to central Europe; (3) from the Near East and the Aegean by sea to the western Mediterranean; and (4) from North Africa to Spain and western Europe. Thus the general direction of cultural movement was from south to north and from east to west; hence at any given moment in time the southern and eastern areas were apt to be enjoying a more advanced form of culture than were the more peripheral regions to the northwest. This is well illustrated by the course developments took in each of the principal periods.

c. 8000– In the Mesolithic period, lasting for several thousand years, the **Tardenoisian culture,** which was most closely related to cultures in Africa and Spain and which was characterized by microlithic implements, spread from the south over most of Europe. At the same time, with the amelioration of the climate, there was a northward movement of peoples following the forests that gradually occupied the steppes and tundras of the North European plain and a forest culture was developed, characterized by the use of the chipped stone axe (Maglemosean and Ertebolle cultures).

c. 7th millennium to 3rd millennium. The full-fledged Neolithic culture in Europe appeared in the Aegean area in the 7th millennium B.C. The earliest villages are known from Thessaly and Macedonia. From Greece the food-producing economy spread to the Balkans, Bulgaria, Roumania, and Yugoslavia not later than the 6th millennium, and gradually into central Europe along the Danube.

The earliest Danubian villages in Czechoslovakia have been dated by Carbon–14 means to the first half of the 5th millennium B.C. Soon after, the Danubian farmers occupied the whole of central Europe between the Netherlands on the west and Moldavia and the western Ukraine on the east. Another wave of

Neolithic diffusion was along the Mediterranean and Adriatic coasts, possibly from southeastern Anatolia, and very likely in the 6th millennium. In the west it reached the southern parts of the Iberian peninsula. In Crete the earliest Neolithic settlement is also dated by Carbon–14 to the 6th millennium B.C. North of the Black Sea local Mesolithic people were converted to a food-producing economy in the course of the 6th and 5th millennia B.C. Northern and western Europe entered the Neolithic stage around 3000 B.C.

c. 3000– The Bronze Age culture began, for Europe, in the Aegean and Greece shortly after 3000 B.C. and copper axes appeared in Hungary a little before 2000 B.C.—in both cases due to Asiatic influence. Other copper influences came into Europe by way of Spain about 2000 B.C. and diffused widely, apparently in association with the Bell Beaker culture. At the same time there were further developments of the Megalithic culture throughout its area. The Bronze Age for Europe as a whole is usually considered to cover the period from about 1800 to 750 B.C. and is divided into three sub-periods: Early, Middle, and Late Bronze Age.

c. 750– The Iron Age began not long after 1000 B.C. with the development of iron metallurgy in Austria and its spread through the rest of Europe. The first part of the Iron Age is usually referred to as the **Hallstatt period** (about 750 B.C. to 450 B.C.), the second part of the **La Tène period** (450 B.C. to 1 A.D.).

(3) Movements of Peoples

It is still uncertain to what extent the spread of all the various cultures was due to trade and borrowing, and to what extent it involved wholesale movements of peoples. The population of Europe in the early part of the Mesolithic period probably consisted largely of the descendants of the food-gathering Upper Paleolithic peoples and was predominantly of the long-headed, white or European stock, sometimes called Atlanto-Mediterranean. Round-headed peoples began to crowd in early in Mesolithic and Neolithic times, from the east (as shown at the site of Offnet in Bavaria) and possibly from Africa (as shown in certain sites in Portugal and Spain). During the succeeding millennia the three fundamental modern European types became established in their respective areas: the Mediterraneans in southern Europe, the Alpines in central and western Europe, and the Nordics in northern Europe. During the latter part of the Bronze Age and especially in the Iron Age we have further witness to great movements of peoples in the **spread of Indo-European languages** over the larger part of Europe. Greek-speaking and Illyrian-speaking peoples came down through the Balkans into Greece, and Italic-speaking peoples into Italy; Celtic-speaking peoples moved west through central and northern Europe as far as France and the British Isles, and were followed over much the same route by Teutonic-speaking and, for part of the way, by Slavic-speaking peoples. We know these

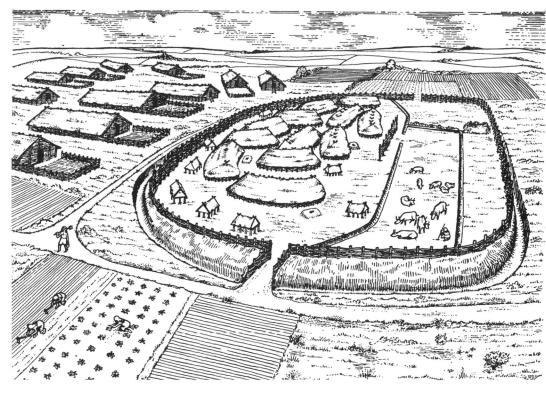

Neolithic village of the Danubian culture

Urn from the La Tène period of the Iron Age

Pottery from the Hallstatt period of the Iron Age

groups were of mixed types, but information about their physical characteristics is inadequate.

(4) Regional Distribution of Cultures

AEGEAN AREA AND GREECE. In Crete a Neolithic culture flourished for at least several millennia. This was followed by a high Bronze Age civilization (with its center at Knossos),

Late Cycladic pottery c. 1600–1500 B.C.

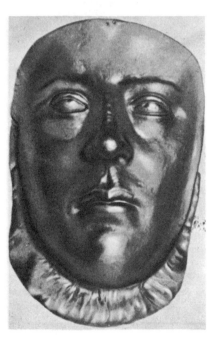

Scythian gold mask, 3rd century B.C.

Scythian clay toy cart, 1st century B.C.

which has been divided into three major periods: **Early Minoan,** 2500–2200 B.C.; **Middle Minoan,** 2200–1550 B.C.; and **Late Minoan,** 1550–1100 B.C. Similar Bronze Age cultures have been reported from Melos and other islands of the Cyclades, namely: **Early Cycladic,** 2800–2200 B.C.; **Middle Cycladic,** 2200–1650 B.C.; and **Late Cycladic,** 1650–1300 B.C. On the mainland of Greece a third series of related cultures flourished in central Greece and the Peloponnesus: Neolithic, before 2800 B.C.; **Early Helladic,** 2800–2100 B.C.; **Middle Helladic,** 2100–1550 B.C.; and **Late Helladic,** 1550–1100 B.C. In Thessaly were two Neolithic cultures, with northern affinities: **Thessalian I,** before 2600 B.C., and **Thessalian II,** 2600–2400 B.C., followed by two of the Bronze Age cultures: **Thessalian III,** 2400–1800 B.C.; and **Thessalian IV,** 1800–1200 B.C. In Cyprus the Neolithic began at least in the 6th millennium, after which developed a series of Bronze Age cultures. During the latter half of the 2nd millennium B.C. the so-called **Mycenaean culture** (Late Helladic), with its center in Mycenae in the Peloponnesus, spread throughout Greece and the whole Aegean area, with extensions to western Asia Minor, Cyprus, and Syria. The Iron Age in Greece began about 1000 B.C. with the Geometric period, the close of which marked the beginning of history in this area.

RUSSIA. North of the Black Sea a local Neolithic culture lasted up to about the middle of the 3rd millennium when it was disturbed by the invasion of the steppe or Kurgan (Barrow) people from beyond the lower Volga. Subsequently, in the whole northern Pontic region and the northern Caucasus, the **Kurgan culture** (also called Ochre-Grave or Pit-Grave) firmly established itself and later spread further to the Caucasus, Anatolia, the Aegean, central, and northern Europe. The enormous Kurgan expansion may have brought the Indo-European language to Europe. During the Bronze Age, the offshoots of the Kurgan culture differentiated into the north Pontic or Cimmerian, the lower Volga or Timber-Grave, and the Fat'janovo in central Russia, the latter closely related to the culture in the East Baltic area and Poland. The most aggressive was the **Timber-Grave** or **Proto-**

Scythian culture which gradually advanced to the Black Sea coasts and ultimately, in the 8th century B.C., to central Europe. The heirs of the Timber-Grave and its sister branch in Siberia, the **Andronovo culture,** are called by the general name Scythians. The Scythian culture, north of the Black Sea, flourished from the 7th to the 4th centuries B.C. Later the Scythians were replaced by another kindred group of eastern origin, the Sarmatians.

In northern Russia and the northern East Baltic area, a large Neolithic or Sub-Neolithic cultural bloc characterized by a primitive pit and comb impressed pottery differentiated during the Bronze Age into the **Turbino culture** in the east, the **Textile Pottery** in northern central Russia, and the **Asbestos Pottery** in Carelia and northwestern Russia. Many local variants emerged from these during the Early Iron Age and continued into history. These northern groups belonged to the Finno-Ugrian and Lapp families.

THE BALKANS AND CENTRAL EUROPE. Throughout the Neolithic period the Balkan peninsula remained intimately related with and was continually influenced by the Anatolian cultures. The basic characteristics are: large stratified tells (mounds), female figurines, and noteworthy pottery, usually painted.

Throughout the millennia many local cultural groups formed, flourished, and declined and new cultural variants arose. The following groups, dating from the 6th to the 4th millennia B.C., can be treated as separate cultures: **Proto-Sesklo** and **Sesklo** in Greece; **Starčevo** in western Bulgaria, eastern Yugoslavia, southern and western Roumania (the earliest full-fledged Neolithic culture in this area); **Veselinovo** in eastern Bulgaria, with strong Anatolian elements, which replaced Starčevo in central Bulgaria and southern Roumania; **Boian** in Roumania, which partly supplanted Starčevo; **Hamangia,** a recently discovered cultural group along the Black Sea coast, mainly in Dobruja; **Gumelnita,** a later Neolithic-Chalcolithic culture, probably derived from Hamangia or Boian, which replaced both Hamangia and Boian; **Vadastra,** a sister branch of Boian in western Roumania, and its later development; **Pre-Tripolye** (c. 5th mil-

Scythian gold ornament, 4th century B.C.

lennium B.C.), between the Dniester and Dnieper, which developed into the **Tripolye Painted Pottery culture** in the 4th and 3rd millennia B.C.

From the end of the 5th and during the 4th millennia B.C. new Anatolian influences caused remarkable changes in the peninsula resulting in the appearance of the Vinca-Tisza-Lengyel bloc in the central Balkans and the middle Danube basin. The Sesklo culture developed in this period into a **Dimini culture.**

In central Europe the so-called **Danubian culture** is held to be an outpost of the Balkan Starčevo culture, but developed its local character due to different climatic and soil conditions. Its eastern part was disturbed by the coming of the Lengyel people. The rest of the culture continued into the beginning of the 3rd millennium B.C. when it was rivaled by the northern European peoples known as **Funnel Beakers** and **Michelsberg.**

These long-lasting cultural groups were disturbed or conquered by the invasion of the Kurgan steppe peoples, very probably Indo-European speaking, around 2300–2200 B.C. This brought the beginning of a new era in Europe characterized by a mixture of cultural elements and the formation of new cultural groups.

The European Bronze Age had its beginnings in the mountainous regions, chiefly in the Carpathians. During the early 2nd millennium remarkable bronze cultures arose, such as the **Unětice** in central Europe followed by the Middle Bronze Age Tumulus and Late Bronze Age Urnfield periods, and the **Otomani** in Transylvania, both of Kurgan origin. The growth and expansions of the Únětice-Tumulus-Urnfield culture brought changes in ethnic configurations, bringing an end, towards the close of the 13th and the 12th centuries B.C., to the Mycenaean period in Greece, to the Hittite empire in Anatolia, and to local cultures in Italy, the Balkans, and eastern France. The central European Bronze Age culture was a cradle of the Celtic, Italic, Venetic, Illyrian, Phrygian, and the Armenian speaking peoples. In eastern Roumania (Moldavia) a distinctive culture called **Monteoru** formed and developed throughout the Bronze Age. South of it on the lower Danube the **Tei culture** flourished. Both

Hallstatt bucket from the Early Iron Age

of these may have been created by ancient Thracians. The first iron artifacts in central Europe appeared in the last centuries of the 2nd millennium B.C., but a true Iron Age started only near the end of the 8th and in the 7th centuries with the beginning of the **Hallstatt culture,** created by the Celts and Illyrians in the Alpine zone and north of the Adriatic Sea. Hallstatt was followed by the Celtic **La Tène,** which continued to Roman times.

ITALY. The earliest Neolithic culture in southern Italy, Sicily, and Liguria is represented by the **Impressed Pottery culture,** called Molfetta, Stentinello, and Arene Candide. It is of east Mediterranean origin and dates back to the 6th or 5th millennia B.C. This was followed by the **Painted Pottery culture** in southern Italy and Sicily with affinities in the east Adriatic area and Greece. The Copper Age started c. 3000 B.C. in Sicily. In eastern Sicily the sequence of Copper Age cultures is characterized by changing painted pottery styles: Conzo, Serraferlicchio, and Malpasso, followed by the Early Bronze Age Castellucio, Middle Bronze Age Thapsos, and Late Bronze Age Pantalica complexes. The local culture of central Italy was interrupted by the appearance of eastern (Kurgan) elements at c. 2000 B.C., which created a hybrid culture called Rinaldone. In the rest of the southern part of the peninsula a local culture called Apennine persisted throughout the greater part of the 2nd millennium B.C.

The Neolithic in northern Italy is little known except for Liguria. Around 2000 B.C. it was reached by the western Bell Beaker people under whose influence the Bronze Age Remedello culture in the Po Valley was formed, succeeded by the Terramare culture which lasted up to the infiltration of central European elements in Italy in the 13th and 12th centuries B.C. After the formative Previllanovian period of the 2nd millennium's last centuries **Villanova culture** (1000–600 B.C.) arose, which maintained intimate relations with central Europe.

ISLANDS OF THE WESTERN MEDITERRANEAN. A remarkable Neolithic development, characterized by massive stone temples and underground structures, took place in Malta. In Sardinia there was a distinctive Chalcolithic culture (Anghelu Ruju) shortly after 2000 B.C., followed by various phases of Megalithic (Giants' Tombs, dolmens, and Nuraghis), much of which dates to the early half of the 1st millennium B.C. There was a related Bronze Age culture, with stone constructions (Navetas and Talayots) in the Balearic Islands.

SPAIN. There were several cultures in the Iberian Peninsula in the Mesolithic period: Final Capsian in the south and center, Tardenoisian and Azilian in the north, and two special developments, the Portuguese Kitchen Middens in the west and the Asturian culture in the northwest. Some of these lasted well into the 3rd millennium B.C. and were succeeded by various Neolithic cultures of which the most important developments were in the southeast (Almerian culture) and in Portugal and Galicia (Megalithic). New trends in the development of the culture in the Iberian Peninsula started with the appearance of eastern Mediterranean colonists in the early 3rd millennium. The **Bell Beaker culture** (about 2000 B.C.) ushered in the Bronze Age, which was marked by a continuation of the Megalithic and, in the southeast, by the development of the **El Argar culture** (middle

Bronze shield, La Tène style

of 2nd millennium B.C.) in southeastern Spain. In the early part of the 1st millennium B.C. there was a local Iron Age culture, with Hallstatt affinities, which lasted until the time of the first Punic and Greek colonies (about 500 B.C.).

WESTERN EUROPE. Two cultures, the Tardenoisian and the Azilian, were dominant in western Europe during the Early Mesolithic period, with the Asturian (Late Mesolithic) partially represented in southern France and the Maglemosean (Early Mesolithic) in northern France and Belgium. Neolithic influences were late in arriving, but by the middle of the 4th millennium B.C., or earlier, there was a Neolithic culture, of Mediterranean origin, in the south. The Bell Beaker culture appeared here shortly after 2000 B.C., while the Megalithic culture spread through the coastal region (especially in Brittany), and influences from central Europe and the Rhine contributed to the development of the Bronze Age in France. Well along in the 1st millennium B.C. this gave way to a western version of the Hallstatt culture, which was followed, as elsewhere in Europe, by the La Tène.

The **British Isles** had a somewhat similar but still more retarded development. In the Mesolithic period a survival of the Upper Paleolithic Creswellian culture was modified in certain

Cult objects, Bell Beaker culture, British Isles

Electrum torque, British Isles, 1st century B.C.

Estonia. The Komsa and Fosna cultures continued in Norway, and Tardenoisian developed further at various points on the North German plain. In the Atlantic period (5500–3000 B.C.) the Ertebolle culture developed out of the Maglemosean, while the Komsa, Fosna, Tardenoisian, and a late version of Maglemosean survived in marginal areas. The beginning of the Neolithic period is synchronous with the beginning of the Sub-Boreal phase, c. 3000 B.C. At about 2500 B.C. the Early Neolithic elements were profoundly modified by the introduction of the Megalithic civilization, which had spread along the Atlantic seaboard, and the eastern Kurgan elements which spread via central Europe. Several distinct but contemporary cultures developed, viz.: Megalithic Battle-Axe or Separate Graves of Kurgan origin, Arctic, and Dwelling-Place cultures. In 1500 B.C. or thereabouts the Scandinavian and Baltic Bronze Age began, which was followed later by the Iron Age.

c. AFRICA

EGYPT. The Mesolithic period witnessed the final stages of the Sebilian culture. The Neolithic period began early in the Nile Valley (probably before 4000 B.C.) and is represented by the Fayum, Merimdean, Tasian, and Badarian cultures. During the 4th millennium B.C., under combined African and Asiatic influences, the important **predynastic culture** developed (Amratian, Gerzean, and Semainian phases), and ended about 3000 B.C. with the establishment of the First Dynasty and the beginning of the historical period.

NORTHWESTERN AFRICA. Mesolithic cultures (final stages of the Mouillian and Capsian) were, at dates as yet undetermined, modified and transformed by the infiltration of Neolithic influences, which spread gradually through Tunisia, Algeria, and Morocco and south across the Sahara. Bronze was late in reaching the Mediterranean coastal regions of this area, and did not penetrate the interior; generally stone did not give way to metal until the Punic Iron Age in the 1st millennium B.C.

EAST AFRICA. Following the close of the Pleistocene in this area the Capsian (formerly called the Aurignacian) penetrated the highlands from the north and two other Microlithic

areas by the introduction of Azilian influences into southwestern Scotland, Maglemosean in southern and eastern England, and Tardenoisian more or less generally. About 3000 B.C., Neolithic features first appeared, in connection with the Windmill Hill culture and the Long Barrows. Bronze came into England some time after 2000 B.C. (Beaker culture, Long Barrows, and Round Barrows). About the end of the 8th century new bronze-using peoples from the continent invaded England, bringing some iron with them. The true Iron Age began about 400 B.C. with an invasion of continental peoples enjoying a predominantly Hallstatt culture (Iron Age A). They were followed, in the 1st century B.C., by La Tène peoples (Iron Age B), the Belgae (Iron Age C), and the Romans. Modified forms of some of these cultures reached Scotland and Ireland but at considerably later dates.

BALTIC REGION. In the early part of the Mesolithic, which corresponds to the Pre-Boreal period (8300–7500 B.C.), tanged-point cultures (Remouchamps, Ahrensburg-Lavenstadt, and Swiderian) occupied the north European plain from Belgium to Poland, with outliers in northern and western Norway (Komsa and Fosna cultures), but there were traces of an early Tar-

denoisian and the beginning of the new forest or axe cultures (Lyngby). In the Boreal period (7500–5500 B.C.), a Mesolithic axe culture, the Maglemosean, with many local variants, spread widely over the whole area from Yorkshire to

Stylized dance group, late Neolithic, Africa

cultures developed (Wilton A and B) and another culture (Elmenteitan), but the dates of all three may be somewhat late as pottery was already present in Elmenteitan. The succeeding cultures (Gumban A and B, Njoroan, Wilton C, and Tumbian) were clearly Early Neolithic in character but not necessarily in date. There was apparently no true Bronze Age in this part of Africa and iron gradually replaced stone during the Christian Era.

SOUTH AFRICA. In what is termed the Later Stone Age of this area, two Mesolithic cultures, Wilton and Smithfield, spread through the greater part of South Africa, beginning at some time after the close of the Pleistocene and continuing with modifications until the Bantu invasions brought iron to the region at a comparatively recent date. South Africa had no true Neolithic period or Bronze Age, although some traces of agriculture and occasional polished stone implements have been found.

CENTRAL AND WEST AFRICA. This also was a marginal region. Mesolithic implements have been found in parts of the Sudan. The Tumbian culture (Mesolithic) was represented in the Congo Basin and persisted after the introduction of polished stone. Various other Neolithic cultures of more fully developed form but uncertain date have been reported from the Sudan and Nigeria. A true Bronze Age is not found here, and iron was late in arriving, but during the Christian Era bronze casting received a special development, notably in Benin.

d. OCEANIA

Australia, New Guinea, and the islands of Melanesia, Micronesia, and Polynesia were uninhabited before the end of the Pleistocene, when Australia and New Guinea were first occupied. The outer islands were reached much later. The first movement of peoples concerned was that of the Australoids from Indonesia along the Lesser Sundas to the Sahul Shelf, which was then out of water, and which connected Australia with New Guinea and Tasmania. This migration required short sea voyages in canoes or rafts.

Australian archaeologists have found various stone tool industries with choppers, chopping-tools, and flakes, and the living aborigines make all of these, plus blades and microliths in a few

Palace of the Chimu princes, Peruvian area

places. Some had learned to grind chopping tools into axes.

At an unknown time Australoids of Papuan type occupied the Melanesian island chain, perhaps as far as New Caledonia and Fiji. Later, probably not long before the time of Christ, predominantly Mongoloid peoples from Indonesia and Southeast Asia introduced garden agriculture, pigs, poultry, and polished stone axes to most of these islands, as well as Melanesian languages, although in the interior and south of New Guinea and the interiors of some of the other islands Papuan is still spoken.

The Polynesians and Micronesians are peoples of largely Mongoloid origin with some Australoid features. This condition is probably due to the fact their ancestors came from the coast of South China, which was a Mongoloid-Australoid frontier before the Chinese expansion forced various coastal peoples out to sea, the Polynesians apparently for the most part

passing by the already occupied regions and pressing east across the Pacific to Micronesia and Polynesia. The date of these movements was comparatively recent. Navigation received its real development in this part of the world in the 1st millennium B.C. The first long voyages into Micronesia and Polynesia probably did not begin until the 4th century A.D., and the farther islands were not settled until some centuries later.

The majority of the peoples who took part in the settlement of Oceania were in a Neolithic stage of culture like that of southeast Asia and Indonesia. There is no concrete evidence to support the view that Polynesia was settled from South America.

e. AMERICA

Studies of the physical characteristics of **American Indians** show these to be predominantly Mongoloid, while there seems to be in both continents a marginal distribution of a stock that may represent the descendants of a group of very early arrivals possibly related in part to the Ainu.

At the time of the first European contact with America in the 16th and 17th centuries A.D., some Indians were still hunters and food-gatherers, like their Paleolithic ancestors, but the great majority were in a Neolithic stage of culture. The fact that they had no cereals that were cultivated in the Old World and no Old World domestic animals except the dog has led to the general opinion that agriculture and the domestication of animals were in this case independent developments after arrival in the New World. Certain polished stone tools, however, and even certain types of pottery show relationship to forms found in northeastern Asia. So two of the four main elements of Neolithic culture may show some evidence of a continuation of Asiatic tradition. In a few

Women running, northern Australian rock painting

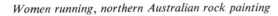

Model of Aztec temple at Tenayuca, Mexico

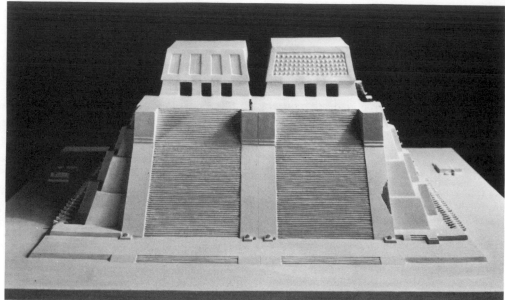

Mayan stone sculpture from Yucatan

Ruins of the Gate of the Sun, Tiahuanaco, Bolivia

cases American Indian groups passed beyond the Neolithic stage, as is indicated by the use of metal.

The first advanced culture in the western hemisphere is believed to have had its origin over two thousand years ago in the Andean region of South America and in the highland region of Central America and Mexico. Here grew up a high civilization, parallel in many striking ways to that of the Old World but probably entirely independent of it. The cultivation of Indian corn (*Zea mais*) was the basis of the new economy. Rich textiles, fine pottery, and magnificent ornaments of gold, silver, and copper were produced. Great city centers arose, with canals and gardens and monumental temples on lofty pyramids. A highly complex social organization was developed, with priest-

emperors, standing armies, schools, courts, and systematized religions. Intellectual progress was marked by astronomical research, the invention of accurate calendars, and—in Yucatan and Mexico—an elaborate hieroglyphic writing.

In the Peruvian area the early Nasca and Chimu cultures were followed by Tiahuanacan and, in immediately pre-Columbian times, by the **Inca civilization.** Influences spread from this center across the Andes into the Amazon Basin and down the Andes to the Argentine region. Farther north, the Chibchan and Chorotegan cultures occupied the intervening area between Peru and Yucatan, where the **Maya civilization,** the climax of native American achievement, developed during the 1st millennium B.C. and reached its culmination shortly before the Spanish Conquest. Similarly, in the

Valley of Mexico the Archaic and Toltec cultures culminated in the **Aztec civilization,** discovered by the Spaniards. The effect of these powerful centers of influence must have been felt in lessening degree throughout much of North America, especially in the advanced cultures of the Pueblo area of the southwest, the southeast, and the Mound Builder area in the Mississippi drainage. Simpler cultures occupied the woodlands area of the northeastern United States and Canada and the Central Plains. California was a marginal region, occupied largely by food-gatherers of a low stage of culture, while the Indians of the northwest coast and the Eskimos of Alaska and northern Canada had, each in their own way, developed highly specialized cultures, which suggest to some extent Asiatic relationships.

II. Ancient History

II. Ancient History

A. Early Kingdoms of Asia and Africa

1. *Mesopotamia, to 333* B.C.

a. THE LAND AND THE PEOPLE

MESOPOTAMIA as a geographical term in its widest sense applies to the lands bordering and lying between the Euphrates and Tigris rivers, reaching from the foothills of the Armenian Taurus range in the northwest to the ancient shore of the Persian Gulf, on the west bounded by the steppes of the Great Syrian Desert, on the east by the barrier of the Zagros Mountains. The lands naturally divide into two sections, Upper Mesopotamia—the Mesopotamia proper of the Greeks, called today the **Jezireh** —and Lower Mesopotamia or Babylonia, the black alluvial plain south of modern Baghdad. In antiquity Upper Mesopotamia had two primary centers of civilization. One was in the country of the Upper Euphrates and included such ancient cities as Carchemish on the Euphrates, Harran on the Balikh and Gozan on the Khabur tributaries of the Euphrates, and further south on the Euphrates, Mari. In this territory arose the Hurrian **kingdom of Mitanni** (15th century) and the Amorite power at **Mari** (18th century). Another center was on the Upper Tigris near the confluences of the Greater and Lesser Zab. This was the country of ancient **Assyria** whose chief cities were Assur, Ninevah, Calah (modern Nimrud), and Dur Sharrukin (modern Khorsabad).

Lower Mesopotamia, the site of ancient **Sumer** and **Akkad,** also falls naturally into northern and southern sections. The northern part centered around **Babylon,** and included such additional cities as Eshnunna on the Diyala, and Sippar, Kutha, Kish, Borsippa, and Isin on the ancient Euphrates or its canals. In the deep south were the old Sumerian cities of **Eridu** and **Ur** with access to the Persian Gulf. The shoreline of the ancient gulf may have reached farther north than at present, or the cities may have been situated on a lagoon; there is conflicting evidence. Farther north

were the cities of **Larsa, Uruk** (biblical Erech), **Lagash** and **Umma. Nippur,** in the middle of the country, was the religious center of Sumer and Akkad. These southern lands were marshy, capable of sustaining a significant population only when elaborate drainage canals and irrigation works were installed in the course of the 4th millennium.

The population of both Upper and Lower Mesopotamia in prehistoric times belonged to the brown, or Mediterranean, race. While this basic stock persisted in historical times, especially in the south, it became increasingly mixed, especially with broad-headed Armenoid peoples from the northeastern mountains, owing to recurrent incursions of mountain tribes into the plain.

The earliest settlers in Mesopotamia known to the historian were the **Sumerians,** who probably created the irrigation culture of Mesopotamia in Chalcolithic (Obeidian) times, beginning not long after 4000 *(p. 18)*. The Sumerians are of unknown origin. They spoke an agglutinative language which has no clear or close

Sumerian finds from Ur

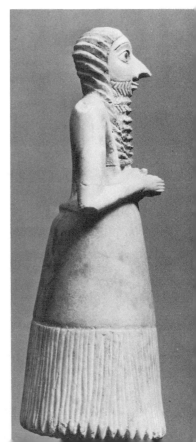

Find from the Protoliterate period of the Mesopotamian civilization

Cuneiform inscription (archaic characters)

relationship to any known family of languages. **Semitic peoples,** presumably from the edges of the desert, and perhaps from the more arid areas of Upper Mesopotamia, were found living side by side with the Sumerians in apparent harmony in earliest historical times. As early as Protodynastic times (2850–2360), dynasts with Semitic names are found in northern Lower Mesopotamia, and the **Akkadians,** as these Semitic-speaking folk came to be called, had become dominant in this district before the rise of the Akkadian dynasty of Sargon (c. 2360–2180). Their Semitic dialect is called Akkadian. From the Old Akkadian of the 3rd millennium developed two major East Semitic dialects, **Assyrian,** spoken on the Upper Tigris, and **Babylonian.** In the course of the 2nd millennium Babylonian became the *lingua franca* of the ancient world, in use in both the Egyptian and Hittite empires.

In addition to the Sumerians and Akkadians, Mesopotamia was occupied by a series of non-Semitic invaders from the northeastern mountains, and by West Semitic tribes from the adjacent deserts. The former include the **Gutians,** who brought to an end the dynasty of Akkad toward 2180 B.C., the **Hurrians** (biblical Horites), whose main movement beginning about 1700 overwhelmed Upper Mesopotamia, and the **Kashshu** (Cossaeans), whose incursions into Babylonia began in the 17th century, and who ruled Babylonia for nearly a half millennium. West Semitic peoples who successfully invaded Mesopotamia include the **Amorites,** who founded the 1st dynasty of Babylon in the 19th century, the **Aramaeans,** whose incursions began toward the end of the 12th century, and the **Chaldeans,** founders of the Neo-Babylonian empire in the 7th century. In Late Assyrian

and Babylonian times, Babylonian gave way to **Aramaic** as the dominant spoken language of Mesopotamia. Aramaic served also as the *lingua franca* of the successive Assyrian, Neo-Babylonian, and Persian empires. Sumerian and Babylonian survived only as learned or religious tongues, dying out finally in Seleucid times.

b. CHRONOLOGY

The chronology of Mesopotamia rests on an extraordinary complex of sources and data which is constantly growing, thanks to archaeological activity. Among the major sources are classical authors, notably the **Canon of Ptolemy** (2nd century A.D.) and fragments of **Berossus** (3rd century B.C.), cuneiform documents including the great Assyrian, Babylonian, and Sumerian king lists, the eponym lists, the Synchronistic Chronicle, building inscriptions; and as well, astronomical data, literary and archaeological synchronisms tying Mesopotamia to Egypt, Syria-Palestine, and Anatolia; and in the early period, Carbon-14 dates.

The major framework of Mesopotamian history is fixed back into the 12th century B.C. within a year or two. Problems or lacunae disturbing calculation exist in the king lists in the 12th, 15th, and 17th centuries especially, and by the 18th century the range of possible error has mounted to more than a half century. Astronomical observations (the **Venus Tablets** of Ammisaduqa) exist for this era and, when sufficient data are in hand, promise to fix the chronology of the 2nd and late 3rd millennia. At present we must choose between two solutions yielded by astronomical calculation, 64 years apart. One gives the *Middle Chronology,* which places Hammurapi's reign in the years 1792–1750; the alternate, the *Low Chronology,* fixes his dates at 1728–1686. Babylonian records are more easily fitted, perhaps, to the Middle Chronology. Carbon-14 dates exclude neither chro-

Ziqqurat excavated at Ur

nology, but tend to favor later dates. The strongest evidence for the Lower Chronology consists of indirect archaeological synchronisms with Egypt, where the chronology is astronomically fixed. For example, the great Middle Bronze Age city at Hazor in Palestine, founded about 1750 following the fall of the Middle Kingdom in Egypt, is well known at Mari in the age brought to an end by the conquests of Hammurapi. Egypt on the other hand goes without mention in the Mari correspondence, a silence that seems incredible if the imperial power of the Middle Kingdom were at its zenith. The Low Chronology appears best at this time and is followed here in giving dates in the 2nd and 3rd millennia.

c. THE RISE OF MESOPOTAMIAN CIVILIZATION

The first great civilization of mankind was created by the Sumerians in Lower Mesopotamia. The formation of the basic lines of this culture took place early, in the **Protoliterate period** (3200–2850 B.C.). As its name suggests this era was marked by the **invention of writing**. The earliest known inscriptions, clay tablets in a pictographic forebear of cuneiform, were found in a temple of Uruk dating from shortly before 3000. The earliest tablets that can be interpreted fully are the archaic texts of Ur, from about 2800. The Protoliterate age witnessed the emergence of the highly organized city state, with its complex of irrigation works elaborated from earlier canal systems. True **ziqqurats,** the towers that dominated the Sumerian temple complex, began to rise from the plain. In much later times the "Tower of Babel," a structure of seven stages topped by a temple, would reach nearly 300 feet into the heavens. The influence of Protoliterate Mesopotamia spread as far as Egypt, stimulating the nascent civilization of the Nile Valley into a burst of energetic growth. This age and the subsequent period of classical Sumer and Akkad created a cultural world of myth and literature, polity, art, and science that dominated ancient Mesopotamia until the demise of the ancient Oriental world, and that ultimately bequeathed a legacy of legal and religious tradition to Israel, and of magical, astronomical, and mathematical lore to Greece.

The city state in earliest Mesopotamia was organized economically and religiously into **temple communities** headed by a priestly representative of the patron deity or deities of the city. A political assembly of citizens or elders also ruled. Later this primitive combination of theocracy and democracy in the cities gave way to rule by an **ensi,** a "governor," holding sway over both the religious and political establishment, or to rule by a **lugal,** "king," a superior title often used by sovereigns claiming wider dominion. In imperial times, highly centralized forms of monarchy emerged.

The **Sumerian gods** in earliest times were closely bound to natural phenomena, the powers of creativity, fertility, and forces confronted in the cosmos. Even at the dawn of history, however, these gods were conceived for the most part in human form and were organized in a cosmic state reflecting the social forms of pre-monarchical Sumer. The world of the gods was a macrocosm of Sumer where earthly temples, counterparts of cosmic abodes of the gods,

forged links between the two realms. The assembly of the gods included four pre-eminent deities, **Anu,** the old god of the sky, titular head of the assembly; **Enlil,** young "Lord Storm," the violent as well as life-giving air; **Ninkhursag** or Ninmakh, the great mother, personification of the fertility of the earth; and **Enki,** god of underground waters, the source of the "masculine" powers of creativity in the earth. Another important triad consisted of **Nanna** (moon), **Utu** (sun), and **Inanna** (Venus). The chief cult-dramas included the cosmogonic battle enacted in the New Year's festival, in which Enlil, later Marduk of Babylon, established order by defeating the powers of chaos, and assumed kingship. Another important cycle of rites had to do with Dumuzi (Tammuz), with laments over his death, celebration of the return to life of the young god and his union (*heiros gamos*) with Inanna (Semitic Ishtar) which assured spring's resurgent life.

d. LOWER MESOPOTAMIA, 3200–1025 B.C.

3200–2850. THE PROTOLITERATE PERIOD. A system of city states dominated by temples emerged. Semitic tribes speaking Akkadian began to settle on the fringes of Sumer, especially in the north. Writing was invented.

2850–2360. THE EARLY DYNASTIC OR CLASSICAL SUMERIAN AGE. The legendary **1st Dynasty of Uruk** may date from the first phase of this period if not earlier. Included in it are the divine or deified heroes of later epic tradition, Enmerkar, Lugalbanda, Tammuz, and Gilgamesh. The Archaic Tablets of Ur also come from early in the era. In the era called **Early Dynastic II,** beginning about 2600, the Akkadians grew increasingly powerful in the north. Several of the dynasts of Kish, for example, bore Semitic names. In the building arts the plano-convex brick was introduced and the great wall of Uruk, some 5½ miles in circumference, was constructed. The Shuruppak Tablets, among them the earliest list of the gods, come from the 26th century. To the same century we probably must assign **Mesilim,** called king of Kish, known both from contemporary and later sources. The last phase of the Early Dynastic period begins about 2500. The **1st Dynasty of Ur** appears to have gained hegemony. Its best known rulers are **Mesannepadda** and **Aannepadda,** and it may be that the rich "Royal Tombs of Ur" are to be attributed to this dynasty. Much more is known of the city state of **Lagash. Urnanshe** founded a vigorous dynasty at Lagash, contemporary with the 1st Dynasty of Ur. His grandson **Eannatum** (c. 2460) was a great warrior, defeating Sumerian cities including Ur in the south and Kish in the north, and extending his power into Elam and as far as Mari. His victory over Umma is recorded on the celebrated **Stele of Vultures.** Lagash's overlordship of Sumer was short-lived, however, and was passed over unmentioned in the canonical king list. At the close of the Early Dynastic Era, **Urukagina** took power in Lagash, instituting the first known social reforms in history. **Lugalzaggisi** (c. 2360), ensi of Umma, defeated Lagash, however, and went on to subdue all of Sumer, ruling as king of Uruk.

2360–2180. THE DYNASTY OF AKKAD.

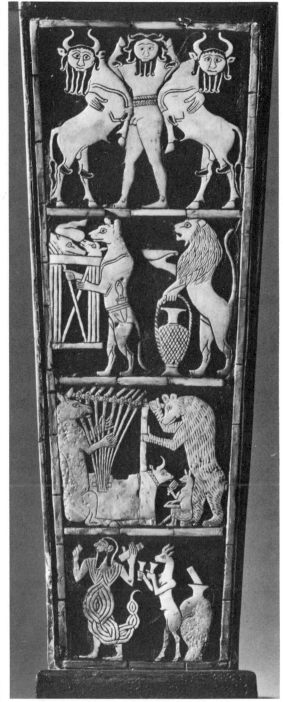

Inlay on the sound box of a harp from the "Royal Tombs of Ur"

Sargon the Great (2360–2305) rose from mean origins in the service of Urzababa, king of Kish. The details of his revolt and achievement of royal rank are not clear. In any case, he built Akkad (Agade) as the new seat of his dynasty, fell on Uruk, defeating and capturing Lugalzaggisi, and in a series of battles reduced the last of the independent states of Sumer. Sargon the Akkadian was able to achieve what no Sumerian of classical times had done: he placed the city states of north and south, Akkad and Sumer, under a highly organized central government. On this base he built the **first world empire.** He gained control of the Persian Gulf, conquered Elam, the mountain lands of Iran, Upper Mesopotamia, and Syria, ruling from "sea to sea." Later legends, including those of the epic tale *King of Battle*, describe Sargon as extending his conquests into Anatolia and even across the sea to Crete. Rimush (2304–2296) and Manishtushu (2295–2281), the sons of Sargon, consolidated the empire. **Naramsin** (2280–2244), Sargon's grandson, brought Akkad to the zenith of its power and peaceful accomplishment. He was the first of the Mesopotamian kings to claim divinity, and to style himself "king of the four quarters" (of the world). The names of Sargon and Naramsin lived on in Babylonian, Hurrian, and Hittite legends as the greatest of Mesopotamian rulers. In the Akkadian era the arts flourished. The Sumerian script was adapted to Akkadian and perfected. Inscriptions and buildings of the dynasty were spread from the Mediterranean to Susa. Trade flourished even with the distant Indus Valley. **Sharkalisharri** (2243–2219), the last of Sargon's line, reigned in a time of troubles, defending his narrowing borders against the blows of surrounding barbarians. After him ephemeral kings held Akkad for some years longer, but the city fell about 2180 to Guti hordes from the Zagros.

c. 2180–2082. The Gutian Dynasty. During the dark interlude of Gutian rule, the Sumerians of the south revived. Utukhegal of Uruk drove out the Guti and re-established the Sumerian kingdom. Urbaba of Lagash flourished.

c. 2060–1950. 3RD DYNASTY OF UR: The Sumerian Renaissance. Urnammu of Ur (c. 2060–2043) seized power from his suzerain Utukhegal, and founded a new Sumerian dynasty. He was a vigorous ruler dedicated to restoring the glories of the Sumerian past. The oldest law code, a forerunner of later Sumerian law and the great code of Hammurapi, comes from his reign. Under the long reign of his son **Shulgi** (2042–1995), the feudal empire of Ur became most highly developed. He governed Elam, Assyria, and northwestern Mesopotamia, and like his Akkadian predecessors, proclaimed himself a god, king of the four quarters of the world. Bursin (1994–1986) and Shusin (1985–1977) maintained the empire. The vast program of temple building and refurbishing initiated by their fathers continued, adding to the brilliance of the Sumerian revival. In the time of Shusin, however, we hear of the building of a line of fortifications on the west to hold at bay the Amorites of the steppe. Fairly early in the reign of **Ibbisin** (1976–1952), the last of the emperors of Ur, the West Semitic Amorite tribesmen swept over Sumer and Akkad, devastating the land. The empire tottered. Later in Ibbisin's reign vassals took advantage of mounting difficulty to proclaim their independence of Ur. Ishbierra, governor of Mari, rebelled, established a kingdom at Isin, and controlled the north. Elam asserted its independence and at last furnished the coup de grâce. Ur was destroyed, an event remembered in a famous lament, and Ibbisin taken prisoner to Elam.

The imperial age of Ur was a golden age of **Sumerian literature.** Most of the surviving myth, epic, and gnomic literature of the Sumerians probably came into final form in this period, to be fixed in writing by copyists of the succeeding Old Babylonian period. **Gudea,** ensi of Lagash (c. 2000), a vassal of Ur, is one of the most brilliant figures of the period. His building inscriptions contain the most extensive and important texts we possess of the Sumerian renaissance.

During this period **Babylonian mathematics** reached its high level with a numbering system based upon the developed sexagesimal system with a place-value notation for both whole numbers and fractions. Also surviving are tables of squares and square roots, of cubes and cube roots, and of the sums of squares and cubes needed for numerical evaluation of cubic equations and exponential functions. Tables of Pythagorean numbers are also extant, showing that Pythagoras's equation was used many years before its formal solution.

The buildings were of mud-brick and although impressive have not survived like those of the Egyptian civilization. The **Hanging Gardens of Babylon** (one of the seven wonders of the Ancient World) was a stepped pyramid structure.

1960–1700. THE ISIN-LARSA PERIOD. The Isin Dynasty (1953–1730) and Larsa Dynasty (1961–1699) struggled for hegemony following the fall of the 3rd Dynasty of Ur.

Upper part of stele with Hammurapi's code

Portrait bust of Gudea, ensi of Lagash

Figurine with inscriptions of Waradsin

Stele of Naramsin

Both were to give way to Babylon. **Ishbierra,** king of Isin (1953–1921), claimed the crown of the four regions of the world as early as 1953, shortly before the final fall of Ur, and held Nippur, Babylonia's central shrine, as early as 1963. He also imitated his Ur predecessors in using titles of divinity. He drove the Elamites from Ur late in his reign and secured the trade routes to Bahrein and the south. Naplanum, the Amorite usurper in Larsa (1961–1941), probably became a vassal of Ishbierra early in the latter's consolidation of the south. Ishbierra was succeeded by Shuilishu (1920–1911), Iddindagan (1910–1890), and Ishmedagan (1889–1871). About this time Larsa began to gain strength under its king **Samium** (1912–1878). However, Ishmedagan is remembered in the great *Ishmedagan Hymn* as a reformer and advocate of justice, and his son, Lipiteshtar (1870–1860) left behind a code of laws. In the time of Ishmedagan, Assyria first gave warning of imperial ambitions. Ilushuma raided Babylonia and is probably responsible for the destruction of Nippur celebrated in a lament of this period.

In the late Isin-Larsa period, Babylonia increasingly fell apart into small independent city states. The succeeding **kings of Isin** were Urninurta (1859–1832), Bursin (1831–1810), Lipitenlil (1809–1805), Erraimitti (1804–1797), Enlilbani (1796–1773), Zambija (1772–1770), Iterpisha (1769–1767), Urdukuga (1766–1764), Sinmagir (1763–1753), and Damiqilishu (1753–1730). **Rulers of the Larsa Dynasty** were Gungunum (1868–1842), Abishare (1841–1837), Sumuel (1830–1802), Nuradad (1801–1786), Sinidinnam (1785–1779), Sineribani (1778–1777), Siniqisham (1776–1772), Silliadad (1771), Waradsin (1770–1759), and Rimsin (1758–1699).

1830–1531. Ist DYNASTY OF BABYLON. In the last years of the Isin-Larsa period Babylon gained independence and began a remarkable climb to power. The 1st Dynasty was founded by the Amorite **Sumuabum** (1830–1817), a contemporary of Sumuel of Larsa. His successors were Sumulael (1816–1781), Sabium (1780–1767), Apilsin (1766–1749), Sinnuballit (1748–1729) and **Hammurapi the Great** (1728–1686). **Rimsin,** scion of the ruling family of Yamutbal, ruled as the last king of Larsa. He brought Larsa to its fullest bloom and, conquering Damiqilishu of Isin, unified south and central Babylonia. He prepared the way of Hammurapi, who, upon his enthronement over the city state of Babylon in 1728, began a series of campaigns of conquest. Isin, Elam, and finally Larsa itself fell to Hammurapi in 1699. One great power, the **Kingdom of Mari,** lay between Hammurapi and the achievement of a new Mesopotamian empire. In 1697 Hammurapi defeated Zimrilim of Mari, and in 1695 razed the city. The **Hammurapi Age** is one of the best known periods of Oriental antiquity, thanks to many thousands of texts from this time, including some 20,000 tablets from Mari alone. Babylonian letters flourished. Akkadian became the common language of the land, Sumerian dying out. **Hammurapi's code** of laws is justly the most famous work of the period. Marduk, god of Babylon, replaced Enlil as king in the Babylonian pantheon. But while Babylonian religion and culture flourished in a new creative period, they remained fundamentally shaped by the mythology and institutions developed by the Sumerians. Shamshuiluna (1685–1648), Hammurapi's son, was unable to hold the empire in unity. The "sea lands" on the Persian Gulf broke free of his rule,

and Ilumailu established the **1st Sea-Land Dynasty** which included twelve kings. Under Abieshu (1647–1620) the decline continued, but Ammiditana (1619–1583), Ammisaduqa (1582–1562), and Shamshuditana (1561–1531) strengthened the empire, forced the rulers of the Sea-Lands back, and controlled the people of Kashshu (the Kassites or Cossaeans), who were streaming into Babylon from the northeast. Disaster struck from an unexpected quarter. **Mursilis,** fourth king of the rising Hittite kingdom in Asia Minor, marched eastward and about 1531 or slightly earlier destroyed Babylon to the ground. He returned home with booty, apparently making little attempt to control the land. The barbarians from the mountains, the Kassites, seized power.

c. 1600–1150. THE KASSITE DYNASTY. The 450 years of Kassite rule in Babylonia was a period of little creative energy or military power. Agum II consolidated Kassite rule upon the fall of the 1st Dynasty of Babylon, but it was not until the time of Ulamburiash (c. 1450) that the Sea-Lands were conquered and Babylonia unified again. **Kurigalzu I,** contemporary of Amenophis III

Boundary-stone, time of Nebuchadrezzar

dian period. However, only small numbers entered northern Mesopotamia and the East Tigris country in the late 3rd millennium. Major invasions of these people began about 1700, and by 1500 they had penetrated into the whole of Mesopotamia, into Syria and eastern Anatolia, and into Palestine. Their language is imperfectly known, but is related to later Urartian. The earliest Hurrian texts are from Mari (18th century). Other texts come from the Hittite archives of Boghazköy (14th–13th centuries), from Ugarit (14th century), and from Egypt (an Amarna letter of the 14th century). Strange to say, the ruling class of the Hurrians bore not Hurrian but Indo-Aryan names. Evidently the Aryans drove both the Hurrians and Kassites before them in the 17th century, overrunning the former and establishing themselves as an aristocracy. Probably they won their position as chariot warriors, since it seems likely that the **horse-drawn chariot,** introduced in the 18th century, and widely used in the 17th century, originated among Aryan peoples. The symbiosis of Hurrian and Indo-Aryan elements at all events is characteristic of Hurrian society wherever we come upon it. The Hurrians rather quickly assimilated Sumero-Akkadian religion and culture. They adopted the cuneiform script both for their own tongue and also for Babylonian, the chief language of diplomatic texts. They seem also to have played a special rôle in transmitting Sumero-Akkadian literature and religion to the Hittites, albeit in highly syncretistic, Hurrian guise.

1500–1380. THE KINGDOM OF MITANNI. Small Hurrian principalities were united toward 1500 into the Kingdom of Mitanni with its capital at Washukkani on the Khabur. At its widest extent it controlled Alalakh and Qatna in Syria on the west, and Nuzu and Arapkha, as well as Assyria, on the east. The earliest of the great kings of Mitanni was

Sudarna I (c. 1500). His grandson **Saushsatar** (c. 1475) probably is to be credited with the consolidation of the kingdom. He established a feudal regime that gave a considerable amount of autonomy to vassal kings of Alalakh, Assyria, etc. In 1475 Tuthmosis III conquered northern Syria and pillaged Mitanni. However, **Egyptian control** did not extend east of the Euphrates, and Saushsatar remained strong. His son Artadama I gave his daughter in marriage to Tuthmosis IV (1425–1417), and apparently by this alliance, held Aleppo and part of northern Syria. Sudarna II (c. 1400) gave his daughter to Amenophis III (1417–1379), and, as we learn from the Amarna correspondence, Sudarna's successor, Tuishrata (c. 1390), also sent a daughter to Amenophis.

1380–1250. THE DECADENCE OF THE HURRIAN STATE. Tuishrata mounted a disputed throne after the murder of his brother, Artasumara. Artadama II, another brother, also claimed kingship, and **Suppiluliumas** (c. 1380), the king of the Hittites, concluded a treaty with him. Tuishrata was forced thereby into a war with the Hittites. Suppiluliumas captured the western holdings of Mitanni and plundered the capital, Washukkani. Egypt, Mitanni's southern ally, made no move to come to Tuishrata's aid. At this point in his war with the Hittites, Tuishrata was killed by one of his sons, perhaps with the connivance of Suppiluliumas. In any case, Sudarna III, son of Tuishrata's rival Artadama, attempted to take power. Suppiluliumas abruptly changed sides, and supported Matiwaza, son of Tuishrata, and succeeded in securing his throne. After Suppiluliumas's death, Assuruballit I of Assyria, an ally of Sudarna III, struck at Mitanni and pillaged it.

1356–1078. THE MIDDLE ASSYRIAN EMPIRE.

1356–1199. The Rise of Assyria. The fall of Mitanni freed Assyria to develop. Under

of Egypt (1417–1379), perhaps was the strongest of the Kassites. He conquered Susa, and entered into **alliance with Egypt.** Burnaburiash II (died c. 1350) protected his realm also by diplomatic marriages with the Egyptian royal house and with the family of Assuruballit I (1366–1331), the monarch of expanding Assyria. Babylonia fell to Tukulti-Ninurta I (1246–1209) and recovered independence only to be reduced again by the Elamites about 1150.

c. 1150–1025. 2ND DYNASTY OF ISIN. A native dynasty arose in the place of the Kassites but had only intermittent life. **Nabukadurriusur I** (Nebuchadrezzar) (c. 1125–1104) was the only important king of the dynasty. He conquered Elam and held Assyria at bay for a time. Babylon then fell to Tiglathpileser I. Aramaean and Chaldean tribes from the Syrian Desert began to sweep into Upper and Lower Mesopotamia in this period breaking Assyrian power and bringing the collapse of Babylonia. Babylon played no significant rôle again in world politics until the appearance of Chaldean kings in the 7th century B.C.

e. UPPER MESOPOTAMIA, 1700–609 B.C.

1700–1500. THE HURRIAN INVASIONS. The Hurrians, biblical **Horites,** began to drift south from the Caucasus as early as the Akka-

Double temple of Anu and Adad in the royal city of Assur

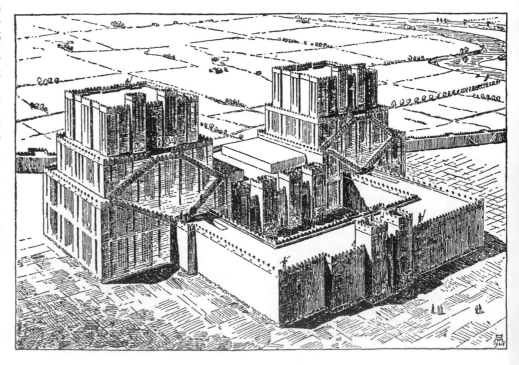

Assuruballit I (1366–1331) Assyria swiftly became a great military power. Its culture was essentially Babylonian, though reflecting some elements of Hurrian and Hittite influence. Enlilnirari I (1330–1321) defeated Kurigalzu II of Babylon. His son, Arikdenilu (1320–1309), fought campaigns in the north and west and built up his royal city, Assur. He is the first of the Assyrian kings to leave military annals. He was succeeded by Adadnirari I (1308–1276) who, after defeating the Kassites, conquered the old cities of Mitanni (now called Hanigalbat in our sources), and finally reached the Euphrates about the time of the clash of the Hittites and the Egyptians at Qadesh in 1298. He now took the title "king of everything." In Assyria he built fortifications in Assur, and built new temples and restored old ones to glorify his capital.

Shalmaneser I (1275–1246) continued the energetic campaigns of conquest. He fought in the far north against Urartu (which appears now as a power for the first time), again crushed the Hurrians and their Hittite auxiliaries, and annexed their lands. He continued west as far as Carchemish. Shalmaneser I made no attempt to expand farther; no doubt the policy was imposed by the new treaty of Khattusilis III and Ramesses II formed in 1283 which divided Syria between the Egyptian and Hittite empires. His son, Tukultininurta I (1245–1209), attacked Kassite Babylon and conquered it, becoming the first Assyrian to be called "king of Babylonia" (*Karduniash*) in his official titulary. Tukultininurta fell victim to his son in 1209 and Assyria entered upon a time of weakness.

1209–1117. Decline of Assyrian Might. The first half of the 12th century was a time of troubles throughout the Ancient World. Confusion reigned in Assur. The Hittite empire fell to Sea Peoples. In Babylon, the 2nd Dynasty of Isin succeeded the moribund Kassite re-gime. Nebuchadrezzar I brought about a brief Babylonian renaissance. Assurreshishi I (1134–1117) halted Babylonia's growing power, and Assyria stirred again, securing its borders.

1116–1078. THE EMPIRE OF TIGLATH-PILESER I. Tiglathpileser I brought the Middle Assyrian empire to its highest level of ascendancy. He was a fierce and clever warrior, and insatiable huntsman. Year after year he led his troops out, conquering the Mushqi, Thraco-Phrygian invaders from Anatolia, the Nairi mountain country north and northeast of Assyria, the Aramaeans who were invading Syria and the lands of the Middle Euphrates, and finally Babylon. The Phoenician city states paid him tribute, and none dared oppose him from sea to sea. His policy of shifting populations, and the ruthlessness of his warfare made him, and Assyria after him, uniquely hated and feared.

1078–935. The Aramaean and Chaldean Invasions. A dark age when Upper Mesopotamia including Assyria was overrun by Aramaeans, Babylonia by Aramaeans and Chaldeans.

935–612. THE NEW ASSYRIAN EMPIRE.
935–860. THE RESURGENCE OF ASSYRIA. Assyrian annals commence again after a century and a half of silence, in the reign of Assurdan II (935–913). Assurdan, his son Adadnirari (912–892), Tukultininurta II (891–885), and Assurnasirapli II (884–860) reestablished the Assyrian empire, fighting repeated campaigns in the west, north, and northwest. Adadnirari II, after defeating the Babylonians, established boundaries and fixed a friendship treaty with the ancient land. A highly centralized bureaucracy emerged in Assyria, and the practices of exchange of population and mass execution became regular policy. Assurnasirapli II was the chief architect of this early phase of the empire. Like Tiglathpileser I he marched to the sea. He built Calah (Kalakh) anew as his capital.

Most important, he handed on to his successor a compact, highly organized state.

859–825. THE REIGN OF SHALMANESER III. Shalmaneser was more ambitious, if possible, than his father Assurnasirapli. He proposed to annex conquered peoples and integrate them into the empire, and to establish regular, annual tribute from other vassals who by reason of their strength or distance could

Statuette of Assurnasirapli II

Alabaster pedestal of Tukultininurta I

Stone tablet, time of Shalmaneser III

not yet be subjugated wholly. The Assyrian armies marched in annual campaigns. Their chief efforts were directed against the far west. In 858 Shalmaneser met a coalition of Aramaean kings (Sam'al, Hattina, Carchemish, and Bît Adini) at Lutibu near Sam'al (modern Zinjirli). Shalmaneser claimed victory, perhaps correctly, though he did not break the power of the allies. In the campaigns of 857–855 he conquered Bît Adini, captured its prince, and annexed the country to Assyria. The west again united against Shalmaneser in 854. The chiefs of the alliance were Irkhuleni of Hamath, Ben Hadad I (Hadadezer) of Damascus, and Ahab of Israel. The forces of Assyria and the west clashed at Qarqar on the Orontes. Despite Shalmaneser's usual claim of victory, it is clear that he was stopped, if not seriously defeated, by the allies. In 850, 849, 846, and 842, Shalmaneser continued pounding against the western forces, finally breaking their power in 842. He then made conquests in Cilicia, and fought against Sardur I, king of Urartu. His reign ended in revolution.

Winged, human-headed bull from the palace of Sargon II

824–746. Assyria and Urartu. Shalmaneser's son, Shamshiadad V (824–812), put down the revolt in Assyria with Babylonian aid, but lost parts of the empire. He was in turn succeeded by Adadnirari III (811–784), who came to the throne as a minor. For four years the queen-mother ruled. Her name was Sammuramat, the **Semiramis** of Greek legend. Adadnirari briefly reimposed tribute on the western states, but increasingly Assyria retreated before the Urarteans. Shalmaneser IV (783–774), Assurdan III (773–756), and Assurnirari V (755–746) were all weak. Urartu expanded under Argishti I (780–756) and Sarduri II (755–735). Under the latter, Commagene, Melitene, and even Carchemish came under Urartian domination.

745–728. THE REIGN OF TIGLATHPILESER III. Tiglathpileser III, a usurper, began a new era, the last and greatest period of the New Assyrian empire. He consolidated his regime at home and pacified Babylonia, leaving Nabunasir (Nabonassar, 747–735) on the throne of Babylon. Then in the years 743–738 Tiglathpileser made his first great western campaign. The Urartian allies were defeated at Arpad, and after a long siege Arpad taken. A coalition of Hamath and coastal cities of north Syria under the leadership of Azariah (Uzziah) of Judah was crushed, and in 738 Tiglathpileser received tribute from the important states of Syria-Palestine including Israel and Damascus. In 735 he stormed Urartu, and in 734–732 launched a second western series of campaigns against Rezin of Damascus, Pekah of Israel, and their allies. Gilead, Galilee, and Damascus were turned into provinces of Assyria. In 731 revolution broke out in Babylon and Tiglathpileser hastened back to stamp it out, naming himself king of Babylon in 729.

726–706. SHALMANESER V AND SARGON II. Shalmaneser V was faced with new rebellion in the west at the beginning of his reign. In 725 he invested Samaria, capital of Israel, and Tyre. Samaria fell in 722 to Shalmaneser (though Sargon later claimed credit for the victory). Sargon II (722–706) mounted his father's throne later in the same year. He turned first to Babylon, meeting Merodach-baladan, pretender to the Babylonian crown, and his Elamite allies in an indecisive battle at Der. He then moved west reconquering Hamath, Samaria, Ekron, and Gaza. Tyre, under siege five years, fell during this campaign, and Judah paid tribute (720). In 717–716, Sargon overthrew and annexed Carchemish, and defeated the Egyptian Pharoah Osorkon at Raphia. In 712 his armies crushed Ashdod, breaking up a conspiracy of Egypt and the southern states of Palestine. In 709 Sargon assumed the kingship of Babylon. Merodach-baladan went into exile, to return to cause mischief in the time of Sennacherib.

Palace of Sennacherib at Nineveh

mains one of our chief sources for knowledge of Babylonian literature. In 667 the Assyrians again ousted Tirhaqah from Memphis, and in 663 destroyed the Ethiopian power in Egypt, capturing Thebes. In the years immediately preceding 652, Shamashshumukin, Assurbanapal's brother, who ruled as king of Babylon, became involved in a gigantic conspiracy to overthrow the kingdom. His allies included the Chaldeans and Aramaeans, Egypt and Elam. Civil war raged from 652 to 648 when Shamashshumukin finally surrendered in Babylon. Susa was sacked in 639. The strife, however, drained away the energies of Assyria.

626-609. The Last Days of Assyria. The Assyrian empire collapsed with extraordinary speed. Assuretililani (626-623?) and the usurper Sinshumlishir (623?) followed Assurbanapal. There was general revolt. Nabopolassar declared himself king of Babylon in 626. Sinsharishkun (622?-612), another son of Assurbanapal, took power. Cyaxares of Media and Nabopolassar joined forces to bring down Assyria. Nineveh fell to the allies in 612, an event celebrated by the *Book of Nahum*. Assuruballit II (611-609) attempted to regroup Assyrian forces in Harran. Harran fell in 610 to the Babylonians. An attempt of Assyrian remnants and Egyptian forces to retake Harran in 609 failed.

705-682. THE REIGN OF SENNACHERIB. In his first years Sennacherib devoted himself to peaceful pursuits, transforming Nineveh, his chosen capital, into a city of unparalleled splendor. Meanwhile Merodach-baladan developed a worldwide conspiracy, and in 702 seized power in Babylon. Sennacherib put down the revolt and subdued the Chaldeans, but for 13 years trouble seethed in Babylonia, leading finally to the **sacking of Babylon** in 689. In the western part of the empire, **Hezekiah of Judah** was a leader in a conspiracy which included Phoenicia, Egypt, and Philistia. In 701 Sennacherib marched west, pacified Phoenicia and Philistia without difficulty, and defeated Egyptian troops of Shabaka at Elteqeh. He then turned on Hezekiah. All of Judah was reduced except Jerusalem. At this point Hezekiah sued for peace. The Assyrians broke off the siege on this occasion. There is some evidence, much disputed, that later in Sennacherib's reign, Jerusalem was again besieged by the Assyrians and escaped intact. Despite these wars, Sennacherib's reign was a relatively peaceful period. No new provinces were added to the realm, and the arts and literature flourished. During this period the domestic water supply was improved and cotton introduced as a supplementary crop.

681-670. The Reign of Esarhaddon. Sennacherib was murdered by one of his sons. **Esarhaddon,** the designated heir, quelled the rebellion. Babylon was gloriously rebuilt and placed under the rule of Shamashshumukin, a son of Esarhaddon. Scythian and Cimmerian hordes appeared on Assyria's northern border and made some inroads into the empire. Esarhaddon was preoccupied, however, with grandiose plans to conquer Egypt. Sidon, an ally of Egypt, was taken in 677. Esarhaddon's first raids into Egypt in 675-674 were indecisive. In 671, Esarhaddon struck with full force, routed Tirhaqah, and took

Memphis. Esarhaddon died in the course of another march on Egypt.

669-c. 627. THE REIGN OF ASSURBANAPAL. The last great king of Assyria was an extraordinary figure, a great general, a sportsman, and a patron of arts and letters. His palace reliefs are the finest examples of Assyrian art. He was a master of cuneiform and gathered a great library of tablets which re-

f. THE NEO-BABYLONIAN EMPIRE, 626-333 B.C.

626-605. THE RISE OF THE CHALDEAN DYNASTY OF BABYLON. Babylonia had become dominantly Chaldean during Neo-Assyrian times. **Nabopolassar** (626-605) finally organized Chaldean power, taking the diadem of Babylon in 626. He spent his

Bas-relief representing Assurbanapal fighting lions

Brick with the name of Nebuchadrezzar II

energies as we have seen finishing off Assyria. In 605 **Nebuchadrezzar** the crown prince commanded the armies of Babylon in the battle of Carchemish against the Egyptian army of Necho. The battle ended in an overwhelming defeat for Necho, and Nebuchadrezzar fell heir to the western empire of Assyria. Shortly after Nabopolassar died. Nebuchadrezzar was crowned king on September 7, 605.

605–561. THE REIGN OF NEBUCHAD-REZZAR (II) THE GREAT. In the years following his accession, Nebuchadrezzar campaigned in Syria-Palestine pacifying his newly won territories. In 601 he marched against Egypt. The clash near the Egyptian border was bloody but indecisive, each side retiring. In 598, Nebuchadrezzar again came west. Judah was crushed and **Jerusalem taken** in 597. After quelling a revolt at home, Nebuchadrezzar came west to put down a rebellion centering in Tyre and Judah. Nebuchadrezzar invested Jerusalem in 588. Hophra sallied out briefly from Egypt but retired in disarray when faced by Nebuchadrezzar's full strength. Jerusalem finally fell in July, 586. The city and its temple were laid waste, and many **Jews taken captive** to Babylon. Tyre, besieged for 13 years, according to Menander, was never taken. Nebuchadrezzar lavished wealth upon Babylon. The city, newly built by Esarhaddon, now became a wonder of the Ancient World.

561–539. THE END OF THE CHALDEAN EMPIRE. Nebuchadrezzar's death in reality was the end of Babylon as a world power. Evil-merodach (Awil-Marduk) ruled two years (561–560) before he was killed by Neriglissar (Nergalsharusur, 559–556). His son Labashi-Marduk (556) was a weakling, shortly replaced by a usurper, Nabonidus (555–539). Nabonidus rallied the country briefly. He was a devotee of the gods, especially Sin of Harran, and an archaeologist and scholar. In his last years he spent much of his time at the Oasis of Teima, leaving his son Belshazzar regent. Meanwhile **Cyrus the Great** had united the Medes and Persians, and defeated the Lydians (547). In 539 he marched on Babylonia. The country fell almost without struggle. Babylon itself opened its gates to Gobryas, Cyrus's general, and on October 29, 539 Cyrus entered the city.

539–332. Mesopotamia under Persian rule.

332–323. Mesopotamia under Alexander the Great.

2. *Egypt, to 332* B.C.

a. THE LAND AND THE PEOPLE

The name **Egypt,** from Homeric Greek *Aiguptos,* applied in antiquity to the lands of the Nile Valley, from the Delta on the Mediterranean southward to the First Cataract of the Nile above Suene (modern Aswan). The Egyptians applied the epithet *Keme (kmt),* the Black Land, to their country in reference to the strip of black alluvial soil laid down by the Nile along its banks. The valley extends for about 550 miles in a straight line, 750 miles as the river flows, never exceeding 13 miles in width, comprising only about 12,500 square miles of cultivable land. Egypt is a land of scant rainfall in the Delta, virtually no rainfall upstream. Cultivation is made possible by the annual inundation of the Nile, which rises late in June, crests in late September, and slowly subsides. The inundation both renews the extraordinary

King wearing the crown of Upper Egypt

Palette of King Na'rmer

The Hunter's Palette, Lower Egypt, c. 3000 B.C.

Lions' Gate at the ruins of Boghazkoy (p.55)

Ruins of the Palace of Minos in Knossos (p.65)

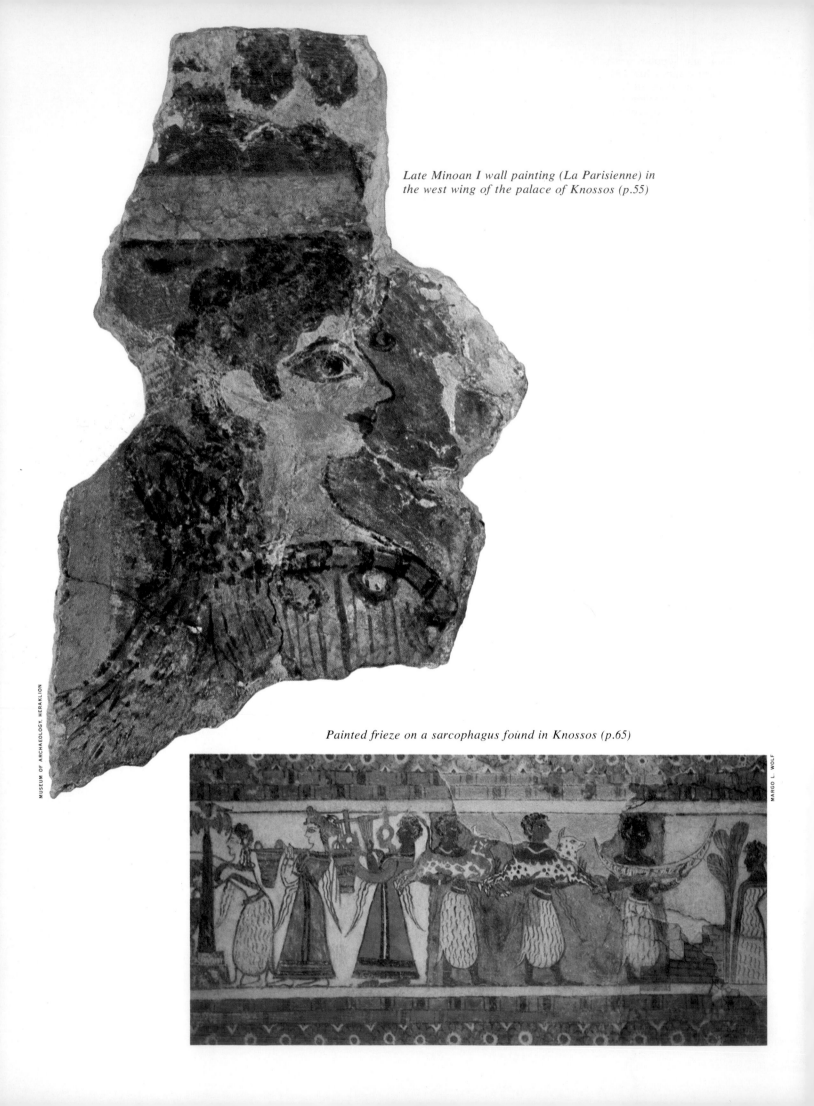

Late Minoan I wall painting (La Parisienne) in the west wing of the palace of Knossos (p.55)

Painted frieze on a sarcophagus found in Knossos (p.65)

fertility of the soil and supplies water for irrigation. From earliest times life in Egypt has been dependent on the flood of the Nile and its elaborate control in irrigation works. The river also made possible easy communication, by either oared or square-sailed boats. Egypt is thus appropriately described as the "gift of the Nile" (Herodotus).

In predynastic times (before 2850 B.C.), **Lower Egypt** (the Delta) and **Upper Egypt** seem to have been organized as distinct kingdoms; in any case an ideology of the duality of "the Two Lands" persisted after the permanent unification of Egypt under Na'rmer until the end of the ancient state. Egypt was further divided into **nomes.** In the fully developed system there were 42 such districts, 20 in Lower Egypt, 22 in Upper Egypt. The principal ancient cities of Lower Egypt included Avaris (later Tanis, biblical Zoan), Sais, Bubastis, Heliopolis (biblical On), and Memphis (biblical Mof or Nof). Those of Upper Egypt, south of the Fayyum, the great depression containing the Lake of Moeris, were Heracleopolis, Hermopolis (Egyptian Khmun), Akhetaten (modern Egyptian 'Amarna), Thinis, Abydos, Thebes (biblical No), and near the First Cataract, Yeb (Greek Elephantine). Egypt's culture was based more on village, agrarian life, than on the city. Capital cities were fixed simply by the residency of the king. While Thebes in Upper Egypt, Memphis-Hikuptah in Middle Egypt,

and Tanis in the Delta were the most important of the capital cities, actually at one time or another, the capital rested in most of the above-named cities.

The **population** of ancient Egypt has been set by scholarly reckoning at about 5,000,000. This figure is little more than a guess, but is to be preferred to the high numbers of Diodorus (7,000,000) and Josephus (7,500,000). The predynastic people of Egypt were slight if well-muscled, long-headed, with little facial hair, a stock sharing many characteristics with the early Semitic folk. While this old strain may be traced throughout dynastic times in Egypt, it became mixed as early as the beginning of the historical period (29th century B.C.) with other stocks, notably with an Armenoid or broad-headed racial strain presumably from the north.

The **language** of ancient Egypt belongs to the rather ill-defined group of Hamitic tongues. It is closely related to Semitic—particularly one stratum of Egyptian—to Berber, and more remotely to the Cushitic family of languages. Egyptian survived into the Middle Ages in late dialects known as Coptic.

b. THE RISE OF EGYPTIAN CIVILIZATION

Toward 3000 B.C. in the last, so-called late Gerzean phase of predynastic times, and in the beginning of dynastic times, Egyptian civiliza-

tion, its art, architecture, and perhaps even its hieroglyphic system of writing, took vast strides ahead under the stimulus of the first great civilization of the Near East then developing in Mesopotamia. While the impact of this old Sumerian culture is quite palpable, it must also be said that the influence of Mesopotamia was ephemeral, serving primarily as an impetus to native Egyptian cultural forms and institutions. The early evolution of Egyptian civilization was swift. In the **Old Kingdom,** in most parts by the 3rd and 4th Dynasties (c. 2615–2440 B.C.), Egyptian cultural patterns reached maturity: the system of divine kingship, the canons of art and architecture, the organization of the funerary cultus, the classical forms of monumental (hieroglyphic) and cursive (hieratic) scripts, and the principal development of mathematics and of certain of the applied sciences. In medicine diagnostic techniques and systematic treatment were established. This classical culture of the Old Kingdom persisted with remarkably slight change through the next two millennia.

c. RELIGION

The origins of Egyptian religion remain relatively obscure. In earliest times we confront a bewildering host of gods in human form, in animal form, and in mixed human and animal form, not to mention deified abstractions and inanimate objects of nature. Attempts to trace

View of a palace at Thebes

Bas-relief from tomb of Ra-hetep, a priest of the 4th Dynasty

Representation of Nut, goddess of Heaven

the historic religion to a prehistoric totemism have wholly failed. No simple evolutionary picture can be drawn. We can say only that the gods easily alter form, in many instances between anthropomorphic and theriomorphic representation or symbolism. Each town or nome had its patron deity or deities, its cult, and "religious community." At the same time the Egyptian was tolerant, quick to identify gods with parallel functions (whether Egyptian or foreign), and saw all of nature, gods, men, and beasts as a continuum. The object of his religion was to find (or establish) the order of the powers manifest in nature, specifically the created order, and in piety and statecraft, in the present and in the world of the dead, to conform to or participate in this order of reality.

Already in the time of the Old Kingdom, one finds basic myths of creation, of divine kingship, of cosmic order. The "Memphite Theology" which can be no later than the beginning of the Old Kingdom, describes the process of creation in which the gods stem from Ptah, patron of Memphis. The pantheon was thus organized in effect as immanations or manifestations of one divine substance according to the order of creation, and can be described as tending toward a nature monotheism, or better, pantheism. The Egyptian state was an integral part of the divine order in the Memphite Theology (which was actually both a cosmology and political program). The king was identified with the god Horus, and Horus, the power of the sky, was fully incarnate in the king. The king's predecessor similarly "became" the dead god Osiris, lord of the Underworld. In Heliopolis the "sun god" Reʿ became the father of the gods, being identified with Atum, a creator god, and Harakhti, "Horus of The Horizon," as Reʿ-atum and Reʿ-harakhti respectively. The sun god in turn was head of the Ennead, which included in its system a series of generations of pairs: Shu and Tefnut, Geb (Earth) and Nut (Heaven), Osiris (god of death and fertility) and Isis (mother goddess, originally the deified throne of the king), Seth (the "storm god," Osiris' enemy) and Nephthys. By the 5th Dynasty the cult of Heliopolitan Reʿ was officially adopted by the king, now entitled "the son of Reʿ," the father ruling the heavens, his counterpart the earth. In the Middle Kingdom, Amun, god of Thebes, emerged as king of the gods. In origin the power in air, he was identified with Reʿ, and in the New Kingdom his cult threatened to absorb all rivals. Egyptians tended, however, to keep both early and late myths and a variety of cosmologies, rituals, and symbols side by side in a rich mass, incompletely unified, perhaps even consciously contradictory. Religious truth for the Egyptian was manifold, arrived at by complementary myths and religious acts. The most rigorous attempt to systematize Egyptian religion was that of **Akhenaten** (and his advisers) in the 18th Dynasty who, as a devotee of the solar disk, suppressed alternate names, cults, and symbols of the sun god, as well as those of other deities. Even the Akhenaten revolution, however, did not discard the traditional centrality of sun worship, its use in the ideology of kingship and in the funerary cult. At all events his innovations in the direction of solar monotheism shortly died out, and Egyptian religion to the end remained a complex and archaic polytheism.

Bust of King Chephren

d. CHRONOLOGY

Manetho, an Egyptian priest (c. 280 B.C.), wrote a history of his country in Greek of which fragments have been preserved in Josephus, Sextus Julius Africanus, Eusebius, and Syncellus. He grouped the kings of Egypt into 30 dynasties beginning with Menes, founder of Dynasty I, ending with the conquest of Egypt by Artaxerxes III in 343 B.C. Despite all its defects, his dynastic arrangement is still used. Valuable ancient sources include the **Palermo Stone,** a chronicle inscribed in Dynasty V, the **Turin Canon,** a hieratic papyrus of Dynasty XIX, and the **Tables of Abydos** (Dynasty XIX), **Saqqarah** (Dynasty XIX), and **Karnak** (Dynasty XVIII).

The earliest fixed date in Egyptian chronology is based on an astronomical observation of the Middle Kingdom in c. 1872 B.C. in the seventh year of Sesostris III (Senwosre). It is a record of the date of the so-called heliacal rising of Sothis (Sirius) which was roughly coeval with the annual rising of the Nile, and hence determined the Egyptian New Year. The civil calendar of 365 days slowly rotated through the year coinciding with the solar calendar each 1460 years. While scholars at one time argued that the Sothic cycle had been recognized during the protodynastic period, or even in predynastic times, it appears likely now that the oldest Egyptian calendar was regulated by the rise of the Nile, and that the device of astronomical observation of Sirius was secondary, perhaps discovered as early as the end of the Old Kingdom.

The **chronology of Egypt,** thanks to annals, monuments, and astronomical observation, is fairly well fixed for the 12th Dynasty, c. 1991–1786 B.C. Even so an error of up to a decade is still possible in the 2nd and early 1st millennia. For the 3rd millennium the chronology becomes highly uncertain, reaching a margin of error of almost a century at the beginning of the historic period. Datings of the early dynasties are projected on the basis of king lists and monuments, certain crucial synchronisms with

The Great Sphinx of Gizeh

Mesopotamia, and so-called Carbon-14 datings. While Mesopotamian chronology is fixed by astronomical observations, multiple solutions, 64 years apart, must be further controlled by other less accurate data. This has given rise to several chronologies for the ancient Near East. Of them, the so-called *Middle Chronology* and *Low Chronology* remain the only probable alternates. We follow here the Low Chronology which sets the first regnal year of Hammurapi in 1728 B.C. Whether one selects the Low Chronology or the alternate chronology 64 years higher (1792 B.C.), the reckoning of early dates in Egypt and elsewhere in the ancient Near East must be raised or lowered together.

c. 3200–2850.   THE GERZEAN CULTURE. Mesopotamian influences stimulated the development of Egyptian civilization in Late Gerzean times (after c. 3000 B.C.).

c. 2850–2615.   THE PROTODYNASTIC PERIOD. Dynasties I–II. **Menes,** no doubt to be identified with Na'rmer, founded the 1st Dynasty uniting Egypt under his single rule. While Manetho termed these dynasties "Thinite," Na'rmer founded his new capital at Memphis.

e. THE OLD KINGDOM, c. 2615–1991 B.C.

c. 2615–2175.   THE OLD KINGDOM. Dynasties III–VII (capital: Memphis). Djoser (Tosorthros), the founder of Dynasty III (c. 2615–2565 B.C.) built the step **pyramid of Saqqarah.** His architect Imhotep (Greek Imouthes) was later deified. With Dynasty IV (2565–2440 B.C.) the Old Kingdom reached its zenith. Snofru (Soris), the founder, fought successful wars with the Nubians and Libyans, and developed a brisk sea trade in cedar with Byblos. His greatest monuments are the two limestone pyramids of Dahshur, each more than 310 feet in height. He was succeeded by Cheops (Khufwey), Chephren (Kha'fre'), and Mycerinus (Menkaure'), who erected the colossal **pyramids of Gizeh,** which involved use of the plumb-lines and A-frame, as well as unlimited manpower. The great pyramid of Cheops originally rose to a height of 481.4 feet. Its base covered an area of about 13 acres. The pyramid of Chephren is only slightly smaller, and to Chephren is probably to be attributed the Sphinx. In the 4th Dynasty, kingship in Egypt reached the apogee of power and centralized authority. The 5th Dynasty (2440–2315 B.C.) witnessed the rise to power of the Heliopolitan priesthood. The kings regularly assumed the title "son of Re'," and built obelisk temples to the sun. The best-known kings are Userkaf (Userchevēs), Sahure' (Sephres), Niuserre' (Rathures), and Unis. Under the last-named the first **Pyramid Texts** appear. The power of the king began to dissipate in the 5th Dynasty, a process which accelerated in the 6th Dynasty (c. 2315–2175 B.C.), especially under the long reign of Pepi II (Phiops, Piopi) (c. 2270–2180 B.C.). In turn the rulers of the nomes assumed independence and power as feudal lords. Dynasty VII, to which Manetho assigned 70 kings reigning 70 days, while evidently fictitious, is symbolic of the decay of the Old Kingdom.

c. 2175–1991. FIRST INTERMEDIATE PERIOD. Dynasties VIII–XI. For much of the period there was strife between competing dynasties, especially between nobles of Heracleopolis in Middle Egypt, and Thebes in Upper Egypt. The victory of Thebes permitted the **reunion of Egypt** under Menthotpe II, the fifth ruler of the 11th Dynasty (2133–1992 B.C.). In this era, the hope of a transfigured life after death was democratized to include non-royal persons. Literature flourished despite civil troubles. Notable are the

Sesostris III

Limestone stele (detail), Thebes, 11th Dynasty

Coffin Texts, the *Instruction for King Merykare',* and the *Admonitions of Ipuwer.*

f. THE MIDDLE KINGDOM, c. 1991–1570 B.C.

c. 1991–1786. THE MIDDLE KINGDOM. Dynasty XII (capital: Lisht near Memphis). Ammenemes I (Amenemhe) (1991–1962) reorganized the country, reduced the power of the nobles, laying the basis again for a strong, stable, and prosperous Egypt. Building, art, literature, and international commerce flourished under him and his successors Sesostris I (Senwosre) (1971–1928), Ammenemes II (1929–1895), Sesostris II (1897–1879), Sesostris III (1878–1843), Ammenemes III (1842–1797), Ammenemes IV (1798–1790), and Sebeknofru (Scemiophris), daughter of Ammenemes III (1789–1786). The **practice of co-regency** was introduced by Ammenemes I and persisted through much of the dynasty. Already in Ammenemes's reign military action began to secure or extend Egypt's boundaries. Lower Nubia was taken, and a punitive campaign carried out against Asiatic nomads. By the reign of Sesostris III the southern border at the Second Cataract had been made secure. The same monarch also marched into Palestine as far north as Shechem. Apparently he made no attempt to set up an Asiatic empire but was content to keep open the routes of Egyptian trade. Under **Ammenemes III** national prosperity reached its peak. He developed the irrigation and land reclamation operations in the Fayyum, probably begun by Sesostris II. Turquoise mining in Sinai was expanded. At Hawara, Ammenemes III built one of his two pyramids and a great funerary temple known later as the *Labyrinth.* One of Egypt's great literary works, the *Story of Sinuhe* was composed in the Middle Kingdom.

c. 1785–1570. SECOND INTERMEDIATE PERIOD. Dynasties XIII–XVII. The 13th (Theban) Dynasty (c. 1785–1647) was a period of declining power of the king. Contemporary with it was the 14th Dynasty, hereditary lords of Xois in the Delta. Dynasty XV (c. 1678–1570) was made up of the **Hyksos** (from Egyptian *hiq-khase,* "chief of a foreign hill country"), invaders from Syria-Palestine. Where their Semitic names are known, they are chiefly Amorite. The Hyksos introduced the horse and chariot into Egypt. Their chief power was in the Delta, their capital at Avaris. Dynasty XVI (Hyksos) apparently was contemporary either with Dynasty XIII or XV. In Dynasty XVII (c. 1600–1570) the native rulers of Thebes regained power and, especially under **Kamose,** began wars against the Hyksos.

g. THE NEW KINGDOM, c. 1570–332 B.C.

c. 1570–1304. THE NEW KINGDOM. Dynasty XVIII (capital: Thebes). Amosis captured Avaris and drove the alien Hyksos out of Egypt. Under Amosis and his son **Amenophis I** ('Amenhotpe) (c. 1545–1525), the Nubian and Libyan borders were secured, and

Queen Hatshepsut

Tuthmosis III

Amenophis III

the power of the central government in Thebes re-established over the nobles of the land. Egypt was re-organized primarily as a military state, dedicated to imperial expansion, headed by a soldier-king. **Tuthmosis I** (Dhutmose) (1525–c. 1512) and **Tuthmosis II** (1512–1504) both fought successful campaigns in Nubia and Syria-Palestine. Tuthmosis II associated his queen **Hashepsowe** (Hatshepsut) with him in his reign, and when he died at a youthful age, Hashepsowe seized power, first as regent of **Tuthmosis II** (1504–1450), later as queen (1503–1482). Meanwhile Tuthmosis grew to manhood in the army, and in 1483 became sole ruler. In the same year he launched his first campaign of **conquest in Syria-Palestine,** and at the **battle of Megiddo** decisively defeated the allies under the king of Qadesh-on-the-Orontes. In 16 campaigns into Asia he succeeded in establishing an empire stretching to the Euphrates. Qadesh, the center of opposition, was destroyed in his sixth campaign (1474); in his eighth campaign (1471) he crossed the Euphrates and pillaged the Hurrian state of Mitanni. In his 42nd year (1462) he ended his Syrian campaigns. In the south he moved the Egyptian banner south to the Fourth Cataract, appointing a viceroy over Nubia. Egypt expanded to its greatest imperial scope and to its greatest power under Tuthmosis. It is in this period that a new title of the king came into use: *per-'o,* literally, "Great House," biblical *pharaoh.* Tuthmosis' son, **Amenophis II** (c. 1450–1424), a great sportsman and warrior, vigorously maintained the Egyptian empire. After the short reign of Tuthmosis IV (c.

1424–1417), **Amenophis III** "the Magnificent" (c. 1417–1379) ruled over a period of unparalleled luxury and peace. He preserved his Syro-Palestinian possessions by diplomacy, among other things by marrying daughters of Sudarna and Tuishrata, kings of Mitanni. He was a fabulous builder whose projects included the great temple of Amun in Luxor, and two statues of himself nearly 70 feet high, the so-called **Colossi of Memnon.** The first signs of trouble in the empire and decadence at home appear in the late reign of Amenophis III, and mount in the reign of Amenophis IV (1379–1362), **Akhenaten.** The disintegration of the empire is graphically reflected in the international correspondence written in Akkadian found at Akhenaten's capital at El-'Amarna. Revolution and revolt spread through Palestine and Phoenicia. The Hittites under Suppiluliumas absorbed parts of the empire in Syria. Egypt under Akhenaten took no action. The king's limited energies were given to **religious innovation** at home. His court officially espoused the worship of Aten, the solar disk, and advocated a doctrine of "truth" (*ma'e*). Under his patronage new naturalistic styles in art and literature matured. The religious revolution was short-lived owing to the disintegration of the dynasty, and the implacable opposition of the priesthood of Amun, supreme god of Egypt under Akhenaten's imperial forbears. A male heir failing, Amenophis IV was succeeded by two sons-in-law, **Smenkhkare'** (c. 1361), and **Tut'ankhamun** (1361–1351). The latter is known chiefly for his richly furnished tomb discovered by Howard Carter in 1922. Ay, an official of the court, seized power, probably before Tut'ankhamun's death, and reigned briefly (1351–1347). He was succeeded by Haremhab (Harmaïs) (c. 1347–1319), general of the armies, who undertook to restore the priesthoods and temples of Amun and the

Akhenaten

other traditional gods, and re-establish strong government.

c. 1319–1200. Dynasty XIX (capitals: Memphis and especially Tanis, rebuilt by Ramesses II). **Ramesses I** (Ra'messe) (c. 1319), a general and later vizier, founded a vigorous new dynasty stemming from Tanis, city of the god Seth. His son **Sethos I** (Seti) (c. 1319–1304) set out to reconquer the lands of the Asiatic empire lost by Akhenaten. He was successful in Palestine and southern Syria extending his list of victories north to Qadesh-on-the-Orontes. Sethos built a great temple at Abydos, and

Ramesses II

Ruins of Hypostyle Hall in Karnak

continued work on the famous Hypostyle Hall in Karnak, completed by his son **Ramesses II,** the Great (1304–1237). Ramesses II had more difficulties in maintaining the empire. In his fifth year, 1298, he marched against the Hittites under Muwatallis. A great battle was fought at Qadesh. Ramesses boasted of his prowess in escaping an ambush and gaining victory. The Hittites, no doubt with more justification, claimed victory. After years of indecisive conflict, Ramesses and Khattusilis III (who had succeeded his brother Muwatallis) made a treaty of peace in 1283. Probably the boundary between the two powers was fixed at the Eleutherus Valley, the traditional northern boundary of "Canaan." Ramesses built prodigiously from Abu Simbel in Nubia to the Delta. In the northeastern Delta he rebuilt Tanis, renamed Pi-Ra'amesse, "House of Ramesses," as his capital, and Pi-Tum (Tell Retabeh). The latter two cities are identical with biblical Raamses and Pithom, the cities where the Israelites were corvée workers (Exodus, 1:11). The **flight of Israelites** from Egypt under Moses must be placed most probably in the reign of Ramesses II. By the fifth year of Merneptah (Ammenephthes) (1237–1225), the son of Ramesses, the Israelites were in Palestine where they suffered defeat at the hand of Merneptah. In the same year, Merneptah defeated a coalition of Libyans and Aegean peoples: Achaeans' (Aqiyawasha), Tyrrhenians (Turusha), Lycians (Luku), Sardinians (Shardina), and Shakrusha. The 19th Dynasty ended in a series of short, confused reigns about 1200, followed by an interregnum.

c. 1190–1065. **Dynasty XX** (capital: Tanis). **Ramesses III** (c. 1188–1156) rallied Egypt to face the deadly menace of another **confederation of Sea Peoples:** Pelast (Philistines), Tjikar (Sicilians?), Danuna (Greek Danaoi), Shardina (Sardinians), Washasha, and Shakrusha. Scenes of his victorious fighting are preserved on the walls of Ramesses's great temple at Medinet Habu. Egypt was saved and the empire held briefly. Some of the Sea Peoples, notably the Philistines and Tjikar, settled the Palestinian coast. Egypt sank into feebleness again under successive Ramessides, Ramesses IV–XI (1156–1065). Her commercial and political empire ceased to function. The priesthood of Amun-re', controlling much of Egypt's land, grew increasingly powerful and arrogant. Hrihor, high priest in Karnak, became effective ruler in Thebes in the time of Ramesses XI. Imperial Egypt's force and spirit were spent. Reflecting these times is the *Tale of Wenamun.*

c. 1065–332. **LATE DYNASTIC PERIOD.** Dynasties XXI–XXXI.

c. 1065–935. **Dynasty XXI** (capitals: in Lower Egypt, Tanis, in Upper Egypt, Thebes). **Smendes** (Nesbanebded), a merchant prince, claimed the kingship on the death of Ramesses XI. He and his successors ruled in Tanis, and the theocratic dynasty of Hrihor governed in Thebes.

c. 935–725. **Dynasty XXII** (capital: Bubastis). Shoshenq I (Sesonchis) (935–914), founder of the dynasty, succeeded in appointing one of his sons high priest of Amun-re', reunifying the land. He is better known as biblical **Shishak.** He stormed Palestine, robbing the Temple in Jerusalem, laying waste many cities of the land (c. 918). His successors were Osorkon I (Osorthon) (c. 914–874), Takelot I (Takelothis) (c. 874–860), and Osorkon II (c. 860–832?), who sent soldiers to fight with the Syro-Palestinian allies against Shalmaneser III at Qarqar in

854. The remaining dynasts were Takelot II (c. 837–823), Shoshenq III (822–770?), Pami (c. 770–765) and Shoshenq IV (c. 765–725?). We know little of Dynasty XXIII (c. 759–715?) and Dynasty XXIV (c. 725–709).

c. 715–656. **Dynasty XXV** (Ethiopian). **Pi'ankhi** (c. 751–710) about 715 invaded Egypt from Napata, his capital at the Fourth Cataract. He easily defeated Tefnakhte, Technactis, a princelet of the 24th Dynasty, and subdued Egypt. His brother and successor was Shabaka (Sabacon) (c. 710–698) who chose to become pharaoh and rule from Thebes. He was succeeded by **Shebteko** (Sebichos) (c. 696–685) and **Taharqo** (Tarcos) (co-regent 689–685; sole ruler 685–663). The power of imperial Assyria now made itself felt in Egypt. **Esarhaddon** (681–670), king of Assyria, attacked Taharqo in 671, conquering Memphis. Taharqo returned, only to be driven out again by **Assurbanapal** (669–627) in 667. Finally in 663, Assurbanapal sacked Thebes and defeated Tanuatamun (663–656).

663–525. **Dynasty XXVI** (capital: Sais). **Neko I** (Nechao, Necho), a governor of Sais, was named king of Egypt first by Esarhaddon and later by Assurbanapal. He was father of **Psammetichus I** (Psamtek, 663–609), real founder of the independent **Saite Dynasty.** Allying himself with Gyges of Lydia, he rebelled successfully against failing Assyria. He began the so-called **Saite revival** in art, painting and architecture, literature, and religion, a nostalgic attempt to re-create the forms and styles of the Old Kingdom. He was followed on the throne by **Neko II** (609–594). In 609 **Neko** marched north, ostensibly to aid Assyria, then being finished off by the founder of the Neo-Babylonian Empire, Nabopolassar. In fact he sought to restore Egypt's ancient empire. On his way northward he was opposed at Megiddo by **Josiah of Judah.** Judah was defeated and

Battle of Memphis, 667 B.C., between Taharqo and Assurbanapal

Detail from sarcophagus of Ramesses III

Bes, statuette, Saite Period, 26th Dynasty

Josiah killed. However, Neko was delayed long enough to prevent his giving aid to the Assyrians. In several campaigns he consolidated his power far north into Syria. However, at Carchemish in 605 he was crushingly defeated by **Nebuchadrezzar,** who succeeded Nabopolassar in the same year. Neko was driven from Syria-Palestine, but lived to defeat Nebuchadrezzar in 601 on Egypt's border. Herodotus records Neko's unsuccessful attempt to link the Nile with the Red Sea by a canal, and tells of a successful exploit, an expedition of Phoenician ships sent to circumnavigate Africa. Neko was succeeded by **Psammetichus II** (594–588), who was in turn followed by **Apries** (Wahibves') (588–568), the biblical Pharaoh Hophra (Jeremiah, 44:30). Apries apparently encouraged Syria-Palestine to revolt against Babylon by promising aid. He proved to be a poor ally. He sallied out briefly against

Nebuchadrezzar during the latter's siege of Jerusalem, but when faced by Nebuchadrezzar's armies retired into Egypt in disarray. Similarly he was defeated by the Greeks of Cyrene when he went to the aid of Libyan allies at the end of his reign. Egypt had become a "broken reed." **Amasis** ('Ahmose-si-neit) (568–526) overthrew Apries. He was a peaceful man and a lover of Greek culture. His son **Psammetichus III** (526–525) mounted the throne only to face the **invasion of Cambyses.** After a hard-fought battle at Pelusium, the Egyptians surrendered.

525–404. Egypt under Persian rule (Dynasty XXVII).

404–399. Dynasty XXVIII consisting of a single king, Amyrtaeus of Sais.

399–380. Dynasty XXIX (capital: Mendes). Achoris (Hakor) (393–380), strongest of the kings of this dynasty, formed an alliance with

Evagoras of Salamis against Artaxerxes II and fought off Persian attack with surprising vigor.

380–343. Dynasty XXX (capital: Sebennytus). The **last native dynasty** of Egypt numbers three kings, Nekhtnebef (Nectanebes) (380–363), Takhos (Djeho) (362–361), and Nekhtharehbe (Nectanebos) (360–343). The first and last enjoyed prosperous reigns and built widely in Egypt. In 373 Artaxerxes II sent a great Persian host against Egypt with no success, and in 350 **Artaxerxes III** sent an expedition against Egypt which failed scandalously, leading to a wave of revolts in the western empire. Artaxerxes himself led his armies against Egypt in 343, and in a brilliant campaign finally reduced Egypt.

343–332. Egypt again under Persian rule.

332. Egypt conquered by Alexander the Great.

(Cont. p. 103.)

3. *Syria-Palestine, to 332* B.C.

a. THE LAND AND THE PEOPLE

Syria, or Syria-Palestine, lay along the eastern Mediterranean coast, south of Mount Amanus, north of the River of Egypt (Wadi 'Arish). In the north its eastern frontier was the Euphrates, in the south the Syrian desert. This region, especially the coastal lands and hill country, was settled by West Semitic peoples speaking an Old Canaanite tongue. The time of their settlement can be no later than the Egyptian Old Kingdom, when Canaanite names are first attested, and probably goes back into the late 4th millennium. Racially these early settlers were Mediterranean with some mixture of other stocks. In the 16th and 15th centuries, the Hurrian invasions added a large element of Alpine traits.

After 1200 the Old Canaanite area was divided into three parts: Palestine, Aram, and Phoenicia. (1) In the south the **tribes of Israel** and associated peoples conquered the area later known as **Palestine.** It comprised Syrian territory south of Mount Hermon. In the course of the 12th century the Sea Peoples, notably the Philistines, took the coastal plain south of Mount Carmel, north of the River of Egypt, pressing Israel's border back into the low hill country (*Shephelah*). (2) The **Aramaean invasions** created a second division, **Aram.** This was the area of the Aramaean city states and later Aramaean empire. Its southern boundary lay below Damascus in the Hauran. Its northern limit was in the district of the Late Hittite city states between the Amanus and the Euphrates. The western border of Aram lay on the eastern side of the coastal range, Mount Bargylus (Jebel Nuseiriyeh) and Mount Lebanon. (3) The name of the third division, **Phoenicia,** is applied to the long narrow strip of land along the Mediterranean Sea from Arvad, north of the Eleutherus River, to Mount Carmel in the south. This was the remnant of the

old Canaanite domain into which the Canaanites were eventually squeezed. By an arbitrary change of terminology, the Canaanites after 1200 are called Phoenicians. Actually "Phoenicia" is merely the Greek translation of "Canaan," "the land of purple (merchants)."

b. THE OLD CANAANITES, TO c. 900 B.C.

33rd to 29th centuries. Early Bronze Age I. City states developed in Syria-Palestine. The Canaanites served as mediators between the Protoliterate culture of Mesopotamia and the Gerzean culture of Egypt.

29th to 27th centuries. Early Bronze Age II. Syria-Palestine developed swiftly in urbanization and in size of population. There is indirect evidence for an Egyptian campaign into Palestine in this period. Egyptian inscriptions begin at Byblos with Nebka (Khasekhemwi).

27th to 22nd centuries. Early Bronze Age IIIA and IIIB. Egypt seems to have exercised commercial if not political control of Palestine in the Old Kingdom (2615–2175). We have direct evidence of military campaigns into Palestine in the 5th Dynasty (2440–2315), and in the 6th Dynasty, Weni, the general of Phiops I (c. 2300), left a report of his Syrian wars. **Sargon the Great** (2360–2305) conquered lands in northern Syria. At the end of this period the Canaanites developed their first indigenous writing system, a syllabary of pictographs based indirectly on Egyptian hieroglyphics.

21st to 19th centuries. Middle Bronze Age I. This era witnessed the great **Amorite movements** into Syria-Palestine, as well as into Babylonia, bringing the end of the Ur Empire (c. 1952). The *Execration Texts* (c. 1925–1825) from the Middle Kingdom in Egypt establish that Egypt claimed suzerainty over southern Syria-Palestine. The latter part of this period has been identified with the Patriarchal

("Abrahamic") age. Transjordan and much of the Syrian hinterland became nomadic in the 20th century.

1850–1500. Middle Bronze Age II. The first phase of this period (IIA, 1850–1750) was a time of settlement of the nomadic Amorites. Egyptian power in Syria-Palestine collapsed in the early 18th century. In many ways, Middle Bronze Age IIB-C (1750–1500) was the **golden age of Palestine.** The early Hyksos (for the most part Syro-Palestinian princes) built enormous fortifications of earthen-work (*terre pisée*), and began building an empire in the west. Hazor, Qatna, and Aleppo were the great centers of power contemporary with the Mari age in Mesopotamia. Yantin'ammu ruled in Byblos (c. 1678–1590), the 15th Dynasty in Egypt (c. 1678–1590), the "Great Hyksos," exercised feudal authority in both Palestine and Egypt. Late in phase IIC of this period (1650–1500), the **Hurrians** streamed into Palestine.

1500–1400. Late Bronze Age I. Syria-Palestine fell under the power of the militant kings of the New Kingdom. Tuthmosis III (1504–1450) established full political control over the whole of Syria. The first extensive epigraphs in the Proto-Canaanite alphabet made their appearance.

1400–1200. Late Bronze Age II. Syria-Palestine continued under **Egyptian control** during the reign of Amenophis III (1417–1379), but the administration of the empire decayed steadily in the time of Akhenaten (1379–1362). This era, the 'Amarna Age, is vividly illuminated by international correspondence, especially the letters of greater and lesser vassal kings of Syria to Egypt. The population of Syria was mixed, Canaanite, Amorite, and Hurrian. The society was feudal, stratified with a nobility of chariot warriors, serfs beneath, and little or no middle class. One segment of the population became freebooters and mercenaries, the so-called **'Apiru.** Their

Syrians bearing tribute to Egypt (tomb painting from Thebes)

condottieri often seized towns or ravaged the countryside. **Ugarit** was one of the great cities of Canaan in the 14th and 13th centuries, alternating under Egyptian and Hittite suzerainty. We possess both Egyptian and Hittite diplomatic correspondence with the Ugaritic kings Ammishtamru I (c. 1380) and Niqmadda II (c. 1365–1325). From the 14th century come the epic and mythological **texts from Ugarit** written in a cuneiform adaptation of the Canaanite alphabet. These include the Ba'al and 'Anat cycle, and the Keret and Dan'el or Aqhat texts. At Ugarit and throughout Canaan in this period, the chief gods of the pantheon were **'El,** creator of heaven and earth, and patriarch in the council of the gods; **Ba'al-Haddu,** the young storm god and effective king of the gods; **Asherah-Elat,** 'El's consort and mother goddess; and **'Anat,** bloody war goddess and heavenly courtesan. International trade flourished in the Late Bronze Age. The Canaanites developed their **purple dye industry** and became famous for it throughout the Ancient World. The Mycenaean Greeks exported pottery to the Levant especially be-

Ritual dish, Ugarit, Late Bronze Age II

Statue of a king, Syria, Late Bronze Age I

David anointed by Samuel

come onto firmer historical ground in the era of **Moses,** contemporary of Ramesses II (1304–1237), though even here our sources derive from religious epic, much of it transmitted orally for longer or shorter periods. Elements of the tribes of Israel escaped from serfdom in the eastern delta of Egypt under the leadership of Moses and his Levitic clansmen. A **Proto-Israelite league** was formed in the wilderness south of Canaan, the clans and disparate peoples being bound into a legal community by a covenant with the god **Yahweh,** mediated by Moses. The new religion had many traits in common with Patriarchal religion: its covenantal form, the conception of Yahweh as leader in war, and the character of Yahweh as creator and judge. In fact, it has been argued plausibly that Yahweh is a cultic name of the old Canaanite and Amorite god 'El. At the same time, the religion of Moses differs from past religious tradition in significant ways from its beginnings. Its cult centered in historical remembrance of Israel's past: the exodus from Egypt and the conquest of Canaan. In memory and re-enactment, the community's covenant was forged anew. In contrast, the Canaanite cults centered in re-enactment of "primordial" events: the battle of creation, the *heiros gamos,* etc. Moreover, there appears to be no trace in our received traditions of a divine consort of Yahweh, the *sine qua non* of the Canaanite nature cults.

The conquest of the land was well advanced when Merneptah in 1232 recorded his defeat of Israel in Palestine, an event not remembered in biblical sources. Once established in Palestine, the league grew rapidly by covenant with new clans and by conquest. A number of Canaanite cities fell to Israelite arms including Hazor, the "head of the kingdom" in the land.

1200–1020. THE PERIOD OF THE JUDGES. While Israel had been successful in her first wave of conquest, a number of large Canaanite cities remained unconquered, and some that had been defeated regained power. Settlement and consolidation was imperiled also by the invasions of other peoples: the Philistines, Moabites, and Midianites in the 12th century, the Ammonites about 1100. Israel's full control of the land was not established until the time of David. The **Judges** of the pre-monarchic period responded to these threats to Israel's life, rallying as many tribes of the loosely knit league as would react to a specific danger. The office of the "judge" in Israel was primarily military and impermanent. In the 12th century **Gideon of Manasseh** led the northern tribes against the Midianites, camel-riding nomads from the Arabian desert. This is the first historical notice of the extensive use of camels, which evidently were domesticated about this time. Perhaps the most serious threat of the 12th century came from a coalition of Canaanite kings in the days of Deborah. The Israelite league was victorious in a battle fought in the Esdraelon Valley about 1125, celebrated in the *Song of Deborah* (Judges 5). The Philistines were not a serious menace to Israel for most of the 12th century. However, border strife intensified in the late 12th and early 11th century, a condition reflected in the legendary cycle of Samson tales. In the course of the 11th century the Philistines united under the king of Gath, and became aggressive. Israel was conquered by

tween about 1375 and 1225. In 1283, Ramesses the Great and Khattusilis III divided Syria between themselves, the boundary at the Eleutherus River (Nahr el-Kebir), a boundary line that persisted in early biblical traditions of the "Promised Land."

Late 13th to 11th centuries. Invasions of Syria-Palestine. Elements of the tribal peoples that were to make up the later nation of Israel left the eastern Delta of Egypt and the southern desert and stormed Palestine in the third quarter of the 13th century. Their presence in Palestine is recorded in the stele of Merneptah (1232). They were joined evidently by kindred folk, as well as by rebellious or dispossessed elements in Palestine's feudal society, in the formation of the early **Israelite league.** About 1180, Sea Peoples, notably the Philistines and Tjikar, settled in the coastal plain of Palestine from Gaza to Mount Carmel. In the early period of their occupation they formed a loose league of five city states governed by "tyrants" (*seranim*): Gaza, Gath, Ashkelon, Ashdod, and Ekron. With the fall of the Hittite Empire, the Hittites, especially Luwian elements, moved into north Syria and formed the **Late Hittite principalities:** a northern group under the hegemony of Carchemish, and a southern group: Ya'diya, Khattina, Arpad, Til Barsip, and Hamath. The southern group became Aramaean states in the course of the late 11th and 10th centuries for the most part: Bit Agusi (Ar-

pad) c. 900 or slightly later, Sam'al (Ya'diya) c. 920, and Bit Adini (Til Barsip) about 1000. As early as the late 12th century the Aramaeans had moved into southern Syria *en masse,* and in the course of the 11th century became dominant in the region of Damascus and Zobah (the valleys of the Anti-Lebanon, south of modern Homs). The Canaanites receded before the blows of these invasions to the narrow strip of coastal land from Tyre northward to Arvad, Phoenicia. Later they expanded south to Carmel, and a number of large Canaanite enclaves remained behind in Israelite, Philistine, and Aramaean country. Sidon and Byblos were the chief city states of the Phoenician coast at the beginning of the 12th century. Ugarit and Tyre had been destroyed by invaders. However, Tyre was refounded in the 12th century by the Sidonians, and shortly became the capital of the Sidonian state.

c. THE ISRAELITES, c. 2000–722 B.C.

2000–1200. ISRAELITE ORIGINS. The beginnings of Israel's religion and historical traditions may be traced back into the Patriarchal period, in the Middle Bronze Age (20th–16th centuries). The sagas preserved in the so-called epic **traditions of the Pentateuch** recall events and persons and in part the religious and social color of this ancient time. We

the Philistines about 1050. The central shrine of the league at Shiloh was destroyed, and the Ark taken as booty. The last of the judges, **Samuel,** failed largely to free Israel from the Philistine yoke. He was forced finally to institute kingship in Israel to bring the tribes under a stronger central authority. **Saul** was annointed king in c. 1020.

1020–961. SAUL AND DAVID. Saul's kingship was sharply limited. The primary title in use by both Saul and David was *nagid,* "military commander." Moreover the rise of a new class of charismatics, the *nabi'im,* "prophets," served as a check on the king, preventing at least for a time the emergence of full-blown Canaanite kingship. Saul's capital was a modest fortress built at Gibeah. He was successful for a time in his wars with the Philistines, but fell at the catastrophic battle of Gilboa. He was succeeded by David (1000–961), Israel's greatest king. David was elected king of Judah upon Saul's death, and shortly gained power also over the northern tribes. He conquered **Jerusalem** and made the neutral city his capital. He carefully preserved the old religious institutions of the league by bringing the Ark to Jerusalem and housing it in a tabernacle, giving his new national shrine the nimbus of the old league sanctuary. He conquered the Philistines and made them a vassal state. He subjugated also the surrounding nations, including the early Aramaean power

to the north, Aram Zobah. David did not conquer Phoenicia, but entered into a treaty with **Hiram of Tyre,** king of the Sidonians (969–936). When he died his kingdom stretched from the Euphrates in the northeast to the Gulf of Aqabah in the southeast. The era of David was also a time of literary activity in Israel. The religious and literary traditions of the era of the Judges were collected at this time and transformed into an epic (the so-called *Yahwistic source*), a major stage in the history of Pentateuchal tradition.

961–922. THE REIGN OF SOLOMON. While David had eschewed outright innovations which seriously violated traditional religious and social institutions, his son Solomon sought to transform Israel into a full-fledged Oriental monarchy. He built a dynastic temple, identical in plan and decoration with Canaanite temples of the period, except that the usual cult statue was replaced in the cella by the Ark. His building operations included a magnificent palace and citadel in Jerusalem, the fortifications of Gezer and Megiddo, and a copper refinery at Ezion-geber. To facilitate tax gathering and the imposition of the corvée, he centralized his control of the state by breaking up the traditional tribal boundaries into arbitrary administrative districts. The standing army was vastly expanded and equipped with chariots. His reign was kept peaceful by treaties and diplomatic marriages

with other dynasties. In partnership with Hiram of Tyre he organized a great fleet of ships for trade in the Mediterranean, and on the Red Sea and Indian Ocean. With Cilicia and Egypt he developed a cartel in horses and chariots, and with the South Arabian kings arranged control of the caravan routes for trade in incense and aromatics.

922. The Disruption of the Monarchy. Rebellion followed immediately upon Solomon's death and the accession of his son **Rehoboam.** Solomon's breach of Yahwistic tradition, and the oppressive tactics of the king and the new nobility, were sorely resented, especially among the northern tribes. **Jeroboam I** became king in the north (Israel), Rehoboam remained king in the south (Judah).

922–722. The (Northern) Kingdom of Israel.

922–900. The Dynasty of Jeroboam I. Civil war between Rehoboam (c. 922–915) and Jeroboam I (c. 922–901) was broken off by the raid of Shishak (Shoshenq I, 935–914) in 918. He devastated Edom, Judah, and much of the Israelite north. Jeroboam organized a new national cult at the Patriarchal sanctuary of Bethel in an attempt to break ties of loyalty of the northern tribes to the sanctuary in Jerusalem. This disruption of the religious unity of Israel was viewed as a grave sin both by traditionalist circles in Shiloh, and, of course, by Judaeans including **Amos** (c. 750) and the Deuteronomistic historian (compiler of Deu-

Tomb of Absalom, son of David, near Jerusalem

Jehu paying homage to Shalmaneser

teronomy, Joshua, Judges, Samuel, and Kings). Jeroboam's son Nadab (901–900) was murdered by Baasha.

900–876. The Dynasty of Baasha. Baasha attempted to re-ignite the smouldering civil war with Judah. Asa of Judah (913–873), however, called upon Ben Hadad I, king of Aram-Damascus (880–842). The latter attacked Baasha, laying waste part of Galilee and annexing territory northeast of the Yarmuk River (878). Baasha's son Elah (877–876) was assassinated by Zimri (876), who in turn was burnt to death in his palace in Tirzah by Omri.

876–842. The Omride Dynasty. Omri established a long-lived dynasty. He built a new capital at Samaria, and renewed alliances with Tyre by the marriage of Jezebel, daughter of Ittoba'al, king of Tyre (887–856) to Ahab, the crown prince. He also reconquered Moab as we learn from the Mesha inscription. Omri was evidently a strong king. The Assyrians called Israel after his name, Bît 'Omri (Khumri). Ahab (869–850) fought defensive wars with Ben Hadad, but when the menace of Shalmaneser III (859–825) became clear after the subjugation of Bît Adini, the two joined against Assyria. In the **battle of Qarqar** in 854, Ahab of Israel, Ben Hadad of Damascus, and Irkhuleni of Hamath headed the coalition that stopped Shalmaneser's march of conquest. Ahab met his end in Transjordan fighting again against Ben Hadad. One of the most vivid figures in Israelite history flourished in this time, **Elijah the prophet.** He battled against the cult of Tyrian Ba'al sponsored by Jezebel, and began a religious revolution against economic injustice that ultimately brought down the house of Omri. Ahab was succeeded by Ahaziah (850–849) and by Joram (849–842).

842–748. The Dynasty of Jehu. In 842, the soldier Jehu at the instigation of Elisha led an open rebellion against the king and his oppressive and pagan nobility. Ahaziah of Judah was killed in the blood purge. In the same year Shalmaneser attacked and defeated Hazael of Damascus (842–806), who had just come to the throne. Jehu weakly paid tribute. Assyrian power was on the wane, however, and Hazael recovered and set out to win an empire. In Jehu's reign he took Transjordan. In the time of Joahaz (814–798), he reduced Israel to a dependency, conquered Philistia, and put Judah under enormous tribute. Meanwhile he had unified the Aramaean states. Hazael died in c. 806, shortly before Assyria returned to fight against Damascus. The campaign of Adadnirari III in 806 left Aram too weak to hold together its empire. Joash (798–782) led Israel in wars against Ben Hadad II (c. 806–750) in which he recovered Israel's lost territories. Later he turned against Judah and defeated Amaziah (797–769), taking Jerusalem and reducing the southern kingdom to vassalage. During the long reign of Amaziah's son **Jeroboam II** (783–748) Israel grew wealthy and powerful. Damascus and Hamath came under Israelite suzerainty for the first time since the days of Solomon. **Amos** and **Hosea** prophesied against the decadence and corruption of the times of Jeroboam. Zechariah (748), the last of the dynasty, was assassinated by Shallum.

748–722. The Last Days of Israel. Shallum (748) was killed in continued civil strife by Menahem (748–738). In his last year Menahem paid tribute to Tiglathpileser III (745–728). Pekahiah (738–736) was killed by the anti-Assyrian party led by Pekah (736–732). Rezin, king of Aram (750–732) and Pekah entered into a league against Assyria, and when Ahaz of Judah refused to join the conspiracy, declared war on Judah. Ahaz appealed to Assyria for aid. Tiglathpileser came west in 734–732, laying waste both Israel and Damascus (732). Much of Israel and the whole of Aram were turned into provinces of Assyria. Hoshea (732–723) was appointed king in Samaria by the Assyrians. About 725 he rebelled, hoping to receive aid from Tefnakhte, an Egyptian ruler of the 24th Dynasty. He was shortly captured by the Assyrians, and in 722 Samaria fell after a three year siege. Sargon II (722–706) claimed to have taken captive 27,290 Israelites.

d. THE KINGDOM OF JUDAH, 922–586

922–842. Rehoboam (922–915) died shortly after Shishak's raid. Civil war continued intermittently through the reigns of Abijah (915–913) and Asa (913–873). **Jehoshaphat** made peace with Ahab of Israel, and joined him in wars against Damascus. Judicial reforms are attributed to Jehoshaphat by the Chronicler. Jehoshaphat was succeeded by his son Jehoram (849–842) and by his grandson Ahaziah (842), who was killed in the Jehu revolution.

842–836. Athaliah, the dowager queen, seized power and tried to secure her throne by destroying the Davidic house. A small son of Ahaziah escaped, however, and in 836 with the backing of the high priest, Jehoash was enthroned and Athaliah killed.

836–769. Jehoash (836–797) came to the throne coeval with Hazael's rise to great power. He was forced to pay a heavy tribute to Aram. His son Amaziah (797–769) did not improve Judah's lot but lost his independence in a war against Joash of Israel.

769–734. THE REIGN OF UZZIAH (Azariah). The fortunes of Judah changed in the course of the rule of Uzziah. His military ventures in Philistia, Edom, and northern Arabia placed important caravan traffic in Judaean control. After the death of Jeroboam, his powerful rival in Israel, Uzziah became head of the western **coalition against Assyria.** He was defeated by Tiglathpileser shortly before 738, but unlike Hamath and his northern allies, escaped with little harm. In his later years Uzziah became a leper and lived in isolation from his court. His son Jotham served as regent (749–734). Jotham survived his father's death only a short while (734).

734–715. Ahaz came to the throne in 734 in time to face attack from the Syro-Ephraimite coalition: Pekah of Israel and Rezin of Aram. Against the prophet Isaiah's advice he appealed to Assyria. The Assyrian destruction of Damascus and Israel followed.

715–687. THE REIGN OF HEZEKIAH. Religious and political reforms were enacted by Hezekiah as part of a general plan to revive the glory of the days of David. Heze-

Isaiah in contemplation

kiah entered into a far-flung coalition against the new king of Assyria, **Sennacherib** (705–682). In 701 Sennacherib marched westward to meet Hezekiah and his Phoenician, Philistine, and Egyptian allies. King Luli of the Sidonians fled in terror to Cyprus. Egyptian forces under Shabaka were easily defeated at Elteqeh, and Philistia fell. Sennacherib then reduced 46 walled cities of Judah according to his own report, and left Hezekiah shut up in Jerusalem "like a bird in a cage." Hezekiah capitulated, paying heavy tribute. Some confusion exists in the biblical sources dealing with Sennacherib's campaign. There is evidence, sharply disputed, that two separate campaigns of Sennacherib, one in the time of Shabaka, one in Taharqo's reign (after 689), are telescoped in the biblical account, and that at the end of Sennacherib's reign, Jerusalem was again besieged by the Assyrians but once more escaped destruction.

687–640. Manasseh (687–642) and his son Amon (642–640) ruled as puppets of Assyria during the brilliant reigns of Esarhaddon (681–670) and Assurbanapal (669–627). Manasseh is particularly remembered in biblical tradition for his syncretistic cults, including, no doubt, the official Assyrian cult, and for child sacrifice.

640–609. The Reign of Josiah. The progressive decay of Assyrian authority in the last years of Assurbanapal and during the reigns of his weak successors is sensitively reflected in Judaean politics. In the eighth year of his reign Josiah, under the guidance of his elders, "began to seek the God of David his father," that is to say, repudiated the gods of his Assyrian overlords. In 627, about the time of Assurbanapal's death, Josiah moved into the old territory of Israel, annexing the Assyrian provinces of Samaria, Gilead, and Galilee. About the same time he established garrisons along the *via maris* in Philistia. In 622 Josiah launched a full-scale politico-religious program for the re-establishment of the Davidic kingdom. A forgotten law book, the nucleus of Deuteronomy, was republished and made the basis of the religious reform. Foreign and syncretistic cults were extirpated. Worship was centralized in Jerusalem. Unfortunately the reign of Josiah and the new golden age of Judah were cut short. In 609 Josiah met his death at Megiddo fighting a delaying action against Neko II, who was hastening to Assyria's aid.

609–586. The Fall of Judah. Jehoahaz II (609) ruled briefly before being removed from the throne by Neko and replaced by Jehoiakim (609–598). Jehoiakim transferred his allegiance to Nebuchadrezzar after the defeat of the Egyptians at Carchemish (605), but rebelled about 601, presumably after Necho's defeat of Nebuchadrezzar on the Egyptian border (601). In 598 Nebuchadrezzar led his forces against Judah. Jehoiakim died (perhaps by violence), leaving his son to pay for his folly. Jehoichin reigned three months (598–597) before Jerusalem fell. He and large numbers of his people were carried captive to Babylonia. Nebuchadrezzar replaced Jehoichin with Zedekiah (597–587). Despite the eloquent protests of Jeremiah, Zedekiah was tempted into revolt in league with Egypt. Nebuchadrezzar laid siege to Jerusalem in January, 588. The city fell and its temple was

Sennacherib's forces during the siege of Lachish, 701 B.C.

The ancient city of Jerusalem, with the Temple

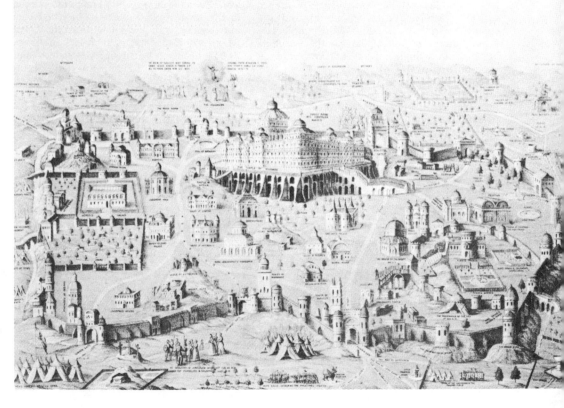

razed in July, 586. A second group of captives was taken to Babylon.

586–539. THE JEWS UNDER BABYLONIAN RULE. Judah was left a desolate land stripped of its leadership. Nevertheless, after the murder of Gedaliah, the governor of the province, the Chaldeans carried out a third deportation (582). In Babylon the Jewish community was treated well. Strange to say the captivity was an extremely creative period in Israel's religious life and literature. The oracles of Ezekiel and Second Isaiah were composed in this period. The Deuteronomic history, first compiled in the time of Josiah, was edited and brought up to date. The so-called Priestly edition of the Pentateuch was also prepared during the Exile.

539–332. Judah under Persian Rule. Babylon

Ezra reveals the text of the Law

fell to Cyrus in 539. The Persian king released the Jews, those who wished, to return to Zion. Many returned in the 6th and 5th centuries. In the years 520–515 the temple was rebuilt at the urging of Haggai the prophet. Nehemiah, a high official of Artaxerxes I (Longimanus, 464–424) took leave of his office to come to the aid of the Jerusalem community. In 445 he came as governor to Jerusalem. He rebuilt the ancient walls of the city in 439, overcoming the opposition of Sanballat, governor of Samaria, and Tobiah, the Jew-

ish governor of Ammon. The date of **Ezra's mission** is disputed. Evidently he was a younger contemporary of Nehemiah, and perhaps his mission is best dated in 438. Ezra instituted cultic and legal reforms with far-reaching effects on the development of Post-exilic Judaism.

332. Palestine conquered by Alexander the Great.

e. THE ARAMAEANS IN SYRIA-PALESTINE, 1300–732 B.C.

1300–1000. Early Aramaean Movements. In the late 14th century cuneiform records begin to mention a new group of nomadic peoples entering Mesopotamia and Syria called the Akhlamu. In the time of Tiglathpileser I (1116–1078) there is specific mention of the *akhlame armaya,* against whom Assyria directed military actions in the region of Palmyra. The relation between the Akhlamu and the later Aramaeans is not wholly clear; the Aramaeans at least replaced the Akhlamu, if they are not to be identified with them. In the course of the 11th century Aramaean bands flooded the Fertile Crescent. One major movement was directed west into Syria, others into Upper Mesopotamia and Babylonia.

1000–900. Early Aram and Israel. The earliest Aramaic states to form, so far as we know, were Zobah (Subatu) and Damascus. Already in the time of Saul (1020–1000) Israel came into conflict with the kings of Aram Zobah. About 970 Hadadezer of Beth Rehob, king of Zobah, headed a league of lesser states including Maacah, Beth Rehob, Tob, and perhaps Geshur and Damascus. On the pretext of aiding Ammon, Hadadezer attacked Davidic territory far south in Transjordan, probably with designs on the trade routes from the south. He was defeated by David in an initial engage-

ment. Later, despite reinforcements from Damascus and farther east, Hadadezer was overcome by Israelite arms. David extended his border north to Hamath, northeast to the Euphrates. Rezon, a captain of Hadadezer, went with troops to Damascus and set himself up as king. Presumably this was shortly after David's death (c. 961), since Rezon is identified as an enemy of Solomon. In the course of the 10th century a number of the Late Hittite city states became Aramaean: Bît Agusi (Arpad), Sam'al (Ya'diya), and Bît Adini (Til Barsip). Carchemish and other northern Hittite states in league with Carchemish were heavily infiltrated by Aramaeans, but kept Hittite dynasties until their incorporation into the Assyrian Empire.

900–842. THE RISE OF DAMASCUS. Ben Hadad I (Hadadezer, 880–842), was the grandson of Hezyon, the son of Tabrimmon (Tabraman). We know little beside the names of Hezyon and Tabraman, and that they ruled in Damascus. Ben Hadad in 878 attacked Baasha at the request of Asa, king of Judah. He ravaged Naphtali and probably at this time annexed the territory of Bashan north of the Yarmuk. The campaigns of Assurnasirapli II (884–860) warned the Aramaean states of the danger of resurgent Assyria. Shalmaneser III (859–825) set out early in his reign to break the power of the Aramaean states. In 858 he engaged a coalition of northern Aramaean and Hittite states at Lutibu in Sam'al. Khayan, son of Gabbar, king of Sam'al, Akhuni of Bît Adini, together with the Hittite kings of Carchemish and Khattina, were defeated but not broken. Shalmaneser returned to the wars against the northern league, finally splitting it up. In the years 857–855 he attacked Akhuni of Bît Adini, the strongest of these princes, and conquered the state. Akhuni was taken captive, and Bît Adini turned into a province of Assyria. About this same time Ben Hadad and Ahab were engaged in

Bronze panel from the gate of the palace of Shalmaneser III, showing the king's expedition against Hamath

warfare. Ben Hadad besieged Samaria with the aid of 32 kings under his hegemony. Apparently Ahab finally fought off the Aramaeans. In the following year after a severe defeat at Aphek, Ben Hadad settled happily for a treaty with Israel.

With the northern coalition broken, Shalmaneser turned against the southern states. Ben Hadad led the coalition of twelve city states which included Ahab of Israel and Irkhuleni of Hamath. At Qarqar in the territory of Hamath the armies met. Shalmaneser was forced to retire to Assyria. The swift growth of Damascene power is illustrated by a stele set up by Ben Hadad about 850 in the vicinity of Aleppo. By the time of the battle of Qarqar, Damascus appears to have been virtually the sole Aramaean power in the south. Evidently all the small Aramaean states of southern Syria were absorbed by Ben Hadad. Shalmaneser returned in four additional campaigns against Aram, finally succeeding in breaking the coalition's power in 842. Ben Hadad was murdered in 842 by Hazael, a commoner, who mounted the throne.

842–806. The Reign of Hazael. After a perfunctory campaign against Damascus in 839, Assyria ceased to intervene in the west for more than 30 years. Hazael was left free to pursue Aram's imperial ambitions. He subjugated Israel, and Philistia in good part, and placed a heavy tribute on Judah. He died in c. 806, shortly before the raid of Adadnirari III on Damascus in the same year.

806–732. The Decline of Aram. Ben Hadad II (Mari, c. 806–750) was unable to hold together the Aramaean empire of Hazael. Early in his reign he led a coalition of north Syrian kings against Zakir, king of Hamath, but failed to subdue him. Joash of Israel fought free of Damascene control, and under Jeroboam II (783–748) Damascus as well as Hamath actually became tributary to Israel. With the decline of Damascus, a northern Aramaean state came to the fore: Arpad or Bît Agusi. Matiel, after becoming a vassal of Assurnirari V in 755, broke faith and led the Aramaean states into a treaty with Ketek, an ally of Urartu, Assyria's most powerful enemy. Tiglathpileser III (745–727) defeated the Urartean allies at Arpad in 743. After a three-year siege Arpad fell. Azariah of Judah, the strongest king left in Syria-Palestine, became leader of the coalition. He was defeated shortly before 738. In 734 Pekah of Israel and Rezin, son of Ben Hadad II, attempted to rally Syria's failing Aramaic states once more. Ahaz, a faithful vassal of Assyria, refused to join the coalition, and when attacked by the two kings, called for aid from Assyria. Tiglathpileser laid waste Israel and Damascus. The whole of Aram-Damascus was divided into Assyrian provinces (732). This was the effective end of Aram as a political entity.

f. THE PHOENICIANS, 1100–332 B.C.

1100–888. The Rise of the Sidonian State. The Phoenicians did not fully recover from the blows that had ravaged their cities and robbed them of nine-tenths of their territory until the beginning of the 10th century. They turned more than ever to the sea, extending

Phoenician seamen and traders

their trade routes and establishing trading colonies. Their expansion into the Mediterranean probably began after David broke the power of the Philistine Empire at the beginning of the 10th century. Colonization proceeded swiftly, evidently to Cyprus first, to Sicily and Sardinia, to Utica on the African coast, and finally to Spain. There is archaeological evidence that Spain was reached no later than the 9th century, and perhaps was colonized as early as 950. This extraordinary development of the Phoenicians as a maritime people must be attributed to **Hiram I of Tyre** (969–936) and his father Abiba'al. Tyre, built on an island, was a superbly defended harbor. After its refounding by Sidonians in the 12th century, it quickly became the capital of the Sidonian state. Hiram ruled the Sidonians in the most brilliant period of Phoenician history. He was a younger contemporary of David (1000–961), with whom he entered into league. His covenant with Israel persisted in the time of Solomon, when Phoenician influence on Israel reached its height. Hiram's workmen designed and built the temple of Solomon. Hiram's and Solomon's joint fleets sailed the Mediterranean Sea and the Indian Ocean. Of particular importance were the Tarshish fleets, ships linking distant mining and refining centers with Levantine ports. In the reign of Hiram the Sidonian state spread southward to Mount Carmel, northward to Arvad, unifying Phoenicia. However, vassal dynasties continued to rule at Byblos and Arvad. From the **kings of Byblos** in this period come a regular series of inscriptions: the sarcophogus inscription of Ahiram (c. 1000) prepared by his son Ittoba'al (c. 975), and dedicatory inscriptions of Yehimilk (c. 950), Abiba'al (c. 930), Eliba'al (c. 920), and Shipitba'al (c. 900). We know little of Hiram's successors: Ba'almazzer I (935–919), Abd'ashtart (918–910), Ashtart (909–898), 'Astartrom (897–889), and Pilles (888).

887–856. Ittoba'al was a priest of Astarte, according to tradition, who, having killed Pilles, initiated a new dynasty. Omri of Israel arranged a marriage between Jezebel, Ittoba'al's daughter, and his own son Ahab. It may be that Ittoba'al was also linked by marriage with the house of Ben Hadad I. Phoenician religious and cultural influence became powerful both in Samaria and in Damascus.

855–774. Ba'al'azor (855–850) succeeded Ittoba'al and in turn was followed by Ba'almazzer II (849–830) who paid tribute to Shalmaneser III in 842. He was succeeded by Mittin (829–821) and by Pu'myaton (Pygmalion, 820–774). Tradition relates that Pygmalion's sister Elissa fled from Tyre and founded the city of Carthage in the king's seventh year (814). The founding date, if not the legend, is almost certainly accurate.

774–701. Hiram II paid tribute to Tiglathpileser in 738. Luli (c. 730?–701) conspired with Hezekiah and the Egyptians to rebel against Sennacherib (705–682). In 701 Sennacherib forced Luli to flee for his life to Cyprus, an event portrayed in Sennacherib's reliefs. Sennacherib set up separate vassal kings in Sidon and in Tyre.

701–627. Ittoba'al II, the appointee of Sennacherib, was at length replaced by 'Abdmilkot, who rebelled against Esarhaddon. In 677 the Assyrian suzerain razed Sidon to the ground and built for himself a new city opposite the old site which he named Kar-Esarhaddon. He caught 'Abdmilkot escaping by sea and cut off his head. Sidon became a province of Assyria. Ba'al, king of Tyre, also rebelled in the reign of Esarhaddon, but soon capitulated. His mainland territories were taken from him and he paid tribute. However, he was still king of Tyre in the reign of Assurbanapal.

627–539. After the death of Assurbanapal, the Phoenicians enjoyed a brief period of independence. However, the Phoenicians were unable to recover fully. Greek coloniza-

Sarcophagus of King Eshmun'azor

Sarcophagus of King Tabnit

tion had ended their near monopoly in the Mediterranean.

The Chaldean rulers did not leave Phoenicia free of oppressors for long. Nebuchadrezzar the Great invested Tyre in the reign of Ittoba'al III in 587, the year Jerusalem fell. After thirteen years of siege, Tyre surrendered in 573. Ba'al II succeeded Ittoba'al III. Tyre then was ruled by judges for a short time after which the monarchy was restored.

539–332. Phoenicia under Persian Rule. In the fourteenth year of the reign of Hiram III, Cyrus the Great came to power in Babylon. Phoenicia became a part of the fifth satrapy. Nevertheless vassal kings still continued to rule in Sidon, Tyre, Arvad, and Byblos. The celebrated inscriptions of Tabnit and Eshmun'azor, kings of Sidon, come from the later part of the 5th century. Phoenician fleets played an important part in Persia's wars with Greece. In c. 350 Tennes led a revolt against the Persians in Sidon. He was crushed by Artaxerxes III with great loss of life.

332. The Conquest of Phoenicia by Alexander. With the exception of Tyre, the Phoenician vassals of Persia attempted no resistance to Alexander. Still confident in his city's protected perch in the sea, **Azemilkos,** the last king of Tyre, refused Alexander entrance. The city was besieged by the Macedonians from January to July/August 332. Alexander threw a mole across from the mainland to the island and finally breached the city's defenses. The siege of Tyre was notorious for the atrocities committed by the Tyrians against Macedonian prisoners, and for the fierce vengeance exacted by Alexander when the city fell. A reported 8,000 were slain and 30,000 sold into slavery.

The main industries of Phoenicia were the manufacture of purple dye, weaving, glass, and metal working. Iron and copper were mined in Cyprus and worked by the Phoenicians, using techniques which originated in Egypt and Babylon.

(Cont. p. 96.)

4. *Anatolia, to 547* B.C.

a. THE LAND AND THE PEOPLE

The peninsula of Anatolia or Asia Minor stretches westward from the Armenian mountains to the Aegean Sea. It is separated from Syria by the Taurus range on the south, and from Upper Mesopotamia by the Anti-Taurus, a chain running northeastward to the Armenian massif. The central highland or plateau is ringed about with mountains, and near its center sinks into a basin which traps drainage waters in a salt lake (Tuz Göl). The people of ancient Anatolia were dominantly broad-headed Armenoids, but owing to repeated invasions became mixed, especially with people of Mediterranean affinities.

b. THE HITTITES, TO c. 1200 B.C.

The founders of the great Hittite state are called after the name of their land Khattu, "Hittites." Actually this designation more appropriately applies to one stratum of the Hittite population, no doubt the predecessors of the Hittites, now called "Proto-Khattians." The **Proto-Khattic language,** known from religious texts, is without affinities to other known language groups. The Hittites themselves spoke a language which belongs to the Indo-European family. They called it **Nesian** after the city of Nesa. Other languages closely affiliated include **Luwian,** the language of southeastern and southwestern Anatolia (ancient Kizzuwatna and Arzawa) and **Palaic,** a northern dialect. A form of Luwian is recorded in the Hittite hieroglyphic script used in inscriptions of the later kings and especially in the monuments of Late Hittite city states. A large part of our knowledge of Hittite history and religion stems from the many thousands of documents found in Khattusas (modern **Boghazkoy**), the capital of the Hittite state located in the bend of the Halys River.

The mixture of peoples in the Hittite homeland was ruled by an Indo-European aristocracy. The great king, called the "Sun" in the later titulary, was military leader, high priest, and judge. The nobility and the state were extensions of his person. **Hittite religion** is peculiarly syncretistic. Proto-Khattic, Hurrian, and Akkado-Sumerian gods and myths are mixed with Luwian and Hittite counterparts in a bewildering fashion. The state cult centered about the sun goddess of Arinna. Her Proto-Khattic name was Wurusemu. In the Empire she was identified with Hurrian Khepat. Her consort was the storm-god, Luwian Tarkhunt, Proto-Khattic Taru, the equivalent of Hurrian Teshup. The chief event of the official cult was the *purulli festival,* evidently a New Year's festival, celebrating the combat of the storm-god with the dragon Illuyankas.

c. 1800–1700. The Cappadocian Texts. Our earliest real historical knowledge of the Anatolian plateau stems from the Assyrian merchant colonies in Cappadocia. At the end of the age of the colonies, contemporary with Shamshi-Adad I of Assyria (1748–1716), we learn of a certain Pitkhana and his son Anit-tas, kings of Kussar. They destroyed Hattusas, and established their capital at Nesa (possibly Kanish, modern Kultepe).

c. 1600–1500. The Old Hittite Kingdom. Tudkhaliyas I and Pusarma, who flourished in the late 17th century, are little more than names. **Labarnas I** (c. 1600) was credited with founding the Hittite kingdom, and his boundaries were said to reach the sea. His name and that of his queen Tawannannas were borne by his successors and their queens as if they were titles. **Khattusilis I** (Labarnas II, c. 1580) evidently shifted the capital to Khattusas. He continued the Hittite expansion, conquering Alalakh and attacking Arzawa. His successor **Mursilis I** (c. 1550–1530) subjugated northern Syria, destroying Aleppo. He then boldly marched on Babylon, pillaged it and brought down the 1st Dynasty of Babylon (c. 1531). He returned home to be assassinated. A time of troubles followed, petty king following petty king: Khantilis, Zidantas, Ammunas, and Khuzzias. **Telepinus** came to the throne about 1500 and halted the decline. He pushed back the Hurrians and made a treaty with Kizzuwatna. Telepinus composed an edict proclaiming a law of succession that stabilized the crown. The Hittite law code also dates from this general period.

c. 1450–1200. THE HITTITE EMPIRE.

c. 1450–1380. The Early Kings. Tudkhaliyas II established a new dynasty destined to build an empire. The reigns of the early kings gave no promise of this. In the reigns of Khattusilis II, Tudkhaliyas III, and Arnuwandas I, the state came into a time of grave danger. It was threatened by the Kingdom of Mitanni on the east, Arzawa on the west, and the hordes of Kashka people on the north. The Kashka actually reached Khattusas and sacked it.

c. 1380–1346. The Reign of Suppululiumas. Suppululiumas, a younger son of Tudkhaliyas, took the throne. He fortified and rebuilt his capital and reorganized the home territories. Then he marched into Syria. His first encounter with Tuishrata of Mitanni resulted in a severe defeat. By adding allies, including Artadama II, a rival of Tuishrata, who also claimed the kingship of Mitanni, Suppululiumas later was able to conquer Washukkani, the Mitanni capital. The little kingdoms of northern Syria now easily fell into his hands. Aleppo and Carchemish became vassal kingdoms under sons of Suppululiumas. Ugarit paid tribute. Suppululiumas fell a victim to plague, and shortly after his son, Arnuwandas II, also died.

c. 1344–1316. The Reign of Mursilis II. In his early reign young Mursilis marched against Arzawa in the southwest, crushed a revolt there and killed Arzawa's king. For many years he fought almost annual campaigns against the Kashka. A revolt in Carchemish was pacified. Mursilis' annals are the most extensive historical work from Boghazkoy.

c. 1315–1295? The Reign of Muwatallis. Muwatallis inherited a powerful, well-organized empire from his father. Egypt, however, under Ramesses II, was ambitious to regain her empire. The inevitable clash between the two for the control of Syria came at Qadesh-on-the-Orontes in 1298. Both sides claimed victory. Ramesses when he returned home filled the walls of his temples with boasts of his valor in the battle. But Muwatallis' claim had more justification in view of the fact that he remained firmly in control of northern Syria.

c. 1295–1260. The Reigns of Urkhiteshup and Khattusilis III. Urkhiteshup (c. 1295–1289), Muwatallis' weak son, was shortly deposed by Khattusilis, Muwatallis' brother. Khattusilis

Ruins of the Lion Gate near Boghazkoy

Hittite ritual standard, Early Bronze Age

III (c. 1289–1260) made treaties with the Kassites and in 1283 made his famous treaty with Ramesses II, setting a boundary favorable to the Hittites between their empires. Evidently these moves were made to counter the growing threat of Assyria under Shalmaneser I (1275–1246).

c. 1260–1200. The Decline and Fall of the Hittite Empire. Tudkhaliyas IV (c. 1260–1240) turned to western Anatolia to meet disturbances caused by the Achaeans (Akhkhiyawa), a portent of the future. A good part of his reign was peaceful, however, given to cultic reforms and the arts. Probably the celebrated **reliefs of Yazilikaya** are to be attributed to Tudkhaliyas. In the reign of Arnuwandas III (c. 1240), the situation in the western provinces abruptly worsened. The final waves of **Sea Peoples** and Phrygians which inundated and destroyed the empire probably came in the succeeding short reign of Suppiluliumas II (c. 1230). The Hittites spread through Syria and Palestine. In northern Syria, Hittite culture survived in a series of Late Hittite city states: Melid (Malatya), Kummukh (Commagene), Gurgum, Carchemish, Unqi, Arpad, Ya'diya (Sam'al), Aleppo, Til Barsip, and Hamath. The southernmost of these became Aramaean in the late 11th and 10th centuries.

c. THE PHRYGIANS, TO 547 B.C.

Civilization. The Phrygians (as well as the Mysians) came from Thrace with the great Aegean migrations, about 1200 B.C., and occupied central Anatolia, west of the Halys. Their language belonged to the Indo-European group. Their capital was **Gordion.** Tumuli (sepulchral mounds) are typical of the Phrygians, although graves cut into the rock also occur.

Religion. The chief deities of the Phrygians were **Cybele** (*Ma,* the Great Mother riding in a chariot drawn by lions), whose orgiastic cult was introduced into Rome in 191 B.C., and **Attis,** the god who died as a result of castration but came back to life; his priests, Galli, were eunuchs.

c. 1000–700. The Kingdom of Phrygia, the history of which is not known, was organized and grew in power. **Midas** (*Mita* of Mushku in the inscriptions of Sargon II of Assyria) ruled about 715.

690. The Cimmerian invasion devastated the kingdom; somehow the Phrygian nation survived until the time of Cyrus (547).

d. THE LYDIANS, TO 547 B.C.

Geography. Lydia, whose capital was Sardis, lies in western Asia Minor, between the Ionian cities on the coast and Phrygia; it borders on Mysia in the north and Caria in the south.

Civilization and Religion. Whereas Phrygia constituted a barrier between Greece and the Orient, Lydia became the link between east and west, culturally and commercially. If the Etruscans, or at least their nobility, came from Lydia (according to a classical tradition going back to Herodotus which modern scholarship is inclined to accept), the Lydians contributed materially to the civilization of ancient Italy. The Lydians were great merchants and expert craftsmen; they probably invented coinage. They were fond of horsemanship in the early period, and later contributed to the development of music and the dance; according to Greek tradition, **Aesop** was a Lydian. Little is known about the religion of the Lydians: the gods **Santas** (*Sandon*) and **Baki** (*Bacchus, Dionysos*) were named in their inscriptions.

680–652. Gyges, founder of the dynasty of the Mermnadae, in alliance with Asshurbanapal of Assyria, defeated the Cimmerians and extended the borders of the kingdom. But after sending Carian and Ionian mercenaries to the help of Psamtik, who drove the Assyrians out of Egypt, Gyges fell in battle against the Cimmerians.

652–547. Dynasty of the Mermnadae: Ardys, Sadyattes, Alyattes, Croesus. After overcoming the Cimmerian menace, Ardys and his successors carried out the conquest of the Greek cities on the coast (begun by Gyges), except Miletus, and of the interior of Asia Minor as far as the Halys, with the exception of Lycia. Lydia reached the zenith of her power under **Croesus,** who attacked the Persian Empire, but was defeated and taken prisoner by Cyrus in 547.

547–333. Asia Minor under Persian rule.

5. *Armenia, to 56* B.C.

a. THE KINGDOM OF VAN (URARTU)

Geography. The borders of Urartu (Ararat) cannot be fixed exactly: in a general way the kingdom was located between the Caucasus and Lake Van.

Population. The basic population seems to have been Hurrian; the Hurrian and Vannic languages seem to be related.

Civilization and Religion. The *Vannic inscriptions,* written in Assyrian cuneiform characters but still very obscure, were chiefly annals recording wars and building operations, particularly hydraulic works (the irrigation

Copper figure of a bison, Van, c. 2300 B.C.

Scythian bronze, c. 5th century B.C.

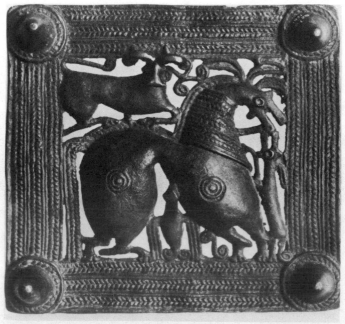

canal of Menuas is still in use). The Vannic people showed special aptitude in industrial arts, particularly metallurgy. At the head of the pantheon, which included numerous deities, stood a triad: **Haldi**, the national god, **Tesheba** (the Hurrian storm-god Teshub), and **Ardini** (a god or goddess of the sun). The temple of Haldi and his consort Bagbartu at Musasir, pictured on a bas-relief of Sargon II of Assyria at Khorsabad, is surprisingly similar to the Greek temples in the Doric style.

c. 1270–850. The Assyrian name for the **Kingdom of Van** (*Uruatri*, later *Urartu*) occurs for the first time in the inscriptions of Shalmaneser I (c. 1275–1246). The lands of the Nairi (east and north of Lake Van) were divided into numerous Hurrian principalities and subject to repeated attacks by the Assyrian kings, particularly by Tukulti-Ninurta I (c. 1245–1209), Tiglathpileser I (c. 1100), Ashurbelkala (c. 1070), Adadnirari II (c. 900), Tukulti-Ninurta II (c. 890), and Assurnasirapli II (884–860).

c. 860–843. Arame, first known king of Urartu, was defeated by Shalmaneser III (859–825), who captured his capital Arzashkun.

c. 832–820. Sarduri I, son of Lutipri, was probably a usurper; he chose Tushpa (Assyrian *Turushpa,* the present Van) as his capital and fortified it. He founded the principal dynasty.

c. 820–800. Ispuini conquered Musasir, appointing his son Sarduri II viceroy there, and was attacked by Shamshiadad V of Assyria.

c. 800–785. Menua, who was at first co-regent with his father Ispuini, enlarged the kingdom considerably, leaving inscriptions over a vast area.

c. 785–760. Argishti I (780–756) annexed the territory along the Araxes and around the Lake of Erivan. Shalmaneser IV of Assyria had no success in his campaigns against Urartu.

c. 760–733. Sarduri III preserved the integrity of the kingdom.

c. 733–612. The last kings of Urartu, Rusas I (c. 733–714) (probably the founder of a new dynasty), Argishti II (c. 714–685), Rusas II (c. 685–650), Sarduri IV (c. 650–625), and Rusas III (c. 625–612), ruled over a much restricted territory. The Cimmerian invasion and the raid of Sargon II of Assyria (714) weakened the kingdom, which met its doom after the Scythian invasion, when the Medes conquered the country (612). The Vannic nation ceased to exist.

b. ARMENIA

The Armenians are mentioned for the first time by Darius (519). They were probably a

Stone relief on the palace at Persepolis

Phrygian tribe and they gradually occupied the territory of Urartu after 612. They adopted the religion of the Persians.

612–549. Armenia under the kings of Media.

549–331. Under the Persian kings, Armenia was a satrapy administered by a member of the royal family.

331–317. Under Alexander and his immediate successors, Armenia continued to be ruled by Persian satraps.

317–211. Ardvates (317–284), one of these Persian satraps, made the country independent of the Seleucids and founded a dynasty that ruled until 211.

211–190. Antiochus III, after removing Xerxes, the Armenian king, by treachery, divided the country into two satrapies, giving the western one (*Armenia Minor*) to Zadriades and the eastern one (*Armenia Major*) to Artaxias.

190–94. After Antiochus was defeated at Magnesia (190), Zadriades and Artaxias made themselves independent rulers, founding two separate dynasties.

94–56. TIGRANES I, a descendant of Artaxias, deposed Artanes, the last king of Armenia Minor, and united the two countries under his rule. From 83 to 69 he was the most powerful king in Asia, ruling over northern Mesopotamia, Syria, and parts of Asia Minor. Defeated by Lucullus in 69, he was stripped of his conquests, but was allowed by Pompey to rule over Armenia as a vassal of Rome.

6. *Iran, to 330* B.C.

Geography. The Iranian plateau extends from the mountains east of the Tigris to the Indus Valley, and from the Persian Gulf and the Indian Ocean to the Caspian Sea and the Jaxartes River. Media (capitals: Ecbatana and Rhagae), Elam (capital: Susa), and Persia (capital: Persepolis) in the west played a much more important historical rôle than Sogdiana, Bactria, Aria, Drangiana, and Arachosia in the east. In the north-central region, the Parthians became Rome's rivals in the Near East.

Population. In the 4th and possibly the 5th millennia B.C., a population of unknown race living at Susa used copper and made pottery decorated with realistic and conventionalized animals. The mountaineers of the Zagros range (Gutium, Lullubu) and the Elamites predominated in the 3rd millennium. The Kas-

Ruins of Persepolis

Zarathustra

sites, who ruled Babylonia from 1550 to 1180, were quite distinct from the Elamites. The Aryans, the Indo-European ancestors of the Indo-Iranians, invaded Iran from the northeast (probably about 1800) and became its basic population.

Religion. The religion of the early Iranians was similar to that of Vedic Indians: the worship of **Mithra** and **Varuna,** of the Asuras (Iranian *Ahura*), and of the Devas (degraded to demons by Zarathustra), the myths about the first man Yama (Iranian *Yima*) and about the killing of the dragon, and the conception of *rita*

(Iranian *asha* or *urta*) or the inflexible order of the world, and the preparation, offering, and divinization of the sacred drink *soma* (Iranian *haoma*) are common to the Aryans of India and Iran and must date back to the time preceding their separation. **Zoroastrianism** was a reform of this ancient Aryan religion and preserved some of its elements even though it took issue with its naturalistic polytheism. **Zarathustra** (Zoroaster: "rich in camels") may have been born in Media about 660 B.C., but seems to have been active in Bactria, where according to tradition he converted King Vishtasp (Hystas-

Representation of the god Ahura Mazda

pes). His teaching is preserved in the Gathas, the oldest hymns in the **Avesta.** The *Avesta* is divided into five parts: the *Yasna* (liturgical hymns including the *Gathas*), the *Vispered* (another liturgical book), the *Vendidad* (a code of ritual and ethical laws), the *Yasht* (mythological hymns in praise of the gods), and the *Khorda Avesta* (a prayer book for private devotions). The great doctrines of the finished Zoroastrian system: monotheism, dualism, individual and universal salvation, are present in the germ in the *Gathas.* In the cosmic battle between good and evil each person should contribute to his own salvation and to that of the world by obeying the will of the good god Ahura Mazda (Ormuzed: "Lord Wisdom"). In the later parts of the *Avesta* the god of evil or supreme devil is called Angro-mainyu or **Ahriman** (the evil spirit). After death the pious cross the Cinvat bridge to their reward, whereas the wicked fall from it and suffer in the "House of Lies."

a. THE ELAMITES, TO 640 B.C.

c. 2850–2180. Sumerians and Akkadians frequently defeated and subjected the Elamites, whose civilization was fundamentally Sumerian. **Dynasty of Awan** (c. 2500–2180).

2180–1830. Dynasty of Simash.

1770–1699. Kudur-mabug of Elam placed his son, Waradsin, on the throne of Larsa. The latter's brother and successor, Rimsin, was deposed by Hammurapi.

1176. Shutruk-nahunte raided Babylonia, taking to Susa the stele of Hammurapi and other monuments.

1150. Kudur-nahunte plundered the Temple of Akkad.

1128–1105. Nebuchadrezzar I of Babylon defeated the Elamites.

721–640. Merodach-baladan of Babylon and Humbanigash of Elam joined forces against Sargon of Assyria, who was defeated at Der by the Elamites (721). Shutruk-nahunte II allowed Sargon to depose Merodach-baladan (709). Hallushu (699–693) carried into captivity Sennacherib's son, who was ruling Babylonia (694). Umman-menanu (693–689), who succeeded Kudur-nahunte, fought at Halule against Sennacherib (691). Umman-haldash I (689–681). Umman-haldash II (681–674) raided Sippar during Esarhaddon's Egyptian campaign. Urtaku (674–664) ruled peacefully. Teumman (664–655) was defeated by Asshurbanapal and his kingdom was occupied by the Assyrians. Ummanigash (655–651) sent his forces to the help of Shamashshumukin, king of Babylon, who had rebelled against his brother Assurbanapal. Ummanigash was assassinated by his cousin Tammaritu. Tammaritu (651–649) was deposed by Indabigash

Impression of the cylinder seal of Darius I

and sought refuge in Nineveh. Umman-haldash III (648–646) was defeated by Assurbanapal, who conquered Susa, and was deposed by Tammaritu II. Tammaritu II was taken prisoner by the Assyrians (646). Umman-haldash III (646–640) returned to the throne, but was taken prisoner by Assurbanapal, who completely devastated the land of Elam and destroyed Susa. The elimination of the Kingdom of Elam facilitated the task of Cyrus, who a century later founded the Persian Empire, with Susa as one of its capitals.

b. THE MEDES, TO 550 B.C.

835–705. Media, divided into small principalities, was attacked successively by Assyrian kings, from Shalmaneser III (in whose inscriptions the Medes are mentioned for the first time) to Sargon II.

705–625. Media under **Assyrian rule.** The two kings Dejoces (700–647) and Phraortes (647–625) mentioned by Herodotus were probably local chieftains.

625–585. Cyaxares was the founder of the Median Empire and of its dynasty. In alliance with Nabopolassar of Babylon (a daughter of Cyaxares was given in marriage to Nebuchadrezzar), Cyaxares destroyed Nineveh (612) and conquered the Assyrian territory east of the Tigris, as also Urartu (Armenia) and eastern Iran.

585–550. Astyages was deposed by Cyrus and

Media became part of the Persian Empire (550).

c. THE PERSIANS, TO 330 B.C.

c. 600–550. Achaemenian kings of Anzan (in Elam): Teispes, Cyrus (I), Cambyses, Cyrus (II) the Great.

550–530. CYRUS THE GREAT deposed his sovereign Astyages of Media (559), conquered Lydia (546) and Babylonia (539), and founded the Persian Empire, which extended from the Indus to the Mediterranean, from the Caucasus to the Indian Ocean.

530–521. Cambyses, son of Cyrus, conquered Egypt (525).

521–486. DARIUS I, son of Hystaspes, after pacifying the empire torn by revolts, notably that of Gaumata or Smerdis, and extending its borders beyond the Indus (521–519), divided it into 20 satrapies. His royal residences were Susa, Persepolis, Ecbatana (Hamadan), and Babylon. Darius was a Zoroastrian. Good roads, with stations for royal messengers, made possible regular communications within the empire. A canal was dug from the Nile to the Red Sea. A general revolt of the Ionian Greeks in Asia ended with the fall of Miletus (500–494), but the war against the European Greeks was unsuccessful (**battle of Marathon, 490**).

486–465. After **Xerxes I** (Ahasuerus) was defeated by the Greeks on the sea at Salamis (480), and on land at Plataea and Mycale (479), Persia abandoned her plans for conquering Greece.

465–424. Athens took the offensive against **Artaxerxes I Longimanus,** by sending troops to aid a revolt in Egypt (456–454) and by attacking Cyprus (450), but finally signed a peace treaty (446). The Persian Empire began to decline.

424–404. Xerxes II was assassinated by his brother Sogdianus (424), who in turn fell at the hands of his brother Ochus or Darius II Nothus (424–404).

Ancient Susa

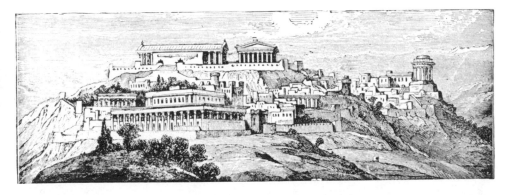

404–358. Artaxerxes II Mnemon defeated his rebellious brother Cyrus, the satrap of Anatolia, near Babylon at Cunaxa (401); Cyrus lost his life in the battle and his "ten thousand" Greek mercenaries, after great hardships, reached the Black Sea (Xenophon's *Anabasis*) in March of the year 400. Another insurrection broke out in Asia Minor under the leadership of Datames, the governor of Cappadocia, and spread to the western satrapies (366–360). Egypt became more or less independent after 404.

358–338. Artaxerxes III Ochus succeeded, through energetic measures, in asserting the royal authority over the satraps. He was followed by Arses (338–336).

336–330. Darius III Codomannus was killed after Alexander the Great, through the victories at Granicus (334), Issus (333), and Gaugamela, near Arbela (331), conquered the Persian Empire.

7. *India, to 72* B.C.

An early urban civilization in the Indus Valley produced the polished stone, metals, incised seals, and pictographs excavated since 1920 at Harappa and Mohenjo Daro. Indian history begins much later with invasion from the Iranian plateau by **Aryans** of uncertain antecedents, who gradually conquered, pushed back, or absorbed the earlier black **Dravidian** and Austro-Asiatic **Munda** populations. The conquest is variously placed at 2000–1200 B.C.

1200–c. 800 B.C. The Indian Aryans worshiped nature-gods. The chief were **Indra,** god of the air and of the storm, **Agni,** the sacrificial fire, and **Soma,** the intoxicant used for libations. **Varuna** was worshiped as guardian of cosmic regularity, including individual human acts. The oldest sacrificial hymns, composed in northern India west of the Ganges (perhaps 1200), are contained in the *Rigveda,* which dates from c. 1000 B.C., possibly two centuries prior to the related *Gathas* in the *Avesta* of Iran; the *Samaveda* which contains antiphonal selections from the *Rig;* the *Yajurveda,* hymns and sacrificial prose; and the *Atharvaveda,* a repertory of magical formulae. The *Rigveda* reveals an Indo-European hieratic literary language remarkable for clarity of structure and wealth of inflection, which was originally transmitted orally. It depicts a patriarchal society, engaged in cattle-raising and agriculture, characterized by usual monogamy, adult marriage, and normal widowhood. The Aryan tribes were frequently at war among themselves and with indigenous tribes. Their attitude toward life was vigorous and objective; the doctrine of reincarnation and the correlated aspiration to release are absent.

800–c. 550 B.C. A transition period during which the Aryans expanded eastward through Magadha (modern Bihar) is known chiefly from the *Brahmanas,* prose commentaries upon the *Vedas* (c. 800–600), and the earlier *Upanishads* or confidential teachings (c. 600–300). Beginning of the Vedic division of Aryan society into three honorable classes: priests (*brahman*), noble warriors (*kshatriya*), and commonalty (*vaisya*), including both farmers and artisans, augmented by a fourth group, the slaves (*sudra*) consisting of non-Aryans with whom the twice-born classes had no ritual community. Progressive **evolution of caste** may be traced to desire of priest and noble to perpetuate supremacy, to diversification of specialized occupation, and to indigenous rules of endogamy and to absorption of the sudras, many of whom improved their servile status. Continual elaboration by the priesthood of an already laborious ritual had become devoid of religious significance. The doctrine of continuous rebirth (*samsara*), conditioned by the inescapable results of former acts (*karma*), was first expressed in the early *Upanishads* (c. 600–550). The *Upanishads,* too, teach that the soul may escape from the suffering inherent in individual existence only by the realization of its identity with an impersonal cosmic soul. Union with the latter is possible through knowledge, but not through Brahman ritual.

550–321. The northern Indian area was divided among many petty states. Sixteen are enumerated in an early list. **Kosala** (King Prasenajit, contemporary of the Buddha) was the largest, extending from Nepal to the Ganges, including modern Oudh. **Magadha** was its small neighbor on the east, south of the Ganges. The King of Avanti ruled at Ujjain. The capital of the Vamsas (King Sedayama) was at Kosambi (on the Jumna below Agra).

The Great Temple at Bodh-Gaya

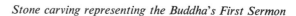

Stone carving representing the Buddha's First Sermon

Ten tribal republics are named in the oldest Pali records.

Dissent from Brahmanism, to abolish authority of its scriptures and rites, was found in many schools, among them the **Jains,** followers of the Jina ("Victorious"), Vardhamana Mahavira (?540–468?), who elaborated the doctrines of an earlier prophet **Parsya,** and in Magadha under Kings Bimbisara (?543–491?) and his parricide son Ajatasatru (?491–459?). Parsya had enjoined four vows: to injure no life, to be truthful, not to steal, to possess no property. **Mahavira** added chastity and rigid asceticism as means to free man's immortal soul from bondage to the material world.

BUDDHISM was founded in the same period and region by **Siddhartha** (?563–483?) of the clan of Gautama and the hill tribe of Sakya, who attained "illumination" (*bodhi*) at Bodh-Gaya after he had convinced himself that Brahman doctrine and asceticism were alike ineffective. He taught the means of escape from the world of suffering and rebirth to **Nirvana,** a state of peaceful release from rebirth, through a twofold way of life, withdrawal for meditation and personal religious experience, combined with strict morality and self-sacrificial altruism. Shortly after the Buddha's death, 500 disciples met at Rajagriha to rehearse together his doctrine (*dharma*) and his code of discipline (*vinaya*) for the monastic community (*sangha*) which he founded. That community served as the instrument for propagation of his religion, which, like Christianity, offers salvation to all who accept the simple doctrine and ethics and seek for personal religious experience. A second **council at Vaisali** a century after the Buddha's death was concerned with the *vinaya.* About this time were formed the four *Nikayas,* earliest extant anthologies from more primitive collections (*Pratimoksa,* etc.).

517–509 B.C. Darius I of Achaemenid Persia seized Gandhara from the disunited Aryans and sent his Greek admiral Skylax to explore the Indus. *Kharoshthi* script, used in northwestern India (5th century), is based on Aramaic of the Persian scribes. It remained confined to the northwest.

The *Sutras* (c. 6th–2nd century B.C.), "Threads" through the **Brahmanas,** compendious manuals designed to be learned by heart, prescribe rules of conduct of various Vedic schools, regions, and periods, for sacrifice and incidentally, for daily life, describe a society in which plural marriage is permitted, child marriage recommended, while numerous taboos mark the beginning of an elaborate theory of caste defilement. **Panini** (c. 400) gives in his *Sutra* the earliest extant Sanskrit grammar, with a wealth of illustration which is augmented by the *Varttikas* or supplementary rules of Katyayana (c. 180) and the rich *Mahabhashya* (Great Commentary) of Patanjali (c. 150 B.C.).

327–325. Alexander the Great invaded the Punjab, crossed the Indus (Feb. 326), was welcomed to the rich and cultured city of Takshasila (Taxila), won a battle on the banks of the Jhelum, and withdrew on demand of his troops, sending Nearchus with a fleet by sea.

c. 321–c. 184. The **MAURYA DYNASTY** was founded by **Chandragupta** (c. 321–c. 297), who first united northern India from Herat to the Ganges delta, with his capital at Pataliputra (Patna), and who defended it against Seleucus Nicator (c. 305). The emperor ruled with aid of a privy council and an elaborate official hierarchy, paid army, and secret service. Administration of public works embraced highways and irrigation.

A Jain high-priest **Bhadrabahu** led a portion of his community south into the Carnatic to escape a 12-year famine in Bengal. On their return (c. 300) the still resident monks in church council at Pataliputra undertook to collect the Jain scriptures, but were unable to record some of the older *purvas.* The canon of the Svetambara sect, the *Siddhanta,* written in its present form at the council of Valabhi (5th or early 6th century A.D.), is consequently incomplete. The returning monks maintained a stricter rule, avoided the council, and, as the **Digambara sect,** have steadily maintained that the true canon is lost. The Jain community had then already begun a westward migration to Ujjain and Mathura.

c. 274–c. 236. ASOKA'S EMPIRE, extended by conquest of Kalinga (Orissa with the Circars, c. 262), embraced two-thirds of the peninsula. As a devout convert he ruled at home and abroad in accordance with Buddhist law. Besides many pious foundations, he engraved on rocks and pillars throughout his empire in true Achaemenid style edicts in vernacular Prakrit exhorting respect for animal life, reverence, and truth, and appointed censors to enforce these injunctions. He sent Buddhist missions to Syria, Egypt, Cyrene, Macedonia, and Epirus, and with much greater success to Burma and Ceylon (c. 251–246; Aryan conquest of Ceylon, traditional date 485 B.C.). The Punjab and Gandhara became a stronghold of the liberal Mahasanghikas, who developed a canonical tradition enriched by legends to bring the life of the Buddha into that region. The canon was then or in the 2nd century in Kausambhi, Sanchi, and Malwa expanded and fixed in Pali to form the *Tripitaka* ("Three Baskets"): *sutra* (doctrine), *vinaya* (monastic code), and *abhidharma* (philosophical discussion). The Pali tradition, which was carried to Ceylon and there preserved intact, says a third church council was held at Pataliputra under Asoka.

The west remained the chief stronghold of **Brahman doctrine** which now reasserted itself. The gradual absorption of substratum cults within the formal brahmanistic framework under the tutelage of the Brahmans gave rise to the complex system of beliefs and practices known as **Hinduism.** As major gods arose **Siva,** personification of cosmic forces of destruction and reproduction implicit in all change; **Vishnu,** god of the sacrifice who was recognized as incarnate in **Krishna,** a hero presented by popular legend at Mathura as romantic lover of cowherd-girls, and on the west coast as a somber warrior. A second avatar or reincarnation of Vishnu was **Rama,** symbol of conjugal devotion. To Vishnu as Preserver and Siva as Destroyer was added **Brahma** the Creator, a personification of the Brahman principle of the *Upanishads.*

The *Mahabharata,* an epic poem composed by several generations of bards, seems to have taken form about the 4th century B.C., although probably revised early in our era. The original 9000 verses were swelled to 100,000 by later accretions, including myths,

Asoka pillar at Naishali

Representation of Siva

legends, popular philosophy, and moralizing narratives. It recounts a feud between the wily Kurus and the fierce Pandus. Krishna takes prominent part in the struggle as counselor of Arjuna, the Pandu chief. Noteworthy within the epic is the *Bhagavadgita* ("Song of the Lord"), which first urges personal love and devotion (*bhakti*) to Krishna. The *Ramayana,* although traditionally ascribed to Valmiki (?6th century B.C.), is, in its present form, later than the *Mahabharata.* It recounts the trials of Rama in rescuing, with an army of apes, his wife, Sita, from a fiend. Both epics are composed in a popular form of Sanskrit.

Entrance to the cave of Ajanta

206. Antiochus III of Syria occupied Gandhara, but shortly lost it to the Greek (Yavana) King Demetrius of Bactria, who (c. 185) seized the Punjab also. Eastward expansion of the Yavanas was halted (after c. 162) by civil war between the houses of Euthydemus, represented especially by the warrior-philosopher Menander, and Eucratides.

c. 184–c. 72. The **SUNGA DYNASTY** was founded in the Ganges Valley and in Malwa by **Pushyamitra,** who overthrew the Maurya, repulsed the Yavanas under Menander, and by a Brahman reaction may have stimulated Buddhist emigration to Bharhut, Sanchi, and Mathura. The dynasty in its later years was overshadowed if not actually displaced by its line of Brahman advisers, the **Kanvas.**

At the same time (c. 100 B.C.–50 A.D.) flourished in Gandhara a school of sculpture which created a Buddha image based on the Greek Apollo. Only a few decadent monuments (mostly 1st century A.D.) bear dates (318, 356, 384 with coin of Kadphises, 399) by reference to a Mauryan era (?322 B.C.) or more probably the Seleucid era of 312 B.C. Stylistic influence of the art of Gandhara was exerted chiefly in Afghanistan (frescoes of Bamiyan and Dukhtar-i-Nushirwan), where it was fused with Sassanian influences, eastern Turkestan, China of the North Wei dynasty, and Japan. But its iconographic formulae were accepted by the entire Buddhist world. Meanwhile, in western India (near Bombay) were cut in rocky cliffs Buddhist *chaityas* or temple halls, of which the earliest (c. 125–100 B.C.) are at Bhaja, Kondane, Pitalkhora, and Ajanta (cave 10); the largest, finest, and latest (1st century A.D.) at Karli. Jain caves in the Udayagiri hills of Orissa are of similar date.

Scythian **Sakas** who, dislodged by the Yueh-chih from the Jaxartes, had overwhelmed the Greeks in Bactria (c. 135 B.C.), only to be expelled thence also by the Yueh-chih (shortly after 128), invaded the Punjab from Baluchistan and Sind (Greek Indo-Scythia).

(Cont. p. 151.)

8. *China, to 221* B.C.

Present information indicates that the Chinese parent people, their language, and their civilization are alike native to North China. It seems probable that, at a primitive stage, they diverged from the Miao-tzu, who now find refuge in the southern mountains, the various T'ai peoples (Dioi, Laotians, Siamese) of Kwangsi and Indo-China, and the Tibeto-Burman peoples (Lolo, Mosso, Shan, and Tibetans) of southwestern China. **Peking Man,** who had some Chinese characteristics, lived in the Tertiary Pleistocene epoch. Paleolithic culture deposits (without skeletal material as yet) are known. Three independent Neolithic cultures are found, characterized by: (1) crude gray pottery with pointed foot; (2) red and black painted pottery similar to that found near Odessa and at Susa; (3) thin black pottery tentatively attributed to a Pacific civilization. The latter is linked with historic China through use of tripod vessels with hollow legs, and bone divination.

During the Shang dynasty the first systematic **astronomical observations** were made (Chinese astronomy represents the longest history of observational science). Use of the gnomon dates from this time, as do the first observations of eclipses and nova (14th century B.C.). By 240 B.C. **Halley's comet** was regularly observed. Mathematics developed to the point that by the 4th century B.C. a fully developed decimal, place-value system was in use. Within the next century Pythagoras' theorem was known and a symbol for zero used. In practical mechanics the balance, steelyard, and scaling ladder were understood. In optics the principles of refraction and reflection from plane and curved surfaces were also understood.

Two literary sources contain genealogies of **the early dynasties,** with chronologies which diverge prior to 841 B.C. Neither earlier chronology has any authority whatever. Nor can historical value be attached to legends which describe a predynastic golden age of fabulous culture-heroes and model rulers. Of the **Hsia Dynasty** we have only the calendar, honorific use of the name, and the putative genealogy of seventeen kings. It was followed by the **Shang** or **Yin Dynasty** of thirty kings, who practiced fraternal succession and who were masters of the Yellow River plain from the mountains of Shansi and the Mongolian plateau to the Shantung massif. Probably the last twelve ruled at An-yang from about the 12th century. The names of twenty-eight kings are found in oracular inscriptions from this site. Advanced pictographic and ideographic script; conventional decoration and perfect casting of bronze vessels; reliance upon ancestral guidance through divination.

c. 1000–950 B.C. The **WESTERN CHOU DYNASTY** established its capital at Hao in the Wei Valley. It exercised actual control over its feudatories only until the murder of King Yu in 771. The king was responsible for sacrifices to his ancestors and to gods of the soil, and for the agricultural calendar, as well as for administration. Tenure of land and office was restricted to a pedigreed aristocracy, whose clan names suggest a possible early matriarchate. The peasantry lived a communal life in the summer fields and winter villages, tilled common land for their prince, and practiced exogamic group betrothals and marriages. The Chinese communities were still surrounded and interspersed with "barbarian," i.e. less cultured, tribes.

770–256. The **EASTERN CHOU DYNASTY** reigned powerless at Loyang with diminishing moral authority over the frequently warring princes of surrounding (nominally) feudal states.

722–481. "**Annals**" **period** of loose confederation. The chief states were Ch'i and Lu, which divided modern Shantung; Sung, west of Lu; Yen, on the northeast; Chin, in modern Shansi; Ch'in, in the former Chou lands to the west; and Ch'u, in the middle Long River Valley.

458–424. **Partition of Chin** among three vassal houses: Han, Chao, and Wei.

412. Institution of **ever-normal granary** by Marquis Wen of Wei.

403–221. **Epoch of the Warring States,** opened

by royal recognition of the partition of Chin.

391. **Change of dynasty in Ch'i,** which, with Chin, had been a chief bulwark of the "middle kingdoms" against the largely non-Chinese states of Ch'u and Ch'in.

334. **Ch'u** expanded eastward, annexing the coastal state of Yueh.

333. "**Vertical**" (i.e. north and south) **alliance of six states,** arranged by Su Ch'in, failed to restrain Ch'in, which conquered Shu (in modern Szechwan) in 316.

307. **Prince Wu-ling** of Chao gained military advantage for his state by adoption of Tatar dress (Iranian trousers, belt, and boots, which now gradually displaced the loose Chinese costume) and enlistment of cavalry archers, but the continual wars of the eastern states weakened them all, paving the way for

230–221. **CONQUEST BY CH'IN OF ALL ITS RIVALS.** Golden age of philosophy in China, as in Greece. Four major **schools of ethics,** which absorbed the practical Chinese to the exclusion of abstract speculation: (1) Coherent teaching embodied in *The Canon of the Way and of Virtue* (5th century or later?), attributed to **Lao-tzu,** of whom nothing is known: Man is part of a harmonious universe governed by transcendent law, and finds his best ethical guide in his own nature. **Yang Chu,** an individualist, sought self-expression in harmless hedonism. **Chuang Chou** (fl. 339–329), the most brilliantly imaginative and subtle of all literary stylists, through parables taught *laissez faire,* mysticism, and relativity of truth. (2) **Mo Ti** (5th–4th century?) taught universal love, pacifism, economy, and the duty of the wise to set up standards. New dialectic method borrowed by all later writers. From him stem the schools of pacifists and sophists. (3) **K'ung Ch'iu** or **Confucius** (551–479 or later?) taught that clear thinking and self-discipline lead the superior man to correct action in all his relationships. Through moral influence and education he should lead the common herd with kindliness and justice; paternalism; golden rule. Having failed as

Gold knife handle, late Chou Dynasty

minister of justice in Lu (500–496) to secure co-operation of his prince, he edited the *Annals* of that state (722–481) to illustrate his monarchical doctrine of political morality. (A much richer chronicle of the feudal states, composed c. 300, is now appended to these *Annals* as part of the *Tso Commentary.*) His precepts were gathered a century later. **Meng K'o** or **Mencius** (fl. 324–314) urged the now independent princes to win the world, i.e. North China, by exemplary conduct, declaring popular welfare to be the objective and condition of royal authority. A humanitarian, he elaborated the moral code to assure proper development of man's beneficent nature. **Hsun K'uang** or **Hsun-tzu** (c. 300–235) taught that man requires education and formation of correct habit to realize his capacity to order nature. He suggested forced conformity to standards. He synthesized earlier doctrines, and, although a muddy writer, so impressed his students that even mutually opposed thinkers for a century claimed succession from him. (4) **Shang Yang,** minister of Ch'in, 359–338, organized strong centralized government, created an official hierarchy, and encouraged agriculture in that state under a severe legal code. His reforms paved the way for the triumph of Ch'in. **Han-fei-tzu** (d. 233) and **Li Ssu** (d. 208), disciples of Hsün-tzu, developed further the legalist doctrine of compulsion to justify Ch'in's use of military force to unify the warring states.

Greek influence, probably traceable to Alexander's invasion of Sogdiana (c. 327), is seen in correct statement of the intervals of the Pythagorean musical scale by **Lu Pu-wei,** prime minister of Ch'in (c. 250), and in diagrammatic illustration of the Pythagorean theorem. *(Cont. p. 155.)*

Bronze wine vessel, Shang Yin Dynasty

1. *The Early Period, to c. 500 B.C.*

a. GEOGRAPHY AND CLIMATE

Mainland Greece is the southern extension and end of the Balkan Peninsula and marks the termination of various mountain ranges running north to south. The coastline is therefore much broken and the neighboring Aegean Islands are actually submerged mountains. The climate is dry and stimulating. Rainfall, which exceeds forty inches per annum in the Adriatic, is only about sixteen in Attica, making drought a constant menace. The weather, though chilly enough in winter, is rarely freezing, while in summer the mid-day heat is hard to bear in the valleys, though sundown invariably brings relief. Thus, the climate and the terrain demand vitality, and reward effort with enough wealth to encourage a robust civilization.

Most of Greece is divided into small compartments by the mountain ranges. This made natural the development of numerous small city states, characteristic of classical Greece. The towns, however, were essentially the dwelling places of an agrarian population, and the city states more or less unions of towns or villages. Boeotia, never really united, had 22 towns according to Homer; classical Athens (i.e. the union of all Attica) was exceptional, being a union of no fewer than about 120 towns and villages.

Over large areas of the country the soil was thin and rocky, making the cultivation of grain difficult, though olives and grapes ripened well

Ruins of the agora *in Athens*

in the rainless summers. Since much of the required grain had to be imported, sea-borne commerce developed at an early stage, the grain being paid for in terms of manufactured goods such as Greek vases, which are found in number throughout the Mediterranean world. But the civilization of ancient Greece at no time depended largely on manufacture or trade; it was basically agrarian.

Greece is almost split in two by the Gulf of Corinth, which runs in from the west, the narrow Isthmus of Corinth being the only link between the southern part, the Peloponnesus ("Island of Pelops"), and the northern. But this geographical division was less important than the difference in the degree of contact with lands of earlier civilization, notably Crete. Crete is the largest and southernmost of the Aegean Islands and its influence spread in mainland Greece through those valleys that faced south and east, such as Messenia and Laconia, the Argolid, Attica, and even Boeotia. Thessaly, more distant, remained somewhat backward, while northern and western Greece, having fewer harbors and being constantly exposed to barbarian invasion from the north, remained savage until, late in Greek history, Alexander and the vigorous Macedonians were able to take over leadership of the Greeks and the government of most of the known world.

Greece's out-of-door climate and town life enabled the inhabitants to engage freely in social activity—gymnastics, politics, litigation, discussion in the agora (forum or market-place), festivals, athletic contests, dancing, drama, and banquets, to say nothing of war. Polis-dwelling became an essential characteristic of every Greek; the Greeks created **politics** and **political theory.**

b. THE MINOAN CIVILIZATION, c. 3000–c. 1100 B.C.

Long before the Greeks arrived in Greece, one of the world's distinctive civilizations had come into being on the largest of the Aegean Islands, Crete. This island (156 miles long) has, in its central and eastern sections, enough small plains and arable valleys, with enough rain in most winters, to enable its inhabitants, when they were reinforced from Asia Minor (not later than c. 2700 B.C.) to emerge into the Bronze Age earlier than any other people of Europe.

The Cretan civilization is called "Minoan" from the name of the legendary King Minos of Knossos, which was always the principal city. The language of the early Minoans remains unknown. Throughout a millennium and a half they were not invaded nor even much affected by outsiders. Their script, when they came to write (c. 1700 B.C.), was almost wholly their own, as was their art. It was a culture marked by color and gaiety. Their art, inspired by direct observation of nature, was freer than any in Europe prior to the 19th century. Their grandest palaces, built of stone, were aggregations of buildings around a large open court, with no insistence on symmetry. The Minoans were devoted to sports, including hazardous bull-jumping, rather than to war; their towns were at all times unwalled.

The form of government was probably monarchical, but for a long time was not highly organized. The king was evidently the chief figure in religious worship and his palace was

Central hall of the palace at Knossos

The two great staircases of the palace at Phaistos (Middle Minoan)

the seat of religious cults. There were also other gods and goddesses, nature-derived and very human, worshiped in caves or at open-air shrines rather than in formal temples. Literature was doubtless oral, and was probably sung. The Minoans seem to have had little love for written records, but crafts such as pottery and painting were highly developed. The palaces reflect comfortable, varied, and refined living. They contained grand suites, commodious storerooms for goods and products paid as taxes (there was no coinage), light-wells with many-storied staircases, and sanitary arrangements superior to any in Europe before recent times.

Minoan civilization went through three main phases of development, each with three subdivisions, making nine successive periods in all. We thus have E(arly) M(inoan) I, II, III; M(iddle) M(inoan), I, II, III; L(ate) M(inoan) I,

II, III. The evidence that distinguishes them is derived mostly from changes in pottery. Indeed, practically all that is known of Minoan Crete is based on the findings of archaeology. The various periods are dated (mostly approximately) from the quite infrequent contacts of Crete with Egypt and the evidence provided by Egyptian records. It suffices to mention

c. 2700–c. 1900 B.C. **Early Minoan**
c. 1900–c. 1600 B.C. **Middle Minoan**
c. 1600–c. 1100 B.C. **Late Minoan,** subdivided into
   c. 1600–c. 1450 Late Minoan I
   c. 1450–c. 1400 Late Minoan II (at Knossos only)
   c. 1400–c. 1100 Late Minoan III (the Mycenaean period)

Clay tablet with Linear A script

Tablet with Linear B script

EARLY MINOAN. This was a period of rapid development compared to the Stone Age, but slow compared to later periods. Stone and bone tools were still in use; bronze was only slowly introduced and, though of crucial importance, was never really abundant. Pottery was still shaped by hand, not on a wheel. People emerged from their cave dwellings and Neolithic hovels and began to live in towns. Some sort of community organization, the first government, must have come into being. Writing of a primitive kind began to appear on seals and as isolated markings.

MIDDLE MINOAN. During this period pottery was thrown on the wheel and was perfected to the point where it could be made as thin as eggshell. Free but well-judged design and profuse color suggest the vitality which led to the founding (in MMI) of the great palaces at Knossos, Phaistos, and Mallia. The process was one of uniting separate buildings. Government evidently was now more centralized: the palace became the royal court and the administrative center, with storerooms for taxes in kind and arsenals for whatever armed forces were maintained. It was also the center for religious observances, an arena for sports and theatrical exhibitions, and the home of the arts and literature.

Minoan Linear A is the name given to the writing of this period, to distinguish it from the earlier signs on images and seals (hieroglyphics) and to distinguish it also from the later **Linear B** script. Linear A took the form of fairly complex signs, most of them representing a consonant plus a vowel, so that it constituted a syllabary rather than an alphabet. Other signs were single symbols, such as for man, woman, sheep, goat, olive, etc., standing for whole words like the modern dollar or pound sterling sign. Counting was by simple signs for units—tens, hundreds, etc. on a decimal system. The numbers can be easily read, as can most of the symbols. But for the syllable signs even the vowels are not positively known in most instances, nor are the meanings of more than a very few words, since even the identity of the language has not yet been determined. Linear A was at first used for short inscriptions signifying ownership and the like. Later it was used for writing accounts on clay tablets. Not much of it survives, for there are fewer than two hundred even of the tablets extant and these are brief and careless. Paucity of the material adds to the difficulty of decipherment.

THE THALASSOCRACY OF MINOS. By MM III the Minoans, who had always carried on some trade with Egypt, the Levant, and more recently with some Aegean Islands (e.g. Melos), began a more aggressive foreign policy. Their

legendary king, Minos, was said to have founded a sea empire (thalassocracy). The proofs that some such empire existed are: (1) the Athenian **Theseus legend,** which, for the purposes of the story, admits that Athens was then tributary to the **Minotaur** (the Minos Bull), i.e. to the ruler of the palace where the bull-sports were held; (2) the fact that no fewer than eleven different places, all seaports, later are known as bearing the name **Minoa.** They were probably trading, raiding, and tribute-collecting posts. The first European empire was doubtless primitive, loosely organized, semi-piratical. Archaeology has as yet discovered only a few actual overseas Minoan settlements, which, like others, were probably not very populous, since Crete hardly had the manpower needed to garrison many foreign establishments. But the tribute and booty collected abroad may well have financed the new palaces, and the thalassocracy, begun perhaps in MM III, continued into the next period, Late Minoan I.

c. THE GREEK MAINLAND IN THE BRONZE AGE

Mainland Greece had had Neolithic settlements, at least in Macedonia, for thousands of years. At the beginning of the Bronze Age, Greece like Crete was invaded by people from

Asia Minor who used names ending in –ssos, such as Knossos, Parnassos, and in –inth, such as Labyrinth, Corinth. Certain names have survived. Narcissus comes to us from their language and Olympos probably meant "high mountain." Neither they nor their Neolithic predecessors spoke the Greek language.

Greek-speakers arrived in Greece at the beginning of the period that corresponds approximately to Early Minoan III in Crete, i.e. about 2200 B.C. They came from the north, wore heavier clothing, and designed their houses for protection against cold. Their pottery, which appeared also in Troy, was smooth-surfaced. But most of their civilization they acquired only in the course of centuries and from the Minoans.

The **Minoan influence** was naturally felt most strongly in the valleys that faced south toward Crete: Messenia, Laconia, the Argolid, Attica, but also Boeotia and certain localities in Thessaly. In time strong towns grew up, the richest and most powerful being **Mycenae,** at the head of the Argolid. The graves discovered by **Heinrich Schliemann** at Mycenae contained hundreds of objects of gold, wrought in a style that shows extensive Minoan cultural domination. But the Minoan thalassocracy never actually ruled Mycenae and even in culture differences remained. Thus each Greek king was buried with a small arsenal of swords; the Greeks were stern and warlike. In time, having greater resources, they would turn against their teachers.

THE GREEKS IN CRETE: LINEAR B. In A.D. 1900 **Sir Arthur Evans** discovered at Knossos large numbers (eventually some thousands) of clay tablets in a script obviously derived from Linear A and hence known as **Linear B.** Numerals, but little else, could be read, yet it was clear that the tablets were all accounts, that the language itself was different from that of Linear A, and that they had been preserved by being burned in a great fire that destroyed Knossos, apparently c. 1400 B.C. When, in 1939, **Carl Blegen** found similar tablets in the palace at **Pylos** (Messenia), scholars still refrained from believing that the language could be Greek, until in 1952 **Sir Michael Ventris** achieved the decipherment and it became evident that the language was undeniably Greek and that it antedated by half a millennium the Homeric epics, hitherto the earliest Greek known.

c. 1450 B.C. The Greeks must have captured Knossos sometime in the 15th century B.C., for their swords, chariots, and pottery as well as their tablets can be recognized at Knossos. They used writing for administrative purposes, the tablets giving us accounts of thousands of sheep and of other riches, likewise of great stores of weapons and also of cults with the names of gods familiar later—most of the Greek pantheon. A highly bureaucratic state was centered in the palace of Knossos and on the mainland at Pylos, at Mycenae, and at other places familiar to us from Homer.

d. THE MYCENAEAN AGE

Late Minoan III was dominated by Mycenae. Pottery shows that her trade extended from the Levant to Sicily. Hittite documents reveal the Greeks as a strong Aegean power and even Egypt felt her influence. This was a period of expansion abroad as well as grandeur at home. At Mycenae huge beehive tombs—their contents long since rifled—attest the manpower and engineering ability of the ancestors of Agamemnon. But wealth brought dangers: the palaces had to be fortified. Mycenae, Tiryns, Athens,

Heinrich Schliemann

Sir Arthur Evans

The Lion Gateway to the citadel, Mycenae

Golden funerary mask of Mycenaean nobleman

Thebes still preserve great walls dating from this period.

Secure for the time at home, the Greeks united in a great joint **attack on Troy** which, once rich, was now poorer and weaker. The Trojans, threatened by siege, stocked their houses and held out for a long time before the city was taken and destroyed by the Greek host under Agamemnon. This was the city called Troy VIIa in the sequence of settlements.

e. THE DARK AGE

The Trojan War was the last effort of Greek expansion before a great invasion of peoples coming down through Asia Minor and going all the way to Egypt, where they fell back. Some among them, the Philistines, settled the country that was later named after them. As for the Greeks, Mycenaean trade was cut off and then Greece itself was invaded. **Pylos** which was never walled, was sacked and burned (c. 1200 B.C.). Unprotected buildings near Mycenae were also destroyed and eventually by about 1100 B.C. Mycenae itself had fallen, as had the other cities, including the half-ruined, half-inhabited palace at Knossos.

The **Dorians** were the new Greek invaders. They came in the age of iron and may have brought iron with them. In any case, the consequences of their invasion were terrific. Overnight the elaborate palace bureaucracies disappeared. Records in Linear B also vanished. The Greeks became illiterate and were reduced to small local communities. Their states had been beheaded and the old title of king (*wanax*) had no bearer. Even Athens, though itself uninvaded, suffered like the rest of the country.

Pottery had long since, in the imperial days of Mycenae, lost its easy naturalism. Forms had hardened; they were now stiff and the pottery style developed in the Dark Age was geometric. Once again pottery was the one continuing element. Archaeology is the method of knowing such details as can be discovered about the Dark Age. There is, however, some additional information available to us. In this period the Greeks, faced by distress and displacement at home, sailed to found cities at promising sites in Asia Minor, on the coast of which the Aeolians established settlements in the north, the Ionians in the center, and even the Dorians in the very south. This was the first massive Greek colonial movement.

f. THE GREEK POLIS

Split up and forced back on local resources, the Greeks now developed the unit that was to be central in the classical period: the **polis,** the roots of which were Mycenaean. Outwardly the poleis of the Dark Age, as earlier, were houses clustered around a palace, which usually stood on some strong hill, called the **Akropolis.** The king (now *basileus*) was the chief of the priests and also the highest judge and the commander of the forces. But there was no longer a bureaucracy nor any great concentration of wealth. There was not even any writing.

Yet Greek society had some organization. In Ionian cities the people were grouped into four tribes, each with its own head and cult. In Dorian cities there were only three tribes. Within the tribes "brotherhoods" (*phratriai*)

appeared, composed of members sufficiently related to each other to certify proper birth, which was the qualification of membership. Hence the phratriai became guardians of citizenship, for which membership in some brotherhood was required. Families of tradition and substance formed smaller units (*gene*), virtually noble. These gene furnished the higher officials and the most eminent of them provided the king. Lesser citizens could attend an assembly, but until heavy-armed infantry learned to stand against cavalry, the horse-owning nobles were superior. Thus the royal powers were far more dependent on community goodwill than were the tight palace bureaucracies of the Mycenaean period. In the new poleis the way was open for royal powers eventually to be divided and shared by the nobles and for the other citizens also to participate in the city's management, as they already did in its defense and in its festivals. Nobles had no special titles or dress, nor any sort of a fenced-off status.

g. EPIC POETRY

Ruinous though the destruction had been, so that even quarrying was a lost art and large statues and stone buildings could not be constructed, memories of the grandeur of the past were still vivid in the impoverished present. Bards sang songs of the ancient heroes and songs preserved what the people loved: not the bureaucracy, but the wealth and might of Mycenae and the other great places, the prowess of the men of old, the names and ancestries of the leaders, the tales of mighty doings. Of all these heroic songs, there are preserved to us two, the *Iliad* and *Odyssey,* products (a) of the traditions handed down about the Bronze Age heroes; (b) of the illiterate Dark Age looking back with yearning and expressing itself in an

The Acropolis of Athens

General view of the ruins of the oracle at Delphi

oral art requiring life practice for mastery; (c) of a new acquisition of literacy in the Greek Renascence that followed the Dark Age.

h. THE GREEK RENASCENCE

The Greek revival was slow in coming, at least 300 years (c. 1100–c. 800 B.C.). Then, quickened by inspiration from the old civilizations of the East and by the accumulation of resources, the Greeks developed rapidly. Pottery shows the change: in **Proto-Corinthian** and **Proto-Attic** the stiffness of geometric design gives way to a new feeling for living, curved forms of men and animals; color reappears; ornament, often symmetrical, is vigorous. A whole new set of vase shapes is invented. Spread by the growing trade with distant places, then by colonies, Proto-Corinthian becomes the luxury pottery of the Mediterranean world.

Coinage, invented in Asia Minor, facilitated trade. Arts and crafts began to flourish as major activities in quarrying were resumed. Progress was made in ship construction, and exploration went beyond trade. The **oracle at Delphi** served as a gathering place for information and helped to guide new ventures.

Contact with the Phoenicians was inevitable, and from them the Greeks learned an alphabet of excellent simplicity and usefulness. A little adaptation made it fully adequate for the Greek language. Its virtue is clear from the fact that the Romans too found it good and passed it on to us. The Greek adaptation was made not earlier than 750 B.C. By the end of the 8th century some scribe, seeing the possibilities, persuaded the (oral) poet **Homer** to dictate his best songs about the heroes of the Trojan War. Homer perceived that, relieved of the urgency of oral composition, he could form his expression at his leisure, and could bring to bear all his incomparable talent. And so we have the *Iliad* and *Odyssey.* "Homeric" hymns and the whole body of **Hesiodic verse** were set down before the oral narrative art vanished.

i. ARISTOCRACY AND TYRANNY. COLONIZATION

c. 900–600. Monarchies were replaced throughout Greece by aristocracies, and the kings vanished or were reduced to a titular office (the *archon basileus* at Athens), save in Sparta, which always continued to have two kings simultaneously, and in Macedonia, where ancient monarchy persisted unbroken. Elsewhere the nobles retained the dominant power in the state through the possession of good iron arms and the acquisition of property at the expense of the poor farmers.

c. 760–550. Love of exploration and adventure, distress and food shortage due to large holdings of land by the nobles led to **colonization,** encouraged first by the aristocrats to get rid of discontent and then by the tyrants for political and commercial advantage. The traditional dates of the more important colonies in east and west, which were entered almost simultaneously, follow: Miletus colonized Cyzicus (757) and Abydos (756) on the Euxine. Through friendship with Psammetichus I of Egypt, Miletus also joined other cities in founding the important trading post of Naucratis, in the Nile Delta (640). Phocaea settled Marssalia (Marseilles) in Gaul (600). Rhodes settled Gela (688) and Gela founded Acragas (580), both in Sicily. Thera colonized Cyrene in North Africa (630). Chalcis and Eretria in Euboea sent colonies to the Chalcidice (northern Aegean) and to Sicily, notably Catana and Leontini (728), Rhegium (730), also Cumae (Bay of Naples, 760). Megara colonized the Hellespont with Chalcedon (660) and Byzantium, as well as settling the Sicilian Megara Hyblaea (728). Corinth occupied the strategic Potidaea (northern Aegean, 609), Corcyra (735), and Syracuse in Sicily (735). In southern Italy (Magna Graecia) Achaea settled Sybaris (721) and Croton (710); while Sparta, occupied with the conquest of Messenia, founded only Taras (Tarentum, 705).

Marble relief, c. 200 B.C., depicting Homer crowned by the World and Time; above are Zeus, Apollo, and the Muses

Head of a poet, bronze, 2nd century B.C.

Athens sent out no colonies until later. In the end. Greek colonies occupied most of the Mediterranean coasts all the way to Gibraltar, wherever the Etruscans. Carthaginians. Egyptians. and Levantines did not exclude them.

Trade had preceded colonization and in turn colonization encouraged trade. since not only the settlers but the peoples among whom they settled desired luxury products (oil, wine, and manufactures) from Greece, which they repaid with raw materials. But the colonies were formally and actually in the main independent. Greater skill in technical processes like metallurgy and pottery allowed the Greeks to compete favorably with the Phoenicians and encouraged the growth of an industrial population, as well as a trading one, in the cities. New farm land was, however, a strong motive. Slavery increased and coined money was introduced from Lydia into Ionia and thence into Greece, traditionally by King Pheidon of Argos (c. 680). The two prominent standards of currency were the Euboean and the Aeginetan.

c. 650–500. Tyrannies arose in Greece, for a variety of causes. The aristocracies refused political equality to the landless traders and manufactures, the peasants were oppressed by the rich and fell into debt and then were reduced to slavery or exile; slaves began to compete with free labor. Ambitious individuals capitalized this discontent to overthrow the constituted governments and establish themselves as tyrants in almost all the Greek cities, with the notable exception of Sparta, whose balanced constitution, organized to dominate the numerous serfs (*helots*), enabled it to preserve its aristocratic form. The tyrants were on the whole popular and successful; they kept the people happy with festivals and public works, they diminished the power of the nobles. and they reduced class and ethnic distinctions. They fostered, especially, the artistic

and intellectual life. **Lyric poetry** flourished; **Archilochus** the father of satire (c. 700); the individual lyric of the Aeolians, **Alcaeus** and **Sappho** of Lesbos (c. 600); the choral lyric of the Dorians, **Stesichorus** (c. 650) and **Arion** (c. 600). Contact with the east led to the eclipse of the geometric style in art by the **oriental** (animal) **style.** Philosophy began with the Milesian school of **Thales** (predicted the eclipse of 585), **Anaximenes**, and **Anaximander**, who began to seek knowledge for its own sake, to find a rational explanation for natural phenomena: they were the first to try to prove any statements that they made, within a logical system. Among the important tyrants were: **Thrasybulus** of Miletus (c. 620); **Polycrates** of Samos (c. 530), noted for his navy, with which he almost dominated the Aegean, his building, and his alliance with Amasis of Egypt; **Cleisthenes** of Sicyon (c. 600); **Theagenes** of Megara (c. 640); **Periander** of Corinth (c. 600), patron of poetry, who recovered control of Corcyra from the oligarchs; and the **Peisistratids** in Athens. The tyrannies generally were overthrown in the second generation, since they had served their purpose, and the tyrants' sons, born to power, tended to become oppressive. Moreover, Sparta consistently opposed them.

j. FORMATION OF THE GREEK STATES

(1) Asia Minor

c. 690. The **Kingdom of Phrygia** (traditional kings Midas and Gordius), which had considerably influenced the Asiatic Greeks, was destroyed by the **Cimmerians,** invaders from southern Russia. Its place was taken by the **Kingdom of Lydia,** in which Gyges founded the active Mermnad Dynasty (c. 685). He and his successors raided the Greek cities, but were prevented from conquest by further in-

cursions of the Cimmerians, who sacked Sardis and slew Gyges (c. 652).

585, May 28. **Alyattes,** third king of Lydia, and **Cyaxares,** king of Media, ended their war by a treaty defining their boundary at the river Halys. Thales is said to have predicted the eclipse which induced them to treat and which, therefore, determines the date. **Croesus** acceded to the Lydian throne (c. 560) and began to reduce the Ionian cities to a tributary condition, save for Miletus. His mild rule, however, did not check their political growth (tyrannies).

547. **CYRUS,** who had united his Persian kingdom with the Median by his defeat of Astyages (550), now defeated Croesus, crossed the Halys, sacked Sardis, and captured Croesus himself. His general, Harpagus, subdued the Ionian cities, save Miletus, which retained its favorable status, and put in pro-Persian tyrants. With the loss of freedom intellectual activity diminished.

(2) The Peloponnese

c. 800. **Sparta** had become mistress of Laconia and had colonized the coast of Messenia. She warred with **Tegea,** chief city of the backward and disunited Arcadians, who maintained a loose religious union centering about the primitive worship on Mt. Lycaeum. Politically, kingship survived in Arcadia into the 5th century. **Corinth,** under the close oligarchical rule of the Bacchiadae, had become commercially important and, until c. 720, dominated its smaller neighbor **Megara. Argos,** though claiming the hegemony of Greece as heir of Mycenae, remained a weak state.

c. 736–716. In the **FIRST MESSENIAN WAR,** Sparta, led by **King Theopompus,** conquered Messenia and divided the rich plain into lots, which the Messenians, as helots, worked for their Spartiate masters. Besides helots and Spartiates, there was a third class of Laconians,

The temple of Poseidon at Paestum, Sicily, c. 460 B.C.

View of the Acropolis of Athens (p.83)

Mycenaean gold mask (p.67)

The School of Plato; Roman mosaic (p.87)

Corinthian wine jug, oriental style, c. 625 B.C.

Ruins of the Acropolis of Corinth

the *perioeci* (dwellers-around), who were free but not possessed of citizen rights. Sparta still, however, had an artistic and intellectual life equal to any in Greece, especially in respect to choral poetry.

c. 680. King Pheidon made Argos for a brief space powerful. He defeated Sparta allied with Tegea in the **battle of Hysiae** (669), and, in support of revolting Aegina, crushed Epidaurus and her ally Athens. Pheidon is said to have introduced coinage into Greece, perhaps with a mint on Aegina. After his death, the powers of the rulers were curtailed and Argos declined.

c. 650–630. In the **Second Messenian War,** Sparta with difficulty crushed her revolting subjects, who were led by Aristomenes, master of Arcadia, and who took refuge on Mt. Eira.

c. 610. By the so-called *Eunomia,* the Spartans, fearing further revolts, completely reorganized the state to make it more severely military. Citizen youth from the age of seven were taken for continual military training. Men of military age lived in barracks and ate at common messes (*syssitia, phiditia*). Five local tribes replaced the three Dorian hereditary ones and the army was correspondingly divided, creating the *Dorian phalanx.* The *gerousia,* comprising 28 elders and the two kings, had the initiative in legislation, though the *apella* of all citizens had the final decision. The chief magistrates, *ephors,* were increased to five, with wider powers especially after the ephorate of **Cheilon** (556). Later ages attributed the reforms to the hero **Lycurgus** in the 9th century, perhaps because the new laws were put under his protection.

c. 560. Sparta finally reduced the Tegeates to the status of subject allies, not helots. She then (c. 546, **battle of the 300 Champions**), took the plain of Thyreatis from Argos. The kings Anaxandridas and Ariston extended the policy of alliances to all the Peloponnesian states save Achaea and Argos to form the **Peloponnesian League,** in which the allies had equal votes on foreign policies, contributed two-thirds of their forces in war, and paid no tax except for war. Sparta's policy was hereafter anti-tyrant; she expelled the tyrants of Sicyon, Naxos, and, later, Athens (510), and sought to do so in Samos (c. 524, Polycrates).

c. 520. The young king **Cleomenes I** tried to reassert the royal power against the ephors. When the expulsion of the tyrants from Athens led not to a pro-Spartan oligarchy but to the democratic reforms of Cleisthenes, he led an expedition into Attica, which, however, failed because of the opposition of the other king, **Damaratus,** and the defection of Corinth through jealousy of Sparta's power. Nevertheless, by his defeat of Argos in the **battle of Sepeia** (494) he so increased the power of Sparta and of himself that he was emboldened to depose Damaratus, despite the opposition of the ephors, on a charge of illegitimacy. Public opinion then turned against him and he fled to Arcadia, whence he forced his return by arms. Traditionally, he soon after (c. 489) went mad, was imprisoned, and committed suicide, but this tale may conceal a real arrest and execution by the ephors. He was succeeded by **Leonidas.** Under Cleomenes the **Spartan League,** most enduring of all Greek leagues, was at its height.

(3) Athens

Attica was gradually unified or reunified by the device of *synoecism,* through which the numerous small independent cities surrendered their local citizenship for that of Athens. This process had by 700 taken in all Attica except Eleusis, which was soon added. Traditionally

Lycurgus

the whole process was accomplished by King Theseus.

In the **Ancient Constitution of Athens** the people were divided into four hereditary tribes (*phylai*), each made up of a number of brotherhoods (*phratriai*), which had common religious ceremonies and gave assistance to members in legal strife and blood feuds. The nobles (*eupatridai*) formed smaller associations of clans (*gene*); the *phratriai* contained eventually both members of these clans (*gennetai*) and common people (*orgeones*), although at first perhaps only the former. Each tribe was divided for administrative purposes into 12 *naucrariai*, which handled the revenue and cared for the navy. The people were grouped, chiefly for military purposes, into three classes: *hippeis* (knights), *zeugitai* (those with a yoke of oxen), and *thetes* (laborers). The nobles gradually restricted the power of the king by giving first his military functions to a *polemarch* and then his civil functions to an *archon.*

683. The hereditary kingship was abolished

GREEK
CITY
STATES

made humane laws affecting private life. By the **Seisachtheia** (shaking-off-of-burdens) all debts on land were canceled; all debt slaves in Attica were freed; those sold abroad were redeemed at state expense; securing of debts by the person was forbidden. By his **judicial reforms** a new and milder code of laws replaced all of Draco's except the laws on homicide; a court of all the citizens, the *heliaea*, was created and a right of appeal to it from decisions of the magistrates was granted. By his constitutional reforms election of magistrates was given to the ecclesia of all freemen; a council (*boulé*) of 400 (100 from each tribe) was created as a deliberative body which had the initiative in all legislation: the assembly could only accept or reject its proposals. The areopagus, hereafter composed of ex-archons, continued as guardian of the laws to have large supervisory powers over the magistrates. Four classes of citizens were defined: *pentacosiomedimnoi* (who had revenues of 500 *medimni* of corn and/or *metretai* of wine or oil); the *hippeis* (300); the *zeugitai* (200); and the *thetes* (all the rest). Some time later these classes were redefined in terms of money, and based on property rather than income. Only the first two classes were eligible to the archonship; the first three to the lower offices; the fourth could participate only in the heliaea and the ecclesia. By his economic reforms, Solon devalued the drachma by about a quarter; weights and measures were increased in size; the exportation of all agricultural produce except oil was forbidden; and immigration of artisans was encouraged.

Solon's reforms were inadequate, perhaps because no provision was made to supply the freed slaves with land or to relieve the *hectemoroi* (sharecroppers), who received only one-sixth of the produce of the land for themselves. Sectional party strife continued immediately after Solon's archonship. The rich nobles of the plain (*pediakoi*) were led by **Lycurgus,** the middle class (*paralioi*) by **Megacles** the Alcmaeonid.

c. 565. Peisistratus acquired fame as the successful general in the **conquest of Salamis** from Megara. He organized a new party, the *diakrioi,* of the small farmers, artisans, shepherds, and other poor folk.

561–527. PEISISTRATUS made himself tyrant, but was almost immediately driven out by Megacles and Lycurgus. In 560–559 he won Megacles over and was restored. About 556 he was again expelled after a break with Megacles. After he had spent some years in gaining wealth from his mines in Thrace, he was restored with aid from Thessaly and Lygdamis of Naxos, whom he had made tyrant (c. 546). Peisistratus's opponents were now exiled and their confiscated lands used to provide for the poor. The *hectemoroi* were made landowners. Peisistratus encouraged industry and trade, and introduced the popular **cult of Dionysius,** in order to break down the power held by the nobles through their hereditary priesthoods. Miltiades and a few Athenians, with Peisistratus's encouragement, set up a tyranny over the Thracians of the Chersonese. Delos was purified. Abroad, Peisistratus pursued a policy of friendship with all near neighbors; at home, he ruled without abolishing existing forms.

527. On the death of Peisistratus his sons **Hip-**

and made into an annual office (*archon basileus*) like the archon and polemarch. Six *thesmothetai* were created to determine the customary law. These, with the *archon eponymous* (civil archon), the archon basileus, and the polemarch, were known as the **nine archons.** They were chosen from the nobles by the **areopagus,** a council of nobles which was the greatest power in the state. The **ecclesia** (assembly of all the citizens) seems not to have had important powers.

632. Cylon, a noble related to Theagenes, tyrant of Megara, attempted to establish a tyranny, but was foiled. Many of his followers were tricked into surrendering and then slaughtered by Megacles of the Alcmaeonid clan ("Curse of the Alcmaeonids").

620. Publication of the law on homicide by **Draco,** the unfairness of the nobles in administering the traditional law having led to a demand for its publication.

c. 600. **Athens** seized Sigeum from Mytilene; the resulting war was arbitrated (c. 590) in favor of Athens by Periander of Corinth.

594. SOLON was made sole archon to remedy the distress caused by the introduction of coined money and high rates of interest; all parties agreed to give this man of the middle class complete powers of reform. He regulated the festivals, basis of the calendar, and

pias and Hipparchus succeeded to the tyranny. Athens protected Plataea against Thebes (519), which was trying to force her into the Boeotian League.

514. An attempt was made by **Harmodius** and **Aristogeiton** to overthrow the tyranny, but only Hipparchus was killed. Hippias was finally expelled by the exiled Alcmaeonids with Spartan aid (510). Party strife followed between the nobles led by Isagoras and the commons led by the Alcmaeonid **Cleisthenes**, who was finally victorious and inaugurated a

508. Structural reform of the Constitution. In order to combat sectionalism, *demes* (townships) were created to a number of over 140, and citizenship was made dependent on membership in one of these rather than as before in a phratria. A new system of 10 local tribes (*phylai*) was created: Attica was divided into three sections: Athens and its vicinity, the coast, and the interior. The demes in each section were associated in ten *trittyes,* and each tribe was composed of one trittys from each section, ordinarily not contiguous. A new council (*boulé*) of 500 replaced the Solonian 400; its members were chosen by lot, 50 from each tribe and from each deme in proportion to its population. The army was reorganized into ten tribal regiments, each of which in 501 was put under an elective general (*strategos*).

507. At the appeal of Isagoras, **Cleomenes** of Sparta invaded Attica, expelled Cleisthenes, and tried to restore the aristocracy. The Athenians rose, expelled the Spartans, and recalled Cleisthenes.

506. A second expedition of Cleomenes was prevented by King Damaratus and by Corinth. The Athenians crushed the Boeotians and Euboeans and annexed part of Chalcis' territory. They disregarded an ultimatum from Darius of Persia that they restore Hippias, whom Darius had made tyrant of Sigeum.

498. The Athenians sent 20 ships to the aid of the revolting Ionians, but after one campaign withdrew and tried to conciliate Persia by electing Hipparchus, a Peisistratid, to the archonship (496).

493/2. Themistocles was elected archon by the anti-Persian party and commenced the fortification of the Piraeus, but his naval policy was opposed by Miltiades, also anti-Persian, who had fled the Chersonese after the failure of the Ionian revolt.

(4) Central and Northern Greece

Some time before 700 the cities of Thessaly had been grouped in four *tetrads,* each under a *tetrarch.* Now they were organized into a loose **Thessalian League,** which elected, when common action was necessary, a general (*tagos*). There was a federal assembly which levied taxes and troops on the members. Until the 6th century this league possessed the strongest army in Greece; Thessalian cavalry was always unsurpassed. The looseness of the organization, however, prevented Thessaly from playing a leading rôle in Greece. Thessaly dominated the **Amphictyony of Anthela,** a religious league that by 600 included all the states of central Greece.

c. 590. In the **FIRST SACRED WAR,** under the leadership of Thessaly, and with help from Sicyon and Athens, the Amphictyony of Anthela defeated and demolished Crisa (Cirrha), in whose territory the shrine of Delphi lay.

Aristogeiton and Harmodius

Theater of Dionysius in Athens

Pindar

Ruins of the Treasury of Athens at Delphi

Mounted warrior, bronze, c. 550 B.C.

The pretext was the tolls levied by Crisa on pilgrims to Delphi. Delphi was put under the administration of the Amphictyones and their headquarters were transferred thither; Athens and the Dorians of the Peloponnese were admitted to membership.

c. 570. In **Euboea** the two states of importance, Chalcis and Eretria, had been very active in colonization and industry (c. 750-650). The Euboean coinage and weights and measures spread through the Greek world.

c. 570. Chalcis, supported by Corinth, Samos, and Thessaly, now became engaged in the **Lelantine War** with Eretria, aided by Aegina, Miletus, and Megara, over the possession of the rich Lelantine plain. Chalcis was victorious.

c. 600-550. Thebes formed a **Boeotian League** by bringing pressure on the other states of Boeotia. After a long struggle the powerful Orchomenos was reduced.

519-506. Plataea refused to join the league and entered into alliance with Athens. In the ensuing conflict, the Boeotians and Euboeans were defeated by the Athenians.

(5) *Sicily and Magna Graecia*

The original people of Sicily were Sicans; these were displaced by the Sicels from southern Italy. Before 800 the Elymians entered, probably from Spain, and occupied the western corner of Sicily. The Phoenician trading posts in Sicily *(p. 53)*, which had covered the coast, were gradually driven out after 735 (foundation of Naxos) by the Greek colonization, except for Motya, Panormus, and Solus, in the west. Meanwhile **Carthage** *(p. 53)* had grown into an imperial power by founding colonies of her own and by protecting the older settlements after Tyre and Sidon were weakened by foreign domination after 669.

c. 580. An attempt of the Spartan **Pentathlus** to colonize western Sicily was defeated by the Elymians.

c. 570-554. **Phalaris,** tyrant of Acragas, pursued a policy of energetic and ruthless expansion, with extreme cruelty at home.

c. 550. The Carthaginian **Malchus** campaigned successfully in Sicily.

Marble frieze, c. 525 B.C., depicting the battle between gods and giants

535. In the naval **battle of Alalia,** off Corsica, the Carthaginians and Etruscans defeated the Phocaean settlers and forced the abandonment of their colony. Shortly after this Massilia defeated Carthage and imposed a treaty limiting Carthaginian influence in the north and west.

510. **Sybaris** was destroyed by Croton, which was at this time ruled by the sect of the Pythagoreans. An attempt of the Spartan Dorieus to colonize western Sicily was prevented by the Carthaginians.

The conquest of Ionia by Persia led to a shift of intellectual and artistic effort to Greece proper and, thanks to their wealth, to the western colonies. **Tragedy** began at Athens with **Thespis** (539); the poets **Pindar, Simonides,** and **Anacreon** flourished c. 500. Attic black-figured vases gave way to red-figured (c. 525). **Sculpture** became more common, in the archaic style (Athens, Delphi). **Heraclitus of Ephesus,** last of the Ionian physicists, advocated "change" against the "one" of **Parmenides of Elea** (*Eleatic School*) in southern Italy. **Pythagoras** founded his sect of mystic philosophers in Croton.

2. *The Persian Wars* *499–478* B.C.

499–494. The Ionians revolted under the leadership of **Aristagoras** of Miletus, against the Persians and the pro-Persian tyrants. Aristagoras made a trip to Greece to solicit aid; Sparta refused, but Athens responded with 20 ships (498) and Eretria with five. The rebels made a dash on Sardis, burned it, and retired to Ephesus. Greek disunion and the desertion of the Samians and Lesbians led to the defeat of the Greek fleet in a battle off the island of **Lade** (494). Darius's control of the sea now enabled him to take and sack Miletus. This practically ended the revolt. Darius subdued all the Greek cities, but did not again force tyrants upon them.

492. **First Persian expedition** under **Mardonius,** sent to punish Athens and Eretria for their aid to the rebel cities. Mardonius subdued Thrace and accepted the submission of Macedonia, but the Persian fleet was dashed to pieces while rounding the rocky promontory of Mt. Athos in a storm. Mardonius thereupon retreated.

490. **Second expedition** of the Persians, across the Aegean, under Artaphernes and Datis. Artaphernes besieged Eretria on Euboea while Datis landed at Marathon, the center of Peisistratid strength. When Eretria fell through treachery, Miltiades, one of the ten generals, persuaded the Athenians to attack. The Athenians won a complete victory in the **BATTLE OF MARATHON** (Sept. 12) and reached Athens in time to prevent its betrayal to Artaphernes by the now pro-Peisistratid Alcmaeonids. The Persians returned to Asia.

Miltiades failed to capture Paros and was condemned to a heavy fine. He died soon after.

489. Athens waged an indecisive **war with Aegina** until c. 483.

488–482. By a **reform of the Athenian constitution** (488/7), the nine archons were hereafter chosen by lot from 500 candidates elected by the demes; at some later time this was changed to ten preliminary candidates elected from each tribe, and still later the preliminary candidates also were chosen by lot. This change naturally reduced the power of the polemarch in favor of the ten elected generals, of whom one might be selected by the people at large as general-in-chief (*strategos autocrator*). To guard against tyranny, the device of **ostracism** was devised. In a meeting in which not less than 6000 votes were cast (*ostraka* were potsherds used for voting), the man with the greatest number was obliged to leave Athens for ten years; he remained a citizen, however, and his property was not confiscated. Hipparchus was ostracized in 487/6; Megacles the Alcmaeonid in 486/5; Xanthippus of the same party in 484/3. The anti-Persian party, of which the noble faction was led by **Aristides** and the commons by **Themistocles,** regained power. Themistocles prevailed upon the people to use a rich new vein of silver found in the state mine at Laurium for the building of 200 **triremes,** a newly invented type of warship. Aristides was ostracized due to his opposition to this measure, and from now on ostracism was used as a measure of party government. By 480 Themistocles headed the state as *strategos autocrator.*

480. **CAMPAIGN OF THERMOPYLAE. Xerxes,** who had succeeded Darius in 486, demanded earth and water (submission) from all the Greek states, most of which refused. Xerxes thereupon led a carefully prepared expedition of about 180,000 men (not the traditional 900,000) into Greece through Thrace and Macedonia. A Greek force sent to hold the pass of Tempe retired when it was found untenable; the Greek army then occupied the **pass of Thermopylae,** and the fleet the Gulf of Artemisium: the plan was for the army to hold the Persians while the fleet won a victory and thus compelled retreat. The naval fighting, however, was indecisive. Under the guidance of the Greek Ephialtes, a Persian company traversed a side path, routed a small Phocian outpost, and turned the Greek position at Thermopylae. Most of the Greeks withdrew, but **Leonidas,** with 300 Spartans and 700 Thespians, refused to retire and they were annihilated. The Boeotians, Phocians, and Locrians immediately "medized"; the Greek army retreated behind a wall built across the Isthmus of Corinth, and the fleet moved to the Saronic Gulf between Athens and Salamis. The Persians occupied Attica and destroyed Athens, whence the citizens had fled to Salamis and the Peloponnese.

BATTLE OF SALAMIS. The Greek fleet was bottled up in the Saronic Gulf by the superior Persian forces. Themistocles craftily warned Xerxes that the Greeks were about to escape by night, and the Persians thereupon rushed into the narrows, became entangled, and were thoroughly defeated. Since it was impossible to force the isthmus merely by assault, this meant the end of the year's campaign. Xerxes returned to Sardis with a third of the army, Artabazus to Thrace with another third, and Mardonius wintered in Boeotia with the rest.

479. **BATTLE OF PLATAEA.** After unsuccessfully trying to detach the Athenians from the Greek cause, Mardonius again invaded Attica. The Peloponnesians, urged by the Athenians, advanced to Plataea under the

Marble gravestone of Xanthippus

Spartan **Pausanias.** Mardonius attacked them as they were confusedly shifting their position, but the day was won by the superiority of the heavy-armed Greek *hoplites* and the discipline and bravery of the Spartans. Mardonius was killed, his camp plundered, and the Persian army routed. The Greeks then took Thebes by siege, and abolished the oligarchy in favor of a democracy. In the meantime, the Spartan **Leotychidas** had sailed with a small fleet to guard the Cyclades against Persia. The Samians and Chians prevailed upon him to attack the Persians, who were at Samos. The Persians, fearing to meet him on the open sea, drew up their ships on land at **Mycale** near Samos. Leotychidas stormed their position, but the Persians succeeded in burning their ships before the Greeks could seize them. The Ionians and several of the island cities (Samos, Lesbos, Chios) now revolted from Persia and joined the Greek fleet, which laid siege to Sestos in the Thracian Chersonese. The Spartans returned home in the fall, but the Athenians and Ionians succeeded during the winter in reducing Sestos (478).

The battle of Plataea

3. *The 5th Century*

a. THE PELOPONNESE, 479–461 B.C.

479. **Pausanias,** in command of the allied fleet, reduced Cyprus and Byzantium. By his domineering he alienated the Ionians and caused the ephors to fear lest his power become excessive; they recalled him and after a first acquittal he was later (c. 471) starved to death in the temple of Athena of the Brazen House. The Ionians refused to recognize his successor Dorcis and went over to Athenian leadership.

Cimon

Thus Sparta's prestige in the Peloponnese fell very low. In 471 Elis united herself under a democratic government by *synoecism* and Tegea deserted Sparta to form an alliance with Argos, probably fostered by Themistocles.

470. After a drawn **battle at Tegea** all of Arcadia except Mantinea joined the anti-Spartan alliance. While Argos was occupied in reducing Tiryns and Mycenae (c. 469), however, Sparta crushed the allies at Dipaea and restored her hegemony.

464. An earthquake in Sparta gave the helots of Messenia a chance to revolt **(Third Messenian War);** after a defeat they retired to Mt. Ithome, where the Spartans besieged them. Unable to take the place, the Spartans called on the aid of their allies, including Athens. Athens sent a force under Cimon which was shortly dismissed (462), probably because many of its members were really hostile to Sparta; this marked the end of the Spartan-Athenian alliance. The fall of Ithome ended the revolt (461), and the Messenians were given safe-conduct to Naupactus, which Athens had just acquired from the Ozolian Locrians.

462. **Megara,** involved in a border war with Corinth, appealed unsuccessfully to Sparta and then made an alliance with Athens.

b. ATHENS AND THE DELIAN LEAGUE, 479–461 B.C.

479. Athens and the Piraeus were fortified by Themistocles, despite the opposition of Sparta.

478–477. The **Ionians,** disgusted with Spartan leadership, made an alliance with Athens for the expulsion of the Persians from all Greek territory. Each ally was to contribute either a quota of ships, or money in lieu of this: the smaller states chose the latter. **Aristides** ("The Just") assessed the tribute, using the old Persian tribute as a guide: the total was probably about two hundred talents at first. The league had a general assembly (*synedrion*) on Delos, which at first controlled league policy, although it was soon dominated by Athens.

476. **Cimon** made an expedition to Thrace and captured the Persian forts along the coast except Doriscus; the siege of Eion occupied the winter. Some time later Carystus in Euboea was compelled to join the league. These successes enabled Cimon to procure the ostracism of Themistocles (471), probably because the latter wished to follow an anti-Spartan policy. Themistocles went to Argos, where he conspired against Sparta; he was later (471) outlawed by Athens and fled to Persia, where Artaxerxes gave him a refuge (464).

467. When **Naxos** attempted to withdraw from the Delian League, though the treaty of alliance made no provision for withdrawal, Athens forced the city to raze its walls, surrender its fleet, and henceforth pay tribute. Athens after this often interfered in the internal affairs of the tributary states, which were soon considered subjects and not equal allies. Commercial disputes between citizens of two subject states or between those of a subject state and Athens, as well as capital criminal cases, were tried in the Athenian courts. Part of the rebels' lands was often taken, especially during Peri-

Terra-cotta chariot from Boeotia

Pericles

cles's supremacy, to establish an Athenian *cleruchy* (colony), serving a military purpose as well as relieving unemployment in Athens. Garrisons were left under military captains (*phrourarchoi*) if necessary; sometimes only civil commissioners (*episkopoi*) were sent. Athenian surveyors (*taktai*) reassessed the tribute, and the Athenian people controlled its use, as well as the use of the contingents of the autonomous allies.

466. Cimon defeated the Persians in a great naval victory at the **Eurymedon River** on the south coast of Asia Minor. He then crushed a revolt of Thasos (465–463). Under the leadership of **Ephialtes,** a man of great probity and ability, a popular party was rising against the domination of Cimon. He was charged with having accepted a bribe from Alexander of Macedon, but was acquitted and prevailed over Ephialtes in having a force sent to Sparta against the helots (462). When the Spartans dismissed Cimon, the strong anti-Spartan feeling in Athens caused him to be ostracized (461). Ephialtes then succeeded in depriving the areopagus of all its powers except the jurisdiction in homicide cases; the other powers were distributed among the ecclesia, the council of 500, and the popular courts, which by this time, owing to the press of imperial business, had been changed from one panel of 6000 to several panels of from 201 up. Ephialtes was murdered shortly afterwards, and **Pericles** (born not long after 500, died 429), on his mother's side an Alcmaeonid, took his place in the leadership of the popular party.

c. THE FIRST PELOPONNESIAN WAR

460. **Inaros,** who had previously raised a revolt in Egypt and defeated a Persian force, appealed to Athens for aid and was sent a fleet (probably not of 200 sail), which took Memphis. Simultaneously war broke out between the Athenians and the Peloponnesians, caused in part by the Megarian alliance of 462, which the Athenians had followed with alliances with Argos and Thessaly.

459. The Athenians were defeated at **Halieis** by the Corinthians and Epidaurians, but their fleet won a victory at **Cecryphaleia.** The Aeginetans joined the Peloponnesians (458), but their combined fleet was defeated by the Athenians in a **battle off Aegina** and the island was invested by a force of Athenians under Leosthenes. The Corinthians raided the Megarid to create a diversion but were defeated by the Athenian old men and boys under Myronides.

457. The **Aeginetans** were forced to surrender, join the Delian League as tributaries, and surrender their fleet.

Sparta then entered the war, sent an army across the Corinthian Gulf, and restored the Boeotian League under the hegemony of Thebes. Athens was defeated at **Tanagra,** but the Spartans returned home, leaving the Athenians to defeat the Boeotians at **Oenophyta** and enroll all the cities except Thebes in her league; Phocis and Opuntian Locris also entered. The Athenians connected the Piraeus with Athens by two long walls.

456. A Persian force under **Megabyzus** defeated the Athenians, who were besieging Leukon Teichos, the citadel of Memphis. The Athenians were in turn besieged on the Nile island Prosopitis.

455. The Athenian **Tolmides** sailed around the Peloponnese, raiding the coast, burning the Spartan shipyard at Gytheum, and gaining Achaea for the Athenian League.

454. **Pericles** crossed the isthmus and made an unsuccessful campaign in the Corinthian Gulf. But meanwhile the Athenians in Egypt were defeated and slaughtered, and a relief squadron met the same fate. As a result the treasury of the Delian League was moved to Athens.

451. After three years of inactivity **Cimon** returned from exile and negotiated a five years' truce with Sparta. Thus, being unprotected, Argos had to make a thirty years' peace with Sparta. Cimon then took a large force to Cyprus (450) but a plague (famine?) caused his death and necessitated the return of the force to Athens. As it was departing, the fleet won a great **victory off Salamis,** a town of Cyprus. An understanding was then reached with Persia (the so-called **Peace of Callias**).

449–448. The **SECOND SACRED WAR** was begun when Sparta took Delphi from Phocis and made it independent; Athens immediately restored it to the Phocians.

447. **Boeotia** revolted and an inadequate Athenian force under Tolmides was crushed at Coronea. Moderate oligarchies were set up in all the Boeotian cities. The Boeotian League was re-established on a federal principle: a total of 11 Boeotarchs was sent by the cities in proportion to their sizes; for each Boeotarch a city was entitled to 60 seats on the federal council. Both local and federal councils were divided into four sections, of which each in turn served as council, while the four together constituted a plenary assembly. There was a federal treasury and coinage. Troops were levied in proportion to population. Phocis and Locris followed Boeotia in quitting the Athenian League.

446. **Euboea revolted** and Pericles crossed over with an army. Simultaneously the Peloponnesians invaded the Megarid and drove out the Athenian garrison. Pericles returned, but not daring a battle retired to Athens and when the Peloponnesians reached Eleusis came to terms satisfactory to the enemy, who withdrew. Pericles then crushed the revolt in Euboea, and established a cleruchy on the territory of Histiaea. Negotiations with the Spartans continued, and during the winter

446/5. The **THIRTY YEARS' PEACE** was concluded: Megara returned to the Peloponnesian League; Troezen and Achaea became independent; Aegina was to be tributary but autonomous; disputes were to be settled by arbitration. Disgust among the Athenian conservatives at the failure of the anti-Spartan policy led to an attempt to ostracize Pericles, but it resulted in the ostracism (445) of their leader Thucydides, son of Melesias (not the historian). Pericles enjoyed undisputed control until 430.

d. ATHENS, 460–431 B.C.

457. Pericles made the zeugitai eligible to the archonship; the thetes were never legally eligible, but in fact were soon permitted to hold the office. Athenian imperialism was extended to the far west by an alliance with Segesta and Halicyae in Sicily (453). An extremely important measure for the development of the democracy was the institution (451) of pay for the *dicasts* (jurors) of the popular courts, which made it possible for the poorest citizens to serve. At the same time Pericles carried a bill restricting Athenian citizenship to those both of whose parents were Athenians (repealed 429, re-enacted 403), and when Athens received a gift of free corn from Egypt in 446/5 the lists were revised and 5000 citizens removed. The western policy was continued with the foundation of Thurii (443) and the alliances made with several Ionic cities of Sicily.

441. Miletus, involved in a war with Samos, appealed to Athens, which replaced the oligarchy in Samos with a democracy.

440. Samos revolted and threw out the democracy, but the Athenians after a long siege took the city (439) which lost its fleet, its walls, and its autonomy, being made tributary. Chios and Lesbos were now the only autonomous allies in the league.

437. A policy of expansion in the north was begun with the foundation of **Amphipolis** in Thrace, controlling the mines of Pangaeus; it also relieved unemployment and served as a garrison against disaffected allies. Perhaps in the same year Pericles made an expedition into the Euxine and established good relations with the princes of Panticapaeum, who exported the grain badly needed by Athens. Athenian settlers were sent to various Pontic cities. In the Corinthian Gulf about this time Phormio made an alliance with some of the Acarnanians.

Etruscan bronze helmet dedicated to Zeus at Olympia by Hieron I after his victory over the Etruscans in 474 B.C.

Athens at the time of Pericles

e. SICILY, 499–409 B.C.

The first decades of the 5th century witnessed the rise of tyrants in the Sicilian cities, of whom the most important were **Theron of Acragas** (488–472) and **Gelon of Gela,** later of Syracuse (485–478). Gelon made Syracuse the first city of Sicily, largely by transporting thither populations from conquered neighbors. He differed from the usual tyrant in favoring the landed nobles (*gamoroi*) at the expense of the commons.

480. Terillus, tyrant of Himera until Theron conquered that city, appealed for Carthaginian help. Carthage, fearing the alliance of Gelon and Theron, responded with a force under Hamilcar, which was utterly defeated at Himera by the allies. Hamilcar was killed and Carthage forced to pay an indemnity.

478–466. Hieron I, brother of Gelon, marks the height of the first Syracusan tyranny. He moved the citizens of Catana to Leontini and resettled Catana with his mercenaries under the name Aetna. In alliance with Aristodemus of Cumae he defeated the Etruscans in a naval **battle off Cumae** (474).

472. Thrasydaeus, a cruel and hated ruler, succeeded his father Theron at Acragas. He immediately became involved in a war with Hieron and was decisively defeated. The people of Acragas and Himera expelled him and set up a democracy.

467/6. Rhegium and Taras were defeated with heavy losses by the native Italian Iapyges. A democracy was established in Taras and the Pythagoreans were expelled from the Italian cities generally.

466. Thrasybulus succeeded his brother Hieron at Syracuse, but was expelled directly; a democracy was established. The attempted tyranny of **Tyndaridas** (Tyndarion) led to the introduction of *petalism,* like Athenian ostracism.

463–460. After a series of conflicts the mercenaries of the deposed Sicilian tyrants were left in possession of **Messana** (formerly Zancle).

459/8. The Sicels united under **Ducetius** and founded a capital at Palice.

453. The Elymian towns of Segesta and Halicyae became involved in a war with Selinus and made an alliance with the aid of Athens.

450. Syracuse and Acragas finally succeeded in defeating Ducetius at Noae; he was exiled to Corinth and the Sicel federation fell apart. As a result of this victory Syracuse and Acragas fell out over the division of territory (c. 445). Syracuse was finally victorious and became the recognized leader of Sicily. In fear of her, Rhegium, Leontini, Catana (?), and Naxos (?) made alliances with Athens (443). Athens at the same time refounded the site of Sybaris as Thurii, calling in colonists from all of Greece.

440/39. Ducetius, who had returned in 446, restored the Sicel federation, and after founding Cale Acte, died; his federation was completely ended; Syracuse destroyed Palice.

427–424. A **general war** broke out in Sicily. Naxos, Catana, Leontini, Rhegium, Camarina, and most of the Sicels opposed Syracuse, which was supported by Gela, Messana, Himera, Lipara, and Locri. Gorgias of Leontini went to Athens and made an appeal for aid, which was granted. After indecisive fighting the aristocrat Hermocrates of Syracuse persuaded the warring cities, which had assembled in the **Conference of Gela,** to make peace and cease to call in the Athenians.

416. Segesta, at war with Selinus, again obtained Athenian aid under the treaty of 453.

415–413. The **Athenian expedition** against Syracuse, during the Peloponnesian War. The Athenians were finally defeated at the Assinarus. A democratic reform was instituted in Syracuse by Diocles (412); privileges of the lower classes were extended and many offices were made elective by lot. Hermocrates, who had commanded a naval squadron in aid of Sparta, was banished after the **battle of Cyzicus** (410).

f. THE GREAT PELOPONNESIAN WAR

Thucydides considered the war of 431–421 (the **Archidamian War**) and that of 414–404 (the **Decelean** or **Ionian War**) to be in reality one, and together they are called the **Peloponnesian War.** Thucydides' incomplete history covers the period to 410. The basic cause of the war was the fact that there existed in Greece two great rival systems of alliances, comprising practically all of continental and Anatolian Greece, each of which was deemed essential by its leader. Thus neither leader could afford to tolerate any

action threatening the solidity of its league, nor could it afford to allow the other to attain power appreciably superior to its own. Hence any minor conflict was bound to involve all Greece, and such a conflict was sure to arise.

435. Corcyra, quarreling with Corinth over the latter's interference in their joint colony Epidamnus, defeated the Corinthian fleet in the **battle of Leucimne.** Corinth began preparation of a great expedition, and the Corcyreans in fear appealed (433) to Athens for an alliance, which was granted, since Athens desired a station on the route to the west (to a small degree for commercial reasons), and especially since she feared Corinth's prospective naval power should the latter acquire the Corcyrean fleet. Ten ships were dispatched to Corcyra. The Corinthians attacked at Sybota, but when it was clear they were winning, the Athenians entered the battle, and the arrival of 20 more ships caused the Corinthians to return home. Athens then demanded that her subject Potidaea, a Corinthian colony, cease to receive her annual magistrate from Corinth, and raze her seaward walls.

432. Assured of Peloponnesian aid, the **Potidaeans** revolted in the spring. An Athenian force won a battle before Potidaea in the fall. Pericles passed a bill barring the Megarians

from all the harbors of the Athenian Empire, ruining them economically; the Peloponnesians alleged that this was contrary to the Thirty Years' Peace, but the truth is uncertain. The Corinthians, Megarians, and Aeginetans forced the Spartans to take action and, although opposed by King Archidamus, the ephor Sthenelaïdas persuaded the Spartan assembly to declare the peace broken. The **Peloponnesian League** was then assembled and declared war. The winter was taken up by fruitless negotiations.

431. The war began when a band of Thebans by treachery entered Athens' ally Plataea; the Thebans were induced to surrender and were then killed.

The strategy of the Athenians, devised by Pericles, was to refuse a land battle, in which they would almost certainly be defeated, remain within their walls, and let their country be ravaged; they could support themselves through their control of the sea, and hoped to wear down the Peloponnesians by coastal raids and destruction of their commerce. They also ravaged the Megarid twice annually, when the Peloponnesian army was not assembled. The strategy of the Peloponnesians was to ravage the land of Attica annually and, if possible, lure the Athenians into battle; they also gave

Naval battle in the harbor of Syracuse, 413 B.C., *during the Great Peloponnesian War*

encouragement and support to revolting allies of Athens.

431. The Athenians expelled the inhabitants of Aegina and replaced them with Athenian cleruchs. Thucydides put in Pericles's mouth the famous *Funeral Oration* for the war dead of this year.

430. A **great plague** broke out at Athens. When an Athenian expedition against Epidaurus failed, it was sent to Potidaea, but returned after infecting the troops there with the plague. Disgusted, the Athenians deposed Pericles. During the winter Potidaea surrendered.

429. The plague continued. Pericles was re-elected *strategos* in the spring, but died soon after. Instead of invading Attica, the Peloponnesians laid siege to Plataea. The Athenians sent Phormio to block the Corinthian Gulf. Off **Naupactus** he won two battles against superior forces.

428. **Cleon** succeeded to the leadership of the radical party in Athens, which favored war; the conservatives, opposed to war, were led by **Nicias.** All Lesbos except Methymna revolted on the promise of Spartan aid. To meet this emergency the Athenians levied the first direct property tax (*eisphora*) since 510 and sent out a large fleet under Paches.

427. **Mytilene** fell before the dilatory Spartan admiral, Alcidas, arrived. The leaders were executed and Athenian cleruchs were sent to the island. Plataea was finally taken by the Spartans; half the garrison had previously escaped; those who remained were executed. The oligarchs in Corcyra, wishing to end the alliance with Athens, opened civil war on the democrats, but the latter, with Athenian help, put down the rebellion; many oligarchs fled to the mainland opposite.

426. The Spartans offered peace to Athens, but it was refused.

425. The Athenian general, **Demosthenes,** in co-operation with the Acarnanians, took Anactorium. He was then sent to reinforce a fleet in Sicily but on the way seized **Pylos,** on the west coast of the Peloponnesus. Demosthenes was left with five ships to use this station to stir up the Messenian helots against Sparta. But the Spartans besieged this force on Pylos by landing a force on Sphacteria, an island in the bay. The Athenian fleet returned, defeated the Peloponnesians, and blockaded Pylos.

Demosthenes

Cleon, in Athens, accused Demosthenes of dilatoriness and, on the motion of Nicias, was sent himself to do better. To everyone's surprise, Cleon and Demosthenes captured the 120 Spartiates on Sphacteria. These were held as hostages to prevent another invasion of Attica.

424. Nicias seized **Cythera.** Cleon almost tripled the tribute assessment; pay for the dicasts was raised from two to three obols a day. Demosthenes and Hippocrates seized Nisaea but were prevented by Brasidas, on his way to Thrace, from taking Megara. **Brasidas,** with 700 helot hoplites and 1000 Argive mercenaries, continued to Thrace, Athens' only vulnerable point, and raised rebellion in several cities. Demosthenes and Hippocrates planned a synchronized invasion of Boeotia from the west and east respectively, to be aided by Boeotian democrats. The Thebans prevented Demosthenes from invading Boeotia from Acarnania and inflicted a heavy defeat on his colleague Hippocrates at Delium. Brasidas took Amphipolis. Thucydides, the historian, commanded a fleet nearby and was exiled at Cleon's instance on a charge of negligence. The fleet in Sicily returned after the **Conference of Gela.**

423. The Athenians made a year's truce with Sparta. Brasidas, however, continued to raise rebellions in the Thracian cities, so the Athenians broke off negotiations.

422. **Cleon** took a force to Thrace, but was routed and killed before **Amphipolis;** Brasidas was also killed: thus the leaders of the war parties on both sides were eliminated and negotiations reopened. Sparta's position in the Peloponnese was being shaken by trouble with Mantinea and Elis, the imminent expiration of the peace with Argos, and the Athenian possession of Pylos, Cythera, and the 120 captives. Athens had exhausted her reserves, which had amounted to 6000 talents in 431.

421. The **PEACE OF NICIAS** was negotiated, to last for 50 years. The Athenians were to keep Nisaea until the Boeotians restored Plataea; the Chalcidian cities were to be auton-

omous but tributary; Amphipolis was to be restored; the captives on both sides were to be freed. The Spartans restored the Athenian prisoners, but Brasidas' successor, Clearidas, refused to give over Amphipolis. The Corinthians, Megarians, Eleans, and Boeotians refused to sign the treaty: the former two because they received no benefits from the whole struggle, the Eleans because of a private quarrel over Lepreum, and the Boeotians because they did not wish to restore Plataea. To protect herself, Sparta made an alliance with Athens for 50 years. Thereupon, Elis, Mantinea, Corinth, and the Chalcidian cities made an alliance with Argos, whose treaty with Sparta had expired. Megara and Boeotia delayed action.

420. Sparta broke the terms of the Athenian alliance by making a separate treaty with Boeotia, whereby Boeotia was to restore Panactum to Athens. The Boeotians, however, first razed Panactum, and the Athenians continued to hold Pylos. The action of Boeotia caused Corinth to quit the Argive League. Athens formed the **Quadruple Alliance** with Argos, Mantinea, and Elis, for 100 years. The two latter states at this time were already at war with Sparta.

418. The Spartans under **Agis** invaded Argos and, after considerable delay, the Athenians sent troops to Argos' support. Agis decisively defeated the Athenians, Argives, and Mantineans (the Eleans dropped out) in the **battle of Mantinea** and restored Sparta's hegemony in the Peloponnese. The Spartans then sent an ultimatum to Argos, which proceeded to repudiate the Quadruple Alliance and make a 50 years' alliance with Sparta. In the spring of 417, the Spartans put an oligarchic government into Argos, but it fell immediately and the democrats renewed the treaty with Athens for 50 years. During the next two years various Spartan armies raided Argos; the Athenians each time sent troops which arrived too late to encounter the Spartans.

416. Athens took by siege the island of Melos, which had refused to join the empire. The men were killed, the women and children enslaved; a cleruchy was established.

Selinus attacked Segesta, which appealed to Athens. Athens had by now a reserve of 3000 talents; the industrial and trading elements desired westward expansion. Against Nicias' opposition an expedition to Sicily was voted, to be commanded by Nicias, Alcibiades (the prime mover), and Lamachus.

415-413. The **Sicilian expedition** set out with a fleet of 134 triremes, carrying 4000 hoplites. Nicias refused Lamachus' proposal to attack Syracuse immediately. Alcibiades was recalled on charges of sacrilege, mutilating the *Hermae*, and profaning the Eleusinian Mysteries. He fled to Sparta. The Athenians won over Naxos and Catana, but accomplished nothing more.

414. Hermocrates was elected to command the defense of Syracuse. The Athenians almost succeeded in enclosing the city by a wall, but were prevented by the arrival of the Spartan Gylippus with a small force; his seizure of the heights called *Epipolae* permanently prevented circumvallation.

413. Reinforcements were sent under Demosthenes. His night attack on Epipolae failed and he advocated immediate return, but was prevented by Nicias' superstitious fear of an eclipse (Aug. 27). When the Athenians finally

Corinth before the Romans

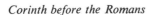

attempted to leave, the Syracusans, who had strengthened their fleet, defeated them in two naval battles. The Athenians withdrew by land; the rear under Demosthenes lagged behind and was defeated; the van under Nicias was crushed at the **Assinarus.** The generals were executed; the prisoners were kept for a time in the stone quarries and then sold into slavery.

414. The Athenians sent a fleet against the coasts of Sparta. The Spartans declared the peace broken.

413. The Spartans seized **Decelea** in Attica. This post was fortified and a garrison kept there continually; the Athenians were thus absolutely prevented from using their own land. The radical party in Athens, led by Peisander and Androcles, fell after the Sicilian defeat and a conservative reform took place. A college of 10 "deliberators" (*probouloi*) received many of the functions of the old council. The imperial tribute was replaced by a 5 per cent import and export levy in all harbors of the empire.

412. A small Spartan squadron stirred up revolts along the coast of Ionia. The Athenians voted to use their last 1000 talents, laid away for extreme emergency, and built rapidly a large fleet, which recovered Lesbos and Clazomenae. The **treaty of Miletus** was negotiated by Alcibiades between Sparta and Tissaphernes, satrap of Sardis. Sparta recognized the Persian king's rights to all lands ever belonging to any of his ancestors, while Persia was to furnish the money to maintain the Peloponnesian fleet.

The Athenians laid siege to **Miletus,** but were forced to withdraw by the arrival of the Peloponnesian fleet. The Athenian fleet at Samos received reinforcements and sent a detachment to blockade Chios. During the winter the Peloponnesian fleet was united at Caunus, but had difficulty in paying its crews, since Tissaphernes' policy, suggested by Alcibiades, was to wear out both sides and let neither win a real victory. The Peloponnesians took Rhodes, where they obtained supplies and money.

411. Sparta made a new treaty with Persia, signed by both Tissaphernes and Pharnabazus, satrap of Phrygia. The king's claims were limited to Ionia.

Alcibiades claimed that he could win Tissaphernes to the Athenians if the democracy were abolished. The oligarchic clubs in Athens (*hetairai*) by terrorism carried a motion to restrict citizenship to about 5000 of the wealthiest Athenians. Pay for public offices was abolished; all citizens except the 5000 were to be completely without political rights. A provisional committee of 400 was to rule until the 5000 had been chosen. The 400, however, continued to rule without choosing the 5000. The crews at Samos, who refused to recognize the new government and constituted themselves as the Athenian people, elected new generals, notably Thrasybulus and Thrasyllus. They forcibly prevented an attempt by Athenian and Samian oligarchs to restore the oligarchy in Samos which had been put down the year before. Alcibiades was recalled and made commander-in-chief; he demanded the abolition of the 400 in Athens, although he approved of the 5000. When the extremists among the 400 seemed ready to surrender to Sparta after four months of rule, the moder-

Destruction of the Athenian army in Sicily, 413 B.C.

Alcibiades' return to Athens, 407 B.C.

ates, led by Theramenes, secured their deposition. Nine thousand citizens were enrolled as councilors, to serve in four sections as in Boeotia (so-called **Government of the 5000**). Pay for civic offices was not restored. This government fell before the beginning of the civil year 410/9, and the democracy was restored, with pay for the dicasts.

Meanwhile the Spartans raised revolts in many Hellespontine and Thracian cities and especially in Euboea. The Athenians under Alcibiades defeated the Spartans at Cynossema and Abydos.

410. In the **battle of Cyzicus,** Alcibiades annihilated the Peloponnesian fleet. Sparta offered peace on the *status quo,* but the radical party in Athens, which had risen again under the leadership of **Cleophon,** rejected the offer.

Pharnabazus paid for the building of a new Peloponnesian fleet.

409. An Athenian expedition under Thrasyllus failed to take Ephesus. Sparta recovered Pylos; Megara had already recovered Nicaea,

408. The Athenians made a truce with Pharnabazus and sent ambassadors to the king, but before they arrived the king had received a Spartan embassy and decided to help Sparta energetically. He sent his son **Cyrus** to replace Tissaphernes. Alcibiades recovered Byzantium.

407. **Thrasybulus** recovered Abdera and Thasos. Alcibiades was elected general and commander-in-chief at Athens and returned to the city in triumph. Cyrus arrived in Asia Minor and formed cordial relations with Lysander, the able Spartan admiral (*nauarchos*).

406. When **Alcibiades** went off to collect

Sophocles

Aristophanes

Hippocrates of Cos

money, his guard squadron at Ephesus was **defeated off Notium** by Lysander. Alcibiades lost all influence and fled to the Hellespont. Callicratidas replaced Lysander, but could not get along with Cyrus. The Athenian Conon was defeated at **Mytilene.** The Athenians with a great effort built another fleet.

406. In the **battle of Arginusae,** Conon won a decisive victory over the Spartan fleet. Eight of the Athenian generals, however, were later tried and, despite Socrates' opposition, sentenced to death for not rescuing the shipwrecked sailors; two fled. The Spartans again offered peace on the *status quo,* but Cleophon again had the offer rejected. On Cyrus' demand, Lysander was sent with the Peloponnesian fleet, nominally as secretary, in reality to command.

405. The Athenians followed Lysander to the Hellespont and, through the gross carelessness of the commanders, the fleet was annihilated while drawn up on the shore at **Aegospotami.** Oligarchies of Ten (*decarchiai*) under Spartan harmosts were set up in all the Athenian subject states.

404. Theramenes negotiated peace after Cleophon, who held out against surrender to the last, was finally tried and executed. Athens was to raze her long walls and the fortifications of the Piraeus, surrender her navy, and make an alliance with Sparta.

404. The Athenian oligarchs, supported by Lysander and led by Theramenes, set up **a Commission of Thirty** which was to make a few immediate reforms and devise a new constitution. Instead of this, the Thirty with Critias at their head seized power and ruled as the **Thirty Tyrants.** They executed Theramenes when he advocated a more moderate course. Finally 3000 of the richest citizens were nominally enfranchised, but never exercised any real power. Many citizens were exiled or fled, and these were supported by Argos and by Thebes, who feared the excessive power of Sparta. In the autumn of 404 Thrasybulus led back some exiles, who occupied Phyle and then the Piraeus. In the beginning of 403, the Athenians deposed the Thirty, who fled to Eleusis, and elected a **Government of Ten.** These, instead of bringing in the democrats from the Piraeus, asked help from Sparta, which sent Lysander.

Then the anti-Lysander party in Sparta replaced Lysander with King Pausanias, who brought about a settlement by which the democracy was restored, and a general amnesty with few exceptions decreed. The decarchies in the former Athenian dependencies were soon abolished.

g. ECONOMIC AND SOCIAL CONDITIONS

The decline of Ionia and the growing prosperity of the western Greeks led, after the Persian Wars, to a shift of trade and industry to Greece proper, toward which converged the routes from both west and east, where the Greeks now sought an outlet for manufactures and a source of raw materials. Corinth and Aegina were the leading commercial states in Greece at the beginning of the 5th century, but they were soon outstripped by Athens. This growth of industry caused a rapid rise in the number of slaves, and many **metics** (*metoikoia,* resident aliens) migrated to the commercial states of Greece, where they were well treated: Athens especially was liberal in granting citizenship from Solon's time until 451. The industrial states were all dependent on the **importation of food.** In Greece itself, only Thessaly, Macedonia, and Sicily exported grains; Sparta, Boeotia, and the backward states of the west and north were self-sufficing. Athens exported wine and oil. The economy of almost all Greek states was now on a **money basis** (e.g. at Athens the Solonian classes had been converted into a money assessment of all property). The Athenian coinage became the predominant medium of exchange. **Prices** had risen tremendously since the 6th century. **Wages** were on a bare subsistence level, and the large number of slaves prevented any increase.

By 500 B.C. the mines at Mt. Laurion were important, economically, to Athens as a rich

Ancient Street of the Tombs, Athens

Parthenon of the Acropolis, Athens

source of lead, silver, zinc, and iron. Mining was extensive, although laborious, the rock being hand cut or the veins being reduced by fire. The mines provided much of the revenue for the wars and financed the building of the Long Wall from Athens to Piraeus, its harbor. The main communications system of Greece was by sea, the terrain being too rugged to build roads; hence the building of harbors became important (e.g., Piraeus, Samos). Water supply was also a problem; towns were usually served by aqueducts, although the remains of pressure lines have been found. Building techniques included the use of timber frames, hoists, pulleys, and hydraulic cement.

Shipping and agriculture remained very primitive. In Sparta and Thessaly great estates existed, but elsewhere ownership of land was much divided, and even in an industrial state like Athens the large majority of the citizens remained landowners. Foreigners were usually prohibited by law from owning land.

Public finance was simple, with no public debt and few surpluses. The chief source of revenue was indirect taxation; Athens profited greatly from her state-owned mines and depended on semi-compulsory contributions by wealthy citizens (*liturgiae*) for such expenses as the equipment of triremes or production of plays. Direct property taxes were used only in case of extreme need. Expenses in most states were correspondingly low; Athens used the rev-

enues from the empire for extensive public works, and also had a large number of citizens on the public payroll. The Peloponnesian War, however, not only exhausted the public finances throughout Greece, but also created economic dislocation, and impoverishment among individuals. These losses must, nevertheless, have been made good rapidly, as the 4th century witnessed a high level of prosperity.

During the 5th century **art and poetry** attained their finest expression in Greece, especially in Athens, whose prosperity favored an artistic life. This was fostered by **Pericles,** who herein, as in other policies, resembled the 6th-century tyrants. In the choral ode, **Pindar** of Thebes (518–442) and **Bacchylides** (c. 480), in the epigram, **Simonides** (556–468), distinguished the early part of the century. At Athens the three great dramatists, **Aeschylus** (525–456), **Sophocles** (?496–405), and **Euripides** (480–406) developed tragedy from a crude choral performance to unsurpassed perfection. **Aristophanes** (c. 448–385), who overlapped into the 4th century, was the acknowledged master of the **Old Comedy.** Prose lagged behind verse, but the Ionian **Herodotus,** writing at Athens (484–425), made the Persian Wars the motif of a delightfully discursive history. **Thucydides** (471–c. 400) perfected history in his account of the Peloponnesian War. In philosophy the conflict of unity against multiplicity was solved by the atomic theories advanced by **Empedocles** in Sicily (c. 444), by

Anaxagoras, an Ionian at Athens (500–425? mind or *nous*), and by **Leucippus** (c. 450?). But philosophy turned from physics to ethics and the **Sophists** became the teachers of Greece and advocates of the subjectivity of standards (*nomos,* convention, against *phusis,* nature). The leading Sophists were **Protagoras, Prodicus, Hippias,** and **Gorgias,** the last of whom came from Leontini in Sicily to Athens in 427.

In medicine **Hippocrates of Cos** (b. c. 460 B.C.) of the cult of Asclepius presented a common sense, natural medicine combined with personal hygiene. A school of medicine developed from his teaching, but the Hippocratic corpus is encyclopaedic, not a canon of medicine; it separated medicine from speculative philosophy, making it an empirical science.

In **architecture,** the heavy and luxurious temples of the early part of the century in Sicily, especially at Acragas (Agrigentum), were succeeded by the perfection of Pericles' Doric and Ionic buildings on the **Acropolis** at Athens, the **Parthenon,** or temple of Athens (447–432), the **Propylaea,** or entrance gate (437–432), and the **Erechtheum** (420–408), or temple of the hero Erectheus. **Sculpture** reached its height in the works of **Myron** (c. 450) and **Polycleitus** (c. 430) of the Argive School and **Pheidias** (500–431) the Athenian. Attic painters of red-figured vases developed line drawing in a series of exquisite styles (to 415), and **Polygnotus** (c. 480) mastered the technique of large-scale painting.

4. *The Rise of Macedon, to 330* B.C.

a. SPARTAN HEGEMONY

401–400. **Darius II** of Persia had been succeeded in 404 by his eldest son, **Artaxerxes II.** A younger son, **Cyrus,** collected 10,000 Greek mercenaries in Asia Minor and marched against his brothers (the *anabasis* or "going up") in 401; he was killed in the **battle of Cunaxa,** and with great difficulty the Greeks, one of whose leaders was the Athenian **Xenophon,** made their way back to the Euxine by 400.

400–394. When **Tissaphernes** besieged Cyme in 400, Sparta sent Thibron to hire a mercenary army and to liberate the Ionians from Persia. Dercyllidas took over the command in 399 and ravaged some Persian territory. A truce was maintained (398–397) while Artaxerxes prepared his fleet and put the Athenian Conon in command. In 396/5 King Agesilaus, succeeding Dercyllidas, ravaged Persian territory. In 394 Agesilaus returned to Greece with most of the troops.

395–387. **The Corinthian War.** In the winter of 396/5 Persia sent Timocrates of Rhodes to bribe the leaders of Athens, Thebes, Corinth, and Argos to attack Sparta. Athens made a defensive alliance with Boeotia which Corinth, Argos, Megara, Euboea, and other states joined. In 394 the Spartans won battles at **Nemea** and at **Coronea,** but their fleet, under Peisander, was annihilated by the Persian fleet, under Conon, at **Cnidus.** Persia granted autonomy to the Asiatic Greek cities and withdrew her garrisons. The Ionians revolted from Sparta and established democracies; the Cyclades followed in 393. Conon returned to Greece, and rebuilt the Athenian long walls. Athens recovered Lemnos, Imbros, Scyrus, and Delos; and made alliances with Chios, Mitylene, Rhodes, Cos, and Cnidus. In 392 an attempt at a general settlement was rejected by the Athenian imperialists, who had just come to power. The Persians deposed Conon, who soon died. In 390 Evagoras of Cyprus revolted from Persia. In 389 the Athenian navy under Thrasybulus recovered Thasos, Samothrace, Tenos, the Chersonese, Byzantium, Chalcedon, *et al.;* garrisons were placed in the more important towns, and 5 per cent harbor tolls levied, which really constituted a **revival of the Athenian naval league.** Thrasybulus was killed in action (388).

387–386. **THE KING'S PEACE.** In 387 the Spartan Antalcidas negotiated with Persia a general Greek settlement. All Greek cities were to be autonomous except those in Asia, which were to belong to Persia. In 386 the Spartan navy forced Athens to accept by blockading the Hellespont; Thebes was frightened into acceptance. Thus the Boeotian and the new Athenian leagues were dissolved.

385–379. Sparta broke Mantinea up into villages (385), seized the citadel, or Cadmeia, of Thebes (382), and captured Olynthus and dissolved its Chalcidian League (379).

379–378. The Theban democratic exiles led by Pelopidas recovered the Cadmeia by a *coup* and established a democracy in Thebes. The raid of the Spartan Sphodrias on the Piraeus caused an Athenian alliance with Thebes (378). Sparta raided Boeotia in 378 and 377.

377. **SECOND ATHENIAN LEAGUE AGAINST SPARTA.** Shortly after 386 Athens had renewed her alliances with several naval powers. In 377 these, Thebes, and many others united in the "second" (really third) league against Sparta. All decisions were to be made jointly by a council (*synedrion*) of the allies, excluding Athens, and the Athenian ecclesia; funds were to be derived from contributions levied by the synedrion and handled by Athens; Athens was to command in war; Athens gave up all claims to its former cleruchies. A fleet was quickly built up. In 376 Chabrias crushed the Spartan fleet off **Naxos,** and gave Athens control of the sea. Meanwhile, Thebes restored the Boeotian League on a democratic basis.

372. Jason, who succeeded his father Lycophron in the tyranny of Pherae, unified Thessaly by having himself made perpetual commander (*tagos*) until his murder in 370.

371. A **general peace settlement** was reached with Sparta in the summer of 371; but when he was not permitted to sign for all Boeotia, the Theban **Epaminondas** withdrew. Sparta immediately sent King Cleombrotus to chastise Thebes, but he was decisively defeated at **Leuctra** by Epaminondas. This shattered Spartan prestige and ended her chance of hegemony over Greece. Thebes withdrew from the Athenian League, and with her Acarnania, Euboea, and the Chalcidian cities.

b. THEBAN HEGEMONY

370. An **Arcadian League** was formed under Theban protection as counterweight to Sparta. Mantinea was restored as a city. The government of the league comprised a general assembly **(the Ten Thousand)** of all free-born citizens, with sovereignty in matters of war, peace, etc.; a council of *damiurgoi,* which gave proportional representation to the member cities; a college of generals (*strategoi*) as civil and military executive; a standing mercenary army (*eparitoi*). The Theban army, under **Epaminondas,** liberated Messenia from Sparta and the city **Messene** was built. In 369 Athens and Sparta made an alliance on equal terms. The Arcadians founded **Megalopolis** as a federal capital. In the following years, Thebes secured the union of all of Thessaly save Pherae under a single ruler (*archon*). The pro-Spartan party of Callistratus in Athens was replaced in power by the party of Timotheus, and peace was made with Thebes on the basis of the *status quo* (365). Pelopidas was killed in battle against Alexander of Pherae (364), whom Epaminondas then defeated (363).

362. Because of financial difficulties, the federal army of Arcadia was disbanded. The oligarchs, who could serve at their own expense, came into control of many cities, which then made peace with Elis. The radicals appealed to Epaminondas, and the league broke up: Tegea and Megalopolis remained pro-Theban, while the others made an alliance with Elis and Achaea; all these jointly made an alliance with Athens; Mantinea was allied with Sparta. Epaminondas faced this coalition at Mantinea, but was killed in battle. A general peace was made on the basis of the *status quo,* but it was not accepted by Sparta, which refused to recognize the independence of Messenia.

359 **Philip II** became regent and, in 356, by the deposition of his ward, **king of Macedon.** Since he was troubled by his unruly barbarian subjects and Athens was involved in war with the Thracian Odrysae, both were glad in 358 to make a treaty by which Philip gave up his claim to Amphipolis and Athens promised to surrender Pydna. Philip now thoroughly reorganized his army, placing more importance on the **phalanx** of infantry, and with it subdued the rebellious barbarians. By agreement with Athens, he conquered Amphipolis (357) to exchange it for Pydna, since Athens was occupied in recovering Euboea from Thebes and the Chersonese from the Thracians.

357–355. The Athenian allies were angry at Athenian policy, e.g. the sending of cleruchies to Samos (365) and Potidaea (361), the subjection of Ceos and Naxos to Athenian jurisdiction (363/2), and especially the arbitrary financial exactions of Athenian generals; further, the decline of Spartan power had removed the league's *raison d'être.* Under encouragement from **Mausolus** (Mausollos, 377–353), who had succeeded Hecatomnus (395–377) as ruler of Caria, the states of Chios, Rhodes, Cos, and Byzantium joined in revolt, known as the **Social War,** i.e. "War of the Allies." After the defeat and death of Chabrias at Chios, the Athenians, under the incompetent Chares, finally withdrew from Ionia and recognized the independence of many of their allies (355). Mausolus in 353 annexed Rhodes and Cos.

c. MACEDON UNDER PHILIP AND ALEXANDER THE GREAT

359–336. **PHILIP II**

355–346. The **THIRD SACRED WAR** began when the Phocians refused to pay a fine levied on certain of their people by the Amphictyonic Council at the instigation of Thebes (355). The Phocians seized Delphi and made alliances with Athens and Sparta. When the Amphictyons declared war, the Phocians used the sacred money of Delphi to recruit a very large mercenary army. Though they were defeated by the Boeotians at **Neon** (354), they seized Thermopylae and Orchomenos (353). When Philip attempted to oppose them in Thessaly, their general Onomarchus twice defeated him,

Macedonian coin with image of Philip II

Assassination of Philip II

Mausolus

Marble statue of Demosthenes

but in 352 Philip defeated and killed Onomarchus. Philip then united Thessaly, which continued loyal to him. His march south was stopped by Athenians, Achaeans, and Spartans at Thermopylae. The war continued indecisively in Phocis until Athens made the **Peace of Philocrates** with Philip (346). Philip then conquered Phocis, prohibited the carrying of arms, and spread the Amphictyonic fine in installments.

356-346. When Athens refused to surrender Pydna to Philip in return for Amphipolis, he conquered the former, kept the latter, made a treaty against Athens with Olynthus, and took Crenides, renamed **Philippi,** from the Odrysae. After the end of the **War of the Allies** (355), Athens was financially exhausted and the imperialist party of Chares and Aristophon was replaced by the pacifists under Eubulus. All financial surpluses were put into a **theoric fund** and used for the entertainment of the citizens. Athens allowed Philip to expand eastward almost unchecked. But in 351 Olynthus, suspicious of Philip, appealed to her for aid. **Demosthenes** appeared as the leader of the anti-Macedonian party, urging action in his three *Olynthiac Orations.* An alliance was made with Olynthus (349), but an attempt to divert the surplus from the theoric to the military fund failed. Philip induced Euboea to revolt from Athens and the latter, against Demosthenes' advice, divided its efforts by sending a force there as well as to Olynthus (348). Phocion was successful in Euboea, but his successor, Molossus, lost the country. Philip took Olynthus, which he razed, and enslaved the citizens (348). Athens could secure no help from the Greeks, and even Demosthenes was in favor of peace.

346. PEACE OF PHILOCRATES. On the motion of Philocrates, ten ambassadors, including himself, Aeschines, and Demosthenes, were sent at Philip's invitation to negotiate a peace: the terms restored the Chersonese, except Cardia, to Athens, canceled Athens' claim to Amphipolis, and left other possessions as they should be when the peace was sworn. Athens could not secure the inclusion of her ally Phocis in the terms. On the return of the ambassadors, the assembly accepted the terms

and sent them back to swear the oaths; they delayed on the way and Philip profited by this to conquer more of Thrace. After the conclusion of the peace, Philip conquered the Phocians, took their seat in the Amphictyonic League, and, as its chairman, presided over the Pythian games; Athens refused to send a delegation until Philip's threats forced her to recognize his membership in the league.

344-339. Despite the friendly attitude of Philip, Demosthenes persuaded the Athenians to make alliances against him in Euboea (341) and the Peloponnese (340), and to help Byzantium repel him (339). Demosthenes, now in control in Athens, urged opposition to Philip in his *Philippic Orations.* He reformed the system of paying for the navy by replacing the individual liturgy (*trierarchia*) with more equitable and efficient groups of contributors (*symmoriae*). He devoted surplus income to the war fund instead of to the theoric. Philip tried to get the Amphictyons to fine Athens for insulting Thebes, but Aeschines cleverly diverted them against Amphissa.

339-338. When this caused the **Fourth Sacred War,** the Amphictyons called in Philip. Athens, terrified at this, made an alliance with Thebes on terms very favorable to the latter. The allies won some minor successes. But Philip annihilated their mercenaries near Amphissa.

338. In the **BATTLE OF CHAERONEA,** Philip crushed the allied citizen armies. He garrisoned Thebes, but let Athens go free. Philip called a **congress at Corinth,** and all states, except Sparta, entered a **Hellenic League.** There was proportional representation in the league council, which was presided over by the king in wartime, otherwise by a chairman; autonomy of the members was guaranteed; existing constitutions were not to be altered and no private property confiscated; no tribute was required and no garrisons left, except in a few places; the king had the military command; the Amphictyonic Council served as a supreme court. Philip announced plans for an Asiatic campaign.

337. A **second congress at Corinth** declared war on Persia, and Philip sent an army under his general, Parmenio, to Asia Minor (336).

336. Philip was assassinated, allegedly at the instigation of his recently divorced wife, Olympias.

336–323. ALEXANDER III, THE GREAT (b. 356), succeeded.

On the rumor that Alexander had died, Thebes revolted with Athens, Arcadia, Elis, and Aetolia, but Alexander swiftly took Thebes, destroyed it, and enslaved the inhabitants. The others submitted (335).

334–331. Alexander, leaving Antipater behind as his governor in Greece, crossed the Hellespont in the spring of 334 with an army of 32,000 infantry and 5000 cavalry, supported by a navy of 160 ships, mostly allied. Memnon of Rhodes, commander of Darius' Greek mercenaries, wished to retreat, laying waste the country, but the satraps, hoping to protect their provinces, forced him to take a stand at the river **Granicus,** where he was completely defeated by Alexander (334).

Most of the Greek cities revolted from Persia. Alexander subdued Caria and (spring 333) Cilicia. Meanwhile, Memnon died and Darius summoned the mercenaries to Syria. Alexander went on to Myriandrus, where he faced Darius, who had raised a large but motley army. Since Alexander feared to come on to the open plain, Darius went behind him to the plain of Issus.

333. BATTLE OF ISSUS. Alexander attacked and completely defeated Darius III. Darius offered to give up all Asia west of the Euphrates and pay 10,000 talents, but Alexander demanded unconditional surrender. All Phoenicia, except Tyre, submitted after Issus, and, by a difficult siege of seven months, Tyre was reduced (332).

332–331. Alexander's **expedition to Egypt** was unopposed; while in Egypt, he founded **Alexandria** and visited the oracle of Ammon.

331. Leaving Egypt in the spring, Alexander met and defeated the Persian army at **Gaugamela** (Oct. 1) and went on to Arbela, where he seized much Persian treasure. Babylonia and Susa surrendered, but at Persepolis resistance was offered, so that the place was looted and burned and immense treasure was taken.

331. Sparta under King Agis III, aided by Persian money and in alliance with Elis, Achaea, and part of Arcadia, defeated a Macedonian force and besieged Megalopolis, but was crushed when Antipater arrived with a greatly superior force.

330. In the spring of 330, Alexander pursued Darius through Media, where Darius was murdered by the satrap Bessus. Alexander subdued the Caspain region and marched southward. When Parmenio's son Philotas had been executed for complicity in a plot, Alexander sent messengers who murdered Parmenio in Media: Alexander feared a revolt and Parmenio was too powerful to be discharged.

329. Alexander went on into Bactria and overcame the Iranians under Spitamenes only with a great deal of trouble (328). Alexander now commenced the **adoption of Persian dress** and court etiquette. In a drunken fury, he murdered his friend Cleitus who had reproached him. He had 30,000 natives trained in Macedonian fashion for the army. He married the Persian **Roxana.** He began to foster a **belief in his divinity** as the best means of dealing with the Greeks as an absolute ruler and yet without offending their sentiments of liberty. Though the Greeks had deified living men before this, Alexander's move met so much opposition that he dropped it temporarily.

327–324. Alexander was invited into **India** by Taxiles against Porus. In the **battle of the Hydaspes** (326), he defeated Porus and advanced as far as the Hyphasis. Here the army refused to go farther. Alexander, therefore, returned via the Hydaspes and Indus to the Indian Ocean (325). Thence **Nearchus** went back with the fleet to explore the Indian Ocean and Alexander returned through the desert of Gedrosia. They met in Caramania and, after a rest, went on to Susa (324).

324–323. In his policy of fusion of the Greek and Asiatic peoples, Alexander had left in office many of the native governors (satraps); most of these, and many of the Macedonian satraps, were now found to have ruled badly; some had enlisted private mercenary armies. These satraps were replaced, usually with Macedonians; the private armies were ordered disbanded. Pursuing the policy of fusion, Alexander, 80 officers, and 10,000 men married native women. Alexander paid all debts of his men. He ordered all exiles recalled by the Greek cities; to give himself a basis for this interference, contrary to the constitution of the Hellenic League, he ordered the Greek states to recognize him as **son of Zeus Ammon.** At Ecbatana Alexander's closest friend, Hephaestion, died.

323, June 13. Alexander died at Babylon. His exploration had fostered commerce; over 25 cities which he had founded served to Hellenize the east, although his policy of direct fusion failed. The organization of his complex empire he left much as he found it, differing in each area. The officers wished to make the unborn son of Alexander and Roxana king, but the privates preferred a Macedonian, the imbecile **Philip III Arrhidaeus,** son of Philip II. When a son, **Alexander IV,** was born to Roxana, a joint rule was established under the regents Craterus and Perdiccas.

330–322. Athens had recouped her strength under the financier **Lycurgus,** who, among other reforms, established compulsory military training for all young men (*epheboi*). In 330, Demosthenes had been acquitted in the trial brought by Aeschines on the justness of the

The battle of Issus (mosaic), Alexander the Great at left, Darius III in the center

award to Demosthenes of a civic crown. In 326 Lycurgus fell from power, and in 324 Demosthenes was exiled for embezzling some of the money which Alexander's treasurer, Harpalus, brought to Athens. On the report of Alexander's death, Athens, led by the radical orator **Hypereides,** organized a new Hellenic League in central Greece and the Peloponnese. The allies under Leosthenes besieged Antipater in Lamia (winter, 323), and eventually forced his retirement to Macedonia. There Craterus joined him from Asia (322).

322. The Athenian fleet was wiped out forever at **Amorgos.** When the allied army was indecisively defeated at **Crannon** the league broke up. Athens received a Macedonian garrison, took back her exiles, and accepted an oligarchic constitution by which only those possessing 2000 drachmas had the franchise, perhaps 9000 out of 21,000 free citizens. Demosthenes, who had been recalled, fled but was caught and committed suicide.

d. THE WEST DURING THE 4TH CENTURY

413–405. After the defeat of the Athenian expedition, **Syracuse** made democratic reforms. In 410 many oligarchs, including Hermocrates, were banished. Then Segesta, warring with Selinus (409), called in the **Carthaginians,** who, despite Syracusan opposition, sacked Selinus and Himera (408) and, in a second expedition, Acragas (406).

405–367. Dionysius I secured his election as one of the ten generals in Syracuse and then made himself tyrant. He made peace with the Carthaginian forces, who were suffering from a plague. He distributed the confiscated land of the oligarchs to the poor and enfranchised the serfs. He conquered Catana (403), Naxos, and Leontini (400). In a **first war with Car-**thage (398–392), he attempted to drive the Carthaginians out, but failed. However, he reduced the Sicels, and then began the conquest of southern Italy (390–379), where he crushed the Italiote League at the **battle of the Elleporus** (389). But he suffered a severe defeat in a **second war with Carthage** (383–381?), which he failed to retrieve in a third (368).

366–344. On the death of Dionysius, his weak son, **Dionysius II,** succeeded under the regency of his uncle **Dion.** Dion brought in Plato to educate Dionysius, but both were forced out (366). Dion regained Syracuse in 357 and ruled tyrannically until his murder in 354. After two more sons of Dionysius I had seized the power and fallen, Dionysius II returned (347), but the Syracusans called in first **Hicetas,** tyrant of Leontini (345), and then **Timoleon** of Corinth.

344–337. Timoleon defeated the Carthaginians at the **Crimissus** (341) and made peace, with the Halycus River as the boundary (339). The tyrants were expelled from the Greek cities, which formed a military league against Carthage. Timoleon established a moderate oligarchy in Syracuse, with the priest (*amphipolos*) of Zeus as chief magistrate and a council of 600 composed of rich citizens. He then retired (337).

338–330. The **Greeks in Italy** (Italiotes), hard pressed by the natives, called in first **Archidamus of Sparta** (338), who was killed, and then **Alexander of Epirus** (334). The latter defeated the natives and made an alliance with Rome, but was finally assassinated during a battle (330).

e. GREEK CULTURE IN THE 4TH CENTURY

The death of Alexander the Great marked the end of the great age of Greece in literature, philosophy, and art. **Xenophon** (431–354),

Marble head of Aphrodite by Praxiteles

Plato

though a writer far inferior to Thucydides, wrote an able continuation of his history from 410 to 362, as well as other historical works. The lesser writers of **Middle Comedy** were followed by **Menander** (343–c. 280), the most outstanding of the writers of **New Comedy,** or comedy of manners. But it was in **oratory** and **philosophy** that the 4th century was most distinguished. Of the ten Attic orators the best known were **Lysias** (445–c. 380), **Demosthenes** (384–322), and the advocate of pan-Hellenism, **Isocrates** (436–338). **Philosophy** was dominated by the figure of **Socrates** (469–399), executed by the Athenians for atheism. His greatest pupil, **Plato** (427–347), founded the **Academy** in the grove of the hero Academus, and **Aristotle** (384–322), the pupil of Plato and tutor of Alexander, founded the **Peripatetic** (walking about) **School** or **Lyceum,** in the grove of the hero Lycus. Plato, under the influence of the number mysticism of the Pythagoreans, established an idealistic ontology with mathematics as the prototype of reality,

Relief from the looted palace at Persepolis, 331 B.C.

The lighthouse (pharos) at Alexandria

while Aristotle, who was primarily a botanist, developed an epistemology using biological models as a prototype for explaining change.

In **sculpture** a refined and less vigorous style was preferred by **Praxiteles** (385–c. 320), **Scopas** (400–c. 340), and **Lysippus** (c. 380–c. 318). The center of activity began to shift to Ionia, as seen in the tomb of Mausolus of Caria (the **Mausoleum**), completed c. 350, and the new **temple of Artemis at Ephesus** (the old one was burned by Herostratus in 356).

Engineering by this time had reached the stage where extensive tunneling could be undertaken by manual excavation. Lake Copias was drained to prevent flooding c. 325 B.C., and the tunnel at Samos was constructed using surveying techniques. The **lighthouse at Alexandria** (Pharos) was built c. 300 B.C. and remained an important navigational aid for 1600 years (one of the seven wonders of the Ancient World).

(Cont. p. 94.)

C. Rome, to 287 B.C.

1. *The Early Period, to 509 B.C.*

a. GEOGRAPHICAL FACTORS

ITALY IS A LONG, narrow peninsula of which the central portion comprises the mountains and isolated valleys of the Apennines. At the northern end, the Apennines swing west and enclose between themselves and the Alps a wide and fertile valley, Cisalpine Gaul, traversed by the Po, which flows east into the head of the Adriatic. The eastern (Adriatic) coast of Italy is infertile and lacks good harbors, while the Adriatic itself, because of prevailing northerly winds, hindered the penetration of the Greeks. Moreover, the rugged opposing shore of Illyria was occupied by wild and piratic tribes, whose forays constituted a continuous threat to commerce. The eastern Italian peoples, therefore, remained backward compared to the western. The western part, though mountainous at the northern end, contains fertile plains in its central portion (Etruria, Latium, and Campania), with good harbors, especially around the Bay of Naples. Its rivers, however (the Arno and the Tiber), are too swift to be readily navigable, so that early civilization sprang up along the coast, while the inland peoples remained rude and simple. The western (Tyrrhenian) sea is enclosed by the islands of Sardinia and Corsica, the former fertile and rich in metals, the latter a wild seat of pirates. Southern Italy, where the mountains begin to fall away, was a land of pastures where later herds moved seasonally from sea to hills under the charge of slave bands of shepherds, whose brigandage formed a constant threat to travelers. Around the Bay of Tarentum, however, the Greek settlers early found a hospitable welcome, and the western toe of Italy afforded ready access, across the narrow Straits of Messana, to the prosperous island of Sicily, whose rich Greek colonies and lavish crops played an important part in Roman history. The western apex of Sicily in turn led towards Africa and the Phoenician colony of Carthage, which became Rome's chief rival for the control of the western Mediterranean.

b. EARLY POPULATIONS OF ITALY

Early Cultures of Italy *(p. 23)*.

c. 900 B.C. The **ETRUSCANS** first appeared in Italy, probably by sea from Asia Minor (Lydia?), in consequence of the break-up of the Hittite Empire. They established themselves north of the Tiber in Etruria, probably as a conquering minority among enserfed Villanovan (?) natives. The power was apparently held by an aristocracy of princes (*lucumones*), whose fortified cities (traditionally twelve, though the precise constituents varied from time to time) formed a loose league, and whose elaborate tombs were at first furnished with bronze utensils and armor, then painted and supplied with imported luxuries, notably Greek vases. They extended into the Po Valley and into Latium and Campania until the end of the 6th century, when the pressure of **Celtic invaders** into the Po Valley cut off their northern settlements and the Cumaeans and Hiero of Syracuse broke their control of the sea and Latium revolted. Thereafter they declined until their absorption by Rome during the 4th century. Their culture preserved its identity until the Sullan land distributions in the 1st century so disorganized it that within a century thereafter it had become dead. The Etruscans made no original contribution to Rome save for certain forms (lictors, curule chair, purple-striped toga of office) and a gloomy religion (perhaps the three divinities Latinized as Jupiter, Juno, and Minerva, and certainly the practice of prophesying by consulting the entrails, *haruspicium*), but they first introduced to Rome Greek culture, though in a debased shape, mythology, the heavy Tuscan temple (from the Doric), and perhaps the alphabet.

c. 760. **GREEK COLONIZATION** began in the Bay of Naples in southern Italy, and in Sicily. The Greeks were prevented from further expansion to the west and north, save for Marseilles (Marssalia), by the Phoenicians and the Etruscans. Despite victories over both peoples by the tyrants of Syracuse in the early 5th century, the Greeks never succeeded in dominating all of Sicily or southern Italy. From the 4th century their fortunes declined until their eventual absorption by Rome during the 3rd. Nevertheless they not only impregnated these areas with a Greek culture which lasted throughout the Roman period, but, by their contact with Rome during the formative period of her national culture, first through the Etruscans and then directly, so Hellenized the Romans that when the latter conquered the Mediterranean world they respected and extended the Hellenistic civilization and, by absorbing it, preserved for later ages the Greek heritage.

c. THE ROMAN MONARCHY

753. **FOUNDATION OF ROME,** according to Cicero's contemporary, the antiquarian Varro. Traditionally the founder, **Romulus,** was son of a princess of Alba Longa, Rhea Silvia, and the god Mars. The kings of Alba Longa, in turn, were descended from **Aeneas,** a fugitive of the Trojan War and son of the goddess Venus (Aphrodite). This tradition dates, however, from the period when Rome was assimilating Greek culture. Actually during the 8th and following centuries small settlements on the Palatine, Esquiline, Quirinal, and Capitoline Hills united into one, with a common meeting place in the valley between, the **Forum.** These peoples may have been of different racial stocks, chiefly Latin but partly Sabine, Etruscan, and perhaps pre-Italic. The importance of Rome is less likely to have been economic (trade up the Tiber or across the ford at this point is not attested by archaeology) than military, an outpost of the Latins against the encroaching Etruscans. This would

Etruscan sarcophagus

Etruscan wall painting, Tomb of the Leopards, Tarquinia

account for the inculcation in the Romans from an early date of habits of obedience, organization, and military drill. The traditions of the four early kings (**Romulus,** 753–715, **Numa Pompilius,** 715–673, **Tullius Hostilius,** 673–641, and **Ancus Marcius,** 641–616) are historically unreliable.

Early government. Rome emerged into history with a **king** (elective, not hereditary), limited by the existence of a **senate** of 100 elders (*patres*) which was advisory, not compulsory, and by a popular assembly of the clans (*curiae*), the **comitia curiata,** which conferred upon the newly elected king his *imperium* and may have had slight legislative power. There were two classes in the state: **patricians,** who alone could belong to the senate, and **plebeians.** Most probably the patricians were simply the more prosperous farmers, who for their own advantage organized themselves in *curiae,* set themselves up as a superior class, and usurped certain privileges. (Another theory is that the plebeians were the conquered native people.) As a result of the plebeians' lack of power to defend themselves, many attached themselves as clients to patrician patrons, who protected them in return for attendance and service.

The **early religion** was simple, chiefly the worship of Mars (an agricultural divinity who only later became god of war) and of animistic forces. Religious ceremonies were simple to the point of being magical; by their proper performance the divine power (*numen*) inherent in gods or objects was compelled to act, and failure to get results indicated some fault in the ceremony.

c. 616. Tarquinius Priscus (616–578) and his successors, **Servius Tullius** (578–534) and **Tarquinius Superbus** (the Proud, 534–510), may represent the Etruscan domination in Rome and emerge more clearly than their predecessors. Tarquin the First was a great builder

Etruscan bronze depicting the legend of Romulus and Remus being suckled by a she-wolf

(*Cloaca Maxima, Temple of Jupiter Capitolinus, Circus Maximus*). To weaken the patrician influence, he is said to have increased the senate to 300. He fought successfully against Sabines, Latins, and Etruscans. **Servius Tullius,** traditionally of slave and Latin descent, fought against Veii and brought Rome into the **Latin League.** His chief achievement, traditionally, was to substitute for the hereditary clans a new military division into **classes** and **centuries,** based on wealth and arms (cf. reforms of Solon in Athens). It may be, however, that this reform should really be dated about 450 and, in any case, the surviving (and

conflicting) descriptions of his arrangements probably portray them in the state which they reached after the 3rd century B.C. Upon this arrangement depended a new assembly, the **comitia centuriata.** Since group voting was taken over from the comitia curiata, the wealthy, who though few in numbers constituted the majority of the centuries, controlled this assembly as, presumably, the patricians had the former. The last, **Tarquin the Proud,** was expelled in a revolt which according to tradition was led by **L. Junius Brutus** and was due to the rape of Lucretia by Sextus Tarquinius, son of the king.

2. *The Early Republic, to 287* B.C.

The **early constitution:** two annual **consuls,** originally called *praetors* (generals), held equally the undivided *imperium* of the king; either could prevent the other from acting, but could not force him to act. They had absolute command of the army in the field, including power over life and death; in the city they were provided with *coercitio,* a sort of summary police power, but with slight civil and no criminal jurisdiction. They were elected by the comitia centuriata, but their *imperium* was conferred by the comitia curiata (*lex curiata*), later represented by 30 lictors.

The **judicial system:** cases of high treason were handled by the *duouiri perduellionis;* all other criminal cases of which the state took cognizance were handled by the *quaestores parricidii* (investigators of murder), later known

simply as *quaestors.* From their collecting of fines, the quaestors became the main financial officers of the state, and in this capacity they became attached to the consuls as comptrollers; later they lost their judicial functions. Civil cases were usually handled by arbitration, but gradually the consuls came to take a larger part, until in 367 there was created a special officer (*praetor*).

In time of crisis the senate could restore unity of command by instructing the consuls to appoint a **dictator** (*magister populi*), who appointed as his assistant a master of the horse (*magister equitum*); the dictator had absolute power in all fields, but had to resign when his task was completed, and in no case could remain in office for more than six months.

The **plebs** seem already to have had an orga-

nization of their own, the *concilium plebis,* with its own officers (?*tribunes* originally commanders of the tribal regiments) and *aediles* (custodians of the temple of Ceres on the Aventine, where were kept the plebeian treasury and archives). When the first 17 rustic tribes were organized shortly after the foundation of the republic (the four urban tribes are ascribed by tradition to Servius Tullius, but may be later), the concilium plebis was reorganized on the basis of these; some time later a *comitia tributa* of the whole people was organized on the same basis, perhaps to break up the power of the hereditary clans (cf. Cleisthenes, at Athens). It is uncertain how long the concilium plebis remained distinct from the comitia tributa; in the later republic the difference was merely technical. A resolution of the plebs alone was called a *plebiscitum,* and was originally binding only on the plebeians, as opposed to a *lex* of the entire *populus,* adopted in a *comitia.*

At the beginning of the republican period, Rome was probably the dominant power in the Latin League, but apparently lost this position because of the continued Etruscan pressure; the next two centuries (to c. 280) were characterized externally by Rome's conquest of the primacy in Italy and internally by the struggle of the oppressed plebs, of which the richer members desired social and political equality with the patricians, while the poorer wanted simply protection from unjust treatment at the hands of the patrician magistrates.

509. TRADITIONAL DATE OF THE FOUNDING OF THE REPUBLIC. L. Junius Brutus and **L. Tarquinius Collatinus** (husband of Lucretia) became consuls. Almost all of the history of the first century of the republic, including the names of the first two or three decades of consuls, is unreliable, but it is not yet possible to establish the truth. The dates given here are those of Cicero's contemporary, Varro, adopted by Livy. They are subject to errors of up to ten years in the first century of the republic, gradually decreasing to become practically certain from c. 300.

A **lex Valeria de prouocatione** is said to have been passed by the *consul suffectus* (filling another's unexpired term), P. Valerius Poplicola, guaranteeing citizens in Rome (not on military service) the right of appeal to the comitia centuriata from a consul who proposed to execute or flog them; probably a retrojection of later legislation, but such a right was recognized by the **Twelve Tables.**

508. A **treaty with the Carthaginians** recognized Carthage's exclusive interests in Africa and Rome's in Latium. Doubt has been cast on the genuineness of this treaty, but probably unjustly.

Lars Porsena of the Etruscan Clusium attacked Rome and probably restored the Etruscan domination for a short time, although Roman tradition claimed he had been turned back by the exploits of **Horatius Cocles** (defense of the *pons sublicius,* or wooden Tiber bridge), Cloelia, and Q. Mucius Scaevola.

496. The dictator A. Postumius, in the **battle of Lake Regillus,** defeated the Latins, who, with the help of Aristodemus of Cumae, had some time before freed themselves from Etruscan rule by the **battle of Aricia.**

494. The **plebeians,** oppressed by debt, **seceded to the Sacred Mount** (probably the Aventine). The patricians were forced to make some concessions before the plebs would return. The latter further protected themselves by swearing to the *leges sacrae,* by which they bound themselves to avenge any injury done to their officials, the tribunes, the aediles, and the *decemuiri stlitibus iudicandis.* These officials were therefore called *sacrosanct.* They were not officials of the state, but officers of a corporate group within the state. But because of the unanimous support of the plebes they had *de facto* great powers, which were never legalized but became gradually respected by custom. The basis of the tribunes' powers was the *ius auxilii,* by which they could intervene to save anyone threatened by the action of a magistrate. This *intercessio* against a specific act of a magistrate developed later (when the tribunes secured admission to the senate) into the right of interposing a veto against any proposed law or decree. They presided over the concilium plebis. The original number of the tribunes was two or four; it eventually became ten. The aediles handled the fines imposed by the tribunes or the concilium, and through the use of this money came to have control of the free distributions of corn to the poor and over the repair of public buildings, etc., which was later extended into a general police power. The *decemuiri stlitibus iudicandis* conducted trials in which the status of persons as slaves or freedmen was in question.

493. A **treaty of Sp. Cassius** with the Latin League provided that booty was to be equally divided; new territory to be colonized in common; the rights of *connubium* and *commercium* (to contract valid marriages between members of different states and to carry on commerce with full legal protection) were restored as they had been before Rome's break with the league (c. 508). The reason for this peace was certainly the increasing pressure of the attacks of the neighboring Volsci and Aequi. The Hernici were later admitted to the alliance on equal terms with the other two members (486).

491. Gn. Marcius Coriolanus traditionally tried to bribe the plebeians with free grain into giving up the tribunate; when he failed and was summoned to trial, he fled to the Volsci and led them against Rome, but was turned back by the prayers of his mother and wife.

Coriolanus receives the delegation of Roman matrons headed by his mother and wife

Etruscan warrior, bronze, c. 5th century B.C.

486. The consul Sp. Cassius attempted to make himself tyrant but was executed. This much may be true, but the story that his method was a proposed division of the public land, which was of insignificant extent for a long time, is probably a retrojection from the Gracchan era.

477. Battle of the Cremera. War had broken out with the Etruscan Veii (483), which was supported by Fidenae, a town controlling the upper Tiber and thus essential to Rome. A large number of Fabii took up a position on the Cremera to prevent the two cities from joining their forces, but were annihilated by the Veientines. Traditionally, only one of 300 escaped. A peace was made in 474.

458. L. Quinctius Cincinnatus, called from his field to assume the dictatorship, rescued a Roman army and defeated the Aequi, who had pressed into the valley of the Algidus.

451. Agitation of the plebs for codification of the law to curb the arbitrariness of the patrician magistrates led to the creation of **ten patrician decemvirs** in place of consuls. According to legend, an embassy had been sent to Athens in 454 to procure the laws of Solon for study. The first decemvirs published ten tables, but since these proved insufficient new decemvirs were created in 450 and drew up two additional tables. Thenceforth the *Twelve Tables* constituted the fundamental law of Rome until the 2nd century. Tradition alleges that this decemviral board continued illegally in office in 449 under the extreme patrician **Appius Claudius.** When he attempted to get for himself by false legal process the maiden Virginia, her father Virginius stabbed her and the plebeians seceded to the Aventine and Sacred Mounts. The decemvirs had to abdicate and Appius committed suicide.

448. The moderate patrician consuls Valerius and Horatius passed a series of **Valerio-Horatian** laws weakening the patrician power. Traditionally, these (1) made the *plebiscita* as valid as *leges;* (2) compelled all magistrates, including the dictator, to allow appeals from their decisions; and (3) affirmed the inviolability of the tribunes and also the aediles. All these changes are probably mere retrojections of later reforms. Two more quaestors were added specially for the military treasury, making a total of four. Though patricians, they were elected in the comitia tributa, and in 421 the quaestorship was opened to the plebeians. The tribunes acquired the right of taking auspices (necessary before any public business and later convenient as a means of blocking action) and the privilege of sitting on a bench inside the senate, though near the door.

445. A law (plebiscite?) of the tribune Canuleius allowed marriage between patricians and plebeians, the children to inherit the father's rank.

444. As a compromise in the face of agitation that the consulate be opened to plebeians, **six (?three) military tribunes with consular power,** who might be plebeians, were substituted for the consuls. Two patrician *censors* were also created to hold office for five (?four) years, later reduced to eighteen months every fifth year. They had no *imperium,* but only a *potestas,* but because usually older and distinguished ex-consuls, they came to outrank even consuls. Their tasks gave them importance, since they made up the citizen lists for tax and military purposes (the *census*), enrolled senators

(*lectio senatus*) and knights (*recognitio equitum*), and examined into public morals (*regimen morum*), so that at the end of their term they could perform the ceremony of purification for the state, the *lustrum,* a word which came to be applied to their five-year cycle. They also made up the state budget, handled its property, and let out contracts for public works.

439. Traditionally, Sp. Maelius was put to death by Servius Ahala, master of the horse for the dictator Cincinnatus, because his free distribution of grain to the people seemed an attempt at a tyranny.

431. The dictator A. Postumius Tubertus decisively defeated the Aequi at the Algidus and drove them out of the valley. The Volsci were then continually driven back and are said to have made peace in 396.

426. Fidenae, which, with Veii, had declared war in 438, was destroyed by the dictator Mamercus Aemilius and the master of the horse A. Cornelius Cossus; thus Veii was forced to make peace for 20 years (425).

405–396. In the **siege of Veii,** tradition alleged that, because the army had to be kept in the field all winter, pay for the troops was introduced. The dictator M. Furius Camillus finally took the town; it was destroyed, and, since the Latins had not contributed to the siege, the territory was annexed directly to Rome and organized in four new tribes. From this time on Rome really outweighed its ally, the Latin League; the Hernici had long been inferior to the other two.

390. Rome was sacked by the Gauls under Brennus, who defeated the defending army at the **Allia** on July 18. According to tradition the Gauls held all of Rome except the Capitol.

T. Manlius Torquatus

Their withdrawal after seven months is attributed to Camillus, but they were probably bought off. The Latins and Hernici broke off their alliance with Rome.

384. The patrician M. Manlius Capitolinus was, according to tradition, convicted of aspiring to a tyranny by releasing plebeian debtors at his own expense, and was executed by being thrown from the Tarpeian Rock.

367. Licinio-Sextian Laws. After ten years of agitation the tribunes C. Licinius and L. Sextius secured the passage of reform measures: (1) some sort of relief was granted to debtors; (2) the amount of public land that one person could hold was limited to 500 iugera (one iugum = ⅝ acre). This provision is almost certainly a retrojection from the Gracchan era; (3) The practice of giving a consular *imperium* to military tribunes was abolished, and one consulship was opened to the plebs. Tradition incorrectly states that both consulships were opened to the plebs, and that one of them had to be filled by a plebeian. At the same time a third praetor was created, to handle the judicial functions of the other two chief magistrates, who thenceforth were usually known as consuls. Two patrician *curule aediles* were created, with functions much like the plebeian aediles. The plebeians were soon admitted to all offices, the last being the religious colleges of *pontifices* and *augures,* by the **lex Ogulnia** of 300. As a result of these changes, a new nobility of office-holding families, both patrician and plebeian, grew up, and the patriciate lost all significance. This nobility soon became quite exclusive, so that a *novus homo* (a man without office-holding ancestors) had great difficulty in obtaining an office.

367–349. Four wars were waged against the Gauls, who made incursions from Cisalpine Gaul into central Italy. In them are supposed to have been fought the single combats against Gallic champions of T. Manlius Torquatus (361) and M. Valerius Corvus (349). Peace was finally concluded c. 334.

362–345. Wars with the peoples immediately around Rome. The Hernici and the revolting Latin cities were forced to rejoin the Latin League on severer terms; southern Etruria was brought under Roman supremacy; and the Volsci and Aurunci were reduced, thus putting Rome in contact with the Samnites.

348. Second treaty between Rome and Carthage; some sources and some modern authorities call this the first treaty.

343–341. The **FIRST SAMNITE WAR** was started by a request for aid from the Samnite tribes in the Campanian plain against the hill tribes. After minor Roman victories the war ended in a draw.

340–338. The **LATIN WAR** began with the revolt of the Latin cities from the league and their demand for complete equality. In the course of the war, P. Decius Mus sacrificed himself for the victory of his army. The consul T. Manlius brought the war to a close in the **victory of Trifanum.** The Latin League was dissolved and its members made dependent on Rome without even *commercium* and *connubium* among themselves. In Rome their inhabitants received private rights but not the vote (*ciuitas sine suffragio,* later called *latinitas*). Some cities ceded land for settlement of Romans, some were made into Roman colonies, others were made dependent states.

The Via Appia today

339. Leges Publiliae, passed by the plebeian dictator Q. Publilius Philo, gave *plebiscita* the force of law provided they obtained the subsequent consent of the senate (*auctoritas patrum*); for regular *leges* it was provided that this consent should now be given in advance, as a pure formality.

326–304. The **SECOND SAMNITE WAR** began when Rome made Fregellae a colony and the first pro-consul (an ex-consul whose *imperium* was extended for carrying on a military command), Q. Publilius Philo, captured Naples (327). The Romans had the support of the Apulians and Lucanians, and later of certain Sabellian cities. After initial successes the consuls Sp. Postumius and T. Veturius were surrounded in the **Caudine Forks** and forced to surrender with their whole army. The Romans only slowly recovered Campania, but in 312 the censor Ap. Claudius began the great military road, the **Via Appia,** from Rome to Capua to secure Campania. The northern Etruscans joined Rome's enemies but were defeated at **Lake Vadimo** in 310. In 308 the

peoples of central Italy, Umbrians, Picentini, Marsians, etc., attacked Rome. The Romans countered by using their first war-fleet in the Adriatic. The Samnites were defeated by M. Fulvius and L. Postumius in 305. In 304 peace was made, slightly to Rome's advantage in that she got sole hegemony of Campania.

313. A law of the consul Poetilius (*lex Poetilia*) secured insolvent debtors against personal imprisonment if they surrendered their property entirely to their creditors.

312. Appius Claudius (later Caecus, "the blind"), as censor, is said to have distributed freedmen not holding land among all the tribes, but in 304 they, and freedmen of small landed property, were confined to the four urban tribes. This may reflect later debates as to the disposition of freedmen. In 304 a freedman of Appius, Gnaeus Flavius, is said to have made public the rules of legal procedure (*legis actiones*), to which he had access as clerk to the magistrates. This completed the work begun by the decemvirs in protecting the poor from manipulation of the law by the rich.

At about this time (or perhaps earlier, after the Gallic sack), the Roman army was reorganized so that in place of a solid phalanx with the long thrusting spear (*hasta*) the legion consisted of small groups, maniples of 120 men in two centuries (now purely titular), arranged in echelon in three lines (*hastati* and *principes* with the throwing javelin, *pilum*, and only the rearmost *triarii* with the spear) for greater mobility in mountainous areas.

During the ensuing years, Rome secured the Apennines by colonies, Sora, Alba Fucens, Carsioli, and Narnia, and built the **Via Flaminia** north to Narnia and the **Via Valeria** to Alba Fucens.

298–290. The **THIRD SAMNITE WAR** was a final effort of the Samnites, aided by the Lucanians, Gauls, and Etruscans, to break the power of Rome. Their capital, Bovianum, was taken in 298, but their army managed to combine with the Gauls, only to be defeated in 295 at **Sentinum,** where a second Decius Mus secured a Roman victory by self-sacrifice, perhaps in fact the only instance. The Gauls scattered, the Etruscans sued for peace in 294, and the Samnites finally made peace as autonomous allies, though the colony of Venusia was planted in the south to watch them, as well as Minturnae, Sinuessa, and Haria farther north. The Sabines, northeast of Rome, were annexed and given Latin rights.

285–282. The Romans, despite defeats, annihilated the Gallic Senones, crushed the Etruscans at Lake Vadimo and Populonia, and occupied the Greek cities in Lucania: Locri, Croton, and Thurii. This advance brought on the war with Tarentum and Pyrrhus.

287. The **lex Hortensia,** passed by the dictator Q. Hortensius, fully equated *plebiscita* with *leges* by requiring the *auctoritas patrum* for the former to be given in advance as well as for the latter; its passage was brought about by another secession of the plebs, this time to the Janiculum. The plebs had thus achieved complete legal equality with the patricians, but the old problem remained in the oppression of the poor by the rich patricio-plebeian nobility, which was in full control of the concilium plebis and the comitia tributa because, since the voting was by tribes, only the rich members of the more distant tribes could afford to come to the meetings in Rome. Further, in the assemblies all initiative was in the hands of the presiding magistrates, and these were now almost always from the nobility and under the control of the senate. As the problems of government became more complex with the expansion of Rome, the control of the senate became still more effective.

Rome had now established her supremacy throughout central Italy. Her relations with the other communities may be summarized as follows:

(1) *Municipia* retained their own municipal administration and enjoyed only the private rights (*connubium* and *commercium*) of Roman citizenship, not the franchise or right of holding office (*ciuitas sine suffragio*).

(2) *Coloniae* were settlements established by Rome for military purposes, usually on land taken from the conquered peoples. Smaller ones, Roman, were real garrisons and their settlers retained full citizenship. At first they may have been administered directly from Rome. Larger ones reflected real attempts to relieve surplus population and included both Latins and Romans, the latter accepting only Latin citizenship, or *ciutas sine suffragio*. They may have had some local government from the beginning. Ultimately, colonies came to have administrations closely modeled on the Roman, with two executive magistrates (*duumuiri*) and a senate or curia whose members were called *decuriones*.

Whatever the original form of government of the various *municipia* may have been, it tended to approximate the oligarchical model of Rome and the *coloniae,* with a small executive, often four (*quattuoruiri*), and a curia. Moreover, recent study suggests that this general pattern of municipality may not be at all early, may, in fact, date only from Caesar's municipal reforms, and that before that both *municipia* and *coloniae* were governed by officials sent out from Rome, as was certainly the case with *municipia* which, by revolt, were deprived of self-government (e.g. Capua later).

(3) *Ciuitates foederatae* were independent allies (*socii*) of Rome, whose obligations were regulated by treaty. They enjoyed freedom from direct interference in their affairs and from taxation (*libertas et immunitas*) and usually provided auxiliary troops or ships rather than legionaries. But their foreign relations were determined by Rome, and, in fact, they suffered considerable control.

(4) There were, in addition, groups or communities which did not have a civic organization and which, consequently, were administered under various names (*fora, conciliabula, uici, pagi*) either directly from Rome, by *praefecti*, or by neighboring cities to which they were attached as *attributi*.

(Cont. p. 104.)

D. The Hellenistic World, to 30 B.C.

(From p. 88)

1. *Cultural Development*

Greek and Amazon, bronze, 4th century B.C.

The **Hellenistic Age** was characterized politically by the **atrophy of the city state.** The cities of Greece were dominated increasingly by their richer or better educated members and the mass of the population lost power. In their external relations the cities either passed under the control of the various monarchs or joined together in leagues, whose attempts at representative federal government marked an advance in government which unfortunately bore no further fruit during the Roman period. Athens was a university town, respected for its past grandeur but of little political weight after 262. Sparta, however, played a lone and considerable hand in the Peloponnese. To offset the decay of Greece itself, the Hellenistic Age witnessed the **spread of Greek culture** by the conquests of Alexander and his successors as far as the Indus Valley, the creation of Greek cities throughout Asia, and the development of monarchical governments. In the new Greek cities, municipal administration and public building reached a high level, as at Priene (Asia Minor) or Alexandria (Egypt). **Social experiments** ranged from state control of the grain supply (Athens) or distribution of grain to citizens (Samos) to extreme agrarian reforms at Sparta. Private or royal munificence benefited the cities on a grand scale, and the cities themselves substituted for political rivalry that of the splendor of games, buildings, and honors. The administration of the three chief kingdoms was conditioned by their background. In **Macedon** the army, representing the Macedonian people, retained considerable influence, and the king was never so absolute as his Asiatic *confrères*. The **Seleucids**

developed a system of provincial administration and of communications based on the Persian satrapies; but their capital, Antioch, never attained the excellence of Egypt's Alexandria and its Hellenism was strongly affected by Syrian emotionalism. The **Ptolemies** administered Egypt as had the Pharaohs, as a state monopoly. They granted a privileged position, however, to Macedonian settlers and to the city of Alexandria, which was kept apart from the rest of Egypt as a Greek city, though it contained also a large Jewish population, for whom, during the 3rd century, a Greek translation was made of the Hebrew *Bible,* called the *Septuagint* from the 70 elders traditionally responsible for it. Alexandria was distinguished by its excellent administration and its splendid buildings, among which were a lighthouse (*pharos*) and an academy of scholars (*museum,* temple of the Muses) with a magnificent library.

The economic life of the eastern Mediterranean was much stimulated by unification in Greek hands, by the opening of new areas, and by improved navigation and communications. The cities became very rich. In particular, the opening of the treasures of the Near East vastly increased the amount of gold and silver in circulation. Two countries were, however, adversely affected. Greece, naturally poor, was drained of men by the opportunities offered for trade or mercenary soldiering in Asia, and could no longer compete with the more fertile areas now opened for exploitation. Egypt's resources, though ample for her self-contained economy, were exhausted by the expenditures of the Ptolemies in their attempt to create an Aegean empire. Nevertheless, in general, the period was one of complacent prosperity throughout the eastern Mediterranean.

Under the great librarians of Alexandria, **Zenodotus** (c. 280), **Aristophanes** of Byzantium (257–180), and **Aristarchus** (217–145), philology, textual criticism, and kindred subjects replaced creative writing. Alexandria became the intellectual center of the world, whose museum not only contained a library but also botanical and zoological gardens, lecture rooms, and dissecting halls. The Hellenistics combined the mathematical emphasis of Plato with the epistemology of

Women gossiping, terra cotta, Asia Minor, 2nd century B.C.

Aristotle to produce a physics that is recognizably modern. Astronomical measurements were made by **Aristarchus,** and the circumference of the earth computed by **Eratosthenes.** Mathematics advanced through the work of **Euclid** (c. 300) and physics through the work of **Archimedes** (287–212, in Syracuse), who must be acknowledged as one of the scientific geniuses of all time. **Herophilos** and **Erasistratos,** physiologists, conducted human as well as animal dissections in their investigations on the function of the brain and the nervous system. Beginning of the building of mechanical contrivances, Ctesibius (fl. c. 283–247) B.C., Hero of

Alexandria (1st century A.D.), and Archimedes, who designed siege instruments.

Literature became imitative, artificial, and overburdened with learning, as in the poetry of **Callimachus** (c. 260), or the epic *Argonautica* of **Apollonius Rhodius** (295–214). Only the pastoral achieved a delicate and spontaneous freshness in the poems of **Theocritus** (c. 270, from Syracuse). The Attalids, notably Eumenes II, tried to make Pergamum into an intellectual rival of Alexandria, but their capital became famous chiefly for its **Pergamene school of art,** whose exaggerated style is best seen in the friezes of the Altar of Pergamum. Another

The Great Library at Alexandria

Archimedes

school flourished in the prosperous island of Rhodes. Much of Hellenistic art dealt with simple subjects of daily life in a realistic fashion, as in the charming pottery figurines from Tanagra, in Greece.

In **philosophy,** the Academy continued the Platonic tradition but with increasing skepticism about the possibility of attaining truth. The **Peripatetics** devoted themselves almost wholly to scientific and historical studies. Two new schools, however, answered the spiritual needs of the time. **Stoicism** was founded by **Zeno** (336–264), a half-Phoenician from Cyprus, who taught in the Painted Porch (*stoa poikile*) at Athens, and **Epicureanism** by **Epicurus** (342–270), who withdrew from the world into his garden. Both sought the same end, a mind which would be so self-sufficient through inner discipline and its own resources that it would not be disturbed by external accidents. The Stoics sought this undisturbed state of mind (*ataraxia*) by modifying the Cynic asceticism to a doctrine of neglect of outward honors and wealth and devotion to duty. A belief that the world was ruled by a universal reason in which all shared led them to a humanitarian view of the brotherhood of men which transcended national, racial, or social differences. This internationalism and the doctrine that the ruler should embody divine reason allowed them to support monarchical government. The Epicureans sought the same end by following the Cyrenaics in advocating an inactive life (*apraxia*) and a moderate, not an excessive, self-indulgence. To free the mind from wrong, they attacked religion and superstition and adopted the atomic metaphysics as a mechanical explanation of the universe.

In **religion,** the Hellenistic Age witnessed a loss of belief in the simple Greek pantheon and a turning to more emotional oriental worships, like those of **Cybele,** the Great Mother of Asia Minor, the Persian **Mithra,** or the Egyptian **Isis.** A fatalistic view of external events led to the personification of Fortune (*tyche*) as a goddess. And a combination of flattery, legalism (since a god could always rule a city without changes in the constitution), skepticism (since many considered that the gods were originally famous men), and real gratitude for the benefits of government introduced the worship of rulers, both dead and living, which the Macedonian monarchs alone refused.

2. *Wars of the Diadochi, 322–275* B.C.

322–315. When **Perdiccas** became regent for Philip III Arrhidaeus, the other generals, Antipater, Antigonus, Craterus, and Ptolemy, refused obedience. Perdiccas was murdered when he attempted to dislodge Ptolemy from Egypt, but his general **Eumenes** defeated and slew Craterus in Asia Minor (321). Antipater and Ptolemy at Triparadeisus in Syria agreed that Antipater should be regent. Antipater sent Antigonus to dislodge Eumenes, who took refuge in the hills (320). When Antipater died (319), he left **Polyperchon** as regent, but Ptolemy defied him and annexed Syria. Antigonus seized Phrygia and Lydia. Polyperchon gave Eumenes command of the troops in Cilicia. Antipater's son, **Cassander,** seized the Piraeus, garrisoned it, and left Demetrius of Phalerum as virtual dictator of Athens (317). Cassander

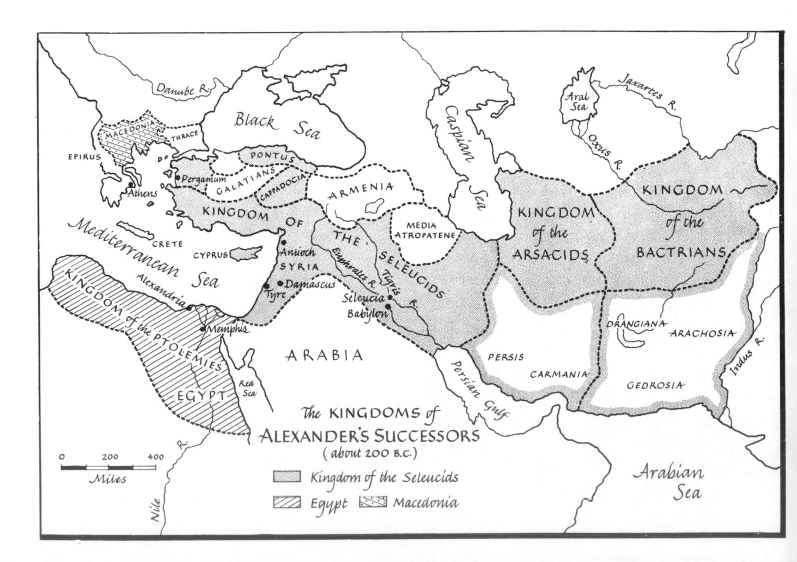

Delphi, ruins of the temple of Apollo

took Macedon from Polyperchon (317), executed Olympias and Philip Arrhidaeus when they attacked him, and imprisoned Roxana with her son Alexander IV, both of whom he put to death in 310. In the meantime, Antigonus, after a drawn **battle at Paraetacene** (317), had defeated Eumenes in Gabiene (316) and executed him. Ptolemy in Egypt, Cassander, and Lysimachus in Thrace formed a coalition against Antigonus (315).

315-307. **Antigonus** seized Syria, but his son, Demetrius, was defeated at Gaza (312) by Ptolemy, who had already occupied the Cyclades (314) and the Peloponnese (313). Ptolemy then sent **Seleucus** to capture Babylon from Antigonus. An attempted settlement in 311 merely allowed Antigonus to continue fighting Seleucus, Cassander to secure the throne of Macedon (above), and Ptolemy to continue his expansion in the Aegean. Antigonus sent Demetrius to Athens, whence he expelled Demetrius of Phalerum and restored the democracy (307).

307. **ANTIGONUS I, MONOPHTHALMOS** ("one-eyed") or Cyclops, and **Demetrius I Poliorcetes** ("besieger") took the title of king,

whereupon Ptolemy and Seleucus, Cassander, and Lysimachus did the same. The unity of Alexander's empire was thus openly ended.

306. Demetrius crushed Ptolemy in a naval battle off Cyprian Salamis but Ptolemy repelled a land attack by Antigonus. Demetrius failed to reduce Rhodes by a year's siege (305-304), but relieved Athens from the **Four Years' War** waged by Cassander (307-304). He then revived the **Hellenic League** of Philip (302).

301. **BATTLE OF IPSUS** (in Phrygia). The allies, Cassander, Lysimachus, and Seleucus, but not Ptolemy, finally crushed and slew Antigonus. Demetrius, who had been recalled by Antigonus, escaped to Corinth. By the division of spoils, Seleucus was given Syria, Lysimachus western and central Asia Minor, Cassander kept Macedon, but his brother Pleistarchus received southern Asia Minor. Ptolemy, however, seized Coele-Syria.

299. **Pleistarchus** was driven out by Demetrius, and Cassander himself died in 298. His eldest son, Philip IV, died also, so that two younger sons, Antipater and Alexander V, divided his realm.

295. **Demetrius,** after a bitter siege, recovered

Athens, where one Lachares had made himself tyrant. He then murdered Alexander V (294) and took Macedon. He mastered northern and central Greece save for Aetolia.

288. A coalition was formed against Demetrius, and Lysimachus and King Pyrrhus of Epirus drove him out of Macedon. He attempted a campaign in Asia Minor, but finally Seleucus captured him in Cilicia (285).

283. Demetrius died in captivity, leaving a son in Greece, Antigonus.

281. Seleucus defeated and slew Lysimachus at the **battle of Corupedium** and became master of Asia Minor. When he tried to seize Macedon, however, he was assassinated by Ptolemy Ceraunus, who acquired control of Macedon. Ptolemy, in turn, was slain in an invasion of Celts (279).

279. The **Celts** ravaged Macedon, defeated the Greeks at Thermopylae, and reached Delphi. A second band ruled Thrace until 210, while a third crossed to central Asia Minor and established the **kingdom of Galatia.**

276-275. Meanwhile, Antigonus recovered Macedon for himself, founding a dynasty that lasted until 168.

3. *Sicily to the Roman Conquest, 216* B.C.

317-289. AGATHOCLES made himself tyrant of Syracuse in consequence of a civil war (c. 323-317) in which he, as democratic leader, expelled the oligarchs with Carthaginian aid and divided their property among the poor. He successfully defended himself against the neighboring cities and the exiled oligarchs until these appealed to Carthage.

311. The Carthaginian general **Hamilcar** defeated Agathocles at the Himera River and besieged Syracuse. In 310, Agathocles slipped across to Africa, where he maintained himself until 307. But his army, under his son, was annihilated during his absence.

305. Agathocles came to terms with Carthage and the oligarchs, and took the title of king.

In the meantime the Tarentines had made peace with the Samnites (c. 320) and Rome (304), but were hard pressed by the Lucanians.

302. When a Spartan commander, Cleonymus, failed to relieve them, the Tarentines called in Agathocles. He also failed to accomplish much and died at Syracuse in 289, bequeathing their freedom to the Syracusans, who restored the democracy. Certain of the Campanian mercenaries of Agathocles, calling themselves **Mamertines** ("sons of Mars"), seized Messana.

282-275. The **Tarentines,** angered by Roman occupation of towns in southern Italy, destroyed a Roman fleet which, in violation of the treaty of 304, had passed the Lacinian promontory. They then drove the Romans from Thurii. When Rome declared war, they called in Pyrrhus. Upon his departure in 275, the Greeks of southern Italy remained under Rome, while those in Sicily passed under Carthaginian power, save for Syracuse.

269-216. Hiero II made himself tyrant of Syracuse and defeated the Mamertines at Mylae. He took the title of king (265), and joined the Carthaginians in besieging the Roman force which occupied Messana in 264. But when he was defeated and besieged in Syracuse, he made peace with Rome (263). At the end of the First Punic War all Sicily save Syracuse and a few other pro-Roman cities passed into Rome's possession. Syracuse was reduced in 211 during the Second Punic War.

4. *Macedon and Greece to the Roman Conquest, 146* B.C.

290. Emergence of the **Aetolian League,** a military federation in western Greece. It had a council with proportional representation and a semi-annual assembly. Affairs were handled by a committee of 100 *apokletoi* and a single general (*strategos*) in wartime. The league expanded into Phocis (254) and Boeotia (245) and dominated Greece from sea to sea. It also included Elis and part of Arcadia (245) and made an alliance with Messene, thus separating Sparta from the Achaean League.

280. Formation of the **Achaean League,** consisting of twelve towns in the northern Peloponnese. It had a general (two until 255), a board of ten *demiourgoi*, a federal council with proportional representation of members. There was also an annual assembly of all free citizens. After 251, Aratus of Sicyon dominated its policy and was *strategos* in alternate years. He extended it to include many non-Achaean cities, especially Corinth (243).

276-239. ANTIGONUS II GONATAS ("knock-kneed"?) had to repel an invasion by **Pyrrhus of Epirus** (274-273). Pyrrhus was then called into Greece by the pretender Cleonymus, who sought to oust King Areus (309-265) from Sparta. Pyrrhus was slain at Argos by the Argives and Antigonus (272). Antigonus established tyrants in several cities of the Peloponnese and made peace with the Aetolian League.

266-262. **Ptolemy II of Egypt** stirred up Athens and Sparta to wage the **Chremonidean War** (from Chremonides, an Athenian leader) against Antigonus. Areus of Sparta was defeated and killed at the isthmus (265) and, when Ptolemy failed to give energetic aid, Athens was obliged to surrender after a two-year siege (262). Antigonus garrisoned several strong points of Attica and imposed a moderate oligarchy on Athens.

258 (?256). Antigonus defeated Ptolemy in a naval **battle off Cos** and took the Cyclades, though he had to reconquer them later in the **battle of Andros** (245).

c. 252. Antigonus' governor of the Peloponnese, Alexander, revolted and held the peninsula until his death (c. 246).

251. **Aratus of Sicyon** recovered that city from Antigonus' tyrant, and then joined the Achaean League, which he soon dominated.

245-235. **Sparta** had fallen into a serious economic crisis because of the excessive concentration of land and wealth in the hands of a few. Coined money had been introduced by King Areus. The number of full citizens who could contribute to their mess-tables (*syssitia*) had fallen to 700. When **King Agis IV** (244-240) tried to redistribute the land into 4500 equal lots, the great landowners executed him. **Cleomenes III,** who married Agis' widow, became king (235).

241. Antigonus sent the Aetolian League to ravage the isthmus.

239-229. Demetrius II succeeded his father, Antigonus. He protected Epirus against Aetolia, so that the latter broke with Macedon and made an alliance with Achaea. Demetrius attacked it in the **War of Demetrius** (238-229), but was recalled by invasions from the north (233). Argos expelled the pro-Macedonian tyrant Aristomachus and joined the Achaean League (229), while Athens asserted her independence.

229-221. Antigonus III Doson ("going to give," i.e. always promising) succeeded his cousin Demetrius as guardian of the latter's nine-year-old son, Philip, whom he deposed in 227 to become king himself. He made peace with Aetolia and drove the barbarians out of Macedon.

228-227. Cleomenes defeated the Achaeans under Aratus. He then seized the power in Sparta, redivided the land, and enfranchised 4000 *perioikoi* and abolished the *ephorate*. With an increased citizen army, he reduced Aratus to appeal to Antigonus (225).

222. Antigonus formed a new Hellenic League and crushed Cleomenes at the **battle of Sellasia** (222). Cleomenes fled to Egypt. Antigonus abolished the Spartan kingship, restored the ephors, and forced Sparta into his league.

221-178. Philip V, son of Demetrius II, succeeded Antigonus III. At his instigation the Hellenic League assembled at Corinth to declare

219-217. The **War of the Allies,** or Social War, against the Aetolians because of the latter's piracy. The Aetolians allied with Elis and Sparta, where an anti-Macedonian faction tried to recall Cleomenes. When he was slain in Egypt, the Spartans nevertheless restored the dual kingship. Philip ravaged Elis (219-218), molested the Aetolian sanctuary of Thermum, and laid waste Laconia.

217. Rhodes and Egypt negotiated the **Peace of Naupactus** between the discouraged Aetolians and Philip, who wanted freedom to act against Rome.

215-205. In the **FIRST MACEDONIAN WAR** Philip V of Macedon attempted to help Hannibal and the Carthaginians against Rome, but a Roman fleet in the Adriatic prevented him from crossing to Italy and the Romans secured the support of the Aetolian League and Pergamum (212), as well as of Elis, Mantinea, and Sparta (210). Sparta in particular, after a period of attempted social reform under King Cheilon (219), had risen to power under Machanidas, regent for the young King Pelops. When the Achaean League under Philopoemen (since the murder of Aratus in 213) slew Machanidas at Mantinea (207), Nabis became regent and soon, by deposing Pelops, king. The Greeks came to terms with Philip in 206 and Rome accepted the settlement by the **Peace of Phoenice** (205).

203-200. Philip, allied with Antiochus III against Egypt (203), began operations in the Aegean, but was defeated by Rhodes and Attalus of Pergamum in the **battle of Chios** (201).

200-196. The **SECOND MACEDONIAN WAR** arose from an appeal by Attalus and Rhodes to Rome (201). When Philip refused to keep the peace, all the Greeks joined Rome (200-198), and Flamininus defeated Philip at **Cynoscephalae** (197), and proclaimed the freedom of Greece at the Isthmian Games (196). Flamininus was forced to check Nabis of Sparta (above), who had carried through agrarian reforms (207-204) and expanded his power in the Peloponnese, especially by acquiring Argos (198). He now lost Argos and much of Laconia, and gave control of his foreign policy to Rome (195). Upon the murder

Philip V

of Nabis (192), Sparta was forced into the Achaean League by Rome, and Messene and Elis soon joined, so that the league controlled all the Peloponnese.

192-189. The **Aetolians declared war on Rome** and secured the support of Antiochus III with a small force. The Achaeans and Philip supported Rome. The Romans drove Antiochus back to Asia in the **battle of Thermopylae** (191), and the Aetolians were finally made subject allies of Rome by M. Fulvius Nobilior (189).

189-181. Philopoemen humbled Sparta but lost his life in suppressing a revolt in Messenia (183). His successor in the Achaean League, Callicrates, was subservient to Rome and allowed Sparta to revive.

179-167. **Perseus** became king of Macedon on the death of his father Philip V. He had already persuaded Philip to execute his pro-Roman brother Demetrius, and now Eumenes II of Pergamum laid charges against him at Rome.

171-167. In the **THIRD MACEDONIAN WAR** Perseus was crushed by Aemilius Paullus at **Pydna** (168). He later died in captivity in Italy and the Antigonids came to an end. Rome made Macedon into four unrelated republics, paying a moderate yearly tribute (167). In Aetolia, 500 anti-Romans were slain. One thousand hostages, including the historian Polybius, were taken from Achaea to Italy.

149-148. The **FOURTH MACEDONIAN WAR** was begun by Andriscus, who pretended to be a son of Perseus. On his defeat, Macedon became a Roman province (148).

146. When the Achaean hostages had returned (151) and Callicrates had died (149), the Achaean League attacked Sparta, but was crushed by the Roman general Mummius (146). The Roman Senate ordered Mummius to abolish the leagues, substitute oligarchies for all democracies, sack Corinth, and place Greece under the supervision of the governor of Macedon. This marked the end of Greek and Macedonian independence, though some Greek states retained autonomy for a long time.

T. Quinctius Flaminius

5. *The Seleucid Empire and Pergamum, 305–64* B.C.

Under the Seleucids there developed, in Mesopotamia, a complex computational method of exact astronomical prediction, although apparently no physical model was used. The zodiac and the constellations against which the planets were seen became important for computational purposes.

305–280. SELEUCUS I NICATOR ("conqueror"), after securing his position against Antigonus (310–306) and assuming the royal title (305), ceded India to **Sandracottus** (Chandragupta) for 500 elephants (304–303). Though Ptolemy took Coele-Syria (301), Seleucus secured Cilicia from Demetrius (296–295). Seleucus failed to reduce **Mithridates I of Pontus,** but got control of western Asia Minor on the defeat of Lysimachus (281).

280–261. Antiochus I Soter ("saviour") succeeded upon the murder of Seleucus. He fought and finally defeated the Galatians (279–275) by terrifying them with his elephants. In the **Damascene War** (280–279) and **First Syrian** (276–272) **War** he lost to Ptolemy II, Miletus, Phoenicia, and western Cilicia.

263–241. Eumenes I made himself virtually independent of Antiochus as ruler of Pergamum, where his uncle, Philetarus, had ruled as governor first for Lysimachus and then for the Seleucids.

261–246. Antiochus II Theos ("god"), son of Antiochus I, secured the support of Antigonus II and Rhodes against Egypt in the **Second Syrian War** (260–255). The succeeding peace restored to Antiochus: Ionia (including Miletus), Coele-Syria, and western Cilicia (255).

250–230. Diodotus I declared himself independent king of Bactria. In 248–247, Arsaces I of the nomad Parni established himself in the province of Parthia and founded the **Parthian Kingdom.**

246–226. SELEUCUS II CALLINICUS ("gloriously victorious"), son of Antiochus II by his divorced wife, Laodice I, succeeded. **Berenice II,** daughter of Ptolemy II, whom Antiochus married in 252, provoked the

246–241. Third Syrian War ("Laodicean War" or "War of Berenice") in favor of her infant son. Though she and her son were murdered in Antioch, her brother, Ptolemy III, invaded Asia and ultimately forced Seleucus to surrender the coasts of Syria and southern Asia Minor (241).

241–197. Attalus I Soter ("savior"), who succeeded his father's cousin Eumenes I, as ruler of Pergamum, took advantage of Seleucus' difficulties to secure for himself western Asia Minor by crushing the Galatians near **Pergamum** (230), after which he took the title king and received the surname *Soter.*

237. Seleucus attacked **Antiochus Hierax** ("falcon"), a younger son of Laodice, whom Seleucus in 241 had recognized as ruler of Asia Minor. Hierax secured the aid of Mithridates II of Pontus and the Galatians. The Galatians crushed Seleucus at Ancyra (236).

229–226. Attalus I of Pergamum drove Hierax out of Asia Minor (229–228), after which Seleucus drove him out of Syria (227) to Thrace, where he died (226).

226–223. Seleucus III Soter or Ceraunus ("thunderbolt"), son of Seleucus II, was murdered during a war with Attalus I (224–221).

223–187. ANTIOCHUS III, THE GREAT, brother of Seleucus III, regained from Attalus most of the territory lost since 241. He recovered the Mesopotamian provinces from the revolting governor, Molon (221). But in the

221–217. Fourth Syrian War, despite initial successes, he finally retained on the Syrian coast only Seleucia, the port of Antioch.

209–204. In a number of campaigns, Antiochus reduced the Parthian Arsaces III Priapatius to vassalship, made an alliance with Euthydemus, who had usurped the Bactrian throne of Diodotus II, and even secured the submission of the Indian rajah Sophagasenus. Thus he restored the Seleucid kingdom to its former extent.

201–195. The **Fifth Syrian War** resulted from the treaty which Antiochus III had made with Philip V of Macedon in 203. The war was decided in 200 by Antiochus' **victory of Panium.** After several campaigns in Anatolia, Antiochus secured from Egypt most of Coele-Syria and southern Asia Minor (save Cyprus). Although Eumenes II Soter of Pergamum (197–159), son of Attalus I, induced Flamininus to order Antiochus out of Asia Minor, Antiochus did not heed, but confirmed his conquests by a peace with Egypt (195).

192–189. WAR WITH ROME, Antiochus continued disregard of the senate led to a war in which he was driven from Greece (191) and his fleet was defeated at **Myonnesus** (190). The Roman army entered Asia Minor and defeated Antiochus himself at **Magnesia** (190). In the peace (189), Antiochus paid a large indemnity, lost his fleet, and surrendered Asia Minor which was divided between Rhodes and Pergamum. This defeat led to the complete breaking away of Armenia (under Artaxias) and of Bactria, where a succession of Greek rulers preserved Hellenism until the invasions of the Sacae (c. 150–125). An offshoot of the Bactrian kingdom flourished in the Punjab (c. 175–c. 40), and though its rulers adopted Buddhism (c. 150) it introduced Hellenistic art and ideas into India.

187–175. Seleucus IV Philopater ("loving his father") succeeded his father, Antiochus III, and during his reign the empire gradually recovered strength. Meanwhile Eumenes II of Pergamum fought against Prusias I of Bithynia (186) and Pharnaces I of Pontus (183–179).

175–163. Antiochus IV Epiphanes ("god manifest") succeeded upon the murder of his brother Seleucus. Though friendly to Rome, he was prevented by the Romans from concluding successfully his war against Egypt (171–168). The Romans also weakened Rhodes by making Delos a free port (167).

168–164. Revolt of the Jews, under **Judas Maccabeus** (d. 160) and his brothers, Jonathan (d. 142) and Simon (d. 135). The Jews achieved religious freedom in 164 and eventually (141) succeeded in liberating Jerusalem. Simon established the **Hasmonean dynasty** and a theocratic state which, under his successors

Tomb of the Maccabees

John Hyrcanus (134–104) and **Alexander Jannaeus** (102–76), took advantage of the weakness of the Seleucid rulers to extend its power over neighboring territories. Eventually the rivalry between Aristobulus II (67–63) and his brother, Hyrcanus II, gave Pompey an excuse for annexing Judaea to the Roman Empire (63). Hyrcanus II remained as high priest and later as ethnarch (63–40). He was supplanted by his nephew, Antigonus (40–37), who, allying himself with the Parthians, incurred the wrath of the Romans. In 37 the Hasmonean dynasty came to an end and **Herod** (the Great, 37–4) was appointed king of Judaea by the Roman senate *(p. 122)*.

163–162. Antiochus V Eupater, young son of Antiochus IV, king, with Lysias as regent.

162–150. Demetrius I Soter ("savior"), son of Seleucus IV, returned from Rome to eject Antiochus V, but was slain in 150 by a pretender, **Alexander Balas** (150–145), who claimed to be the son of Antiochus IV and was supported by Attalus II Philadelphus ("loving his brother") of Pergamum (159–138) (who had succeeded his brother Eumenes II), by Ptolemy VI of Egypt, and by Rome. Ptolemy, however, soon invaded Syria in favor of Demetrius II, the son of Demetrius I, who slew Balas in 145.

145–139. Demetrius II Nicator ("conqueror") won several victories (140) over Mithridates I of Parthia, who had seized Media (c. 150) and Babylon (c. 141). Mithridates, however, captured Demetrius by treachery in 139. In the meantime, a son of Alexander Balas, Antiochus VI Epiphanes Dionysus ("god manifest"), had held Antioch from 145 to 142, when he was expelled by the mercenary leader Diodotus, who took the title of King Tryphon (142–139). He was expelled in 139.

139–127. Antiochus VII Euergetes Eusebes Soter Sidetes ("benefactor, pious, savior") did much to restore the Seleucid power. However, after several victories over Phraates II of Parthia, he was finally defeated and killed at Ecbatana (127).

138–133. Attalus III Philomater ("loving his

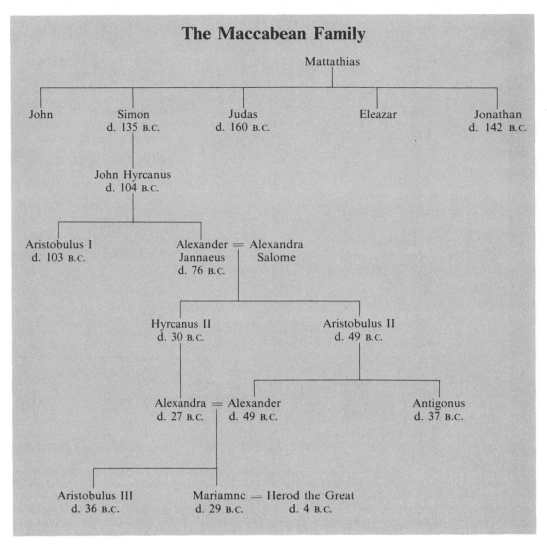

The Maccabean Family

Mattathias
— John
— Simon d. 135 B.C.
— Judas d. 160 B.C.
— Eleazar
— Jonathan d. 142 B.C.

Simon → John Hyrcanus d. 104 B.C.
John Hyrcanus → Aristobulus I d. 103 B.C.
John Hyrcanus → Alexander Jannaeus d. 76 B.C. = Alexandra Salome

Alexander Jannaeus → Hyrcanus II d. 30 B.C.
Alexander Jannaeus → Aristobulus II d. 49 B.C.

Hyrcanus II → Alexandra d. 27 B.C. = Alexander d. 49 B.C.
Aristobulus II → Antigonus d. 37 B.C.

Alexandra = Alexander → Aristobulus III d. 36 B.C.
Alexandra = Alexander → Mariamne d. 29 B.C. = Herod the Great d. 4 B.C.

mother") **of Pergamum,** a son of Eumenes II, succeeded his uncle, Attalus II. In his will, he bequeathed his kingdom to Rome, apparently in order to protect his subjects from absorption by their neighbors. Rome had to suppress the pretender Aristonicus before it could make the kingdom of Pergamum into the province of Asia (129).

129–125. Demetrius II was sent back to Syria by Phraates II in 129 and was slain in 125 by

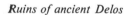

Ruins of ancient Delos

a pretender with Egyptian support, Alexander Zabinas. Demetrius' son, **Seleucus V,** assumed the diadem but was put to death at once by his mother, Cleopatra Thea.

125–96. Antiochus VIII Epiphanes Philomater Callinicus "Grypus" ("god manifest, loving his mother, gloriously victorious, hook-nosed"), a younger son of Demetrius II, reigned with Cleopatra until her death (c. 120). The pretender, Alexander Zabinas, was killed in 123. In 117 Antiochus was forced into retirement by a half-brother, **Antiochus IX Philopater, "Cyzicenus"** ("loving his father, of Cyzicus"), son of Cleopatra and Antiochus VII. After an indecisive series of battles (113–112), they divided the realm in 111 and both reigned until Antiochus VIII was murdered in 96 by his favorite, Heracleon.

95–64. Seleucus VI, son of Antiochus VIII, defeated and killed Antiochus IX (95). The son of the latter, **Antiochus X,** defeated and killed Seleucus VI, but the latter's brother, Demetrius III, seized Damascus. Another son of Antiochus VIII, **Antiochus XI,** was defeated and killed, but his brother, Philip I, continued the war with Antiochus X. The latter was killed in 93 fighting the Parthians in Commagene. Demetrius III and Philip I engaged in civil war until Demetrius was captured by the Parthians in 88. **Antiochus XII,** another son of Antiochus VIII, seized Damascus, which he held until he was killed on an expedition against the Nabataeans in 84. An insurrection expelled Philip I from Antioch, and Tigranes of Armenia seized Syria and held it until he was defeated by Lucullus in 69. **Antiochus XIII,** son of Antiochus X, was installed at Antioch (68) and soon had to fight with Philip II, son of Philip I. The Arabian prince of Emesa slew Antiochus XIII by treachery in 67; Philip was unable to secure his rule. In 64 Pompey made Syria a Roman province.

6. *Parthia, 312* B.C.–*77* A.D.

331–323. Rule of Alexander the Great.

305–280. Seleucus I founded the dynasty of the Seleucids, ruling over Babylonia and Syria; he built the city of Seleucia near Ctesiphon on the Tigris.

248–212. Arsaces I founded the **kingdom of Parthia,** including at first only Parthia and Hyrcania, between the Seleucid kingdom in the west and the Bactrian kingdom in the east. In 238 Arsaces was expelled by Seleucus II, but returned when the latter withdrew to deal with a revolt in Syria.

212–c. 190. Arsaces II withstood the attacks of Antiochus III, the Great, in 209; he was followed by Arsaces III (Priapatius, 190–175) and Arsaces IV (Phraates I, 175–171).

171–138. Mithridates I conquered Babylonia and Media from the Seleucids; later he added to his kingdom Elam, Persia, and parts of Bactria, thus founding the Parthian Empire. Ctesiphon-Seleucia became the capital.

138–124. Phraates II (138–127) defeated Antiochus VII in Media (129), and as a result the Seleucids were permanently excluded from the lands east of the Euphrates; but he died in battle fighting the Tochari (the Scythians or *Sacae* of the Greeks), a tribe driven forth from Central Asia by the Yue-chi. The kingdom was devastated and Artabanus I (127–124) fell likewise fighting against the Tochari.

124–88. MITHRIDATES II, THE GREAT, defeated the Scythians and also Artavasdes, king of Armenia Major. In 92 he made a treaty with Rome.

88–70. Parthia suffered a collapse and was greatly reduced in territory by Tigranes I of Armenia.

70–57. Phraates III restored order, but was not strong enough to resist the Roman advance, led by Lucullus and Pompey.

57–37. Orodes I defeated Crassus at **Carrhae** (53) and regained Mesopotamia.

37–32. Phraates IV defeated Antony in 36, but could not prevent him from conquering Armenia in 34. After a period of dynastic disturbances

A.D. 51–77. Vologesus I, after a war with Rome, obtained recognition of his brother Tiridates as king of Armenia (63), thus establishing an Arsacid dynasty in that country. In Parthia itself the utmost confusion prevailed after 77, with two or more kings (all of them little known) ruling at the same time and constantly challenged by other claimants.

(Cont. p. 133.)

Phraates III

7. *Bactria, 328–40* B.C.

328–323 B.C. Bactria under the rule of Alexander. A mutiny of Greek auxiliaries after Alexander's death was crushed at once by Perdiccas.

323–302. Bactria under Perdiccas (d. 321), Antipater (d. 319), Eumenes (d. 316), Antigonus (d. 301). In his wars against Antigonus, Seleucus I conquered the eastern provinces (311–302).

302–c. 250. Bactria under the Seleucids.

c. 250–c. 139. Diodotus, the satrap of Bactria, made himself an independent ruler and conquered Sogdiana. He founded a dynasty that withstood the attacks of the Seleucids.

After the defeat of Antiochus III at Magnesia (190), Euthydemus and his son Demetrius began the **conquest of the Indus Valley.** But Eucratides made himself king of Bactria (c. 170) while Demetrius was founding a kingdom in the Punjab. About 150 the Tochari (Scythians) occupied Sogdiana, and about 139 Bactria. The line of Eucratides maintained itself in Kabul until about 40 B.C., but most of the region was ruled by Scythian dynasties.

Temple of Athena at Delphi (p.69)

Greek theater at Taormina, Sicily (p.78)

Tachara (Central Hall) of the Palace of Darius at Persepolis, destroyed by Alexander the Great (p.86)

Ruins of the Gate of Xerxes at Persepolis

Detail of capital of Central Palace at Persepolis

8. Ptolemaic Egypt to the Roman Conquest, 305–30 B.C.

(From p. 46)

305-283. PTOLEMY I SOTER ("savior"), the son of Lagus (hence the "Lagid" house), had been governor of Egypt since 323 and king since 305. He had seized Coele-Syria in 301, and acquired from Demetrius, Pamphylia and Lycia (296–295), and Caria and the island of Cos (286).

285-246. PTOLEMY II PHILADELPHUS ("lover of his sister") adopted a Pharaonic practice by marrying his sister Arsinoe II (276), founder of the museum at Alexandria. He explored the upper Nile and extended his power along the Red Sea and into northern Arabia (278) for commercial purposes.

280-272. In the **Damascene War** (280–279) and **First Syrian War** (276–272), he suffered initial defeat from Antiochus I and the revolt of his half-brother Magas in Cyrene. But he finally defeated both and secured Miletus, Phoenicia, and western Cilicia. He subsidized Pyrrhus against Antigonus (274), aided Athens and Sparta in the Chremonidean War (266–262), and incited Alexander II of Epirus to attack Macedon (264). He likewise incited Eumenes of Pergamum to revolt from Antiochus (262) and supported the seizure of Ephesus (262–259) by his own son, Ptolemy "the Son." These activities brought Antiochus II, Antigonus II, and Rhodes together to wage

The building of the temple of Horus at Edfu was started during the reign of Ptolemy III

Ptolemy II discussing with architects the plans for the Alexandrian library

260-255. The **Second Syrian War** (260–255), in which Antigonus defeated Ptolemy in the **battle of Cos** (258 or 256). Though by the resulting peace he lost Cilicia and western Pamphylia (255), he later recovered the Cyclades (250) and also Cyrene (c. 248), which had become independent in 258.

246-221. Ptolemy III Euergetes ("benefactor") supported his sister Berenice II in the **Third Syrian War** (246–241) and acquired the coasts of Syria and southern Asia Minor, as well as some Aegean ports, including Ephesus. But he lost the Cyclades to Antigonus through the **battle of Andros** (245). Height of the Ptolemaic power.

221-203. Ptolemy IV Philopater ("loving his father") was a weak monarch, dominated by his minister, Sosibius. In the **Fourth Syrian War** (221–217) he at first lost much of the Syrian coast to Antiochus III, but the victory of **Raphia** (217) brought the recovery of all save the port of Seleucia.

203-181. Ptolemy V Epiphanes ("god manifest"), a young boy, succeeded his father. While the Egyptian natives revolted in the Delta (201–200) Antiochus III attacked him in

201-195. The **Fifth Syrian War,** as a result of which Ptolemy retained only Cyprus of his Asiatic possessions. When he came of age (195), he succeeded in suppressing the native revolts.

Cleopatra VII

181–145. Ptolemy VI Philomater ("loving his mother") followed Ptolemy V under the regency of his mother, Cleopatra I. In consequence of Ptolemy's cowardice during the war with Antiochus (171–168), the people of Alexandria forced him to associate his brother, **Ptolemy VII**, in the rule. Rome prevented Antiochus from capturing Alexandria (168). When Ptolemy VI was expelled by his brother (164), the Roman Senate restored him and gave Cyrene and Cyprus to Ptolemy VII, who, however, secured only Cyrene (163). Ptolemy VI expelled Demetrius I from Syria (152–151) and supported Demetrius II against Alexander Balas (147–145), but was slain in the war.

145–116. Ptolemy VII Euergetes II ("benefactor") or Physcon ("fat-bellied") reunited the empire after his brother's death and restored order. At his death, he left Cyrene separately to his son Apion, who willed it to Rome in 96, though it was not actually annexed until 75. Another son, Ptolemy IX, received Cyprus, which was ultimately bequeathed to Rome and annexed in 58.

116–47. Ptolemy VIII Soter II ("savior") or Lathyrus, son of Ptolemy VII, was eventually expelled by his brother **Ptolemy IX Alexander I** (108–88). The people of Alexandria, however, slew Ptolemy IX and restored Ptolemy VIII (88–80). **Ptolemy X Alexander II,** son of Ptolemy IX, succeeded but was at once slain by the people of Alexandria (80), who set up an illegitimate son of Ptolemy VIII, **Ptolemy XI Auletes** ("flute-player") or **Neos** ("new") **Dionysos.** Though expelled in 58, he bribed the "first triumvirate" to send Gabinus to restore him (55). On his death in 51, he left his throne jointly to his children, **Cleopatra VII** and **Ptolemy XII** (51–47). When Ptolemy expelled his sister, Caesar forced her restoration (48) and, since Ptolemy died during the fighting about Alexandria (48–47), Caesar joined with Cleopatra a younger brother, **Ptolemy XIII** (47–44), whom Cleopatra murdered on Caesar's death (44).

47–30. Cleopatra VII sought to restore the Ptolemaic Empire by winning to her support Caesar and later Antony (41), with whom she sought to establish a Hellenistic monarchy (36). Upon Antony's suicide after Actium (31), she sought to fascinate the young Octavian, but failed and committed suicide rather than adorn his triumph (30). This brought to an end the last of the Hellenistic monarchies.

E. Rome, The Republic, to 31 B.C.

(From p. 94)

1. *The Punic and Macedonian Wars, 282–132 B.C.*

During the 3rd and 2nd centuries B.C. Rome's internal history was marked by the consolidation of the rule of the patricio-plebeian aristocracy. The extension of Rome's external relations and the consequent complexity of her internal problems raised questions impossible of settlement in the unwieldy and uninformed *comitia,* which came more and more to surrender the initiative in government to the senate, composed as it was of ex-magistrates, urban, military, and provincial, who had the necessary background and experience. They, in their turn, had come to regard government and office as a prerogative of themselves and their children. This distinction was furthered by the increased opportunities for wealth opened to the ruling group through conquest and provincial government. Since custom, confirmed by a *lex Claudia* of 218, forced senators to invest chiefly in land, they built up large estates, partly by renting public land, which through long tenure they came to regard as their own, and partly by acquiring the holdings of poorer farmers. The poorer farmers, in turn, subjected to the devastations of the Hannibalic Wars, and to the demands of long-term military service abroad, found it difficult to exist, and tended either to emigrate, remain in the army, or congregate as an idle mob in Rome. The political, social, and economic problems thus raised finally caused the ruin of the senatorial republic by the Gracchan troubles.

The republic saw notable achievements in **engineering.** These were based on abundant materials, superb organization, and cheap labor (freemen and legionaires as well as slaves were used). In road building no attention was paid to topography; the straight Roman roads, contrary to legend, were paved only through and along the approaches to cities. Aqueducts, which, from the 4th century B.C., supplied Rome with water, were continually enlarged and improved (e.g., the high-level aqueduct Marcia was added, 144 B.C.). Other techniques developed include the use of the arch (in vaulting and aqueducts), improvements in mine drainage and extraction of metals from ores, and the use of timber piles and hydraulic cement (*pozzulano*) for building foundations.

Rome's position in Italy became increasingly strong during these centuries. In consequence, the senatorial class began to act with increasing arbitrariness toward Rome's Italian allies and to impose on them the burdens of conquest while reserving the rewards for themselves or using them as sops to the Roman citizens. The citizens, who found that citizenship paid in privilege, in some share in the public land, in free entertainment at Rome, eventually in a government-controlled food supply, and probably in the indirect benefits of bribery and corruption, became unwilling to extend the franchise. The discontent of the Italians found ultimate expression in the Social War, which won for them Roman citizenship.

In the Mediterranean, Rome, without really

so desiring, was forced to extend her sway, *imperium,* more and more widely. The senate, like such landed aristocracies as Sparta, was not imperialistic. Nor, on the whole, was the *populus.* But the fear of attack from strong powers led Rome to attack such as might threaten her, and experiments in allowing her rivals a feeble and divided independence (*diuide et impera,* divide and rule) proved unsatisfactory. Either her creations quarreled among themselves and forced her to intervene, or they became the willing or unwilling prey of stronger powers. Hence Rome was forced into annexation. But conquest led ultimately to the corruption of both senate and people, to the creation of a financial group, the *equites,* interested in imperialism, and to opportunities for self-aggrandizement on the part of generals and governors. In consequence, the discontented peoples of Asia supported Mithridates, the equestrian class became a possible rival to the senate, and the way was opened for the domination of the state by military commanders.

282–272. WAR WITH PYRRHUS arose from an attack by the Tarentines on Thurii and their destruction of a Roman fleet which entered the harbor in violation of a treaty forbidding Roman warships from sailing east of the western promontory of the Gulf of Tarentum. Tarentum called in **Pyrrhus of Epirus** *(p. 98).* In 280, with an army of 25,000 men and 20 elephants, he won a hard-fought victory over the Romans at **Heraclea.** Though the Bruttians, Lucanians, and Samnites then joined Pyrrhus, the senate, instigated by Ap. Claudius, the blind ex-censor, rejected the peace offers of Pyrrhus' ambassador Cineas. In 279 Pyrrhus won his second victory at **Ausculum,** but with losses so great that he exclaimed, "Another such victory and we are lost" (a "Pyrrhic victory"). Pyrrhus then crossed to Sicily. Rome rejected peace with Pyrrhus and made one with his enemy, Carthage. Pyrrhus returned to Italy after two years but was

defeated at Beneventum in 275 and returned to Greece. His general, Milo, then surrendered Tarentum to the Romans (272), who destroyed its military resources, but left it its own municipal administration. Rome rounded out her subjugation of Italy by the recapture in 270 of Rhegium from the Mamertines and the reduction of the Bruttians, Lucanians, Calabrians, and Samnites.

264–241. The FIRST PUNIC WAR arose from the fact that certain of the Campanian mercenaries, or Mamertines, who were holding Messana against Hiero II of Syracuse appealed to Rome while others appealed to Carthage. The Roman assembly, though the senate hesitated, sent a fleet and army which found the Carthaginians already in possession. The Romans drove them out and were in turn besieged by the Carthaginians. In 264 the consul Ap. Claudius Pulcher relieved them, but failed to take Syracuse. During the following year two Roman armies invaded Sicily and Hiero shifted to a Roman alliance.

262. The Romans defeated the Carthaginian general Hanno and took Agrigentum (Acragas).

260. After losing the consul Cn. Cornelius Scipio with 17 ships off the Lipara Islands, the Romans under C. Duilius won the **naval victory of Mylae,** west of Messana.

257. The Romans sent 330 ships under the consuls M. Atilius Regulus and L. Manlius Vulso to carry troops from Sicily and effect a landing in Africa. This fleet defeated the Carthaginians off the south coast of Sicily at **Ecnomus** (256) and landed just east of Carthage. Regulus, left with half the troops, offered such stringent terms that Carthage continued her resistance under the leadership of the Spartan mercenary Xanthippus.

255. Xanthippus captured Regulus and part of his army. The Romans sent a fleet which took off the remainder, but was lost in a storm, as happened again two years later.

254. Rome seized Panormus and, in 251, de-

feated the new Carthaginian general, **Hasdrubal,** son of Hanno. On the advice, traditionally, of Regulus, who had been sent to negotiate an exchange of prisoners with the Carthaginians, they refused to do so and Regulus returned to die in Carthage.

249. The consul Claudius Pulcher, after throwing the sacred chickens overboard because they refused to give a good omen by eating grain, lost his fleet at **Drepana.** The Romans were unable to dislodge the Carthaginian **Hamilcar Barcas** ("lightning") from the strong promontory of Eryx, whence his ships harried their coasts.

241. At the **Aegates Islands,** off Lilybaeum, the Romans annihilated the Carthaginian fleet. Carthage received peace on condition of the surrender of Sicily and the payment of 3200 talents in ten years. Rome left eastern Sicily to Hiero of Syracuse but undertook to govern the remainder herself as her **first province,** regularly constituted in 227.

241–217. Some time during this period the comitia centuriata suffered a radical reform,

Pyrrhus of Epirus

Claudian Aqueduct near Rome

probably because the centuries had lost their military significance. The centuries of *equites* lost the right of first vote, which was hereafter determined by lot among the centuries of the first class. The number of centuries was increased to harmonize in some way with the

Hannibal

tribal divisions and divided into seniors and juniors. Perhaps there was one century each of seniors (over 46) and juniors from each of the five classes in each of the 35 tribes, i.e. $2 \times 5 \times 35 = 350$, $+ 18$ of knights and 5 of propertyless persons $= 373$. Though the reform passed for democratic, its basis remained one of property and age, since the first class (wealthy) probably had a proportion of centuries (almost one-fifth) in excess of its proportion of population and since the elders, naturally fewer than the younger, had nearly half of the centuries. At the same time (241) the final two tribes were added, making a total of 35. Thereafter new citizens were enrolled in the existing tribes, so that these lost their geographical significance.

238. **Rome seized Sardinia,** rich in minerals, during a revolt of the mercenaries in Carthage. It later (227) formed a province with Corsica.

235. The first recorded closing of the temple of Janus since its foundation by Numa indicated that Rome was at peace with all nations.

229–228. **The first Illyrian War.** Rome sent a fleet of 200 vessels to suppress the pirates of Queen Teuta. The grateful Hellenes admitted the Romans to the Isthmian Games and the Eleusinian Mysteries and thus recognized her as a civilized power. In a second war (219), Rome defeated Teuta's successor, Scerdilaidas.

225–222. Large hordes of **Celts** moved from the Po Valley to Etruria. The Romans surrounded and slew a considerable body at **Telamon** (225) and gradually reduced the Insubres, around Milan. In the **battle of Clastidium** (222) M. Claudius Marcellus slew a Gallic chief in single combat. The Romans founded the fortress colonies of Placentia, Cremona, and Mutina, and extended the Via Flaminia from Spoletum to Ariminum.

218. A *lex Claudia* forbade senators to own a ship of more than 300 *amphorae* (225 bushels), only enough to care for their farm produce; they were thus forced to invest in land rather than in industry or commerce.

218–201. The **SECOND PUNIC WAR** arose from Rome's jealousy of Carthaginian expansion in Spain, where Hamilcar Barcas (236–228) and, after his death, his son-in-law Hasdrubal (228–221) had established themselves. Rome made Carthage promise not to attack Saguntum or Emporiae, Greek foundations south of the Ebro, or to cross that river. After the assassination of Hasdrubal, his 25-year-old successor **Hannibal** destroyed Saguntum in 219, perhaps without the full support of his home government, the conservative element in which was jealous of the power and independence of the Barcids. Carthage, however, refused to disown him.

218. Hannibal executed a daring land march through southern France and by an undeter-

Hannibal's army crossing the Rhone River

mined Alpine pass advanced into the Po Valley. The Roman consul **Publius Cornelius Scipio** reached Marseilles with his fleet too late to stop Hannibal. He therefore sent his brother Cnaeus with most of the fleet to Spain and returned himself to meet Hannibal, who had perhaps 26,000 men and a few elephants, at the **Ticinus,** a branch of the Po. He was defeated, as was his colleague soon after at the **battle of the Trebbia,** another branch of the Po. As the Romans took refuge in Placentia and Cremona, the Gauls rallied to Hannibal.

217. Hannibal crossed the Apennines west of two new Roman armies posted at Ariminum and Arretium. The consul C. Flaminius followed him from the latter place and was led into an ambush and annihilated at **Lake Trasimene.** The Romans, terrified, appointed **Quintus Fabius Maximus** dictator. Hannibal moved east again to the Adriatic and then south, in hopes of a general Italian rising. The cities, however, refused to receive him, and Fabius, without joining battle (hence his title *Cunctator*), harried his army. The Romans were dissatisfied with this policy.

216. The consuls L. Aemilius Paullus (conservative) and C. Terentius Varro (popular) led an army of 86,000 Romans and Italians against Hannibal. Consuls, when together, now commanded on alternate days, and Varro, on his day, unwisely attacked Hannibal at **Cannae,** in Apulia. The Romans, including Paullus, were practically annihilated, though Varro escaped. When, during the same year, a legion was destroyed in Cisalpine Gaul, a rift appeared in the allegiance of Italy to Rome. Capua deserted, along with the Samnites, Lucanians, and other peoples of southern Italy. The Romans checked all public grief, refused Hannibal's terms, and sent out an army under M. Claudius Marcellus. Carthage made alliances with Philip V of Macedon, and Hieronymus, grandson of Hiero of Syracuse, who died in 217. Hannibal wintered at Capua.

215. **Marcellus,** now pro-consul, defeated Hannibal at **Nola** and forced him into Apulia. The government at Carthage gave Hannibal almost no support and he was unable to receive aid from his brother Hasdrubal in Spain.

218-211. Publius Scipio had rejoined his brother Cnaeus in Spain and between them, with varying fortune, they kept Hasdrubal busy and stirred up Syphax, king of western Numidia, against Carthage.

215-205. By using a few troops for the **First Macedonian War,** the Romans prevented the irresolute Philip from helping Hannibal. In 211 they organized a Greek alliance, under the lead of the Aetolians (**treaty of Naupactus)** including even Thracians, Illyrians, and Pergamum, against him. After her Greek allies quit in 206, Rome was forced to make the disadvantageous **peace of Phoenice.**

214-210. Marcellus carried the war into Sicily, where he defeated a Carthaginian army and sacked Leontini. Though Hieronymus had been murdered, the Syracusans renewed their alliance with Carthage (213), but, despite the ingenious defensive machinery devised by Archimedes, **Marcellus reduced Syracuse** in 211. The rest of Sicily quickly fell again under Roman control.

212. Hannibal seized Tarentum, save for the citadel. He compelled the Romans to raise the siege of Capua, defeated two armies, but retired again to Tarentum. Both Scipios were slain in Spain by the Carthaginians, who drove the Romans to the Ebro.

211. Hannibal returned to relieve Capua. The Romans this time refused to abandon the siege, so he marched to within a mile of Rome, but as they did not falter, he again had to retire. **Capua surrendered to Rome** and was deprived of all self-government. As Hannibal seemed unable to weaken Rome or reduce the citadel of Tarentum, his prestige sank and his Italian allies went back to Rome.

210. P. Cornelius Scipio, son of the late general, was sent to Spain with proconsular powers, though only 25 and a mere ex-aedile. In Sicily, the Romans reduced Agrigentum.

209. Scipio captured New Carthage in Spain. Marcellus defeated Hannibal and Fabius reduced Tarentum. In the following year, Hasdrubal evaded Scipio and reached the Po Valley.

207. In the **battle of the Metaurus River** (Sena Gallica), the consul M. Livius Salinator, supported by his colleague G. Claudius Nero, who had made forced marches from the south, where he was holding Hannibal in check, defeated and slew Hasdrubal. Hannibal withdrew to Bruttium.

206. Scipio drove the Carthaginians out of Spain and made a secret treaty with their ally Massinissa, king (in 208) of eastern Numidia. He returned to Italy and was elected consul under age, for 205.

205-178. Spain was divided into two provinces (197), Hither Spain (*Hispania Citerior*) in the Ebro Valley, and Farther Spain (*Hispania Ulterior*) in the south around Gibraltar and the Guadalquivir River. Constant warfare, however, was necessary to subdue the Lusitanians.

204. Scipio took a force to Africa and, with Massinissa's help, defeated the Carthaginians and Syphax (203). Carthage was forced to recall Hannibal, who attempted in vain to negotiate.

202. In the **battle of Zama,** Scipio annihilated the Carthaginian army, though Hannibal escaped.

201. Carthage accepted **Rome's terms:** surrender of Spain and all other Mediterranean islands; transfer of the kingdom of Syphax to Massinissa; payment of 200 talents a year for 50 years; destruction of all except 10 warships; promise not to make war without Rome's permission. Scipio, now entitled *Africanus,* celebrated a splendid triumph. The unfaithful Italian allies were in part forced to cede land, in part deprived of independence. Rome founded many colonies in southern Italy.

200-191. The resubjugation of the Po Valley required considerable effort. Rome founded colonies and built the Via Aemilia as a continuation of the Via Flaminia from Ariminum to Placentia.

The newly acquired **overseas territories** could not be governed either from Rome or, as had been just possible in Sicily, by creating new praetors. This last method was tried in Spain, but it became more economical to retain the governors there for two years so that their *imperia* were "prorogued" for another year. The device of extending an *imperium* without renewing the corresponding magistracy was apparently first employed to keep

M. Claudius Marcellus

Scipio Africanus

the experienced commander Philo in command against Naples. As the number of provinces grew, this custom was regularly applied to the consuls and praetors, who came to expect a profitable year (for governorships were reduced to this) in a province to recoup themselves for the heavy expenses entailed in securing election (bribery) or incident to the tenure of office (games, etc.). A further effect of the transmarine provinces was that it became necessary to maintain a **standing army.** In the 2nd and 1st centuries B.C. the soldier not only could not return to his farm for harvest or the winter—that had long been impossible—but he could not look for a discharge at the end of a year of service, for the government could not afford to send new armies each year across the sea. Though the fiction of annual re-enlistment and the requirement of a property qualification were maintained, the soldiers became in fact professional and served for 20 years or more. They could not then return to farms which would have passed into other hands or

The attack on Carthage, 146 B.C.

Ruins of the Roman baths at Carthage

fallen into decay, and so they had either to be settled in colonies or allowed to congregate in Rome. As they looked to their commander for rewards in war and protection of their interests at home, they shifted their loyalty, and oath (*sacramentum*), from the state to him. It is therefore extraordinary that for nearly a century the corporate class consciousness of the *nobiles* was sufficient to prevent disloyalty to the senatorial government.

200–197. Rome was drawn into the **SECOND MACEDONIAN WAR** by an appeal from Pergamum, Rhodes, and Athens, which were harried by Philip and Antiochus III of Syria. The senate, fearful of Philip's growing power, frightened an unwilling comitia centuriata into declaring war by visions of a renewed invasion of Italy. **T. Quinctius Flamininus,** supported by both the Aetolian and Achaean Leagues, finally (197) defeated Philip at **Cynoscephalae** in Thessaly and forced him to make peace (196) on the following terms: surrender of Greece; payment of 1000 talents in 10 years; reduction of his forces to 5000 men and 5 ships; promise not to declare war without permission of Rome. At the ensuing Isthmian Games, Flamininus proclaimed the **independence of the Greek cities.** Rome sought to balance the Achaean League by curtailing but not destroying the power of King Nabis of Sparta.

192–189. THE SYRIAN WAR. Antiochus III, invited by the Aetolians, invaded Greece, but the consul, M. Acilius Glabrio, landed in Epirus, moved into Thessaly and, with M. Porcius Cato, repeated the maneuver of Xerxes at Thermopylae to rout Antiochus (191).

190. The Roman fleet, helped by the Rhodians, won two victories. The Roman army, under **L. Cornelius Scipio** (later *Asiaticus*) and his brother Scipio Africanus, crossed the Hellespont and defeated Antiochus in the **battle of Magnesia,** near Smyrna. Antiochus was obliged to make peace on the following terms: surrender of all European and Asiatic possessions as far as the Taurus Mountains; payment of 15,000 talents in 12 years; surrender of Hannibal, who had fled from his enemies at Carthage (195). Though Hannibal escaped, he finally poisoned himself (183) at the court of Prusias I of Bithynia, who was about to betray him. Rome divided the Anatolian territory of Antiochus between Pergamum and Rhodes and aided Eumenes II of Pergamum against the Galatians (189). In Greece, Rome subjected the Aetolians, but left the other cities free. Philip was not rewarded as he had hoped.

171–167. The **THIRD MACEDONIAN WAR** was waged against Rome by Perseus, the successor of Philip V. After several unsuccessful campaigns, the Romans sent L. Aemilius Paullus.

168. Battle of Pydna. Paullus utterly defeated Perseus and brought him back in his triumphal procession. So much booty accrued from his victory that Roman citizens were thereafter relieved of direct taxation, the *tributum.* Mace-

donia was broken up into four wholly distinct confederacies. Illyria was reduced to three tributary confederacies, and Epirus was devastated. From the Achaean cities 1000 of the chief citizens were taken as hostages and kept in Italy for 16 years. Rome likewise dictated to Eumenes of Pergamum, to Rhodes, and to Antiochus IV, who was prevented by the ambassador C. Popilius Laenas from making war on the Ptolemies of Egypt.

153. On account of an uprising in Spain, the consuls entered office on Jan. 1 instead of Mar. 15. Thus Jan. 1 became established as the beginning of the civil year.

151. A law forbidding re-election to the consulship superseded an earlier one of 342 which had imposed a 10-year interval between two tenures. It lasted, with some exceptions, until Sulla revived the older law. Possibly the same law raised the minimum ages for the tenure of all magistracies from those established by a *lex annalis* of the tribune Villius (180) to those of Cicero's time: quaestorship after the 30th year, aedileship after the 36th, praetorship after the 39th, and consulship after the 42nd.

149. The tribune L. Calpurnius Piso enacted a *lex Calpurnia* which set up a permanent commission to hear the suits of provincials to recover from governors money unjustly collected (*quaestio de rebus repetundis*). This commission differed from previous specially created boards of investigation (*quaestiones*) or panels of special judges (*reciperatores* or *iudices*) in being made always available (*perpetua*) without special legislation. Like its predecessors, the membership for different cases was drawn by lot from a panel of senators and the board met under the presidency of a praetor. The new court soon became an instrument whereby the senate could discipline governors. Decisions were motivated not by justice but by class selfishness. It is probable that further courts of this type were established before the revision of the system of Sulla.

149-146. The **THIRD PUNIC WAR** arose from alarm among conservative Romans over Carthage's revival, typified in the phrase with which Cato expressed his opinion on any question which was discussed in the senate: *ceterum censeo Carthaginem esse delendam* ("but I declare that Carthage must be destroyed"). The occasion was an attack by Carthage (150) on Rome's ally, the now aged Massinissa. When a Roman army landed in Africa, the Carthaginians offered submission, but refused to vacate the city. With almost no resources they withstood a siege until **Scipio Aemilianus** captured and **destroyed Carthage** (146). The Romans organized a small area around Carthage as the province of Africa, but left the rest to the sons of Massinissa (d. 149).

149-148. THE FOURTH MACEDONIAN WAR. A pretended son of Perseus, Andriscus, who called himself Philip, provoked the war, but was defeated by Q. Caecilius Metellus. In 148 Macedonia became a Roman province.

146. When the 300 surviving hostages returned to Achaea, the **Achaeans made war on Sparta.** Their leaders, Critolaus and Diaeus, were defeated by Metellus and L. Mummius. The latter took Corinth, sent its art treasures to Rome, sold its inhabitants into slavery, and burned the city (at the order of the Roman senate). The territory of Corinth passed in part to Sicyon, in part became Roman public land. The remaining Greek cities retained a certain measure of autonomy under the governor of Macedonia, though they paid tribute. Not until later (127) did they become organized as the Province of Achaea.

143-133. Continuous unrest in Spain grew into a **war in Lusitania,** led by Viriathus (assassinated 139, thanks to Roman bribery), and in northern Spain, where the city of Numantia took the lead. Numantia fell in 133 and all Spain, except the northwestern part, passed under Roman domination.

135-132. The **First Servile War** broke out when the ill-treated slaves of the large Sicilian estates revolted under the Syrian Eunus, who called himself King Antiochus. Eunus held Henna and Tauromenium against Roman armies, but was finally captured and his supporters brutally executed.

Rome now possessed **eight provinces:** Sicilia (241), Sardinia (238) with Corsica (c. 230?), Hispania Citerior (205), Hispania Ulterior (205), Gallia Cisalpina (191?), Illyricum (168), Africa (146), Macedonia and Achaea (146). The first four were initially governed by praetors and then, as these became useful at Rome for the new standing courts and as the system of proroguing *imperia* became regular, they were governed by pro-praetors (in the less important or "praetorian" provinces) or pro-consuls (in the more important or "consular"). After the middle of the 2nd century, consuls and praetors less frequently took command of a province or army while in office, though this was probably never forbidden by law. Wars were conducted either by the governors or by commanders specially endowed with an *imperium* and ranking usually as pro-consuls, even though they had not held the consulship.

Provinces were generally organized by their conqueror with the aid of a commission of ten senators sent out by Rome. The charter of organization was called a *lex data,* as it was authorized in advance by the comitia but not brought before it (*rogata*). Usually the senate rather than the comitia confirmed such arrangements. The Romans tended to leave undisturbed existing arrangements where they could; e.g. the charter of Sicily incorporated

Corinth, Roman agora with Acrocorinthus

the usages of Hiero of Syracuse, the *lex Hieronica.* Moreover, organized cities were left to themselves for purposes of local government. The Roman governor was chiefly concerned with warfare and general police duties, with settlement of disputes between cities, of important native trials, of all cases involving Roman citizens, and with the public land and tax-collections. Since, however, Rome had no elaborate administrative organization, the actual management of such lands (when not distributed to Roman citizens) and the collection of taxes were auctioned off at Rome (but not the taxes of Sicily), as were contracts for public works, every fifth year by the censors to companies of private capitalists (*publicani*), whose members came to be called *equites* because they had the census requisite for membership in the centuries of knights. (The actual cavalry, composed usually of sons of senators and distinguished by the grant from the state of a horse, the *equus publicus,* had been abolished by Scipio Aemilianus at the siege of Numantia). The evils of the publican system lay not so much in extortionate collections, since the rates were laid down in the contract, as in the fact that on the one hand, a bad year might endanger the revenues, except in Sicily, and lead to undue hardship in the collection, and that on the other the municipalities, who were responsible to the publicani for the payments, might fall into arrears and have to borrow, which they did from the same publicani (acting

Terence

as bankers, *negotiatores*) at very high rates. Once behindhand, they found it hard to get out of debt. The rates on such loans were in time laid down by law, but the governor, who

was often a silent partner in the company (a senator could openly invest only in land), would connive at illegal practices, especially since for a time after the Gracchi, and again after 70 B.C. he would be likely to be called to account for his own administration before a court composed of equites.

Roman literature began with the production in 241 of a translation of a Greek play by **Livius Andronicus,** who had been captured at Tarentum in 272. The most important early writers, all strongly under Greek influence, were: for verse, **Naevius** (269–199), who wrote plays and an epic on the First Punic War (*Bellum Punicum*); **Plautus** (254–184), writer of comedies; **Ennius,** who dabbled in many fields and produced in quantitative (Greek) dactylic hexameters (instead of the old, native, accentual "Saturnians") an epic on all Roman history, the *Annales;* **Pacuvius** (220–130), a tragedian; **Caecilius** (d. 166) and **Terence** (190–159), authors of comedy; and **Lucilius** (180–103), the "inventor" of satire; for prose, a number of historians who wrote in Greek, like **Fabius Pictor** (c. 200), on the Second Punic War, and **Polybius; Cato** (234–149), "founder" of Latin prose with his *Origines* (Italian history) and his work on agriculture. Despite the conservative opposition Greek rhetoric and philosophy were studied by the liberals who gathered about Scipio Aemilianus, whose "Scipionic circle" included Polybius, Terence, Laelius, and the Stoic Panaetius of Rhodes.

2. *Domestic Strife and Eastern Conquest, 133–31* B.C.

133. Ti. Sempronius Gracchus, a noble, was elected tribune on a platform of social reform. Traditionally his motive was to stop the spread of great estates (*latifundia*) at the expense of the small peasants, but since this tendency was restricted to Etruria and Campania, he was more probably motivated by the problem of the proletariat in Rome. He proposed an **agrarian law** (perhaps only a re-enactment of a law of 367) limiting holdings of public land to 500 iugera (312 acres) per person, with an additional 250 for each of two sons. This measure hurt both the great nobles and certain Italian cities. The senate persuaded a tribune, M. Octavius, to veto the measure, but Gracchus violated custom and had the assembly depose Octavius; the bill was then passed. A commission of three (Tiberius Gracchus, his brother Gaius, and his father-in-law Ap. Claudius) was appointed to recover land held in violation of this law and distribute it in inalienable lots of 30 iugera. To obtain funds for the new settlers Gracchus again violated custom, which left provincial affairs to the senate, and proposed that the people accept Attalus' legacy of the kingdom of Pergamum; probably this measure was not passed. Again contrary to custom, Tiberius stood for a second tribunate, on an even more radical program.

The *optimates* (reactionary party of the nobles, contrasted with the democratic *populares*), led by **P. Cornelius Scipio Nasica,** murdered him and 300 of his followers during the election, and afterwards the senate had more of his partisans executed as public enemies.
133-129. Apparently the commission carried out in part the redistribution of the public land. In 129, Scipio Aemilianus, who had married a sister to Tiberius and, espousing a middle course, perhaps favored some concession to the increasing bitterness of the Italians, was found dead with suspicions of murder.
129. After the defeat of the pretender Aristonicus, Pergamum became the **province of Asia.**
125. The senate balked the attempt of the democratic consul **M. Fulvius Flaccus** to extend the franchise to all Italians and sent him to Liguria, where, by helping Marseilles against the Gauls, he began the conquest of southern Gaul. The **revolt of Fregellae,** a town which despaired of peaceful means, was ruthlessly suppressed. In 123 the **Balearic Islands** were conquered and in 121 southern Gaul became the province of **Gallia Narbonensis,** so-called from the newly established colony of Narbo Martius (Narbonne).
123. Gaius Gracchus, the more forceful brother

of Tiberius, became tribune. To the motive of social reform was added that of revenge, and in this and the following year, when he secured a second tribunate, he put through a far more extreme program than Tiberius had envisaged. The precise order and interrelation of his measures is uncertain, but the most important were the following: by a *lex iudiciaria* (probably the surviving *lex Acilia repetundarum*) he transferred membership in the court on extortion (*quaestio de rebus repetundis,* and any others that existed) from senators to equestrians. He also passed a law reorganizing the province of Asia, and particularly changing the tax rate into a tithe on produce, as in Sicily. The collection was to be auctioned off to the publicani, as heretofore. The two measures were probably intended to relieve the provincials, but they only served to separate the equestrians from the senate; the former were now able to avenge themselves on a governor who sought to check their rapacity or divert the profits to his own account.

In behalf of the proletariat Gaius passed three measures: (1) a revival of his brother's **land law;** (2) the foundation of **three commercial colonies** (Capua, Tarentum, and Carthage) to take care of veterans and Oriental freedmen, who comprised the majority of the Roman proletariat and who, it was recognized, would not make good farmers; (3) a **law obliging the government to provide grain at a fair price** (probably not below the average market level) to protect the poor against famine and speculation. The transmarine colonies failed because the proletarians preferred the pleasures of Rome to life in remote provinces. The **state control of the grain supply** became a means whereby demagogues could win popular support (by reducing the price and by increasing the number of eligible beneficiaries). Less important bills mitigated the conditions of military service and reaffirmed the laws against execution without appeal to the people. Finally, Gracchus planned to extend the full franchise to Latin cities and to grant Latin rights to all other Italians. This measure was naturally unwelcome to the Roman *populus,* now fully conscious of the advantages of citizenship. The senate took advantage of Gracchus' absence in Africa to undermine his influence, and he was defeated in the election for his third tribunate. When a riot ensued over the repeal of his colonization bill, the senate invoked a right based on recent custom and of dubious validity, to declare a state of emergency and to call upon the consuls and other magistrates to see to it, even by use of force, that the state suffered no harm (*senatus consultum ultimum: ut consules . . . opera dent ne quid res publica detrimenti capiat*). This was a substitute for the dictatorship, the last effective use of which had been made in 216. In the ensuing struggles, Gaius Gracchus and many of his supporters were slain.

121–111. A series of measures, ending with the *lex agraria* of 111, recognized the failure of the land distributions by discontinuing them, by relieving the lots of rent, and by making them alienable. After various experiments, the courts also were completely restored to the control of the senate.

111–105. The **Jugurthine War** resulted from the usurpation of the African kingdom of Massinissa's descendants by King Micipsa's nephew, **Jugurtha.** The latter murdered one rival, bribed a senatorial commission to support his claim, and captured Cirta (Constantine), capital of the surviving son of the king. The death of some Italians at Cirta led Rome to declare war, but Jugurtha again bought peace. A second murder led to hostilities, waged with varying success by Q. Caecilius Metellus.

107. Gaius Marius, a self-made man and legionary commander (*legatus*) of Metellus, appealed to the Roman people over the head of a hostile senate and secured the consulship, with command in the war. Since the senate refused to grant him an army, he called for volunteers and took men without the requisite property qualification. There resulted a thorough **reform of the military system,** carried through by P. Rutilius Rufus in 105. For the manipular system with its three ranks was substituted a division of the legion (6000 men, gradually sinking to about 4500 during the 1st century) into 10 cohorts, each composed of three maniples; the old military tribunes lost their importance and the command was held by a delegate of the general (*legatus*); the backbone of the legion became the centurions (commanders of the maniples); to each legion was attached an equal number of auxiliary troops, levied from the subject peoples and usually organized in their own fashion; about 300 professional cavalry replaced the old noble *equites,* abolished by Scipio Aemilianus; from the time of Scipio the general had also a special bodyguard (called from his headquarters *praetorium*), the *cohors praetoria* or praetorian guard.

107–105. Marius' aristocratic quaestor, **L. Cornelius Sulla,** secured the surrender of Jugurtha by the latter's ally and father-in-law, Bocchus, king of Mauretania. Marius triumphed in 105, Jugurtha died in prison, and his kingdom was divided between Bocchus and a grandson of Massinissa.

105. The **CIMBRI,** a German (or Celtic) people originally located east of the Rhine, who in 113 had moved into the Alpine regions and across the Rhone, ravaged Gaul and defeated two Roman armies at Arausio, on the Rhone.

Marius was elected consul for the second time, and then continuously for four more annual terms (contrary to the law of 151).

The Cimbri, defeated in Spain and again in northern France by native tribes, joined with the Germanic Teutons and other peoples. Most of the Cimbri then moved on Italy, while the Teutons, some Cimbri, and others advanced into southern Gaul to approach Italy from the west.

104. By a *lex Domitia* the pontiffs and augurs were made elective, but by a minority (17) of the 35 tribes, chosen by lot so that the gods

Flight of Gaius Gracchus

Gaius Marius

Tombstone of Aristion

102. Marius, having deflected the invading barbarians from the Little St. Bernhard Pass and having followed them to Aquae Sextae (Aix in Provence), annihilated them there. He then returned to the support of Catulus in northern Italy, which had been invaded by the main body of Cimbri coming over the Brenner Pass.

101. Marius and Catulus defeated the Cimbri at **Vercellae** (Campi Raudii). Marius became the national hero.

100. Marius, consul for the sixth time, but despised by the senate, turned to the demagogues C. Servilius Glaucia (a praetor) and L. Appuleius Saturninus (a tribune) to secure land with which to reward his veterans. A number of extreme bills were passed, including one which defined treason no longer as internal revolt (*perduellio*) but as impairing the "majesty" of the Roman people (*lex Appuleia de maiestate imminuta*—later *laesa*). When Glaucia secured the murder of his rival for the consulship, the senate passed the *senatus consultum ultimum* and Marius was obliged to besiege and kill his former supporters on the Capitoline. Marius then left for a tour of the east.

91. The tribune, **M. Livius Drusus,** son of an opponent of the Gracchi, brought forward several liberal bills: to compromise the problem of the courts by adding 300 equites to the senate; to distribute land; to cheapen the price of grain; and to extend the citizenship to all Italians. The first three measures were passed as one bill, whereupon the senate, in virtue of a recent law against such omnibus bills (*lex Caecilia Didia* of 98), declared them void.

91-88. The **Social War** (i.e. War of the Allies). The disappointed Italians, save for Latins, Etruscans, Umbrians, and some southern cities, flared into open revolt. They formed a republic, **Italia,** with a capital at Corfinium. Though Marius and Gn. Pompeius Strabo succeeded in suppressing it in the north, the consul **L. Julius Caesar** suffered reverses in the south.

90. The danger of the secession of the Etruscans and Umbrians led to the passage by Caesar of a *lex Iulia* by which citizenship was granted to all Italians who had remained faithful.

89. The war in the north was concluded and L. Cornelius Sulla won successes in the south. The two new consuls moved a *lex Plautia Papiria* which extended **citizenship to all Italians** who applied for it within 60 days, but enrolled them in only eight designated tribes, to prevent them from dominating the assemblies. Cities in Cisalpine Gaul received Latin rights by a *lex Pompeia,* though the precise status of the region between the Po and the Alps, the Transpadanes, remained a matter of dispute until 49. This concession brought the war to a close in 88 and showed that the Italians preferred to remain with Rome rather than to be independent. It also frankly recognized that citizenship was no longer a right, since personal participation in the assemblies at Rome was impossible for most Italians and no system of representation was devised, but a privilege which ensured to its possessors the special protection of Rome, favored treatment in the provinces, and a share in the profits of conquest.

88-84. FIRST MITHRIDATIC WAR. Contemporaneously with the Social War, **Mithridates IV Eupator,** ambitious king of Pontus since 120, made war on Rome. He had absorbed Colchis at the east end of the Pontus (Euxine, Black Sea), the kingdom of the Bosporus in the Tauric Chersonese (Crimea), Paphlagonia, and Cappadocia. He then came into conflict with Nicomedes of Bithynia, in northwestern Asia Minor, who was supported by the Romans. Mithridates routed both Nicomedes and the Romans, overran the province of Asia, and is said to have commanded the natives to put to death 80,000 "Romans" (Italian traders?) on a single day. Sulla, consul for 88, joined his army at Nola to start for Asia.

88-82. But **civil war** broke out in Rome. The demagogue **P. Sulpicius Rufus** carried several measures by violence, notably one distributing the new Italian citizens among all the tribes, and another conferring the eastern command on Marius. Sulla marched his troops to Rome, stormed the city, and slew Sulpicius and others. Marius fled to Africa. Sulla put through conservative reforms, which did not last, and went as pro-consul to Asia in 87.

87-84. The demagogic consul **L. Cornelius Cinna** turned to violence against the optimates under the other consul, Gn. Octavius. He was driven from the city, raised an army, and secured the support of Marius, who returned from Africa. They seized Rome, instituted a reign of terror, a **"proscription" of the optimates,** who were either slain or, if they escaped, lost their property. Cinna and Marius became consuls for 86 (Marius' seventh consulship). Marius soon died and his successor, **L. Valerius Flaccus,** went out to command in the east. Cinna tyrannized at Rome until his death in a mutiny in 84.

87-84. In the meantime, Sulla, in Greece, drove the generals of Mithridates, Archelaus and Aristion, back into the Piraeus and Athens respectively. When, in 86, Athens fell, Archelaus retired from the Piraeus by sea to Boeotia, where he was defeated by Sulla at **Chaeronea** and, in 85, at **Orchomenos.**

84. Sulla, supported by a fleet collected in Asia and Syria by **L. Licinius Lucullus,** moved around the Aegean into Asia, where Mithridates made peace on the following terms: evacuation of all his conquests, surrender of 80 warships, and an indemnity of 3000 talents. Sulla then won over the troops of the democratic general G. Fimbria, who had secured command by murdering Flaccus and now committed suicide. Sulla left these two legions to police Asia and to help Lucullus collect an immense fine of 20,000 talents from the Asiatic cities, while he himself returned to Italy.

83-79. Sulla made a cautious advance from Brundisium against the successors of Cinna, in the course of which the army of the consul Lucius Scipio deserted him after the defeat of the other consul, C. Norbanus. After wintering at Capua, Sulla conducted a brilliant campaign against the various opposing forces which culminated in the **battle of the Colline Gate** (Nov., 82), when he repulsed from Rome a large force of Samnites, who had taken advantage of the civil war to revolt. Sulla punished severely the cities that had sided with his opponents, and then had himself appointed dictator for the purpose of restoring the state (*rei publicae constituendae*).

might exercise their influence. This law was repealed by Sulla but revived by Caesar in 63 to secure his election as chief priest (*pontifex maximus*).

103-99. A **Second Servile War** in Sicily, under Tryphon and Athenion, was suppressed with difficulty by the consul, M. Aquillius.

Sulla's dictatorship was only in name a revival of the old institution. It was not an "emergency" office and was not limited in time, so that actually it was a tyranny. Sulla's objective was to restore the old senatorial system. To this end he sought, by a series of laws (*leges Corneliae*), to subordinate to the senate all those powers that had been set up against it: magistrates, governors, knights, and people. The size of the senate was increased from 300 to 600 by the addition of new members, probably equestrians; admission became automatic for those who held the quaestorship, whose numbers had increased to 20. Thus the censors lost the control they had hitherto had over admissions to the senate, though probably Sulla only confirmed what had already become a general practice. But he also deprived the censors of the right to remove unworthy members. The *lex annalis* was revived, with permission for re-election to the consulship after ten years. The number of praetors was increased to eight. Governors were forbidden to take troops outside their province by a law that made such action treason. The number of **standing courts** (*quaestiones perpetuae*) was increased to at least seven: *de rebus repetundis*, *de maiestate*, *de ui* (violence), *de peculatu* (embezzlement), *de ambitu* (corrupt electioneering), *de falsis* (fraud), and *inter sicarios* (assassination). Membership was definitely restricted to senators, thus depriving both magistrates and people of judicial power. The **tribunes' veto** was confined to the protection of individuals (*auxilium*) and they were probably forbidden to bring any measure before the people without previous approval of the senate. Moreover, election to the tribunate disqualified a man for further political office, so that men of ambition would avoid it. The public distribution of grain, an instrument of demagoguery, was perhaps abolished.

Of these reforms, the only one of enduring importance was that of the **judicial system.** Though sentimentally the Laws of the Twelve Tables continued to be regarded as the fountainhead of the Roman law, in actual fact the *leges Corneliae* laid the foundations of Roman criminal law by defining the types of crime (which had naturally increased as Rome grew) and by providing a more expeditious system of court trial than the hearings before the *populus*. The importance of the praetors, who

(except the *urbanus* and *peregrinus*) normally presided over the courts, was thus vastly increased. During this same period, by the *lex Aebutia* (probably c. 150), the civil law was liberated from the restraints of the old, ritualistic, narrow "actions at law" (*legis actiones*) by the recognition of the praetor's *formulae*. The formulae, borrowed by the urban praetor from the peregrine (i.e. praetor for foreigners), were general definitions of civil wrongs not covered by specific laws, for which remedies would be granted. Such formulas were published by the praetor either on special occasions (*edicta repentina*) or in the edict with which he assumed office (*edictum perpetuum*). A large body of such material was naturally passed on from praetor to praetor and became "tralatician" (*edictum tralaticium*). Thus the praetors, until the time of Hadrian, could widen the scope of civil law to meet new needs, and the praetor's edict became the chief authority for civil law.

As soon as his reforms were completed, Sulla voluntarily retired from public life (79) He died in the following year.

83–81. The **SECOND MITHRIDATIC WAR** resulted from a Roman invasion of Cappadocia and Pontus. After victory, peace was renewed on the terms of 84.

80–72. Q. Sertorius, the democratic governor of Hither Spain (83), was expelled by Sullan troops. When the Lusitanians invited him back in 80, he established an independent state modeled on Rome. He soon extended his sway over much of Spain and held the Romans at bay until he was murdered in 72 by a jealous subordinate, M. Perperna. Pompey, who had been sent to Spain in 77, quickly defeated and executed Perperna.

78–77. The democratic consul **M. Aemilius Lepidus** sought to undo Sulla's work. When he was blocked, he raised in Etruria an army of the discontented. He was defeated before Rome by his colleague Q. Lutatius Catulus and the remnant of his army was wiped out in

northern Italy in 77 by the brilliant young Roman commander **Gnaeus Pompeius** (Pompey), son of a general in the Social War and a protégé of Sulla.

74. Cyrene, which had been tentatively bequeathed to Rome in 154 and again in 96, finally became a province.

73–71. Third Servile War. The Thracian gladiator **Spartacus** and other gladiators started a war by seizing Mt. Vesuvius, to which rallied many fugitive slaves. The praetor **M. Licinius Crassus** (b. 112), a favorite of Sulla who had enriched himself by buying the property of the proscribed, defeated Spartacus twice, and Pompey, returning from Spain, finished off the stragglers. For his achievements during this period, Pompey became known as "the Great" (*Magnus*).

70. Crassus and Pompey openly deserted the optimate cause and used their troops to win for themselves the consulship for 70, though both were under the age set in 151. As consuls, they secured the restoration to the tribunate of the privileges of which Sulla had deprived it. Already, in 75, the disqualification of tribunes for higher office had been abolished and, in 72, the censors had recovered the privilege of removing unworthy senators. Thus Sulla's restoration of the senate was largely undone. The prosecution of the corrupt pro-praetor of Sicily, Verres, by Cicero in 70 brought to a head discontent with the senatorial courts and the praetor L. Aurelius Cotta introduced a *lex Aurelia* under which the senators retained only one-third membership on the juries and the other two-thirds were filled from the equites and a group of slightly lower property census, the *tribuni aerarii,* whose origin is uncertain but whose sympathies were equestrian.

68–67. Defeat of the Mediterranean pirates by Q. Caecilius Metellus Pius. There had been a rapid increase of piracy (especially kidnapping for the slave market at Delos) in the eastern Mediterranean after the defeat of Carthage,

M. Aemilius Lepidus

Roman architecture in Cyrene

Cicero, at left, during one of his orations in the Roman Senate

Rhodes, and Syria and during the civil wars in Italy. The centers were Crete and Cilicia and the situation began to interfere seriously with Rome's grain supply. Efforts to suppress the pirates met with little success until Metellus took Crete (68). It was made a province (67) and later joined to Cyrene.

67. The tribune A. Gabinius secured the passage of the *lex Gabinia,* which conferred upon Pompey for three years the command of the Mediterranean and its coasts for 50 miles inland, equal to that of the governors in each province (*imperium aequum*). Thus enabled to mobilize all available resources, Pompey in three months cleared the sea of pirates and pacified Cilicia.

74-64. The **THIRD MITHRIDATIC WAR.** Mithridates, encouraged by Rome's troubles at home, supported his son-in-law, **Tigranes I of Armenia,** in the annexation of Cappadocia and Syria.

74. **Nicomedes III** of Bithynia bequeathed his kingdom to Rome, presumably to protect it against Mithridates, who nevertheless occupied it. The consul for 74, **L. Licinius Lucullus,** gradually drove Mithridates back and occupied Pontus (73). Mithridates fled to the court of Tigranes.

69. Lucullus defeated Tigranes at **Tigranocerta** and started to push on into the mountains of Armenia. His troops, many of them brought out twenty years before by Flaccus, mutinied and forced him to retire to Asia (68). This failure and his efforts to relieve Asia by wholesale reduction of the indebtedness of the publicani, to say nothing of his optimate sympathies, made him unpopular at Rome.

66. The tribune C. Manilius moved a bill (*lex Manilia*), which was supported by the rising orator, **M. Tullius Cicero** (b. 106), that gave Pompey a command over all Asia equal to that of the governors and valid until the conclusion of the war (*imperium aequum infinitum,* i.e. without time limit).

Pompey quickly drove Mithridates to the east end of the Black Sea, after which he captured Tigranes at Artaxata and deprived him of all territories save Armenia, besides imposing a fine of 6000 talents.

65. Pompey pursued Mithridates until the latter fled to the Crimea, where he committed suicide on hearing of the revolt of his son (63).

65-62. **Reorganization of Asia and Syria by Pompey.** He formed four provinces: Bithynia-Pontus (excluding eastern Pontus), which became a client kingdom; Asia, the old province, which was again heavily taxed; Cilicia, including Pamphylia and Isauria; and Syria, the region about Antioch. As client kingdoms he left eastern Pontus, Cappadocia, Galatia (under King Deiotarus), Lycia, and Judaea.

64. Pompey took **Jerusalem,** in order to pacify Judaea. He left in charge the Maccabean high-priest Hyrcanus and a civil adviser, Antipater, from the non-Jewish district of Idumaea.

Pompey's reorganization of Asia had enduring significance. He followed the Roman practice of making cities the responsible agencies of local government and founding new ones wherever advisable. In order to keep the support of the equestrian class, he extended the pernicious publican system throughout the east. The senate was loath to confirm his arrangements or look after his veterans, but he did not turn against the government. Instead, he dismissed his army at Brundisium (61) and entered Rome as a private citizen.

64-63. **Conspiracy of Catiline.** The discontented classes at Rome (debtors, veterans, ruined nobles, those proscribed by Sulla, etc.) found a leader in **L. Sergius Catilina.** He may at first have had the support of Crassus and of Crassus' demagogic agent, **G. Julius Caesar** (b. 102 or 101). Caesar belonged to a poor branch of the patrician *gens Iulia,* but his aunt had been the wife of Marius and his (Caesar's) wife was a daughter of Cinna. Catiline tried to run for the consulship on a radical program

in 66, but could not get his name presented to the comitia centuriata, as he was threatened with prosecution for extortion while pro-praetor in Africa. After a plot to murder the consuls failed (65), he ran again in 64, but was defeated by Cicero. Catiline turned to even more extreme methods (sedition in Rome and levying a force in Etruria). Then, if not before, Crassus and Caesar abandoned him. The plot was detected, and Cicero, in virtue of a *senatus consultum ultimum,* arrested the conspirators. With the senate's approval he had them put to death as *hostes* without appeal, despite the law of Tiberius Gracchus. The forces in Etruria were dispersed. Cicero's famous *Orations against Catiline.*

60. THE FIRST TRIUMVIRATE. Caesar returned from a pro-praetorship in Spain and brought his master Crassus into alliance with Pompey, who had fallen out with the senate because of the unwillingness of the latter to confirm his eastern arrangements. This informal union became known as the first triumvirate.

59. **Caesar, as consul,** put through the program of the trio: distribution of the Campanian land to Pompey's veterans; confirmation of Pompey's eastern settlement; grant to himself (*lex Vatinia*) for the unprecedented period of five years of the province of Cisalpine Gaul, with Illyria. To this was added later Gallia Narbonensis, with the possibility of action throughout Transalpine Gaul. The political union was cemented by the marriage of Caesar's daughter Julia to Pompey.

58-51. **CONQUEST OF GAUL** by Caesar, both to enrich himself and to forge for himself an army and a military reputation to rival Pompey's. He used as an excuse the attempt of the Helvetii to move from Switzerland into Gaul. His plan of campaign was to move down the Rhine, separate the Gauls from the Germans, and then turn back on the Gauls. In 58 he defeated the **Helvetii** at **Bibracte** (Autun) and the German Ariovistus near Vesontio (Besancon). He then reduced the Belgae (57), including the stubborn Nervii, in northwestern Gaul. He defeated the **Veneti** on the southern coast of Brittany and the **Aquitani** in southwestern Gaul (56). After he had repulsed the Germanic Usipetes and Tencteri, Caesar built a wooden bridge over the Rhine near Coblenz to make a two weeks' demonstration in Germany (55). He also tried with little success to invade Britain.

58. To remove opposition at Rome, the triumvirs secured the mission of the irreconcilable **M. Porcius Cato** (the younger) to investigate the affairs of Cyprus, and allowed the violent demagogue and tribune **P. Clodius** to move a bill against Cicero for the execution of Roman citizens without appeal. Cicero voluntarily withdrew to Epirus, the bill was passed, and his property was confiscated. Clodius also made the distribution of grain free to a large number of poor, perhaps 300,000.

57. An optimate tribune, **T. Annius Milo,** secured the recall of Cicero, and organized a following to oppose that of Clodius. The optimates summoned up enough courage to attack Caesar's land bill.

In consequence of the shortage of grain, the senate conferred on Pompey the supervision of the grain supply (*cura annonae*) and an *imperium aequum* over the areas concerned, but without what he really wanted, viz. military force.

56. Worried by the revival of opposition, Caesar, Pompey, and Crassus met at Luca, on the southern boundary of Caesar's province, and laid plans for the future.

55. In pursuance of these plans, Pompey and Crassus became consuls. By a consular *lex Pompeia Licinia,* Caesar's command in Gaul was prolonged for five years. By a tribunician law (*lex Trebonia*), Crassus was given Syria and Pompey both Spains for the same period. Crassus hurried east, but Pompey, contrary to custom, remained near Rome and governed Spain through his *legati.*

54. **INVASION OF BRITAIN.** Caesar was

Portrait bust of Caesar

Vercingetorix surrenders to Caesar

more successful than in 55 and defeated King Cassivellaunus somewhere north of the Thames, perhaps at Wheathampstead near Verulamium (St. Albans). Nevertheless, he withdrew to Gaul without any permanent result save to open Britain somewhat to the penetration of trade and Roman influence. In 53 he made a second demonstration across the Rhine.

54-51. Breakup of the Triumvirate. This began with the death of Julia in 54.

53. Crassus was utterly defeated and slain by the Parthians at Carrhae in Mesopotamia.

52. All Gaul flared into revolt under **Vercingetorix.** Caesar failed to take Gergovia (Clermont in Auvergne) and was himself surrounded while besieging Vercingetorix in Alesia (Alise near Dijon), but finally won a complete victory and captured Vercingetorix. He spent the year 51 ruthlessly suppressing the remaining insurgents.

52. Milo's ruffians killed Clodius in a street fight at Bovillae.

As it had not yet been possible to elect magistrates for this year, the senate passed a *senatus consultum ultimum* and illegally appointed **Pompey sole consul,** i.e. in fact dictator. Milo, tried in a special court under Pompey's presidency, was condemned despite Cicero's faltering defense. Pompey then made the optimate Metellus Scipio, father of his new wife, Crassus' widow, his colleague, thus openly returning to the side of the senate. Afraid, however, of a decisive break with Caesar, he tried, by a series of indirect moves, to jockey him out of office long enough to leave him open for prosecution in the courts. Since prosecutions could not be brought against one in office, Caesar had so arranged his tenure of Gaul (the details are uncertain) that, by being allowed to canvass in absence during 49, he could proceed direct to the consulship in 48.

49. The senate finally passed a *senatus consultum ultimum* which declared Caesar a public enemy unless he should disband his army (Jan. 7). The tribunes favorable to him fled to Ravenna, where he was waiting. During the night of Jan. 10-11, Caesar with one legion crossed the **Rubicon** (*alea iacta est*, "the die is cast"), the brook south of Ravenna on the Adriatic which marked the limit of his province. He thus broke not only Sulla's law on treason, but also an old custom by which a general could bring armed forces into Italy only for a triumph. He justified his action as aimed to protect the sacrosanct tribunes.

49-46. Pompey, fearful of the legions in Gaul, left Italy for Greece, where he might have the resources of the east behind him. Most of the senate went with him. Caesar, after failing to trap Pompey at Brundisium, turned to Spain, where he defeated the latter's commanders at **Ilerda** (Lerida) north of the Ebro. Marseilles surrendered to him on his way back to Italy.

48. Caesar landed in Epirus and defeated Pompey at **Pharsalus.** Pompey fled to Egypt, where he was treacherously slain by order of the minister of the young king, Ptolemy XII.

48-47. When Caesar reached Alexandria in pursuit of Pompey, he was besieged by Ptolemy and the natives during the winter, until he was rescued by an army from Asia. Since Ptolemy perished, Caesar made his sister **Cleopatra** and a younger brother, Ptolemy XIII, joint rulers of Egypt. Cleopatra soon disposed of her brother and set herself to restore the power of the Ptolemies with Roman aid. She charmed Caesar into remaining three months with her and perhaps siring her son Caesarion.

47. Caesar advanced into Syria to meet a son of the great Mithridates, Pharnaces, who had invaded Pontus. On Aug. 2 Caesar defeated him at **Zela** (*ueni, uidi, uici*).

46. On his return to Rome Caesar subdued a mutiny of his devoted Tenth Legion. He then crossed to Africa and defeated the Pompeians, led by Pompey the Great's son Sextus, at **Thapsus** (Apr.). Cato committed suicide at Utica (hence called *Uticensis*). A part of Numidia, whose Pompeian king, Juba, had committed suicide, was added to the province of Africa; the rest was left to the king of eastern Mauretania. After four simultaneous triumphs in Rome (July) Caesar went to Spain, where Sex. Pompey had joined his brother Gnaeus.

45. Caesar utterly routed them at **Munda** (Mar.). He then returned to Rome (Sept.).

Caesar's position was that of an absolute monarch. In 49 he had been dictator for 11 days to hold elections. In 48 he was consul for the second time. After Pharsalus he was given the consulship for a five-year term and was given the dictatorship annually; perhaps also some of the tribunician powers (*tribunicia potestas*), since being a patrician he could not be tribune. In 46 he was consul for the third time with Lepidus. After Thapsus he was made dictator for ten years and *praefectus morum* (supervisor of morals). In 45 he was sole consul. After Munda he was made consul for ten years; in 44, dictator and *praefectus morum* for life; his tribunician power was extended to include *sacrosanctitas*. Thus his position was essentially a revival of the Sullan dictatorship. His plans for the future are not definitely known, but while he certainly planned to continue as monarch, it is doubtful that he planned to take the crown or move the capital to Ilium.

The **senate was increased to 900** by enrolling ex-centurions and provincials, as much to weaken it as to make it representative of the empire. To provide for its maintenance at this size Caesar doubled the number of quaestors and praetors (to 40 and 16 respectively); the quaestors were later reduced. His agrarian and colonization program was like that of all reformers since the Gracchi. The citizenship was considerably extended, beginning in 49 with the confirmation of the Transpadanes' long disputed claim. The *lex Iulia municipalis* may perhaps have been a measure to give to the cities in the west something of the autonomy enjoyed by those in the east. The **calendar was reformed** in the light of Egyptian knowledge on the nearly correct basis of $365\frac{1}{4}$ days per year; this system continued in use in some countries into the 20th century. The number of those receiving free grain was reduced from 320,000 to 150,000. The publican system was somewhat restricted, since Caesar had considerable concern for the provinces and none for the *equites*.

44. ASSASSINATION OF CAESAR. Caesar's greatest weakness was an inability to choose trustworthy subordinates. A conspiracy

Caesar crossing the Rubicon

Caesar preparing to take Marseilles

of such people, together with the high-minded patriots and disgruntled optimates, led by M. Junius Brutus, Decimus Brutus, and G. Cassius Longinus, assassinated him in the senate on the Ides (15th) of March. The famous *Et tu Brute* ("Thou too, Brutus") may have been addressed to Decimus, not Marcus.

The conspirators had no organization ready to take charge. **M. Antonius** (Mark Antony), formerly Caesar's master of horse, got control, in part by appealing to the sympathies of the proletariat by his funeral oration and in part by seizing Caesar's papers and treasure. The conspirators fled, Decimus Brutus to Cisalpine Gaul, Marcus Brutus to Macedonia, and Cassius to Syria, provinces already assigned to them, and over which the senate now gave them commands superior (not equal) to those of other governors (*imperia maiora*), so that they could raise armies against Antony. Antony secured from the people the transfer of Cisalpine Gaul and Macedonia to himself and Syria to his colleague, P. Cornelius Dolabella. In the meantime, Caesar's eighteen-year-old great-nephew, **Gaius Octavius,** whose mother, Atia, was daughter of Caesar's sister, Julia, and who had been named as heir and adopted in the will of Caesar, came to Rome to claim his inheritance. Antony refused to give him the money and prevented the passing of the *lex curiata* necessary to ratify his adoption. Octavius nevertheless called himself **Gaius Julius Caesar Octavianus.** He borrowed money and, illegally, as a private citizen, levied a force among Caesar's veterans in Campania.

43. Antony marched north to dislodge Decimus Brutus from Mutina (Modena). The senate sent the new consuls Hirtius and Pansa to relieve Decimus and joined to them Octavian with the command (*imperium*) of a pro-praetor. In two battles, **Forum Gallorum** and **Mutina,** Antony was forced to retire westward toward Gaul. But the consuls were killed. Octavian, marching to Rome (July), forced the senate to hold special elections in which he and Pedius were elected to replace the dead consuls. He had his adoption duly confirmed. By a *lex Pedia* vengeance was declared on the conspirators who had assassinated Caesar. In the meantime, **Marcus Lepidus,** governor of Transalpine Gaul, had allied with Antony, and Decimus had been slain. Octavian thereupon changed his support from the senate to Antony in a meeting at Bononia (Bologna).

43, Nov. SECOND TRIUMVIRATE. A tribunician *lex Titia* confirmed their arrangements: Antony, Lepidus, and Octavian were appointed a comission of three to establish the state (*triumuiri rei publicae constituendae*), which amounted to a Sullan dictatorship in commission and differentiated this second triumvirate from the first by recognizing it legally. The triumvirs proceeded with a widespread proscription inspired both by political hatred and by the need for money and lands with which to reward their troops. Octavian acquiesced in the **execution of Cicero** by Antony's agents (Dec. 7).

Temple of Caesar (*the three columns at right*) *erected in 42* B.C. *on the Forum*

Mark Antony delivering the funeral oration over the dead body of Caesar

Mark Antony

42. The triumvirs secured the erection of a temple to Caesar in the Forum, where he had been burnt, and his deification. The magistrates were forced to take an oath to support all Caesar's arrangements (*acta*). Antony and Octavian then crossed to Thrace, where they met the combined forces of Cassius and Brutus at **Philippi.** Cassius, defeated by Antony and misled by a false report of Brutus' defeat, committed suicide. Brutus, though actually victorious over Octavian, was finally defeated 20 days later and also killed himself. Antony betook himself to the eastern provinces, where he met Cleopatra at Tarsus in the summer of 41. Either fascinated by her charms or desiring to get control of her resources, he remained with her in Egypt for a year.

41–40. Octavian, who shared the western provinces with Lepidus, had a difficult war against Antony's wife Fulvia and brother Lucius Antonius before finally reducing them at **Perusia** (Perugia) in 40.

40. By a pact made at Brundisium, Antony married Octavian's sister Octavia (since Fulvia had recently died). Octavian took Gaul from Lepidus, who was left only Africa.

39. Sextus Pompey, who had conducted a piratical career since Munda, was now a power to be reckoned with, as he controlled Sicily and his fleet could interrupt Rome's grain supply. His possession of Sicily, Sardinia, Corsica, and the Peloponnese was recognized by the triumvirs in the **pact of Misenum.** Octavian divorced his second wife, Scribonia, and married **Livia,** previously wife of Tib. Claudius Nero.

37. Octavia engineered a **second pact at Tarentum.** Octavian gave troops to Antony for his Parthian War and Antony supplied ships for use against Pompey. The triumvirate was renewed for five years more, though the precise date set for its termination is uncertain.

36. Octavian's fleet, under his general **M. Vipsanius Agrippa,** defeated Pompey, who fled to Miletus, where he died. Lepidus, after landing in Sicily ostensibly to help Octavian, tried to secure the island. When, however, his troops deserted to Octavian, the latter annexed his rival's territory but, because Lepidus himself had become chief pontiff (*pontifex maxi-*

mus) on the death of Caesar, kept him in honorable captivity at Circeii until his death in 13. Octavian spent the following years consolidating Roman power in the Alps and Illyria.

36. Antony suffered a severe defeat from the Parthians in 36, but managed to retreat to Armenia. He openly married Cleopatra (though already married to Octavia).

34. At Alexandria he established her as a Hellenistic monarch and distributed Roman provinces to her children as subordinate rulers. How far he intended to be her consort cannot be determined, but Octavian made the most of such a probability.

32. When Antony prepared to attack Octavian, the latter had the support of the west, which was both terrified by fear of an oriental domination under Cleopatra and angry at Antony's high-handed disposition of Roman territory. After the consuls, friends of Antony, fled to him, Octavian had the *imperium* of Antony under the triumvirate annulled by the *comitia*. He published a will purporting to be Antony's in which the Roman possessions in the east were bequeathed to Cleopatra. Italy, and perhaps all the western provinces, took a military oath (*coniuratio Italiae*) to support Octavian. In virtue of this, since he no longer had any legal *imperium* himself if the triumvirate was at an end, he levied troops, outwardly to meet Cleopatra. Antony formally divorced Octavia.

31, Sept. 2. BATTLE OF ACTIUM. The rival fleets met outside the bay. The course of the battle is uncertain, but Cleopatra fled to Egypt, followed by Antony, whose army then surrendered to Octavian. In the following year,

30. Antony, on hearing a false report of Cleopatra's suicide, killed himself. Upon Octavian's arrival at Alexandria, Cleopatra tried to win him as she had his predecessors. When she failed, she committed suicide (the story of the asp is perhaps false) lest she have to grace his triumph. Egypt passed finally into Rome's possession.

29. Octavian celebrated three triumphs and by closing the temple of Janus, something recorded only twice before (by Numa and in 235), signalized the restoration of peace throughout the Roman world.

If the crossing of the Rubicon marked the final fall of the republic, the battle of Actium signalized the final triumph of the empire. The last century of the republic was characterized by the collapse of popular government because of the wide extension of citizenship, the considerable adulteration of the citizen body at Rome by the introduction of un-Romanized Orientals, chiefly through the manumission of slaves, the growth in Rome of an unemployed proletariat, the rise of demagogues, and the complexity of the problems of government. The increasingly corrupt senate had lost control of the assemblies, the armies, and the generals. The financiers, as well as the governors, saw in the provinces only a field for exploitation. Italy had been exhausted by civil war, proscriptions (which especially reduced the upper classes), recruitment, and land confiscations.

The last century of the republic witnessed a vigorous **literary activity** at Rome. Hellenism, thoroughly absorbed into Roman education, formed a constituent element in thought rather than something imposed from without. At the same time the native talent of the Romans adapted Hellenism to their own particular needs. **Lyric poetry** found expression in **Catullus** (87–54) from Verona, who, besides his imitations of the Alexandrine poets, produced strongly personal and intense lyrics on his hates and loves. The Epicurean **Lucretius** (99–55), wrote his epic "On the Nature of Things" (*de Rerum Natura*) to expound a materialistic atomism. **Caesar's** (102–44) *Commentaries* on the Gallic Wars, continued by his officers for the other campaigns, are, despite their apologetic purpose, admirably clear and impartial. Minor writings which have survived are the historical monographs on Catiline and the Jugurthine War by **Sallust** (86–35) and the *Lives* by **Nepos** (100–29). Outstanding among antiquarians was **Varro** (116–27), while the **Scaevolae,** father and son, in the Sullan period, were outstanding students of jurisprudence. But the figure who gave his name to the age was **Cicero** (106–43). In spite of his active public life, he not only published his forensic and judicial speeches but wrote extensively on philosophy, rhetoric, and politics. He passed on to the Middle Ages much of value from Greek thought, especially from Plato, the Stoics, and the New (Skeptic) Academy. But he added thereto a Roman color and much of his own thought and experience. Finally, his correspondence, published after his death, gives a deep insight into both the writer and his times.

Roman art began during this century to emerge with a definite character. Though buildings still preserved the heavy lines and ornament of the Etruscans, they acquired majesty and splendor under direct Greek influence. Portrait sculpture, though executed by Greeks, portrayed the individual to a degree unknown in idealizing Hellenic art.

Livia

F. The Roman Empire, to 527 A.D.

1. *The Early Empire, 31* B.C.–*192* A.D.

[*For a complete list of the Roman emperors see Appendix I.*]

27 B.C.–14 A.D. IMPERATOR CAESAR OCTAVIANUS (b. Sept. 23, 63), later called **Augustus,** established his government in 27 (Jan. 23), with some modifications later, especially after a serious illness in 23. He proclaimed that he would "restore the republic," i.e. resign his extraordinary powers and put the senate and Roman people again at the head of the state. He held the consulship annually until 23, but only twice thereafter for a short part of the year. He also received, and retained after 23, a proconsular command superior to those of other senatorial pro-consuls and unlimited in time, though actually renewed at intervals (*imperium proconsulare maius infinitum*). Although he received a special dispensation to retain his *imperium* within the *pomoerium*, it is uncertain to what extent he could actually exercise it over Rome or even Italy, the sphere of the consuls. However, in virtue of the *imperium,* he controlled all the armed forces of the state and appointed as legionary commanders his own senatorial delegates (*legati*). He also divided the provinces between the emperor and the senate. Augustus himself took charge of all provinces in which the presence of troops was required and appointed to govern them other senatorial delegates, called in this case *legati pro praetore.* The senate sent pro-consuls to the pacified provinces where troops were no longer needed. Thus Augustus hoped to prevent that rivalry of independent commanders that had brought about the downfall of the republic. He also sought to assure better government in the provinces by the payment of salaries to all governors, senatorial and imperial. Two major districts received special treatment. The command of the legions on the Rhine was given to a special legate, independent of the imperial government of the Gallic provinces, and only later did this command develop into two territorial provinces. Egypt was administered by Augustus as a private estate under an equestrian praefect (*praefectus Aegypti*) appointed by himself, who directed the elaborate machinery inherited from the Pharaohs and Ptolemies for the benefit of the new imperial treasury (*fiscus*), which was distinct from the old senatorial treasury (*aerarium Saturni*). Smaller districts were governed, not by senatorial *legati,* but by equestrian procurators or praefects. Imperial governors of all sorts tended to have longer terms than the senatorial and thus to perform their task better. Since, however, the imperial *legati,* in both provinces and the army, were drawn from the senate and usually held pro-consulships later, no sharp distinction was drawn between the republican and imperial administration in the upper ranks.

A distinct **imperial civil service** did, however, grow up among the equestrians, partly in the provinces where, besides the minor governorships above mentioned, they held financial posts as stewards (*procuratores*) of the emperor or of his treasury (*fiscus*) and partly in various administrative posts in Rome and Italy, of which the chief were those with which Augustus supplemented the inadequate republican administration of the city of Rome. The most important officer was a consular senator, the *praefectus urbi,* who had general supervision of the city with three "urban cohorts" of soldiers for police. This office, however, may have become permanent only under Tiberius. The other three major officials were equestrian. A *praefectus annonae* had charge of the grain supply for Rome. A *praefectus uigilum* had seven cohorts of freedmen as firemen, one for every two of the 14 regions into which Augustus divided the city. And a *praefectus praetorio* had charge of the nine cohorts of the imperial or "praetorian" guard (praetor-general), which Augustus kept scattered through Italy, but which Sejanus later concentrated in a camp at Rome. Because of the importance of this post, later emperors frequently divided it between two incumbents.

In 23 B.C. Augustus secured the consolidation and extension of certain tribunician privileges which had been granted to him because, as a patrician, he could not be a tribune. The value of this tribunician power (*tribunicia potestas*) was in part its traditionally popular appeal and in part the privileges of sacrosanctity, *auxulium*, veto, direct jurisdiction in Rome, consultation of the senate, and, most important, the initiation of legislation. Augustus, during his reign, initiated a series of far-reaching laws (*leges Iuliae*) in an attempt to reform the criminal law, regulate social classes, and revive morality and family life. With respect to the social order, he purified the senate of Caesarian intruders by a series of "selections" (*lectiones*); he restricted severely the freeing of slaves and the attainment of full citizenship by freedmen; and he bestowed the

Imperator Caesar Octavianus (Augustus)

citizenship on provincials very grudgingly. However, he did increase the recipients of free grain from Caesar's 150,000 to 200,000. The final law in his effort to restore morality was the consular *lex Papia Poppaea* of 9 A.D., which supplemented his own *lex Iulia de maritandis ordinibus* of 18 B.C. These laws encouraged marriage in the senatorial and equestrian orders by penalizing the unmarried and offering privileges to the fathers of children, especially of three (*ius trium liberorum*).

Augustus likewise held a number of minor offices or titles. Though he did not become chief priest (*pontifex maximus*) until after the death of Lepidus in 13, he undertook to revivify the old Roman religion in the face of an influx of exotic eastern cults. He also allowed the worship of his genius, allied often with the goddess Roma, in Italy and the provinces. After his death he, like Caesar, was deified and temples were erected to him as *diuus Augustus;* but the official worship of living emperors

during the early empire is questionable. Besides revising the rolls of senate, knights, and people either as censor or with censorial powers, he controlled admission to the senate by various methods. He alone could grant the wide stripe (*latus clavus*), the sign of a senatorial career, to those who did not inherit it as sons of senators. He appointed to the minor military posts which were a necessary qualification for the republican magistracies. And the privilege of either recommending (*nominatio*) or requiring (*commendatio*) the election of certain candidates for office allowed him to advance those whom he thought most fit. The republican magistracies continued with only minor changes save that the term of the consulship suffered progressive diminution until it averaged two months. When the opening pair of consuls (*consules ordinarii*) left office, there followed a succession of *consules suffecti*. Finally, in virtue either of specific enactments or of his general authority (*auctoritas*), Augustus undertook many improvements throughout the empire: roads, buildings, colonies, etc.

The title by which he is best known, **Augustus,** was bestowed on him by the senate in 27 (Jan. 16) and expressed a semi-religious feeling of gratitude for his achievements. He did not, however, set himself up outwardly as a monarch, and the term which he himself used

The "Gemma Augustea," cameo depicting the glorification of Augustus, with Roma and Tiberius

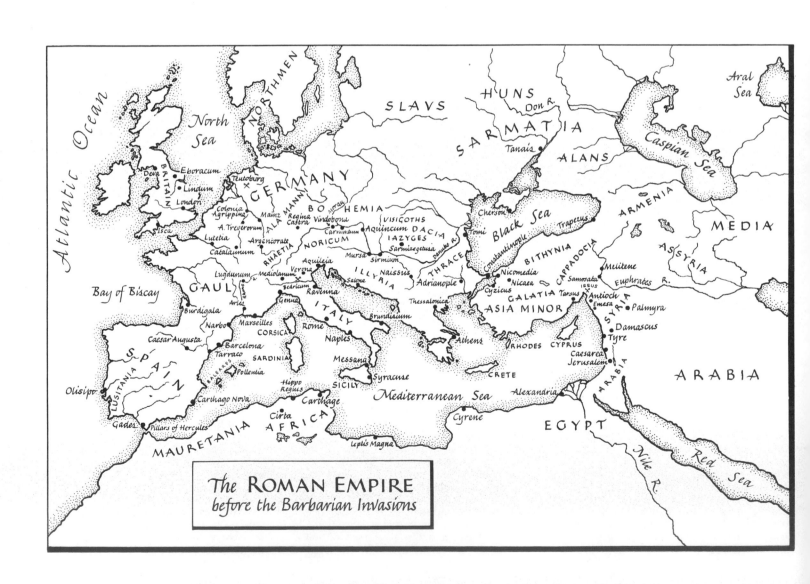

Remains of the Forum of Augustus and the temple of Mars Ultor

informally, though not as an official title, to describe himself was **princeps**, chief among equals.

29. The **closing of the temple of Janus** for the first time since 235 signified the achievement of longed-for peace throughout the empire (cf. year 9, below).

20. By a **treaty with Parthia**, Augustus recovered the standards lost by Crassus and Antony and thereby vindicated Roman honor.

17. A celebration of the *ludi saeculares*, religious ceremonies, concluded the fifth era (*saeculum*) since the founding of Rome.

16–15. The **defeat of Lollius** by the Germans necessitated the presence of Augustus in Gaul and Tiberius in Germany. Rhaetia, Noricum, and Vindelicia were annexed so that the frontier reached the upper Danube.

12–9. **Tiberius** was summoned to Pannonia by a severe revolt. Drusus fought against the Germans until his death in 9.

9. The **altar of Peace** (*ara pacis*), voted by the senate four years before, was dedicated (cf. year 29, above).

9–7. Tiberius carried on the conquest of Germany, but was sent to Armenia in 6. For some reason now unknown, he retired to Rhodes until the death of the sons of Agrippa and Augustus' daughter, Julia, made him the only possible successor to Augustus. He returned to Rome in 2 A.D., on the death of Lucius Caesar at Marseilles, and was adopted in 4 A.D., after the death of Gaius Caesar in Asia.

4. B.C. Probable date of the **birth of Jesus,** following shortly the death of **Herod the Great** (37–4 B.C.), king of Judaea. Herod, who had rebuilt the temple in Jerusalem, was strongly disliked by the principal factions among the Jews: Saducees, Pharisees, Zealots, Essenes. He was succeeded by his sons **Archelaus** as ethnarch of Samaria (4 B.C.–6 A.D.); **Antipas** as tetrarch of Galilee (4 B.C.–39 A.D.); and **Philip** as tetrarch of Batanaea (4 B.C.–34 A.D.). Judaea itself was put under an imperial procurator. After the brief reign of **Herod Agrippa** (41–44 A.D.) and his son **Herod Agrippa II** (50–100), all Palestine was under direct Roman rule. The revolts of the Jews in 66–70 and 132–135 led only to the destruction of Jerusalem and the dispersal of the Jewish people.

The **DEAD SEA SCROLLS.** Much light has been cast recently on the religious and political life of the Jews in the centuries before and after Christ by the discovery of large numbers of scrolls and manuscripts in several localities to the west and north of the Dead Sea. These finds are without precedent in the history of modern archaeology and are of supreme importance for the understanding of primitive Christianity.

1. The **Qumran manuscripts,** the first of which were found in 1947 by a goatherd near **Khirbet Qumran,** site of the communal center of the **Essene sect.** In the sequel (1947–1956) further manuscripts and fragments, some 600 in number, were discovered by bedouin and archaeologists in eleven caves in the same general area, Cave IV containing the largest number. The finds include early texts, in Hebrew or Aramaic, of practically all books of the Old Testament, Apocrypha, commentaries, rules, laws, prayers, hymns, and psalms, dating from the late 3rd century B.C. to 68 A.D., when the community was destroyed by the Romans.

2. The **finds in the Wadi Murabba-at,** 18 km. south of Qumran, first made by bedouin in 1951. These records were left behind by fugitives of the army of **Bar Cocheba** (Bar Kokhba), who led the revolt of the Jews against Roman rule in 132–135. They consist of fragmentary biblical writings and legal documents in Hebrew, Aramaic, and Greek, but contain also a Hebrew papyrus of the 7th century B.C., the earliest yet known.

3. The **finds of Nahal Hever and Se-elim,** near En Geddi, in Israeli territory. The documents found here since 1952, like those of the Murabba-at caves, belong largely to the period of Bar Cocheba and the Jewish revolt.

4. Finds of the Wadi Daliyeh, 14 km. north of ancient Jericho, 1962–1964, consisting largely of papyri fragments dated 375–335 B.C. left in the cave by Samarians fleeing before the army of Alexander the Great in 331 B.C. They

Altar in the Temple of Augustus, Pompeii

Bethlehem, Square and Church of the Nativity

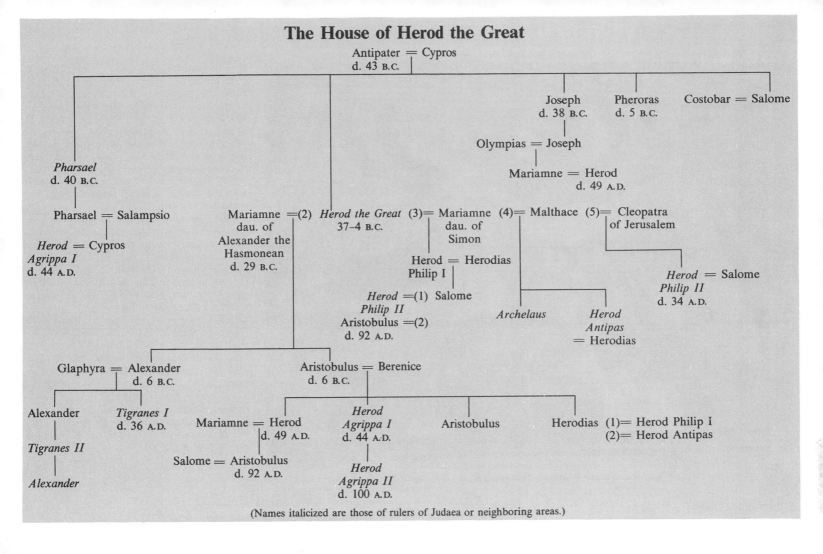

The House of Herod the Great

Antipater = Cypros
d. 43 B.C.

Joseph
d. 38 B.C.

Pheroras
d. 5 B.C.

Costobar = Salome

Olympias = Joseph

Mariamne = Herod
d. 49 A.D.

Pharsael
d. 40 B.C.

Pharsael = Salampsio

Herod = Cypros
Agrippa I
d. 44 A.D.

Mariamne =(2) *Herod the Great* (3)= Mariamne
dau. of   37–4 B.C.   dau. of
Alexander the   Simon
Hasmonean
d. 29 B.C.

(4)= Malthace (5)= Cleopatra
                    of Jerusalem

Herod = Herodias
Philip I

Herod =(1) Salome
Philip II
Aristobulus =(2)
d. 92 A.D.

Archelaus   *Herod*
                Antipas
              = Herodias

Herod = Salome
Philip II
d. 34 A.D.

Glaphyra = Alexander
            d. 6 B.C.

Aristobulus = Berenice
              d. 6 B.C.

Alexander   *Tigranes I*
                d. 36 A.D.

Mariamne = Herod
            d. 49 A.D.

Herod
Agrippa I
d. 44 A.D.

Aristobulus

Herodias (1)= Herod Philip I
         (2)= Herod Antipas

Tigranes II

Salome = Aristobulus
          d. 92 A.D.

Herod
Agrippa II
d. 100 A.D.

Alexander

(Names italicized are those of rulers of Judaea or neighboring areas.)

Dead Sea Scrolls, fragments from the Book of Isaiah

Mosaic floor of the Hamath-Tiberias synagogue, 3rd–4th century

the sacraments of baptism and communion owe much to earlier Jewish institutions and liturgical practices of the Essene type. On the other hand, the early Christian community stood far closer to the Pharisaic societies than to the Essene sectaries in its freedom from priestly domination and in its participation in the ordinary life of the world. Again there is no real parallel between the place of the inspired Righteous Teacher in Essene doctrine and the central role of Jesus as Messiah in Christian teaching

The **Christian Era** begins with the year 1 A.D., which follows directly on the year 1 B.C., since no year is numbered 0. Hereafter dates A.D. (*anno Domini,* "year of our Lord") will appear without designation and dates B.C. (before Christ) will be indicated as such.

4–6. Upon his adoption, Tiberius was sent again to Germany. From there he was recalled to suppress revolts in Pannonia and Dalmatia until 9. He finally established the frontier on the middle Danube. At the same time (6) the creation of the province of Moesia and the reduction of Thrace to a client state advanced the frontier to the lower Danube.

6. Augustus set up a special treasury, the *aerarium militare,* to pay bonuses to retiring legionary veterans. Though land grants to veterans occurred thereafter, this bonus system finally solved the problem of caring for veterans. Augustus reduced the number of legions

Rock fortress of Masada

constitute the earliest extensive group of papyri to have been found in Palestine.

5. Finds at Masada, in the Judaean wilderness, in 1963–1964. This ancient fort was the site of the last stand of the Zealots against Rome (73 A.D.). The finds include valuable fragments of biblical writings.

After years of scholarly controversy paleologists and archaeologists are now generally agreed that the Qumran documents stem from the Essene sect that centered on that site. Secular records show this desert community to have been founded around 130 B.C. and to have existed until 68 A.D. It derived from the Pious (**Hasidim**) and seceded from the main Jewish community in protest against the policies and practices of Jonathan and Simon Maccabee, as did the Pharisees and Saducees. Persecuted by Simon, the Essenes, under their leader "The Righteous Teacher," fled into the wilderness, turned to apocalyptic visions, and looked forward to the establishment of their community as the true Israel, the Elect of God, in the dawning Messianic Age. Apparently many Essenes, like the more militant Zealots, took up arms against the Romans in 66–70 A.D. and were annihilated almost without leaving a trace.

In the light of the documents from the wilderness of Judah, early Judaism now appears far richer and more varied than scholars had previously suspected. The Essenes appear to have been the bearers, and in no small part the creators, of the late **Apocalyptic tradition.** Furthermore, the primitive Christian community is now shown to have stood in the same tradition of Jewish sectarianism. Its institutions, including its early practice of religious communism, its church organization, and even

Triumphal return of Germanicus to Rome

from 70 or more to 27 or 28 at his death. These, with about an equal number of auxiliary troops, gave a total army of some 300,000 men.

9. The legate, **P. Quinctilius Varus,** with three legions, was annihilated by the German Arminius in the **battle of the Teutoburg Forest,** perhaps near Paderborn. This defeat put an end to Augustus' plans for the conquest of Germany to the Elbe and established the Rhine as the future border between Latin and German territory. Augustus discontinued his conquest because of the financial difficulties involved in replacing the lost legions and levying enough additional forces to subdue Germany permanently.

14. AUGUSTUS DIED at Nola on Aug. 19. Legally, his position could not be inherited, since the various powers and offices composing it ceased with his death and could be received by another only from the senate and Roman people. In fact, however, Augustus had throughout his life sought so to indicate a successor as to insure the perpetuation of the principate. In this attempt he tried to combine inheritance, by either blood, marriage, or adoption, with selection of the best available man, through the bestowal of a secondary proconsular *imperium* and the tribunician power. After several possible successors had predeceased him, he selected **Tiberius,** son of his wife Livia by her first husband. Though, at the death of Augustus, Tiberius held the tribunician power and an unusually extensive

imperium, he perhaps sincerely laid before the senate the option of restoring the republic. The senate, however, realized the impossibility of such a step or, according to ancient authorities, found its freedom of action impeded by the hypocrisy of Tiberius. Revolts of the legions in Pannonia and Germany showed the need of a single strong commander to prevent a recurrence of the civil wars of the later republic. Tiberius already occupied too strong a position for anyone else to be chosen. The senate therefore conferred on him the powers and titles of Augustus.

14-37. TIBERIUS Claudius Nero (b. 42 B.C.), emperor. He transferred the elections from the assemblies to the senate. Already the passage of laws in the assemblies had become a formality and though continued until the time of Nerva, the assemblies hereafter had no official share in the government save to confirm the grant of the *imperium* and *tribunicia potestas* to a new emperor. The Roman mob, however, continued by its frequent riots to exert a pressure upon the government out of proportion to its importance.

14-16. The **revolt of the Pannonian legions** was suppressed by Tiberius' son, the younger Drusus. The son of Tiberius' brother Drusus, who is known by his father's title, **Germanicus,** and whom Augustus had forced Tiberius to adopt as a possible successor, suppressed the German mutiny and campaigned in Germany with some successes. He defeated Arminius, whose kingdom then broke up, and recovered

Battle of the Teutoburg Forest, 9 A.D.

the eagles of Varus' legions. He was, however, recalled, probably not because Tiberius begrudged his victories, but because he found them too costly.

The Julian-Claudian House

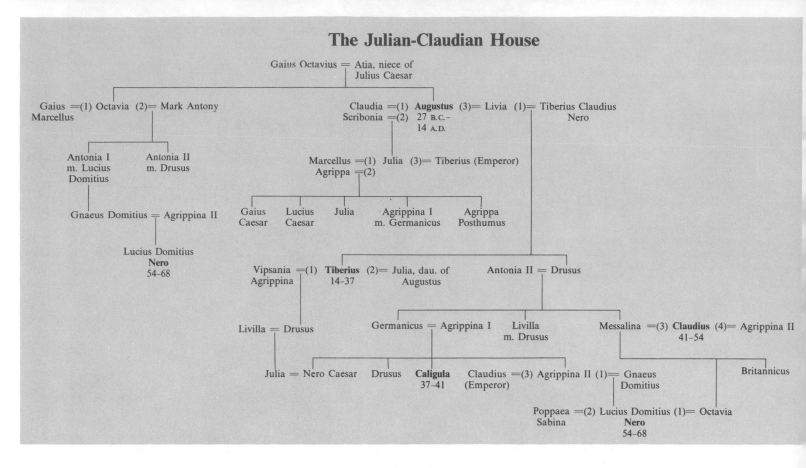

17. On the death of their kings, Cappadocia and Commagene became a province.

17-19. Germanicus, sent to install a king in Armenia, conducted himself in a high-handed manner both in Syria and in Egypt. When, however, he died in Syria the enemies of Tiberius rallied about his wife Agrippina, and charged the legate of Syria, Piso, before the senate with having poisoned him. Piso's consequent suicide gave color to the probably unjust suspicion that Tiberius, or even Livia, had encouraged the supposed poisoning.

19. Maroboduus, who had built up a strong kingdom in Bohemia, was forced by internal dissensions to take refuge with the Romans. Thereafter, the Romans were not seriously threatened on the Rhine or upper Danube until the time of Marcus Aurelius.

21. A revolt broke out in Gaul among the Treveri, led by Julius Florus, and the Aedui, led by Julius Sacrovir. Though soon suppressed by the commander in upper Germany, Gaius Silius, it showed that anti-Roman feeling was still strong in Gaul, even among the chiefs who had received Roman citizenship, as these Julii from Caesar or Augustus.

23-31. Tiberius fell increasingly under the influence of the ambitious and treacherous equestrian praefect of the guard, **Sejanus,** who quartered the praetorian cohorts in one camp outside Rome. He encouraged the gathering of information against those hostile to Tiberius by unscrupulous informers (*delatores,* many of whom were of the nobility) and the prosecution of the accused under the law of treason (*lex de maiestate imminuta*), since actions against the person of the emperor were regarded as harmful to the majesty of the state. When such trials involved senators or important equestrians, they were heard by the senate, which came increasingly to act as a court under the presidency of the emperor or the consuls. Ancient writers have, however, much exaggerated the abuse of this law under Tiberius. In 23, Sejanus probably poisoned Tiberius' son Drusus, in order to intrigue for his own succession.

26. Sejanus persuaded Tiberius to retire from the annoyances of an increasingly hostile Rome. Tiberius eventually settled on **Capreae** (Capri), an island in the Bay of Naples, where the popular imagination, probably wrongly, pictured him as giving way to the most abominable vices. Actually, Tiberius was of rigid morality and of the utmost conscientiousness in governing the empire and in carrying out the policies of Augustus.

29. Livia, accused of attempting to dominate the empire after Augustus' death, died. Sejanus secured the exile of **Agrippina,** wife of Germanicus (she died in 33), and the arrest of his two eldest sons, Nero (d. 31) and a third Drusus (d. 33).

(30). PONTIUS PILATE, procurator of Judaea (26-36), ordered the **crucifixion of Jesus** of Nazareth, called the Christ (the Greek *Christos* is a translation of Messiah, "anointed" in Aramaic), accused of sedition.

31. The plots of Sejanus finally came to the notice of Tiberius, who engineered his arrest and execution. Tiberius remained in rigid seclusion in Capreae.

36. Artabanus, king of Parthia, made peace with Rome. Rome was saved from a serious Parthian threat throughout this period by dynastic quarrels within Parthia and by disputes over the possession of Armenia.

37. Tiberius, dying at Misenum (Mar. 16), indicated as his successors his young grandson, **Tiberius Gemellus,** and the surviving son of Germanicus, **Gaius Caesar** nicknamed *Caligula* ("Little Boot"). Gaius at first favored Tiberius Gemellus, but soon put him to death.

37-41. Gaius CALIGULA (b. 12), emperor. If not insane at his accession, Caligula was at least a megalomaniac and soon became unbalanced. Though the follies ascribed to him may be exaggerated, his conduct was extremely irrational. Behind it may have lain the desire for an absolute monarchy after the pattern of his great-grandfather, Antony. He established many client kings, including Julius Agrippa I, wrongly called Herod Agrippa, a grandson of Herod the Great. He had himself worshiped as a god, though his attempt to erect a statue of himself in the temple of Jerusalem was blocked by the legate of Syria, Petronius.

39. Caligula's **campaign into Germany** was stopped by a conspiracy led by Gaetulicus.

40. A campaign against Britain was also a fiasco.

41, Jan. 24. Caligula was assassinated by conspirators led by Cassius Chaerea.

An attempt by the senate to revive the republic was frustrated when the praetorian guard found in the palace a scholarly, neglected younger brother of Germanicus, Claudius. Being loyal to the family, the guard imposed him upon the senate as emperor.

41-54. Tiberius CLAUDIUS Drusus (b. 10 B.C.), emperor.

He was regarded at Rome as a driveling imbecile, subject to the whims of his wives and freedmen. Of the former he had four. The third, **Messalina** (a great-granddaughter of Antony) used her power to gratify her lusts until her enemies, the freedmen, secured her execution in 48. The last wife was Claudius' niece, Agrippina the Younger. She used her power to insure the succession to Lucius Domitius Ahenobarbus, her son by a former husband. The most prominent of Claudius' freedmen were **Narcissus,** secretary for the imperial correspondence (*ab epistulis*), and **Pallas,** financial secretary (*a rationibus*). Henceforth these secretaryships and others like them, on petitions (*a libellis*), on legal precedents (*a studiis*), etc., which had hitherto been simply posts in the imperial household inherited from the establishments of the republican nobility, became real offices of state, heads of a great bureaucracy. Though they never again conferred such power as they had under Claudius, their administrative importance grew and they were later filled by equestrians. In fact, for all his domestic weaknesses, Claudius took a real and intelligent interest in the administration of the empire. Without departing widely from Augustan precedents, he extended the citizenship and opened the senate to noble Gauls (48). He incorporated the client provinces of Mauretania Tingitana and Mauretania Caesariensis (42), Lycia with Pamphylia (43), and Thrace (46). Though he made Agrippa king of all Judaea in 41, he resumed it as a procuratorial province on Agrippa's death in 44. He restored Macedon and Achaea to the senate in 44.

43. Aulus Plautius invaded Britain. The precise motives for the Roman conquest are unknown. Claudius himself visited the island to receive the surrender of Camulodunum (Colchester in Essex) in the same year. Thereafter the conquest proceeded slowly north to Lindum (Lincoln) and west to Deva (Chester) and

Caractacus before Claudius

Isca Silurum (Caerlon, i.e. *Castra Legionum*) on the Welsh border. The British leader **Caractacus** was finally captured in 51.

47. Claudius revived the censorship and celebrated secular games (*ludi saeculares*).

48. On the execution of Messalina, Claudius was permitted by a special senatorial enactment to marry his niece Agrippina. In 50 he adopted her son, Lucius Domitius Ahenobarbus, who took the name **Nero** and ousted from the succession Claudius' son by Messalina, Britannicus (b. 41 or 42 and inheriting his name from his father's British triumph). In 53

Nero married Claudius' daughter by Messalina, Octavia.

53. Claudius secured a decree of the senate by which jurisdiction was granted to imperial procurators in financial cases. This marked an important stage in the increase of the importance of imperial officials at the expense of senatorial.

54. Claudius died (Oct. 13), reputedly from poison administered in a dish of mushrooms by Agrippina. When Agrippina secured the

recognition by the praetorian guard of **Claudius Nero Caesar** as successor, the senate had to confer on him the imperial powers.

54–68. NERO (b. 37), emperor. He began his rule well under the guidance of the philosopher **Seneca** and the praefect of the guard Burrus. But in spirit he was an actor and wished to play the monarch in the grand manner. He discharged the freedman financial secretary (*a rationibus*) Pallas and poisoned Britannicus in 55. He deserted Octavia, first

Roman coins with, on the obverse side, the heads of the twelve Caesars: Julius Caesar, Augustus, Tiberius, Caligula, Claudius, Nero, Galba, Otho, Vitellius, Vespasian, Titus, Domitian

for the freedwoman Acte and then for Poppaea Sabina, the wife of his friend Otho. Finally he murdered his mother Agrippina in 59. After the death of Burrus in 62, he divorced, exiled, and murdered Octavia, and married Poppaea.

55-63. The general **Corbulo,** who had been successful under Claudius in Germany, was sent to settle the Parthian problem. After spending three years building up the morale of his troops, Corbulo successfully invaded Armenia and took Artaxata (58) and Tigranocerta (59). In 61, however, Nero replaced him with Paetus, who was thoroughly defeated at **Rhandeia** (62). In 63, therefore, Corbulo's solution, peace without conquest, was accepted by Nero, whose vanity was satisfied when the Parthian Tiridates came to Rome in 66 to receive his crown.

56. By a decree of the senate, the tribunes were forbidden to usurp the judicial functions of higher magistrates and the power to fine of the tribunes and aediles was limited. At the same time the senatorial treasury (*aerarium Saturni*) was put under special praetorian prae-

Boudicca

Josephus

fects chosen by the emperor. The senatorial treasury constantly required subventions from the emperor. In 61 there is evidence that the city praefect (*praefectus urbi*), originally a military or police official, had acquired a jurisdiction which was competing with that of the city praetor (*praetor urbanus*). These instances show how even in Rome the imperial officials were gaining power at the expense of the republican.

60. **St. Paul,** before his conversion to Christianity a Jew of Tarsus named Saul belonging to the rigid sect of the Pharisees, was brought to trial before the procurator of Judaea, Felix, and appealed to the emperor.

61. While Suetonius Paulinus, governor of Britain since 59, was engaged in the subjugation of the Druidical center, Mona (Anglesey, an island off northwest Wales), the queen of the Iceni (Norfolk), **Boudicca** (not *Boadicea,* as usually spelled) led a determined revolt and sacked Camulodunum (Colchester), Verulamium (St. Albans), and Londinium (London). Paulinus succeeded in defeating and killing Boudicca.

64. **A great fire destroyed most of Rome.** Nero's "fiddling," if genuine, was singing to the lyre a poem on the burning of Troy. When suspected of having set the fire himself, Nero found convenient culprits in the new and despised sect of the **Christians,** already a considerable group in Rome, with their prophecies of an imminent second advent of Christ and a world-wide conflagration. They were put to death with refined tortures.

65. A widespread conspiracy was organized to put **Gaius Calpurnius Piso** into the principate. Its noble leaders conducted it with such pusillanimity that it was discovered and many senators including Seneca, his nephew Lucan the poet, Faenius Rufus (successor to Burrus as praetorian prefect), and Petronius (the writer and friend of Nero), were executed or forced to commit suicide.

66-70. **REVOLT IN JUDAEA,** resulting from misgovernment by a succession of Roman procurators. When the governor of Syria failed to suppress it, **Vespasian** was sent as special legate with three legions (67). He slowly reduced the country, took prisoner the pro-Roman Jewish historian, **Josephus,** and laid siege to Jerusalem (69). After his proclamation as emperor, Vespasian left his son **Titus** to continue the siege against the Zealot leader, John of Giscala, who had removed his rival Eleazar. Jerusalem fell (7 Sept. 70). Titus celebrated a triumph in 71, which is commemorated on the surviving Arch of Titus at Rome. Some of Judaea was given to Marcus Julius ("Herod") Agrippa II, son of Agrippa I, but most of it became imperial domain. The temple was destroyed, the sanhedrin (Jewish national council) and high-priesthood abolished, the two-drachma tax paid by Jews to the temple was diverted to a special account in the imperial treasury (*fiscus Iudaicus*), and a legion under a senatorial legate superior to the procurator, was quartered in Jerusalem.

67. Nero undertook an artistic tour in Greece, in the course of which he executed Corbulo, and two ex-legates of Germany.

68. On Nero's return to Italy, he heard that **G. Julius Vindex,** legate of Gallia Lugdunensis, had revolted. Though the revolt was put down by the legate of upper Germany, L. Verginius Rufus, who refused to be saluted as emperor (*imperator*) by his troops, the two legions in Hispania Tarraconensis, on the suggestion of Vindex, had already (Mar.) saluted as emperor their elderly legate, **Servius Sulpicius Galba.** When the praetorian guard, under the praefect Nymphidius Sabinus, recognized Galba, the senate declared Nero a public enemy (*hostis*). He committed suicide in a villa outside Rome (*"what an artist I perish"*) and the Julio-Claudian line came to an end.

68-69. **Servius Sulpicius GALBA** (b. 5 or 3 B.C.), emperor. By the recognition of Galba the helpless senate admitted that, in the words of Tacitus, "emperors could be made elsewhere than at Rome." The success of Augustus' compromise depended on the loyalty of the troops to the person to whom the senate might grant the powers of the principate. It had already been made clear that the senate could not resist accepting a candidate of the praetorian guard; now the provincial legions, disabused of their loyalty to the Julio-Claudian house by the unwarlike conduct of Nero, and jealous of the privileges of the praetorians, asserted themselves during this year of the four emperors (Galba, Otho, Vitellius, and Vespasian).

69, Jan. 1. The eight legions on the Rhine refused allegiance to Galba, and on Jan. 3 the four in lower Germany saluted as emperor their legate **Aulus Vitellius** (b. 15). He was also accepted by the four legions of upper Germany under Hordeonius Flaccus. Galba, whom Tacitus called "in the judgment of all capable of ruling if he had not ruled" (*capax imperii nisi imperasset*), had reached Rome where he adopted as his successor the aristocrat Piso Licinianus.

Thereupon, **Marcus Salvius Otho** (b. 32), the dissolute friend of Nero, who had been made legate of Lusitania so that Nero could marry his wife Poppaea and had returned with Galba, secured the support of the praetorians and had Galba and Piso murdered (Jan. 15). The helpless senate then recognized him.

Meanwhile, the troops of Vitellius approached Italy in two divisions under Valens and Caecina. They met in the plain of the Po and defeated the forces of Otho (Apr. 19) in the **first battle of Bedriacum** (near Cremona), whereupon **Otho** committed suicide. The senate immediately recognized Vitellius, who presently reached Rome himself.

In the meantime (July 1) the praefect of Egypt, Tiberius Julius Alexander, proclaimed as emperor, **Vespasian,** legate in Judaea. Mucianus, legate of Syria, lent his support. Antonius Primus, commander of the seventh legion in Pannonia, rallied all the Danubian legions to Vespasian and moved rapidly into northern Italy. There he defeated the forces of Vitellius in the **second battle of Bedriacum** and sacked Cremona (late Oct.). When Antonius approached Rome, Vespasian's brother seized the Capitol, which was burnt in the ensuing struggle. The Vitellians fought bitterly in the city streets, but Vitellius was finally slain (Dec. 20). The senate immediately recognized Vespasian. When Mucianus reached Rome in Jan. (70), he ruled it until Vespasian arrived during the summer.

69–79. Titus Flavius VESPASIANUS (b. 9), emperor and founder of the Flavian dynasty. He was the son of a humble tax collector from the Italian municipality of Reate. Vespasian was confronted with the task not only of restoring the principate but of equating him-

Titus Flavius Vespasianus

self with his aristocratic Roman predecessors. He himself, with his son Titus, held the opening consulship of every year of his reign save

73 and 78. A surviving law (*lex de imperio Vespasiani*) may be part of an inclusive measure whereby all the powers accumulated by preceding emperors were conferred specifically and together on Vespasian. Such events as the restoration of the Capitol (70, dedicated by Domitian in 82), the triumph of Titus (71), the erection of a temple of peace (71–75), the closing of the temple of Janus (71), the destruction of Nero's extensive "Golden House" and parks, on the site of which a vast public amphitheater, the Coliseum (or Colosseum, *amphitheatrum Flavianum*), was begun, served to surround the new dynasty with material glamor. To reorganize the senate, Vespasian felt compelled to revive the censorship with Titus in 73, instead of tacitly assuming the right of enrollment (*adlectio*) exercised by his predecessors. In 74 he granted Latin rights to all of Spain. He reorganized and rigidly controlled the finances.

69–71. The revolt of some Batavian auxiliaries under their native commander, Julius Civilis, won the support of some of the legions of Germany. This inflamed the Gallic Treveri under Julius Classicus and Julius Tutor and the Lingones under Julius Sabinus. Hordeonius Flaccus was slain at Novaesium (Neuss) on the lower Rhine. Petillius Cerealis, with six legions, took advantage of disagreements between Gauls and Batavians to crush the revolt piecemeal. The movement, though ostensibly begun in the interests of Vespasian, had in reality aimed at the establishment of

Spoils from the temple in Jerusalem (marble relief on the arch of Titus at Rome)

an independent Gallic empire, the last instance of dangerous national separatism during the early empire. Thereafter auxiliaries were not employed in the country of their origin and the corps soon came to be composed of recruits of different nationalities. By this time the praetorian guards were alone recruited in Italy; the legions drew from Roman settlers in the provinces or Romanized provincials, to whom citizenship was often granted to secure their enlistment. Thus the army had become less Italian, more provincial in its sympathies. After the revolt, Vespasian disbanded at least four disloyal legions.

70. By putting Cappadocia in charge of the imperial governor of Galatia, by moving the eastern legions from Syria to forts on the upper Euphrates (Satala, Melitene, and Samosata), and by absorbing a number of small native principalities in Asia and Syria, Vespasian consolidated the eastern frontier against Armenia and Parthia and prepared the way for Trajan's expansion.

71. **Titus,** though a senator, was made praetorian praefect, a post hitherto equestrian. He also received both the proconsular command (*imperium*) and the tribunician power (*tribunicia potestas*), whereby Vespasian made it clear that he would follow the hereditary principle of succession.

73-74. Vespasian began the conquest of the territory east of the upper Rhine and south of the Main, the later *agri decumates* (or *decumathes;* the meaning is uncertain). He furthermore reorganized the defenses of the upper and lower Danube.

73. At about this time Vespasian banished Helvidius Priscus, son-in-law of Thrasea and his successor as leader of the Stoic opposition

Vespasianus planning the new Roman Coliseum

to the empire. He also banished the professors of philosophy, perhaps because their doctrines encouraged disloyalty.

77-84. **Conquest of Britain. Cn. Julius Agricola** (40–93) as imperial governor continued the conquest carried on by his predecessors Cerialis (72–74) over the Brigantes around Eboracum (York) and Frontinus (74–77) over the Silures in Wales. In 83 he fought a successful engagement against the Caledonians at **Mt. Graupius** (not *Grampius*), possibly near Aberdeen in Scotland, the farthest point reached by Roman arms. But Domitian recalled him in the following year, due to the fact that troops were needed for the German war. Despite later revolts Romanization progressed rapidly thereafter in Britain.

79-81. **TITUS** Flavius **Vespasianus** (b. 39) emperor, succeeding on the death of his father, Vespasian (June 24). Though popular, Titus was more concerned with playing the prince charming than with the economical administration of the empire. Public opinion forced him to put away the Jewish princess Berenice, already thrice married sister of Agrippa II.

79. An **eruption of Mt. Vesuvius,** on the Bay of Naples, buried the cities **Pompeii** and **Herculaneum.** In 80 a severe fire occurred in Rome. During this year, however, Titus dedicated magnificently the Coliseum and some elaborate public baths (*thermae Titianae*).

81-96. **Titus Flavius DOMITIANUS** (b. 51) succeeded upon the death of his older brother, Titus (Sept. 13).

Naturally of a suspicious, perhaps cruel, temperament, Domitian had apparently borne with ill grace the favor and preference shown to his brother and came to the throne determined to rule without respect for others, especially the senate. Nevertheless, despite the hatred which his reign aroused, he appears to have been an able administrator and general. He legislated against immorality and strictly controlled the governors.

83. Domitian crossed the Rhine at Mainz to **campaign against the Chatti.** His victory allowed him to begin the construction of a series

of forts connected by a road and later by an earth rampart surmounted by a wooden palisade which served to prevent the infiltration of barbarians into Roman territory and as a base for offensive or defensive operations, though it would not have withstood a full-fledged invasion. This system, which later extended along the central Rhine, then from Mainz outside the *agri decumates* to the upper Danube so as to straighten the dangerous reentrant angle of the frontier at that point, and along the upper Danube north of Rhaetia, was known as the *limes.*

84. Through his election as consul for ten years and censor for life, Domitian openly subordinated the republican aspect of the state (senate and magistrates) to the monarchical. By increasing the pay of the troops by one-third (probably in itself a needed reform), he secured their loyalty. And with lavish shows and buildings, he ingratiated himself with the Roman mob. He revived the excessive use of the law of treason with its attendant encouragement of informers. After the abortive **revolt of Saturninus,** legate of upper Germany, in 88, he proceeded bitterly against the opposition; expulsion of the philosophers in 89 was followed in 93 by the execution of Herennius Senecio, Junius Arulenus Rusticus, and Helvidius Priscus. Flavius Clemens, a first cousin of Domitian, was executed in 95 on a charge of atheism (Christianity?), though perhaps the real ground was fear of him as a possible rival. Domitian, besides widening the cult of his deceased father and brother, had himself addressed as "lord and god" (*dominus et deus*), in the tradition of Gaius and perhaps Antony.

85-89. An **invasion of the Dacians** across the Danube into Moesia in 85 was repulsed by Domitian in person. In 89, however, the complete reduction of Dacia was prevented by his defeat at the hands of the Marcomanni and Quadi, who had occupied Bohemia, west of Dacia. Domitian made a somewhat humiliating peace with the Dacian king, **Decebalus,** who retained his independence and defeated, but did not crush, the Marcomanni, Quadi.

Air view of the Coliseum

Temple of Apollo in the ruins of Pompeii, Mt. Vesuvius in the background

and Iazyges (a Sarmatian people) in 92. Thus the situation on the middle and lower Danube remained dangerous.

88. In consequence of the revolt of Saturninus, Domitian ceased the quartering of more than one legion in one camp to prevent any commander from gaining excessive power. The individual legions became permanently fixed in separate camps and no longer highly mobile, as they had been meant to be by Augustus.

96. Assassination of Domitian (Sept. 18) in a palace plot. The senate decreed the removal of his name from all public inscriptions (*damnatio memoriae*) and cancellation of his arrangements (*rescisio actorum*). Thus ended the Flavian house.

Since the conspirators, wisely, had a candidate ready to receive the senate's grant of powers, the armies remained quiet and **Nerva,** an elderly and distinguished senator, acceded without difficulty. This marked the last attempt at self-assertion on the part of the old republican element in the principate. Already the old aristocratic families had become exhausted by persecution and race suicide. Their places had been taken by a new nobility of families elevated from the cities of Italy or the provinces through the imperial (equestrian) organization to senatorial rank. Despite a sentimental attachment to the traditions and forms of the Republic, the new generation admitted that the emperor was master, not, as Augustus had pretended, servant of the senate.

96-98. Marcus Cocceius NERVA (b. 35), emperor. He was forced to recognize that the wishes of the army should be consulted by adopting in the autumn of 97 as his successor the victorious general **Trajan.** Since Nerva and his three successors had no sons of their own, the principle of adoption, triumphing over heredity, secured a succession of capable rulers known as **the five good emperors** (Nerva, Trajan, Hadrian, Antoninus Pius, Marcus Aurelius). Nerva's two important contributions were to shift from the cities to the imperial treasury the cost of the postal service maintained for government dispatches (*cursus*) and to supplement existing private charity by a system of state aid for orphans (*alimenta*) supported by government grants or, under Trajan, by the interest of permanent loans to small farmers. Both reforms are symptomatic of the gradual breakdown of local economy and the municipal system. The last reference to

The first six panels of the column of Traianus

legislation in the assemblies is to an agrarian law (*lex agraria*) in his reign. Nerva died Jan. 25, 98.

98–117. Marcus Ulpius TRAIANUS (b. 53), emperor. At the time he was in command in lower Germany, but was accepted at Rome without difficulty, though he was the first provincial emperor (born near Seville) and though he did not visit Rome until 99. On one Rhine frontier, Trajan continued the boundary palisade (*limes*) begun under Domitian.

101–107. In two **Dacian Wars** (101–102, 105–107), whose precise chronology is uncertain, Trajan first seriously exceeded the limits set to the empire by Augustus. Upon the death of Decebalus, Dacia, north of the Danube, became a Roman province. The war was commemorated by a column, covered with a spiral band of continuous reliefs in the magnificent Forum of Trajan in Rome. Trajan had many fine structures erected throughout the empire.

111–112. Pliny the Younger was sent by Trajan as special legate with proconsular power to reorganize the senatorial province of Bithynia. The appointment of Pliny is symptomatic of a spreading bankruptcy of municipalities, particularly in the Greek east, which necessitated imperial interference. The emperor not only sent special legates to senatorial provinces but appointed special supervisors for cities (*curatores rei publicae*). Extravagance and increased cost of administration, both municipal and imperial, thus started locally the crisis which disrupted the whole empire during the third century. Further indications of financial stringency appear in the enlargement of the alimentary system and in the burning of records of unpaid taxes in the forum. During his governorship, Pliny corresponded with Trajan on many problems, including the treatment of Christians, toward whom Trajan instructed him to be lenient.

Marcus Ulpius Traianus

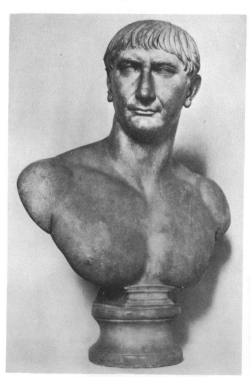

Castel Sant'Angelo, Rome, tomb of Hadrianus

Publius Aelius Hadrianus

113-117. Parthian War. When the Parthian monarch **Chosroes** set up his puppet in Armenia, thus violating the compromise reached under Nero, Trajan declared war on Parthia. In 114, on the death of the Parthian puppet, he annexed Armenia. As he advanced, he formed the provinces of Mesopotamia (115) and Assyria (116) and made the Tigris the eastern boundary of the empire. He was, however, recalled from the Persian Gulf by a widespread **revolt of the Jews** and of the newly conquered areas. Both were suppressed with great severity. In 117 Trajan was repulsed from the desert town of Hatra. He died at Selinus in Cilicia (June 22 or July 9) after having adopted on his deathbed (some suspected his wife Plotina of having invented the adoption) his ward and cousin, **Hadrian,** at the time legate of Syria. Trajan's conquests, though spectacular, were of no permanent value and probably hastened the financial collapse by increasing the military expenses.

117-138. Publius Aelius HADRIANUS (b. 75), emperor. He was recognized as emperor by the senate on Aug. 11. Almost immediately he abandoned the new provinces across the Euphrates. His lack of military ambition may have been responsible for the serious conspiracy, in 118, of four generals of consular rank, whom the senate put to death. Hadrian then took an oath, which had become a test of constitutionalism, not to execute senators without trial by their peers. Under him the appointment of equestrians rather than freedmen to the important posts in the imperial secretariat became regular. He spent most of his reign (121-126, 129-134) traveling through the provinces, where he erected many buildings. He especially favored the Greek cities, notably Athens. In Britain he built (122-127) the elaborate combination of road, ditches, and stone wall from the Tyne to the Solway which consituted a boundary (*limes*) between the Roman province and the unconquered Caledonians. In Numidia he completed the extensive permanent camp of the Third Augustan Legion at Lambaesis.

In the collection of taxes, the companies of *publicani* had given way to individual collectors (*conductores*) under municipal supervision. Like his predecessors, Hadrian lightened or remitted certain taxes. Yet the economic difficulties continued. He had to deal with the problem of deserted farm lands (*agri deserti*), an indication that peasants were finding agriculture unprofitable, and with complaints from tenants (*coloni*) on the imperial estates in Africa. The replacement of slaves by tenants

Roman coin with head of Antoninus Pius

on large estates had begun when the cessation under Augustus of wars of conquest put an end to large supplies of cheap slaves. The oppression of tenants on both private and imperial estates by rising rents, heavier taxation, and forced labor rendered their lot ever more wretched.

131. The **Praetor's Edict** was definitively codified by the jurist Salvius Julianus under Hadrian's orders. Since no praetor could thereafter alter it, the extension of legal procedure by praetorian *formulae* ended. Senatorial decrees became only a confirmation of the imperial speech (*oratio principis*) that initiated them. The tribunician privilege of introducing business had been extended to the first five motions in any meeting so that the emperor presented all important matters. The only source of law was now the **edicts of the emperor.** The emperor hereafter summoned to his advisory council (*concilium*) distinguished jurists, who profoundly influenced the development of law.

132-135. The **Jews of Judaea revolted** upon the founding of a Roman colony (Aelia Capitolina) in Jerusalem and the dedication of a temple to Jupiter Capitolinus on the site of

Marcus Aurelius

Antoninus Pius column (detail), erected by Marcus Aurelius

their temple. Their leaders were the rabbi **Akiba** and the fanatic **Simon Bar Cocheba.** The suppression of the revolt all but depopulated Judaea and thereafter Jews could enter Jerusalem but once a year. This completed the denationalization of the Jews begun by Vespasian. Until 1919 the Jews of the Dispersion (*Diaspora*), scattered among other peoples and generally despised, possessed only a racial and religious unity. The great edition of the *Talmud* was prepared in Babylon in the late 5th century.

138. Upon the death (Jan. 1) of his first choice for successor, **Lucius Ceionius Commodus,** Hadrian adopted (Feb. 25) the competent Titus Aurelius Fulvius Boionius Arrius **Antoninus,** who received the imperial powers and took the name Imperator Titus Aelius Antoninus. He, in his turn, had to adopt the young son of Commodus, Aelius Aurelius Commodus (later Lucius Aurelius Verus) and his own nephew, Marcus Annius Verus, henceforth called Marcus Aurelius Antoninus. Hadrian died on July 10.

138-161. **Titus Aurelius ANTONINUS PIUS** (b. 86), emperor. Warned by Hadrian's unpopularity with the senate, he spent his reign in Rome. For his filial piety in securing the deification of Hadrian from a hostile senate, he received the title *Pius.* His uneventful reign marked the culmination of the happy age of the Antonines.

142-143. **Quintus Lollius Urbicus,** legate of Britain, suppressed a revolt of the Brigantes in Yorkshire and, along the temporary line of forts built by Agricola from the Forth to the Clyde, constructed a turf wall north of Hadrian's. This, however, was soon abandoned.

146. **Marcus Aurelius,** who had married Faustina, daughter of Antoninus, received the imperial powers. Antoninus apparently passed over the younger and incompetent Verus.

155. A brief **war with Vologesus of Parthi**a ended in an inconclusive peace.

161-180. MARCUS AURELIUS Antoninus (b. 121) became emperor on the death o Antoninus (Mar. 7). Loyal to the wishes o Hadrian, he shared the imperial powers in ful equality with **Lucius Aurelius Verus** (b. 130) This constitutes the first sure instance of com plete collegiality in the imperial position, sav for the office of chief pontiff (*pontifex maxi mus*), which remained unshared until Pupienu and Balbinus.

The reign of Marcus represents the **triump**h of Stoicism. Politically, the emperor was re garded as the human counterpart of the guid ing reason of the universe and as obliged t rule for the good of his subjects. In law, th doctrine of the universal brotherhood of man transcending limits of city or station, empha sized the humanizing trend which had lon been operative, especially in legislation or slaves and women. Socially, the municipa and provincial aristocracy, which had appeare in the senate through the imperial service had wholly replaced the old Roman nobilit and worked in complete loyalty with the em peror. Economically, the empire most nearl approximated unification. Italy had yielde her economic supremacy to the increased pros perity of the provinces and was losing it favored political position. It received from th emperor four special judges (created by Ha drian, abolished by Antoninus, revived b Marcus).

162-165. **Verus** was sent by Marcus to com mand in the east against Parthia, adumbratin the later territorial division of the empire Though Verus dissipated at Antioch, his gen erals sacked Artaxata, Seleucia, and Ctesiphon put a Roman puppet on the throne of Arme nia, and made part of Mesopotamia a prov ince.

Ritual Dance, detail of an Etruscan wall painting on a tomb in Tarquinia (p.89)

Etruscan silver plate

*Interior of a villa with house altar
at Herculaneum (p.130)*

Grain mill and bakery in Pompeii (p.130)

166-167. The troops of Verus brought from the east a terrible plague, which seriously depopulated the empire.

166-175. The upper Danube was crossed by hordes of **Marcomanni** from Bohemia, with kindred tribes. Marcus created his young sons, Lucius Aelius Aurelius Commodus and Marcus Annius Verus, Caesars. He himself, with his colleague Verus, set out at once for the north. Verus died in 169. Just when Marcus had settled with the Marcomanni and had set an extremely important precedent by importing (172?) considerable numbers of them to occupy areas in the empire which had been depopulated by the plague, the **Sarmatians** attacked the lower Danube frontier.

175. **Avidius Cassius,** a distinguished general and legate of Syria, revolted, perhaps misled by a false report of Marcus' death. Though his revolt was crushed before Marcus could reach the east, it prevented a final settlement of the Sarmatian war.

177. Marcus' eldest son, **Commodus,** became Imperator, then Augustus, coequal with his father. The younger son had died in 169. Marcus is said to have issued a severe **rescript against the Christians.** In any case, they were subjected to increasingly bitter and far-reaching persecution, probably as fomenters of trouble by their prophecies of evil, and as disloyal to the state because they would not swear oaths to the emperor or offer incense to his statues or serve in the army.

178-180. The Marcomanni again opened war so that Marcus and Commodus had to go to the Danube. The wars of Marcus were commemorated on a column in Rome. Marcus died at Vindobona (Vienna) Mar. 17, 180.

180-192. Marcus Aurelius **COMMODUS Antoninus** (b. 161), as Marcus' son was now called, was the first emperor since Domitian to succeed by birth rather than by adoption. He made a peace with the Marcomanni which, though temporarily satisfactory, lost him favor with the troops. He returned to Rome, where he gave himself up to pleasure. The government was at first managed by the capable prae-torian praefect **Perennis,** but on his unwarranted execution in 185, at the request of a deputation of mutinous soldiers from Britain, it fell to the mercenary freedman **Cleander,** who, in turn, was sacrificed in 189 to the Roman mob, which blamed him for a grain shortage. Commodus, already hostile to the senate in consequence of an abortive conspiracy in 182, became extravagantly despotic. He identified himself with Hercules and lavished wealth acquired from the treasury or by confiscation on his favorites, the praetorians, whose pay he increased by a quarter, and on hunts of beasts, in which he participated. On Dec. 31, 192, his concubine Marcia, his chamberlain Eclectus, and the praetorian praefect Laetus had him strangled by a wrestler named Narcissus. Thus ended the Antonine line.

The **important trends in the early empire** were: **politically,** the transformation of the *princeps,* agent of the republican senate and Roman people, into a Stoic king, head of a state in which all good men co-operated for the common weal; **administratively,** the subordination of the republican magistracies and organs to the will of the emperor and the growth of the imperial secretariat and equestrian civil service; **socially,** the substitution for the irreconcilable republican nobility of a new aristocracy drawn from the better classes throughout the empire, which, though sentimentally republican, accepted the empire if the emperor was good; **economically,** the financial breakdown of the municipal system, which was accompanied by a loss of local pride, and the increased burdens of the imperial government; and **militarily,** greater and more constant pressure on both frontiers, north and east, at the same time.

The **literature of the early empire** falls into two periods; the **Augustan Age,** which, with the preceding Ciceronian Age, forms the **Golden Age;** and (after 14) the **Silver Age** of the Julio-Claudians, Flavians, and Antonines. Under Augustus, the chief figures gathered around his friend, their patron **Maecenas: Publius Vergilius Maro** or Virgil (70–19 B.C.) author of the *Bucolica, Georgica,* and the *Aeneid,* and **Quintus Horatius Flaccus** or Horace (65–8 B.C.), author of *Odes, Epodes, Sermones* (satires), and *Epistolae.* Besides these, **Albius Tibullus** (54–19 B.C.) and **Sextus Propertius** (50–15 B.C.) wrote erotic elegies and **Publius Ovidius Naso** or Ovid (43 B.C.–17 A.D.) composed the erotic *Amores, Heroides, Ars Amatoria,* etc., and the longer *Metamorphoses, Fasti, Tristia, Epistolae ex Ponto,* etc. **Titus Livius,** or Livy (59 B.C.–17 A.D.) composed his *History of Rome (Libri ab urbe condita),* a prose glorification comparable to the *Aeneid.* The writers of the Silver Age are numerous and less outstanding: **Aulus Persius Flaccus** (34–62 A.D.) and **Decimus Iunius Juvenalis** (55–138) wrote satire, and **Marcus Valerius Martialis** (40–104) composed satirical epigrams. **Lucius Annaeus Seneca** the Philosopher (4 B.C.–65 A.D.), son of Seneca the Rhetorician (55 B.C.–40 A.D.), and his nephew, **Marcus Annaeus Lucanus** (39–65), author of the epic *Pharsalis,* belong, like Martial, to the Spanish group of authors prominent in the 1st century, as does also **Marcus Fabius Quintilianus** (35–100), teacher of rhetoric and author of an *Institutio Oratoria.* **Gaius Petronius Arbiter** (d. 66), the Epicurean friend of Nero, probably composed the *Satyricon,* a picaresque novel. **Publius Cornelius Tacitus** (55–118?), author of the *Dialogus de oratoribus,* the life of his father-in-law *Agricola,* the *Germania,* the *Annales,* and the *Historiae,* **Gaius Plinius Caecilius Secundus** (61–113?), whose *Letters* are preserved, and nephew of the erudite Gaius Plinius Secundus (23–79), the author of the *Historia naturalis,* who died in the eruption of Vesuvius, and the biographer **Gaius Suetonius Tranquillus** (70–121?), whose *De vita Caesorum* extend from Caesar through Domitian, belonged to the literary circle that flourished under Trajan. Under Hadrian began a revival of interest in pre-Ciceronian Latin language and literature, while under the Antonines a school of African writers introduced a florid and exaggerated style. Its chief exponent was **Lucius Apuleius** (124–?), whose *Metamorphoses*

Marcus Aurelius Commodus Antoninus

Publius Virgilius Maro

Marcus Valerius Martialis

Synagogue at Capernaum, site of Jesus' preaching

Porch of the Pantheon, Rome

and other writings cast light on the mystery religions and neo-Pythagoreanism. The surviving writings of emperors, apart from administrative edicts, etc., are the succinct account of his life by Augustus, preserved on inscriptions at Ancyra (Ankara, *Monumentum Ancyranum*) and, in fragments, elsewhere; some speeches and letters of Claudius in inscriptions or papyri; and the *Meditations,* in Greek, of Marcus Aurelius.

In **philosophy,** Stoicism remained dominant throughout the period and claimed among its chief exponents the statesman **Seneca** (1–65), the slave **Epictetus** (60–140), and the emperor **Marcus Aurelius.** But it had to compete with mystical tendencies which found expression in astrology, in such **oriental religions** as those of the Egyptian **Isis,** the Persian **Mithras,** and the Jewish **Jesus Christ,** and in a revival of the early Greek mystical philosophy of Pythagoras. **Christianity,** which had begun as a Jewish sect but was universalized and widely spread by the ardent convert **Paul,** soon developed both an organization and a literature. The organization consisted of independent churches governed by boards of elders (*presbyters*) among whom one frequently secured preeminence as bishop (*episcopos,* overseer). Those churches that traced their foundation to the immediate associates of Christ, the **Apostles,** or which arose in big cities, tended to overshadow the less important ones and their bishops, especially, in the west, the bishop of Rome, became authorities in ecclesiastical quarrels. Heresies appeared from the beginning, like **Gnosticism** and, about 150, **Montanism.** Christian literature commenced with the *Gospels* and *apostolic* (or pseudo-apostolic) *writings.* The early martyrs, **Ignatius of Antioch** (d. 117?) and **Polycarp of Smyrna** (d. 155?), as well as the Greek bishop, **Irenaeus of Lyons** (c. 130–200), who attacked the heretical transcendentalism of the Gnostics, wrote largely for Christians. But the increasing hostility of the public and government occasioned apologetic writings addressed to non-Christians, like those of **Justin Martyr** (153?) and others.

Augustan art, like Augustan literature, achieved a happy blend of native Roman realism and Greek idealism, as best appears in the sculpture of the *Ara pacis* or the famous "Prima Porta" statue of Augustus. Julio-Claudian art aped the manner without attaining the excellence of Augustan. Under the Flavians, a certain heaviness and materialism, characteristic of the period, appeared. But two relief techniques were perfected, that of illusionism, the attempt to represent space, as on the panels of the Arch of Titus, and the continuous style, by which a series of events was represented in an unbroken sequence, as on the Column of Trajan. Hadrian's reign witnessed a revived interest in and copying of Greek archaic art. Under the Antonines, a crudeness appears on the Column of Marcus, though not in the reliefs from his arch. Mention should be made of the **wall-paintings** of all periods from the 2nd century B.C. to 79 A.D. preserved at Pompeii and of the common red pottery with appliqué reliefs known as

Galen

Arretine ware (modeled on the Greek Samian ware) made first in Italy, at Arretium (Arezzo), and then progressively at various places in Gaul and even in Britain.

In **science,** in outlying districts of the empire, the Greek scientific tradition was strong. **Galen** of Pergamon (c. 130–200) was a brilliant anatomist and physiologist who wrote prolifically on medicine and developed an all-embracing theory of medicine. **Ptolemy** (c. 85–165) collected the writings on astronomy into the *Almagest,* which also contained writings on optics and geography. Indigenous Roman science was little more than popular handbook science depending heavily on Greek sources, epitomized but not understood. The best of these was the *Historia naturalis* of **Pliny** (23–79), an uncritical compendium of good and bad information from a variety of sources, on technology as well as science.

In **architecture,** the grandeur of the Augustan Age, as in the porch of the Pantheon or the Maison Carrée at Nîmes, gave way to massiveness, as in the temple of Venus at Rome and the Coliseum. But the Roman engineers produced at all periods substantial and useful structures: aqueducts, theaters, circuses, baths, harbors, roads, etc. From the Augustan Age dates a treatise on architecture by Marcus Pallio **Vitruvius** (fl. in the Augustan Age), who described the instruments and techniques of surveying, hydraulic works, and bridge-building. Also included in the treatise are descriptions of war machines. Roman technology was empirical. Her engineers carried out vast and important projects; one such was **Agrippa** (c. 63–12 B.C.), who was director of Augustus' massive construction program. **Frontius** (fl. 35–103) wrote on the aqueduct system of Rome.

2. *The 3rd Century, 192–284* A.D.

The 3rd century is characterized by the complete collapse of government and economics throughout the Mediterranean. Upon the death of Commodus, the armies asserted themselves against the senate as they had in 68. The ultimate victor, **Septimius,** finally and frankly unmasked the military basis of the imperial power. After an attempted revival of "constitutional" government under Alexander, the imperial position became the reward of successful generals of increasingly provincial and uncultured origins. The one ideal that still dominated the armies was the preservation of the frontiers against the Germans and Persians. Even the separatist movements were aimed, not at independence, but at the preservation of the *imperium Romanum.* To secure this end and their own support, the troops made and unmade emperors and drained the scanty resources of the civilians by taxation, depreciation of coinage, and exactions of food, quarters, etc. The military wholly absorbed the civil administration. Intellectual life ceased, inscriptions became rare, and archaeological finds show a rapid decline in skill and taste.

193. Publius Helvius PERTINAX, emperor. He was chosen by the senate, but his strict and

economical rule led to his murder (Mar. 28) by the praetorian guard, which then auctioned off the empire to him who promised them the highest gift of money, **M. Didius Severus Julianus** (b. 133?). The British legions proclaimed as emperor the legate, **D. Clodius Septimius Albinus;** the Pannonian, the legate of Upper Pannonia **L. Septimius Severus** (April or May); and the Syrian, the legate **C. Pescennius Niger Justus.** Severus at once seized Rome, where the senate deposed and executed Julianus (June 1).

193–211. L. SEPTIMIUS SEVERUS (b. 146, at Leptis in Africa), emperor. He dissolved the existing praetorian cohorts, composed of recruits from Italy, and enrolled new ones from deserving legionary veterans. He kept Albinus quiet by recognizing him as Caesar (i.e. heir). He then defeated Niger in **battles at Cyzicus** and **Nicaea** and at **Issus** (the Cilician Gates), and put him to death near Antioch (194). Byzantium held out until 196, when it was sacked and reduced to the status of a village. Albinus, who now claimed full equality, was defeated and slain (197, Feb. 19) at Lugdunum (Lyons), which was also sacked and never recovered its prosperity.

L. Septimius Severus

Severus created three new legions, one of which was quartered on the Alban Lake in Italy, hitherto free from the presence of legionary troops. He appointed equestrians to command these legions contrary to the Augustan rule and also put the new province of Mesopotamia under an equestrian. He thus initiated the replacement of senators by equestrians in military posts which culminated under Gallienus. Military marriages were recognized, since the immobilization of the legions had made these usual. Auxiliaries were settled on public land in return for military service and the legionary pay was raised. Severus humiliated the senate, which had supported Albinus, and put equestrian deputies to watch senatorial governors. When he closed down the now almost defunct courts (*quaestiones*), he transferred the jurisdiction over Rome and the area within 100 miles to the praefect of the city and over the rest of Italy to the praetorian praefect, who also exercised jurisdiction on appeal from the provinces. After the fall of the single and powerful praetorian praefect Palutianus (205), Severus returned to the practice of having two, one of whom was the distinguished jurist Papinian. In the criminal law, a distinction was drawn between the privileged classes (*honestiores*), who were treated favorably, and the ordinary people (*humiliores*). The emperor began the subdivision of provinces into smaller units, which culminated under Diocletian, and extended the organization of municipalities as the basis of tax-collecting even to Egypt, which shows how valueless municipal status had become. He created a new treasury in addition to the *fiscus* (the original imperial treasury) and the *patrimonium Caesaris* (originally the ruler's private property, then crown property), namely the *res privata*, his personal funds. He depreciated the silver content of the *denarius* to 60 per cent. Despite all of these difficulties, his administration was good.

197-198. In a successful **Parthian war** Severus advanced as far as Ctesiphon and reconstituted the province of Mesopotamia under an equestrian governor with two legions.

205-211. A recurrence of **troubles in Britain,** which had suffered from invasion in 155 and revolt in 180, required the presence of Septimius himself to fight the Caledonians. He definitely withdrew from the wall of Antoninus to that of Hadrian, which he rebuilt. He died at Eboracum (York) on Feb. 4, 211

211-217. CARACALLA (properly Caracallus), so named from a Gallic cloak which he wore. He was the oldest son of Septimius and had been associated with him as Augustus (198). To strengthen the bond between the Severi and the Antonines he had changed his name from Septimius Bassianus to Marcus Aurelius (Severus) Antoninus (197). Upon his accession, he murdered his colleague (since 209) and younger brother, P. (originally L.) Septimius (Antoninus) Geta (b. 189), along with the jurist Papinian and many others. He increased the pay of the troops to a ruinous degree and called them all *Antoniniani*. To meet the consequent deficit he issued a new coin, the *antoninianus,* with a face value of two *denarii* but a weight of only one and two-thirds. He erected at Rome the vast **Baths of Caracalla** (*thermae Antoninianae*).

212. The **EDICT OF CARACALLA** (*constitutio Antoniniana*) extended Roman citizenship to all free inhabitants of the empire save a limited group, perhaps including the Egyptians. His motive has been much disputed; citizenship now meant so little that this step was a natural culmination of the leveling down of distinctions that had been continuous throughout the empire. Moreover, he may

have hoped to extend to all inhabitants the inheritance tax paid by Roman citizens.

213-217. Caracalla successfully defended the northern frontier against the Alamanni in southern Germany and the Goths on the lower Danube (214), and in the east he annexed Armenia (216). But as he was preparing an invasion of Parthia, he was murdered by a group of his officers (217, Apr. 8).

217-218. M. Opellius (Severus) MACRINUS (b. 164?), emperor. He was a Mauretanian who had risen from the ranks to be praetorian praefect, and was the first equestrian emperor. He surrendered Caracalla's eastern gains and sought to reduce the pay of the troops, who set up as a rival (218, May 16) at Emesa in Syria a grandnephew of Julia Domna, the Syrian wife of Septimius. Macrinus fell on June 8, 218.

218-222. ELAGABALUS (Heliogabalus, b. c. 205), emperor. He derived his cognomen from the Emesa god, whose priest he was. To legitimize his rule, he changed his name from (Varius) Avitus to Marcus Aurelius Antoninus and claimed to be a son of Caracalla. While Elagabalus surrendered himself to license and introduced the worship of his god to Rome, the empire was really ruled by his forceful mother, **Julia Maesa.** She obliged him to adopt his cousin (Gessius) Bassianus (Alexianus?), son of her sister, Julia Mamaea. The praetorians murdered Elagabalus (222, Mar. 11).

222-235. Marcus Aurelius SEVERUS ALEXANDER (b. c. 208), emperor. He was the adopted son of Elagabalus and was dominated by his mother, Mamaea. She established a regency committee of senators and used the

Baths of Caracalla

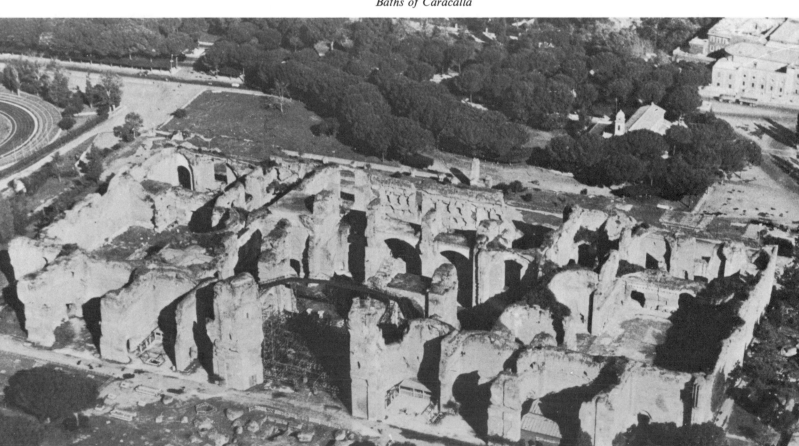

Elagabalus

Rock sculpture near Shapur representing the capture of Valerianus

advice of the jurists Paulus and Ulpian. The new rule was an attempt to revive the Antonine monarchy. It was marked, however, by an extension of governmental control over the trade guilds (*collegia*) and further depreciation of the coinage.

227. The **New Persian (Sassanid) Empire** was founded by **Ardashir** (Artashatr, Artaxerxes), a Persian who overthrew the Parthian Arsacids, Artabanus V and Vologesus V. The strength of the new empire lay in a revival of **Zoroastrianism.**

234-235. Alexander was forced to buy peace from the Alamanni on the Rhine. The disgruntled troops murdered him (235, Mar.). With his death the last attempt to preserve a civil or "constitutional" government came to an end and military anarchy began.

235-238. **G. Julius Verus MAXIMINUS** "Thrax" (b. c. 172), a Thracian peasant of huge size and no culture, was elevated by the Rhine legions, but was not recognized by the senate, which put forward the senators **M. Clodius Pupienus Maximus** and **D. Caelius Calvinus Balbinus.** In the meantime (238), the African legions proclaimed the 80-year-old pro-consul **Marcus Antonius Gordianus I** and his son **Gordianus II.** The former committed suicide after his son was defeated and slain by the praefect of Mauretania. However, the populace of Rome forced the senate to join the grandson, **Gordianus III,** with Pupienus and Balbinus. Maximin was slain by his troops while besieging Aquileia (238, June) and the praetorians murdered Pupienus and Balbinus (238, June?).

238-244. **Marcus Antonius GORDIANUS III** (b. 225) was dominated by the wise praetorian praefect **C. Furius Timesitheus** (Misitheus?), whose daughter he married (241). Timesitheus drove the son of Ardashir, Shapur (Sapor), out of Antioch (241-243) but died of disease. The new praetorian praefect, and Arabian, made himself co-Augustus, then murdered Gordian (early in 244).

244-249. **M. Julius PHILIPPUS "ARABS"** bought peace with the Persians and, at Rome, celebrated the *ludi saeculares* for Rome's thousandth birthday (248). He was killed at Verona (249) in battle against his commander in Dacia, Decius.

249-251. **G. Messius Quintus Traianus DECIUS** (b. 200?), instituted the first general **persecution of the Christians,** and perhaps of all who would not sacrifice to the emperor. Emperor-worship seems now to have become a requirement of all loyal subjects, which indicates a growing belief in the actual divinity of the emperor. Decius was slain by the Goths in Dacia (251) because of the disloyalty of the legate of Moesia, Gallus.

251-253. **G. Vibius Trebonianus GALLUS** (b. c. 207) put to death his co-Augustus, **Hostilianus,** son of Decius. In his reign began a 15-year plague. When he marched against his successor in Moesia, the Moor M. Aemilius Aemilianus, his own troops slew him (before Oct., 253).

253. **M. Aemilius Aemiliamus,** emperor.

253-259. **P. Licinius VALERIANUS** (b. c. 193), commander in Germany, became emperor, with his son Gallienus as co-Augustus. He fought unsuccessfully against the Franks, who crossed the Rhine in 256, the Alamanni, who reached Milan, and the Goths. As the frontiers ceased to hold, cities within the empire began to build walls. Valerian recovered Antioch again from Shapur (256-258) but was treacherously seized at a parley (259?) and died a captive at an uncertain date.

259-268. **P. Licinius Egnatius GALLIENUS** (b. 218) continued to reign alone, though pretenders appeared throughout the empire and the period has been called that of the **"thirty tyrants."** He completed the substitution of equestrians for senators as legionary commanders and as governors.

The **Goths,** who had broken through to the Black Sea, harried Asia and the Aegean area from ships.

258-267. **Odenathus,** ruler of Palmyra in the Syrian Desert, kept the Persians out of Asia (260), but his queen and successor, **Zenobia,** declared her independence (267).

259-268. **Postumus** set himself up as emperor in Gaul. **Gallienus** was finally murdered by his own troops before Mediolanum (Milan),

P. Licinius Egnatius Gallienus

where he was besieging the pretender **Aureolus** (before Sept., 268). Aureolus in his turn was slain by Claudius II.

268-270. **M. Aurelius CLAUDIUS II "Gothicus"** (b.?) was the first of a series of capable Illyrian emperors who prepared the way for Diocletian. He repelled a Gothic invasion of the Balkans (269, whence his title) at **Naissus** (Nisch) and settled numbers of Goths in the vacant lands of the Danubian provinces. Upon his death from plague, his brother Quintillus was proclaimed as

270. **Marcus Aurelius Claudius QUINTILLUS,** Deserted by his troops, he committed suicide, and was succeeded by an associate of Claudius II.

270–275. **L. Domitius AURELIANUS** (b. c. 214?) was rightly entitled "restorer of the world" (*restitutor orbis*). He abandoned trans-Danubian Dacia and settled its Roman inhabitants in a new Dacia carved out of Moesia. He repulsed the Alamanni from Italy (271) and built the existing walls of Rome (271–276).

271–272. **Probus,** and then Aurelian himself, defeated and captured Zenobia and, upon a second revolt, sacked Palmyra (273).

273 or 274. Aurelian recovered Gaul from the successor of Postumus, Tetricus, in a **battle at Châlons.** Both Zenobia and Tetricus adorned his magnificent triumph in Rome (274). He was murdered by some officers while preparing to invade Persia (275).

275–276. **M. Claudius TACITUS,** an elderly senator, was appointed emperor against his will by the senate. Though he defeated the Goths and Alans, who had invaded Asia Minor, the troops slew him.

276. **Marcus Annius FLORIANUS,** brother of Tacitus, was slain soon after assuming the purple.

276–282. **M. Aurelius PROBUS,** an Illyrian, was saluted by the eastern armies (276). He repelled from Gaul the Franks and Alamanni and other peoples, who had inflicted great devastation. He also strengthened the Danube frontier, quieted Asia Minor, and suppressed pretenders in Gaul. When he tried to use the troops in works of peace, e.g. clearing the canals in Egypt, they murdered him (282, autumn?).

282–283. **M. Aurelius CARUS,** an Illyrian (?) and praetorian praefect to Aurelian, succeeded and campaigned successfully against the Persian monarch Varahran. He perished in 283,

Roman relief showing the sacrifice of a bull in honor of Mithras

Origen

and his son Marcus Aurelius Numerius **Numerianus,** co-Augustus with him, was murdered (284, autumn). A second son, M. Aurelius **Carinus** (emperor, 283–285), tried to hold the west against **Diocletian,** an officer whom the eastern army had elected emperor, but he was slain by his own troops during the battle at the river Margus in Moravia (285, summer?).

The **troubles of the 3rd century** had two main causes: the increased pressure on the frontiers from the new Germanic tribes and from the vigorous Persian Empire, and the economic collapse within, the causes of which cannot be wholly established. In part, at least, the economic crisis was due to the heavy burdens of government and defense and to the oppressive and erratic system of taxation; in part, perhaps, to a "fatigue of spirit." Literature ceased almost entirely. Of art and building notable examples survive, like the Arch of Septimius, the Baths of Caracalla, and the Walls of Aurelian at Rome, but these are imitative and uninspired. **Roman law,** however, reached its heights under the Antonines and Severi. Though the two great schools of jurisprudence, the **Sabinians** and the **Proculians,** originated under Augustus or Tiberius, the great jurists were **Salvius Julianus** under Hadrian, who dealt with the **Praetor's Edict, Gaius** under the Antonines, whose *Institutes* became a standard textbook, and the triumvirate of **Papinian, Paulus, and Ulpian** under the Severi, whose various works provided most of

the material for Justinian's *Institutes.* In **philosophy,** neo-Pythagoreanism gave way to neo-Platonism, whose chief exponents were **Plotinus** (204–270), **Porphyrius** (233–306), and, later, **Iamblichus** (d. 333?).

Despite the persecutions under the Antonines, Severus, Maximin, and Decius, the **Christian Church** grew in numbers and power. Its chief competitor was the cult of the Persian **Mithras,** a god popular with the troops. The major internal problems of the church in the 3rd century were the heresy called Montanism (an extreme asceticism) and the acute question of the treatment of those who lapsed from their faith during persecutions (*lapsi*) or betrayed the sacred books (*traditores*). Those who had confessed their faith in the face of persecution (*confessores*) opposed the readmission of backsliders to full communion, while the church as a whole, led in the west by the bishop of Carthage, **Cyprian,** and the bishop of Rome, **Stephen,** advocated a milder policy. The extremists were called **Novatians** in the 3rd century and **Donatists** in the 4th, after a certain Donatus, whose riotous bands of schismatics (*circumcelliones*) terrorized the province of Africa. Christian apologetics gave way to homiletic and theological writings in the hands of the African **Tertullian** (150–225) and **Cyprian** (200–258) and the Alexandrians **Clement** (d. 215) and **Origen** (182–251), the last two of whom combined Platonism with Christianity in the manner of contemporary neo-Platonism.

3. *The Later Empire, 284–527* A.D.

284-305. G. Aurelius Valerius DIOCLETI-ANUS (b. 245, saluted as emperor 284, Nov. 17?), was of humble Illyrian stock. Faced with the task of bringing order out of chaos, he desired to emulate Augustus, to revive the happy days of the early empire, but he succeeded only in creating an oriental despotism.

Since it is difficult to distinguish how far the reorganization of the empire was due to Diocletian and how far to Constantine, a brief outline will be given here. In general, all these reforms were merely a regularization and crystallization of practices developed in the 3rd century. Although the senate continued to meet and the higher republican magistrates survived to varying dates, e.g. the consulship in the east until its abolition by Justinian, and although two provinces, Asia and Africa, still received senatorial pro-consuls, nevertheless the whole administration was organized in a pyramid of interlocking bureaus emanating from the emperor.

According to Diocletian's system, which operated only sporadically, there were to be two coequal emperors (*Augusti*), as in the case of Marcus and Verus. Now, however, **the empire was divided** for practical administrative purposes into two spheres, eastern and western, the line between which ran from the Danube to the Adriatic south of Dalmatia. Each part was administered by one of the Augusti. But the edicts of the emperors were issued conjointly and they might on occasion command in one another's spheres.

The emperors ruled absolutely, in virtue of selection by the troops and without the consent of the senate (since 282). Each surrounded himself with the pomp of an oriental court. No longer was he the first citizen among equals (*princeps*), but since Aurelian, "lord" (*dominus*). All connected with him was "sacred" (the "sacred court," *sacra aula*, appeared under the Severi). Each emperor chose an assistant and successor (*Caesar*).

Under these four rulers, praetorian praefects, now wholly civilian magistrates, administered the four praefectures, Gaul, Italy, Illyrium, and the east. Each praefecture was divided into several dioceses under vicars (*uicarii*) independent of the praefects and directly responsible to the emperor. The dioceses were subdivided into provinces under presidents (*praesides* or *rectores*). These provinces were subdivisions of those of the early empire and their number increased from 60 to 116.

The military power, which during the 3rd century had absorbed all the functions of government, was now wholly separated from the civilian. Each province had a duke (*dux*) or count (*comes*) in charge of its permanent garrison, which was not, as in the early empire, concentrated in large camps, but scattered in smaller posts along the frontier, often in the guise of soldier-peasants (*limitanei, riparienses,* border or riverbank men). In each praefecture, under masters of the infantry and of the horse (*magistri peditum, equitum*), were mobile forces that could be rushed to strengthen threatened points (*comitatenses,* companions of the emperor). The emperors, moreover, had large bodies of special guards (*protectores* or *domestici*). The old legions were split into smaller, more mobile but less highly trained units of about 2000 men. Heavy armed cavalry (*cataphractarii*) played a large part in warfare. The auxiliary troops were mostly mercenary bands of barbarians, whose chiefs became extremely influential. The total forces now numbered about 500,000 men, an increase over the Augustan 300,000, which accounts in part for the financial problems of the later empire.

Besides the separate and elaborate administration for each territorial unit, the emperors had an extensive central bureaucracy, the various "offices" (*officia*) under such officials like the quaestor of the sacred palace (*quaestor sacri palatii,* the chief judicial officer), the chancellor (*magister memoriae,* master of records), and the personnel manager (*magister officiorum,* master of the offices, very powerful because he had a finger in every department). These men automatically belonged to the senate, and other high officials had the titles of honor formerly reserved for equestrians, who vanished as a class. The senators also now formed a class of dominant and very wealthy landowners

Palace of Diocletian near Solin, Dalmatia

G. Aurelius Valerius Diocletianus

throughout the empire, who might seldom actually attend the senate, but who enjoyed privilege and exemption. The rest of the population were crushed by heavy taxes, which were largely collected in kind (*annona*) after the collapse of the currency, and which were reassessed every 15th year by an "indiction" (*indictio*). Both labor and property were evaluated in terms of a unit of wheat-producing land (*iugum*). The taxation bore especially heavily on the members of the municipal senates (*curiales, decuriones*), who continued to be held responsible for the collection of taxes and the payment of arrears, and on the small landowners, who had to provide recruits for the army and see that waste lands (*agri deserti*) were kept under cultivation. Thus freemen found it wisest to flee the country, enter monasteries, or become serfs (*coloni*) on large estates. Craftsmen and tradesmen were rigorously confined to their professions. The whole caste system was arranged to insure the maintenance of the administration and the army. Since, therefore, it benefited no one but the great landlords or imperial officials, the vast majority of the population lost interest and either accepted the barbarian invasions supinely or even welcomed relief from oppression. Whether, however, this lethargy, which pervaded not only the political and economic life but also the intellectual, save in the Christian Church, resulted from the system or whether the unwieldy and inflexible system indicated the poor mental caliber of the rulers, so many of whom were of peasant or barbarian origin, and the effeteness of the hereditary upper class, cannot be determined.

285. Upon the defeat of Carinus, Diocletian chose as his colleague (Caesar in 285, Augustus in 286) the Illyrian **M. Aurelius Valerius Maximianus** (b. c. 240?), who was a harsh, uneducated man but a competent general. They assumed the titles respectively of *Jovius* and *Herculius*. Diocletian took up his residence in the east, at Nicomedia in Bithynia, from which the main road to the upper Euphrates frontier began, while **Maximian,** in the west, lived mostly at Mediolanum (Milan) in northern Italy, which was a better center for the defense of the northern frontier than Rome. Despite its sentimental pre-eminence, Rome thereafter declined in practical importance. But the departure of the imperial court gave the bishop of Rome increased scope.

293, Mar. 1. Diocletian chose as Caesar **G. Galerius Valerius Maximianus** (b. c. 250), who became his son-in-law and received the government of Illyricum; Maximian chose **Flavius Valerius Constantius** (misnamed Chlorus) (b. ?) who divorced his wife Helena to marry Maximian's daughter Theodora; he received the praefecture of Gaul. He at once drove out the rebel Carausius from Boulogne and subdued the Franks.

294. A revolt was raised in Egypt by Achilleus, whom Diocletian besieged in Alexandria (295) and captured.

296. **Narses,** king of Persia, invaded Roman Mesopotamia and defeated Galerius, but the latter gathered reinforcements in the winter and returned to defeat Narses (297) and recover Mesopotamia; Roman influence was restored in Armenia, whose king became Christian.

297. Constantius crossed to Britain and his lieutenant defeated and killed Allectus, who had murdered and replaced Carausius.

298. Constantius returned to Gaul and defeated the Alamanni.

301. An edict limiting prices of goods and labor was passed by Diocletian in an attempt to end the economic distress caused by the collapse of the currency; no attempt was made to enforce it in the west, and in the east it soon proved impracticable.

303, Feb. 23. Galerius persuaded Diocletian to declare a **general persecution of the Christians,** which, however, Constantius did not enforce in his praefecture. The persecution was stopped in the entire west in 306 but raged in the east until 313.

305, May 1. Diocletian and Maximian abdicated; Galerius and Constantius became Augusti; Diocletian and Galerius selected as Caesars **Flavius Valerius Severus** under Constantius, receiving the praefecture of Italy, and for Galerius his own nephew **Galerius Valerius Maximinus Daia,** who received Syria and Egypt. The hereditary claims of Maximian's son Maxentius and Constantius' son Constantine were neglected.

306–337. Flavius Valerius CONSTANTINUS I THE GREAT (b. 288? of Constantius and Helena) fled from Galerius to his father in Britain. On the death of the latter (July) Constantine was saluted as emperor by the troops, but made an agreement with Galerius by which he became Caesar and Severus became Augustus. In Rome the praetorians and the people proclaimed **Maxentius Augustus** (Oct. 28); he called his father Maximian to be Augustus and temporarily took the title of Caesar. When the Emperor Severus came with an

Arch of Galerius at Saloniki

Constantinus the Great, colossal bust on the Capitoline Hill, Rome

himself near Rome at the **Milvian Bridge** (Saxa Rubra) (Oct. 28). Before the battle he is said to have seen in the sky a cross and the device *in hoc signo vinces.* Sometime later he became a Christian. He dissolved the praetorian guard. At a meeting with Licinius in Milan (early 313?) equal rights were proclaimed for all religions and the property confiscated from the Christians was restored by the **Edict of Milan.**

313. Daia crossed to Europe, but was defeated by Licinius at **Tzirallum** and fled to Tarsus, where he died soon after. Licinius now held the entire east and Constantine the west.

314. After a brief war, in which Licinius was defeated at **Cibalae** (Oct. 8), a peace was made giving Constantine all of the Balkans except Thrace.

323. Relations between the two were strained by Licinius' anti-Christian policy, and war finally broke out. Licinius was defeated at **Adrianople** (July 3), his fleet was defeated by Constantine's son Crispus, and Licinius was again defeated at Chrysopolis in Anatolia (Sept. 18). He surrendered and was executed in the next year.

324–337. CONSTANTINE REUNITED THE EMPIRE under his sole rule He had already interfered in the affairs of the Church (at its invitation) when in 316 he tried to settle the Donatist schism.

325. He now summoned the **first ecumenical** (world-wide) **council of the Church,** to meet at **Nicaea** in Asia Minor. It was to settle a controversy that had arisen in Alexandria between the priest **Arius,** who maintained that Christ was of different substance from God (*heterousios*), and the Bishop Alexander (succeeded in 328 by **Athanasius,** who supported the doctrine that they were of the same substance (consubstantiality, *homo-ousios*). The council agreed on a creed favorable to Alexander (not the present "Nicene" creed); in addition it adopted certain canons giving privileges to the bishops (patriarchs) of Alexandria, Antioch, and Rome. Constantinople later acquired similar rights. The **primacy of Rome,** although in a very restricted sense, had been generally recognized in the west since the **Council of Arles** in 314. The prominent part taken by Constantine in this council laid the basis for the later supremacy of the emperor in the eastern Church. Though Arius died a horrible death in 336, Constantine and his successors swung the

Maxentius Augustus (Roman gold coin)

army, it deserted and he surrendered to Maximian and was later executed by Maxentius. In fear of Galerius, Maximian went to Constantine in Gaul; Constantine recognized him as senior Augustus and married his daughter, Fausta. Galerius attempted an invasion of Italy (307), but disloyalty in his army forced its abandonment. Maxentius took the title of Augustus (308) and Maximian fled to Constantine; for four years Maxentius ruled in Italy very oppressively. Galerius induced Diocletian to preside over a conference at Carnuntum, where it was decided that Maximian should

abdicate, **Valerius Licinianus Licinius** was to be Augustus in the west; and Constantine was to return to the rank of Caesar. Constantine refused and Galerius gave him and Daia the rank of *filius Augusti;* both were still unsatisfied, and were finally given the rank of Augustus (310). Maximian attempted to revolt, but Constantine killed him. When Galerius died of disease (311, May), Daia seized Asia Minor, leaving the Balkans to Licinius.

312. Constantine suddenly invaded Italy and after winning a battle over Maxentius' general at Verona defeated and killed Maxentius

Church increasingly toward Arianism, and strife in the Church on this subject was not ended until the reign of Theodosius I. The west remained firmly Athanasian.

330, May 11. Constantine dedicated as his capital **CONSTANTINOPLE,** which he had spent four years in building on the site of Byzantium, commanding the strategic center of the east, the Bosporus.

337, May 22. Constantine died at Nicomedia. He had been induced (326) by his wife Fausta to execute Crispus, his son by his first wife. His heirs were three sons and two nephews. Of the sons, all Augusti, Constantinus II (b. 317) received the praefectures of Italy and Gaul; Constantius II (b. 317) took the east; and Constans (b. 323?) got Illyricum and part of Africa. The nephews, Dalmatius and Annibalianus, were at once executed by Constantius.

337–361. RULE OF CONSTANTINE'S SONS. While Constantius carried on an indecisive war against Persia, Constantinus attacked Constans, but was slain at Aquileia (340). Constans was killed by the pretender **Magnus Magnentius** (350, Jan.).

351, Sept. 28. Constantius defeated Magnentius at **Mursa,** near the confluence of the Danube and Drave. The latter slew himself at Lugdunum (353) and the empire was once more united.

351, Mar. 15. Constantius chose his cousin Gallus as Caesar, but had him executed in 354.

355, Nov. 6. Constantius chose as Caesar the half-brother of Gallus, **Julian,** who was given command against the Alamanni and Franks.

360. Julian marched against Constantius, who died before Julian reached the east (361).

361–363. JULIANUS, "the Apostate," (b. 332). He is known chiefly for his attempt to substitute paganism for Christianity and to organize a pagan church. After continuing his successes against the Franks, he campaigned against the Persians, but died on his way back from an attack on Ctesiphon (363, July 36). With him ended the line of Constantine.

363–364. JOVIANUS (b. c. 331), was elected

Constantinus II (contemporary gold coin)

Magnus Magnentius (contemporary gold coin)

by the troops. He surrendered Mesopotamia to the Persians and died soon after (364, Feb. 17).

364–375. FLAVIUS VALENTINIANUS I (b. 321) was the next choice of the troops. He ably defended the west against the barbarians and made his brother **Valens** co-Augustus in the east (364, Mar. 28).

367. Valentinian made his son **Gratian** co-emperor in the west. Valentinian died on an expedition against the Quadi and Sarmatians (375, Nov. 17).

375–383. GRATIANUS (b. 359) named his half-brother **Valentinian II** (b. 371) co-Augustus in the west.

376. The **Visigoths** (West Goths) crossed the Danube. Valens fell in battle against them at **Adrianople** (378, Aug. 9). The Goths continued to ravage the Balkan region.

379, Jan. 19. Gratian appointed as co-Augustus for the east, **Theodosius,** son of a successful general in Britain.

382. Gratian, at the request of Bishop Am-

brose, removed from the senate-house the pagan altar of victory and gave up the title of *pontifex maximus.*

379–395. FLAVIUS THEODOSIUS "THE GREAT" (b. 346). He supported orthodoxy (i.e. Athanasianism) in the east, and came to terms with the Goths by settling them as military allies (*foederati*) in the Balkans.

383. The British legions proclaimed **Magnus Maximus,** who seized Gaul. Gratian was slain at Lugdunum (Aug. 25). Theodosius recognized Maximus.

387. When Maximus drove Valentinian II from Italy, Theodosius captured and executed him at Aquileia (388, July 28).

390. Theodosius cruelly massacred 7000 people at Thessalonica in revenge for an insurrection. Bishop Ambrose of Milan forced him to do penance for this act and emphasized thereby the independence of the western church from imperial domination.

392, May 15. The Frankish count (*comes*), **Arbogast,** murdered Valentinian II at Vienne

Triumphal arch of Constantinus I at Rome

Attalus

and set up as emperor the pagan rhetorician **Eugenius.**

394, Sept. 5. Theodosius defeated and slew Eugenius and Arbogast at the Frigidus, just east of Aquileia. The empire was reunited for a brief space.

395, Jan. 17. Theodosius died at Milan. The empire was divided between his elder son **Arcadius** (made Augustus in the east in 383) and the younger son **Honorius** (made Augustus in the west in 393). The division proved to be permanent, though at the time the unity of the empire was fully accepted in theory and was always envisaged as a practical possibility. One consul regularly held office in Rome (until 472) and one in Constantinople (until 541).

395–408. ARCADIUS (b. 377), emperor of the east. He married Eudoxia, daughter of the Frank, Bauto (395). The praetorian praefect, Rufinus, managed to check the inroads of the Visigoths in the Balkans until his murder by the troops, but thereafter the eunuch Eutropius failed to prevent the invasions of the Visigoths or of the Huns, who overran Asia.

395–423. HONORIUS (b. 384), emperor of the west. He fell wholly under the influence of the Vandal **Stilicho** who, as master of the

Theodosius "the Great"

Honorius and Maria

troops (*magister militum*), commanded all the forces and married his daughter Maria to Honorius (398).

396–397. Stilicho drove the Visigoths, led by Alaric, out of Greece.

402, Apr. 6. He frustrated their efforts to invade Italy (victory of the Romans at **Pollentia**).

406, Aug. 23. Stilicho at Florence broke up a miscellaneous force of barbarians which Radagaisus had led into Italy.

At about this time Gaul was overrun by Vandals, Alans, Suevi, and Burgundians.

407. EVACUATION OF BRITAIN by the Romans. Constantine, whom the troops in Britain had proclaimed emperor, crossed to Gaul with his forces and it is probable that Roman troops were never sent back. The Romanized natives were left to deal as best they could with the inroads of Caledonians (Picts) from the north and of various German tribes

coming by sea. The Saxons seem to have secured a permanent footing at the mouth of the Thames about 441.

408, Aug. 22. Murder of Stilicho, at Honorius' order.

408–450. THEODOSIUS II (b. 401), emperor of the east. He was the son of Arcadius and was a weak ruler dominated by his sister Pulcheria. With Valentinian III, Theodosius issued the earliest collection of existing laws, the **Theodosian Code** (438).

The Huns, under Attila, continued to ravage the empire and extort tribute.

409. Alaric again invaded Italy and set up a usurper, **Attalus** (praefect of Rome, the last pagan "emperor"). Alaric soon deposed him again.

410, Aug. 14 or 24. ALARIC SACKED ROME. He died soon after in southern Italy. His brother-in-law Ataulf led the Visigoths into

Gaul (412) and thence began the conquest of Spain from the Vandals (415). There **Wallia** (416–419), successor of Athaulf, established the first recognized barbarian kingdom (419).

411. Constantine was defeated by Honorius' commander Constantius, near Arles.

423–425. Johannes usurped the purple on the death of Honorius at Ravenna (which he had made the capital in place of Milan).

425. Forces sent from the east by Theodosius II captured Johannes and put him to death.

425–455. VALENTINIAN III (b. 419), emperor of the west. He was the son of Honorius' half-sister Galla Placidia and the general Constantius, who had been made Augustus in 421, but had died almost at once. Valentinian was recognized by Theodosius II and married his daughter Eudoxia (437).

429. The general **Bonifatius** tried to set himself up as independent in Africa, with the aid of the Vandals, who crossed from Spain under **Gaiseric** (Genseric). But the Vandals seized Africa for themselves after a two-year siege of

Pillage of Rome by the Vandals, 455

Hippo Regius (430–431) during which the bishop, **St. Augustine,** died (430, Aug. 28).

430. Aëtius, master of the troops, disposed of his rivals, Felix and Bonifatius (recalled from Africa in 432). He then devoted himself to clearing Gaul of barbarians, which he did by a resounding victory over the Visigoths (436) and by suppressing an uprising of the peasants and slaves (*Bagaudae,* 437).

435. The **Vandal kingdom in Africa** was recognized. The Vandals took Carthage in 439.

450–457. MARCIAN, emperor of the east. Pulcheria, sister of Theodosius II (d. 450), had married Marcian, an able general. He allowed the Ostrogoths (east Goths) to settle as military allies (*foederati*) in Pannonia.

450. Attila, leader of the Huns, decided to bring his people from the east into Gaul.

451, June. Aëtius, aided by the Visigothic king, Theodoric I (*Theoderich, Theoderid*), defeated the Huns in the **battle of Châlons** (actually the *campi Catalauni* or Mauriac plain, near Troyes).

452. Attila invaded Italy, but turned back, traditionally because warned by Pope Leo I, but probably because well paid. Attila died in 453 and his hordes broke up.

454, Sept. 21. Valentinian rewarded Aëtius by murdering him with his own hand.

455, Mar. 16. Valentinian was murdered by two of Aëtius' guards. End of the house of Theodosius.

455–472. A succession of puppet rulers in the west. In 455 Eudoxia, widow of Valentinian, set up **Petronius Maximus** at Rome. On his murder, in the same year, she called the Vandals from Africa.

455, June 2–16. Gaiseric and the Vandals sacked Rome. By the thoroughness of their destruction they attached a permanent stigma to their name.

456. Avitus advanced from southern Gaul to Rome, but was deposed by his able general, the Suevian **Ricimer.** Ricimer retained power by securing the consent of the eastern emperors to his nominees, who were **Majorianus** (457–461), **Severus** (461–465), and after a two-year interregnum, **Anthemius** (467–472), and **Olybrius** (472). When in 472 both Ricimer and Olybrius died, the eastern emperor, Leo I, appointed **Glycerius** (473), and **Julius Nepos** (473–475).

457–474. LEO I (b. ?), a Thracian (?), succeeded Marcian as emperor of the east. To offset his master of the troops, the Alan Aspar, he married his daughter Ariadne to Zeno, an Isaurian from the mountains of southern Asia Minor (467) and made Zeno's son, Leo, his colleague (473).

474. Leo II, who succeeded on the death of Leo I. His father, Zeno, made himself his colleague. Leo died the same year.

474–491. ZENO (b. 426), disposed of the pretender Basiliscus, brother-in-law of Leo I (475). He then tried to control the Goths by setting the rival chiefs, Theodoric, son of Strabo, and Theodoric the Amal, against each other.

475. The master of the troops, **Orestes,** removed Nepos in favor of his own son, whose name combined those of the founder of Rome and of the empire,

475–476. ROMULUS AUGUSTUS (nicknamed *Augustulus*).

476, Sept. 4. After defeating and killing Orestes at Pavia, the Herulian **Odovacar** (*Odoacer*) deposed Romulus Augustulus, the last emperor of the west, at Ravenna. **Traditional end of the Roman Empire.**

The eastern emperor, **Zeno,** apparently recognized Odovacar as "patrician" (*patricius* had become the title of honor for barbarian commanders). Nepos retained titular claim as emperor until his death in 480 and after that date the empire was theoretically reunited under the eastern emperors, but actually Odovacar ruled as an independent king in Italy.

481. On the death of Theodoric, the son of Strabo, Zeno recognized his rival as patrician and master of the troops. His people were established in Moesia as foederati.

488. Theodoric, ostensibly as **Zeno's** agent, invaded Italy.

493, Feb. 27. After a three-year siege of Ravenna, Odovacar surrendered. He was soon after murdered by Theodoric. Italy was united under Theodoric the Great (b. c. 455) as the kingdom of the Ostrogoths.

491–518. ANASTASIUS I (b. 431), emperor of the east. He married Zeno's widow and removed the Isaurians from power, thus causing a serious revolt in Isauria (suppressed only in 497).

The inroads of the Slavic Getae forced him to protect Constantinople by a wall.

502–506. The emperor waged a long war with the Persians.

514–518. Conflict with the pretender Vitalian, commander of the Bulgarian foederati. Anastasius died in 518 (July 1).

518–527. JUSTINUS I (b. 450?), a humble Illyrian who had risen to be commander of the imperial bodyguard. He took as his colleague his able nephew Justinian (527) and died the same year.

527–565. JUSTINIAN. (For his reign see Byzantine Empire. *(p. 195).*

Diocletian and his successors managed to delay, but not to stop, the decay that had attacked the empire during the 3rd century. The administrative reforms added to the burdens of taxation without stopping the military domination and rivalry for the purple. The army became increasingly barbarized and immobilized by settlement on the land as peasant militia or barbarian foederati. The active defense was entrusted to barbarian mercenaries under their powerful chiefs, who came to dominate the state. Thus, the empire in the west did not fall: it petered out; and the establishment of the barbarian kingdoms simply recognized the end of a gradual process. In the east the empire, in Greek garb, maintained itself, at times as a very great and splendid power, until the conquest of Constantinople by the crusaders in 1204 and the definitive fall of the city into the hands of the Turks (1453).

In **architecture,** the later empire continued the able engineering of earlier days, as in the Baths of Diocletian at Rome, his palace at Spalato, or the Basilica of Maxentius and Constantine at Rome. But **art** showed a rapid decline, e.g. in the frieze of the Arch of Constantine at Rome.

The second half of the 4th century witnessed a revival of pagan **Latin literature** in **Symmachus,** the praefect of the city who vainly urged Valentinian II to restore the altar of victory (384), the Gallic poet **Ausonius,** consul in 379, and the Alexandrian **Claudius,** court

"Donation of Constantine" (13th-century fresco)

poet of Honorius and Stilicho. **Boethius,** the last classical philosopher, compiled an elementary treatise on mathematics and translated the logic of Aristotle into Latin; whether he was pagan or Christian, he wrote the *De consolatione philosophiae* in prison before his execution by Theodoric the Ostrogoth, 524. **John Philopponus** (fl. first half of the 6th century) wrote critical commentaries on Aristotle widely quoted through the late Middle Ages.

Active intellectual life, however, appeared chiefly in the Church. The great Latin fathers were: **Lactantius** (d. c. 325), **Ambrose** (340–397), bishop of Milan (374), **Jerome** (340–420), who retired from Rome to Bethlehem, where he translated the Bible into Latin (the *Vulgate*), and **Augustine** (354–430), bishop of Hippo Regius in Africa (395), who founded Christian theology on Platonism. The important Greek fathers were: **Basil** of Caesarea (330–379), his brother **Gregory** of Nyssa (d. c. 394), and **Gregory** of Nazianzus (329–389), all three Cappadocians, and **John Chrysostom** (329–389), patriarch of Constantinople (381). **Eusebius** (264–340), orthodox bishop of Caesarea (315), who should be distinguished from the contemporary Arian, Eusebius of Nicomedia, is noted for his *Historia ecclesiastica* and other historical works.

During the 5th and 6th centuries the eastern Church was torn by the **monophysite heresy,** whose doctrine was that Christ had a single nature. The orthodox doctrine, that Christ combined divine and human, had the support of Pope Leo of Rome and was approved at the **Council of Chalcedon** (451), but the eastern emperors on the whole were mono-

physite. In the west, as imperial authority weakened, and as rival bishoprics passed into barbarian hands, the bishop of Rome—or **pope** (*papa*) as he came to be known—became supreme, and such great popes as **Damasus** (pope, 366–383) and **Leo I, "the Great"** (pope, 440–461) became temporal as well as spiritual leaders of their people. A claim of territorial sovereignty began to be based on a fictitious **"Donation of Constantine"** to Pope Sylvester of the lands around Rome. A significant missionary effort of the Church was the sending of **Ulfilas to the Goths** (c. 340–348), who converted them to Arianism. But the chief feature of the Church during this period was the introduction of **monasticism.** In the east, the single solitary had long been common and **St. Antony** first gathered some of them together for a common life (*coenobite*) in Egypt in about 285. **Basil of Caesarea** established a monastic rule popular in the east. Monasticism spread to the west under the efforts of **Martin of Tours** (362) and **Jerome. Cassian of Marseilles** (c. 400) wrote *Institutes* for his monastery, but the rule that became dominant was that of **St. Benedict** (*regula Sancti Benedicti*), who founded his monastery at Monte Cassino, near Naples, in 529. His rule was adopted by Cassiodorus (480–575), secretary to Theodoric the Ostrogoth, who founded a monastery at Beneventum in 540. The closing of the schools at Athens by Justinian, the execution of Boethius, and the founding of Benedict's monastery mark the transition from classical to medieval intellectual life.

(Cont. p. 165.)

G. The Empires of Asia

1. *The Neo-Persian Empire of the Sassanians, 226–651* A.D.

(From p. 139)

226–240. Ardashir I (*Artaxerxes, Artashatr*), son of Papak, a vassal-king of the Parthian Empire ruling in Fars (Persia proper), revolted against Artabanus, last king of the Arsacid dynasty of Parthia, and defeated him finally at **Hormuz** (226–27), where Artabanus was slain.

Merv, Balkh, and Khiva conquered by Ardashir; submission of the kings of Kushan, Turan, and Makran received; India invaded and tribute levied on the Punjab.

229–232. War with Rome. Rome summoned to evacuate Syria and the rest of Asia. Armenia, the real objective of Ardashir's campaign, subjugated after the murder of its Arsacid king, Chosroes.

Under Ardashir a strongly centralized nation supported by the priesthood created; Zoroastrianism revived and the privileges of the Magi restored; collection of the text of the *Zend Avesta* under Arda-Viraf. He was succeeded by

240–271. Shapur I (*Sapor, Shahpuhri*). Revolts in Armenia and Hatra crushed (240).

241–244. FIRST WAR WITH ROME. Shapur invaded Mesopotamia and Syria, took

Shapur II (gold coin)

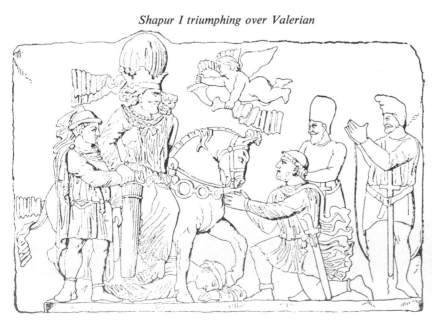

Shapur I triumphing over Valerian

Shapur I (6th-century bronze statuette)

Nisibis and Antioch, but was finally driven back across the Euphrates and defeated at Resaina by the Emperor Gordian. Gordian was murdered and peace was concluded by his successor, Philip. In the east, Balkh apparently independent.

258-260. SECOND WAR WITH ROME. Shapur again invaded Mesopotamia and Syria, taking Nisibis, Edessa, and Antioch, and defeating and capturing near Edessa the Emperor Valerian, who remained a captive until his death (265-66). Asia Minor also invaded, Caesarea Mazaca in Cappadocia taken, but no attempt made to consolidate and hold the conquered territory.

260-263. Palmyra. In a brilliant campaign **Odenathus,** the Arab prince of Palmyra, drove the Persians back across the Euphrates, defeated Shapur and besieged Ctesiphon, seized and occupied Mesopotamia, Syria, and other provinces west of the Euphrates, and was recognized by Gallienus as co-regent for the east.

Palmyra had, by the mid-century, supplanted **Petra** as the chief junction of the caravan routes. Striking ruins of Petra, first described by Burckhardt in 1812: buildings and tombs hewn from rose-colored rock, some dating back to 5th century B.C.

Shapur's later years were devoted to public works, of which the greatest was the dam at Shuster. He also founded many cities, among them Nishapur. In his reign appeared Mani (215-273), founder of **Manichaeism,** whom Shapur at first favored, then banished.

271-293. Shapur was succeeded by his son, **Hormisdas I** (271-272), who was followed by his brother, **Varahran I** (272-275). Mani executed. Insufficient support given to **Zenobia of Palmyra,** the widow of Odenathus, against Aurelian, whose Persian expedition came to an end with his murder (275). Varahran succeeded by his son, **Varahran II** (275-293). An eastern campaign, in which the Sakae of Sistan were subdued, was brought to a close by a Roman invasion of Persia under the Emperor Carus, who conquered Mesopotamia and took Ctesiphon (283). The mysterious death of Carus ended the war (284). Armenia seized by Tiridates, the son of the murdered Chosroes,

with the help of the Emperor Diocletian (286). **Varahran III,** son of Varahran II, reigned four months, and was succeeded by his brother.

293-301. Narses, who finally worsted his brother and rival, Hormisdas, and drove Tiridates from Armenia (296).

296-297. WAR WITH ROME. The Roman army under Galerius routed near **Carrhea** (296). The Persian army surprised by Galerius in the following year and almost annihilated. Peace concluded (297). Terms: (1) cession to Rome of the five provinces west of the Tigris; (2) the Tigris to be the boundary instead of the Euphrates; (3) cession to Armenia of Median territory up to the fort of Zentha; (4) Iberia (*Georgia*) to be a Roman protectorate.

Abdication of Narses and accession of his son, **Hormisdas II** (301-309), noted for his activity in building and for setting up a court of justice at which the poor were encouraged to make complaint against the oppression of the rich. Upon his death his natural heir, Hormisdas, was set aside by the nobles, who elected his posthumous son, the famous

309-379. SHAPUR II.

309-337. His minority and early campaigns. Persia invaded by the Arabs of Bahrain and Mesopotamia; Ctesiphon sacked. At the age of 17 Shapur grasped the reins of state, adopted an active policy, invaded Arabia, and exacted a terrible revenge upon the Arabs.

337-350. FIRST WAR WITH ROME. The Romans were defeated in the field, but Shapur was unable to capture the Roman strongholds. Nisibis invested three times in vain (338, 346, 350). Constantius routed at Singara (348). Persecution of the Persian Christians (from 339 on). **Treaty with Armenia** (341), but in 351 Armenia went over to Rome. Successful campaigns in the east against the Huns, Euseni, and Gilani (350-357).

359-361. SECOND WAR WITH ROME. Syria invaded, Amida taken after a heroic defense (359). Singara and Bezabde captured (360). Constantius attempted in vain to recapture the latter place, and died in the following year. His successor, Julian, invaded Persia, forced the passage of the Tigris, defeated the Persians north of Ctesiphon, but retreated

before investing that city and was mortally wounded in a battle near Samarra (363). His successor, Jovian, concluded peace with Shapur for 30 years. Terms: (1) restoration of the five provinces ceded by Narses; (2) surrender of Nisibis, Singara, and a third fortress in eastern Mesopotamia to Persia; (3) Armenia declared to be outside the Roman sphere of influence. Conquest of Armenia by Shapur and invasion of Iberia.

371-376. THIRD WAR WITH ROME. No decisive results and an obscure peace. Persian power at its zenith at the death of Shapur II. His immediate successors weak and unenterprising. **Ardashir II** (379-383) and **Shapur III** (383-388). Shapur concluded a peace with Rome (384) by the terms of which Armenia was partitioned between Rome and Persia. **Varahran IV** (388-399). Khusru (*Chosroes*), the satrap of Persian Armenia, who had revolted, was deposed and succeeded by Varahran's brother. Varahran was killed in a mutiny and succeeded by his son,

399-420. Yezdigird the Wicked. A peaceful reign. A firman issued permitting Christians to worship openly and rebuild their churches (409), a decree as important to the eastern church as the **Edict of Milan** to the church of the west. The **Council of Seleucia** adopted the decrees and the creed of the **Council of Nicaea.** Yezdigird possibly contemplated baptism and persecuted the Magians, but returning to his old faith he authorized the destruction of the Christian sect. A terrible persecution for four years. Yezdigird succeeded by his son,

420-440. Varahran V. Brought up among the desert Arabs who supported him against his cousin, Khusru, the choice of the nobles, who finally accepted him peacefully. He continued persecution of the Christians and declared war on Rome (420), when the Christians crossed the border seeking Rome's protection. Varahran was defeated and peace concluded (422): Christians to be allowed to take refuge in the Roman Empire, persecution of the Christians to cease. Declaration of the independence of the eastern church at the **Council of Dad-Ishu** (424). Persian Armenia reduced to a satrapy (428). Campaign of Varahran against the White Huns or Ephthalites (*Haytal*), of Turkish stock probably, in Transoxania. They invaded Persia, but were surprised and defeated by Varahran, who crossed the Oxus and forced them to sue for peace. Varahran succeeded by his son,

440-457. Yezdigird II. War declared upon Rome and peace concluded the same year (440). Successful campaigns against the Ephthalites of Transoxania (443-451). Armenia forcibly converted to Zoroastrianism (455-456), after the defeat of the Christian party at the hands of the Persians and their Armenian supporters. Persecution of Christians spread to Mesopotamia. Khorasan again invaded by the Ephthalites, who inflicted a severe defeat upon Yezdigird, after he had driven them across the Oxus. At his death his younger son, Hormisdas, seized the throne, but the elder son,

459-483. Firuz (*Perozes*), defeated and captured Hormisdas with the aid of the Ephthalites. A famine of several years; wise measures adopted by Firuz. Unsuccessful campaigns against the Ephthalites ending in a humiliating peace (464-480?). A further

Varahran IV engaged in battle

defeat at the hands of the Kushans of the maritime provinces of the Caspian Sea (481) led to the revolt of Iberia and of Armenia under Vahan (481–483). This was still smoldering when Firuz, breaking his troth, attacked the Ephthalites, was defeated and slain. Succeeded by

483–485. Balas (Vologesus), his brother. Tribute paid by Persia to Khush-Newaz, the Ephthalite Khan, for about two years. Conciliation of Armenia. **Edict of toleration** granted Christians, after **Vahan** aided Volagases in a civil war. Thereupon Armenia and Iberia contented provinces of the empire. Nestorian Christological doctrine of the two natures in Christ established by **Bar-Soma** in the Persian Church with royal authority; the college of Edessa driven out by Zeno and set up at Nisibis by Bar-Soma (489). Repudiation by Armenia of the **Council of Chalcedon** (491). Volagases succeeded by his son,

485–498. Kobad (first reign), who had taken refuge with the Ephthalites after an abortive attempt to seize the throne. Successful campaign against the Khazars, dwelling between the Volga and the Don. Many converts gained for his communistic and ascetic doctrines by **Mazdak,** a high priest of Zoroastrianism, among them the king. Unrest in Armenia and Persia owing to the intolerant proselytism of the Mazdakites, leading to a conspiracy of the Chief Mobed, nobles, and army against Kobad, who was deposed and succeeded by his brother **Zamasp,** who reigned from 498 to 501. Kobad escaped to the Ephthalites, who espoused his cause with vigor. Zamasp resigned the crown voluntarily.

501–531. Kobad (second reign). Official support withdrawn from Mazdak.

503–505. FIRST WAR WITH ROME. Cause: non-fulfillment of the Eastern Empire's agreement to pay a share of the expenses of the defense of the pass of Derbend, the usual route taken by nomadic tribes in their invasions of Persia and the Eastern Empire. Roman Armenia invaded; Theodosiopolis taken; sack of Amida in northern Mesopotamia (502).

Khusru Parviz during a boar hunt

An Ephthalite raid forced Kobad to conclude peace on the basis of the *status quo ante.*

503–523. Successful and final campaign against the Ephthalites (503–513). Massacre of the Mazdakites (523). Rebellion in Iberia.

524–531. SECOND WAR WITH ROME. Cause: Erection of the fortress of Daras within a day's march of Nisibis by the Emperor Anastasius. The first campaign ended in the defeat of the Romans (526), who were again defeated in 528, but were finally victorious in the **battle of Daras** (528) under Belisarius. An indecisive battle near Callinicum brought the war to a close. Kobad was succeeded by

531–579. ANUSHIRWAN THE JUST (*Chosroes*), his son. The most illustrious member of the Sassanian dynasty. Succession disputed. Execution of all his brothers and their male offspring with one exception. Massacre of Mazdak and his followers. Conclusion of the **Endless Peace with Rome** (533). Terms: (1) Rome to pay 11,000 pounds of gold toward the upkeep of the Caucasian defenses; (2) Rome to keep Daras as a fortress, but not as its headquarters in Mesopotamia; (3) restoration on both sides of captured strongholds in Lazica; (4) eternal friendship and alliance. Within seven years, however, Anushirwan, alarmed at Justinian's successes in Africa and Italy (533–539) and prompted by the Ostrogoths and Armenians, began a defensive war.

540–562. WAR WITH ROME. Syria invaded. Antioch sacked. Terms of peace agreed upon and ratification of the treaty received by Anushirwan at Edessa. He nevertheless extracted ransoms from the cities along the route of his return march, whereupon Justinian denounced the treaty.

540–557. Campaigns in Lazica. Lazica (ancient *Colchis*), a Roman protectorate since 527, appealed to Anushirwan for help to throw off the Roman yoke. Petra taken by the Persians (540). Lazica a Persian province. Petra retaken by the Romans (550), and the Persians driven out of the country (555). A truce agreed upon (557). **Definitive peace with Rome** (562). The terms included: (1) cession of Lazica to

Rome; (2) payment by Rome of 30,000 pieces of gold annually; (3) free exercise of their religion guaranteed to the Christians of Persia; (4) commercial intercourse restricted to certain roads and marts; (5) Daras to remain a fortified town; (6) arbitration of all disputes and free diplomatic intercourse; (7) inclusion in the treaty of the allies of either party; (8) the defense of the Caspian gate to be undertaken by Persia alone; (9) the peace to hold for 50 years.

554. Subjugation of the Ephthalites with the aid of the Turks and the division of their territory with the Oxus as boundary. Successful campaign against the Khazars.

572. Declaration of war on Persia by Justin. Syria ravaged by Anushirwan and Daras taken (573). Abdication of Justin. A peace purchased by Tiberius.

576? Arabian campaign. The Abyssinians driven out of southern Arabia, which became a Persian province.

576–578. Alliance of the Turks with the Eastern Empire. Ill-success of their invasion of Persia. Armenian campaigns. An Indian campaign also reported.

Under Anushirwan the administration was reorganized. The empire was divided into four great satrapies: the east comprising Khorasan and Kerman; the west including Iraq and Mesopotamia; the north comprehending Armenia and Azerbaijan; and the south containing Fars and Khuzistan. A fixed land tax was also substituted for the former variable tax on produce, and its collection placed under the supervision of the priests. Irrigation and communications were improved, the army reformed, foreigners protected, agriculture encouraged, laws revised, the Christians granted toleration, learning subsidized, Indian tales and chess introduced. Anushirwan was succeeded by his son,

579–589. Hormisdas IV (*Hormazd*). War with Rome continued. The Persians were defeated at Constantia (581) and again at Arzanene near Martyropolis (588). In 589 the Persians took Martyropolis and defeated the Romans, who, however, gained a signal victory near Nisibis soon thereafter.

589. Invasion of Persia by Arabs, Khazars, and Turks. The advance of the Turks constituted a real danger, but they were defeated by the great Persian general, Varahran (*Bahram*). **Bahram** was then ordered to invade Lazica, but was met and defeated by the Romans on the Araxes. Superseded and insulted by the king, he rebelled. Hormisdas was deposed and murdered, and succeeded by his son,

589–628. KHUSRU PARVIZ (*Chosroes II*), the last famous king of the Sassanian dynasty. Under him the Neo-Persian Empire reached its greatest extent and suffered also a sudden downfall. Defied by Bahram, Khusru was forced to flee to Constantinople, whereupon Bahram seized the throne and reigned as Bahram (*Varahran*) VI (590–591). Restoration of Khusru with the aid of the Emperor Maurice. Flight of Bahram to the Turks, by whom he was assassinated.

603–610. A victorious **war against Phocas,** the murderer of Maurice. Capture of Daras, Amida, Harran, Edessa, Hieropolis, Berhoea (Aleppo), etc. Armenia, Cappadocia, Phrygia, Galatia, and Bithynia ravaged.

610. A Persian force defeated by the Arabs at

Dhu-Qar, a famous day in the annals of the tribes.

610–620. Accession of Heraclius as Roman emperor. War with Rome continued. Sack of Antioch and Apamea (611) by the Persians. Invasion of Cappadocia (612). Capture of Damascus (614). Sack of Jerusalem and capture of the "True Cross" (615). Capture of Pelusium and Alexandria by Shahr-Baraz. Subjugation of Egypt (616). Chalcedon taken. The Persians within a mile of Constantinople (617). Ancyra and Rhodes captured (620). Khusru had now restored the empire of Darius I, and the condition of the Roman Empire was desperate. Thrace was overrun by the Avars. Heraclius decided to flee to Carthage, but was prevented by the citizens of Constantinople. He determined as a forlorn hope to make use of his one great advantage, the possession of sea power, and carry the war to enemy territory.

622–627. The famous **campaigns of Heraclius.** Disembarkment at Issus and defeat of Shahr-Baraz (622). Expedition to Lazica and invasion of Armenia (623). Retreat of Khusru and wintering of Heraclius in Albania. The second invasion of Armenia. Surprise and defeat of Shahr-Baraz (624). Invasion of Arzanene and the recovery of Amida and Martyropolis. Campaign in Cilicia. Indecisive **battle of the Sarus.** Retreat of Shahr-Baraz (625).

626. THE SIEGE OF CONSTANTINOPLE. Alliance between Khusru and the Avars. Two Persian armies placed in the field, one against Heraclius in Asia Minor, the other to co-operate with the Avars in the siege of Constantinople. The first under Shahen, the captor of Chalcedon, was defeated by the emperor's brother, Theodore. The second was prevented by the Roman command of the sea from assisting the Avar assault on Constantinople, which failed.

627. Invasion of Assyria and Mesopotamia by Heraclius. Defeat of the Persians near Nineveh. Flight of Khusru. Heraclius marched on Ctesiphon, but did not besiege it. His retreat to Canzaca. Mutiny of the Persian troops in Ctesiphon under Gurdanaspa, their commander. Imprisonment and murder of Khusru, he was succeeded by

628–629. Kobad II (*Siroes*), who made peace with Heraclius on the basis of an exchange of conquests and prisoners and the surrender of the "True Cross." The massacre of his brothers and his death by plague (629). The usurpation of Shahr-Baraz and his murder by his own troops (629). The reign of **Purandukht** and that of **Azarmidukht,** daughters of Khusru Parviz, followed by a period of anarchy, in which pretender after pretender aspired to the throne and perished almost immediately (629–634).

634–642. Yezdigird III, grandson of Khusru Parviz, and last Sassanian king of Persia, whose story is that of the expansion of the Muslim caliphate eastwards.

633–651. Arab invasion of Iraq under Khalid ibn al-Walid. Hira and Obolla taken. The Arab advance checked temporarily at the **Battle of the Bridge.** The Persians under Rustam were decisively defeated by the Arabs under Sa'd ibn-abi-Waqqas at **Qadisiya** (637). Mesopotamia invaded by Sa'd and Ctesiphon (*Madain*) captured. Defeat of the Persians at Jalula (637). Invasion of Susiana and Fars (639). Defeat of the Persians at Ram Hormuz; Shuster taken; conquest of Khuzistan (640). Final defeat of the Persians under Firuzan at **Nehawand** (642). Conquest of the Persian provinces and their incorporation into the caliphate. Flight of Yezdigird to Balkh; his appeal for help to the Emperor of China; his murder in a miller's hut near Merv (651).

2. *India, 72* B.C.–*500* A.D.

a. NORTHERN INDIA

1st century B.C. Dating of the known Saka rulers, the **"Great King Moga"** or Maues, Azes, and Azilises, raises a complex chronological problem affecting the whole epoch from 100 B.C. to 200 A.D. It springs from multiplicity of eras, which are hardly ever explicitly identified.

The **Pahlavas** (Parthians closely related to the Scythians) under Vonones and his brother Spalirises became independent in eastern Iran with the title of "King of Kings" sometime (c. 30? B.C.) after the death of Mithridates II (88 B.C., supposed by L. de la Vallée Poussin to begin a Pahlava era). **Azes II,** son of Spalirises, succeeded the Sakas in the Punjab. Pacores was the last to rule as suzerain, although others probably continued as satraps.

The Kushana **Kujula Kadphises** forcibly united the five tribes of Yüeh-chih in Bactria (end 1st century B.C.) and seized from the Pahlavas the Kabul Valley and adjacent regions. His son **Vima Kadphises** conquered northwestern India and ruled it by deputy till his death at 80. An inscription near Panjtar speaks of a "Gushana Great King" under date "122" which is 64 or 34 A.D. by the Azes or Pahlava systems. The inscriptions of "136" similarly belongs to 78 or 48 A.D.

c. 78–176+ A.D. A second Kushana dynasty was founded by

c. 78–96+ A.D. KANISHKA, who extended his rule from Benares and Kabul to the Vindhyas, and established his capital at Peshawar. Whether or not the era he founded is the "Saka" era of 78 A.D., he probably came to the throne near that date. The Chinese *Later Han History* says:

84. A Yüeh-chih king was allied to Sogdiana by marriage, and by presents to him Pan Ch'ao secured the help of the latter against Kashgar.

88. The king presented precious stones and lions with a request for a Chinese princess, peremptorily refused by Pan Ch'ao.

90. A punitive army of 70,000 sent across the Pamirs under the Yüeh-chih viceroy Hsieh was starved into surrender by Pan, the ablest strategist of his time, who exacted payment of annual tribute. Although the king is not named, only a powerful ruler could have played so strong a hand across the mountains. Some scholars identify Kanishka rather with King Chien of Khotan, who was killed in error by a Chinese envoy in 152 A.D. The Chinese source does not, however, suggest any connection of this king with the Yüeh-chih or with India.

Kanishka appears to have been tolerant in religion, and built a great stupa at Peshawar over relics of the Buddha. A fourth church council, unknown to the Pali sources, was apparently convoked at Jalandhara in the Punjab by the powerful Sarvastivadin, a realist sect of the conservative Theravacla. It probably supervised translation into Sanskrit of the canon which had been fixed in Prakrit in Mathura, the Punjab, and Kashmir in the last centuries B.C. The earliest and most vigorous classical Sanskrit is found in Asvaghosha's *Saundarananda* ("Conversion of Nanda") and the *Buddhacharita,* an artistic versified life of the Buddha, together with a work long supposed to be his *Sutralamkara,* which is now identified as the *Kalpanamanditika* of Kumaralata, a junior contemporary.

2nd century A.D. Kanishka's successors with their inscriptions (dated in terms of his reign) are: his son Vasishka (24, 28, 29); the latter's son Kanishka II (41); his younger brother Huvishka (29 or 33–60); Vasushka, son of Kanishka II (68, 74); and Vasudeva (76–98).

Asoka's inscriptions name three **Tamil states** in the Carnatic: Pandya (extreme south), Chola (southeast), and Chera or Kerala (southwest coast, chief port Muziris). These competed with Maesolia at the mouth of the Kistna and especially with the rich western port of Barygaza (Broach) in thriving trade with the Roman Empire. An embassy to Augustus (c. 22 B.C.) was sent by a king "Pandion" who may have been a Pandya. Strabo (d. 21 A.D.) speaks of fleets of 120 ships from Egypt to India, and Pliny (23–79) values annual imports from India at 50 million sesterces.

The **DECCAN** was dominated (from c. 100 B.C. to c. 225 A.D.) by a dynasty called **Andhra** by the late *Puranas* but **Satavahana** or **Satakani** in their own Prakrit inscriptions. Founded by Simuka on the ruins of the Sunga-

INDIA, 72 B.C.–500 A.D. 151

Gold coins of the Kushana and Kushana-Sassanian Dynasties: 1. Vima Kadphises; 2. Kanishka; 3. Huvishka; 4. Vasudeva; 5. Kanishka II; 6. Hormisdas; 7. Bahram; 8. Bahram II

Kanva power, with capital at Pratishthana (Paithan) on the upper Godavari, its early conquests to north and northwest were appropriated by the Saka satraps. A Saka satrap **Bhumaka** established Scythian power on the northwest coast (c. 70 A.D.). Nahapana, junior to him, ruled many years over Surashtra (Kathiawar) and the adjacent coast with capital probably at Junnar, east of Bombay. Named Mambanos in the *Periplus* (c. 89), his inscriptions are dated "41–46" (?119–124 A.D.), probably with reference to the Saka era of 78.

c. 109–132+. **Gotamiputa Siri Satakani** conquered Surashtra from Nahapana, and in an inscription at Nasik (18th year of his reign, c. 126) claimed not only the Deccan from the Vindhyas to Banavasi, but less probably Malwa as well. Very likely by this epoch the Satakani had extended control over the properly Andhra Telugu (Dravidian) lands of the Godavari and Kistna deltas. The Prakrit poems of the *Sattasai* in part date from this time. Liberal toward all religions, the Satakani especially exalted the Brahmans.

Sculptures about the great Buddhist stupa of Amaravati on the lower Kistna reveal union of Hindu traditional style with its crowding and naturalism, already more refined than at Bharhut and Sanchi, with Greco-Buddhist motifs which were borrowed from Gandhara and in turn transmitted to Malaya, Sumatra-Java, Cambodia, and Champa.

c. 120–c. 395. A **DYNASTY OF WESTERN SATRAPS** of Ujjain in Malwa was founded by Bhumaka's son Chashtana (Tiastanes of Ptolemy, c. 150).

c. 170. **Rudradaman,** Chashtana's grandson, in a Sanskrit inscription at Girnar in Kathiawar, records repair of a dam which broke in 150 A.D., defeat of northern tribesmen, and repeated rout of the southern Satakani.

Ujjayini (Ujjain) became a center of Sanskrit learning, and was taken as meridian by Indian astronomers. At Mathura, where sculpture early resembled that of Bharhut and Sañchi, and later imitated the forms of Gandhara, the heavy drapery of the Hellenistic school was rendered transparent, and schematized in decorative ridges, creating the so-called *Udayana Buddha,* carried to China and Japan.

The Buddhist community was now divided between two means to salvation: the **Hinayana** or Lesser Vehicle, which retained much of the primitive simplicity of the *Dharma,* "Law" by which Buddhism was then named; and the **Mahayana** or Great Vehicle, which emphasized personal devotion to Sakyamuni and exalted Bodhisattva (future Buddhas) as saviors. Although practically deified in the *Lalitavistara* (2nd century ?, Chinese trans. 308) and *Saddharma-pundarika-sutra,* "Lotus of the Good Law" (Chinese trans., 265–316), Buddha is regarded as but the human representative (*manushi-buddha*), for the current epoch, of an infinite series of buddhas. Popular bodhisattvas are Avalokitesvara (*Lotus Sutra,* ch. 24), Manjusri (*Avatamsaka-sutra,* 2nd–3rd centuries, Chinese trans. 317–420), Samantabhadra, and Kshitigarbha, all of whom have deferred their own illumination to succor struggling mankind. The goal of effort is no longer sainthood or final absorption in nirvana, but direct attainment of buddhahood or rebirth to indefinite residence in a celestial paradise. Nagarjuna (2nd century), founder of the *Madhyamika Sutra* teaches that all sensory and mental experience is illusion, and comments on the *Prajñaparamita,* "Perfect Wisdom" (Chinese trans. 160) which consists in recognition of the Buddhist law as sole reality.

Already before our era Indian writers recognized and wrote treatises about three phases of human existence: *dharma,* religious and moral duty; *artha,* politics and practical life; and *kama,* love. The *Artha-sastra* (compounded from earlier materials c. 300–330) aims to teach a prince the whole science of successful rule according to accepted principles. It assumes autocratic monarchy, justification of all means by the end (personal aggrandizement), and chronic war. It advocates use of spies in all quarters; deception, intimidation, false witness, and confiscation to obtain money; cunning, and assassination. Virtuous rule is described because desirable to win affection of a conquered people. The *Kamasutra* ("Laws of Love") by Vatsyayana Mallanaga (c. 4th century or later) imitates the *Artha-sastra* in both form and morals.

320–c. 535. The **GUPTA DYNASTY** united northern India after five centuries' division.

320-c. 330. Chandragupta I ruled from Pataliputra (Patna), having strengthened his position by marriage into the ancient Lichchavi tribe. His son

c. 330-c 375. Samudragupta completed the conquest of the north (Aryavarta) and won glory by traversing Telugu lands to force homage of the Pallava. Claiming to receive tribute from southeastern Bengal, Assam, and Nepal, with presents from the Kushan "son of Heaven and king of kings" (now actually vassal of the Sassanids) in Kabul-Kapisa-Gandhara, the satrap of Ujjain, the King Meghavanna (352-379) of Ceylon (who founded a monastery at Gaya for his subjects), he revived the Vedic horse-sacrifice which sanctified claim to the title of "universal monarch." He was a patron of poetry and music.

c. 375-c. 415. Chandragupta II Vikramaditya (on throne in 379) ended the satrapy of Ujjain by conquest of Malwa, Gujerat, and Surashtra (between 388 and 401). He moved his capital to Ayodhya (in Oudh) and then to Kausambi on the Jumna.

c. 415-455. Kumaragupta I probably founded the monastic community at Nalanda which was the principal Buddhist seminary till it burned c. 988.

455-c. 467. Skandagupta repulsed the White Huns, as heir apparent and as emperor (455).

477-495+. Budhagupta, one of the last emperors of the dynasty, ruled from northern Bengal to eastern Malwa, perhaps to Surashtra. After c. 500 the chief branch of his house ruled as kings of Magadha till the 8th century.

The **Brahman legal writers** defined the social structure and ritual obligations. The *Dharma Sastra* of **Manu** (1st century B.C.?) was respected and freely utilized by later writers. The *Dharma Sutra* of **Vishnu** (3rd century A.D.), like the epics, recognized *suttee,* widow-burning, though it is not yet recommended. The days of the week were named from Greek sources. **Yanjavalkya** (4th century) admitted documentary evidence, and recommended use of ordeals of ploughshare, scales, and poison in addition to Manu's fire and water. **Narada** (5th century) first omitted religious and moral precepts from legal discussion. **Brihaspati** (c. 600 or 700) cited nine ordeals. Punish-

Traditional Hindu statue, sandstone, 1st century

Sculpture from Gandhara, Greco-Buddhist style

Buddhist gold reliquary, 2nd–3rd century

Detail of the stone carving on the Kapaleeswarar Temple at Mylapore, built by Dravidians

ments: impalement, hanging, burning, mutilation, fines, and outcasting were adjusted to caste. A plaintiff might enforce justice by fasting to death on a debtor's premises. Fa-hsien, pioneer Chinese Buddhist pilgrim at the height of Gupta power, stated that fines were usually imposed, and that mutilation was reserved for brigands and rebels. He was enthusiastic about the peace and happiness of northern India (401–409) and Ceylon (410–411).

Six **schools of Hindu philosophy** (or rationalized religion) developed during the first centuries before and after Christ. They enjoy orthodox status in that all recognize the primordial and eternal character of the *Veda*, although in fact they do not derive from it. None is concerned primarily with ethics, but all seek freedom from bondage through deeds to rebirth. Escape for the soul is found in knowledge and cessation of thought. The *Purvamimamsa* is a systematization of rules for sacrifice. The *Vaiseshika-sutras* are variously dated from the 2nd century (Masson-Oursel) or 4th–5th centuries (Stcherbatsky). They elaborate an analysis of matter as composed of atoms combined in molecules under influence of time and direction. Souls are bound through linkage to such matter. The Nyaya is a system of logic calculated to attain that knowledge necessary to freedom. The *Yogasutras* (5th century?) teach rigid concentration of mind and body, a method open to all and regarded as valuable by many diverse religious groups. The *Samkhya-karika* is attributed to Isvarakrishna (3rd or 4th century? Chinese trans. c. 560). It sets forth a dualistic system teaching that the eternal soul can be freed by realization that it is not material like the world about it. The *Brahma Sutra* (c. 350–400) gives the first clear expression of the Vedanta *darsana,* or "point of view," developed continuously from the older *Upanishads:* God is every-

thing, the soul is God, and it is the task of the high-caste Brahman to realize in contemplation this identity.

Vasubandhu (c. 300–350), leading philosopher of Hinayana Buddhism, in his *Abhidharmakosa sastra* gave a classic summary of the Vibhasha and of the Vaibhashika school based upon it, with illuminating comments on the competing Sautrantika school founded by Kumaralabdha (c. 150–200) and developed by Harivarman. Vasubandhu was converted to the Mahayana by his brother Asanga, founder of the Vijñanavadin (Idealist) or Yogachara (Mystic) school, which explains phenomena as mere reflections of ideas and exalts the bodhisattvas, in particular Maitreya. The active translator to Chinese, **Kumarajiva** (c. 344–413), and the logician **Dignaga** (c. 5th century) were both adherents of this school, which developed important branches at Valabhi and Nalanda (6th–7th centuries). Fa-hsien first reported Mahayanist monasteries separate from those of the Hinayana.

Literary studies at Ujjain blossomed under the Guptas into the **golden age of classical Sanskrit. Arya Sura** in the *Jatakamala* (Chinese trans. 428) put into elegant *kavya* verse tales of former births of the Buddha which had been best known through the *Divyavadana* (Chinese trans. in part, 265). Secular fables gathered into the *Panchatantra* passed through Pehlvi (531–570), Syriac (570), and Arabic (750) into the languages of Europe. The *Sakuntala* and *Vikramorvasi* of **Kalidasa** (c. 400–455) rank first among Indian dramas (Greek influence), his *Meghaduta* equally high as a lyric poem, while his *Kumarasambhava,* and *Raghuvamsa* mark the apogee of *Kavya,* scholarly epic poetry. Literary taste survived the Gupta Empire: witness **Sudraka's** drama, *Mrichchakatika* ("Little Clay Cart"), and **Dandin's** romance *Dasakumaracharita* (both 6th

century) and **Santideva's** brilliant poem of Mahayanist altruism, *Bodhicharyavatara* (late 7th century).

As in literature, so in **art** the Gupta period is one of dignity, restraint, and refinement: classicism in a land given to exaggeration.

Indian medicine largely parallels the Greek, but was limited, and surgery atrophied, by objection to dissection. An ethical code like the Hippocratic oath appears in works of Charaka and Susruta (prior to 4th century, though present texts date from 8th and 11th). Greek origin is clear for many astronomical ideas in the (4th century?) treatises summarized in **Varahamihira's** *Panchasiddhantika* (c. 550). Zodiacal division of the ecliptic replaces the (Babylonian?) Nakshatras; planetary motion is explained by epicycles; parallax and eclipses are calculated, etc. But many Indian inconsistencies suggest that Greek astronomy was known imperfectly, perhaps through rule-of-thumb manuals. **Aryabhata** (499) taught rotation of the earth and the value of π as 3.1416 (epic value 3.5). **Brahmagupta** (b. 598) systematized the rules of astronomy, arithmetic, algebra, and geometry. His integral solution of an indeterminate equation, with another method given by **Bhaskara** in his *Siddhantasiromani* (1150) is called by Hankel the finest thing in numerical theory before Lagrange (1736–1813). The abacus was described in the *Abhidharmakosa* from 1st-century sources long before its use in China (1303–1383). More important, the zero (actually a superscribed dot) is attested in Indian literature (600), and the decimal position in a Sanskrit inscription in Cambodia (604) before they passed to the Arabs of Syria (662), and thence to the Europeans.

b. SOUTHERN INDIA

The whole Indian peninsula south of the Vindhyas, save for a part of Maharashtra (Nasik and Pratishthana) easily accessible from Malwa and already Aryanized before our era, was occupied by **Dravidians:** Canarese on the northwest, Telugu on the east, and Tamil in the Carnatic. Jainism, brought to Sravana Belgola in Mysore under Chandragupta (end 4th century B.C.), flourished in the Digambara, "naked clergy," form which the north rejected. Buddhism with its stupas and sculpture was brought to Amaravati and Mysore under Asoka. Sanskrit and Hindu culture were carried from the south to Cambodia about the opening of our era. Sanskrit influence is clear in the early Tamil grammar *Tolkappiyam,* and the *Kural* of Tiruvalluvar, lofty songs of a priest of pariahs (2nd–3rd centuries A.D.). Brahman colonies with Hinduism and the caste system were at various periods imported from the Ganges Valley and endowed by local rulers, as was done also in Bengal.

The south, however, placed its own impress on what it received, and developed lingaworship, *bhakti* devotion to Vishnu and Siva, organization of Saiva monasteries and laymen, occasional violent religious intolerance, and municipal and corporate life with a sacrificial spirit of personal loyalty.

c. 225. Breakup of the Satakani Empire led to establishment, in Maharashtra near Nasik, of a
c. 250–c. 500. **Traikutaka dynasty,** probably founded by chiefs of the pastoral Abhira tribe.

c. 300-c. 500. **The Vakatakas,** extended their power from the fortress of Gawilgarh in northern Berar to Nagpur, Bundelkhand, and Kuntala, probably limiting Gupta expansion to the south.

Farther south the **Chutu branch of the Satakani,** called Andhrabhrityas in the Puranas, ruled at Banavasi (c. 200–c. 250) where they were succeeded by

c. 350-c. 500. The **Kadamba dynasty,** founded by a Brahman rebel from the Pallava. His great-grandson **Kakutsthavarman** (c. 435–475) married his daughters to a Gupta, a Vakataka (445), and a Ganga of Mysore.

In the Telugu lands, the Andhras were succeeded by the **Ikshvaku dynasty** (3rd century), notable for donations to a Buddhist stupa on the Nagarjunikonda (hill), on the Kistna above Amaravati; by the

c. 300-450. **Salankayana of Vengi;** and by the
c. 400-611. **Vishnukundins,** a dynasty of at least ten kings at the same place.

c. CEYLON

Ceylon traditionally received Buddhism from Asoka under

?247-?207 B.C. **Devanampiya Tissa,** who founded the Mahavihara or Great Monastery at his capital Anuradhapura. The Pali *Tripitaka,* which reflects Theravadin tradition, was written under

89-40 or 29-?17 A.D. **Vattagamani,** who founded the rival Abhayagiri Monastery. His epoch is supported by the geography (c. 90–200 A.D.) of the *Mahaniddesa,* a commentary admitted late to the Canon. Under

412-434. **Mahanaman,** Buddhaghosha of Magadha, author of the *Visuddhimagga* or "Way of Purity," recorded in Pali Singhalese traditions.

(Cont. p. 349.)

3. *China, 221 B.C.–618 A.D.*

(From p. 63)

221-207 B.C. The **CH'IN DYNASTY** established by the self-styled "First Emperor" (**Shih Huang Ti,** b. 259; acceded 247; d. 210), advised by **Li Ssu.** Territorial reorganization into 36 *chün,* each under civil, military, and supervisory officials. Disarmament by melting down weapons. Standardization of law, weights and measures, and axle length to facilitate interstate commerce.

214. Earlier ramparts linked by convict labor to form the **Great Wall** against the Turkish Hsiung-nu or Huns. Strategic roads. Wholesale transportation of families, especially criminals, to strengthen defenses and weaken particularism. Central South China conquered, from T'ai and Miao tribes, as far as the Southern Mountains and Canton, with the help of a new canal at Hsing-an, from present-day Hunan into Kwangsi.

213. **Proscription of books** that had been employed by enemies of the new order. Exception made for all scientific works and for

Section of the Great Wall of China

those in the hands of 70 official scholars. Introduction of roll silk as writing material led to improvement of hair brush (attributed to Gen. Meng T'ien, d. 209) and to standardization and simplification of script (attributed to Li Ssu). Old complex characters were quickly forgotten.

206. **Epic struggle of Hsiang Yü against Liu Pang** (posthumous temple name [Han] Kao Tsu), who founded

202 B.C.–9 A.D. The **FORMER OR WESTERN HAN DYNASTY,** with capital at Ch'ang-an. Classic illustration of the typical Chinese dynastic pattern: foundation by rude warrior and administrator; gradual weakening of ruling line; renascence under a strong successor whose reign reveals cultural progress; further degeneration of dynasty, weakening of control over officials, oppression, revolts, dissolution. In general the Han continued the Ch'in system of administration, gradually increasing the *chün* from 36 to 108.

The study of number theory continued (concepts of negative numbers, fractions, and rules for measuration contained in a treatise that dates from 120 B.C.). In astronomy the sundial was introduced during the Han dynasty and first observations on sunspots were made (28 B.C.). The first maps also date from this period.

200. The emperor was surrounded for seven days by the Hsiung-nu, who had formed the first Turkish Empire in Mongolia during the preceding decade. The gift of an imperial princess as consort (repeated in 173), with other presents, secured peace till 166.

196. **Chao T'o** was recognized as king of southern Yüeh (the modern Kwang provinces), which he had conquered for the Ch'in in 218–214. An expedition against him in 181 ended in disaster.

191. Withdrawal of proscription of conservative literature permitted private scholars in the cultured East to begin its restoration and (equally vital) to transcribe it into modern characters.

155-130. **Liu Teh,** prince of Ho-chien, collected a library of archaic texts. His cousin, Liu An, prince of Huai-nan (d. 122), directed an inclusive compilation of early (especially Taoist) philosophy.

140-87. The **reign of Wu Ti,** "The Martial Em-

Painted lacquer toilet box, Han Dynasty

Watchtower of green-glazed pottery, Han Dynasty

peror," was notable alike for foreign conquests and for the establishment of Confucian scholarship in control of civil administration.

140. **Tung Chung-shu** advocated Confucian training for a civil service, and urged limitation of private holding of land and slaves to remedy undue concentration of wealth resulting from commerce and mining on a national scale. As result of his efforts the emperor appointed in

136. **Doctors of the Five Classics.** These were the *I* or Changes (an early divination manual); the *Shih* or Odes; the *Shu* or History (documents compiled in the 6th century); the *Ch'un Ch'iu* or Annals of Confucius; and the *Shih-li* (now *I-li*) or Rituals. All were studied in terms of moralistic and ritual commentaries. The Han had followed the bad precedent of the Chou by granting fiefs to relatives and assistants, and found that direct efforts to weaken them resulted in revolt of seven princes (154).

127. **Chu-fu Yen** solved the problem by suggesting that younger sons should share by inheritance one-half of their father's fief. He thus also demonstrated the utility of the scholars.

126. **Chang Ch'ien** returned empty-handed, but with new knowledge of Central Asia and India, from a mission (138) to secure help against the Hsiung-nu from the **Yüeh-chih,** an Indo-European people who had been driven by the Hsiung-nu west from the Chinese border into Ili, and had thence invaded Hellenistic Bactria.

124. **Creation of a Grand College** to train officials for civil service through study of what was now fast becoming Confucian orthodoxy.

121-119. The Hsiung-nu were driven north of the Gobi by **Ho Ch'ü-ping** (d. 117, aged 22). They then split into northern and southern divisions (54).

111-110. **Subjugation of eastern Yüeh** and southern Yüeh (along the coast from modern Chekiang to Tonkin), and of the southwest. These conquests rounded out the frontiers of modern "China proper," and gave the Chinese all the best lands in their known world. During the next century Chinese officials traveled on the coasting vessels of local southern merchants at least as far as the Indian Ocean, exchanging gold and silk for glass and pearls.

110. **Wu Ti inaugurated the sacrifice to Heaven** which has since been the primary prerogative and obligation of imperial office.

108. **Conquest of Ch'ao Hsien,** a border kingdom of Korea.

102. **Conquest of the petty states of the Tarim Basin** and **Ferghana** (Ta Yüan) by Li Kuang-li and a large army. Indo-European languages were spoken throughout this region: Tokharian and Kuchean in the northern oases, Eastern Iranian or Shaka in those of the south, while Sogdian served as *lingua franca.*

Imperial finances, drained by war, were replenished by sale of military titles (123), monopolies of salt and iron (119), forced contributions by the nobility (112), and commutation by fines of judicial sentences (97). They were inflated by debasement of currency (119). The government, guided by Sang Hung-yang, entered the grain business (110), buying cheap and selling dear until exactions of greedy officials led to repeal under Chao Ti (86–73).

The *Shih Chi* or Historical Memoirs, first general history of China and a model for later dynastic histories, was compiled by **Ssu-ma Ch'ien** (d. c. 87). **Tai Teh** and **Tai Sheng** compiled standard repertories of early ritual texts, the *Ta Tai Li-chi* and *Li-chi.* **Liu Hsiang** (79–8) prepared a series of reports on the contents of the imperial library. His son **Liu Hsin** (d. 23. A.D.) digested these to form the first classified inventory of extant literature, and rescued from archaic script several important texts, notably the *Tso-chuan* (cf. supra) and the *Chou-li* or Chou Ritual.

1-8. A.D. **Wang Mang** served as regent for child-emperors.

6. All candidates for office were required to take **civil service examinations.** Tribute of a live rhinoceros was presented on request by the distant but unidentified southern state of Huang-chih.

9-23. **WANG MANG** reigned as emperor of the **Hsin Dynasty,** and undertook radical reforms: nationalization of land with division of large estates and manumission of slaves had to be repealed (12); a tax on slaveholding was substituted in 17. To monopolies of salt, iron, and coinage was added one on wine, and other mining profits were taxed. Seven regional commissions were directed to establish annual high, low, and mean price levels for staple products; to buy surplus goods at cost; and to peg the market by sales above the seasonal index. To curb usury, loans were offered free up to 90 days for funerals, and at 3 per cent a month or 10 per cent a year for productive purposes. Merchants and capitalists employed as administrators provoked revolts, in one of which Wang was killed.

25–220. LATER OR EASTERN HAN DYNASTY, founded by a collateral imperial scion, (Hou Han) Kuang Wu Ti (25–57), reigned at Loyang. **Buddhism** was introduced by missionaries from Central Asia and later from India, probably about the time of Christ. In 65 A.D. the presence of monks and lay believers at his brother's court was favorably mentioned in a decree by Emperor Ming (58–75). The story of official introduction following a dream of this emperor has been shown by Maspero to be a pious legend, completed in its main outlines by the end of the 2nd century.

43. Ma Yüan conquered Tonkin and Annam, much of which remained (except for brief revolts) under Chinese control until 939. A few natives adopted the Chinese classics, Confucianism, and Buddhism; but the masses retained their own language and customs. Commercial relations through the southern seas were gradually extended. "Java" (perhaps then Sumatra) sent tribute early in 132, and traders from the Roman Empire reached Cattigara or Chiao-chih (now Tonkin) in 166 and 226. A newly organized Malay people, the Chams, occupied Quangnam, the region of Tourane, c. 192; but when they came farther north they were repelled (270, 360, and 446).

74–94. Pan Ch'ao, by personal diplomacy and strategy, brought into submission all the petty states of Turkestan, opening the way for extensive silk trade with the Roman Orient **(Ta Ch'in).** His lieutenant Kan Ying penetrated to the Persian Gulf (97). Even the Yüeh-chih, who had recently founded the Kushana Kingdom in the Indian Punjab, sent tribute in 90. The northern Hsiung-nu, as a result of successive defeats by the southern Hsiung-nu (85), by the Mongol Sien-pi (87), and by the Chinese general Tou Hsien (89), in part submitted, in part migrated westward, leaving their lands to the Sien-pi, who in 101 in turn began raiding the frontier. To the west the Ch'iang Tibetans disturbed the peace of modern Kansu for several decades until repulsed by Chao Chung, 141–144.

After only two vigorous reigns the court was dominated by women, by their relatives, and by eunuchs by whom they were surrounded.

82. Empress Tou altered the succession, and, with her family, ruled as dowager (88–97).

105–121. Empress Teng ruled as dowager for her infant son and his boy successor till her death, when her most prominent relatives chose suicide.

124. A change in succession made by Empress Yen was violently reversed in the same year.

132. Empress Liang secured honors for her father, and ruled for three youthful emperors from 144 until her death in 150. A younger empress of the same family survived until 159.

159. Emperor Huan finally compassed the death of Liang Chi, brother of the elder empress.

184. Rebellion of the Yellow Turbans, provoked by the rapacity of the eunuchs, against whose influence and ruthless murder of scholars opposed to them there had been vigorous protests in 135–136.

189. Massacre of the eunuchs by Yüan Shao

190–220. Emperor Hsien, last of the Later Han dynasty, never really governed, the actual power having passed to competing military dictators.

Insecurity of life and property contributed to the popularity of **religious Taoism,** a cult of mysticism and occultism which promised longevity or even immortality as a reward for support, faith, and monastic austerity. Its founders, **Chang Ling** (according to tradition he ascended into heaven in 156 at the age of 123) and his son **Chang Heng,** claimed authority from Lao-tzu and philosophic Taoism, but followed the practices of alchemy, breath-control, and magic inherited from charlatans who had infested the courts of Ch'in Shih Huang Ti and Han Wu Ti. Their successors slavishly imitated Buddhism by creation of a divine hierarchy, a voluminous textual canon, and a monastic community.

Cultural tradition was maintained by **Pan Ku** (32–92), who compiled the dynastic *History of the Former Han,* his sister **Pan Chao,** whose *Lessons for Women* codified the standard of feminine morality, and **Hsü Shen,** who completed in 100 the first lexicon of archaic script, *Shuo wen chieh tzu.* The rhymed and rhythmic prose-form *fu* was developed at this time. In 105 the eunuch **Ts'ai Lun** presented to court **paper** made of vegetable fibers: bark, hemp, fish nets, and rags. Paper rolls now rapidly supplanted bamboo or wooden slips strung with cords, and the costly roll silk and silk floss paper. The first mathematical text *Chou Pei Suan Ching* dates from the 3rd century and counting rods from the 5th century (rod numerals in evidence from the 1st century). The applications of mathematics are illustrated through the practical examples used in the texts. The first accurate figure for π is that of **Tsu Ch'ung-chih** and was computed between 430–501 A.D. In the 3rd century the first charts of the heavens appear and the astrolabe is used as an astronomical instrument. During the 5th century the foot stirrup was invented either in China, or Korea. **Ma Jung** invented the device of double-column commentary (138–140). Six classics were first engraved on stone (175–183) to perpetuate the academic victory of the conservative school of commentators, who accepted only the earliest renderings into modern script. Figure painting (portraits of 28 generals) and calligraphy (text for stone classics written by Ts'ai Yung) emerged as fine arts. Mortuary chapel of Wu Liang decorated with stone flat reliefs (151).

220–264. THREE KINGDOMS divided the empire, each claiming imperial status.

220–264. Wei dynasty formally founded by Ts'ao P'ei, son of Ts'ao Ts'ao, who had dominated the court since 196. Loyang remained the capital. Eunuchs excluded from government. Families of empresses excluded from future exercise of regency (222). Three classics cut in stone (240–248) to establish versions sponsored by the Archaic Text School, founded by Liu Hsin.

221–264. Shu or Shu-Han dynasty founded in the west by Liu Pei (d. 223), antagonist of Ts'ao Ts'ao since 194. Capital at Ch'eng-tu. Chuko Liang chief minister 221–234. Rapid development of Szechwan.

222–280. Wu dynasty founded by Sun Ch'üan in the lower Long River Valley with capital at Chien-K'ang (modern Nanking).

c. 245–250. K'ang T'ai mission to Fu-nan, Khmer state in southern Cambodia (first tribute 243), learned details of southern Asia from the envoy of the Indian king.

265–317. Nominal reunion under weak **Western Chin dynasty,** established by rebellion of Ssu-ma Yen against the Wei. Institution of the censorate.

317–589. Southern and Northern dynasties divided the empire. Six dynasties (counting the eastern Wu) ruled at Chien-K'ang. The later five are considered legitimate:

317–420. Eastern Chin dynasty.

420–479. Former (or Liu) **Sung dynasty,** so called from the eight emperors of the Liu family.

479–502. Southern Ch'i dynasty.

502–557. Southern Liang dynasty.

557–589. Southern Ch'en dynasty. Meantime a series of barbarian dynasties was established in the north by invasion and infiltration of diverse peoples who avidly sought Chinese culture, followed Chinese precedents, and were rapidly absorbed.

304–439. Sixteen kingdoms established along the northern marches by three Chinese and leaders of five northern peoples: three Turkish Hsiung-nu, five Mongol Sien-pi, three Ti, one Chieh, and one Tibetan Ch'iang.

386–534. Northern Wei dynasty, founded at Ta-t'ung by the Toba Tatars, who spoke a Mongol dialect strongly palatalized by contact with the Tungus. In 495 the capital was transferred to Loyang.

534–550. The **Eastern Wei dynasty** ruled at Ye (present An-yang) as did their successors,

550–557. The **Northern Ch'i.** Meanwhile at Ch'ang-an

535–556. The **Western Wei** were succeeded by

General Kuan Yu, Shu-Han Dynasty
(Hokusai drawing)

557-581. The **Northern Chou,** who overthrew the Northern Ch'i in 577.

This long epoch of political division retarded cultural progress. Pseudo-reconstruction of texts which had been added to the *Canon of History* by K'ung An-kuo in the 2nd century B.C., but lost in the 1st century A.D., was probably carried out c. 250, and was presented to the throne in 317-322. Thirteen texts, including the *Bamboo Annals,* were recovered (281) from a tomb which was closed in 299 B.C. Gen. **Wang Hsi-chih** (321-379) provided the classic models (cut in stone) for formal and cursive calligraphy. **Ku K'ai-chih** (c. 344-c. 406) perfected the technical refinement of episodic figure-painting.

Buddhism flourished in China already by the close of the Han. The splendor of the Buddhist pantheon and ritual, with its novel conceptions which embraced 10 heavens, 10 hells, rebirth, and salvation of individual souls of common men, proved irresistible. Sutras were translated in terms borrowed from philosophic Taoism chiefly by Indian and Central Asiatic missionaries, among whom the most prolific was **Kumarajiva** (c. 344-413, to China 383), son of an Indian and of a princess of Kucha. Indian sectarian divergencies became reflected especially in versions of the monastic law (*vinaya*). Desire for direct intelligence of authoritative texts led at least 82 Chinese pilgrims to visit India during the period 200-600 (61 in the 5th century alone). Fa-hsien blazed the desert trail across Central Asia and returned by sea (399-414), and Sung-yun followed the land route to and from Udyana and Gandhara (518-522). Most popular text of the 6th century was the *Parinirvana-sutra,* which recounts the birth, illumination, first teaching, and death of the Buddha. Unfavorable Confucian appraisal of Indian asceticism, parasitic practices (celibacy, monasticism, mendicancy), and unrestrained imaginative metaphysical literature, together with hostility of the competing Taoist priesthood, led to brief persecution by the Northern Wei (446) and by the Northern Chou (574).

The Northern Wei cut **cave temples** in the Yün-kang cliffs near Ta-t'ung and decorated them with Buddhist sculpture in imitation of the "Caves of a Thousand Buddhas" at Tunhuang, then the point of bifurcation of trade routes north and south of the Tarim basin. After 495 new caves were cut at Lung-men near Loyang. The various Buddhas, bodhisattvas, Lohan (Skt. Arhat or Saints), and militant guardians of the law reflect Indian iconography given form by Greek artisans in Gandhara, as well as Iranian influence.

In Central Asia the Juan-juan or Avars founded the **first Mongol Empire** throughout Mongolia (407-553). Revolt by the T'u-chüeh in the Altai (551) led to establishment in imitation of it of a Turkish Empire which shortly (572) split into eastern and western divisions. The Western Turks assailed Sassanian Persia from the east, and by weakening it contributed to the triumph of Islam a few decades later.

581-618. The **Sui dynasty** was founded at Ch'ang-an by Yang Chien (Wen Ti), chief minister (580) of the Chou.

585 and 607-608. Reconstruction of the Great Wall (as in 543 by the Eastern Wei and in 556 by the Northern Ch'i), against the Eastern Turks of the Orkhon.

589. REUNION OF THE EMPIRE by conquest of the southern Ch'en dynasty.

Active patronage of Buddhism, the common religion of north and south, multiplied shrines and images. Chinese Buddhists increasingly neglected the intangible goal of Indian theology, the eventual ending of the perpetual chain of sentient existences by nihilistic absorption into nirvana; and stressed more pratical objectives: immediate response to prayer by the protective Bodhisattva Kuan-yin (Avalokitesvara), direct rebirth into the Western Happy Heaven (Sukhavati) of O-mi-t'o (Amitabha), and salvation by the coming Buddha Mi-lo-fo (Maitreya). Early Chinese philosophic divergencies reappeared within Buddhist sectarian doctrine. Taoist thought was reflected in the increasingly influential **Ch'an sect,** which taught that the Buddha-nature is in every man, and that illumination is to be sought solely through meditation, to the exclusion of prayer, asceticism, and good works. Confucian reaction was evident in the emphasis by the **T'ien-t'ai school,** founded (575) in the mountains of Chekiang by Chih-i (531-597), upon education as necessary to realization of the Buddha-nature. Strongly synthetic, approval was given to ecstasy, ceremonial, discipline, and to a variety of texts that were interpreted as corresponding to stages in the Buddha's teaching. Perfection was reached in the Lotus (*Saddharmapundarika*) Sutra, which thenceforth surpassed all others in popular favor.

602-605. **Liu Fang** suppressed rebellion in Annam, repelled the Chams, and sacked their capital Indrapura (near Tourane). The Chams now paid tribute for a century and a half. They controlled (until the 10th century) the trade in spices for China, and in silk and porcelain for the Abbasids, which was largely in the hands of Persian merchants. Probably before this time the Cambodian kingdom of Chen-la overthrew its suzerain Fu-nan, and now resumed tribute missions to China (616 or 617).

605-618. **Yang Ti,** a parricide (604), was ruined by extravagance at home and fruitless foreign wars.

605. The **Grand Canal** was formed by linking existing waterways from the sumptuous new capital at Loyang (604) to the Long River. It was extended to Cho-chün (near modern Peking) by a million laborers in 608, and to Hangchow in 610.

606. The **National College** was enlarged and the doctoral *chin-shih* degree first awarded. The first Japanese embassy was received from the Empress Suiko.

607. Appointment of P'ei Chü to command in the west led to defeat (608) of the Mongol T'u-yü-hun, who had entered the Koko-nor region in the early 4th century, and submission of minor kingdoms (609), but provoked the Eastern T'u-chüeh, who invested the emperor in Yenmen (615).

610. The king of the Liu-ch'iu Islands (or Formosa?) was killed by Ch'en Leng.

611-614. **Disastrous wars with Kao-li** in the Liao Basin and Korea completed exhaustion of the empire and provoked

613-618. **Domestic revolts** which led to murder of Yang Ti.

618-907. The **T'ang dynasty** was founded.

(Cont. p. 356.)

4. *Korea, 300* B.C.–*562* A.D.

Korea is a mountainous peninsula 100 to 150 miles wide and about 400 miles long, extending southward from Manchuria toward the western tip of Japan. High mountains and the cold Japan Sea have retarded the development of the east coast, but the milder climate and more suitable terrain of the west coast facing China and the south coast opposite Japan have made these regions the natural centers of Korean history.

The people since prehistoric times seem to have been closely related racially, linguistically, and culturally to the ancient peoples of Manchuria and Siberia as well as to the Japanese, but their post-Neolithic civilization came largely from China.

c. 300-200 B.C. A semi-Sinicized state called **Chosŏn** (Japanese: Chōsen) developed in the northwest, and other less civilized states appeared in the south and east.

108 B.C. **Emperor Wu Ti** of the Han dynasty of China conquered Chosŏn and established four prefectures covering central and western Korea and centering around Lo-lang near the modern P'yŏng-yang (Chinese Ping-yang, Japanese Heijo), where an extensive Chinese colony grew up.

c. 150 A.D. Koguryŏ, founded over 100 years earlier in Manchuria and northern Korea, and other states in the south and east asserted their independence of the Chinese colony.

c. 210. The **Kung-sun family** of southern Manchuria obtained control of Lo-lang and established Tai-fang to the south of it.

c. 238. The **Wei dynasty** of China captured Lo-lang and Tai-fang by sea.

c. 250. Northern invaders established the state of **Paekche** in the southwest.

313. The last remnants of the Chinese colonies were extinguished by native states, and Chinese civilization was diffused throughout the peninsula by the dispersed Chinese colonists. This marked the beginning of

313–668. THE THREE KINGDOMS PERIOD. After the elimination of China, Korea remained for several centuries divided between Koguryŏ in the north, Paekche in the southwest, and Silla, established probably in the 2nd or 3rd century, in the southeast.

c. 360–390. Period of greatest **Japanese influence** and activity in Korea through their foothold on the coast between Silla and Paekche.

372. Koguryŏ received Buddhism from China.

413–490. King Changsu brought Koguryŏ to the height of its power and moved the capital from the banks of the Yalu River to P'yŏng-yang (427).

528. Silla adopted Buddhism. The last of the Korean states to do so and culturally the most backward, Silla at this time began to make rapid progress and to expand at the expense of the Japanese sphere.

554. Silla won an outlet on the East China Sea in central Korea, giving her easy sea communications with China.

562. Silla destroyed Japan's sphere in Korea.

(Cont. p. 365.)

5. *Japan, 230–645* A.D.

GEOGRAPHY. Japan proper consists of a group of islands running eastward from the southern tip of the Korean peninsula for some 700 miles and then turning abruptly northward for about the same distance, approaching the Asiatic mainland once more off the coast of the Maritime Province of Siberia. The cold Japan Sea enclosed by this island arc gives the inner side of the archipelago a cold, damp climate, but because of the Japan Current the Pacific coast of southwestern Japan enjoys a warm, temperate climate. Consequently, here the main centers of civilization have developed. Four main islands account for most of the land area of Japan. Hondō, the largest, extends for the greater part of the arc. The next largest, Hokkaidō or Ezo, lies to the north of Hondō. Kyūshū at the southwestern extremity and Shikoku east of it, together with the westernmost portion of Hondō, almost surround a long narrow strip of water known as the Inland Sea. Among the many lesser islands Tsushima and Iki are of most significance, for they lie in the straits between Korea and Japan.

The two most important areas of Japan are the group of small plains lying in Hondō at the eastern end of the Inland Sea and the great Kantō Plain around Tōkyō Bay in eastern Hondō. The Inland Sea, as an artery of communications, and northern and western Kyūshū, which face the Asiatic mainland, are also important regions.

The rivers are all short and shallow and are consequently of little significance. Mountains cover almost the entire area and are particularly high in central Hondō. Many of them are volcanic, and eruptions and earthquakes are frequent. The climate is temperate throughout the land, and rain is abundant. Since antiquity rice has been the principal crop.

ETHNOLOGY. The origin of the Japanese people is still in question. Archaeology and physical anthropology indicate a close connection with the Koreans and the Tungusic peoples of northeastern Asia. Linguistic evidence, though more hotly disputed, tends to support this. However, ethnographical evidence and mythology suggest South Chinese, Malaysian, or even Polynesian origin. Furthermore, the Ainu (also called Ezo and Emishi), possibly a proto-Caucasian people, originally inhabited the northeastern half of Japan and undoubtedly contributed to the racial composition of the Japanese. One may conclude, therefore, that, though the early Japanese seem to have been primarily a Mongolian people, there was probably some admixture of blood from southeastern Asia and from the Ainu.

RELIGION. The primitive religion of Japan was a simple worship of the manifold manifestations of the powers of nature combined with a system of ritualistic observances, notable among which was an insistence on physical and ritual purity. The deities tended to become

Emperor Jimmu

Vessel of shell-mound culture, Japan

anthropomorphic and to merge with memories of past heroes. They were also affected by attempts to explain the origins of man and society in mythological terms. This eventually resulted in an organized mythology centering around the sun-goddess (Amaterasu) and her descendants, the imperial family. After the introduction of Buddhism this combination of nature-worship, ritualistic observances, and ancestor-honoring mythology was given the name of **Shintō** to distinguish it from the Indian religion.

CIVILIZATION. Japan's earliest known civilization was a Neolithic shell-mound culture, which before the Christian era gave way to a culture featured by sepulchral mounds over dolmens containing pottery and iron and bronze objects which show a predominantly north Asiatic influence. Prehistoric Japanese civilization seems to have come from what is known linguistically as the Altaic region and seems early to have been influenced strongly by the much higher Chinese civilization.

HISTORY. The first authentic historical accounts of Japan occur in Chinese histories of the 3rd century A.D., and picture western Japan, if not all of Japan, as divided among a great number of small political units, among which feminine rule was not uncommon. Some of these petty states had direct relations with the Chinese colonies in Korea, and embassies from Japanese states to the Chinese capital are recorded from 57 to 266.

Japanese historical mythology commences with the accession of the first emperor, **Jimmu,**

Men of Shinra submit themselves to the Empress Jingō

in 660 B.C., a date arbitrarily chosen, probably over thirteen centuries later. The mythology hints at the migration of the future imperial clan from Kyūshū up the Inland Sea to the plain of Yamato or Nara, and a successful contest for supremacy with another clan in Izumo on the Japan Sea. The Izumo clan seems to have had a rather distinctive culture and to have had close relations with Korea. During the first four centuries of the Christian era the imperial clan in Yamato seems gradually to have established its suzerainty over most of central and western Japan in a long series of wars with neighboring clans and with the Ainu in the east and the Kumaso in the west, a people apparently of alien and quite possibly of southern origin.

c. 230 A.D. With the accession of the tenth emperor, **Sujin,** Japanese records begin to contain some material of probable historical accuracy. The victories of the half-legendary **Prince Yamatodake** over the Kumaso and the Ainu seem to reflect a period of rapid expansion in the early decades of the 4th century.

c. 360. The story of the **conquest of Korea** by the Empress Jingō, ruling in the name of her deceased husband and later in the name of her son, probably refers to Japanese campaigns in the peninsula. Korean records mention Japanese inroads during this century, and a Korean inscription of 391 proves that their armies were widely active in the peninsula at that time. From this period probably dates the establishment of a Japanese protectorate over a group of miniature states in southern Korea known as Kara or Imna (Japanese, Mimana), which had for long constituted a Japanese sphere of influence, and at the same time a semi-protectorate over Paekche, a larger state in southwestern Korea. Japan in the 5th century claimed suzerainty over all of Korea, but in reality her power was on the wane even in the south, as Silla, a vigorous kingdom in the southeast, gradually rose to supremacy. The chief significance of the Korean contacts was that Japan through them was able to imbibe deeply of Chinese civilization and was able to open the way once more for direct relations with China, which was accomplished in 413.

About the end of the 4th century or early in the 5th, scribes able to read and write Chinese are said to have come from Korea. This implies the official **adoption of Chinese writing,** but not the first knowledge of it in Japan. Writing spread slowly, but was early used for historical records, for by the first half of the 6th century the traditional Japanese chronology becomes reasonably accurate.

Japan's **social organization** as it emerged at that time was that of a large group of clans (*uji*) under clan chiefs (*uji-no-kami*). The members of a single clan all claimed descent from a common ancestor, often the clan god (*ujigami*). The clan chief acted as high priest to the clan god, and his political rule was tinged throughout with a sacerdotal flavor. The chief and his immediate family often had one of several hereditary titles (*kabane*), which

Hōryūji monastery

in time came to be grouped hierarchically. Below the clans were hereditary occupational groups (*be* or *tomo*), often called guilds or corporations. They were the economic foundation of the clan system. Below them in turn was an inconsiderable number of slaves.

The **imperial clan** at first was little more than hegemon among the various clans. Its chief was the emperor, and its clan god was made the national deity. Its rule over the country was extremely loose and feeble. The clans with the two most important hereditary titles, *Omi* and *Muraji,* were controlled through a chief *Omi* (*Oomi*) and a chief *Muraji* (*Omuraji*). *Tomo-no-miyatsuko* were placed over the imperial clan's hereditary occupational groups and *Kunino-miyatsuko* over its rice lands. Chieftains of the Kume, Otomo, and Mononobe clans served as imperial generals and those of the Nakatomi and Imube (also pronounced Imibe and Imbe) clans were in charge of the court religious ceremonies.

The **importation of Chinese civilization** and an influx of Korean immigrants seriously shook the clan system. In imitation of China there developed a greater centralization of power in the hands of the imperial clan and its ministers, who at times even aspired to the throne themselves. Imperial lands were gradually extended, and imperial authority grew, eventually leading to a complete political and economic reorganization of Japan on the Chinese model.

? 527. A serious **revolt in Kyūshū** prevented the crossing of an army to Korea to aid Imna. Dissension among the Japanese and the treason of some of their officers in Korea seriously reduced their prestige in the peninsula and opened the way for the conquest of Imna by Silla.

? 552. The official introduction of **Buddhism** from Paekche, which itself had received it in 384, marked the beginning of a new epoch in Japan. There probably were Buddhist converts in Japan prior to 552, but at this time Buddhism first began to play a significant rôle in Japanese history and to stimulate the influx of Chinese civilization by way of Paekche. Supported by the powerful Soga clan and strengthened by the arrival of clerics from Korea, Buddhism made headway at court, but soon a temporary proscription of it was brought about by the Nakatomi and Mononobe clans, the political rivals of the Soga. It was presently restored, and the Emperor Yōmei (585–587?) embraced the faith shortly before his death.

? 562. Silla drove the Japanese out of Imna, ending their long direct control of a portion of Korea.

? 587. The Soga crushed their rivals in a short civil war, thereby establishing their political supremacy and the right of Buddhism to an unhampered development in Japan.

592. **Soga Umako** (d. 626) had his nephew, the Emperor Sushun (587–592), murdered.

593–628. **Suiko,** the first officially recognized empress, ruled over the land at the crucial period when Buddhism was taking root and the importation of Chinese civilization was strongly influencing the basic forms of Japanese government and society. The leading spirit during her reign was the crown prince, **Shōtoku** (d. 621 or 622), who was the real establisher of Buddhism in Japan, the pioneer in laying the foundations for the Sinicized

Polychromed wooden angel from Hōryūji monastery, second half of 7th century

form of government of the next several centuries, and the founder of such great monasteries as the Shitennōji (593), the Hōkōji (588–596), and the Hōryūji (607?).

604. **Prince Shōtoku** issued the so-called **Seventeen Article "Constitution,"** a moral code consisting of somewhat vague injunctions imbued with Confucian ethics and the Chinese political theory of a centralized imperial government. Thus it served as an ideological basis for political centralization. The constitution was also strongly influenced by Buddhism and shows that the prince was aware of its moral and philosophical import and not merely of its supposed magical powers, which chiefly attracted the contemporary Japanese. In this same year, in imitation of China, official grades known as "cap ranks" (*kan'i*), an official calendar, and regulations for court etiquette were adopted.

607. **Ono Imoko,** the first official envoy from the central government, was dispatched to the Sui court in China. This and a second embassy to the Sui in 608 were followed in the course of the next two and a half centuries by twelve embassies to the T'ang. Since Japanese students, scholars, and monks accompanied the envoys to China and sometimes remained there for prolonged periods of study, these embassies were a very important factor in the importation of Chinese civilization to Japan.

630. First embassy to the T'ang.

643. Prince Yamashiro no Oe, the heir of Prince Shōtoku, was forced to commit suicide by Soga Iruka (d. 645), the son of Emishi (d. 645), the kingmaker of the period. The prince had twice been overlooked in the imperial succession by the Soga, whose obvious imperial aspirations brought about

645. The **DOWNFALL OF THE SOGA** in a *coup d'état* led by the future Emperor Tenchi (661–672) and by Nakatomi Kamatari (d. 669), the founder of a new clan, the Fujiwara. This incident gave the progressive element at court a chance to begin a series of sweeping reforms along Chinese lines, which mark the beginning of a new era in Japan.

(Cont. p. 366.)

Haniwa falconer, clay funerary figure, Yamato era, c. 600

III. The Middle Ages

III. The Middle Ages

A. The Early Middle Ages

I. *Western Europe*

(From p. 147)

a. CONDITIONS OF LIFE

SCIENCE AND TECHNOLOGY were separate from one another during this period. The science was based on the work of the early Latin Encyclopaedists, Pliny, Boethius, Cassiodorius, Isidore of Seville. Thought was profoundly influenced by Neo-Platonism; and observational science was abandoned since nature was seen as vivid symbols of moral realities. Technological developments were slow and came in small steps, which however added up to the increased pulse of life of the 11th century. Communication was difficult; roads and harbors were unused and in disrepair until about the 8th century, when commerce began again on a more than local basis. Building was stagnant; the art of bricklaying appears to have been lost; scarcely any stone buildings were erected in northern Europe. Metal working was still important, although stamping was unskilled and hence coins were crude. Precious metals were worked with enamel decorations, while silver and bronze could be cast. Unlike the light Mediterranean soils, those of northern Europe could not be pulverised for farming purposes; these heavy soils had to be "sliced, moved to one side and turned over." This was impossible until the introduction of the iron, wheeled plowshare, with

moldboard. The basic farm tools evolved during this period: rake, spade, fork, pick, balanced sickle, scythe. Development of the horse collar was very important, for an efficient draft animal relieved the small, work force. With an effective harness and stirrup (the latter depicted in a drawing c. 900) and tandem rather than fan-hitched teams of horses or oxen, men were freed of even more work. Another important source of power was water: the Roman water mill (in use 536) spread throughout Europe.

b. THE EARLY PAPACY, TO 461

[*For a complete list of the Roman Popes see Appendix IV.*]

The Church before the emergence of the bishops of Rome. The center of gravity was in the east. Possession of the Holy Places and the presence of the emperor gave the east political and ecclesiastical supremacy.

Rise of the episcopate. The bishops, originally overseers (*episcopus*), thanks to their consecration, the tradition of apostolic succession, and their control of the sacraments, were distinguished among the clergy. Each church was originally independent, but the evolution of an ecclesiastical counterpart to the centralized civil state gave the bishop a clearly monarchical

Papal coat of arms

quality in the 3rd century. The lay and ecclesiastical states met in the person of the emperor, and the original loose autonomy of the independent churches began to be lost in a centralized system. The precedence of **metropolitans** (i.e. the bishops of the great sees) was recognized (341), without reducing the accepted superiority of the **patriarchs.** The five patriarchates (ecclesiastical equivalents of exarchates) were (save for Rome) in the east—Jerusalem, Antioch, Alexandria, Constantinople. The west (including Rome) was either poorly represented or not represented at all at the ecumenical councils in the east. Vague precedence in honor was conceded to Rome, but no more.

Ecumenical councils settled general problems of dogma and discipline. These councils were called by the emperor and presided over by him in person or by legate. Local problems were dealt with in synods.

EMERGENCE OF THE BISHOPS OF ROME. *Papa* was a title applied to all bishops until c. 425, and did not take on its present meaning until the 7th century. **Bishop Victor** of Rome (c. 190) exercised a kind of spiritual sovereignty which was continued in the 3rd century. Gradually the recession of the Church of the east, the loss of Africa, and the rise of powerful churches in the east, left Rome iso-

Agriculture in the Early Middle Ages

St. Peter crucified (detail from the 15th-century bronze doors of St. Peter's Cathedral, Rome)

lated in the west. As the sole western apostolic see, the scene of the martyrdom of Peter, and guardian of the tombs of Peter and Paul, Rome enjoyed a unique spiritual prestige, and until the reign of Diocletian (284–305) it was the administrative center of the empire. After that the capital was at Milan, and this see at times was almost equal to Rome in influence. With the removal of the imperial capital to Constantinople (330), Rome lost prestige, especially in the east. On the other hand, between 330 and 395, since there was no emperor permanently resident in the west, the bishop of Rome had no political rival.

(1) The emperors supported the Roman cam-paign against paganism and against heresy (e.g. Arians and Donatists) with civil penalties, and confirmed and deprived bishops.

(2) The Roman See, as early as the days of Diocletian, was rich, and was further enriched by the emperors until it was the wealthiest in the Church; the bishop of Rome enjoyed the "presidency in charity" throughout Christendom.

(3) Sporadic intervention (usually on appeal) was made outside his direct jurisdiction by the bishop of Rome, but until after 1000 he rarely pronounced on doctrinal points on his own au-thority, nor did he interfere between a bishop and his flock in ordinary diocesan affairs or collect money except within his own immediate episcopal jurisdiction.

(4) The **Petrine theory,** on the basis of Mat-thew 16: 18, 19, asserts that Peter was designated by Christ as the founder of the Church, and that Christ conferred the "power of the keys," i.e. "the power to bind and loose," upon Peter, who transmitted it to his successor, the bishop of Rome, through whom it passed to all bishops. This theory was given currency by **Pope Celes-tine I** (422–432). In effect this abandoned the original concept of the bishop of Rome as *episcopus inter episcopos* for the more radical monarchical concept of the Roman bishop as *episcopus episcoporum.* Early writers give no

The Forum Romanum at Rome (pp.89 & 114)

Roman aquaduct at Segovia, Spain, attributed to Trajan (p.132)

*Harpist; terracotta figurine
from T'ang dynasty (p.168)*

indication of such interpretations, and Cyprian (d. 258) in a famous passage avers that the bishop of Rome is no more than a bishop among other bishops.

340. The introduction of **eremitical monasticism** into the west by Athanasius marked the beginning of a strong ascetic reaction against the corruption of western life. Supported by Jerome, Ambrose, and Augustine, this development led to a great growth of monasticism. Bishop Eusebius of Vercelli (d. 371), by insisting that his clergy lead a monastic life, began a practice that led to the general ordination of monks. Martin of Tours founded (c. 362) a cenobitic community of monks near Poitiers.

343. The **Council of Sardika** apparently recognized the right of appeal from a provincial synod to the bishop of Rome.

The oldest extant decretal dates from the episcopacy of **Siricius** (c. 384–399).

THE LATIN FATHERS OF THE CHURCH. Jerome (c. 340–420), a Dalmatian, devoted to pagan learning despite his keen ascetic convictions. The first great western exponent of monasticism. One of the greatest scholars of the Latin Church, his translation of the *Bible* into Latin (the *Vulgate*) is still authoritative in the Roman Church today. This excellent ver-

Innocent I (early fresco)

sion exerted stylistic and theological influence throughout the Middle Ages. **Ambrose** (c. 340–397) of Trier, a Roman provincial governor, elected (374) archbishop of Milan before he was baptized. His *Duties of the Clergy* (based largely on Cicero, *de Officiis*) was for centuries the standard work on ethics, and is probably the chief single source of the Stoic tradition in early western thought. He made Milan almost the equal of Rome in prestige, and forced the Emperor Theodosius to do penance, maintaining that in ecclesiastical matters a bishop was superior to an emperor. **Augustine** (354–430) of Hippo, greatest of the western fathers. Converted to Christianity after ventures in Neo-Platonism and Manichaeism, he was founder of western theology, the link between the classical tradition and the mediaeval schoolmen. Through him a great stream of Platonic and Neo-Platonic thought came into the Church. For a thousand years all thought was influenced by Augustine, and theology betrays his influence to this day. He gave wide currency to the doctrines of original sin, predestination, salvation through divine grace, and his influence was felt by Calvin and Luther. His *City of God* presents a dualism of the heavenly city (identified with the Christian Church) and the earthly city (Rome), and is written to prove that the misfortunes of Rome (e.g. the sack of 410) were not due to Christianity. The *Confessions* set the fashion in spiritual autobiography.

All knowledge was used as symbolic allegory. A model of this is seen in the *Physiologos,* where animals, real and imaginary, form the keys to moral teachings; in medicine the doctrine of signatures was popular; the external appearance of the plant held the key to its use.

401–417. INNOCENT I asserted that the pope was custodian of apostolic tradition and claimed universal jurisdiction for the Roman Church.

440–461. LEO THE GREAT, the first great pope, a highly cultivated Roman, vigorous foe of the Manichaean heresy. He procured an edict from Emperor Valentinian III (445) declaring that papal decisions have the force of law. Leo was probably the first pope to enunciate the theory of the mystical unity of Peter and his successors, and to attribute all their doings and sayings to Peter. Leo, repudiating the decrees of the Robber Council of Ephesus (449) at the Council of Chalcedon (451), dic-

St. Augustine in his study (fresco by Sandro Botticelli)

tated without discussion, and with imperial support, his solution of the greatest doctrinal controversy since 325. His *Tome* promulgated the doctrine of the union of the two natures. He refused to accept the decree of the council that the patriarch of Constantinople was supreme in the Church. The tradition of his miraculous arrest of Attila's advance and his efforts to stop Gaiseric's attack (455) won the papacy tremendous prestige in later days.

(Cont. p. 171.)

c. INVADERS OF THE WEST, TO 532

ORIGINS OF THE INVADERS. The Germanic race was established in Scandinavia (Denmark) and between the Elbe and Oder as early as the 2nd millennium B.C. Eastward lay the Balts (Letts) and to the west of the Elbe were the Celts.

EXPANSION. (1) The West Germans (Teutons) displaced (c. 1000 B.C.) the Celts, moving up the Elbe and Rhine (the Main reached c. 200 B.C.). South Germany was occupied (c. 100 B.C.); Gaul threatened (cf. Caesar's *Commentaries*). These invaders were a pastoral, agricultural folk, tending to settle down. By the time of Tacitus' (c. 55–c. 117 A.D.) *Germania* they were wholly agricultural. Later new tribal names and a new kind of federated organization appeared. (2) The East Germans (Scandinavians) crossed the Baltic (c. 600–300 B.C.) and pushed up the Vistula to the Carpathians. (3) The North Germans remained in Scandinavia.

NEW GROUPINGS AMONG THE WEST GERMANS. Alamanni (of Suevian stock) on the upper Rhine; **Franks** (i.e. "free" of the Romans) and **Saxons** between the Weser and the Elbe, inland to the Harz; **Thuringians,** south of the Saxons.

GOVERNMENT. All were tribal democracies, some under kings, others under *grafs.* In each case the head of the state was elected by the assembly of free men, the kings chosen from a royal house, e.g. Amals (Ostrogoths), Balthas (Visigoths), Mervings (Franks), the *grafs* without such restriction.

PROGRESS OF MIGRATIONS. The East Germans (Bastarnae, Burgundians, Gepids, Goths, Heruls, Rugians, Sciri) moved toward the Black Sea where they had arrived by 214 A.D. The division of Visigoth (West Goth) and Ostrogoth (East Goth) probably arose after their arrival at the Black Sea.

(1) The Huns

The **Huns,** nomadic Mongols of the Ural-Altaic race group, probably under pressure from the Zhu-Zhu Empire in Asia, swept into Europe in the 4th century and halted for some fifty years in the valley of the Danube and Theiss.

372. They defeated the Alans and Heruls, destroyed the Ostrogothic empire of Hermanric, absorbed the Ostrogoths for a time in their own empire, routed the Visigoths under Athanaric on the Dniester River, and then began a new thrust to the west.

445–453. Height of the Hun power under **Attila.** Honoria, sister of Valentinian III, to escape an unwelcome marriage, sent her ring to Attila and asked for aid. Attila claimed this to be an offer of marriage. About the same time Gaiseric the Vandal was intriguing to induce Attila to attack the Visigoths. By a clever pretense of friendliness to both sides, Attila kept the Romans and Goths apart, and set out westward with a great force (451) which included Gepids, Ostrogoths, Rugians, Scirians, Heruls, Thuringians, Alans, Burgundians, and Ripuarian Franks. Metz was taken and the Belgic provinces ravaged. To meet Attila the Roman Aëtius mustered a force of Salian Franks, Ripuarians, Burgundians, Celts, and Visigoths under Theodoric I, as well as his own Gallo-Romans. Attila apparently declined battle near Orleans and turned back.

451. Aëtius overtook him at an unknown spot near Troyes, the so-called *Lacus Mauriacus* **(Châlons),** and a drawn battle was fought. Attila continued his withdrawal. Still claiming Honoria, Attila turned into Italy, razed Aquileia, ravaged the countryside (foundation of Venice) and opened the road to Rome. Pope Leo, one of a commission of three sent by the emperor, appeared before Attila. Attila retreated after plague had broken out in his force, food supply had run low, and reinforcements arrived from the east for the Roman army. Attila's death (453) was followed by a revolt of his German vassals led by the Gepids, and (454) the defeat of the Huns on the Nedao (in Pannonia). The remnant of the Huns settled on the lower Danube, the Gepids set up a kingdom in Dacia, the Ostrogoths settled in Pannonia.

(2) The Visigoths

After their defeat by the Huns, the Visigoths (perhaps 80,000 in number) sought refuge in the Roman Empire.

376. The Emperor **Valens** ordered them disarmed and allowed to cross the Danube in order to settle in Lower Moesia. Faced with the unprecedented problem of these refugees, the Roman government bungled the administration, failed really to disarm the Goths, and ultimately had to fight a two-year war with them.

378. The Visigoths, under **Fritigern,** defeated and killed **Valens** near Adrianople, thereby making the first decisive break in the Rhine-Danube frontier. This defeat of the Roman infantry by mounted warriors forecast the revolution in the art of war which determined the military, social, and political development of Europe throughout the Middle Ages.

Fritigern, hoping to carve a Visigothic empire out of the Roman provinces, ravaged Thrace for two years, but could not take Adrianople. After his death (379), the Emperor **Theodosius** arranged a pacification of the Visigoths as part of a general policy of assimilation. He won over some of the chieftains, including **Alaric** of the royal house of Balthas who hoped for a career in the Roman service. Alaric, disappointed in his hopes at the death of Theodosius, was elected king by the Visigoths, and ravaged Thrace to the gates of Constantinople. Arcadius, emperor of the east (395–408), was helpless until the arrival of Stilicho, *magister utriusque militiae* (field marshal of both services) in the east.

Stilicho, a Vandal by blood, married to Theodosius' sister, was guardian of Theodosius' sons, Arcadius and Honorius. He faced Alaric in Thessaly and the Peloponnesus, avoiding battle, apparently on orders from

Leo the Great (miniature from St. Basil's Calendar of Saints)

East German migrants cross the Rhine frontier, 406

Honorius. Alaric was made *magister militum* in Illyricum, and Stilicho, out of favor in Constantinople, was declared a public enemy.

401. Alaric began a thrust into Italy, probably because of the triumph of an anti-German faction in Constantinople, and ravaged Venetia. Simultaneously Radagaisus (an Ostrogoth) began an invasion of Raetia and Italy. Stilicho, firmly against any Germanic invasion of the west, repulsed Radagaisus.

402. Pollentia, a drawn battle between Stilicho and Alaric, was a strategic defeat for Alaric. Alaric's next advance was stopped, probably through an understanding with Stilicho. Halted again (403) at Verona, the Visigoths withdrew to Epirus.

406 The **Rhine frontier,** denuded of troops for the defense of Italy, was crossed by a great wave of migrants, chiefly East Germans: Vandals, Sueves, and Alans (non-German). The usurper **Constantine** having crossed from Britain to Gaul, Alaric in Noricum was paid a huge sum of gold by the senate, as a sort of retainer for his services against Constantine. Stilicho, his popularity undermined by these events and by the hostility of Constantinople, was beheaded (408). There is no evidence of treason by Stilicho. His execution was followed by a general massacre of the families of the barbarian auxiliaries in Italy, and some 30,000 of them went over to Alaric in Noricum.

410. ALARIC TOOK ROME after alternate sieges and negotiations. He sacked it for three days, and then moved south toward Africa, the granary of Italy. Turned back by the loss of his fleet, Alaric died and was buried in the bed of the Busento. His brother-in-law Ataulf was elected to succeed him. Ataulf, originally bent on the destruction of the very name of Rome, now bent his energies to the fusion of Visigothic vigor and Roman tradition.

412. Ataulf led the Visigoths north, ravaged Etruria, crossed the Alps, ravaged Gaul, and married (against her brother Honorius' will) Galla Placidia (414) after the Roman ritual. He was forced into Spain (415), where he was murdered. **Wallia** (415–c. 418), after the brief reign of Sigeric, succeeded him.

Ulfilas (311–381), a Gothic bishop of Arian convictions, invented the Gothic alphabet for his translation of the *Bible*. This translation, the first literary monument of the German invaders, had enormous influence, and recalls the wide extent of the **Arian heresy,** which won every important Germanic invader except the Franks, a development with the greatest political consequences, since the lands where the Germans settled were peopled by orthodox Roman Catholics.

Spain had already been overrun by a horde of Vandals, Sueves, and Alans (409), and the Roman blockade made food hard to get.

Wallia planned to cross to the African granary, but lost his ships, was forced to make terms with Honorius and restore Galla Placidia to her brother. He agreed to clear Spain of other barbarians. Succeeding in this he received the grant of *Aquitania Secunda* (i.e. the land between the Loire and the Garonne) with Toulouse as a capital. Thus began the

419–507. KINGDOM OF TOULOUSE. The Visigoths received two-thirds of the land, the remainder being left to the Roman proprietors. A Gothic state was created within the Roman state. Honorius, hoping to counteract alien influences, revived a Roman custom of holding provincial councils, decreeing an annual meeting of the leading officials and the chief landowners for discussion of common problems. The most important rulers of Toulouse were

419–451. Theodoric I, who fell in the **battle of Châlons,** and

466–484. Euric, whose reign marked the apogee of the kingdom. He continued the pressure of the Visigoths upon Gaul and Spain, and by 481 extended his domain from the Pyrenees to the Loire and eastward to the Rhone, securing Provence from Odovacar (481). Euric first codified Visigothic law, but the *Breviary of Alaric* (506), a codification of Roman law for Visigothic use, had tremendous influence among the Visigoths and among many other barbarian peoples. Under Visigothic rule the administration in general remained Roman and the language of government continued to be a Latin vernacular. The Gallo-Roman population and clergy were hostile to the Visigoths as Arians, and this hostility opened the way for the **Frankish conquest** (507), which reduced the Visigothic power to its Spanish domains.

507-711. The **Visigothic Kingdom of Spain** dragged out a miserable existence under more than a score of rulers, some mere phantoms, until the arrival of the Moslems *(p. 185)*.

554. Belisarius' invasion of Spain, part of Justinian's reconstruction of the Roman Empire *(p. 171),* was a brilliant campaign, but reduced only the southeast corner of Spain, later regained by the Visigoths, who also reduced the Sueves in the north.

(3) The Vandals

406. The **Vandals** (Asding and Siling), allied with the Sciri and Alani, crossed the Rhine near the Main, followed the Moselle and Aisne (sacking Reims, Amiens, Arras, Tournai), then turned southward into Aquitaine, and crossed the Pyrenees into Spain (409).

429-534. THE VANDAL KINGDOM IN AFRICA. The Vandals and Alani had been established in southern Spain under Gunderic. His brother **Gaiseric** received an appeal from Bonifatius, the revolted Roman governor of Africa, following which the Vandals (perhaps 80,000 in number) crossed into Africa (429).

430. The **first siege of Hippo** failed, but Bonifatius, now reconciled to the regency of Galla Placidia, was annihilated, and the city fell (431). **St. Augustine,** Bishop of Hippo, died during the siege. The creation of a great Vandal power in Africa, supported as it soon was by a powerful navy, distracted the attention of the Roman government from the new barbar-

ian kingdoms of the west and had a decisive effect of a negative kind.

In Africa the Vandals spared nobody and nothing and the treaty made with the Romans was no restraint. After the arrival of a fleet from Constantinople, a second treaty was made. Eudocia, daughter of Valentinian, was betrothed to Gaiseric's son, Huneric, and the Vandals received most of the Roman territory except the region about Carthage.

439. Gaiseric took Carthage from the Romans, and made it his capital and naval base.

455. Gaiseric attacked Rome, on the invitation (according to tradition) of Valentinian's widow Eudoxia. He took it easily, and for two weeks pillaged the city, scientifically and ruthlessly, but without wanton destruction.

In Africa the Vandals were hated as Arians, and they had to deal with serious **Berber revolts,** but their power was not broken until the

533-548. Vandalic Wars of Justinian. Belisarius quickly defeated the Carthaginian power of the Vandals; the ensuing Berber revolt was not put down until 548.

(4) The Burgundians

411-532. The **Burgundians,** arriving from the Oder-Vistula region, moved along the Main athwart the Rhine, entered Gaul under King Gundicar, and finally settled as federates of the Roman Empire in upper Burgundy (i.e. the lands including Lyons, Vienne, Besançon, Geneva, Autun, Macon). King **Gundibald** (d. 516) codified Burgundian law in the *Lex Gundobada.* The Burgundians were finally conquered by the sons of Clovis (c. 532), but the Burgundian state remained separate under Frankish control with Merovingian princes until 613. After 613 it was a province of the Frankish Empire.

Theodoric the Great receiving the keys of Ravenna

d. THE OSTROGOTHS IN ITALY, 489-554

On the breakup of the Hunnic Empire (after Nedao, 454), the Ostrogoths settled in Pannonia (their first settlement inside the Roman frontier) as federates of the empire. Under the Huns the emergence of a single ruler had been impossible. Thiudareiks (ruler of the people), corrupted into Theodoric, educated as a hostage at Constantinople, was elected (471) merely a *gau* king, but soon became leader of his people on a march into the Balkan Peninsula where he forced the Emperor Leo to grant them lands in Macedonia. His ambition for imperial appointment was realized (483) when he was made *magister militum praesentalis* and (484) *consul.* He quarreled with the emperor and marched on Constantinople. To get rid of him the emperor commissioned him (informally) to expel Odovacar from Italy. Arriving in Italy (489) the Ostrogoths triumphed over Odovacar, but did not reduce Ravenna until 493. Theodoric killed Odovacar with his own hands and had his troops massacred.

489-526. THEODORIC THE GREAT. In general Theodoric continued Odovacar's policy, substituting Ostrogoths for Odovacar's Germans, and assigning one-third of the Roman estates (as Odovacar had probably done) to his people. Theodoric's rule was officially recognized (497) by Constantinople. Together with the emperors he named the consuls in the west, but never named an Ostrogoth. Theodoric was the only member of his people who was a Roman citizen; constitutionally the others were alien soldiers in the service of the empire. No Roman was in military command, no Ostrogoth in the civil service. Imperial legislation and coinage continued. The so-called *Edictum Theodorici* is a codification of Theodoric's administrative decrees rather than a body of legislation, as none of Theodoric's "laws" were anything more than clarifications of imperial legislation. Theodoric's secretary of state was the learned Italian, **Cassiodorus,** and the dual state was paralleled by a dual religious system. Theodoric was tolerant of the orthodox Catholics and a protector of the Jews. His chief aim was to civilize his people under the Roman environment and to keep peace.

Theodoric's co-operation with the other Germanic peoples was close, and he cemented his associations by marriage alliances (one daughter married Alaric II, the Visigoth, another Sigismund the Burgundian, and he himself married Clovis' sister). He intervened to protect the Alamanni from Clovis and tried to save the Visigoths. Provence was acquired from Burgundy and annexed to Italy. He was regent and protector of his grandson Amalaric after Alaric II's death, and virtually ruled the Visigothic Kingdom until his death (526).

To the Italians Ostrogothic rule was alien and heretical and they resented it. The end of Theodoric's reign was marked by a growing ill-feeling and suspicion that may have been due to this. **Boethius,** the Roman philosopher and commentator on Aristotle, author of the *De consolatione philosophiae,* an official of Theodoric's government, and his father-in-law, the brilliant and polished Roman **Symmachus,** were both executed (c. 524) on a charge of treasonable conspiracy.

535–554. RECONQUEST OF ITALY BY THE EMPEROR. Justinian, as part of his grandiose reconstitution of the Roman Empire, dispatched **Belisarius** and later **Narses,** who reduced the stubborn Ostrogoths and drove them over the Alps to an unknown end.

After the expulsion of the Ostrogoths the **Exarchate of Ravenna** was established under the Emperor Maurice (582–602). The exarch had military and civil powers and received full imperial honors. He exercised imperial control over the church, including the bishopric of Rome. War and pestilence had completely ruined northern Italy; Rome, in ruins, had sunk from her imperial position to be a provincial town; the way was open for the Lombard invaders.

Ravenna had been the capital of the west (c. 402–476) and was the home of Theodoric's brilliant court. The architecture of the city offers a unique series of examples of Roman and Romano-Byzantine buildings begun under the emperors and continued by Theodoric. The name and glory of Theodoric have survived in German tradition in Dietrich von Bern (i.e. of Verona, where he had a palace).

PROGRESS OF THE PAPACY. Gelasius (492–496) was the first pope to proclaim the independence of the Papacy from both emperor and church council in matters of faith. He asserted that two powers rule the world, the *sacerdotium* and the *imperium.* The *sacerdotium,* since it is the instrument of human salvation, is superior to the *imperium.*

As soon as Italy ceased to be a ruling state, there began a long effort to create national unity and to establish national independence. The barbarian invasions had isolated Italy, accentuated the break with the empire, and left the pope as the sole native representative of ancient unity and Italian hegemony. At the same time the Ostrogoths (half romanized as they were) did not destroy Italian culture, but allowed the Church to transmit the Greco-Roman tradition (linguistic, social, cultural, administrative, and religious) in the west.

529. Western monasticism, representing a wide ascetic reaction against current corruption in life and supported by Jerome, Ambrose, and Augustine, had expanded rapidly in the 6th century and reached a chaotic condition ranging from extremes of eremitical asceticism to the laxest kind of cenobitic worldliness. **Benedict** of Nursia, scandalized at conditions, withdrew to Monte Cassino where he founded a colony and gave it (traditionally in 529) the famous *Benedictine Rule.* This rule, which dominated western monasticism for centuries, was a remarkable and characteristic Roman compromise adapted to the average man. It placed the monks under the control of an abbot, made each house autonomous in a loose federation (not strictly an order at all), and provided for careful recruiting and probation. Discipline was efficient but not extreme, and great stress was laid on labor, especially in the open air (*laborare est orare*). The individual was merged in an ascetic, self-contained, self-sufficient corporation. The spread of the Benedictines was rapid, and soon the only important survival of eremitical monasticism was in the Irish monks of St. Columban. The order became the chief instrument for the reform of the Frankish (Gallic) Church, and for the conversion and civilization of England and Germany. In the course of history it gave the Church 24 popes, 200 cardinals, 5000 saints, 15,000 writers and scholars.

Ruined by invasion, its aqueducts cut, **Rome** was reduced in population from a half million to perhaps 50,000. Its aristocracy had fled, and mediaeval decay had replaced pagan

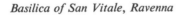

Basilica of San Vitale, Ravenna

Symmachus

grandeur. The city was not revived until the Renaissance.

554. Justinian's Pragmatic Sanction restored the Italian lands taken by the Ostrogoths and made a *pro forma* restoration of government, but agricultural lands were depopulated and grown into wilderness, the rural proprietors were sinking into serfdom. Town decline was

The Merovingian Kings

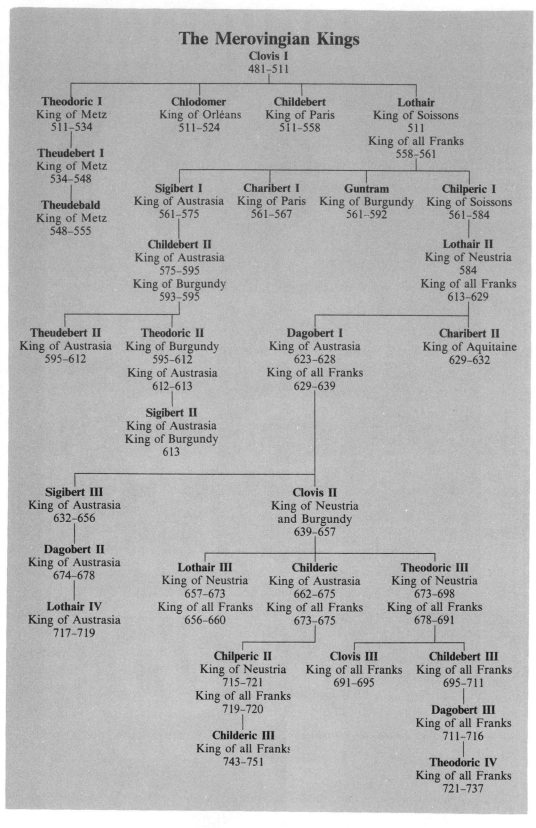

Clovis I
481–511

Theodoric I
King of Metz
511–534

Chlodomer
King of Orléans
511–524

Childebert
King of Paris
511–558

Lothair
King of Soissons
511
King of all Franks
558–561

Theudebert I
King of Metz
534–548

Theudebald
King of Metz
548–555

Sigibert I
King of Austrasia
561–575

Charibert I
King of Paris
561–567

Guntram
King of Burgundy
561–592

Chilperic I
King of Soissons
561–584

Childebert II
King of Austrasia
575–595
King of Burgundy
593–595

Lothair II
King of Neustria
584
King of all Franks
613–629

Theudebert II
King of Austrasia
595–612

Theodoric II
King of Burgundy
595–612
King of Austrasia
612–613

Dagobert I
King of Austrasia
623–628
King of all Franks
629–639

Charibert II
King of Aquitaine
629–632

Sigibert II
King of Austrasia
King of Burgundy
613

Sigibert III
King of Austrasia
632–656

Clovis II
King of Neustria
and Burgundy
639–657

Dagobert II
King of Austrasia
674–678

Lothair IV
King of Austrasia
717–719

Lothair III
King of Neustria
657–673
King of all Franks
656–660

Childeric
King of Austrasia
662–675
King of all Franks
673–675

Theodoric III
King of Neustria
673–698
King of all Franks
678–691

Chilperic II
King of Neustria
715–721
King of all Franks
719–720

Clovis III
King of all Franks
691–695

Childebert III
King of all Franks
695–711

Childeric III
King of all Franks
743–751

Dagobert III
King of all Franks
711–716

Theodoric IV
King of all Franks
721–737

---

similar. The Roman senate ceased to function after 603 and the local curiae disappeared at about the same time.

Duces were appointed, probably over each *civitas,* as part of the imperial administration, but they gradually became great landowners and their military functions dominated their civil duties. A fusion of the ducal title and landownership ensued and a new class of hereditary military proprietors emerged beside the clergy and the old nobles. The details of

this process are, of course, hard to determine, the more so as evidence is scant.*(Cont.p.174.)*

e. THE FRANKISH KINGDOM, 481–752

The **Franks** first appear as settlers on the lower Rhine in two divisions, the **Salians** (dwellers by the sea, *sal*) and the **Ripuarians** (dwellers by the riverbank, *ripa*). By the end of the 4th century the Salians were established in the area between the Meuse and the Scheldt as federates of the Roman Empire; the Ripuarians in the tract between the Rhine and Meuse. They formed no permanent confederations, and, unlike the other Germanic peoples, did not migrate as a nation, but expanded.

431–751. THE SALIAN FRANKS UNDER THE MEROVINGIANS.

451. Chlodio (son of Merowech) invaded Artois, and was defeated by Aëtius. Salian Franks were in the Roman forces at the battle of Châlons. **King Childeric** (d. 481) fought as a federate of the empire at Orleans when Aëtius defeated the Visigoths, and he later defeated the Saxons on the Loire. His tomb was found (1653) at Tournai, the "capital" of the Salians.

481–511. CLOVIS (Chlodovech), son of Childeric, in the service of Julius Nepos and Zeno. He defeated the Gallo-Roman general Syagrius at Soissons (486), expanding Salian power to the Loire. The story of the **Soissons vase** is significant of the friendly relations between Clovis and Bishop Remigius. Sigebert, the Ripuarian, defeated an Alamannic invasion at Tolbiac (496) with Salian support. Clovis in the same year defeated the Alamanni (Strasburg?) and later, after election as king of the Ripuarians, emerged as master of the Franks on both sides of the Rhine.

496. The traditional date of the **conversion of Clovis** to Roman Catholicism is 496. He had previously married a Burgundian, Clotilda, who was of the Roman communion. The Burgundians in general were Arians, and Clovis' choice may have been deliberate. In any case his conversion won him powerful papal and episcopal support and opened the way to wide conquests from the heretic (i.e. Arian) German peoples. Burgundy was conquered (after 500), the Visigoths defeated at Vouillé (507), and their whole kingdom north of the Pyrenees (except Septimania and Provence) was soon subjugated. These conquests were warmly supported by the Gallo-Roman clergy as a religious war. Clovis founded the Church of the Holy Apostles (Ste. Geneviève) at Paris, and shortly moved his "capital" from Soissons to Paris. He was made an honorary consul by the Emperor Anastasius, a proceeding that brought the Franks technically into the empire.

511–628. Divisions of the Frankish lands after the death of Clovis: (1) His four sons established four capitals—Metz, Orleans, Paris, Soissons. Expansion eastward continued along the upper Elbe; Burgundy was added, and the territory of the Ostrogoths north of the Alps. After a period of ruthless conflict, only **Lothair** (Chlothar) survived, and for a brief time (558–561) the Frankish lands were under one head again. (2) Lothair's division of his lands among his four sons led to a great feud from which three kingdoms emerged: **Austrasia** (capital Metz) lying to the east (Auster) and mostly Teutonic; **Neustria** (the "new land" as the name implies) (capital Soissons), Gallo-Roman in blood; **Burgundy,** which had no king of its own but joined Neustria under a common ruler. The prince of Neustria exterminated the rival house in Austrasia, but the local baronage preserved the kingdom's identity. Under **Lothair II** all three kingdoms were united again (613) under one ruler.

629–639. Dagobert (Lothair's son), the last strong ruler of the Merovingian house, made wide dynastic alliances and found wise advisers in **Bishop Arnulf** and **Pepin of Landen.** His firm rule led to a revolt. Under the *rois fainéants* following Dagobert the **mayors of the palace** emerged from a menial position to a dominant rôle in the government both in Austrasia and Neustria.

Merovingian government retained the Roman civitas as a unit of administration and set a count (*comes* or *graf*) over it. The source of law was not the king, but local custom administered by the graf with the aid of local landowners. Military leaders of large districts were the duces who were over several counts. Land grants were made in lieu of pay to officials.

Gregory, bishop of Tours (c. 540–594), a Frank, wrote in Latin the *Historia Francorum,* the best single source on the history of the Merovingian period.

Decline of the royal power under the last of the Merovingians, and beginning of **feudal decentralization.** (1) Concentration of landownership in the hands of a few (i.e. a landed aristocracy of which the mayors of the palace were representative). (2) The breakdown of the old clan and tribal organization without an effective state to replace it, leading to personal and economic dependence on private individuals rather than on the state (e.g. commendation, *beneficium,* immunity). (3) Military service on horseback became attached to the benefice as early as the 8th century; for example, Martel's cavalry (see *infra*) for service against the Saracens. Since these grants involved church lands to a considerable degree, Martel in effect compelled the Church to help support national defense. (4) The royal domain was exempt from visitation except by the king's personal administrators. This immunity was extended to royal lands granted to others, and then to lands never in the royal domain. The upshot of the system was complete decentralization by the delegation of the royal powers to local officials who tended to become entirely independent.

Emergence of the Carolingians in Austrasia. The son of Arnulf married the daughter of **Count Pepin I** (of Landen, d. 640). mayor of the palace, founding the line later called Carolingian.

656. Pepin's son, Grimoald, made a premature effort to usurp the crown, which cost him and his son their lives, and led to a reaction in favor of the Merovingians.

678–681. Ebroin, mayor in Neustria, united the mayoralties under one house; he was murdered (681).

687. Pepin II (of Heristal), grandson of Pepin I, gained supremacy in Austrasia and Neustria by his victory at Tertry. The kingdom was on the verge of dissolution (ducal separatism), and Pepin began an effort to reduce the landed aristocracy from which he himself had sprung.

714–741. Charles Martel (i.e. the Hammer), Pepin's son, an ally of the Lombards, supported Boniface's mission in Germany (Boniface testified that his achievements would have been impossible without Martel's aid).

732. Martel's great **victory at Tours** arrested the advance of the Moslems in the west, and was followed by their final retreat over the Pyrenees (759).

Pepin's **conquest of the Frisians** was continued, five wars were waged against the Sax-

The battle of Tours, 732

The House of Pepin (640–814)

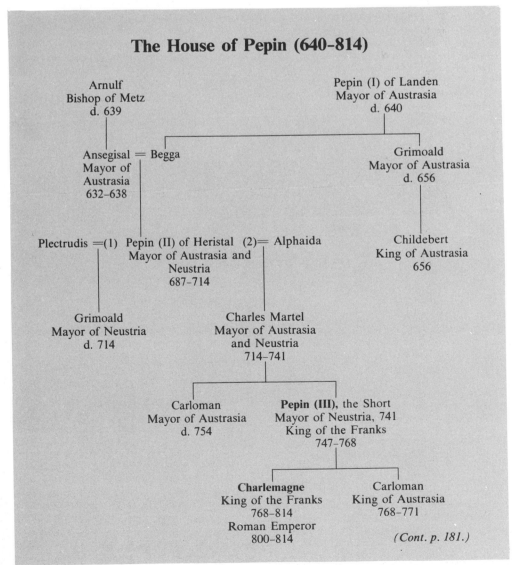

Arnulf
Bishop of Metz
d. 639

Pepin (I) of Landen
Mayor of Austrasia
d. 640

Ansegisal = Begga
Mayor of
Austrasia
632–638

Grimoald
Mayor of Austrasia
d. 656

Plectrudis =(1) Pepin (II) of Heristal (2)= Alphaida
Mayor of Austrasia and
Neustria
687–714

Childebert
King of Austrasia
656

Grimoald
Mayor of Neustria
d. 714

Charles Martel
Mayor of Austrasia
and Neustria
714–741

Carloman
Mayor of Austrasia
d. 754

Pepin (III), the Short
Mayor of Neustria, 741
King of the Franks
747–768

Charlemagne
King of the Franks
768–814
Roman Emperor
800–814

Carloman
King of Austrasia
768–771

(Cont. p. 181.)

Pope Gregory III asks Charles Martel for protection

The Lombard conquest of Italy

ons, and powerful decentralizing forces (notably in Burgundy and Alamannia) were broken down.

739. Pope Gregory III, threatened by the Lombards, sent an embassy to Martel, and offered the title of *consul* in return for protection. Charles, an ally of the Lombard king, ignored the appeal. At the end of his life Martel, like a true sovereign, divided the Merovingian lands between his sons, Austrasia and the German duchies going to Carloman, Neustria and Burgundy to Pepin. Carloman and Pepin ruled together, 741–747; Pepin ruled alone, 747–768.

(Cont. p. 176.)

f. THE LOMBARDS AND THE POPES, 568–774

(From p. 172)

[*For a complete list of the Roman popes see Appendix IV.*]

Under the Emperor Augustus the Lombards were still established on the lower Elbe (Bardengau) and were defeated (5 A.D.) by the Romans. Their history for the next 400 years is confused and often blank. They were members of the Hunnic Empire and were subdued by the Heruls (505), whom they then destroyed (508).

They were probably Arians by this time. Resistance to the Gepids began (c. 546). They were given land by Justinian in Noricum and Pannonia and aided (553) the imperial attacks on the Ostrogoths. The Avars arrived (c. 560) from the Volga, entered Thuringia (562), were defeated by the Franks, and allied themselves (c. 565) with the Lombards against the Gepids, who were annihilated. The Lombards moved on toward Italy and the Avars occupied Dacia. Alboin (d. 573), the Lombard king, killed the Gepid king, Cunimund, with his own hand and married his daughter Rosamund (story of Cunimund's skull as a drinking-cup). The Lombards took part in Belisarius' conquest, and soon they began to move south toward Italy.

568. THE LOMBARD CONQUEST OF ITALY. Italy, worn out by the Gothic wars, famine, and pestilence, offered little resistance. Constantinople was indifferent, and the conquest was easy. The Lombards, always few in numbers, had associated other peoples (including 20,000 Saxons, who soon departed, and some Slavs) in their invasion, but even then they were not numerous enough to occupy the whole peninsula. Rome and Naples were never held, and Ravenna only briefly. The coast was not really mastered. The Lombards (unlike even the Vandals) did not enter into a compact with the empire, and Italian feeling against them was bitter. Pavia became the capital (Italy, until 774, had always two and usually three capitals: Rome, the papal capital; Ravenna, the Byzantine capital; and Pavia, the Lombard capital after 573) and the peninsula was a mosaic of Byzantine, papal, and Lombard jurisdictions.

Lombard occupation (virtually military rule at first) covered inland Liguria, inland Tuscany, inland Venetia, the duchy of Spoleto and the duchy of Benevento. **Imperial Italy** comprised Venice and the land from north of Ravenna to the south of Ancona, and included the duchy of Rome and the duchy of Naples, as well as the toe and heel of Italy. *Hospitalitas* was revived and one-third the produce of the land (not one-third the land) was given to the Lombards. Lombards also took the lands of the dead and the exiled. At first lands were assigned with a full title, but Liutprand introduced (713, 735) leases, and the grant of estates without permanent tenure.

The Lombards took Roman titles and names, and in the end accepted Roman Catholicism. By the time of **Liutprand** (712–744) their speech was clearly Italian, but the natives were loyal to their past, and remained sharply divided from the Lombards. Legally there was a dual system of private law, and in Lombard territories there was a dual episcopal system (i.e. Arian and Roman).

573–584. Alboin's murder was followed by the rule of Cleph (d. 575) and then by ten years of anarchy and private war under a loose federation of dukes (some 36 in number). Roman Catholic opposition and papal negotiations with the Franks alarmed the Lombards, and led to the election of

584–590. Authari, a grandson of Alboin, who was endowed with half the baronial lands as royal domain. The dukedoms were gradually absorbed (the marches like Fruili, Trent, Turin, survived longest).

Authari's widow Theodolinda, a devoted Roman Catholic, bidden to choose a husband who should also be king, selected a Thuringian.

590-615. Duke Agilulf, of Turin, who was friendly to the Roman Church and the true founder of the Lombard state. Gregory the Great blocked an Italian conspiracy against the Lombards. **Rothari** (636–652) became a Roman Catholic. He collected Lombard customary law in Latin and began the consolidation of Lombard power. Eventually Roman law triumphed and Lombard law survived only in the schools (e.g. Pavia).

The Italian bishops since 476 had been the leaders of the peaceful civilians in the cities, the protectors of the oppressed, and the dispensers of charity. Under the Lombards a system of **episcopal immunities** emerged which made the bishops virtually local temporal sovereigns and enabled them to preserve the local spirit of municipal independence and organization (e.g. consuls, guilds). The urban population was free of feudal bonds, and the town walls (often built by the bishops) were refuges. Milan resumed her greatness and almost equaled Rome. These developments prepared the way for the great assertion of Italian town independence against Roman clerical and German feudal encroachments. **Paul the Deacon** (c. 720–c. 800), the first important medieval historian, wrote the *Historia gentis Langobardorum.* **Martianus Capella** (fl. c. 600), encyclopaedist, formulated the seven arts (grammar, logic, rhetoric, geometry, astronomy, arithmetic, music) which were to guide education down to the Renaissance.

590-604. GREGORY THE GREAT. Of medium height, good figure, large, bald head, brown eyes, aquiline nose, thick red lips, prominent bearded chin, with exquisite tapering hands. His family was a rich senatorial house and Gregory was prefect of Rome (573). He founded (c. 574) six monasteries in Sicily and one at Rome (St. Andrews) into which he immediately retired as a monk. Embassy to Constantinople (c. 579–586). As abbot of St. Andrews (586) his rule was severe. Elected pope (590) against his will, he began a vigorous administration. Discipline within his patriarchate was rigorous (stress on celibacy, close watch on elections, insistence on exclusive clerical jurisdiction over clerical offenders). Church revenue was divided into four shares for the bishop, the clergy, the poor, and church buildings. His administration of the wide estates of the Church was honest and brilliant, and the revenue was expanded to meet the tremendous demands on Rome for charity. The pope continued the old imperial corn doles in Rome and elsewhere, aqueducts were repaired, urban administration, especially in Rome, reformed.

Outside his immediate patriarchal jurisdiction Gregory expanded the influence and prestige of the pope, maintaining that the pope was by divine designation head of all churches. Appeals to Rome were heard even against the patriarch of Constantinople, whose claim to the title of universal bishop was denied. Gregory boldly assumed the rôle of the emperor in the west, and the powers of a temporal prince, counterbalancing the prestige of Constantinople. From his administration date the foundations of later **claims to papal absolutism.** Gregory was the real leader against the Lombards, appointing governors of cities, directing the generals in war, and receiving from Constantinople pay for the army.

As the first monk to become pope, Gregory made a close alliance between the Benedictines and the papacy (at the expense of the bishops). The monks were given charters and protected from the bishops, the Benedictine Rule was imposed, and a great missionary campaign was begun with monkish aid: (1) the mission to Britain (596) under **Augustine of Canterbury** and the conversion of England provided a base from which the Frankish (Gallic) Church was later reformed and the German people converted; (2) campaigns against paganism in Gaul, Italy, and Sicily, and against heresy in Africa and Sicily.

Gregory was the last of the four great Latin Fathers, and first of the medieval prelates, a link between the classical Greco-Roman tradition and the medieval Romano-German. Not a great scholar, he was a great popularizer, and spread the doctrines of Augustine of Hippo throughout the west. At the same time he gave wide currency through his *Dialogorum libri* to the popular (often originally pagan) ideas of angels, demons, devils, relic worship, miracles, the doctrine of purgatory, and the use of allegory. Gregory reveals the clerical contempt for classical Latin which profoundly influenced the Latin of the Middle Ages. His *Regulae pastoralis liber* remained for centuries an essential in the education of the clergy. There

Pope Gregory the Great

was a school of music at Rome, but how much Gregory had to do with it, and how much with the introduction of the Gregorian chant, is doubtful.

Gregory introduced the papal style, *Servus Servorum Dei.*

CONTINUED ALIENATION OF ITALY FROM THE EAST. (1) The **Monothelite controversy:** condemnation by the **Lateran Synod** (649) of Emperor Heraclius' *Ecthesis* (of 638) and Emperor Constans II's *Typos* of 648. Arrest (653) by the exarch of Pope Martin I (649–655), who died in exile in the east. The **Council of Constantinople** (680–681) compromised on the controversy, taking a position in favor of Rome. The Council of Constantinople (692) reasserted the equality of the patriarchates of Constantinople and Rome. (2) **Emperor Leo the Isaurian's** (717–740) attempt to bring Italy back to obedience: heavy taxation to reduce the great landowners angered Pope Gregory II (the largest landowner in Italy) and Leo's iconoclastic decree (726) aroused all Italy. Gregory III excommunicated all Iconoclasts (731). Gregory's defeat and final humiliation weakened the pope and opened the way for the final Lombard advance.

Nicholas I (detail from an 11th-century fresco)

712–744. DESTRUCTION OF THE LOMBARD KINGDOM. Liutprand, fearing Frankish, Slavic, Hungarian, Byzantine, and papal hostility, began to consolidate his kingdom, reducing the duchies of Benevento and Spoleto. Ravenna was taken temporarily During the Iconoclastic controversy Liutprand's sincere efforts at rapprochement with the papacy met a brief success.

749–756. Aistulf continued Liutprand's policy of consolidation. The pope, alarmed at Lombard progress, had already (741) made overtures to Charles Martel. Martel, busy with the Moslems, remained faithful to his alliance with the Lombards, but Aistulf's continued advance brought a visit (753) from Pope Stephen II. Stephen had already begun negotiations with Pepin, and the mutual needs of the rising papacy and the upstart Carolingian dynasty drew them into alliance.

754, 756. Pepin in two expeditions forced Aistulf to abandon the Pentapolis and Ravenna (bringing the Lombards virtually to their holdings of 681). Legally the lands involved in the **Donation of Pepin** (756) belonged to the Eastern Empire. The Donation was a tacit recognition of implicit claims of the popes to be the heirs of the empire in Italy. Most important from the papal point of view was the fact that the Church had won a powerful military ally outside Italy. Henceforth the Carolingians maintained a protectorate over the papacy in Italy.

774. Charlemagne, heir to the traditions of Pepin, having repudiated the daughter of the Lombard king, Desiderius, appeared in Italy to protect the pope. After a nine-month siege Pavia was taken, Spoleto and Benevento were conquered, Charles absorbed the Lombard Kingdom into the rising Frankish Empire, and assumed the crown of the Lombards. On a visit (774) to Rome (the first of any Frankish monarch), Charlemagne confirmed the Donation of Pepin, but made it plain that he was sovereign even in the papal lands. At no time did Charlemagne allow the pope any but a primacy in honor (in this respect following the strict Byzantine tradition). The Donation of Pepin was the **foundation of the Papal States** and the true beginning of the temporal power of the papacy. Henceforth there was neither the Lombard menace nor the overlordship of the exarch to interfere with the rising papal monarchy. In this sense the fall of the Lombard Kingdom was decisive in papal history. It was equally decisive in Italian history, for the papal victory over the Lombards terminated the last effective effort to establish national unity and a national government until the end of the 19th century. For the Carolingian monarchy the episode was equally significant.

Under the successors of Charlemagne the emperors continued to participate in the papal elections and did what they could to protect Italy against the attacks of the Moslems from Africa.

827–831. The Moslems conquered Sicily.

837. They attacked Naples, pillaged Ancona (839) and captured Bari (840).

846. In the **battle of Licosa,** Duke Sergius of Naples defeated the Moslems at sea.

847–848. Construction of the **Leonine Wall** by Pope Leo IV (847–855) to defend St. Peter's from the Moslems.

POPE NICHOLAS I (858–867), one of the few great popes between Gregory I and Gregory VII, was the arbiter of western Christendom. Elected by the favor of Louis II. Three great controversies: **(1) Support of Ignatius,** patriarch of Constantinople, resulting in the excommunication (863) of Ignatius' rival, Photius. Photius' futile deposition (867) of Nicholas. This controversy brought the eastern and western churches closer to the final rupture (1054). (2) **Discipline of King Lothair** of Lorraine because of the divorce of his wife Theutberga. Lothair had been allowed (Synod of Aix) by his pliant bishops to remarry, and Nicholas reopened the case at the Synod of Metz (863), which found for Lothair. Nicholas (supported by Charles the Bald) quashed the entire proceeding, disciplined the bishops, and, despite the invasion (864) of the Leonine City by Louis II, compelled Lothair to submit. (3) **Vindication of the right of appeal to Rome** by a bishop against his metropolitan—humiliation of the powerful Archbishop Hincmar of Reims. First papal citation (865) of the *Forged Decretals* (brought to Rome, 864). Emergence of the theory that no bishop may be deposed or elected without papal approval.

867– Decline of the papacy, after the pontificate of Nicholas and the death of Louis II. As the popes had no powerful protectors outside Italy until 961, they fell increasingly under the dominance of the Roman and Italian feudal aristocracy. The lapse of the imperial power left room for the insinuation of a new **doctrine of papal autonomy,** well formulated in the *Forged Decretals.* Outside Italy the relaxation of papal control and the decline of papal prestige, accompanied by the rise of dominant local feudal lords, accentuated the power of the bishops and made the unity of the western Church a mere shadow until the papacy, having learned to cope with feudalism in the second half of the 11th century, once again made its supremacy felt in the Church.

875–877. The Emperor **Charles the Bald** continued to support the papacy against the invader and came to Rome (875) to be crowned, having forced Charles the Fat to retreat and having induced his brother Carloman to sign a truce and withdraw. He was then elected king of Italy by the local magnates.

888. Berengar of Friuli was crowned king of Italy at Pavia.

894. Guido of Spoleto was consecrated emperor with his son Lambert as co-emperor and co-king.

893. Zwentibold (illegitimate son of Arnulf) was sent to Italy in response to an appeal from Pope Formosus (891–896), but he accomplished nothing. Arnulf then came in person (894) and received an oath of fealty from the Italian magnates, but Guido continued as emperor and was succeeded by

892–898. Lambert. Arnulf embarked upon a second expedition, took Rome, and was formally crowned (896). *(Cont. p. 235.)*

g. THE EMPIRE OF CHARLEMAGNE AND ITS DISINTEGRATION, 747–886

747–768. PEPIN THE SHORT, who attempted to conciliate the Church by granting and restoring lands to it.

752. Pepin was elected king by the Frankish

Charles the Great (Carolingian bronze statuette)

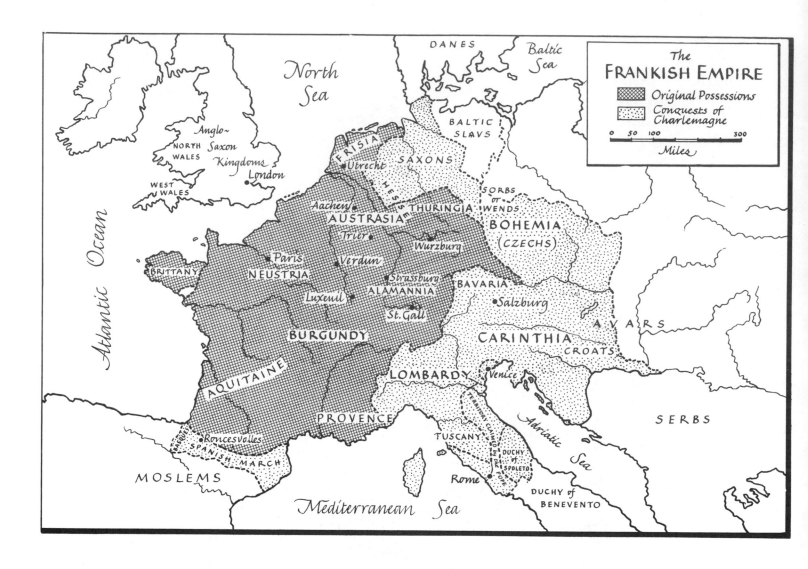

magnates. Both the house of Pepin and the papacy (in the act of usurping political control from the emperor at Constantinople) needed each other's support. The immediate need of the popes was protection against the expanding Lombard monarchy. **Aistulf,** king of the Lombards, had taken Ravenna (751), the seat of the exarch, besieged Rome, and exacted tribute.

754. Pope Stephen II arrived in Gaul, annointed Pepin, and by conferring the title *Patricius* (which could legally come only from Constantinople) designated him in a sense regent and protector of Italy. The net result was to give some shadow of authority to Pepin's new title as king of the Franks.

754. Pepin marched into Italy, defeated the Lombards, and required them to hand over the exarchate and Pentapolis to the pope. The Lombards failed to do so.

756. Pepin returned and, after defeating the Lombards again, made his famous Donation. The **Donation of Pepin** (which Pepin had no legal right to make) established the Papal States (*Patrimonium Petri*) and began the temporal power of the papacy. It also established the Franks, a distant, non-Italian power, as the allies and defenders of the papacy.

759. Pepin conquered Septimania, disciplined Aquitaine, and so brought effective Frankish rule to the Pyrenees. On his death his lands were given to his sons: Charles receiving Aus-

trasia, Neustria, and northern Aquitaine; Carloman, southern Aquitaine, Burgundy, Provence, Septimania. The brothers ruled together, 768–771; Charles alone, 771–814.

771–814. CHARLES THE GREAT (Charlemagne), a reign of the first magnitude in European history. Charles was a typical German, well over six feet tall, a superb swimmer, of athletic frame, with large, expressive eyes and merry disposition. He understood Greek, spoke Latin, but could not learn to write. He preferred the Frankish dress. In general he continued the Frankish policy: (1) expansion of Frankish rule to include all the Germans was completed (omitting only Scandinavia and Britain); (2) close understanding with the papacy; (3) support of church reform (which settled the foundations of medieval Christian unity).

Italian conquest and reduction of German tribes: Already overlord of the Lombards, Charles married King Desiderius' daughter, soon repudiated her, conquered

773–774. Lombard Italy, and became king of the Lombards, whose kingdom was absorbed into the Frankish Empire. Charlemagne also established his rule in Venetia, Istria, Dalmatia, and Corsica.

787–788. Bavaria was incorporated, its duke, Tassilo, first made a vassal and then deposed.

785. Saxony, after a costly and bitter struggle of 30 years, involving 18 campaigns, was con-

quered, and Christianity forcibly introduced despite stubborn pagan resistance. Foundation of the bishopric of Bremen (781).

795–796. The Avars (on the lower Danube) were reduced.

801. After the Frankish defeat at **Roncesvalles** (778), the Moslems in northeastern Spain were gradually reduced (Barcelona taken, 801), and the Spanish March created.

Establishment of marks (after c. 782) to hold the conquests: Dane Mark, the Altmark (against the Wends), Thuringian Mark, Bohemian Mark, Ostmark (against the Avars), Friulian Mark (on the Italian border), and the Spanish March. These marks were also centers of colonization and germanization.

Relation to the Church. Charlemagne held it to be his duty to defend the Church and the pope, and to maintain the faith. He treated the pope like any Frankish bishop, but recognized his unique spiritual prestige. His visit (774) to Rome was the first of a Frankish sovereign: the Donation of Pepin was confirmed, but the terms are not clear. The pope crowned Charles' son, Pepin, king of Italy (781), his son Louis, king of Aquitaine.

REVIVAL OF THE ROMAN EMPIRE IN THE WEST. Pope Leo III, a submissive pontiff, notified Charlemagne of his election to the Holy See, and dated his pontificate by Charlemagne's regnal years. Driven from Rome (799) by a conspiracy and riot, he sought refuge at Charlemagne's court and was restored by Frankish troops.

800. Charlemagne arrived in Rome, allowed Leo to clear himself of a series of charges by oath (avoiding the trial of a pope), and was crowned emperor in St. Peter's on Christmas Day. According to Einhard, Charlemagne avowed his regret at the coronation. He cannot have been unaware of the general plan, and his feeling may have been due to modesty or concern at Byzantine reactions or hostility to papal pretensions. Charlemagne disregarded the imperial title in a partition of the empire (806), and arranged to have his son Louis crown himself (813). Theoretically the coronation of 800 marked a return to the dualism of Theodosius I (i.e. two emperors over an undivided empire). In fact the Frankish Empire was more German than Roman in population and institutions. Byzantium regarded Charlemagne as a usurper; Charlemagne seems to have meditated a marriage with the Empress Irene as one solution of the difficulty. The papal coronation, an act of rebellion in Byzantine eyes, marked a definite **break between Rome and Constantinople.** The Emperor Michael I recognized (812) Charlemagne's title in the west in return for sovereignty in Venice, Istria, Dalmatia.

GOVERNMENT. (1) **In the Church:** Charlemagne's rule was a theocracy, and he insisted on supremacy over the Frankish Church, legislating on all subjects, settling dogmatic questions, deciding appointments, presiding at synods. (2) **In the Frankish state:** centralization continued; taxation in the Roman sense (which survived only under local and private auspices) was replaced by services in return for land

Alcuin

grants (the economic basis of Carolingian society). Such services included forced labor on public works among the lower ranks, the provision of food for the court and public officials on duty, and judicial and military obligations (primarily among the upper ranks). Charlemagne's continuous campaigns reduced the small farmers, accentuating the tendency to serfdom. Charlemagne tried to offset this tendency by allowing groups of poorer farmers to cooperate in sending a single soldier, and by excusing the poorest from ordinary field service. Systematization of the army and of military service was also begun. Commendation and immunity continued, and the basis of later feudal development was firmly established.

Administration: The tribal dukes were largely eliminated and government was carried on by counts, appointed for life, but frequently removed. This system was extended to Italy, Bavaria, and Saxony. To prevent the counts establishing an hereditary tenure, and to limit local abuses, the *missi dominici* (usually a bishop and count) were introduced (802) as officers on circuit in a given district. The missi held their own courts, had power to remove a count for cause, and were charged with the supervision of financial, judicial, and clerical administration. They formed an essential link between the local and central government. Under the counts were viscounts and vicars (*centenarii*). Margraves (*Mark Grafen*) were set over the marks with extended powers to meet the needs of their position. Local administration of justice was reformed by the introduction of *scabini*, local landowners appointed by the counts to sit as permanent judiciary officers.

The Carolingian **revival of learning:** Charlemagne, perhaps out of concern for the improvement of ecclesiastical education, set up the Palace School under **Alcuin** from the School of York, later abbot of Tours. Various clerics were also given liberal grants that they might establish local schools, though no general system of education was introduced in the Frankish Em-

Charlemagne destroying the column of Irmin, sacred to the Saxons

Coronation of Charlemagne by Pope Leo III (illumination from a 14th-century manuscript)

monasteries, he allowed himself to be crowned again by the pope (816). Ineffectual as a soldier and ruler. Louis and his heirs concentrated on a long struggle (leading to civil war) over territorial questions, to the neglect of government, foreign policy, and defense, a program which hastened the breakup of the empire.

817–838. A significant series of **partitions** involving Louis' sons: Lothair (d. 855), Louis the German (d. 876), Pepin (d. 838), and their half-brother, Charles the Bald (d. 877).

The division of 817: Aquitaine and parts of Septimania and Burgundy went to Pepin as sub-king; Bavaria and the marches to the east were assigned to Louis the German as sub-king undivided; Francia, German and Gallic, and most of Burgundy were retained by Louis and his eldest son Lothair. Italy went to a third sub-king.

The division of 838: Charles the Bald was assigned Neustria and to this was added Aquitaine on the death of Pepin. Charles' holding, which had no name, approximated (accidentally) medieval France and was mainly Romance in speech.

840–855. LOTHAIR I (emperor). On the death of Louis the Pious the three heirs contained their struggle, and after the indecisive **battle of Fontenay** (841) Carolingian prestige sank to a new depth. Charles the Bald and Louis the German formed an alliance against Lothair (who was supported by the clergy in the interests of unity) in the bilingual (Teutonic and Romance) **Oaths of Strassburg** (842), sworn by the rulers and their armies, each in their own vernacular. They then forced a family compact upon Lothair at Verdun.

Louis the Pious does penance

pire. In general, the source of inspiration was Latin rather than Greek. **Einhard,** for example, who came to the Palace School from Fulda, wrote his biography of Charlemagne in the manner of Suetonius. At Charlemagne's court were gathered scholars and literary men of almost every nationality, including **Peter of Pisa,** the grammarian, the Visigothic poet **Theodulf,** the Lombard historian, **Paul the Deacon** (*Historia gentis Langobardorum*). Great care was given to the copying of texts, and the refined Carolingian minuscule was evolved.

814–887. THE DISINTEGRATION OF THE CAROLINGIAN EMPIRE.

Such efficiency as the Carolingian government possessed under Charlemagne derived rather from his personality than from permanent institutions. Local administration was carried on by unpaid officials whose compensation was a share of the revenue. Local offices tended to become hereditary. The tentative partitions of the empire in Charlemagne's lifetime followed Frankish tradition, and had no relation to any racial or national elements. One son, Louis the Pious, survived, and the empire was passed on to him (quite by accident) undivided. The decisive stage in the partition of the empire came under Louis and his heirs.

814–840. LOUIS the Pious (emperor), educated at the Palace School, crowned in his father's lifetime. Sincerely religious, a reformer of his court, the Frankish Church, and the

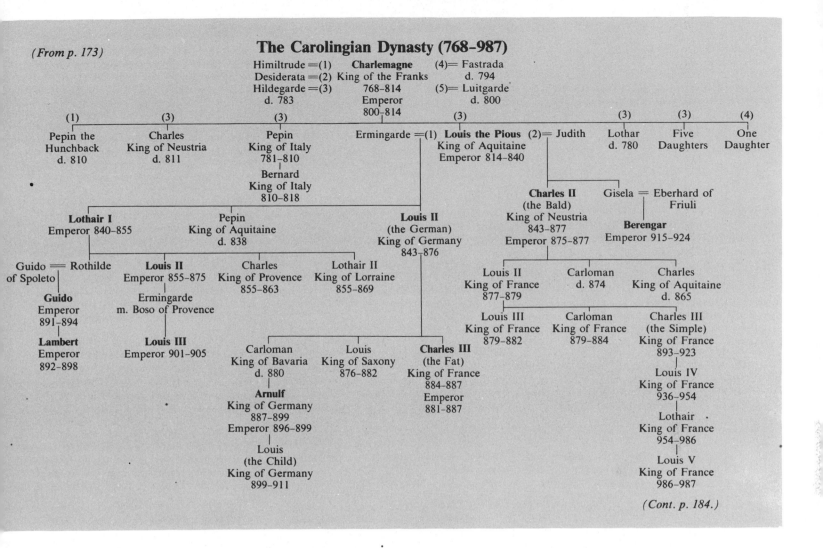

(From p. 173)

(Cont. p. 184.)

843. The **TREATY OF VERDUN** divided the administration and control of the Carolingian Empire as follows: (1) **Lothair** kept the (empty) title of emperor, and was king of Italy and of an amorphous territory (the "middle kingdom") which was bounded roughly by the Scheldt, the upper Meuse, Saône, and Rhone on the west, and by the Rhine and Frisia on the east (i.e. the territory of Provence, Burgundy, and what was later called *Lotharingia*); (2) **Louis the German,** as king of the (East) Franks, ruled a realm essentially Teutonic in blood, speech, and geography, extending from the Rhine (except Frisia) to the eastern frontier of the empire; (3) **Charles the Bald,** as king of the (West) Franks, received a realm (loosely called Carolingia for a time) made up of West Francia and Aquitaine, Gascony, Septimania, etc., mainly Romance in speech, approximating medieval France in general outline.

855–875. **LOUIS II** (emperor). At Lothair I's death his lands were divided as follows among his sons: Louis II received Italy, Charles (d. 863), the newly formed kingdom of Provence (centered around the city of Arles), and Lothair II the inchoate aggregate (from Frisia to the Alps and from the Rhine to Scheldt) which began to be called *Lotharii regnum* or *Lotharingia* (modern Lorraine).

870. **Treaty of Mersen,** following the death (869) of Lothair II, king of Lorraine. Louis the German forced Charles the Bald (crowned king of Lorraine, 869) to divide equally and solely on the basis of revenue the lands of Lothair outside of Italy. Thus Louis gained a strip of land which brought his frontier west of the Rhine.

875–877. CHARLES THE BALD, emperor.

877–881. Anarchy and interregnum in the empire.

879. The **kingdom of Burgundy** (Cisjuran Burgundy) was established by Boso of Provence.

888. The **kingdom of Juran Burgundy** (i.e. Besançon, Basel, Lausanne, Geneva, etc.) was erected by Rudolf I. It passed to the empire by bequest in the time of Conrad II.

c. 787–925. THE 9TH-CENTURY INVASIONS:

(1) **In the north.** Bands of Northmen (Scandinavians, *p. 194),* under pressure of population and resentful at the rise of local kings, pushed outward from Scandinavia. The Swedes penetrated into Russia, the Norwegians and Danes moved into the northern islands (including the British Isles) and south to the Continent. Within a half century of the first raid (c. 787) on England, the British Isles had been flooded. Masters of the sea in the west, the Northmen pushed inland from the mouths of the great rivers (e.g. Rhine, Scheldt, Somme, Seine, Loire), sacking the cities (e.g. Utrecht, Paris, Nantes, Bordeaux, Hamburg, Seville). "Normandy" was invaded (841) and a simultaneous attack made (845) on all three Frankish kingdoms. The Mediterranean was entered (843). In the east Constantinople was attacked by Swedes (*Rus*), who came down from Russia. A great attack on Paris (885) was heroically met by Count Odo (Eudes), son of Robert the Strong. Raids were pushed farther into France and the Mediterranean in the course of the 9th century.

(2) **In the east.** Bulgarian expansion produced a great Bulgar state between the Frankish and Byzantine Empires. The Bulgars were converted to the Greek communion (870). Hungarians (Magyars), closely followed by Pechenegs, crossed the Carpathians and the lower Danube, pushing into Venetia, Lombardy, Bavaria, Thuringia, Saxony, the Rhineland, Lorraine, and Burgundy (925).

(3) **In the Mediterranean.** Moslem domination of Sicily, Corsica, Sardinia, and the Balearic Islands made the Mediterranean virtually a Moslem lake. Raids were almost continuous, Rome was attacked (846) and later Monte Cassino.

852–886. Under the combined influence of the disruption of the Carolingian Empire and the pressure of the 9th-century invasions, the **great fiefs** of France began to appear as the only effective centers of local resistance to invasion, and feudalism may be said to have struck root.

Feudalism. Its origins may be traced to the German *comitatus* and the proprietary system of the later Roman Empire. Essentially it was an informal system of contracts for the disposal of land and honorable services, and was in no sense a form of government. Inseparable from it was the agricultural organization (**manorialism**), which rested on servile tenures and contracts for manual labor and services. Antedating feudalism, manorialism was also derived from the Roman proprietary system. The feudal system evolved in each country under local conditions and followed a different development. The feudalism of France is ordinarily regarded as typical.

h. THE WEST FRANKS UNDER THE CAROLINGIAN KINGS, 843-987

843-877. CHARLES THE BALD (emperor, 875-877). His kingdom under the **treaty of Verdun** was roughly equivalent to modern France with additions in the north and south and a restricted frontier on the east. Charles was effective master of Laon, but his sway over Neustria was nominal, his control sporadically maintained by war and intrigue. Charles granted three great fiefs as a buffer for his frontiers: the county of Flanders to his son-in-law, Baldwin Iron-Arm (862); Neustria to Robert the Strong as "duke between Seine and Loire"; the French duchy of Burgundy to Richard, count of Autun. Brittany (Amorica) was semi-independent under its own dukes and counts in the 9th century and continued so virtually to the end of the Middle Ages. Aquitaine, joined to Neustria for Charles (838), soon emerged as a duchy and was consistently hostile. The duchy of Gascony was joined to Aquitaine in 1052. From Neustria were carved the counties of Anjou (870) and Champagne. Septimania remained refractory.

870. Carloman, Charles's son, emerged from monastic retirement and led a series of intrigues which ended when he was blinded and fled to his uncle, Louis the German. He died in 874. Charles was further weakened by his intrigues in Lorraine and Italy, and by his efforts to win the imperial crown, leaving France open to invasion, anarchy, and brigandage.

The crown, impotent and virtually bankrupt, commanded no respect from magnates or prelates, and the **Capitulary of Mersen** (847) shows clear evidence of the progress of essentially feudal ideas; every free man is to choose a lord; none may quit his lord; each must follow his lord in battle. It must be noted that this was purely a military measure. France was already divided into *comtés* under counts theoretically removable by the king.

875. Expedition of Charles to Italy and imperial coronation.

877. The **Capitulary of Kiersy** made honors hereditary, but lands were still granted only for life.

877-879. Louis II (the stammerer), son of Charles the Bald, maintained himself with difficulty despite the support of the Church. His sons

879-882. Louis III and

879-884. Carloman divided their heritage, Louis taking Neustria, Carloman Aquitaine, Septimania, and Burgundy, and reduced their rivals to impotence. Louis' victory over the Northmen (Saucourt, 881) did not stop their raids.

884-887. Charles the Fat, son of Louis the German, already king of the East Franks (879) and

emperor (881-887), was chosen king of the West Franks instead of Charles the Simple, the five-year-old brother of Louis and Carloman. Charles the Fat, having failed (886) to aid the gallant Odo (Eudes) against the Northmen, was deposed (887).

888-898. Odo (Eudes), count of Paris, marquis of Neustria (son of Count Robert the Strong, whence the name *Robertians* for the line before Hugh Capet) was elected king of the West Franks by one faction of magnates to avoid a minority on the deposition (887) of Charles the Fat. Another faction chose Charles III, the Simple, son of Louis II (Carolingian). Despite five years of civil war

893-923. Charles III ruled from Laon, the last Carolingian with any real authority in France. Charles, unable to expel the Northmen from the mouth of the Seine, granted (911) **Rollo** (Hrolf the Ganger, d. 931), a large part of what was later Normandy, for which Rollo did homage.

Formation of Normandy. Rollo was baptized (912) under the name **Robert,** acquired middle Normandy (the Bessin, 924) and the western part of the duchy (Cotentin and Avranche, 933). The colony was recruited with fresh settlers from Scandinavia for the best part of a century, and was able to retain a strong local individuality. Yet soon after 1000 the duchy was French in both speech and law. Between this period and the accession of Duke William I (the Conqueror) Norman history is fragmentary.

923-987. The French kingship. Robert, count of Paris, duke between the Seine and Loire, won the West Frankish crown with the aid of his sons-in-law, Herbert, count of Vermandois,

Hugh Capet

and Rudolf, duke of Burgundy, but was killed (923), leaving a son (later Hugh the Great) too young to rule.

929-936. Rudolf followed Robert as the foe of Charles the Simple, and ruled with no opposition after Charles' death. **Hugh the Great,** master of Burgundy and Neustria, declined the crown, preferring to rule through the young Carolingian heir,

936-954. Louis IV, a son of Charles the Simple. Hugh's title, Duke of the French, seems to have implied governmental functions as much as territorial sovereignty, and he held most of the northern barons under his suzerainty.

954-986. Lothair succeeded his father Louis IV. On the death of Hugh the Great, his son Hugh, known as *Capet*, succeeded him (956).

978. Lothair's effort to gain Lorraine led to an invasion by Emperor Otto II to the walls of Paris. Hugh Capet, in alliance with Emperor Otto III, and aided by Gerbert of Reims, reduced Lothair's rule at Laon to a nullity. Lothair's son

986-987. Louis V was the last Carolingian ruler of France.

987. ELECTION OF HUGH CAPET, engineered by Adalbero, bishop of Reims, and by Gerbert. Hugh was crowned at Noyon with the support of the duke of Normandy and the count of Anjou. His title was recognized by the Emperor Otto III in exchange for Hugh's claims to Lorraine. The emergence of the new house of Capet was not the victory of a race, a nationality, or a principle, but the triumph of a family, already distinguished, over a decadent rival. *(Cont. p. 245.)*

i. GERMANY UNDER THE CAROLINGIAN AND SAXON EMPERORS, 843-1024

[For a complete list of the Holy Roman emperors see Appendix V.]

843-876. LOUIS THE GERMAN. Increasing Slavic and Norse pressure (general Norse attack, 845, on Carolingian lands). Louis had three sons: Carloman (d. 880), Louis (d. 882), and Charles the Fat. Carloman was assigned Bavaria and the East Mark; Louis, Saxony and Franconia; Charles, Alamannia. Contest with Charles the Bald for Lorraine. By the **Treaty of Mersen** (870) Louis added a strip of land west of the Rhine.

876-887. CHARLES THE FAT. He blocked Charles the Bald's advance toward the Rhine. Emergence of the kingdom of Cisjuran Burgundy (i.e. Dauphiné, Provence, part of Languedoc) under Boso (879). Expedition to Italy and coronation by John VIII (881). Negotiations (882) with the Northmen, now permanently established in Flanders. While Charles was in Italy settling a papal election, a great Norse invasion burst on France (Odo's defense of Paris, 886). **Deposition of Charles** by the Franconian, Saxon, Bavarian, Thuringian, and Swabian magnates at Tribur (887).

887 (896)-899. Arnulf (illegitimate son of Carloman, grandson of Louis the German). A certain supremacy was conceded to Arnulf by the various rulers of Germany and Italy who rendered a kind of homage to him. Victory over the Norse on the Dyle (Löwen, 891); resistance to the Slavic (Moravian) advance (893), with Magyar aid. Magyar raids after

King Henry I receives the imperial insignia

911–918. Conrad I. Magyar raids and ducal rebellions in Saxony, Bavaria, and Swabia met vigorous but futile resistance from Conrad. Lorraine passed (911) temporarily under the suzerainty of the West Frankish ruler, Charles the Simple. Conrad nominated his strongest foe, Henry, duke of Saxony, as his successor, and he was elected.

919–1024. THE SAXON (OR OTTONIAN) HOUSE.

919–936. KING HENRY I (called *the Fowler,* supposedly because the messengers announcing his election found him hawking). Tolerant of the dukes, he forced recognition of his authority; cool to the Church, he avoided ecclesiastical coronation.

920–921. Reduction of the duke of Bavaria; alliance with Charles the Simple.

923–925. Lorraine restored to the German Kingdom and unified into the **duchy of Lorraine,** a center of spiritual and intellectual ferment. Henry's daughter married the duke of Lorraine (928).

924–933. Truce (and tribute) **with the Magyars,** fortification of the Elbe and Weser Valleys (Saxony and Thuringia), palisading of towns, villas, monasteries, etc., establishment of *Burgwarde,* i.e. garrisons (which later often became towns like Naumburg, Quedlinburg), where one-ninth of the Saxon effectives were on duty and trained as horsemen each year.

928. Saxon expedition across the frozen Havel River **against the Wends:** Branibor (Brandenburg) stormed; the Wends driven up the Elbe; creation of the marks of Branibor, Meissen, and (later) Lusatia as guardians of the middle Elbe.

933. Henry ended the Magyar truce with his **victory at Riade** on the Unstrut River, the first great defeat of the Magyars. Occupation of the land between the Schlei and the Eider (Charlemagne's Dane Mark), and erection of the mark of Schleswig, guardian of the Elbe mouth; the Danish king was made tributary and forced to receive Christian missionaries. Henry had prepared the way for his son, whose election was a formality, the succession becoming virtually hereditary.

936–973. KING OTTO I (the Great). Otto

King Otto I (contemporary French miniature)

900. Arnulf dared not leave Germany to answer the appeal of Pope Stephen V (885–891) for aid. His illegitimate son Zwentibold was sent on the call of Pope Formosus (891–896), but accomplished nothing (893). Arnulf went to Italy in person (894), was crowned king and received an oath from most of the magnates. On another appeal from Formosus (895) he took Rome and was crowned emperor (896).

899–911. Louis the Child (born 893), last of the Carolingians, elected king by the magnates at Forchheim (900). Increasing Norse, Slavic, and Magyar pressure and devastation.

The **weakening of the royal power** as the East Frankish kingdom of the Carolingians declined, and the survival of tribal consciousness left the way open for the emergence of the stem (German *Stamm,* a tribe) duchies. These duchies preserved the traditions of an-

cient tribal culture, and their independent development under semi-royal dukes (beginning in the 9th century) ensured the disruption of German unity for a thousand years. These stem duchies were: **Franconia** (the Conradiners ultimately drove the Babenbergers into the East Mark, later Austria); **Lorraine** (not strictly a stem duchy but with a tradition of unity); **Swabia** (the early ducal history is obscure); **Bavaria** (under the Arnulfings; repulse of the Magyars, acquisition of the mark of Carinthia); **Saxony** (under the Liudolfingers; repulse of the Danes and Wends, addition of Thuringia); **Frisia** (no tribal duke appeared).

911. End of the East Frankish line of the Carolingians, with the death of Louis the Child (911); the German magnates, to avoid accepting a ruler of the West Frankish (French) line, elected Conrad, duke of Franconia.

The Saxon and Salian Emperors (919–1125)

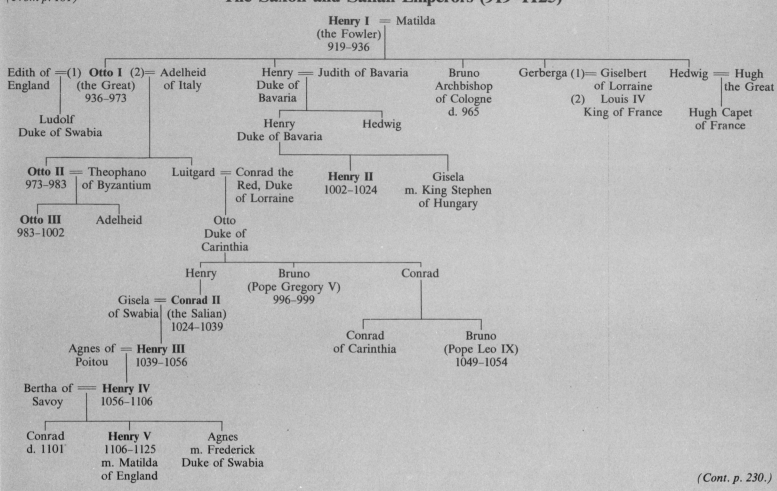

Henry I = Matilda
(the Fowler)
919–936

Edith of =(1) Otto I (2)= Adelheid | Henry = Judith of Bavaria | Bruno | Gerberga (1)= Giselbert | Hedwig = Hugh
England | (the Great) | of Italy | Duke of | Archbishop | of Lorraine | the Great
| 936–973 | | Bavaria | of Cologne | (2) Louis IV
| | | | d. 965 | King of France | Hugh Capet
Ludolf | | Henry — Hedwig | | of France
Duke of Swabia | | Duke of Bavaria

Otto II = Theophano | Luitgard = Conrad the | Henry II | Gisela
973–983 | of Byzantium | | Red, Duke | 1002–1024 | m. King Stephen
| | | of Lorraine | | of Hungary

Otto III — Adelheid | Otto
983–1002 | Duke of
| Carinthia

Henry — Bruno — Conrad
(Pope Gregory V)
996–999

Gisela = Conrad II
of Swabia | (the Salian)
| 1024–1039 | Conrad — Bruno
| | of Carinthia | (Pope Leo IX)
Agnes of = Henry III | | 1049–1054
Poitou | 1039–1056

Bertha of == Henry IV
Savoy | 1056–1106

Conrad — Henry V — Agnes
d. 1101 | 1106–1125 | m. Frederick
| m. Matilda | Duke of Swabia
| of England

(Cont. p. 230.)

revived the policy of Arnulf, was crowned and anointed at Aachen, Charlemagne's capital; his coronation banquet revived the Carolingian coronation banquet (of Roman origin) at which the duke of Franconia served ceremonially as steward, the duke of Swabia as cup-bearer, the duke of Lorraine as chamberlain, and the duke of Bavaria as marshal.

Otto's vigorous **assertion of royal authority** (a three-year war reduced the dukes of Bavaria, Franconia, Lorraine, and Saxony). He followed the policy of keeping the great duchies (except Saxony) in his own hands or those of his family. Taking Conrad, the boy king of Arles (Provence and Burgundy), under his protection (937), Otto forced the recognition of his overlordship (forestalling Hugh of Provence); Conrad's sister, Adelheid, married Lothair, one of the claimants to the crown of Italy, and later Otto himself. The Bavarians defeated Otto (944) at Wels, but Otto conquered (950) Duke Boleslav of Bohemia and put the duchy under the suzerainty of Bavaria.

951–952. Otto's first expedition to Italy to keep the passes through the mountains open. Marriage to Adelheid and assumption of the crown of Italy; the pope refused him imperial coronation; Berengar of Ivrea, forced into vassalage, ceded the marks of Verona, Friuli, Istria (the keys to the passes), to Otto's brother Henry, duke of Bavaria.

953. Revolt of Otto's son (Ludolf, duke of Swabia), his son-in-law Conrad (duke of Lorraine), and others (suppressed, 955).

955. BATTLE OF THE LECHFELD. Otto, with an army recruited from all the duchies, ended the Magyar menace by a great victory. Defeat of the Wends on the river Recknitz. Re-establishment and colonization with Bavarians of Charlemagne's East Mark (Austria).

968. The bishoprics established among the Slavs (e.g. Brandenburg, Merseburg, Meissen, Zeitz) were consolidated under the new **archbishopric of Magdeburg.** German bishoprics were everywhere filled with bishops loyal to the monarchy, marking the alliance of the king and the Church against feudal opposition.

961–964. Otto's second expedition to Italy on the appeal of Pope John XII for protection. Assumption of the crown of Italy at Pavia.

962. IMPERIAL CORONATION BY THE POPE: REVIVAL OF THE ROMAN EMPIRE IN THE WEST. Otto put a temporary end to feudal anarchy in Rome, deposed one pope and nominated another, and compelled the pope to recognize the emperor's right to approve or reject papal elections.

966–972. Otto's third expedition to Italy: deposition of one pope, restoration of another; nomination of a new pope; punishment of the Romans. Imperial coronation (967) of the future Otto II and assertion of suzerainty over Capua and Benevento (967). Betrothal of **Theophano** (probably a niece or grandniece of the Byzantine Emperor, John Tzimisces) to the future Otto II (969); coronation of Theophano (972) and marriage to Otto (supposedly bringing Greek Italy as her portion).

Otto, with the able assistance of his brother Bruno, archbishop of Cologne, began a cultural revival (the so-called **Ottonian Renaissance**) in the manner of Charlemagne; late in life, he learned to read, but not to speak, Latin; Bruno knew Greek. The cosmopolitan court literary circle included Irish and English monks, and learned Greeks and Italians, notably **Liutprand of Cremona** (*Historia Ottonis; Legatio Constantinopolitana*). Great literary activity of the monasteries: **Widukind of Corvey** (*Res Gestae Saxonicae*); **Roswitha,** the nun of Gandersheim, author of the *Carmen de Gestis Ottonis* and of learned Latin comedies in a bowdlerized Terentine style, celebrating saintly virginity; the vernacular *Heliand* (9th century), a Christian epic; **Ekkekard of St. Gall's** *Waltherius,* inspired by German legends.

The German rulers and nobles of the 9th century had regarded the monasteries as their personal property and prepared the way for a strong clerical reaction toward reform supported by the regular clergy (e.g. Cluny), opposed by the seculars who were rapidly passing under feudal influences.

973–983. Otto II. The revolt of Henry the Wrangler, duke of Bavaria, in alliance with Boleslav of Bohemia, and others, required five years to put down; Henry was banished (978). Repulse of a Danish incursion.

978. Lothair, king of the West Franks, invaded Lorraine and was forced to abandon his claims by Otto's invasion of France (980).

981-982. Otto's campaign in southern Italy, to expel the Saracens and reduce the Byzantine power, ended in defeat.

983-1002. Otto III (an infant of three years). Rule of his brilliant mother Theophano (983-991), his grandmother Adelheid, and Archbishop Willigis of Mainz (991-996). Under Theophano's influence his education was in the Byzantine tradition; his tutor **Gerbert of Aurillac,** one of the most learned men of his day, whose brilliance won him the nickname *Stupor Mundi.* Henry the Wrangler proclaimed himself king, but was forced to submit.

996. Otto's first expedition to Italy ended Crescentius II's sway in Rome; Otto designated his cousin Bruno as pope (Gregory V).

998. Returning to Rome on his **second expedition to Italy,** Otto deposed the Crescentine pope, John XVI, and decapitated Crescentius. Otto made Gerbert of Aurillac pope, as Sylvester II. Sylvester shared Otto's devotion to the Carolingian tradition of an intimate union and co-operation of pope and emperor. Otto's romantic antiquarianism led him to a plan of reform through universal imperial overlordship independent of the German crown. He settled down at Rome and began a theatrical restoration of the splendors of the city: palace on the Aventine, Byzantine court and Byzantine titles, futile revival of ancient formulae (seals inscribed *Renovatio imperii romani,* etc.); rapid alienation of the Roman populace. He left no heir and was buried by his own orders beside Charlemagne at Aachen.

1002-1024. Henry II (son of Henry the Wrangler, cousin of Otto, great-grandson of Henry the Fowler) emerged from the contest for the throne, and was crowned emperor at Rome (1014). Devout (canonized with his wife, St. Kunigunde), but a political realist and firm with the Church, he concentrated his attention on Germany. Against episcopal objections he founded (1007) the great bishopric of Bamberg, endowed it richly as an outpost of German culture against Slavdom; the cathedral, one of the glories of German architecture, contains his tomb. Vigorous (Gorzian) monastic reform with many confiscations.

1002. Successful **revolt of Ardoin** in Lombardy (reduced temporarily in 1004, and finally in 1014).

1003-1017. A long, unsuccessful struggle with Boleslav Chrobry (992-1025) of Poland, duke of Bohemia, who had acquired Lusatia and Silesia.

1006-1007. Unrest in Burgundy and **revolt of Baldwin of Flanders** (suppressed, 1007).

In practice Henry had no choice but to allow the great fiefs to become hereditary. He relied heavily on the clergy to supply advisers and administrators, and looked to the Church also for military and financial support, but he dominated the Church in Germany through his control of the episcopal appointments. Extensive secularization and reform of the monasteries of the Church resulted.

(Cont. p. 227.)

j. SPAIN

(1) The Visigothic Kingdom, 466-711

[For a complete list of the Caliphs see Appendix III.]

In the time of **Euric** (466-484) the Visigothic rule extended from the Loire to Gibraltar and from the Bay of Biscay to the Rhone. The capital was Toulouse.

507. Clovis' victory in the **battle of Vouillé** obliged the Visigoths to withdraw over the Pyrenees, retaining only Septimania north of the mountains. The new capital was Toledo.

The Visigoths in Spain were a small minority (about one in five) and were rapidly romanized (e.g. the *Breviary of Alaric*). The conversion of King Reccared (587) from Arianism to Roman orthodoxy brought an end to their religious separateness, accelerated the process of romanization and initiated the domination of the clergy over the monarchy. The **Synod of Toledo** (633) assumed the right to confirm elections to the crown. After 600 the Jews were forced to accept baptism, for which reason they later on welcomed the Moslem invasion. Visigothic speech gradually disappeared and the current vernacular was of Latin origin. Roman organization and tradition survived to a marked degree. **Isidore of Seville** (c. 560-636), a bishop, theologian, historian, man of letters, and scientist, produced in his *Etymologiae* a general reference work that re-

mained a standard manual for 500 years and was a medium for transmitting much ancient knowledge to the medieval world.

(2) Moslem Spain, 711-1031

711-715. THE MOSLEM CONQUEST. In 711 a mixed force of Arabs and Berbers, led by the Berber **Tariq** (whence Gibraltar—*Gebel al-Tariq*) crossed from Africa. Roderick, the last Visigothic king, was completely defeated in the **battle on the Guadalete** (Rio Barbate), whereupon his kingdom collapsed. The Moslems took Córdoba and the capital, Toledo. Tariq was followed (712) by his master, **Musa,** who took Medina Sidonia, Seville, Merida, and Saragossa. The Moslems soon reached the Pyrenees (719), having driven the remnants of the Christians into the mountains of the north and west.

732. In the **battle of Tours** the Moslems, having crossed into France, were decisively defeated by Charles Martel and the Franks. By 759 they had been entirely expelled from France.

756-1031. THE OMAYYAD DYNASTY OF CÓRDOBA.

756-788. Abd ar-Rahman I, emir. He was the grandson of the Omayyad caliph of Damascus, and was the founder of the Moorish state in Spain. Christians were given toleration in return for payment of a poll tax. The Jews were very well treated. But Abd ar-Rahman met with vigorous opposition from the Arab nobility, which was supported from abroad by Pepin and Charlemagne.

777. Invasion of Spain by Charlemagne, checked by the heroic defense of Saragossa. Annihilation of his rear-guard by Basques at Roncesvalles (778—*Song of Roland*). Wars with the Franks continued throughout the rest of the century, Charlemagne ultimately conquering northeastern Spain as far as the Ebro River (capture of Barcelona, 801).

788-796. Hisham I, son of Abd ar-Rahman, emir, during whose reign Malikite doctrines were introduced in Spain.

796-822. Al-Hakam I, son of Hisham, emir. Revolts in Córdoba (805, 817) and Toledo (814). The Córdoban rebels, expelled from Spain, went to Alexandria and thence to Crete, which they reconquered.

822-852. Abd ar-Rahman II, son of Al-Hakam. During his reign Alfonso II of Leon invaded

Coronation of Otto III

Aragon. He was defeated and his kingdom destroyed. The Franks too were driven back in Catalonia. The Normans first appeared on the coasts. In 837 a revolt of Christians and Jews in Toledo was suppressed, but Christian fanatics continued to be active, especially in Córdoba.

852–886. Muhammad I. He put down another Christian uprising in Córdoba, and carried on extensive operations against the Christian states of Leon, Galicia, and Navarre (Pampeluna taken 861).

886–888. Al Mundhir.

888–912. Abdallah, brother of Al Mundhir.

912–961. Abd ar-Rahman III. The ablest and most gifted of the Omayyads of Spain, who assumed the titles of *Caliph* and *Amir al-Mu'minin* in 929, thus asserting supremacy in Islam as against the Abbasid caliphs of Bagdad. Abd ar-Rahman's reign was marked by the pacification of the country, by completion of governmental organization (centralization), by naval activity, by agricultural advance, and by industrial progress. Development of huge paper mills by the 12th century. **Córdoba** (population c. 500,000) became the greatest intellectual center of Europe, with a huge paper trade, great libraries, and pre-eminent schools (medicine, mathematics, philosophy, poetry, music; much translation from Greek and Latin).

The height of **Moslem learning** was reached by **Averroës** (ibn Rushd, c. 1126–1198), philosopher, physician, and commentator on Plato and Aristotle, master of the Christian schoolmen.

The aristocracy, by this time almost extinguished, was replaced by a rich middle class and feudal soldiery. The Christians and Jews continued to enjoy wide toleration.

Abd ar-Rahman continued the wars with Leon and Navarre, which extended over most of his long reign. By the **Peace of 955** with Ordono III of Leon, the independence of Leon and Navarre was recognized and the Moslem

Averroës

frontier withdrawn to the Ebro; on the other hand, Leon and Navarre recognized the suzerainty of the caliph and paid tribute. This peace was soon broken by Ordono's brother Sancho (957) who, after his defeat, was expelled by his subjects but restored by the caliph (959).

961–976. Al-Hakam al Mustansír. He continued the wars against Castile, Leon, and Navarre and forced their rulers to sue for peace (962–970). At the same time he waged successful war against the Fatimid dynasty in Morocco, which was brought to an end (973) and replaced by the Omayyad power.

976–1009. Hisham II al Muayyad, whose reign marked the decline of the Omayyad dynasty. Power was seized by Muhammad ibn Abi'-Amir, with the title of *Hajib al-Mansur* (European: *Alamansor* = the Victorious Chamberlain), a brilliant reforming minister (army and administration). He carried on successful campaigns against Leon, Navarre, Catalonia, and Mauretania, and temporarily checked the religious and racial separatism which later on brought about the collapse of the Omayyad Caliphate. On his death in 1002 he was succeeded by his son, Abdulmalik al-Muzaffar (the Victorious), who several times defeated the Christians, and was followed by his brother, Abd ar-Rahman, named Sanchol. The latter obliged Hisham to proclaim him his heir, whereupon a revolt took place in Córdoba under the leadership of Muhammad, a member of the royal family. Hisham was compelled to abdicate in favor of Muhammad II al-Mahdi 1009–1010, and Sanchol was executed. In the meanwhile the Berbers nominated Sulaiman al-Mustain as caliph 1009–1010, 1013–1016. Civil war ensued, reducing Spain to more than a score of petty kingships (*taifas*) and making easier the Christian reconquest.

1027–1031. Hisham III, the last Omayyad caliph.

(3) Christian Spain, Castile and Leon, 718–1065

718–737. Pelayo, successor to Roderick the Visigoth, created the **kingdom of the Asturias,** a theocratic elective monarchy in the Visigothic tradition. Beginning of the reciprocal alliance of kings and clergy under

739–757. Alfonso I, who assigned to the Church a generous share of the lands conquered from the Moslems and used the clergy as a counterweight to the aristocracy.

899. Miraculous discovery of the bones of **St. James the Greater** and erection of the first church of Santiago de Campostella, which became the center of the Spanish national cult and one of the most influential shrines in Europe.

910–914. García, king of Leon, began a rapid expansion of his domain to the east (construction of numerous castles, hence the name *Castile*).

c. 930–970. Count Fernán González, count of Burgos (later Castile), marked the rise of the counts of Burgos. By intrigue and alliance with the Moslems he expanded his domains at the expense of Leon, and made the country of Castile autonomous and hereditary. His progress was arrested by Sancho the Fat of Leon (d. 966), who was in alliance with Abd ar-Rahman III.

970–1035. Sancho the Great of Navarre effected a close union of Castile and Navarre and began the conquest of Leon.

1035–1065. Ferdinand (Fernando) I, of Castile, completed the work by conquering Leon (1037) and assuming the title of king of Leon.
(Cont. p. 253.)

k. THE BRITISH ISLES

(1) England, to 1066

Prehistoric Britain. The prehistoric inhabitants of Britain (called *Celts* on the basis of language) were apparently a fusion of Mediterranean, Alpine, and Nordic strains which included a dark Iberian and a light-haired stock. Archaeological evidence points to contacts with the Iberian Peninsula (2500 B.C.) and Egypt (1300 B.C.).

1200–600 B.C. The true **Celts** are represented by two stocks: Goidels (*Gaels*), surviving in northern Ireland and high Scotland, and Cymri and Brythons (*Britons*), still represented in Wales. The Brythons were close kin to the Gauls, particularly the Belgi. Their religion was dominated by a powerful, organized, priestly caste, the druids of Gaul and Britain, who monopolized religion, education, and justice.

55 B.C.–c. 450 A.D. ROMAN OCCUPATION began with Julius Caesar's conquests in Gaul and Britain (57–50 B.C.); Emperor Claudius' personal expedition and conquest (43 A.D.) were decisive in the romanization of Britain. Reduction of the "empire" (5–40 A.D.) of Cymbeline and suppression (61) of the national revolt of Boudicca (*Boadicea*). Conquest of Wales (48–79). Construction of the great network of Roman roads began (eventually five systems, four centering on London). Bath emerged as a center of Romano-British fashion.

78–142. Roman conquests in the north began under Agricola; results north of the Clyde-Forth line were not decisive. The Emperor Hadrian completed the conquest of Britain in person: construction of **Hadrian's Wall** (123) from Solway Firth to Tyne mouth. Firth-Clyde rampart (c. 142).

208. Emperor Septimius Severus arrived (208), invaded Caledonia (Scotland), restored Roman military supremacy in the north, and fixed Hadrian's Wall as the final frontier of Roman conquest.

300–350. Height of villa construction in the plain of Britain. Chief towns: Verulamium (St. Albans), Colchester, Lincoln, Gloucester, York. The skill of the artisans and clothworkers of Britain was already famous on the Continent in the 4th century. The island south of the wall was completely romanized.

c. 350. Piratic raids of Irish (*Scoti*) and **Picts** were common, and the Teutonic conquest of Gaul cut Britain off from Rome in the 5th century, leaving the Romano-British to defend themselves against Saxon attacks on the south and east which soon penetrated the lowlands.

410–442. Withdrawal of the Roman legions and the end of the Roman administration coincided with an intensification of Nordic pressure and the influx of **Jutes, Angles, and Saxons,** which permanently altered the racial base of the island. By c. 615 the Angles and Jutes had reached the Irish Channel and were masters of what is virtually modern England. A

Celtic recrudescence appeared in the highlands of the west and northwest. The history of Britain for two centuries (c. 350–597) is obscure. Christianity had not made much progress under the Romans.

Seven Anglo-Saxon kingdoms, the *Heptarchy,* emerged after the Teutonic conquest: Essex, Wessex, Sussex (probably prevailingly Saxon as the names suggest); Kent (Jutes); East Anglia, Mercia, Northumbria (Angles).

560–616. The supremacy of **Ethelbert of Kent** in the Heptarchy coincided with the

597. Arrival of **Augustine the Monk** and the conversion of Kent to the Roman Church. The hegemony in the Heptarchy passed eventually to **Edwin of Northumbria** (which had also been converted).

Remains of Hadrian's Wall in Britain

Bronze helmet, Britain, probably 1st century B.C.

Stonehenge on the Salisbury Plain, prehistoric assemblage of stones in England

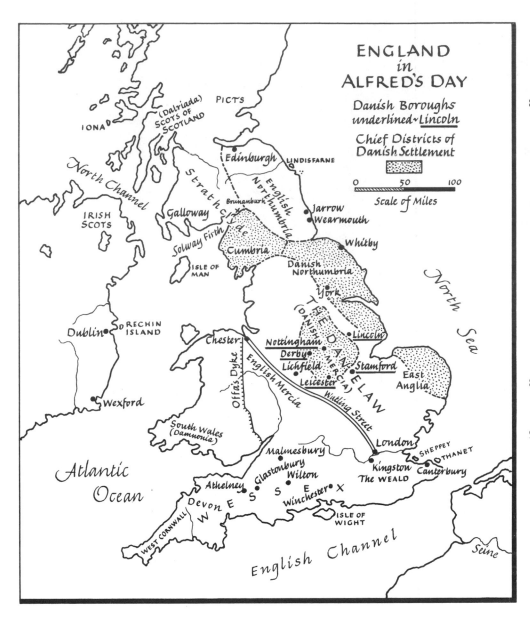

ENGLAND in ALFRED'S DAY

Danish Boroughs
underlined~Lincoln

Chief Districts of
Danish Settlement

0   50   100

Scale of Miles

Danes and forced the **peace of Wedmore**, whereby Guthrun the Dane became a Christian and divided England with Alfred. The *Danelaw,* north of the Thames-Lea line, went to Guthrun; the south, together with London, went to Alfred.

878–900. The Danes were masters of the northeast, and under Danish pressure **Scotland** began to take on shape and unity.

Alfred proceeded to organize the defense of his kingdom. London was walled and garrisoned with burghers charged with its defense. Earth forts (*burhs*) of the Viking type were thrown up and garrisoned. The *fyrd* and the fleet were reorganized, the army increased, the *thegns* began to be used as a mounted infantry. All citizens of the requisite wealth were forced to thegnhood, i.e. to join the military class attached to the royal household. A Danish reaction (892–896) was firmly suppressed.

Alfred's **patronage of learning.** Foreign scholars and learned refugees were welcomed at court. Alfred translated Bede's *Historia,* Orosius, and Boethius' *Consolatio* into the vernacular. To provide trained administrators, Alfred established schools for the sons of thegns and nobles. The *Anglo-Saxon Chronicle* was started.

899–924. **Edward,** Alfred's son, succeeded him, and with his sister, Ethelfleda of Mercia, began the conquest of the Danelaw, which was completed under

924–940. **Ethelstan,** Edward's son. The descendants of Alfred were the first true kings of England; his great-grandson **Edgar** (959–975) was recognized as such. Archbishop Dunstan, Edgar's chief counselor, was a great ecclesiastical reformer (simony and morals) of the Church and the people. He followed a policy of fusion and conciliation toward the Danes, and Oda, a full-blooded Dane, became (942) archbishop of Canterbury. The absorption of the Danelaw by Wessex left the Celtic fringe in Scotland and Wales independent under a vague kind of vassalage to the king.

As the Danelaw was absorbed, the shire system was extended to it with the old Danish boroughs as a nucleus. The administration was often in the hands of men of Danish blood. The Anglo-Saxon farmers had no love for war, and the thegns began to emerge as a professional soldier class. The old tribal and clan organization was superseded by a system of

633. The defeat and death of Ethelbert's brother-in-law Edwin at the hands of the heathen Mercians ended the Northumbrian primacy and temporarily overwhelmed the Roman Church. A period of anarchy ensued.

633. **Oswald of Northumbria** called Aidan from Iona, whose mission began the great influence of Celtic Christianity, which for a time threatened to replace the Roman Church.

664. The **Synod of Whitby** turned Britain back into the orbit of the Roman Church and the Continent, and prepared the way for the decisive rôle of

669–690. **Theodore of Tarsus,** archbishop of Canterbury. Theodore introduced a strictly Roman parochial system and a centralized episcopal system which became the model for the secular state and created a new concept of kingship. National synods brought the rival kingdoms together for the first time, and began the long evolution destined to create English nationality and national institutions, and to spread them through the civilized world.

Theodore's episcopate was marked by the reintroduction of Greco-Roman culture and the permanent establishment of a new cultural

tradition which produced **Bede** (673–735), the father of English literature, and culminated in the wide influence of the great school at York, which extended to the Continent (e.g. **Alcuin** at the court of Charlemagne). The archbishopric of York was founded, 735. Romance ecclesiastical architecture and church music flourished.

757–796. **Under Offa II** the kingdom of Mercia, supreme south of the Humber, reached its maximum power, after which it broke up.

787. The first recorded **raid of the Danes** in England was followed by the Danish inundation of Ireland. In the pause before the great wave of Viking advance, Wessex under

802–839. **Egbert,** who had been in Charlemagne's service, emerged supreme (conquering Mercia), exercised a vague suzerainty over Northumbria, and received the homage of all the English kinglets.

856–875. Full tide of the **first Viking assault.** Wessex was the spearhead of resistance.

871–899. **ALFRED THE GREAT** purchased peace until he could organize his forces and build up a navy. Almost overwhelmed by the winter invasion of 878, he finally defeated the

Alfred the Great (9th-century manuscript)

quasi-feudal form whereby each man had a lord who was responsible for him at law. The great earldoms were beginning to emerge.

No common law existed; shire and hundred courts administered local custom with the free-man suitors under the king's representative-ealdorman, shire-reeve, or hundred-reeve. From the days of Edgar, the feudal element tended to encroach on royal authority, especially in the hundred courts. The old monasticism had been destroyed by the invasions, and the Church in England fell into corruption and decadence, only reformed by the influence of Cluny and Fleury and the Norman conquest.

991. An ebb in Viking raids was followed by a fresh onset during the reign of **Ethelred the Redeless** (978–1016), led by Sven I (Forked Beard), king of Denmark. *Danegeld* had been sporadically collected under Alfred; now it was regularly levied and used as tribute to buy off the invaders. This tax, and the invasions, led to a rapid decline of the freeholders to a servile status. Under Canute, the Danegeld was transformed into a regular tax for defense. Collection of the Danegeld, originally in the hands of the towns, fell increasingly to the lord of the manor, and it was only a step from holding him for the tax to making him lord of the land from which the tax came.

1013–1014. **Sven I** (d. 1014) was acknowledged by the English, and Ethelred fled to Normandy, the home of his second wife, Emma.

1016–1035. **King Canute** (Cnut), one of the two sons of Sven, elected by the witan. The witan was a heterogeneous body of prelates, magnates, and officials without any precise constitutional status. Canute was "emperor," on the model of Charlemagne, over a northern empire which included Denmark, Norway, and England, and, but for his early death, might have played a more important rôle. His reign was marked

Anglo-Saxon Chronicle, late 11th century, recording Alfred's defeat of the Danes

Danish warriors c. 750

by conciliation and fusion. The Church was under Anglo-Saxon clergy. Canute maintained a good navy, and his standing army included the famous *housecarls,* which soon had an Anglo-Saxon contingent. The four great earldoms, Wessex, East Anglia, Mercia, Northumbria, and seven lesser earldoms can be distinguished in this period. The greatest of the earls was **Godwin of Wessex.** Canute's sons were incompetent, and his line ended, 1042.

Godwin was chiefly responsible for the election of the successor to Canute's line, Edward, son of Emma and Ethelred, who married (1045) Godwin's daughter.

1042–1066. **Edward the Confessor,** of the line of Alfred, was under Godwin's domination. Brought up at the Norman court, speaking French, he tried to Normanize the English court. Godwin's influence led to the deposition of the Norman archbishop of Canterbury and the selection of the Saxon Stigand by the witan. As Stigand had supported an anti-pope, Alexander II favored the Normans, as did Hildebrand, the power behind the papal throne. Godwin's son, **Harold,** succeeded (1053) him as earl of Wessex, and dominated Edward as his father had. Another son of Godwin, Tostig, became earl of Northumbria. Harold (c. 1064) was driven ashore on the Channel, fell into

King Edgar offering up the foundation charter of the Abbey at Winchester (11th-century manuscript)

The Anglo-Saxon Kings of England (802–1066)

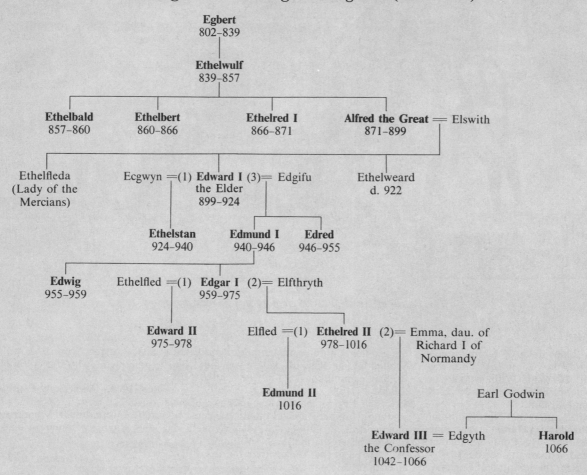

Egbert
802–839

Ethelwulf
839–857

Ethelbald
857–860

Ethelbert
860–866

Ethelred I
866–871

Alfred the Great = Elswith
871–899

Ethelfleda
(Lady of the
Mercians)

Ecgwyn =(1) Edward I (3)= Edgifu
the Elder
899–924

Ethelweard
d. 922

Ethelstan
924–940

Edmund I
940–946

Edred
946–955

Edwig
955–959

Ethelfled =(1) Edgar I (2)= Elfthryth
959–975

Edward II
975–978

Elfled =(1) Ethelred II (2)= Emma, dau. of
978–1016   Richard I of
                  Normandy

Edmund II
1016

Earl Godwin

Edward III = Edgyth
the Confessor
1042–1066

Harold
1066

The Danish Kings of England (1013–1066)

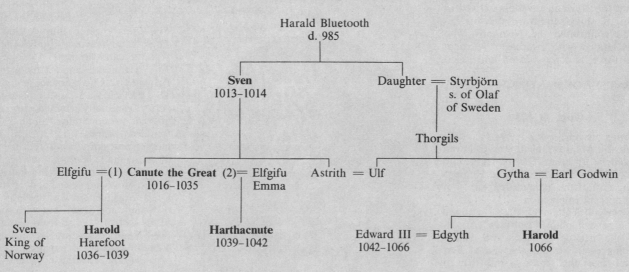

Harald Bluetooth
d. 985

Sven
1013–1014

Daughter = Styrbjörn
           s. of Olaf
           of Sweden

Thorgils

Elfgifu =(1) Canute the Great (2)= Elfgifu
            1016–1035   Emma

Astrith = Ulf

Gytha = Earl Godwin

Sven
King of
Norway

Harold
Harefoot
1036–1039

Harthacnute
1039–1042

Edward III = Edgyth
1042–1066

Harold
1066

(Cont. p. 220.)

The Battle of Hastings, 1066, panel from Bayeux Tapestry

the hands of William, duke of Normandy, a cousin of Edward the Confessor, and was forced to take an oath to aid William to attain the crown of England, which William declared Edward had promised him.

1066. Tostig, exiled after the Northumbrian revolt (1065), returned with **Harald Haardraade** to attack Northumbria. The Confessor died in January (1066) and William at once began vigorous preparations for the conquest of England.

1066. On Edward's death **Harold was chosen king** by the witan and was guarding the coasts of England against William when Tostig and Haardraade appeared in the north. After a brilliant dash northward, Harold defeated them at **Stamford Bridge** in September, at the very moment that the Norman invaders arrived in the Channel. Rushing southward after his victory, Harold confronted the Normans, who had already landed, with a reduced, wearied, and shaken force, and was beaten and killed in the

OCT. 14. BATTLE OF HASTINGS, or Senlac.
(Cont. p. 213.)

(2) Scotland, to 1034

Racial origins obscure. A wave of Neolithic peoples from the Mediterranean was followed by Celts, Goidels, Brythons, Saxons in the 6th century B.C., and then by Picts. The Romans arrived at the end of the 1st century, A.D., but made no permanent impression.

450–600. Four **political nuclei: Picts** (Pentland Firth to the central plain); **Dalriada** (Argyllshire and the islands of Jura and Islay); **"Welsh" refugees** in Strathclyde; **Ida of Bernicia's realm** (from the Tweed to the Firth of Forth).

c. 565. COLUMBA arrived from Iona and converted the king of the Picts to the Celtic Church, giving Scotland her first cultural contact with the civilized world.

664. The **Synod of Whitby** turned England to

the Roman Church and temporarily isolated Scotland. The Picts ultimately went into the Roman communion (c. 700) and Iona itself followed (716).

685. The English power was broken on the southern frontier, and Scotland began her independent evolution. Under **Kenneth I** (d. 858) began the first Scottish union.

794. Arrival of the Norse. Iona burned (802); a series of devastations followed.

921. Edward, son of Alfred the Great, was acknowledged lord of Scotland. Ethelstan enforced the bond in arms (934) and a Scottish effort to revolt was crushed (937).

1005–1034. Under **Malcolm II,** Lothian was

Duncan

added to the Scottish crown and Strathclyde completed (1034) the union of the four nuclei under

1034–1040. Duncan, but without a homogeneous racial or political basis. The isles and the north were under Scandinavian dominance, and England aimed to make Scotland her vassal.
(Cont. p. 223.)

(3) Ireland, to 1171

Racial origins. The Neolithic inhabitants, followed by Celts and Goidels (c. 600–500 B.C.). The "fifths" (i.e. Ulster, Leinster, Connaught, East and West Munster) may date from the Goidel arrival. Belgic and other Brythonic migrations (300–150 B.C.) probably in the southeast. Supremacy of the Brythonic **kingdom of Tara** in the 4th century of the Christian Era. The **Picts** pushed into Antrim and Down. There is an enormous body of legend dealing with the early origins.

431. Traditional date for the arrival of **Bishop Palladius** and his mission.

432. PATRICK, a pupil of Germanus of Auxerre, especially trained for this mission, arrived to continue Palladius' work. He founded churches in Meath, Ulster, Connaught, and probably established the bishopric of Armagh. Chieftains were converted, but much paganism survived. Patrick began the education of the priesthood. Patrick's ecclesiastical organization was probably close to that of Britain and Gaul, but with the withdrawal of the Roman legions from the latter countries the Roman connection was cut, and there was a recrudescence of paganism. The diocesan organization of Patrick apparently slipped back into the native system.

Chieftains, on their conversion, made donations of land to the Church, and at first the ecclesiastical offices seem to have remained in the hands of the sept, with the *coarb* (inheritor) as bishop or abbot. The cenobitic organization of the 5th century was that of a sept, whose chief was a Christian. Later there was a rigorous form which separated the sexes. As the earlier diocesan organization declined, the number of bishops rose to fantastic figures. There was a great exodus of Irish scholars and monks to Europe during the 8th and 9th centuries.

. 500–800. The **Golden Age of Irish monastic scholarship** occurred in the 6th to the 9th centuries. A great school founded by **Eudo,** prince of Oriel (c. 450–540), at Aranmore drew scholars from all Europe. Establishment of the monastery of **Clonard** (c. 520) under Welsh inspiration. Here there were said to be 3000 students living in separate, wattled huts under open-air instruction. From Clonard went forth the so-called **Twelve Apostles of Ireland,** founding schools all over Ireland and later the Continent.

. 533. True monasticism began with the work of Columba. Columba founded Iona (563), the mother Church of Scotland, whence Aidan, the apostle of England, founded Lindisfarne (635) for the conversion of Northumbria. The *Book of Kells* and the flowering of Gaelic vernacular poetry date from this period.

590. Columban of Leinster, from Bangor, began his mission to Europe, founding Luxeuil and a great series of other foundations (e.g. Gall, Würzburg, Salzburg, Tarantum, Bobbio). The 8th century saw a great wave of missions from the Rhine-Meuse area inland to the Rhone-Alps line. This powerful advance of Celtic Christianity at one time seemed destined to win northern Europe from Rome. The chief formal differences from Rome were in tonsure, the date of Easter, the consecration of bishops. In the 7th century the Irish Church conformed to Roman usage, but the bond with Rome was not close.

723. Boniface (Winfred) the Anglo-Saxon arrived on the Continent to begin the organization on Roman lines of the Celtic establishments among the Franks, Thuringians, Alamanni, and Bavarians.

Before the coming of the Norse there were no cities, no stone bridges in Ireland, and no foreign trade of importance.

795. The first Norse attack. Dublin (840), Waterford, and Limerick founded as centers of Norse trade with the Continent. Soon a mixed race, the Gallgoidels (whence Galloway) arose, and a Christian decline set in. The Scandinavians remained chiefly in the ports.

1002–1014. Brian of Munster established his supremacy. A period of road- and fort-building. At Clontarf (1014) Brian defeated the Norse, ending the domination of Dublin, though the Norse remained in their cities. Brian fell in the battle and anarchy followed— the struggle of the O'Brians of Munster, the O'Neils of Ulster, the O'Connors of Connaught—which ended in an appeal to King Henry II of England by Dermond (or Dermot) MacMurrough.

Boniface converting the heathen

1152. The **Synod of Kells** established the present diocesan system of Ireland, recognized the primacy of Armagh, and the archbishoprics of Cashel, Tuam, Dublin. Tithes were voted.

1167–1171. The Norman Conquest. Henry II, on his accession, had the idea of conquering Ireland. John of Salisbury records that on his request as Henry's envoy (1155), Pope Adrian IV sent Henry a letter granting him lordship of Ireland, and a ring as the symbol of his investiture. Henry seems never to have availed himself of the papal grant.

1167. On the appeal of Dermond MacMurrough, Henry issued a letter allowing Dermond to raise troops in England for his cause. Dermond came to terms with Richard of Clare, a Norman, earl of Pembroke, and with other Normans, most of whom were related to one another. A series of expeditions to Ireland brought into the island a group of Norman families (e.g. Fitzmaurices, Carews, Gerards, Davids, Barries, *et al.*), who began to establish a powerful colony. This greatly alarmed Henry.

1171. HENRY II, with papal sanction, landed in Ireland to assert his supremacy and to reconcile the natives. The **Synod of Cashel,** at which Henry was not present, acknowledged his sovereignty. *(Cont. p. 224.)*

I. SCANDINAVIA, TO 981

Origins. References in Pytheas, Pomponius Mela, Pliny the Elder, Tacitus, Ptolemy, Procopius, Jordanes. Archaeological remains indicate Roman connections in the 3rd century after Christ, but there is no evidence for close continental relations until the Viking period.

VIKING PERIOD. Scandinavia developed in isolation during the barbarian migrations until the 2nd century after Christ. The Viking expansion from Scandinavia itself prolonged the period of migrations in Europe for four hundred years. The traditional participation of Scandinavia was as follows: (1) **Norwegians** (outer passage): raids in Scotland, Ireland, France (Hrolf the Ganger, i.e. "Rollo"); (2) **Danes** (the middle passage): British Isles, France, the Low Countries; (3) **Swedes** (eastward passage): across Slavdom to Byzantium (foundation of Novgorod 862, Kiev, c. 900). There never was a mass migration, and probably all stocks shared in the various movements to some degree. **Causes:** (1) pagan reaction, including renegade Christians; (2) pressure of population; (3) tribal warfare and vassalage of the defeated, especially after 872 (this is the traditional explanation for Rollo's migration, 911); (4) love of gain; (5) fashion and love of adventure.

NORWEGIAN COLONIZATION. (1) **Ireland:** the Norwegian conquest began c. 823 and centers were established at Dublin (the kingdom endured until 1014), Waterford, and Limerick. Exodus of learned monks to Europe **(Scotus Erigena?).** Attacks by the Picts and Danes. The subsequent colonization of the Scottish Islands drew Norwegians from Ireland and accelerated the celtization of the colonists who remained there. (2) **The Islands:** Hebrides, Man, Faroes, Orkneys, Shetlands. (3) **Iceland:** reached by Irish monks c. 790; discovered by the Norsemen in 874 and colonized almost at once; establishment of a New Norway, with a high culture. (4) **Greenland:** visited by Eric the Red of Iceland (981) and colonized at once; expeditions from Greenland to the North American continent *(p. 382)*. The Norse settlements in Greenland continued until the 15th century.

CIVILIZATION. Large coin hoards indicate the profits of raids and trade with the British Isles, Mediterranean, Byzantium, and Moslem Asia. Export of furs, arms (to eastern Europe), and mercenary services to rulers (e.g. bodyguards of Ethelred, Cnut, Slavic princes, Byzantine emperors). Trade eastward was cut off by the Huns and Avars (5th and 6th century), but resumed after Rurik's expedition (862) reopened Russia.

Runes (from a Scandinavian root, meaning to inscribe) were already ancient in the Viking period, and probably are modified Roman letters. The *Eddas,* dramatic lays (prose and verse) of the Norwegian aristocracy (especially in Iceland) dealing with gods and heroes (many in the German tradition, e.g. Sigurd and the Nibelungs), are the highest literary production of heathen Scandinavia.

Scandinavian society rested on wealth from raids and commerce and consisted of a landed aristocracy with farmer tenants with the right and obligation to attend local courts; there were

Head of the wooden stem-post of a Viking ship

Viking helmet, 7th century, reconstructed

few slaves. The only general assembly was the *Allthing* of Iceland (established 930), the oldest continuous parliamentary body in existence.

Mythology and religion. The Norwegians had a more complicated mythology than any other Teutonic people: giants, elves, dwarfs, serpents, succeeded by the triumph of **Odin,** his wife **Friga,** and his son **Thor.**

Conversion to Christianity. The first Christians (probably captives) appeared in the 6th century. The first Christian missionary was the Anglo-Saxon, **Willibord** (c. 700), who accomplished but little. A Carolingian mission (c. 820) was welcomed by King Bjorn of Sweden. A few years later (c. 831) the archbishopric of Hamburg was established and became at once the center for missionary work in the north.

(Cont. p. 224.)

2. *Eastern Europe*

a. THE BYZANTINE EMPIRE, 527–1025

[*For a complete list of the Byzantine emperors see Appendix II.*]

527–565. JUSTINIAN. A Macedonian by birth and the chief adviser of his uncle, Justin, since 518. Justinian was a man of serious and even somber temperament, but of strong, even autocratic character, sober judgment, grandiose conceptions. He was strongly influenced by his wife **Theodora** (d. 548), a woman of humble origin, probably unduly maligned by the historian Procopius. Theodora was cruel, deceitful, and avid of power, but a woman of iron will and unusual political judgment. Justinian's whole policy was directed toward the establishment of the absolute power of the emperor and toward the revival of a universal Christian Roman Empire. The entire reign was filled with wars in the east and in the west, punctuated by constant incursions of the barbarians from the north.

527–532. The **first Persian War** of Justinian. His commander, **Belisarius,** won a victory at Dara (530), but was then defeated at **Callinicum.** The conflict ended with the **Perpetual Peace** of 532, designed to free the imperial armies for operations in the west.

532. The **Nika Insurrection** (so called from the cry of the popular parties, *nika = victory*). This was the last great uprising of the circus parties and led to great violence and incendiarism. Much of Constantinople was destroyed by fire. Justinian was deterred from flight only through the arguments of Theodora. Ultimately Belisarius and the forces put down the insurrection with much cruelty (30,000 slain). Therewith the period of popular domination ended and the epoch of absolutism began.

533–534. CONQUEST OF NORTH AFRICA. Belisarius, with a relatively small force, transported by sea, defeated the Vandal usurper, Gelimer, and recovered the whole of North Africa for the empire.

535–554. THE RECONQUEST OF ITALY. Belisarius landed in Sicily, overran the island, conquered southern Italy from the Ostrogoths, and took Rome (Dec. 9, 536). The Ostrogoth king, **Witiges,** besieged the city for a whole year (537–538), but failed to take it. In the following year Belisarius advanced to the north, took Ravenna, and captured Witiges, but, after the recall of Belisarius, the new Ostrogoth leader, **Totila,** reconquered Italy as far as Naples (541–543). He took Rome (546) and sacked it. Belisarius returned, captured the city, but then abandoned it to the Goths (549). He was later replaced by **Narses,** who invaded Italy by land from the north with a large army composed chiefly of barbarian mercenaries. He defeated the Ostrogoths decisively in the **battle of Tagina** (552) and brought all of Italy under imperial rule.

540. The **Huns, Bulgars,** and other barbarian tribes crossed the Danube and raided the Balkan area as far south as the Isthmus of Corinth.

540–562. The great **Persian War against Khusru I** (Chosroes). The Persians invaded Syria and took Antioch, after which they attacked Lazistan and Armenia and raided Mesopotamia. In 544 they besieged Edessa, but in vain. A truce was concluded in 545, but hostilities were soon resumed in the Transcaucasus region. The Persians took Petra (549), but lost it again (551). By the fifty-year **Peace of**

Theodora (detail from 6th-century mosaic in the Church of San Vitale, Ravenna)

Justinian I (detail from 6th-century mosaic in the Church of San Vitale, Ravenna)

562, Justinian agreed to pay tribute, but Lazistan was retained for the empire.

542–546. Constantinople and the empire were visited by a very severe and disastrous epidemic of the bubonic plague.

554. The **conquest of southeastern Spain** by the imperial armies. Cordova became the capital of the province.

559. The **Huns and Slavs,** having advanced to the very gates of Constantinople, were driven off by Belisarius.

JUSTINIAN AND THE CHURCH. Peace had been made with Rome in 519 and Pope John I had visited Constantinople in 525. Justinian made a great effort to maintain the unity of the western and eastern churches, but this led him into trouble with the **Monophysites** of Syria and Egypt. He attempted to reconcile them also, but with indifferent success. The cleavage between Latin and Greek Christianity became ever more marked. Justinian suppressed all heresies and paganism (closing of the Neo-Platonic Academy at Athens, 529). Extensive missionary work was carried on among the barbarians and in Africa. For the rest, the emperor, with a great taste for dogma, set himself up as the master of the Church and arrogated to himself the right to make binding pronouncements in even purely theological matters.

ADMINISTRATION. The emperor insisted on honesty and efficiency. He abolished sale of offices, improved salaries, united the civil and military powers of provinicial authorities, etc. In order to hold back the barbarians, he built hundreds of forts along the frontiers and established a regular system of frontier forces (*limitanei*). Financially the empire suffered greatly

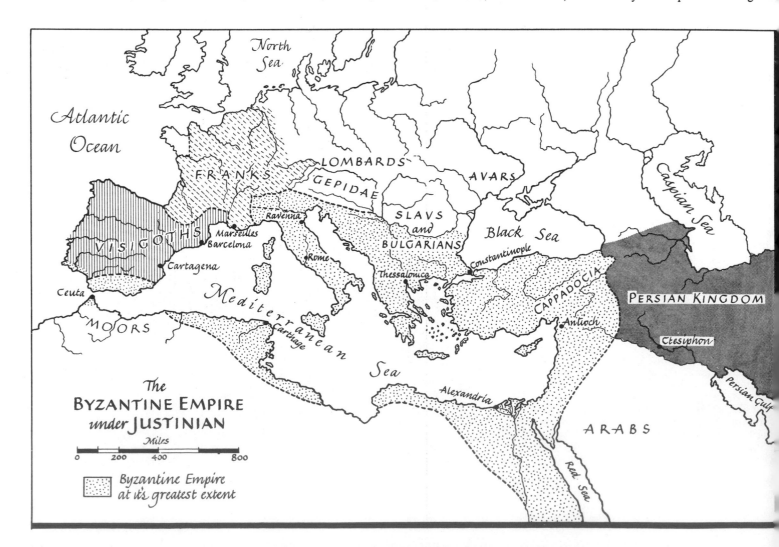

The
BYZANTINE EMPIRE
under JUSTINIAN

Miles

0   200   400   800

Byzantine Empire
at it's greatest extent

Church of St. Sophia, Istanbul, built during Justinian's reign

from the extensive military operations and from the great building activities of the court.

LAW REFORM. In order to clarify the law, Justinian appointed a commission headed by the jurist, **Tribonian.** This commission collected and ordered all the constitutions promulgated since the time of Hadrian and published them as the *Codex Justinianus* (529). There followed the collection of opinions of the jurists, the *Digest* or *Pandects* (533), and a general textbook of the law, the *Institutes.* Justinian's own legislation was collected in the *Novellae* (565). By this great work of codification Justinian assured for the Roman Law an immense prestige and far-reaching influence, but at the same time diminished its chances of further development.

BUILDING ACTIVITY. The period was one of unexampled construction, ranging from whole towns to public baths, palaces, bridges, roads, and forts, as well as countless churches and cloisters. It was a period of much free experimentation and originality, resulting in unusual variety of types, all of them, however, marked by grandeur and splendor. The **Church of St. Sophia** (constructed between 532–537 by Anthemios of Tralles and Isidoros of Miletus) is the greatest of the many monuments of Justinian's reign.

LITERATURE. An age of revival. The *Anekdota* (*Secret History*) of **Procopius;** the historians **Agathias** and **John of Ephesus.** Renascence of Greek classical poetry; creation of religious poetry by **Romanos.**

565–578. JUSTIN II, nephew of Justinian, who seized the throne with the aid of Tiberius,

commander of the guard. Justin was a careful, economical ruler, who continued the policies of his predecessor, but attempted to concentrate attention upon the economic plight of the empire and the growing danger from the barbarians. In 574 he became insane, after which the empire was ruled by Tiberius, in conjunction with the Empress Sophia.

568–571. The **Lombard invasion of Italy** led to the loss of most of the imperial possessions in the north and center, though Ravenna, Rome, and Naples were retained.

572–591. War with Persia, growing out of an insurrection in Armenia, which was supported by the emperor. The Persians took Dara (573) and devastated Syria. In 575, Khusru ravaged the country as far as Cappadocia, but was finally driven back by the imperial commander, Maurikios.

578–582. TIBERIUS, emperor. His reign was marked by a great inundation of the Slavs, who advanced into Thrace and Greece and settled in large numbers, thus changing profoundly the ethnographic composition of the Balkan populations.

582–602. MAURICE (Maurikios), emperor. Like his forerunner, Justin, he pursued a policy of retrenchment, which only made him unpopular in the capital. The reign was marked by constant disturbances and by widespread dissatisfaction.

583. The **Avars,** grown to be a formidable power, took the forts along the Danube.

589–591. Last phase of the Persian War. Khusru I had died in 579. In 589 a military re-

volt led to the deposition of Khusru II, who fled to Constantinople. The emperor, espousing his cause, led a great army to the east (591) and restored him to the throne. In return the emperor received Dara and the larger part of Armenia.

591. The Avars raided to the very gates of Constantinople.

593. The imperial armies, under **Priscus,** proceeded against the Avars. The latter were defeated at **Viminacium** (601) after which Priscus pushed on to the Tisza River.

602. A **mutiny of the troops on the Danube,** led by Phocas, resulted in a march to the capital, the outbreak of popular insurrection in the city, and the flight of the emperor.

602–610. PHOCAS, emperor. He was an untutored soldier, cruel and utterly incompetent. Maurice was captured and executed with his sons. All his supporters met with a like fate.

606–608. Resumption of the Persian War. The Persians again captured Dara and overran Syria and Mesopotamia (608) advancing through Anatolia as far as Chalcedon.

610. Conspiracy against Phocas, led by Priscus and supported by the exarch of Africa. The latter sent an army by land which conquered Egypt, while a fleet from Carthage arrived at Constantinople. The mob thereupon rose, slew Phocas, and proclaimed Heraclius, the son of the exarch, as emperor.

610–641. HERACLIUS I, founder of a new dynasty, in whose reign the empire became definitely a Greek (Byzantine) monarchy. Heraclius found the empire in a perilous state, threatened from the north by the Avars and from the east by the Persians. But he showed himself an able organizer, general, and statesman, and found in the Patriarch Sergius a courageous supporter.

611–622. The Persian advance. They took Antioch, Apameia, Emesa, and Kaisareia; Damascus (613); Jerusalem (614), which was sacked, the inhabitants and the Holy Cross being transferred to Ctesiphon. In 615 the Persians were at Chalcedon. In 619 they conquered Egypt.

616. The imperial possessions in Spain were lost to the Visigoths.

619. The **Avars appeared at Constantinople,** which was threatened on the Asiatic side by the Persians. Heraclius was deterred from flight to Africa only by the influence of the patriarch.

622–630. DEFEAT OF THE PERSIANS. Heraclius, with a newly organized army and supported by a tremendous outburst of religious enthusiasm (the *Byzantine Crusade*), took the offensive against the Persians and carried on three brilliant campaigns in the Transcaucasian region, refusing to allow himself to be distracted by the constant attacks of the Avars in the Balkans. In the **battle of Nineveh** (Dec. 12, 627) he won a decisive victory, which enabled him to advance to Ctesiphon (628). The death of Khusru (628) and dynastic disorders in Persia made possible the conclusion of a victorious peace. All the Persian conquests were returned and the Holy Cross restored to Jerusalem.

626. The Avars and Slavs attacked Constantinople by land and sea, but were unable to storm the walls. This marked the height of the Avar power.

634–641. The Arab conquests *(p. 207).* They took Bostra (634); Damascus (635); by the **battle of Yarmuk** (636) gained all Syria; forced the surrender of Jerusalem (637); overran Mesopotamia (639) and conquered Egypt (640–642).

635. Alliance between the emperor and Kuvrat, king of the Bulgars, intended to break the power of the Avars.

638. The *Ecthesis,* a formula elaborated by the Patriarch Sergius and other churchmen in the hope of reconciling the Monophysites, who were welcoming rather than opposing the Islamic advance. The formula recognized one will in the two natures of Christ (*monothelitism*), but failed to win acceptance in Syria and Egypt. On the contrary, it called forth much opposition in the strictly orthodox Italian and African possessions.

641. HERACLIUS CONSTANTINUS III, son of Heraclius, became emperor, but died in a few months under suspicious circumstances.

641. HERACLEONAS, younger son of Heraclius, emperor, under his mother's tutelage. He was almost at once overthrown by the army.

641–668. CONSTANS II (Constantinus), grandson of Heraclius, emperor. He was an energetic and able ruler, who did his utmost to check the Arab advance. With this object in view he reorganized the provincial administration by establishing **themes** (*themata*) under military governors with wide powers (*strategio*) and authority over the civil officials. This system greatly strengthened administrative control and was the basis of the imperial organization for centuries.

643. The Arabs took Alexandria, last outpost of the Greeks in Egypt.

647–648. Arab invasion of North Africa.

648. The Arabs, having assembled a fleet, took Cyprus.

649. Pope Martin condemned the teaching of the *Ecthesis,* but was soon arrested by the exarch of Ravenna (653) and sent to Constantinople.

653. The Arab advance continued. Armenia was conquered (653) and Rhodes plundered (654). In 655 the Arab fleet defeated an imperial armada under the emperor's own command off the Lycian coast. But in 659 a truce was concluded with the Arab commander in Syria.

663–668. Transfer of the court to Italy. Constans was intent on blocking the Arab conquest of Sicily and Italy and had dreams of restoring Rome as the basis of the imperial power. But he failed to make any conquests in Italy at the expense of the Lombards and in his absence the Arabs annually invaded and devastated Anatolia.

668. Constans was murdered in the course of a mutiny at Syracuse.

668–685. CONSTANTINE IV (Pogonatus), the son of Constans, a harsh character, but an able soldier. He had been in charge of affairs and had come to Sicily to put down the revolt that had resulted in his father's death. On his return to Constantinople, the troops obliged him to accept his brothers Heraclius and Tiberius as co-rulers, but after 680 Constantine was sole emperor. His reign witnessed the high point of the Arab attack, accompanied, as usual, by repeated incursions of the Slavs in the Balkans.

673–678. The **Arab attacks on Constantinople.** After a siege by land and sea (Apr.–Sept. 673), the assailants blockaded the city and attacked it every year for five years. The city was saved by the strength of its walls and by the newly invented **Greek fire,** which raised havoc with the Arab fleet. In 677 the Greeks destroyed the Arab fleet at **Syllaeum** and secured a favorable thirty-year peace (678). Never again did the Arab menace become so pressing. The empire had proved itself a formidable bulwark of Europe.

675–681. Repeated assaults of the Slavs on Thessalonica. The city held out, but the settlement of Thrace and Macedonia and northern Greece by Slavic tribes continued uninterruptedly.

679. Appearance of the **Bulgar menace.** The Bulgars, a people of Turkish race, had pressed westward through southern Russia and settled in Bessarabia. The emperor failed in his efforts to defeat them there. They crossed the Danube, settled in the region between the river and the Balkan Mountains, gradually fused with the Slavs and became largely Slavicized, and founded the first coherent Slavic power in the Balkans.

680–681. The **sixth ecumenical council** at Constantinople condemned the monothelite heresy and returned to pure orthodoxy. Since the loss of Syria and Egypt, there was no longer any need for favoring the monophysite view. The return to orthodoxy was a victory for the papal stand and was probably intended to strengthen the Byzantine hold on Italy. In actual fact the patriarch of Constantinople (now that the patriarchs of Antioch, Jerusalem, and Alexandria were under Moslem power) became more and more influential in the east and the primacy of the Roman pope was hardly more than nominal.

685–695. JUSTINIAN II, the son of Constantine and the last of the Heraclian dynasty. He ascended the throne when only sixteen and soon showed himself to be harsh and cruel, though energetic and ambitious like most members of his family.

689. The emperor defeated the Slavs in Thrace and transferred a considerable number of them to Anatolia.

692. The Byzantine forces were severely defeated by the Arabs in the **battle of Sevastopol.**

695. A revolt against the emperor, led by Leontius and supported by the clergy and people, initiated a period of twenty years of anarchy. Justinian was deposed and exiled to the Crimea (Cherson).

Heraclius I

Front cover of the Lindau Gospels

Two details from the Bayeux Tapestry (p.247)

Constantinople attacked by Persians (illustration from a 14th-century manuscript)

The Arab fleet was destroyed in 673 with the help of the then newly invented "Greek fire" (14th-century manuscript)

695-698. LEONTIUS, emperor. His reign was marked by the domination of the army.

697-698. The Arabs finally took **Carthage** and brought to an end the Byzantine rule in North Africa.

698-705. TIBERIUS II, made emperor by another revolt in the army. The reign was distinguished by an insurrection against Byzantine rule in Armenia and by constant Arab raids in eastern Anatolia.

705-711. JUSTINIAN II, who returned to the throne with the aid of the Bulgar king. He took an insane revenge on all his enemies and instituted a veritable reign of terror.

711. The emperor failed to suppress a serious **revolt in the Crimea,** supported by the Khazars. The insurgent troops, under Philippicus, marched on Constantinople and finally defeated and killed Justinian in an engagement in northern Anatolia.

711-713. PHILIPPICUS, emperor. He proved himself quite incompetent and was unable to check the raids of the Bulgars (reached Constantinople in 712) or the ravages of the Arabs in Cilicia (they took Amasia, 712).

713-715. ANASTASIUS II, emperor, the creature of the mutinous Thracian army corps. He attempted to reorganize the army, but this led to new outbreaks.

715-717. THEODOSIUS III, an obscure official put on the throne by the army. He was helpless in the face of the Arabs, who in 716 advanced as far as Pergamon. The invaders were finally repulsed by the strategos of the Anatolian theme, Leo, who forced the abdication of the emperor and was enthusiastically proclaimed by the clergy and populace of the capital.

717-741. LEO III (the Isaurian), founder of the **Isaurian dynasty,** an eminent general and a great organizer. Leo used drastic measures to suppress revolts in the army and re-established discipline by issuing new regulations. The finances were restored by heavy, systematic taxation, but steps were taken, by an **agrarian code,** to protect freemen and small holders. By the *Ecloga* (739) the empire was given a simplified law code, distinguished by the Christian charity of its provisions. In the administrative sphere Leo completed the **theme organization,** dividing the original units and making seven themes in Asia and four in Europe.

717-718. Second great siege of Constantinople by the Arabs. The siege, conducted by land and sea, lasted just a year and ended in failure, due to the energetic conduct of the defense.

726. Beginning of the great **iconoclastic controversy.** Leo found the empire generally demoralized and a prey to superstition and miracle-mongering. Like many devout persons (especially in the Anatolian regions), he disapproved of the widespread image-worship, which he proceeded to forbid. Behind these measures there undoubtedly lay the desire to check the alarming **spread of monasticism,** which withdrew thousands of men from active economic life and concentrated great wealth in the cloisters, which were free from taxation. The first measures led at once to a revolt in Greece (727), whence a fleet set out for Constantinople with an anti-emperor. This was destroyed by the Greek fire of the imperial fleet. The pope at Rome (Gregory II) likewise declared against the emperor's iconoclasm and

the population of the exarchate of Ravenna rose in revolt and made an alliance with the Lombards. Only with the aid of Venice were a few crucial stations held by the imperial forces. A fleet from the east failed to restore Byzantine authority (731). In revenge the emperor in 733 withdrew Calabria, Sicily, and Illyria from the jurisdiction of the pope and placed them under the Constantinople patriarch.

739. The Byzantine forces won an important victory over the Arab invaders of Anatolia in the **battle of Akroinon.**

741-775. CONSTANTINE V (Kopronymos), the son of Leo and for years associated with him in the government. Constantine was autocratic, uncompromising, and violent, but withal able and energetic as well as sincere. A revolt of his brother-in-law, Artavasdos, was supported by the idolaters and by part of the army. It took fully two years to suppress it

745. The emperor, taking the offensive against the Arabs, carried the war into Syria.

746. The Greek destroyed a great Arab armada and reconquered Cyprus.

746. The empire suffered from the greatest **plague epidemic** since the time of Justinian.

751-752. The emperor led a successful campaign against the Arabs in Armenia. The Arabs were weakened by the fall of the Omayyad Caliphate and the removal of the capital from Damascus to Baghdad *(p. 212).*

751. The Lombards conquered the exarchate of Ravenna. The pope thereupon called in the Franks and was given the former Byzantine territory by Pepin (**Donation of Pepin,** 756) *(p. 176).*

753. The **Church Council of Hieria** approved of the emperor's iconoclastic policy. Therewith began the violent phase of the controversy. The monks offered vigorous resistance, but the emperor was unbending. The monks were imprisoned, exiled, and some even executed; monasteries were closed and their properties confiscated; images were destroyed or whitewashed.

755-764. Nine successive **campaigns against the Bulgars.** The emperor won important vic-

tories at Marcellae (759) and Anchialus (763), and, despite some reverses, forced the Bulgars to conclude peace (764).

758. The Slavs were defeated in Thrace and a large number of them settled in Asia.

772. Renewal of the **war with the Bulgars,** marked by further victories of the emperor.

775-780. LEO IV, the son of Constantine. In religious matters he simply continued his predecessor's policy.

778-779. Victory over the Arabs at **Germanikeia** (778) and their expulsion from Anatolia.

780-797. CONSTANTINE VI ascended the throne as a child, wholly under the influence of his ambitious, unscrupulous, and scheming mother, **Irene,** and her favorites. Irene, anxious to secure support for her personal power, devoted herself almost exclusively to the religious question. The Arabs, who again advanced to the Bosporus (782), were bought off with heavy tribute (783). On the other hand, the general, Staurakios, carried on a successful campaign against the Slavs in Macedonia and Greece (783).

787. The **Council of Nicaea** abandoned iconoclasm and ordered the worship of images. Tremendous victory for the monkish party, which soon advanced far-reaching claims to complete freedom for the Church in religious matters.

790. The army, opposed to the monks, mutinied and put Constantine in power. Irene was forced into retirement. The emperor set out on campaigns against the Arabs and Bulgars, but met with indifferent success.

792. Constantine recalled his mother and made her co-ruler. She took a vile advantage of him and, after his divorce and a remarriage arranged by her (795), put herself at the head of a party of the monks in opposing the step. A rising of the army put her in control and she had her son taken and blinded (797).

797-802. IRENE, the first empress. Though supported by able generals (Staurakios and Aëtios), she preferred to buy peace with the Arabs (798) and devote herself to domestic intrigue.

800. Resurrection of the empire in the west,

The second Council of Nicaea, 787

200   THE EARLY MIDDLE AGES

through the coronation of Charlemagne. The Eastern Empire refused to recognize the claim.

802–811. NICEPHORUS, who was put on the throne by a group of conspiring officials of the government. Irene, deposed, died in 803. Nicephorus was a firm ruler, who carried through a number of much-needed financial reforms.

803. The emperor made **peace with Charlemagne,** the Eastern Empire retaining southern Italy, Venice, and Dalmatia.

804–806. The Arabs resumed their raids in Anatolia and ravaged Cyprus and Rhodes, ultimately forcing the conclusion of a humiliating peace.

809. Banishment of the monks of Studion, who, under **Theodoros of Studion,** took the lead in advancing claims to church freedom. They went so far as to appeal to the Roman pope and offer to recognize his primacy.

809–813. War with Krum, the powerful king of the Bulgars. The emperor was defeated and killed in a great battle (811).

811. STAURAKIOS, son of Nicephorus, was emperor for a few months.

811–813. MICHAEL I (Rhangabé), brother-in-law of Staurakios, emperor. He proved himself quite incompetent, being unable to check the advance of Krum to Constantinople, or the success of the party of monks in domestic affairs.

813–820. LEO V (the Armenian), called to the throne by the army. Though personally not much moved by the religious controversy, he could not avoid taking up the challenge of the monks.

815. The **COUNCIL OF ST. SOPHIA** marked the return to iconoclasm and the beginning of the second period of active and violent persecution of the monks.

817. The emperor won a great victory over the Bulgars at **Mesembria,** Krum having died (814). The Bulgars were obliged to accept a thirty-year peace.

820–829. MICHAEL II (Phrygian dynasty), succeeded to the throne after the murder of Leo by conspirators.

822–824. Insurrection of the general, **Thomas,** in Anatolia. This was supported by the lower classes and encouraged by the Arabs. Thomas attempted twice to take Constantinople, but was ultimately defeated and executed in Thrace.

826. Crete was seized by Moslem freebooters from Spain and until 961 remained the headquarters of pirates who ravaged the eastern Mediterranean.

827–878. Conquest of Sicily by Moslems from North Africa.

829–842. THEOPHILUS, emperor. He was an arrogant, theologizing fanatic who promulgated a new edict against idolaters (832) and pushed persecution to the limit.

837–838. War against the Arabs. The Byzantine armies, after invading the caliphate, were repulsed. After a long siege, Amorion, one of the key positions on the frontier, was taken by the Moslems (838).

842–867. MICHAEL III, for whom his mother Theodora was regent. Advised by her brother, **Bardas,** she decided to end the religious controversy.

843. Image-worship was restored. This was a great victory for the opposition party, but only in the matter of doctrine. Politically the power

Ruins of the Greek theater in Taormina, Sicily

of the emperor over the Church remained unimpaired, if not strengthened.

849. Reduction of the Slavic populations of the Peloponnesus, followed by their conversion.

856. Theodora was obliged to retire, but her brother Bardas, an able but unprincipled politician, remained the real ruler of the empire by exploiting to the full the weaknesses of the emperor.

860. First appearance of the Russians (Varangians) at Constantinople.

863–885. Missionary activity of **Cyril** and **Methodius** of Thessalonica among the Slavs of Moravia and Bohemia. They invented the **Glagolitic** (i.e. Slavic) **alphabet** and by the use of Slavic in the church service paved the way for the connection of Slavic Christianity with Constantinople.

865. Tsar Boris of Bulgaria (852–889) allowed himself to be baptized. Although Michael III acted as godfather, the Bulgarian ruler was for a time undecided between the claims of Rome and Constantinople to religious jurisdiction in Bulgaria.

866. Bardas was murdered by Michael's favorite, Basil.

867. Michael himself was deposed and done away with at Basil's order.

867. Schism with Rome. The great patriarch, **Photius,** had replaced **Ignatius** in 858, whereupon the latter had appealed to the pope for an inquiry. Photius came to represent the Greek national feeling in opposition to Rome. He took a strong stand towards the papal claims and the **Council of Constantinople** (867) anathematized the pope, accused the papacy of doctrinal aberrations, rejected the idea of Rome's primacy, etc.

867–886. BASIL I, founder of the Macedonian dynasty (he was really of Armenian extraction, though born in Macedonia). His reign initiated what was probably the most glorious period of Byzantine history. The empire had by this

time become a purely Greek monarchy, under an absolute ruler. Settlement of the iconoclastic controversy released the national energies and there followed a period of brilliant military success, material prosperity, and cultural development. An important departure was the recognition of the idea of legitimacy and of an imperial family. This was paralleled by the gradual emergence of a feudal system.

Basil I was himself an intelligent, firm, and orderly ruler, a good administrator and general, whose ambition was to restore the empire both internally and externally. He rebuilt the army and especially the navy, and did much to revise the legal system: the *Procheiros Nomos* (879), a compilation of the most important parts of the Justinian code; the *Epanagoge* (886), a manual of customary law.

869. The eighth ecumenical synod. Photius had been banished (867) and Ignatius recalled. The latter made peace with Rome on papal terms, but conflict and friction continued.

871–879. Campaigns in the east. Border warfare with the Arabs was chronic, but the campaign against the Paulicians (Christian purists hostile to the empire) was a new departure. The imperial armies advanced to the upper Euphrates and took Samosata (873). In 878–879 victorious campaigns were carried through in Cappadocia and Cilicia. By land the Byzantine forces were gradually taking the offensive against the Moslems, wracked by internal dissensions.

875. The Byzantine forces seized **Bari** in southern Italy. Some years later (880) they took Tarentum and then (885) Calabria, establishing two new themes in southern Italy, which became a refuge for Greeks driven from Sicily by the completion of the Saracen conquest (Syracuse taken, 878; Taormina taken, 902).

877. Photius was restored as patriarch and the break with Rome was renewed.

880–881. A number of naval **victories over the**

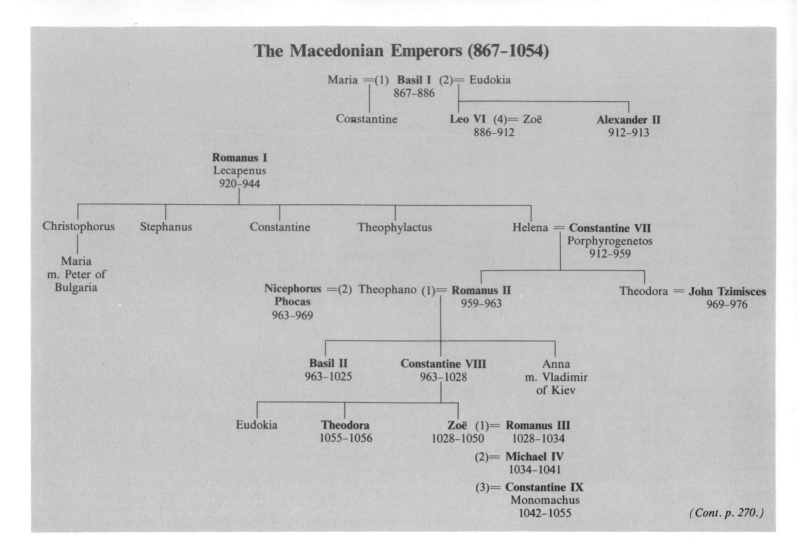

The Macedonian Emperors (867–1054)

Maria =(1) **Basil I** (2)= Eudokia
867–886

Constantine — **Leo VI** (4)= Zoë   **Alexander II**
886–912   912–913

Romanus I
Lecapenus
920–944

Christophorus   Stephanus   Constantine   Theophylactus   Helena = **Constantine VII**
Porphyrogenetos
912–959

Maria
m. Peter of
Bulgaria

Nicephorus =(2) Theophano (1)= **Romanus II**   Theodora = **John Tzimisces**
Phocas   959–963   969–976
963–969

Basil II   **Constantine VIII**   Anna
963–1025   963–1028   m. Vladimir
of Kiev

Eudokia   **Theodora**   Zoë (1)= **Romanus III**
1055–1056   1028–1050   1028–1034

(2)= **Michael IV**
1034–1041

(3)= **Constantine IX**
Monomachus
1042–1055

(Cont. p. 270.)

Moslem pirates of the eastern Mediterranean marked the beginning of a long campaign against this scourge.

886–912. LEO VI (the Wise), a somewhat pedantic philosopher, but nevertheless a determined ruler with a high sense of his office and obligations. He deposed Photius at once and put the Ignatians back in power. The result was a renewal of the **union with Rome** (900), which, however, could hardly be more than external. The reign of Leo was marked also by further legislative work. The *Basilika* (887–893) provided a series of 60 new law books, consisting largely of a compilation of decrees since the time of Justinian.

889– War with the Bulgarians, who now entered the period of greatness under **Tsar Symeon** (893–927). The emperor encouraged the Hungarians to attack by way of diversion and most of Symeon's reign was taken up with continued campaigns against this enemy. Symeon was educated at Constantinople and was deeply impressed by Greek culture, which he introduced in Bulgaria.

904. The Saracen corsair, **Leo of Tripoli,** stormed Thessalonica, plundered it, and carried off some 20,000 of the inhabitants.

907. The **Russians,** under their prince, Oleg, appeared again at Constantinople and secured rights of trade.

912–913. ALEXANDER II, the brother of Leo, emperor for less than a year.

912–959. CONSTANTINE VII (Porphyrogenetos) ascended the throne as a child, with a regency composed of his mother Zoë, the

Patriarch Nikolas, and John Eladas. Constantine was a learned man of artistic tastes. He never really governed, leaving the actual conduct of affairs to strong men who were associated with him.

913–917. The Bulgarian threat. Tsar Symeon, who had established a brilliant capital at Preslav (seat also of the Bulgarian patriarchate), styled himself Emperor of the Romans, and undoubtedly hoped to possess himself of the imperial crown. In 913 he appeared at Constantinople; in 914 he took Adrianople, only to lose it again. But in 917 he defeated a Byzantine army at Anchialus. The war continued, indecisively, for years. In 924 Symeon again appeared at Constantinople.

915. A Byzantine victory over the Arabs at **Garigliano** assured the empire of its possessions in south Italy.

920–944. ROMANUS LECAPENUS, co-emperor with Constantine. He was the emperor's father-in-law, an able but ruthless Armenian, whose whole policy was designed to strengthen his own control and establish that of his family.

920–942. Brilliant campaigns of the Byzantine general, **John Kurkuas,** in the east. He took the modern Erzerum (928) and Melitene (934), and extended the imperial power to the Euphrates and Tigris.

920. Official reunion with Rome.

924. The piratical fleets of **Leo of Tripoli** were completely defeated off **Lemnos.** Nevertheless, the Moslem pirates continued to be the scourge of the Mediterranean.

927. The empire suffered from a **great famine,**

which probably explains the stringent legislation of the government to prevent the purchase of small holdings by the great landed magnates.

941. A great armada of Russians, under **Prince Igor,** was signally defeated by the Greeks.

944. The **Emperor Romanus** was seized and imprisoned (d. 948) by the very sons whose interests he had attempted to serve. The Emperor Constantine became officially the sole ruler, but governed with the aid of the great general, **Bardas Phocas,** and under the influence of the Empress Helena and her favorite, Basil.

955. Visit to Constantinople and baptism of **Princess Olga** of Russia.

959–963. ROMANUS II, the young and dissipated son of Constantine.

961. Reconquest of Crete from the Saracen pirates. A great armada was sent out under Nicephorus Phocas. Candia was stormed, the Moslems expelled from the island or converted to Christianity.

962. Otto I, Roman emperor in the west, claimed suzerainty over the Lombards in southern Italy, initiating a period of friction with Constantinople, which was only temporarily broken by the marriage of Otto II and the Byzantine princess, Theophano (972).

963–1025. BASIL II, an infant at the death of his father. The principle of legitimacy was carefully respected, but before Basil II really assumed power, the empire was governed by two great generals associated with him.

963–969. NICEPHORUS II PHOCAS, who

had carried on a successful campaign in the east. He seized control and married the widowed Empress Theophano. Never popular, especially with the clergy, Nicephorus, by his victories in the field, helped to raise the empire to its greatest glory.

964–968. Victorious campaign in the east. Adana was taken (964) and then Tarsus (965). Cyprus was reconquered and in 968 northern Syria was invaded. **Aleppo** and even **Antioch** fell into the hands of the Greeks.

966–969. The **Bulgarian campaign,** carried through with the aid of Sviatoslav and the Russians. The latter, with their fleets, were so successful on the Danube that the Greeks made peace with the Bulgars.

969. Nicephorus Phocas was overthrown by a conspiracy of officers led by his own nephew

969–976. JOHN I TZIMISCES, an Armenian by birth and one of the greatest of Byzantine generals.

969. Sviatoslav, the Russian, crossed the Balkan Mountains and took Philippopolis. John Tzimisces marched against him, defeated him near Adrianople, and, with the aid of the Byzantine fleet on the Danube, forced him to evacuate Bulgaria (972). John thereupon annexed eastern Bulgaria as far as the Danube to the empire. The patriarchate of Preslav was abolished.

971. A great feudal insurrection, led by Bardas Phocas, was put down only with difficulty.

972–976. Continuation of the campaigns in the east. John took Edessa and Nezib (974), Damascus and Beirut (976), and advanced to the very gates of Jerusalem, where he was halted by the Moslem forces from Egypt.

976. Sudden **death of John Tzimisces,** at the early age of 51.

976. BASIL II (Bulgaroktonos = Slayer of the Bulgarians) now became sole emperor. He was only 20 years old, but serious and energetic, cynical and cruel. Until 989 he was much influenced by Basil the Eunuch, the illegitimate son of Romanus Lecapenus. The reign of Basil began with another great feudal upheaval, led by **Bardas Skleros,** who marched his armies from the east through Anatolia and to Constantinople. Basil appealed to Bardas Phocas, defeated leader of the earlier rising, to save the situation, which he did by defeating Skleros at Pankalia (979).

976–1014. Tsar Samuel of Bulgaria. He built up another great Bulgarian empire, with its capital at Ochrid, extending from the Adriatic to the Black Sea and from the Danube to the Peloponnesus. In 981 he defeated Basil near Sofia.

987. Rising of Bardas Phocas and Bardas Skleros against Basil and the imperial authority. The great feudal barons overran Anatolia. In 988 they threatened Constantinople, but the movement collapsed with the defeat of Phocas at Abydos (989) and his subsequent death. Skleros then submitted.

989. Conversion of Prince Vladimir of Russia, at Cherson. This initiated the general conversion of the Russians to eastern Christianity and the close connection between Kiev and Constantinople.

992. Extensive trade privileges in the empire were granted to **Venice,** by this time quite independent of imperial control, but in close co-operation with Constantinople in the Adriatic.

995. Victorious campaigns of the emperor in the east. Aleppo and Homs were taken and Syria incorporated with the empire.

996. Land legislation of Basil II. Many of the great estates were confiscated and divided among the peasants, and provision made to prevent the further development of feudalism.

996–1014. THE GREAT BULGARIAN CAMPAIGNS. In 996 Basil defeated Samuel on the Spercheios River and reconquered Greece. In 1002 he overran Macedonia. Samuel recovered, however, reconquered Macedonia, and sacked Adrianople (1003). In 1007 Basil subdued Macedonia again and after years of indecisive conflict annihilated the Bulgarian army at **Balathista** (1014). He sent several thousand blinded soldiers back to Samuel, who died of the shock. The Bulgarians finally submitted (1018), but were left their autonomy and an autocephalous church at Ochrid. Many of the Bulgarian noble families settled in Constantinople and merged with the Greek and Armenian aristocracy.

1018. The Byzantine forces won a great victory over the combined Lombards and Normans at **Cannae,** thus assuring continuance of the Greek domination in southern Italy.

1020. The **king of Armenia,** long in alliance with the Greeks against the Arabs, turned over his kingdom to Basil to escape the new threat from the Seljuk Turks. Thereby the empire became firmly established in Transcaucasia and along the Euphrates.

BYZANTINE CULTURE reached its apogee in the late 10th and early 11th centuries. The empire extended from Italy to Mesopotamia

Madonna and Child, Byzantine ivory carving

and its influence radiated much farther. Constantinople, indeed, was the economic and artistic center of the Mediterranean world.

Government. The emperor was an absolute ruler, regarded almost as sacred. Under the Macedonian emperors the idea of legitimacy became firmly established. The imperial court reflected the emperor's power and splendor. There was an extensive and elaborate ceremonial (cf. the *Book of Ceremonies* of Constantine Porphyrogenetos); the administration was highly centralized in Constantinople and was unique for its efficiency; the treasury was full and continued to draw a large income from taxes, customs, and monopolies; the army and navy were both at the peak of their development, with excellent organization and leadership; the provinces were governed by the strategoi; there were by this time 30 themes (18 in

St. Luke, 11th-century Byzantine medallion, cloisonné enamel on gold

St. George, Byzantine ikon, detail

Asia and 12 in Europe), but throughout this period there was a steady growth in the number and power of the provincial magnates (*dunatoi*), feudal barons who acquired more and more of the small holdings and exercised an ever greater influence, even challenging the emperor himself. All the legislation of the Macedonian emperors failed to check this development.

The **Church** was closely connected with the throne, but during this period it too became more and more wealthy and gradually produced a clerical aristocracy. The union with Rome, when it existed, was a purely formal thing. The Greek patriarchate in practice resented the Roman claim to primacy and the popular dislike of the Latins made any real co-operation impossible

Economic life. This was closely controlled by the state, which derived much of its income from the customs and monopolies. Yet it was a

period of great commercial development, Constantinople serving as the entrepôt between east and west. It was also a great center of the industry in luxuries (organization of trades in rigid guilds, etc.).

Learning. The university of Constantinople (opened c. 850) had quickly become a center of philosophical and humanistic study, in which the emperors took a direct interest. In the 11th century there appeared the greatest of the Byzantine scholars, **Psellus,** reviver of the Platonic philosophy and universal genius. In the field of literature there was a conscious return to the great Greek models of the early Byzantine period; historians, **Constantine Porphyrogenetos, Leo the Deacon,** etc. The great popular epic, *Digenis Akritas,* describing the heroic life of the frontier soldiers (*Akritai*), dates from the 10th century.

Art. The period was one of extensive construction, especially in Constantinople; full exploitation of the St. Sophia type in church architecture; mosaics; ikons; gold and silver work. Byzantine influence in this period permeated the entire Mediterranean world, Moslem as well as Christian. *(Cont. p. 268.)*

b. THE FIRST BULGARIAN EMPIRE, TO 1018

The Bulgarians, first mentioned by name in 482 as a people living to the northeast of the Danube, were members of the Finno-Tatar race, probably related to the Huns and at first ruled by princes of Attila's family. They were organized on the clan system, worshiped the sun and moon, practiced human sacrifice, etc.

584-642. Kurt, or **Kubrat,** of the Dulo family, the first authenticated ruler. His dominions lay in the eastern steppes, from the Don to the Caucasus. In 619 he visited Constantinople to secure aid against the Avars, at which time he became converted to Christianity, though this step seems to have had no consequences for his people.

643-701. Isperikh (Asperuch), the son or grandson of Kurt. The old Great Bulgaria was disrupted by the attacks of Avars and Khazars, and various tribes of Bulgars moved westward into Pannonia and even into Italy. Those under Isperikh crossed the Danube (650-670) and established a capital at Pliska. In 680 they defeated a Byzantine army and occupied the territory between the Danube and the Balkan Mountains. At the same time they still held Wallachia, Moldavia, and Bessarabia. The amalgamation with the Slavic inhabitants was probably very gradual, the upper, military classes remaining strictly Bulgar for a long time.

701-718. Tervel, to whom the Emperor Justinian II paid a subsidy or tribute, but only after the imperial forces had been defeated at Anchialus (708) and after Tervel had advanced to the very gates of Constantinople (712).

718-724. Ruler unknown.

724-739. Sevar, during whose reign the peace with the empire was maintained. The Dulo dynasty came to an end with Sevar, whose death was followed by an obscure struggle of noble factions.

739-756. Kormisosh, of the Ukil family. Until the very end of his reign he maintained peace with the empire, until further domestic disorders gave the signal for Byzantine attacks (755 ff.).

756-761. Vinekh, who was killed in the course of an uprising.

761-764. Telets, of the Ugain family. He was defeated at Anchialus by the Byzantines (763) and put to death by the Bulgarians.

764. Sabin, of the family of Kormisosh. He was deposed and fled to Constantinople.

? 764. Pagan, who finally concluded peace with the emperor.

766. Umor, who was deposed by

766. Tokt, who was captured and killed by the Greeks. This entire period is one of deep obscurity, the years 766-773 being a complete blank.

? 773-777. Telerig, whose family is unknown. The Greeks renewed their attacks, which were on the whole successful and resulted in the subjugation of Bulgaria.

777-791. Ruler unknown.

? 791-797. Kardam, whose reign marked the turning of the tide. He took advantage of the confusion in the empire to defeat the Greeks at **Marcellae** (792) and to rebuild the foundations of the state. What happened after his death is unknown.

808-814. KRUM, one of the greatest Bulgarian rulers. He appears to have been a Pannonian Bulgar, who rose to power as a result of his victories over the Avars. During his short reign he organized the state and encouraged the Slav elements at the expense of the Bulgar aristocracy. His objective seems to have been the establishment of the absolute power of the khan. For four years (809-813) he carried on war with the Byzantine Empire. The Greeks sacked Pliska (809; 811), but Krum defeated and killed the emperor in a battle in the mountains (811). In 812 he took the im-

portant fortress of Mesembria and in 813 won another victory at Versinicia. In the same year he appeared at Constantinople. The city was too strong for him, but he retired, devastating Thrace and taking Adrianople.

814-831. Omortag, the son of Krum. After a defeat by the Greeks (815), he concluded a thirty-year peace with them (817), returning Mesembria and Adrianople. Construction of the earthwork barrier (the Great Fence) on the Thracian frontier. Founding of the new capital, **Great Preslav** (821). During the peace in the east, the Bulgars began systematic raids into Croatia and Pannonia (827-829).

831-852. Malamir, the son of Omortag, the period of whose reign is vague, excepting for gradual expansion into upper Macedonia and Serbia (839).

852-889. BORIS I. He continued the cam-

Nicephorus leads army against Krum (top) and, hands bound, is taunted by Krum

paigns in the west, but suffered severe defeats by the Germans (853) and a setback from the Serbs (860). Boris' reign was important chiefly for his

865. Conversion to Christianity. The way had undoubtedly been prepared by numerous prisoners of war, but Boris was induced to take the step under pressure from Constantinople, where the government was eager to frustrate a possible German-Roman advance. Boris had all his subjects baptized, which led to a revolt and the execution of a number of noble leaders. For some time Boris was undecided whether to lean toward Rome or toward Constantinople. To counteract the aggressive Greek influence he accepted the primacy of Rome (866), but then turned to Constantinople (870) when the pope refused to appoint an archbishop for Bulgaria. In 885 the Slavonic liturgy was introduced among the Slavs of Bulgaria by the successors of Cyril and Methodius. In 889 Boris voluntarily retired to a monastery.

889–893. Vladimir, the son of Boris, who was soon exposed to a violent aristocratic, heathen reaction.

893. Boris re-emerged from retirement, put down the revolt, deposed and blinded his son, completed the organization of the church, and made the Slavonic liturgy general in its application. The capital was definitely moved to Preslav. Boris then returned to his monastery, where he died (907).

893–927. SYMEON I, another son of Boris, the first Bulgarian ruler to assume the title *Tsar*. Symeon had been educated at Constantinople, as a monk. He was deeply imbued with Greek

Baptism of Bulgarians by immersion, 865 (14th-century manuscript)

Fresco in the Church of St. Sophia at Ochrid

Church of St. Sophia at Ochrid

culture and did much to encourage translations from the Greek. Splendor of Great Preslav and Symeon's court; development of a second cultural center at Ochrid, under St. Clement and St. Nahum.

894–897. Symeon's reign was filled with **wars against the Byzantine Empire,** which grew originally out of disputes regarding trade rights and ultimately developed into a contest for possession of the imperial throne. The war began in 894, with the defeat of a Greek army. The emperor thereupon induced the Magyars, located on the Pruth River, to attack the Bulgarians in Bessarabia (895). Symeon induced the Greeks by trickery to withdraw and then defeated the Magyars, after which he returned and fell on the Greeks at Bulgarophygon. Peace was made in 897, the emperor paying tribute.

In the meanwhile the **Magyars,** driven westward by the Patzinaks (Pechenegs), advanced into Transylvania and Pannonia, which were lost to the Bulgars.

913. Symeon, taking advantage of the dynastic

troubles in the empire, advanced to Constantinople, but withdrew with many presents and the promise that the young emperor, Constantine Porphyrogenitus, should marry one of his daughters. Symeon evidently hoped to attain the crown for himself, but was frustrated by the seizure of power by Zoë. He thereupon made war (914), raiding into Macedonia, Thessaly, and Albania. But the Patzinaks, instigated by the Greeks, invaded and occupied Wallachia (917), while Symeon defeated the Greeks near **Anchialus** (917). In 918 Symeon defeated the Serbs, who had also been aroused by the empress.

919-924. Symeon four times advanced to the Hellespont and Constantinople, but was unable to take the city because of his lack of a fleet. In 924 he had an interview with the Emperor Romanus Lecapenus and finally made peace.

925. Symeon proclaimed himself **Emperor of the Romans and the Bulgars.** The Greek emperor protested, but the pope recognized the title.

926. Symeon set up Leontius of Preslav as a patriarch.

926. Conquest and devastation of Serbia.

927-969. Peter, the son of Symeon, a pious, well-intentioned but weak ruler, who married the granddaughter of Romanus Lecapenus. Peace with Constantinople was maintained, the Greek emperor recognizing the Bulgar ruler as emperor and acknowledging the Bulgarian patriarchate. Bulgaria was, during this period, occupied by the constant threat from the Magyars (raids, 934, 943, 958, 962) and the Patzinaks (great raid of 944). Internally the period seems to have been one of unrest and religious ferment (founding of monasteries; St. John of Rila; beginning of the **Bogomil heresy,** c. 950, a dualistic creed possibly inspired by the Paulicians settled in the Thracian region by the Byzantine emperors).

967. Invasion of Bulgaria by Sviatoslav and the Russians. Tsar Peter roused the Patzinaks, who attacked Kiev in 968 and forced Sviatoslav to withdraw.

969-972. Boris II. The reign was filled with the second invasion of Sviatoslav, who took Preslav and captured Boris and his family (969). The Greeks, in alarm, sent an army against him and defeated him at **Arcadiopolis** (970). In 972 the Emperor John Tzimisces attacked the Russians by land and sea. He took Preslav and destroyed it, besieged Sviatoslav at Dristra on the Danube, and finally forced him to evacuate Bulgaria. Boris was obliged to abdicate, the patriarchate was abolished, and Bulgaria came to an end as a separate state.

976-1014. SAMUEL, son of a governor of one of the western districts, which had been unaffected by the Russian invasion, set himself up as ruler. He soon expanded his domain to Sofia, and re-established the patriarchate (ultimately fixed at Ochrid, which was the center of the new state).

986-989. Samuel took Larissa after several annual raids into Thessaly and c. 989 took also Dyrrhacium on the Adriatic coast. In the east he extended his power to the Black Sea.

996-1014. The **campaigns of Basil II** (Bulgaroktonos = Slayer of the Bulgarians) against Samuel. Basil proceeded to reduce one stronghold after another. Samuel avoided open battle as much as possible, but throughout suffered from defection of his leaders, who were bribed by attractive offers by the emperor. The crowning defeat of the Bulgarians at Balathista (1014) and the sight of his 15,000 blinded warriors brought on Samuel's death.

1014-1016. Gabriel Radomir (or Romanus), the son of Samuel. He tried to make peace, but was murdered by his cousin

1016-1018. John Vladislav, who continued the war, but was killed in a battle near Dyrrhacium. He left only young sons. The Bulgar leaders thereupon decided to submit. Bulgaria was incorporated into the Byzantine Empire (themes of Bulgaria and Paristrium); the patriarchate was abolished, but the Archbishop of Ochrid retained practical autonomy. The Bulgarian aristocracy settled in Constantinople and merged with the leading Greek families.

(Cont. p. 267.)

3. *The Moslem World*

a. MUHAMMAD AND ISLAM, 622-661

[For a complete list of the caliphs see Appendix III.]

Arabia before the time of Muhammad was inhabited by tribes of Semitic race, those in the desert areas (Bedouins) of nomadic, pastoral habits, those in the coastal valleys along the Red Sea (Hijaz, Yemen) much more settled, engaged in agriculture and trade. The towns of Mecca and Medina were centers of considerable commercial and cultural development, in which Greek and Jewish influence was probably quite marked.

570-632. MUHAMMAD. He was the posthumous son of Abdallah of the Hashimite sept of Mecca. Having lost his mother when about six, he was brought up by his grandfather, Abd al Muttalib, and his uncle, Abu Talib. Muhammad became a merchant in the caravan trade, serving Kadijah, a widow of means whom he married when he was about 25, thus achieving for himself a modest independence. Given to religious meditation and affected by Christian and Jewish ideas and practices, he began his prophetic career about 612, preaching the One God, the Last Judgment, alms, prayers, and surrender to the will of God (Islam). Gaining a few adherents, but rejected and persecuted by his townsmen, he and his followers fled to Medina, on July 2, 622.

622, July 16. The traditional (though erroneous) date of **Muhammad's flight** (*Hijrah, Hegira*). This date has been adopted as the beginning of the Moslem era.

622-632. In Medina, Muhammad organized the **commonwealth of Islam** by welding together the Meccan fugitives and the Medinan tribes in and around the town (the Aus and the Khazraj)—expelling or devoting the Jewish tribes—into a community based on the will of God as revealed to his prophet, and on the common law of the tribesmen. At the same time he carried on war against the Meccans.

624-630. The Moslems defeated the Meccans at **Badr** (624), but were themselves defeated at Ohod (625). The Meccans thereupon besieged Medina (627) but were repulsed. By the **treaty of Hudaybiya** (628), Muhammad and his followers were granted permission to make the pilgrimage to Mecca. When the treaty was broken by the allies of the Meccans, the war was resumed and Muhammad took Mecca (630). Many of the Arab tribes were subdued before Muhammad's death (632).

The **essential articles of the Moslem faith** are: Belief in the One God, **Allah,** in his

Muhammad

Entrance of Omar into Jerusalem, 638

angels, and in his prophet, **Muhammad,** the last of the prophets; belief in his revealed books, of which the *Koran* is the last and the only one necessary; belief in the Day of Resurrection, and in God's predestination, which determines the fate and the actions of men.

The **six fundamental duties** are: the recitation of the profession of faith; attesting the unity of God and the mission of Muhammad; the five daily prayers; the fast in the month of Ramadhan; the pilgrimage to Mecca; and the Holy War.

632–661. The **Orthodox Caliphate,** including the first four caliphs.

632–634. Abu Bakr, the first caliph or vicegerent of the prophet, chosen by acclamation. Defeat of the so-called false prophets, Tulayha and Musaylima; reduction of the rebellious tribes (632).

632–738. EXPANSION BEYOND ARABIA. First incursion into Iraq under **Khalid ibn al-Walid** (633). Hira, the ancient Lakhmid capital, and Obolla taken and put to ransom. The main advance, however, was against Syria. Defeat of Theodore, brother of the Emperor Heraclius, at Ajnadayn (Jannabatayn) between Gaza and Jerusalem (634). Death of Abu Bakr, who appointed as his successor

634–644. Omar, who first assumed the title of *Amir al-Mu'minin* (Prince of the Faithful) and established the primacy of the Arabs over their taxpaying subjects.

Conquest of Syria. Defeat of the Byzan-

tines under Baanes at Marj al-Saffar, near Damascus, by Khalid (635). Damascus and Emessa taken, only to be given up, however, under the pressure of superior forces. Decisive defeat of the Byzantines at **Yarmuk,** south of the Lake of Tiberias (636). Damascus and Emessa retaken. Subjugation of northern Syria, Aleppo and Antioch taken. Capitulation of Jerusalem (638). Caesarea captured (640). The seacoast occupied. Northern boundary of the caliphate the Amanus Mountains. Subjugation of Mesopotamia (639–641).

Conquest of Persia. After a disastrous defeat at the **battle of the Bridge,** the Moslems resumed their attack on Persia. Invasion and occupation of Iraq (635–637). Defeat of the Persians under Mihran at Buwayb by Muthanna (635). The Persian chancellor, Rustam, defeated by Sa'd ibn-abi-Waqqas at **Qadisiya** (637). Al-Madain (Ctesiphon) taken (637). Persians defeated again at Jalula, fifty miles north of Madain (637). Invasion and occupation of central Persia (638–650). Final defeat of the Persians at Nehawand (642).

Conquest of Egypt. Invasion of Egypt by the Arabs under Amr ibn al-'As (639). Pelusium taken (640). Byzantine defeated at Heliopolis (640). Death of the Emperor Heraclius (641). Capture of Babylon (642). Capitulation of Egypt arranged by Cyrus, patriarch of Alexandria (642). Terms: security of person and property guaranteed to the inhabitants on payment of a tribute and free exercise of

their religion. Omar assassinated (644). His successor was chosen by a body of electors.

644–656. Othman, a member of the Omayyad family of Mecca, notorious for his nepotism. The official redaction of the *Koran* made by Zayd ibn Thabit in this reign.

Occupation of Barqa and the Pentapolis (642–643). Revolt of Alexandria, inspired by the appearance of the Byzantine fleet (645). The city retaken by assault (645). Creation of an Arab fleet by Abdallah ibn Sa'd, governor of Egypt. Capture of Cyprus (649) and Aradus (650). Expedition against Constantinople, annihilation of the Byzantine fleet at Dhat al-Sawari on the Lycian coast (655). Disaffection of Arab troops in Iraq and Egypt owing to Othman's nepotism, led to the assassination of Othman in Medina. He was succeeded by

656–661. Ali, the prophet's cousin and son-in-law, whose succession was disputed.

First civil war. Revolt of Talha and Zobayr, two old companions of the prophet, and Aishah, the prophet's favorite wife, in Iraq They seized Basra, but were defeated by Ali ir the **battle of the Camel,** near that town.

Revolt of Muawiya, Omayyad governor of Syria, who demanded revenge for the murder of his kinsman, Othman. Indecisive battle of **Siffin** (657). Hostilities suspended by an agreement to arbitrate the dispute. Arbitration of Adhroh (658). Rejection of the decision by Ali, who was deserted and opposed by a party of his followers, the Kharijites, whom he decimated at Nahrawan. Egypt taken for Muawiya by its first conqueror, Amr (658). Murder of Ali by a Kharijite.

b. THE OMAYYAD CALIPHATE, 661–750

[For a complete list of the caliphs see Appendix III.]

661–680. Muawiya, founder of the Omayyad dynasty.

Hasan, Ali's eldest son, was proclaimed caliph, but abdicated in the face of Muawiya's advance on Iraq. Muawiya, who had been proclaimed caliph in Jerusalem in 660, moved the seat of government to Damascus. Expedition against Constantinople, Chalcedon taken, Constantinople besieged (669). Ifriqiya (North Africa from the eastern limits of Algeria to the frontiers of Egypt) invaded and the conquest consolidated by the founding of Qairawan by 'Oqba ibn Nafi' (670). In the east under Muawiya's brilliant viceregent, Ziyad ibn Abihi, Sind and the lower valley of the Indus were overrun by Muhallib. Eastern Afghanistan invaded. Kabul taken (664). The Oxus was crossed and Bokhara captured (674). Samarkand taken (676). Moslem advance to the Jaxartes.

Blockade of Constantinople by the Moslem fleet (673–678). Failure of the Moslem attack.

Peace concluded for thirty years (678). Death of Muawiya, who had proclaimed as his successor in 676

680–682. Yazid I.

The second civil war. Husayn, the second son of Ali, was invited by the Kufans in Iraq to assume the caliphate. Advancing from Mecca he was basely deserted by the Kufans, defeated, and slain at the famous **battle of Kerbela** (680), whence the Shi'ite celebration of the martyrdom of Husayn each year in the month of Muharram.

Revolt of Abdallah ibn Zubayr, the candidate for the caliphate supported by the Meccans and Medinans. Defeat of the Medinans on the Harra near the town. Siege of Mecca; the Ka'ba burned. Death of Yazid.

The son and successor of Yazid, **Muawiya II,** died some months after his father. **Ibn Zubayr's** caliphate accepted in Arabia, Iraq, Egypt, and by the adherents of the Qais tribe in Syria. The Omayyad party with its adherents of the Kalb tribe chose **Marwan ibn al-Hakam,** a distant cousin of Muawiya I. The Qais were defeated with great slaughter at Marj Rahit (684), north of Damascus, which began the disastrous feud between the so-called northern and southern Arabs, which was largely responsible for the fall of the Arab kingdom of the Omayyads.

684–750. THE MARWANIDS.

684–685. Marwan I. Proclaimed caliph in Syria. Egypt was recovered from **Ibn Zubayr.**

Muhammad with Ali, Husayn, and Hasan

Ruins of Caesarea

Ruins of the winter palace of Omar near Jericho, built in the 8th century

Death of Marwan. He was succeeded by his son,

685-705. Abdalmalik, creator of the Arab administration of the empire.

Inroads of the Mardaites of the Amanus, encouraged by the Byzantines, occupied Abdalmalik's first years. His rival, Ibn Zubayr, was occupied by Shi'ite and Kharijite revolts in Kufa and Basra, Arabia and Persia.

The **Shi'ite sect** were supporters of the claims of the "House of the Prophet," the descendants of the Caliph **Ali,** and of the prophet's daughter, Fatima. Later they developed the dogma of the **Imamate,** that the Imam (the leader of the people) was the representative or incarnation of the deity and the only seat of authority both religious and civil.

The **Kharijites** held that any Moslem in good standing could be elected by the community as caliph. They held that works were an essential part of religion and that those who committed mortal sins were unbelievers. Both sects were bitter opponents of both the Omayyad and the Abbasid dynasties.

Mus'ab, Ibn Zubayr's brother and governor in Iraq, was defeated by Abdalmalik on the Tigris (690). Medina was captured by Abdalmalik's general, Hajjaj, later his governor in Iraq (691). Mecca was besieged and captured (692). Ibn Zubayr was killed and Abdalmalik became undisputed master of the empire. The Kharijites (Azraqites) were crushed in Iraq and Persia by Muhallib (693-698). A rebellion in the east under Ibn al-Ash'ath, who was

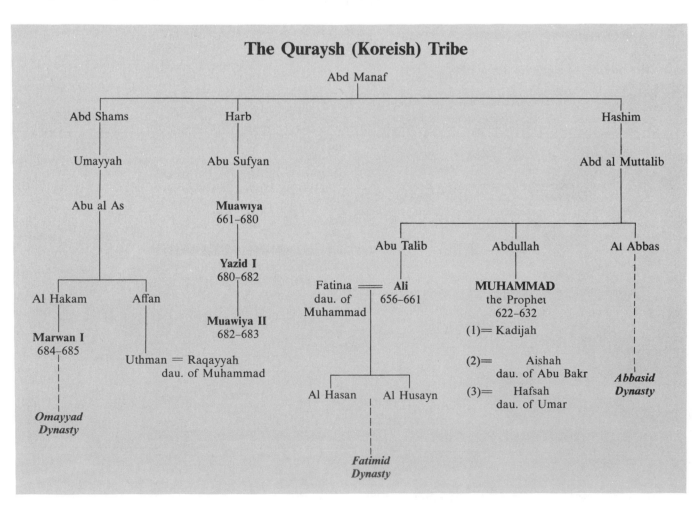

The Quraysh (Koreish) Tribe

Abd Manaf

Abd Shams — Harb — Hashim

Umayyah — Abu Sufyan — Abd al Muttalib

Abu al As — **Muawiya** 661-680

Yazid I 680-682

Abu Talib — Abdullah — Al Abbas

Fatima dau. of Muhammad = **Ali** 656-661

MUHAMMAD the Prophet 622-632

Al Hakam — Affan

Muawiya II 682-683

(1)= Kadijah

Marwan I 684-685

Uthman = Raqayyah dau. of Muhammad

(2)= Aishah dau. of Abu Bakr

Abbasid Dynasty

Al Hasan — Al Husayn

(3)= Hafsah dau. of Umar

Omayyad Dynasty

Fatimid Dynasty

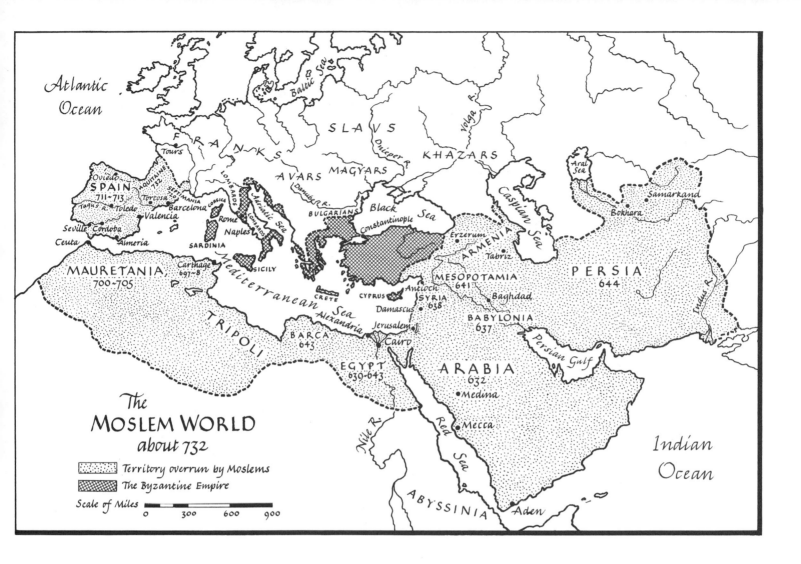

The
MOSLEM WORLD
about 732

Territory overrun by Moslems
The Byzantine Empire

Scale of Miles
0   300   600   900

proclaimed caliph, was put down by Hajjaj (699). Kabul retaken.

In Africa **Oqba ibn Nafi,** now a saint, had raided as far as Tangier, but had met death on his return march (683). Carthage, however, was finally taken (698), and peace concluded with the Berbers, after they had defeated the Arabs under Hassan ibn No'man near Mons Aurasius (703). Thereupon the Berbers became allies of the Arabs. Death of Abdalmalik. He was succeeded by his son,

705-715. Walid I, who built the cathedral mosque at Damascus. Conquest of Transoxania under Qutayba (705-715). Bokhara taken (709), Samarkand (712), Ferghana (714). It is reported that Qutayba invaded China and reached Kashgar (c. 713). Conquest of Sind and part of the Punjab by Mohammed ibn Qasim (708-715).

Invasion of Cilicia (710-711) **and of Galatia** (714). Preparations for a grand attack on Constantinople by land and sea. Subjugation of the western Berbers and pacification of North Africa by Musa ibn Nusayr (708-711).

711-715. CONQUEST OF SPAIN. Invasion of Spain by a mixed force of Arabs and Berbers under Tariq, a freed slave of Musa (711). The Goths under their king, Roderick, were totally defeated in Wadi Bekka, near Rio Barbate (not at Xeres de la Frontera) (July, 711). Fall of Ecija, Córdoba, and the capital, Toledo. Tariq master of half of Spain. The advance of Musa himself (712). Capture of Medina Sidonia, Carmona, Seville (712), Merida (713),

and Saragossa. Resistance to Arab arms continued only in the mountains of Asturias. Death of Walid. He was succeeded by his brother,

715-717. Sulaiman. Conquest of Jurjan (Hyrcania) and Tabaristan by Yazid ibn Muhallib (716). Siege of Constantinople by the caliph's brother, Maslama (717-718), which failed. The crossing of the Pyrenees and invasion of southern France by Hurr, the successor of Musa. Sulaiman succeeded by his cousin,

717-720. Omar ibn Abdul-Aziz, who attempted to reorganize the finances of the empire. Members of the subject races, who had become Moslems, were placed on the same footing as the Arabs in respect to taxation. Narbonne in southern France taken by Samh, the successor of Hurr. Omar was succeeded by the third son of Abdalmalik,

720-724. Yazid II. Samh was defeated and killed by Duke Eudo before Toulouse (721). Revolt of Yazid ibn Muhallib in Iraq. His defeat at Akra on the Euphrates by Maslama. Outbreak of internecine strife between the Yemenites (Kalb) and Modharites (Qais) (the so-called southern and northern Arabs) throughout the empire, especially in Khorasan and Transoxania, where propaganda for the Abbasids (descendants of the prophet's uncle, Abbas) also began. Yazid was succeeded by his brother,

724-743. Hisham. Defeat of the Khazars, conquest of Georgia (727-733).

732. Invasion of southern France by Abd ar-

Rahman, governor of Spain; his defeat at Poitiers (Tours) by Charles Martel.

738. Kharijite revolts in Iraq, insurrection of Sogdians and Arabs in Khorasan supported by the Turkomans of Transoxania, was quelled by Khalid ibn Abdallah al-Kasri, governor of Khorasan.

740. Shi'ite revolt in Iraq under Zayd, grandson of the martyred Husayn; his defeat and death. Hisham was succeeded by his nephew,

741-742. The **revolt of the Kharijites and Berbers** in North Africa was put down by Hanzala, the viceroy in North Africa.

743-744. Walid II, who was killed in a Yemenite revolt led by his cousin, who succeeded him as **Yazid III,** only to die a few months later. He was succeeded by the last Omayyad,

744-750. Marwan II, the grandson of Marwan I. Insurrections in Syria at Homs and in Palestine. Kharijite revolt in Mesopotamia (745), and in Arabia (745-746). Mecca and Medina seized by the rebels. Shi'ite insurrection in Iraq and Persia under Abdallah, grandson of Ali's brother, Ja'far, which was joined by Kharijites and Abbasids (745-747). The black standard of the Abbasids was raised by **Abu Muslim** in Khorasan (747). Marwan's governor of Khorasan, Nasr, was defeated at Nishapur and Jurjan by Abu Muslim's general, Kahtaba, who routed the Omayyad forces again at Nehawand and Kerbela. Marwan himself was defeated at the **battle of the Zab,** and was pursued to Busir, Egypt, and killed (750). Slaughter of the Omayyad princes. Few

Jabir (Gebir)

escaped, but among those was Abd ar-Rahman, grandson of Hisham, who later founded the Omayyad Kingdom of Córdoba in Spain (755).

c. THE ABBASID CALIPHATE, 750–c. 1100

750–1258. THE ABBASID CALIPHATE. Spain never recognized it, nor did Morocco. Abbasid authority was re-established in the province of Africa as far as Algiers in 761, but only for a short period.

750–754. Abu-l-Abbas al-Saffah, the first Abbasid caliph. Omayyad revolts in Syria and Mesopotamia. Byzantine raids into the northern provinces. First paper mill of the Moslem world established (c. 751). Abu al-Saffah was succeeded by his brother,

754–775. AL-MANSUR, the real founder of the dynasty. The revolt of his uncle, Abdallah, governor of Syria, was crushed by Abu Muslim, who was then murdered at Mansur's orders (754). Revolt of Abu Muslim's followers in Khorasan (755). A Byzantine invasion was repulsed with great slaughter. Cappadocia reoccupied; Malitia (Melitene), Mopsuestia, and other cities rebuilt and fortified against Byzantine raids (758). Annexation of Tabaristan (759); Shi'ite revolt in Iraq and Medina under the Hasanids, Muhammad and Ibrahim (762). Foundation of Baghdad (762). Khazar invasion of Georgia repelled (762). Insurrection of Ustad Sis in Khorasan and Sistan (767). Rise of the **Barmecides** to power as vizirs of the realm (752–803). Mansur was succeeded by his son,

775–785. AL-MAHDI, noted for his improvement of the communications of the empire, his fortification of important centers, his founding of towns and schools, and his encouragement of the arts.

Hindu scientific works, including the *Siddhautas, Charaka, Sustrata,* were translated into Arabic. Jabir (fl. 776) known as Gebir to the West, recorded the chemical methods of his time, many of which were concerned with alchemy. He described chemical apparatus, techniques—refining of metals and the distillation of alcohol, and glassmaking. A school of chemists and a corpus of chemical writings arose.

Persecution of the Manichaeans. Revolt of the veiled prophet, **Mokanna,** in Khorasan (775–778). Rise of a communistic, nihilistic sect, the Zindiqs, in Khorasan, western Persia, and Iraq. Invasion of the Byzantines, who were routed. Moslem advance against Constantinople; the Empress Irene forced to sue for peace (783–785). Mahdi was succeded by his son,

785–786. Al-Hadi, who reigned only a year and was succeeded by

786–809. HARUN AL-RASHID (of *Arabian Nights'* fame). Kabul and Sanhar were annexed to the empire (787). Khazar invasion of Armenia (799). Fall of the Barmecides (803). Kharijite revolts. A collection of original Greek manuscripts ordered.

791–809. War with the Byzantines. Defeat of Nicephorus at Heraclea or Dorylaeum (798). The peace, which was concluded, was broken by Nicephorus, and the Moslems invaded Asia Minor led by the caliph in person. Capture of Tyana (806). Advance to Ancyra. Meanwhile Cyprus (805) and Rhodes (807) were ravaged by the Moslem fleet. Iconium and Ephesus in Lydia captured, Sideropolis, Andrasus, and Nicaea reduced. Heraclea Pontica on the Black Sea taken by storm. Nicephorus again invaded Moslem territory in 808, but troubles in Khorasan compelled Harun to march east, where he died. In his reign the **Hanafite school of law** began to assume a systematic form. He was succeeded by his son,

809–813. AL-AMIN, against whom his brother Mamun rebelled and was accepted as caliph in Persia. Siege of Baghdad by Mamun's general, Tahir (813). Amin was murdered after surrendering on terms.

813–833. AL-MAMUN (MAMUN THE GREAT). His reign probably the most glorious epoch in the history of the caliphate. A **House of Knowledge** was set up in Baghdad, where translations of philosophical, literary, scientific works from Greek, Syriac, Persian, and Sanskrit were made. The translations were scholarly, especially those, with commentaries, that were made on the works of Aristotle. **Hunayn Ibn-Ishaq** (c. 809–877) translated the works of Galen and some of those of Ptolemy, Hippocrates. Astronomical observatory was set up by **Al-Farghani** (d. c. 850) whose work was continued by **Al-Battani** (c. 858–929) and **Thabit Ibn-Quarra** (c. 826–901), who also translated Greek mathematical and physical texts Apollonius, Ptolemy, Euclid). **Al-Khwarizmi** (d. 835) introduced Hindu numerals and calculation methods to the Moslem world. **Al-Rhazi** (Rhazes in the West d. c. 924), was a physician and an encyclopaedist; he added his own observations in gynaecology, obstetrics, ophthalmic surgery. **Ibn-Sina** (Avicenna) wrote a comprehensive canon of medicine. Many of the above men became important to the West, as indicated by their Latinized names, since they preserved the knowledge of the Greeks, transmitted to the West by the Arab world. A liberal religious attitude adopted. **Mu'azilitism** became the established faith. The Mu'tazilites maintained, like the Qadarites of the later Omayyad period, man's free will, also that justice and reason must control God's action toward men, both of which doctrines were repudiated by the later orthodox school of the Ash'arites.

Transference of the capital by Mamun from Merv to Baghdad, owing to Omayyad and Shi'ite revolts in Arabia, Iraq, and Mesopotamia. To meet this crisis he had proclaimed as his heir-apparent, Ali al-Ridha, a descendant of the caliph Ali (817).

Conquest of Crete (from Egypt) by Arabs who had been expelled from Spain by the Omayyads (825); of Sicily by the Aghlabites of North Africa (827). Palermo taken (831). Only Syracuse and Taormina left in Byzantine hands.

Terrorization of the northern provinces by the Magian, **Babek,** leader of the communistic Khurramites, from his stronghold in Azerbaijan (816–833). Byzantine invasions in his support were repulsed by Mamun in person (829–833). In his reign the Tahirids of Khorasan became practically independent (820–872). Mamun was succeeded by his brother,

833–842. Al-Mu'tasim. Transference of the capital to Samarra (836). Formation of a standing military corps composed of Turkish slaves and mercenaries, of whom the later caliphs were the mere puppets.

Revolt of the Jats or **Gypsies** on the lower Tigris (834). Babek was defeated by Afshin and put to death (837–838). **War with Byzantium** (837–842). Defeat of the Byzantines at Anzen on the Halys, Ancyra destroyed; Amorium, the place of origin of the Byzantine dynasty, captured (838). Preparations for the siege of Constantinople. Arab fleet destroyed by a tempest. Death of Al-Mu'tasim (842) and his succession by his son,

842–847. Al-Wathiq, who continued his father's policy of aggrandizing the Turks at the expense of the Arabs and Persians. Interchange of prisoners between the Byzantines and Moslems. Al-Wathiq's reign marks the beginning of the decline of the caliphate. He was succeeded by his brother,

847–861. Al-Mutawakkil, who sought to re-establish the traditional Moslem faith. Mu'tazilite doctrines were abjured, their professors persecuted. Shi'ites, Jews, and Christians also persecuted. The mausoleum of Husayn, the martyr of Kerbela, was razed to the ground. Damietta in Egypt was taken and Cilicia ravaged by the Byzantines. Al-Mutawakkil was murdered by his Turkish guard and was succeeded by his son,

861–862. Al-Muntasir, who reigned only six months, when he was deposed by the Turkoman chiefs of his guard, who raised to the throne another grandson of Al-Mu'tasim, **Al-Musta'in** (862–866), who escaped from the Turks to Baghdad, but was forced by them to abdicate and was later murdered by an emissary of his successor, **Al-Mu'tazz** (866–869), in whose reign Egypt became virtually independent under **Ahmad ibn Tulun,** founder of the Tulunid dynasty. Al-Mu'tazz was murdered by his mutinous troops and succeeded by **Al-Muqtadi** (869–870), a son of Al-Wathiq, who was compelled to abdicate by the Turks, who chose as his successor the eldest surviving son of Al-Mutawakkil,

870–892. Al-Mu'tamid, who transferred the court to Baghdad; and for this and the next two reigns the power of the Turkish guard was successfully checked.

The **Zenj rebellion** in Chaldaea (869–883), which devastated this region for fifteen years, was put down finally by the caliph's brother, Al-Muwaffiq. A Byzantine invasion of Syria was repelled by the Tulunid governor of Tarsus.

In this reign the caliphate lost its eastern provinces. The **Saffarid dynasty** was founded by Ya'qub ibn Layth, who established himself in Sistan, drove out the Tahirids of Khorasan, and became master of the whole of modern Persia. The dynasty lasted from 870 to 903, when it was extinguished by the Samanids of Transoxania, who had succeeded the Tahirids there (872), and who, after the overthrow of the Saffarids, ruled from the borders of India to Baghdad and from the Great Desert to the Persian Gulf. Their power was finally broken by the Ilak Khans of Turkestan (999), who then ruled over Transoxania, Kashgar, and eastern Tatary from Bokhara (932–1165). Under the Samanids, Bokhara was the intellectual center of Islam.

Al-Mu'tamid was succeeded as caliph by his nephew,

892–902. Al-Mu'tadid, who restored Egypt to the caliphate and reformed the law of inheritance. His successor, Al-Muqtafi (902–908), brought Egypt under his direct control and repulsed the Byzantines, storming Adalia.

891–906. The Carmathian revolt. These communistic rebels overran and devastated Arabia, Syria, and Iraq, took Mecca, and carried away the sacred **Black Stone.** Al-Muqtafi was succeeded by

908–932. Al-Muqtadir, his brother, during whose reign occurred the **conquest of North Africa** by the Fatimid, Obaydullah al-Mahdi, who also drove out the last Aghlabite, Ziyadatullah, from Egypt. Establishment of the Zi-

yarids in Tabaristan, Jurjan, Isfahan, and Hamadan as independent sovereigns (928–1024). **Rise of the Buwayhids** (932–1055) under the patronage of the Ziyarids. Conquest and division of Persia and Iraq by the three Buwayhid brothers, Imad al-Dawla, Rukn al-Dawla, and Mu'izz al-Dawla. Mu'izz granted the title of Amir al-Umara (Prince of the Princes) by the caliph Al-Mustaqfi (945). The caliphs became puppets of the Amir al-Umara. The Buwayhid dominions fell piecemeal to the Ghaznavids, the Kakwayhids of Kurdistan (1007–1057), and the Seljuks, owing to divisions among the Buwayhid rulers.

During the first half of the 10th century the **Brotherhood of Purity** was organized. A secret organization, it sponsored educational projects and artisans' guilds, and was influential in publicizing the work of the alchemists.

962–1186. THE GHAZNAVIDS. Founder of the dynasty was **Subaktagin,** a Turkish slave of Alptagin, himself slave and commander-in-chief of the Samanids in Khorasan and independent prince of the petty fief of Ghazni in the Sulayman mountains. Subaktagin defeated the Rajputs and received Khorasan from the Samanids (994). His successor, **MAHMUD** (the Idol-Breaker), one of the greatest figures in the history of Central Asia, became master of Khorasan (1000) and invaded India several times. His court was the resort of famous scholars and poets, such as Beiruni and Firdausi. The Ghaznavids were overthrown by the Seljuks.

929–1096. In Syria and Mesopotamia four Arab dynasties and one Kurdish held sway.

929–1003. The Hamdanids of Mosul and Aleppo, the most famous of whom, **Sayf al-Dawla,** took Aleppo from the Ikhshidids of

Egypt (944) and warred successfully against the Byzantines. His court was one of the brilliant centers of Islam in the 10th century. The great Arab poet, **Mutannabi,** was its chief ornament. The Hamdanids were descendants of the Arab tribe of Taghlib. Their dominions were absorbed by the Fatimids and the Buwayhids.

1023–1079. The **Mirdasids of Aleppo,** of the Arab tribe of the Banu Kilab, engaged in continual warfare with the Fatimids and the Buwayhids, and were finally driven out by the

996–1096. 'Uqaylids of Mosul, a division of the Banu Ka'b tribe, who succeeded the Hamdanids in Mosul, and whose dominions under **Muslim ibn Quraysh** extended from the neighborhood of Baghdad to Aleppo. Their domain was ultimately merged in the Seljuk Empire.

990–1096. The **Marwanids of Diyar-Bakr,** established by the Kurd, Abu-l Ali ibn Marwan, ruled over Amid, Mayyarfariqun, and Aleppo. They too fell before the Seljuks.

995. Under the Fatimid caliphate a House of Science was established in Cairo. Among the scholars there were Al-Hazen (c. 965–1038), who worked on optics; Al-Mushudi (d. 957), who wrote an encyclopaedia of natural history, containing the first description of a windmill; Ibn al-Nafis (1210–1288), who described the lesser circulation of the blood. The first block-printing in the West occurred in Egypt between 900 and 1350.

1012–1050. Mazyadids of Hilla, a tribe of the Banu Asad. The fourth ruler of this dynasty, the Sadaqa, was one of the great heroes of Arab history. The state was ultimately absorbed by the Zangids.

(Cont. p. 272.)

B. The Age of the Crusades

I. *Western Europe*

a. THE BRITISH ISLES

(From p. 192)

(1) *England, 1066–1307*

[*For a complete list of the kings of England see Appendix VI.*]

1066–1087. WILLIAM I (the Conqueror), of medium height, corpulent, but majestic in person, choleric, mendacious, greedy, a great soldier, governor, centralizer, legislator, innovator.

1066–1072. Rapid collapse, speedy submission or reduction of the south and east. The Confessor's bequest, acceptance by the witan, and coronation "legalized" William's title. Reduction of the southwest (1068). Reduction of the rest of England (1067–1070): a series of local risings leniently dealt with; construction by forced native labor of garrison castles (Norman mounds). Great **rising of the north** (Edwin and Morca's second) with Danish aid (1069) put down by William in person. The "harrying of the north" (1069–1070), a devas-

tation (often depopulation) of a strip from York to Durham (the consequences survived to modern times) ended Scandinavian opposition in England. **Reduction of Hereward's last stand** (the "last of the English") in the Isle of Ely (1070–1071); raid into Scotland (1072).

Norman fusion, conciliation, innovation: (1) **Feudalization** on centralized Norman lines (on the ruins of the nascent Saxon feudalism) followed military reduction and confiscation of the rebel lands (1066–1070). Theoretically every bit of land in England belonged to the crown; in practice only the great estates changed hands and were assigned to William's followers on Norman tenures. The king retained about one-sixth of the land; less than a half of the land went to Normans on feudal tenures. Except on the border few compact holdings survived; the earldoms, reduced in size, became chiefly honorific. Some 170 great tenants-in-chief, and numerous lesser tenants emerged. A direct oath (the *Oath of Salisbury*) of primary vassalage to the crown was exacted from all vassals, making them directly responsible to the crown (1086). Construction of castles (except on the borders) subject to royal license; coinage a royal monopoly; private war prohibited. (2) The **Anglo-Saxon shires** (34) and hundreds continued for local administration and for local justice (bishops no longer sat in the shire courts and the earls were reduced) under the sheriffs (usually of baronial rank), retained from Anglo-Saxon days, but subject to removal by the king. The sheriffs were an essential link between the (native)

Great Seal of Henry I

William II

The coronation of William the Conqueror (15th-century manuscript illumination)

local machinery and the central (Norman) government. Communities were held responsible for local good order; sporadic visitations of royal commissioners. Anglo-Saxon laws little altered. (3) Early grant of a charter to London guaranteeing local customs. (4) **Innovations of the centralizing monarch:** a royal council, the **great council** (*curia regis*), meeting infrequently (three stated meetings annually) replaced the Anglo-Saxon witan and was of almost the same personnel: tenants-in-chief, the chancellor (introduced from Normandy by Edward the Confessor), a new official, the justiciar (in charge of justice and finance, and William's viceroy during his absences), the heads of the royal household staff. This same body, meeting frequently, and including only such tenants-in-chief as happened to be on hand, constituted the **small council,** a body which tended to absorb more and more of the actual administration.

The **church** retained its lands (perhaps a

fourth of the land in England). Pope Alexander II had blessed William's conquest, and William introduced the (much-needed) Cluniac reforms. Archbishop Stigand and most of the bishops and great abbots were deprived or died, and were replaced by zealous Norman reformers; **Lanfranc** (an Italian lawyer, a former prior of Bec), as archbishop of Canterbury, carried through a wide reform: celibacy enforced, chapters reorganized, new discipline in the schools, numerous new monastic foundations. By royal decree episcopal jurisdiction was separated from lay jurisdiction and the bishops given their own courts, a decisive step in the evolution of the common law as an independent force. William refused an oath of fealty to Pope Gregory VII for his English conquests, and (despite the papal decree of 1075) retained control of the appointment of bishops and important abbots, from whom he drew his chief administrators (thereby making the church, in effect, pay for the administration of the state). No papal bull or brief, no papal legate might be received without royal approval and no tenant-in-chief or royal officer could be excommunicated without royal permission. The king retained a right of veto on all decrees of local synods. The great prelates were required to attend the great council, even to do military service.

1086. The great **Domesday survey:** royal commissions on circuit collected on oath (sworn inquest) from citizens of the counties and vills full information as to size, resources, and present and past ownership of every hide of land. The results, arranged by counties in *Domesday Book,* gave a unique record as a basis for taxation and administration.

Royal finance: (1) non-feudal revenues: Danegeld, shire farms, judicial fines; (2) the usual feudal revenues.

Military resources of the crown: (1) (non-feudal) the old Anglo-Saxon *fyrd* (including *ship fyrd*) was retained (i.e. a national non-feudal militia, loyal to the crown, was used, e.g. against the Norman rebellion of 1075); (2) (feudal) about five thousand knights' fees owing service on the usual feudal terms. The prosperity of England under Norman rule was great and an era of extensive building (largely churches, cathedrals, and monasteries) began under the Conqueror and continued even through the anarchy of Stephen and Matilda.

1087–1100. WILLIAM II (Rufus), a passionate, greedy ruffian, second son of the Conqueror, designated by his father on his death-bed (Robert, the eldest, received Normandy; Henry, cash). A Norman revolt (1088) was put down, largely with English aid, and William firmly settled on the throne. Justice was venal and expensive, the administration cruel and unpopular, taxation heavy, the Church exploited. On Lanfranc's death (1089), William kept the revenues of the see of Canterbury without appointing a successor until he thought himself dying, when he named (1093)

Anselm (an Italian, abbot of Bec, a most learned man, and a devoted churchman), who clashed with William over the recognition of rival popes; Anselm maintained church law to be above civil law and went into voluntary exile (1097). William, deeply hated, was assassinated (?) in the New Forest.

1100–1135. HENRY I (Beauclerc, Lion of Justice), an educated, stubborn, prudent ruler, a good judge of men, won the crown by a dash to the royal treasury at Winchester and a quick appeal to the nation by his so-called *Coronation Charter,* a promise of reform by a return to the good ways of the Conqueror (a promise often broken). Henry married Edith (of the line of Alfred), whose name became Matilda out of deference to the Norman's difficulties with Saxon names. Anarchy in Normandy under Robert's slack rule, an invitation from the revolting Norman barons, and the victory of **Tinchebray** (1106), gave Henry Normandy (Robert remained a prisoner until his death), and made a later struggle between the new English kingdom and the rising Capetian power in France inevitable. **Anselm,** faithful to the reforming program of the revived papacy, on his recall from exile refused homage for the archiepiscopal estates (i.e. he refused to recognize lay investiture) and refused to consecrate the bishops who had rendered such homage. Henry temporized until firmly on the throne, then seized the fiefs and exiled Anselm. Adela, Henry's sister, suggested the **Compromise of 1107,** which terminated the struggle by establishing clerical homage for fiefs held of the king, while the king allowed clerical investiture with the spiritual symbols. The crown continued to designate candidates for the great prelacies.

This reign was marked by a notable expansion, specialization, and differentiation of function in the royal administration (e.g. the exchequer, influenced by accounting methods from Lorraine or Laon). Extension of the

jurisdiction of royal courts: growing use of royal writs, detailing of members of the small council as judges on circuit (hitherto a sporadic, now a regular practice), who not merely did justice but took over increasingly the business formerly done by the sheriffs (e.g. assessment and negotiation of aids and other levies), and brought the curia regis into closer contact with shire and hundred courts.

Prosperity was general and trade in London attracted Norman immigrants. The **Cistercians** arrived (1128) and began an extensive program of swamp reclamation, mill and road building, agricultural improvement, and stock-breeding. Henry began the sale of charters to towns on royal domain.

Influence of the Conquest on English culture: (1) architecture: wide introduction of the Norman (Romanesque) style (e.g. St. John's Chapel in the Tower of London, end of the 11th century; Durham Cathedral, c. 1096–1133); (2) **literary:** Anglo-Saxon, the speech of the conquered, almost ceased to have a literary history, rapidly lost its formality of inflections and terminations, and became flexible and simple if inelegant. Norman French, the tongue of the court, the aristocracy, the schools, the lawyers and judges, drew its inspiration from the Continent until the loss of Normandy (1204). The Normans then began to learn English, and the Anglo-Saxon was enriched with a second vocabulary of Norman words, ideas, and refinements.

Anglo-Norman culture: (1) **historical writing: Geoffrey of Monmouth,** *History of the Kings of Britain* (written in Latin, before 1147), created the tale of Arthur for Europe; **Walter Map** (c. 1140–c. 1200), author of Goliardic verse, welded the Grail story into the Arthurian cycle, giving it a moral and religious slant; **Wace** (c. 1124–c. 1174) *Roman de Brut* and *Roman de Rou;* **Marie de France;** all three were at the court of Henry II. (2) **Science: Walcher of Malvern** observed the eclipse of 1092 and attempted to calculate the difference in time between England and Italy; Walcher began to reckon in degrees, minutes, and seconds (1120); **Adelard of Bath,** a student of Arabic science, in the service of Henry II, observed and experimented (e.g. the comparative speed of sound and light), translated Al-Khwarizmi's astronomical tables into Latin (1126) and introduced Al-Khwarizmi's trigonometric tables to the West; **Robert of Chester** translated Al-Khwarizmi's algebra into Latin (1145); **Alexander Neckham** (1157–1217), encyclopedist, wrote on botany and on the magnet. (3) **Philosophy: John of Salisbury** (d. 1180), pupil of Abelard, the best classical, humanistic scholar of his day, attached to the court of Henry II, and later bishop of Chartres, wrote the *Policraticus,* etc. **Beginnings of Oxford University** (c. 1167) on the model of Paris, a center of national culture.

1135–1154. STEPHEN. Henry's son drowned on the White Ship (1120), and Henry had had his daughter **Matilda** (widow of the Emperor Henry V) accepted as his heir and married to Geoffrey of Anjou, as protector. Stephen of Blois (son of Henry's sister Adela) asserted and maintained his claim to the throne at the price of a dynastic war (till 1153) with Matilda, the climax of feudal anarchy, and the ruin of English prosperity. Archbishop Theobald fi-

Arrival of Queen Matilda at Winchester

nally negotiated a compromise (1153) whereby Matilda's son Henry should succeed to the crown on Stephen's death. The reign was remarkable for a tremendous amount of ecclesiastical building.

1154–1399. THE HOUSE OF PLANTA-GENET (Angevin).

1154–1189. HENRY II. Master of a hybrid "empire" (England, Normandy, Anjou, Maine, Touraine, by inheritance; Poitou, Aquitaine, Gascony, by marriage with Eleanor of Aquitaine [1152]; Brittany [acquired, 1169], and Wales, Ireland, and Scotland [on a loose bond]

without unity save in the person of the ruler). **Dynastic marriages:** daughter Eleanor to the king of Castile, Joan to the king of Sicily, Matilda to Henry the Lion. King Henry was a man of education, exhaustless energy, experience as an administrator, a realist, violent of temper.

Restoration of England to the good order of Henry I: dismissal of mercenaries, razing of unlicensed castles (1000?), reconquest of Northumberland and Cumberland from the Scots, resumption of crown lands and offices alienated under Stephen. Reconstitution of

Henry II

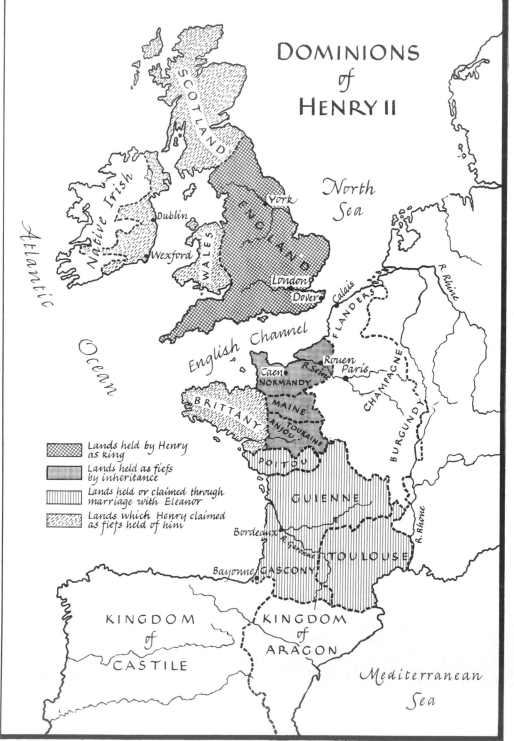

the exchequer and great council. After 1155 Henry felt free to leave England, and spent less than half his reign in the realm.

1155–1172. Struggle to reduce clerical encroachment on the royal courts: Under Stephen anarchy and the theories of Roman law had favored the expansion of clerical courts, extending benefit of clergy to include even homicides. **Thomas Becket** (a close friend of Henry's at the time of his elevation to the chancellorship, 1155) resigned as chancellor when he became archbishop of Canterbury (1162), and clashed at once with Henry over the criminous clerks. The *Constitutions of Clarendon* (1164), largely a restatement of old customs (including the Conqueror's), provided (*inter alia*) for the indictment of clerics in royal courts, their trial in ecclesiastical courts, and their degradation, followed by their sentence and punishment in royal courts. They also extended royal (at the expense of clerical) jurisdiction, and asserted royal rights of control in episcopal elections. Becket yielded, was dispensed from his oath by the pope, violated the *Constitutions,* and fled to France. Reconciled (1170) with Henry, Becket returned, excommunicated certain bishops friendly to Henry, and was murdered in the cathedral of Canterbury by four knights of Henry's court, spurred by Henry's outbreak of fury against Becket, but not by Henry's orders. Henry escaped excommunication by promising to abide by the papal judgment, and was reconciled with the papacy (1172) after an oath denying all share in the crime. After this incident Henry had no choice but to tolerate benefit of clergy, which continued to be an increasing scandal in England until the reign of Henry VII. Henry retained the right of presentation and virtual control over episcopal elections. The *Assize of Clarendon* (1166) contains the first civil legislation on heresy since Roman days.

1170. Extensive replacement of the (baronial) sheriffs with men of lower rank, trained in the royal service. Henceforth the barons ceased to hold the shrievalty.

1173–1174. Reduction of the last purely feudal revolt; Henry's only use of mercenary troops in England.

1181. The Assize of Arms. By this reorganization of the old *fyrd* every freeman was made

(Map)
DOMINIONS of HENRY II

SCOTLAND
Native Irish
Dublin
Wexford
York
ENGLAND
WALES
London
Dover
North Sea
Calais
FLANDERS
R. Rhine
Atlantic Ocean
English Channel
Rouen
Paris
Caen
NORMANDY
R. Seine
CHAMPAGNE
BRITTANY
MAINE
ANJOU
TOURAINE
BURGUNDY
POITOU
GUIENNE
R. Rhône
Bordeaux
R. Garonne
Bayonne
GASCONY
TOULOUSE
KINGDOM of CASTILE
KINGDOM of ARAGON
Mediterranean Sea

Lands held by Henry as king
Lands held as fiefs by inheritance
Lands held or claimed through marriage with Eleanor
Lands which Henry claimed as fiefs held of him

responsible, according to his income, for his proper share in the defense of the realm. The king thus ensured a national militia for the defense against the baronage.

Henry was not a great legislator, but he initiated a remarkable series of innovations in government which fixed the political framework of national unity.

Judicial Reforms: (1) Increasing concentration of judicial business in the small council. (2) Designation (1178) of five professional judges from the small council as a **permanent central court;** extension of the transfer of judicial business to royal courts by the increase and specialization of royal writs (the fees a valuable source of revenue); formalization and regularization (c. 1166) of the itinerant justices (*justices in eyre*), the great source of **Common Law** (a law universal in the realm). One of the judges, **Glanvil,** wrote the *Treatise on the Laws and Customs of the Kingdom of England,* the first serious book on the common law, revealing the formal influence of Roman law, but English in substance. The itinerant judges were charged with cases dealing with crimes like murder, robbery (soon forgery and arson), and with financial business as well as judicial. (3) **Expansion of the sworn inquest** (probably of Roman origin, introduced into England by the Conqueror): statements by neighbors (freeholders) under oath in the shire courts: (a) *jury* (12 members) *of presentment in criminal cases* (Assize of Clarendon, 1166), a process which expanded (after 1219), replacing the ordeal; and (b) the use of juries (recognitions) instead of ordeal to determine landownership.

Reorganization of the exchequer: Nigel, bishop of Ely (nephew of the original organizer, Roger of Salisbury), restored the exchequer to the general form of Henry I. **Innovations in the raising of revenue:** (1) *tallage,* levied by local negotiations (i.e. by the itinerant justices) with boroughs and tenants: (2) *hidage* (*carucage*) replaced the Danegeld; (3) *scutage,* levied by Henry I on the clergy, now extended to knights' fees in lieu of military service (due to Henry's need of non-feudal levies across the Channel); (4) *personal property taxes* (the first, 1166), Saladin tithe (1188), assessed by neighborhood juries. *The Dialogue of the Exchequer* written by one of the officials of the exchequer.

Extension of trade: German merchants were well established in London by 1157; there was a large Italian business in wool; and there was extensive development of domestic trade.

Foreign affairs: (1) **Norman penetration of Wales** since the Conquest bred a sporadic national resistance; Henry by three expeditions reduced Wales to nominal homage to the English crown; (2) **Ireland,** despite a brilliant native culture, was in political chaos under rival tribal kinglets and economically exhausted. Pope Adrian IV, hoping that Henry would reform the church in Ireland, "gave" Ireland (1154) to Henry. Richard of Clare's (Strongbow) expedition (1169–1170) established a harsh rule; Henry landed (1171), temporarily reduced the rigors of the baronial administration, and reformed the Irish Church (Synod of Cashel, 1172). **John Lackland** (Henry's son) was appointed lord of Ireland (1177), arrived (1185), but was soon recalled for incompetence. Intrigues and revolts (beginning 1173) of

Assassination of Thomas Becket in 1170 (12th-century miniature)

Henry's sons, supported by their mother Eleanor, King Louis VII, and later Philip II of France, as well as by disgruntled local barons.

The ruling class continued to speak French during this reign, but the establishment of primogeniture as applied to land inheritance insured that younger sons would mingle with the non-aristocratic sections of society and accelerate the fusion of Norman and native elements. Manor houses began to appear in increasing numbers as domestic peace continued. Numerous Cistercian houses spread new agricultural methods and especially improved wool-raising.

1189–1199. Richard I (Coeur de Lion). Nei-

ther legislator, administrator, nor statesman, but the greatest of knights errant, an absentee ruler who spent less than a year of his reign in England, visiting his realm only twice, to raise money for continental ventures. Taxation was heavy. The government remained in the hands of ministers largely trained by Henry II, but there appeared a tendency toward a common antipathy of barons and people toward the crown. Richard (having taken the Cross, 1188) went on the Third Crusade with Frederick Barbarossa and Philip II, his most dangerous foe. On his return trip Richard was captured by Duke Leopold of Austria and turned over to the Emperor Henry VI,

Kex anglie d'morre oradrois accusar quod abnegas
se ensina mann excusaturu pmitre.

tandē uenia petēs ut absoluat

The arrest of Richard the Lionhearted by the Duke of Austria

who held him for a staggering ransom. John and Philip bid for the prisoner, but Richard finally bought his freedom (1194) with a ransom raised partly by taxation in England. The crusade gave Englishmen their first taste of eastern adventure, but drew few except the adventurous portion of the baronage. The domestic reflection was a series of anti-Semitic outbreaks. John Lackland (despite his known character) was given charge of several coun-

ties; his plot against Richard was put down by **Hubert Walter** with the support of London. Hubert Walter, archbishop of Canterbury and Justiciar (1194–1198), ruled England well, maintained the king's peace, and began a clear reliance on the support of the middle class in town and shire. Charters were granted towns (London received the right to elect its mayor)—and the knights of the shire were called on to assume a share of county business as a balance to the sheriffs. Knights (elected by the local gentry) served as coroners and chose the local juries, a departure looking to the day when local election and amateur justices of the peace would be the basis of government. The first known merchant guild, 1193.

1194–1199. Richard's continental struggle against Philip II, in which Richard more than held his own. Château Gaillard, a new departure in castle architecture based on eastern lessons, built by Richard on the Seine, as an outpost against Philip.

1199–1216. JOHN (Lackland, Softsword), cruel, mean, licentious, faithless, weak of will, without counterbalancing virtues. Crowned with the support of the Norman barons against his nephew Arthur's claims (by primogeniture), he became Arthur's guardian.

1202–1204. John's first contest with Philip (to protect his French possessions): struggle over Brittany, Maine, Anjou (temporary acceptance of John's title by Philip, 1200). John's marriage to Isabella of Angoulême (already betrothed to his vassal Hugh of Lusignan) led Hugh to appeal to Philip II as their common overlord. John ignored Philip's summons to judgment (1202); his French fiefs were declared forfeit, and Philip began a war with rapid successes. The death of Arthur (1203), possibly by John's own hand, ruined John's cause, and Philip, already master of Anjou, Brittany, and Maine, took Normandy (1204) and soon Touraine. John's vassals in southern France (preferring an absent Angevin to an encroaching Capetian) resisted Philip's advance south of the Loire. John's loss of the lands north of the Loire reduced the power and prestige of the English crown, cut the Norman baronage in England from their French connections, and turned their interests back to the island, with decisive constitutional and social consequences.

1205–1213. John's struggle with Pope Innocent III: after a double election to the see of Canterbury, Innocent rejected both elections (including John's nominee) and named (1207) **Stephen Langton,** a noted scholar and theologian. John refused to accept Langton, confiscated the estates of the see, expelled the monks of Canterbury; Innocent laid an interdict on England (1208). John confiscated the property of the English clergy who obeyed Innocent's ban without arousing serious public opposition. Innocent excommunicated John (1209), but John, holding as hostages the children of some of the barons, weathered the storm. Innocent deposed John (1213) and authorized Philip II to execute the sentence. John, aware of treason and mounting hostility, promised indemnity to the clergy, did homage to the pope for England and Ireland, agreed to an annual tribute, and was freed of the ban.

1213–1214. Final contest with Philip II (to regain the lands north of the Lorie): John's great coalition (including his nephew, Emperor Otto IV, and the Count of Flanders) against Philip; most of the English baronage held aloof. Crushing defeat of the coalition at **Bouvines** (1214) ended all hope of regaining the lands north of the Loire (formal renunciation of English claims, 1259).

1215. MAGNA CARTA. The first politico-constitutional struggle in English history: in origin this struggle resulted from an effort of the feudal barons, supported by Archbishop Langton (notwithstanding papal support of John) and public opinion, to enforce their rights under their feudal contract with the king; it did not aim to destory the monarchy or the royal administration. Preliminary demands of the barons (1213); John's concessions to the Church and negotiations with Pope Innocent; civil war. London opposed John (despite his liberal charter to the city). John's acceptance of the **great charter** at Runnymede. Magna Carta was essentially a feudal document, exacted by feudal barons from their lord but with national implications in its reforms: (1) concessions to the barons: reform in the exaction of scutage, aid, and reliefs, in the administration of wardship and in the demands for feudal service; writ of summons to the great council to be sent individually to the great magnates, collectively proclaimed by the sheriffs to the lesser nobles (i.e. knights); (2) concessions to the agricultural and commercial classes: Mesne tenants granted the privileges of tenants-in-chief; uniform weights and measures; affirmation of the ancient liberties of London and other towns; limitation on royal seizure of private property; reform of the forest law; reform of the courts; (3) concessions to the Church (in addition to John's charter of 1214): promise of freedom and free elections.

The **most significant provisions of the great charter:** (1) chapter 12: no scutage or aid (except for the traditional feudal three) to be levied without the consent of the great council; (2) chapter 14: definition of the great council and its powers; (3) chapter 39: "*No freeman shall be arrested and imprisoned, or dispossessed, or outlawed, or banished, or in any way molested; nor will we set forth against*

King John of England hunting deer (early 14th-century manuscript)

Facsimile of part of the articles of the Magna Carta containing the demands of the barons

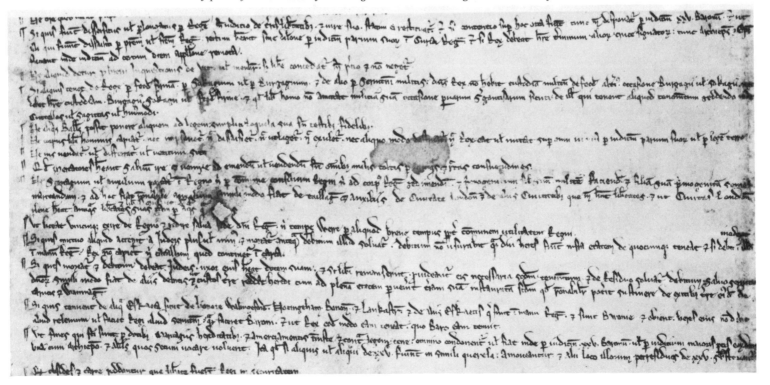

(From p. 191)

England: The Norman and Plantagenet Kings (1066–1377)

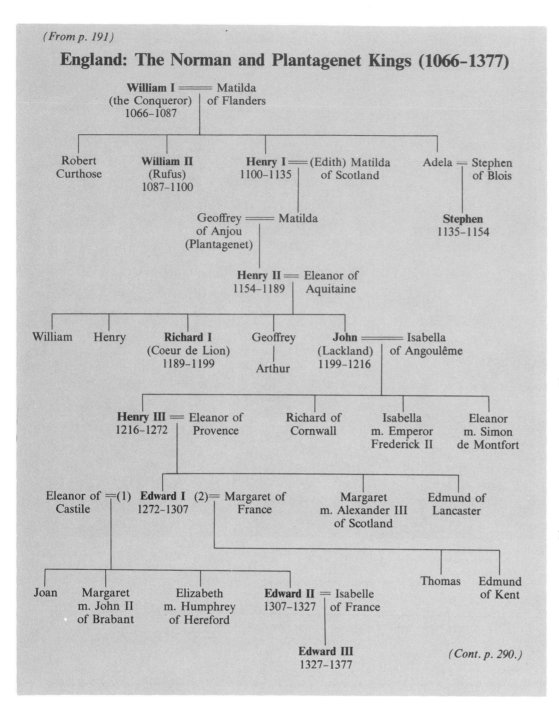

```
                    William I ═══ Matilda
                   (the Conqueror)  of Flanders
                     1066–1087

        ┌──────────────┬────────────────────────┬──────────────┐
      Robert       William II            Henry I ═══ (Edith) Matilda    Adela ═══ Stephen
      Curthose      (Rufus)              1100–1135    of Scotland               of Blois
                   1087–1100
                                              │                             Stephen
                              Geoffrey ═══ Matilda                          1135–1154
                              of Anjou
                             (Plantagenet)

                              Henry II ═══ Eleanor of
                              1154–1189    Aquitaine
        ┌─────────┬──────────────┬─────────────┬──────────────────┐
      William   Henry      Richard I        Geoffrey          John ═══ Isabella
                          (Coeur de Lion)      │           (Lackland)  of Angoulême
                           1189–1199         Arthur        1199–1216

              ┌──────────────────┬──────────────────┬──────────────────┐
        Henry III ═══ Eleanor of    Richard of       Isabella          Eleanor
        1216–1272    Provence       Cornwall         m. Emperor        m. Simon
                                                     Frederick II      de Montfort

   ┌──────────────────────────────┬──────────────────────┐
 Eleanor of ═(1) Edward I (2)═ Margaret of    Margaret          Edmund of
 Castile        1272–1307      France         m. Alexander III  Lancaster
                                              of Scotland
   ┌──────────┬──────────────┬──────────────┐                   ┌──────────┐
 Joan    Margaret      Elizabeth      Edward II ═══ Isabelle   Thomas   Edmund
         m. John II    m. Humphrey    1307–1327    of France            of Kent
         of Brabant    of Hereford

                                     Edward III
                                     1327–1377
```

(Cont. p. 290.)

---

him, nor send against him, unless by the lawful judgment of his peers and by the law of the land." Even these clauses were feudal and specific in background, but centuries of experience transformed them into a generalized formula of constitutional procedure, making them the basis of the modern English constitution. At the time their chief significance lay in the assertion of the supremacy of law over the king. Careful provisions were made for the enforcement of the charter by the barons, even by force of arms, but in practice such enforcement was impossible. The charter was repeatedly reissued by succeeding rulers. The pope, as John's feudal suzerain, declared the great charter void. Civil war followed; a Francophile section of the barons called Louis, son of Philip II, to the throne (1216). John opportunely died; his young son Henry, with the support of the Anglophile barons, succeeded him, and Louis abandoned his pursuit of the crown (1217).

1216–1272. Henry III (a boy of nine). Guardianship (1216–1219) of **William Marshal,** Earl of Pembroke; an able, patriotic regime: two reissues (1216, 1217) of the (modified) great charter; elimination of French influence and interference, opposition to papal encroachments, reduction of feudal castles. William Marshal had designated the pope as Henry's guardian, and the government passed on his death (1219) to the papal legate Pandulph, the justiciar Hubert de Burgh, and Peter des Roches, tutor to Henry. Arrival of the **Dominicans** (1220) and the **Franciscans** (1224). Henry's personal rule (1227–1258) was marked by a major constitutional crisis.

Growth of national consciousness. After a futile but expensive effort (1229) to recover Aquitaine, Henry, always devoted to the papacy, gave free reign to papal exactions. At the same time the increase of papal provisions filled the English Church with alien (usually absentee Italian) appointees, to the exclusion of natives. A bitter anti-papal outbreak (perhaps supported by de Burgh) drove de Burgh from office; des Roches succeeded him (1232–1234), filling the civil offices with fellow Poitevins. Henry's French marriage increased the alien influx and public opinion grew bitter. The papal collector was driven out (1244), and the great council refused (1242) a grant for Henry's effort to recover Poitou, which failed. Henry's acceptance of the crown of Sicily from the pope for his second son Edmund (1254), and his permission to his brother, Richard of Cornwall, to seek election as emperor (1257), both costly ventures, added to public ill-feeling. Finally, in a period of great economic distress, Richard asked the great council for one-third of the revenue of England for the pope. This grant was refused and the barons set out to reform the government with public approval (1258). A committee of twenty-four, representing king and barons equally, brought in a proposal.

1258. The **PROVISIONS OF OXFORD,** a baronial effort to restore the charter, with strong clerical and middle-class support; creation of a council of fifteen (containing a baronial majority) with a veto over the king's decisions; the great council to be superseded by a committee of twelve, meeting thrice a year with the permanent council of fifteen; the chancellor, justiciar, and treasurer were to be chosen annually by the council. All officials, including the king and his son, took an oath of loyalty to the Provisions.

1260–1264. The **knights,** alienated by the baronial oligarchy, appealed to Edward (Henry's eldest son). Gradually there emerged a group of progressive reformers (younger barons, many of the clergy and knights, townsmen, notably of London and Oxford); the more conservative barons turned to the king. Henry obtained papal release from his oaths (1261) and replaced the council of fifteen with his own appointees; chaos was followed by civil war (1263). Papal exactions continued. Louis IX (asked to arbitrate the Provisions of Oxford), in the *Mise of Amiens* (1264), decided in favor of the king. This decision was rejected by London and the commercial towns, and civil war soon broke out.

1264. Simon de Montfort (son of Simon of the Albigensian crusade), Henry's brother-in-law, of French blood and education, a friend of Grosseteste, bishop of Lincoln (a lifelong champion of ecclesiastical and governmental reform), emerged as leader of the reforming group. This group, ahead of its time, manifested strong religious fervor, and even traces of democratic ideas. Simon's victory at **Lewes** (1265), capture of Henry, and exaction of the *Mise of Lewes* (a return to the reforms of 1258).

In the course of this reign the great council came to be called **Parliament** (c. 1240) and at various times knights of the shire were summoned to share in its deliberations. Parliament was still as much concerned with administration and justice as with "legislation"; its membership, control of finance, and specific

Parliament of Edward I (engraving from 1794)

functions were by no means precisely defined. The summoning of the knights in effect merely transformed the negotiation of shire business into a collective negotiation by the same men who managed it locally.

1265. De Montfort's Parliament: two knights from each shire, and two burgesses from each borough were summoned, probably the first summons to townsmen in parliamentary history.

1265. Edward, now leader of the baronial, conservative opposition, defeated de Montfort at **Evesham** (death of de Montfort).

Henry's return to power was formal, as Edward was the real ruler, and Edward and the barons were aware of the need of reform. Edward, on a crusade with Louis IX when Henry died, was proclaimed king while still absent, spent a year in Gascony on the way back, and was not crowned until 1274.

1272–1307. EDWARD I (Longshanks; the English Justinian), an able ruler and a great legislator, fit to rank with Frederick II, Louis IX, and Alfonso the Wise. He observed his motto, *Pactum serva* (Keep troth), but tempered it with realism. The first truly English king, he surrounded himself with able ministers and lawyers. The reign was marked by a frequent consultation of the knights and townsmen, not always in parliament. The institutions of the English state began to take shape.

EXTERNAL AFFAIRS

1276–1284. Reduction of Wales. Wales during the reign of Henry III had gotten out of hand, and a national revival had set in (bardic poetry and tribal union under the Llewelyns around Snowdon in the north). **Llewelyn,** prince of Wales, joined de Montfort's opposition, refused homage (1276), and, with his brother David, renewed war with the English (1282). Edward marched into Wales, killed Llewelyn, and executed David (1283), asserting the full dominion of the English crown. In these wars Edward became aware of the efficiency of the Welsh longbow. Edward's fourth son, Edward (later Edward II), was born at Carnarvon (1284), and with him began the customary title, **Prince of Wales,** bestowed on the heir to the English throne. Local government was organized in Wales, and the *Statute of Wales* settled the legal status of the newly disciplined Welsh.

1285–1307. Scotland. William the Lion had purchased freedom from homage to the English king from Richard I in 1189, but his successors continued to do homage for their English lands. The Scottish nobility were largely Normanized. Margaret, the *Maid of Norway* (daughter of Erik of Norway), was granddaughter and heir of King Alexander III of Scotland. After Alexander's death (1286), Edward arranged a marriage for her with the Prince of Wales (1290), but she died on her way to England and Edward's hope of a personal union of the two crowns vanished. There were three collateral claimants to the Scottish crown: **John Baliol, Robert Bruce, John Hastings.** Edward, asked to arbitrate, demanded (1291) homage and acknowledgment of paramountcy from the Scots, which was given (the commons protested). He awarded the crown to Baliol (1292), who did homage for Scotland. Edward's insistence on appellate jurisdiction alienated the Scots and disposed them toward France, and an alliance began (1295) which endured intermittently for 300 years. Edward invaded Scotland, defeated Baliol at **Dunbar** (1296), declared himself king of Scotland, received the homage of the nobles, took away the coronation stone of Scone. Oppressive administration by Edward's officials led to the rising of **William Wallace** (1297), who was supported by the gentry and commonalty, but got little aid at first from the nobles. Wallace won a victory at Stirling. Edward, using the longbow to open the way for a cavalry charge, defeated Wallace at **Falkirk** (1298), drove him into exile, and completed his second conquest

of Scotland (1304). Wallace was taken (1305) and executed and Scotland incorporated under the English crown. Scottish law was retained, Scottish representatives sat in parliament, but the nobles had to yield their fortresses, and an English lieutenant was sent to rule Scotland with a council and with power to amend the laws. Scottish nationalism found a leader in **Robert Bruce** (grandson of the claimant to the crown), who was crowned at Scone. Edward died (1307) on an expedition against Bruce.

1293–1303. France. Ill-feeling between sailors from the Cinque Ports (Sandwich, Dover, Rommey, Hythe, Hastings, and [later] Rye and Winchelsea) and the French, culminated in a victory for the Anglo-Gascon fleet (1293) and Edward's summons to the court of his French overlord, King Philip IV. Under a *pro forma* compromise (1294), Edward turned over his Gascon fortresses to Philip, who refused to return them, and declared Gascony forfeited. Futile expeditions of Edward (1294, 1296, and 1297, in alliance with the count of Flanders) against Philip. Philip, busy with his contest against Boniface VIII and other matters, returned Gascony to Edward (1303).

DOMESTIC AFFAIRS

1290. Expulsion of the Jews: Hitherto the Jews had been protected by the kings, as they were important sources of loans. By this time public opinion was hostile to the Jews, and the Italian houses, like the Bardi and Peruzzi, were ready to finance royal loans. Foreign trade, like banking, was in the hands of foreigners, and there were few native merchants, except for wool export, where Englishmen did about 35 per cent of the business, Italians 24 per cent. The English wool staple was established in Antwerp under Edward.

1296. The **clash with Pope Boniface VIII: Winchelsea,** archbishop of Canterbury, in accordance with the bull *Clericis laicos,* led the clergy in refusing a grant to the crown. Edward, with the general support of public opinion, withdrew the protection of the royal courts, and thus promptly brought the clergy to an evasion of the bull through "presents" to the crown; the lands of recalcitrant clergy were confiscated, the pope soon modified his stand, and the victory of Edward was complete.

Institutional and "legislative" developments: (1) The parliament of 1275 granted (hitherto permission had not been asked) an increase of the export duty on wool and leather to the king, to meet the rising cost of government. (2) **Distraint of knighthood:** various enactments (beginning in 1278) to insure that all men with a given income (e.g. £20 a year from land) should assume the duties of knighthood. Probably primarily an effort to raise money, the acts also ensured a militia under royal control. (3) *Statute of Gloucester* (1278), providing for *quo warranto* inquests into the right of feudal magnates to hold public (i.e. not manorial) courts. (4) *Statute de religiosis* (statute of mortmain, 1279), forbade gifts of land to the clergy without consent of the overlord (a usual policy elsewhere in Europe). Such consent was often given; the statute frequently evaded. (5) Second *Statute of Westminster* (*De donis conditionalibus,* 1285) perpetuated feudal entail (i.e. conditional grants of lands), and led to the later law of trusts. It also reorganized the militia and provided for care of the roads. (6) Third *Statute of Westminister* (*Quia emptores,* 1290) forbade new sub-infeudations of land. Land could be freely transferred, but the new vassal must hold direct of the king or from a tenant-in-chief.

1295. The Model Parliament. The writs of summons included (probably by accident) the famous phrase, *quod omnes tangit ab omnibus approbetur* (let that which toucheth all be approved by all). Bishops, abbots, earls, barons, knights, burgesses, and representatives of the chapters and parishes were summoned. The clergy did not long continue to attend parliament, preferring their own assembly (*Convocation*) and left only the great prelates, who sat rather as feudal than ecclesiastical persons.

1297. The **Confirmation of Charters** (*Confirmatio cartarum*), a document almost as impor-

Robert Bruce

Duns Scotus

tant as Magna Carta, extorted by a coalition of the barons (angered by taxation and the Gascon expedition) and the middle classes (irritated by mounting taxes) under the leadership of Archbishop Winchelsea. In effect the Confirmation included Magna Carta (and other charters) with the added provision that no non-feudal levy could be laid by the crown without a parliamentary grant. Edward left the actual granting of this concession to his son Edward as regent, and Pope Clement V later dispensed Edward from the promise in exchange for the right to collect (for the first time) annates in England. Edward did not surrender tallage, despite the so-called statute *de tallagio non concedendo.*

1303. The *carta mercatoria* granted the merchants full freedom of trade and safe conduct, in return for a new schedule of customs dues.

1305. The petition from the barons and commonalty of the parliament of Carlisle to end papal encroachments, notably in provisions and annates. Edward enforced the petition except in the matter of annates.

The reign is remarkable for frequent consultation of the middle class (in parliament and out), for the encouragement of petition to parliament (now one of its chief functions), and for frequent meetings of parliament, which educated the nation not merely in the elements of self-government but in ideas, and kept the crown in close contact with public opinion. The word *statute* as used of this reign means any formal royal regulation intended to be permanent, and does not imply formal parliamentary enactment.

Judicial developments. Under Edward the differentiation of the great common law courts is clear: (1) **Court of King's Bench** (concerned with criminal and crown cases); (2) **Court of Exchequer** (dealing with royal finance); (3) **Court of Common Pleas** (handling cases between subjects). The **King's Council** (small council) still remained supreme as a court by virtue of its residual and appellate jurisdiction, and the councilors were expected to take the councilor's oath to the king. Edward began the practice of referring residual cases which did not readily come within the jurisdiction of the common law courts to the chancellor with a committee of assessors from the council. This chancellor's court tended to absorb the judicial business of the council and finally emerged as a court of equity. The **Year Books,** unofficial, verbatim reports in French (the language of the courts) of legal proceedings, a record unique for completeness in the period, began in this reign. Coherence and continuity of tradition among the lawyers was greatly facilitated by the establishment of the **Inns of Court** under the three Edwards. Here the lawyers assembled their libraries, lodged, and studied, transmitting with increasing strength the living force of the common law, to the virtual exclusion of Roman law.

PROGRESS OF ENGLISH CULTURE

Architecture. Early English Gothic (under French influence): Canterbury, begun 1175; Lincoln, 1185–1200; Salisbury, 1220–1258. Decorated Gothic: Choir of Lincoln, 1255–1280; York, west front, 1261–1324.

Painting and minor arts. St. Albans at the

Salisbury Cathedral

opening of the 13th century was the greatest artistic center in Europe (manuscript painting by Matthew Paris). The court of Henry III was a mecca for European craftsmen, especially Frenchmen.

Literature. Orm's *Ormulum* (early 13th century), a translation into English of portions of the Gospels; the *Ancren Rewle,* rules for the ascetic life tinged with the cult of the Virgin (c. 1200); **Layamon's** *Brut,* an English verse translation of Wace's *Brut.* Political songs and satires of the Barons' War, etc. (e.g. *Song of the Battle of Lewes;* the *Husbandman's Complaint*). **Matthew Paris** (c. 1200–1259), a friend of Henry III, monk of St. Albans, in his compilation, the *Historia Maior,* covered the history of the world, but in the portion dealing with the years 1235–1259 produced a work of original research in which he glorified England and things English.

Foundation of Cambridge University (1209). Foundation of University College (1249); Balliol (1261); Merton (1264) began the collegiate system of Oxford.

Science and learning. Bartholomew Anglicus (c. 1230), *On the Properties of Things,* a popular encyclopedia influenced by Pliny and Isidore, combining accurate observation (e.g. the domestic cat) with discussion of the fantastic (e.g. the griffin).

The English Franciscans at Oxford. Robert Grosseteste (d. 1253), bishop of Lincoln: insistence on the study of the sources (the Fathers and the Bible); knew Greek and Hebrew, a precursor of the Christian humanists; student of

philosophy, mathematics, astronomy, physics, teacher of Roger Bacon. **Roger Bacon** (d. 1292), greatest mediaeval exponent of observation and experiment. Foresaw the application of mediaeval power to transport, including flying; "formula" for gunpowder; author of the *Opus Maius* and *Opus Minus.*

Opponents of the Thomist rationalists. Duns Scotus (c. 1270–1308) and **William of Occam** (c. 1300–1349). *(Cont. p. 284.)*

(2) Scotland, 1034–1304

1034–1286. Racial and political turmoil. Duncan I was followed by his murderer, the usurper

1040–1057. Macbeth, and his son and avenger

1057–1093. MALCOLM CANMORE. Malcolm was forced to do some kind of homage by William the Conqueror (1072) and by William Rufus (1091), and Anglo-Norman penetration began. Malcolm's wife (Saint) Margaret (sister of Edgar Aetheling, grandniece of Edward the Confessor) was a masterful and remarkable woman whose Anglicizing influence on Scottish culture, on the national life, and the native Church was profound. Her three sons, especially

1124–1153. DAVID I, continued the so-called "bloodless Norman conquest," and the new Anglo-Norman aristocracy (e.g. Baliols, Bruces, Lindsays, Fitz Alans, i.e. Stewarts) became the bulwark of the crown.

1153–1286. The new four reigns were notable for the consolidation of Scotland, and for signs

King Canute and Queen Aelgifu crowned by angels (11th-century manuscript)

of impending collision with the English monarchy. William the Lion, captured in a raid by the English, accepted (1174) the feudal lordship of the English crown and did ceremonial allegiance at York (1175). Richard I weakened England's position, John tried to restore it.

1249–1286. ALEXANDER III did homage (1278) to the English king for his English lands, "reserving" his Scottish fealty. All of Alexander's issue were dead by 1284, leaving only his granddaughter Margaret, the *Maid of Norway*. Margaret's death (1290) made impossible the personal union of England and Scotland (by Margaret's marriage to Edward I's heir). Thirteen claimants to the Scottish crown were narrowed down to the candidacy of **Robert Bruce** and **John Baliol.** Edward I of England, called upon to arbitrate, awarded the crown to Baliol (1292), but when Baliol ignored a summons to attend Edward and instead embarked upon an alliance with France (1295), the English invaded the country and, after some years of warfare, reduced it in 1304 *(p. 222)*. *(Cont. p. 293.)*

(3) Ireland, 1171–1307

(From p. 194)

The period following the **expedition of Henry II** (1171) was marked by a steadily developing conflict between the feudal system of the incoming Normans and the old tribal organization of the Irish. In its later phases this struggle bred centuries of discord and bloodshed. Henry's authority was precariously maintained by a viceroy who had orders to be fair to the natives, a policy which estranged the Norman elements.

1185. Henry's son, John Lackland, returned to England after a short and inglorious rule as lord of Ireland, but his authority was maintained by his representative, **William Marshal,** earl of Pembroke, who married the daughter of Richard of Clare.

1213. John abandoned Ireland, along with England, to Pope Innocent III.

1216–1272. Under Henry III the power and possessions of the Anglo-Norman colony expanded rapidly: bridges and castles were built, towns prospered and guilds were formed.

1272–1307. Edward I's revolutionary legislation in England was extended to Ireland, which continued to prosper, at least in the Anglo-Norman sections. But the cleavage between the two races had become very marked and the native clans remained restive.

(Cont. p. 294.)

b. SCANDINAVIA

(From p. 195)

(1) Denmark, 950–1320

c. 950–985. Harald II (Bluetooth), whose reign saw a steady advance of Christianity and expansion of Danish power over Schleswig, the Oder mouth, and Norway. But the kingship was of little importance until the reign of

985–1014. SVEN I (Forked-beard). He defeated the Norwegians, Swedes, and Wends and conquered England (1013).

1014–1035. CANUTE II, THE GREAT (Knut), Sven's son, was king of Denmark, Norway (1028), and England (1016–1035), the first "northern empire." Canute's conversion completed the conversion of his people. He imported priests, architects, and artisans from his English realm, and new influences spread from Denmark to Norway and Sweden. On his death Norway broke away, England passed to Edward the Confessor.

1157–1182. Under **WALDEMAR I, THE GREAT,** the founder of the **Waldemarian dynasty,** a great expansion eastward took place at the expense of the Wends; Copenhagen was established as the capital.

1182–1202. CANUTE VI made conquests in (Slavonic) Mecklenburg and Pomerania.

1202–1241. WALDEMAR II (the Conqueror) led crusading expeditions into Livonia, Estonia (Reval founded), and penetrated the Gulf of Finland, making the southern Baltic a Danish lake (the second "northern empire"). This empire collapsed in 1223, and the advance was in fact more in the nature of a crusade than of permanent imperial expansion. The monarchy was now dominant, the nobles largely feudalized, the clergy (with royal grants) powerful, the bourgeoisie vigorous (fisheries and cattle-raising), the yeoman class strong and independent.

1241–1250. ERIC IV (Plowpenny), whose reign was taken up with civil war against his brothers Christopher and

1250–1252. ABEL, who was supported by his brother-in-law, the count of Holstein, and also by the Swedes and by the city of Lübeck.

1252–1259. CHRISTOPHER I. His effort to tax the Church opened a struggle that lasted nearly a century.

1259–1286. ERIC V (Glipping). He was forced by the nobility to sign a charter, the **Danish Magna Carta** (1282), recognizing the national assembly and initiating the subordination of the king to the law. He continued the contest with the clergy, fought against dynastic rivals, planned expansion in Mecklenburg and Pomerania, and lost Scania and North Halland to Sweden.

1286–1319. ERIC VI (Menved), during whose reign the conflict between the crown and the Church came to a head. By a compromise (1303) the rights of the Church were guaranteed, but the king's right to levy military service on church lands was upheld.

(Cont. p. 329.)

(2) Sweden, 993–1319

The origins of the Swedish kingship are obscure, but the kingdom may be dated back to the **union of Gothia and Svealand** (prior to 836). The conversion of the country to Christianity took place in the 9th century and

993–1024. OLAF SKUTKONUNG was the first Christian ruler. He was the son of Eric the Conqueror, the founder of the Northern Kingdom, and brought to Sweden many Anglo-Saxon workers. His wars with St. Olaf of Norway led to some conquests, which were soon lost. The century following his death was marked by wars between the Goths and the Swedes and by what appear to have been religious conflicts.

1134–1150. SVERKER. Amalgamation of the Swedes and Goths with alternation of rulers from the two peoples (an arrangement which continued for a century). The monarchy gradually became established on a firm basis and the progress of Christianity was marked by the foundation of many bishoprics (including Uppsala, 1163). The first monasteries also belong to this period.

1150–1160. ERIC IX (the Saint), whose reign was a short golden age. He led a crusade into Finland, the first real expansion of Sweden. The line of St. Eric ended with

1223–1250. ERIC XI (Laespe), whose reign was dominated by his brother-in-law, Jarl i.e. Earl) **Birger Magnusson,** the greatest statesman of mediaeval Sweden. He controlled the government from 1248–1266 and had his son elected king in 1250, thus founding the **Folkung line.**

1250–1275. WALDEMAR. As regent, Jarl Birger abolished judicial ordeal by fire, ended

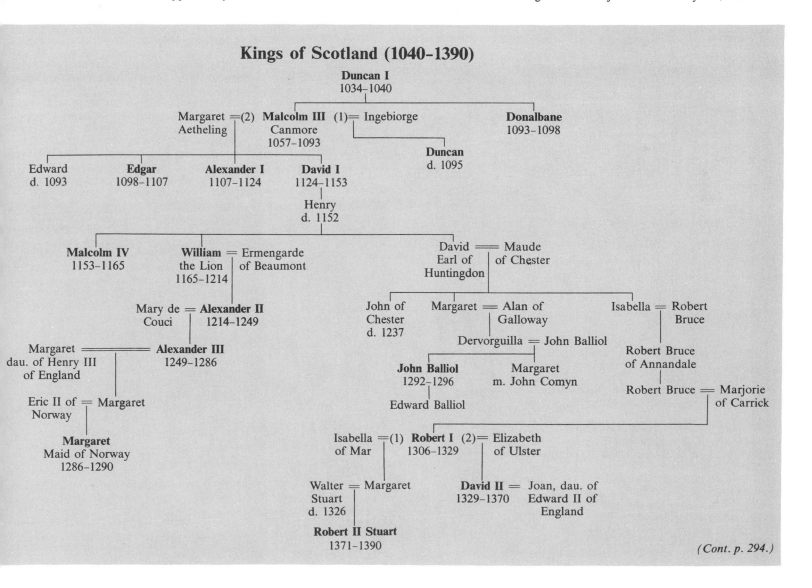

Kings of Scotland (1040–1390)

Norse sea-king of the 11th century

serfdom by choice, encouraged commerce, favored the settlement of German artisans, checked the power of the baronage. He attempted to introduce typical European feudalism, setting up his other sons in quasi-independent duchies.

1279-1290. MAGNUS LADULOS, who had dethroned and imprisoned his brother Waldemar. Magnus continued his father's feudal innovations, extended the powers of the clergy, and set up an hereditary nobility. Town charters became numerous as the burghers became prosperous through trade and mining.

1290-1319. BIRGER (son of Magnus). His rule was chaotic, due to civil war with his brothers, whom Birger ultimately captured and executed. This led to a popular uprising and the expulsion of Birger, who was followed by his three-year-old nephew. *(Cont. p. 329.)*

(3) Norway, 872-1319

Norway was a region with little natural unity, which in the earlier mediaeval period was ruled by numerous petty kings.

872-930. HAROLD I (Haarfager) began the unification of the country by deposing many of the chieftains (traditionally including Hrolf of Rollo). It was in this period that the Norsemen supposedly made their conquests in Iceland, the Faroes, Shetlands, Orkneys, Hebrides, Scotland, and Ireland.

935-961. HAAKON I (the Good), who attempted, prematurely, to convert the country to Christianity.

995-1000. OLAF I, TRYGVESSON, who with the aid of English clergy, converted Norway, Iceland, and Greenland. He was defeated by the kings of Denmark and Sweden, who supported the Norwegian nobility. There followed a period of feudal disruption.

1016-1028. OLAF II (St. Olaf) reunited the country and established Christianity on a firm footing.

1046-1066. HARALD III, HAARDRAADE, who was defeated by King Harold of England in the **battle of Stamford Bridge** *(p. 190)*. There

followed another period of confusion, marked by constant wars of succession, and by a struggle against the growing power of the clergy. Nevertheless the expansion of trade brought increasing prosperity.

1184-1202. SVERRE. He was able to maintain a strong monarchy in the face of aristocratic and clerical opposition, thanks to support from the small landowners. Nevertheless Norway continued to be troubled with dynastic conflict.

1223-1263. HAAKON IV, a strong king, who temporarily restored order, conquered Iceland, but was defeated in a war with Scotland.

1280-1299. ERIK II (the Priest-Hater), whose reign was marked by a war with the Hansa towns, in which he suffered a reverse. As a result he was obliged to grant the towns full privileges in Norway and to join the Hanseatic League.

1299-1319. HAAKON V, marking the culmination of decline of the royal power.

The crown in Scandinavia depended on its vassals for soldiers and for administration. The introduction of cavalry (first recorded in Denmark, 1134) accentuated this feudal tendency, and a new nobility emerged. This nobility was a professional military class always ready for war, exempt from taxes; it quickly became a governing class receiving local offices and lands as a reward for military services. From Denmark this new society spread to Norway and Sweden. Henceforth the nobles added a further complication to dynastic wars, causing a series of crises, and restricting the normal evolution of royal power.

German capital and German merchants began to penetrate Scandinavia, achieving by the second half of the 13th century a dominating position. The growth of the Hanseatic League delayed the progress of the native bourgeoisie, but commerce led to the active growth of towns and town life. Population was increasing rapidly, lands were cleared, the arts were advancing in distinction and perfection under the patronage of wealthy kings and prosperous prelates.

The **heroic age of the Icelandic** *skalds* (court poets) in the 10th and 11th centuries brought the art to an involved perfection and a concentration on war that ultimately killed it. Meantime the kings, interested in politics as well as war (notably Sverre of Norway, 1185) began to patronize the Norwegian story-tellers, particularly the Icelanders, and the **Sagas** emerged. The greatest master of the new form was an Icelander, **Snorri Sturleson** (1179-1241), an active political figure in both Iceland and Norway. Snorri's *Younger Edda* (*Edda Snorra Sturlusonar*) in prose and verse,

Henry III presiding at the Synod of Sutri

containing the rules of versification, the old myths, and a collection of ancient Icelandic poems, is unique. History was written by **Saxo Grammaticus** (c. 1208), whose *Historia Danica* is the chief source for the Hamlet story. Both Snorri and Saxo were preoccupied with the ideals of national unity, strong royal power, and resistance to baronial particularism.

(Cont. p. 330.)

c. GERMANY UNDER THE SALIAN AND HOHENSTAUFEN EMPERORS, 1024–1268

(From p. 185)

[*For a complete list of the Holy Roman emperors see Appendix V.*]

1024–1125. THE FRANCONIAN (or Salian) **HOUSE.** Dawn of the great imperial age.

1024–1039. CONRAD II (the Salian). He continued the general policy of Henry: personally interested only in the churches of Limburg and Speyer, he was firm in his dealings with the Church in general and relied on the lesser nobles to balance the clergy and magnates. The *ministeriales,* laymen of humble or even servile origin, were used to replace the clergy in many administrative posts; regalian rights were retained and exploited. Dukedoms were not regranted as they fell vacant, but were assigned to Conrad's son Henry, who on his accession to the crown held all but the duchies of Lorraine and Saxony. By encouraging the making of fiefs heritable Conrad weakened the dukes and got the support of the lesser nobles, but insured the ultimate feudalization of Germany. Conrad's imperial coronation (1027), one of the most brilliant in mediaeval Rome, was witnessed by two kings, Canute the Great and Rudolf III of Burgundy. Burgundy, willed to Conrad by Rudolf III, guardian of one road to Italy, was reincorporated (1033) in the empire on the death of Rudolf. Failure of an expedition (1030) against Stephen of Hungary; successful disciplinary expedition (1031) against the Poles; recovery of Lusatia; payment of homage by the Poles.

1039–1056. HENRY III (the Black). Imperial authority at its height. A period of great town prosperity, due to development of trade. His wife, Agnes of Poitou, was an ardent devotee of Cluny; Henry, an honest reformer, abandoned simony, purified the court along Cluniac lines, but retained a firm hold on the Church. Strongest of the German emperors, he asserted his mastery in Poland, Bohemia, and Hungary; Saxony was the only duchy to keep a trace of its original independence; resumption of the dangerous practice of granting duchies outside the royal house made Germany a feudal volcano; use of the *ministeriales* in administration, but retention of the bishops as principal advisers and administrators. Henry's reforms alienated the bishops, the magnates, and the nobles.

1043. Henry proclaimed the **"Day of Indulgence,"** forgiving all his foes and exhorting his subjects to do likewise; Brětislav of Bohemia forced (1041) to do homage; pagan reaction in Hungary put down (1044); final peace in Hungary (1052), which became a fief of the German crown. Homage of Denmark, repudiated soon after.

Detail of the opening page of Pope Gregory's Dictatus Papae, *1075*

1046. Synods of Sutri and Rome. Deposition at Henry's instigation of three rival popes and election of his nominee, Clement II, the first of a series (Clement, Leo IX, and Nicholas II) of reforming German popes; reaffirmation of the imperial right of nomination to the papacy.

1047. Godfrey the Bearded, duke of Upper Lorraine, disappointed at Henry's refusal to award him Lower Lorraine, stirred up serious disaffection, and finally joined Baldwin of Flanders in a revolt at first supported by Henry of France (1047); he married (1054) Beatrice, widow of Boniface, marquis of Tuscany, one of the most powerful Italian supporters of the popes.

1056–1106. HENRY IV. (Aged six at his accession; nine-year regency of his pious, colorless mother, Agnes.) During the regency lay and clerical magnates appropriated royal resources and sovereign rights with impunity, and dealt a fatal blow to the German monarchy.

1062. Anno, archbishop of Cologne, kidnaped the young king and with **Adalbert,** archbishop of Hamburg-Bremen, governed in his name, dividing the monasteries (one of the chief resources of the crown) between themselves.

1066. The **Diet of Tribur,** thanks to the reaction of the clergy and nobles against Adalbert, freed Henry from Adalbert and his personal government began.

Henry was a remarkable but undisciplined man, intelligent, resolute, ill-balanced, and headlong, with the odds against him from the start; under papal pressure he was reconciled (1069) with his wife Bertha, reformed his personal life, and began a vigorous rule. His

policy was a return to the Ottonian habit of using the Church as a major source of revenue; simony was open, and the reforming party appealed to Rome against Henry. Henry began the recapture, reorganization, and consolidation of royal lands and revenues, especially in Saxony, and probably planned to consolidate the monarchy in the Capetian manner around a compact core of royal domain in the Harz-Goslar region.

1073. A great **conspiracy of the leading princes** led to a rising of virtually all Saxony. Henry came to terms with the pope, played one faction off against the other, won the South German baronage, and finally defeated the rebels (1075).

1074. Charter of Worms, the first imperial charter issued direct to citizens without episcopal intervention.

Theophilus the Presbyter (fl. second half of the 11th century) described the techniques of building a cathedral, including the making of stained glass.

1075–1122. THE STRUGGLE OVER LAY INVESTITURE. The German bishops, alarmed at Hildebrand's reform policy *(p. 237),* opposed his confirmation as pope, but Henry, in the midst of the Saxon revolt, sanctioned it, and apparently promised reforms in Germany. The sudden abolition of lay investiture would have reduced the emperor's power in Germany and would have made government impossible. With the end of the Saxon revolt Henry's interest in reform vanished.

1075. Pope Gregory, at the Lenten Synod, issued a rigorous reform program and later sent a stern warning to the emperor and the

German episcopate. Henry, under pressure from his bishops, called

1076. **The Synod of Worms.** The bishops repudiated their allegiance to Pope Gregory, addressed a list of (ridiculous) charges to him, and declared him deposed. Henry's letter to the pope associated him with the charges and demanded Gregory's abdication in the most insolent and violent terms. Public opinion was shocked at the letter, but the North Italian bishops at Piacenza supported Henry. Gregory at the Lenten Synod (1076) in Rome, suspended and excommunicated the German and Lombard prelates involved, and deposed and excommunicated Henry, absolving his subjects from allegiance and producing political and ecclesiastical chaos in Germany. Henry was isolated, the Saxon rebellion broke out again, and a powerful coalition of German magnates eager to regain power was formed against him. The **Diet of Tribur** (October) compelled Henry to humble himself and agree to stand trial and clear himself of Gregory's charges before Feb. 22, 1077, on pain of the withdrawal of their allegiance. The princes called a synod to meet at Augsburg, inviting Gregory to preside; Gregory accepted and started for Germany.

1077. Henry, after a midwinter dash across the Alps with his wife, was welcomed by the North Italians and avoided the humiliation of a public trial in Germany by presenting himself as a penitent at Canossa (Jan. 21). Gregory, outmaneuvered, hesitated three days, and finally, on the appeals of the Countess Matilda and Abbot Hugh of Cluny (Henry's godfather), accepted Henry's promises and solemn oaths of contrition, and absolved him. The **penance at Canossa** is hardly mentioned by contemporaries, and made much less impression in Germany than the excommunication; the chief source on the episode is Gregory's letter of justification to the disappointed German nobles; Gregory, after some months of waiting for a safe conduct into Germany, turned back.

1077. A faction of the nobles elected an anti-king, **Rudolf of Swabia,** with the approval of Gregory's legates, but without papal confirmation.

1077–1080. **Civil war** ensued, but Henry, loyally supported by the towns, gained strength steadily; Rudolf of Swabia was defeated and killed (1080); Gregory again excommunicated and deposed Henry, but a synod of German and North Italian prelates then deposed Gregory, naming as his successor Guibert of Ravenna, a reforming bishop and former friend of Gregory (1080).

1083. Henry, at the end of a series of expeditions to Italy (1081–1082), besieged Rome; after futile efforts at reconciliation he gained entrance to the city and Gregory called in his Norman allies. Henry, crowned at Rome by his anti-pope, invaded Apulia; **Robert Guiscard** expelled him from Rome and sacked (1084) the city. The horrors of the Norman sack made it impossible for Gregory to remain in Rome and he departed with his allies, dying as their "guest" in Salerno (1085). The papal position was justified by **Manegold of Lautenbach's** theory that an evil ruler violates a contract with his subjects and may therefore be deposed by the pope, who is responsible for the salvation of mankind. Henry's advocate, **Peter Crassus,** based his denial of this right on historical precedent backed by citations of Justinian (one of the earliest examples of such quotations).

1093–1106. Gregory's successors, unbending champions of reform, supported the revolts of Henry's sons in Germany and Italy: **Conrad** (1093), and the future **Henry V** (1104). Henry was elected king, but his father retained the loyalty of the towns to the end. Henry V shamefully entrapped and imprisoned his father, who abdicated, escaped, and was regaining ground when he died.

1106–1125. **HENRY V** (married to Matilda, daughter of Henry I of England in 1114). A brutal, resourceful, treacherous ruler, Henry continued his father's policies. Skillfully pretending to be dependent on the princes, he continued lay investiture, opposed papal interference in Germany, and retained the support of the lay and clerical princes; meantime, relying on the towns and *ministeriales,* he built up the nucleus of a strong power. Wars against Hungary, Poland, and Bohemia (1108–1110).

1110–1111. Imposing **expedition to Italy** to secure the imperial crown, universally supported in Germany. In Italy the Lombard towns (except Milan) and even the Countess Matilda yielded to Henry. Pope Paschal II (1099–1118) offered to renounce all feudal and secular holdings of the Church (except those of the see of Rome) in return for the concession of free elections and the abandonment of lay investiture, a papal humiliation more than equal to the imperial mortification at Canossa. At Henry's coronation the clergy repudiated Paschal's renunciation, there was a scuffle, Henry took the pope and cardinals prisoners, and forced the pope to acknowledge the imperial powers. The net result was nil, but papal prestige was badly damaged.

1114–1115. A series of revolts (Lorraine, along the lower Rhine, in Westphalia, and soon in East Saxony and Thuringia). Henry was saved by the loyalty of the South Germans.

1115. **Matilda, countess of Tuscany,** who had made over all her vast holdings to the papacy, retaining them as fiefs with free right of disposition, willed these lands to Henry on her death, and Henry arrived in Italy to claim them (1116–1118).

Both pope and emperor were weary of the investiture controversy, Europe was preoccupied with the Crusades *(p. 273),* and the time was ripe for compromise. The first important compromise negotiated by the pope was with Henry I of England (1107) and provided that the king should not invest with the spiritual symbols (the ring and the staff), but that he was to be present or represented at all elec-

Henry IV and his anti-Pope, Clement III, expelling Pope Gregory VII from Rome by force of arms (top of illustration) and (below) the death of Gregory at Salerno in 1085 (illumination from a 12th-century chronicle)

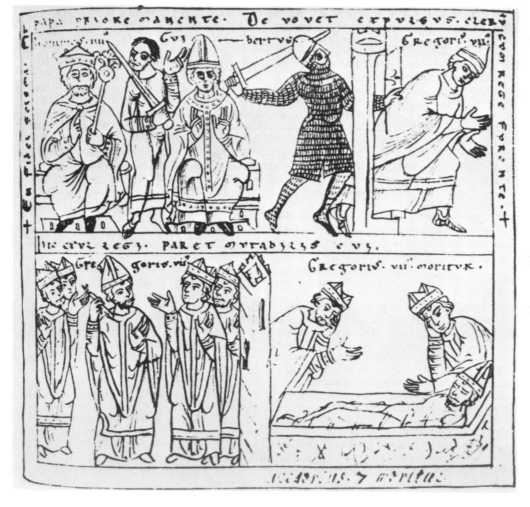

Henry IV presenting himself as a penitent at Canossa, 1077

clerical Salian line, cleverly prevented, with papal aid, the election of the nearest heir, Frederick of Swabia, of the house of Hohenstaufen, on the ground that the hereditary principle was dangerous, and Lothair of Supplinburg, duke of Saxony, was chosen, opening the great struggle of Welf and Waiblinger (Hohenstaufen) in Germany (**Guelf** and **Ghibelline** in Italy).

1125–1137. LOTHAIR II. Elected with the support of the clergy, he remained loyal to the Church, was the first German king to ask papal approval of his election, and did not exercise his rights under the Concordat of Worms for some years. Bitter civil war against the Hohenstaufens (1125–1135); vigorous policy of German expansion among the Wends and Scandinavians; renewal of Wendish conversions (1127).

1133. Influenced by Bernard of Clairvaux, Lothair decided in favor of Pope Innocent II (against Anacletus II) and went to Italy to settle the papal schism; he was crowned, had the Concordat of Worms confirmed, and received the lands of Matilda as fiefs.

1135. The **"year of pacification"** in Germany—general peace proclaimed. Lothair apparently planned to create a vast dynastic holding for his son-in-law, the Welf Henry the Proud, to include Bavaria, Swabia, Saxony, the allodial

Holy Roman Emperor Henry V forcing Pope Paschal II to crown him in St. Peter's in 1111 (illumination from a German manuscript)

tions. After due homage the king should then invest with the symbols of temporal authority. In France a similar compromise was reached in practice with Philip I (c. 1108). Pope Calixtus II convinced Henry that neither Henry of England nor Philip of France had suffered by their compromise.

1122. At the Synod of Worms, under the presidency of a papal legate, the **Concordat of Worms** was drawn up in two documents of three brief sentences each which provided that: (I) elections in Germany were to be in the presence of the emperor or his representative, without simony or violence; in the event

of disagreement the emperor was to decide; the emperor was to invest with the temporalities before the spiritual investiture; (2) in Italy and Burgundy consecration was to follow within six months of election; the emperor to invest with the regalia after homage. This concordat ended the investiture struggle, but not the bitter rivalry of pope and emperor, for the papacy, now clearly the independent spiritual leader of Europe, could not long tolerate an imperial rival.

1125. Henry left no direct heir, and at the bitterly fought election of 1125 the archbishops of Mainz and Cologne, foes of the anti-

lands and fiefs of Matilda of Tuscany, and to secure him the imperial crown. Lothair died suddenly on his return from an expedition against King Roger II of Sicily, and in the election (1138) the clergy, led by Adalbert of Trier, had the Waiblinger, Conrad of Hohenstaufen, chosen. Conrad almost at once put Henry the Proud under the ban, gave Saxony to Albert the Bear, Bavaria to Leopold of Austria, his half-brother, and reopened the civil war.

1138–1268. THE HOUSE OF HOHENSTAUFEN (from Staufen, their Swabian castle). The first German dynasty to be conscious of the full historical implications of the imperial tradition and the significance of Roman law for imperial pretensions. Their consequent devotion to a policy of centralization and to the aggrandizement of the lay imperial power in the face of the new spiritual supremacy and political aspirations of the Papacy precipitated a second great struggle between the popes and the emperors, centering in Italy but turning upon a sharp conflict between rival spiritual and political concepts.

1138–1152. CONRAD III, a gallant, knightly, attractive, popular hero, but no statesman. The Welf, **Henry the Lion** (son and successor of Henry the Proud), acknowledged Conrad's title, but regained Saxony by force and was granted it by the peace (1142); the struggle of Welf and Waiblinger reduced Germany to chaos and Conrad left on the Second Crusade. On his return Conrad found Germany in worse confusion.

The most significant development of the reign was the renewal of **expansion against the Slavs and Scandinavians** (chiefly on the initiative of Albert the Bear and Henry the Lion): a regularly authorized German crusade against the Slavs (1147); colonization of eastern Holstein; foundation of Lübeck (1143); conversion of Brandenburg and Pomerania; Albert the Bear began to style himself margrave of Brandenburg; Henry the Lion began the creation of a principality east of the Elbe. Conrad took no share in these developments; was the only king since Henry the Fowler not to attain the imperial title. Alienated from the Church toward the end of his life, Conrad was preparing a more vigorous assertion of the imperial position, and supported the strong imperialist Frederick of Swabia, his nephew, as candidate for the throne. On Conrad's death anarchy was so prevalent in Germany that even the magnates favored a strong ruler, and Conrad's candidate, Frederick, duke of Swabia, was unanimously elected.

1152–1190. FREDERICK I (Barbarossa, i.e. Red Beard), a handsome man with flowing golden hair, who could both frighten and charm, the embodiment of the ideal medieval German king. A close student of history and surrounded with Roman legists, he regarded himself as heir to the tradition of Constantine, Justinian, and Charlemagne (whom he had canonized by his anti-pope), and aimed at restoring the glories of the Roman Empire. He began the style *Holy Roman Empire.*

Policy of consolidation and expansion of royal lands. Burgundian lands regained by marriage (1156) with Beatrice, heiress of the county of Burgundy; purchase of lands from the Welfs in Swabia and Italy; exploitation of regalian rights.

Conciliation of the magnates. (1) **Henry the Lion,** recognized as virtually independent beyond the Elbe; confirmed in Saxony; regranted Bavaria (1156). (2) **Austria made an independent duchy** (1156), granted to Henry of Austria in return for Bavaria. (3) **Alliance with the episcopate.** Free exercise of rights under the Concordat of Worms; reforming bishops replaced with hard-headed appointees of the old school, loyal to the crown. Administration delegated to the *ministeriales.* Successful maintenance of public order; Frederick won the title *pacificus.*

Expeditions to Italy*(p. 240, seq.).* (1) 1154–1155; (2) 1158–1162; (3) 1163–1164; (4) 1166–1168; (5) 1174–1177; (6) 1184–1186.

1156–1180. Henry the Lion's "principality" beyond the Elbe: military progress against the Slavs and colonization (Hollanders, Danes, Flemings); Bremen taken from the archbishop (1156), Lübeck from Adolf of Holstein

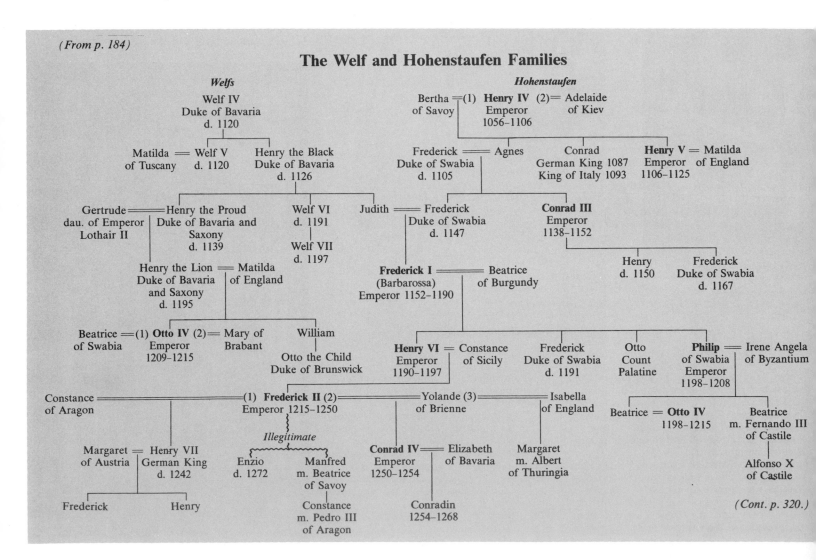

(From p. 184)

The Welf and Hohenstaufen Families

Welfs　　　　　　　　　　　　　　　*Hohenstaufen*

(Cont. p. 320.)

*Pope Boniface VIII (p.242), detail
of fresco, School of Giotto*

St. Francis of Assisi (p.241) by Cimabue

The Defense of Jerusalem (p.275), illuminated page from medieval manuscript

Henry the Lion submitting to Frederick I, 1180

(1158); commercial relations with Denmark, Sweden, Norway; alliance with Waldemar II of Denmark; reduction of Slavic pirates; colonization of Mecklenburg, extension of Christianity; war with Albert the Bear; refusal of aid to Frederick in Italy (1176); confiscation of Henry's holdings and exile (1180); dismemberment of Saxony.

1156. Diet of Regensburg. Emergence of the **prince electors** as a substantive body in the German state.

1157. Diet of Besançon. Emissaries from Rome, France, England, the Spanish princes, Apulia, Tuscany, Venice, and the Lombard towns did honor to Frederick. Frederick savéd the life of the papal legate, Cardinal Roland, whose statement of papal claims enraged the German nobles (translation of *beneficia* as "fiefs"). Boleslav, duke of Bohemia, granted the style of "king" (1158).

1174–1177. Frederick's fifth expedition to Italy. Vain siege of Alessandria, futile efforts at reconciliation with the pope.

1176. LEGNANO. Decisive defeat of Frederick by the Lombard League, the first major defeat of feudal cavalry by infantry, herald of the new rôle of the bourgeoisie.

1183. Final peace of Constance between Frederick, the pope, and the Lombard towns: restoration of all imperial confiscations during the papal schism confirmed, recognition of general imperial suzerainty in Italy; the Lombard towns virtually autonomous city states under a loose administration by imperial legates and vicars. Frederick retained the Matildan lands without a specific definition of their status. Henceforth there was no shadow of unity in the empire, as Germany and Italy followed a divergent development.

1184. Great Diet of Mainz. A tremendous medieval pageant for the knighting of Frederick's two sons in the presence of a great concourse, 70 (?) princes, 70,000 (?) knights.

1186. Marriage of the future Henry VI to Constance (daughter of Roger II of Sicily), heiress of King William II; possibly arranged in the hope of permanent peace with the empire. The net result of the marriage was the transfer of the center of gravity in the struggle between the popes and the emperors to Sicily, the final destruction of German unity, and the ruin of the house of Hohenstaufen. The pope refused imperial coronation to Henry.

1186. Triple coronation at Milan. Frederick as king of Burgundy; Henry as *Caesar* (a deliberate revival of the title), and Constance as queen of the Germans.

1186. Frederick took the Cross, and until his death led the Third Crusade *(p. 275)* in the traditional rôle of the emperor as the knightly champion of Christendom.

1190–1197. HENRY VI (already Caesar and regent, crowned emperor, 1191). The medieval empire at its maximum, ideally and territorially. Henry was not robust, and lacked the usual Hohenstaufen good nature. A good soldier, learned, practical, a shrewd diplomat, stern, cruel, but of heroic and original mind.

1190–1195. Intermittent struggles with the Welfs in Germany under Henry the Lion.

1191–1194. Restoration of order in Sicily. Struggle with the Norman anti-king, Tancred of Lecce (d. 1194); coronation of Henry as king of Sicily (1194); birth of Frederick (later Frederick II) at Jesi (1194).

1192–1194. Henry used the captivity of King Richard I of England to make the crown of England a fief of the empire, and to extort an enormous ransom.

Henry's plans to unite the German and Sicilian crowns, and to crown Frederick without election, thereby establishing the heredity of the German crown, were blocked by powerful German and papal opposition. Frederick was elected king of the Romans (1196). Plans (traditional with the Norman kings of Sicily) for the foundations of a Mediterranean empire on the ruins of the Byzantine Empire as the basis for a universal dominion; dynastic marriage with the Greek imperial house; active preparations for a crusade; advance in central Italy and conciliation of northern Italy. Sicilian outbreak against the German administration brutally crushed. Henry's sudden death was followed by a bitter anti-imperial reaction in Italy, by fourteen years of civil war in Germany.

1197–1212. Civil war in Germany, chaos in the empire. Rival kings; Henry's brother, the Waiblinger **Philip of Swabia** (supported by King Philip II of France) and the Welf **Otto of Brunswick,** son of Henry the Lion (supported by King Richard I of England). The German nobles played one side off against the other. Chaos in Sicily, where Pope Innocent III acted as guardian of Frederick (after 1198). Otto's title validated by Innocent (1201); assassination of Philip (1208); imperial coronation of Otto (1209); papal break with Otto (1210) and support of Frederick (with Philip II); Frederick's second election (1211) and dash to Germany.

1212-1250. FREDERICK II (Stupor Mundi), a valetudinarian of middle height, courteous, amiable, charming, pitiless, arrogant; the most brilliant ruler and one of the most learned men of his day; a legislator of the first order, able soldier, diplomat, skeptic, one of the leading scientific investigators of his time; an astrologer with the mind of a Renaissance rationalist; Sicilian by taste and training, half Norman by blood, with little of the German about him. Crowned: king of the Romans, 1212; king of the Germans, at Aachen, 1215; emperor, at Rome, 1220.

1212. Alliance with King Philip II of France.

1213. The **Golden Bull of Eger:** Frederick, who had already sworn an oath to keep his two crowns separate and to support the pope, abandoned the German church to Innocent (conceding the free election of bishops, the right of appeal to Rome) and undertook to support the pope against heretics.

1214. The **battle of Bouvines** *(p. 250):* Frederick and Philip II completed the defeat of Otto and the Welfs. On the death of Innocent III (1216) Frederick's personal rule may be said to have begun.

1216-1227. Frederick on tolerable terms with Pope Honorius III, his old tutor: election (1220) of Frederick's son Henry as king of the Romans (a violation of Frederick's promise); Frederick allowed to retain Sicily during his lifetime; renewal of his crusading oath; grant of generous privileges (1220) to the clergy: exemption of the Church from taxation and of clerics from lay jurisdiction, making clerical princes virtually independent territorial princes; support of the bishops against the towns; promises to suppress heresy. Crusade postponed until 1225.

1223. First appearance of the Mongols in Europe *(p. 281);* capture of Cracow (1241); defeat of the Hungarians and Silesians.

1226. The **conversion of Prussia** undertaken by the Teutonic Order *(p. 235).*

Gregory IX (mosaic from the old Basilica of St. Peter, Rome)

A knight of the Teutonic Order

1226-1232. Renewal of the ancient imperial claims in Lombardy, formation of the **Second Lombard League,** and appearance of the **First League of the Rhineland;** town leagues in central Italy; Pope Gregory alienated.

1227-1229. Frederick's crusade *(p. 276):* return of Frederick due to illness; first excommunication (1227); resumption of crusade (1228); violent papal and imperial propaganda and recrimination; the Teutonic Knights under Hermann of Salza remained faithful to Frederick. Aware of the commercial value of Moslem friendship Frederick negotiated a ten-year truce (1229) with El-Kamil, sultan of Egypt, which restored Jerusalem, Nazareth, and Bethlehem to Christian hands. Frederick crowned himself king of Jerusalem. Papal war (1228-1229) of devastation in Apulia (first known papal mercenaries, the *soldiers of the keys*); Frederick on his return expelled the papal forces and threatened the *Patrimonium Petri* with invasion.

1230. Hollow **peace of San Germano** with Pope Gregory IX: Frederick promised to protect the papal domains, confirmed papal rights over Sicily, and was absolved. In preparation for the next struggle Frederick concentrated on Italy, especially Sicily. Frederick's son Henry on his majority (1228) devoted himself to Germany, and favored the towns. Frederick, like Barbarossa, had leaned heavily on the German episcopate, especially Engelbert of Cologne, and had increased the independence of the lay princes and ministeriales; administrative offices tended to become hereditary, and after Engelbert's death (1225) the administration had become less efficient. Settlement of the Teutonic Knights in Prussia: union (1237) with the Livonian Brothers of the Sword and eastward expansion: foundation of Thorn (1231), Kulm (1232), and Marienwerder (1233).

1231. Privilege of Worms. Hoping for German support for his Italian policy, Frederick extended to the lay princes his generous grants of 1220 to the clergy, giving them control over local justice, minting rights, roads, and streams,

Excomunication of Frederick II by Pope Gregory, 1239 (painting by Giorgio Vasari)

etc. From this grant dates a clear emergence in Germany of the territorial sovereignty of both lay and clerical princes. The **Decree of Ravenna** (1232) allowed expansion of the power of the princes at the expense of the towns. Henry objected, revolted (1234), and tried to win the German and Italian towns to his side.

1231. Completion of the **reorganization of Sicily:** clean sweep of private titles and royal privileges in the Norman manner; resumption of royal domain; destruction of private garrisons and feudal castles; ban on private war; criminal jurisdiction transferred from feudal to royal courts; towns deprived of magistrates and put under royal officers; clergy taxed and excluded from civil office. Sicily reduced to order (1221-1225): feudal revolts put down, towns brought to heel; large Saracen garrison-colonies (loyal to Frederick and indifferent to papal threats) established at Lucera and Nocera. Recognizing in Sicily the true source of his strength in money and men, Frederick

aimed to unify Sicily and Italy into a kingdom of the empire. Local risings (1228-1230 and 1232) in Apulia and Sicily; unrest (1234) in southern Italy.

1231. The **Constitutions of Melfi,** the most conspicuous and constructive single piece of "legislation" in the Middle Ages, completed the Sicilian reorganization: an efficient divine right absolutism (much of it a return to the policy of Roger II) profoundly influenced by Roman law; centralization under an expert departmentalized bureaucracy; clerical jurisdiction limited to ecclesiastical matters; heresy a civil crime; simony in civil office a capital offense; gift or sale of Church land forbidden. Feudal, clerical, and municipal administration replaced by royal officials; supreme court at Capua; justices on annual circuits; careful financial organization. The University of Naples (the first European university on a royal charter) founded (1224) to train state officials, and given a monopoly of higher education; Salerno revived as a school of medicine.

Advanced economic policy in Sicily based on Arab practice: abolition of internal tolls; mercantilistic regulation, state monopolies. Replacement of feudal dues by fixed payments; direct taxation in crises, efficient customs collection and internal prosperity.

1235-1237. Frederick's last visit to Germany. Deposition, arrest, and imprisonment of Henry, who committed suicide in prison (1242) and was succeeded by his brother Conrad (1237); conciliation and peace with the Welfs strengthened Frederick in Germany. Great reform **Diet of Mainz** (the German Melfi, 1235); issue of the model *Landfrieden*. Frederick was unable to stem the steady progress of towns (resting on expanding commerce) in Germany or Italy.

1237. Frederick at **Cortenuova** smashed the Second Lombard League and humiliated Milan.

1239. Pope Gregory's **second excommunication of Frederick,** followed by a tremendous battle of pamphlets and preaching: Frederick painted as a heretic, rake, anti-Christ. He retorted with a demand for reform of the Church and an appeal to the princes of Europe, proposing a league of monarchs against the papacy.

Beginning of the amalgamation of northern and central Italy with the imperial administration on Sicilian lines: a system of general vicariates under imperial vicars, each city with an imperial *podestà* (generally Apulians, and often relatives of Frederick).

1241. Gregory's call for a **synod at Rome** to depose Frederick. Frederick ravaged papal territory, almost took Rome, and his fleet captured a large delegation of prelates off Genoa on their way to the synod; annexation of papal Tuscany to the empire. Gregory's death (1241). Celestine IV (1241). During the two-year interregnum in the Papacy Frederick intrigued for a friendly pope, and welcomed

1243. The **election of Sinibaldo de'Fieschi** (Innocent IV), who turned out to be the architect of his ruin.

1244. **Frederick's invasion of the Campagna** and vain efforts at reconciliation with the pope; Innocent's flight to Lyons, and call for a synod.

1245. **The Synod of Lyons.** Appeal to the Germans to revolt and elect a new king; deposition of Frederick; Louis IX's efforts at conciliation and Frederick's offers rebuffed by the pope: Innocent unleashed the Franciscans and Dominicans in a war of propaganda and proclaimed a crusade against Frederick. Henry Raspe, duke of Thuringia (d. 1247), was set up (1246) as an anti-king in Germany, followed by

1247-1256. **William of Holland,** who was supported by a newly formed **league of Rhenish towns.** Innocent's ruthless but vain campaign against Frederick's episcopal allies in Germany; bitter warfare in northern Italy with extreme cruelty on both sides; Italian conspiracy to assassinate Frederick (probably with Innocent's knowledge) put down in cold blood; Piero della Vigne, Frederick's most trusted official, supposedly implicated. He was arrested, blinded, and died a suicide (1249); capture of Frederick's son Enzio (1249), who died in prison (1272).

1248. The **defeat of Frederick** after a long siege of Parma did not destroy his hold on northern Italy.

1250. Sudden **death of Frederick**; burial in the cathedral at Palermo, where his sarcophagus still remains.

1250-1268. **Relentless persecution of the Hohenstaufens by the popes:**

1250-1254. **CONRAD IV,** king of Germany, and king of Sicily by the will of his father, Frederick; **Manfred,** his illegitimate half-brother, regent of Sicily; Pope Innocent IV's offer (1253) of the Sicilian crown under papal suzerainty to Edmund (son of Henry III of England); renewal of Conrad's excommunication and proclamation of a crusade against him; papal invasion of the kingdom (i.e., southern Italy and Sicily).

1254-1273. **THE GREAT INTERREGNUM.** An epilogue to the medieval struggle of the popes and the emperors, marks the end of the medieval Holy Roman Empire and the failure of imperial efforts to establish German unity; it was a prologue to the complete triumph of particularism which dominated German life until well into the 19th century.

1255-1261. **Manfred** regained southern Italy (1255) and Sicily (1256), was crowned king of Sicily (1258), and after the Sienese (Ghibelline) victory over Florence at Montaperto (1260) almost dominated Italy; Alexander IV's peace offers were rejected by Manfred (1261).

1257. **Double election in Germany** of two foreigners: **Richard of Cornwall** (brother of Henry III of England, brother-in-law of Frederick II), and **Alfonso X** of Castile.

1266. **Charles of Anjou** (brother of Louis IX of France), accepting Urban IV's offer (1262) of the Sicilian crown under papal suzerainty, invaded southern Italy in accordance with papal plans and with his own ambitions to create a Mediterranean empire. He defeated Manfred, who fell in the battle (**Benevento,** 1266), ending any hope of a native ruler for Italy.

1268. **Conradin** (Conrad IV's son, aged 15), called from Germany by the Italian Ghibellines, was defeated at **Tagliacozzo,** betrayed to Charles of Anjou, and beheaded at Naples with at least the tacit approval of Pope Clement IV. European public opinion was shocked, and Henry III of England and Louis IX of France were aroused. The heir of the house of Hohenstaufen was Constance, daughter of Manfred, whose husband, Pedro III of Aragon, was destined to become the first Aragonese king of Sicily (1282-1285) *(p. 303)*.

The imperial title remained (1268-1806) an appendage of the German monarchy, but as the Germans were little interested in the title the way to the imperial throne was opened to ambitious foreigners. The bitter struggle of the Hohenstaufens and the popes, followed by removal of the Papacy to French soil, alienated the German people from the Roman popes and bred a lasting suspicion of the Latin Church that bore fruit in the nationalism of the Reformation.

The princes of Germany, busy consolidating their own power, were not eager to elect a king, and there was no election until Pope Gregory X, alarmed at the progress of Charles of Anjou and the degeneration of Germany, which reduced papal revenue and indirectly strengthened France, and needing an imperial leader for the crusades, threatened to name an emperor.

SIGNIFICANT ELEMENTS IN 13TH-CENTURY GERMANY

I. **Great tenants-in-chief:** (1) Four ancient princely houses: the **Ascanians** (Brandenburg and eastern Saxony with the ducal title); the **Welfs** (Brunswick); the **Wittelsbachs** (Upper Bavaria, the County Palatine of the Rhine, Lower Bavaria); the **Wettins** (Saxony after the 15th century); (2) **Ottokar,** king of the Slavic kingdom of Bohemia (1253-1278), with claims to Austria, Styria, Carinthia, Carniola.

II. **Great ecclesiastical tenants-in-chief:** especially in the Rhineland (notably the archbishops of **Mainz, Trier,** and **Köln**).

III. **Three minor houses** about to emerge into importance: (1) **Luxemburgs,** (2) **Hapsburgs,** (3) **Hohenzollerns.**

IV. **Lesser tenants-in-chief** (the so-called *Ritterschaft*), who regarded the central power as their defense against the great princes.

V. **Imperial cities** (*Reichsstädte*), growing richer and more powerful and disposed to support the

crown against the princes. Tendency of the cities to organize as leagues.

The informal (until the 14th century) constitution of the German monarchy: (1) Election of the king (originally by tribal chieftains) devolved upon the tenants-in-chief, then upon a group of them; election to be followed by ratification by the others. In the 13th century the group election became final election and was confined to a body of **seven electors** (of varying personnel).

(2) The ancient feudal *Reichstag* (*curia regis*) became (in the 13th century) the German Diet (equivalent to parliament or the estates-general) divided into two houses: princes and electors. Its functions remained vague and amorphous. Towns were admitted in 1489.

The great ecclesiastical states of the Rhineland and their feudal satellites reached the zenith of their power in the 13th century, and strove to maintain their position in the face of the rising lay states to the east (Saxony, Brandenburg, Austria, and Bohemia) by electing to the monarchy feeble princes who could pay well for election and would remain amenable. The lay states became dynastic principalities primarily concerned with their own fortunes and anti-clerical in policy.

Epic poetry flourished in the Middle High German period, in national epics such as the *Nibelungenlied* (c. 1160) and *Gudrun* (c. 1210-1220); court epics, the romance of chivalry, as sung by **Hartmann von Aue, Wolfram von Eschenbach** (c. 1200), **Gottfried von Strassburg** (*Tristan*), and **Conrad von Würzburg** (1220-1287). The art of the *Minnesang* reached its peak with **Walther von der Vogelweide** (c. 1165-1230) and **Neidhart von Reuenthal** (c. 1215-1240).

(1) *The Teutonic Knights, 1190-1382*

1190-1191. **Crusading origin.** Merchants of Lübeck and Bremen founded a hospital at Acre which soon became attached to the German church of Mary the Virgin in Jerusalem.

1198. The brethren of this hospital were raised to a military order of knighthood (as the *Order of the Knights of the Hospital of St. Mary of the Teutons in Jerusalem*) by the Germans gathered for Henry VI's crusade. Henceforth membership in the order was open only to Germans, and knighthood only to nobles. Pope Innocent III gave them the rule of the Templars. Headquarters were successively at Acre (1191-1291), Venice, and (after 1309) Marienburg, clear evidence of the new orientation of the Knights. Intense rivalry existed between the order and the Templars and Hospitalers in the Holy Land until the failure of the crusades turned them to other fields of action. The robes of the Teutonic Knights were white with a black cross.

Reconstitution of the order and **transfer to the eastern frontier** of Germany. The eastward advance (*Drang nach Osten*) of the Germans, begun under Charlemagne, had never wholly ceased, and colonization with Netherlandish farmers and German merchants, coupled with Cistercian efforts during the days of Adolf of Holstein, Albert the Bear (self-styled margrave of Brandenburg), and Henry the Lion of Saxony, established the Germans firmly in Mecklenburg and Brandenburg. Lübeck (founded 1143) early became an important commercial center. The foundation of Riga (1201), as a crusading and missionary center, the establishment of the Livonian *Brothers of the Sword,* and an influx of Westphalian nobles and peasant immigrants insured the continued advance of Germanization and the progress of Christianity (largely under Cistercian auspices) in Livonia. The defeat of the Danes at Bornhöved (1227) by the combined princes of North Germany, cost them Holstein, Lübeck, Mecklenburg, and Pomerania, leaving only Estonia to Denmark. The Poles had already begun the conversion of the Prussians and East Pomeranians.

1210-1239. Under **HERMANN VON SALZA,** the first great grand master, the order, at the invitation of Andrew of Hungary, was established (1211-1224) in Transylvania as a bulwark against the Comans (Cumani) until their progress alarmed the Hungarian monarch.

Hermann was an intimate friend of Emperor Frederick II, and was the real founder of the greatness and prosperity of the (still relatively poor and insignificant) order.

1226. By the **Golden Bull of Rimini,** Frederick laid down the organization of the order (on Sicilian lines) and prepared the Knights for a new career as pioneers of Germanization and as Christian missionaries on the eastern frontier. Frederick repeatedly made them generous gifts, used them for his own crusade, and employed individual knights on important missions. The grand master was given the status of a prince of the empire.

Organization of the order. Districts, each under a commander; a general chapter, acting as advisers to the grand master; five chief officers; the grand master elected for life by the Knights. The order was nominally under the pope and the emperor, but in the days of its might only strong popes exerted any influence.

1229. The call of Prussia. (The name *Prussia* is probably derived from a native word *Prusiaskai* and not from *Bo-Russia*.) An appeal (1225-1226) from Conrad of Masovia, duke of Poland, for aid, coinciding with Frederick's reorganization, was accepted by Hermann von Salza, and the Knights embarked on a unique crusade comparable only with that in the Iberian Peninsula, as champions of Christianity and Germanism. Conrad gave (1230) them Kulmerland, and promised them whatever they conquered from the Prussians. Frederick confirmed their rights.

1234. The Knights transferred all their holdings to the pope, receiving them back as fiefs of the church and thus had no other lord than the distant Papacy.

1237. Union with the Livonian Brothers was followed by notable progress in Livonia and plans for the conversion of the Russians from the Greek Church to the Roman, which led to a serious defeat for the order. Courland was also gained and Memel founded (1252) to hold the conquests. Eventually the southern Baltic coast from the Elbe to Finland was opened by the order to the missions of the Church and the trade and colonies of the Germans.

A great era of town foundations (some 80 in all) opened under the order: Thorn (castle, 1231), Kulm (castle, 1232), Marienwerder (1233), Elbing (castle, 1237), Memel (1252), Königsberg (1254), *et al.*

1242-1253. A **Prussian revolt** was put down, and the conquest of Prussia continued with aid from Ottokar of Bohemia, Rudolf of Hapsburg, Otto of Brandenburg.

1260. The **battle of Durben,** a disastrous defeat of the order by the Lithuanians, was followed by another Prussian revolt which had national aspects and was put down with Polish aid. The suppression was marked by deliberate extermination and the virtually complete Germanization of Prussia ensued. Castle Brandenburg was built (1266) and the reduction of Prussia completed (1285).

The order allowed great freedom to the towns (especially after 1233); no tolls were collected, only customs dues. The large commercial towns joined the Hanseatic League *(p. 327).* The Knights were also generous (after 1236) in charters to German (and Polish) nobles, the peasants were well treated, and mass migrations into territories of the Knights became common.

1263. The pope granted the order permission to trade, not for profit, a concession later expanded (by devious means) into full commercial freedom. As a result the order, founded as a semi-monastic crusading society, eventually became a military and commercial corporation of great wealth and selfish aims, and a serious competitor of the very towns it had founded. The Knights escaped the fate of the Templars, though temporarily on the defensive.

Great state was kept at the headquarters in Marienburg, and under Grand Master Winrich (1351-1382) the order was the school of northern chivalry, just as later it became a great cultural influence through the foundation of schools everywhere in its domains and the maintenance of its houses as centers of learning.

(Cont. p. 328.)

Hermann von Salza

(From p. 176)

d. ITALY AND THE PAPACY, 888-1314

[For a complete list of the Roman popes see Appendix IV.]

The Papacy was a local and secular institution until 1048; Italy was without effective native rule.

888-924. Berengar I, last of the phantom "emperors" (vacancy in the empire, 924-962), was the grandson of Louis the Pious. Surviving rival "emperors" were Guido of Spoleto, Lambert his son, and Louis of Provence (901-905). **Raids of Saracens** (c. 889) and **Magyars** (c. 898) into Lombardy; a Saracen stronghold at Freinet controlled the Alpine passes; Saracen settlements in southern Italy, and the **Moslem conquest** (827) **of Sicily** began the isolation of that area; Italian urban life had become almost extinct; the invasions were checked, not by the shadowy monarchs, but by the rise of feudal defenders.

914-963. The **nadir of the Papacy** (the *pornocracy*): the landed aristocracy of Rome, under the leadership of the senator Theophylact, his wife Theodora, and his daughter Marozia (mistress of Pope Sergius III, and mother of Sergius' son John, later Pope John XI) dominated the curia.

928. Marozia, having imprisoned Pope John XI, took control of Rome until her son

932-954. Alberic II assumed power; the *Patrimonium Petri* was a plaything of the **Crescentii** (Marozia's family), who maintained an intermittent supremacy in Rome during the 10th century. The Papacy was without political power or spiritual prestige and the western Church for all practical purposes became a loose organism under its bishops, who gave "national churches" such coherence as they had, and acknowledged a vague kind of allegiance to Rome.

924. Rudolf of (Juran) Burgundy elected king, followed by

926-945. Hugh of Provence.

945. Lothair II (d. 950), Hugh's son and co-regent, was declared sole king, Lothair's rival,

950-961. Berengar II, imprisoned his widow, Adelheid, who appealed (according to tradition) to Otto the Great.

951-952. Otto the Great's first expedition to Italy.

961-964. Otto's second expedition to Italy, in answer to the appeal of the profligate pope, John XII, for protection against Berengar. Otto's coronation at Pavia as king of Italy and his coronation by the pope as Roman emperor, marked the

962. REVIVAL OF THE ROMAN EMPIRE. Otto confirmed his predecessors' grants in the *Patrimonium Petri* (probably with additions), but made careful reservation of the imperial right to sanction papal elections, and treated the pope like a German bishop (i.e. subject to the state). Otto also exacted a promise from the Romans not to elect a pope without imperial consent. He established a precedent by calling a synod at Rome which deposed (963) Pope John XII for murder and other crimes, and selected a (lay) successor, Leo VIII (963-964). This synod opened a period of about a hundred years when the papacy was dominated by the German emperors and by

Pope Sylvester II, 999–1003

the counts of Tusculum, vassals of the emperors, with the title of *patricius* in Rome. In the same period the bishops in the west lost the position they had won in the 9th century, and became increasingly dependent on the kings and feudal nobility, and increasingly secular in outlook. The homage of Pandolf I for Capua and Benevento (967) and his investiture with the duchy of Spoleto mark the beginning of the long imperial effort to include southern Italy in the empire.

964. **Leo VIII** was expelled by the Romans shortly after his election, and **Benedict V** was (964) elected by the Romans without imperial consent.

966–972. **Otto's third expedition to Italy.** Otto held a synod which deposed Benedict. **Pope John XIII** (elected with imperial co-operation) was soon expelled by the Romans, and Otto, after a terrible vengeance on Rome, restored him. Imperial coronation of the future Otto II (967) by John XIII, coronation of Theophano and her marriage to Otto in Rome (972).

980–983. **Otto II's expedition to Italy.** Otto crushed Crescentius I, duke of the Romans, restored Pope Benedict VII (981), and was utterly defeated in his effort to expel the Saracens from southern Italy by a Greco-Moslem alliance (982). Otto nominated **Pope John XIV** (983–984).

983. Great **Diet of Verona.** Remarkable unity of the Italian and German magnates; resolve on a holy war against the Moslems; election of the future Otto III as successor to his father. Venice, already profiting by her Moslem trade, refused ships and defied the emperor.

996. **Otto III,** on his first expedition to Italy deposed the *Patricius,* Crescentius II, and (at the request of the Roman people) nominated as pope his cousin Bruno, **Gregory V** (996–999), the first German pope, an ardent Cluniac. Gregory and Otto compelled Gerbert to yield the archbishopric of Reims to the German Arnulf, and forced the French episcopate to acquiesce. Gregory censured King Robert of France. As the successor of Pope Gregory, Otto named **Gerbert of Aurillac.**

999–1003. SYLVESTER II (Gerbert of Aurillac), the first French pope, a man of humble origin, one of the most learned men of his day (Arabic, mathematics, and science). An intriguer and diplomat who co-operated with Otto in his mystic renewal of the empire; he was a moderate reformer, asserting that simony was the worst evil of the Church.

1012–1046. The **Tusculan popes** were either the relatives or the creatures of the counts of Tusculum: **Benedict VIII** (1012–1024), something of a reformer; **John XIX** (1024–1033), his brother, and **Benedict IX** (1033–1045), a debauchee who sold the Papacy for cash (i.e. the Peter's Pence from England) to his godfather, a priest, **Gregory VI** (1045–1046), who bought the See of Peter in order to reform it. The emperors, preoccupied with German affairs, made only rare visits to Italy.

Notable local efforts were made by the Church to reform itself and society:

(1) Local synods decreed clerical celibacy (e.g. Augsburg, 952; Poitiers, 1000; Seligenstadt, 1023; Bourges, 1031), attacked simony.

(2) Foundation (910) of the **Abbey of Cluny** by William the Pious, duke of Aquitaine, as a reformed Benedictine house, wholly free of feudal control, directly under the Holy See. Centralization of all daughter and affiliated houses (priories) under a single abbot of Cluny; rapid spread of Cluniac organization (France, Lorraine, Germany) and ideas of reform into western Europe: celibacy of the clergy; abolition of lay investiture and of simony.

(3) Gerard, lord of Brogne, founded (923) a monastery on his own estate which became a center of ecclesiastical reforms among existing foundations in Flanders and Lorraine.

(4) **Synods in Aquitaine and Burgundy** (where monarchical opposition to feudal anarchy was weak) pronounced (c. 989) anathema on ravagers of the Church and despoilers of the poor, initiating a long series of clerical efforts throughout Europe to force feudal self-regulation, which go by the name of the **Peace of God.** These decrees, repeatedly renewed and extended, were supplemented (after c. 1040) by the **Truce of God,** an effort to limit fighting to certain days and seasons of the year.

(5) An effort to restore the central authority of the Church by reference to past decrees, of which the most notable were the so-called *Isidorean* (or Forged) *Decretals,* attributed to Isidorus Mercator, and produced (c. 850) by a Frankish cleric. A combination of authentic and forged papal decrees, they aimed to establish the authority and power of the bishops and the position of the pope as supreme lawgiver and judge, and to make him supreme over councils.

(6) Notable increase in new ascetic orders in Italy and monastic schools north and south of the Alps; outstanding individual reformers (e.g. **Peter Damian,** d. 1072; **Lanfranc,** d. 1089; **Anselm,** d. 1109).

ITALY AT THE OPENING OF THE 11TH CENTURY. Sicily was in the hands of the Saracens; Apulia and Calabria under the feeble rule of Constantinople; Gaeta, Naples, Amalfi, were city republics; Benevento, Capua, and Salerno the capitals of Lombard principalities. Norman pilgrims arriving (1016) at the shrine of St. Michael on Monte Gargano began the penetration of the south by Norman soldiers of fortune in the service of rival states: the first permanent Norman establishment was at Aversa (c. 1029); the sons of the Norman Tancred of Hauteville (including Robert Guiscard) appeared (after c. 1035), and their steady advance at the expense of the Greeks led Benevento to appeal for papal protection (1051). Feudal anarchy prevailed in the north.

1027. **Conrad II,** in Italy for his coronation, restored order in the north, reducing the Lombard nobles.

1037. On a second expedition he disciplined Archbishop Aribert of Milan, restored order in the south; his *constitutio de feudis* made Italian fiefs hereditary.

1045–1046. GREGORY VI purchased the papal throne to reform the Papacy, but the end of his reign saw three rival popes (Gregory, Sylvester III, and Benedict IX). All three were deposed by the **Synods of Sutri and of Rome** (1046) under pressure from the reforming emperor, Henry III, who made Suitgar,

The Abbey of Cluny, founded 910, as it appeared in 1220

bishop of Bamberg, pope as **Clement II** (1046–1047), the first of a series of German pontiffs: Damasus II (1048), Leo IX (1049–1054), Victor II (1055–1057), representing strong Cluniac influences. Henry pacified southern Italy, reaffirmed the imperial right of nomination to the Papacy, and left Italy in sound order.

1049–1085. Restoration of the independence of the Papacy, resumption of papal leadership in the Church and of spiritual supremacy in the west.

1049–1054. LEO IX (Bruno of Toul, a kinsman of Henry III) began the identification of the Papacy with Cluniac reforms, and the restoration of the spiritual primacy of the Holy See. He insisted on his own canonical election to the papal throne, reorganized the chancery on the imperial model, reformed the Church by personal or legatine visitation, giving reform reality in the west. The **Synod of Rome** (1047) had issued stern decrees against simony and clerical marriage.

1052. Henry III granted the duchy of Benevento to the Papacy.

1053. Leo, in his personal effort to enforce papal rights in the south, was utterly defeated by the Normans at Civitate.

1054. The long doctrinal **controversy with the Greek Orthodox Church,** which really hinged on fundamental divergences between east and west, ended with the final schism between the eastern (Orthodox) and western (Roman) Church *(p. 269)*.

1055–1057. VICTOR II. Elected at the urging of Hildebrand (later Gregory VII), who dominated this pontificate and the following one and who made the Papacy the leader in reform. Beatrice, mother of Matilda, and widow of Count Boniface of Tuscany, married (1054) Godfrey the Bearded, duke of Upper Lorraine, Henry's most dangerous foe in Germany, as Boniface had been in Italy. Henry arrested Beatrice and her daughter Matilda, Boniface's heiress; Godfrey fled; Matilda remained all her life a powerful ally of the Papacy, and kept middle Italy loyal to the popes.

1057–1058. STEPHEN IX (brother of Godfrey the Bearded), a zealous Cluniac. The **Pataria** (c. 1056), a popular movement (the result of a preaching campaign), gained wide currency in the Milan region for its demands of clerical celibacy, the end of simony, and for apostolic simplicity among the clergy. It came into sharp conflict with the bishop and clergy. Peter Damian, sent by the pope, maintained the papal position (1059), and brought the archbishop to terms; there was a later outbreak of the Pataria.

1058–1061. NICHOLAS II.

1059. The **Synod of the Lateran,** by its electoral decree, replaced the vague traditional rights of the Roman clergy in papal elections by an electoral **college of cardinals:** the prerogative voice in the election went to the seven cardinal bishops; the cardinal clergy represented the clergy and people at large; a Roman prelate (if worthy) was to be preferred; the election to be at Rome if possible. Henry's rights were provided for, but the provision seems to have been personal rather than general.

1059. Under Hildebrand's influence an alliance was made with the Norman, Richard of Aversa, and Nicholas after exacting an oath

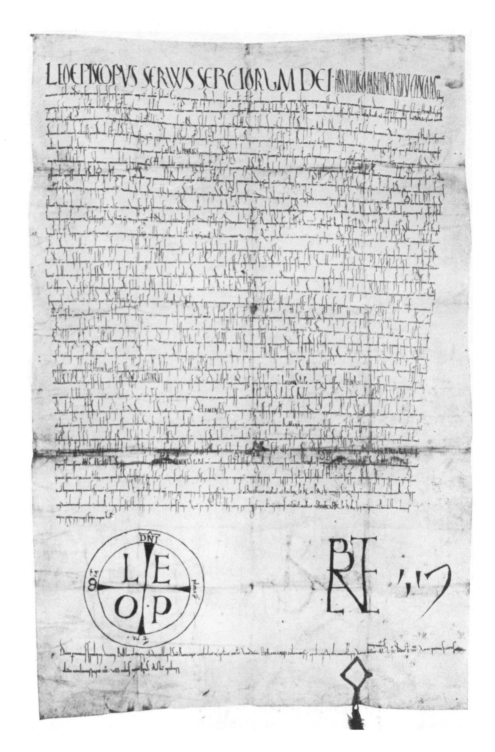

Bull of Pope Leo IX, November 16, 1052

later invested Robert Guiscard with the duchy of Apulia and Calabria, and promised him Sicily if he could conquer it, thereby establishing papal suzerainty over southern Italy, the first great expansion of temporal suzerainty by the popes. The **Synod of Melfi** condemned (1059) the marriage of clergy.

1061–1073. ALEXANDER II. His election without consultation of Henry IV created serious tension; the **Synod of Basel** declared the election invalid, and chose an anti-pope. Alexander, on friendly terms with William the Conqueror, blessed the Norman conquest of England.

1071. Robert Guiscard (d. 1085) captured Bari, ending the Greek power in Italy; his capture of Palermo (1072) began the

1072–1091. Norman conquest of Sicily. Roger I (d. 1101) succeeded Guiscard as lord of southern Italy (except Capua, Amalfi, and papal Benevento).

1073–1085. GREGORY VII (Hildebrand). Short, corpulent, with glittering eyes, the son of an Italian peasant educated at Rome under strong Cluniac influence. Inspired by Gregory the Great, Gregory VI, and the study of the Decretals, he was neither an original thinker nor a scholar, but was intensely practical and

Pope Gregory VII (woodcut from 1592)

of lofty moral stature. After a brilliant career in the Curia he was acclaimed pope by the Romans before his election. German bishops protested the election, and Gregory postponed his consecration, awaiting Henry's decision in a sincere effort to live up to his ideal of perfect co-operation between pope and emperor in the interest of peace, reform, and the universal monarchy of the Papacy. His program was summed up by his *Dictatus,* an informal memorandum which asserted: (1) the Roman Church has never erred, can never err; (2) the pope is supreme judge, may be judged by none, and there is no appeal from him; (3) no synod may be called a general one without his order; (4) he may depose, transfer, reinstate bishops; (5) he alone is entitled to the homage of all princes; (6) he alone may depose an emperor.

1075-1122. THE INVESTITURE STRUGGLE. Vindication of the spiritual supremacy and leadership of the Papacy *(p. 227).*

The Emperor Henry IV after his Saxon victory forgot his promises of reform in Germany. The **Synod of Rome** (1075) passed severe decrees against simony, clerical marriage, and (for the first time) against lay investiture, providing deposition for clerical offenders, excommunication for laymen. Gregory's letter of remonstrance and rebuke to Henry was ignored, and Henry, on the urging of the German bishops, called a **Synod at Worms** (1076). This synod deposed Gregory. Henry's first excommunication and the so-called humiliation at Canossa (1077) profited neither party; Henry's second deposition (1080) was without serious effect. After a series of invasions (1081-1084), Henry entered Rome and was crowned by his anti-pope, only to be expelled by Gregory's Norman ally, Robert Guiscard, with a motley army which included Saracens; the atrocity of the Norman sack made it impossible for Gregory to remain and he died a virtual exile, almost a prisoner of his allies at Salerno, leaving Henry and his anti-pope master of Rome for the time.

Gregory was on excellent terms with William the Conqueror and responsible for Alexander's blessing of the Conquest (1066), but William, true to the Norman conception of strong monarchy, ignored Gregory's pressure to make England a fief of the Papacy, and forbade the circulation of papal bulls in England without his permission. Gregory asserted papal suzerainty over Hungary, Spain, Sardinia, and Corsica. After a vacancy of a year, a close friend of Gregory was elected pope, **Victor III** (1086-1087), an aged, unwilling pontiff, soon driven from Rome by Henry's partisans.

1088-1099. URBAN II. A Frenchman of noble blood, long intimate with Gregory; handsome, eloquent, learned, he continued Gregory's policy of maintaining the complete independence of the Papacy and vigorous opposition to the emperors. Urban arranged the marriage of Countess Matilda and the son of the (Welf) duke of Bavaria (1089).

Henry invaded northern Italy successfully, but Matilda held out in the hills; Urban, profiting by the anarchy in Germany, urged Henry's son Conrad to a revolt (1093) which was taken up by half of Lombardy. Urban

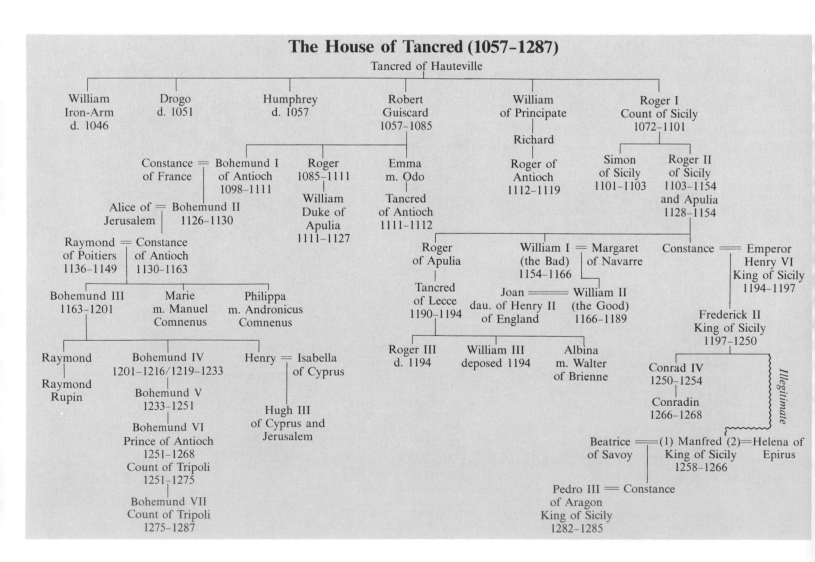

The House of Tancred (1057-1287)

Tancred of Hauteville

- William Iron-Arm d. 1046
- Drogo d. 1051
- Humphrey d. 1057
- Robert Guiscard 1057-1085
- William of Principate
- Roger I Count of Sicily 1072-1101

Constance of France = Bohemund I of Antioch 1098-1111

Roger 1085-1111

Emma m. Odo

Richard → Roger of Antioch 1112-1119

Simon of Sicily 1101-1103

Roger II of Sicily 1103-1154 and Apulia 1128-1154

Alice of Jerusalem = Bohemund II 1126-1130

William Duke of Apulia 1111-1127

Tancred of Antioch 1111-1112

Raymond of Poitiers 1136-1149 = Constance of Antioch 1130-1163

Roger of Apulia

William I (the Bad) 1154-1166 = Margaret of Navarre

Constance = Emperor Henry VI King of Sicily 1194-1197

Bohemund III 1163-1201

Marie m. Manuel Comnenus

Philippa m. Andronicus Comnenus

Tancred of Lecce 1190-1194

Joan dau. of Henry II of England = William II (the Good) 1166-1189

Frederick II King of Sicily 1197-1250

Raymond

Raymond Rupin

Bohemund IV 1201-1216/1219-1233

Henry = Isabella of Cyprus

Roger III d. 1194

William III deposed 1194

Albina m. Walter of Brienne

Conrad IV 1250-1254

Bohemund V 1233-1251

Hugh III of Cyprus and Jerusalem

Conradin 1266-1268

Bohemund VI Prince of Antioch 1251-1268 Count of Tripoli 1251-1275

Beatrice of Savoy = (1) Manfred (2) = Helena of King of Sicily Epirus 1258-1266

Illegitimate

Bohemund VII Count of Tripoli 1275-1287

Pedro III of Aragon King of Sicily 1282-1285 = Constance

at the **Synod of Piacenza** (1095) renewed the decrees against simony and clerical marriage, added a ban on clerical homage to laymen, and received the appeal of the Byzantine emperor for help against the Turks at the **Synod of Clermont** (1095). Urban excommunicated King Philip I of France for adultery, and proclaimed the **First Crusade,** directing his appeal to the nobles and peoples rather than the monarchs, most of whom were hostile to the Papacy. On a visit to southern Italy Urban made Roger of Sicily his legate (1098), thus exempting him from the visits of an ordinary legate. At the **Synod of Bari,** Urban was as much interested in keeping the papal leadership in the crusade as he was in the debates on the procession of the Holy Ghost. The First Crusade was the first great victory for the reformed Papacy; the papal dominance of the military effort to defend Christendom is significant of the new prestige of the Papacy and the decline of the emperors.

1099-1118. PASCHAL II renewed the excommunication of Henry IV; intrigued with Henry, his son; Anselm waged the investiture battle in England (1103-1107), ending in a compromise (1107), followed almost at once by the lapse of lay investiture in France (formerly one of the worst offenders). Paschal's humiliating renunciation (1111) of papal fiefs and secular revenues, his repudiation by his clergy, and his arrest by Henry V made a much more profound impression in Europe than Canossa. Paschal recalled (1112) his concessions.

1115. The **Countess Matilda,** having made a donation (1086 and 1102) of her allodial lands (the second great addition to papal holdings) to the Papacy (subject to free testamentary disposition), willed them at her death (1115) to Henry V, who came and occupied the Matildine lands (1117), destined to be a bone of contention between the popes and emperors for a century.

1118-1119. GELASIUS II was forced to flee Rome; Henry V appointed his own pope; Gelasius, having excommunicated (1118) Henry, was finally driven to France.

Pope Innocent II

1119-1124. CALIXTUS II, a Burgundian, related to half the rulers of Europe and a skilled diplomat, arranged the **Concordat of Worms** (1122), which closed the investiture controversy with a compromise. The **Synod of Reims** (1119) renewed the decrees against simony, clerical marriage, and lay investiture, as well as the excommunication of Henry V.

1130-1138. **Papal schism.** Precipitated by the corrupt election of the (Cluniac) Cardinal Pierleone (son of a rich converted Jewish banker of Rome), as **Anacletus II** (1130-1138), and the hostility of the rival houses of Corsi and Frangipani. The rival pope, **Innocent II** (1130-1143), supported by Bernard of Clairvaux and most of Europe, was given military support by Lothair in return for confirmation of his rights under the concordat of 1122, imperial coronation, and investiture with the Matildine lands. Anacletus confirmed Roger II's title as king in return for his support.

1139. The **Second Lateran Council** (the tenth general council in the west) was attended by a thousand bishops. It marked the end of the schism.

1143. The **Commune of Rome** established in opposition to the non-Roman pope, it defied three feeble popes (Celestine II, Lucius II, Eugene III). **Arnold of Brescia,** pupil of Abelard, emerged as the eloquent leader with bitter denunciations of clerical wealth and papal bloodshed and burning appeals for a return to apostolic poverty and simplicity. Temporary restoration of the ancient Roman state, appeal to the emperor's protection. **Ber-**

nard of Clairvaux agreed with Arnold's indictment (cf. *De Consideratione,* addressed to Pope Eugenius), but saw salvation for the Church in purification from within, not in diminution of its great powers, and opposed Arnold as he had Abelard.

1147-1149. The Second Crusade *(p. 274).*

1154-1159. Adrian IV (Nicholas Breakspear, the only English pope). Son of a poor man, learned, kindly, of high character, he had risen by his own merits; Roman anarchy ended by a stern interdict. Arnold expelled; alliance with **Frederick Barbarossa** against William, king of Sicily; altercation with Frederick over his haughty refusal of ceremonial service to the pope (stirrup episode). The bitter hostility of the Romans to pope and emperor forced a surreptitious coronation and hurried departure from Rome.

1155. Frederick executed Arnold as a heretic, but abandoned Adrian to the Normans and forced him to an independent Italian policy (i.e. alliance with an anti-Norman league of southern barons and with Constantinople) which brought William of Sicily to his knees as the pope's vassal. Adrian accepted the Roman Commune and returned to Rome.

1158-1162. Frederick's second expedition to Italy: the **League of Pavia** (Brescia, Cremona, Parma, Piacenza) supported Frederick; Milan and its league were reduced to submission. The great **Diet of Roncaglia:** Frederick, using Roman law to justify an extreme assertion of imperial rights and a brusque resumption of imperial regalia, substituted an imperial *podestà* for the consuls in the Lombard cities,

Pope Urban II

drove Milan into open revolt (1159–1162), and turned the towns to alliance with the pope. Renewal of the papal alliance with Byzantium; formation of an alliance of Lombard towns under papal auspices.

1159–1181. ALEXANDER III (imperialist anti-popes: Victor IV, Paschal III, Calixtus III). Frederick, citing precedents from Constantine, Charlemagne, and Otto the Great, held a synod at Pavia to adjudicate the claims of Alexander III and Victor IV. Alexander ignored the synod, Victor was recognized. Alexander, after an exile in France, returned and excommunicated Frederick (1165). Renewal of the town leagues (1164); Milan rebuilt, expulsion of imperial *podestàs.*

1167–1168. Frederick's **fourth expedition to Italy:** Alexander's flight to the Normans; Frederick's capture of Rome; renewal of the Lombard League (1168): promises of mutual aid; organization for federal administration; erection of Alessandria, a great fortress city (named for the pope), to guard the passes (1168); Italy virtually independent.

1174. Frederick's **fifth expedition to Italy:** vain siege of Alessandria, complete **defeat at Legnano** (1176); preliminary peace of Venice (1177, the centenary of Canossa).

1179. The **Third Lateran Council** decreed a two-thirds vote of the conclave to be necessary for a valid papal election.

Pope Innocent III

Saint Dominic handing a book containing an account of the true faith to an envoy of the Albigensian crusaders (detail from a painting by Fra Angelico)

1181–1198. A series of unimportant popes, often exiled from Rome by local anarchy until 1188, when papal recognition of the Commune of Rome made peaceful residence again possible.

1183. Peace of Constance: imperial suzerainty in Italy recognized; resumption by the Lombard towns of all regalia they had ever enjoyed, including the right to maintain an army, to fortify, to keep the league or expand it, full judicial jurisdiction, control of their own coinage, abolition of the imperial *podestàs.* The only relic of imperial control was the reservation of the emperor's right to confirm elected consuls, the right of appeal to the imperial court, and the retention of the *fodrum* as a contribution to military needs. The Lombard towns were autonomous for all practical purposes under a very loose system of imperial legates and vicars.

1184. Frederick's **sixth expedition to Italy:** utilizing the split in the Lombard League (after 1181) and local feuds in Tuscany and Bologna, Frederick created a strong imperial party in middle Italy and by a liberal charter (1185) even won over Milan.

1189–1192. The Third Crusade *(p. 275).*

1198–1216. INNOCENT III. A tough-minded Italian patrician of German blood (whose family provided the Church with eight popes), chosen by the cardinals to restore the political power of the Papacy. Animated by an historical mysticism, he looked on Christendom as a single community in which he aimed to combine moral unity with a world-state under papal guidance. He deduced the papal powers from the *Petrine Theory,* the *Old Testament,* the *Donation of Constantine,* and from the duty of the pope to insure justice, maintain peace, prevent and punish sin, and aid the unfortunate. With a clear grasp of essentials, he never lost sight of this concept, but his frequent opportunism destroyed his moral grandeur. Insistence, not on moral or theological, but on historical grounds (i.e. the Translation of the Empire) on the right (claimed by Gregory VII) to pass on imperial elections. A brilliant administrator, he first brought the papal chancery into systematic organization (division into four sections under experts, careful systematized treatment of documents) and made a great collection of canons and decretals. This pontificate was the zenith of the medieval Papacy.

Restoration of the Papal States (Spoleto, Ancona, Romagna regained); many towns succeeded in escaping and keeping their local autonomy. Tuscany: an anti-imperial league under papal auspices; towns like Florence, Lucca, and Siena retained their appropriations of the Matildine lands (a partial foundation of their later power); the rest of the Matildine lands were regained by the Church. Innocent used his position first as protector, then as guardian of Frederick II, in an attempt to alienate Sicily from the Hohenstaufens.

Steady **insistence on a crusade.** The Fourth Crusade *(p. 275)* combined opportunity to attack the infidel with a chance to reunite the Roman and Orthodox Churches; Innocent reconciled himself to the sack of Constantinople by the organization of the new Latin church of Constantinople. The **Albigensian Crusade** *(p. 250),* directed against the spreading heresy of southern France, drenched that region with blood and exterminated one of the most advanced local cultures in Europe, under revolting circumstances of feudal cynicism and clerical intolerance. Simon de Montfort nullified Innocent's efforts to divert the crusaders' ardor to Spain against the Moslems.

Vindication of the political claims of the Papacy. (1) Asserting his right to pass on imperial elections, Innocent rejected the Hohenstaufen claimant (Philip of Swabia) to the imperial crown, ignored the undoubted rights of Frederick, crowned and supported Otto (in return for large promises of obedience to papal authority), and then procured (in alliance with King Philip II) the election of Frederick II. (2) By excommunicating Philip II (1198) he forced him to a formal recognition of his wife Ingeborg, but was coldly rebuffed when he intervened in Philip's struggle with the Angevins. (3) Maintaining the rights of his nominee to the See of Canterbury (Langton), Innocent forced King John of England (interdict, 1208) to cede England to the Holy See and receive it back as a fief (1213). (4) Innocent received the homage as papal vassals of the following states: Aragon, Bulgaria, Denmark, Hungary, Poland, Portugal, Serbia, and brought the Roman Church to its closest approximation to an ideal Christian, universal commonwealth.

The struggle against urban heresy. The Church, long organized to deal with a predominantly rural society, was increasingly out of touch with the rising bourgeoisie and urban proletariat as town life revived and expanded; the anti-clericalism of the cities had become a major problem. The Italian, **Francis of Assisi,** and the Spaniard, **Dominic,** organized the spontaneous response within the Church to this crisis: Francis (d. 1226), a converted gilded youth, as the joyous "troubadour of religion" began preaching the beauties of humbleness, poverty, simplicity, and devotion, of the brotherhood of man, of man and the animals, of man and nature. His cheerful vernacular hymns won tremendous success in the towns of Italy. Founded as a brotherhood, whence the name **Friars Minor** (Minorites, Grey Friars, also Cordeliers), the **Franciscans** won cautious support from Innocent, but not formal ratification as a corporation until 1223.

The second of the mendicant orders, the **Dominican,** born of Dominic's campaign against the Albigensian heresy, was sanctioned by Innocent (1215). Organized as a preaching order, the Dominicans (Friars Preachers, Black Friars, or Jacobins in Paris) patterned their constitution on the Franciscan. These two mendicant orders were not monastic, rural monks, but town-dwellers devoted to preaching and charity. The conduct of the Inquisition was entrusted to them (1233) and their direct influence on education (especially that of the Dominicans) was enormous.

The Fourth Lateran Council, 1215 (woodcut from a 1255 chronicle)

1215. The **Fourth Lateran Council** was the climax of Innocent's pontificate (attended by 400 bishops, 800 abbots and priors, and the representatives of the monarchs of Christendom) and its decrees were of tremendous significance: (1) the Church was pronounced one and universal; (2) the sacraments were decreed the channel of grace, and the chief sacrament, the Eucharist; (3) the dogma of transubstantiation was proclaimed; (4) annual confession, penance, and communion were enjoined; (5) careful rules were made as to episcopal elections and the qualifications of the clergy, and (6) injunctions for the main-

Meeting of St. Francis (left) and St. Dominic (glazed terra-cotta relief by Andrea della Robbia)

Pope Innocent III granting St. Francis the right to preach (fresco by Giotto)

tenance of education in each cathedral and for theological instruction were formulated; (7) the Albigensian and Catharist heresies were condemned; (8) trial by ordeal and by battle forbidden; (9) relic worship regulated, and (10) rules of monastic life were made more rigorous. Finally, another crusade was proclaimed.

1216–1227. HONORIUS III, a high-minded noble of conciliatory disposition who managed to keep on relatively good terms with Frederick II.

1227–1241. GREGORY IX, a relative of Innocent III, aged and fiery, he never relaxed his relentless pressure on Frederick. **Canonization of Francis of Assisi** (1228) and **Dominic** (1234).

Leonardo of Pisa (Fibonacci) (c. 1170–1240), the mathematician, who wrote the first rigorous, systematic demonstration of Hindu mathematics. He also wrote treatises on geometry and algebra, including quadratic and cubic equations.

1243–1254. INNOCENT IV, a canon lawyer.

Supposedly friendly to Frederick, he continued the uncompromising attack on the emperor, and encompassed the final ruin of the Hohenstaufen.

1271–1276. GREGORY X (Visconti), a high-minded pope with three aims: to pacify Italy, to check Charles of Anjou and the rising power of France, and to pacify Germany. At the **Synod of Lyons** (1274) he provided for the seclusion of conclaves to avoid corruption. His successors were occupied with Italian affairs (the war of Naples and Sicily, baronial anarchy in Rome, etc.), and the advancement of their own houses: **Nicholas III** (Orsini) (1277–1280), a foe of Charles of Anjou; **Martin IV** (1281–1285), a puppet of Charles of Anjou; **Honorius IV** (Savelli) (1285–1287); **Nicholas IV** (1288–1292). The rivalries of the great houses were so close that two years were required to elect Nicholas' successor, a hermit dragged unwilling (as a result of Cardinal Malabranca's dream) to the Holy See, **Celestine V** (1294), who never saw Rome, a

puppet of Charles of Anjou and Cardinal Gaetani. Induced (probably) by Gaetani (the midnight voice, a megaphone over the papal couch) he resigned (*The Great Refusal,* Dante, *Inf.* III, 60) and was kept a prisoner by his successor, Boniface VIII (Gaetani).

1294–1534. THE SECULARIZED PAPACY. Absorption in secular politics to the exclusion of spiritual leadership.

1294–1303. BONIFACE VIII (Gaetani). Surpassed all his colleagues in the Sacred College as lawyer, diplomat, and man of affairs. A skeptic in religion, but a believer in amulets and magic, well-read in the pagan classics, he was the last pope to claim the universal authority of the papacy as asserted by Gregory VII and maintained by Innocent III. Addicted to low company, he was not as vicious as contemporary propaganda painted him. Handsome and vain, he substituted on occasion imperial dress and regalia for papal vestments (*I am pope, I am Caesar*). Rude beyond belief, domineering and well-hated, his chief aim was the aggrandizement of the Gaetani family. An intelligent patron of architecture and art: Giotto in Rome.

1295. Bent on regaining Sicily for the papacy, Boniface continued the support of the Angevin claimant, Charles II of Naples, arranged the **Peace of 1295,** by which James of Aragon exchanged Sicily for the investiture of Sardinia and Corsica, and the extinction of French claims in Aragon.

1296. The **Bull** *Clericis laicos,* designed to bring the kings of France and England to accept papal intervention, forbade the payment of taxes by the clergy to lay rulers without papal consent (a vain attempt to maintain a medieval custom in the face of rising national states). Philip IV of France answered with an embargo on the export of bullion; Edward I of England with outlawry of the clergy; both were supported by public opinion expressed in their national assemblies (*pp. 222, 252.*)

1297. Angered by the Colonna, their insistence on the validity of Celestine V's election, their appeal to a general council, and their support of the Aragonese in Sicily, the pope began a veritable crusade which exiled the Colonna (Palestrina, the family stronghold, razed).

Recognition of the rights of Robert (second son of Charles II) in Naples. Beginning of the formation of a Gaetani state as a threat to the barons.

1300. The **GREAT JUBILEE,** zenith of the pontificate, one of the magnificent pageants of the medieval Papacy, managed with tremendous pomp by Boniface; huge donations (raked over public tables by papal "croupiers"); the proceeds intended by Boniface for the second Gaetani state to be formed in Tuscany and for the subjection of Sicily.

1302. Charles of Valois' failure to dislodge Frederick, the Aragonese claimant in Sicily, forced Boniface to the **Peace of 1302** which ended the War of the Sicilian Vespers, left Frederick king, and provided for the ultimate reunion of Naples and Sicily under the Aragonese.

1302–1303. Boniface's defeat and humiliation by the national states.

The **Bull** *Unam sanctam* (1302) marked the

Pope Gregory IX (fresco by Raphael)

Pope Boniface III (detail of fresco by Giotto)

climax of papal claims to superiority over national states and lay rulers. Philip IV (his appeal for a compromise rejected) dispatched Nogaret to bring the pope to French soil for trial by a general council called by Philip.

1303, Sept. 8. The **"Terrible Day at Anagni."** Nogaret and Sciarra Colonna penetrated to the papal apartment, found Boniface in bed, threatened him with death, tried to force his resignation, took him prisoner. Faced with a public reaction against them as foreigners, Nogaret and Colonna fled, and Boniface died shortly of humiliation. The papacy, so lately triumphant over the empire, found itself defeated by a new force, national feeling supporting national monarchy, and the defeat vindicated the claim of the new states to tax clerics and to maintain criminal jurisdiction over them.

1303–1304. BENEDICT XI. Exiled to Perugia by the anarchy in Rome, he promulgated a bull condemning the principals in the affair at Anagni, and died almost immediately (reputedly by poison). The cardinals, almost evenly divided for and against Boniface, after a conclave of ten months, chose a compromise candidate, the French archbishop of Bordeaux, Bertrand de Got (supposed to be a bitter foe of Philip IV), who assumed the name

1305–1314. CLEMENT V. Clement never entered Italy and became friendly (bribed?) to Philip. The **Synod of Vienne** (1311–1312) exonerated Boniface's memory despite Philip's pressure, but Philip had his way with the Templars (1307). Italy was in anarchy, but Clement was bent on returning there as soon as he had made peace between England and France and launched a crusade. To escape Philip, Clement established the papal **court at Avignon.** (Avignon was an enclave in the Venaissin, which was papal territory). *(Cont. p. 305.)*

(1) The Norman Kingdom in South Italy and Sicily, 1103–1194

1103–1154. The Norman count **Roger II of Sicily** (1103–1154) succeeded the Norman duke William of Apulia (1111–1127) and assumed the title of king of Sicily, Apulia, and Capua with the approval of anti-Pope Anacletus II. Excommunicated by Pope Innocent II (1139) for his alliance with Anacletus, he defeated Innocent (1140), took him prisoner, and forced recognition of his title. By skillful diplomacy he prevented a joint invasion of Sicily by the Greek and Roman emperors. Planning a Mediterranean commerical empire, Roger established an extensive North African holding (at its maximum, 1153).

1154–1166. William I, continuing Roger's policy, defeated (1156) the Byzantine allies of Pope Adrian IV and compelled Adrian to recognize his title in Sicily, Apulia, Naples, Amalfi, and Salerno. He supported Pope Alexander III against Frederick I.

1166–1189. WILLIAM II continued this policy, but as he planned a Mediterranean empire and wished a free hand, he welcomed the marriage (1186) of Constance (Roger II's daughter), his heiress, to the future emperor Henry VI. He himself married Joan, sister of King Richard I of England, and intended to lead the Third Crusade as part of his imperial plans. On his death,

1190–1194. Tancred of Lecce (son of Roger, duke of Apulia, the brother of Constance) led a vigorous native resistance to the emperor Henry VI (king, 1194–1197) with the support of the pope and Richard I. Henry reduced Sicily, southern Italy, and part of Tuscany, with the aid of Pisa and Genoa, retained the Matildine lands in central Italy, organized an imperial administration of his holdings, and planned a great empire with Italy as its base. Purely Norman rule ended with Tancred.

The Norman kingship in southern Italy and Sicily was theocratic, on Byzantine lines; the administration was an efficient, departmentalized bureaucracy. Tremendous prosperity and efficient taxation made the Sicilian monarchs perhaps the richest in Europe. Dealing with a cosmopolitan kingdom containing Italian, Greek, and Saracen elements, and needing settlers, the Norman rulers practiced a tolerant eclecticism which provided for wide racial divergences in law, religion, and culture.

Roger II's cosmopolitan court and generous patronage of the learned produced a brilliant circle including the Arab geographer **Edrisi,** **Eugenius,** the translator of Ptolemy's *Optics,* and **Henry Aristippus,** translator of Plato's *Phaedo* and Book IV of Aristotle's *Meteorologica.*

(2) The Development of Italian Towns

No continuous tradition of medieval and classical town government in Italy can be traced. The post-Carolingian anarchy left defense in local hands and rural refuges and town walls were the work of local co-operation. The bishops in Lombardy, traditional guardians of their flocks, with large episcopal and comital powers delegated from the monarchs, played a decisive rôle in communal organization for defense (e.g. Bergamo, 904). The first cases of true urban autonomy were in Amalfi, Benevento, and Naples (1000–1034), a development cut short by the advent of the Normans.

The great urban evolution took place in the north, and particularly in Lombardy, where sworn municipal leagues and urban associations appeared (probably) in the 10th century. In these cities the nobles (since ancient times town-

dwellers for at least part of each year) played an important part, though they were always balanced by the bishops. The emperors, busy in Germany or preoccupied with the popes, made wide grants of regalian rights over local coinage, tolls, customs dues, police powers, and justice (diplomas of Henry I, Lothair II, and Conrad II); there were also considerable delegations of local episcopal powers. Full-fledged communes appeared in the 11th and 12th centuries (e.g. Asti, 1093; Pavia, 1105; Florence, 1138; and Rome itself, by papal charter, 1188). Expansion in the great maritime and commercial republics was rapid (e.g. Pisa's new walls, 1081; Florence's second wall, 1172–1174; Venetian expansion in the Adriatic after the capture of Bari from the Saracens, 1002).

As a result of revolt and negotiation the towns of Lombardy were largely self-governing communes by the opening of the 12th century, and the consulate or its equivalent was in full activity by the end of the century. Typical town organization: an assembly (legislation, declaration of war and peace, etc.); the consuls, core of the magistracy, usually four to twenty in number, serving a one-year term, and chosen from the leading families; the town council and minor magistrates.

The development of the merchant and craft guilds led to a vigorous class warfare as the rising bourgeoisie asserted itself, and brought in the podestate (the *podestà*), a kind of local dictator, during the last quarter of the 12th century.

In Tuscany the towns treated the counts as the Lombards had treated their bishops. Venice, thanks to her peculiar circumstances, evolved a unique commercial oligarchy.

(3) The Rise of Venice, to 1310

Fugitives from the Huns found refuge among the fishing villages of the lagoons; the permanent establishment of Venice seems to date from the Lombard invasion (568). Venetian aid to Belisarius began the formal connection between Venice and Constantinople and a (largely) theoretical connection with the Eastern Roman Empire. The *tribuni maiores* (a central governing committee of the islands) dated from c. 568.

687. Election of the first doge. A salt monopoly and salt-fish trade were the sources of the first prosperity of Venice. Two great parties: (1) pro-Byzantine aristocrats favoring an hereditary doge; (2) democrats friendly to the Roman church and (later) the Franks. Venice offered asylum to the exarch of Ravenna fleeing from Liutprand, and gained trading rights with Ravenna. When Charlemagne ordered the pope to expel the Venetians from the Pentapolis and threatened the settlement in the lagoons, Venice turned again to Constantinople, and in a treaty

810. Charlemagne and Nicephorus recognized Venice as Byzantine territory and accepted her mainland trading rights.

1000. After a 200-year expansion in the Adriatic, Venice completely reduced the Dalmatian pirates, and the doge took the title of duke of Dalmatia. Venice was mistress of the sea route to the Holy Land (commemorated in the wedding of the doge and the sea).

1032. The aristocratic effort to establish an hereditary doge was defeated. Establishment of a council and senate.

1043. The construction of the **church of St. Mark** begun; one of the most notable and influential examples of Byzantine architecture in the west.

1063. The first three crusades established Venetian trading rights in a number of Levantine ports (e.g. Sidon, 1102, Tyre, 1123) and founded the power of a wealthy ruling class. A war with the Eastern Empire (financed by the first known government bonds) was unsuccessful, and led to the institution of a deliberative assembly of 480 members (the germ of the **great council**).

1171. Appointment of the doge was transferred to this council, a complete triumph for the commercial aristocracy.

1198. A coronation oath (in varying terms) began to be exacted of the doge.

1204. In the **FOURTH CRUSADE** (*p. 275*) Venice gained the Cyclades, Sporades, Propon-

Church of St. Mark, Venice, begun in 1043

Port of Tyre, 1123

tis, the Black Sea coasts, Thessalian littoral, and control of the Morea. She administered this vast empire on a kind of feudal tenure, portioning it out to families charged with defense of the seaways. Venice had also gained a further foothold in Syrian ports.

From this period dates a great epoch of building and increasing oligarchic pressure as the government began to become a closed corporation of leading families.

1253-1299. The **STRUGGLE WITH GENOA** for the Black Sea and Levantine trade. The feud of Genoa and Venice was ancient, and trouble began at Acre (1253). The first war with Genoa ended in the complete defeat (1258) of the Genoese.

1261. The Greeks seized Constantinople during the absence of the Venetian fleet; they favored Genoa, turning over Galata to her.

1264. The Venetians destroyed the Genoese fleet at **Trepani,** and soon returned to their old status in Constantinople.

1289-1299. The **advance of the Turks** (capture of Tripoli, 1289, of Acre, 1291) led Venice to a treaty with the new masters of Asia Minor. Genoa met this by an effort to close the Dardanelles, and won a victory (1294) at Alexandretta; Venice forced the Dardanelles and sacked Galata. The Genoese defeated the Venetians at **Curzola** (1299), but Matteo Visconti negotiated an honorable peace (1299) for them.

1284. The **first ducat** was coined.

1290-1300. The perfection of the great galleys. Establishment of the **Flanders galleys** (1317).

1297. The **great council** was restricted in membership to those who had been members within the preceding four years. A commission added other names and then the council was closed to new members (except by heredity). In effect this excluded a large section of the citizens from any share of the government in favor of a narrow, hereditary, commercial oligarchy. Popular reaction led to a revolt (1300), the leaders of which were hanged.

1310. **Tiepolo's rebellion,** the only serious uprising in Venetian history, was crushed. This seems to have been a patrician protest against the extreme oligarchy, and led to the creation of an emergency committee of public safety, the **council of ten,** which soon became permanent (1335).

The **Venetian government** thus consisted of: the great council (i.e. the patrician caste); the senate (a deliberative and legislative body dealing with foreign affairs, peace, war, finances, trade); the council of ten, a secret, rapidly acting body concerned with morals, conspiracy, European affairs, finance, the war department, which could override the senate; the *collegio* or cabinet (the administrative branch); the doge and his council, which, sitting with the ten, made the council of seventeen. *(Cont. p. 317.)*

e. FRANCE, 987-1314

(From p. 182)

[*For a complete list of the kings of France see Appendix VII.*]

987-1328. DIRECT LINE OF THE CAPETIAN HOUSE (the dynasty continued until 1792).

987-996. **HUGH** (called *Capet*, from the cloak he wore as abbot of St. Martin de Tours). At Hugh's accession the kingship was at its nadir; such power as Hugh had was feudal; the royal title meant little more than an hegemony over a feudal patchwork, an ill-defined area called France, and the prestige of ancient monarchical tradition sanctified by ecclesiastical consecration. Hugh's own feudal domain consisted of the Île de France (extending from Laon to Orleans, with its center at Paris) and a few scattered holdings. The great barons of the so-called royal fiefs recognized Hugh as their suzerain, but never did homage nor rendered service. Hugh's special interest was to maintain his control over his chief resources, the archbishopric of Reims and the great bishoprics (Sens, Tours, Bourges) and abbeys of the Île de France, and to wean northeastern France away from the Carolingian and imperial interest. Despite clerical pressure, he avoided submission to imperial suzerainty, a policy that facilitated the demarcation between

(*From p. 181*)

France: The Capetian Kings (987–1328)

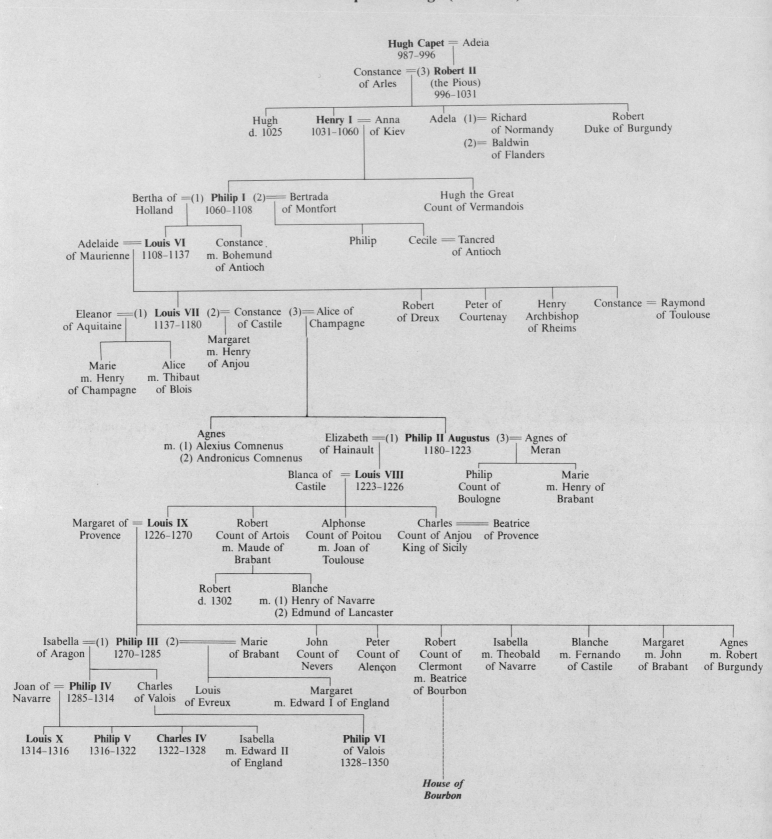

(*Cont. p. 296.*)

The Battle of Hastings, Oct. 14, 1066, panel of the Bayeux Tapestry

France and Germany. In defiance of pope and emperor he forced his own candidate into the archbishopric of Reims. Hugh crowned his son shortly after his own coronation and began a practice (*co-optation*) which the early Capetians continued (until Philip II no longer felt it necessary), thus insuring the succession, and weakening the principle (dear to the feudality) of elective kingship.

996–1031. ROBERT II (the Pious), an active, well-educated, polished, amiable ruler, a good soldier, supported by the duke of Normandy in constant wars against his neighbors, and by the religious houses of Burgundy in attacks on the dukes of Burgundy. The duchy of Burgundy escheated to the crown, and was given to Robert, a younger son. Robert the Pious, like his father, supported the Cluniac reformers. Minor territorial additions signify the revival of royal power.

1031–1060. HENRY I, an active, brave, indefatigable ruler, whose reign nevertheless marked the lowest ebb of the Capetian fortunes. The rebellion of his brother Robert, supported by Eudes, count of Chartres and Troyes, was put down with the aid of the duke of Normandy, and Robert was pacified by the grant of the duchy of Burgundy (which continued in his family until 1361). Henry supported the duke of Normandy (1047), but led a coalition against him two years later, and was defeated. He boycotted the pope and his synod at Reims, and, like his son and successor, opposed the reform movement in the church. The *prévôts* were introduced to administer justice and taxation in the royal lands. The kingdom of Burgundy passed (1032) to the empire.

1035–1066. RISE AND EXPANSION OF NORMANDY. William I became duke (1035) and until 1047 faced a series of baronial revolts. With the aid of his feudal suzerain, King Henry of France, William defeated his revolting barons (1047) and razed their castles. The union of Normandy and Maine was completed (1063) against powerful opposition from the counts of Anjou. William's alliance with Henry was broken (1053), and Henry ravaged the heart of Normandy (1058). Normandy was now a fully developed feudal state under firm ducal control. Military service, assessed in knights' fees, was attached to specific pieces of land, no castles could be built or maintained without ducal license. Private warfare and blood feud were strictly limited. Coinage was a ducal monopoly. The legal jurisdiction of the duke was wide, local government was under the duke's representatives (the *vicomtes*), who commanded the local forces, guarded the castles, did justice, collected the revenue (a large part of which was cash). The Church had been revivified, but here too the duke was supreme, naming bishops, most of the abbots, and sitting in provincial synods.

Norman **relations with England** had grown closer, and this tendency culminated (1002) in the marriage of Duke Robert's sister Emma with King Ethelred. The son of this marriage, Edward the Confessor, educated largely at the Norman court, came to the throne of England (1042), and died without heirs (1066). The witan at once elected Harold, Earl Godwin's son. **William I** of Normandy with a volunteer force (perhaps 5000–6000) collected from Normandy and the Continent, defeated Harold in the **Battle of Hastings** (Oct. 14) and was crowned king of England on Christmas Day (*p. 192*). The *Bayeux Tapestry* forms a unique and probably contemporary record of this expedition.

1060–1108. PHILIP I, enormously fat, but active and vigorous; excommunicated and unpopular with the clergy as the result of an adulterous marriage (1092) and because of his hostility to clerical reform. He defeated (1079) Duke William of Normandy (the Conqueror) and steadily supported **Robert Curthose,** William's son, against Anglo-Norman pressure. Systematic expansion of the resources of his house, and regular annexations to its domains in the face of stubborn feudal resistance. The *Chanson de Roland,* the national epic of France, was probably composed during this reign.

The growth of feudalism tended to diminish anarchy and to improve the general security of life, and ultimately led to decisive economic recovery in western Europe, a trend toward urban economy, and the emergence of a bourgeoisie who were beginning to accumulate capital. This development was a determining factor in the economic, social, and monarchical evolution of the 13th century. The **Peace of God** in the 10th century, and the **Truce of God** (first mentioned, 1027), promoted by the Church with Capetian support, were significant rather than effective attempts to reduce warfare.

1108–1328. A period in which the Capetians reduced the great feudatories north of the Loire and began the transformation of the vague ecclesiastical, judicial, and military rights derived from Carolingian tradition into royal powers over the French people as a whole.

1108–1137. LOUIS VI (the Fat). A brave soldier, of tremendous physique, intelligent, affable, avaricious, but liked by the peasantry, commercial class, and clergy, the first popular Capetian. Consolidation of his Norman frontier (wars with Henry I of England: 1109–1112; 1116–1120), and steady reduction of his lesser vassals as far as the Loire. His charters to colonizers (*hôtes*) of waste lands, and frequent if inconsistent support of the communes, especially on the lands of the Church and the baronage, began the long alliance of the Capetians with bourgeois interests; Louis's *charter of Lorris,* widely copied in town charters, was a significant sign of the great **urban development** setting in all over Europe in this period. As protector of the Church, Louis gained a foothold in the lands of his vassals. Careers

Geoffrey, count of Anjou (Limoges champlevé enamel from his tomb in Le Mans, c. 1155)

at court were opened to talented clergy and bourgeois: great influence of **Suger** (see below). Louis's compromise with the Church over feudal patronage and investiture initiated the king of France's effective rôle as *eldest son of the Church.* He was the first Capetian to intervene effectively outside his own feudal lands. He defeated the alliance of Henry I of England with the Emperor Henry V, and stopped (1124) a German invasion. The marriage (1137) of his son Louis to Eleanor, heiress of William X of Aquitaine (i.e. Guienne [*Aquitania Secunda*] and Gascony), marked the Capetian effort to balance the Anglo-Norman menace in the north by additions of territory south of the Loire. The Anglo-Norman danger had appeared in aggravated form when in 1129 Geoffrey became count of Anjou, Maine, and Touraine. He had in 1128 married Matilda (daughter of Henry I of England), and proceeded (1135) to conquer Normandy.

DEVELOPMENT OF ROYAL ADMINISTRATION under the early Capetians. The court of the king, usually known as the *curia regis,* consisting as it did of magnates, royal vassals, and court officials (mainly chosen from the baronage), was essentially feudal in spirit and tradition. Meeting at royal summons and relatively frequently, its early duties were undifferentiated, its functions judicial, advisory, legislative. The royal administration was in control of the great officers of the crown whose aim was to concentrate power in their own hands, a process which culminated in a virtual monopoly of such power by the **Garlande family** early in the 12th century. Louis VI, after a struggle (1128–1130), terminated their dominance, and thenceforth the Capetians relied increasingly on lesser and more docile nobles, clerics, and bourgeois men of affairs. Such men were career men devoted to the crown rather than to feudal ambitions, and their presence in the *curia regis* began the differentiation of its functions and its subjection to royal rather than feudal influences. Most notable of these careerists was **Suger,** Louis's old tutor, a cleric of humble origin, who became abbot of St. Denis (1122). An able statesman, his influence was decisive in the reign of Louis and his son Louis VII. Suger began (c. 1136) the new abbey church of St. Denis, the first edifice wholly Gothic in design.

1100–1400. RISE OF TOWNS. The economic revival of western Europe was paralleled by a resumption of town life and development throughout the west, which was most notable in France, where the movement reached its apogee in the 12th century, before the consistent advance of the Capetian monarchy began to retard its progress. Types of town development were by no means uniform, but important general categories can be distinguished: (1) The *commune* proper, a collective person endowed with legal rights and powers (e.g. financial, judicial), able to hold property. As a feudal person the commune could have vassals, render and exact homage, establish courts for its tenants, and even declare war and make treaties. Symbols of its independence were the belfry, town hall, and seal. Typical communes of northern France and Flanders were the *communes jurées* (e.g. Beauvais, St. Quentin [chartered before 1080], Rouen [chartered 1145], and Amiens [chartered in the 12th century]); in southern France the corresponding communes were called *consulates,* which enjoyed even greater rights than in the north, especially in Roussillon, Provence, Languedoc, Gascony, and Guienne. In the south the nobles took an active part in the formation of consulates and shared in their government. (2) *Villes de bourgeoisie* (or *communes surveillées*) had elements of communal powers in varying degrees, but lacked full political independence (i.e. they were privileged but unfree). They were found all over France, but especially in the center, and were the prevailing type on the royal domain. Citizens enjoyed specific privileges, but the crown retained judicial and other powers in varying degrees. (3) *Villes neuves* (characteristic of the commercial north) and *bastides* (typical of the south, and usually strongholds) were small rural creations of kings or feudal lords, given a charter from the first, establishing their status. (4) *Peasant associations* and village federations (influential in the north) which sought to define and guarantee the rights of their citizens. Governmentally town development seems to have been hardly the result of conscious effort to introduce a new political dispensation. It was rather an attempt to establish and define the rights of non-feudal groups, and aimed at economic prosperity and personal security. The movement constantly enjoyed royal support, but royal policy toward it was governed by immediate political or financial considerations, and the crown always strove to reduce or control town independence in the interest of its own power. Ultimately monarchy triumphed, but not before the bourgeois groups and the serfs had gained substantial advantages.

1137-1180. LOUIS VII (the Young), not a strong king, but pious and therefore popular with the clergy. He remained under the influence of Suger until the latter's death in 1151. A papal interdict on the royal lands, resulting from Louis's insistence on his feudal rights, led to intervention by Bernard of Clairvaux.

1147. Louis inspired the **Second Crusade** *(p. 274)*. He induced the German king, Conrad III, and Bernard of Clairvaux to join him and, leaving the kingdom in the hands of Suger, he set out for the east. He returned (1149) beaten, humiliated, and estranged from his wife Eleanor, who had accompanied him. The marriage was annulled (1152), probably due to lack of a male heir. This step cost the Capetians the territories of Poitou, Guienne, and Gascony, for Eleanor at once married Henry, duke of Normandy, who in 1151 had succeeded his father as count of Anjou, Maine, and Touraine. The acquisition of Eleanor's domains made Henry master of more than half of France and put him in a position to bring pressure on the holdings of the king of France both from the north and the south. When Henry in 1154 became king of England, the so-called Angevin Empire extended roughly from the Tweed to the Pyrenees.

1165-1170. Louis supported **Thomas Becket** *(p. 216)* against Henry II of England, and was saved from Henry's wrath only through the mediation of the pope, Alexander III, a refugee in France against whom the Emperor Frederick had raised an anti-pope. It was in Louis's interest to support the anti-imperial party, because of the emperor's pressure upon Burgundy.

During the reign of Louis VII the appointment of non-feudal experts to the *curia regis* continued, and their influence on the adminis-

Louis VII

tration began to be decisive. Grant of town charters also continued. The period was, moreover, one of marked

Cultural progress: The guild of masters (germ of the University of Paris) was recognized (c. 1170) and a number of eminent scholars appeared on the scene: **St. Bernard of Clairvaux** (1091-1153), member of the Cistercian Order, a great preacher, fervent reformer, and dominant spiritual figure of the west; **Roscellinus** (died c. 1121), champion of nominalism; **Anselm** (d. 1109), abbot of Bec, later archbishop of Canterbury, champion of realism; **Peter Abélard** (d. 1142), eminent master at Paris (after about 1115), supporter of conceptualism, a middle ground in the great controversy over universals. Abélard's *sic et non* presented without solution the conflicting the-

ological arguments on 158 important problems. **John of Salisbury** (d. 1180), bishop of Chartres, favored the humanistic rather than the dialectical approach to knowledge. Before the rise of the University of Paris, Chartres was the cultural center where Ptolemaic astronomy and Aristotelian logic were taught. **Thierry of Chartres** put forward a rational explanation of the creation, within the Mosaic framework, as well as a cosmology based on the Aristotelian pattern. **Peter Lombard,** bishop of Paris (1159), in his *Sententiae* offered a cautious solution of theological and philosophical problems that became a standard text of the Paris schools. In literature the period produced the *chansons de geste* such as *Chanson de Roland,* the epics of poets like Chrétien de Troyes, and the troubadour lyrics.

1180-1223. PHILIP II (Augustus). He began his rule at fifteen and had no time for education (he knew no Latin). A calculating realist, perhaps the outstanding figure of his time, he was the consolidator of the monarchy and the founder of the organized state. As the "maker of Paris" he paved the streets, walled the city, and began the building of the Louvre.

1180. A six-year alliance with King Henry II of England enabled Philip to defeat Philip of Artois and the counts of Champagne, to crush a baronial league against him, and to gain recognition for his title to Artois and Vermandois. Philip intrigued with the sons of Henry, welcomed the rebellious Richard (1187), and, joining him, defeated Henry (1189), who died the same year.

1191. Philip, under pressure of public opinion, joined King Richard on the **Third Crusade;** eclipsed by Richard, he quarreled with him, returned to France, and intrigued against him with John during his (Richard's) captivity (1192-1194).

1194-1199. Richard, in a pitiless war of venge-

Death of Richard I, 1199

ance, built Château Gaillard on the Seine and restored the Angevin power in northern France.

1198. Excommunicated by Pope Innocent III for his divorce of Ingeborg of Denmark, Philip was forced by public opinion to a reconciliation, but sharply refused Innocent's offer of mediation with John, who succeeded Richard (1199).

1202–1204. The final duel with John for, and conquest of, the Angevin lands north of the Loire. On King John's refusal to stand trial as Philip's vassal on charges by Philip's vassal, Hugh of Lusignan, Philip declared John's French fiefs forfeited (1203), and supported John's nephew, Arthur of Brittany. The murder of Arthur (1203) cost John his French support, Château Gaillard was lost (1204), Normandy and Poitou followed, and Philip emerged master of the Angevin lands north of the Loire.

New royal officials, the *baillis* (*sénéchaux* in the south), paid professionals (often Roman lawyers), superseded the now feudalized *pré-*

Battle of Bouvines, July 27, 1214

Knight of the royal army

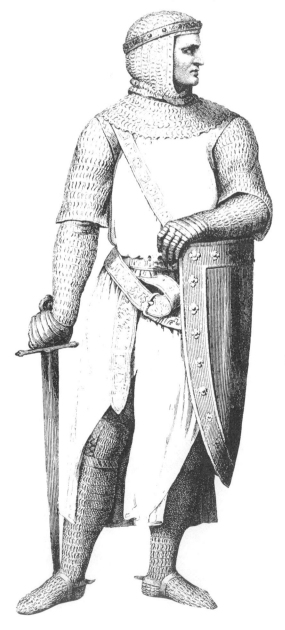

vôts as the chief local administrators (financial, judicial, military) on the Capetian lands (c. 1190). In the course of the 13th century baillis began to be assigned to regular districts (*baillages*), but they continued responsible to and removable by the king. As the royal domain expanded, royal administration was extended to it, and the foundation laid for a national, specialized, professional system.

Philip, henceforth master in the north, left the conquest of the south to his successors and devoted himself to statecraft rather than war. He played the barons off against each other, used his position as protector of the Church to weaken them further, and sought the support of the towns and rich bourgeoisie as a balance to the feudality. Part of this process involved the systematization of the royal finance, the regular exaction of feudal aids and obligations due to the crown as well as the systematic collection of customs, tolls, fines, and fees, though as yet there was no such thing as taxation in the modern sense. The levy of the Saladin tithe (1188) was, however, a forerunner of true taxation. Philip's reign also saw the formation of a semi-permanent royal army.

1208–1213. The Albigensian-Waldensian Crusade. The Albigensians (Catharists of Albi) and the Waldensians (followers of Peter Waldo) represented originally a reaction of the lower classes against clerical corruption, but the movement was soon espoused by the nobles, who saw in it a chance to appropriate church lands. Innocent III, after a vain appeal to Philip, proclaimed a crusade against these heretics. Philip took no direct part in the action, but allowed his northern vassals to begin the penetration of the south and thus prepare the way for the advance of the Capetian power. **Simon de Montfort** (the elder), a baron of the Île de France, emerged as the leader of the crusaders. His **victory at Muret** (1213) sealed the fate of the brilliant Provençal culture, of the leading southern barons, and of the heretics. After a long chapter of horrors the conquest was finally completed in a campaign by Louis VIII (1226). In the reign of Louis IX

the county of Toulouse passed under Capetian administration and the royal domain was extended to the Mediterranean.

1213–1214. The great **anti-Capetian Alliance** (John of England, Emperor Otto IV, the counts of Boulogne and Flanders, and most of the feudality of Flanders, Belgium, and Lorraine).

1214, July 27. BATTLE OF BOUVINES. Philip, in alliance with Emperor Frederick II, defeated the coalition near Tournai and thereby established the French monarchy in the first rank of the European powers, at the same time ruining John of England, assuring Frederick II of the imperial crown, and bringing Flanders under French influence. Militarily speaking the battle was a triumph of Philip's professional cavalry and bourgeois militia over the older infantry.

1223–1226. LOUIS VIII, a pallid reflection of his father. The first Capetian king not crowned in his father's lifetime.

1224. Temporary conquest of the lands between the Loire and the Garonne; the English soon regained all but Poitou, the Limousin, and Perigord (1225).

1226. Renewal of the Albigensian Crusade and Louis's **conquest of the south.** Louis began the dangerous practice of bestowing great fiefs as appanages on the princes of the blood, a practice which later had almost fatal consequences to the monarchy (the case of Burgundy).

1226–1270. LOUIS IX (St. Louis, canonized 1297). The most chivalrous man of his age and the ideal medieval king. Handsome and lofty in character, Louis's careful education prepared him for a unique reign, in which ethics dominated policy. His justice won him national support and made him the arbiter of Europe. His reign was the golden age of medieval France.

1226–1234. Minority of Louis IX and regency of his able and devout mother, Blanche of Castile. With the support of the Church, the royal officials, and the people, Blanche was able to suppress a number of feudal rebellions

(1226–1231). By the **treaty of Paris** (1129) Raymond of Toulouse surrendered, and his heiress was betrothed to Louis's brother, Alphonse. Louis himself was married to Margaret of Provence and thus began the severance of that province from the empire.

233. As part of the campaign against heresy, Pope Gregory IX granted independent authority to investigate heresy to the **Dominicans,** requiring the bishops to co-operate with them. Louis later supported the **Inquisition,** despite episcopal objections.

241. Louis induced the Emperor Frederick II to release the prelates and delegates captured off Genoa while en route to a synod at Rome but, without directly attacking the Church, he associated himself with Frederick's grievances against the pope and refused to intervene against the emperor (1247).

242. Invasion of France by Henry III of England, in coalition with the rebellious feudal lords of southern France. The whole movement collapsed and was followed by the final submission of Aquitaine and Toulouse (1243).

244. Louis took the Cross, against his mother's advice, and sailed on his first crusade (1248). His aim was to free Palestine by the capture of Egypt, but the expedition was poorly managed, Louis was captured (1250), and most of his army was put to the sword. Louis himself was ransomed and returned to France.

258. The **treaty of Corbeil,** representing a peaceful adjustment of conflicting claims between France and Aragon, to the advantage of France. Louis's son, Philip, was betrothed to Isabella of Aragon.

259. Treaty of Paris. Louis, in the interest of amity, yielded Perigord and the Limousin to the king of England, despite protests from both provinces. In return he received the renunciation of English claims to Normandy, Maine, Poitou. Henceforth Guienne became distinct from Aquitaine. This pacific gesture displeased opinion in both countries and weakened the French position in the south as the Hundred Years' War approached.

265. Louis permitted his brother, Charles of Anjou, to accept the crown of Sicily, a step which later involved France in Italian problems, with decisive consequences.

270. Louis's second crusade. Probably influenced by Charles of Anjou, who cherished far-reaching Mediterranean ambitions, Louis set out for Tunis. He died of pestilence without accomplishing anything.

Louis's reign was marked by rigorous insistence on inherent royal rights even at the expense of the Church, and despite episcopal protests. Royal justice was notably efficient and was constantly expanded. The right of appeal from feudal to royal courts was clearly established. The old *curia regis* had already become somewhat differentiated: a *chambre des comptes* and a *parlement* (i.e. high court) were already recognizable. Louis introduced the *enquêteurs,* itinerant investigators, to supervise the baillis and sénéchaux, but he made few other administrative innovations. Many of his diplomats, baillis, and other officials were chosen from the royal household, notably from the so-called *chevaliers du roi,* and from the clergy. Assemblies of royal vassals, irregularly held, gave such "national" sanction as there was to royal policy. Louis was the first king to issue *ordonnances* (i.e. legislation)

for the whole realm on his sole authority. By ordonnance he outlawed private warfare, the carrying of arms, and trial by battle as part of the royal judicial process, and extended the royal coinage to the whole realm. By 1270 the communal movement was already in decline and the crown profited by enforcing a more rigorous control over the towns. Only one new charter (to the port of Aigues Mortes) was granted during the reign. The bourgeois oligarchy of the towns got on increasingly bad terms with the lower orders, often reducing the town finances to chaos. Louis took advantage of this state of affairs to introduce a town audit (1262). The country at large was prosperous in this period, but the financing of the two crusades and of the grandiose schemes of Charles of Anjou led to complaints that royal taxation was leading to bankruptcy and formed a bad precedent for Philip IV.

A brilliant **cultural advance** accompanied the general material and political progress of the time of Philip II and Louis IX; perfection of the **French Gothic:** Cathedral of Chartres (c. 1194, Romanesque and Gothic); Amiens (c. 1200); Reims (1210); Louis IX's *Sainte Chapelle;* progress of naturalism in Gothic sculpture. **University of Paris:** foundation charter (1200); regulations of Innocent III (1215); endowment of Robert de Sorbon (hence Sorbonne) in 1257. Advance of **vernacular literature: Villehardouin's** (d. c. 1218) *Conquête de Constantinople* (the first vernacular historical writing); **Chrétien de Troyes** and the Arthurian romances; Goliardic verse (with pagan touch); *fabliaux* (risqué, semi-realistic bourgeois tales); *Aucassin et Nicolette* (a *chante fable* marked by irony and realism); **Jean de Meun's** (d. 1305) completion of William of Lorris's *Roman de la Rose* (a satire on the follies of all classes, especially women and clergy); **Jean de Joinville's** *Histoire du roi Saint Louis* (1309), the first vernacular classic of lay biography. Paris the center of **13th century philosophy:** harmonization of the Greek philosophy, especially Aristotle (newly recovered during the Renaissance of the 12th century in Latin translations, with

Cathedral of Chartres, Romanesque and Gothic

Albertus Magnus

Christian orthodoxy: **Vincent of Beauvais's** (d. 1264) *Speculum Maius* (a compendium of contemporary knowledge); **Albertus Magnus** (a German, d. 1280), chief of the great Dominican teachers in Paris; **Thomas Aquinas** (an Italian, d. 1274), the pupil of Albertus Magnus. Thomas Aquinas' *Summa Theologiae* reconciled reason and religion, completed the integration of the classical learning and the Christian theology, and remains to this day the basis of all Catholic theological teaching. Also at Paris was **Jordanus Nemorarius** (d. 1237), a German, who wrote arithmetical and geometrical treatises as well as working in physics.

1270–1285. PHILIP III (the Bold), a hasty, ill-balanced king, victim of his favorites. The death of Philip's uncle, Alphonse of Poitiers, brought Languedoc under royal sway and established the royal power firmly in southern France (1272). The walls of Carcassonne and Aigues Mortes were built, the latter place giving access to the Mediterranean. Unsuccessful candidacy (1273) of Charles of Anjou for the imperial crown. Crusade (1282) against the king of Aragon, Philip acting as papal champion against the successful rival of the house of Anjou in Sicily.

1281–1285. The pontificate of Martin IV brought to an end an anti-French period of papal policy; papal support of Charles of Anjou's ambitious dreams of Byzantine conquest until the **Sicilian Vespers** *(p. 310)*. There followed another period of papal opposition to French ambitions.

1285–1314. PHILIP IV (the Fair). His reign had a distinctly modern flavor and was marked by ruthless expansion of the royal power and notable consolidation of the monarchy: royal finance superseded the feudal; Roman lawyers (trained at Bologna and Montpellier) rather than clerics dominated the government; papal pretensions were reduced and the national Church made virtually autonomous under royal domination.

1286. Edward I of England did homage for Guienne.

1293. Philip treacherously confiscated Gas-cony, which had been temporarily surrendered by Edward as a pledge, after a Gascon-Norman sea-fight.

1294–1298. War with Edward I over Guienne. Philip announced a war levy on the clergy and followed a protest with a violent anti-papal pamphlet campaign. To finance the war Philip debased the coinage. He first made an **alliance with the Scots** (1295) and excluded English ships from all ports. In 1297 Edward invaded northern France, in alliance with the count of Flanders, but the war was brought to a close by a truce negotiated by Pope Boniface VIII.

1296–1303. Philip's **conflict with Pope Boniface VIII,** who put forward extreme claims to papal supremacy. The bull *Clericis laicos* (1296) forbade secular rulers to levy taxes on the clergy without papal consent. Philip retorted by forbidding the export of precious metals (a serious threat to the papal finances) and by a vigorous propaganda campaign. Boniface, engaged in a feud with the Colonna in Rome and absorbed in Sicilian affairs, gave way and practically annulled the bull (1297). But the great papal jubilee of 1300 was followed by a resumption of the quarrel, culminating in 1302 in the bull *Unam sanctam,* the most extreme assertion of the doctrine of papal theocracy in the Middle Ages. On the **"Terrible Day"** of Anagni (1303, *(p. 243)*, Nogaret and Sciarra Colonna attacked the papal palace, demanded the resignation of the pope, and had a violent scene with Boniface. The death of the aged pontiff followed shortly.

1302. The first well-authenticated convocation of the **estates-general,** including representatives of the towns in their feudal capacity. The meeting was called mainly to insure national support for the king's struggle with the pope.

Philip III

1302, July 11. Battle of the Spurs (at Courtrai), brought about by the troubles in Flanders. Philip had antagonized the count of Flanders by his efforts to penetrate his territory, and the count had turned to Edward I of England for support. The Flemish nobility betrayed him (1300) and he lost both his liberty and his county. But French rule soon alienated the independent burghers and led to the massacre of the French (*Matin de Bruges*) followed by the **battle of Courtrai,** in which the burghers defeated the flower of the French chivalry.

1305. Election of Clement V (a Frenchman) as pope. Clement reluctantly accepted French royal domination, lingered in France after his election, and finally took up his residence at Avignon, thus beginning the **Babylonian** or **Avignonese Captivity** of the Papacy *(p. 305)*. During the captivity (1305–1376) the French monarchy exercised an important influence on the Papacy. Clement was obliged to quash the bulls of Boniface, to absolve the assailants of Anagni, and to support Philip's suppression of the Knights Templar (see below). Philip may properly be called the founder of **Gallicanism** (i.e. of the autonomy of the French Church).

1306. The Jews were arrested, despoiled, and expelled from France.

1307. The **Order of the Knights Templar,** a rich, decadent organization which acted as banker to the popes and was a creditor of Philip, had become almost a state within the state. Philip now launched an attack upon it. He had its lands occupied by royal officers and its property sequestrated. The country was stirred up against the Order by a vigorous propaganda campaign and by an appeal to the estates-general (1308). Clement was obliged to co-operate and the Inquisition was made use of in the trial, the entire affair being conducted with unparalleled ruthlessness and horror (torture freely used to extort confessions).

1312. The Order of the Templars was abolished by the **Synod of Vienne.** Its property was transferred to the Hospitalers (except in Spain and in France, where it passed to the crown). Philip made the Temple treasury a section of the royal finance administration.

New economic and social alignments. The rapid expansion of France, and especially the wars of Philip III and Philip IV against England and Flanders, raised an acute financial problem. Philip IV tried every device to raise money (feudal *aides,* war levies to replace military service, tallage of towns, special levies on clergy and nobles, "loans" and "gifts," the *maltôte* or sales tax, debasement of the coinage, attacks upon the Jews and Templars), but without finding an adequate solution. It was this situation primarily that explains the emergence of the

Estates-General. Levies on the nobles and clergy had long been arranged in meetings of representatives of these two orders; by negotiations between the towns and the royal agent the burghers had been brought to contribute. Provincial estates had been called frequently during the 13th century. The convocation of the estates-general simply meant the substitution of national for provincial or local negotiation, and implied no principle of consent or control over royal taxation. The royal revenue was increased perhaps tenfold between the time of Louis IX and the time of Philip IV, but this meant overtaxation of all classes, harmful effects upon economic life, and estrangement of public opinion. Anti-tax leagues were organized and local assemblies drew up lists of grievances. Philip was obliged to call the estates-general again in 1314, but as the bourgeoisie and the nobility distrusted each other, no effective measures were taken and no permanent constitutional development took place. Characteristic of the period was

Pierre Dubois's *De Recuperatione Sanctae Terrae* (c. 1306), ostensibly an appeal to Philip to undertake a crusade to recover the Holy Land from the Saracens, in reality an extensive program of reform in the interests of stronger national monarchy. Dubois envisaged the formation of a European league to enforce peace through common military action and economic boycott, disputes between parties to be settled by judicial methods. He called also for a system of universal education and for the secularization of Church property.

(Cont. p. 294.)

f. THE IBERIAN PENINSULA, 1037–1284

(From p. 186)

(1) Moslem Spain

1037–1086. THE MULUK AL-TAWA'IF (i.e. *Party Kings*). These were petty dynasties founded on the ruins of the Omayyad caliphate: the Hammudids of Malaga (from 1016 onward) and of Algeciras (1039–); the Abbadids of Sevilla (1031–); the Zayrids of Granada (1012–); the Jahwarids of Córdoba (1031–); the Dhul-Nunids of Toledo (1035–); the Amirids of Valencia (1021–); the Tojibids and Hudids of Saragossa (1019– and 1031–). Most of these dynasties were absorbed by the most distinguished of them, the **Abbadids,** who summoned the Almoravids from Africa to aid them against Alfonso VI of Castile.

1056–1147. The **ALMORAVIDS,** a Berber dynasty, founded by the Berber prophet **Abdullah ibn Tashfin.** They conquered Morocco and part of Algeria and were called into Spain by the Abbadids to help in the defense against the Christians. They defeated Alfonso of Castile at **Zallaka** (1086) and proceeded to annex Moorish Spain, with the exception of Toledo and Saragossa.

1130–1269. The **ALMOHADES,** a dynasty founded by the Berber prophet **Mohammed ibn Tumart.** His successor, Abdul-Mu'min, annihilated the Almoravid army (1144), after which Morocco was conquered (1146).

1145–1150. The Almohades invaded and conquered Moorish Spain, after which they conquered Algeria (1152) and Tunis (1158). They were finally defeated by the Christian kings of Spain in

1212, July 16. The **battle of Las Navas de Tolosa,** which was followed by their expulsion from Spain. Thereafter only local Moslem dynasties remained, of which the **Nasrids of Granada** (1232–1492) alone offered much resistance to the Christians until union of the Christian states brought about their defeat.

(2) Castile

1072–1109. ALFONSO VI, of Castile. He captured Toledo from the Moors (1085) and

Battle of Courtrai, 1302

Coronation of Pope Clement V, 1305

created his son-in-law, Henry of Burgundy, count of Portugal (1093).

1086. The Moslems, alarmed by Alfonso's progress, called from Africa the great **Yusuf ibn Tashfin** (d. 1106), leader of the newly dominant sect of Berber fanatics, the Almoravids. Ibn Yusuf landed at Algeciras (1086), and with the support of Sevilla began a successful counter-thrust against the Christians (defeat of Alfonso at **Zallaka,** 1086). Yusuf, recalled by the African situation, did not at once exploit his advantage, but on his return to Spain his energetic, puritanic reforms strengthened the Moslems and brought them into an integral relation (c. 1091) with his great African empire which was centered in Morocco. This empire quickly disintegrated on Yusuf's death.

Alfonso resumed the Christian reconquest

The Cid during one of his conquests

with the aid of **Rodrigo (Ruy) Diaz** of Bivar, the **Cid** (*Cid* as applied by the Moslems means *lord* or *master*). Alfonso's style of "emperor" represented personal prestige and a vague hegemony rather than political reality.

The **Cid,** a Castilian originally in the service of Sancho II of Castile, later passed to that of Alfonso VI; was exiled (1081); returned to Castilian service (1087–1088); went over to the Moslem king of Saragossa after his second exile. Eventually he became ruler of Valencia. The Cid served both sides, was cruel, selfish, and proud. Despite these characteristics the legendary figure of the man became the great national hero of Spain. On his death

(1099) Valencia was soon abandoned to the Almoravids.

In the course of the 11th century French influence began to penetrate the peninsula. The Cluniacs, already (1033) strong in Catalonia, Castile, and Aragon, reinforced French influence, and stimulated clerical reform and the reconquest. A literary reflection of this is to be found in the *Cantar de mio Cid* (c. 1140), which already shows French elements in the cycle of the Cid (a cycle which continued into the 15th century).

1126–1157. ALFONSO VII, crowned "emperor" (1135) on the basis of military ascendancy and an intense feeling of equality with

rival monarchs, especially the Holy Roman emperors. The weakening of the Almoravids by luxury, and the rise of rivals (the Almohades) in Africa (c. 1125), made possible a resumption of the reconquest (1144–1147) with wide raids into Andalusia. The Almohades, summoned from Africa (1146), completed (1172) the second **restoration of Moslem unity,** and made Moslem Spain a province of their African empire, reducing the Arab influence in Spain to nothing in favor of Berber fanatics. Alfonso's death was followed by a minority and an eight-year dynastic crisis from which his son Alfonso VIII finally emerged as master.

1158–1214. ALFONSO VIII. After a series of successful attacks on the Moslems, Alfonso was overwhelmingly defeated (**Alarcos,** 1195) by the Almohades, then at the zenith of their power. Leon and Navarre promptly invaded Castile, but Alfonso triumphed over them, and, with the aid of Pope Innocent III and the clergy, began the preparation of a unified general assault on the Moslems which led to the greatest victory of the reconquest, **Las Navas de Tolosa** (1212), soon followed by the decline of the Almohade power in Spain and Africa and by Christian dissension.

1179. Portugal's independence and royal title were recognized by Pope Alexander III.

1217–1252. FERDINAND III ended the dynastic war in Castile and attacked the Moors in the Guadalquivir Valley, taking Córdoba (1236) and Sevilla (1248). On the appeal of the Almohade emperor he sent aid to him, gaining in return a line of African fortresses, and permission to establish a Christian church at Marrakah. His plans for an invasion of Africa were cut short by death. After the capture of Jaen (1246), the emir was allowed to establish himself at Granada, the last Moorish stronghold, as Ferdinand's vassal.

The long history of guerrilla warfare in Castile disorganized tillage, made the people averse to agriculture, led to a concentration of population in the towns, and accounts for the poverty of Castilian agriculture, the tremendous influence of municipalities in medieval Castile, the development of a race of soldiers, and the isolation of Spanish thought from general European currents. In general the Moors were not disliked, and intermarriages were not unusual until the 13th century. Then the preaching of crusades as part of the reconquest and papal propaganda prepared the Spanish mind for the burst of intolerance and fanaticism which began in the second half of the 15th century.

The war of Christian reconquest gave birth to three great native military orders, modeled partly on Moorish societies for border defense, partly on the international crusading orders, notably the Templars, already established in the Peninsula. Some members took the regular monkish vows, others did not. Two Cistercian monks assumed (1158) the defense of Calatrava (when the Templars gave it up), and the **Order of Calatrava** which grew up was confirmed by the pope (1164). The **Order of Santiago** (established 1171) was the largest and richest, the **Order of Alcántara** (founded c. 1156), an offshoot of Calatrava, was the most clerical in type. By 1493 these orders had grown to stupendous size (the largest, Santiago, having 700,000 members and vassals, and a vast annual income.

In the period following 1252 fear of the infidel was no longer a dominant force in Iberian politics and the nobles turned from assaults on the Moors to attacks upon the monarchy. The struggle between crown and baronage (which found a parallel all through Europe) was notable in Spain for the depth of governmental degradation which it produced. The new elements in the situation were clearly indicated in the reign of

1252–1284. ALFONSO X (the Learned), a versatile savant, distinguished as an astronomer (*Alfonsine Tables*), poet, historian, patron of learning, a pre-eminent lawyer and codifier (*las Siete Partidas*), devoted to the Roman ideal of centralized absolute monarchy, but a futile, vacillating monarch. Lavish concessions to the nobles (1271) to avoid civil war established the aristocracy in a position from which it was not dislodged until the reign of Ferdinand and Isabella. Debasement of the coinage to relieve poverty produced economic crises; alternate alliance and war with the vassal king of Granada, and hostilities with Aragon, accomplished nothing. The kingdom of Murcia was regained (1266) with the aid of James I of Aragon, and was then incorporated with Castile.

In foreign affairs Alfonso abandoned the long peninsularity of Spanish sovereigns, made a series of dynastic alliances, and attempted to give Castile an important European position. **1263–1267.** Efforts to rectify the Portuguese boundary with advantage to Castile ultimately produced an actual loss of territory (in Algarve); Alfonso began the long effort to regain Portugal, which finally succeeded under Philip II (1580). Claims to (English) Gascony were revived (1253) and abandoned (1254); desultory wars fought with France. A twenty-year effort to win the crown of the Holy Roman Empire (despite papal opposition and public opinion) met with two defeats (1257 and 1273). The death of Alfonso's eldest son Ferdinand (1275) led at once to a bitter struggle over the succession organized by Alfonso's son Sancho.

(3) Barcelona and Catalonia

The **Spanish Mark** was established as a result of the conquest of Catalonia by Charlemagne (785–811). The county of Barcelona (erected 817) under the Frankish crown became independent, perhaps as early as the 9th century. By the beginning of the 12th century the counts of Barcelona had large holdings north of the Pyrenees (notably in Provence), to which they added for a brief period (1114–1115) Majorca and Iviza, and permanently Tarragona. **1137.** The **union of Catalonia and Aragon,**

Alfonso X, 1252–1284

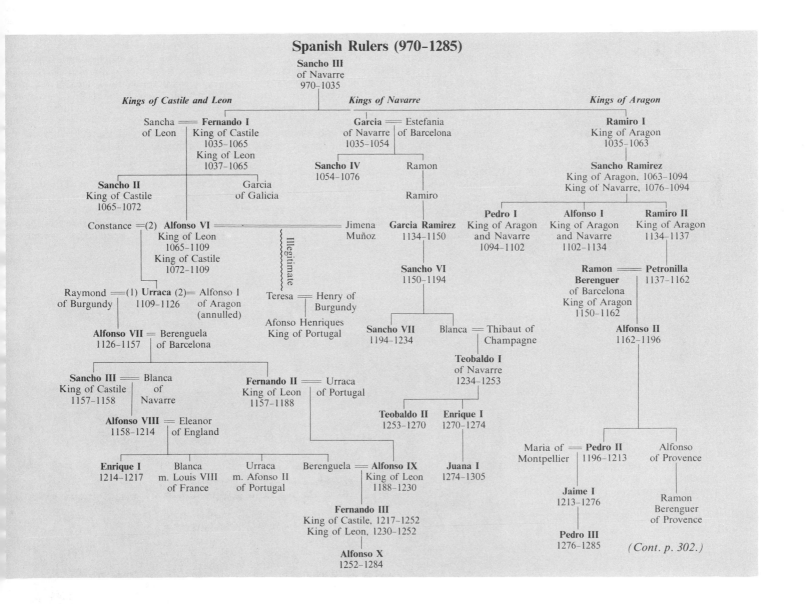

Spanish Rulers (970–1285)

(Cont. p. 302.)

Ramon Lull

Moses ben Maimon

terranean (Sicily and the Greek Archipelago), gave Barcelona further commercial advantages and made it one of the most active Mediterranean ports.

Ramon Lull (1232–1315) was the greatest Catalonian intellectual figure of the Middle Ages, a vernacular poet, novelist, missionary, mystic, educator, reformer, logician, scientist, and traveler.

(4) Navarre

Navarre gained its independence from Carolingian rule in the 9th century and fell heir to the Carolingian rights in Aragon, which was absorbed by Navarre in the 10th century. **Sancho the Great** (970–1035) secured the succession of Castile, conquered most of Leon and temporarily united the Iberian kingdoms. By his will Aragon passed to his son Ramiro (d. 1063) and the union came to an end. On the death of **Alfonso the Warrior** (1104–1134), Navarre returned to its old ruling house until it passed under French control (1234) for two centuries.

(5) Aragon

Aragon, beginning as a county on the river Arago under Carolingian control, emerged from Carolingian domination in the middle of the 9th century, passed under the control of Navarre, and then became independent under Ramiro (d. 1063). The period from 1063 to 1134 is marked by confusion, intrigue, some progress against the Moors, and the annexation of Navarre (1076).

1102–1134. ALFONSO I (the Warrior) advanced to the Ebro, captured Saragossa (1118), and made raids to the Mediterranean. On Alfonso's death, Aragon chose his brother, **Ramiro,** a monk who emerged from retirement long enough to marry and produce a daughter, Petronilla, whom he betrothed to Ramon Berenguer IV (1131–1162), count of Barcelona. He then returned (1137) to his monastery, leaving Petronilla under the guardianship of Ramon. On his marriage to Petronilla in 1150, Ramon became king of Aragon. The resulting **union of Catalonia and Aragon** was a decisive event in Spanish history.

After the union the Aragonese kings, preoccupied with Spanish affairs, let Provence drift, and on the death of Alfonso II (1162–1196) it passed to his son Alfonso, nominally under the suzerainty of his brother Peter **(Pedro) II** (1196–1213), but, in fact, lost for good. Alfonso tried to keep his Provençal holdings clear of the Albigensian heresy, but Raymond, count of Toulouse, a supporter of the heresy, sought to win Peter II to his views. Peter went to Rome (1204) for a papal coronation, declared himself a vassal of the Holy See, and bore an honorable part at Las Navas de Tolosa, but was forced by the horrors of the Albigensian Crusade and the legitimate appeals of his vassals to oppose Simon de Montfort at Muret, where he fell.

1213. The **battle of Muret** marked the real end of Aragonese interests north of the Pyrenees.

1258. By the **Treaty of Corbeil** the king of France renounced his claims to Barcelona, Urgel, etc., Cerdagne, Roussillon, etc. Aragon ceded: Carcassonne, Foix, Béziers, Nîmes, Narbonne, Toulouse, etc. All rights in Provence passed to Margaret, wife of Louis IX; a marriage was arranged between Louis's son Philip and Isabella, daughter of James I of Aragon.

1213–1276. JAMES (Jaime) I (the Conqueror). After the weakness and anarchy of his minority, James, one of the greatest soldiers of the Middle Ages, conquered Valencia in an intermittent campaign (1233–1245), took the kingdom of Murcia for Castile (1266), and freed the Aragonese frontier of the Moslem menace. James also attempted to establish his overlordship over Tlemcen and Bugia in North Africa, and to secure a hold in Tunis. Against the will of his Aragonese nobles, but with the support of his Catalonian and French vassals, James conquered the Balearic Islands (1229–1235), thus beginning the creation of an Aragonese Mediterranean empire.

SPANISH CULTURE in the Middle Ages was very largely conditioned by external influences. The Moslem tradition of scholarship continued and the translations from the Arabic to the Latin made Spain the avenue by

The great mosque of Córdoba

begun by Ramon Berenguer IV of Catalonia, was epochal, for it created a powerful state with access to the sea. Catalonian territories included Cerdagne, a large part of Provence, etc., with the later addition of Roussillon (1172), Montpellier (1204, under French suzerainty), Foix, Nîmes, Béziers (1162–1196).

1213. The **battle of Muret** (see below) definitely turned Catalonia back into the Spanish orbit.

In the 13th century **Barcelona,** utilizing the skill of her native sailors and the local (mostly Jewish) accumulations of capital, and profiting by Italian commercial pioneering, began an extensive slave trade in Moorish prisoners. Aragonese imperial expansion in the Medi-

which the knowledge of antiquity came to the West. **Gerard of Cremona** translated the works of Ptolemy, Euclid, Galen, and the Hippocratic corpus. Toledo, which had been a center of learning of the Arabic world, became a center for the translation of Arabic and Greek works into Latin. **John of Sevilla** (fl. 1135–1153), also at Toledo, translated Arabic texts on mathematics, astronomy, and philosophy into Latin and the vernacular. Abraham bar-Hiyya (d. 1136) **(Sarasorda)** was one of the earliest to introduce Moslem mathematics to the West. Moses ben Maimon **(Maimonides)** (1135–1204), born in Córdoba, who became one of the most influential thinkers of the West, also translated medical and astronomical texts from Arabic. **Ibn-Rushd** (1126–1198), born in Córdoba, was known as "the commentator," through whom the West relearned the works of Aristotle.

Architecture: (1) **Pre-romanesque** architecture revealed traces of Visigothic, Carolingian, Persian, Byzantine, and Moslem traditions. (2) **Romanesque** architecture showed particularly the influence of Auvergne and Languedoc (e.g. second church of Santiago de Compostella). (3) The **Gothic** was marked by strong elements of the Burgundian style, brought by the Cluniacs. The full tide of the Gothic was probably introduced by the Cistercians (e.g. cathedrals of Toledo, c. 1230; Burgos 1126; Leon, c. 1230). Catalan Gothic shows German influences (cathedrals of Barcelona, 1298; Gerona, 1312). The later Spanish Gothic revealed French, German, and Flemish currents (e.g. cathedral of Sevilla, begun 1401; west towers of Burgos cathedral, 1442). (4) **Moorish** architecture had a development of its own: the great mosque of Córdoba (completed 1118), the Alcazar, Sevilla (c. 1181), and the Alhambra (mostly 14th century).

Foundation of the first universities: Valencia (1209); Salamanca (1242). *(Cont. p. 301.)*

(6) Portugal

1055– Reconquest from the Moors of much of present-day Portugal by **Ferdinand the Great** of Leon and Castile. Ferdinand organized the

The inner court of the Alcazar, Seville

Court of Lions in the Alhambra, Granada

territory as a county, with Coimbra as the capital.

1093–1112. Henry of Burgundy, a descendant of King Robert of France, came to Spain with other knights-adventurers, to fight against the Moors. In return the king of Castile granted him the county of Portugal and gave him the hand of his (illegitimate) daughter, Teresa. Henry himself was a typical crusader, restless and enterprising, whose main hope appears to have been to establish a dynasty in Castile.

1112–1185. AFONSO HENRIQUES, the founder of the Portuguese monarchy and of the Burgundian dynasty. Afonso was only three years old at the death of his father. His mother Teresa ruled as regent, but soon became involved in a struggle with Galicia and Castile. Being defeated, she agreed to accept Castilian domination, but

1128. Afonso assumed authority, repudiated the agreement, and, after defeating the Spaniards, drove his mother into exile.

1139. Afonso, one of the most famous knights

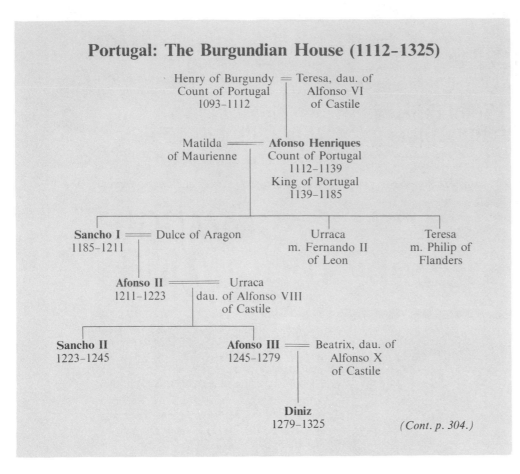

Portugal: The Burgundian House (1112–1325)

```
Henry of Burgundy ══ Teresa, dau. of
Count of Portugal        Alfonso VI
   1093–1112              of Castile

   Matilda ══════ Afonso Henriques
of Maurienne          Count of Portugal
                        1112–1139
                      King of Portugal
                        1139–1185

Sancho I ══ Dulce of Aragon          Urraca              Teresa
1185–1211                          m. Fernando II      m. Philip of
                                     of Leon             Flanders

  Afonso II ══════ Urraca
  1211–1223        dau. of Alfonso VIII
                     of Castile

Sancho II                Afonso III ══ Beatrix, dau. of
1223–1245                1245–1279        Alfonso X
                                          of Castile

                           Diniz
                         1279–1325        (Cont. p. 304.)
```

Wedding of Henry of Burgundy and Teresa of Castile

of his age, began a long series of struggles against the Moors by defeating them in the **battle of Ourique.**

1143. Afonso was proclaimed king by the cortes. The pope arranged the **Treaty of Zamora** between Portugal and Castile, the latter recog-

nizing Portuguese independence, while Portugal accepted the suzerainty of the pope.

1147. The Portuguese took Lisbon and established a frontier on the Tagus.

1169. Further conflicts with Castile led to Afonso's attack on Badajoz. He was defeated and captured, but soon released.

1185–1211. SANCHO I, the son of Afonso Henriques. His reign was noteworthy for the development of towns and for the establishment of military orders of knighthood. Sancho did much to settle colonists on the lands that were won back in the prolonged wars against the Moors.

1211–1223. AFONSO II. Beginning of the king's conflict with the clergy, which led to interference by the pope and to restlessness among the nobility.

1223–1245. SANCHO II. His trouble with the clergy and nobility led ultimately to his deposition by the pope, who offered the crown to

1245–1279. AFONSO III, the brother of Sancho II and count of Boulogne. His title being weak, Afonso was much dependent on the cortes, in which the commons were for the first time represented. **War with Castile** was ended by a peace in 1253. *(Cont. p. 304.)*

g. DEVELOPMENTS IN EUROPEAN TECHNOLOGY

The increased pulse of life in the later Middle Ages was felt throughout society as well as in literature, science, and technology. The technological developments are known, but sparsely and not chronologically recorded. The water mill was used for fulling, stone cutting, and wood cutting after the introduction of the geared wheel. The windmill (documented from the 12th century), was more complex than that used in the East, due to the more variable winds of Europe. As a fuel, coal was being used as the forests were depleted (coal was mined in Liège during the 13th century). Communications improved partly because bridge and road building was considered a Christian duty and partly because of the more effective use of animal power. Communication by sea was improved by the Lateen sail, in use in Italy in the 11th century, and by the sternpost rudder and compass (the latter was introduced in the 13th century). Along with the increase in the building of stone bridges came an increase in the number of stone buildings and greater empirical knowledge of building techniques (e.g., improvements in the arch and the knowledge of the distribution of roof weight). The textile industry developed employing wool, linen, cotton, and silk. The spinning wheel dates from the 13th century and is the first example of belt power transmission. Soap was also invented and produced on a large scale by the 12th century. Mining had declined from the end of the Roman Empire to the 10th century after which it increased rapidly both with the discovery of new sources and by the conquest of the Spanish mines from the Moslems. The most important development was in the discovery of iron-casting techniques; tools and weapons could be more efficiently produced. Gunpowder, although known in Europe in the 13th century, did not become revolutionary until the 14th century, when it was first used to propel missiles.

(Cont. p. 446.)

2. Eastern Europe

a. THE SLAVS

The Slavs, an eastern branch of the Indo-European family, were known to the Roman and Greek writers of the 1st and 2nd centuries A.D. under the name of *Venedi* as inhabiting the region beyond the Vistula. The majority of modern scholars agree that the "original home" of the Slavs was the territory to the southeast of the Vistula and to the northeast of the Carpathian Mountains, in the upper basins of the Western Bug, the Pripet, and the Dniester. In the course of the early centuries of our era the Slavs expanded in all directions, and by the 5th century, when they were known to Gothic and Byzantine writers as *Sclaveni*, they were apparently already separated into three main divisions: (1) the western Slavs (the present-day Poles, Czechs, Slovaks, and Moravians); (2) southern Slavs (the Bulgarians, Serbs, Croats, and Slovenes); (3) the eastern Slavs (the Russians, subsequently subdivided into the Great Russians, the Little Russians or the Ukrainians, and the White Russians).

Closely related to the Slavs were the Lithuanians who, together with the Letts and the ancient Prussians, formed the Baltic branch of the Indo-European family. They inhabited the southeastern coast of the Baltic Sea, between the present location of Memel and Estonia.

b. BOHEMIA AND MORAVIA, TO 1306

The earliest recorded attempt at the construction of a Slavic state was that made by

c. 623-658. Samo, who appears to have been a Frankish tradesman traveling in central Europe. Probably taking advantage of the defeat of the Avars by the Greeks in 626, he managed to unite the Czechs and some of the Wends, and succeeded in repulsing not only the Avars, but also the Franks under King Dagobert (631). But on the death of Samo the union of the tribes disintegrated.

833-836. Mojmir, founder of the Moravian state, maintained himself against pressure from the East Franks.

846-869. Rastislav, prince of Moravia, made an alliance (862) with **Michael III,** the Byzantine emperor, to counteract the close relationship between the East Franks and the Bulgarians.

863. Conversion of the Moravians by Cyril (Constantine, 826-869) and **Methodius** (815-885), two monks from Saloniki sent at Rastislav's request. Beginning of Slavic church language and liturgy. **Cyrillic alphabet.**

869. Rastislav captured and blinded by Carloman.

870-894. Sviatopluk, a Moravian prince, succeeded in uniting under his authority Moravia, Bohemia, and present-day Slovakia, and managed to maintain his position as against the Germans. During his reign the western Slavs were converted to Christianity by Cyril and Methodius but in the last years of the century the German clergy redoubled its efforts and won Bohemia and Moravia for the Latin Church, thus establishing the ecclesiastical dependence of the western Slavs on Rome.

906. The **kingdom of Moravia** was dissolved as the result of a great defeat by the Hungarians.

920-929. St. Wenceslas, duke of the Premysl house. He was murdered in 929 at the instigation of his brother Boleslav, leader of the heathen reaction, who ascended the throne as

929-967. BOLESLAV I. He seems to have carried on constant warfare against the encroaching Germans, until forced (950) to accept German suzerainty. To the eastward he made many conquests and included Moravia, part of Slovakia, part of Silesia, and even Cracow in his kingdom. Furthermore, he appears to have established a fairly strong royal power over the old tribal chiefs.

967-999. BOLESLAV II, son of the preceding. He apparently continued the policies of his father and saw to the final victory of the Christian faith (foundation of the bishopric of Prague, 973). Missionaries from Bohemia took an active part in the conversion of Hungary and Poland.

The entire 11th and 12th centuries were filled with chronic dynastic conflicts between members of the Premysl family and the various claimants appealing to Poland and more particularly to the German emperors for support. The result was an ever-increasing German influence and the gradual integration of Bohemia with the empire.

999-1000. Boleslav the Brave of Poland took advantage of the anarchy in Bohemia to conquer Silesia, Moravia, and Cracow. In 1003 he became duke of Bohemia, but was driven out in the next year by a German army. There followed another period of disorder, marked only by

1031. The reacquisition of Moravia, which thenceforth remained connected with Bohemia.

1034-1055. BŘETISLAV I (the Restorer), who overran Silesia, took Cracow (1039) and for a time ruled Poland, which had now entered upon a period of disruption.

1041. Emperor **Henry III,** alarmed by the expansion of the Bohemian power, invaded the country and advanced to Prague. Bratislav agreed to give up his Polish conquests and pay tribute to the emperor.

1055-1061. Spytihnev, son of Břetislav, whose reign was uneventful.

1061-1092. VRATISLAV II, who, throughout his reign, loyally supported the German emperor, Henry IV, in his struggle with the Papacy and took part in the Italian campaigns. He was rewarded by Henry with a crown (1086), but only for his own person.

1092-1110. Břetislav II.

1111-1125. Vladislav I.

1125-1140. Sobeslav I.

1140-1173. VLADISLAV II. Like his predecessors, he supported the German emperors in the main, and was rewarded (1156) by Frederick Barbarossa with an hereditary crown for his aid against the Italian cities.

1173-1197. Another period of dynastic conflict, during which there were some ten rulers.

1198-1230. OTTOKAR I. He took full advantage of the struggles for the succession which now began to wrack the German Empire. Siding now with one party, now with another, he made the Bohemian king (an imperial elector since the early 12th century) one of the decisive powers in German affairs. On the other hand, a long-drawn conflict with the clergy (1214-1221) led to the almost complete independence of the Church.

1212. The **Golden Bull** of Frederick II recognized the right of the Bohemian nobility to elect its own ruler.

1230-1253. WENCESLAS (VACLAV) I. His reign was marked by large-scale immigration of Germans, encouraged by the ruler, possibly to counteract the growing power of the nobility. Germans had been coming in for a long time (chiefly clergy and nobility), but they now began to open up large forested tracts and to build cities, which were given practical autonomy under German (Magdeburg) law.

1247-1250. Rising of the nobility against the king, possibly in protest against the favor shown the Germans.

1251. The Austrian estates, after the death of the last Babenberg duke, elected Ottokar, son of Wenceslas, as duke.

1253-1278. OTTOKAR II (the Great) whose reign marked the widest expansion of Bohemian power and was characterized by great prosperity (opening of the famous silver mines, which made Bohemia one of the wealthiest countries in the later Middle Ages).

1255. Ottokar carried on a successful campaign in support of the Teutonic Knights against the heathen Prussians.

1260. After defeating the Hungarians, Ottokar took from them the province of Styria.

1267. A second northern campaign, against the Lithuanians, achieved little.

1269. Ottokar, taking advantage of the interregnum in the German Empire, extended his power over Carinthia, Carniola, and Istria.

1273. Election of **Rudolf of Hapsburg** as king of Germany. Ottokar refused to recognize him. The Diet of Regensburg (1274) therefore declared all Ottokar's acquisitions void. The king, supported by the Hungarians and by some of the Bohemian nobility, attacked Ottokar, who agreed to give up all but Bohemia and Moravia, and to recognize Rudolf's suzerainty even over these.

1278. New war between Rudolf and Ottokar. Ottokar was decisively defeated on the **Marchfeld** (Aug. 26) and killed.

1278-1305. Wenceslas II, a boy of seven, for whom Otto of Brandenburg at first acted as regent.

1290. Wenceslas was elected and crowned king of Poland.

Bohemia: The Premyslid Kings (1198-1378)

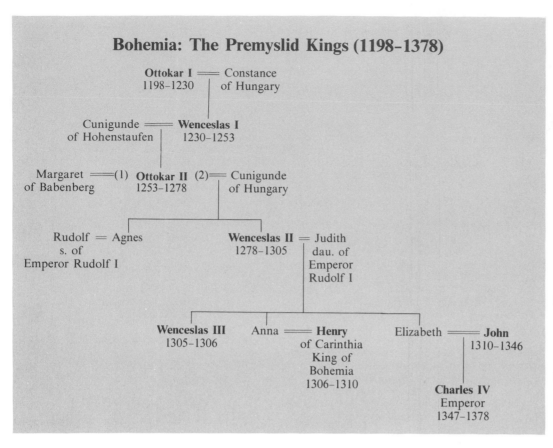

1301. His son, Wenceslas, was elected king of Hungary (ruled to 1304).

1305-1306. Wenceslas III. He gave up the claim to Hungary and was murdered while en route to Poland to suppress a revolt of the nobles. **End of the Premyslid line.**

(Cont. p. 323.)

c. POLAND, TO 1305

The Polish state emerged in the 10th century, the result of the unification of some six tribes under the **Polani,** who were ruled by the members of the semi-mythical **family of Piast.** From the outset the Poles were obliged to fight against the encroachment of the Germans from the west, the Prussians from the north, the Bohemians from the south, and the Hungarians, also in the south.

c. 960-992. MIESZKO I, of the house of Piast, the first historical ruler. He conquered the territory between the Oder and the Warthe Rivers, but was defeated by Markgraf Gero and obliged to recognize German suzerainty (973).

966. Mieszko was converted to Christianity by Bohemian missionaries, probably for political reasons, to deprive the Germans of any further excuse for aggression. The acceptance of Latin Christianity meant the connection of Poland, like Bohemia and Hungary, with western European culture.

992-1025. BOLESLAV I (Chrobry = the Brave). He ascended the throne at 25 and was the real organizer of the Polish state. An energetic, but at times treacherous and cruel ruler, he built up an efficient military machine, laid the basis for an administrative system (*comites* = *castellani* = *Burggrafen,* with civil and military powers), organized the Church

(establishment of Benedictine monasteries, etc.). Politically his aim appears to have been the union of all western Slavs under his rule. He conquered eastern Pomerania and gained access to the Baltic (992-994), added Silesia, Moravia, and Cracow to his domain (999), and induced Otto III to erect an independent archbishopric of Gnesen (1000). On the death of Otto he took advantage of the confusion in Germany to occupy Lusatia and Meissen, and in 1003 made himself duke of Bohemia. The new emperor, Henry II, carried on long wars against Boleslav to break his power (1004-) and ultimately forced the abandonment of Bohemia and Lusatia (1005). But by the **treaty of Bautzen** (1018) Boleslav was given Lusatia as an imperial fief, and just before his death he was able to make himself king of Poland (1025).

1025-1034. MIESZKO II, a much weaker ruler. The Poles, like the other Slavs, divided the domain among the various sons of a deceased king, thus creating endless dynastic conflict and ample opportunity for intervention by neighboring rulers. During Mieszko's reign most of the territorial gains of Boleslav were lost: St. Stephen of Hungary conquered Slovakia (1027); Bretislav of Bohemia took Moravia (1031); Yaroslav of Russia acquired Ruthenia (1031); Canute of Denmark took Pomerania (1031). In 1032 the Emperor Conrad actually divided Poland between Mieszko and two of his relatives.

1034-1040. A period of violent dynastic struggle and general insurrection, including a heathen reaction (burning of monasteries, massacre of the clergy) and a peasant uprising against the landlords. Meanwhile Bretislav of Bohemia seized Silesia (1038).

1038-1058. CASIMIR I (the Restorer), who suc-

ceeded, with the aid of the Emperor Henry III, in reconquering his domain, re-establishing Christianity, and restoring order. Silesia was recovered (1054). In return Casimir was obliged to give up the royal title (becoming merely a *grand duke*) and to make numerous concessions to the nobility and clergy, thus initiating a baneful practice.

1058-1079. BOLESLAV II (the Bold), one of the great medieval rulers. In the great struggle between the emperor and the pope he consistently supported the latter, as a counterweight to German influence. At the same time he did his utmost to throw off the pressure of the nobility. In his countless campaigns he reconquered upper Slovakia (1061-1063) and marched as far as Kiev to put his relative upon the Russian throne (1069). In 1076 he reassumed the royal crown, with the pope's approval. But his entire policy estranged the nobility, which ultimately drove him from his throne.

1079-1102. Vladislav I (Ladislas), **Hermann,** an indolent and unwarlike ruler, brother of Boleslav. He resigned the royal title and attempted to secure peace by supporting the Emperor Henry IV, as well as by courting the nobility and clergy.

1102-1138. BOLESLAV III (Wry-mouth), who acquired the throne only after a violent struggle with his brother Zbigniew. He was one of the greatest Polish kings, who defeated the Pomeranians (**battle of Naklo,** 1109) and, by the incorporation of Pomerania (1119-1123), re-established the access to the sea. At the same time he defeated the Emperor Henry V (1109, **battle of Hundsfeld,** near Breslau) and checked the German advance. On the other hand, his campaigns in Hungary (1132-1135) had no permanent results.

Boleslav completed the organization of the state, in which the great landlords (*nobiles* = magnates), gentry (*milites* = knights = *szlachta*) had become well-defined social classes, the peasantry having steadily lost in the periods of confusion. The Church was reorganized under the archbishop of Gnesen, by the papal legate Walo. In order to avoid dispute, Boleslav fixed the royal succession by seniority. Poland was divided into **five principalities** (Silesia, Great Poland, Masovia, Sandomir, Cracow) for his sons; Cracow was established as the capital, and was to go, with the title of *grand duke,* to the eldest member of the house of Piast. In actual fact this arrangement by no means eliminated the dynastic competition, but introduced a long period of disruption, during which the nobility and clergy waxed ever more powerful and the ducal or royal power became insignificant. Only the weakness of the neighboring states saved Poland from destruction.

1138-1146. Vladislav II (Ladislas).

1146-1173. Boleslav IV, an ineffectual ruler, during whose reign the Germans, under Albert the Bear and Henry the Lion, supported by Waldemar of Denmark, drove back the Poles from the entire territory along the Baltic and west of the Vistula (1147). The Emperor Frederick Barbarossa intervened and forced the humble submission of Boleslav (1157).

1173-1177. Mieszko III, a brutal and despotic prince who antagonized the nobility and was soon driven out by them.

1177-1194. CASIMIR II (the Just) was, practically elected by the magnates, who extorted privileges from him. In the **Assembly of Lenczyca** (1180) the clergy was also given far-reaching concessions. Casimir attempted to preclude further strife by making the principality of Cracow hereditary in his own line.

194-1227. **Leszek I** (the White), whose reign was punctuated by constant wars against Mieszko III, who attempted to regain the throne (d. 1202), and against the latter's son Vladislav Laskonogi (1202-1206). The period was one of complete feudal anarchy, with the nobility and clergy controlling the situation.

227-1279. **Boleslav V,** whose unhappy reign was marked by complete disruption and by constant aggression by neighboring states.

228. Arrival of the **Teutonic Knights,** called to Prussia by Duke Conrad of Masovia *(p. 234).* Within the next 50 years they conquered Prussia and erected a most formidable barrier to Polish access to the sea.

241. Beginning of the great **Mongol invasions** (p. *266),* of which there were constant renewals throughout the rest of the century. The Poles managed to stave off Mongol domination, but the country was devastated. One result was the calling in of large numbers of German settlers, some of whom cleared forest land

The Scandinavian chieftain Rurik

and colonized new areas in Silesia and Posen, others of whom settled in the towns. In all cases large concessions in the direction of autonomy were made (Magdeburg law). The German influence meant greater and more efficient exploitation of the soil, development of trade, cultural advance.

1279-1288. **Leszek II** (the Black).

1288-1290. Further dynastic and feudal warfare, with the brief reign of Henry Probus.

1290-1296. **Przemyslav II.** He was crowned king with the consent of the pope (1295), but was murdered soon afterward.

1300-1305. **Wenceslas I,** son of the king of Bohemia, elected by the nobility but challenged by claimants of the Piast family. He soon resigned the position and returned home.

(Cont. p. 331.)

d. RUSSIA, TO 1263

The **eastern Slavs** settled on the territory of present-day European Russia in the period from the 5th to the 8th century A.D. Little is known of their political history during these centuries, but undoubtedly there were attempts at political organization in the shape of both tribal principalities and city states formed around

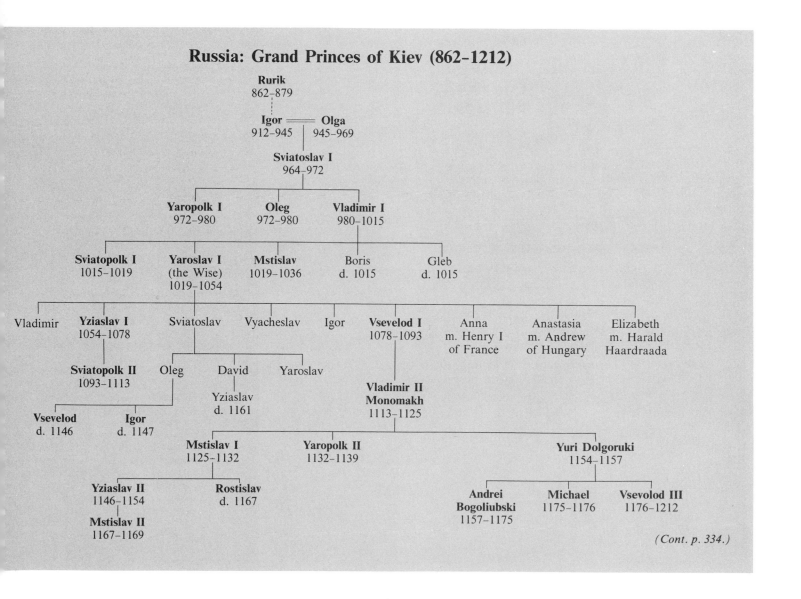

Russia: Grand Princes of Kiev (862–1212)

Rurik
862–879

Igor ═══ **Olga**
912–945 │ 945–969

Sviatoslav I
964–972

Yaropolk I 972–980 — **Oleg** 972–980 — **Vladimir I** 980–1015

Sviatopolk I 1015–1019 — **Yaroslav I** (the Wise) 1019–1054 — **Mstislav** 1019–1036 — Boris d. 1015 — Gleb d. 1015

Vladimir — **Yziaslav I** 1054–1078 — Sviatoslav — Vyacheslav — Igor — **Vsevelod I** 1078–1093 — Anna m. Henry I of France — Anastasia m. Andrew of Hungary — Elizabeth m. Harald Haardraada

Sviatopolk II 1093–1113 — Oleg — David — Yaroslav

Yziaslav d. 1161

Vladimir II Monomakh 1113–1125

Vsevelod d. 1146 — **Igor** d. 1147

Mstislav I 1125–1132 — **Yaropolk II** 1132–1139 — **Yuri Dolgoruki** 1154–1157

Yziaslav II 1146–1154 — **Rostislav** d. 1167

Andrei Bogoliubski 1157–1175 — **Michael** 1175–1176 — **Vsevolod III** 1176–1212

Mstislav II 1167–1169

(Cont. p. 334.)

important commercial centers. In the 8th century some of the eastern Slavs were under the protectorate of the **Khazars,** a Turkish tribe which established a strong and prosperous state along the lower Volga. After the end of the 8th century the northern part of Russia began to be penetrated by the Scandinavian Vikings called in the old Russian chronicles **Varangians** or *Rus* (hence the name of *Russia*). In the course of the 9th century the Varangians constantly moved southward along the main waterway leading from the Baltic to the Black Sea, gradually establishing their political domination over the Slav communities. According to tradition, the Scandinavian chieftain **Rurik** ruled in Novgorod in the 860's. Later he was recognized as the founder of the Russian princely dynasty.

860. The first recorded appearance of the Russians (Varangians) at Constantinople. This was a raid not unlike those of the Norsemen on Britain and France in the same period.

c. 880–912. PRINCE OLEG, who succeeded in uniting under his control both Novgorod and Kiev (on the Dnieper River). Kiev subsequently became the political center of a loose federation of Russian states.

911. The Russians again appeared at Constantinople and extracted trade privileges from the Byzantine emperor. Trade became a lead-

ing occupation of the Russian princes, who, with their followers (*druzhina*) protected the merchant ships. Russians also began to take service with the Greek emperors in considerable number and came to play an important rôle in the mercenary corps.

945. Further trade agreements with the Greek Empire testify to the ever closer economic connections and no doubt to an increasing cultural contact.

957. The Russian princess, **Olga,** visited Constantinople and was converted to the Christian faith. This was, however, a personal conversion, and may in fact have been Olga's second.

964–972. SVIATOSLAV, the son of Olga. He was the first of the great conquering princes. In 965 he defeated the Khazars on the lower Volga and proceeded to establish a Russian state in place of the Khazar Empire. Called to the Balkans to aid the Greek emperor against the powerful Bulgars, he carried on a successful campaign (967) and decided to establish himself on the lower Danube. At this time his power extended from Novgorod in the north to the Danube in the southwest and to the lower Volga in the southeast. He was forced to abandon Bulgaria in order to resist the **Patzinaks** (Pechenegs), who had entered southern Russia from the east and were threat-

ening Kiev. Having repulsed them (968), Sviatoslav returned to Bulgaria, but he was no more welcome to the Greeks than were the Bulgars. In 971 he was defeated and driven out by the Emperor John Tzimisces *(p. 207)* Sviatoslav was defeated and killed by the Patzinaks on his way back to Kiev (972).

972–980. A dynastic struggle between the sons of Sviatoslav ended in the victory of

980–1015. VLADIMIR THE SAINT, in whose reign (c. 990) the Russians were converted in mass to Christianity in the eastern (Byzantine) form. The Russian church was organized on the Greek pattern and was considered to be under the canonical authority of the patriarch of Constantinople. From this time on the cultural relation between Constantinople and Kiev was very close.

1015–1019. Further dynastic conflict between the sons of Vladimir.

1019–1054. YAROSLAV (the Wise), the greatest ruler of Russia in the Kievan period. He was finally successful in the struggle with his brother Sviatopolk, but was obliged to leave to another brother, Mstislav, that part of the principality east of the Dnieper River until Mstislav's death in 1036. Yaroslav was then supreme ruler of all Russia. Extensive building activity at Kiev (Cathedral of St. Sophia)

Vladimir the Saint (center) *c. 990 (from an ancient banner)*

Vladimir Monomakh, 1113–1128, in council with his advisers (carved wood panel, 1551)

of contention between the princes of Volynia and Suzdal.

1147. First mention of **Moscow** in one of the chronicles.

1157–1174. **ANDREI BOGOLIUBSKI,** prince of Suzdal. He repressed the rising power of the nobles (*boyars*), united a large block of territory, and established his capital at Vladimir.

1169. Andrei conquered Kiev, which became part of the Vladimir principality. But the new state underwent a marked decline on the death of the ruler.

1199–1205. **Zenith of the Galician principality** under Prince Roman.

1201. Foundation of Riga, which became the center of German missionary enterprise and commercial expansion.

1202. Foundation of the German Order of Swordbearers by Bishop Albert of Livonia (Latvia).

1219. **Conquest of Estonia** by Waldemar II of Denmark.

1223. **BATTLE OF THE KALKA RIVER,** near the Sea of Azov. The Mongols (Tatars, *see p. 281*), under Subutai, invaded southern Russia from the Transcaucasus region and completely defeated a coalition of Russian princes and Cuman leaders. They retired, however, without pressing their conquests.

Andrei Bogoliubski's warriors before Novgorod (detail from an ikon)

Religious activity (Metropolitan Hilarion and the Monastery of the Caves). Promotion of education. Revision of the *Russian Law* (the earliest known Russian law code), under Byzantine influence. Dynastic alliances with western states (Yaroslav's daughter, Anna, married Henry I of France).

The period following the death of Yaroslav the Great was one of disintegration and decline. Technically the primacy of Kiev continued and the power remained concentrated in the family of Yaroslav. Actually Kiev continued to lose in importance, and authority became divided between members of the princely family on a system of seniority and rotation, leading of necessity to much dynastic rivalry and countless combinations, sometimes with Poles and Hungarians.

At the same time the Kievan state was subjected to ever greater pressure from the nomads (Patzinaks and Cumans) moving into southern Russia from the east. The period witnessed also a shifting of the older trade routes, due to the decline of the Baghdad Caliphate and the conquest of Constantinople (1204) by the Latin crusaders.

Emergence of new political centers: Galicia and Volynia in the southwest, principalities characterized by a strongly aristocratic form of government; Novgorod the Great, in the north, controlling territory to the east to the Urals. In Novgorod the assembly of freemen (*Vieche*) reached its fullest development; Suzdal-Vladimir in central Russia, the precursor of the grand duchy of Moscow. In this region the princely power was dominant.

1113–1125. **VLADIMIR MONOMAKH,** prince of Kiev. He carried on numerous campaigns against the Cumans of the steppes and his reign marked the last period of brilliance at Kiev, which soon thereafter became a bone

1226. The **Teutonic Knights** *(p. 234)* were commissioned to conquer and convert Prussia. They united with the Swordbearers in 1237.

1236-1263. ALEXANDER NEVSKI, prince first of Novgorod and after 1252 of Vladimir.

1237-1240. The **MONGOL CONQUEST,** under the leadership of Batu. The great armies of the invaders swept over southern and central Russia and into Europe, coming within 60 miles of Novgorod. They took Kiev (1240) and ultimately established themselves (1242) at Sarai on the lower Volga. The **Khanate of the Golden Horde** for two centuries thereafter acted as suzerian of all Russia, levying tribute and taking military contingents, but for the rest leaving the princes in control, respecting the Russian church and interfering little.

1240. Alexander Nevski defeated the Swedes under Birger Jarl on the Neva River and thus broke the force of the Swedish advance.

1242. Alexander defeated the Teutonic Knights in a **battle on Lake Peipus.**

1252. As prince of Vladimir, Alexander Nevski did his utmost to prevent insurrections against Tatar rule and built up a system of protection based upon submission and conciliation.

1253. Daniel of Volynia attempted to organize a crusade against the Tatars. In order to secure papal aid he accepted the union of the Russian church with Rome, but his efforts came to nothing.

1263. Death of Alexander Nevski on his way back from the Golden Horde.

RUSSIAN CULTURE in this period was still primarily religious and largely Byzantine in character. Noteworthy churches were built at Kiev, Novgorod, and Cernigov in the 11th and 12th centuries, decorated with fine frescoes. Church literature was voluminous and there appeared further the first chronicles and epics of fights against the nomads. *(Cont. p. 333.)*

St. Stephen's crown, 1001

Battle on Lake Peipus, 1242

e. HUNGARY, TO 1301

896. The Hungarians, organized in a number of tribes, of which the **Magyar** was the leading one, occupied the valley of the middle Danube and Theiss (Tisza). Under **Arpad** (d. 907) they had come from southern Russia by way of Moldavia, driven on by the Patzinaks (Pechenegs) and other Asiatic peoples. The Hungarians were themselves nomads of the Finno-Ugrian family. For more than half a century after their occupation of Hungary they continued their raids, both toward the east and toward the west.

906. The Hungarians destroyed the rising Slavic kingdom of Moravia.

955. Battle of Augsburg, in which Emperor Otto I decisively defeated the raiding Hungarians. From this time on the Hungarians began to settle down and establish a frontier.

972-997. Geza, duke of the Magyar tribe, and the organizer of the princely power. He began to reduce the tribal leaders and invited Christian missionaries from Germany (Pilgrin of Passau, 974; **St. Adalbert of Prague,** 993). Christianization had already begun from the east, and was furthered by large numbers of war prisoners.

997-1038. ST. STEPHEN (I), greatest ruler of the Arpad dynasty. He suppressed eastern Christianity by force and crusaded against paganism, which was still favored by the tribal chiefs. Stephen took his stand definitely by the west, married a Bavarian princess, called in Roman churchmen and monks (Benedictines), and endowed them with huge tracts of land. With the help of the clergy he broke the power of the tribal chieftains, took over their land as royal domain, administered through counts (*Ispan*), placed over counties (*Comitat*). The counts and high churchmen formed a royal council. Every encouragement was given to agriculture and trade and a methodical system of frontier defense was built up (large belt of swamps and forests, wholly uninhabited and protected by regular frontier guards; as time went on this frontier was gradually extended).

1001. Stephen was crowned with a crown sent by the pope. He was canonized in 1083.

1002. Stephen defeated an anti-Christian insurrection in Transylvania.

1030. Attacks of the Germans under Conrad II, who tried to enforce German suzerainty over Hungary, were repulsed.

1038-1077. A period of dynastic struggles over the succession, every member of the Arpad family claiming a share of the power, and sometimes calling in the Germans for support.

1038-1046. Peter Urseolo, son of Stephen's sister and the doge of Venice, succeeded to the throne. He called in German and Italian favorites, aroused the hostility of the Hungarians, and was driven out (1041). For a few years Samuel Aba, the brother-in-law of Stephen, occupied the throne, but he in turn was expelled by Peter, who returned with the Emperor Henry III, to whom he swore fealty.

1046. Peter was overthrown in the course of a great **pagan rising** of the tribal chiefs under Vatha, who massacred the Christians and destroyed the churches. This was the last serious revolt of the kind.

1047-1060. **Andrew I,** who managed to restore the royal power.

1049-1052. The three campaigns of Emperor Henry III against the Hungarians. Andrew managed to hold his own, and in 1058 the emperor recognized Hungary's independence of the empire.

1061-1063. **Bela I,** brother of Andrew and popular hero of the campaigns against the Germans.

1063-1074. **Solomon,** the son of Andrew, the

candidate of the German party. He was defeated by his cousin

1074-1077. **Geza I.**

1077-1095. **ST. LADISLAS I** (canonized 1192), the first great king after St. Stephen. He supported the pope in his conflicts with the emperor, and at home restored order and prosperity.

1091. Ladislas conquered Croatia and Bosnia,

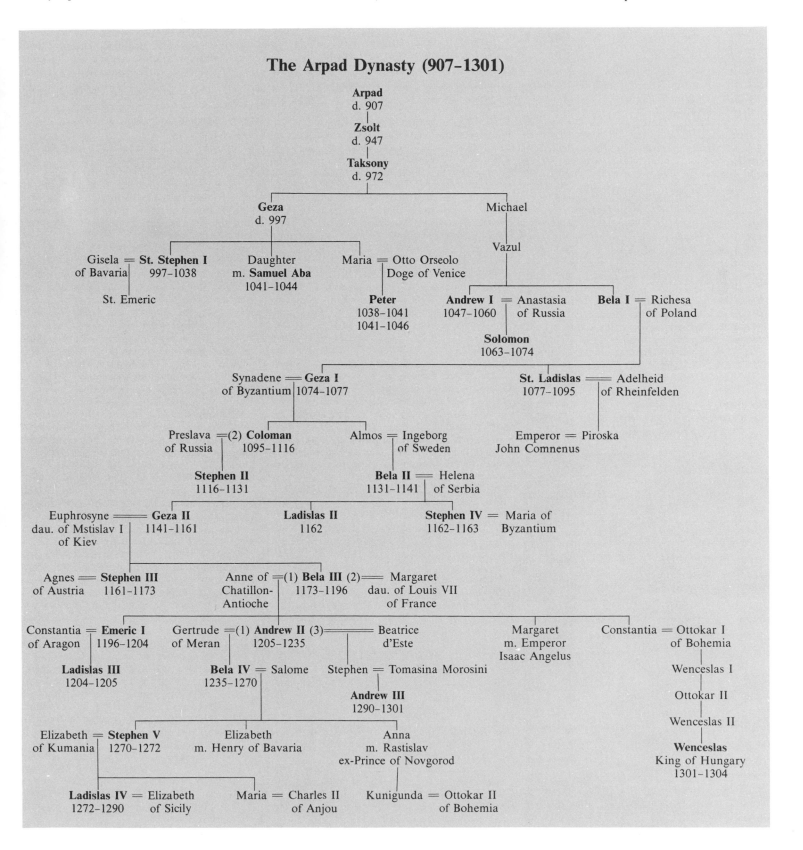

The Arpad Dynasty (907-1301)

Arpad d. 907

Zsolt d. 947

Taksony d. 972

Geza d. 997 — Michael

Vazul

Gisela of Bavaria = **St. Stephen I** 997-1038 — Daughter m. **Samuel Aba** 1041-1044 — Maria = Otto Orseolo Doge of Venice — **Andrew I** 1047-1060 = Anastasia of Russia — **Bela I** = Richesa of Poland

St. Emeric

Peter 1038-1041 1041-1046

Solomon 1063-1074

Synadene of Byzantium = **Geza I** 1074-1077 — **St. Ladislas** 1077-1095 = Adelheid of Rheinfelden

Preslava of Russia = (2) **Coloman** 1095-1116 — Almos = Ingeborg of Sweden — Emperor John Comnenus = Piroska

Stephen II 1116-1131 — **Bela II** 1131-1141 = Helena of Serbia

Euphrosyne dau. of Mstislav I of Kiev = **Geza II** 1141-1161 — **Ladislas II** 1162 — **Stephen IV** 1162-1163 = Maria of Byzantium

Agnes of Austria = **Stephen III** 1161-1173 — Anne of Chatillon-Antioche = (1) **Bela III** (2) 1173-1196 = Margaret dau. of Louis VII of France

Constantia of Aragon = **Emeric I** 1196-1204 — Gertrude of Meran = (1) **Andrew II** (3) 1205-1235 = Beatrice d'Este — Margaret m. Emperor Isaac Angelus — Constantia = Ottokar I of Bohemia

Ladislas III 1204-1205 — **Bela IV** 1235-1270 = Salome — Stephen = Tomasina Morosini — Wenceslas I

Andrew III 1290-1301 — Ottokar II

Wenceslas II

Elizabeth of Kumania = **Stephen V** 1270-1272 — Elizabeth m. Henry of Bavaria — Anna m. Rastislav ex-Prince of Novgorod — **Wenceslas** King of Hungary 1301-1304

Ladislas IV 1272-1290 = Elizabeth of Sicily — Maria = Charles II of Anjou — Kunigunda = Ottokar II of Bohemia

but left these regions self-government under a *ban.*

1095-1116. **Coloman** (Kalman) **I.** Another strong ruler, who, in

1097-1102. Conquered Dalmatia from the Venetian Republic.

1116-1131. **Stephen II,** in whose reign the dynastic struggles were resumed.

1131-1141. **Bela II.** He had been blinded by Coloman, and now took a horrible revenge on his opponents.

1141-1161. **Geza II.** The intestine conflicts were greatly complicated by the efforts of the Greek emperor, Manuel I, to extend his sway over Hungary. But a number of campaigns carried out to this end (1097-1102) led to no success, though at one time (1156) the Hungarians recognized Byzantine suzerainty.

1150. **Saxon** (i.e. Germans from the Moselle region) **settlement** in the Zips and southern Transylvania regions. They were called in to help defend the frontiers against Poland and against the Greeks, and had much to do with developing agriculture, trade, and town-building. In this period many Pechenegs and Szeklers were also established for frontier protection.

1161-1173. **Stephen III.**

1173-1196. **BELA III,** who had been educated at Constantinople. He married the sister of Philip Augustus of France and established a close dynastic connection with France. Bela was a strong ruler who successfully defended Dalmatia against Venice.

1196-1204. **Emeric I,** whose position was challenged by his brother Andrew.

1204-1205. **Ladislas III,** dethroned by Andrew.

1205-1235. **ANDREW II.** The most disastrous

The Marriage at Cana, detail from a fresco in the monastery of Studenica, built by Stephen Nemanya

reign in the Arpad period. Andrew was renowned for his extravagance and for his generosity to his foreign favorites. A crusade to the Holy Land (1217) cost him much money, which he raised by alienating huge tracts of the royal domain, facilitating the emergence of large landed magnates or oligarchs.

1222. The **GOLDEN BULL,** forced upon Andrew by the lesser nobility or gentry, led by Andrew's own son, Bela. This document became the charter of feudal privilege. It exempted the gentry and the clergy from taxation, granted them freedom to dispose of their domains as they saw fit, guaranteed them against arbitrary imprisonment and confiscation, and assured them an annual assembly to present grievances. No lands or offices were to be given to foreigners or Jews.

1224. The privileges of the Transylvanian Saxons were set down. They were given practical self-government, directly under the king.

1235-1270. **BELA IV.** A strong ruler who tried desperately to make good the losses of the preceding reign. The magnates, in reply, attempted to set up a rival ruler, and Bela in turn allowed some 40,000 families of the Cumans, who were driven westward by the Mongol invasions, to settle in the Theiss region in the hope of securing support against the magnates.

1241. The **GREAT MONGOL INVASION,** which took the country by surprise in the midst of its dissensions. Bela's army was overwhelmingly defeated at Muhi on the Theiss and he was obliged to flee to the Adriatic. The Mongols followed him, but suddenly gave up their conquests when news arrived of the death of the Great Khan. But the Mongol invasion left the country devastated. For defense purposes the nobility was allowed to build castles and these soon became bases for feudal warfare and for campaigns against the king himself.

1246. Bela defeated Frederick of Austria, the last of the Babenbergs, who had taken advantage of the Mongol invasion to appropriate some of the western provinces.

1265-1270. Wars of Bela against Ottokar II of Bohemia.

1270-1272. **Stephen V,** a weak ruler.

1272-1290. **Ladislas IV.** His efforts to curb the feudal aristocracy were of little avail, but in alliance with Rudolf of Hapsburg he succeeded in breaking the power of Ottokar in the **battle of Dürnkrut** (1278).

1290-1301. **Andrew III,** last of the native dynasty. He continued the struggle against the domination of the feudal aristocracy, but with little success. *(Cont. p. 334.)*

f. SERBIA, TO 1276

650. Approximate date of the completion of the Slav occupation of the Balkan area. Part of the Slav people extended as far west as Carniola and Carinthia, but these (the Slovenes) were conquered by the Franks in the early 9th century and were thenceforth part of the German Empire.

818. The **Croats,** who had also been conquered by the Franks, revolted, but were again subdued.

924. **Tomislav** became king of Croatia, accepting his crown from the pope. He ruled over later-day Croatia and over the territory as far

south as Montenegro, though the coastal towns were mostly under Byzantine control.

960. **Death of Chaslav,** who had made the first effort to unite the Serbs. The Serbs, inhabiting a mountainous area, were divided into tribes and clans, under headmen or *zupans.* The grand zupan held an honorary pre-eminence. Technically the territory was under Byzantine suzerainty, which, when the Eastern Empire was strong, was effectively exercised. By the end of the 10th century the inhabitants of present-day Serbia and eastern Bosnia had for the most part accepted eastern Christianity, while western Bosnia and Croatia leaned toward Roman Catholicism. But the conflict of the churches drew the southern Slavs this way and that, becoming frequently an important political as well as religious issue.

1077. **Mikhail of Serbia** was crowned by a papal legate.

1081-1101. **Bodin** established a Serbian state in Zeta (i.e. Montenegro).

1102. **Croatia** was joined with Hungary in a dynastic union, after the defeat of the last ruler, Petar, by King Ladislas. This involved the definitive victory of the western orientation in Croatia and the separation from the other southern Slavs.

1168-1196. **STEPHEN NEMANYA,** founder of the Nemanyid dynasty in the Raska (i.e. *Rascia* or Serbia proper). Though only grand zupan, Stephen appears to have made considerable progress in uniting the various clans. He definitely adopted the Greek Orthodox faith and persecuted the **Bogomils,** who were forced across the frontier into Bosnia, which at that time was ruled by a strong prince, Kulin (d. 1204). The death of Manuel I Comnenus (1180) and the subsequent decline of the Eastern Empire gave Stephen an opportunity to establish his independence of Constantinople and to conquer extensive territories to the south. In 1196 he retired to a monastery on Mt. Athos which had been founded by his son, **St. Sava.** Stephen died in 1200.

1196-1223. **STEPHEN NEMANYA II,** the son of the preceding. The beginning of his reign was marked by a struggle with his elder brother, Vukan, to whom Montenegro had been assigned. The Hungarians, who became an ever greater meance to Serbia, supported Vukan, and Stephen was forced to flee to the Bulgarian court. He returned with an army of Cumans supplied by Kaloyan (see below), who appropriated for himself most of eastern Serbia, including Belgrade and Nish. Stephen's brother, St. Sava, finally mediated between the two contestants and Stephen became ruler of Serbia proper.

1217. Stephen was crowned king by a papal legate (hence Stephen the First-Crowned).

1219. St. Sava, fearful of the Roman influence, visited Nicaea and induced the Greek patriarch to recognize him as archbishop of all Serbia and as head of an autocephalous church.

1222. Stephen was recrowned by St. Sava with a crown from Nicaea, thus re-establishing the eastern orientation.

1223-1234. **Radoslav,** the son of Stephen, a weak ruler, who was deposed by his brother

1234-1242. **Vladislav.** He married a daughter of Tsar John Asen II of Bulgaria and during this period much of eastern Serbia was under Bulgarian domination.

1242-1276. **Urosh I,** brother of the preceding

Bogomil tombstones in Bosnia

Vladislav, 1234–1242 (13th-century fresco)

two rulers. He married a daughter of the deposed Latin emperor, Baldwin II, and established an alliance with Charles of Anjou, heir of the Latin claims to Constantinople.

1254. The Hungarians, who already held part of northern Serbia, established their suzerainty over Bosnia and Herzegovina. *(Cont. p. 335.)*

g. THE SECOND BULGARIAN EMPIRE, TO 1258

(From p. 207)

Following the collapse of the First Bulgarian Empire in 1018, Bulgaria was, for 168 years, an integral part of the Byzantine Empire. The more stringent taxation and other grievances led to a serious revolt in 1040, led by **Peter Delyan,** a son of Gabriel Radomir, and confined to the northwest and western parts of the former empire. Delyan had himself proclaimed *tsar,* but the movement suffered from his rivalry with Tikhomir of Durazzo. In 1041 Delyan was defeated and captured by the im-

perial troops. Another uprising, led by **George Voitech,** in 1072–1073, never assumed the same proportions and was suppressed without much difficulty. During the Byzantine period the country was constantly exposed to marauding raids by the Patzinaks (1048–1054), many of whom settled in northeastern Bulgaria, and by invasions of the Cumans (1064). The **Bogomil heresy** continued to spread, despite persecution by the government (1110 ff.). Under the leadership of the monks it became to a certain extent a reaction to the Greek influence exerted by the higher clergy.

1185. RISING OF JOHN AND PETER ASEN, two Bulgarian lords from the vicinity of Tirnovo. Defeated by the Emperor Isaac II Angelus (1186) they fled to the Cumans and returned with an army of the latter. After raiding into Thrace, they accepted a truce which left them in possession of Bulgaria north of the Balkan Mountains.

1189. The Asens attempted to effect an alliance with Frederick Barbarossa and the leaders of the Third Crusade, against the Greeks.

This came to nothing, but the Bulgarians resumed their raids into Thrace and Macedonia. An imperial army under Isaac Angelus was completely defeated in **a battle near Berrhoe.**

1196. Peter Asen succeeded to leadership of the movement after the murder of John by boyar (i.e. noble) conspirators.

1197. Peter himself fell a victim to his boyar rivals.

1197-1207. KALOYAN (Joannitsa), the younger brother of John and Peter. He made peace with the Greeks (1201) and then engaged (1202) in campaigns against the Serbs (taking of Nish) and the Hungarians, whom he drove back over the Danube.

1204. The **collapse of the Byzantine Empire** (p. 271) gave Kaloyan an excellent opportunity to reaffirm his dominion. By recognizing the primacy of the pope, he succeeded in securing the appointment of a primate for Bulgaria and in getting himself crowned king by the papal legate. At the same time he took over the whole of western Macedonia.

1205. Supported by the Cumans and the local Greeks, Kaloyan completely defeated the Frankish crusaders near Adrianople and captured the Emperor Baldwin I.

1206. Kaloyan put down a revolt of the Greeks and besieged Adrianople and Thessalonica. He was murdered in 1207.

1207-1218. Boril, the nephew of Kaloyan, whose position was not recognized by all other leaders, some of whom attempted to set up independent principalities.

1208. Boril was completely defeated by the Franks under Henry I in the **battle of Philippopolis,** and ultimately (1213) was obliged to make peace.

1217. Ivan (*John*) **Asen,** son of Kaloyan, supported by the Russians, began a revolt in northern Bulgaria. He besieged and took Tirnovo, and captured and blinded Boril (1218).

1218-1241. JOHN ASEN II, whose reign marked the apogee of the Second Bulgarian Empire. John was a mild and generous ruler, much beloved even by the Greek population.

1228-1230. Owing to the youth of the Emperor Baldwin II, a number of Frank nobles at Constantinople projected making John Asen emperor and thereby securing themselves against the aggression of Theodore of Epirus (p. 280). The scheme was opposed by the Latin clergy and ultimately came to nothing.

1230. John Asen defeated Theodore of Epirus at **Klokotnitsa** on the Maritza River and captured him. He then occupied all of western Thrace, Macedonia, and even northern Albania, leaving Thessalonica and Epirus to Theodore's brother Manuel, who became his vassal.

1232. John broke with Rome and the Bulgarian church became independent.

1235. Alliance of John with the Greek emperor of Nicaea against the Franks. The Greeks recognized the patriarch of Tirnovo. Together the allies besieged Constantinople, which was relieved by a fleet and forces from Achaia.

1236. The Hungarians, instigated by the pope, began to threaten the Bulgarians and forced John to withdraw from operations against the Latin Empire.

1241-1246. Kaliman I, the son of John Asen II. His reign was distinguished chiefly by the great incursion of the Mongols, returning from the expedition into central Europe (1241).

1246-1257. Michael Asen, the youngest son of John, and a mere child. The Nicaean emperor, John Vatatzes, took advantage of the situation to conquer all southern Thrace and Macedonia, while Michael of Epirus appropriated western Macedonia.

1254. On the death of John Vatatzes, Michael Asen attempted to recover the lost territories, but was badly defeated by Theodore II Lascaris at **Adrianople** and later (1256) in Macedonia.

1257-1258. Kaliman II, who, with support of the boyars, drove out Michael Asen, only to be deposed and expelled in his turn. He was the last ruler of the Asen dynasty.

(*Cont. p. 337.*)

3. *The Near East*

a. THE BYZANTINE EMPIRE, 1025-1204

(*From p. 205*)

[For a complete list of the Byzantine emperors see Appendix II.]

The period of the later Macedonian emperors (to 1050) and the succeeding thirty years was a period of decline, marked by the rule of women, barbarian invasions in the Balkans, the advance of the Normans in Italy, and the expansion of the Seljuk Turks (p. 272) in Anatolia. Within the empire there was a steady development of the clerical and bureaucratic nobility in the capital and of the feudal baronage in the provinces, leading ultimately to sharp conflict between the two interests.

1025-1028. CONSTANTINE VIII, the younger brother of Basil II, a man suspicious of the military commanders, who granted many high offices to court favorites.

1027. The **Patzinaks,** who had invaded the Balkans, were finally driven back over the Danube by the general, Constantine Diogenes.

1028-1050. ZOË, empress. She was the third daughter of Constantine and, though 48 years old at her accession, married three times, associating her husbands in the imperial office.

1028-1034. ROMANUS III (Argyropolus), an official 60 years old, first husband of Zoë. He made great efforts to gain popularity by catering to the populace, the nobility, and especially the church. The patriarchate was permitted to persecute the Monophysites of Syria, thousands of whom fled to Moslem territory. The hatred engendered by this policy helps to explain the Seljuk advance in subsequent years.

1030. Romanus suffered a severe defeat in a campaign against the Moslem emirs who attacked Syria.

1031. The situation was saved by the victories of **Georgios Maniakes,** greatest imperial general of the period.

1032. A combined Byzantine-Ragusan fleet completely defeated the Saracen pirates in the Adriatic.

1034-1041. MICHAEL IV (the Paphlagonian), second husband of Zoë. He was a man of lowly origin, who promptly established his brothers (mostly men of energy and ability) in high office.

1034-1035. The Byzantine fleets, manned by the Norseman Harald Haardraade and Scandinavian mercenaries, repeatedly defeated the Saracen pirates off the Anatolian coast and ravaged the coasts of North Africa.

1038. Maniakes and Haardraade with Scandinavian and Italian mercenaries and with the support of the Byzantine fleets, stormed Messina and defeated the Sicilian Saracens, first at **Rametta** (1038), then at **Dragina** (1040).

1040. Revolt of the Bulgarians under Peter Delyan, a descendant of Tsar Samuel. The revolt was directed against the harsh fiscal policy of the government. The Bulgars attacked Thessalonica, but the city held out. Ultimately the movement collapsed, as the result of dissension among the leaders. Bulgaria was then incorporated in the empire and the autocephalous church of Ochrid became a prey of the patriarchal hierarchy.

1041-1042. MICHAEL V (Kalaphates), one of Zoë's favorites. He attempted to secure sole power by shutting the empress in a cloister, but this led to a rising of the Constantinople nobility and to the incarceration of Michael in a monastery.

1042-1055. CONSTANTINE IX (Monomachus), the third husband of Zoë, a scholarly person, wholly out of sympathy with the army and with the military aristocracy. He systematically neglected the frontier defenses and the forces.

1042. Maniakes totally defeated the Normans, who had begun the attack on southern Italy, in the **battle of Monopoli** (near Naples).

1043. Revolt of Maniakes, representing the disaffection of the military classes. Maniakes landed at Durazzo and prepared to march on the capital, but he was accidentally shot and killed on the way.

1046. The Byzantine forces occupied Ani and took over the government of Armenia, which became another field for clerical exploitation.

1047. Another military uprising, led by Leo Tornikios, failed.

1048. The imperial generals defeated the advancing Seljuk armies at **Stragna.**

1050. **Death of Zoë.** Her husband Constantine continued to reign alone.

1051. Expulsion of the Patzinaks from Bulgaria, after years of ravaging and unsuccessful Byzantine campaigns.

1042–1056. **THEODORA,** empress. She was the elder sister of Zoë, an intelligent, vigorous, and popular ruler, but already advanced in age.

1054. **Final schism between Rome and Constantinople.** The long-standing friction between the Papacy and the eastern patriarch had come to a head with the conquest of parts of southern Italy by the Normans, who were supported by the Papacy. The Patriarch Michael Kerularios disputed the claim of Pope Leo IX to jurisdiction in southern Italy. Negotiations were opened, but each side assumed an uncompromising attitude and the rift became unbridgeable. The enmity it left behind was of the utmost importance for the development of the following years.

1056–1057. **MICHAEL VI** (Stratioticus), who was overthrown almost at once by a revolt of the Anatolian feudal barons.

1057–1059. **ISAAC I COMNENUS,** proclaimed by the insurgents. He was an able and energetic army man, who promptly abolished a host of sinecures, undertook the reform of the finances, etc. Isaac, already advanced in years, soon found his work too arduous and abdicated in favor of

1059–1067. **CONSTANTINE X** (Dukas), a high official of the finance department. Constantine introduced a period of domination by the civil officials, church, and scholars, during which the army was viewed with suspicion, neglected, and driven into hostility.

1060. The Normans took Rheggio, completing the conquest of Calabria.

1064. The Seljuks, under Alp Arslan, took Ani and ravaged Armenia.

1065. The Cumans, having crossed the Danube, flooded the Balkan area as far as Thessalonica. They were finally driven back by local forces.

1068–1071. **ROMANUS IV DIOGENES,** who, on Constantine's death, married the widowed empress, Eudoxia. Romanus was an ambitious soldier, who did his best to check the advance of the enemy in the east and the west.

1068. The Normans took Otranto, and then Bari (1071), the last Byzantine outpost. This marked the **end of the Byzantine rule in Italy.**

1068–1069. Romanus succeeded in repulsing the Seljuks, though they repeatedly raided through the whole of eastern Anatolia.

1071. **BATTLE OF MANZIKERT** (north of Lake Van). Romanus had concentrated huge forces for a decisive battle, and he rejected all offers of a settlement. In the course of a hard-fought battle he was deserted by Andronicus Dukas and other Byzantine magnates. Romanus was defeated and captured, but then released by the Seljuks. He attempted to

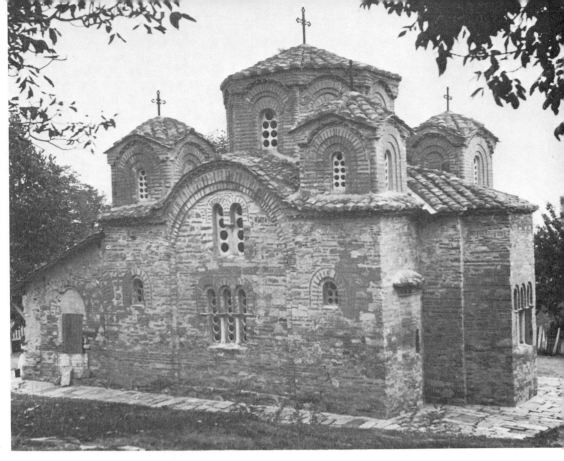

The Nerezi, church built near Skopje in 1164 by Alexius Comnenus

regain the Byzantine throne, but was defeated by his opponents and blinded. He died soon afterward.

1071–1078. **MICHAEL VII** (Parapinakes), a son of Constantine X. His elevation meant another victory for the bureaucratic group. Michael made the great scholar **Michael Psellus** his chief adviser and devoted himself to the pursuit of learning. The military system was again allowed to fall into neglect.

1074. The emperor concluded a **treaty with the Seljuks** in order to secure their aid against his uncle, who had set himself up as a pretender. The Seljuks defeated the pretender, but took advantage of the situation to spread themselves over a large part of Anatolia.

1078. Revolt of Nicephorus Briennius in Albania. Another military revolt broke out in Anatolia, led by Nicephorus Botaniates, who was supported by the Seljuks.

1078–1081. **NICEPHORUS III** (Botaniates), emperor after Michael's abdication. His accession was met by a number of insurrections in various parts of the army, but these were suppressed by the able general Alexius Comnenus.

1081. Revolt of Alexius Comnenus himself. He seized Constantinople with a force of mercenaries, who thereupon plundered the capital. The victory of Comnenus meant the final success of the military aristocracy and the beginning of a new period of military achievement.

1081–1118. **ALEXIUS I COMNENUS,** an able general, vigorous administrator, conscientious ruler, and shrewd diplomat. Having to rely upon the great feudal families, he attempted to win their support by lavish grants of honors and ranks. At the same time he tried to use the high clergy to counterbalance the influence of the nobility. He reformed the judicial and financial systems and systematically used his

resources in money to buy off the enemies he could not conquer.

1081–1085. The war against the Normans under **Robert Guiscard.** The latter landed in Epirus with a large force and besieged Durazzo (Dyracchium). Alexius bought the support of the Venetians with extensive trade privileges (1082), but Guiscard defeated the emperor in the **battle of Pharsalus,** after which he took Durazzo. The war was continued by Robert's son, Bohemund, who again defeated Alexius and in 1083 conquered all Macedonia as far as the Vardar. But the advance was broken by the resistance of Larissa, by the guerrilla tactics of the natives (who hated the heretical Latins), and by the Seljuk cavalry employed by the emperor. In 1085 the combined Byzantine and Venetian fleets defeated the Normans near Corfu. The death of Robert Guiscard at the same time led to dissension among his sons and the abandonment of the Balkan project.

1086–1091. **Revolt of the Bogomils** in Thrace and Bulgaria. The heretics were supported by the Patzinaks and Cumans and were able to defeat Alexius and a large army (**battle of Drystra** or Dorostolon, 1087). The Cumans then ravaged the entire eastern Balkan region as far as Constantinople until Alexius bought them off, took them into imperial service, and used them (1091) to annihilate the Patzinaks (**battle of Leburnion**).

1092. Death of Malik Shah, ruler of the Seljuk empire of Iconium, which controlled almost all of Anatolia. The death of Malik led to disputes as to the succession and paved the way for the partial reconquest of Anatolia.

1094. **Constantine Diogenes,** a pretender to the throne, crossed the Danube with an army of Cumans and besieged Adrianople, but was then defeated in the battle of **Taurocomon.**

The Comneni and Angeli (1057–1204)

(From p. 202)

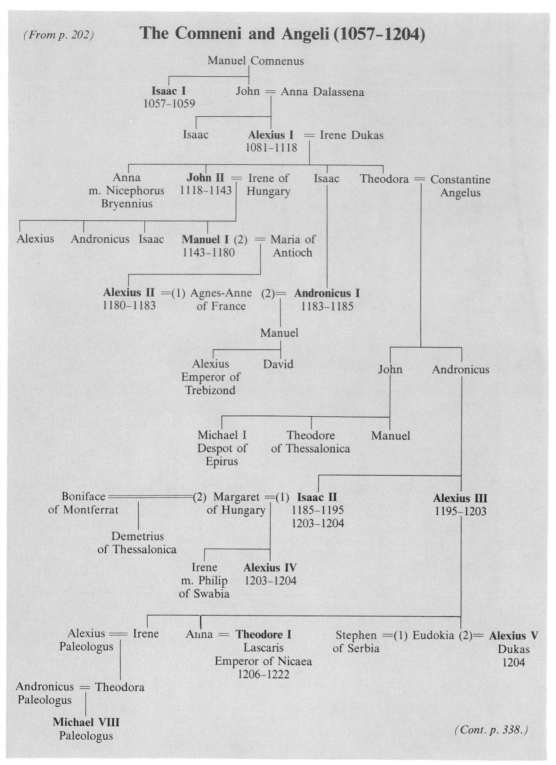

Manuel Comnenus

Isaac I 1057–1059 — John = Anna Dalassena

Isaac — **Alexius I** 1081–1118 = Irene Dukas

Anna m. Nicephorus Bryennius — **John II** 1118–1143 = Irene of Hungary — Isaac — Theodora = Constantine Angelus

Alexius — Andronicus — Isaac — **Manuel I** (2) 1143–1180 = Maria of Antioch

Alexius II 1180–1183 =(1) Agnes-Anne of France (2)= **Andronicus I** 1183–1185

Manuel

Alexius Emperor of Trebizond — David

John — Andronicus

Michael I Despot of Epirus — Theodore of Thessalonica — Manuel

Boniface of Montferrat =(2) Margaret of Hungary =(1) **Isaac II** 1185–1195 1203–1204 — **Alexius III** 1195–1203

Demetrius of Thessalonica

Irene m. Philip of Swabia — **Alexius IV** 1203–1204

Alexius Paleologus = Irene — Anna = **Theodore I** Lascaris Emperor of Nicaea 1206–1222 — Stephen of Serbia =(1) Eudokia (2)= **Alexius V** Dukas 1204

Andronicus Paleologus = Theodora

Michael VIII Paleologus

(Cont. p. 338.)

1096–1097. THE FIRST CRUSADE (p. 273) The crusaders, of whom Bohemund was one of the leaders, were looked upon with great suspicion in the east, where there was little interest in a movement organized by the heretical Latin pope. But Alexius was unable to stop the crusaders, and therefore devoted himself to managing the movement. He induced them to promise to do homage to the empire for all territory reconquered from the infidel. The crusading **victories at Nicaea** and **Dorylaeum** (1097) enabled Alexius to recover the entire western coast of Anatolia.

1098–1108. Second war with the Normans. The crusaders, having regained Antioch (lost to the Turks only in 1085), turned it over to Bohemund, who refused to recognize Alexius' suzerainty. War broke out. Bohemund returned to Italy and raised a huge army, with which he appeared in Epirus (1104). He failed in his siege of Durazzo, and Alexius wisely avoided open battle. Ultimately (1108) Bohemund agreed to make peace, recognizing Byzantine suzerainty over Antioch.

1110–1117. War against the Seljuks, who again advanced to the Bosporus. In 1116 Alexius won a resounding victory at **Philomelion**, which induced the Turks to make peace at **Akroinon** (1117); they abandoned the entire coastal area of Anatolia (north, west, and south) and all of Anatolia west of a line from Sinope through Ancyra (Ankara) and Philomelion.

1111. Trade privileges granted to the Pisans. This was part of the emperor's effort to draw the Pisans away from the Normans and at the same time to counterbalance the extensive trade position of the Venetians in the empire.

1118–1143. JOHN II COMNENUS, a ruler of high moral integrity, mild, brave, and sincere. He devoted his attention chiefly to the east, with the object of recovering the old frontier of the Euphrates and of subjecting the Latin states of Syria to the empire.

1120–1121. In a successful campaign against the Seljuks, John recovered southwestern Anatolia. He was diverted from further conquests by continued incursions of the Patzinaks in the Balkans.

1122. The Patzinaks were completely defeated and thenceforth did not threaten the empire.

1122–1126. War with Venice, resulting from John's refusal to renew the extensive trading privileges, which the Venetians had been exploiting to the full. The Venetian fleets ravaged the islands of the Aegean, occupied Corfu and Cephalonia, and ultimately (1126) forced John to renew the privileges.

1124. Intervention of the emperor in behalf of Bela II in Hungary, initiating a policy which continued throughout the century. The objective of the Comneni was to prevent the Hungarians from establishing control over the Slavic regions of Dalmatia, Croatia, and Serbia. By the **Peace of 1126** the emperor secured Branicova, a vital bridgehead on the Danube.

1134–1137. Conquest of Cilician (Little) Armenia, which was allied with the Latin kingdom of Antioch. John forced Raymond of Antioch to do homage for his domain.

1143. John died from a wound incurred while hunting. He was just about to renew his campaigns in Syria.

1143–1180. MANUEL I COMNENUS, the son of John, a noble, intelligent, chivalrous idealist, and yet an adroit statesman and ambitious soldier. He was the greatest of the Comneni and the most splendid. In his reign Constantinople came to be accepted as the capital of the world and the center of culture. Its brilliant art was imitated in the east as in the west. Manuel married a Latin princess (Maria of Antioch) and throughout his career cherished the hope of resurrecting a universal empire. Hence his association with and employment of Latin nobles, who intermarried with the Greek aristocracy, his constant toying with the idea of reunion with Rome, his designs on Italian territory, and his antagonism to the Hohenstaufen emperors. All this tended to arouse much hostility among the Greeks (accentuated by the high-handed activities of the Italian traders), cost the empire inordinate sums of money, and involved repeated conflict with the Normans. The emperor's preoccupation in the west at the same time forced him to neglect the east, where the Seljuk sultanate of Iconium (Rum) was able to effect a marked recovery.

1147–1158. War with Roger of Sicily. The Norman fleets ravaged Euboea and Attica, took and plundered Thebes and Corinth, carried away large numbers of the silk-workers, who were established at Palermo. The emperor, having neglected the Byzantine fleet, was obliged to buy the aid of Venice with extensive trading rights (1148). The Venetians helped to reconquer Corfu (1149) and paved the way for the Byzantine conquest of Ancona (1151). But efforts to extend the Greek power in Italy met with failure (1154) and Manuel in the end had to agree to an inconclusive peace (1158).

1147-1149. THE SECOND CRUSADE (p. *274*). The crusaders, having plundered the Balkan region, almost came to blows with the Greeks at Constantinople, but Manuel by diplomacy prevented a clash. The Greeks did nothing to prevent the defeat of the crusaders in Anatolia.

1152-1154. Successful war against the Hungarians, who attempted to make good their claims to Serbia and Bosnia. Peace was made in 1156, the Hungarians recognizing the emperor's suzerainty.

1155. Trade privileges granted to Genoa, the emperor hoping thereby to counteract the domination of the Venetians.

1158-1159. An expedition against Raymond of Antioch forced the latter to renew his homage.

1161. Kilidj Arslan IV, sultan of Rum, made peace with the empire, recognizing the emperor's primacy.

1165-1168. War with the Hungarians. The imperial forces took Dalmatia and in the final peace (1168) received also part of Croatia. The following years Manuel interfered actively in Hungarian dynastic affairs. Bela III was practically his vassal.

1170-1177. War with Venice, the natural result of the Byzantine acquisitions in Dalmàtia and in Italy. The emperor arrested all Venetian traders in Constantinople and confiscated their goods, but with a neglected fleet he was able to do little. The Venetians conquered Ragusa (1171) and Chios (1171), though they failed in an attack on Ancona (1173). In 1175 the Venetians made an alliance with the Normans against the empire and thereby forced Manuel to yield. By the **Peace of 1176** the trade privileges were renewed and the emperor paid a heavy indemnity.

1176-1177. War against the Seljuks. The Byzantines were defeated at **Myriocephalon** (1176), but in the next year Manuel defeated the enemy in Bithynia, while John Vatatzes drove them out of the Meander Valley.

1180-1183. ALEXIUS II COMNENUS, the son of Manuel, who ruled under the regency of his mother, Maria of Antioch. The regent relied almost entirely upon Latins in her service.

1182. Revolt of the populace of Constantinople against the Latins, officials, and traders, who were brutally cut down in a great massacre. The mob forced the proclamation of

1183-1185. ANDRONICUS I COMNENUS, an uncle of the boy-emperor, who ruled first as co-emperor, but in 1183 had Alexius strangled and became sole ruler. Andronicus had intrigued innumerable times against Manuel and was renowned for his lack of principle. But he was a man of great personal charm, intelligent, vigorous, unscrupulous, and cruel. Through persecution, confiscations, and executions he cleaned the court circle, got rid of the hated Latins, abolished sale of offices, sine-

cures, etc.; reformed the judiciary, lightened the taxes. All this was a policy directed against the powerful official and landed aristocracy and might, had it been carried through, have led to a thoroughgoing reform of the empire.

1185. The Norman attack. The Normans took Durazzo, sent an army and a navy against Thessalonica, which they stormed, and massacred the Greeks. This attack led to a revolt of the Greek nobility against Andronicus, who was deposed, tortured, and executed.

1185-1195. ISAAC ANGELUS, leader of the insurgents. His accession meant a return of the old negligence and corruption. Within a brief space the entire empire began to disintegrate. In the provinces the powerful feudal families (i.e. Sguros in Greece; Gabras at Trebizond) began to set up as independent potentates.

1185. Victory of the Byzantine general, Alexius Branas, over the Normans at Demetritsa. By 1191 the Normans were driven out of the Balkans and even out of Durazzo and Corfu.

1185-1188. The **great insurrection in Bulgaria,** led by Peter and John Asen. This was due primarily to the extortion of the imperial fiscal agents. The revolt was supported by the Cumans and resulted in the devastation of much of the Balkan region, with the annihilation of much of the Greek population. Though at times successful, the Greek commanders were unable to suppress the movement, which resulted in the formation of a new Bulgarian state north of the Balkan Mountains (1188).

1187. Fall of Jerusalem. Isaac, in fear of another crusade, allied himself with Saladin.

1189. THE THIRD CRUSADE *(p. 275)*. Frederick Barbarossa was welcomed in Bulgaria by John Asen, who offered him an army for use against the empire. But Frederick avoided friction as well as might be, and Isaac did not

oppose the crossing of the crusaders into Anatolia. The death of Saladin (1193) relieved the danger from the east.

1190-1194. Continuation of the war in Bulgaria. The Byzantine forces were defeated at Berrhoe (1190) and at Arcadiopolis (1194).

1195-1203. ALEXIUS III, the brother of Isaac, whom he deposed and blinded.

1196. The western emperor, Henry VI, heir to the Norman domains, demanded Durazzo and Thessalonica. Alexius settled for a huge money payment, and Henry's death (1197) removed the immediate threat from that quarter.

1201. Peace with the Bulgars, who were allowed to retain most of the eastern Balkan area, under the younger brother of the Asens, John (Joannitsa, Kaloyan, 1197-1207).

1202-1204. THE FOURTH CRUSADE (p. *275*). The leaders were the Venetian doge, **Enrico Dandolo,** and **Boniface of Montferrat.** Alexius, the son of Isaac, appealed for aid against his uncle and promised great concessions. Dandolo succeeded in diverting the expedition against Constantinople. The crusaders took Durazzo (1203) and arrived at Constantinople (June, 1203). The emperor thereupon fled to Adrianople (July). His deposed brother, Isaac, was set upon the throne with his son, the accomplice of the crusaders.

1203-1204. ALEXIUS IV. He was wholly under the control of the crusaders and was forced to pay a heavy tribute. Popular discontent led to

1204, Jan. 25. A revolution and the proclamation of

1204. Alexius V (Dukas). Alexius IV was killed. The new ruler refused payments to the crusaders and demanded their withdrawal.

Apr. 12. The crusaders stormed the city, which was given over to a merciless sack. The emperor succeeded in escaping. *(Cont. p. 279.)*

Battle between the Turks and the Crusaders, 1148

b. THE SELJUK TURKS, 1037-1109

(From p. 213)

1037. The **Seljuks,** a sept of the Ghuzz Turks, under the brothers Tughril Beg and Chagar Beg, invaded Khorasan and defeated the Ghaznavid armies. They then conquered Balkh, Jurjan, Tabaristan, and Khwarezm.

1055. Entry of Tughril Beg into Baghdad, where he was proclaimed sultan, with the title *King of the East and the West.* Invasion of Byzantine Cappadocia and Phrygia by Tughril Beg.

1063-1072. Alp Arslan, brilliant nephew of Tughril, succeeded the latter. He conquered Georgia and Armenia.

1071. BATTLE OF MANZIKERT (Malaz Kard). Alp Arslan defeated the Byzantine emperor, Romanus IV Diogenes, and virtually destroyed the Byzantine power in Asia Minor.

1073-1092. Malik Shah, son of Alp Arslan. His vizir, **Nizam al-Mulk,** was one of the ablest administrators of Oriental history. At the same time he was a patron of learning, founder of colleges in Baghdad (the Nizamiya) and other principal cities. Under him the calendar was reformed by the last of the intellectuals of the Baghdad school, **Omar Khayyam** (d. 1123), poet and mathematician (worked on cubic equations).

1084. The Seljuks took Antioch.

1090. Rise of the Ismailian fraternity of the **Assassins,** founded by Hasan Sabbah, a schoolfellow of Nizam al-Mulk, and a Fatimid propagandist. He captured the mountain stronghold of Alamut in the Elburz range in Mazandêran. The Assassins later became masters of many mountain fortresses in northern Persia, Iraq, and Syria. The crusaders came into contact with the Syrian branch.

1091. Nizam al-Mulk was murdered by one of Hasan's emissaries, after two expeditions against the Assassins had failed.

1094-1104. Barkyaruk (Rukn al-Din), son of Malik Shah, sultan. Civil war broke out between the new ruler and his brother, Mohammed, over Iran and Khorasan, and separate branches of the Seljuk family attained virtual independence in different parts of the empire, although the main line still preserved the nominal sovereignty down to 1157. The **Seljuk Empire of the East** ultimately fell before the attack of the Khwarezm shah (1157). The Seljuks of Kirman (1041-1187) were overthrown by the Ghuzz Turcomans; the Seljuks of Syria (1094-1117) by the Burids and Ortuqids; the Seljuks of Iraq and Kurdistan (1117-1194) by the shahs of Khwarezm. The Seljuks of Rum (Iconium, Koniah), who ruled most of Anatolia, absorbed the Danishmandid princedom in Cappadocia, but were ousted by the Mongols and the Othmanli (Ottoman) Turks *(p. 341).*

1100-1200. During the 12th century the whole of the Seljuk Empire, excepting Rum, fell into the hands of captains of the Seljuk armies, the so-called *Atabegs* (regents). The **Burid dynasty** of Damascus (1103-1154) was founded by Tughtugin. The **Zangid dynasty** of Mesopotamia and Syria (1127-1250) by Imad al-Din Zangi, whose son, Nur al-Din, was famous as an opponent of the crusaders. The Zangids absorbed the Burids (1154). The **Ortuqid dynasty** of Diyar-Bakr (Diarbekr) was founded by Ortuq ibn Akrab (1101), whose sons, Sukman and Il-Ghazi, both won renown in the wars against the Latin princes of Palestine. The dynasty lasted until 1312. Sukman Qutbi was the first of the shahs of Armenia (1100-1207). The Atabeg house of Azerbaijan (1136-1225) was founded by Ildigiz, whose son, Mohammed, was the actual ruler of the Seljuk kingdom of Iraq. The Salgharids held Fars (1148-1287), the Hazaraspids Luristan (1148-1339); and Anushtigin, a Turkish slave of Balkatigin of Ghazni, was the grandfather of the first independent shah of Khwarezm, Atsiz. At one time the rule of the Khwarezm shah was almost co-terminous with the Seljuk Empire.

1095. The crusaders, having invaded the dominions of the sultan of Rum, took Antioch, with frightful slaughter. They stormed Jerusalem (1099) and founded the Latin kingdom of Jerusalem. By 1109 Caesarea, Tripoli, Tyre, and Sidon were captured. Constant warfare between the crusaders and the Moslems (Fati-

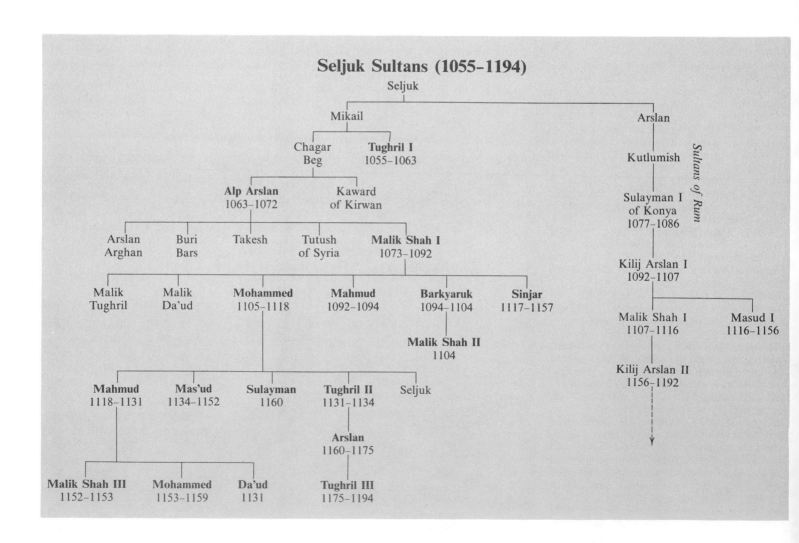

Seljuk Sultans (1055-1194)

mids, Burids, Zangids, Ortuqids, and finally Saladin, the sultan of Egypt). *(Cont. p. 341.)*

c. THE CRUSADES, 1096–1291

Precursors of the Crusades

(1) **Penitentiary pilgrimages** probably dating from the days of Helena, mother of Constantine the Great; after the Arab conquest of Jerusalem (638) the Holy City was a joint shrine of Christian and Moslem; protectorate of Charlemagne over the Holy Places (recognized by Harun al-Rashid, 807); abrogated by the mad Caliph Hakim (1010); (2) **Charlemagne's war** of Christian reconquest in Spain; (3) the **Cluniac revival** and its stress on pilgrimages led to a steady increase of pilgrimages (117 known in the 11th century) without serious opposition from the tolerant Moslems until the advent of the Seljuks; (4) **wars of Christian reconquest** in the west began European reaction to Moslem pressure; Pisan reconquest of Sardinia (c. 1016) with papal support; alliance of Castile and Aragon in the reconquest of Spain (c. 1050); Norman reconquest of Sicily (1060–1090).

1087. Genoa and Pisa, by capture of Mahdiyah in Africa, gained command of the western Mediterranean from the Moslems. Appeal of the Greek emperor after Manzikert (1071) to Pope Gregory VII; preparation of an army (alliance with Roger Guiscard) by Gregory (1074) to aid the Greeks.

Transformation by Pope Urban II of military assistance to Constantinople into a new kind of holy war (a sort of ecclesiastical imperialism) under the auspices of the revived and regenerated Papacy.

1095. Appeal from the Greek emperor at the **synod of Piacenza;** Urban's call at the **synod of Clermont** (1095): Urban, a Cluniac and a Frenchman, speaking to Frenchmen, recited the glorious deeds of the French and tales of Moslem atrocities, made open allusions to the chances of profit and advancement, attacked feudal violence at home, and brought the audience to wild enthusiasms; he himself distributed crosses. Urban's propaganda journeys and the preaching of **Peter the Hermit** and others stirred the west, but had the greatest effect in France and Lorraine, the area most under Cluniac influence. The great rulers were all at odds with the Papacy or busy at home; the rest of Europe indifferent, and the Crusades began as they continued, largely under French auspices.

1096–1099. THE FIRST CRUSADE. Five popular, aimless mass migrations (1096), emptying whole villages and often accompanied by pillage and anti-Semitic outbreaks, of which two (perhaps 7000 under Peter the Hermit and perhaps 5000 under Walter the Penniless) reached Asia Minor and were annihilated. The Norman-French baronage flocked to the Cross and converged in three divisions on Constantinople: the Lorrainers under **Godfrey of Bouillon** and his brother Baldwin, via Hungary; the Provençals under **Count Raymond of Toulouse** and the papal legate, Adhemar of Puy, via Illyria; the Normans under **Bohemund of Otranto** (the most effective leader) via Durazzo by sea and land. Perhaps they were 30,000 in all.

The Greek emperor, Alexius I Comnenus, expecting mercenaries and unprepared for

Peter the Hermit and Walter the Penniless leading the First Crusade

Early 18th-century reproduction of stained glass with the story of the Crusades

back home. The Norman effort to dominate the government through their patriarch Dagobert led to his deposition by the anti-Norman party and Jerusalem became a feudal kingdom rather than theocracy under papal domination. The government (as revealed by the *Assizes of Jerusalem*, the most complete feudal code extant) was narrowly feudal, the king a feudal suzerain, not a sovereign, the tenants-in-chief dominant. Besides the feudal organization there were burgher and ecclesiastical organizations, with their own courts.

Continued divisions among the Moslems and the weakness of the Greeks favored the progress of the Latin states: the **kingdom of Jerusalem,** in close commercial alliance with the Italian towns (Genoa, Pisa, and later Venice), profited by the commerce through its ports and extended south to tap the Red Sea trade. The other states: the **county of Edessa** (established by Baldwin), the **principality of Antioch** (established by Bohemund), and the **county of Tripoli** (set up by Raymond of Toulouse), were fiefs of Jerusalem (divided into four great baronies and into lesser fiefs). The departure of the main body of the crusaders left the Franks without enough forces to prevent their orientalization and decline. After the capture of Jerusalem (1187) the kingdom of Jerusalem ceased to be an organized state.

Moslem unification in Syria was completed by the Atabegs of Mosul and signalized by the capture of Edessa (1144). Mosul soon mastered Egypt; Saladin emerged supreme in Egypt (1171), quickly reduced Damascus and Aleppo, and brought Syria and Egypt under a single efficient rule.

1147–1149. THE SECOND CRUSADE. Bernard of Clairvaux, persuaded by Pope Eugenius III, somewhat against his will, preached (1145) the Second Crusade. Conrad III and King Louis VII of France took the Cross. To avoid conflicts the two monarchs went by separate routes; there never was coherent direction or unity of command. The Norman Roger of Sicily profited by the Second Crusade to seize the Greek islands and to attack Athens, Thebes, and Corinth. Nothing

Saladin, Sultan of Egypt and Syria

Godfrey of Bouillon at the Holy Sepulcher

crusaders, provided food and escort and punished the plunderers. He exacted an oath of fealty from the leaders (Raymond refused) in an effort to insure his title to any recovered "lost provinces" of the Greek Empire.

The **Moslem opposition:** the Seljuks had merely garrisoned Syria and were not popular with the native population. Moslem unity in Asia Minor ended with the death of Malik Shah (1092), and Syria was divided politically, racially, and theologically (Sunnite *vs.* Shi'ite; the Fatimite capture of Jerusalem (1098) from the Sunnites).

1097. Nicaea, the Seljuk capital in Asia Minor, taken by the combined Greek and crusading force; defeat of the Moslem field army at Dorylaeum; excursion of Baldwin and Tan-

cred, and rivalry in Cilicia; Bohemund established himself in the Antioch area. Siege and capture (by treachery) of Antioch (1097–1098); countersiege of the Christians in Antioch by the emir of Mosul; election of Bohemund as leader. Baldwin's conquest of Edessa (1097); death of Adhemar of Puy (1098); Christian divisions: rivalry of Norman and Provençal (the *Holy Lance*).

1099. March to Jerusalem (Genoese convoy and food supply); siege, capture, and horrors of the sack. The death of the papal legate left the organization of the government of Jerusalem to feudal laymen. **Godfrey of Bouillon,** elected king, assumed the title of *Defender of the Holy Sepulcher* (for pious reasons). The main body of the crusaders soon streamed

The Crusaders' Wall at Acre

of importance was achieved by the Second Crusade and the movement was discredited throughout Europe.

1184. Saladin's steady advance led to a great appeal to the west; King Philip II of France and Henry II of England declined the crown of Jerusalem, but levied a **Saladin tithe** (1188) to finance a crusade. Christian attack on a caravan (said to be escorting Saladin's sister) provoked Saladin's holy war (1187–1189): **capture of Jerusalem** (1187) without a sack (Saladin's humanitarianism) and reduction of the Latin states to the cities of Antioch, Tyre, Tripoli, and a small area about each.

1189–1192. THE THIRD CRUSADE. Precipitated by the fall of Jerusalem, a completely lay and royal affair despite the efforts of the Papacy to regain control. It was supported partly by the Saladin tithe, and was led by the three greatest monarchs of the day: (1) **Frederick Barbarossa** (a veteran of the Second Crusade) as emperor, the traditional and theoretical military leader of Christendom, headed a well-organized and disciplined German contingent starting from Regensburg (1189), which marched via Hungary, entered Asia Minor, and disintegrated after Frederick was drowned (1190); (2) **King Richard I of England** and (3) **King Philip II of France,** who went by sea. Already political rivals, they quarreled in winter quarters in Sicily (1190–1191); Richard turned aside in the spring and took Cyprus which he sold to Guy de Lusignan. The quarrels of Philip and Richard continued in the Holy Land, and Philip returned to France after the capture of Acre (1191). Richard's negotiations with Saladin (Richard proposed a marriage of his sister Joan to Saladin's brother, who was to be invested with Jerusalem) resulted (1192) in a three-year truce allowing the Christians a coastal strip between Jaffa and Acre and access to Jerusalem. Captivity of Richard (1192–1194) and heavy ransom to the Emperor Henry VI. The Third Crusade ended the golden age of the crusades.

1202–1204. THE FOURTH CRUSADE. Emperor Henry VI, king of Sicily (by virtue of his marriage to the Norman Constance) and heir of the traditional Norman plan of creating an empire on the ruins of the Greek Empire, was determined to continue his father

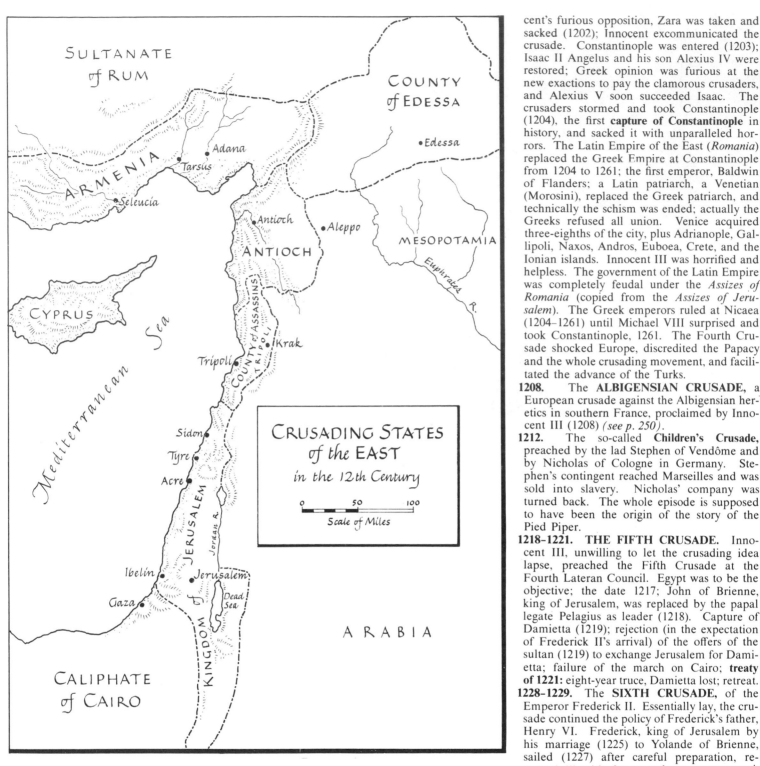

CRUSADING STATES
of the EAST
in the 12th Century

0   50   100

Scale of Miles

cent's furious opposition, Zara was taken and sacked (1202); Innocent excommunicated the crusade. Constantinople was entered (1203); Isaac II Angelus and his son Alexius IV were restored; Greek opinion was furious at the new exactions to pay the clamorous crusaders, and Alexius V soon succeeded Isaac. The crusaders stormed and took Constantinople (1204), the first **capture of Constantinople** in history, and sacked it with unparalleled horrors. The Latin Empire of the East (*Romania*) replaced the Greek Empire at Constantinople from 1204 to 1261; the first emperor, Baldwin of Flanders; a Latin patriarch, a Venetian (Morosini), replaced the Greek patriarch, and technically the schism was ended; actually the Greeks refused all union. Venice acquired three-eighths of the city, plus Adrianople, Gallipoli, Naxos, Andros, Euboea, Crete, and the Ionian islands. Innocent III was horrified and helpless. The government of the Latin Empire was completely feudal under the *Assizes of Romania* (copied from the *Assizes of Jerusalem*). The Greek emperors ruled at Nicaea (1204–1261) until Michael VIII surprised and took Constantinople, 1261. The Fourth Crusade shocked Europe, discredited the Papacy and the whole crusading movement, and facilitated the advance of the Turks.

1208. The **ALBIGENSIAN CRUSADE,** a European crusade against the Albigensian heretics in southern France, proclaimed by Innocent III (1208) *(see p. 250)*.

1212. The so-called **Children's Crusade,** preached by the lad Stephen of Vendôme and by Nicholas of Cologne in Germany. Stephen's contingent reached Marseilles and was sold into slavery. Nicholas' company was turned back. The whole episode is supposed to have been the origin of the story of the Pied Piper.

1218–1221. THE FIFTH CRUSADE. Innocent III, unwilling to let the crusading idea lapse, preached the Fifth Crusade at the Fourth Lateran Council. Egypt was to be the objective; the date 1217; John of Brienne, king of Jerusalem, was replaced by the papal legate Pelagius as leader (1218). Capture of Damietta (1219); rejection (in the expectation of Frederick II's arrival) of the offers of the sultan (1219) to exchange Jerusalem for Damietta; failure of the march on Cairo; **treaty of 1221:** eight-year truce, Damietta lost; retreat.

1228–1229. The **SIXTH CRUSADE,** of the Emperor Frederick II. Essentially lay, the crusade continued the policy of Frederick's father, Henry VI. Frederick, king of Jerusalem by his marriage (1225) to Yolande of Brienne, sailed (1227) after careful preparation, returned ill with fever, and was excommunicated. He sailed again (1228); the pope proclaimed a crusade against Frederick's Sicilian lands and renewed the excommunication; Hermann von Salza, master of the Teutonic Order, remained loyal to Frederick. Frederick, the first crusader to understand the Moslems, negotiated a treaty (1229) with Malik al-Kamil, nephew of Saladin, sultan of Egypt; peace for ten years, grant of Nazareth, Bethlehem, Jerusalem, etc., and a corridor from Jerusalem to the coast for the Christians. The patriarch of Jerusalem opposed Frederick at every turn, and Frederick had to crown himself king (1229) in the Church of the Holy Sepulcher. He returned home at once to repel the papal

Frederick's crusade, and began to encroach on the Greek lands: homage of Cyprus and Lesser Armenia (1195); the marriage of Henry's brother Philip to Irene, daughter of the deposed Emperor Isaac II Angelus, established a Hohenstaufen claim to the Greek throne. Henry died 1197.

Pope Innocent III, determined to regain control of the crusading movement, and hoping to unite the Greek and Latin churches, issued a call to the monarchs; it was ignored (Philip II and King John of England were at odds, Germany in chaos, the Spanish rulers

busy with the Moors), and the brunt fell again on the French baronage. Egypt, the objective, could only be reached by water; negotiations with Venice (1201): terms, 85,000 marks and half the booty. **Meeting of Hagenau (1201)** between Philip (brother of Henry VI), Boniface of Montferrat, and (?) Alexius; decision to divert the crusade to Constantinople (a return to the plans of Henry VI); Venice may have shared in the decision. As it was impossible to raise 85,000 marks, Venice agreed to fulfill her bargain if the Christian city of Zara were taken by the crusade. Despite Inno-

crusade in his lands. The capture of Jerusalem by a rush of Moslem mercenaries (1244) led to the crusades of King Louis IX of France, but Jerusalem was not again in Christian hands until General Allenby captured it (1917).

The **crusades of Theobald of Navarre** (1239) and **Richard of Cornwall** (1240–1241) were forbidden by the pope and were fruitless.

1248–1254. The **SEVENTH CRUSADE,** the first of King Louis IX of France. Poorly organized; Damietta taken without a blow; march to Cairo (1249); rout of the army; capture of Louis; massacre of the army; loss of Damietta. Louis, ransomed, spent four years on a pilgrimage to Jerusalem (1251–1254).

1267. Charles of Anjou, aiming at the conquest of Constantinople, became heir (by treaty) to the Latin Empire. He planned to unite Sicily and Jerusalem, but was balked by the Sicilian Vespers (1282).

Ruins of Crusader castle in Upper Galilee

Dominican friar preaching a Crusade

Crusaders storm Constantinople, 1204

1269. James the Conqueror, of Aragon, under papal pressure, made a futile crusading expedition to Asia Minor.

1270. The **EIGHTH CRUSADE,** the second of King Louis IX and Edward of England (the last of the western crusaders who arrived [1271] and did nothing permanent). Attack on Tunis, possibly at the insistence of Charles of Anjou; death of Louis; the expedition continued by Charles; nothing accomplished.

1274. Preaching of a crusade at Lyons by Pope Gregory X; every ruler took the Cross; Gregory's death ended the project. Acre fell, 1291.

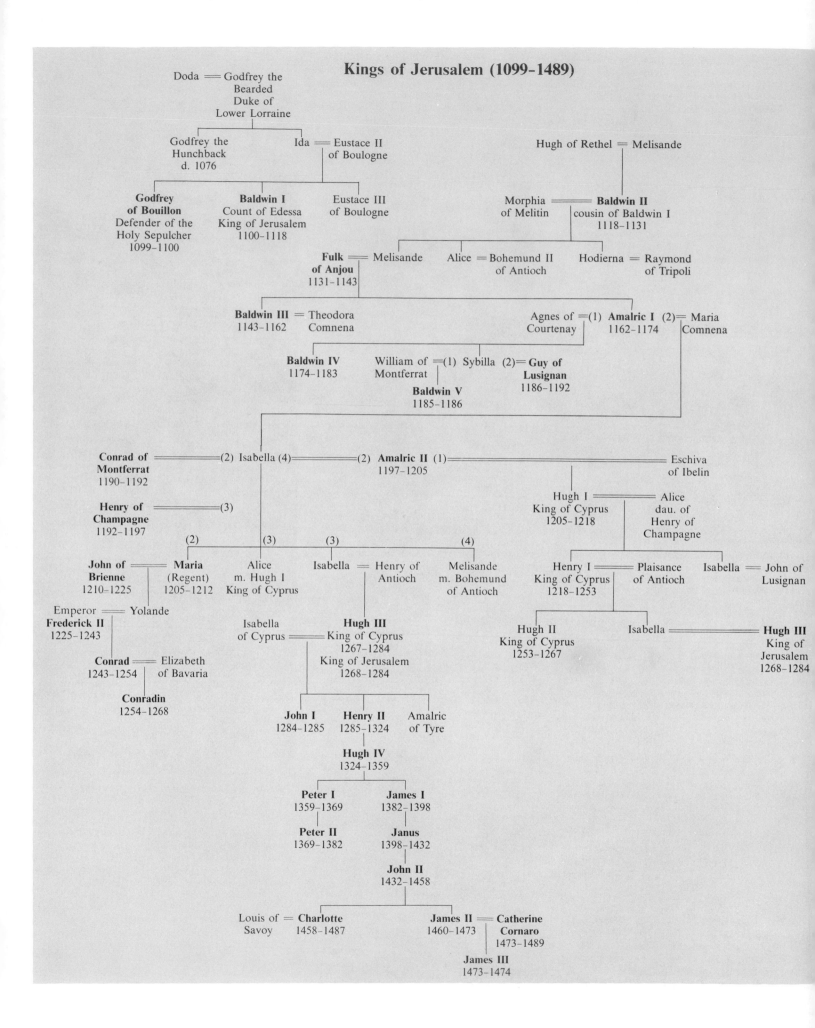

Kings of Jerusalem (1099–1489)

Doda ═ Godfrey the Bearded Duke of Lower Lorraine

Godfrey the Hunchback d. 1076

Ida ═ Eustace II of Boulogne

Hugh of Rethel ═ Melisande

Godfrey of Bouillon Defender of the Holy Sepulcher 1099–1100

Baldwin I Count of Edessa King of Jerusalem 1100–1118

Eustace III of Boulogne

Morphia of Melitin ═ **Baldwin II** cousin of Baldwin I 1118–1131

Fulk of Anjou 1131–1143 ═ Melisande

Alice ═ Bohemund II of Antioch

Hodierna ═ Raymond of Tripoli

Baldwin III 1143–1162 ═ Theodora Comnena

Agnes of Courtenay ═(1) **Amalric I** 1162–1174 (2)═ Maria Comnena

Baldwin IV 1174–1183

William of Montferrat ═(1) Sybilla (2)═ **Guy of Lusignan** 1186–1192

Baldwin V 1185–1186

Conrad of Montferrat 1190–1192 ═(2) Isabella (4) ═(2) **Amalric II** (1) 1197–1205 ═ Eschiva of Ibelin

Henry of Champagne 1192–1197 ═(3)

Hugh I King of Cyprus 1205–1218 ═ Alice dau. of Henry of Champagne

John of Brienne 1210–1225 ═ (2) **Maria** (Regent) 1205–1212

(3) Alice m. Hugh I King of Cyprus

(3) Isabella ═ Henry of Antioch

(4) Melisande m. Bohemund of Antioch

Henry I King of Cyprus 1218–1253 ═ Plaisance of Antioch

Isabella ═ John of Lusignan

Emperor **Frederick II** 1225–1243 ═ Yolande

Isabella of Cyprus ═ **Hugh III** King of Cyprus 1267–1284 King of Jerusalem 1268–1284

Hugh II King of Cyprus 1253–1267

Isabella ═ **Hugh III** King of Jerusalem 1268–1284

Conrad 1243–1254 ═ Elizabeth of Bavaria

Conradin 1254–1268

John I 1284–1285

Henry II 1285–1324

Amalric of Tyre

Hugh IV 1324–1359

Peter I 1359–1369

James I 1382–1398

Peter II 1369–1382

Janus 1398–1432

John II 1432–1458

Louis of Savoy ═ **Charlotte** 1458–1487

James II 1460–1473 ═ **Catherine Cornaro** 1473–1489

James III 1473–1474

Local and specific crusading expeditions were subsequently undertaken under various circumstances at different times; there was a revival of crusading zeal with the fall of Constantinople (1453) under papal urging, but the true crusades were over.

The crusades gave rise to great orders of knighthood which combined chivalry and monasticism.

The **KNIGHTS OF ST. JOHN** or the Hospitalers (black mantle with a white cross), originally an order founded at Jerusalem by Amalfitan merchants (c. 1070) to care for the Hospital of St. John; militarized (c. 1130) on the model of the Knights Templar; transferred to Cyprus (1291); to Rhodes (1310–1522) (the **Knights of Rhodes**) and then to Malta (**Knights of Malta**). Noble blood was a requisite to knighthood in the order.

The **KNIGHTS OF THE TEMPLE** (their house in Jerusalem stood near the Temple) or Templars (white mantle with a red cross) founded (c. 1120) by Hugh of Pajens to guide and protect pilgrims; confirmed by the **synod of Troyes** (1128) and Pope Honorius II. Bernard of Clairvaux drew up their rule, a modification of the Cistercian; they took the threefold monastic vows of poverty, chastity, and obedience, and their rule in general was that of the canons regular. The Order consisted of knights, men-at-arms, and chaplains. Admission to knighthood in the order was open only to those of noble blood. Organization: by commanderies under a grand master. Transferred to Cyprus (1291), the order was dissolved by the **synod of Vienne** (1312).

The other great orders were associated with national or racial influences, and do not represent the older international aspects of knighthood:

The **Knights of the Hospital of St. Mary of the Teutons** in Jerusalem (Teutonic Knights) (white mantle with a black cross) founded (c. 1190); headquarters at Acre. (For their history in Germany, *(see p. 234)*.

The great Spanish orders: **Calatrava** (founded, 1164); **Avis** (Portuguese, founded 1166); **St. James of Compostella** (founded 1175); **Alcantara** (founded, 1183).

Famous orders of chivalry of royal foundation: the **Order of the Garter** (English), founded c. 1344; the **Order of the Star** (French), founded 1351, replaced by the **Order of St. Michael** (1469–1830); the **Order of the Golden Fleece** (Burgundian), founded 1429, became Hapsburg 1477.

d. LATIN AND GREEK STATES IN THE NEAR EAST, 1204–1261

(From p. 271)

Division of the Eastern Empire after the fall of Constantinople: A council, composed equally of crusaders and Venetians, decided to award the imperial crown to **Count Baldwin of Flanders,** while a Venetian (Pier Morosini) was made patriarch of Constantinople. **Boniface of Montferrat** was made king of Thessalonica and the remaining parts of the empire were assigned to various feudal barons as vassals of the emperor. In Anatolia the crusaders were never able to establish themselves excepting in a part of Bithynia near the Bosporus. In Europe they were

A knight of St. John

constantly exposed to the attacks of the Bulgarians. The kingdom of Thessalonica at first extended over part of Thrace, Macedonia, and Thessaly, but to the westward the Greek, **Michael Angelus Comnenus,** set himself up as despot of Epirus and soon began to expand his dominion eastward. Attica and the Peloponnesus were conquered by crusading barons in a short time, and these territories were organized on a feudal basis as the **lordship of Athens** (Otto de la Roche, 1205–1225; Guy I, 1125–1263; John I, 1263–1280), and the **principality of Achaea** (conquered by Guillaume de Champlitte and Geoffroy de Villehardouin in 1205). Achaea was in turn divided into twelve feudal baronies, a perfect example of the French feudal system. Under the Villehardouin family (Geoffroy I, 1209–1218; Geoffroy II, 1218–1246; Guillaume, 1246–1278) it was well-governed and popular with the Greco-Slavic population, which was considerately treated.

The **Venetians** took as their share of the empire most of the islands and other important strategic or commercial posts. They kept for themselves part of Constantinople, Gallipoli, Euboea, Crete, the southwestern tip of the Peloponnesus (Coron and Modon), Durazzo, and other posts on the Epiran coast, as well as the islands of the Ionian and Aegean Seas. For the most part these possessions were granted as fiefs to the leading Venetian families (triarchies of Euboea, duchy of the Archipelago, etc.).

1204–1205. BALDWIN I, Latin emperor.

1204–1214. MICHAEL ANGELUS COMNENUS, despot of Epirus.

1204. Theodore Lascaris, with most of the Byzantine leaders, established himself in Bithynia; Theodore Mancaphas set himself up at Philadelphia; Leo Gabalas took over Rhodes; Manuel Maurozomes established himself in the Meander Valley; Alexius and David Comnenus organized a state on the north coast of Anatolia, with David at Sinope and Alexius at Trebizond, thus founding the **empire of Trebizond,** which lasted until the Ottoman conquest of 1461.

1204–1222. Theodore I (Lascaris) became founder of the Nicaean Empire. In 1204 he made an alliance with the sultan of Rum and with Mancaphas of Philadelphia to resist the advance of the crusaders into Anatolia, but was defeated by the latter under Peter of Bracheuil.

1205. The **Bulgars,** under Kaloyan, defeated Emperor Baldwin and Doge Dandolo in **battle near Adrianople.** Baldwin was captured and died in captivity. The Bulgars then overran much of Thrace and Macedonia, exterminating a large part of the Greek population.

1205–1216. HENRY I, Latin emperor. He was the brother of Baldwin, and the ablest of the Latin emperors.

1207. Kaloyan and the Bulgarians besieged Thessalonica, but in vain. Kaloyan died suddenly, probably murdered.

1207. Theodore Lascaris, allied with the Seljuks of Rum, defeated David Comnenus and drove him back to Sinope. Theodore then concluded a truce with the Emperor Henry, in order to oppose the advance of Alexius of Trebizond, who was now allied with the Seljuks.

1209. Theodore repulsed a second attempt by

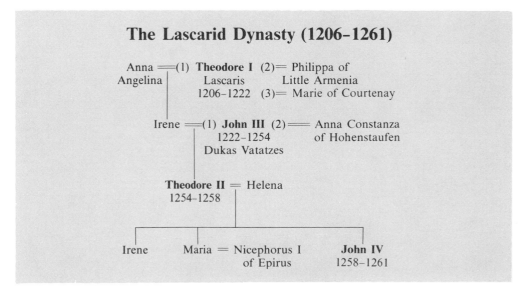

The Lascarid Dynasty (1206–1261)

Anna ══(1) **Theodore I** (2)══ Philippa of
Angelina   Lascaris   Little Armenia
        1206–1222 (3)══ Marie of Courtenay

Irene ══(1) **John III** (2)════ Anna Constanza
      1222–1254   of Hohenstaufen
    Dukas Vatatzes

Theodore II ══ Helena
1254–1258

Irene   Maria ══ Nicephorus I   **John IV**
              of Epirus   1258–1261

Peter of Bracheuil and the crusaders to conquer Bithynia.

1210. The **Parliament of Ravennika,** at which the feudal lords of Greece finally recognized the suzerainty of the emperor at Constantinople. In practice this meant little, and the emperor was left to shift for himself, with such support as the Venetians saw fit to give him.

1211. Theodore Lascaris defeated Alexius of Trebizond and the sultan of Rum, both of whom were captured. As a result a large part of the Anatolian coast was added to the empire of Nicaea.

1212. Henry I defeated Theodore at Luparcos and began the invasion of Anatolia. Theodore made peace, abandoning to the Latin Empire part of Mysia and Bithynia.

1214–1230. Theodore Dukas Angelus, nephew of Michael, became despot of Epirus. He began the work of expansion at the expense of the Latins and Bulgars, taking Durazzo and Corfu from the Venetians (1214).

1216–1217. PETER OF COURTENAY, Latin emperor. He was the brother-in-law of Baldwin and Henry and was in Europe when Henry died. On the way from Durazzo to Thessalonica he was captured by Theodore Dukas of Epirus. He died in 1218.

1217–1219. Regency of Yolande, the wife of Peter of Courtenay.

1219–1228. ROBERT OF COURTENAY, Latin emperor. His domain was reduced to Constantinople and he spent most of his time soliciting aid in the west.

1222. Theodore Dukas of Epirus captured Thessalonica and extinguished the kingdom. He then had himself proclaimed Emperor of the West, and before long had extended his conquests to the vicinity of Philippopolis and Adrianople.

1222–1254. JOHN III (Dukas Vatatzes), emperor at Nicaea. He proved himself a great ruler as well as an able general. During his reign agriculture was encouraged, trade and industry developed, the finances reformed. The Nicaean Empire enjoyed a period of real prosperity and power.

1224. John Vatatzes defeated the Franks at Poimanenon. In succession he took the islands near the Anatolian coast (Samos, Chios, Lemnos) and subjected Rhodes. An army was even sent across the Straits to capture Adrianople.

1224. Theodore of Epirus defeated an army of the Latin emperor at Serres and then drove the invading Nicaean army away from Adrianople.

1228. On the death of Robert of Courtenay, it was proposed that a regency be established under the Bulgarian ruler, John Asen II (1218–1241), but this suggestion was frustrated by the Latin clergy.

1228–1261. BALDWIN II, Latin emperor. He was the eleven-year-old son of Peter of Courtenay. The reign was a helpless one, during which the emperor was reduced to the point of peddling the Constantinople relics through Europe.

1229–1237. Regency of John of Brienne, former king of Jerusalem, for the boy-emperor. John became co-emperor in 1231.

1230. Theodore of Epirus was defeated and captured by John Asen in the **battle of Klokotnitsa.** The Bulgarian ruler thereupon appropriated most of the eastern sections of the Empire of the West. Thessalonica and Thessaly passed to

1230–1236. MANUEL, the brother of Theodore.

1235. An expedition sent by John Vatatzes against the Venetians in Crete failed to achieve anything.

1236. An attack of the Nicaean Greeks, allied with John Asen of Bulgaria, on Constantinople. The city was saved by the Venetians and by a force sent by the duke of Achaia.

1236–1244. JOHN, the son of Theodore Dukas of Epirus, became despot of Thessaly and Emperor of the West.

1236–1271. MICHAEL II, despot of Epirus.

1242. John Vatatzes, in company with Theodore, who had been liberated by the Bulgarians, set out with an army and besieged Thessalonica. He failed to take the city, owing to his lack of seapower, but John, the despot of Thessaly, was obliged to give up the title Emperor of the West and to recognize the suzerainty of the Nicaean emperor.

1244. The **Mongol invasion** of Anatolia, after the defeat of the Seljuks in the **battle of Erzinjan.** The Mongols reached Ancyra (Ankara). John Vatatzes established friendly relations with them and succeeded to much of the Seljuk territory in central Anatolia.

1246. Second expedition of John Vatatzes to the Balkans. He conquered northern Macedonia and finally took Thessalonica, deposing Demetrius Angelus, despot since 1244.

1254. Michael II, of Epirus, recognized Nicaean suzerainty, after a defeat by the forces of John Vatatzes.

1254–1258. THEODORE II (Lascaris), Greek emperor at Nicaea.

1255. Theodore defeated the Bulgarian armies of Michael Asen in northern Macedonia.

1257. Revolt of Michael II of Epirus, who managed to defeat the Nicaean forces sent against him.

1258–1261. JOHN IV (Lascaris), emperor. He was a mere child and his accession led to a military uprising, led by Michael Paleologus, who became regent and then (1259) co-emperor.

1259–1282. MICHAEL VIII (Paleologus), who was first co-emperor with the boy John, whom in 1261 he had imprisoned and blinded. Michael was an able and energetic general, whose great objective was to re-establish the Greek power at Constantinople.

1259. Michael II of Epirus, allied with the king of Sicily and with the prince of Achaea, attacked Thessalonica, but was defeated and

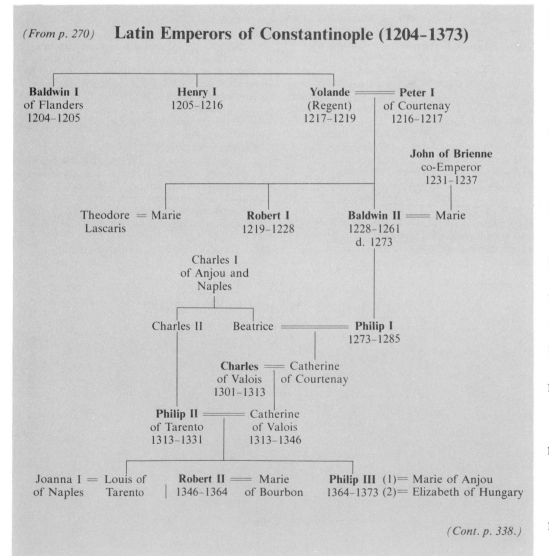

Latin Emperors of Constantinople (1204–1373)

(From p. 270)

- **Baldwin I** of Flanders 1204–1205
- **Henry I** 1205–1216
- Yolande (Regent) 1217–1219 ═══ Peter I of Courtenay 1216–1217

  - John of Brienne co-Emperor 1231–1237

  - Theodore Lascaris ═ Marie
  - **Robert I** 1219–1228
  - **Baldwin II** 1228–1261 d. 1273 ═══ Marie

    - Charles I of Anjou and Naples

      - Charles II
      - Beatrice ═══ **Philip I** 1273–1285

        - **Charles** of Valois 1301–1313 ═ Catherine of Courtenay

          - **Philip II** of Tarento 1313–1331 ═══ Catherine of Valois 1313–1346

            - Joanna I of Naples ═ Louis of Tarento
            - **Robert II** 1346–1364 ═ Marie of Bourbon
            - **Philip III** 1364–1373 (1)═ Marie of Anjou (2)═ Elizabeth of Hungary

(Cont. p. 338.)

driven back by the Nicaeans (**battle of Pelagonia**).

1261. RECONQUEST OF CONSTANTINOPLE. Michael made an alliance with the Bulgarians and concluded the **treaty of Nymphaion** with Genoa, promising the Genoese all the privileges hitherto enjoyed by the Venetians. On July 25 a Greek army under **Alexius Stragopulos,** taking advantage of the absence of the Venetian fleet, crossed the Bosporus and retook Constantinople without much difficulty. Baldwin II fled (d. 1273). End of the Latin Empire. *(Cont. p. 337.)*

e. THE MONGOLS, 1206–1349

Under the last caliphs, the Caliphate had regained its temporal power in Iraq, Mesopotamia, and Fars, and its spiritual authority was greater than at any time since the death of Wathiq (847), but the Caliphate was soon threatened by the Mongols, who, in the late 12th century, had advanced from Mongolia.

1206. The Mongol chief, **Temujin** (1162–1227), was proclaimed supreme ruler, *Jenghiz Khan* (Very Mighty King), of all the Mongols. Under his leadership the Mongol armies swept over northern China and over Azerbaijan, Georgia, and northern Persia. Transoxania was invaded and Bokhara taken (1219); Samarkand captured (1220) and Khorasan devastated. Destruction of Merv and Nishapur. Capture of Herat.

1223. Battle of the Kalka River, in southern Russia. The Mongols defeated a strong force of Russians and Cumans, but after their victory returned to Asia.

1237–1240. Mongol armies under **Batu** (actually commanded by Subutai) overran and

Jenghiz Khan

Battle of Liegnitz, 1241 (illustration from ancient chronicle)

conquered southern and central Russia and then invaded Poland and Hungary.

1241. The Mongols defeated the Poles and Germans in the **battle of Liegnitz** (Wahlstatt) in Silesia, while another army defeated the Hungarians. But because of political complications arising from the death of the Great Khan, Batu withdrew from western Europe, subjugating, on the way back, Bulgaria, Wallachia, and Moldavia. Subsequently he settled on the lower Volga, where a Mongol (Tatar) state was organized under the name of **Golden Horde,** with Sarai as the capital. The Golden Horde, like other Mongol khanates, recognized the supreme authority of the Great Khan, whose capital was first at Kara-Korum in Mongolia, then at Khanbalyk (present-day Peip'ing) in China. But after the death of **Kublai Khan** (1294) the unity of the empire was purely nominal.

1245–1253. Continued ravages of the Mongols in Mesopotamia, Azerbaijan, Armenia, and Georgia.

1256–1349. THE ILKHANS OF PERSIA. Hulagu, the grandson of Jenghiz Khan, was sent by his brother, Mangu, to crush the Assassins and extirpate the Caliphate.

1256. Suppression and **extinction of the Assassins.**

1258. CAPTURE AND SACK OF BAGH-

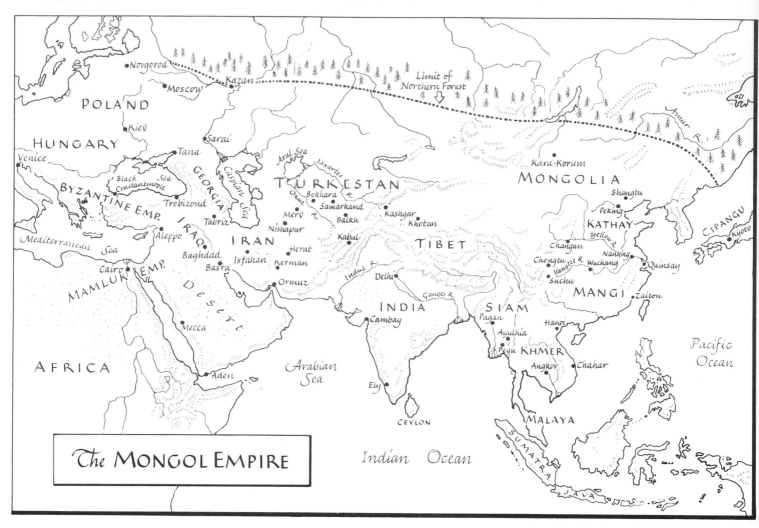

The MONGOL EMPIRE

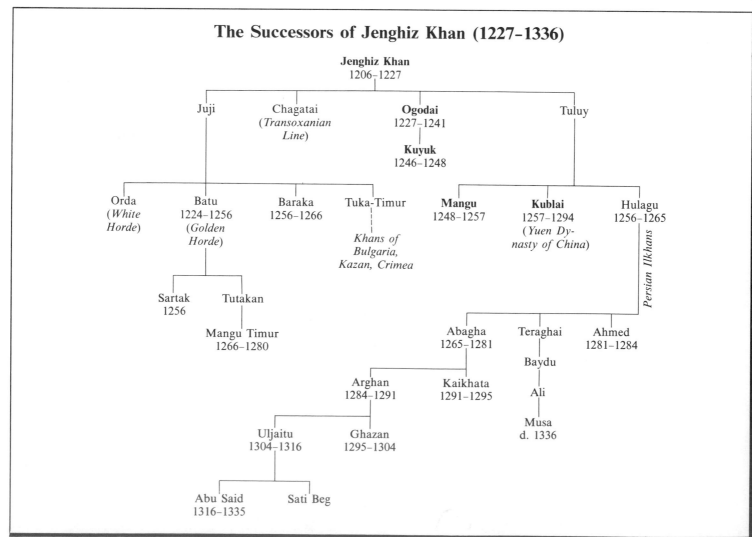

The Successors of Jenghiz Khan (1227–1336)

Jenghiz Khan
1206–1227

Juji — Chagatai (*Transoxanian Line*) — **Ogodai** 1227–1241 — Tuluy

Kuyuk 1246–1248

Orda (*White Horde*) — Batu 1224–1256 (*Golden Horde*) — Baraka 1256–1266 — Tuka-Timur

Khans of Bulgaria, Kazan, Crimea

Mangu 1248–1257 — **Kublai** 1257–1294 (*Yuen Dynasty of China*) — Hulagu 1256–1265

Persian Ilkhans

Sartak 1256 — Tutakan

Mangu Timur 1266–1280

Abagha 1265–1281 — Teraghai — Ahmed 1281–1284

Baydu

Arghan 1284–1291 — Kaikhata 1291–1295

Ali

Uljaitu 1304–1316 — Ghazan 1295–1304

Musa d. 1336

Abu Said 1316–1335 — Sati Beg

DAD. Hulagu executed the caliph, Musta'sim. He then invaded Syria and took Aleppo.

1260. Great victory of the Mamluks of Egypt, under Baybars, at **Ain Jalut.** This victory checked the Mongol advance and saved Egypt, the last refuge of Moslem culture. **Baybars** revived the Caliphate by inviting to Cairo Ahmad Abu-l-Qasim, a scion of the Abbasid house, who was acknowledged as caliph under the title of *Mustansir l' Jllah.*

1344–1349. **Reign of Nushirwan,** last of the Ilkhans of Persia. The dynasty was succeeded by a number of lesser families. *(Cont. p. 348.)*

f. MOSLEM EGYPT, 868–1193

From p. 213)

[For a complete list of the caliphs see Appendix III.]

868–905. **Dynasty of the Tulunids.**

934–969. **Dynasty of the Ikhshidids.** Both these dynasties also ruled Syria.

968–1171. The **FATIMID DYNASTY,** under which Egypt became the most brilliant center of Moslem culture. The Fatimids claimed to be descendants of the Caliph Ali, and of Fatima, the daughter of the Prophet. They rose to power as a result of Shi'ite (Ismailian) propaganda among the Berbers, begun about 894 and directed from Yemen. Abu Abdallah, an Ismailian missionary, had won over the powerful Kitama tribe and had overthrown the

Aghlabids (909). Obaydullah, son of the Ismailian hidden Imam, then appeared and was proclaimed caliph and mahdi in Qairowan (909–934). In 922 he reduced the Idrisids, but an attempt to conquer Egypt failed. His son, Al-Qaim (934–945), was defeated again and again and was besieged in his capital by the Kharijite, Abu Yazid Makhlad. Al-Qaim's son, **Al-Mansur** (945–952), finally defeated Abu Yazid (947), and brought the whole of North Africa, Sicily, and Calabria under Fatimid rule, though he lost Morocco to the Omayyads of Spain. He was succeeded by his son, Al-Muizz (952–975). The latter recovered Morocco and drove the last Byzantine forces out of Sicily (966).

968. **Al-Muizz** took Egypt and transferred the seat of government to Cairo (founded 969).

975–996. **Al-Aziz,** son of Al-Muizz, sultan. He conquered Syria and part of Mesopotamia, and ruled from the Euphrates to the Atlantic.

996–1021. **Al-Hakim,** son of Al-Aziz, sultan. He was known as the *Mad Caliph,* having affirmed his own divinity. He tried to make Shi'ism the orthodox religion of Egypt. The cult of Hakim as an emanation of deity still survives among the Druses of Syria.

1021–1036. Reign of **Az-Zahir,** marking the beginning of the decline of the Fatimid power. Most of Syria was lost.

1036–1094. Reign of **Al-Mustansir.** The holy cities of Mecca and Medina disclaimed their allegiance (1047) and North Africa threw off

Baybars

the Fatimid yoke. On Al-Mustansir's death civil war broke out among his sons, Nizar and Ahmad. Nizar was defeated and killed, and Ahmad reigned as

1094–1101. **Al-Mustadi.** He lost Jerusalem to the crusaders (1099). The Fatimid power continued to decline.

1167. **Shirkuh,** general of the Zangid Nur al-Din of Damascus, entered Egypt to assist the

The Horns of Hittin, where Saladin in 1187 destroyed the crusading Kingdom of Jerusalem

second-last Fatimid caliph, Al-Adid (1160–1171). Shirkuh was appointed vizir, in which office he was succeeded by his nephew, **Salah al-Din** (Saladin), who founded the

1169–1250. Ayyubid dynasty. Saladin ruled at first as viceroy of Nur al-Din, but on the latter's death (1173) asserted his independence and consolidated his power over Egypt, part of Nubia, Hijaz, and Yemen.

1172. Saladin drove the Normans from Tripoli.

1174. Invasion of Syria and conquest of Damascus. Aleppo taken (1183).

1185–1186. Saladin seized Mosul and reduced Mesopotamia.

1187. Battle of Hittin. Saladin destroyed the crusading kingdom of Jerusalem.

1190–1193. Saladin defended his conquests against the Third Crusade. *(Cont. p. 439.)*

g. MOSLEM DYNASTIES OF NORTH AFRICA, 788–1470

788–985. The **Alid dynasty** of the Idrisids in Morocco, founded by Idris ibn Abdallah, a great-grandson of the Caliph Ali's son Hasan, overthrown by the Miknasa and Berbers.

801–909. The **Aghlabid dynasty** in Tunis, founded by Ibrahim ibn Aghlab, the Abbasid governor of Africa. This dynasty conquered Sicily (827–878), took Malta and Sardinia and invaded southern Italy. The dynasty was ultimately destroyed by the Fatimids.

1056–1147. The **Almoravids,** a Berber dynasty founded by Abdallah ibn Tashfin, conquered Morocco and part of Algeria and intervened actively in the affairs of Spain.

1130–1269. The **ALMOHADES,** another Ber-

ber dynasty founded by the prophet, Mohammed ibn Tumart. His successor, Abdul-Mu'min, annihilated the Almoravid armies (1144). Morocco was conquered (1146) and Spain invaded. Algeria was subjugated in 1152, and the Normans driven out of Tunis (1158). Tripoli too was annexed. But in 1235 the Almohades were defeated and gradually ejected from Spain.

1228–1534. The **Hafsid dynasty,** which succeeded the Almohades in Tunis.

1235–1339. The **Ziyanids,** successors of the Almohades in Algeria. They were ultimately absorbed by the

1296–1470. Marinids of Morocco, a dynasty founded in 1195 which took the Moroccan capital from the Almohades in 1296.

(Cont. p. 439.)

C. The Later Middle Ages

I. *Western Europe*

a. THE BRITISH ISLES

(From p. 223)

(1) England, 1307–1485

[*For a complete list of the kings of England see Appendix VI.*]

1307–1327. EDWARD II. Married to Isabelle, daughter of Philip IV of France. Ignorant of his task and bored with the business of kingship, Edward was dominated by his favorite, **Piers Gaveston,** a Gascon. The Scottish war was continued in desultory fashion. The baronage, angered by Gaveston, followed the leadership of Edward's nephew, Thomas, duke of Lancaster, an ambitious, incompetent person. They forced Edward to accept a committee of reform, the twenty-one **Lords Ordainers** (1310), whose reform ordinances, suggestive of the Provisions of Oxford, were confirmed by parliament (1311). The ordinances required a baronial consent to royal appointments, to a declaration of war, and to the departure of the king from the realm, this consent to be given through parliament. Gaveston was captured and slain (1312).

1313–1314. The Scottish War. By 1313 only the castle of Stirling remained in the hands of the English. Edward set out (1314) to relieve the castle; Lancaster and the baronial party refused to support the expedition. At **Bannockburn** (1314) Edward was overwhelmingly defeated, and Scottish independence won.

In Gascony the French kings began a policy

Edward II

of egging Edward's vassals on to resistance, a process which culminated in the French conquest of Gascony and its retention by the French with the consent (1327) of the regents who ruled after Edward's abdication.

1314–1322. Supremacy of Lancaster. Lancaster offered no opposition to Scottish raids; private wars broke out in England; Edward was under a new favorite, Hugh le Despenser. Parliament exiled Despenser (1321). Edward defeated Lancaster at **Boroughbridge** (1322) and beheaded him. The parliament of York repealed the ordinances.

1322–1326. Rule of the Despensers, father and son: Scottish truce (1323); decline of the popularity of the Despensers; alienation of Queen Isabelle. Isabelle went to France (1325), arranged the marriage of her son, the future Edward III, to Philippa of Hainault, and returned (1326) with Mortimer and foreign troops. Supported by the barons, Isabelle gained London, the Despensers were hanged, and the **parliament of Westminster** (1327), dominated by Isabelle and by Edward's enemies, forced an abdication that was tantamount to deposition. Edward was brutally murdered in prison eight months later.

Baronial reform was cynical and selfish in aim, but made no effort to destroy the monarchy. Burgesses and knights sat in the parliaments of 1311, 1322, and 1327, and retained a share in the grant of taxes.

1327-1377. EDWARD III (aged fifteen at his accession). Council of regency and rule (1327–1330) under Mortimer, Isabelle's paramour; Bruce's invasion of England forced the acknowledgment of Scottish independence (1328). Edward led the baronial opposition to Mortimer (hanged, 1330) and opened his personal rule (1330)

1338. Outbreak of the **HUNDRED YEARS' WAR.** Edward did homage (1329) for his French lands and renewed it (1331). French support of Scottish aggression continued and Edward, profiting by civil war in Scotland, supported Baliol; after a series of expeditions he avenged Bannockburn at **Halidon Hill** (1333). French intrigues to alienate Aquitaine continued; Edward sought allies in the emperor, the German princes, and his wife's relatives in Hainault and Holland, but could not win the count of Flanders, the vassal of Philip VI. The economic interdependence, due to the wool trade, of England and the Flemish cities made an English alliance with them inevitable. Philip continued his advance into the English lands south of the Loire (1337) and open hostilities broke out (1338). Edward ravaged northern and eastern France without a decisive battle. Urged on by the Flemings, Edward proclaimed himself king of France (in right of his mother Isabelle), and enabled the Flanders towns under Jan van Arteveldt to support him without violating their oaths.

1340. The **naval victory of Sluys** transferred the mastery of the Channel from France to England (until 1372). Intermittent truces (1340–1345) were followed by Edward's invasion of France, and

1346, Aug. 26. Great victory at **CRÉCY** where English longbowmen, supported by dismounted horsemen, routed the undisciplined chivalry and mercenary crossbowmen of France. This tactical innovation, the result of English experiences in Wales and Scotland, began the joint participation of the yeomanry and the aristocracy in war, and gave the English a unique military power and new social orientation.

Isabelle of France and her troops (14th-century Flemish manuscript)

Battle of Crécy, August 26, 1346

Edward III

Queen Philippa interceding for the lives of the burghers of Calais, 1347

1346. The invasion of Philip's Scottish allies was halted at **Neville's Cross,** and the king of Scotland captured.

1347. Calais was taken after a long siege in which artillery was used. (Philippa's intervention in behalf of the burghers of Calais.) Calais remained an English military and commercial outpost in France until 1558.

1347–1355. A series of truces with France was ended by the expedition of Edward's son, **the Black Prince,** to Bordeaux, followed by ruthless plundering raids from there as a base, which enriched the English and alienated the populace.

1356, Sept. 19. BATTLE OF POITIERS. The Black Prince, using the tactics of Crécy, defeated King John, capturing him, his son, and the king of Bohemia, as well as the flower of French chivalry.

1359–1360. Edward's last expedition to France penetrated to the walls of Paris; the south had been so devastated that the English could hardly find food.

1360. PEACE OF BRETIGNY, ending the first period of the war. (1) France, utterly exhausted and in chaos, surrendered the full sovereignty of Aquitaine, Calais, Ponthieu; and (2) fixed John's ransom; (3) Edward waived his claims to the crown of France.

THE BLACK PRINCE IN THE SOUTH. The Black Prince, ruling as duke of Aquitaine, supported Pedro the Cruel of Castile against Henry of Trastamara (allied with Charles V and aided by Du Guesclin). Having defeated Du Guesclin and Henry (**Navarrete,** 1367), the Black Prince, disgusted at Pedro's character, his army dissipated by illness, and seriously ill himself, withdrew. Taxation in Aquitaine to pay for the expedition led the southern baronage to appeal to Charles V, who summoned the Black Prince to answer to him as his feudal lord (alleging a technical defect in the **peace of Bretigny**). The prince defied Charles, and parliament advised Edward to resume his claims to the French crown. Du Guesclin avoided open battle, pursuing a warfare of attrition which wore out the Black Prince and alienated the Aquitanians from the English. After the hideous **sack of Limoges** (1370) the Black Prince returned to England (1371) and was replaced (1372–1374) by his brother, **John of Gaunt,** duke of Lancaster, an incompetent soldier, who lost town after town until only Calais, Cherbourg, Brest, Bayonne, and Bordeaux remained in English hands (1375).

Edward's personal rule and domestic developments in England. Edward, a majestic, affable man, opened his reign with generous concessions to the baronage, and a courteous welcome to the complaints of the middle class. He grew steadily in popularity. He was fond of war and the war was popular; the nation backed him.

Progress of parliament. The necessities of war finance played into the hands of parliament, and (after 1325) the knights and burgesses began to establish a privileged position for their common petitions. Without immediate redress when the king broke promises of reform, they were able to apply financial pressure in crises. The king could still legislate outside parliament by ordinances in council, but parliament was gaining the initiative: non-feudal levies and changes in levies require parliamentary sanction (1340); a money grant made conditional on redress, and auditors of expenditure appointed (1340–1341); all ministers of the king declared (1341) to be subject to parliamentary approval (soon repealed); demand that a grant be spent as directed (1344); a specific grant voted for defense against the Scots (1348); appointment of parliamentary treasurers and collectors (1377). Parliament continued to sit as a single body, but deliberated in sections: the magnates and prelates sitting in the parliament chamber with the king's council (thus forming the **Great Council**); tne knights and burgesses met separately until 1339–1349, when they began joint sessions (i.e. emergence of the **Commons**) and designated (before 1377) a representative, the speaker, to voice their views in debate. Royal officials ceased to attend the council-in-parliament, leaving the council to the prelates and magnates (now sitting virtually by hereditary right). The outline of the **house of lords** began to appear.

Development of **justices of the peace.** The conservators of the peace established under

Henry III to keep the peace had no judicial powers; the statute of 1327 allowed them to receive indictments for trial before the itinerant judges. In 1332 their jurisdiction was made to include felonies and trespass. Established as police judges in each county (1360), they were also charged with price and labor regulation. By 1485 they had absorbed most of the functions of the sheriffs. Chosen from the local gentry, under royal commission, they constituted an amateur body of administrators who carried on local government in England until well into the 19th century.

1348–1349. The ravages of the **Black Death** probably reduced the population one-third; coupled with tremendous war prosperity, this dislocated the wage and price structure, producing a major economic and social crisis. Wages and prices were regulated by a royal ordinance (1349) followed by the **Statute of Laborers** (1351), fixing wages and prices, and attempting to compel able-bodied unemployed to accept work when offered. The labor shortage accelerated the transition (already begun) from servile to free tenures and fluid labor; the statute in practice destroyed English social unity without markedly arresting servile emancipation or diminishing the crisis.

War prosperity affected everybody and led to a general surge of luxury (e.g. the new and generous proportions of contemporary Perpendicular Gothic). Landowners, confronted with a labor shortage, began to enclose for sheep-raising, and the accumulation of capital and landholdings founded great fortunes, which soon altered the political and social position of the baronage. The yeomanry, exhilarated by their joint military achievement with the aristocracy, and their share of war plunder, lost their traditional passivity, and a new ferment began among the lower sections of society.

Growth of national and anti-clerical (anti-papal) **feeling.** Hostility to the francophile Papacy at Avignon: **statute of Provisors** (1351), an effort to stem the influx of alien clergy under papal provisions (renewed several times); **statute of Praemunire** (1353), forbidding appeals to courts (i.e. Avignon) outside England (renewed several times); rejection (1366) by parliament of the papal request that

The Black Prince

John's tribute (intermitted by Edward, 1333) be renewed, and declaration that no king could make England a papal fief without parliament's consent; parliament declared bishops unfit for state offices (1371). **Progress of the vernacular.** English became, by statute (1362), the language of pleading and judgment in the courts (law French retained in documents). English began to be taught in the schools (1375). Parliament was opened (1399) with a speech in English.

c. 1362. Growth of social tension. Langland's *Piers Plowman*, a vernacular indictment of governmental and ecclesiastical corruption, and an appeal (unique in Europe) in behalf of the poor peasant. Langland, a poor country parson, typical of the section of the church directly in contact with public opinion, was the voice of the old-fashioned godly England bewildered and angered by a new epoch. Preaching of scriptural equalitarianism by various itinerant preachers (e.g. John Ball); growing bitterness against landlords and lawyers.

c. 1376. JOHN WICLIF, an Oxford don and chaplain of Edward, already employed (1374) by the government in negotiations with the Papacy over provisions, published his *Civil Dominion*, asserting in curious feudal terms that, as Christians hold all things of God under a contract to be virtuous, sin violates this contract and destroys title to goods and offices. Wiclif made it plain that his doctrine was a philosophical and theological theory, not a political concept, but extremists ignored this point. A remarkable precursor of the Reformation, Wiclif advocated a propertyless Church, emphasizing the purely spiritual function, attacked the Caesarian clergy, and insisted on the direct access of the individual to God (e.g. abolition of auricular confession, reduction of the importance of the sacraments, notably penance) and the right of individual

Battle of Poitiers, September 19, 1356

judgment. He also was responsible (with Purvey and Nicholas of Hereford) for the first complete, vernacular **English Bible.** He wrote pamphlets, both in Latin and English, and carried on a wide agitation through his poor priests for his doctrines (**Lollardy**) until it was said every fourth man was a Lollard.

1369–1377. Edward, in his dotage, was under the domination of Alice Perrers; the Black Prince (after his return, 1371) was ill and lethargic; government in church and state was sunk in the depths of corruption, society in an orgy of luxury.

1374. John of Gaunt, returning from France, struck a bargain with Alice Perrers, became the leader of the state, set out to use the strong anti-clerical feeling and social unrest for his own ends, and probably aimed at the succession.

1376. The Black Prince, awakened from his lethargy, led the **Good Parliament** in a series of reforms: the commons refused supply until an audit of accounts; two notorious aristocratic war profiteers (Lyons and Latimer) were impeached before the king's council (i.e. the future Lords), the first impeachment of officials by parliament in English history.

1377. After the death of the Black Prince (1376) John of Gaunt's packed parliament undid the reforms and passed a general poll tax (4*d.*).

1377. Gaunt, aiming at the confiscation of clerical estates, supported Wiclif, but the bishops, unable to touch Gaunt, had Wiclif called to account. A violent scene between Gaunt and Bishop Courtenay ended with public opinion on the bishop's side and Gaunt in flight. Attempts to discipline Wiclif failed because of public opinion, but his denial of transubstantiation (1380) alienated Gaunt and his aristocratic supporters.

ART, LITERATURE, AND SCIENCE

Perpendicular Gothic: Gloucester, transepts and choir (1331–1335); cloisters (1351–1412). Minor arts: *Louterell Psalter* (opening of the 14th century), illuminations. English influence on craftsmen of the Rhineland, Paris, Lorraine

Popular songs: Anti-French songs in celebration of victories at Halidon Hill, Sluys, the capture of Calais, etc., c. 1377 first mention of Robin Hood. Popular performances of miracle and mystery plays.

Historical writing: Higden's *Polychronicon* (before 1363), a brilliant universal history in Latin; Walsingham of St. Albans' (end of the 14th century) *Chronicle,* in Latin, rivaling Froissart in brilliance of description. English translation (1377) of the fictional account of the *Travels of Sir John Mandeville* by Jean de Bourgogne

The Pearl, a mystical poem of lament for a dead daughter, influenced by the *Roman de la Rose,* and suggestive of Dante's mystical visions

Geoffrey Chaucer (c. 1340–1400), son of a London burgher, a layman, attached to the circle of John of Gaunt, a diplomat, active at court, later member of parliament, combined observation with learning. Translator of Boethius' *Consolatio,* etc. Representative of the new cosmopolitanism of English society, he was under Italian and French influences; probably knew Petrarch. Creator of English versification; recaster of the English vocabulary by adding continental grace to the ruder Anglo-Saxon word-treasury. The influence of Wiclif, Oxford, Cambridge, the court, and above all, Chaucer fixed Midland English as the language of the English people. The *Canterbury Tales* are a witty, sympathetic, sophisticated, realistic picture of contemporary society (omitting the aristocracy). John Gower (d. 1408), last of the Anglo-Norman poets, wrote in both Latin and French, and later (perhaps due to Chaucer) in English: *Confessio Amantis; Vox Clamantis* (expressing the alarm of a landowner at the Peasants' Revolt).

Foundation of Winchester College (St. Mary's College) by William of Wykeham (1393). **Merton College,** Oxford, became a center for scientific investigations, especially in mechan-

Illumination from the Louterell Psalter

Woodcut of the Knight in Chaucer's Canterbury Tales, *1490 edition*

cs. **Robert Grosseteste, Roger Bacon, Richard Swineshead, Thomas of Bradwardine** began a tradition of logical analysis and experiment which remained influential until the Renaissance.

377-1399. RICHARD II (son of the Black Prince, aged ten at his accession).

377-1389. Minority. Marriage to Anne of Bohemia (1382); rule by the council under the domination of John of Gaunt; activity of parliament: insistence by the commons on the nomination of twelve new councillors. Renewal of war in France (1383): loss of the Flanders trade, complaints at the cost by parliament. Poll taxes (1370 and 1380); sporadic violence, growing tension in the lower orders of society.

381. PEASANTS' REVOLT. Efforts by the landlords to revert to the old servile tenures culminated in a peasant rising, the burning of manors, destruction of records of tenures, game parks, etc., assassination of landlords and lawyers, and a march (100,000[?] men) from the south and east of England on London led by **Jack Straw, Wat Tyler,** and others (release of John Ball from prison). London admitted the marchers; lawyers and officials were murdered, their houses sacked, the Savoy (John of Gaunt's palace) burned. Significant **demands:** commutation of servile dues, disendowment of the Church, abolition of game laws. The Tower was seized, Archbishop Sudbury (mover, as chancellor, of the poll taxes) was murdered. Richard met the rebels (Mile End), rapidly issued charters of manumission, and started most of them home. After the murder of Wat Tyler, Richard cleverly took command of the remnant (possibly 30,000), deluded them with false promises, and dispersed them. Cruel reaction ensued: Richard and parliament annulled the charters; terrible repression followed, and a deliberate effort was made to restore villeinage. This proved impossible and serfdom continued to disappear.

381. Passage of the first **Navigation Act,** followed by clear signs of growing national monopoly of commerce.

382. Wiclif, who had alienated his upper-class supporters by a denial of transubstantiation, was discredited by the Peasants' Revolt, and condemned by the Church, and withdrew to Lutterworth (1382-1384), where he continued to foster Lollardy until he died (1384). His body, by order of the council of Constance, was dug up and burned (1428).

382. Archbishop Courtenay purged Oxford of Lollardy, thus separating the movement from the cultured classes and destroying academic freedom, with serious results alike for reform and education in England. Parliament refused to allow persecution of the Lollards. The position of the English church was not wholly due to its own corruption nor to the paralysis of the Avignonese Captivity, but was partly a result of the fact that secular learning, secular society, and the secular state had overtaken the position of the Church.

385. Futile **expedition of Richard to Scotland;** threatened French invasion (1386); general demands for reform in government. Parliament blocked Richard's effort (1385) to set up a personal government, and appointed a commission of reform. The lords appellant (led by Richard's uncle, the duke of Gloucester) secured the impeachment and condemnation

John Wiclif

(1388) of five of Richard's party (in the *Wonderful,* or *Merciless Parliament*).

1389-1397. Richard's personal and constitutional rule. Truce with France (1389), peace negotiations, marriage to Isabelle, infant daughter of Charles VI (1396). Richard was on good terms with parliament, England prosperous and quiet. Livery and maintenance forbidden by statute (1390); re-enactment of the statutes of: provisors (1390); mortmain (1391); praemunire (1393).

1397-1399. Richard's attempt at absolutism. Richard, furious at a parliamentary demand for financial accounting, had the mover (Haxey) condemned for treason (not executed). In the next parliament (commons, packed for Richard; lords friendly) three of the lords appellant were convicted and executed for treason, Richard was voted an income for life (1398) and the powers of parliament delegated to a committee friendly to Richard. Heavy taxation, ruthless exactions, and a reign of terror opened the way for the **conspiracy of Henry of Bolingbroke** (exiled son of John of Gaunt).

1399. Bolingbroke landed while Richard was in Ireland, got him into his power on his return, and forced him to abdicate. Richard was thrown into the Tower and later died (murdered?) in prison (1400). Parliament accepted the abdication and, returning to the ancient custom of election, made Henry king. Henry's title by heredity was faulty; his claim was based on usurpation, legalized by parliament, and backed by public opinion.

1399-1461. THE HOUSE OF LANCASTER.

1399-1413. HENRY IV. The reign, in view of the nature of Henry's title to the throne, was inevitably a parliamentary one. Henry, an epileptic, was not a great king, but a national monarch was now a necessity to England. To retain the support of the Church, Henry opposed the demand (1404) of the commons (perhaps a reflection of Lollardy) that church property be confiscated, and applied to poor relief. The request was renewed (1410). The statute, *de Heretico Comburendo* (1401), increased the power of the Church over heresy

Battle of Agincourt, October 25, 1415

(primarily, of course, against Lollardy) and was the first law of its kind in England.

1400-1406. Rebellions and invasions: (1) revolt in behalf of Richard (1400); (2) Scottish invasion (1402) stopped by the Percies, the leading barons of Northumberland, at **Homildon Hill;** (3) Owen Glendower's revolt in Wales (1402-1409) joined by (4) the revolt of the Percies (1403-1404); (5) French landing in Wales (1405); (6) archbishop (of York) Scrope's rebellion (1405); (7) attack by the duke of Orléans in Guienne (1406).

1413-1422. HENRY V, a careful king, whose military achievements brought England to the first rank in Europe. Bent on the revival of the Church, he led a strong attack on Lollardy: **Sir John Oldcastle** (Lord Cobham), the leading Lollard, was excommunicated by Archbishop Arundel, but escaped; a Lollard plot against the king's life was discovered; Henry attacked (1414) and captured a Lollard group, most of whom were hanged; anti-Lollard legislation allowing seizure of their books; Oldcastle, the last influential Lollard, executed (1417). Henceforth Lollardy was a lower-class movement driven undergound until the Reformation.

1415. Henry, in alliance with Burgundy, reasserted his claims (such as they were) to the throne of France. Relying on the anarchy in France and hoping by military successes to unite the English behind the house of Lancaster, he advanced into France.

1415, Oct. 25. BATTLE OF AGINCOURT. Henry's great victory over vastly superior forces opened the way to

1417-1419. The **reconquest of Normandy** and an advance to the walls of Paris (1419). The temporary union of the Armagnac and Burgundian factions in France was broken by the assassination (1419) of the duke of Burgundy, followed by the renewal of Anglo-Burgundian alliance and

1420. The treaty of Troyes. The dauphin (later Charles VII) was disinherited; Henry V was designated regent of France and successor to the mad Charles VI, was given control of northern France, and was married to Charles's

Henry V

Henry VI

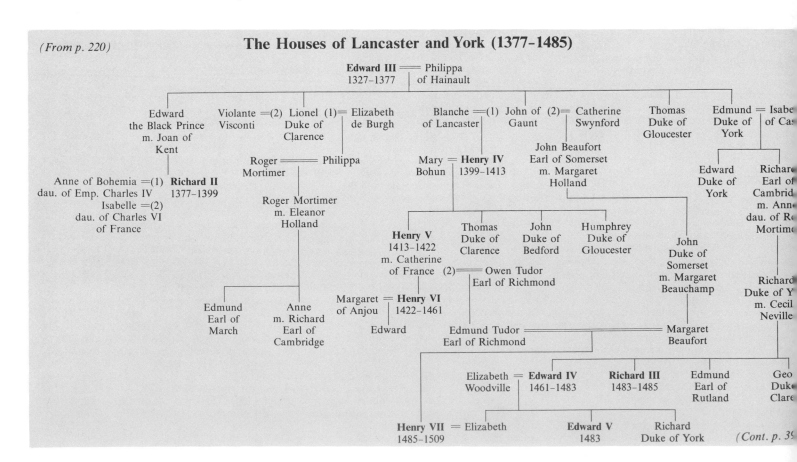

(From p. 220)

The Houses of Lancaster and York (1377–1485)

Edward III === Philippa
1327–1377 | of Hainault

Edward
the Black Prince
m. Joan of
Kent

Violante ==(2) Lionel (1)== Elizabeth
Visconti | Duke of | de Burgh
| Clarence

Blanche ==(1) John of (2)== Catherine
of Lancaster | Gaunt | Swynford

Thomas
Duke of
Gloucester

Edmund == Isabe
Duke of | of Cas
York

Roger === Philippa
Mortimer

Mary = **Henry IV**
Bohun | 1399–1413

John Beaufort
Earl of Somerset
m. Margaret
Holland

Edward
Duke of
York

Richar
Earl of
Cambrid
m. Ann
dau. of Ro
Mortime

Anne of Bohemia ==(1) **Richard II**
dau. of Emp. Charles IV | 1377–1399
Isabelle ==(2)
dau. of Charles VI
of France

Roger Mortimer
m. Eleanor
Holland

Thomas
Duke of
Clarence

John
Duke of
Bedford

Humphrey
Duke of
Gloucester

John
Duke of
Somerset
m. Margaret
Beauchamp

Henry V
1413–1422
m. Catherine
of France (2) === Owen Tudor
| Earl of Richmond

Richard
Duke of Y
m. Cecil
Neville

Edmund
Earl of
March

Anne
m. Richard
Earl of
Cambridge

Margaret = **Henry VI**
of Anjou | 1422–1461

Edward

Edmund Tudor ============ Margaret
Earl of Richmond | Beaufort

Elizabeth = **Edward IV**
Woodville | 1461–1483

Richard III
1483–1485

Edmund
Earl of
Rutland

Geo
Duke
Clare

Henry VII = Elizabeth
1485–1509

Edward V
1483

Richard
Duke of York

(Cont. p. 39

daughter Catherine. Henry, busy in the reconquest of France, died suddenly, followed shortly by Charles VI (1422).

422-1461. Henry VI (aged nine months on his accession), acclaimed king of France; his uncle, the duke of Gloucester, regent (under the council) in England; another uncle, the duke of Bedford, regent in France.

424. Bedford defeated the French at **Verneuil,** but his ally, the duke of Burgundy, was angered by Gloucester's foolish invasion of Hainault. Bitter feud of Gloucester and Beaufort, bishop of Winchester and chancellor.

428-1429. English failure at Orléans; coronation of Charles VII at Reims (1429).

431. The English burned **Joan of Arc** *(p. 299)* at Rouen and crowned Henry VI king of France in Paris. Steady advance of Charles VII; unpopularity of the war in England; parliamentary resistance to grants; loss of the Burgundian alliance (1435) and of Paris (1436).

436-1437. Richard, duke of York (heir to throne), regent in France. He was replaced, after a few successes, by the earl of Warwick (1437-1439), but later returned to France (1440-1443). Continued rivalry of Beaufort and Gloucester. Beaufort, supported by the king, who liked his peace policy, attended the conference of Calais (1439).

442. French conquest of Gascony except Bordeaux and Bayonne.

444. The king's new favorite, the duke of Suffolk, arranged the marriage of Henry and Margaret of Anjou, concluded a truce of two years, and promised to surrender Maine to Charles VII. Margaret was unpopular in England and Maine was not turned over.

448. Charles VII, in a vigorous renewal of

the war, took Maine, completed the conquest of Normandy (1450), and regained Bordeaux and Bayonne (1451). The English effort to reconquer Gascony failed (1453), leaving only Calais in English hands at the end of the Hundred Years' War.

Domestic disorders. Henry, declared of age (1437), was unfit to rule; the council continued in power, factions and favorites encouraged the rise of disorder. The nobles, enriched by the war and the new sheep-farming and progress of enclosures, maintained increasing numbers of private armed retainers (livery and maintenance) with which they fought one another, terrorized their neighbors, paralyzed the courts, and dominated the government. The government lost prestige; Gloucester, arrested (1447) for treason, died in prison, Suffolk (impeached 1450) was killed as he sailed into exile.

1450. Cade's rebellion: a revolt of perhaps 30,000 men of Kent and Sussex, including many respectable small landowners, who marched on London to demand reform in government and the restoration of the duke of York to power. Admitted to London, the marchers were finally crushed after they resorted to violence. **Richard of York** returned from Ireland and forced his admission to the council (1450). York was regent during Henry's periods of insanity (1453-1454; 1455-1456), but on his recovery (1454) Somerset returned to power.

1455-1485. THE WARS OF THE ROSES. A dreary civil war between the houses of Lancaster and York (the Yorkists wearing a white rose, the Lancastrians [later] a red rose). The nation as such took little part. **Battle of St.**

Albans (1455): Somerset defeated and killed. **Battle of Northampton** (1460): the Yorkists defeated the royal army and took Henry prisoner. York asserted his hereditary claim to the throne, and the lords decided that he should succeed Henry on his death (excluding Henry's son, Edward).

1460. Queen Margaret raised an army in the north, defeated Richard of York, who fell on the field (Wakefield, 1460). Southern England rallied to Richard's son Edward (aged nineteen) who defeated the Lancastrians at **Mortimer's Cross** (1461), but was defeated at the **second battle of St. Albans** (1461), and lost possession of King Henry. London stood firm against Margaret, admitted Edward to the town, and after his victory at Towton acclaimed him king (1461).

Growth of the powers of parliament under the Lancastrians: Profiting by the cloud on the royal title and by the pressing needs for war supply, parliament reached the zenith of its influence: (1) Grant of supply delayed until the end of the session after redress of grievances; agreement by the king not to alter petitions when drafted into statutes. Petitions began to take the form of bills, which when approved by the king became statutes in the modern sense. (2) Beginnings of the commons' control over the initiation of financial legislation. (3) Enforcement of reform (1404) in the royal administration; members of the council named in parliament; appointment of the new council enforced (1405). (4) Parliament forced a reversal of the Haxey judgment (1399), establishing its right to freedom of speech in debate. (5) Opposition to packing began to develop and a statute was passed

Soldiers pillaging a house during the French conquest of Gascony, 1442 (contemporary manuscript illumination)

Edward IV and his court

Richard III

defining the franchise for elections (1430); this statute was in force until the great reform bill of 1832.

The king could still legislate by ordinances in council. Under Henry VI the autocratic council ruled, and in the end dominated parliament; finally the chaos of the Wars of the Roses saw the temporary eclipse of parliament as well as of ordered government.

1461–1485. THE HOUSE OF YORK.

1461–1483. EDWARD IV. Parliament declared the three Lancastrian kings usurpers and Henry VI, his wife, son, and chief adherents, traitors. Edward closed the session with a speech of thanks to the commons, the first time an English king had addressed that body. The mass of Englishmen now wanted a monarch to keep order in the state, and allow them to attend to trade, industry, and agriculture. Civil war continued intermittently, and Henry VI was finally captured (1465) and put in the Tower. Edward's marriage to the commoner, Elizabeth Woodville, and the beginnings of the creation of a new nobility, angered the older nobles, especially the earl of Warwick. Edward's sister Margaret was married to Charles the Bold, duke of Burgundy, and master of the Netherlands (1468). Warwick abandoned the king for his brother, the duke of Clarence, and began to foment trouble for Edward, now increasingly unpopular (1469–1470). Edward's victory (partly due to artillery) at **Stamford** (1470) was followed by the flight of Warwick and Clarence.

1471. Warwick next turned to the Lancastrians (under the astute guidance of King Louis XI of France), returned to England with Lancastrian support. Edward's victory at Barnet (1471), where Warwick was killed. Edward then turned on Queen Margaret at Tewksbury and defeated her. Henry VI died (in all probability murdered) in the Tower. The only surviving claimant to the crown was Henry earl of Richmond, an exile aged 14, descended from John of Gaunt and his mistress, Catherine Swynford.

Edward's vigorous plans for war against Louis XI: parliamentary grants were too small, so he began a new practice—benevolences (supposedly free, but in fact forced gifts).

1475. Landing in France, Edward got no support from Charles the Bold, and was bought off by Louis XI. Charles the Bold was killed (1477) and Edward was left without an ally.

1483. EDWARD V, aged twelve. **Richard, duke of Gloucester,** Edward's uncle, an able man, good soldier, cruel and cynical, skilled at winning popular support, had been appointed guardian by Edward's will. Fearing the Woodvilles (family of Edward's mother) Richard struck at them, taking Earl Rivers and Sir Richard Grey prisoners; the queen mother took sanctuary at Westminster; assassination of Lord Hastings (a supporter of the queen); execution of Grey and Rivers; attacks on the legitimacy of Edward; parliament declared Gloucester the heir and he was crowned Richard III. Edward was sent to the Tower.

1483–1485. RICHARD III. The duke of Buckingham, a former supporter of Richard, led (under the skilled direction of Morton, bishop of Ely) a rebellion in behalf of Henry, earl of Richmond. The rebellion failed, Buckingham was beheaded, Edward and his brother were murdered in the Tower (1483), and universal indignation was aroused. Richard and the earl of Richmond were both candidates for the hand of Elizabeth of York, daughter of Edward IV, now heiress to the throne. As she was Richard's niece, even his own followers were shocked.

1485. Henry, earl of Richmond, landed at Milford Haven, there were open defections from Richard by the nobles, and Henry defeated Richard on **Bosworth Field** (Aug. 22), where Richard fell. The crown of England was found on a bush and passed to the first ruler of the great **house of Tudor,** by virtue of his victory in arms and a later act of parliament.

Cultural movements. The Italian humanist, Poggio Bracciolini's visit (1418–1423) to England. *The Paston Letters* (1422–1509), a remarkable collection of the correspondence (in the vernacular) of a middle-class English family. *The Libel of English Policie* (c. 1436), a militant nationalistic exposition of the economic value of sea power. **Eton founded** by Henry VI.

Humphrey, duke of Gloucester (d. 1447), influential patron of classical learning and Italian humanism, was the donor of 279 classical manuscripts to Oxford, the nucleus of the university library. **Sir John Fortescue** (d. c. 1476), chief justice of the king's bench, a Lancastrian exile during the anarchy of the Wars of the Roses, wrote *On the Governance of the Kingdom of England,* and *De Laudibus Legum Angliae,* contrasting the "political" (i.e. constitutional) spirit of the English common law with the absolutism of the Roman law, and comparing the French monarchy unfavorably with the English. Many of his ideas foreshadowed the policies of Henry VII, in form if not in spirit.

Trade guilds and other lay groups gradually took over production of miracle plays and later morality plays.

Caxton's printing press set up at Westminster (1476) under the patronage of Edward IV. Malory's *Morte Arthure* printed (1484), the first book in poetic prose in the English language. *(Cont. p. 389.)*

(2) Scotland, 1305–1488
(From p. 224)

1305. The conquest of Scotland by Edward I of England saved the country from civil war. Edward's plan of union seemed possible for a brief period until the emergence of Bruce's great-grandson, Robert, who turned against the English and maintained himself until the incompetence of Edward II gave him a chance to extend the opposition to the English.

1311–1313. Bruce began a great advance into England and besieged Stirling (1314).

1314, June 24. BATTLE OF BANNOCKBURN. Bruce completely defeated the English and established himself on the throne, thus postponing for centuries the union with England. Bruce's daughter, Margaret, married Walter "the Steward" and became the founder of the house of Stuart.

1315–1318. Edward Bruce, brother of the king, led an unsuccessful invasion of Ireland.

1323. A truce of five years with England was followed by the **treaty of Northampton,** which recognized Robert Bruce's title and provided for the marriage of his son David to Joan, daughter of Edward II.

1329–1370. DAVID II, son of Robert, king. His minority was followed by an incompetent rule.

1332. Edward Baliol, with English support, was crowned, and Bruce fled to France. After Baliol's recall to England, Bruce returned and was defeated and captured at

1346. The **battle of Neville's Cross,** in an effort to aid France by invading England. He was not ransomed until 1357.

This futile reign gave the Scottish parliament its chance; the burghs had sent representatives to the parliament of 1326, but the practice was not a regular one until 1424. On at least two occasions the parliamentary majority went home (1367, 1369), leaving the session to commissions, thus establishing the **Lords of Articles,** who assumed deliberative functions and soon became tools of the crown. Nevertheless, parliament managed to establish a considerable control over royal acts, and kept its hand on the declaration of war and peace and the coinage. The lower clergy began sending representatives to parliament (e.g. 1367, 1369, 1370).

1356. Edward Baliol handed over his crown to Edward III.

1363. David Bruce's scheme for a union with England if he died childless was blocked by parliament's refusal to approve it (1364).

1371. The **STUART LINE** was established on the Scottish throne by the accession of

1371–1390. ROBERT II, grandson of Robert Bruce. The family maintained itself for three centuries despite a succession of futilities and minorities. The rival **house of Douglas** was finally extinguished (1488).

William Caxton

Henry, on white horse, during the Battle of Bosworth Field, 1485

1390–1424. ROBERT III, king. The arrival of **James I** (1424) after a long imprisonment (since 1405) in England began a vigorous, if premature, reform, reduction of violence, restoration of the judicial process, and new legislation which ended anarchy and disciplined the church. The country lairds were given representation in parliament as a support to the crown (1428). James was assassinated, 1437. St. Andrew's University founded.

1437–1460. JAMES II. From James I to Charles I (1625) every sovereign was a minor on his accession. The reduction of the earls of Douglas (1452), followed by confiscation of their lands, enriched the crown. Rosburgh was taken from the English, leaving only Berwick in alien hands.

1460–1488. JAMES III, a feeble figure, was kidnaped (1466) by Lord Boyd, who ruled as governor (by vote of parliament). The Orkneys and Shetlands were acquired from Norway (1472). France kept Scotland in contact with the Continent. *(Cont. p. 389.)*

Louis X

Philip V

(3) Ireland, 1315–1485

(From p. 224)

1315. Edward Bruce, brother of Robert Bruce of Scotland, landed in Ireland and, with the aid of native chieftains, had himself crowned (1316). But he was able to maintain himself only until 1318.

The Anglo-Norman colony began to weaken from internal quarrels while Edward III was preoccupied with the Hundred Years' War. The chieftains thereupon seized their opportunity to encroach still further upon the position of the outsiders. From this period dates the gradual ebb of English influence. The Black Death (1348–1349) made matters even worse.

1366. The **statute of Kilkenny** (passed during the viceroyalty of Lionel, duke of Clarence) had two aims: (1) to maintain the allegiance of the English colony and keep it to the English tradition, and (2) to reduce the grounds of racial conflict. Marriages with the Irish were forbidden, though this was not an entirely new measure. English was enjoined as the speech of the colonists, and English law was insisted on. Nevertheless, the viceroys and governors were unable to maintain order.

1398. Expedition of Richard II to reduce Ireland. This was without permanent results. Under Henry V misery in Ireland reached a new peak and perhaps half of the English colony returned home. The danger in this situation is mentioned in the *Libel of English Policie* (c. 1436). Fear that Ireland might pass into other hands was widespread.

1449. Richard of York arrived as viceroy and ingratiated himself equally with colonists and natives. He departed to England in 1450, but on his return made Ireland virtually independent, with the approval of the Irish parliament. English rule was repudiated and a separate coinage established. Richard continued this policy until his death, but Edward IV resumed a harsh and anarchic policy. Under Richard III the strongest figure in Ireland was **Kildare,** leader of the Yorkists. *(Cont. p. 389.)*

b. FRANCE, 1314–1483

(From p. 253)

[For a complete list of the kings of France see Appendix VII.]

1314–1316. LOUIS X (the Quarrelsome). The real ruler was Louis's uncle, Charles of Valois.

(From p. 225)

The House of Stuart (1370–1625)

Robert II = Elizabeth
1371–1390   Muir

Annabella = **Robert III**
Drummond   1390–1424

James I = Joan
1424–1437   Beaufort

Margaret
m. Louis XI
of France

James II = Mary of Guelders
1437–1460

Margaret = **James III**
of Denmark 1460–1488

Alexander
Duke of Albany
d. 1485

John
Earl of
Mar

Thomas
Earl of
Arran

John, Duke
of Albany
(Regent)

Margaret, == **James IV**
dau. of Henry VII 1488–1513
of England

Madeleine ==(1) **James V** (2)= Mary of
dau. of Francis I 1513–1542   Guise
of France

Francis II ==(1) **Mary Stuart** (2)== Henry,
of France   1542–1567   Lord Darnley

James, Earl ==(3)
of Bothwell

James VI
1567–1625
King of England
1603–1625

(Cont. p. 450.)

Doge Leonardo Loredano (p.318) by Giovanni Bellini

The Battle of Nancy (p.326) by Ferdinand Delacroix

Michael VIII (Paleologus; p.337) by Benozzo Gozzoli

Naval battle of Sluys, 1340 (14th-century manuscript illumination)

A reaction against the monarchy forced concessions from the king.

1316. Louis was succeeded by his posthumous son, John I, who lived only a few days. Louis's daughter by his first wife, Jeanne, was also an infant. A great national council therefore decreed that there could be no queen regnant in France (so-called) and awarded the crown to Louis's brother.

1316–1322. PHILIP V (the Tall). There were frequent meetings of assemblies which included burghers. Philip, in an enormous number of royal ordinances, gave definitive form to the Capetian government. He left no male heir.

1322–1328. CHARLES IV (the Fair), the last Capetian of the direct line, succeeded his brother Philip, to the exclusion of Edward III of England, grandson of Philip IV. This established the principle, later called the **Salic Law,** that the throne could pass only through males. On Charles's death, an assembly of barons declared that "no woman nor her son could succeed to the monarchy."

1328–1498. In this period the **Capetian house of Valois** freed the soil of France from the alien occupation of the English; completed the creation of French national unity and the establishment of a strong national monarchy; prepared France for its brilliant political and cultural rôle in the Renaissance, and began French expansion south of the Alps.

1328–1350. PHILIP VI (nephew of Philip IV, son of Charles of Valois), the nearest male heir. Jeanne, daughter of Louis X, became queen of Navarre. Edward III did homage for his French fiefs (1329 and 1331). Brittany, Flanders, Guienne, and Burgundy remained outside the royal sway. The Papacy was located in France under powerful French influence; rulers of the Capetian house of Anjou were seated on the thrones of Naples, Provence, and Hungary; French interests were firmly established in the Near East; French culture was dominant in England and northern Spain, and was making headway on the fringes of the empire; Dauphiné, the first important

imperial fief added to French territory, was purchased (1336). The king had become less accessible; the kingdom, regarded as a possession rather than an obligation, was left to the administration of the royal bureaucracy.

1338–1453. THE HUNDRED YEARS' WAR. English commercial dominance in Flanders precipitated a political crisis. The communes made the count of Flanders, Louis of Nevers, prisoner (1325–1326); Philip marched to his relief, massacred the burghers on the field of Cassel (1328), and established French administration in Flanders. Edward III retorted with an embargo on wool export from England (1336); the weavers of Ghent, under the wealthy Jan van Arteveldt, became virtual masters of the country and made a commercial treaty with England (1338). On van Arteveldt's insistence, Edward declared himself king of France; the Flemings recognized him as their sovereign, and made a political alliance with him (1340).

1338. Philip declared Edward's French fiefs forfeited and invested Guienne. Edward was made vicar of the empire and his title as king of France was recognized by the emperor. Thus began the **Hundred Years' War,** really a series of wars with continuous common objectives: the retention of their French "empire" by the English, the liberation of their soil by the French.

1340. Philip, by dismissing two squadrons of Levantine mercenary ships, lost his mastery of the Channel until 1372 and was overwhelmingly defeated by Edward at the **naval battle of Sluys** (June 24). This opened the Channel to the English and gave them free access to northern France.

1341–1364. A dynastic contest in Brittany, in which both Edward and Philip intervened.

1341. First collection of the *gabelle* (salt tax) in France; increasing war levies and mounting dissatisfaction.

1346. Edward's invasion of Normandy and overwhelming **VICTORY AT CRÉCY,** Aug. 26 (10,000 English defeated some 20,000 French). The French military system was outmoded, the

people unaccustomed to arms, and the chivalry inefficient. Blind King John of Bohemia was slain. Artillery came into use (1335–1345). Continued war levies led to open refusal (1346) of a grant by the estates-general of Langue d'Oïl, and a demand for reforms. The king attempted some reforms.

1347. Edward's siege and **capture of Calais** gave the English an economic and military base in France that was held until 1558.

1348–1350. The **Black Death** penetrated northern Europe, reducing the population by about a third, and contributing to the crisis of 1357–1358 in France.

1350–1364. JOHN II (the Good Fellow), a "good knight and a mediocre king," a spendthrift who repeatedly debased the currency.

1355. English **renewal of the war** in a triple advance: into Brittany; from the Channel; and from Bordeaux by the Black Prince. Virtual collapse of French finance. The estates-general of Languedoc and Langue d'Oïl (the latter under the leadership of **Etienne Marcel,** the

Capture of Calais, 1347

Massacre of the Jacques, an episode of the Jacquerie, 1358

richest man in Paris, provost of the merchants) forced the king (ordinance of 1355) to agree to consult the estates before making new levies of money, a policy already in practice, and to accept supervision of the collection and expenditure of these levies by a commission from the estates. John cleverly induced the estates to adjourn, debased the coinage in the interest of his treasury, and organized his opposition to the estates.

1356. The **Black Prince** (the English "model of chivalry") defeated John, the last "chivalrous" king of France, at **Poitiers** (Sept. 19). King John, his son Philip, and two brothers were taken prisoner with a multitude of the French aristocracy. The royal authority in France was reduced to a shadow; civil chaos reigned. Charles, the eighteen-year-old son of John, became regent.

1357. Climax of the power of the **estates-general:** The estates-general again had to be called and passed the **Great Ordinance** which provided for supervision of the levy and expenditure of taxes by a standing committee of the estates, regular and frequent meetings of the estates, poor relief, and many other reforms, but did not attempt to reduce the traditional powers of the monarchy. The estates had met too frequently, were divided, and had no real coherence or skill in government. They were discredited by Marcel's alliance with Charles the Bad of Navarre (a son of Jeanne, daughter of Louis X), who had a better claim to the throne than Edward III. The regent Charles fled from Paris and created a powerful

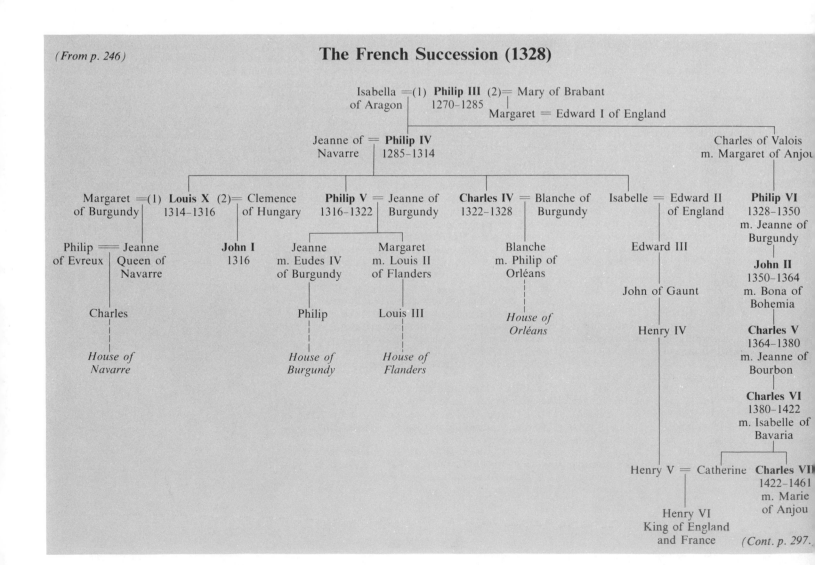

(From p. 246)

The French Succession (1328)

Isabella =(1) **Philip III** (2)= Mary of Brabant
of Aragon   1270–1285
      Margaret = Edward I of England

Jeanne of = **Philip IV**   Charles of Valois
Navarre   1285–1314   m. Margaret of Anjou

Margaret =(1) **Louis X** (2)= Clemence   **Philip V** = Jeanne of   **Charles IV** = Blanche of   Isabelle = Edward II   **Philip VI**
of Burgundy   1314–1316   of Hungary   1316–1322   Burgundy   1322–1328   Burgundy   of England   1328–1350
                                                                m. Jeanne of

Philip = Jeanne   **John I**   Jeanne   Margaret   Blanche   Edward III   Burgundy
of Evreux   Queen of   1316   m. Eudes IV   m. Louis II   m. Philip of
        Navarre   of Burgundy   of Flanders   Orléans   **John II**
                                                                           1350–1364

Charles   Philip   Louis III   John of Gaunt   m. Bona of
                                                             Bohemia

House of   *House of*   *House of*   *Blanche*   Henry IV   **Charles V**
Navarre   *Burgundy*   *Flanders*   m. Philip of   1364–1380
                                 Orléans   m. Jeanne of
                                     House of   Bourbon
                                     Orléans

Charles VI
1380–1422
m. Isabelle of
Bavaria

Henry V = Catherine   **Charles VII**
                            1422–1461
                            m. Marie

Henry VI   of Anjou
King of England
and France   *(Cont. p. 297.)*

coalition against the estates and Charles the Bad.

1358. The *Jacquerie* (a violent peasant reaction against war taxes, the weight of the ransoms of the captives at Poitiers, and the pillage of the free companies) led to a merciless reaction by the nobles. Marcel, already distrusted, was further discredited by intrigues with the revolted peasantry and with the English. Charles, after the murder of Marcel (1358), returned to the capital, repressed disorder with a firm hand, and refused to approve John's preliminary peace (1359), which virtually restored the old Angevin lands in France to Edward.

1360. The **PEACE OF BRETIGNY** (Calais) (virtually a truce of mutual exhaustion): Edward practically abandoned his claims to the French crown; Charles yielded southwestern France (Guienne), Calais, Ponthieu, and the territory immediately about them, and promised an enormous ransom for John. King John was released on partial payment of the ransom, but returned after the flight of a hostage to die in his luxurious and welcome captivity in England. The southern provinces protested their return to English rule, and there were clear signs of national sentiment born of adversity.

1361. The **duchy of Burgundy** escheated to the crown, and John handed it to his son Philip as an appanage (1363). Charles negotiated (1369) the marriage of Duke Philip to Margaret, daughter and heiress of Louis de Male, last count of Flanders, in order to keep Flanders out of English hands. As Margaret brought Flanders, the county of Burgundy, Artois,

Charles V

Nevers, and Rethel under control of the dukes of Burgundy, this marriage added a new danger on the east and north to the Plantagenet threat in the west. Philip further strengthened his house by marriage alliances with the children of the Wittelsbach, Albert of Bavaria, which added holdings in Hainault, Holland, and Zealand.

1364–1380. CHARLES V (the Wise), neither strong of body, handsome, nor chivalrous; a pious, refined, realistic statesman of modern cast. He saved France and made it plain to the nation that national well-being depended on the monarchy rather than on the estates-general.

The reign opened with a bad harvest, plague, and pillage by the free companies (discharged soldiers). The Breton, **Bertrand Du Guesclin,** the first great soldier on the French side in the Hundred Years' War, was sent with some 30,000 of these men to support Henry of Trastamara against Pedro the Cruel of Castile, who had become an ally of the Black Prince.

Charles managed to dominate the new financial machinery set up by the estates-general, continued the war levies (e.g. hearth-tax, *gabelle*, sales taxes) and utilized the peace for general reform and reconstruction: castles were rebuilt, and royal control of them strengthened; permanent companies of professional cavalry and infantry were established; artillery was organized and supported by pioneers and sappers; a military staff and hierarchy of command established in the army (1374); the navy was reorganized, and French sea power restored. New walls were built around Paris.

The government and finance were reorganized and the general frame of the financial structure fixed until 1789. The grant of the estates-general of Langue d'Oïl (1360) for John's ransom had been for a term of six years; their grant of a hearth-tax (1363) was without a time limit. Following these precedents,

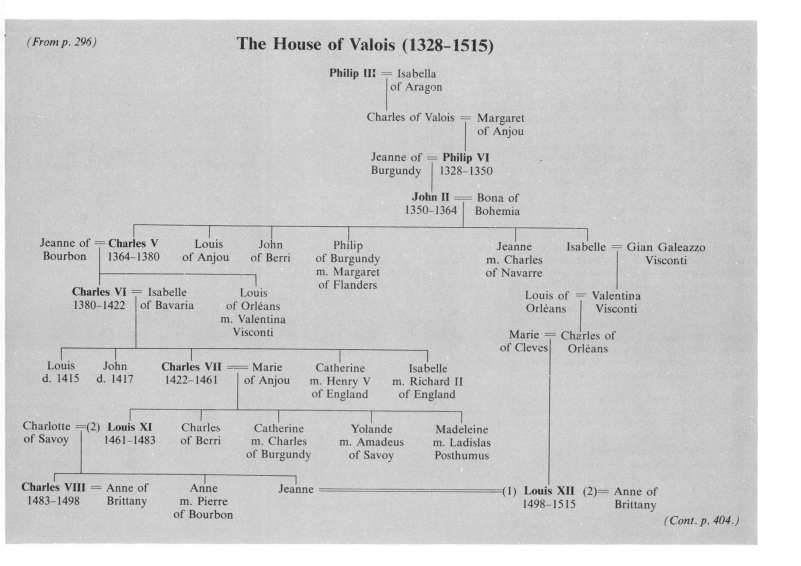

(From p. 296)

The House of Valois (1328–1515)

Philip III = Isabella of Aragon

Charles of Valois = Margaret of Anjou

Jeanne of Burgundy = **Philip VI** 1328–1350

John II 1350–1364 = Bona of Bohemia

Jeanne of Bourbon = **Charles V** 1364–1380 — Louis of Anjou — John of Berri — Philip of Burgundy m. Margaret of Flanders — Jeanne m. Charles of Navarre — Isabelle = Gian Galeazzo Visconti

Charles VI 1380–1422 = Isabelle of Bavaria — Louis of Orléans m. Valentina Visconti

Louis of Orléans = Valentina Visconti

Marie of Cleves = Charles of Orléans

Louis d. 1415 — John d. 1417 — **Charles VII** 1422–1461 = Marie of Anjou — Catherine m. Henry V of England — Isabelle m. Richard II of England

Charlotte of Savoy =(2) **Louis XI** 1461–1483 — Charles of Berri — Catherine m. Charles of Burgundy — Yolande m. Amadeus of Savoy — Madeleine m. Ladislas Posthumus

Charles VIII 1483–1498 = Anne of Brittany — Anne m. Pierre of Bourbon — Jeanne =(1) **Louis XII** 1498–1515 (2)= Anne of Brittany

(Cont. p. 404.)

The fall of Rouen, 1419

Charles was able (1369) to induce the estates to agree to the general principle that old grants of funds need not be renewed by the estates unless their terms were to be changed. This freed the king from control by the estates unless new taxes were needed and meant that the estates no longer had a vital function. The financial control established by the estates (1357) was transferred to the royal *chambre de comptes* in Paris.

1369. The appeal of the count of Armagnac to Charles against the Black Prince and the Black Prince's refusal to appear at Charles's court served as an excuse for the **resumption of the war.** Du Guesclin became (1370) constable of France (a title usually reserved for great nobles), abandoned chivalrous tactics, and allowed the English to parade through France. Avoiding pitched battle, he harassed the invaders with a picked force. The reconquest of Poitou and Brittany (1370–1372) was followed by the death of the Black Prince (1376); the French fleet, supported by the Castilian, regained control (La Rochelle, 1372) of the Channel, and blocked English transport in the north. By 1380 the English held only Bordeaux, Bayonne, Brest, Calais, Cherbourg, Valais, and their immediately surrounding territory. France was cleared of the enemy, but was in ruins.

1378. With the end of the Avignonese Captivity (1376) the **Great Schism** in the Church began; Charles and his successors supported the French line of popes. On his deathbed Charles forbade the hearth-tax.

1380–1422. CHARLES VI. A minority reign accompanied by the disruptive rivalry of the king's uncles (the dukes of Anjou, Berri, and Burgundy, the "Princes of the Lilies"), who exploited France for their own ends. This was followed by the intermittent insanity of the king, and paralysis in the government.

General economic distress, popular unrest, and general revolts, usually against taxes (vigorously repressed): the *Tuchins* (1381) in Languedoc; the *Maillotins* (1382) in Paris, and elsewhere; and the outbreak in Flanders (1382) under Philip (son of Jan) van Arteveldt. The French feudality, under leadership of the duke of Burgundy, ended this revolt by the victory of **Roosebeke** (1382), following it up with atrocious repression. Flanders on the death of the count (1384) passed to Burgundy; its pacification was completed in 1385. The hearthtax was renewed and taxation remained heavy.

1388. The death (1384) of the duke of Anjou had left the duke of Burgundy in a position of great power, and Charles, angered at Philip of Burgundy's policies, began his personal rule by replacing the duke by his own brother, Louis, duke of Orléans, and by restoring (1389) his father's old advisers, men of humble birth (whence their nickname, the *Marmousets*). Louis of Orléans was a refined, talented spendthrift, unpopular in Paris, and Philip of Burgundy (supported by Queen Isabelle) was able to pose as a reformer and lead the opposition, bringing the rivalry of Burgundy and Orléans into the open.

1392. Charles's first (brief) **attack of insanity** was soon followed by longer seizures; Philip of Burgundy (as regent) replaced Louis of Orléans in power and the situation returned to what it was before 1389.

1396. Twenty-year truce with England; annihilation of the French knights on a crusade to free Hungary from the Turk (Nicopolis, *p.342*).

1404. John (the Fearless), an able, ambitious man, became **duke of Burgundy.** After the sudden transfer of Isabelle's support to Louis of Orléans, John's orders led to the assassination of Louis, duke of Orléans (1407). John became the hero of Paris, but caused the emergence of two great factions in France and began the civil war of the **Armagnacs** against the Burgundians. The Armagnacs, named for their head, the count of Armagnac (father-in-law of Charles, the new duke of Orléans), were strong among the great nobles, drew their power from the south and southeast, were a reactionary, anti-English, war party. The Burgundians, supported by the people, the University of Paris, and the Wittelsbachs, were strong in the north and northeast, favored peace, were pro-English, and supported Pope Clement VII and his papal successors.

1413. The **Cabochian revolt** (named for the skinner, Simon Caboche) in Paris forced attention to reform, and led to the **Cabochian Ordinance** (1413), inspired by the University of Paris and aimed at efficiency in government rather than democracy. It provided for three councils to conduct public business, and a general detailed program of reform. The Armagnacs returned to control in Paris and led a feudal reaction, which destroyed all hope of reform and opened the way for the English. The duke of Armagnac (Constable, 1415) repeated the traditional military errors of the feudal class, which understood tournaments but not war.

1415, Oct. 25. THE BATTLE OF AGINCOURT. Henry V, with 10,000 men, defeated three times that number of French; the duke of Orléans was taken prisoner; **Normandy was reconquered** by the English, undoing for the time the work of Philip Augustus; the dauphin (later Charles VII) fled to the south of France (1418); the Burgundians returned to power and there was a massacre of Armagnacs in Paris (1418).

1419. Rouen fell; the Burgundians, alarmed at the English advance, began negotiating with the Armagnacs; John of Burgundy was assassinated at a conference with the dauphin at the bridge of Montereau, and the Burgundians returned to the English alliance.

1420. Charles, under Burgundian influence, and supported by his wife Isabelle, accepted the **treaty of Troyes** (which repudiated the dauphin as illegitimate), adopted Henry V of

The Battle of Agincourt, 1415

England as his heir and immediate regent (with the approval of the University of Paris and the estates-general, 1421). Charles's daughter, Catherine, was married to Henry V and, also under the treaty, the English were allowed to retain all their conquests as far as the Loire. King Henry V drove the forces of the dauphin across the Loire and began the steady conquest of France which continued uninterrupted until his death (1422). The dauphin remained at Bourges (whence his nickname, *the Roi de Bourges*).

1422–1461. CHARLES VII (the Roi de Bourges, not crowned until 1429). Physically weak, bowed and lethargic from misfortune, the puppet of unscrupulous advisers until the advent of a better group (including Dunois, Richemont, brother-in-law of the duke of Burgundy, La Hire, *et al.*), after 1433, when he became known as "Charles the Well-Served." **Regency of the duke of Bedford** (1422–1428) for the infant Henry VI of England, who was recognized as king of France in the north, supported by the Burgundians, and crowned in Paris (1436).

1424. Bedford's decisive **victory at Cravant** was followed by the defeat of the Armagnacs and the Scots at Verneuil.

1428. The English began the **siege of Orléans. Jeanne d'Arc** (Joan of Arc, The Maid of Orléans), born in 1412 at Domrémy, was of comfortable village family, illiterate, but a good seamstress. A devout mystic, she began to have visions at the age of thirteen.

1429. Jeanne presented herself to the king at Chinon, and was allowed to lead an army (with the empty title of *Chef de Guerre*) to the relief of Orléans. The relief of the city, followed by **Charles's coronation** (1429) at Reims, was the turning point of the war and marked a decisive change in the spirit of the king and the nation. Jealous ministers (*e.g.* La Trémoille) of Charles soon undermined Jeanne's position, despite the progress of the royal cause.

1430. Jeanne was captured at Compiègne by the Burgundians, ransomed by the English. Without intervention by Charles on her behalf, she was tried for witchcraft. The process was probably a typical ecclesiastical trial. After her confession and its repudiation she was burned (1431) by the English at Rouen ("We have burned a saint"), and Charles returned to his old ways.

1432. Charles favored the **council of Basel,** which was pro-French and anti-papal.

1435. Separate **peace of Arras,** reconciliation with Burgundy: Charles agreed to punish the murderers of Duke John of Burgundy and recognized Philip as a sovereign prince for life. Burgundy was to recognize Charles's title; the Somme towns were to pass to Burgundy (subject to redemption). The English refused to make peace on acceptable terms. **Charles recovered Paris** (1436).

1436–1449. Period of military inaction, utilized by Charles for reforms of the army paid for from the *taille*. The estates-general agreed to permanent taxation for support of the army. Charles entered Paris and was welcomed (1437).

1437–1439. Famine, pestilence, the anarchy of the *écorcheurs,* but steady progress against the English.

1438. THE PRAGMATIC SANCTION OF

Monument to Jeanne d'Arc at Bonsecours, France

BOURGES. Assertion that a church council is superior to a pope; suppression of the annates; provision for decennial councils; maintenance of the autonomy of the French national church (*Gallicanism*) and its isolation from Rome.

1440. The **Praguerie,** part of a series of coalitions of great nobles against the king, with support from the dauphin (later Louis XI), was put down; the dauphin was ordered to the Dauphiné, where he continued his intrigues.

1445–1446. Army reforms: establishment of the first permanent royal army by the creation of 20 companies of élite cavalry (200 *lances* to a company, six men to a *lance*) under captains chosen by the king; a paid force, the backbone of the army, assigned to garrison towns; regularization of the auxiliary free archers (*francs-archers*), a spontaneous body dating from the reign of Charles V (opposed by the nobles), under royal inspection (1448) and under territorial captains (1451). Establishment of artillery (the Bureau brothers).

1444. Louis the dauphin made a treaty of **alliance with the Swiss cantons.** The alliance was strengthened (1452) and an alliance made with the towns of Trier, Köln, *et. al.* (1452), and with Saxony, as part of a developing anti-Burgundian policy. Intermittent support for the house of Anjou in Naples and the house of Orléans in Milan. Under **Jacques Coeur,** the merchant prince of Montpellier, royal finances were reformed, control of the public revenue by the king established, and French commer-

cial penetration of the Near East furthered (c. 1447).

1449–1461. Expulsion of the English: Normandy and Guienne regained; Talbot slain (1453).

1456. Retrial and **rehabilitation of Jeanne d'Arc,** to clear Charles's royal title.

1461–1483. LOUIS XI (the Spider), of simple, bourgeois habits, superficial piety, and feeble, ungainly body, the architect of French reconstruction and royal absolutism. He was well-educated, a brilliant diplomat, a relentless statesman, an endless traveler throughout his kingdom. He perfected the governmental system begun under Charles V (revived by Charles VII), and established the frame of the constitution until 1789. The recognized right of the king to the taille, the aides, and the gabelle made a good revenue available for defense and diplomacy. Louis improved and perfected the standing army with added emphasis on the artillery, but seldom waged war. Feudal anarchy and brigandage were stopped; a wise economic policy restored national prosperity despite grinding taxes.

1461. Louis's first step in the reconstruction of the kingdom was a rapprochement with the Papacy by the formal **revocation of the Pragmatic Sanction of Bourges.** Little of the royal power was sacrificed, and the national church remained under the firm control of the crown. Louis steadily reduced urban liberties and began the extinction of local and provincial

administrative independence in the interests of royal centralization.

1462. Acquisition of Cerdagne and Roussillon; redemption of the Somme towns (1463) revealing the resumption of national expansion.

1465. League of the Public Weal, a conspiracy against Louis by the dukes of Alençon, Burgundy, Berri, Bourbon, Lorraine.

1465. Louis's defeat by the league at Montl'héry. The **treaty of Conflans** restored the Somme towns to Burgundy, and Normandy to the duke of Berry. Louis began to evade the treaty at once, and split the league by diplomacy.

Louis's greatest rival was **Duke Philip the Good** of Burgundy. Philip was head of the first union of the Low Countries since the days of Charlemagne, a curious approximation of the ancient Lotharingia, which included: the duchy and county of Burgundy, Flanders, Artois, Brabant, Luxemburg, Holland, Zealand, Friesland, Hainault. The dukes lacked only Alsace and Lorraine and the royal title.

1467. The accession of **Charles the Bold** as duke of Burgundy opened the final duel with Burgundy.

1468. Anglo-Burgundian alliance; marriage of Charles the Bold to Margaret of York.

1468. The **affair at Péronne:** Charles, assuming Louis's treachery in the revolt of Ghent, arrested him at a conference at Péronne.

1469. The Duke Sigismund ceded Charles's rights in Alsace; Charles occupied Alsace and Lorraine (1473). Louis formed an alliance with the Swiss (1470) and seized the Somme towns (1471).

1474. Louis formed the **Union of Constance** (a coalition of the foes of Burgundy, under French subsidies) which opened the war on Charles.

1475. Edward IV, an ally of Charles, invaded France; Louis met him at Piquigny and bought him off.

1476. Charles's conquest of Lorraine and war on the Swiss cantons: defeat of Charles at **Grandson** and **Morat.**

1477, Jan. 5. DEFEAT AND DEATH OF

The Battle of Montl'héry, 1465

Duke Philip the Good

CHARLES AT NANCY (triumph of the Swiss pikeman over cavalry); end of the Burgundian menace. Louis united the duchy of Burgundy to the crown and occupied the county of Burgundy (Franche Comté). Flanders stood by the daughter of Charles, Mary of Burgundy, and was lost to France forever. Mary hurriedly married the Hapsburg Archduke Maximilian, the "heir" to the empire.

1480. On the **extinction of the house of Anjou,** Anjou, Bar, Maine, and Provence fell to the French crown. Bar completed Louis's mastery on the eastern frontier.

The most significant internal fact of the reign was the development of a clear basis for royal absolutism. Only one meeting of the estates-general was held (1469), and on that occasion the estates asked the king to rule without them in future. Legislation was henceforth by royal decree, a situation which facilitated Louis's thoroughgoing reform of the government and administration.

CULTURAL DEVELOPMENTS

Jean Froissart (1337–1410) wrote his *Chroniques,* a colorful history of his times.

Philippe de Commines, (1447–1511), a Fleming who left the service of Charles the Bold for that of Louis, produced in his *Mémoires* the finest piece of critical history since the days of the great historians of antiquity, and was a precursor of Machiavelli.

François Villon (1430–1470), a lyric poet of the first rank.

Jan (d. 1441) **and Hubert van Eyck** (d. 1426), Flemish painters in the service of the court of Burgundy, perfected oil technique; religious painting; portraiture, raising the painter's art to the highest stage of proficiency and perfection.

The Burgundian school of music flourished under the patronage of Charles the Bold: **Gilles Binchois** (d. 1470); **Guillaume Dufay** (d. 1474). *(Cont. p. 403.)*

The only professional engineering document of the Middle Ages is the notebook of **Villard de Honnecourt** (fl. late 14th century), a French architect who worked in Cambrai, Laon, Reims, Meaux, Chartres, as well as in Hungary. His notebook contains architectural plans, practical geometry, descriptions of machines. In France around the University of Paris arose a school of mechanists who developed the ideas of the group at Merton College. **Jean Buridan** (d. 1358) used the concept of impetus as an explanation for motion and acceleration. **Nicole Oresme,** College of Navarre, used geometrical diagrams to display the variation of physical quantities under various conditions.

c. THE IBERIAN PENINSULA

(From p. 257)

(1) Castile, 1312–1492

The successors of Alfonso X were not conspicuous for capacity. Frequent minorities and constant dynastic contests still further weakened the authority of the crown. Most outstanding of the Castilian rulers in this period was

1312–1350. ALFONSO XI, who decisively defeated the joint attack of the Spanish and Moroccan Moslems. His **victory at Rio Salado** (Oct. 30, 1340) ended the African menace

forever and was the chief battle in the whole history of the reconquest.

Throughout the **Hundred Years' War** Castile supported France, but attempted to avoid hostility with England as much as possible.

1350–1369. PETER (Pedro, the Cruel). His reign was in fact little more than a nineteen-year dynastic conflict with his half-brother, the bastard **Henry of Trastamara.** The French, alienated by Peter's outrageous treatment of his wife, Blanche of Bourbon, supported Henry and sent Du Guesclin to Spain. The English (the Black Prince) supported Peter. Henry was defeated at **Navarrete** (1367), but the English were soon estranged by Peter's vicious character. Ultimately Henry defeated and killed Peter (1369).

1369–1379. HENRY (ENRIQUE) II (Trastamara), who renewed the alliance with France. The Castilian fleet, by its victory over the English in the **battle of La Rochelle** (1372), restored command of the Channel to the French. Peace between Castile on the one side and Portugal and Aragon on the other concluded at **Almazan** (1374).

1375. Rapprochement of Castile and Aragon, through the marriage of Henry's son, John, to Eleanor, daughter of Peter IV of Aragon.

Castilian leadership in the reconquest of Moslem Spain led to a maximum of local and municipal self-government between the middle of the 12th and the middle of the 14th centuries. The cortes apparently originated from

Jean Froissart

Illustration (1489) for a poem by Villon

Shield of parade, Flemish, 1477

councils of nobles dating from Visigothic days. The Castilian rulers freely granted *fueros* (charters of self-government) to towns in the early stages of the reconquest, and definite elements of democracy appeared in municipal government in this period. By calling the burghers to the cortes, the kings found allies against the baronage, and this process began in Castile and Leon at least as early as 1188

(From p. 255)

The House of Castile (1252–1504)

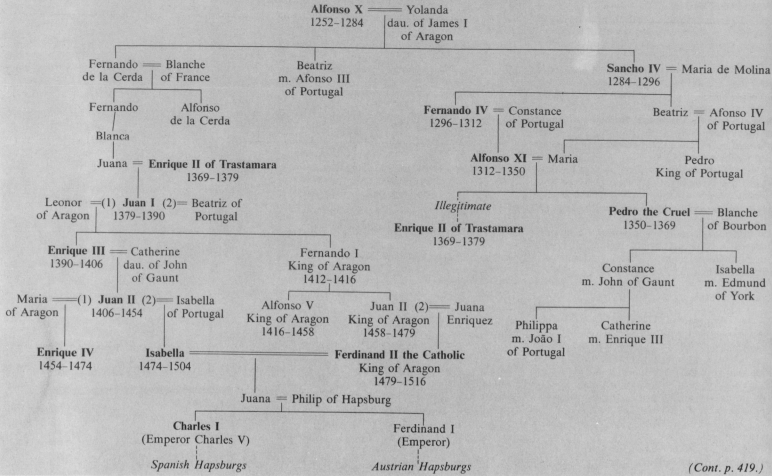

Alfonso X === Yolanda
1252–1284 dau. of James I of Aragon

Fernando === Blanche de la Cerda of France

Beatriz m. Afonso III of Portugal

Sancho IV === Maria de Molina
1284–1296

Fernando — Alfonso de la Cerda

Fernando IV === Constance of Portugal
1296–1312

Beatriz === Afonso IV of Portugal

Blanca

Alfonso XI === Maria
1312–1350

Pedro King of Portugal

Juana === **Enrique II of Trastamara**
1369–1379

Illegitimate

Enrique II of Trastamara
1369–1379

Pedro the Cruel === Blanche
1350–1369 of Bourbon

Leonor ===(1) **Juan I** (2)=== Beatriz of
of Aragon 1379–1390 Portugal

Enrique III === Catherine
1390–1406 dau. of John of Gaunt

Fernando I King of Aragon 1412–1416

Constance m. John of Gaunt

Isabella m. Edmund of York

Maria ===(1) **Juan II** (2)=== Isabella
of Aragon 1406–1454 of Portugal

Alfonso V King of Aragon 1416–1458

Juan II (2)=== Juana
King of Aragon Enriquez
1458–1479

Philippa m. João I of Portugal

Catherine m. Enrique III

Enrique IV
1454–1474

Isabella ======= **Ferdinand II the Catholic**
1474–1504 King of Aragon
1479–1516

Juana === Philip of Hapsburg

Charles I
(Emperor Charles V)

Ferdinand I
(Emperor)

Spanish Hapsburgs

Austrian Hapsburgs

(Cont. p. 419.)

(From p. 255)

The House of Aragon (1276–1516)

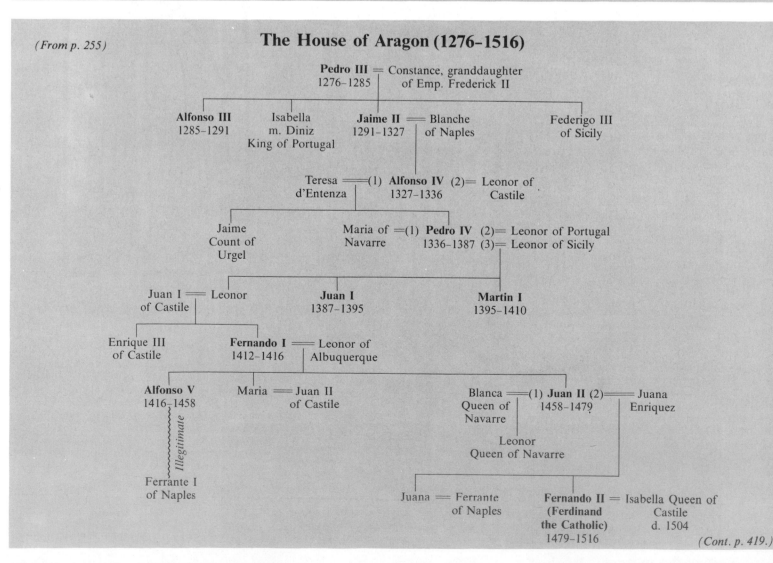

Pedro III === Constance, granddaughter
1276–1285 of Emp. Frederick II

Alfonso III
1285–1291

Isabella
m. Diniz
King of Portugal

Jaime II === Blanche
1291–1327 of Naples

Federigo III of Sicily

Teresa ===(1) **Alfonso IV** (2)=== Leonor of
d'Entenza 1327–1336 Castile

Jaime
Count of
Urgel

Maria of ===(1) **Pedro IV** (2)=== Leonor of Portugal
Navarre 1336–1387 (3)=== Leonor of Sicily

Juan I === Leonor
of Castile

Juan I
1387–1395

Martin I
1395–1410

Enrique III
of Castile

Fernando I === Leonor of
1412–1416 Albuquerque

Alfonso V
1416–1458

Illegitimate

Ferrante I
of Naples

Maria === Juan II
of Castile

Blanca ===(1) **Juan II** (2)=== Juana
Queen of 1458–1479 Enriquez
Navarre

Leonor
Queen of Navarre

Juana === Ferrante
of Naples

Fernando II === Isabella Queen of
(Ferdinand Castile
the Catholic) d. 1504
1479–1516

(Cont. p. 419.)

(in Aragon probably not before 1250). The córtes reached its zenith in the 14th and 15th centuries, but petitions to the crown were received and embodied in legislation as early as the 13th century.

Urban groups, the *hermandades* (brotherhoods), sworn to defend the laws of the realm and the lives and property of their members, were clearly developed in the 13th century (e.g. Sancho's, 1282, directed against his father, Alfonso X) and usually supported the kings in periods of crisis (minorities, succession struggles, baronial assaults). The decline of the hermandades is associated with the municipal decline and the appearance of the royal *corregidores* (mayors) in the towns (14th century), but it is not clear whether the crown hastened the decay of the towns and the brotherhoods or sought to stave it off.

Despite all this support, the battle of the kings with the aristocracy, firmly entrenched during the early stages of the reconquest, was a losing one. The nobles were exempt from taxes and from many laws; in general the same was true of the clergy, and some of the great bishops were virtual sovereigns.

The status of the lower classes of Castile was, however, far from desperate: Jew and Moslem were protected for their economic value, though the tendency toward jealousy and toward the segregation of the Jews was already appearing and the Jewish population was declining. The status of rural workers and serfs tended to improve by the definition and limitation of the landlord's rights. Slavery had probably disappeared by the 15th century.

1454-1474. HENRY (ENRIQUE) IV, during whose reign the feudal anarchy reached its apogee. The monarchical power was saved primarily through the support of the towns.

1469. Marriage of Isabella, half-sister and heiress of Henry IV, to **Ferdinand,** heir of the king of Aragon.

1474. ISABELLA succeeded to the Castilian throne. Isabella's succession was challenged by the daughter of Henry IV, supported by Afonso V of Portugal. But the córtes of Segovia (1475) recognized Isabella and Ferdinand and the latter defeated the Portuguese in 1476 **(battle of Toro).**

1479. FERDINAND (FERNANDO) succeeded to the rule of Aragon, Catalonia, Valencia. A form of dyarchical government was set up for the united Castilian and Aragonese crowns. Rule of the **Catholic kings** (Ferdinand and Isabella). Restoration of the royal power in Castile: by revising the town charters, the towns were made centers of resistance to feudal aggression; formation of the *Santa Hermandad,* a union of Castilian towns in the interest of royal authority and order. The great feudal magnates were deprived of many of their possessions and rights and a royal administration was gradually established. The *Libro de Montalvo* (1485), an early codification of Spanish law. **Concordat of 1482** with the pope, carefully restricting the power of Rome over the Spanish church: the king became grand master of the powerful religious orders of knighthood. The **Inquisition** (established in 1478) wholly under royal control, used primarily for the persecution of the Marranos (converted Jews secretly practicing their old faith). Confiscations of property did much to increase the financial power of the rulers and to

Ferdinand and Isabella (1502 woodcut)

Expulsion of Jews from Spain, 1492

strengthen them in the work of subduing the feudal opposition.

1492. Fall of Granada, marking the end of the reconquest of Spain from the Moors. This was speedily followed by a spiritual reconquest, the work of the Inquisition. The **expulsion of the Jews** (possibly as many as 200,000) in 1492 was followed by that of the Moors in Castile (1502).

Art and literature. Castilian painting showed the influence of the school of Giotto (after c. 1380), and in the 15th century came under Flemish inspiration (visit of Jan van Eyck, 1428-1429). In general literature and learning followed the same foreign tendencies as architecture and painting: French influence came in early, followed later by Italian and English (notably Dante, Petrarch, Boccaccio, Gower). Introduction of printing at Valencia (c. 1474) and in Castile (c. 1475).

(2) Aragon, 1276-1479

1276-1285. PETER (PEDRO) III, who was married to Constance, daughter of Manfred and heir of the Hohenstaufen. In 1282 he sailed on a long-planned expedition for the **conquest of Sicily** (which he disguised as an African crusade). He landed at Collo, was called to the throne, defeated Charles of Anjou, and became Peter I of Sicily (1282-1285), refusing to do homage to the pope for his island kingdom. This expansion of the Aragonese kingdom gave Aragon for a time predominance in the western Mediterranean. But it estranged the Aragonese aristocracy, as well as the towns. The nobility therefore formed the **Union for Liberty** and, in the cortes of 1283, extorted from Peter a **General Privilege** which defined the rights and duties of the nobles, affirmed the

principle of due process of law, and provided for annual meetings of the córtes.

1285-1291. ALFONSO III was obliged to make a sweeping re-grant of the Privileges of Union (1287), the so-called **Magna Carta of Aragon.**

1291-1327. JAMES II (king of Sicily, 1285-1295). He exchanged the investiture of Sardinia and Corsica for that of Sicily (1295), which thereupon passed to his brother Frederick, who established the separate Sicilian dynasty. James began the expulsion of the Genoese and Pisans from Sardinia (1323–1324), a process not finally completed until 1421. For a period Aragon held the duchy of Athens (first indirectly through Sicily, 1311–1377, then directly, to 1388), thanks to the activity of the **Grand Catalan Company** *(p. 338)*.

1327–1336. ALFONSO IV.

1336–1387. PETER (PEDRO) IV. He was virtually a prisoner of the revived union of the nobility and had to confirm their privileges. But, after a victory over the union (at **Epila**, 1348), he broke up the coalition and gradually restricted the power of the aristocracy in Aragon and Valencia. The clergy and the towns had far less power than in Castile, while the rural workers and serfs suffered a much harder lot.

1377. On the death of Frederick II of Sicily, Peter IV, as the husband of Frederick's sister, sent his son Martin as viceroy to Sicily.

1387–1395. John (Juan) king.

1395–1410. Martin, king. He reunited Aragon and Sicily (1409). On his death the native dynasty came to an end after a period of dynastic struggle.

1412–1416. Ferdinand (Fernando) I, of Castile, a grandson of Peter IV, succeeded to the throne.

1416–1458. ALFONSO V (the Magnanimous). His attention was engrossed by the desire to conquer Naples. After long diplomatic in-

trigues and occasional combats, he succeeded (1435) in being recognized as king by the pope in 1442. Alfonso, a lover of Italy and passionate devotee of the Renaissance, shifted the center of gravity of the Aragonese empire and subordinated the interest of Aragon to that of Naples. Aragon was ruled by his brother John, as viceroy. On the death of Alfonso, Naples passed to his son Ferrante (1458–1494).

1458–1479. John (Juan) II, king.

1479–1516. FERDINAND (FERNANDO) II, king. **Union of Aragon with Castile.**

(Cont. p. 408.)

(3) Portugal, 1279–1495

(From p. 258)

1279–1325. DINIZ (the Worker), the best-known and best-loved king of medieval Portugal. An ardent poet, he did much to raise the cultural level of the court. His interest in agriculture and constant effort toward economic development (commercial treaty with England, 1294) resulted in greater prosperity. Beginning of **Portuguese naval activity** (under Venetian and Genoese guidance). Foundation (1290) of the University of Lisbon, which was soon (1308) moved to Coimbra.

1325–1357. AFONSO IV (the Brave), whose reign was scarred by dynastic troubles. The **murder of Inez de Castro** (1355), the mistress

and later the wife of Afonso's son Peter, at the behest of Afonso. This episode, the subject of much literature, led to a revolt of Peter.

1340. The Portuguese, in alliance with Castile defeated the Moors in the **battle of Salado.**

1357–1367. PETER (PEDRO) I (the Severe) a harsh and hasty, though just, ruler, who continued his predecessor's efforts in behalf of the general welfare.

1367–1383. FERDINAND (FERNÃO) I (the Handsome), a weak ruler whose love for Leonora Telles led him to repudiate his betrothal to a Castilian princess and so bring on a war with Castile.

1383. Regency of Queen Leonora in behalf of Ferdinand's daughter, Beatrice, who was married to John I of Castile. This arrangement led to strong opposition among the Portuguese who detested both the regent and her lover and resented all control from outside.

1385–1433. JOHN (JOÃO) I, an illegitimate son of Peter I, established the **Avis dynasty** after leading a successful revolt and driving the regent out of the country. He was proclaimed king by the cortes of Coimbra, but his position was at once challenged by the Castilians, who twice invaded Portugal and besieged Lisbon

1385, Aug. 14. The **BATTLE OF ALJUBARROTA,** in which the Portuguese defeated the Castilians. A decisive date in the history of

Kings of Portugal (1248–1521)

(From p. 258)

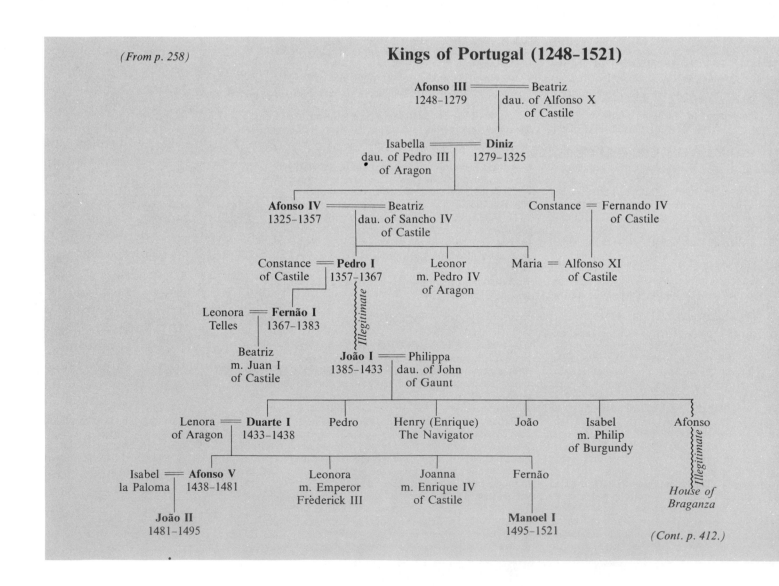

(Cont. p. 412.)

Diniz (the Worker), 1279–1325

the country, this battle established the **independence of Portugal** beyond all possibility of challenge. With the Avis dynasty Portugal entered upon the greatest period of her history. The king himself was an able and enlightened ruler, who enjoyed the aid of five outstanding sons, of whom **Henry the Navigator** (1394–1460) became the greatest figure in the history of the epoch-making discoveries of the 15th century *(p. 377).*

1386, May 9. The **treaty of Windsor,** by which England and Portugal became permanently allied. King John married Philippa, the daughter of John of Gaunt. The dynasty thereby became part English.

1411. **Peace was finally concluded with Castile.**

1415, Aug. 24. The Portuguese took **Ceuta** from the Moors, thus initiating a policy of expansion on the African mainland.

1433–1438. **Edward (Duarte) I,** a learned and intelligent prince, eldest son of John. His short reign was marked by a terrific epidemic of the plague and by

1437. The **disaster at Tangier,** where the Portuguese were overwhelmingly defeated. They were obliged to promise to return Ceuta, and to leave in Moorish hands the youngest brother of the king, **Ferdinand** (the Constant Prince), who died in captivity after five years of suffering. Ceuta was not returned.

1438–1481. **AFONSO V** (the African), an attractive and chivalrous ruler, but lacking the hard-headed realism of his predecessors. The reign began with the regency of the king's mother, Eleonora, a Spanish princess, who again was confronted with Portuguese opposition to a Spanish connection. The nobility revolted, the regent fled, and the king's uncle, Peter, was made regent. His able and enlightened rule came to an end when the king, having reached his majority, allowed himself to be persuaded by favorites to make war on Peter. The latter and his son were defeated and killed in the **battle of Alfarrobeira** (1449).

1446. The *Ordenaçoes Affonsinas,* the first great law code of the Portuguese, representing an amalgam of Roman, Visigothic, and customary law.

1463. Campaigns against the kingdom of Fez. The Portuguese captured Casablanca and

1471. Tangiers.

1476. **Battle of Toro.** Defeat of the Portuguese by the Castilians, after Afonso, who had married a sister of Isabella, attempted to dispute the latter's succession to the throne.

1481–1495. **JOHN (JOÃO) II,** an energetic prince who at once undertook to restrict the property and power of the nobility, which had become very great during the preceding reign. This led to a revolt of the nobles, led by **Ferdinand of Braganza** and supported by the Catholic kings of Castile and Aragon. The revolt was suppressed in 1483; Braganza and many of his followers were executed. The royal power thenceforth was more firmly established than ever before. *(Cont. p. 411.)*

d. ITALY AND THE PAPACY

(From p. 243)

(1) The Papacy, 1305–1492

[*For a complete list of the Roman popes see Appendix IV.*]

1305–1378. **THE AVIGNONESE PAPACY** (Babylonian Captivity): during seven pontificates the popes, exiled from the spiritual capital of the West, preferred to contend against the pressure of the French crown rather than face the disorder of Rome and Italy.

1310–1313. **Expedition of the Emperor Henry VII** to Italy *(p. 318).* Henry asserted his independence of the spiritual power and claimed control of Italy. Clement V and Philip IV (opposed to him as a rival of the Angevins) combined against him.

1316–1334. **JOHN XXII,** who supported the Angevins in Naples. His attempt to decide the validity of Emperor Louis IV's title led to a long struggle (1323–1347). Louis was supported by the German people, who resented the Avignonese Papacy, and by the Franciscans. John was unable to return to Italy because of the continued anarchy.

1334–1342. **Benedict XII,** and

1342–1352. **CLEMENT VI,** whose pontificate was marked by the

1347. **REVOLUTION OF COLA DI RIENZI** at Rome. With the support of the populace, Cola overthrew the rule of the patricians, set himself up as tribune of the people, and summoned an Italian national parliament. Expelled by his opponents (1348), he returned in 1352 and was appointed senator by the pope (1354), but was in the same year slain by his baronial opponents. The lords of the Papal States resumed control and were, to all intents

Pope John XXII (contemporary silver coin)

Coronation of Pope Boniface IX, 1389

Pope Urban VI

and purposes, independent of papal authority. **1352-1362. INNOCENT VI.** He sent the Spanish cardinal, Albornoz, to Italy and the latter succeeded in reducing the powerful barons to obedience, thus making possible an eventual return of the pope.

REFORM OF THE CURIA during the Avignon period. General work of centralization and departmentalization: (1) the *camera apostolica;* (2) the chancery; (3) justice; (4) the penitentiary (punishments and dispensations). Centralization put important clerical appointments throughout Europe under direct papal control through an extraordinary extension of the papal rights of reservation and provision; made a virtual end of local elections, filled ecclesiastical offices with aliens and strangers, and outraged public opinion everywhere. A parallel reorganization and departmentalization of the papal financial administration led to a new efficiency in the levy and collection of papal taxes, fees, etc., which bore hard on the clergy, and drained large sums from the national states, stirring public opinion still further, especially in England. Significant items of the budget of John XXII: war, 63.7 per cent; upkeep and entertainment, 12.7 per cent; alms, 7.16 per cent; stables, 0.4 per cent; art, 0.33 per cent; library, 0.17 per cent.

Vying with the growing magnificence of the monarchies of Europe, the Avignonese popes and cardinals became proverbial for their pomp and luxury, and these tendencies spread to the episcopate despite the thunders of the Franciscans and the decrees of local synods. The insubordination of outraged reformers like the **Fraticelli,** the Bohemian preachers, and **Wiclif** soon penetrated to the masses.

Virtually every pope (notably Clement V and John XXII) made serious and honest efforts to combat these alarming developments, but the general anarchy in Europe made success impossible. There was a notable **expansion of missions to the Far East:** China (an archbishop and ten suffragans, 1312; fifty Franciscan houses, 1314; missions to Persia). Rome, the ancient spiritual center of the West, was reduced to an anarchic, poverty-stricken, provincial city, and clamored for the return of the popes. Petrarch's extreme denunciations of the Avignonese popes had little justification.

1362-1370. URBAN V. Return to Rome with the co-operation of Emperor Charles IV; the city a dismal ruin; return to Avignon on the entreaties of the cardinals (a majority of whom were French).

1370-1378. GREGORY XI visited Rome and died before he could leave. The conclave, under threat of personal violence from the Roman mob, yielded to demands for an Italian pope, electing

1378-1389. URBAN VI, a blunt, avaricious man, who alienated the cardinals by announcing that his reform of the Church would begin with the sacred college.

1378-1417. The **GREAT SCHISM:** the papacy divided and dishonored. Thirteen cardinals, meeting at Anagni, elected
1378-1394. CLEMENT VII, thus dividing western Christendom into obediences:

The Roman Line	The Avignonese Line
Urban VI	**Clement VII**
(1378–1389)	(1378–1394)
Boniface IX	**Benedict XIII**
(1389–1404)	(1394–1423)
Innocent VII	
(1404–1406)	
Gregory XII	
(1406–1415)	

Allegiance to the rivals was determined partly by practical considerations, but often was settled after careful study of the claims of each and consultation with the clergy (e.g. King Charles V of France, John of Castile); England's decision was based largely on hostility to France; Scotland's on its hostility to England; in Naples and Sicily the rulers and their subjects took opposite positions.
EMERGENCE OF THE CONCILIAR MOVEMENT. The basic ideas were inherent in such writers as **Marsiglio of Padua;** specific arguments that a general council is superior to a pope, can be called by a king, and is competent to judge a pope or call a new conclave, were advanced in 1379 (**Henry of Langenstein**) and from then on grew in importance. King Charles VI of France (influenced by the Uni-

versity of Paris) called a **national synod** (1395), which voted overwhelmingly to urge the resignation of both popes. The Avignonese cardinals approved with only one negative; the popes refused to resign. The French clergy voted (1398) to withhold papal taxes and dues, and were endorsed by the king. Benedict's cardinals deserted him in panic and he fled, producing a reaction of public opinion against the king of France. Two Roman popes were elected with the understanding that they would resign if Benedict XIII would do so. The two colleges of cardinals joined in a call for a general council to meet at Pisa, 1409.
1409. The **COUNCIL OF PISA,** attended by 500 prelates and delegates from the states of Europe. Two parties: (1) a moderate majority with the sole aim of ending the schism; (2) radical reformers (including d'Ailly and Gerson from Paris), who were compelled to accept postponement of reform to a council supposed to meet in 1412. After hearing specific charges against both popes, the council deposed both. The conclave chose **Alexander V** (d. 1410) and then the ecclesiastical *condottiere,* Cardinal Baldassare Cossa, a man without spiritual qualities. Neither the Roman nor the Avignonese pope resigned, and the schism became a triple one.
1410-1415. JOHN XXIII, expelled from Rome by Ladislas of Naples, was forced by the Emperor Sigismund to issue a call for the **Council of Constance** (1414) in return for protection.

This marked the passing of the initiative in reform from the king of France to the Roman emperor, a return in theory to the days of the Ottos.
1414-1417. The **COUNCIL OF CONSTANCE:** one of the greatest assemblies of medieval history; three aims: (1) **restoration of unity to the Church;** (2) **reform in head and members;** (3) **extirpation of heresy,** particularly the Hussite heresy *(p. 322).* Following university practice, voting was by nations and the numbers of the Italian prelates did no good to Pope John. John, seeing a chance to divide the council and the emperor, allowed the imprisonment of Hus (in violation of the imperial safe-conduct).
Hus, heard three times by the whole council (and cleverly induced to expand his doctrine that sin vitiates a clerical office to include civil office as well), lost Sigismund's support, was condemned and executed (1415) as was his companion, Jerome of Prague (1416).
John XXIII, having agreed to resign if his rivals did so, fled the council, was brought back, tried, and deposed (1415); **Gregory XII** resigned (1415); Sigismund, unable to induce Benedict XIII to resign, won away his supporters, and isolated him. Reform was again postponed, but two decrees are significant: *Sacrosancta* (1415), asserting that a council is superior to a pope; and *Frequens* (1417) providing for stated meetings of general councils.
The conclave elected Cardinal Colonna as

Jan Hus at the Council of Constance, 1415

Martin V. Christendom ignored the obstinate Benedict, and the schism was over.

1417–1431. MARTIN V (Colonna), a Roman of Romans, declared it impious to appeal to a general council against a pope and dissolved the council of Constance. Evasion of general reform and the threat of general councils supported by powerful monarchs, through the negotiation of concordats with the heads of states (i.e., by dealing with the bishops through lay rulers, a complete negation of the theory of a universal papal absolutism, and a virtual recognition of national churches). **Recovery of the Papal States:** most of the cities were under their own lords who bore *pro forma* titles as papal vicars but were in fact independent. Concentration on Italian political problems at the expense of the universal spiritual interests of Christendom.

1431–1447. EUGENE IV, an obstinate Venetian who favored summoning the **council of Basel.**

1431–1449. The **COUNCIL OF BASEL,** dominated by strong anti-papal feeling. Dissolved by Eugene because of negotiations with the Hussites, the council ignored the order and decreed (with the support of the princes) that no general council can be dissolved without its consent, continued in session, and summoned Eugene and the cardinals to attend. Eugene ignored the summons, but was forced (1433) to accept the council. Temporary compromise with the Hussites registered in the *Compactata.* **Reforms voted:** abolition of commendations, reservations, appeals to Rome, annates, etc.; provision for regular provincial and diocesan synods; confirmation of the right of chapter elections; appeal from a general council to a pope pronounced heresy. Already divided over these reforms, the council split over reunion with the Greek church. Eugene and his cardinals ignored a second summons, were pronounced contumacious; Eugene dissolved the council and called another to meet at Ferrara; the papalists left Basel. The rump council continued to meet, deposed Eugene (1439), elected Amadeus of Savoy,

1439–1449. FELIX V, because he could pay his own way. Moved to Lausanne, the council continued with dwindling numbers and prestige.

1438–1445. The **COUNCIL OF FERRARA-FLORENCE** (under the presidency of Eugene). After months of futile discussion (over the *filioque* question, unleavened bread at the sacrament, purgatory, and papal supremacy), the Greeks were forced to accept the Roman formula for union (1439) and the schism between East and West, dating from 1054, was technically healed. As the Greeks at home repudiated the union, it was of no effect. Isidore of Kiev and Bessarion remained as cardinals of the Roman church.

1438. A **French national synod** and King Charles VII accepted the *Pragmatic Sanction of Bourges* embodying most of the anti-papal decrees of the council of Basel (basis for the Gallican liberties). It checked the drain of money from France to the Papacy.

1439. The **diet of Mainz** accepted the *Pragmatic Sanction of Mainz,* abolishing annates, papal reservations, provisions, and providing for diocesan and provincial synods.

Enea Silvio de'Piccolomini, sent to win Germany back for the Papacy, came to an agreement with Emperor Frederick III on such cynical terms that the German princes flocked to Felix V, but a provisional concordat, embodying the Pragmatic of 1439 enabled Enea Silvio to detach the princes one by one.

1448. Concordat of Vienna, Eugene's greatest triumph, accepted the supremacy of a general council, but restored the annates and abandoned most of the restrictions on papal patronage.

1449. Dissolution of the Council of Basel: abdication of Felix V (who became a cardinal). Papal celebration of the triumph over the conciliar movement in the **Jubilee of 1450.** Postponement of moderate reform made the radical Reformation of the 16th century inevitable.

1447–1455. NICHOLAS V, former librarian of Cosimo de' Medici, scholar, humanist, collector of manuscripts, founder of the **Vatican Library.** Rome temporarily a center of humanism: Nicholas' circle included: **Poggio Bracciolini, Alberti,** and **Lorenzo Valla** (a scientific humanist and critic who had just demolished the *Donation of Constantine* as a forgery). Plans for a new St. Peter's.

1453. The **Turkish capture of Constantinople** (*p. 345*) ended the Greek Empire of the East

SWISS CONFEDERATION

HUNGARY

DUCHY OF SAVOY

DUCHY OF MILAN

Como
Milan
Verona
Pavia
Padua
Venice
Turin
Saluzzo
PO
M. OF MANTUA
D. OF FERRARA

VENETIAN REPUBLIC

Pola

DALMATIA

Adriatic Sea

REP. OF GENOA
Genoa
D. OF MODENA
Bologna
Ravenna
Rimini
REP. OF LUCCA
REP. OF FLORENCE
Pisa
Arno
FLORENCE
Urbino
Siena
REP. OF SIENA
Assisi
STATES OF THE CHURCH
Tiber
ELBA (to Naples)
CORSICA (to Genoa)
Rome
The KINGDOM OF NAPLES
Capua
Naples
Benevento
Bari
Salerno
Taranto
KINGDOM OF SARDINIA
Cagliari
Tyrrhennian Sea
Palermo
KINGDOM OF SICILY

ITALY in the 15th CENTURY

Mediterranean Sea

Pope Eugenius IV (detail from a fresco by Francesco Salviati)

and removed all serious rivalry by the patriarch to the position of the Roman pope.

1455-1458. CALIXTUS III (an Aragonese), an aged invalid, anti-humanist, energetic supporter of war against the Turk, an ardent nepotist (three Borgia nephews, one of them later Pope Alexander VI).

1458-1464. PIUS II (Aeneas Sylvius Piccolomini). In his youth a gay dog; in later life austere; most brilliant and versatile of the literary popes, a humanist, lover of nature, eloquent essayist, orator, and Latin stylist. A short, bent man with smiling eyes, a fringe of white hair, seldom free of pain, a tireless worker, always accessible. Advocate of papal supremacy, obstinate foe of conciliar reform. His appeals for a crusade ignored by a preoccupied Europe, he gallantly took the Cross himself to shame the princes of Christendom, and died at Ancona. His family was large and poor and he was a nepotist.

1464-1471. PAUL II, a Venetian, rich, kindly, handsome, a collector of jewels and carvings, founder of the Corso horse-races. A strong centralizer, supporter of the Hungarian crusade. The Turkish victory at **Negroponte** (1470) gave the Turks mastery of Levantine waters.

1471-1484. SIXTUS IV (della Rovere) aimed to consolidate the Papal States and reduce the power of the cardinals; methodical nepotist (three nephews, the Riarios, one of them later Pope Julius II).

1475. Rapprochement with Ferrante of Naples; alienation of the Medici who were replaced as papal bankers by the Pazzi. The Riarios organized with Sixtus' knowledge, if

Coronation of Pope Pius II, 1458

not approval, the **Pazzi Conspiracy** (assassination of Giuliano de' Medici, 1478). This destroyed the alliance of Florence, Naples, Milan, to maintain the Italian balance of power and led to a war involving most of Italy; the war was terminated by the capture of Otranto (1480) and by the diplomacy of Lorenzo de' Medici. Sixtus' coalition with Venice led to the Ferrarese War (1482-1484). Sixtus and Julius II were the great beautifiers of Rome: **Sistine Chapel** (c. 1473), paving and widening of streets and squares; patronage of **Ghirlandaio, Botticelli, Perugino, Pinturicchio,** *et al.*

1484-1492. INNOCENT VIII, a kindly, handsome Genoese, a compromise cipher, the first pope to recognize his children and to dine publicly with ladies. A baronial revolt (1485-1487) in Naples (supported by Innocent and, secretly, by Venice) led to a revival of the Angevin claims to Naples. Florence and Milan, fearing French intervention in Italy, opposed the war, and peace and amnesty were arranged. Ferrante's cynical violation of the amnesty led the exiles (on Ludovico Sforza's advice) to call in King Charles VIII of France. Sforza struck an alliance with Charles to protect Milan and opened the road into Italy to this alien invader (1494). Italy was not again to know full independence from foreign domination until the end of the 19th century.

Girolamo Savonarola (1452-1498), a Dominican, prior of San Marco in Florence (1491), eloquent reforming preacher and precursor of the Reformation, was already denouncing the new paganism of the Renaissance, the corruption of the state and the Papacy, and foretelling the ruin of Italy.

(Cont. p. 415.)

(2) Sicily and Naples, 1268-1494
(From p. 243)

1268-1285. CHARLES I (Angevin) king of Naples and of Sicily (1268-1282). His grandiose scheme for the creation of a Mediterranean empire in succession to the Byzantine (a revival of the Latin Empire under French auspices) was frustrated by the **Sicilian Vespers** (1282) and the war in Sicily which continued until 1302. Sicily maintained its independence and offered the crown to **Peter III of Aragon** (husband of Constance, heiress of the Hohenstaufen), an ally of Constantinople against Charles. Peter accepted the offer (1282), ejected the Angevins, and established the house of Aragon on the throne.

1282- SICILY UNDER ARAGONESE RULE: Peter (1282-1285); **James** (1285-1295). James exchanged the investiture of Sardinia and Corsica for that of Sicily, and Sicily passed to his brother, **Frederick** (1295-1337). Frederick brought to a close the war with Naples (**Peace of Caltabelotta,** 1302), marrying the daughter of Charles I and accepting the stipulation that the Sicilian crown should pass to the Angevins on his death. This agreement was not fulfilled, with the result that the struggle continued until, in 1373, Joanna of Naples abandoned Sicily to the Aragonese in return for tribute. Sicily was ruled as a viceroyalty until the reunion with Aragon in 1409.

1285-1309. Charles II (Angevin) of Naples.

1309-1343. Robert (Angevin) of Naples. He was the leader of the Italian Guelfs and, having been appointed imperial vicar on the death of Emperor Henry VII, planned to create an Italian kingdom.

1343-1382. Joanna (Giovanna) I, queen of Naples.

1382-1386. Charles III, a grandnephew of Robert.

1386-1414. Ladislas, son of Charles III, finally succeeded in establishing some measure of order in the kingdom and began a vigorous campaign of expansion in central Italy. In 1409 he bought the States of the Church from Pope Gregory XII, but his designs were blocked by Florence and Siena.

1414-1435. JOANNA (GIOVANNA) II, sister

Tomb of Innocent VIII, St. Peter's, Rome

of Ladislas. The amazing intrigues of this amorous widow with her favorites, successors designate, and rival claimants to the throne kept Italian diplomacy in a turmoil, and culminated in a struggle between **René,** the Angevin claimant (supported by the pope), and **Alfonso V of Aragon** (supported by Filippo Maria Visconti). This conflict ended in the triumph of Alfonso, who secured Naples in 1435 and was recognized as king by the pope in 1442.

1435–1458. ALFONSO (the Magnanimous) reunited the crowns of Naples and Sicily and made Naples the center of his Aragonese Mediterranean empire *(p. 304)*. He supported Filippo Maria Visconti of Milan, who apparently willed his duchy to him on his death. Alfonso avoided arousing Italy by claiming the duchy, but Ferdinand of Aragon later revived the claim. Alfonso's pressure drove Genoa into the arms of France. Loyal to the pope, Alfonso supported Eugene IV against Francesco Sforza. He centralized the administration, reformed taxation, and arranged a series of dynastic marriages in Italy. But he failed to subdue his barons entirely. He preferred Italy to Aragon, was a passionate devotee of Italian culture and acted as a Renaissance Maecenas, the patron of Lorenzo Valla. The **Academy of Naples** was composed mostly of poets. Alfonso divided his domain, Aragon and Sicily passing to his brother, John, and Naples (correctly called the kingdom of Sicily) going to his illegitimate son

1458–1494. FERRANTE (FERDINAND I), one of the most notoriously unscrupulous Renaissance princes. He triumphed in his struggle for the succession with the aid of Francesco Sforza and Cosimo de' Medici (who was alarmed at the presence of the French in Genoa). Ferrante generally supported the triple Italian alliance except for the period 1478–1480. Pope Innocent V, angered at Ferrante's suspension of tribute, supported the Angevin pretender, and Ferrante made a hollow peace until he could crush a baronial revolt. Then, supported by the Colonna and Orsini in Rome, he turned on Innocent, who was saved only by Lorenzo de' Medici. Innocent (1492) guaranteed the succession in Naples. Alexander VI stood by the bargain, and opposed Charles VIII's demand for investiture.

The **CLAIMS OF THE VALOIS KINGS** to Naples. Based on (1) the marriage of Margaret (daughter of Charles II of Naples) and Charles of Valois, the parents of King Philip VI; and on (2) the claims of the so-called "second" house of Anjou founded by Duke Louis I (d. 1384) of Anjou, count of Provence. Louis was grandson of Philip VI, and grandfather of (1) Maria, wife of Charles VII of France, mother of Louis XI; and of (2) Duke Louis III (d. 1434) and his brother René of Lorraine (d. 1468).

(Cont. p. 419.)

Charles de Valois

(3) Florence, to 1492

EARLY HISTORY. The **margraviate of Tuscany,** set up by the Carolingians, extended from the Po to the Roman state under the Margrave Boniface (d. 1052), whose daughter, the great **Countess Matilda** (1052–1115), was probably the strongest papal supporter in Italy. Associated with her in the government was a council of *boni homines,* whose administration during her frequent absences, and after her death, laid the foundation for the emergence of the commune. Florence, already a great commercial center, opposed the Ghibelline hill barons, who preyed on her commerce. The burghers continued Guelf in sympathy; trade and financial connections with France made them Francophile and friendly to Charles of Anjou. Under Matilda the **guild organization** emerged, which came to form the basis of the city government. Control of the government was concentrated in the hands of the great guilds (one of which included the bankers). Consuls appeared after 1138. The populace was divided into two great groups, the *grandi* (nobles) and the *arti* (guilds). Consuls were chosen by the grandi.

On the breakup of the margraviate following Matilda's death, Florence began her advance, and by 1176 was master of the dioceses of Florence and Fiesole. The institution of the *podestate* (magistrates) after 1202 was favored by the feudal elements and the lesser guilds. Intermittent rivalry of the noble houses continued. Wars were fought with Pisa, Lucca, Pistoia, Siena. Under the *podestà* the commune developed a strong organization paralleled by the growth of the *popolo* (populace) under its *capitano* (chief).

The great struggle of **Guelf and Ghibelline** was reflected in Florentine civil strife. After a Guelf régime, Frederick of Antioch (son of Frederick II) as imperial vicar instituted the first mass expulsion in Florentine history by driving out the Guelfs (1249).

1252. The first **gold florin** was coined, and soon became the standard gold coin in Europe.

1260. Siena, with the aid of Manfred and the Florentine Ghibellines, inflicted a great defeat on the Florentine Guelfs **(Montaperti),** beginning a Ghibelline dominance that lasted until Manfred's death (1266). This was followed by a reaction, and the expulsion of the Ghibellines. Under the Ghibelline régime the popolo lost all share in the government.

In the reaction following the Ghibelline régime, Ghibelline property was confiscated to support persecution of the Ghibellines.

The Martyrdom of Savonarola in Florence, 1498

(From p. 246)

The House of Anjou (1266–1435)

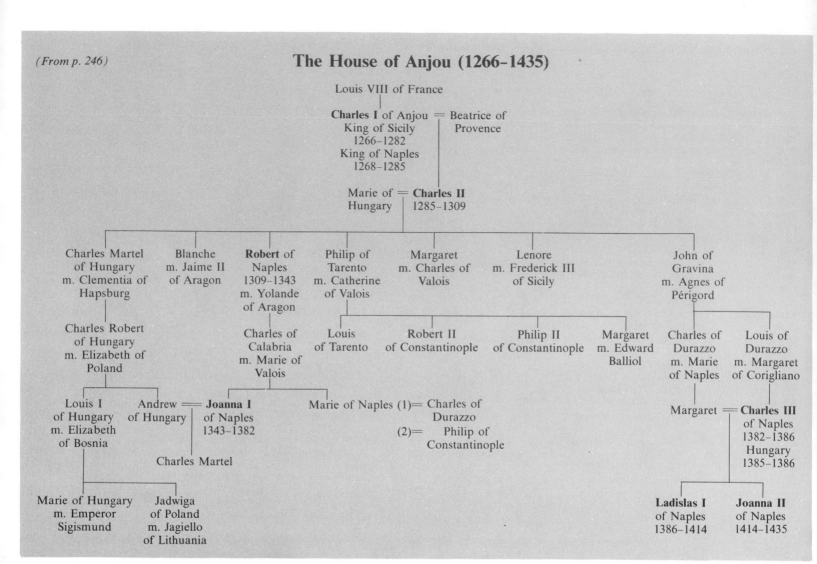

Louis VIII of France

Charles I of Anjou = Beatrice of
King of Sicily   Provence
1266–1282
King of Naples
1268–1285

Marie of = **Charles II**
Hungary   1285–1309

Charles Martel | Blanche | **Robert** of | Philip of | Margaret | Lenore | John of
of Hungary | m. Jaime II | Naples | Tarento | m. Charles of | m. Frederick III | Gravina
m. Clementia of | of Aragon | 1309–1343 | m. Catherine | Valois | of Sicily | m. Agnes of
Hapsburg | | m. Yolande | of Valois | | | Périgord
| | of Aragon | | | |

Charles Robert   Charles of   Louis   Robert II   Philip II   Margaret   Charles of   Louis of
of Hungary   Calabria   of Tarento   of Constantinople   of Constantinople   m. Edward   Durazzo   Durazzo
m. Elizabeth of   m. Marie of   Balliol   m. Marie   m. Margaret
Poland   Valois   of Naples   of Corigliano

Louis I   Andrew = **Joanna I**   Marie of Naples (1)= Charles of   Margaret = **Charles III**
of Hungary   of Hungary   of Naples   Durazzo   of Naples
m. Elizabeth   1343–1382   (2)=   Philip of   1382–1386
of Bosnia   Constantinople   Hungary
          Charles Martel   1385–1386

Marie of Hungary   Jadwiga   **Ladislas I**   **Joanna II**
m. Emperor   of Poland   of Naples   of Naples
Sigismund   m. Jagiello   1386–1414   1414–1435
          of Lithuania

Dante Alighieri, 1265–1321

Illustration for Boccaccio's Decameron

FRANCESCO PETRARCA.

Petrarch, 1304–1374

Under Charles of Anjou the formulae of the old constitution were restored; the party struggle continued. The Sicilian Vespers (1282) weakened Charles, strengthened the commune, and the Florentine "republic" became in effect a commercial oligarchy in the hands of the greater guilds.

1282. By the **Law of 1282** nobles could participate in the government only by joining a guild. The last traces of serfdom were abolished (1289) and the number of guilds increased to 21 (seven greater, 14 lesser).

1293. The **ordinance of 1293** excluded from the guilds anyone not actively practicing his profession, and thus in effect removed the nobles from all share in the government.

Two factions arose: the **Blacks** (*Neri*), extreme Guelfs led by Corso Donati; the **Whites** (*Bianchi*), moderate Guelfs (and later Ghibellines) under Vieri Cerchi. The Neri favored repeal of the ordinance of 1293.

Emperor Henry VII was unable to capture Florence, but

1320–1323. **Castruccio Castracani,** lord of Lucca, humiliated the city in the field. Growing financial troubles, partly the result of Edward III's repudiation of his debts to the Florentine bankers, culminated in the failures of the Peruzzi (1343) and Bardi (1344), and damaged Florentine banking prestige. The government was discredited and civil war ensued. **Walter of Brienne** (duke of Athens) was called in, reformed the government, began a usurpation, and was expelled (1343). The restored commune was under the domination of the business men who had three objectives: access to the sea (hence hostility to Pisa), expansion in Tuscany (to dominate the trade roads), and support of the popes (to retain papal banking business). Social conflict continued and grew as the oligarchy gained power and the Guelfs opposed the increasing industrial proletariat. The lesser guilds were pushed into the background, the unguilded were worse off. The first social revolt came in 1345.

1347–1348. Famine followed by the **Black Death** reduced the population seriously.

1351. The commutation of military service for cash marked the decline of citizen militia and the golden age of the *condottieri* (mercenary captains). War with Milan resulted (1351) from Giovanni Visconti's attempt to reduce Florence and master Tuscany.

1375–1378. Papal efforts to annex Tuscany led Florence into a temporary alliance with Milan.

1378. Continued pressure by Guelf extremists to exclude the lesser guilds led to a series of violent explosions. **Salvestro de' Medici,** gonfalonier, ended the *admonitions,* which were the basis of the Guelf terrorism, and a violent **revolt of the ciompi** (the poorest workmen) broke out. The ciompi made temporary gains, but Salvestro was exiled, and by 1382 the oligarchy was back in the saddle and even the admonitions were revived.

FLORENTINE CULTURE: Precursors of the Renaissance. (1) Dante (1265–1321): *Vita Nuova,* in the Tuscan vernacular; the *Divina Commedia,* a brilliant poetic synthesis of medieval ideas and culture which established Tuscan as the literary vernacular of Italy; *De Vulgari Eloquentia,* a defense of the vernacular, written in Latin. **Petrarch** (1304–1374), of Florentine origin, greatest of Italian lyrists, brilliant Latinist, the first great humanist; interested in every

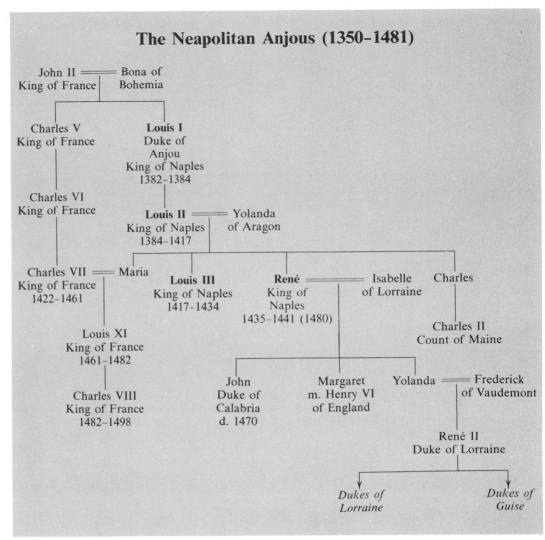

The Neapolitan Anjous (1350–1481)

John II, King of France ═══ Bona of Bohemia

— Charles V, King of France
— Louis I, Duke of Anjou, King of Naples 1382–1384

Charles VI, King of France
Louis II, King of Naples 1384–1417 ═══ Yolanda of Aragon

Charles VII, King of France 1422–1461 ═══ Maria
Louis III, King of Naples 1417–1434
René, King of Naples 1435–1441 (1480) ═══ Isabelle of Lorraine
Charles

Louis XI, King of France 1461–1482
Charles II, Count of Maine

Charles VIII, King of France 1482–1498
John, Duke of Calabria d. 1470
Margaret m. Henry VI of England
Yolanda ═══ Frederick of Vaudemont

René II, Duke of Lorraine

Dukes of Lorraine   Dukes of Guise

---

aspect of humanity; a lover of nature; a universal mind. **Boccaccio** (1313–1375), friend of Petrarch, knew both Greek and Latin, the first modern student of Tacitus, collector of classical manuscripts, first lecturer on Dante (1373). His *Decameron,* an epitome of bourgeois sophistication. Founder of Italian prose. **Giotto** (1276–1337), architect (employed on the cathedral), sculptor, painter, revealing Renaissance tendencies. **Villani** (d. 1348), *Chronicon Universale* with clear bourgeois elements. **Chrysoloras** (called from Constantinople), the first public lecturer on Greek in the West (1396–1400); he had many famous humanists as pupils.

1382–1432. A half-century of oligarchic domination in Florentine politics, in many ways the **zenith of Florentine power.** Constitutional reform (1382) broadened popular participation in government, but nothing much was done for the ciompi, and sporadic revolts continued as the Guelfs slowly regained power.

1393. **Maso degli Albizzi's** long control of the government began with the exile or disenfranchisement of the Alberti and their supporters. Capitalism had destroyed the guild organization as a vital political force, and Albizzi ruled for the advantage of his own house and the *Arte della Lana* (wool) with which he was associated. Democratic elements in the state had vanished.

1397–1398. Florence resisted the Visconti advance into Tuscany.

1405. **Pisa was bought** and reduced to obedience (1406), giving Florence direct access to the sea. Livorno (Leghorn) was purchased (1421) and the *Consuls of the Sea* established. Filippo Maria Visconti's drive into Tuscany led Florence to declare war. The peace party was led by **Giovanni de' Medici,** a wool dealer and international banker, probably Italy's richest man. Several defeats of Florence were accompanied by a decline of Florentine credit and a number of serious bankruptcies. Alliance with Venice and defeat of the Visconti, who accepted peace on onerous terms (1429); Venice monopolized the gains of the war.

1427. **Taxation reform,** the *catàsto,* an income tax intended to be of general and democratic incidence, supported (?) by the Medici.

1433. The fiasco of the war on Lucca (1429–1433) led to Cosimo (son of Giovanni) de' Medici's imprisonment as a scapegoat, and his sentence to ten-year exile. The next election to the signory (governing body) favored the Medici, and Cosimo was recalled (1434). Rinaldo degli Albizzi, Rodolfo Peruzzi, *et al.,* were in turn exiled, and the Medici dominance in Florence began, opening three centuries of close identity between the fortunes of the family and those of Florence. Cosimo, with-

The Medici Family (1434–1737)

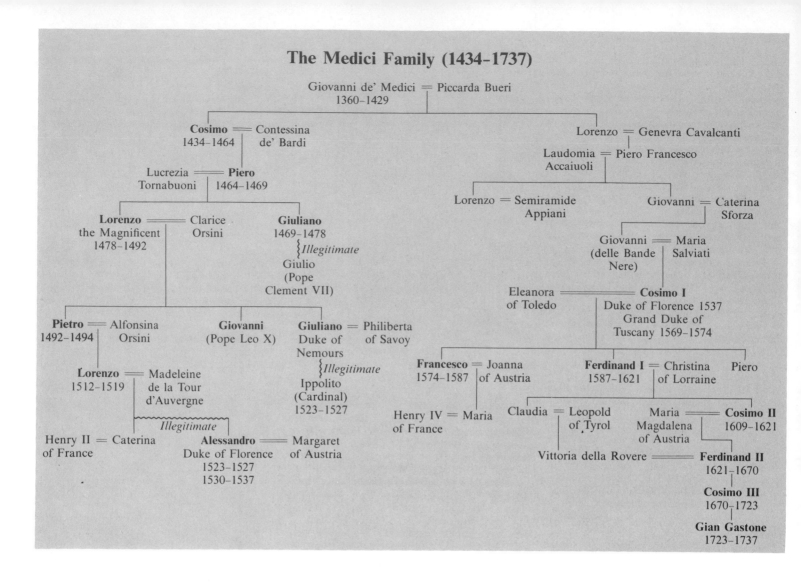

Giovanni de' Medici = Piccarda Bueri
1360–1429

Cosimo = Contessina
1434–1464   de' Bardi

Lorenzo = Genevra Cavalcanti

Laudomia = Piero Francesco
Accaiuoli

Lucrezia === **Piero**
Tornabuoni   1464–1469

Lorenzo = Semiramide
Appiani

Giovanni = Caterina
Sforza

Lorenzo === Clarice   **Giuliano**
the Magnificent   Orsini   1469–1478
1478–1492
{*Illegitimate*
Giulio
(Pope
Clement VII)

Giovanni = Maria
(delle Bande   Salviati
Nere)

Pietro = Alfonsina   **Giovanni**   **Giuliano** = Philiberta
1492–1494   Orsini   (Pope Leo X)   Duke of   of Savoy
Nemours
{*Illegitimate*
Ippolito
(Cardinal)
1523–1527

Eleanora === **Cosimo I**
of Toledo   Duke of Florence 1537
Grand Duke of
Tuscany 1569–1574

Lorenzo = Madeleine
1512–1519   de la Tour
d'Auvergne

Francesco = Joanna   **Ferdinand I** = Christina   Piero
1574–1587   of Austria   1587–1621   of Lorraine

Illegitimate

Henry II = Caterina   **Alessandro** === Margaret
of France   Duke of Florence   of Austria
1523–1527
1530–1537

Henry IV = Maria
of France

Claudia = Leopold
of Tyrol

Maria === **Cosimo II**
Magdalena   1609–1621
of Austria

Vittoria della Rovere === **Ferdinand II**
1621–1670

Cosimo III
1670–1723

Gian Gastone
1723–1737

---

out holding office, dominated the government, determining who should hold office.

1434–1494. DOMINATION OF THE MEDICI.

1434–1464. COSIMO (Pater Patriae).

1440. Florence and Venice in alliance defeated Filippo Maria Visconti at **Anghiari.** The catàsto was replaced by a progressive income tax designed to lighten the burdens of the poor (i.e. the Medici adherents). Cosimo supported Francesco Sforza's contest for the duchy of Milan and aided him in his war with Venice. For commercial reasons he favored France, but backed Ferrante of Naples against the Angevin claims. He was thus the real creator of the **triple alliance** of Florence, Milan, and Naples in the interest of the Italian equilibrium and security.

1464–1469. Piero the Gouty, son of Cosimo, a semi-invalid who was opposed by Luca Pitti.

1469–1478. Lorenzo and Giuliano de' Medici, and

1478–1492. LORENZO DE' MEDICI (the Magnificent) alone. Lorenzo continued the general policy of Cosimo. He enjoyed the power and prestige of a prince, though he had neither the title nor the office. His marriage to Clarice Orsini was the first princely marriage of the Medici.

1471. Lorenzo's effort to conciliate Pope Sixtus IV netted him a confirmation of the Medici banking privileges and the appointment as receiver of the papal revenues.

1474. Pope Sixtus and Ferrante of Naples were asked to join the alliance of Florence, Venice, and Milan (concluded in 1474), but Ferrante, feeling isolated, and Sixtus, angered at Lorenzo's opposition to his nephews, the Riarios, drew together. Italy became divided into two

Lorenzo de' Medici (terra cotta by Verrocchio)

camps. The Pazzi family, rivals of the Medici, were given the lucrative position as receivers of the papal revenues.

1478. The Pazzi Plot. The Riarios (apparently not without Sixtus' knowledge), plotted to have Lorenzo and Giuliano assassinated in the cathedral at Easter Mass. Giuliano was killed, Lorenzo wounded. The Medici almost exterminated the Pazzi and hounded the fugitives all over Italy. Sixtus laid an interdict on Florence, excommunicated Lorenzo; Alfonso of Calabria invaded Tuscany. Venice and Milan stood by Florence, Louis XI sent Commines as his representative. Ferrante engineered a Milanese revolt, the Turks diverted Venice at Scutari, plague broke out. Desperate, Lorenzo visited Ferrante (the cruelest and most cynical despot in Italy), and by his charm and the threat of a revival of Angevin claims, arranged (1480) a peace. Florence suffered considerable losses, but Lorenzo was a popular hero and succeeded in establishing the council of seventy, a completely Medici organ, the instrument of *de facto* despotism, but a source of real stability in government.

Lorenzo's brilliant **foreign policy** was costly; he had neglected the family business and apparently used some of the state money for Medici purposes; he also debased the coinage. Florentine prosperity, under the pressure of rivals, heavy taxation, and business depression, was declining. Nonetheless, Lorenzo, the leading statesman of his day, brought a twelve-year

Leonardo da Vinci, self-portrait

Florence, center of the Italian Renaissance. For over a century the Medici were the greatest patrons of the Renaissance, and led the rich bourgeoisie of Florence in fostering the most brilliant development of culture since the days of Pericles. **Cosimo** was an enthusiastic patron of manuscript collectors, copyists, and humanists, established the **library of San Marco** and the **Medici library.** The council of Ferrara-Florence sat in Florence (1439) and brought a number of learned Greeks who stimulated Platonic studies. Under Cosimo's auspices **Ficino** was trained to make his great translation of Plato (still ranked high) and the **Platonic Academy** was founded. **Lorenzo,** a graceful poet (carnival songs, etc.),

Gold enamel ornament made by Ghiberti for Cosimo de' Medici

calm before the storm to Italy, resuming the Medici alliance with Naples and Milan to balance the Papacy and Venice, and to keep a united front against alien invasion. Florence, on good terms with Charles VIII, regained most of her Tuscan losses. **Savonarola,** prior of San Marco (1491), had already begun his denunciations of Florentine corruption and his attacks on Lorenzo *(p. 310).*

1492. PIERO succeeded Lorenzo on his death. Son of an Orsini mother, married to an Orsini, he supported Naples, angered Milan, and threw Ludovico Sforza into alliance with the Neapolitan exiles who summoned Charles VIII.

1494. Charles's invasion began the age-long subjugation of Italy to alien invaders who dominated the national evolution until 1870. Piero, alarmed at public opinion, fled the city.

The Creation of Adam, *detail of fresco by Michelangelo on the ceiling of the Sistine Chapel*

Masaccio (right), *self-portrait in a fresco at Florence*

Marsilio Ficino

ardent champion of the vernacular, and lover of the countryside, a generous patron, drew about him a brilliant circle. He continued the support of Ficino. Florentine leadership in Renaissance: (1) **painting: Masaccio** (1401–1429?), **Botticelli** (1444–1510), **Leonardo da Vinci** (1452–1519) (sculptor and polymath); (2) **architecture: Brunelleschi** (1377–1446); **Alberti** (1405–1471); (3) **sculpture: Donatello** (c. 1386–1466), **Ghiberti** (1378–1455); **Verrocchio** (1435–1488); **Michelangelo** (1475–1564) (also painter, poet, architect); (4) **history and political theory: Machiavelli** (1469–1527); **Guicciardini** (1485–1540); (5) **romantic poetry: Pulci** (1432–c. 1487). *(Cont. p. 419.)*

(4) Milan, to 1500

EARLY HISTORY. Milan, ancient center of the agriculture of the Lombard plain, self-sufficient in food, master of important passes (Brenner, Splügen, St. Gothard) of the Alps, was for a long time surpassed in wealth only by Venice.

Establishment of Pavia as the Lombard capital (569). Emergence of Milan as the center of Italian opposition in the Lombard plain to alien and heretical domination. Rise of the archbishop as defender of native liberty and orthodoxy laid the basis for the evolution of archiepiscopal temporal power (military, administrative, judicial) exercised through his viscounts. The end of Lombard domination (774), followed by Carolingian destruction of the great Lombard fiefs, strengthened the episcopal power still further.

The spirit of municipal independence emerged from intense rivalries for the archiepiscopal see and the necessities of defense;

Milan became an island of safety and justice in the Lombard plain, a populous, self-sufficient, city-state. Under **Archbishop Heribert** (1018–1045) the *carroccio* (arc of municipal patriotism) was set up; expansion in the Lombard plain began (reduction of Lodi, Como, Pavia). The moat was dug after Emperor Frederick I's destruction (1162); the city was rebuilt by its allies, Bergamo, Brescia, Mantua, and Verona. (For the Lombard League and the wars with Frederick, *see p. 239.)* Rapid growth, extension of the walls (after 1183). Chief industry: armor manufacturing and the wool trade, later silk manufacture; irrigation made the plain productive.

Government: (1) *parlamento* (*consiglio grande*) (membership successively reduced to 2000, 1500, 800); (2) *credenza,* a committee of twelve for urgent and secret business; (3) *consuls* (the executive) elected for a year, responsible to the assembly.

Bitter warfare between populace and nobles led to the rise of two great families, the Della Torre (lords of the tower, i.e. castle) and the Visconti (i.e. the viscounts).

1237–1277. Rule of the (Guelf) **DELLA TORRE.** Martino established the catàsto, a tax of democratic and uniform incidence. The title *signore,* i.e. lord of Milan, established (1259); defeat and capture of the (Ghibelline) Visconti and their adherents. Milan established her power over Bergamo, Lodi, Como, and Vercelli.

1277–1447. Rule of the **VISCONTI.** Established by Archbishop Otto Visconti. Brief restoration of the Della Torre (1302) in a Guelf reaction with outside support. Establishment (1312) of the Visconti supremacy (Matteo designated *imperial vicar*). Ruthless Visconti rule

and expansion over northern Italy (including Genoa). Stefano's sons, Bernabò, Galeazzo, Matteo, divided the domains but ruled jointly until Matteo was assassinated (1355) by his brothers. Intolerably harsh joint rule of Bernabò (1354–1385) at Milan and Galeazzo (1354–1378) at Pavia; ostentatious patronage of learning and art.

1378–1402. GIAN GALEAZZO succeeded his father Galeazzo and did away with Bernabò (1385), thereafter ruling alone (1385–1402). Gian Galeazzo married Isabelle, daughter of King John of France. one of his daughters, Valentina, married Louis of Orléans (the source of Louis XII's claims to Milan). Gian Galeazzo began the creation of a northern Italian kingdom: mastery of Verona, Vicenza, Padua (1386–1388); Tuscan advance blocked by Florence (1390–1392) and by the rebellion of Padua. Created hereditary duke (1395) by Emperor Wenceslas, he added Pisa and Siena (1399), Assisi and Perugia (1400) to his domains, and routed (1401) Elector Rupert III (in Florentine pay). The *Certòsa* (Charterhouse) and *Duomo* (Cathedral) were begun. Gian Galeazzo's death (1402) saved Florence and opened a period of anarchy in Milan under his sons Gian Maria, (1402–1412) and Filippo Maria (1402–1447), which undid much of their father's work.

1402–1447. FILIPPO MARIA, after the assassination (1412) of Gian Maria, regained Gian Galeazzo's lands (even Genoa). Venice joined Florence against Filippo and took Bergamo, Brescia (1425). Filippo, last of the Visconti, was followed by

1447–1450. The **Republic** and the supremacy of Francesco Sforza, son-in-law of Filippo, who fought his way to mastery, defeating Venice and conquering the Lombard plain.

1450. **Francesco Sforza** was invested with the ducal title by popular acclaim.

1450-1500. Rule of the **SFORZA.** Francesco, eager for peace, came to terms with Cosimo de' Medici and Naples (the so-called triple alliance for the Italian balance of power). Louis XI was on intimate terms with Francesco and made him his political model. Francesco completed the Certósa and the Duomo with Florentine architects under Renaissance influence and began the *Castello* (Castle). Patron of the humanist **Filelfo,** Francesco gave his son Galeazzo and his daughter Ippolita a humanist education; Ippolita was famous for her Latin style. His court was full of humanists and learned Greeks.

1466-1476. **GALEAZZO MARIA SFORZA** was assassinated after a cruel but able rule. His son

1476-1479. **GIAN GALEAZZO,** husband of Isabella of Naples, under the regency of his mother, supported Florence against Naples after the Pazzi conspiracy (1478). Gian Galeazzo's uncle Ludovico usurped the duchy (1479).

1479-1500. **LUDOVICO** (il Moro), alarmed at his isolation after the death (1492) of Lo-

renzo de' Medici, supported the appeals of Neapolitan refugees to Charles VIII of France, whose expedition (1494) began the destruction of Italian independence. In Charles's train came Louis of Orléans, who, as Louis XII (1498-1515), added claims to Milan to his other Italian claims, took Milan (1499) and captured Ludovico (1500), who ended his days (1508) as prisoner of Louis.

Ludovico's generous patronage marked the **golden age of the Renaissance in Milan.** Ludovico, an artist, man of letters, economist, and experimenter, beautified the city, improved irrigation, bettered agriculture. He was the patron of Bramante and Leonardo.

(Cont. p. 418.)

(5) Venice, 1310-1489

(From p. 245)

In the early 14th century Venice already dominated the trade of the Adriatic and possessed many colonies throughout the Near East. Her position in the eastern trade was challenged primarily by Genoa, at that time at the height of her power.

1353-1355. **War between Venice and Genoa.** The Venetians were defeated at **Sapienza** (1354) and suffered the loss of their fleet. Peace was mediated by Milan.

1378-1381. The **WAR OF CHIOGGIA** between Venice and Genoa. This grew out of the grant, by John V Paleologus, of the island of Tenedos, key to the Dardanelles. Luciano Doria, the Genoese admiral, defeated the Venetians at **Pola,** seized Chioggia and blockaded Venice. The Venetians, under **Vittorio Pisano,** blocked the channel and starved out the fleet of Pietro Doria, forcing its surrender. From this blow Genoa never recovered. Henceforth Venice was mistress of the Levantine trade, which made an outlet for her goods over the Alpine passes more urgent than ever. The war with Genoa had demonstrated the importance of a mainland food supply and thereby inaugurated an inland advance which had a decisive influence on Italian politics. Venice had already taken Padua from the Scaligers of Verona (1339), but by agreement had turned it over to the Carrara family. Treviso and Belluna, however, were retained.

1388. **Treaty of the Venetians with the Ottoman Turks,** the first effort to assure trade privileges despite the rise of the Turkish power.

1405. Venice seized Padua, Bassano, Vicenza, and Verona after the breakup of the Visconti domains (1402) and the defeat of the Carrara family.

1416. **First war of Venice against the Ottoman**

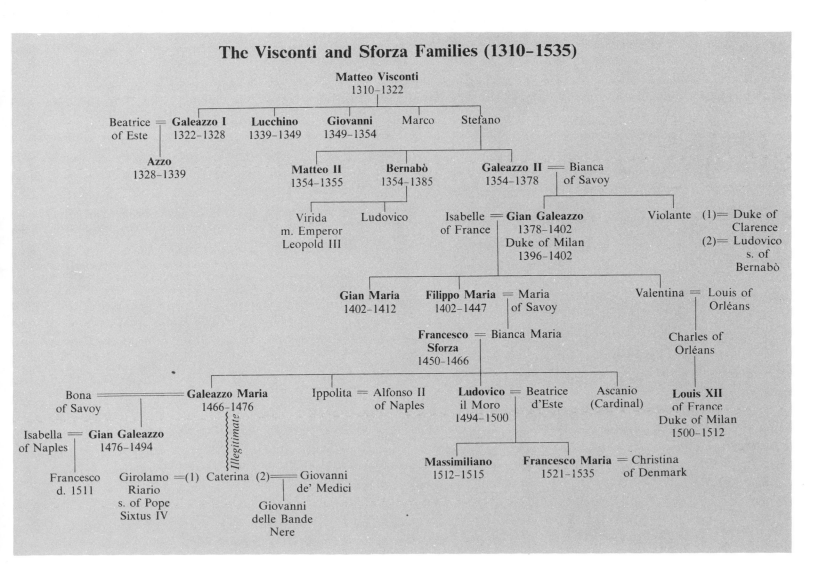

The Visconti and Sforza Families (1310-1535)

Matteo Visconti
1310-1322

Beatrice = **Galeazzo I**   **Lucchino**   **Giovanni**   Marco   Stefano
of Este   1322-1328   1339-1349   1349-1354

Azzo
1328-1339

Matteo II   **Bernabò**   **Galeazzo II** = Bianca
1354-1355   1354-1385   1354-1378   of Savoy

Virida   Ludovico   Isabelle = **Gian Galeazzo**   Violante (1)= Duke of
m. Emperor   of France   1378-1402   Clarence
Leopold III   Duke of Milan   (2)= Ludovico
   1396-1402   s. of
   Bernabò

Gian Maria   **Filippo Maria** = Maria   Valentina = Louis of
1402-1412   1402-1447   of Savoy   Orléans

Francesco = Bianca Maria   Charles of
Sforza   Orléans
1450-1466

Bona = **Galeazzo Maria**   Ippolita = Alfonso II   **Ludovico** = Beatrice   Ascanio   **Louis XII**
of Savoy   1466-1476   of Naples   il Moro   d'Este   (Cardinal)   of France
   1494-1500   Duke of Milan
Isabella = **Gian Galeazzo**   *Illegitimate*   1500-1512
of Naples   1476-1494

Francesco   Girolamo =(1) Caterina (2)= Giovanni   **Massimiliano**   **Francesco Maria** = Christina
d. 1511   Riario   de' Medici   1512-1515   1521-1535   of Denmark
   s. of Pope
   Sixtus IV   Giovanni
   delle Bande
   Nere

Turks, the result of Turkish activity in the Aegean. The **Doge Loredano** won a resounding victory at the Dardanelles and forced the sultan to conclude peace.

1423. The Venetians took over Thessalonica as part of a plan of co-operation with the Greek emperor against the Turks.

1425–1430. Second war against the Turks. The Turkish fleets ravaged the Aegean stations of the Venetians and took Thessalonica (1430). The Venetians were obliged to make peace in view of

1426–1429. The **war with Filippo Maria of Milan,** by which the Venetians established a permanent hold over Verona and Vicenza, and gained in addition Brescia (1426), Bergamo (1428), and Crema (1429).

1453. Participation of the Venetians in the **defense of Constantinople** against Mohammed II *(p. 345).* After the capture of Constantinople, Mohammed proceeded to the conquest of Greece and Albania, thus isolating and endangering the Venetian stations.

1463–1479. The great **WAR AGAINST THE TURKS.** Negroponte was lost (1470). The Turks throughout maintained the upper hand and at times raided to the very outskirts of Venice. By the **treaty of Constantinople** (1479) the Venetians gave up Scutari and other Albanian stations, as well as Negroponte and Lemnos. Thenceforth the Venetians paid an annual tribute for permission to trade in the Black Sea.

1482–1484. War with Ferrara, as a result of which Venice acquired Rovigo. This marked the limit of Venetian expansion on the mainland. The frontiers remained substantially unaltered until the days of Napoleon.

1489. Acquisition of Cyprus (partly by gift, partly by extortion), from Catherine Cornaro, widow of James of Lusignan.

Venetian culture in the Renaissance. Preoccupied with her commercial empire, her ex-

Doge Leonardo Loredano

Rudolf I

pansion on the mainland, and the advance of the Turk, Venice, despite her wealth, unique domestic security, and the sophistication of wide travel, long stood aside from the main currents of the early Renaissance. Her architecture remained under Gothic and Byzantine influences until the end of the 15th century, and the Palazzo Vendramini (1481) is perhaps the first important example of the new style. The **Bellinis** (Jacopo, 1395–1470, and his two sons) were the most notable early Venetian painters, but there was little promise of the brilliant if late achievement of the 16th century. The printing press apparently appealed to the practical Venetian nature and the senate decreed (1469) that the art should be fostered. Much of the finest early printing issued from the Venetian presses of the 15th and 16th centuries. *(Cont. p. 418.)*

e. THE HOLY ROMAN EMPIRE, 1273–1486

[*For a complete list of the Holy Roman emperors see Appendix V.*]

(From p. 235)

1273. The election fell to **Rudolf of Hapsburg** (b. 1218), who ranked as a prince, wished to restore and retain in his family the duchy of Swabia, and had three daughters to marry off. The Hapsburgs or Habsburgs (from *Habichts-Burg,* Hawk-Castle) originally (10th century) of the district of Brugg (junction of the Aar and Reuss) had steadily expanded their lands in the Breisgau, Alsace, and Switzerland, emerging as one of the leading families of Swabia.

1273–1291. RUDOLF I. Indifferent to the Roman tradition, he concentrated on the advancement of his own dynasty, and founded the greatness of the Hapsburgs on territorial expansion of the family holdings and dynastic marriages. Edicts for the abolition of private war and support of local peace compacts (*Landfrieden*).

1276–1278. Struggle with Ottokar, king of Bohemia, over the usurped imperial fiefs of Austria, Styria, Carinthia, Carniola. Rudolf expelled Ottokar from Austria by force (1276),

but allowed him to retain Bohemia and Moravia (after homage) as a buffer against Slavdom; dynastic alliance with the Hapsburgs. Ottokar was ultimately defeated and killed (1278, Aug. 26, **battle of the Marchfeld**); investiture of Rudolf's sons with the imperial fiefs of Austria, Styria, Carniola (1282) established the Hapsburgs on the Danube until 1918.

Rudolf threw away the last remnants of Frederick II's great imperial fabric: confirmation of papal rights in Italy and Angevin rights in southern Italy (1275); renunciation of all imperial claims to the Papal States and Sicily (1279).

1291. Alarmed at the rapid rise of the Hapsburgs to first rank, the electors passed over Rudolf's son, choosing instead **Adolf of Nassau** in return for substantial considerations.

1291. Revolt of the three Forest Cantons, Uri, Schwyz, and Unterwalden, and formation of a (Swiss) confederacy *(p. 325).*

1292–1298. ADOLF, a strong imperialist, and able. He supported the towns and lesser nobles and entered into alliance with Edward I of England against Philip IV of France to protect the imperial fiefs of Franche Comté, Savoy, Dauphiné, Lyonnais, and Provence, long under French pressure; the alliance came to nothing, as the German princes were indifferent. The princes, alarmed at Adolf's advance in Meissen and Thuringia, deposed him (1298), electing Rudolf's rejected son Albert.

1298–1308. ALBERT (ALBRECHT) I. Firm reduction of the ecclesiastical electoral princes (aid of the French and the towns); double dynastic marriage with the Capetians; acquisition of the crown of Bohemia (on the extinction of the Premyslids, 1306); Albert supported the Angevin Carobert's acquisition of Hungary; the Rhineland was filled with Francophile clerical appointees of the pope, and the election of 1308 was dominated by French influence. Charles of Valois procured the election of Henry of Luxemburg, brother of the archbishop of Trier.

1308–1313. HENRY VII (Luxemburg), Francophile, devoted to Italian culture, and bent on restoring the empire. The marriage of his son John to the sister of King Wenceslas of Bohemia brought the throne of Bohemia to the house of Luxemburg (1311–1489).

1310–1313. Expedition to Italy at the urging of Pope Clement V and the Ghibellines; order restored, Milan, Cremona, Rome reduced; imperial coronation (1312); alliance of the pope and King Philip IV of France to save Naples from Henry.

1314–1347. LOUIS IV (Wittelsbach). A Hapsburg anti-king, **Frederick the Handsome,** and civil war (until 1325). Bitter papal opposition (1323–1347, refusal of confirmation of Louis's title to the empire); Louis, backed by the German people, against the Avignonese pope. Violent war of propaganda: **Marsiglio of Padua** (*Defensor Pacis,* 1324) and **William of Occam,** defending the imperial position, gave wide currency to pre-Reformation ideas; **Dante's** *De Monarchia;* papal supporters, **Augustino Trionfans** and **Pelagius.**

1327–1330. Louis's futile expedition to Italy and "lay" coronation (1328); his demand for a general council welcomed by the Italian Ghibellines.

Effort to give the German monarchy a formal constitution.

The Crown of the Holy Roman Empire

1338. The Day at Rense: formation of a strong electoral union (*Kurverein*); declaration by the electors that election by a majority of the electors without papal confirmation is valid. The **diet of Frankfurt:** declaration (the *Licet juris*) that the electors are competent to choose an emperor (i.e. papal intervention is not nec-

essary); in effect the Holy Roman Empire was divorced entirely from the Papacy.

1346. Louis was deposed, but fought against his successor, Charles (son of King John of Bohemia, who had been elected after an open alliance with the pope).

1347–1378. CHARLES IV (Luxemburg). Con-

centration on the advancement of his dynasty (in Silesia, the Palatinate, Lusatia, Brandenburg) and on the progress of Bohemia. Prague became one of the chief cities of the empire (the university founded, 1348). The **Black Death** (1348–1349); the Flagellants; anti-Semitic massacres. Promulgation of the Swa-

Coronation of Sigismund, 1433 (15th-century relief from St. Peter's, Rome)

bian League and numerous *Landfrieden* reduced private warfare. Dauphiné and Arles continued to drift into the French orbit.

Further elaboration of a formal constitution of the empire.

1356. The **GOLDEN BULL** (in force until 1806) transformed the empire from a monarchy into an aristocratic federation, to avoid the evils of disputed elections. Seven **electors,** each a virtual sovereign: the archbishops of Mainz, Trier, and Köln, the count palatine of the Rhine, the duke of Saxony, the margrave of Brandenburg, the king of Bohemia. Secular electorates to be indivisible and pass by primogeniture. Elections to be by majority vote and without delays; urban leagues forbidden without specific license; other restrictions on the towns. No mention of papal rights or claims. The electors to exercise supervision over the empire, a new function. The crown to remain in the house of Luxemburg.

Charles openly regarded the empire as an anachronism, but valued the emperor's right to nominate to vacant fiefs.

1364. **Treaty of Brünn** with the Hapsburgs, whereby either house (Luxemburg or Hapsburg) was to succeed to the lands of the other upon its extinction.

Little improvement in internal anarchy; climax of localism and the *Faustrecht;* the only islands of order and prosperity were the walled towns; the only basis of order were the town

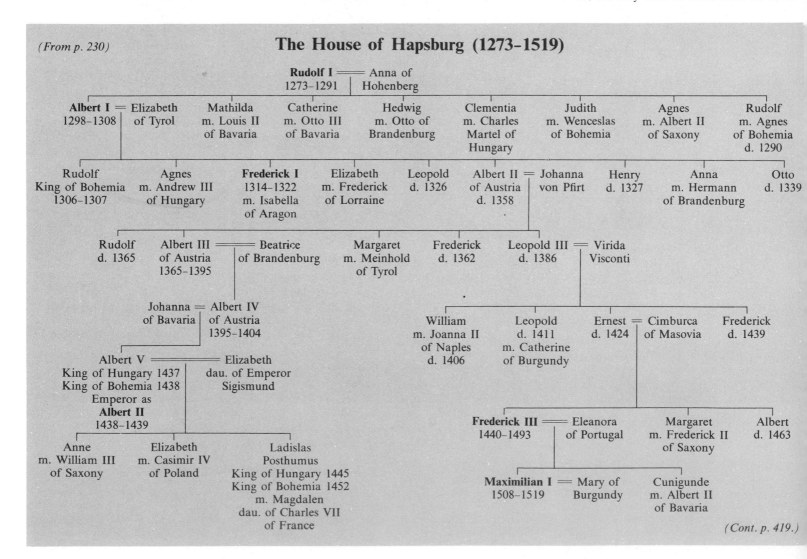

(From p. 230)

The House of Hapsburg (1273–1519)

Rudolf I === Anna of
1273–1291 | Hohenberg

Albert I = Elizabeth | Mathilda | Catherine | Hedwig | Clementia | Judith | Agnes | Rudolf
1298–1308 | of Tyrol | m. Louis II | m. Otto III | m. Otto of | m. Charles | m. Wenceslas | m. Albert II | m. Agnes
| | of Bavaria | of Bavaria | Brandenburg | Martel of | of Bohemia | of Saxony | of Bohemia
| | | | | Hungary | | | d. 1290

Rudolf | Agnes | **Frederick I** | Elizabeth | Leopold | Albert II = Johanna | Henry | Anna | Otto
King of Bohemia | m. Andrew III | 1314–1322 | m. Frederick | d. 1326 | of Austria | von Pfirt | d. 1327 | m. Hermann | d. 1339
1306–1307 | of Hungary | m. Isabella | of Lorraine | | d. 1358 | | | of Brandenburg |
| | of Aragon | | | | | | |

Rudolf | Albert III ====== Beatrice | Margaret | Frederick | Leopold III = Virida
d. 1365 | of Austria | of Brandenburg | m. Meinhold | d. 1362 | d. 1386 | Visconti
| 1365–1395 | | of Tyrol | | |

Johanna = Albert IV | | William | Leopold | Ernest = Cimburca | Frederick
of Bavaria | of Austria | | m. Joanna II | d. 1411 | d. 1424 | of Masovia | d. 1439
| 1395–1404 | | of Naples | m. Catherine | | |
| | | d. 1406 | of Burgundy | | |

Albert V ====== Elizabeth
King of Hungary 1437 | dau. of Emperor
King of Bohemia 1438 | Sigismund
Emperor as
Albert II
1438–1439

Anne | Elizabeth | Ladislas | **Frederick III** ===== Eleanora | Margaret | Albert
m. William III | m. Casimir IV | Posthumus | 1440–1493 | of Portugal | m. Frederick II | d. 1463
of Saxony | of Poland | King of Hungary 1445 | | | of Saxony |
| | King of Bohemia 1452 | | | |
| | m. Magdalen | **Maximilian I** = Mary of | Cunigunde
| | dau. of Charles VII | 1508–1519 | Burgundy | m. Albert II
| | of France | | | of Bavaria

(Cont. p. 419.)

The Imperial Orb of the Holy Roman Empire

(From p. 230)

Luxemburg Rulers (1308–1437)

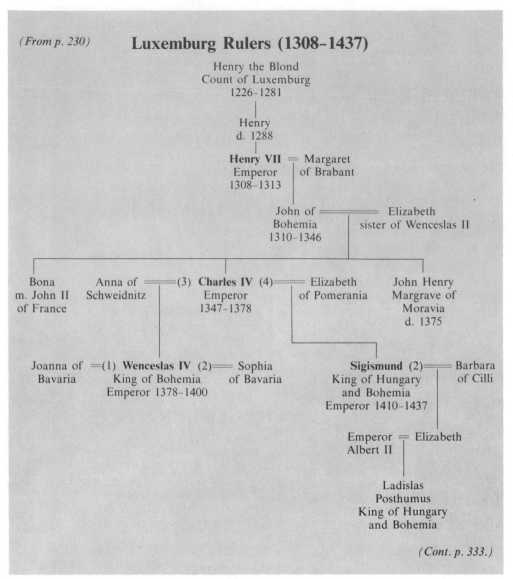

(Cont. p. 333.)

leagues (e.g. revival of the **Rhine League** [1354]; the **Swabian League**); bitter warfare of classes, and princely opposition to the towns. Charles's vain appeal to the princes of Europe to resist France and end the Avignonese Captivity.

Apogee of the **Hanseatic League** (*p. 326*).

1378–1400. WENCESLAS (Wenzel, son of Charles IV, king of Bohemia, 1378–1419). Formation of the **Knights' League** (*League of the Lion*) followed by a series of political quarrels between the knights and lords on one side and the towns on the other, ending in the town war (1387–1389) and the defeat of the towns, but not their ruin. Rising Bohemian nationalism: revolts, 1387–1396.

1400. Deposition of Wenceslas for drunkenness and incompetence. He refused to accept the decision, and the result was that at the end of the confused period (1400–1410) there were **three rival rulers** (Sigismund, Jobst, and Wenceslas) to correspond to the three rival popes.

1410–1437. SIGISMUND (Luxemburg; king of Bohemia, 1419–1437; king of Hungary by marriage). His main concern was to end the Great Schism, and he succeeded the king of France as protagonist of conciliar reform by forcing Pope John XXIII to call the **council of Constance** (*p. 307*). Establishment of the **house of Wettin** in Saxony (1423); the **Hohenzollerns (Frederick)** in Brandenburg (1415). Sigismund's failure at Constance not merely alienated Bohemia, but also ended any hope of German unification.

1410. Utter **defeat of the Teutonic Knights** by the Polish-Lithuanian army at **Tannenberg;** beginning of the decline of the Teutonic Knights.

1411. Peace of Thorn, halting of the Slavic advance.

1420–1431. Emergence of **Bohemian Nationalism** and the **Hussite Wars** (*p. 323*).

1433. Called to the **council of Basel** (*p. 308*), the Hussites finally accepted the *Compactata* (which embodied the *Four Articles*), but the Church by its devious dealings alienated them, and they began a final break. Bohemian nationality asserted itself increasingly in the 15th century, and Bohemia never returned to the German orbit.

Sigismund struggled against the Turkish advance (1426–1427) and was crowned at Rome (1433). In the election of 1438, Frederick of Brandenburg (candidate of the political reformers in Germany) withdrew, making the choice of Albert of Hapsburg (Sigismund's son-in-law) unanimous. Albert also succeeded Sigismund on the thrones of Hungary and Bohemia. Henceforth the imperial crown in practice became hereditary in

1438–(1740) 1806. THE HOUSE OF HAPSBURG.

1438–1439. ALBERT II.

1439. The **Pragmatic Sanction of Mainz** (abolition of annates, papal reservations, and provisions), a preliminary agreement between the Papacy and the emperor, left the German church under imperial and princely control and postponed reform until the days of Martin Luther.

1440–1493. FREDERICK III. The last emperor crowned (1452) at Rome by the pope; a handsome, placid *fainéant*, amateur astrologer, botanist, mineralogist, he ignored the existence of diets, debates, and appeals for crusades.

Ladislas Posthumus (d. 1457), ward of Frederick, became duke of Austria (1440), was acknowledged king of Hungary (1445) and elected king of Bohemia (1452) with a council of regency. **George Podiebrad** (champion of the *Compactata*) emerged (1452) from the Bohemian civil war (Catholics vs. Utraquists) as regent of Bohemia, and later king (1458–1471) (*p. 324*).

1448. The **Concordat of Vienna:** a compromise on cynical terms between the pope and the emperor on the reform issue: the Papacy triumphed over the conciliar movement for reform, by dividing profits with the princes and emperor; external episcopal jurisdiction was excluded, the princes retained rights of presentation, obtained a share in episcopal taxation, and established an authority over the German church which survived even the Reformation.

1453. The **capture of Constantinople** (*p. 345*) and end of the Eastern Empire left the Holy Roman Empire without a rival and brought the Turkish menace to the frontier of Germany.

1454. Traditional date for the **invention of printing** from movable metal type. This invention is usually attributed to **Johann Gutenberg** (?1400–1468) of Mainz, printer of the so-called **Mazarin Bible** (1456). Printing had been in process of development for many years and was probably perfected not only by Gutenberg, but by others like **Lourens Coster** at Haarlem (1440), Albrecht Pfister of Bamberg, Peter Schoeffer and Johann Fust of Mainz.

Schools sprang up, especially in South Germany, to teach the art of *Meistergesang* in accordance with very strict and complicated rules.

1456. John Hunyadi (without imperial support) repulsed the Turk from Belgrade.

1458. Election of Hunyadi's son **Matthias Corvinus,** king of Hungary (to 1490) and **George Podiebrad,** king of Bohemia (to 1471), the climax of national spirit in Bohemia and Hungary.

1462. Pius II's **annulment of the Compactata** and the excommunication and deposition (1466) of Podiebrad reopened the Bohemian religious wars. **Ladislas** (elected 1468) succeeded on Podiebrad's death as king of Bohemia (1471–1516), becoming king of Hungary in 1490 (see below).

1473. Frederick, faced with the threat of (French) Burgundian expansion in the empire, avoided giving Charles the Bold, duke of Burgundy, the royal title *(p. 300)*, and married his son Maximilian to Charles's daughter Mary (1477), bringing the Hapsburg fortunes to their zenith, and giving reality to his own monogram: **A.E.I.O.U.** (*Austriae est imperare orbi universo,* or, *Alles Erdreich ist Oesterreich unterthan.*)

1485. Expelled from Vienna by Mathias Corvinus, Frederick became a cheery imperial mendicant.

1486. Maximilian, elected king of the Romans, became the real ruler of Germany and began the creation of the Hapsburg dynastic empire. *(Cont. p. 419.)*

(1) Bohemia, 1306–1471

(From p. 260)

1306. The **Premyslid dynasty** came to an end with the death of Wenceslas (Vaclav) III. There followed an interregnum, during which the Bohemians were driven out of Poland. The interregnum ended with the election of

1310–1346. JOHN OF LUXEMBURG, son of the Emperor Henry VII. The circumstances of his accession forced John to issue a charter guaranteeing the rights and privileges of the nobility and clergy. Thus limitations of the royal power were fixed by written law. At the same time the national diet, theretofore called only on special occasions, became a regular institution. During this reign Bohemian overlordship over Upper Lusatia and Silesia was established.

John supported the Teutonic Knights against the Lithuanians and participated in three campaigns (1328, 1337, 1346). For a time (1331–1333) he ruled western Lombardy, as well as the Tyrol (1336–1341). John was killed in the **battle of Crécy,** where he fought on the side of the French. While he had shown little concern for Bohemian domestic affairs, he had made Bohemia a power in international politics.

1346–1378. CHARLES I (Charles IV as German Emperor), the son of John of Luxemburg. His reign is regarded as the "golden age" of Bohemian history. A series of charters issued in 1348 established an order of dynastic succession and determined Bohemia's place in the Holy Roman Empire. Moravia, Silesia, and Upper Lusatia were to be indissolubly connected with the Bohemian crown. By the **Golden Bull** (1356, *see p. 320)* the king of Bohemia was given first place among the empire's secular electors. At the same time Bohemia's internal independence was guaranteed. Acquisition of Lower Lusatia (1370) and Brandenburg (1373). Charles ruled as a constitutional king and spared no effort to promote material well-being and cultural progress. A new code of laws, the *Maiestas Carolina,* was published. Prague was rebuilt and beautified. The **University of Prague** founded (1348), the first university in central Europe.

1378–1419. WENCESLAS (Vaclav) IV, son of Charles. Gradual weakening of the connection with the German Empire. Loss of Brandenburg (1411). Continued conflicts with the barons. This was hastened by the develop-

Jan Hus led to the stake (illustration from a 1450 chronicle)

ment (since the end of the 14th century) of a national-religious movement which culminated in **Hussitism. JOHN HUS** (1369–1415), a professor at the University of Prague and a popular preacher in the vernacular, was deeply influenced by the teaching of Wiclif and the Lollards in England. He attacked sale of indulgences, demanded reforms in the Church, challenged the primacy of the pope, and emphasized the supreme authority of the Scriptures. He also supported the native element in the university in the struggle which ended in the exodus of the alien Germans (1409), becoming rector of the university. Excommunicated by the pope and eager for vindication, he went to the **council of Constance** (1415) under a safe-conduct from the emperor. His arrest in violation of this guaranty, his trial and burning (July 6), identified religious reform with Bohemian nationalism and split the empire in the

1420–1433. HUSSITE WARS. Refusal to recognize Sigismund as king. The reformers divided into two groups: (1) The moderate **Calixtines,** with the university as a center, favored separation of religious and political

reform and formulated their program in the **Four Articles of Prague** (1420): full liberty of preaching, the cup to the laity (*Utraquism*), exclusion of the clergy from temporal activity and their subjection to civil penalties for crime. (2) The radical **Taborites,** under extreme Waldensian, Catharist, and Wiclifite influences, with a program of democracy and apostolic communism. The papal proclamation of a **Bohemian Crusade** (not opposed by the Emperor Sigismund) united the nation behind **John Ziska,** a brilliant soldier, who led the Hussites in a series of victories (1420–1422). Ziska's "modernization" of tactics: improved, mobile artillery, use of baggage wagons for mobile cover. Ziska's death (1424) did not affect the movement. Under a priest, **Procop the Great,** the Hussites defeated one crusade after another (1426, 1427, 1431) and carried the war into neighboring regions of Germany, on one occasion (1432) advancing as far as the Baltic. Then civil war broke out between the Calixtines and the Taborites (led by Procop the Great), the latter suffering defeat (1434).

1431–1436. The council of Basel. The Huss-

Battle of Morgarten, November 15, 1315

ites finally accepted a compromise, the *Compactata* (1436), recognizing them as true sons of the Church and conceding them the cup in the communion.

1436. Sigismund was finally accepted as king by all parties. He attempted a Catholic reaction, which was cut short by his death in the following year. Disputes continued between the Catholics and the Hussites, complicated by factional struggles between Hussite moderates and radicals and by social tension between nobility, townsmen, and peasantry.

1437–1439. ALBERT OF AUSTRIA (son-in-law of Sigismund), elected king. An opposition group chose Ladislas, king of Poland. Albert died in the course of a civil war.

1439–1457. LADISLAS POSTHUMUS, the son of Albert. The Emperor Frederick III acted as his guardian, and for many years kept him from Bohemia. In the midst of continued factional conflict, a young nobleman, **George Podiebrad,** rose to power.

1448. George seized Prague and became head of the Hussites. He was recognized as administrator of the kingdom (1452) and devoted himself to the task of reconciling Catholics and Hussites. The radical wing of the latter was completely suppressed by the **capture of Tabor** (1452). George ultimately succeeded in bringing the young king to Prague, but Ladislas died before he could accomplish much in behalf of the Catholics.

The House of Wittelsbach, Main Line (1180–1508)

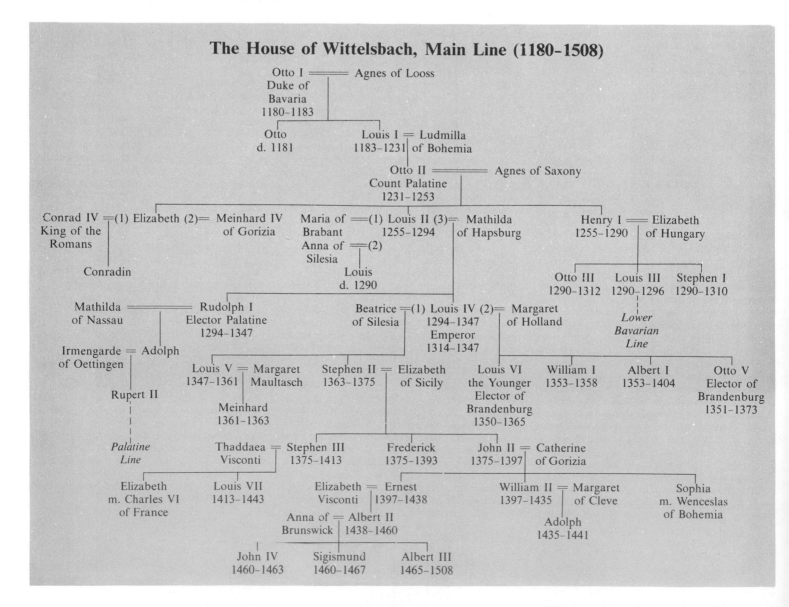

1458–1471. GEORGE PODIEBRAD elected king. Policy of conciliation: vigorous persecution of the **Bohemian Brotherhood,** a puritanical sect with outspokenly democratic leanings, dating from the teaching of **Peter of Chelchich** (d. 1460), and, like the Taborites, rejecting all subordination to Rome. George, an avowed Hussite of the moderate school, was technically a heretic and soon found himself in conflict with the pope.

1462. The pope denounced the agreements of Basel, and deposed George (1465). Thereupon the Catholic nobility of Bohemia elected **Matthias of Hungary** as king. George defeated him in a series of engagements, but the issue was undecided when George died.

(Cont. p. 437.)

(2) The Swiss Confederation, to 1499

Lake Lucerne and the original **Forest Cantons** belonged to the duchy of Swabia, and the expansion of powerful Swabian families during the Great Interregnum led the Forest Cantons to a determined effort to replace feudal allegiances to various nobles with a single direct allegiance to the emperor. Most powerful of the Swabian families was the rising **house of Hapsburg** (whose original lands expanded in the 13th century into the Aargau, Breisgau, and Alsace). **Rudolf I** (b. 1218) of Hapsburg sought to restore the duchy of Swabia under his house.

The **Forest Cantons of Uri** (already acknowledged independent of any but a loose imperial allegiance in 1231), **Schwyz,** and **Unterwalden,** emerged as champions of local independence and masters of the St. Gothard Pass into Italy. Rudolf during the Interregnum expanded his suzerainty, but as emperor was too busy to assert it.

1291. First (known) **League of the Three Forest Cantons,** an undertaking for mutual defense, a kind of constitution, but not an independent federal league, as the cantons did not claim independence. Emperor Adolf confirmed the status of Uri and Schwyz, Henry VII that of Unterwalden, and henceforth the three Forest Cantons were thought of as a unit. The Swiss sent Henry VII three hundred soldiers for his Italian expedition, the first recorded use of Swiss troops outside their own borders.

1315, Nov. 15. Battle of Morgarten. Leopold of Austria, in an effort to crush the Swiss and punish them for support of Louis IV against the Hapsburg Frederick the Handsome, was thoroughly beaten at Morgarten, a battle which began the brilliant career of the Swiss infantry in Europe. Renewal and strengthening of the league and its confirmation by Louis IV.

1332–1353. Additions to the three Forest Cantons: canton of Lucerne (1332); canton of Zürich (1351); canton of Glarus (1352); canton of Bern (1353), bringing the number to

seven, half of which were peasant cantons, the other half urban.

1386, July 9. BATTLE OF SEMPACH. The confederation, supported by the Swabian League, defeated the Hapsburg Leopold III of Swabia. In 1388 another victory was won at **Näfels.**

1394. Twenty-year truce between the confederation and the duke of Austria. Austria abandoned claims on Zug and Glarus. The confederation became solely dependent on the empire, which amounted to practical independence.

The confederation was controlled by a **federal diet** (1393), but the cantons retained the widest possible autonomy. Throughout the succeeding period there was but little evidence of union. The various cantons followed their own interests (Lucerne and Schwyz looked to the north; Bern to the west; Uri to the south) and wrangled among themselves. Only the threat from Austria invariably united them against the common enemy. Meanwhile the 15th century was marked by continual struggles and conflicts with neighbors, as a result of which further territories were brought into the confederation and some approach was made to natural frontiers.

1403. The canton of Uri began expansion southward, to get control of the passes to the Milanese. In 1410 the whole Val Antigorio was conquered, with Domodossola. The Swiss

Battle of Sempach, July 9, 1386

were driven out by the duke of Savoy in 1413, but in 1416 regained mastery of the country.

1415. Conquest in the north of the Aargau, from Frederick of Austria, at the behest of his rival, the Emperor Sigismund.

1419. Purchase of Bellinzona, which, however, was seized by the Visconti of Milan (1422).

1436–1450. Civil war between Zürich and some of the neighboring cantons over the succession to the domains of the count of Toggenburg. Zürich allied itself with Emperor Frederick III (1442), but was defeated by Schwyz (1443); Zürich besieged (1444). Frederick called in the French, but after a defeat near Basel, the French withdrew. The emperor made **peace at Constance** (June 12, 1446) and in 1450 peace was made within the confederation. The general effect of the war was to strengthen the confederacy.

1460. Conquest of the Thurgau from Austria gave the confederation a frontier on Lake Constance.

1474–1477. The great war against **Charles the Bold of Burgundy,** whose designs on Alsace were regarded as a menace to the confederation. The Swiss allied themselves with the South German cities. This combination was joined by the emperor (perpetual peace, Mar. 30, 1474: Austria again renounced claims to Swiss territory). Louis XI of France also joined, but in 1475 both the emperor and the king withdrew again. Great victories of the

Swiss at **Grandson** (Mar. 2, 1476), **Morat** or **Murten** (June 22, 1476), and at **Nancy** (Jan. 5, 1477) sealed the fate of Charles's plans and established the great military reputation of the Swiss, who were thenceforth sought far and wide as mercenaries.

1478. War with Milan. Victory of the Swiss at **Giornico** (Dec. 28). Alliance with the pope, who was allowed to engage Swiss forces.

1481. Solothurn and Fribourg were admitted to the confederation after a long dispute among the members. The **diet of Stans** drew up a covenant by which federal relations were regulated until 1798. Henceforth the urban cantons were in a majority.

1499. War with the emperor over disputed territories in the east. The emperor was supported by the South German cities, while the Swiss enjoyed the support, especially financial, of the French. The Swiss won a series of victories (especially **Dornach,** July 22) and forced the emperor to conclude the **treaty of Basel** (Sept. 22) which granted the confederation independence of the empire in fact, if not formally (this came only in 1648). By the inclusion of **Basel** and **Schaffhausen** (1501) and later **Appenzell** (1513), the confederation rounded out its northern frontier.

The Swiss at the end of the 15th century enjoyed immense military prestige, but within the confederation there was much social unrest, especially among the peasants, and a good deal of demoralization in the towns. **Hans**

Waldmann, bürgermeister of Zürich (1483–1489), was only the most outstanding of the typical ruthless, mercenary, cynical figures which dominated the scene and remind one of the contemporaneous Italian despots.

(Cont. p. 430.)

(3) The Hanseatic League, 1000–1669

Hansa (Old French *Hanse;* Med. Latin *Hansa*), meaning a group, company, or association.

Associations (*Hansas*) and partial unions of North German towns date from the 13th century and were an important aspect of the great town development of Germany in that period.

c. 1000. German traders were established on the island of Gothland and in London.

c. 1150–c. 1250. Revival of the German river trade, notably along the Rhine, centering in the towns of Köln, Dortmund, Soest, and Münster. At the same time the German expansion toward the Slavic east extended the sphere of German trade along the Baltic coasts. In the later 12th century the German settlement on Gothland **(Wisby)** became autonomous and established an offshoot at **Novgorod** (*St. Peter's Yard*) which became the focus of the important Russian trade.

1226. Lübeck (founded 1143) secured an imperial charter from Frederick II. Hamburg followed in 1266–1267.

1237. Wisby secured trading rights in England, and soon afterward in Flanders.

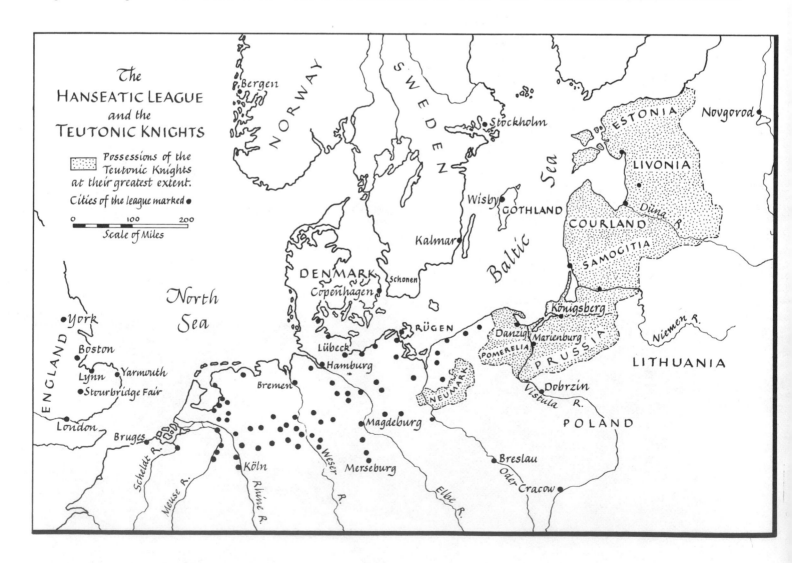

The
HANSEATIC LEAGUE
and the
TEUTONIC KNIGHTS

Possessions of the
Teutonic Knights
at their greatest extent.
Cities of the league marked ●

0   100   200
Scale of Miles

Petrarch (p.313)
by Justus of Ghent

Meeting between Emperor Frederick III (p.310) and his Fiancée,
Eleanor of Portugal, by Pinturicchio

1241. Lübeck and Hamburg formed an alliance to protect the Baltic trade routes.

1256. The **Wendish towns** (Lübeck, Stralsund, Wismar, Rostock, Greifswald, and later Lüneburg), held their first recorded meeting. Lübeck began to emerge as the dominant North German town, a position it retained throughout the history of the Hanseatic League. Most of the commercial towns followed the *Code of Lübeck,* which was an early source of unity between them. By the end of the century the Wendish towns had taken the leadership from the Gothland merchants.

1282. The **Germans in London** formed a corporation and established their own guildhall and steelyard. Other German yards were opened at York, Bristol, Yarmouth, Lynn, and Boston. The London trade was dominated by Köln, but the yards at Lynn and Boston were under the control of Lübeck and Hamburg.

THE HANSEATIC LEAGUE. No date can be fixed for its organization, which was evidently the result of the lack of a powerful German national government able to guarantee security for trade. Its formation was no doubt facilitated by the medieval affinity for co-operative action and for monopoly. The term *Hanseatic League* was first used in a document in 1344. The exclusion of Germans abroad (1366) from the privileges of the Hansa indicates a growing sense of unity, but league members spoke of the association merely as a *firma confederatio* for trade, and throughout its history it remained a loose aggregation. This looseness of organization allowed a maximum of independence to its members and was not modified until the league was put on the defensive in the 15th century. The league never had a true treasury or officials in a strict sense; its only common seal was that of Lübeck; it had no common flag. Assemblies of the members (*Hansetage*) were summoned by Lübeck at irregular intervals and were sparsely attended, except in time of crisis. The objectives of the league were mutual security, extortion of trading privileges, and maintenance of trade monopoly wherever possible. The chief weapon against foreigners or recalcitrant members was the economic boycott and (rarely) war. Primarily concerned with the North European trade, the Hansa towns dealt chiefly in raw materials (timber, pitch, tar, turpentine, iron, copper), livestock (horses, hawks, etc.), salt fish (cod and especially herring), leather, hides, wool, grain, beer, amber, drugs, and some textiles. The four chief *kontors* were Wisby, Bergen, London, and Bruges.

1340-1375. WALDEMAR IV of Denmark, who freed his country of the German domination and took up the struggle against the powerful Hansa towns. He threatened the Hanseatic monopoly of the herring trade by his seizure of Scania, and in 1361 cut the Russian-Baltic trade route by his capture of Wisby. In 1362 he defeated the German fleets at **Helsingborg.** By the **peace of Wordingborg** (1365) the Hansa was deprived of many of its privileges in Denmark.

1367. The **CONFEDERATION OF KÖLN (COLOGNE),** effected by a meeting of representatives of 77 towns, organized common finance and naval preparations for the struggle. Reconstruction of Scandinavian alliances to meet the threat from Waldemar. After a series

Roland pillar, a symbol of independence in the Hanseatic city of Bremen

of victories, the German towns extorted from the Danish *Reichsrat*

1370. The **PEACE OF STRALSUND,** which gave the league four castles in Scania (dominating the Sound), control of two-thirds of the Scanian revenues for 15 years, and the right to veto the succession to the Danish throne unless their monopoly was renewed by the candidate. The treaty marked the **apogee of Hanseatic power** and virtually established control over the Baltic trade and over Scandinavian politics. The Baltic monopoly was not finally broken until 1441, after a war with the Dutch. Wisby itself never recovered from

Waldemar's sack, and was long a nest of pirates (e.g. the famous **Victual Brothers**).

FLANDERS. The Germans in Bruges received a special grant of privileges in 1252, which allowed them their own ordinances and officials. They later (1309) established exemption from the usual brokerage charges levied on foreigners and eventually won an influential voice in the affairs of the city, notably in foreign policy. The revised statutes of the Bruges kontor (1347) recognized the division of the Hanseatic League into thirds: the Wendish-Saxon, the Prusso-Westphalian, and the Gothland-Livland thirds. Bruges was the most ardent champion of Hanseatic unity, and, with Lübeck, was the chief source of such cohesion as the League attained. A boycott in 1360 brought the town into complete submission to the League.

ENGLAND. The Hansa towns, by maintaining friendly relations with the crown, were able to ignore the growing national hostility to alien traders (directed at first mainly against the Italians) and to avoid granting reciprocal privileges to the English in return for their own exclusive rights (notably those claimed under Edward I's *Carta Mercatoria* of 1303). One source of Hanseatic influence derived from loans to the crown, especially during the Hundred Years' War. The English themselves began to penetrate into the Baltic (c. 1360) and growing public resentment against the League led to increased customs dues, but Richard II in 1377 renewed the privileges of the League, thus firmly establishing the Hanseatic power in England. The Sound was opened to the English in 1451, and the League, profiting by the Wars of the Roses, secured full title to the steelyard in London (1474) and the renewal of rights in Boston and Lynn. Not until the days of Elizabeth were the Hanseatic privileges finally reduced.

DECLINE OF THE LEAGUE. Externally the league was weakened by the disorders of the Hundred Years' War; by the rise of Burgundy and the new orientation thereby given to Dutch trade (e.g. Brill wrested the monopoly of the herring trade from the League); and by the great discoveries and the opening of new trade routes. But above all, the monopolistic policies of the League aroused ever sharper opposition in the countries where the League operated (notably in England, Holland, Scandinavia, and Russia; Ivan III destroyed the Novgorod kontor in 1494). **Internally** the League continued to suffer from lack of organization. The inland towns held aloof from the Baltic policy and Köln sent no representatives to the assembly until 1383. The assembly itself was summoned only at irregular intervals. The delegates were strictly bound by their mandates and their votes were subject to review by their home towns. Decisions were not binding on all members until 1418. In the 15th century the League was further weakened by the struggle within the member towns between the democratic guildsmen and the patrician oligarchy. The League threatened the expulsion of "democratic" towns. The German princes (notably the Hohenzollerns of Brandenburg) gradually reduced the freedom of various powerful members of the League and rivalries broke out within the League itself (Köln and the Westphalian towns stood together, as did Danzig and the Prussian towns, especially after 1467). The South German towns opened direct trade relations of their own with Flanders, Breslau, Prague, and other centers, and began to establish their own fairs. Leipzig, for example, replaced Lübeck as the center of the fur trade.

1629. The assembly entrusted the guardianship of the common welfare to Lübeck, Hamburg, and Bremen.

1669. The last assembly (attended by six towns) was held. The League by this time was the merest shadow of its former self, but its kontors survived in Bergen until 1775, in London until 1852, and in Augsburg until 1863.

(4) The Teutonic Knights, 1382–1561
(From p. 235)

The 14th century marked the apogee of the power of the **Teutonic Order** in eastern Europe. The knights began the penetration of Poland, where Germans settled some 650 districts and where the middle class of the towns became German in speech and law, much to the alarm of the rulers and nobles. At the same period the knights advanced into Lithuania, a huge region extending from the Baltic to the Black Sea, the last heathen area in Europe. German colonization and town-building first opened and civilized this region.

1326–1333. The **FIRST POLISH WAR**, marking a sharp reaction to German penetration and putting the Order for the first time on the defensive. With the aid of John of Bohemia, Louis of Hungary, Albert of Austria, Louis of Brandenburg, and others, the Order emerged triumphant and the Poles were obliged to conclude a truce.

1343. PEACE OF KALISCH. The Poles, despite papal support of their claims to Pomerelia, were obliged to recognize the Order's possession of the territory, in return for a promise of aid against the Lithuanians. Poland was thus cut off from the Baltic.

1343–1345. The **Estonian Revolt**, one of the worst *jacqueries* of the Middle Ages. Estonia was taken by the Order from the Danes in 1346.

1385. Union of Poland and Lithuania under Jagiello and Jadwiga, thus creating a strong barrier to the further advance of the Germans and, indeed, sealing the ultimate fate of the Order.

1410, July 15. Defeat of the Knights in the **battle of Tannenberg** by a huge army of Poles and Lithuanians. Poland, unable to exploit the victory, concluded

1411. The **FIRST PEACE OF THORN**, which cost the Knights only Samogitia and an indemnity.

1454. The **Prussian Revolt**, a great uprising against the oppressive rule of the Order in which the Prussian nobility and towns took part. The movement was supported by the Poles, and Casimir of Poland declared war on the Order.

1466. SECOND PEACE OF THORN: Prussia was divided: (1) **West Prussia** (including Danzig, Kulm, Marienwerder, Thorn, and Ermeland) went to Poland, thus cutting East Prussia off from the rest of Germany and securing for Poland access to the sea. (2) **East Prussia** was retained by the Order, with Königsberg as capital. East Prussia, Brandenburg, and Memel were all to be held as Polish fiefs. The Order was opened to Polish members. This peace marked the definitive end of the German advance until the partitions of Poland. The **decline of the Order** continued (growing commercialization, exclusiveness, lack of new blood, loss of discipline, Slavic pressure) despite efforts at reform by various grand masters.

1525. East Prussia was finally secularized by

Bruges (Town Hall), the most ardent champion of Hanseatic unity

Waldemar IV regains Iceland, 1346

the grand master, Albrecht (Hohenzollern) of Brandenburg, and became a fief of the Hohenzollerns under the Polish crown.

1561. The Livonian holdings were similarly transformed and became the duchy of Courland.

The Order itself survived in Germany until 1809 and was later revived in 1840 under Hapsburg auspices with its original functions (e.g. ambulance service in war).

f. SCANDINAVIA

(1) Denmark, 1320–1387

(From p. 225)

The active and on the whole successful reign of **Eric Menved** (1286–1319) was followed in Denmark by a period of weakness and decline, marked by the ascendancy of the nobility and the constant advance of German influence.

1320–1332. CHRISTOPHER II, elected king after a capitulation, the first in Danish history, limiting the royal power in the interest of the nobility and clergy. The Hansa towns, having acquired a monopoly of trade in Denmark, soon became dominant in Danish politics.

1332–1340. A period of complete anarchy. Christopher was driven from the throne by Gerhard, count of Holstein, who parceled out the territories of the crown, established Ger-

man nobles in all the important fortresses, and gave the German traders full rein. Gerhard was murdered in 1340.

1340–1375. WALDEMAR IV, the youngest son of Christopher and one of the greatest Danish kings. At home he did his utmost to break the German influence and to restrict the power of the nobility and the clergy. The Church was subordinated to the royal power and the nobles and towns obliged to perform their military obligations. Abroad Waldemar devoted himself to the reconquest of the territories lost by his father. In wars with Sweden, Holstein, and Schleswig he regained Zeeland (1346), most of Fünen and Jutland (1348), and Scania (1360). His seizure of Gothland (1361) brought him into direct conflict with the powerful Hansa towns, which were supported by Sweden.

1361–1363. First War against the Hansa. Copenhagen was sacked, but Waldemar defeated the Hansa fleets at **Helsingborg** (1362) and forced the Hansa to accept peace (1363) which greatly curtailed their privileges.

1368. A revolt against heavy taxation led to Waldemar's flight. His return (1370) was purchased by tremendous concessions. Meanwhile

1368–1370. The **SECOND WAR WITH THE HANSA** had broken out. The German towns were supported by Sweden, Norway,

Holstein, Mecklenburg, and even by some of the Danish nobles. Waldemar, badly defeated, was obliged to accept

1370. The **PEACE OF STRALSUND,** renewing the privileges of the German Hansa, turning over the larger part of the revenues of four places, and accepting interference in the royal succession. This treaty marked the **ascendency of the Hansa** in the Baltic.

1376–1387. Olaf, grandson of Waldemar, who, until his death, ruled with his mother Margaret as regent.

1387–1412. MARGARET, mother of Olaf, was queen, ruling at the same time Norway and Sweden and thus uniting Scandinavia.

(Cont. p. 431.)

(2) Sweden, 1319–1387

(From p. 226)

1319–1365. MAGNUS II (Smek), aged three at his accession and, until 1333, ruler under the regency of his mother. He was a weak and ineffectual ruler, but through his mother succeeded (1319) to the Norwegian crown and, during the troubled period in Denmark, managed to acquire, temporarily, Scania, Halland, and Bleking (given up again in 1360, to Waldemar IV). His long minority and his reliance on unworthy favorites led to a striking weakening of the royal power and an equally striking rise of the aristocratic party (first *Riksdag,*

Scandinavian Rulers (1263–1533)

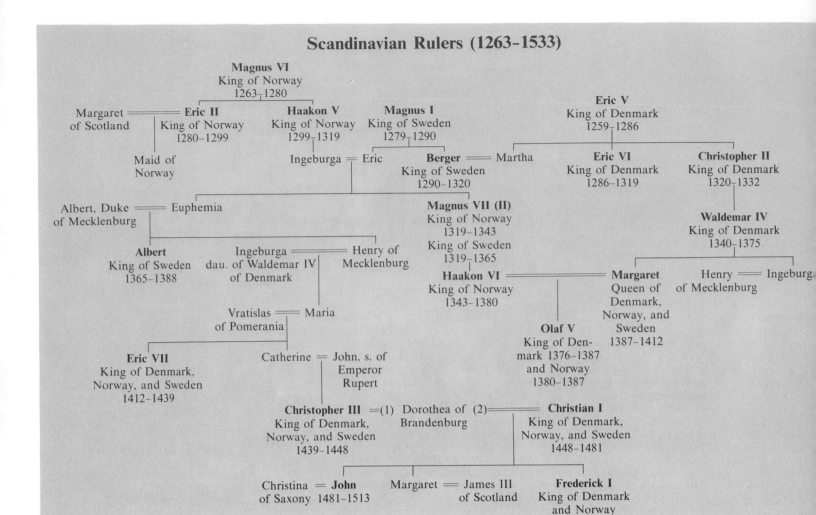

including burghers 1359). Magnus was ultimately deposed and was succeeded by

1363–1388. Albert of Mecklenburg, who from the outset was merely a tool of the nobility. The magnates eventually deposed him and defeated him, calling to the throne

1387–1412. MARGARET, the regent of Denmark. *(Cont. p. 431.)*

(3) Norway, 1320–1387

(From p. 227)

1319–1343. Magnus VII, who was also king of Sweden. In 1343 he turned over Norway to his son

1343–1380. Haakon VI, who was married (1363) to Margaret of Denmark.

1380–1387. Olaf, the son of Haakon and Margaret, already king of Denmark, succeeded to the throne. His death ended the Norwegian line.

1387–1412. MARGARET, mother of Olaf, was elected to the throne, thus introducing into Norway the system of election already in practice in Denmark and Sweden. *(Cont. p. 431.)*

(4) The Union of Kalmar, to 1483

1387–1412. MARGARET OF DENMARK, ruler of all three Scandinavian kingdoms. She had her grand-nephew, Eric of Pomerania, elected king of all three countries, but retained effective power herself.

1397. Coronation of Eric. Margaret presented a draft for the union of the three kingdoms. Vague and incomplete, the plan provided for a single king, established rules of succession, and set up a system of common defense. It was never ratified by the councils of the three kingdoms, but as long as Margaret lived, it worked relatively well. The union left the internal government of each kingdom much as it was. Margaret, an able despot (the Lübeck delegates called her "the lady king"), repressed the nobles, maintained order, and began the recovery of the Danish royal domain. In general the Danes profited by the union, and Danes and Germans were gradually insinuated into power in Sweden and Norway. Effective government of Scandinavia was centered in Denmark.

1412–1439. ERIC, Margaret's successor, proved himself less able. His efforts to regain control in Schleswig led to a long contest with the dukes of Holstein, who, in alliance with the Hansa towns, finally conquered Schleswig completely (1432). At the same time much unrest developed among the peasantry (especially in Sweden, where **Engelbrecht Engelbrechtson** emerged as a leader of the lower classes).

1434. Engelbrecht marched through eastern and southern Sweden, seizing castles and driving out bailiffs, until the **diet of 1435** recog-

nized his demands, electing him regent. This diet included representatives of all four orders and for four hundred years continued to be an important institution. The movement of revolt spread to Norway, where it was taken up and controlled by the nobles. Eric finally took flight and the Danish council called in

1439–1448. CHRISTOPHER (of Bavaria), nephew of Eric, who again ruled all three countries (elected in Sweden, 1440; in Norway 1442). His reign marked the **nadir of the monarchy,** for Christopher was entirely dependent on the Hansa towns and was obliged to renew all their privileges, despite protests from the Danish burghers.

1448–1481. CHRISTIAN I (of Oldenburg) was elected by the Danish council under a capitulation which left all real power in the hands of that body. He had to accept a similar engagement on assuming the crown of Norway. The Swedish nobility, on the other hand, elected **Knut Knutsson** as king with the title of **Charles VIII** (1449–1457). Charles tried to secure the throne of Norway, but was ousted by Christian.

1457. Charles was driven out of Sweden by a revolt inspired by the Church. Christian I was then crowned, but the real power was in the hands of the **Stures** (Sten, Svante, and Sten the Younger). Christian kept a great state, but his court, like that of Christopher and Eric, was filled with Germans, and he was financially dependent on the Hansa cities. The **union of Schleswig and Holstein,** each autonomous under the crown of Denmark, was arranged in 1460. Christian founded the **university of Copenhagen** (1479).

Sweden in the later 15th century: The crown was a plaything of the nobles, while the clergy supported the king of Denmark. A rising commerce and industry was, however, creating a burgher class which was soon to assert itself. **Sten Sture the Younger,** who came into power

with the death of Charles VIII, repulsed Christian of Denmark (1471) with the aid of the towns (especially Stockholm) and returned to the reforms of Engelbrecht. The **university of Uppsala** was founded (1477) and **printing** was introduced soon afterward. *(Cont. p. 431.)*

2. *Eastern Europe*

a. POLAND, 1305-1492

(From p. 261)

The history of Poland in this period was concerned chiefly with the efforts of the kings to reunite the various duchies and to establish the royal power. This policy was opposed, with success, by the nobility, which, as elsewhere in Europe, managed to extract countless privileges and to erect a type of oligarchical government. Externally the Poles were involved in a long struggle with the Teutonic Knights, designed to secure an outlet to the Baltic. This conflict alternated with a policy of expansion to the southeast toward the Black Sea.

1305-1333. VLADISLAV IV (Lokietek), under whom Poland regained its independence after a brief period of Bohemian domination. Vladislav was obliged to continue the struggle against Bohemia, and was not crowned until 1320. For protection he concluded dynastic alliances with Hungary (his daughter married Charles Robert of Anjou) and Lithuania (his son Casimir married the daughter of Gedymin). He did much to reunite the various duchies and established a new capital at Cracow. But he failed to secure Pomerania, which in 1309 passed from Brandenburg to the Teutonic Order. A papal decision in 1321 awarded the region to Poland, but the Knights ignored the order to turn it over, and continued their raids into Polish territory (1326-1333).

1333-1370. CASIMIR III (the Great), an astute and cautious statesman. He introduced an improved administration, reduced the influence of the German town law (a new law code published), developed national defense, and promoted trade and industry (extensive privileges to the Jews, 1334). In 1364 he founded a school at Cracow, which became a university in 1400 and the chief intellectual center of eastern Europe. Here **Johannes Dlugosz** (1415-1480) wrote the first critical history of the country. There was a printing press in Cracow as early as 1474.

In **foreign affairs** Casimir abandoned claims to Silesia and Pomerania, turning his attention toward the southeast, where dynastic problems in the Ukraine called forth dangerous rivalry between Poles, Lithuanians, and Hungarians. By an agreement with Hungary (1339), Casimir, who had no direct heir, promised that on his death the Polish crown should pass to Louis, the son of Charles Robert of Hungary. Louis was to reconquer the lost territories and to respect the privileges of the Polish nobility. This marks the beginning of the disastrous elective system, which gave the magnates an unequaled opportunity for extracting further rights (first real diet—*colloquia*—in 1367). In 1340 Casimir seized Halicz, Lemberg, and Volhynia. War ensued with Lithuania over Volhynia, and ultimately the Poles retained only the western part (1366).

1370-1382. LOUIS (of Anjou). He paid but little attention to Poland, which he governed through regents. To secure the succession to his daughter Maria (married to Sigismund, son of Emperor Charles IV) he granted to the nobility the *Charter of Koszyce* (Kaschau), the basis of far-reaching privileges.

1382-1384. Opposition to Sigismund led to the formation of the **confederation of Radom** and civil war between the factions of the nobility.

1384-1399. JADWIGA (Hedwig), a daughter of Louis, was elected queen.

1386. Marriage of Jadwiga to Jagiello, grand duke of Lithuania, who promised to become a Christian and to unite his duchy (three times the size of Poland) with the Polish crown. As a matter of fact, though the marriage prepared the way for union, Jagiello was obliged to recognize his cousin, **Witold,** as grand duke of Lithuania, and the connection continued to be tenuous.

1386-1434. JAGIELLO (title **Vladislav V**). He had great difficulty in keeping his fractious nobility in order and in 1433 was obliged to grant the *Charter of Cracow*, reaffirming and extending their privileges.

1410, July 15. BATTLE OF TANNENBERG (Grünwald), a great victory of the Poles, using Bohemian mercenaries under John Ziska and supported by the Russians and even the Tatars, against the Teutonic Knights. The Poles thereupon devastated Prussia, but Jagiello, unable

Battle of Tannenberg, July 15, 1410

POLAND, LITHUANIA and RUSSIA in the 15th Century

0 100 200 300 400 500

Scale of Miles

to keep his vassals in order, concluded the

1411, Feb. 1. FIRST PEACE OF THORN, which left matters much as they were and failed to secure for the Poles an access to the Baltic.

1434-1444. VLADISLAV VI, son of Jagiello, succeeded to the throne. Since he was only ten years old, the country was ruled by a regency. Vladislav's brother, Casimir, was offered the Bohemian throne by the Hussites (1438); Vladislav himself became **king of Hungary** (1440). Thenceforth he devoted himself

to Hungarian affairs, leaving Poland in the hands of the magnates. Vladislav lost his life in 1444 at the **battle of Varna** *(p. 345)* against the Turks.

1444-1447. An interregnum, followed by the reign of

1447-1492. CASIMIR IV, brother of Vladislav. He was able to make use of a rift between the great nobles (magnates) and the gentry *(szlachta)*. The *statute of Nieszawa* greatly limited the power of the former and granted substantial rights to the latter (no laws

to be passed, no war to be declared without their consent). At the same time the independence of the Church was curtailed (bishops to be appointed by the king).

1454-1466. War against the Teutonic Order. The Poles took advantage of the Prussian Union (Prussian nobles and towns in opposition to the Order). The war was carried on in desultory fashion, marked by constant shifting of the feudal forces and of the mercenaries from side to side, but the Poles ultimately gained the upper hand and secured

1466, Oct. 19. The **SECOND PEACE OF THORN,** by which Poland finally secured an outlet to the Baltic. Poland acquired Kulm, Michelau, Pomerania, Marienburg, Elbing, and Christburg. The Order became a vassal of the Polish crown, and half its membership became Polish.

1471-1516. Vladislav, the son of Casimir, became king of Bohemia, which involved a long and indecisive war with Hungary (1471-1478). Eventually Vladislav became king of Hungary as Ladislas II (1490). *(Cont. p. 433.)*

b. LITHUANIA, 1240-1447

Of the early history of Lithuania little is known. The numerous heathen tribes were first brought to some degree of unity by the threat of the German Knights (after 1230).

c. 1240-1263. Mindovg, one of the Lithuanian chieftains, in order to deprive the Knights of their crusading purpose, accepted Christianity and was given a crown by Pope Innocent IV. He later broke with the Teutonic Order (1260) and relapsed into paganism. He was killed by one of his competitors. Of the following period almost nothing is known.

1293-1316. Viten re-established a Lithuanian state.

1316-1341. GEDYMIN, the real founder of Lithuania. Blocked by the Germans on the Baltic, he took advantage of the weakness of the Russian principalities to extend his control to the east and south (acquisition of Polotsk, Minsk, and the middle-Dnieper region). **Vilna** became the capital of the new state.

1341-1377. OLGERD, the son of Gedymin, was the ablest of the dynasty. Defeated by the Knights (1360), he too turned eastward. Siding with Tver in the dynastic conflicts of Russia, he advanced several times to the very outskirts of Moscow. During his reign the domain of Lithuania was extended as far as the Black Sea, where Olgerd defeated the Tatars (1368).

1377-1434. JAGIELLO, the son of Olgerd, married Jadwiga of Poland (1386) and established the **personal union with Poland.** Through him Lithuania became converted to Roman Catholicism and the Polish and Lithuanian nobility gradually became assimilated. In 1387 and 1389 Moldavia and Wallachia, and in 1396 Bessarabia, accepted Lithuanian suzerainty.

1398. Jagiello was obliged to recognize his cousin, **Vitovt** (Witold) as grand duke of Lithuania. Vitovt hoped to re-establish the independence of the country from Poland, but his failure in a crusade against the Tatars greatly weakened him.

1447. Casimir IV of Poland, having been grand duke of Lithuania before his accession, once again united the grand duchy and the Polish kingdom. *(Cont. p. 433.)*

c. RUSSIA, 1263–1505

(From p. 264)

The period following the death of **Alexander Nevski** (1263) was marked by the continued and repeated disruption of the Russian lands, due to the complicated and unfortunate system of succession in the princely family. Russia was under the **suzerainty of the Tatars,** who played off one candidate against another, thus increasing the confusion and perpetuating the weakness of the country. The **rise of Moscow** (first mentioned 1147) to prominence among the Russian principalities was perhaps the most important development looking toward the future. Centrally located, Moscow was in the most favorable position to serve as nucleus for a revived Russian state.

1328–1340. IVAN I KALITA (Moneybag), grand prince of Moscow. His was the first of a series of noteworthy reigns. Extremely cautious and parsimonious, Ivan bought immunity from Tatar interference and was ultimately entrusted by the Tatars with the collection of tribute from the other princes.

1340–1353. Simeon I continued the policy of his predecessor and was placed, by the Tatar overlord, above all the other princes.

1353–1359. Ivan II Krasnyi (the Red).

1359–1389. DMITRI DONSKOI (of the Don), who ascended the princely throne at the age of nine. His reign was filled with a struggle against **Michael of Tver,** his chief rival, who was supported by Olgerd of Lithuania. At the same time he began the conflict with the Tatars, whose power was fading, but who also enjoyed the support of Lithuania.

1380, Sept. 8. THE BATTLE OF KULIKOVO. Dmitri completely defeated the Tatar armies before the Lithuanians arrived. The victory was in no sense decisive, for the Tatars on several occasions thereafter advanced to the very gates of Moscow. But Kulikovo broke the prestige of the Tatar arms and marked the turning point.

Ivan III, 1462–1505

(From p. 322)

Rulers of Hungary, Poland, and Lithuania (1205–1492)

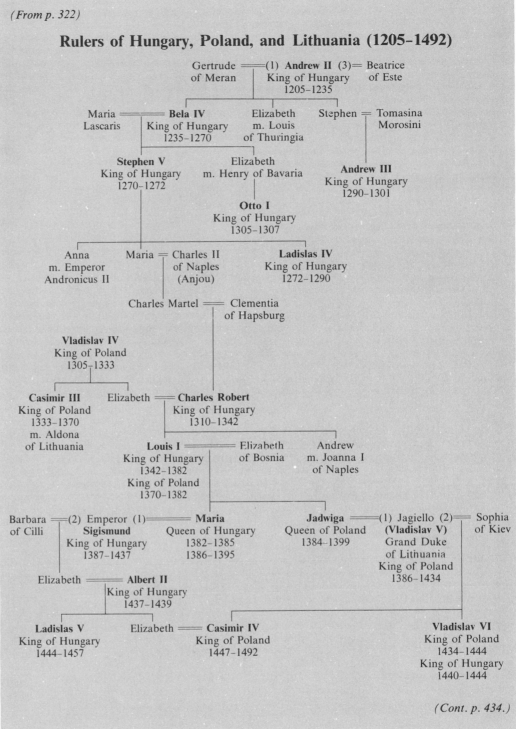

(Cont. p. 434.)

1389–1425. Basil I (Vasili). He annexed Nishni-Novgorod and continued the struggle with the Tatars and the Lithuanians, without forcing a decision.

1425–1462. Basil II, whose reign was distinguished by a relapse into anarchy. A long civil war with his rivals, Yuri and Shemyaka, was followed by Tatar invasion (1451, the Tatars beaten back from Moscow). Nevertheless the Moscow principality managed to maintain itself. In 1439 Basil refused to accept the union of the eastern and western churches, arranged for at the council of Florence. Thenceforth the Russian metropolitan, who had moved to Moscow in the time of Ivan Kalita, became more and more the head of an independent Russian church.

1462–1505. IVAN III (the Great), who may be regarded as the first national sovereign of Russia. By a cautious but persistent policy he annexed most of the rival principalities and, after a series of wars, subjected Novgorod, where the patrician elements tended to side with Lithuania. In 1471 Novgorod was obliged to renounce the alliance of Lithuania and to pay tribute. After a second war, in 1478, **Novgorod's independence was ended** and the troublesome upper classes were deported to central Russia. In 1494 Ivan drove out the German merchants and closed the Hanseatic kontor. Thus he acquired the huge territory of Novgorod, extending eastward to the Urals. Indirectly he greatly reduced the danger of Lithuanian interference. The **annexation of Tver** (1485) put an end to the most formidable rival of Moscow.

1472. Marriage of Ivan with Zoë (Sophia), niece of the last Greek emperor of Constantinople. This was arranged by the pope in the hope of bringing the Russians into the Roman church, but all efforts in that direction failed. The marriage was of importance in establishing the claim of Russian rulers to be the successors of the Greek emperors and the protectors of Orthodox Christianity (theory of the Three Romes, of which Moscow was to be the third and last). It also served to introduce into Moscow the Byzantine conception of the autocrat (Ivan took the title of *Tsar*, i.e. Caesar) and the practice of court ceremonial. Rebuilding of the grand ducal palace (Kremlin) with the assistance of Italian architects brought in by Zoë. The court hierarchy (precedence in rank of princes and nobles, etc.).

1480. Ivan threw off the Tatar yoke after a last Tatar advance on Moscow. Ivan avoided open warfare, but took advantage of the Tatars' disunion. Mengli Girai, the khan of the Crimea, joined him against the Lithuanians.

1492. Invasion of Lithuania, made possible by dynastic troubles in Lithuania and Poland. A **second invasion** (1501) led to the conclusion of peace in 1503, which brought Russia many of the border territories of White Russia and Little Russia. Moscow had by this time become an important factor in European affairs and enjoyed a considerable prestige. Resumption of active diplomatic relations with western countries. The art of icon-painting reached its apogee in the 15th century: Master **Andrew Rublyor** (1370–1430) *(Cont. p. 435.)*

d. HUNGARY, 1301–1490

(From p. 266)

At the beginning of the 14th century Hungary was already an essentially feudal country, in which the great magnates and the bishops, richly endowed with land, ruled as virtually independent potentates ("little kings"), while the lower nobility, organized in the *Comitats* (provincial governments), had, to a large degree, control of the administration. The nobility, freed of taxation, was responsible for defense, but acted only as it saw fit.

1301–1308. The **extinction of the Arpad dynasty** led to a period of conflict, during which Czech, German, and Italian parties each attempted to put their candidates on the throne. **Wencelas,** son of the king of Bohemia, thirteen years old, was first elevated, but could not maintain himself, nor could **Otto of Bavaria.**

1310–1342. CHARLES I (Charles Robert of Anjou), a grandson of Maria, the daughter of Stephen V, was elected and founded the brilliant and successful **Anjou line.** Charles established his capital at Visegrad and introduced Italian chivalry and western influences. After 15 years of effort he succeeded in subduing the "little kings" of whom **Matthias of Csak** and **Ladislas of Transylvania** were the most powerful. Recognizing the hopelessness of suppressing the nobility entirely, he regulated its position and obliged it to furnish specified contingents to the army. Regulation of taxation (first direct tax); encouragement of towns and trade. Charles left the royal power well entrenched, but only as part of an avowedly feudal order.

1342–1382. LOUIS (the Great), the son of Charles, a patron of learning who established a brilliant court at Buda. He attempted to solidify the position of his house in Naples and embarked on a successful expedition to Italy to avenge the murder of his brother Andrew (1347). In conjunction with Genoa he carried on a long struggle with Venice, which ended in the **peace of 1381:** Venice ceded Dalmatia and paid tribute. In the east the Hungarian power made itself felt throughout the Balkans:

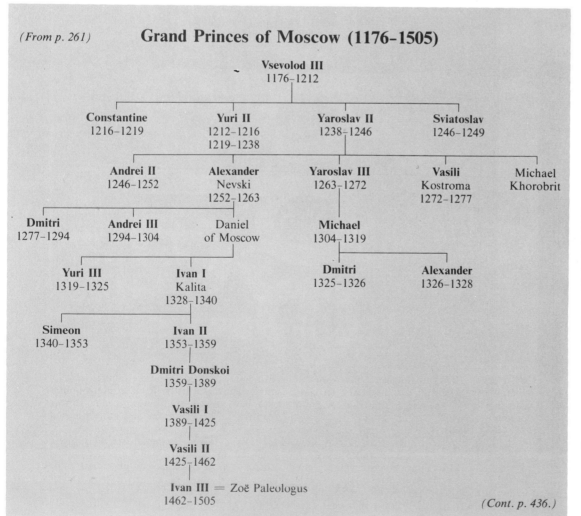

(From p. 261)

Grand Princes of Moscow (1176–1505)

Vsevolod III
1176–1212

Constantine 1216–1219

Yuri II 1212–1216 1219–1238

Yaroslav II 1238–1246

Sviatoslav 1246–1249

Andrei II 1246–1252

Alexander Nevski 1252–1263

Yaroslav III 1263–1272

Vasili Kostroma 1272–1277

Michael Khorobrit

Dmitri 1277–1294

Andrei III 1294–1304

Daniel of Moscow

Michael 1304–1319

Yuri III 1319–1325

Ivan I Kalita 1328–1340

Dmitri 1325–1326

Alexander 1326–1328

Simeon 1340–1353

Ivan II 1353–1359

Dmitri Donskoi 1359–1389

Vasili I 1389–1425

Vasili II 1425–1462

Ivan III = Zoë Paleologus 1462–1505

(Cont. p. 436.)

Double-headed eagle, symbol of the marriage of Ivan and Zoë, 1472

Serbia, Wallachia, and Moldavia recognized the suzerainty of Louis; foundation of the border districts (*banats*) south of the Danube and the Save, as protection against the Turkish advance. **War against the Turks:** Hungarian victory in northern Bulgaria (1366).

1370. Louis became king of Poland but paid little attention to his new obligations. In Hungary he continued the work of his father: the *jus aviticum* (1351) restricted the freedom of the great magnates to dispose of their property.

1382-1385. Maria of Anjou, queen. She was married to Sigismund of Luxemburg, who became guardian of the kingdom. His position was challenged by Charles of Durazzo and Naples, who had many adherents, especially in southern Hungary and Croatia.

1385-1386. Charles II (of Naples). He was assassinated after a very brief reign, which led to a new revolt in Croatia.

1387-1437. SIGISMUND (of Luxemburg), who became German emperor in 1410 and king of Bohemia in 1436. His reign marked a great decline in the royal power, due in large measure to Sigismund's constant absence from the country and his practice of selling royal domains in order to get money for his far-reaching schemes elsewhere. In general Sigismund relied on the towns and lesser nobility against the great magnates (who imprisoned him for four months in 1401). Hence the grant of ever greater rights to the comitats.

1396. The disastrous **crusade of Nicopolis** against the Turks *(p. 342)*. Loss of Dalmatia to the Venetians. Hussite invasions of Hungary, resulting from Sigismund's attempts to gain the Bohemian throne.

1437-1439. Albert (Albrecht) of Hapsburg, son-in-law of Sigismund, also German emperor and king of Bohemia. He was obliged to sign far-reaching capitulations (nobles not obliged to fight beyond the frontiers).

1437. First victory of John Hunyadi over the Turks. Hunyadi was a powerful frontier lord of uncertain origin.

1440-1444. Vladislav I (Vladislav VI of Poland), a weak ruler, whose reign was distinguished chiefly by the continued victories of Hunyadi (1443). Crusade against the Turks.

1444, Nov. 10. Disaster at Varna and death of Vladislav.

1444-1457. Ladislas V, the son of Albert of Hapsburg, also king of Bohemia. He was only four years old at his accession and Hunyadi was therefore appointed governor of the kingdom until 1552.

1456. Crusade against the Turks, preached by John of Capistrano and led by Hunyadi. The Turks were turned back from the siege of Belgrade, but Hunyadi died in the same year.

1458-1490. MATTHIAS CORVINUS (the Just), the son of John Hunyadi and one of the greatest of the Hungarian kings. He was fifteen at his election, but soon distinguished himself as a soldier, statesman, and patron of art and learning. Intelligent, firm, crafty, yet just and noble, he re-established the power of the crown and made Hungary the dominant power in central Europe, if only for the brief space of his reign. He once again broke the power of the oligarchs and drew on the support of the lesser nobility. Development of a central administration; regulation and increase of the taxes. Great wealth and luxury of the court. The *Bibliotheca Corvina,* consisting

Decani Monastery, built by Stephan Dechanski, 1321-1331

of more than 10,000 manuscripts and books, many beautifully illuminated by Italian artists. Matthias the patron of Renaissance learning. Famous law code (1486). University of Buda (c. 1475) re-founded 1635. Development of Magyar literature. Creation of a standing army (Black Troop), composed first of Bohemian, Moravian, and Silesian mercenaries. This gave Matthias one of the most effective fighting forces in the Europe of his day. **Matthias' aims:** to secure the Bohemian throne and ultimately the empire and then to direct a united central Europe against the Turks. Long struggles against **George Podiebrad** of Bohemia ended with George's death in 1471, after Matthias had been proclaimed king of Bohemia (1470). Equally prolonged struggle against Emperor Frederick III, who had been elected king of Hungary by a faction of nobles in 1439. Frederick was finally bought off (1462), but trouble continued. Matthias, disposing of much greater funds and forces than Frederick, conquered not only Silesia and Moravia, but also lower Austria. His capital established at Vienna (1485). Matthias died at 47, leaving Hungary the dominant state in central Europe and a decisive factor in European diplomacy. *(Cont. p. 438.)*

e. THE SERBIAN STATES, 1276-1499

(From p. 267)

By the end of the 13th century the Serbian states, like others of eastern Europe, had evolved a strong secular and clerical aristocracy which, to a large extent, controlled even the more outstanding rulers. In view of the general unsettlement of the law regarding succession and inheritance, the tendency toward dynastic conflict and territorial disruption was very pronounced. In the western Balkans the situation was further complicated by the rivalry of the western and eastern forms of Christianity, to say nothing of the persistence of the heretical Bogomil teaching, especially in Bosnia.

1276-1281. Dragutin, with the aid of the Hungarians, seized the Serbian throne from his father, **Urosh I.** Having been defeated in battle by the Greeks, he abdicated after a short rule.

1281-1321. Milyutin (Stephen Urosh II), the brother of Dragutin. He was a pious and yet dissolute ruler, but above all a political and religious opportunist. Taking full advantage of the growing weakness of the Byzantine Empire, he gradually extended his possessions in Macedonia, along the Adriatic, and, in the north, toward the Danube and the Save.

1321-1331. Stephen Dechanski (Stephen Urosh III), the illegitimate son of the preceding. His reign was marked chiefly by the great victory of the Serbs over the Greeks and Bulgarians near **Küstendil** (Velbuzhde) in 1330. The Serbs now held most of the Vardar Valley.

1331-1355. STEPHEN DUSHAN (Stephen Urosh IV), the greatest of the Serbian rulers in the Middle Ages. Dushan began his career by deposing his father, who was strangled soon afterward. For most of his reign he attempted to maintain friendly relations with Hungary and Ragusa, in order to have a free hand to exploit the dynastic war in the Byzantine Empire between the Palaeologi and John Cantacuzene. By 1344 he had subjected all of Mace-

Stephen Dushan, 1331–1355

1371–1389. Lazar I, of the Hrebelyanovich family, became prince of Serbia.

1375. The Greek patriarch finally recognized the patriarchate of Peč.

1376. TVRTKO I, lord of Bosnia from 1353–1391, proclaimed himself *King of Serbia and Bosnia*, taking over parts of western Serbia and controlling most of the Adriatic coast, excepting Zara and Ragusa. Tvrtko was the greatest of the Bosnian rulers and made his state for a time the strongest Slavic state in the Balkans.

1389 (traditional June 15). **BATTLE OF KOSSOVO,** a decisive date in all Balkan history. **Prince Lazar,** at the head of a coalition of Serbs, Bosnians, Albanians, and Wallachians, attempted to stop the advance of the Turks under **Murad I.** Murad was killed by a Serb who posed as a traitor, but his son Bayazid won a victory. Lazar was captured and killed, due to the reputed desertion of Vuk Brankovich. Henceforth Serbia was a vassal state of the Turks.

1389–1427. STEPHEN LAZAREVICH, the son of Lazar I. He was a literary person, but withal an able statesman. During the early years of his reign he loyally supported the Turks, being present with his forces at the **battles of Nicopolis** (1396) and **Angora** (1402). In return the Turks recognized him as *despot of Serbia,* and supported him against Hungary and other enemies.

1391. Death of Tvrtko I of Bosnia; gradual disintegration of the Bosnian Kingdom.

1392. Venice acquired Durazzo, beginning the process of establishment on the Dalmatian and Albanian coasts. Scutari was acquired in 1396, and when, in 1420, Venice secured **Cattaro,** she possessed practically all the fortified coast towns.

1393. Hungary recovered Croatia and Dalmatia from the Bosnian Kingdom. Hungarian campaigns against Bosnia itself continued for years, until the native elements in 1416 called in the Turks.

1427–1456. GEORGE BRANKOVICH, the nephew of Stephen Lazarevich, despot of Serbia. He built himself a new capital at Semendria (Smederovo) on the Danube and attempted, with Hungarian support, to hold his own against the Turks. This policy led to a Turk invasion (1439) and conquest of the country, the Hungarians, however, saving Bel-

Seat of the patriarchate at Peč, 1346

donia, Albania, Thessaly, and Epirus. His daughter was married to the Bulgarian tsar and Bulgaria was under Serbian supremacy.

1346. Dushan set up his capital at Skoplye (üsküb) and proclaimed himself *Emperor of the Serbs, Greeks, Bulgars, and Albanians.* At the same time he set up a Serbian patriarchate at Peč (Ipek), for which he was anathematized by the Greek patriarch. Dushan established a court wholly Byzantine in character, with elaborate titles and ceremonial. In the years 1349–1354 he drew up his famous law code (*Zabonnik*), which gives an invaluable picture of Serbian conditions and culture at the time.

1349. Attack upon Dushan by the ruler of Bosnia. This led to the invasion of Bosnia by the Serbs, who found much support among the Bogomils, resentful of the Catholic proclivities of their rulers. The conquest of Bosnia was not completed because of Dushan's diversion elsewhere.

1353. Dushan defeated Louis of Hungary, who had been instigated by the pope to lead a Catholic crusade. The Serbs now acquired Belgrade.

1355. Dushan died at the age of 46 as he was en route to Constantinople. Thus perished his hope of succeeding to the imperial throne and consolidating the Balkans in the face of the growing power of the Ottoman Turks *(p. 341).*

1355–1371. Stephen Urosh V, a weak ruler who was faced from the outset by the disruptive ambitions of his uncle Simeon and other powerful magnates. He was the last of the Nemanyid house.

1358. Hungary obtained most of Dalmatia, after defeating Venice. Ragusa became a Hungarian protectorate.

1371. Battle of the Maritza River, in which the Turks, having settled in Thrace, defeated a combination of Serbian lords.

1371. Zeta (Montenegro) became a separate principality under the Balsha family (until 1421).

Prinze Lazar, 1389 (contemporary fresco)

grade. But in 1444 Brankovich, with the aid of **John Hunyadi** *(p. 344),* recovered his possessions and the Serbian state was recognized in the **treaty of Szegedin.** Thereafter Brankovich deserted Hunyadi and tried to maintain himself through close relations with the Turks.

1456-1458. Lazar III, the son of George Brankovich. On his death he left his kingdom to

1458-1459. Stephen Tomashevich, the heir to the Bosnian throne. Stephen, as a Roman Catholic, was much disliked by the Serbs, who consequently offered less resistance to the Turks.

1459. The Turks definitively conquered and incorporated Serbia with the empire.

1463. The Turks overran and conquered Bosnia.

1483. Turkish conquest of Herzegovina (Hun).

1499. Conquest of Zeta (Montenegro) by the Turks.

f. THE BYZANTINE EMPIRE, 1261-1453

(From p. 281)

After the recapture of Constantinople by the Greeks in 1261, the **empire of the Paleologi** was still a relatively small domain, consisting of the former Nicaean Empire, the city of Constantinople and its immediate surroundings, the coastal part of Thrace, southern Macedonia with Thessalonica, the islands of Imbros, Samothrace, Lesbos, and Rhodes. In Anatolia the northeastern part was still held by the Greek **empire of Trebizond,** which in the course of the 13th century had managed to hold a balance between the Seljuk Turks and the Mongols and had become the great entrepôt of the eastern trade coming to the Black Sea by way of Persia and Armenia. The city and the court reached their highest prosperity and brilliance under the Emperor **Alexius II** (1297-1330), whose reign was followed by a period of dynastic and fac-

tional struggle, marked by unbelievable degeneracy and cruelty. The reign of **John Alexius III** (1350-1390) marked a second period of splendor, but the 15th century was one of decline. The empire of Trebizond ended with the Ottoman conquest in 1461 (last ruler, **David,** 1458-1461).

The European territories of the earlier empire were divided between the Greek despotate of Epirus and the Greek duchy of Neopatras (Thessaly, Locris), the Latin duchy of Athens, the Latin principality of Achaea, and the Venetian duchy of the Archipelago.

1259-1282. MICHAEL VIII (Paleologus). He was the ablest of the Paleologi, a man who devoted himself to the restoration of Byzantine authority throughout the Balkan area, persisting despite many setbacks.

1261. Michael established a foothold in the southeastern part of the Peloponnese (Morea), which was widely expanded in the ensuing period. **Mistra** (Misithra) became the capital of a flourishing principality and one of the great centers of late-Byzantine culture.

1262. Michael II of Epirus was forced to recognize the suzerainty of the Constantinople emperor. In a series of campaigns much of the despotate was regained for the empire (Janina taken, 1265).

1264-1265. Constant raids of the Bulgars into Thrace led to a formidable campaign against them and the reconquest of part of Macedonia.

1266. Charles of Anjou became king of Sicily.

He made an alliance with Baldwin II, the last Latin emperor, and, through the marriage of his son with the heiress of the Villehardouins, extended his authority over Achaea. He soon became the most formidable opponent of the Greeks, for by the **treaty of Viterbo** (1267) he took over the claims of Baldwin II.

1267. Michael permitted the Genoese to establish themselves at Galata, across from Constantinople. This was part of his policy of encouraging the Genoese at the expense of the Venetians, to whom, however, he had to grant privileges also (1268).

1271. Death of Michael II of Epirus. Charles of Anjou had already taken Corfu (1267) and now undertook the conquest of the Epiran coast, the essential base for any advance on Thessalonica and Constantinople. Durazzo was taken in 1272. **John Angelus,** driven out of Epirus, set up as lord of Neopatras (to 1295). **Nicephorus I** was the titular ruler of a much-reduced Epiran state (to 1296). Charles of Anjou proclaimed himself *king of Albania* and entered into alliance with the Serbs, who had begun the construction of a large state by advancing down the Vardar Valley.

1274. THE COUNCIL OF LYON. Michael, in order to escape from the Angevin danger, accepted the Roman creed and the primacy of the pope, thus effecting the **reunion with Rome.** This move, purely political in intent, met with vigorous resistance on the part of the Orthodox Greek clergy and in the long run

Sketch for a study of the opening battle formations of Serbian (upper left) *and Turkish* (lower right) *armies at the Battle of Kossovo, 1389*

only served to accentuate the antagonism of Greek and Latin.

1274. Campaigns of Michael against the Angevins in Epirus. These campaigns were carried on year after year, with varying success.

1278. The death of William of Villehardouin, prince of Achaea, gave the Greeks an opportunity to expand their holding in the southeastern part.

1281. Michael VIII won a great victory over the Angevins at **Berat.** Thereupon Charles made an alliance with the papacy and with Venice, with which the Serbs and Bulgars were associated. Michael in reply effected a rapprochement with Peter of Aragon.

1282. The Sicilian Vespers (*p. 310*). This blow at the Angevin power in Sicily served to relieve the pressure on the Greek Empire.

1282–1328. ANDRONICUS II, the son of Michael, a learned, pious, but weak ruler, whose first move was to give up the hated union with Rome and conciliate the Orthodox clergy.

1285. Venice deserted the Angevin alliance and made a ten-year peace with the Greeks.

1295–1320. MICHAEL IX, son of Andronicus, co-emperor with his father.

1296. The Serbs, continuing their advance, conquered western Macedonia and northern Albania. Andronicus was obliged to recognize these losses (1298).

1302. Peace between the Angevins and the Aragonese. Andronicus, once again exposed to Angevin ambition, engaged **Roger de Flor** and 6000 Catalan mercenaries (the Catalan Company) to fight against the Italians. They raised havoc at Constantinople, where 3000 Italians are said to have been killed in the disorders.

1304. The Catalans repulsed an attack of the Turks on Philadelphia, but they then turned and attacked Constantinople (1305–1307), without being able to take it.

1305. Murder of Roger de Flor. The Catalan Company became a veritable scourge, roaming through Thrace and Macedonia and laying the country waste.

1311. The Catalans, having advanced into Greece, took the duchy of Athens, where they set up a dynasty of their own.

1321–1328. Civil war between the emperor and his grandson Andronicus. In the course of the struggle much of the empire was devastated.

1325. Andronicus was obliged to accept his grandson as co-emperor.

1326. RISE OF THE OTTOMAN TURKS in northwestern Anatolia. In 1326 they took Brusa (Bursa) from the Greeks, and in 1337 Nicomedia (*p. 341*).

1328–1341. ANDRONICUS III, the grandson of Andronicus II, who finally forced the emperor's abdication (d. 1332). Andronicus III was a frivolous and irresponsible ruler, wholly unequal to the great problems presented by the rise of the Turkish and Serb powers (Sultan Orkhan, 1326–1359; Tsar Stephen Dushan, 1331–1355).

1329. The Greeks managed to take the important island of Chios from the Genoese.

1330. The Serbs defeated the Bulgars in a decisive battle and put an end to the Bulgar power.

1334–1335. Andronicus conquered Thessaly and part of Epirus from the despot, John II Orsini.

1336. The Greeks reconquered Lesbos.

1340. Stephen Dushan, having conquered the Albanian coastal territory (as far as Valona) from the Angevins, drove the Greeks out of the interior and took Janina.

1341–1376. JOHN V, the son of Andronicus III, ascended the throne as a child, under the regency of his mother, Anna of Savoy.

1341–1347. CIVIL WAR IN THE EMPIRE

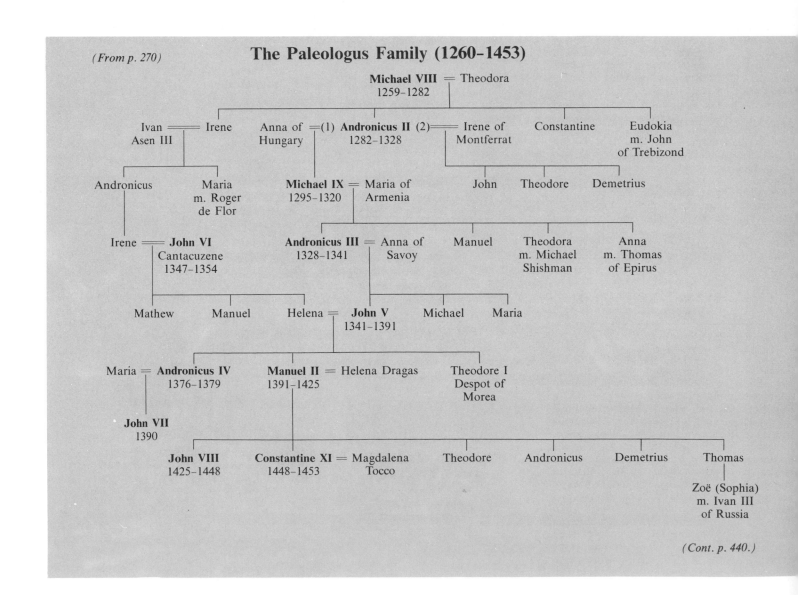

(From p. 270)

The Paleologus Family (1260–1453)

Michael VIII = Theodora
1259–1282

Ivan = Irene — Anna of = (1) **Andronicus II** (2) = Irene of — Constantine — Eudokia
Asen III — Hungary — 1282–1328 — Montferrat — — m. John of Trebizond

Andronicus — Maria m. Roger de Flor — **Michael IX** = Maria of Armenia 1295–1320 — John — Theodore — Demetrius

Irene = **John VI** Cantacuzene 1347–1354 — **Andronicus III** = Anna of Savoy 1328–1341 — Manuel — Theodora m. Michael Shishman — Anna m. Thomas of Epirus

Mathew — Manuel — Helena = **John V** 1341–1391 — Michael — Maria

Maria = **Andronicus IV** 1376–1379 — **Manuel II** = Helena Dragas 1391–1425 — Theodore I Despot of Morea

John VII 1390

John VIII 1425–1448 — **Constantine XI** = Magdalena Tocco 1448–1453 — Theodore — Andronicus — Demetrius — Thomas

Zoë (Sophia) m. Ivan III of Russia

(Cont. p. 440.)

John Cantacuzene, supported by the aristocratic elements, set himself up as a rival emperor. John V was supported by the popular elements. In the ensuing war much of Thrace and Macedonia was ravaged. The war was the undoing of the empire, since both sides freely called in Serbs or Turks to support them.

1341-1351. The **HESYCHAST CONTROVERSY** in the Greek church, which added to the confusion. The controversy was really a conflict between the mystic teachings emanating from the monasteries of Mt. Athos (founded 962 ff.) and the rationalism of the clergy. The Hesychasts (Zealots) supported Cantacuzene and were victorious with him. In the interval the dispute led to a great popular, almost socialistic **rising in Thessalonica,** where the extremists set up an almost independent state (1342–1347).

1343. The Venetians, taking advantage of the civil war, seized Smyrna.

1346. Stephen Dushan was crowned emperor of the Serbs and the Greeks and made preparations to seize Constantinople and replace the Greek dynasty.

1347. Cantacuzene managed to take Constantinople, through treachery.

1347-1354. **JOHN VI** (Cantacuzene), sole emperor. He made his son Manuel despot of the Morea (1348). The Serbs held all of Macedonia.

1351. Stephen Dushan besieged Thessalonica.

1353. The **Ottoman Turks,** called in by Cantacuzene, defeated the Serbs.

1354. The Turks established themselves in Europe, at Gallipoli, thus beginning their phenomenal career of expansion *(p. 341).*

1354. John V took Constantinople and forced the abdication of Cantacuzene (d. 1383). At the same time Dushan, having taken Adrianople, was advancing on the capital. His sudden death (1355) led to the disintegration of the Serb Empire and to the removal of a great threat to the Greeks. On the other hand, it left the Christians an easier prey to the advancing Turks.

1365. The Turks, having overrun Thrace, took Adrianople, which became their capital.

1366. John V, who had been captured by Tsar Shishman of Bulgaria, was liberated by his cousin, Amadeus of Savoy.

1369. John V appeared before the pope at Avignon and agreed to union of the churches, in order to secure the aid of the west against the Turks.

1376-1379. **ANDRONICUS IV,** the son of

Rossikon Monastery on Mt. Athos

John V, who dethroned his father with the aid of the Genoese.

1379-1391. **John V,** supported by the Turks, managed to recover his throne.

Ruins of the palace of Michael VIII at Mistra

John VIII, 1425–1448 (detail of a fresco by Benozzo Gozzoli)

1386. The Venetians recovered Corfu, which they held until 1797.

1388. The Venetians purchased Argos and Nauplia.

1389. Battle of Kossovo *(p. 336).* End of the great Serb Empire.

1390. John VII, a grandson of John V, deposed the latter, but after a few months the old emperor was restored by his second son, Manuel.

1391–1425. MANUEL II, an able ruler in a hopeless position. By this time the empire had been reduced to the city of Constantinople, the city of Thessalonica, and the province of Morea. The Turks held Thrace and Macedonia.

1391–1395. The Turks, under Bayazid I, blockaded Constantinople, and only the Christian crusade that ended in the disastrous **battle of Nicopolis** (1396) gave the Greeks some respite.

1397. Bayazid attacked Constantinople, which was valiantly defended by Marshal Boucicaut. This time the advance of the Tatars under Timur distracted the Turks. The defeat and capture of Bayazid in the **battle of Angora** (1402), led to a period of confusion and dynastic war among the Turks *(p. 344).*

1422. The Turks again attacked Constantinople, because of Manuel's support of the Turkish pretender Mustapha, against Murad II.

1423. The Venetians bought the city of Thessalonica.

1425–1448. JOHN VIII, the son of Manuel, whose position was, from the outset, desperate.

1428. Constantine and Thomas Paleologus, brothers of the emperor, conquered Frankish Morea, with the exception of the Venetian ports. In these last years the Morea was the most extensive and valuable part of the empire.

1430. The Turks took Thessalonica from the Venetians.

1439. THE COUNCIL OF FLORENCE. John VIII, having traveled to Italy, once again accepted the union with Rome and the papal primacy. As on earlier occasions this step raised a storm of opposition among the Greeks and to some extent facilitated the Turk conquests.

1444. A second crusade from the west ended in disaster when the Turks won a decisive victory at **Varna.**

1446. The Turks frustrated an attempt of the Greeks to expand from the Morea into central Greece. Corinth fell into Turkish hands.

1448–1453. CONSTANTINE XI, the last Byzantine emperor.

1453. The siege and **capture of Constantinople** by **Mohammed the Conqueror** *(p. 345)*. **End of the Byzantine Empire** after a thousand years of existence.

1460. Conquest of the Morea by the Turks. End of the rule of the Paleologi in Greece.

1461. Conquest of the empire of Trebizond, the last Greek state, by the Turks.

BYZANTINE CULTURE in the time of the Paleologi. The territorial and political decline of the empire was accompanied by an extraordinary cultural revival, analogous to the Renaissance in Italy. The schools of Constantinople flourished and produced a group of outstanding scholars (philosophy: **Planudes, Plethon, Bessarion**). In theology the dominant current was one of mysticism (**Gregory Palamas** and the Hesychasts; **George Scholarius**). Historical writing reached a high plane in the work of **John Cantacuzene, Nicephorus Gregoras,** and, in the last years of the empire, of **Phrantzes, Ducas,** and **Chalcocondylas.** Art, especially painting, was distinctly humanized and three different schools (Constantinople, Macedonia, and Crete) cast a flood of splendor over the closing years of the empire. **Mistra,** the capital of the Morean province, became in the early 15th century the center of a revived Greek national feeling and a home of scholars and artists.

g. THE OTTOMAN EMPIRE, 1300–1481

(From p. 273)

The presence of the Turks in central Asia can be traced back to at least the 6th century (**Orchon inscriptions,** in Turkish, dealing with the period 630–680). These Turks, of the Oghuz family, were conquered by the Uighur Turks in 745 and continued under their rule until 840, when the Uighurs in turn were conquered by the Kirghiz Turks coming from the west. In the 9th and 10th centuries the Turks were converted to Islam, and in the 11th century, having pushed their advance into southeastern Russia and Iran, they began to attack the Byzantine Empire. The **Seljuks,** a branch of the Oghuz Turks, took **Baghdad** in 1055, and in the following two centuries built up an imposing empire in Anatolia and the Middle East *(p. 272)*.

1243. The **Mongols** defeated the Seljuks at **Kösedagh.** Anatolia under Mongol suzerainty; disintegration of the Seljuk Empire in Anatolia.

1260–1300. Foundation of new **Turkish principalities** on the Aegean coast, which was conquered from the Byzantines by Turkish chiefs or lords of the border. The influx of Turkish population, the revival of the Holy War, as well as the withdrawal of the Byzantine frontier guards to the Balkans were the main reasons for this development.

1290 (?)–1326. OSMAN, son of one of the border chiefs, was the founder of the principality called Osmanli (Ottoman) in Bithynia.

The immigration into these frontier states consisted not only of semi-nomadic tribesmen, but also of civilized townsmen from central Anatolia. Osman allied himself with the **Akhis,** members of a fraternity, who became the first organizers of the Ottoman state, with the traditional Islamic institutions.

1317–1326. Siege of Brusa (Bursa) by the Ottoman Turks. The town was finally starved into submission (April 6).

1326–1361 (?). ORKHAN I struck the first Ottoman coin and took the title of sultan of the **Ghazis** (warriors of the faith). His dominions came to extend from Ankara in central Anatolia to Thrace in Europe.

1329, June 10. The Turks defeated a Byzantine force under Andronicus III at **Pelekanon,** near the present Maltepe.

1331, March 2. Nicaea (Iznik) taken by the Turks. The first Turkish college was established there.

1337. Nicomedia (Ismid) taken by the Turks.

1345. The **Ottoman Turks first crossed into Europe,** called in by the Emperor John Cantacuzene to support his claims against the Empress Anna. Orkhan married Theodora, daughter of Cantacuzene.

1352. The Ottoman Turks again called in by Cantacuzene, this time to aid him against the Serbian conqueror, **Stephen Dushan.** The first Turkish settlement in Europe made in the vicinity of Tzympe, on Gallipoli.

1354, March. Gallipoli taken by the Ottomans.

They then spread rapidly over Thrace. On Orkhan's death the Ottoman state was already well organized and the Turkish ruler was able to dictate to the Byzantine emperors.

1359. Angora (Ankara) submitted to the Ottomans.

1361 (?)–1389. MURAD I. In his time the Ottoman state became the leading power in Anatolia and the Balkans. **Adrianople** (Edirne) was taken in 1362, and after 1402 became the capital of the empire. Organization of the **Janissary corps** (date uncertain), composed of captives taken in war, and later of levies of Christian children. Economic development: commercial treaty with the Genoese.

1366. Crusade of Amadeus of Savoy. He took Gallipoli, which the Turks recovered seven years later.

1366–1370. Turkish expansion northward to the Balkan range, under Lala Shahin, and toward Macedonia under Evrenuz (Evrenos) beg.

1371, September 26. Defeat of the allied Serb princes of Macedonia at **Chernomen** (Chirmen) on the Maritza. The rulers of Bulgaria, Macedonia, and the Byzantine Empire recognized the sultan's suzerainty.

1377–1386. Ottoman expansion in central Anatolia; first clash with the **Karamanids of Koniah** (siege of Koniah in 1387).

1385. Capture of Sofia by the Turks; defeat and submission of the Albanian lords at the **battle of Voissa.**

Mosque of Osman

Conquests of the OTTOMAN TURKS to 1481

1386. **Capture of Nish. Lazar of Serbia** became a Turkish vassal.

1387. **Capture of Saloniki** (Thessalonica); Turkish raids into Greece and the Morea.

1388. Defeat of the Turks in Bosnia; coalition of Serbia, Bosnia, and Danubian Bulgaria against the Ottomans. Invasion of Bulgaria by the Ottoman general, Ali Pasha (winter of 1388–1389).

1389, June 15. **BATTLE OF KOSSOVO.** The Ottomans defeated the allied forces of the Serbs and Bosnians. Murad was assassinated by a Serb, and Lazar was executed by Bayazid's order.

1389–1402. **BAYAZID I.** Chosen sultan on the battlefield of Kossovo, he had his brother Yakub strangled. Disorders broke out in Rumelia and Anatolia; Saloniki was lost. Bayazid reached an agreement with the Serbs and turned his attention to Anatolia.

1390. Bayazid first occupied the emirates of Saruhan, Aydin, Mentezhe, then captured Philadelphia. He defeated Ali beg, the Karamanid ruler, thus re-establishing Ottoman authority in Anatolia.

1391–1392. After two expeditions, Bayazid annexed **Kastamonu** and **Amasia** in northern Anatolia. Manuel II Paleologus participated in these operations as vassal of the sultan.

1393. Bayazid's **fourth expedition to Anatolia** and clash with **Kadi Burhâneddin,** the ruler of Sivas. Final occupation of Trnovo, capital of Bulgaria. **Tsar Shishman** was executed two years later when **Nicopolis** was taken by the Ottomans.

1394. Bayazid summoned his European vassals to Serez. The threat of **Timur and the Mongols** in eastern Anatolia encouraged them to resist Bayazid's demands. Coalition between Bayazid, Egypt, and the Golden Horde against Timur.

Bayazid I, 1389–1402

1395, April. **Bayazid invaded Hungary** and fought against **Mircea,** the voyvod of Wallachia, on the Argesh. He started the **blockade of Constantinople,** which continued for seven years. Preparations in the west for a crusade against the Turks.

1396. **CRUSADE OF NICOPOLIS,** led by **Sigismund of Hungary,** supported by Balkan princes and by French, German, and English knights, as well as by both the Roman and Avignon popes. Venice and Genoa negotiated with both sides. The crusading forces assembled with great pomp at Buda and advanced along the Danube to Nicopolis, pillaging and slaying as they went. On September 25 they met the Turks about four miles south of Nicopolis. The knights ignored all advice and pressed forward; after an initial success they were completely overwhelmed and many were captured. The forces numbered about 20,000 on each side.

1397. The **siege of Constantinople** pressed more vigorously by the sultan, while Evrenuz made further conquests in Greece. Bayazid again defeated the Karamanids and occupied Konia.

1398–1399. The sultan took **Sivas** and annexed the entire area west of the Euphrates, thus incurring the enmity of the sultan of Egypt. At the same time depossessed Turkish emirs called Timur into Anatolia.

1400. **Timur took and sacked Sivas.** War be-

وَيُحَمِّلُ الْقَفَصَ وَالْحِبَالَةَ وَالْفَسَرَ وَالذُّبَالَةَ أَنَّهَا لَضَنِنْتُ عَلَى بَالِهِ فَأَضَاعَتْ نِصْفَ مَنْ جَهَا

فَتَشُدُّ مِنْ وَزْرِهَا فَلَمَّا دَانِنِي قَوَّتْ بِالرَّقْعَةِ دِرْهَمًا وَقِطْعَةً وَقُلْتُ لَهَا أَرَغِبْتَ فِي الْمَشُوفِ الْمُعَلَّمِ

وَاسْتَرْنَ إِلَى الدِّرْهَمِ فَوَجَّى بِالسِّرِّ الْمُدَهَّمِ وَأَنَّ ابْنَانِ نَتَرَجَّى خُذِي الْقِطْعَةَ وَأَبِيرُجَنْ

... أَتْ إِلَى اسْتِخْلَاضِ الْبَدْرِ الْتَنِّمِ وَالْأَبْلَجِ الْهَمِّ وَقَالَتْ دَعْ جِدَّالَكَ وَبَايِعْمَا بَدَالَكَ فَأَسْطَعَ

طَلَعَ الشَّيْخُ وَبَلَدِهِ وَالسِّعْرِ وَنَايِجُ بُرْدَتِهِ فَقَالَتْ أَنَّ الشَّيْخَ مِنْ أَهْلِ نَرُوجَ وَهُوَ الَّذِي وُشِّى

Ottoman standard bearers (from a 14th-century manuscript)

Bayazid captured by Timur in the Battle of Angora, July 28, 1402

tween him and Bayazid became inevitable when the latter retaliated by taking **Erzinjan.**

1402, July 28 (not 20). **BATTLE OF ANGORA** (Ankara). Bayazid, deserted by most of his Turkish vassals, was completely defeated and captured. Timur restored many of the Turkish emirs and himself advanced as far as Smyrna and Bursa. The Ottoman Empire on the verge of dissolution. Dispute of Bayazid's sons for the succession.

1403–1413. Civil War. Bayazid died in captivity (1403) and his three sons, **Isa** in Bursa, **Suleiman** in Edirne, **Mehmed** in Amasia, began to fight each other for control of Bursa and Edirne and for the acquisition of supreme power.

1404. Mehmed defeated Isa and took Bursa, whereupon Suleiman intervened.

1405. Suleiman crossed to Anatolia and drove Mehmed into the mountains. Most of the emirs restored by Timur were reduced to obedience.

1409. Mehmed sent his brother **Musa** to Wallachia to threaten Suleiman's European possessions.

1410. Suleiman returned to Europe and defeated Musa near Constantinople. Meanwhile Mehmed reoccupied Bursa.

1411, June 5. Suleiman was attacked by Musa, who was joined by the warlike frontier elements and by the Serbs. Suleiman was defeated and killed at Edirne, but Musa's radical policy soon alienated his supporters.

1413. Musa threatened Constantinople and the Serbs who had allied themselves with Mehmed. The latter finally defeated and killed Musa and thereupon was able to reunite the Ottoman possessions.

1413–1421. Mehmed I (the Restorer *or Kirishdji*). He conciliated the Serbs and the Byz-

antine emperor, who held as a hostage **Mustafa,** Mehmed's elder brother and a pretender to the throne.

1414. Mehmed defeated the Karamanids and restored the Ottoman overlordship over the emirs of Anatolia. Nonetheless, the Karamanids remained restless for some years to come.

1415. Mustafa attempted to overthrow Mehmed. A great social-religious rising led by **Sheikh Bedreddin** was put down with difficulty in 1416.

1416. First war with Venice, due chiefly to Turkish activity in the Aegean. The Venetian admiral, **Giovanni Loredano** (later doge), destroyed a Turkish fleet off Gallipoli, whereupon the sultan made peace.

1417. Mehmed invaded Wallachia to punish Mirčea, who had supported both Mustafa and Bedreddin.

1421–1451. MURAD II proclaimed sultan in Bursa.

1421. Mustafa, released by the Byzantine emperor, was proclaimed sultan in Adrianople. In 1422 he attempted to take Bursa, but was taken prisoner and executed. Murad, to revenge himself on the Greek emperor, undertook a serious **siege of Constantinople,** but when his brother Mustafa rose against him in Anatolia he had to abandon the siege (June–August). A treaty of peace with the Greek emperor was signed in February 1424.

1439. Murad annexed the whole of Serbia, whose prince (despot), **George Brankovich,** fled to Hungary.

1440. Murad's vain **siege of Belgrade,** which had been in Hungarian possession since 1427.

1441–1442. Two Ottoman armies were defeated in Transylvania by its governor, **John Hunyadi,** who became famous as the Christian champion in defense against the Turks.

1443. Battle of Zlatica (Izladi). An army under **Vladislav,** king of both Hungary and Poland, supported by Hunyadi and by George Brankovich, took Nish and Sofia and was stopped in its advance only at Zlatica (a Bal-

Mohammed II, 1451–1481

The Castle of Europe, 1452

kan pass) by Murad. This daring campaign evoked great enthusiasm and agitation for a crusade in the west.

1444, June 12. Truce of Adrianople (Edirne), which was ratified in Szegedin (Hungary) in August. Under its terms Brankovich was restored to his despotate. Murad also made **peace with Karaman** and then voluntarily abdicated in favor of his twelve-year-old son, Mehmed (August). **THE VARNA CRUSADE.** The Hungarians, encouraged by the papal representative, thereupon broke the truce and renewed the crusade (September). They advanced through Bulgaria to the coast at Varna. Murad was called from his retirement to take command of the army. The Venetian fleet, cruising in the Dardanelles, tried to prevent the Ottoman forces from crossing from Asia to Europe, but was foiled when Murad crossed the Bosporus and defeated the crusaders (only

the Hungarians and the Wallachians took part) at **Varna** on November 10. Vladislav was killed and a great many knights taken prisoner.

1444–1446. Mohammed (Mehmed) II, whose first short reign was unsuccessful.

1446–1451. Second reign of Murad II. An insurrection in Adrianople, instigated by grand vizir **Khalil**, brought Murad back to the throne.

1448. Turkish expedition against **Scanderbeg** (George Castriota), an Albanian chieftain, followed by the **second battle of Kossovo,** where Murad defeated Hunyadi.

1450. Second Turkish expedition against Scanderbeg, again without decisive result.

1451–1481. MOHAMMED II (the Conqueror). He can be considered as the real founder of the Ottoman Empire with its centralist administration and its firm territorial basis in Rumelia and Anatolia. In this huge area he put an end to all local dynasties, and drove out the

Hungarians and the Venetians. Mohammed was at once an inexorable conqueror and a broad-minded ruler, who assembled at his court Muslim, Greek, and Italian scholars.

1451. Mohammed campaigned in Anatolia to reassert Ottoman authority over the rebellious Turkish emirs.

1452. Mohammed completed the **Castle of Europe** (*Rumili Hisar*) at the narrowest point of the Bosporus, opposite the older **Castle of Asia** (*Anadoli Hisar*). This assured him freedom of passage between Anatolia and Rumelia and at the same time enabled him to control the supply of Constantinople. Its construction led at once to war between Mohammed and the last Greek emperor, Constantine (June).

1453, Apr. 6–May 29. SIEGE AND FALL OF CONSTANTINOPLE, at that time largely depopulated and very poor. Constantine had only some 10,000 men at his command and was unpopular because of his efforts to reunite the eastern and western churches. He received some aid from the Venetians and Genoese, but his chief asset was the tremendous system of fortifications which had defended the city for a thousand years. The Turks concentrated between 100,000 and 150,000 men outside the city. Though the sultan had a substantial fleet, this was shut out from the Golden Horn by a great iron chain. The most important role was played by the Turkish artillery, especially by the huge guns built by a Hungarian renegade, **Urban.** The walls were continuously bombarded, but for a long time the defenders managed to close the breaches. Finally Mohammed had some 70 small ships dragged overland from the Bosporus to the Golden Horn, thereby forcing the defenders to divide their attention. On May 29, the Turks delivered a great attack on the Romanos Gate and forced an entry. **Constantine was killed** in the ensuing melée and many of the defenders took refuge on the Venetian and Genoese ships. The city was given up to pillage for three days. Mohammed tried at first to populate it with Turks but then began to settle Greeks and other Christians, chiefly artisans. He gave the patriarch, **Gennadios,** considerable civil as well as religious authority over the Orthodox inhabitants of the entire empire. Somewhat later similar authority over the Armenian and Jewish communities was conferred upon the Armenian patriarch and the Grand Rabbi (*millet system*). Constantinople (Istanbul) soon became the Ottoman capital, with a population of some 70,000 at the end of the reign. Churches were transformed into mosques (notably *Santa Sophia*) and palaces built (*Old Serai,* completed 1458; *New Serai,* completed 1467). The seat of government now became firmly fixed and the Ottoman administrative system was developed, with an elaborate system of training (palace school; slave household). Some of the court ceremonial could be traced to the Greeks, but most institutions were fundamentally Turkish and Islamic.

1455. Mohammed annexed southern Serbia; treaty with the despot.

1456. The sultan besieged **Belgrade,** which was relieved by Hunyadi shortly before his death (Aug.).

1458–1459. The Turks annexed the rest of Serbia, with Smederovo.

1458–1460. Conquest of the Morea.

1461. Conquest of the Black Sea coast, with the principality of **Kastamonu** and the **empire of Trebizond.**

1463–1464. Mohammed invaded Bosnia and Herzegovina, while the Hungarians recaptured Yaiche, the Bosnian capital.

1463–1479. GREAT WAR BETWEEN THE TURKS AND THE VENETIANS, resulting from Turkish interference with Venetian privileges in the Levant trade, and from Venetian apprehension about the future of the outposts on the Greek and Albanian coasts. The humanist pope, **Pius II,** attempted to organize a crusade and Hungary did in fact join Venice. But only a small, miscellaneous force of crusaders was assembled at Ancona. In 1470 a huge Turkish fleet and landing force took Euboea (Negroponte) from the Venetians, but in 1472, a Venetian-Papal fleet burned Smyrna (Izmir) and Adalia and tried to supply firearms to Venice's ally, **Uzun Hasan** of the Akkoyunlu. On August 11, in the critical **battle of Otluk-beli** (on the upper Euphrates) Mohammed defeated Hasan and not only assured his own rule over Anatolia, but deprived Venice of its most formidable ally. In 1477 Turkish raiders reached the very outskirts of Venice, and in 1478 Mohammed took **Kroia, Alessio** and **Drivasto** from the Venetians. Scutari held out. On January 25, 1479, peace was concluded: the Venetians gave up Scutari and the other Albanian stations, but kept Dulcigno, Antivari, and Durazzo; they accepted the loss of Negroponte and Lemnos and thenceforth paid an annual tribute of 10,000 ducats for trade privileges in the Ottoman Empire.

1480, Aug. 11. A Turkish force occupied **Otranto** in southern Italy. On the other hand, Mohammed failed to take **Rhodes,** which was besieged from May until August and valiantly defended by the Knights of St. John.

1481, May 3. Mohammed died as he was about to begin another campaign in Anatolia.

(*Cont. p. 439.*)

*Sultanahmet Mosque, Istanbul (*Constantinople*)*

D. Africa During the Middle Ages

(For the history of Mediterranean Africa see p. 283.)

THE EARLIEST HISTORY of Africa is shrouded in obscurity. In the north the original inhabitants appear to have been of some white stock (the ancestors of the Berbers), while south of the Sahara the country was populated by Negrillos, a small race of Negroes of whom the Pygmies, Bushmen, and Hottentots are probably the descendants. The Negrillos were evidently pushed to the northwest and south by a great invasion (possibly c. 30,000 B.C.) of a larger Negro race arriving from the other side of the Indian Ocean and landing on the central part of the eastern coast. From the newcomers the Bantu derive. A second great invasion from overseas followed and pushed the Negrillos even farther to the west, though there seems to have been much intermixture in the region north of the equator, forming the various Sudanese tribes. In all likelihood there was also a good deal of infiltration of Semitic stocks into the northern part of the continent, both west (Carthage) and east (Syria). The earlier inhabitants were chiefly hunters, but the Negro invaders brought pastoral and agricultural pursuits and introduced polished stone and iron. Very few monuments of the earlier ages have survived. The great stone ruins **(Zimbabwe)** of Rhodesia have been variously dated from the 10th century B.C. to the 15th century A.D. They may have been built by the Bantu, though the weight of expert opinion seems to favor the Sabaeans from the Yemen (10th century A.D.) or Dravidians from India.

c. 1st to 6th centuries A.D. The **kingdom of Axum** in northern Ethiopia and in southwestern Arabia (obelisks of Axum); direct contact with the Greek world; conversion of the country to Christianity by **Frumentius** (early 4th century). The connection with the Christian east was broken by the Arab conquests (640–).

640–710. CONQUEST OF NORTH AFRICA BY THE ARABS, beginning with Egypt and spreading westward *(p. 208 et seq.).*

c. 980. Settlement of Arabs from Muscat and Persians from Shiraz and Bushire along the eastern coast, south as far as Cape Corrientes. They founded Mogdishu, Melinde, Mombasa, Kilwa (Quiloa), and Sofala and traded with the interior natives in slaves, ivory, and gold that was shipped to India and Arabia.

10th century. Apogee of the kingdom of Ghana (capital Kumbi), which had been founded in the 4th century, supposedly by people of Semitic extraction. It extended from near the Atlantic coast almost to Timbuktu and was an essentially Negro state consisting of a group of federated tribes with a surprisingly developed culture (visits of the Arabs Ibn Haukal and Masudi in the late 10th century). There appears to have been an active trade with Morocco by way of the Sahara.

1054. Beginning of the **Islamic conquest** of West Africa by the Almoravids under Abdallah ben Yassin. Several of the native dynasties

Zimbabwe stone ruins of Rhodesia

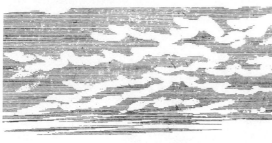

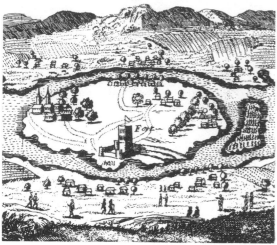

Magical Sofala in Mozambique

were converted, though the masses appear to have retained their original beliefs.

1076. The Almoravids pillaged Kumbi, the capital of Ghana, which never entirely recovered. Its decline was evidently hastened by the growing barrenness of the region. The **breakup of the Ghana Empire** led to the formation (11th century) of succession states (Diara, which existed till 1754, Soso, the two Mossi states south of the bend of the Niger, and Manding). Both the rulers of Manding and Songhoy were converted to Islam, Songhoy being a great empire which rose (c. 690) on the middle Niger and came to divide West Africa with Manding.

1203. **Sumanguru,** greatest of the rulers of Soso, plundered Kumbi.

1224. Sumanguru conquered and annexed Manding.

1235. **Sun Diata,** powerful king of the Mandingos, defeated the ruler of Soso and re-established his independence. In 1240 he destroyed Kumbi.

1307–1332. **Apogee of the Mandingo Empire** under **Gongo Musa,** who extended his dominions until they covered most of West Africa, after defeating and subjecting the Songhoy Empire (1325). Brilliant culture of Timbuktu (founded 12th century).

1352–1353. The great Arab traveler, **Ibn Batuta,** having crossed the Sahara, visited the Mandingo Empire, of which he wrote a description.

1433. The Tuaregs from the Sahara took and sacked Timbuktu.

1433. The **Portuguese explorers** first rounded Cape Bojador, beginning a long series of expeditions along the coast *(p. 377).*

1468. The Songhoy ruler recaptured Timbuktu from the Tuaregs.

1471. The Portuguese founded the post of San Jorge d'el Mina on the Guinea coast.

1490. The Portuguese ascended the Congo for about 200 miles and converted the king of the Congo Empire (14th century–). They established a post at **São Salvador** and exercised a wide influence in the region until the end of the 16th century.

1493–1529. **Greatness of the Songhoy Empire** under **Askia Mohammed,** who conquered the larger part of the Mandingo Empire and pushed his conquests to the east beyond the Niger. Visit of Leo Africanus (1507).

1505–1507. The Portuguese took Sofala and Kilwa from the Arabs and founded Mozambique. In 1513 they ascended the Zambezi, establishing posts at Sena and Tete. Missionaries probably penetrated much of the hinterland, but details are not known.

(Cont. p. 543.)

E. Asia During the Middle Ages

1. *Persia, 1349–1497*

(From p. 283)

1349. The end of the troubled reign of **Nushirwan** was also the end of the dynasty of the Il-Khans of Persia. They were succeeded by

1336–1411. The Jalayrs, in Iraq and Azerbaijan;

1313–1393. The Muzaffarids in Fars, Kirman, and Kurdistan;

1337–1381. The Sarbadarids in Khorasan. The Muzaffarids and Sarbadarids were overthrown by Timur, and the Jalayrs by

1378–1469. The **Turkomans of the Black Sheep,** who ruled Azerbaijan and Armenia until they were succeeded by

1387–1502. The **Turkomans of the White Sheep.**

1369–1405. **TIMUR** (Tamerlane), the vizir of the Mongol Chagatay Khan Suyurghatmish,

usurped the power of his master. Between the years 1380 and 1387 he overran Khorasan, Jurjan, Mazandaran, Sijistan, Afghanistan, Fars, Azerbaijan, and Kurdistan. In 1391 he completely defeated Toqtamish, the khan of the Golden Horde.

1393. **Timur took Baghdad** and reduced Mesopotamia. After an invasion of India (1397) he marched against Anatolia and routed the Ottoman Turks at **Angora** *(p. 344).* The empire of the Timurids (until 1500) was soon restricted to Transoxania and eastern Persia.

1404–1447. **SHAH RUKH,** fourth son of Timur, whose reign was noted for its splendor. He carried on successful campaigns against Kara Yusuf, head of the Turkoman dynasty of the Black Sheep (1390–1420), who ruled Azerbaijan, Shirvan, and other regions of the north-

Timur's wars, 1380–1387

west. Kara Yusuf was obliged to recognize the suzerainty of the Timurids, though Kara Yusuf and his successor, Kara Iskender (1420–1438), and Jehan Shah (1435–1467) were effective rulers of all northwestern Persia. Jehan Shah for a brief period (1458) held even Herat.

1452–1469. Abu Said, last of the Timurid dynasty. This period was marked by the great expansion of the Turkoman power under

1453–1478. UZUN HASAN, of the dynasty of the White Sheep. This dynasty had established itself under Hasan's grandfather, Osman Beg Kara Iluk (d. 1435) and ruled the territory about Diabekr. Hasan rapidly extended his authority over Armenia and Kurdistan. His defeat by the Ottoman Turks (1461) turned his attention eastward, and led to five large-scale raids into Georgia.

1467. Uzun Hasan defeated and killed Jehan Shah of the Black Sheep and took over his territories.

1469. Uzun defeated, captured, and killed Abu Said, the Timurid sultan, who had marched against him. Thereupon Hasan became effective ruler of Armenia, Kurdistan, Azerbaijan, and Iran. He entered with Venice into a treaty directed against the Ottoman Turks, but the artillery that was sent him never reached him, and he was defeated by Mohammed II in

1473. The battle of Erzinjan (Otluk-beli). On his death he was succeeded by his son

1478–1490. JAQUB, who continued his father's policies and gave the country firm and enlightened rule.

1492–1497. RUSTAM SHAH, who succeeded to the throne after a severe dynastic conflict. His death was followed by confusion and by the emergence of the new Safavid dynasty, under Shah Ismail *(Cont. p. 545.)*

2. *India*

(From p. 154)

a. NORTHERN INDIA, 500–1199

The **White Huns** or Hephthalites, a branch of the Mongol Juan-juan who dominated Central Asia (407–553), had occupied Bactria (425) and, after defeat by Sassanid Bahram Gor (428), Gandhara. Victory over Sassanid Peroz (484) freed them for raids from the Punjab into Hindustan.

c. 500–502. Toramana ruled as far as Eran.

502–c. 528. Mihirakula from Sialkot controlled Gwalior and Kashmir. Bhanugupta probably expelled him from Eran (510). Yasodharman of Mandasor (?) boasts (533) of victory over him. Although the Huns in Central Asia were crushed by Turks and Sassanians (553–567), their chiefs kept rank in the Punjab and Rajputana till the 11th century.

606–647. HARSHA, fourth king of Thanesar, north of Delhi (new era Oct. 606), succeeded his brother-in-law as king of Kanauj (royal title 612), and quickly conquered an empire across northern India, to which he left no heir. He received an embassy (643) from the Emperor T'ang T'ai-tsung. A poet and dramatist, he patronized men of letters. He is well known through **Bana's** poetic romance *Harshacharita,* and by the *Hsi yü chi (Record of Western Lands)* of his guest, the pilgrim **Hsüan-tsang,** whose exact observations in India (630–643) have given priceless guidance to modern archaeology.

Tantrism meanwhile sought to secure for its adepts in magic arts, through esoteric texts (*tantra*) and charms, rapid attainment of Buddhahood or at least supernatural powers. Partial syncretism with Sivaism led to a cult of Vairochana and various new divinities, largely terrible or erotic. Spells (*dharanis*) appear early (Chinese trans. 4th century), but the *Panchakrama* is in part the work of Sakyamitra (c. 850). Tantrism seems to have flourished chiefly along the northern borderland. Buddhism, however, progressively disappeared from India from the 9th century, lingering in Bengal and Bihar until the Moslem conquest (1202). It was largely absorbed by Hinduism.

Marriage of Siva and Parvati, 10th-century stone from Pala

647. A second Chinese embassy, under Wang Hsüan-tse, having been attacked by a usurper on a local throne (Tirhut, north of Patna ?), secured 7000 troops from Amsuvarman, king of Nepal, and 1200 from his son-in-law, Srong-tsan-sgampo, king of Tibet; captured the malefactor, and haled him to Ch'ang-an (648).

c. 730–c. 740. YASOVARMAN, king of Kanauj, an author, patronized the Prakrit poet **Vakpatiraja** and **Bhavabhuti,** a Sanskrit dramatist ranked by Indian criticism next to **Kalidasa.**

c. 725–1197. The Pala Buddhist kings ruled Bengal (till c. 1125) and Magadha. Leading rulers: Dharmapala (c. 770–c. 883), and Deva-pala (c. 881–c. 883), who endowed a monastery founded at Nalanda by Balaputradeva, king of Sumatra.

c. 1125–c. 1225? **Senas** from the Carnatic gradually advanced from North Orissa into Bengal.

c. 1169–c. 1199. Lakshmanasena patronized Jayadeva, whose *Gitagovinda,* mystic call to love of Krishna, is considered a Sanskrit masterpiece. Tightening of caste restrictions was accompanied by origin of **kulinism:** prohibition of marriage of any girl below her own caste, which led to infanticide; and rise in caste by marriage to man of higher caste, which led to polygamy of high-caste husbands to collect dowries.

b. WESTERN INDIA, 490–1490

Western India, thanks to many impregnable fortresses in Rajputana, was usually divided among local dynasties from the time of the Gupta power to the advent of the Moslems.

c. 490–766. A dynasty of **Maitrakas,** foreigners of the Rajput type, usually independent at Valabhi in Surashtra, created a Buddhist scholastic center which rivaled Nalanda. Their gifts reveal that Buddhist images were honored with *puja* of the kind devoted to Hindu gods.

c. 550–861. The **GURJARA** horde of central Asiatic nomads established a dynasty of twelve kings at Mandor in central Rajputana. Two retired to Jain contemplation, and a third to self-starvation.

712– **Arab raids** from Sind devastated Gujarat and Broach (724–743) and finally shattered the Maitraka dynasty (766).

c. 740–1036. The **GURJARA-PRATHIHARA DYNASTY,** by uniting much of northern India, excluded the Moslems till the end of the 10th century. Prominent early rulers were Nagabhata I (c. 740–c. 760), who defeated the Arabs; Vatsaraja (c. 775–c. 800); and Nagabhata II (c. 800–836), conqueror of Kanauj.

746–c. 974. The Chapas (or Chapotkatas), a Gurjara clan, founded Anahillapura (or Anandapura, 746), the principal city of western India until the 15th century.

831–1310. A Dravidian dynasty of **Chandellas** (in present Bundelkhand) built numerous Vaishnava temples, notably at Khajuraho, under Yasovarman (c. 930–954) and Dhanga (954–1002).

c. 840–c. 890. **Mihira,** or Bhoja, devoted to Vishnu and the Sun, ruled from the Sutlej to the Narmada, but failed to subdue Kashmir.

c. 950–c. 1200. The **Paramaras of Dhara,** near Indore, were known for two rulers: Munja (974–c. 994) who invaded the Deccan, and Bhoja (c. 1018–1060), author of books on astronomy, poetics, and architecture, and founder of a Sanskrit college.

c. 974–c. 1240. The **Chalukya** or Solanki Rajput clan, led by Mularaja (known dates 974–995) ruled from Anahillapura over Surashtra and Mt. Abu.

977–1186. The **Ghaznavid** (Yamini) **dynasty** ruled at Ghazni and Lahore. It was founded by **Subaktagin** (977–997), a Turkish slave converted to Islam, who extended his rule from the Oxus to the Indus and broke the power of a Hindu confederacy which included King Jaipal of Bhatinda, the Gurjara-Prathihara king of Kanauj, and the Chandella King Dhanga.

998–1030. **MAHMUD OF GHAZNI** made 17

INDIA *to the* MOSLEM CONQUEST

plundering raids into the Punjab (defeat of Jaipal, 1001) to Kangra (1009), Mathura and Kanauj (1018–1019), Gwalior (1022), and Somnath (1024–1026). Vast destruction, pillage of immensely rich Hindu temples, and wholesale massacre resulted only in enrichment of Ghazni and annexation of the Punjab. Ghazni, heir to the rich artistic heritage of the Samanids of northeastern Persia, was now one of the most brilliant capitals of the Islamic world. **Alberuni** (973–1048) of Khiva, the leading scientist of his time, followed Mahmud to the Punjab, learned Sanskrit, and wrote the invaluable *Tahkik-i Hind* (*Inquiry into India*).

1093–1143. The Chalukya ruler, **Jayasimha Siddharaja,** a patron of letters, although himself a Saiva, organized disputations on philosophy and religion, and favored a Jain monk, **Hemachandra,** who converted and dominated

1143–1172. **Kumarapala.** As a good Jain, he decreed respect for life (*ahimsa*), prohibited alcohol, dice, and animal fights, and rescinded a law for confiscation of property of widows without sons. He also built (c. 1169) a new

edifice about the Saiva temple of Somanatha, which had been reconstructed by **Bhimadeva I** (1022–1062) after destruction by the Moslems.

1151–1206. The Shansabani Persian princes of Ghur (Ghor) having burned Ghazni (1151), drove the Yamini to the Punjab and deposed them there (1186).

1172–1176. **Ajayapala,** a Saiva reactionary, ordered the massacre of Jains and sack of their temples until he was assassinated, when Jain rule was restored under a mayor of the palace whose descendants displaced the dynasty (c. 1240).

Two Jain temples at Mt. Abu are the work of a governor, **Vimala Saha** (1031), and a minister, **Tejpala** (1230). Built of white marble with a profusion of ornamented colonnades, brackets, and elaborately carved ceilings, they are the most elegant version of the northern or Indo-Aryan architectural style.

Kashmir, already (c. 100 A.D.) an important home of the Sarvastivadin Buddhist sect, remained a center for Buddhist studies (till the 10th century; degenerate before the Moslem conquest, 1340) and of Sanskrit literature (until today). Its history from c. 700 is rather fully known through the *Rajatarangini*, the only extant document by **Kalhana** (c. 1100), the sole early Indian historian, who consulted literary sources and inscriptions but accepted even absurd tradition without criticism.

1175-1206. Mohammed of Ghur, Mu'izz-ud-Din, undertook conquest of Hindustan by capture of Multan and Uch. He ruled from Ghazni as governor for his elder brother, **Ghiyas-ud-Din Mohammed,** whom he succeeded as ruler of Ghur (1203).

1192. A battle at Tararori (14 miles from Thanesar) decisively crushed a new Hindu confederacy led by the Chauhan king of Ajmer and Delhi. Cumbersome traditional tactics, disunited command, and caste restrictions handicapped the Hindu armies in conflict with the mounted archers from the northwest. Victory led to occupation of Delhi (1193), to conquest of Bihar, where the organized Buddhist community was extinguished (c. 1197), Bengal (c. 1199), and the Chandella state in Bundelkhand. Mohammed appointed **Kutb-ud-din Aibak,** a slave from Turkestan, viceroy of his Indian conquests, and left him full discretion (1192, confirmed 1195).

1206-1266. A dynasty of slave kings, the first of six to rule at Delhi (until 1526), was founded by Aibak (killed playing polo, 1210).

The numerically weak early Moslem rulers in India were forced to employ Hindu troops and civilian agents, welcome allegiance of Hindu landholders, and afford their native subjects much the same limited protection (including tacit religious toleration) and justice to which they were accustomed. Rebels, both Hindu and Moslem, were slaughtered with ruthless barbarity.

1211-1236. Shams-ud-din Iltutmish, ablest slave and son-in-law of Aibak, succeeded to his lands in the Ganges Valley only, but recovered the upper Punjab (1217), Bengal (1225),

the lower Punjab with Sind (1228), and Gwalior after a long siege (Feb.–Dec. 1232). He advanced to sack Ujjain (1234).

1229. He was invested as sultan of India by the Abbasid caliph of Baghdad.

Islamic architects brought to India a developed tradition of a spacious, light, and airy prayer chamber covered by arch, vault, and dome, erected with aid of concrete and mortar, and ornamented solely with color and flat linear, usually conventional, decoration. This formula was applied with recognition of local structural styles and of the excellence of Hindu ornamental design. Aibak built at Delhi (1193-1196) with the spoils of 27 temples a mosque of Hindu appearance to which he added (1198) an Islamic screen of arches framed with Indian carving. He began (before 1206) a tower for call to prayer, which was finished (1231-1232) and named *Kutb Minar* to honor a Moslem saint (d. 1235) by Iltutmish, who also enlarged the mosque in strictly Islamic style.

Upon the death of Iltutmish actual power passed to a group of 40 Turks who divided all offices save that of sultan, and controlled the succession.

1266-1290. A new dynasty at Delhi was founded by **Balban** (d. 1287), a slave purchased by Iltutmish (1233); made chamberlain (1242), father-in-law and lieutenant (1249-1252 and 1255-1266) of King Mahmud (1246-1266). Balban as king, aided by an effective army and corps of royal news-writers, repressed the 40 nobles, ended highway robbery in south and east, and rebellion in Bengal. His son repelled the Mongols established in Ghazni (since 1221), but was killed by them (1285).

The **tomb of Balban** is the first structure in India built with true arches instead of Hindu corbelling.

1290-1320. The **Khalji dynasty of Delhi** was founded by **Firuz** of the Khalji tribe of Turks, long resident among the Afghans. Senile mild-

Buddha, 7th-8th-century Kashmir

ness led him to release in Bengal 1000 Thugs (murderers in honor of Siva's consort Kali) captured in Delhi.

1296-1316. Ala-ud-din, his nephew and murderer, bought allegiance with booty secured by surprise attack upon Devagiri in Maharashtra (1294-1295). He consolidated the empire.

1297. He conquered and despoiled Gujarat with its rich port Cambay. Frequent revolts prompted a program of repression which included espionage; confiscation of wealth (especially of Hindus), endowments, and tax-exempt lands; prohibition of liquor and all social gatherings. Mongol invasions (1299 and 1303) led to

1303. Decrees which by fixing low prices for all products permitted reduction of army pay and increase of strength to nearly 500,000 cavalry. Mongol armies were destroyed (1304 and 1306) and expeditions, usually led by a eunuch, Kafur, entitled Malik Naib, effected

1305-1313. Conquest of Malwa (1305) and the Deccan: Devagiri (1306-1307, annexed 1313), Warangal (1308), the Hoysala capital at Dvarasamudra and that of the Pandyas at Madura (1310-1311), and the central Deccan (1313), with enormous treasure.

The *Alai Darwaza* (1311), southern gateway of a proposed vast enlargement of Aibak's mosque, represents the finest ornamental architecture of the early Delhi sultanate, fortunately continued in Gujarat. **Amir Khusrav** (1253-1325), greatest Indian poet to write in Persian, was son of a Turk who had fled before Jenghiz Khan to Patiala. He was prolific as court poet to Ala-ud-din and later in religious retirement. Another excellent Persian poet of Delhi was **Hasan-i-Dihlavi,** who died at Daulatabad (1338).

1320-1413. The **Tughluk dynasty** was founded

Tughlakabad, built by Ghiyas-ud-din Tughluk, 1320-1413

by the old but vigorous **Ghiyas-ud-din Tughluk** (d. 1325), a pure Turk who boasted 29 victories over the Mongols. He reduced to provincial status Warangal (1323) and eastern Bengal (1324). He encouraged agriculture, corrected abuses in tax collection, and perfected a postal system by which runners covered 200 miles a day. At Multan he erected a splendid octagonal tomb of Persian character for the saint, Rukn-i-Alam. Increasing austerity marked the architecture of his house.

1325-1351. Mohammed Tughluk hastened to the throne by deliberate parricide. A military genius, his administrative measures were warped and defeated by his own unwisdom, inordinate pride, inflexibility, and ferocious cruelty. Revolt of a cousin in the Deccan (1326) led to

1327. Transfer of the capital to Devagiri, renamed Daulatabad, handsomely rebuilt with European feudal fortifications about an impregnable rock citadel. As a punitive measure

1329. All remaining citizens of Delhi were forced to move thither. He raised taxes so high in the Doab as to force rebellion and then destroyed both fields and cultivators.

1330. Emission of copper fiat money equivalent to the silver *tanga* of 140 grains failed because of easy counterfeiting.

1334. Ibn Batuta, a Moorish traveler, was welcomed with fantastic gifts like other foreigners who might help in world conquest. He left on a mission to China (1342).

1334-1378. Madura revolted under a Moslem dynasty, ended by Vijayanagar.

1337-1338. An army of 100,000 horse, sent through Kangra into the Himalaya to conquer Tibet and China, was destroyed by rains, disease, and hill-men; and with it resources needed to avert

1338. Loss of Bengal to the house of Balban, independent until 1539. Moslem architects used at Gaur, its capital, local brick and terra cotta to build, e.g., the bold *Dakhil Gateway* (1459-1474?).

1340. Mohammed sought recognition (received 1344) from the caliph in Egypt. He vainly tried to restore prosperity by redistricting, and appointing undertakers to supervise fixed (unscientific) crop rotation, and to maintain a mounted militia. Increased penal severity culminated when he began

1344-1345. Wholesale extermination of his centurions, revenue collectors who usually failed to meet his quotas. Rebellion begun by them in Gujarat led to permanent loss of the whole south.

1346-1589. Shah Mirza (1346-1349) founded a Moslem dynasty in Kashmir. He substituted the usual land tax of one-sixth for the extortionate rates of the Hindu kings.

1347-1527. The **Bahmani dynasty,** founded by rebels against Mohammed Tughluk, who elected **Bahman Shah** (1347-1348), at first ruled four provinces: Gulbarga, Daulatabad, Berar, and Bidar. The capital at Gulbarga and many other fortresses were built or strengthened with European science to serve against Gujarat, Malwa, and Khandesh in the northwest, the Gonds, Orissa, and Telingana in the northeast, and Vijayanagar in the south.

1351-1388. Firuz Tughluk (b. 1305) restored rational administration. He exacted tribute from Orissa (1360), Kangra (1361), and Sind (1363). He refused to disturb the Bahmani kingdom of the Deccan, its tributary Warangal, or the rebels from it, the khans of Khandesh between the Tapti and Narbada (independent 1382). He built several towns, notably Jaunpur north of Benares (1359), many mosques, palaces, hospitals, baths, tanks, canals, and bridges; but with cheap materials and little artistic quality. His successors were too weak to prevent further dissolution of the empire.

1358-1375. The Bahmani **Mohammed I** gave lasting organization to the government of the new dynasty.

1363-1364. Warangal was forced to cede Golconda, with much treasure.

1367. Victory of the Bahmani over immense but ineffectual armies of Vijayanagar. It was the first of several successes and was won with artillery served by Europeans and Ottoman Turks. The subsequent massacre of 400,000 Hindus led to agreement to spare noncombatants. The **Great Mosque at Gulbarga** was completely roofed with domes.

1392-1531. Malwa (formally independent in 1401) was ruled by the Ghuris and the Khaljis (1436). **Hushang Shah** (1405-1435) fortified the capital at Mandu above the Narbada, and erected there the durbar hall *Hindola Mahall,* together with a great mosque. These buildings are impressive through structural design rather than surface ornament.

1394-1479. Jaunpur, with Oudh, became independent under the Sharki (eastern) dynasty, founded by the eunuch, Malik Sarvar, and his adopted sons, probably of African Negroid descent. The second ruler, **Ibrahim Shah** (1402-1436), was a cultured and liberal patron of learning.

1396-1572. Gujarat prospered under a Moslem Rajput dynasty.

1398-1399. INVASION OF TIMUR (Tamerlane) of Samarkand, who had already conquered Persia, Mesopotamia, and Afghanistan *(p. 348).* He desolated the whole kingdom of Delhi. Crossing the Indus (Sept. 24), he marched 80 miles a day for two days (Nov. 6-7) to overtake fugitives at Bhatnair, massacred 100,000 Hindu prisoners before Delhi (Dec. 12), sacked the city (Dec. 17), stormed Meerut (Jan. 9), and fought his way back along the Himalaya to the Indus (Mar. 19).

1411-1442. Ahmad Shah built Ahmadabad as a capital and beautified it with the *Tin Darwaza* (Triple Gateway) and *Great Mosque,* one of the most imposing structures in the world.

1414-1526. The **KINGDOM OF DELHI,** reduced to the Jumna Valley, with tenuous control over the Punjab, was ruled by the Sayyids, who laid nebulous claim to Arab descent from the Prophet, but could collect their revenues only by force. Later the Afghan **Buhlul Lodi** (1451-1489) founded the Lodi dynasty.

1420-1470. Zain-ul-Abidin, learned and tolerant, recalled the exiles, permitted Brahman

Rock temple by the sea near Madras, last remaining edifice of the Pallava culture

Descent of Ganga, *7th-century rock relief at Mahabalipuram, south of Madras*

rites, employed convicts on public works, and exacted communal responsibility for order.

1422-1436. Ahmad Shah enrolled 3000 foreign mounted archers, who, like the Turks, Arabs, Mongols, and Persians, when employed as ministers, earned by superior qualities and disdain the envy and hostility (massacre 1446) of the native-born Deccanis, Africans, and Muwallads, half-breed offspring of the latter.

1429. Bidar, rebuilt under Persian decorative influence, became capital.

1458-1511. Mahmud I, called Begarha (Two Forts) because of his conquest of Girnar (with Kathiawar, 1469-1470) and Champanir (near Baroda, 1483-1484), when 700 Hindu Rajputs preferred ritual death (*jauhar*) to Islam. He built magnificently and in exquisite taste: the great mosque at Champanir; the palace at Sarkhej; the step-well at Adalaj; and the pierced stone window-screens of Sidi Sayyid's mosque. The tiny Rani Sipari mosque at Ahmadabad (1514) displays harmonious perfection of the ornamental style.

1463-1482. Mohammed III conquered the Konkan and Telingana to both coasts. He died at 28 of drink, the curse of nearly all his house, and of remorse at having slain (while drunk) his best minister, Mahmud Gavan, the builder of the large quadrangular college at Bidar.

1490. Ahmadnagar (1490-1633), Bijapur (1490-1686), and Berar (1490-1574) became in fact independent of Mahmud (1482-1518), the incompetent prisoner of his minister, Kasim Barid, whose dynasty mounted the throne of Bidar in 1527 (till 1619). *(Cont. p. 548.)*

c. SOUTHERN INDIA, 100-1565

100-200. King Karikalan of early Tamil poems is credited with construction of a great irrigation dam on the Kaveri River, east of Trichinopoly.

c. 300-888. The **Pallava warrior dynasty** of foreign (Pahlava?) origin, using Prakrit and later Sanskrit, held from Kanchi (near Madras) hegemony of the Deccan, which it disputed with the Chalukyas of Vatapi (550-753), the Rashtrakutas of Malkhed (753-973) and the Chalukyas of Vengi (611-1078).

c. 500-753. The **first Chalukya dynasty** in Maharashtra advanced from Aihole on the upper Kistna to near-by Vatapi (or Badami, c. 550) and to Banavasi (566-597) at the expense of the Kadambas. Construction of the earliest temples at Aihole was followed by that of Mahakutesvara (c. 525) and completion of the cave-temple to Vishnu at Vatapi (578).

c. 575. The Pallava **Simhavishnu** seized the Chola basin of the Kaveri, which his family held until after 812.

c. 600-625. The Pallava **Mahendravarman I,** converted from Jainism to Sivaism, destroyed a Jain temple, but dug the first (Saiva) cave-temples in the south (at Trichinopoly, Chingleput, etc.). From his reign date **Buddhist monasteries** (in part excavated) and *stupas* on the Samkaram Hills (near Vizagapatam).

609-642. The Chalukya **Pulakesin II** placed his brother on the throne of Vengi, where he ruled as viceroy (611-632), repulsed an attack by Harsha of Kanauj (c. 620), sent an embassy to Khosroes II of Persia (625), and enthroned a son, who headed a branch dynasty in Gujarat and Surat (c. 640-740). Hsüan-tsang (641) describes the prosperity of the country just before the Pallavas pillaged the capital (642), a disaster that was avenged by pillage of the Pallava capital, Kanchi, by Vikramaditya (c. 674).

611-c. 1078. The **Eastern Chalukyas** of Vengi (independent after 629-632), were continually at war with Kalinga on the north, the Rashtrakutas on the west, and the Pandyas on the south.

c. 625-c. 645. The Pallava **Narasimhavarman** defeated Chalukya Pulakesin II (c. 642) and took Vatapi. He defeated also his southern neighbors and enthroned Manavalla in Ceylon (?). He improved the port of Mamallapuram, near Kanchi, and cut there the first of five *raths,* monolithic sanctuaries in the form of cars, the earliest monuments of the Dravidian style; also the cliff-relief depicting the descent of the River Ganges from Heaven.

c. 675-c. 705. The Pallava **Narasimhavarman II** built in stone and brick the Shore temple at Mamalla, and the central shrine of the Kailasa temple at Kanchi, completed by his son.

c. 700. Conversion of King Srimaravarman to Sivaism by Tirujnana Sambandhar, the first of 63 *nayanmars* or Tamil saints, led the king to impale 8000 Jains at Madura in a single day, since celebrated by the Saivas. Another saint, Manikka Vasagar (9th century), wrote poems of his own religious experience which correspond to our *Psalms.* The Tamil Vaishnavas, too, had their saints, twelve *alvars*, who also expressed emotional religion and whose works were collected c. 1000–1050.

733–746. The Chalukya **Vikramaditya II** thrice took Kanchi, and distributed presents to the temples. He imported Tamil artists and his queen commissioned Gunda, "the best southern architect," to build the temple of Virupaksha. The **frescoes of Ajanta caves** 1 and 2 are believed to date from this period. So too the Saiva and Vaishnava sculptures of the Das Avatara cave-temple at Ellora.

c. 735–c. 800. Nandivarman II, a collateral kinsman twelve years of age, accepted the Pallava throne offered him by the ministers and elders, who defended him against rival claimants.

753–973. The **Rashtrakuta dynasty** of Canarese kings, already enthroned in North Berar (631) and in Gujarat (c. 700) was elevated to empire by Dantidurga, who soon overthrew the Chalukyas.

758–772. Rashtrakuta **Krishnaraja I** cut from the cliff and decorated with Saiva sculpture the Kailasa (natha) temple at Ellora to rival that of Kanchi. To the same Canarese dynasty if not to the same reign belong the equally classic Saiva sculptures of the **cave-temples at Elephanta** (an island in Bombay harbor). The successors of Krishnaraja were Govinda II (779) and Dhruva (783), who defeated the Pallava Nandivarman II and the Gurjara Vatsaraja.

774–13th century. The **Eastern Gangas** ruled Kalinga, waging constant war with the Chalukyas of Vengi and the princes of Orissa.

c. 788–c. 850. Samkara of Malabar revitalized the Vedanta, creating an unobtrusively new but consistent synthesis of tradition, which he speciously traced to the *Upanishads* and to Badarayana, author of the *Brahma sutra*. His doctrine became accepted as orthodox Brahmanism. He taught a rigorous monism (*advaita*) which admits release for the soul only in union with *brahman* through the higher knowledge that the phenomenal world (and individual personality) do not exist save for those who think objectively. For these latter, however, engrossed in worldly phenomena (*maya*), he recognized that a simpler kind of knowledge was necessary; and for them he was a practical apostle of Sivaism. Although he denounced Buddhism he imitated its moral teaching by opposition to sectarian extravagance, its ecclesiastical strength by organization of an ascetic order for zealous youth (hitherto debarred till later life from religious activity). He founded four scholastic monasteries (*maths*) which still survive at Sringeri (Mysore), Puri (Orissa), Badrinath (the Himalaya), and Dwaraka (western Kathiawar). **Ramanuja** (c. 1055–1137) of Kanchi (Conjeeveran, near Madras) also interpreted the Vedanta. For him souls are distinct from *brahman*, whose representatives they are, and from the material world with which they are entangled. It is through piety toward Vishnu and his saving grace that they may recover their divine nature.

c. 790. The Chalukya **Vikramaditya II** was defeated by the Rashtrakuta Dhruva (779–794).

794–813. Rashtrakuta **Govinda II** seized Malwa with Chitor from the Gurjaras, and enthroned his brother as head of a second Rashtrakuta dynasty in Gujarat (till c. 900). He took from the Pallava (c. 800) tribute and territory as far as the Tungabhadra.

c. 812–844. Pallava **Nandivarman III** helped Govinda III to crown Sivamara II as Ganga king of Mysore. At the same time

c. 812– Pandya **Varaguna I** imposed suzerainty on the Pallavas.

817–877. Rashtrakuta **Amoghavarsha I** moved the capital from Nasik to Malkhed, the better to carry on war against the Vengi. He abdicated and died in saintly Jain fashion. The last of his line found death in Jain starvation (982).

c. 825–1312. The **Yadavas,** early suzerains of a score of petty vassal kings, occupied in turn three capitals: (modern) Chandor and Sinnar (1069), both near Nasik, and the fortress of Devagiri (c. 1111) renamed Daulatabad (1327).

Raja in Procession, *fresco in Cave One at Ajanta*

They fell heir to the northern possessions of the Chalukyas of Kalyani.

843-1249. The **Silaharas,** another petty dynasty, under Chalukya or Rashtrakuta suzerainty, provided 45 kings in three different areas along the west coast north of Goa. The Parsis (Parsees), refugees in Kathiawar, had probably already reached Thana near Bombay during the 8th century.

844-888. Gunaga **Vijayaditya III** fought successfully against western and northern enemies and by the defeat of the Pallava Aparajita and the Pandya Varaguna II helped the rising Chola to supersede both. His association of two brothers as kings-consort led ultimately to succession struggles which placed eight kings on the throne in ten years (918–927).

c. 844-870. Pallava **Nripatungavarman** recovered Tanjore and obtained the submission of Varaguna II (862–) and of Ganga Prithivipati I.

c. 870-888. Pallava **Aparajitavarman,** with Ganga Prithivipati, crushed Varaguna II, but was himself defeated and killed by the Chola Aditya I. Numerous Pallava chiefs continued to rule locally. Perungina, in the Tamil South, claimed imperial titles for at least 31 years.

888-1267. The **Chola dynasty of Tamil kings** from Tanjore, under **Aditya I** (870–c. 906), with the aid of the Chalukyas of Vengi, replaced the Pallavas at Kanchi. The Chola territory extended along the east coast from Telugu to the Pandya lands.

927-934. A royal inscription is the earliest extant specimen of Telugu literature. It records the erection of a Saiva temple and sectarian hostel.

973-c. 1190. The Chalukyas of Kalyani (near Bombay) were restored to power by Taila II (or Tailapa), who spent his reign fighting the Cholas and Paramaras.

985-1014. Chola **Rajaraja I** acquired hegemony over the Deccan.

994. Conquest of the Cheras and Pandyas justified the title *Thrice-crowned Chola,* marking the first historical union of the southern peninsula.

999. The conquest of Vengi drove a usurper from the East Chalukyan throne and was extended (1000) to Kalinga.

1001-1004. A successful **invasion of Ceylon**

Statue of Siva, from Elephanta cave-temples

Sculptures in the temple at Ellora

permitted assignment of Singhalese revenues to the Saiva great pagoda of Rajarajesvara, which Rajaraja I built at Tanjore, the masterpiece of baroque Dravidian architecture. He also endowed a Buddhist monastery built at Negapatam by a king of Srivijaya (Sumatra).

1014-1042. Rajendra Choladeva, who had helped his father since 1002.

1014-1017. A second invasion of Ceylon secured the regalia and treasure of the Pandya kings, so that a son of the Chola could be consecrated king of Pandya.

1024. An **invasion of Bengal** enabled the Chola to assume a new title and establish a new capital near Trichinopoly.

c. 1030. By use of sea power, the Chola exacted tribute from Pegu, Malaiyur (Malay Peninsula), and the empire of Srivijaya.

1040-1068. (Chalukya) **Somesvara I** founded Kalyani, the capital until c. 1156. He drowned himself with Jain rites in the Tungabhadra, a sacred river of the south.

1042-1052. Chola **Rajadhiraja I,** who had aided his father since 1018. He was killed in battle at Koppam against Somesvara I of Kalyani.

1062-1070. Chola **Virarajendra** defeated the Chalukyas and gave his daughter to Vikramaditya VI. He founded a vedic college and a hospital. His two sons fell into conflict and extinguished their line by assassination (1074).

1073-1327. The **Hoysalas,** at first a petty dynasty, ruled at Dvarasamudra (Halebid) in Mysore.

1074-1267. The **Chalukya-Chola dynasty,** founded by Rajendra, son and grandson of Chola princesses, king of Vengi (1070–), who took the vacant throne of Kanchi (1074) and thenceforth ruled Vengi through a viceroy. His authority was recognized by the Ganga king of Kalinga.

1075-1125. **Vikramaditya VI** of Kalyani began a new era in place of the Saka era, but with small success. One of his many inscriptions is at Nagpur in the northern Deccan, while in the south one of his generals repelled the Hoysalas. His people enjoyed unwonted security. He built temples to Vishnu, but made gifts also to two Buddhist monasteries which must have been among the last in the south to withstand Hindu reaction and absorption. **Bilhana of Kashmir,** in return for hospitality, a blue parasol, and an elephant, wrote the *Vikramankacharita* in praise of his host.

1076-1147. **Anantavarman Codaganga** extended his authority from the Ganges to the Godavari, and built at Puri (south of Cuttack) the temple of Jagannath (Vishnu) which, at first open to all Hindu castes, is now barred to fifteen. The great Sun temple, in form of a solar car, known as the *Black Pagoda*, at Konarak, may be earlier than its attribution to Ganga Narasimha (1238-1264).

1111-1141. **Bittideva,** independent, fought successfully against Chola, Pandya, and Chera. As viceroy before accession he was converted from Jainism to Vishnu by Ramanuja, at that time a refugee from Saiva persecution by the Cholas. He began construction at Belur and Halebid of temples in a distinctively ornate Hoysala style, featured especially by a high, richly carved plinth of stellate plan.

c. 1150-1323. The **Kakatiyas** reigned in the east at Kakati or Warangal between the Godavari and the Kistna. They held an important kingdom under **Ganapati** (1197-1259) and his daughter (1259-1288), whom Marco Polo knew.

c. 1156-1183. A revolt against the Chalukya ruler **Taila III** (known dates 1150-1155) led to usurpation by a general who was soon assassinated by Basava, who was in turn compelled to commit suicide. Basava created and organized the Lingayat sect of fanatic, anti-Brahman worshipers of Siva under a phallic emblem. The movement at the outset appeared in the form of a religious and social (equalitarian) war.

1183. Taila's son **Somesvara IV** regained Kalyani, but was unable to resist the Hoysalas (last date 1189).

1292-1342. The Hoysala ruler **Viraballala III** inherited an empire comprising most of southern India.

1327. After sack of Halebid by **Mohammed Tughluk,** Viraballala moved his capital to Tiruvannamalai (South Arcot).

c. 1335-1565. **Vijayanagar** (present Hampi), founded by two brothers from the region of Warangal, fought steadily against the Moslem sultans north of Kistna and Tungabhadra. It became an important center for Brahman studies and for Dravidian nationalism and art. **Madhava** wrote at Sringeri (c. 1380) the *Sarva darsana samgraha,* which remains the classic summary of the various Brahman philosophical points of view.

1520. Division of the Moslems into five rival sultanates (late 15th century) gave Krishnadeva (c. 1509-1529) a chance to win a victory over the sultan of Bijapur.

1542-1565. Ramaraja sought to profit by further division of the Moslems but provoked a coalition which crushed him and razed Vijayanagar.

d. CEYLON, 846-1284

846. The capital was moved south to Polonnaruva to escape Tamil invasions, which later culminated in

1001-1017. The **two great invasions** (1001-1004 and 1014-1017) by Chola Rajaraja and his son Rajendra.

1065-1120. **Vijayabahu** ruled prosperously despite further incursions (1046, 1055).

1164-1197. **Parakramabahu I** repelled the Tamils (1168), invaded Madura, and united the two rival monasteries.

1225-1260. **Parakramabahu II** repelled two attacks (c. 1236 and c. 1256) by a king of Tambralinga (Ligor on the Straits of Malacca), with Pandya help.

1284. The king sent a relic of the Buddha to Kublai Khan.

(Cont. p. 548.)

3. *China, 618–1471*

(From p. 158)

618-907. The **T'ANG DYNASTY,** founded by
618-626. **LI YÜAN** (T'ai Tsu) and his son Li Shih-min. The T'ang used Loyang and Ch'ang-an as eastern and western capitals. Sui institutions were in general retained. The central administrative organization remained essentially unchanged from this time until 1912. The emperor ruled through daily audience with a grand council composed of (1) heads of a secretariat and chancery, which for safety divided transaction of business (a feature later discarded); (2) representatives of the six ministries of civil office, finance, ceremonial, war, justice, and public works; and (3) specially appointed dignitaries. The censorate and nine independent offices, notably a clan court and a criminal high court, together with three technical services including the national college and flood-prevention bureau, reported to him directly. Although the empire was divided into ten (627), later fifteen (733), districts for supervisory purposes, the prefectures (*chou*) depended directly from the central administration, the prefect being responsible for duties corresponding to those of the six ministries. Each prefecture sent an annual quota of candidates to join graduates of two state universities in civil service examinations. These led to the eighth or ninth (bottom) ranks in the official hierarchy. Appointment to a corresponding office depended on a further searching examination before each term until the sixth rank was reached. Promotion was based on performance.

627-649. The reign of **T'AI TSUNG** (Li Shih-min) is illustrious not alone because of the military conquests which established stimulating contacts with Iranian and Indian civilizations, but still more for the liberal, tolerant spirit of the emperor and his patronage of art and letters.

630. The eastern Turks, who had attacked Ch'ang-an in 624 and 626, were crushed.

631-648. Chinese suzerainty was acknowledged by the petty states of western and eastern Turkestan. The western Turks were divided and defeated (641).

635. A Nestorian missionary, A-lo-pen, was officially welcomed to Ch'ang-an; and given (638) both freedom of the empire and an imperial church at the capital.

641. A Chinese princess was married to the first king of Tibet, Srong-tsan-sgam-po, and helped convert Tibet to Buddhism, later (after 749) modified by Padmasambhava toward Tantrism.

645. **Hsüan-tsang,** returned from a pilgrimage to India, recorded his precise observations, and headed a commission which translated 75 books in 1335 volumes, creating for the purpose a consistent system for transcription of Sanskrit. He introduced the scholastic doctrine of **Vasubandhu** (which still survives), that the visual universe is only a mental image. The **Pure Land** or **Lotus School** of Buddhism for the next seventy years enjoyed far more popular favor. Based on texts translated in the 2nd and 5th centuries, it is called the *Short-Cut School* because it teaches direct salvation by faith in Amitabha and invocation of his name. Religious **Taoism,** fully organized on the Buddhist model, now also received imperial patronage on the ground that Lao-tzu, whose surname legend gives as Li, was the ancestor of the ruling house. A 4th century apocryphal text, *Hua Hu Ching,* which claims Lao-tzu to be a prior avatar of Buddha, was actively debated. It was proscribed (668) but again tolerated (696). Imperial commissions completed or newly compiled eight standard histories to bring the series down to date from the Three Kingdoms. Another prepared the first literary encyclopedia, *I Wen Lei Chü.*

657-659. **Dispersal of the western Turks** (T'u-chüeh), some of whom eventually migrated across southern Russia to Hungary while others followed Mahmud of Ghazni to India.

671-695. I-ching made the pilgrimage to India

Emperor T'ai Tsung and horse, 7th-century stone bas relief

Painted funerary pottery, T'ang Dynasty

Glazed lion, T'ang Dynasty

Hsüan-tsang, 645

by sea, stopping to learn Sanskrit in Srivijaya (southeastern Sumatra), a state which became tributary (670–673), and remained powerful until the close of the 14th century.

684–704. **Empress Wu** temporarily altered the dynastic title to *Chou* (690–704), and decreed use of capriciously deformed written characters.

712–756. **HSÜAN TSUNG,** popularly known as Ming Huang, ruled over a court of brilliant High Renaissance literary and artistic attainment. He founded the **Academy of Letters** (725) and established schools in every prefecture and district in the empire (738). **Li Po** (705–762) and **Tu Fu** (712–770) created and excelled in lyric verse. In painting, continuous composition was substituted for episodic treatment. **Wu Tao-hsuan** (c. 700–760) ranks foremost among figure-painters. **Li Ssu-hsün** (651–c. 720) and **Wang Wei** (698–759) created two of the first and most influential landscape styles. Slackening of genuine religious enthusiasm is conspicuous alike in the tone of Buddhist votive inscriptions and in the monumental realism of the sculpture which becomes increasingly secular, then perfunctory. T'ang potters freely borrowed forms of Iranian flask and ewer, Indian ritual drinking vessel, and Greek amphora. They made these resplendent with new colors in soft lead glaze applied over slip with new technical versatility. From about this time dates probably also the first true porcelain with high-fired felspathic glaze. **I-hsing** (c. 725), a Buddhist astronomer, invented the first known clock-escapement. The Buddhists, too, now enlarged the seal and produced wood blocks for **printing on paper** (earliest extant printed book dated 868).

732. **Manichaeism** was condemned as perverse doctrine, but was permitted to Persians and Tokharians who had introduced it (694 and 719) and who were favored for their competence in astronomy and astrology.

738. The title *King* was conferred on a T'ai ruler who (730) united six principalities as **Nan-chao** with capital at Ta-li (741). After two disastrous efforts at conquest (750 and 754), the T'ang made peace (789–794), leaving the kings of Nan-chao full autonomy. They still had to be repelled, twice from Cheng-tu (829 and 874), once from Hanoi (863).

745. Uighur Turks overthrew the eastern Turks and set up their own empire on the Orkhon, ruling from Ili to Tibet and the Yellow River. Their *kaghan* was given a title and a Chinese princess (758).

747. **Kao Hsien-chih** led an army across the Pamirs and Hindukush, but

751. **Defeat by the Arabs** at Talas lost Turkestan to China.

751–790. Wu-k'ung made the pilgrimage to India through Central Asia on the eve of displacement of Buddhism by Islam.

755. **Revolt of An Lu-shan,** a Turkish adventurer who had been adopted by the emperor's favorite concubine, Yang Kuei-fei, and had united three military commands, plunged the empire into particularly sanguinary and destructive civil war.

756–757. The emperor fled to I-chou (renamed Cheng-tu) which was developed rapidly as a cultural center. He there abdicated in favor of his son. Despite gradual suppression of the rebellion by Kuo Tzu-i and Li Kuang-pi, power remained in hands of territorial military leaders.

762–763. The Uighur kaghan sacked the eastern capital at Loyang, then in rebel hands, but was himself there converted to Manichaeism, which became the Uighur state religion.

763. The Tibetans, by a surprise attack, sacked Ch'ang-an. Through fear of the Uighur, who tried to convert the T'ang, Manichaeans were allowed to build temples in the capitals (768) and seven other cities (771 and 807). The kaghans were given rich gifts of silk, and a princess (821).

840–846. **Overthrow of the Uighur Empire** by the Turkish Kirghiz and Karluk led to migration of many tribes from the Orkhon to the Tarim basin, where they carved out a second Uighur Empire in which the Turkish language extinguished the Indo-European dialects.

841–846. The reign **of Wu Tsung,** under Taoist influence, was filled with persecution of Manichaeans (843), Buddhists, Nestorians, and Mazdeans (845). Buddhism alone was now naturalized and able to survive. The most prominent place in an epoch of increasing anarchy was taken by the **Ch'an** (Sanskrit, *Dhyana,* Japanese, *Zen*) **sect** which offered refuge in introspective contemplation. **Bodhidharma,** an aged Persian who had come to Loyang from India prior to 534, was now hailed as fabulous founder of the school, although in fact he was still obscure as late as 728.

CULTURAL PROGRESS continued despite military alarms. **Wei Pao** was commanded (744) to prepare an authentic version of the *Canon of History* by collation of variant manuscripts. It was included, together with all three competing rituals and all three commentaries on the *Annals,* among twelve classics which were cut in stone at Ch'ang-an (836–841). **Han Yü** (768–824) not only wrote excellent poetry, as did **Po Chü-i** (772–846), but created and set the classic model for the essay style. The first historical encyclopedia, the *T'ung Tien,* was compiled (766–801) by **Tu Yu;** and the practice of writing monographs on individual prefectures and districts was begun.

907–959. **FIVE DYNASTIES** of short duration asserted imperial authority but seldom exercised it outside the Yellow River Basin: Later Liang (907–923), Later T'ang (923–936), Later Tsin (Chin) (936–947), Later Han (947–950), and Later Chou (951–960). Among ten competing secession states the most considerable were southern Han at Canton (904–971), and southern T'ang, which from Nanking ruled much of the east and south (937–975).

932–953. **Nine classics were first printed** from wood blocks, as cheap substitute for stone engraving, at the Later T'ang capital at Loyang by **Feng Tao,** who had seen the process in Shu (Szechwan). The text was that of the stone inscriptions of 836–841.

907–1123. **KHITAN MONGOLS** under their dynastic founder Ye-lü A-pao-chi (907–926) conquered all Inner Mongolia, the kingdom of Po Hai in the Liao Valley, and 16 northern districts of China. His suzerainty was recognized even by the Uighurs. His son Ye-lü Te-kuang (927–947) first helped set up the Later Tsin dynasty at Ta-liang (modern Kaifeng) and then destroyed it. He took Yen-ching (Peking) as his own southern capital (938), and adopted the Chinese dynastic name *Liao* with periodic reign-titles (947–1125).

960–1279. The **SUNG DYNASTY** marks the advent of modernity, not only in governmental and social organization, but in thought, belief, literature, and art; not least in the diffusion of learning through print. It was an age of humanism, of scholar statesmen who were at once poets, artists, and philosophers. The first half of the dynasty is often distinguished as the Northern Sung (960–1127) when the capital was at Kaifeng, then variously called Ta Liang, more properly Pien-liang, or Pien-ching.

960–976. **Chao K'uang-yin** or (Sung) T'ai Tsu gradually restored unity and order under accustomed forms with the help of a paid army.

965. The Annamese secured independence before South China could be subdued and shortly (c. 982) sacked the Cham capital Indrapura before Chinese pressure forced them to peace. Although the Chams (c. 1000) moved

The Diamond Sutra, *earliest block-printed book*, 686

Mayan Calendar Pyramid at Chichén Itzá, Yucatan, Mexico (p.379)

Head of a Mayan warrior, terracotta

Toltec caryatid figures at Tula, Mexico (p.379)

Aztec temple of Quetzalcoatl at Teotihuacán, Mexico (p.379)

their capital south to Vijaya (Cha-ban, near Binh-dinh), the Annamese resumed the war (1043) and sacked it also.

967. The emperor deliberately refused to invade the territory of the native kings of Nanchao in Yünnan, a policy observed by his successors. He permitted temporary autonomy to the king of Wu Yüeh (modern Chekiang) who had retained his throne (897–978) by pledging loyalty to each Chinese dynasty.

972 ff. The **Buddhist canon** was printed in Szechuan by imperial order from 130,000 blocks. It was reprinted with additions in Fukien (1080–1104), and elsewhere thereafter.

976–997. **T'ai Tsung** completed reunion of the empire (979), but was twice repulsed from Peking by the Liao (979 and 986).

997. Division of the empire into 15 provinces (*lu*), later extended to 18 (1023–1031) and 23 (1078–1085).

990–1227. The **western Hsia** (Hsi Hsia) kingdom of Tangut on the northwest frontier with capital at Ning-hsia appealed often to arms (996, 1001–1003, 1039–1042) despite grant of the imperial surname *Chao* and office (991, 997, 1006) and royal investiture (1044).

1004. An invasion by the Liao reached the Yellow River near Pien-liang. They were granted annual tribute. These payments, increased in 1042, and the hire of a large standing army bade fair to bankrupt the treasury.

1006. Granaries for emergency relief were established in every prefecture. In 1069 grain so stored was valued at 15 million strings of cash.

1069–1074. **WANG AN-SHIH** (1021–1086) carried out a program of radical reform with the full confidence of Shen Tsung (1068–1085), and in face of bitter opposition of conservative statesmen.

Through a new **financial bureau** (1069) he cut the budget 40 per cent and raised salaries to make honesty possible for ordinary officials. To avoid excessive transport costs and to control prices he empowered the chief transport officer to accept taxes in cash or kind, to sell from the granaries, and to buy in the cheapest market, using capital of 5 million strings of cash. Further to protect poor farmers against usurers and monopolists, loans of cash or grain were offered in spring against crop estimates to be repaid in autumn with interest of 2 per cent a month (moderate in China). Ambitious officials forced these loans upon merchants and others who did not want them. Objection to both principle and administration of these measures, which were accompanied by alarming centralization of power and disregard for precedent, led to wholesale resignations and transfers of the best officials, whose help alone might have made them successful. **Conscript militia** were organized (1070) and trained for police purposes and national defense. The standing army of over a million inefficient men was gradually cut in half. By 1076 the militia, volunteer guards, and border bowmen numbered over 7 million men. **Cash assessments** graded in proportion to property were substituted (1071) for compulsory public services which had borne too heavily upon thrifty rural families. The exemption of officials, clergy, and small families was reduced by half. Necessary local services were now performed by paid volunteer agents. **State banking** and barter offices were opened

Taoist deity, wood, Sung Dynasty, 960–1279

(1072) first at the capital and later in every prefecture, with the object of controlling prices for the popular benefit.

1074–1085. The reform program was continued, despite complaints of excessive cash levies and other malpractices, until the emperor's death, for a time (1075–1076) by Wang himself.

1085–1093. Regency of the hostile grand dowager empress (under the reign title Yüan Yu)

and recall of Ssu-ma Kuang, Su Shih, and the conservative faction to rescind the whole of the reform scheme (1085–1086). Extreme reaction in turn provoked reaction. On the death of his grandmother,

1093–1100. Che Tsung again favored reform, as did his younger brother

1101–1125. **Hui Tsung,** who permitted Ts'ai Ching to proscribe (1102) 98 of the Yüan-Yu partisans, finally (1104) 309 conservatives, living and dead, headed by Ssu-ma Kuang. Eventually much that was good in the measures of 1070 and 1071 was retained. Hui Tsung, himself an able painter, was an active patron of the arts and letters. He founded the **Imperial Academy of Painting,** and sponsored catalogues of his collections of painting and of archaic bronzes, some of which were obtained by excavation.

The Northern Sung period was the golden age of **landscape painting,** when compositions of majestic breadth and exquisite detail were rendered in monochrome and color on long rolls or broad panels of silk. **Tung Yüan** (late 10th century) and **Kuo Hsi** (c. 1020–1090) combined mastery of continuous composition and linear technique with that of suggestion of atmosphere through gradations of ink-tone. **Li Kung-lin** (c. 1040–1106) excelled in vigorous contrasts of light and shade, of broad and delicate line, and in airy architectural renderings in ruled and measured style. **Mi Fei** (1051–1107) used hardly any lines, building mountains and forests from graded accumulations of blobs of ink.

Scholarship flourished no less. Two great encyclopedias were compiled by imperial order, the *T'ai Ping Yü Lan* (977–983) and the *Ts'e Fu Yüan Kuei* (1005–1013). **Ou-yang Hsiu** (1007–1072), a prominent statesman, prepared the *New History of the T'ang,* the first repertory of early inscriptions, and a monograph on the peony. **Ssu-ma Kuang's** greatest work was an integrated history of China, 403 B.C.–959 A.D., compiled 1066–1084. **Su Shih** (1036–1101), better known as **Su Tung-p'o,** was distinguished as an independent statesman, and one of China's greatest essayists, poets, and calligraphers. **Wang An-shih** held his own with these as a brilliant writer of state papers and classical expositor.

Use of tea, first mentioned as substitute for wine under the Wu dynasty (222–280), spread through North China.

It is not known when or by whom the **principle of magnetic polarity,** known to the Chinese at least since the 1st century A.D., was applied in the mariner's compass with floating needle. The Malays in the 16th century employed, like the Chinese, a compass rose with 24 points, in contrast to the Arab rose of 32 points; which suggests, but does not prove, that the Malays received both compass and rose from the north. The compass is plainly mentioned by Chinese writers of the early 12th century. The volume of **maritime commerce** swelled greatly as Arabs in the 9th and 10th centuries entered into competition with Persians at Canton and Ch'üan-chou (Zayton), later at Lin-an. It was trade in cotton goods that brought 70 families of Jews from Persia and India to settle at the capital Pien-liang, where they remained unmolested until gradually absorbed.

1114–1234. **Jürchen Tungus tribes** overthrew

Boating by Moonlight, *attributed to Ma Yüan*

their Khitan rulers in Manchuria (1114–1116) and, with short-sighted Chinese aid, seized all the Liao lands in China (1122–1123). Ye-lü Ta-shih of the Khitan led the remnant of his people to found a new state, Kara-Khitai, in eastern Turkestan (1130) and Turkestan proper (1141–1211). Meantime

1122. The Jürchen prince declared himself emperor of the **Chin** (or Kin) **dynasty.** He attacked the Sung so vigorously that although

1125. Hui Tsung abdicated in favor of his son,

1126. Ch'in Tsung and his father were both captured with the entire court in the capital. Hui Tsung died in captivity (1135).

1127–1279. THE SOUTHERN SUNG. A junior prince fled southeastward across the Long River from city to city, even by sea to Wen-chou; but, when the Chin retired north of the Long River (1130) and set up the puppet buffer state of Ch'i (1130–1137), the capital was established (1135) at Lin-an (modern Hangchow). The gallant general Yüeh Fei won several successes until put to death by Ch'in Kuei who made

1141. A peace dictated by economic exhaustion, accepting as frontier the line of the Huai and upper Han Rivers.

1161. Explosives were used by **Yü Yün-wen** in defeating the Chin at Ts'ai-shih (in Anhuei near Nanking). The Chin, like the Liao before them, avidly absorbed and adopted Chinese culture.

Early **Chinese philosophers** devoted nearly all their effort to the practical study of ethics. Buddhism, however, insistently raised the problems of ontology and epistemology. It is the merit of the Sung philosophers to have achieved a synthesis of ancient ethics with a new rationalized metaphysics. **Chou Tun-i** (1017–1073) revived a diagram of the ancient diviners to illustrate his conception of causation: emergence of paired forces from primal unity and differentiation of natural phenomena by their interaction. **Ch'eng Hao** (1032–1085), the leading member of a commission which initiated the valuable public services act of 1071, was in philosophy a mystic synthesist who found benevolence in all things. His brother **Ch'eng I** (1033–1107) was an analyst who discovered in the *Li Chi* the *Ta Hsüeh* or "Great Learning," a short work on method which stresses knowledge as essential to self-improvement on which all human welfare depends. Ideas of the school were systematized and crystallized by **Chu Hsi** (1130–1200), who equated as universals primary unity, an impersonal but just and benevolent heaven, and righteousness, which correspond to the physical, metaphysical, and ethical spheres. From these proceed as co-ordinates the dual modes of production, the decrees of heaven, and the processes of self-improvement. The final products are, respectively, the diversity of natural phenomena, conscience, and character. All these activities of parallel evolution are expressions of a universal divine law. Acceptance of knowledge as an element in self-improvement, and consequent emphasis on objective study, pointed the way toward scientific research; but this tendency was promptly combated by **Lu Chiu-yüan** (1139–1192), who stressed the teaching of Mencius that goodness springs from within.

Painters under the Southern Sung reproduced most often the mild misty landscapes of the Hang-chow region rather than the beetling crags found south of Ch'ang-an that had often inspired northern artists. **Ma Yüan** (1190–1224), **Hsia Kuei** (c. 1180–1230), and their school placed special emphasis on economy of line and representation of mists and clouds. Secular painters came increasingly under domination of conventions which grew up in the academy founded by Hui Tsung, and elegance, charm, and impeccable taste tended to replace more virile virtues; but religious painters, both Buddhist and Taoist, continued to produce vigorous work until the close of the dynasty. **Ch'en Jung** (c. 1235–1255) ranks as China's greatest painter of dragons.

Sung **ceramists** applied to pottery and porcelain in forms of subtle and sophisticated elegance both incised and molded decoration, together with a wide variety of high-fired glazes, some of which have never since been equaled. Although most wares were ostensibly monochrome, the potters learned to control color-transmutation of their pigments. The potters of Tz'u-chou for the first time employed penciled decoration both under and over glaze.

Science developed so that in mathematics the complete properties of the circle were known. Astronomical instruments became very large, to increase the accuracy of the measurements. The calendar month had been computed to be 29.53 solar days. By 1200 the first windmills appeared in China, spreading there from Afghanistan.

c. 1190–1294. THE MONGOLS. In central Asia, **Temujin** (c. 1162–1227) created a new Mongol empire which was rapidly expanded by strategy and a military machine employing discipline, extreme mobility, espionage, terrorism, and superior siege equipment.

1194. The **Yellow River,** after repeated alterations of its bed, flowed south of the Shantung massif until 1853.

1206. Temujin was proclaimed *Jenghiz Khan* ("Emperor within the Seas") at Karakorum. He employed as chancellor a Uighur scholar Tatatonga, who applied to Mongol the Uighur script that was derived from Phoenician through Aramaic, Old and New Sogdian. Enforcement of peace and order within the empire promoted both commerce and cultural exchanges.

1211–1222. The Chin were driven south to the Yellow River (from Yen-ching, 1215).

1227. After several campaigns (1205, 1207, 1209) the Hsi Hsia Kingdom was destroyed, with massacre at Ning-hsia. Temujin bequeathed the empire to a grandson and three sons: to **Batu,** son of his eldest, Juchi, Kipchak in Russia; to **Chagatai,** the former Kara-Khitai empire; to **Ogadei,** Outer Mongolia; and to **Tului** (regent 1227–1229), eastern Mongolia and North China.

1229–1241. Ogadei was elected khan by plenary kuriltai on the Kerulen.

1231. Ye-lü Ch'u-ts'ai (1190–1244), a sinicized scion of the Khitan royal house and adviser to Temujin since 1215, proved his ability to collect taxes in China by traditional methods, and was appointed chancellor. Korye (Korea) conquered and placed under 72 Mongol residents.

1233. Pien-liang fell after a flanking campaign by Tului through Hanchung and Szechwan (1231–1232), and a long siege by Subutai in which the Chin defenders used explosive bombs.

1234. The Chin Empire was annexed. Belated Chinese attack provoked Mongol seizure of Szechwan (1236–1238).

1237. Ye-lü Ch'u-ts'ai secured 4030 scholars one-quarter of whom were freed from slavery through civil service literary examinations, and restored full civilian administration.

1237–1241. Subutai subjugated Russia and led an invasion through Hungary to Cattaro which was recalled only by death of Ogadei *(p. 266)*.

1246–1248 or 1249. Guyuk, son of Ogadei and his widow Turakina (regent 1242–1246), was elected khan in presence of Plano Carpini, envoy of Innocent IV.

1251–1259. Mongka, son of Tului, was elected over the son of Guyuk's widow (regent 1249–1251).

1252–1253. Mongka's brother Kublai crushed Nan-chao. The king was named *maharaja* and hereditary administrator under the eyes of a Mongol garrison commander and Chinese resident. More autonomy and an imperial princess were conferred in 1284.

1254. Mongka, the son of a Nestorian woman and employer of a Nestorian chancellor, told William of Rubruck, envoy of Louis IX of France, that religions are like the fingers of one hand. He yet favored Buddhism, and after public disputation (1255) proscribed Taoist books for forgery. Kublai shortly followed this example (1258).

1257. The capital was transferred to Shang-tu, north of present Peking.

1258. The Mongols pillaged Hanoi, while, at the other end of the empire, Hulagu with a Nestorian wife and general destroyed the Abbasid caliphate of Baghdad.

1260–1368. The **YÜAN DYNASTY** (as distinguished from the Mongol Empire) was effectively founded when **Kublai** (1214–1294) had himself elected khan by his own army at Shang-tu (1260), although he adopted the dynastic title only in 1271. He ruled in China according to Chinese precedents. His dynastic name is Shih tsu.

1264. The **Mongol Empire** was reunited by capture of Kublai's brother Arikboga, who had been proclaimed khan at Karakorum (1260). Twice (1277 and 1287–1288) its unity was defended against Khaidu, head of the house of Ogadei. Kublai's authority was respected by his brother Hulagu and the succeeding ilkhans of Persia, and in theory by the Golden Horde on the Volga. He transferred (1264) the winter capital to Yen-ching where he constructed Khanbalig, modern Peking (1267). He erected an astronomical observatory on the city wall, wherein were installed bronze instruments cast by Kuo Shou-ching (1279).

1268–1273. A siege of Hsiang-yang and Fan-ch'eng on the Han was ended after four years five months only by engineers and machines from Mesopotamia. Thereafter the Mongols were free to descend toward the sea.

1276. Capitulation of the empress-regent and boy-emperor at Lin-an (Hangchow) was followed by capture of Canton (twice, 1277) and destruction of a fleet carrying the last youthful Sung pretender (1279).

1281. Disastrous **attack upon Japan.** An assault in 1274 having failed, a Mongol army of 45,000 from Korea joined (June) a tardy armada with 120,000 men from the southern Chinese coast in landing at Hakozaki Bay. The invaders were repulsed by the well-prepared Japanese until (Aug. 15) a typhoon destroyed their fleets, leaving them to death or slavery.

1282–1283. An army sent by sea from Canton to subdue Champa took the capital Vijaya, but was forced by epidemics to withdraw.

1285 and **1287–1288.** Abortive expeditions against Annam and Champa by land and sea were massacred and repulsed, but secured admission of vassalage.

1287. The Mongols pillaged Pagan, capital of Burma, received homage (1297), and returned (1300) to pacify competing Shan chiefs.

1292–1293. A naval **expedition to Java,** after temporary success, was forced to re-embark.

1294. Tribute was received from the Siamese kingdoms of Xieng-mai and Sukhotai.

1295–1307. **Temur Oljaitu,** grandson of Kublai, was the second and last effective ruler of the Yüan dynasty.

1296. A Mongol embassy accompanied by Chou Ta-kuan found Chen-la (Cambodia) much weakened by the attacks of Sukhotai, which had now become a powerful state under its second ruler Rama Kamhing.

ECONOMIC DEVELOPMENTS. Kublai devoted special attention to economic matters: the grand canal was restored (1289–1292) from the former Sung capital, Lin-an at Hangchow (the Kinsay of Marco Polo), now a great and rich city, to the Huai River, and carried north to the outskirts of Peking. Imperial roads were improved, and postal relays of 200,000 horses

Kublai, Khan of the Mongols, 1214–1294

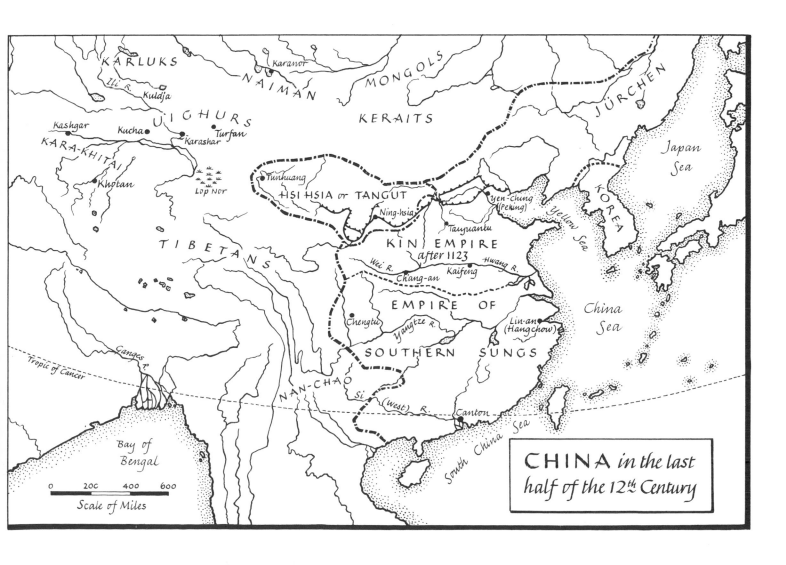

CHINA *in the last half of the 12th Century*

Tiger, *by Mu Ch'y, late 13th century*

1292), traveled widely in Cathay (from Khitai, hence North China), and Manzi (South China), and to Burma *(p. 376)*. Through his "Division of the World" he first brought detailed and accurate knowledge of eastern Asia to Europe. In his time, and even in that of the Arab, Ibn Batuta (c. 1345), Zayton (Ch'üan-chou) was the busiest deep-sea port in the world, leading Kinsay (Lin-an), Foochow (Fu-chou), and Canton in shipping silks and porcelains to Java, Malaya, Ceylon, India, and Persia in exchange for spices, gems, and pearls. The itineraries given by Chao Ju-kua (1225) imply in the precision of their bearings the use of a compass needle mounted on a dry pivot.

The **MOSLEM COMMUNITIES** of Persian and Arab traders at these ports were small compared to those which now grew up in North China and in Yünnan. Saiyid-i Edjill as governor of Yünnan (1274–1279) built the first two mosques in what became a stronghold of Islam. Most popular religion with all the Mongols was Buddhism. Kublai welcomed a gift of relics of the Buddha from the raja of Ceylon. He conferred the title *Teacher of the State* upon a Tibetan lama Phags-pa, whom he employed to convert the Mongols and to whom he entrusted government of the three provinces of Tibet.

NESTORIAN CHRISTIANS enjoyed full protection. The patriarch of Baghdad created an archbishopric at Peking (1275); churches were built in Chen-kiang (1281), Yang-chou, and Hangchow; and a special bureau was created (1289) to care for Christianity. **Mar Yabalaha,** pilgrim from Peking to Jerusalem, was elected patriarch (1281), and his companion Rabban Sauma was sent by him and Argun, ilkhan of Persia, to Rome and France. He negotiated with Pope Nicholas IV an entente between the Nestorian and Roman churches.

John of Montecorvino was the first of several Roman missionaries to China (1294–1328). He baptized 5000 converts and was named by the pope (1307) archbishop of Peking. He received a three-year visit from **Oderic of Pordenone** who reported to Europe the custom of foot-binding, which had spread through South China under the Southern Sung, but which was unknown to the Chin and early Yüan.

SCIENCE AND TECHNOLOGY. Meteorology developed to the extent that by the 14th century the correlation between the climatic changes and the sunspot cycle was known. By 1500 a rotary disc-cutter was being used to cut jade, highly valued in China since the 13th century B.C. By 1593 a modern form of the abacus was in use.

LITERATURE. The Mongol period introduced the novel and the drama, the latter accompanied by raucous percussion music. Although neither was at once admitted as a form of polite letters, both are now recognized to possess artistic merit.

PAINTING. One group of artists continued traditions of the Southern Sung while another boldly swept away the mists which had shrouded landscape. **Ch'ien Hsüan** (1235–c. 1290) is perhaps the greatest painter of flowers and insects. **Chao Meng-fu** (1254–1322) was particularly adept at depicting the horses and other livestock that were prominent in Mongol economy. Yüan porcelain reveals in arabesques no less than in the technique of penciling in cobalt blue directly on clear white paste the debt of Chinese potters to Persian models. From these also is derived the Byzantine form of cloisonné enamel.

1368–1644. The **MING DYNASTY** was founded by **Chu Yüan-chang** (Ming T'ai Tsu, 1328–1398), a monk turned insurgent amidst anarchy, who seized Chiang-ning (Nanking) in

Military watchtower of the Ming Dynasty

established. Charitable relief was organized (1260) for aged scholars, orphans, and the sick, for whom hospitals were provided (1271). Imperial inspectors every year examined crops and the food supply with a view to purchase when stocks were ample for storage against famine.

The T'ang first employed paper money orders, to which the Sung and Chin added various bills of exchange. When issue of paper currency was suggested to Ogadei (1236), Ye-lü Ch'u-ts'ai secured limitation to value of 100,000 ounces of silver. Under Kublai, a Mohammedan financier, Saiyid-i Edjill Chams al-Din Omar (1210–1279), kept annual issues at an average of 511,400 ounces (1260–1269). His successor Ahmed Fenaketi increased emissions (1276–1282) to 10,000,000 ounces annually. After Ahmed's murder, inflation increased until a Uighur, Sanga, reduced the rate of printing to 5,000,000 ounces (1290–1291). Circuit stabilization treasuries (1264 and 1287) were given reserves inadequate to redeem the flood of bills at $2\frac{1}{2}$ per cent discount, the official rate of 1287. The issue of 1260 depreciated until replaced 1 for 5 by that of 1287, which again was replaced 1 for 5 in 1309. All printing was discontinued in 1311; but the credit, financial and moral, of the dynasty was already on the wane. The southern provinces of the empire rapidly fell from its control.

Marco Polo, in the service of the khan (1275–

1356, set up there an orderly government, and proceeded to annex the holdings of surrounding southern war-lords until in 1368 he was strong enough to drive the Mongols from Peking with Shensi, Kansu (1369), and Szechwan (1371). Like all the emperors of this and the following dynasty he ruled under a single reign-title, *Hung-wu* (1368–1398), which is accordingly often used instead of his personal name.

1382. Yünnan was completely conquered, and its prince executed at Nanking. The whole territory of China was now under direct government.

1388. The Mongols were driven from Karakorum and defeated on the Kerulen.

1392–1910. The **Li dynasty** was founded in Korea upon the ruins of that of Wang, which had reigned since 918 *(p. 365)*.

1403–1424. The **Yung Lo reign** of Ch'eng Tsu was established by violence against his nephew, who disappeared in a palace fire (1402).

1403–1433. A series of **naval expeditions** through the southern seas was motivated by desire for commerce and military prestige, but also by uneasiness lest the deposed nephew emerge thence to claim his throne. Secret inquiry by Hu Jung within the empire also was protracted (1407–1416, 1419–1423). A claimant actually appeared in Honan in 1440.

1405–1407. **Cheng Ho,** the chief eunuch (a Moslem whose real surname was Ma), brought back in chains the prince of Palembang (Sumatra), who had been defeated in battle, as he did

1408–1411. The **king of Ceylon** and his family, who had attacked the mission. As a result of

1412–1415. A third cruise as far as Hormuz, sixteen southern states sent tribute. Cheng Ho was appointed to lead three more embassies

during this reign: 1416–1419 (as far as Aden), 1421–1422, and 1424. Other eunuchs led additional missions.

1410, 1414, 1422–1424. Campaigns into Outer Mongolia were directed at destruction of whatever chieftain or group momentarily possessed sufficient prestige to threaten recreation of the Mongol power.

1421. Transfer of the capital to Peking was mooted in 1409, decreed in 1420. Wisdom of the move is reflected by the fact that the northern frontier was never successfully violated during the five centuries Peking remained capital, save when the Manchus were invited in.

1428–1788. The **later Le dynasty in Annam,** after a quarter century of fighting, secured recognition of independence (1431) from Hsüan Tsung in the Hsüan Te reign (1426–1435). The royal title was conferred in 1436.

1431–1433. Cheng Ho led a seventh and final embassy to twenty states. As result tribute was sent by Mecca and ten others.

1449. Emperor Ying Tsung (1436–1449 and 1457–1464) was captured in battle by the chief of a new Mongol confederation (Oirat) of four tribes. Although released next year, he recovered his throne from his brother Ching Ti only in 1457.

c. 1470–1543. Dayan, a descendant of Jenghiz, restored unity to Mongolia, but then divided it among his own descendants.

1471. Annam finally annexed its southern neighbor, Champa. *(Cont. p. 554.)*

a. BURMA, 1044–1365

From early times Burma was under Indian influence. By the 3rd century A.D. expanding Hindu peoples had established commercial settlements on the Tenasserim coast and at the

principal river mouths which developed into small kingdoms in contact with the Tibeto-Burman tribes of the Irrawaddy Valley. Commercial relations with China were less influential, although an embassy from a Burmese state reached Ch'ang An in 802.

1044. Anawrata seized royal power at Pagan and by his patronage of Hinayana Buddhism and conquests, both north and south, made it the political, religious, and cultural center of Burma; the Burmese written language was developed and Buddhist scriptures translated; architectural monuments followed the inspiration of Ceylon and southern India; able rulers succeeded Anawrata.

1106. A Burmese embassy at the Sung capital in China was received as from a fully sovereign state.

1287. Following the rejection of Mongol demands for tribute (1271 and later), Burmese raids into Yünnan, and the death of Narathihapate (who ruled 1254–1287), **Mongol forces looted Pagan** and destroyed its power. The invasion of Shan tribes, forced southward by the Mongols, led to the division of Burma into a number of petty states, chief among them being Toungoo (established 1280), Pegu in southern Burma, and Ava in the middle and lower Irrawaddy Valley (established as capital 1365). *(Cont. p. 559.)*

b. SIAM, to 1557

During the early centuries of the Christian Era, the **Khmer** peoples of the Menam Valley came under the influence of Hindu civilization, and about the 6th century there was organized, in the region of Lopburi, the **kingdom of Dvaravati,** which was Buddhist rather than Brahman in religion, and from which during the 8th cen-

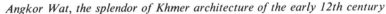

Angkor Wat, the splendor of Khmer architecture of the early 12th century

Giant sculptures on the Bayon temple of Angkor Wat

tury migrants to the upper Menam Valley established the independent and predominantly Buddhist **kingdom of Haripunjaya,** with its capital near the present Chiengmai. Early in the 11th century Dvaravati was annexed to Cambodia; but Haripunjaya retained its independence. Splendor of Khmer architecture; vast funerary temples for the god-kings (**Angkor Wat,** early 12th century). In the 13th century Haripunjaya was overrun by a migration of Tai, or Shan, peoples from the north. This migration, accelerated by the Mongol conquest of the Tai state of Nan-chao (in modern Yünnan and southern Szechwan) in 1253, led eventually to the suppression of the Khmer kingdoms and the setting up of the Tai Kingdom of Siam with its capital at Ayuthia, founded by Rama Tiboti in 1350.

The early Siamese state was from the first under the influence both of Hinayana Buddhism and of Chinese political institutions. Toward the end of the 13th century a form of writing had been invented for the Siamese language.

1350–1460. Siamese **invasion of Cambodia** finally led to the abandonment of Angkor (1431) and collapse of the Khmer Empire.

1371. A Siamese embassy at Nanking inaugurated tributary relations with the newly founded Ming dynasty.

1376–1557. Intermittent friction between Siam and the Tai state of Chiengmai in the northern Menam Valley ended only with the destruction of Chiengmai by the Burmese.

During the 14th and 15th centuries strong Siamese influence was exerted over the dis-

united states of Burma and the northern part of the Malay Peninsula. *(Cont. p. 559.)*

c. MALAYSIA, to 1407

Early Indian commercial settlements in Sumatra and Java, at first Brahman in religion and later influenced by Buddhism, became the centers of organized states. Toward the end of the 7th century A.D., **Srivishaya** became the dominant state of Sumatra and built up a commercial empire which at its height (c. 1180) controlled the Straits of Malacca and of Sunda, all of Sumatra and the Malay Peninsula, and the western half of Java; its authority was recognized as far away as Ceylon and Formosa, and in many colonies throughout the East Indies.

The **Sailendra dynasty**, rulers of Srivishaya, were ardent patrons of Buddhism, as is shown in the great Borobudur victory monument in central Java. The consolidation of petty Javanese states, begun after the middle of the 9th century, led to the rise of **Singosari** in eastern Java, which under Kartanagara (who ruled 1268–1292) challenged and finally destroyed the power of Srivishaya.

1293. A Mongol expedition, sent to avenge insult offered by Kartanagara, was forced out of Java by a new kingdom, **Madjapahit**, which during the 14th century built up a commercial empire with authority extending over Borneo, Sumatra, and parts of the Philippines and of the Malay Peninsula, and profited by an extensive trade with China, Indo-China, and India. After the

1389. Death of Hayam Wuruk, the power of Madjapahit disintegrated.

1405–1407. The first Chinese expedition under Cheng Ho established tributary relations between many Malay states and the Ming Empire; and the authority of Madjapahit rapidly gave way to that of the Moslem Arabs. During the 15th century Moslem commercial operations, based chiefly on Malacca, were extended to the whole archipelago, and some twenty states accepted Islam as the state religion. (*Cont. p. 559.*)

Borobudur, 8th-century victory monument in central Java

4. *Korea, 612–1451*

(*From p. 159*)

612. Emperor Yang-ti of the Sui dynasty of China invaded Koguryŏ but was repulsed.

645–647. Two T'ang expeditions against Koguryŏ failed.

663. The T'ang destroyed Paekche.

668. The T'ang and Silla together destroyed Koguryŏ.

670. Silla robbed the T'ang of Paekche and southern Koguryo, but did not break its allegiance to China.

670–935. SILLA PERIOD.

670–780. Height of Silla power and culture, when Buddhism and art flourished, particularly at the capital near the modern Kyŏngju (Japanese Keishū).

780–935. Period of political decline, but of closer relations with and increasing imitation of China.

c. 880. Serious rebellions broke out.

918. The state of **Koryŏ** was founded in west central Korea.

935. Silla peacefully submitted to Koryŏ.

935–1392. KORYŎ PERIOD.

935–1170. Height of Koryŏ power and culture centering around the capital, Kaesong (modern Sŏngdo; Japanese, Kaijō), in west central Korea and P'yŏngyang, the secondary capital.

936. Koryŏ destroyed Later Paekche, thus uniting Korea once more.

996. The **Khitan** (Liao dynasty) forced Koryŏ to recognize them, and not the Sung dynasty of China, as overlords of Korea.

1044. A great wall was completed across northern Korea as a defense against the Manchurian peoples.

1123. The **Jürchen** (Chin dynasty) forced Koryŏ to recognize their suzerainty.

1170. Military officers seized the government and proscribed Buddhism.

1196. The **Ch'oe family** established its control over the government with the title of *Kongnyŏng*.

1223. Beginning of over 200 years of attacks on coastal regions by Japanese pirates.

1231. The **Mongols** invaded Korea, and the Ch'oe removed the government to the island of Kanghwa off the west coast.

1258. The Im (Lim; Japanese, Rin) family supplanted the Ch'oe as *Kongnyŏng*.

1259. Koryŏ submitted to the Mongols, and the Koryŏ kings through intermarriage became merely a branch of the Mongol imperial family and their representatives in Korea. This situation and the rise of Confucianism at this time led gradually to the unquestioning acceptance of Chinese suzerainty and leadership in political and cultural matters.

1356. Koryŏ revolted successfuly against the Mongols.

1356–1392. Period of great disorder. The Koryŏ kings, who had depended on Mongol prestige for their authority, were unable to suppress their unruly vassals, and the Japanese pirates were at their worst.

1369. Koryo submitted to the Ming dynasty of China.

1392. I (Li; Japanese, Ri) **Sŏnggye** declared himself king after a series of *coups d'état* and assassinations, thus founding the

1392–1910. I (Li; Japanese, Ri) **DYNASTY** with its capital at Kyŏnsŏng (modern Sŏul [Seoul]; Japanese, Keijō). This new dynasty based its claims to legitimacy on its championing of the Ming cause as opposed to the Mongols, considered by them not to be the legitimate rulers of China. Like their predecessors they remained unswervingly loyal and subservient to China.

1392–1494. Period of greatest prosperity and cultural development.

1419–1451. King Sejong was a patron of learning, and in his time the native phonetic script called *ŏnmun* was introduced. During this reign the Japanese pirates ceased to ravage the Korean coast, and the northeastern corner of present-day Korea was brought under Korean rule.

(*Cont. p. 560.*)

5. *Japan, 645–1543*

(From p. 162)

645–784. PERIOD OF THE IMITATION OF CHINA. An edict outlining the general principles of national reorganization was promulgated as early as 646 (the *Taika Reform*), but it was only in the course of several decades that the principles were put into practice and even then the reforms often remained on paper. The major features of the new system were: (1) the nationalization of the land, in theory; (2) the adoption of the T'ang system of land distribution and taxation; (3) the reorganization of local government and other measures intended to increase the authority of the central government in the provinces and its income from them, and (4) the reorganization of the central government. The principles and many of the details of the reforms were borrowed directly from China, but in Japan, dominated as it was by an hereditary aristocracy, it was well-nigh impossible to carry them out in full, and from the start they were basically modified in practice. (1) Although the land was nationalized in theory, in actuality the large hereditary estates of the clan chiefs were returned to them as lands held as salary for their official positions and ranks. (2) The land was to be periodically divided among the agriculturalists in accordance with the membership of each family as determined by census, and uniform taxes were to be levied on all alike. These were (a) the land tax (*so*), paid in rice; (b) the corvée (*yōeki*), often commuted at a fixed rate into a textile tax; and (c) the excise (*chō*), levied on produce other than rice. The system was too closely patterned after the Chinese and functioned badly in Japan from the beginning. Powerful families and institutions, hungry for land, were always ready to deprive the public domain of taxpaying lands, and the peasants, impoverished by taxes, were often anxious to transfer themselves and their lands from the taxpaying public domain to the care of privately owned manors (*shōen*). As a result the history of economic development during the next several centuries is primarily the story of the return of the land into private hands and the emergence of large tax-free estates owned by the court nobility and great religious institutions. (3) The improvement of means of communication helped in the centralization of government and in the collection of taxes, but, although the officials of the provincial governments were to have been appointees of the central government, in practice local leaders retained their supremacy by occupying the lower posts, and it soon became the accepted custom for the high provincial officials to remain at the capital and to delegate their powers to underlings in the provinces. (4) An essential and permanent feature of the reforms was the complete reorganization and great elaboration of the central government. A department of religion (*jingikan*) and a great council of state (*dajōkan*) were established as two parallel organs controlling the spiritual and political aspects of the state. Below the great council were eight ministries, and below them in turn many smaller bureaus. The organization was too ponderous for the Japan of that day. Moreover, with the collapse of the economic supports of the central government through the growth of tax-free estates, this elaborate organism was literally starved to death. Although in theory it continued little changed until the 19th century, actually during most of that period it was merely a skeleton devoid of most of its former substance. In adopting the Chinese form of government the Japanese made one significant change: the official hierarchy of Japan remained a hereditary aristocracy and, with rare exceptions, there was little opportunity for the able or learned of low rank to rise far in this hierarchy.

This period was the **classic era of Japanese culture.** Poetry and prose in pure Chinese were composed, and native Japanese poetry reached an early flowering. Japan in the preceding century had already been imitating continental artistic styles, and now the art of T'ang China found fertile soil in Japan and produced there many of the greatest extant examples of Far Eastern art of that day in the fields of architecture, sculpture, painting, and the applied arts.

663. The **Japanese withdrew from Korea,** after the defeat of a Japanese army and fleet, sent to the aid of Paekche, by a combined force from China and Silla (662). Thus ended the first period of Japanese continental expansion. The fall of Paekche in 663 and of Koguryŏ (a North Korean kingdom) in 668 left Silla supreme in the peninsula and resulted in a great immigration of Korean refugees into Japan.

697. The **Empress Jitō** (686–697) abdicated in favor of her grandson, **Mommu** (697–707). This was the first case of the accession of a minor and the second of the abdication of a ruler, but both were soon to become the rule.

702. New **civil and penal codes** known as the *Taihō Laws* were promulgated. This may have been the first complete codification of the laws embodied in the reforms commenced in 646, although there is mention of an earlier code. These laws, together with a revision of 718 (*Yōrō Laws,* not enforced until 757), have come down to us only through later commentaries, the *Ryō no Gige* of 833 and the *Ryō no Shūge* of 920. A supplementary code, the *Engishiki,* was completed in 928.

710. **Heijō** (or Nara) was laid out on the model of Ch'ang-an, the T'ang capital, as the first permanent capital of Japan. The period during which it was the capital is known as

710–784. THE NARA PERIOD.

712. The *Kojiki,* which records the history of the imperial line since its mythical origins, was written in Chinese characters (used to a

Japanese wooden dance mask, Tempyō Period

large extent phonetically) to represent Japanese words. This is Japan's oldest extant book.

720. The *Nihonshoki* (or *Nihongi*), a more detailed history of Japan written in Chinese, was compiled. It was continued to 887 by five other official histories written in Chinese, which together with it constitute the **Six National Histories** (*Rikkokushi*).

724–749. Shōmu's reign, which included the brilliant Tempyō year period (729–748). This and the period during which Shōmu dominated the court as the retired emperor (749–756) marked the apogee of the Nara Period and its classic semi-Chinese culture.

737. The death of the four grandsons of Kamatari delayed for several decades the complete domination of the imperial court by the Fujiwara clan.

741. Government monasteries and convents (*Kokubunji*) were ordered erected in each province.

752. The dedication of the **Great Buddha** (*Daibutsu*) at Nara marked the completion of the devout Shōmu's most cherished project. The 53-foot bronze figure of the Buddha Rushana (Sanskrit, *Vairocana*) and the huge hall built over it was a tremendous undertaking for the Japanese court and gave witness to the great Buddhist fervor of the time. Many of the objects used in the dedication service together with the personal belongings of Shōmu form the basis of the unique collection of 8th century furniture and art preserved at the imperial treasury in Nara (the *Shōsōin,* commenced in 756).

Shortly before the erection of the Great Buddha the famous monk, **Gyōgi** (670–749), is said to have propagated the concept that Buddhism and Shintō were two aspects of the same faith. Such beliefs served as a justification for the growing amalgamation of the two religions, which was to lead by the 12th century to the development of **Dual Shintō** (*Ryōbu Shintō*), in which Shintō gods were considered to be manifestations of Buddhist deities. Faced with a highly developed foreign religion backed by all the prestige of the more advanced Chinese civilization, the simple native cult became for a period of almost 1000 years the handmaiden of Buddhism in an unequal union.

754. The Chinese monk **Ganjin** (also pronounced Kanshin, etc.; Chinese, *Chien-chên,* d. 763), after five unsuccessful attempts to reach Japan, finally arrived at Nara, where he set up the first ordination platform (*kaidan*) and firmly established the **Ritsu** (Sanskrit, *Vinaya*) **Sect,** which stressed discipline rather than doctrine. The Ritsu Sect together with five other sects formed the so-called **Nara Sects,** the oldest sectarian division of Japanese Buddhism. These others were the **Sanron** (Sanskrit, *Madhyamika*) **Sect,** said to have been introduced in 625; the **Hossō** (Sanskrit, *Dharmalaksana*) **Sect,** brought from China by Dōshō (d. 700), who had gone there to study in 653; the **Kegon** (Sanskrit, *Avatamsaka*) **Sect,** which was largely responsible for the cult of Rushana, the universal and omnipresent Buddha; the **Kusha** (Sanskrit, *Abhidharmakosa*) **Sect;** and the **Jōjitsu** (Sanskrit, *Satyasiddhi*) **Sect;** which last two may never have existed as independent religious bodies in Japan.

759. The *Man'yōshū,* a collection of over 4000 poems in pure Japanese, composed largely by the court nobility between 687 and 759, was compiled shortly after the latter date. It was followed in later centuries by similar anthologies. In 751 the *Kaifusō,* a small collection of poems in Chinese, had been compiled; it likewise was continued by similar works.

764. A clash for power between **Fujiwara Nakamaro** (also known as Emi Oshikatsu), the leading statesman during Junnin's reign (758–764), and Dōkyō, the monk favorite of the retired nun empress, Kōken (749–758), led to the death of Nakamaro, the exile of Junnin, his subsequent assassination and the reascension to the throne of Kōken as the Empress Shōtoku.

764–770. Dōkyō was all-powerful during Shōtoku's reign and may even have aspired to the throne. Strong opposition and Shōtoku's death led to his ultimate downfall. Perhaps because of the memory of Dōkyō's influence over Shōtoku, for almost nine centuries thereafter no woman occupied the throne.

781–806. The reign of the energetic **Kammu** witnessed the conquest of much of northern Hondō in a prolonged but successful border struggle with the Ainu. After several initial failures the natives of this region, both Ainu and intractable Japanese frontiersmen, were definitely brought under the imperial sway by **Sakanoue Tamuramaro** (d. 811). His campaigns concluded centuries of slow advance into Ainu territory. After a final outbreak in 812 the Ainu menace in the north never again assumed major proportions.

794. Kammu moved the capital from Nagaoka, where it had been since 784, to Heian, the modern Kyōto, where it remained until 1868. The reasons for his abandoning of Nara are not definitely known but were probably: (1) a desire to make a new departure politically and economically; (2) a desire to escape the oppressive influence of the powerful Nara monasteries; (3) the superior location of Nagaoka and Kyōto, which had better water communications with the sea; and (4) the influence of the Hata family (?), which had lands in that region. The reasons for the sudden removal of the capital from Nagaoka to Kyōto, a few miles farther inland, are still more obscure, but may have been connected with Kammu's fear that the first site had incurred the curse of certain spirits. The establishing of the capital at Kyōto marked the beginning of

794–1185. The **HEIAN PERIOD,** a long era marked by few violent upheavals but one in which the transition from the period of the imitation of China to the feudal and more strictly Japanese Kamakura period was slowly made. These centuries were characterized by a somewhat effete dilettantist court society, becoming increasingly divorced from political and economic realities; the gradual decline and collapse of the economic and political system borrowed from China; the growth of tax-free manors; the slow emergence of a new military class in the provinces; the full glory and subsequent decline of the Fujiwara family; the appearance and development of the Buddhist sects and cults that dominated much of Japan's religious history; a sounder understanding of the borrowed Chinese civilization and a greater ability to synthesize it with what was natively Japanese, or to modify it to fit the peculiar needs of Japan; a resultant growing cultural independence of China, and the reappearance of more purely Japanese art and literature.

800–816. New offices in the central government, which were to affect profoundly the whole administration, appeared at this time. These were: (1) the *kageushi* (audit office) (c. 800), which in time usurped the prerogatives of the original audit and revenue offices; (2) the *kurōdo-dokoro* (bureau of archivists) (810), which gradually attained control of palace affairs and became the organ for issuing imperial decrees; (3) the *kebiishichō* (police commission) (c. 816), which in time became the primary law enforcement organ of the state and eventually created outside of the official codes its own code of customary law.

The Great Buddha at Nara, 752

804. **Tendai** and **Shingon,** the two leading sects of the Heian period, were founded by **Saichō** (Dengyō Daishi 767–822) and **Kūkai** (Kōbō Daishi 774–835) respectively. Both monks accompanied the eleventh embassy to the T'ang in 804. Saichō returned to Japan the next year to found the Tendai Sect, named after Mt. T'ien-t'ai in China. The syncretistic inclusive nature of the philosophy of the sect appealed to the Japanese, and its central monastery, the Enryakuji, which Saichō founded on Mt. Hiei overlooking Kyōto (788), became the center from which sprang most of the later significant movements in Japanese Buddhism. Kūkai returned from China in 806 bringing with him the Shingon or Tantric Sect, a late esoteric and mystic form of Indian Buddhism. Because of his tremendous personality and the natural appeal of Shingon to the superstitious propensities of the people, the new sect won considerable popular support, and the Kongōbuji monastery on Mt. Kōya, which Kūkai founded (816), became one of the great centers of Buddhism. Tendai and Shingon were more genuinely Japanese in spirit than were the Nara sects, and the Shingon Sect in particular furthered the union of Shintō and Buddhism.

838. The twelfth and **last embassy to the T'ang** was dispatched. When in 894 Sugawara Michizane (845–903) was appointed to be the next envoy, he persuaded the court to discontinue the practice on the grounds that China was disturbed and no longer able to teach Japan. Although some unofficial intercourse continued between the two countries, this brought to an end the three centuries of the greatest cultural borrowing from China and marked the beginning of a period in which peculiarly Japanese traits asserted themselves increasingly in all phases of Japanese life.

858. The complete **domination of the Fujiwara clan** over the imperial family was achieved by Yoshifusa (804–872) when he became the *de facto* regent of the child-emperor, Seiwa (858–876). In 866, after Seiwa had attained his majority, Yoshifusa assumed the title of regent (*sesshō*), becoming the first non-imperial regent. Seiwa was the first male adult emperor to have a regent. The typical inner family control which the Fujiwara exercised over the emperors can be seen in the relationship that existed between Seiwa and Yoshifusa, for the latter was both the grandfather and the father-in-law of the young ruler. It was the definite policy of the Fujiwara to have a young imperial grandson of the head of the clan occupy the throne and to have him abdicate early in favor of another child. The period of the domination of the Fujiwara family is often called

866–1160. THE FUJIWARA PERIOD.

880. **Fujiwara Mototsune** (836–891) became the first civil dictator (*kampaku*), a post thereafter customarily held by the head of the clan when an adult emperor was on the throne, while the post of regent came to be reserved for the clan head in the time of a minor emperor.

889. The branch of the warrior **Taira clan** which was to rule Japan for part of the 12th century was founded when a great-grandson of Kammu was given this surname. The clan was established in 825 by another imperial prince. In 814 the rival military **clan of Minamoto** was founded by other members of the imperial clan, and in 961 the princely progenitor of the later Minamoto rulers received this surname. The descendants of such imperial princes, reduced to the rank of commoners, often went to the provinces to seek their fortunes, and there some of them merged with the rising class of warriors, who were soon to dominate the land.

891. The **Emperor Uda** (887–897), who was not the son of a Fujiwara mother, made a determined effort to rule independently without Fujiwara influence and refused to appoint a new civil dictator after Mototsune's death. To further this end he used the brilliant scholar, **Sugawara Michizane** (845–903), as his confidential minister, but after Uda's abdication (d. 931) Fujiwara Tokihira (871–909) managed to obtain the removal of Michizane to a provincial post, where he soon died. He was posthumously loaded with honors and deified because it was believed that his vengeful spirit had caused certain calamities. Tokihira throughout his official career strove valiantly but in vain to stem the tide of governmental corruption and disintegration.

905. The *Kokinshū,* an anthology of over a thousand poems in Japanese, was compiled by imperial order in a revival of interest in Japanese poetry. For over a century almost all literary effort and scholarship had been devoted to prose and poetry in the Chinese language, but **Ki Tsurayuki** (d. 946) wrote the preface to the *Kokinshū* in Japanese and followed it in 935 by a travel diary (*Tosa Nikki*) also in Japanese. Within the short compass of a century Japanese prose was to rise to great heights of literary achievement. An important contributing factor to the revival of Japanese literature at this time was the fact that in the preceding century a simple syllabary for writing Japanese phonetically had been evolved from the complicated Chinese characters.

930. The offices of regent and civil dictator were revived after a lapse of four decades when **Fujiwara Tadahira** (880–949) became regent in 930 and civil dictator in 941.

935–941. Civil strife in the provinces broke out on an unprecedented scale, giving witness to the rise of the provincial military class. From 936 until his death in 941 Sumitomo, a member of the Fujiwara clan and a former provincial official, controlled the Inland Sea as a pirate captain, while in eastern Japan an imperial scion, Taira Masakado, after waging war on his relatives and neighbors, declared himself emperor (940), but was presently killed.

949. The **Emperor Murakami** (947–967) did not appoint a successor to Tadahira, but after the former's demise

967–1068. The successive heads of the Fuji-

Lacquer mask, late Fujiwara Period

Daigoji pagoda, 951

wara clan occupied the posts of regent and civil dictator almost uninterruptedly for a full century. This was the heyday of the Fujiwara clan and the core of the so-called Fujiwara period. Court life was ostentatious and extravagant and was characterized by amatorial dilettantism and moral laxity. At the same time petty jealousies and intrigues disrupted the Fujiwara clan, members of the provincial warrior class began to appear on the capital stage as petty military officers and came to be used by the court nobles in their disputes, manors continued to grow apace, further limiting government resources, and the general collapse of the central government continued unabated.

985. The *Ojōyōshū* by the monk **Genshin** (942–1017) gave literate expression to new religious currents that were stirring the nation. A belief had sprung up that the age of *mappō* ("the latter end of the law"), a period of degeneracy to come 2000 years after the Buddha's death, had already commenced. There was a growing belief in the **Pure Land** (*Jōdo*), Paradise of Amida (Sanskrit, *Amitabha*) and salvation through his benign intervention in favor of the believer and not only through one's own efforts, as earlier Buddhism had taught. Emphasis was increasingly placed on *nembutsu*, the repetition of Amida's name or a simple Amidist formula. **Kūya** (903–972), an itinerant preaching monk, was the first articulate voice to express this new religious movement, and Genshin gave it sound literary formulation. It continued to develop, and in the 12th and 13th centuries produced important new Buddhist sects.

995–1028. FUJIWARA MICHINAGA'S (966–1028) rule over clan and state saw the zenith of clan power and some of the most brilliant decades of artistic and literary achievement of the epoch. Although he was never officially civil dictator and was regent for only a short period prior to his official retirement in 1017, he was perhaps the most powerful leader the Fujiwara produced. At this time the classic prose literature of Japan reached its height in the *Genji Monogatari* (c. 1008–1020), a long novel by **Murasaki Shikibu,** a court lady, and in the *Makura no Sōshi* (Pillow Book) (c. 1002), a shorter miscellany by another court lady, **Sei Shōnagon.** The refined and somewhat feminine art of the epoch also was at its height. **Jōchō** (d. 1057), a famous Buddhist sculptor, was already active, and Michinaga's successor, **Yorimichi** (992–1074, regent 1017–1020; civil dictator 1020–1068), built the *Byō-dōin,* the outstanding architectural work remaining from the age.

1039. Armed Enryakuji monks invaded Kyōto to force their will upon the government, but were driven off by Taira troops at Yorimichi's command. Such descents upon the capital, known as "forceful appeals" (*gōso*), were common during the 11th and later centuries and sometimes led to actual fighting. The turbulence of the monks, who fought fiercely among themselves as well as with the court, made it necessary for the court to appeal to the Taira and Minamoto for military aid, and the warrior clans consequently became more influential at court.

1051–1062. In the **Earlier Nine Years' War**

Minamoto Yoriyoshi, on imperial command, destroyed the **Abe,** a powerful military clan of northern Japan. Thereby he firmly established the prestige of his branch of the Minamoto clan in eastern and northern Japan. Yoriyoshi's ancestors had already started the military renown of the house, and its status at court as "the claws and teeth of the Fujiwara" greatly increased its power.

1068–1073. The **Emperor Sanjō II,** who was not the son of a Fujiwara mother, ruled directly without the interference of the Fujiwara. Although the latter continued to occupy the posts of regent and civil dictator, they never again gained full control of the government. Sanjō II established a records office (*kirokujo*) to examine title deeds of manors in an effort to check their growth, but in this attempt he was blocked by the opposition of the Fujiwara.

1083–1087. In the **Latter Three Years' War** Minamoto Yoshiie (1041–1108) destroyed the Kiyowara family of northern Japan, thereby increasing Minamoto prestige in that region.

1086–1129. The **Emperor Shirakawa** (1073–1086) continued to rule after his abdication as a retired emperor (*jōkō*) and after 1096 as a priestly retired emperor (*hōō*). He built up a complete governmental organization of his own (*insei,* camera government) which was continued during much of the next two and a half centuries by other retired emperors and priestly retired emperors, but after 1156 they lost control of the government to the warrior clans.

1129–1156. The **Emperor Toba** (1107–1123) ruled after Shirakawa's death as a priestly retired emperor.

1156. Civil war (the *Hōgen no Ran*) broke out between the reigning emperor **Shirakawa II** (1155–1158), and the retired emperor, Sutoku (1123–1142). Both were supported by prominent members of the Fujiwara, Minamoto, and Taira clans. Shirakawa II's partisans, among whom were numbered Minamoto Yoshitomo (1123–1160) and Taira Kiyomori (1118–1181), were victorious. Sutoku was exiled, and many of his supporters were executed. This war brought no lasting peace and was soon followed by

1160. A **second civil war** (*Heiji no Ran*), in which Minamoto Yoshitomo and an adventurous young Fujiwara noble, Nobuyori (1133–1160), gained temporary control of the capital by a successful *coup d'état,* but were soon crushed by the Taira. This war left

1160–1181. Taira Kiyomori in control of the nation. The two wars of 1156 and 1160 had not been a struggle for power between the court and the military clans, but the result had been to make a single victorious warrior, backed by personal troops, the dominating figure in Japanese politics. Shirakawa II as retired emperor (1158–1192) had some influence in the government, but in 1167 Kiyomori had himself appointed prime minister (*dajō-daijin*), and gave important posts in the central and provincial governments to his clansmen. Kiyomori married his daughters into both the imperial and the Fujiwara families. In 1180 his infant grandson, Antoku, was placed on the throne. Thus he attained the same hold over the imperial family that the Fujiwara had once had.

1175. The **Pure Land** (*Jōdo*) **Sect** was founded by Genkū (Hōnen Shōnin) (1133–1212). It

Representation of the Paradise of Amida

Byōdōin temple, Kyōto, 992–1074

was the first of the Amidist Sects, and this event marked the beginning of a great new sectarian movement.

1179. The **death of Shigemori** (1138–1179), Kiyomori's eldest son and perhaps the wisest of the Taira, removed a stabilizing check on Kiyomori, whose desire for more power was leading him to excesses which were alienating the sympathies of the imperial family, the court nobility, and the Buddhist monasteries. The rapid adoption on the part of Kiyomori and his family of the customs and mentality of the court nobles also estranged many of the provincial supporters of the clan.

1180. An abortive uprising against the Taira led by an imperial prince and by Minamoto Yorimasa (1106–1180), together with certain monasteries, started a general uprising of the remnants of the Minamoto clan under the leadership of Yoshitomo's son, Yoritomo (1147–1199), backed by Taira and other clansmen of eastern Japan.

1183. The Taira were driven out of Kyōto by Yoshinaka (1154–1184), a cousin of Yoritomo. A long campaign in the Inland Sea region followed and culminated in

1185. The **battle of Dan no Ura,** at the western outlet of the Inland Sea, where Yoritomo's younger brother, Yoshitsune (1159–1189), annihilated the Taira. The child-emperor, Antoku, whom the fleeing Taira had taken with them, died in the battle. The elimination of the Taira left Yoritomo, as head of the Minamoto clan, the virtual ruler of the nation and marked the beginning of the first period of feudal rule in Japan known as

1185–1333. THE KAMAKURA PERIOD. The outstanding feature of the era was the clear division between the now powerless civil and religious government of the imperial court at Kyōto and the military government (*Bakufu*) of the Minamoto established at Kamakura, near the clan estates in eastern Japan and away from the enervating influence of the court nobility. The transition from civil to feudal military rule had begun with the Taira and was not completed until centuries later, but it was in the Kamakura period that the most drastic changes occurred and the political and economic institutions of the next several centuries began to take shape.

Feudalism. The usurpation of the powers of the imperial court was largely unconscious and developed naturally out of the economic and political conditions of the late Heian period. Primary factors in this evolution were: (1) The wars of the 11th century had hastened the transfer of the prerogatives of ownership of the great manors of the nobles to the military men who resided on these manors as bailiffs or wardens and who often had feudal ties with the warrior clans. The actual ownership of the estates usually remained unchanged, but ownership was robbed of most of its meaning by a complicated series of feudal rights (*shiki*) which ranged from rights to cultivate the land up through an ascending scale of rights to the income from it. (2) Because of the breakdown of the old centralized government and the need for self-defense feudal military groups had grown up in the provinces with their own "house laws," governing the conduct and the relations of the members of a single group. Moreover, a feudal code of ethics had been developed which emphasized personal loyalty to a feudal chief rather than to a political ideal. (3) Minamoto prestige had for long induced landed warriors to commend themselves and their lands to the Minamoto for the sake of protection. The victory over the Taira greatly increased Minamoto feudal authority both through new additions of this sort and through the confiscation of vast Taira lands. The single Minamoto feudal union consequently had grown so large that it now controlled the nation, and its military government, not the impotent Kyōto adminis-

The holy Buddhist Nakura, color on silk, 12th century

Yoritomo, 1185–1199

traditional style (*Wayō*), and (3) the perfection of the narrative picture scroll (*emakimono*). Significant literary trends were: (1) the increasing use of Japanese in preference to Chinese; (2) the revival of native poetry in the *Shinkokinshū*, an imperial anthology of 1205, and (3) the popularity of historical military tales written in rhythmical prose.

Religion. The Kamakura period was one of great religious and intellectual ferment. It witnessed the birth and development of new sects growing out of the popular movements of the late Heian period. It saw the introduction of the **Zen Sect** from China and the growth of a military cult glorifying the sword, Spartan endurance, and loyalty. From these two elements was born the combination of the aesthetic and mystical penchants of the Zen monk with the qualities of the Kamakura warrior—a combination which remains one of the chief characteristics of the Japanese people.

1185–1199. Yoritomo, as the feudal military dictator, organized the new military government with the aid of Kyōto scholars like Ōe Hiromoto (1148–1225). Already in 1180 he had created a *Saburaidokoro* to perform police duties and to control affairs of the warrior class. In 1184 he had established an administrative board, renamed the *Mandokoro* in 1191. In 1184 the *Monchūjo* had also been established as a final court of appeal. Impartial administration of justice characterized the rule of the Kamakura military government and was one of the chief reasons for its long duration.

In 1185 Yoritomo appointed constables (*shugo*) in some of the provinces and placed stewards (*jitō*) in many of the large manors. A few such appointments had been made in preceding years, but now this system was expanded in order to strengthen his influence in regions over which he had hitherto had no direct control. The constables were special military governors in charge of the direct vassals of the Minamoto. The stewards, who represented Yoritomo on estates not otherwise under his control, levied taxes on the estates for military purposes. Thus the fiscal immunity of the manors was violated, and Kamakura retainers were scattered in key positions all over the country. The constables and stewards gradually grew in importance in the economic and political life of the provinces and in time developed into the feudal lords of later centuries.

1189. Yoshitsune was killed at the orders of Yoritomo, who apparently was jealous of the fame the latter had won as the brilliant general responsible for the greatest victories over the Taira. Yoritomo similarly disposed of other prominent members of the family, including his cousin Yoshinaka (1184), who as a warrior ranked next only to Yoshitsune, his uncle Yukiie (1186), who was one of the prime movers in the Minamoto uprising, and his brother Noriyori (1193), who also was one of the clan's great generals. His cruel treatment of his own relatives contributed to the early extinction of the family.

1189. Yoritomo crushed the powerful Fujiwara family of northern Japan on the grounds that they had killed Yoshitsune, albeit at his own command. The northern Fujiwara in the course of the previous century had become a great military power and had made their capi-

tration, was the real government of the land.

Foreign Relations. For four and a half centuries only a few Japanese monks had gone abroad, and foreign trade had been in the hands of the Koreans and Chinese, but in the Kamakura period the Japanese once more began to take part in foreign commerce. At the same time they began to raid and plunder the coasts of both Korea and China, and in time they became a serious nuisance and occasionally even a national menace to both countries.

Art. Kyōto, though remaining the scene of a colorful court life, was forced to share honors with Kamakura as a center of art and culture. Many Kyōto scholars moved to Kamakura to aid in the civil administration of the military government, and the warrior class brought a new creative energy to art and literature, which were approaching sterility in the late Heian period. Significant artistic trends were: (1) a final great flowering of sculpture before its gradual extinction in following centuries; (2) the introduction from China of two new architectural styles known as the Chinese (*Karayō*) and the Indian (*Tenjukuyō*) styles, which came to blend with the

tal, Hiraizumi, a brilliant center of culture. Their elimination removed a serious menace to Minamoto supremacy.

1191. Eisai (1141–1215) propagated the Rinzai branch of the Zen (Sanskrit, *Dhyana*) Sect after his return from a second study trip to China. The Zen Sect enjoyed the official patronage of Kamakura and the special favor of the warrior class in general.

1192. **Yoritomo** was appointed *Seiidaishōgun* ("barbarian-subduing great general"), or *shō-gun* for short. He was not the first to bear this title, but he was the first of the long line of military dictators called *shōgun*.

1199–1219. **Transition period from Minamoto to Hōjō rule.** Yoritomo was succeeded as head of the Minamoto by his eldest son, Yoriie (1182–1204), who was not appointed *shōgun* until 1202, but his mother, Masako (1157–1225), actually ruled with the aid of a council headed by her father, **Hōjō Tokimasa** (1138–1215). The latter, though a member of the Taira clan, from the start had cast his lot with Yoritomo and had exercised great influence in the Kamakura councils before Yoritomo's death. The Hōjō, though loyal to the military government, unscrupulously did away with Yoritomo's descendants and crushed their rivals among the other Minamoto vassals.

1203. Yoriie was exiled and his younger brother, Sanetomo (1192–1219) was made *shōgun* by Tokimasa. The following year Yoriie was murdered.

1205. Tokimasa was eliminated from the government by Masako. His son, Yoshitoki (1163–1224), then became regent (*shikken*) of the *shōgun*, a post held by successive Hōjō leaders, who were the real rulers.

1219. The Minamoto line came to an end when Sanetomo was assassinated, probably with Hōjō connivance, by his nephew, who in turn was executed.

1219–1333. The **PERIOD OF HŌJŌ RULE** as regents for weakling *shōgun* of Fujiwara and imperial stock was characterized by administrative efficiency and by justice.

1221. An uprising under the leadership of the retired emperor, **Toba II** (1183–1198), was the gravest menace the Hōjō had to face, but was quickly crushed. Two prominent Hōjō leaders were left in Kyōtō as joint civil and military governors of the capital region (*Rokuhara Tandai*). The estates confiscated from the defeated partisans of Toba II gave Kamakura much needed land with which to reward its followers, and the abortive uprising gave the Hōjō a chance to extend the system of constables, stewards, and military taxes to regions hitherto unaffected by it.

1224. **Shinran Shōnin** (1173–1262), a disciple of Genkū, founded the **True Pure Land** (*Jōdo Shin*) **Sect** as an offshoot from the Pure Land Sect of his master. The True Pure Land Sect introduced innovations such as marriage for the clergy. It was destined to become the most popular of all Japanese Buddhist sects with Zen its only close rival.

1226–1252. Fujiwara nobles as figurehead *shōgun.*

1229. **Dōgen** (1200–1253) introduced the Sōtō branch of the Zen Sect after his return from study in China.

1232. The *Jōei-shikimoku*, a law code based primarily on custom rather than on earlier sinicized law codes, was adopted for all those directly under the feudal rule of Kamakura. It remained the basis of law codes until modern times.

1252–1333. Imperial princes as figurehead *shōgun.*

1253. **Nichiren** (1222–1282) founded the **Lotus** (*Hokke*) **Sect,** popularly known as the Nichiren Sect. In it the Lotus Sutra was venerated much as the Amidist Sects venerated Amida. A fiery religious and political reformer, Nichiren was an ardent nationalist, and his writings illustrate the gradual emergence of a definite national consciousness at this time. Imbued with the turbulent nature of its founder, the sect had a stormy career.

1274. FIRST MONGOL INVASION. The Mongols, already masters of Korea and most of China, repeatedly sent embassies (1268–1273), enjoining the Japanese to submit, but the Kamakura government under the bold leadership of the regent, Hōjō Tokimune (1251–1284), refused. Finally in 1274 the Mongols dispatched an expedition aboard a Korean fleet. The islands of Tsushima and Iki were reduced, a landing was made in Hakata (Hakozaki) Bay in northern Kyūshū, and an inconclusive encounter, in which superior weapons and military organization gave the Mongols the advantage, was fought with the local warriors. But the same night, because of their insecure position and the threat of a storm, the invaders set sail for Korea.

1281. SECOND MONGOL INVASION. Mongol envoys sent to Japan in 1275 and again in 1280 were summarily executed, and the military government hastily prepared defense works in western Japan. In 1281 the Mongols embarked a huge force on two large fleets, one Korean and one Chinese, and again, after capturing Tsushima and Iki, landed in northern Kyūshū. Although the invaders numbered some 150,000, the Japanese checked their advance on land with walls they had prepared for this emergency and worsted them on the sea because of the greater mobility of their smaller craft in close quarters. After almost two months of fighting a terrific storm destroyed a large portion of the invading armada, and the remainder departed with serious losses. The Mongols continued plans for another invasion of Japan until the death of their emperor, Kublai (1294), and the Japanese continued their defense preparations still longer.

Higashi-Honganji Temple of the True Pure Land Sect in Kyōto

The Mongol invasions no doubt spurred on Japan's nascent national consciousness, but it also contributed greatly to the final collapse of the Kamakura government. Military preparations against the Mongols had seriously taxed the nation's resources, and at the end of the two invasions the military government, lacking land confiscated from the enemy, was without the usual means of rewarding its vassals for their valiant efforts. This state of affairs helped undermine the loyalty of the warrior retainers of Kamakura. At the same time the monasteries were becoming increasingly unruly, the court nobility was beginning again to intrigue with disaffected warriors against the Hōjō, and the latter themselves had lost the virtues of frugality and justice that had once characterized the family.

The Hōjō during the final decades of their rule began to resort to **Acts of Grace** (*Tokusei*) cancelling certain indebtedness in an effort to save the lands of their vassals from mortgages, but such obviously unfair measures antagonized certain powerful interests and failed adequately to protect the Kamakura vassals.

1331–1333. The **IMPERIAL RESTORATION** of **Daigo II** and the fall of the Hōjō. The energetic and able emperor, Daigo II (1318–1339), after bringing to an end in 1322 the domination of the court by retired emperors, organized an abortive plot to overthrow the Hōjō as early as 1324. In 1331 open warfare broke out between Daigo II, supported by his able sons, some of the large monasteries in the capital region, and various local nobles and warriors like **Kitabatake Chikafusa** (1292–1354) and **Kusunoki Masashige** (1294–1336), the two outstanding patriot heroes of medieval Japan. The following year the emperor was captured and exiled to Oki, but in 1333 he escaped. Most of western Japan declared for the imperial cause. Ashikaga Takauji (1305–1358), one of the two chief generals dispatched by the Hōjō from eastern Japan, deserted to Daigo II's standards, and the sudden capture of Kamakura by another prominent Hōjō vassal, Nitta Yoshisada (1301–1338), brought the military government of Kamakura to an end.

1333–1336. **Daigo II** in a short period of personal rule, failing to face economic and political realities, attempted to revive the civil imperial rule of the 8th century. However, he did make his able son, Morinaga (1308–1335), *shōgun* and appointed his leading generals military governors of large sections of the land. Because of his dissatisfaction with his share of the spoils in northeastern Japan,

1335. **Takauji** revolted against the throne. Defeating the Nitta, Kitabatake, and other loyal families,

1336. Takauji drove Daigo II out of Kyōto and set up a new emperor from a branch of the imperial family which had been jealously contending the throne with Daigo II's branch for several decades. He thereby became the virtual dictator of the central government, and, although he was not appointed *shōgun* until 1338, with his capture of Kyōto commenced

1336–1568. **THE ASHIKAGA** (or Muromachi) **PERIOD.** The Ashikaga *shōgun* continued the outward forms of the military rule of the Minamoto and Hōjō, but during most of the first and last centuries of the period open warfare disrupted the nation, and at best the Ashikaga exercised only a shadowy control over the great feudatories who made their appearance at this time. The age was characterized by quickly shifting allegiances and by political instability, which at times amounted to anarchy. There was a general redistribution of feudal and economic rights, and the Kyōto nobility, which now lost most of its few remaining lands and provincial sources of income, was reduced to penury. The complicated feudal relations of the Kamakura period broke down into simpler, more compact divisions with practically independent lords, often the former provincial constables, ruling large territories, which were in turn subdivided into smaller units administered by their direct vassals. The collapse of clan unity and an organized feudal system necessitated stronger solidarity within the smaller family and feudal units. The division of patrimonies among heirs was abandoned, and women were reduced to a subordinate status. Lords exercised a closer paternalistic supervision over their vassals, and the latter in turn served their lords with greater personal loyalty.

The **overseas trade** and pirate enterprises of the Japanese increased in the Ashikaga period; the central government once more established official relations with China; and another important period of borrowing from abroad commenced. Foreign trade stimulated the growth of towns and provincial ports, such as Sakai (part of the modern Ōsaka), Hyōgo (the modern Kōbe), and Hakata (part of the modern Fukuoka). Despite political disruption and incessant warfare, a phenomenal economic development took place. Nascent industries grew and expanded, and trade guilds (*za*), usually operating under the patronage of some religious institution, appeared and flourished. However, the unrestricted multiplication of various levies and of customs barriers proved a serious curb to the development of trade.

Kyōto was once more the undisputed political and cultural capital, and there the warrior class and the court nobility tended to fuse. Constant warfare made the period in some respects the intellectual dark ages of Japan, but political disunity helped to diffuse learning throughout the land. Zen monks dominated the intellectual and artistic life of the nation and through their intimate contacts with China, where many had lived and studied, expanded Japan's intellectual and artistic horizons. Although this was a great age of Zen, the other sects, particularly the Amidist sects, flourished and sometimes developed powerful military organizations. It was still a thoroughly Buddhist age, but intellectual life began to free itself from the bonds of Buddhism, Sung Confucian philosophy was introduced from China, and stirrings of new life appeared in Shintō, where for the first time systematic syncretic philosophies were developed.

Despite the violent internecine strife of the early and late Ashikaga period, in the middle decades literature and art, ruled by Zen standards of restraint and refinement, flourished. The *Literature of the Five Monasteries*, as the Zen school at Kyōto was called, revived poetic composition in Chinese, and a great lyric drama called *Nō* appeared. The Sung style of painting, often in monochrome and usually of landscapes, reached its height in Japan with such great masters as **Shūbun** (c. 1415) and **Sesshū** (1420–1506), and the two greatest Japanese schools of painting, the **Tosa** and **Kano**, flourished. The independent architectural styles of the Kamakura period were blended to form a composite style. Minor arts like landscape gardening and flower arrangement grew up, and the tea ceremony was popular among the upper classes. Under Zen tutelage there developed a refined simplicity of taste and a harmony with nature that has had a lasting influence on Japanese art and psychology.

1336–1392. **CIVIL WARS OF THE YOSHINO PERIOD.** When Takauji drove Daigo II out of Kyōto and set up a rival emperor, Daigo II and his partisans, the Kitabatake, Kusunoki, and others, withdrew to the mountainous Yoshino region south of Nara, where Daigo II and three imperial successors maintained for almost six decades a rival court, called the *Southern Court* because of its location. During this period, known as the *Yoshino period* or the *Period of the Northern and Southern Dynasties,* civil war convulsed Japan. In support of the legitimacy of the southern court

1339. **Kitabatake Chikafusa** wrote the *Jinnō-shōtōki,* a history of Japan imbued with extreme nationalistic and patriotic sentiments. It is an important landmark in the growth of a national consciousness and the imperial cult.

1392. **The reunion of the two courts.** Although at times the Yoshino warriors even captured Kyōto, the hopes of the southern court gradually waned. Eventually in 1392 peace was made, and Kameyama II (1383–1392) of the southern line abdicated in favor of **Komatsu II** (1382–1412) of the northern line, with the understanding that the throne should henceforth alternate between members of the two branches of the imperial family, as it had done for several reigns preceding that of Daigo II. However, the northern line never yielded the throne to its rivals despite futile uprisings in their behalf. Official history regards the southern line as the legitimate rulers during the Yoshino period.

1395–1408. **Rule of Yoshimitsu** as retired *shōgun.* Yoshimitsu, the third Ashikaga *shōgun* (1369–1395), after crushing his principal opponents, uniting the two imperial courts, and bringing the Ashikaga power to its apogee, passed on the title of *shōgun* to his son and retired as a monk to his Kitayama estate on the outskirts of Kyōto. The **Golden Pavilion** (*Kinkaku*) he erected there is the outstanding remaining architectural work of the day, and his coterie of artists was the center of the artistic movements of the most creative epoch of the Ashikaga period. There **Kan-ami** (1333–1384) and his son **Se-ami** (1363–1444) perfected the highly refined *Nō* drama from earlier dramatic and terpsichorean performances. The luxurious but artistically creative life of the Kitayama estate was continued for several decades after Yoshimitsu's death by his successors.

1449–1490. **Rule of Yoshimasa** as *shōgun* (1449–1474) and retired *shōgun.* This was the second great creative period of Ashikaga art. In his Higashiyama estate on the edge of Kyōto, Yoshimasa built the **Silver Pavilion** (*Ginkaku*), which as an architectural work

The Golden Pavilion, erected by Yoshimitsu in Kyōto

ranks second only to the Golden Pavilion of Yoshimitsu, and here he and a brilliant group of artists and aesthetes, presided over by Nō-ami (1397–1476), enjoyed a life of luxury and artistic elegance.

At the same time the complete collapse of what little authority the Ashikaga exercised over the nation became apparent, and there was great social unrest, resulting in numerous popular uprisings. Under the pressure of popular demands, Yoshimasa, like other Ashikaga *shōgun,* repeatedly issued Acts of Grace (*Tokusei*), which, unlike those of the Kamakura period, were sweeping debt cancellations for the benefit of the whole debtor class.

1465. The monks of the Enryakuji destroyed the Honganji, the central monastery of the True Pure Land Sect in Kyōto. Such affrays between the great monasteries were common at this time. Rennyō (1415–1499), the eighth hereditary head of the sect, fled to the region

north of Kyōto, where his teachings met with great success and his numerous followers built up a military organization to defend their interests.

1467–1477. The **Ōnin War,** ostensibly a contest over the succession in the Ashikaga and other great military families, was actually a reshuffling of domains and power among the feudal lords, who divided into two camps under the leadership of two great war lords of western Japan, **Yamana Mochitoyo** (Sōzen) (1404–1473) and his son-in-law, **Hosokawa Katsumoto** (1430 [1425?]–1473), long the chief minister (*kanryō*) of the military government (1453–1464, 1468–1473). Kyōto was soon laid waste, but both leaders died in 1473, and exhaustion eventually brought peace in 1477. However local struggles went on unabated. In fact, the Ōnin War was merely the prelude to over a century of almost uninterrupted warfare. This period, which is aptly called the

Epoch of a Warring Country, witnessed a continual shifting of fiefs and power, the elimination of many of the old feudal families, and the emergence of a new group of territorial lords, now known as *daimyō.*

1488. The **True Pure Land Sect** believers north of Kyōto defeated and killed a local lord. This is considered the first of the *Ikkōikki,* or Uprisings of the Ikkō Sect, another name for the True Pure Land Sect. Such uprisings became increasingly common and acted as a medium for popular manifestations of discontent.

1493. **Hosokawa Masamoto** (1466–1507) drove the *shōgun,* Yoshitane (1490–1494, 1508–1521) out of Kyōto and set up a puppet *shōgun* (1494), acts which were repeated by his adopted son, Takakuni (1484–1531), in 1521. Yoshitane's successors suffered similar indignities as the prestige of the Ashikaga dwindled further.

(Cont. p. 561.)

F. The Great Discoveries

1. Asia

THE CRUSADES left Europe with a greatly expanded horizon, with much more extensive trade interests and connections, and with an accentuated hostility toward Islam. The great conquests of the Mongols in the 13th century (**Jenghiz Khan,** 1206–1227; period of greatness under **Kublai Khan,** 1259–1294), in uniting most of Asia, the Near East, and eastern Europe under one sway opened direct communication between Europe and the Orient and raised the prospect of an alliance against the Moslems.

1160–1173. Rabbi **Benjamin of Tudela** (in Navarre) traveled through Persia, central Asia, and to the very confines of China, but for religious reasons his records had little influence on Christian Europe. The same was true of the researches of the great Arab geographer **Yaqut,** who lived in the late 12th and early 13th centuries and wrote a great geographical dictionary.

1245–1247. Travels of **John of Pian de Carpine,** an Umbrian sent to the court of the Great Khan to propose an alliance against Islam and if possible to convert the Mongols. Traveling by way of southern Russia and the Volga, Carpine crossed central Asia and reached the Mongol court at Karakorum. Though well received his mission proved abortive.

1253–1255. Mission of **William of Rubruck,** a Fleming sent by St. Louis to the court of the Great Khan. Rubruck followed much the same route as Carpine and left one of the finest travel accounts of the Middle Ages.

1255–1266. First journey of the Polo brothers, Nicolo and Maffeo, Venetian traders in the Black Sea, who traveled to central Asia, spent three years in Bokhara and proceeded thence to China. They returned to Acre in 1269, bearing letters to the pope from the Mongol ruler.

1271–1295. Second journey of the Polos, accompanied this time by Nicolo's seventeen-year-old son, **Marco,** greatest of all medieval travelers. They took the route Mosul-Baghdad-Ormuz-Kerman-Khorasan-Pamir-Kashgar and thence across the Gobi Desert to the court of the Great Khan. The Mongol ruler was so favorably impressed that he took them into his service. During the next fifteen years Marco became acquainted with much of China, Cochin-China, Burma, and India. The Polos returned by sea by way of Sumatra, India, and Persia. Marco's famous *Book of Various Experiences* was dictated, probably in 1297, while he was a prisoner in Genoa. It was almost immediately popular and colored the whole geographic outlook of the succeeding period. Marco died in 1324.

1290–1340. During this period lively trade relations sprang up between Europe and Asia. Specific records are few, but such as they are they indicate the existence of commercial colonies and missionary groups in Persia (Tabriz), in India (Gujerat and Malabar coast), and in China (Peking and other cities). The great trade routes from Central Asia through southeastern Russia and the Black Sea, and from Trebizond through Persia were wide open. Embassies were constantly passing between western rulers and the ilkhans of Persia, whose emissaries on various occasions came as far as England (1287, 1289, 1290, 1307).

1289. The pope sent out Friar **John of Montecorvino** to take charge of the newly established archbishopric of Peking. John remained at his post until his death in 1328 and seems to have built a flourishing Christian community.

1324–1328. Friar **Oderic of Pordenone** traveled to China, leaving one of the best accounts of the country.

1328. The pope established a bishopric of Quilon and sent out **Jordanus of Severac** to take charge.

1338–1346. **John Marignolli** was sent out to Peking as legate of the pope.

1340. **Francesco Pegolotti,** a Florentine trader at the Genoese station at Kaffa (Black Sea, founded 1266), wrote his *Merchants' Handbook (Della Pratica della Mercatura),* most valuable business manual of the time, which gives an unrivaled account of the commercial communications with Asia.

1368. Overthrow of the Mongol domination in China. Under the succeeding Ming dynasty foreigners were again excluded. The conquests of Timur the Great, shortly after, served to block the Near Eastern trade channels once more.

2. Africa

During the Middle Ages much of Africa was familiar to the Arabs. **Ibn Batuta,** greatest of Arab travelers, between the years 1325 and 1349 journeyed from his home in Morocco across northern Africa, through Egypt, the Near East, Arabia, eastern Africa, and thence to India. Later he traveled northward to the Crimea and thence through central Asia to India. After spending eight years at Delhi, he went on to Ceylon and China. On his return to Morocco in 1349, he set out across the Sahara and visited Timbuktu and the Niger region. His remarkable journeys serve to record not only the Arab trade from Egypt down the east coast to Africa and to India and beyond, but also the regular caravan trade from southern Morocco across the desert to the **kingdom of Ghana** (i.e. Guinea) in Nigeria.

1225. Under the tolerant rule of the Almohades and Marinides in Morocco, the Franciscans and Dominicans were allowed to establish their missionary centers in the country. By the end of the 13th century Christian, and more particularly Jewish, European merchants were engaged in the trans-Saharan trade, dealing chiefly in gold and ivory. In 1447 the Genoese Antonio Malfante penetrated far to the south.

1316. Having heard of a Christian king in East Africa (legend of **Prester John,** widespread in Europe after the spurious letter of 1165), the pope sent eight Dominicans to Ethiopia. Others seem to have been sent in the course of the century.

1402. An **Ethiopian embassy** reached Venice. There were others in 1408 and 1427. In 1452 Ethiopian emissaries arrived at Lisbon and in 1481 at Rome. The object of these embassies, and of those sent in return (especially by the pope in 1453) was to establish a Christian alliance against the Moslem Mamluks in Egypt and later against the Ottoman Turks. Nothing came of this project, but the exchange of missions served to acquaint Europe with that part of Africa.

1270. Beginning of **Portuguese exploration** of the west coast of Africa. The Portuguese Malocello visited the Canary Islands (1340–1341). These were assigned by the pope to the crown of Castile (1344).

1291. The two Genoese, Doria and Vivaldo, set out to find a route to India by sea; they never returned and nothing is known of their explorations.

1394–1460. PRINCE HENRY THE NAVIGATOR, the greatest patron of cosmography and discovery. Prince Henry, as general of the *Order of Christ,* was able to turn the crusading enthusiasm as well as the funds of the order into the fields of science and discovery. From 1418 onward he sent out, almost annually, expeditions carefully prepared and ably conducted. There can be little doubt that the religious factor dominated the work of the prince, though the scientific and commercial factors were hardly less important. That Prince Henry hoped to open up direct communications with Guinea by sea is clear. That he hoped ultimately to find a sea route to Ethiopia and thence to India has been questioned by some, but is reasonably certain.

1418–1419. Exploration of the **Madeira Islands,** some of which had been known before. The **Azores,** some of which appear on the *Medi-*

Prince Henry the Navigator, 1394–1460 (16th-century line engraving)

Marco Polo (1477 woodcut)

cean Portolano of 1351, but probably as imaginary islands, were discovered by Diogo de Sevilla in 1427–1431.

1425. Expedition sent by Prince Henry to conquer the **Canaries** from Castile. Thereafter the prince tried hard to secure the islands by negotiation and so exclude Castile from any share in the West African trade. Further attacks were made upon them in 1450–1453, but by the **treaty of Alcacovas** (1480, Mar. 6) they were definitely assigned to Castile, while West Africa, Guinea, and the islands of the ocean were assigned to Portugal.

1433. After more than ten years of repeated efforts, the Portuguese (under Gil Eannes) succeeded in doubling **Cape Bojador.** The advance then became rapid. Gold and natives were brought back and slave-raiding (later forbidden by Prince Henry) began.

1444. Nuño Tristam reached the Senegal River.

1445. Dinis Dias rounded Cape Verde. By this time the most barren part of the coast

was passed and a lively trade with West Africa (c. 25 caravels a year) developed.

1455–1457. Alvise da Cadamosto (Ca da Mosto), a Venetian in the service of Prince Henry, explored the Senegal and Gambia Rivers and discovered the Cape Verde Islands.

1469. After the death of Prince Henry there was a slackening of activity and the king, Afonso V, for financial reasons leased the Guinea trade for five years to **Fernão Gomes,** with the stipulation that exploration be carried forward at least 100 leagues annually.

1470–1471. Under Gomes' auspices, **João de Santarem** and Pedro de Escolar reached Mina on the Gold Coast, where the Portuguese established a factory (fort, 1482) and did a rich trade in gold.

1472. Fernando Po discovered the island which bears his name. Lopo Gonçalves crossed the equator and Ruy de Sequeira reached latitude 2° south.

1481. With the accession of **John (João) II**

Covilhã and Dias. He rounded the Cape in Nov. 1497, reached Quilimane (Jan. 1498), Mozambique (Mar.), and then Mombasa. Despite trouble with the jealous Arab traders, he was finally able to get a pilot from Melindi. He reached Calicut on the Malabar coast (May 22). He started for home in August 1498, touched Melindi (Jan. 1499) and rounded the Cape (Mar.). The exact date of his arrival at Lisbon is disputed.

1500, Mar. 9.–1501, June 23. VOYAGE OF PEDRO CABRAL, who set out with 13 ships to establish Portuguese trade in the east. After touching Brazil he went on to India, which he reached in September. The fleet loaded pepper and other spices and arrived safely in Lisbon. From this time on Portuguese trading fleets went regularly to India, and Lisbon soon became the chief entrepôt in Europe for oriental products.

1501. Vasco da Gama was sent out with 20 ships to punish the Arabs and to close the Red Sea, in order to cut the trade route through Egypt to Alexandria.

1505. Francisco de Almeida sent out as first governor of the Indies. He took Quiloa and Mombasa on the African coast and established forts at Calicut, Cananor, and Cochin on the Malabar coast.

1509, Feb. 2. Almeida destroyed the Moslem fleet in the **battle of Diu,** definitely establishing Portuguese control in Indian waters.

1509–1515. Governorship of **Afonso de Albuquerque,** who in 1507 had conquered Ormuz on the Persian Gulf. He made Goa the capital of the Portuguese possessions (1510), and in 1511 took Malacca. He opened communication with Siam, the Moluccas, and China.

1513. Jorge Alvarez first landed near Canton.

1517. Fernão Peres de Andrade appeared with a squadron at Canton.

1542. Antonio da Mota and two companions, driven by a storm, first reached Japan.

1557. The Portuguese established themselves

Vasco da Gama's audience with the Samorin at Calicut in 1498 (1747 line engraving)

Bartolomeu Dias

(1481–1495) the crown once more took in hand the work of exploration, and with greater energy than ever.

1482–1484. Diogo Cão reached the mouth of the Congo River and Cape St. Augustine. In 1485–1486 he advanced to Cape Cross and Cape Negro.

1487. King John organized expeditions by land and by sea in the hope of reaching Ethiopia and India. **Pedro de Covilhã** and Afonso de Paiva were sent out by way of Cairo and Aden. Covilhã reached India and on his return followed the east coast of Africa as far south as the mouth of the Zambezi.

1487, Aug.–1488, Dec. VOYAGE OF BARTOLOMEU DIAS. Having followed the Afri-can coast, Dias was driven by a great storm (Dec.–Feb.) south of the tip of Africa. He turned east and soon discovered hills running to the northeast, showing him that he had rounded the **Cape of Good Hope.** He followed the east coast of Africa as far as Mossel Bay and the Great Fish River and then was obliged by his crew to return.

1497, July 8–1499, Aug. 29 or Sept. 9. VOYAGE OF VASCO DA GAMA. This would have been undertaken sooner, excepting for internal troubles in Portugal and disputes with Castile arising from the discoveries of Columbus. Da Gama left with four ships to find the way to India, the feasibility of the route being perfectly clear after the discoveries of

at Macão (near Canton) and initiated regular trade with China.

The opening of the direct route to India at once began the revolution in the conditions of trade between Europe and Asia. The Mamelukes in Egypt had controlled the main routes, from the Persian Gulf to Syrian ports and from the Red Sea to Alexandria, and from these ports the Venetians shipped to western Europe. The Egyptian sultan kept the consignments small (210 tons of pepper per year) and the prices were therefore high. By 1503 the price of pepper in Lisbon was only one-fifth what it was in Venice. When the Portuguese succeeded in blocking the Red Sea route, the Egyptian-Venetian trade was more or less ruined. The conquest of Syria and Egypt by the Turks (1516–1517), though frequently described as a stimulus to the discovery of new routes, had almost nothing to do with the situation. On the contrary the Turkish sultans (notably Suleiman, 1520–1566) did what they could to reopen the Near Eastern routes.

(Cont. p. 543.)

3. *America*

Aztec sacrificial knife

a. PRE-COLUMBIAN AMERICA

The aborigines of America, varying among themselves in certain racial characteristics, migrated from Asia to North America in successive waves by way of the Bering Strait. These migrations began at a very early date, and apparently continued until relatively recent times. The migrants, when they arrived, were in a very primitive state. Becoming isolated from other peoples, they slowly expanded throughout both continents and developed autochthonous cultures which ranged from savagery to a relatively high degree of civilization. Many groups at a comparatively early date attained the agricultural stage, and the Inca of Peru achieved the use of bronze. The use of iron and the principle of the wheel were unknown. The dog universally, the turkey, the duck, and, in the Peruvian highlands; the llama, alpaca, and guanaco were the only existing domestic animals, the llama being the sole beast of burden.

At the time of the discovery the peoples of highest culture, most complex society, and greatest political importance were the **Aztec,** with their center in the Valley of Anáhuac; the **Maya** of Yucatan and portions of Mexico and Central America; the **Chibcha** of the Colombian plateau; and the **Inca,** whose empire centered in the highlands of Peru. Between the higher civilizations of Mexico, Yucatan, and Central America and between those of the Andean region there was extensive interchange of culture over a lengthy period, and it is possible that there was cultural interchange between the peoples of Central America and those of the Andean region. The civilizations of the Aztec and the Inca were built upon preceding cultures of a high order.

The **AZTECS** were originally a minor tribe of the great Nahua group. This group evolved the high **Toltec civilization** which, receiving through cultural transmission mathematical and astronomical knowledge and a calendar from a lowland people, possibly the Maya, reached its height in the 13th century and declined thereafter, being followed by the transitional Chichimec culture. Reaching the shores of Lake Tezcuco in 1325, the Aztecs erected an impregnable capital, **Tenochtitlán,** in the marshes of the lake and, through superior political and military capacity and alliance, extended their control over central and southern Mexico from the Gulf to the Pacific and established colonies

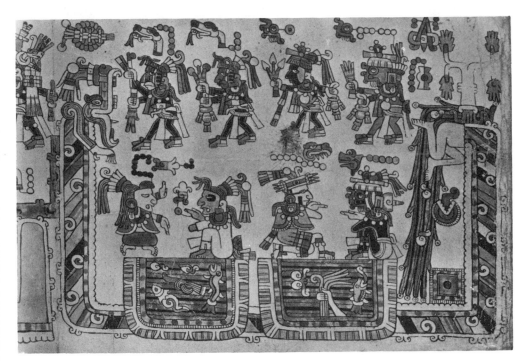

Pre-Columbian Mixtec pictographic manuscript

in Central America. In 1519 Tenochtitlán was a city of some 60,000 house-holders and the Aztec Empire included perhaps 5,000,000 inhabitants. The government was relatively centralized, with an elective monarch, provincial governors appointed by the central authority, a well-organized judicial system, and a large and efficient army. The Aztecs attained a high degree of development in engineering, architecture, art, mathematics, and astronomy. Principal buildings were of mortar and rubble faced with stucco. There existed a body of tradition, history, philosophy, and poetry that was orally transmitted. Picture writing which was rapidly approaching phonetic was evolved. Music was rudimentarily developed. Agriculture was far advanced and commerce and simple industry flourished. The working of gold and silver and the production of pottery and textiles were highly developed. The religion of the Aztecs was polytheistic, and although it included many lofty concepts the deity of war, Huitzilopochtli, was the principal god and his worship led to the development of one of the most extensive systems of human sacrifice that has ever existed. The priesthood constituted a powerful group, political as well as religious. Certain of the peoples subjected by the Aztecs were restive under their domination and were prepared to rebel at the first opportunity. In the mountains to the east of Lake Tezcuco there existed the powerful republic of **Tlaxcala,** which, main-

Aztec pectoral ornament, turquoise mosaic in the form of a double-headed serpent, 14-15th century

Toltec andesite mask

Mayan goddess

taining its independence, regarded the Aztec as hereditary enemies. These conditions created a situation favorable to the Spaniards during the conquest.

The **MAYAS**, before the Christian Era, established themselves in the peninsula of Yucatan, Tabasco, Chiapas, northern, central, and eastern Guatemala, and western Honduras. They developed a civilization which, reaching its apogee well before 1000 A.D., was in certain cultural aspects the highest in the New World. The Maya culture in the earlier period extended with considerable uniformity throughout the greater part of their general area, but after about 1000 A.D., tended to center in the northern part of the peninsula of Yucatan. During the period of highest development the Mayas did not evolve a unified empire, the area being divided into city states governed by politico-religious rulers or ruling groups. Art, architecture, mathematics, engineering, and astronomy were far advanced, and the Mayas had evolved the conception of zero, a vigesimal numerical system, and a calendar more accurate than the Julian. Temples and other major buildings were constructed of stone and mortar and were faced with carved stone. A system of causeways existed. Codices were formed for religious and astronomical purposes, but writing did not exist. A body of traditions, history, and religious prophecies were orally preserved. Religion was polytheistic and relatively humane, and the priestly class, exercising

political authority as well as religious, possessed, with the ruling groups, a monopoly of learning. Widespread commerce existed, and weaving and pottery-making were well developed. Agriculture was on an exceedingly high level. Civil war occurred during the 13th century and certain Mexican groups conquered the Mayas of northern Yucatan. Mexican cultural influences were consequently introduced, especially in art and religion. In the same century a greater degree of political cohesion appears to have been established in the northern part of the peninsula, and this resulted in a period of peace which endured until the 15th century, when internecine strife led to the destruction of Mayapan in 1451 and the abandonment of the great cities Chichen Itzá and Uxmal. The Mayan civilization was decadent culturally and politically when the Spaniards arrived, although certain of the independent provinces were relatively powerful militarily. The Mayas of Yucatan numbered perhaps 400,000 to 500,000 on the eve of the Spanish conquest.

The **CHIBCHAS.** The political organization of the Chibchas, who numbered some 1,000,000, was comparatively cohesive. The Zipa at Bacatá and the Zaque at Tunja were the political rulers, and supreme religious authority was held by the high-priest known as the *Iraca*. The Chibchas possessed a well-developed calendar and numerical system and employed pictographs. Extensive commerce and simple industry existed, ceramics and textiles being highly

Mayan observatory at Chichen Itzá

Lintel from House G in the ancient Maya ceremonial center at Menche, Guatemala

The Inca city of Macchu Pichu, Peru, discovered in 1911

Inca gold beaker

developed. In gold-working the Chibchas were in certain respects unequaled. They employed wood and thatch in the construction of buildings.

The **INCAS,** with their capital at Cuzco, successors to the high coastal and upland cultures of Chimú, Nasca, Pachacamac, and Tiahuanaco, which flourished during the early centuries of the Christian Era, extended their control over the area from Ecuador to central Chile along the coast and inland to the eastern slopes of the Andes including the Bolivian plateau. Expansion was particularly rapid from the 14th century onward and one of the greatest of the conquerors, **Huayna Capac,** lived until the eve of the Spanish conquest. The empire, with a population of perhaps 6,000,000 to 8,000,000, was a thoroughly organized, absolute, paternal, socialistic, and theocratic despotism. All power emanated from the Inca as the ruler and representative of the Sun Deity, whose worship constituted the religion of the Incas. There existed a close-knit and graduated system of provincial and local administration. Each individual had a fixed place in society, and the state benignly provided for the welfare of all. The army was large and well organized, and a system of post and military roads extended to all portions of the empire. In mathematics and astronomy the Incas were not as accomplished as the Mayas and Aztecs, but in engineering, architecture, and the production of textiles and ceramics they were far advanced. The Incas did not evolve writing, but possessed a device to aid memory in the form of the *quipu,* through which governmental records were kept, tradition was preserved, and messages were sent. In gold-working a high degree of skill was attained. Commerce, entailing extensive navigation along

the coast, was well developed. A great body of oral tradition and poetry existed, and music was comparatively well developed. Principal buildings were of stone. Politically the Incas were the most advanced of the peoples of the New World. At his death Huayna Capac, contrary to practice, divided the empire between Huáscar, his son by a lawful wife, and Atahualpa, his son by a concubine. A civil war followed, in which Atahualpa, shortly before the arrival of the Spaniards, triumphed and imprisoned his half-brother.

b. PRE-COLUMBIAN DISCOVERIES

790. **Irish monks,** searching for religious retreats and for new fields of missionary enterprise, reached **Iceland,** after discovering the Faroe Islands in the 7th century.

874. The **Norsemen** (Normans, Vikings) arrived in Iceland and settled.

981. The Norsemen, under **Erik the Red,** discovered **Greenland** and settled on the southwest coast (985–986).

1000. **LEIF ERICSSON,** returning from Norway to Greenland, was driven onto the American coast. In 1963 a Norwegian expedition under **Dr. Helge Ingstad** discovered and excavated nine buildings near L'Anse aux Meadows, at the northern tip of Newfoundland. The settlement dated from c. 1000 A.D. and was incontrovertibly Norse. It was therefore in all probability the *Wineland* (*Vinland*) mentioned by Leif Ericsson.

1003–1006. THORFINN KARLSEFNI set out from Greenland with three ships to settle Wineland. He and his party spent three winters on the American continent. There is no general agreement regarding the localities visited by him, which have been placed by different authorities as far apart as Labrador and Florida. One writer puts the *Helluland* (Flatstone Land) of the Greenlandic-Icelandic sagas in northeastern Labrador; *Markland* (Wood Land) in southern Labrador; *Furdustrand* (Wonder Strand) on the north side of the Gulf of St. Lawrence; *Straumfjord* (Stream Fjord), where the first and third winters were spent, on Chaleur Bay (New Brunswick); and *Hop* (Lagoon) on the New England coast, either north or south of Cape Cod. Another writer is convinced that Karlsefni visited only the Labrador coast and both sides of the northern peninsula of Newfoundland, Straumfjord being, perhaps, in the vicinity of Hare Bay. Wineland was first mentioned in the *Hamburg Church History* of **Adam of Bremen** (1074 ff.), but most of our knowledge derives from the Norse sagas written down in the 14th century. Supposed Norse remains on the American continent (Dighton Rock, Old Stone Mill at Newport) have all been rejected by scholars as spurious, as has also the Kensington Stone, found near Kensington, Minnesota,

in 1898, under the roots of a tree. The stone contains a long runic inscription purporting to record the presence there of a group of Norsemen in 1362. Though long the subject of heated disputation, the stone is now generally held to be a forgery.

How long the Norsemen continued to visit America is an open question. The last definite mention is for 1189 A.D., but there is some reason to believe that they came at least as far as southern Labrador for ship's timber as late as 1347. After that date the Greenland colonies declined, though the West Colony (in southeast Greenland) continued to exist until at least the mid-15th century and ships appear to have gone there periodically, probably trading in walrus hides and tusks.

1470-1474. Between these years two Germans in the Danish service, **Didrick Pining** and **Hans Pothorst,** undertook a voyage to Iceland and the west, supposedly at the request of the king of Portugal. Pining was a great seaman and the terror of the English; from 1478 to 1490 he was governor of Iceland. There is no reason why he should not have been able to reach America, but the evidence does not show

that he and Pothorst went beyond Greenland. On a map of 1537 it is stated that a famous pilot, **Johannes Scolvus** (claimed by some to have been a Pole—Jan Szkolny), reached Labrador at this time. It has been held by some scholars that he must have accompanied Pining and Pothorst, but, since Labrador at this time was a name generally used for Greenland, it seems unlikely that Scolvus went beyond the old Norse settlements. From the Portuguese connection with the expedition it has been concluded by some that **João Vaz Corte Real** went along. There is no satisfactory evidence of this, but in 1474 Corte Real was rewarded with the captaincy of one of the Azores Islands for having made a voyage to the "Land of the Codfish" (?Newfoundland), so that some scholars are well-disposed toward the theory that he may have reached America. But the markings on early maps make it seem likely that he too failed to get beyond Greenland. It is not unlikely, though there is no real evidence, that Breton, Gascon, or Basque fishermen regularly visited the Grand Banks in this period. In any event there is no conclusive proof of any pre-

Ruins of the Inca fortress of Sacsahuaman, Cuzco, Peru

Christoforo Colombo, *by del Piombo*

Columbian discovery, or of any influence on later attempts.

A great many theories have been advanced in recent years, notably by the Portuguese, but also by others, to show that the Portuguese knew of the existence of America before Columbus sailed. Most of the theories rest upon conjecture and clever deductions. All that can be said is that, after the translation of Ptolemy's *Geography* into Latin (1410), the idea of the sphericity of the earth (never entirely lost during the Middle Ages, cf. Roger Bacon's *Opus Maius* of the late 13th century) spread rapidly in scientific circles and revived the idea of reaching Asia by sailing westward. Prince Henry the Navigator, for all his interest in the African route, sent expeditions to the west. In 1427–1431 Diogo de Sevilla discovered seven of the Azores, which may have been known to the Italians as early as 1351. Flores and Colvo were discovered in 1451–1452. The map of Andrea Bianco (1448) shows land of the proper conformation where Brazil lies. It is clear that after 1450 many Portuguese expeditions set out in search of legendary islands (St. Brandan's, Brazil, Antillia, Island of the Seven Cities, etc.) and, according to some scholars, the Lisbon government enforced a policy of rigorous secrecy with regard to new findings. Nevertheless, no present evidence of Portuguese knowledge of America before 1492 can be regarded as conclusive.

c. THE VOYAGES OF COLUMBUS

1451, bet. Aug. 26 and Oct. 31. CRISTO-FORO COLOMBO (Spanish Cristóbal Colón) born near Genoa, the son of Domenico Colombo, a weaver. Almost nothing definite is known of his youth (general unreliability of the biography by his son Fernando). He was probably himself a weaver and probably went to sea only in 1472, when he made a trip to Scio. He seems to have come to Portugal in 1476 and to have made a voyage to England in 1477 (the story of his visit to Iceland is

rejected by almost all authorities). In 1478 he appears to have made a voyage to the Madeiras and in 1482 possibly to the Guinea coast. In 1480 he married the daughter of Bartholomew Perestrello, hereditary captain of Porto Santo, near Madeira. By this time Columbus must have learned much about Portuguese discoveries and certainly about the ideas current in Lisbon. His appeal to the great Florentine geographer, **Paolo Toscanelli**, and the latter's reply (1474) urging a voyage to the west, have been called in question by some writers and may be spurious. In any event the idea of seeking India or China in the west was not novel.

1483 or 1484. Columbus appealed to King João II of Portugal to finance a voyage to the west, but whether to seek new islands or a route to Asia is not clear. At this very time the king was authorizing self-financed expeditions to the west of the Azores (1486, Ferman Dulmo) and he might have licensed Columbus had the latter been willing to finance himself. Others maintain that the Portuguese already knew that Asia could not be reached in this way. Apparently Columbus, whose geographical knowledge appears to have been very incomplete, was regarded as a vain boaster. His project was rejected.

1486. Columbus, through the mediation of some Franciscan monks, was able to submit his project to **Ferdinand and Isabella** of Spain. His religious fervor and personal magnetism impressed the queen, but the project was again rejected by experts. In the following years Columbus met the three Pinzón brothers, wealthy traders and expert navigators, from whom he doubtless learned much.

1492. After being recalled to court, Columbus finally induced the queen to finance his expedition. It is not yet clear whether he set out to discover new islands and territories, or whether his object was to find a route to the Indies. He was made admiral and governor of the territories to be discovered, but also carried letters to the great khan, which makes it probable that his purpose was twofold.

1492, Aug. 3–1493, Mar. 15. THE FIRST VOYAGE. Columbus left Palos with three ships, of which Martin Pinzón commanded one, and the famous pilot Juan de la Cosa another. He left the Canaries (Sept. 6) and reached land in the Bahamas (probably Watling Island) (Oct. 12), naming it *San Salvador*. He then discovered Cuba, which he thought was the territory of the great khan, and Santo Domingo (Española). A post, Navidad, was established on Santo Domingo, after which Columbus returned (1493, Jan. 4), touching at the Azores (Feb. 15), landing at Lisbon (Mar. 4) and finally reaching Palos (Mar. 15). He announced that he had discovered the

Columbus landing on San Salvador, October 12, 1492

Indies, news of which spread over Europe with great rapidity and caused much excitement.

1493, May 4. The Line of Demarcation. At the instance of the Spanish rulers, who feared counterclaims by Portugal, Pope Alexander VI granted to the Catholic kings exclusive right to and possession of all lands to the south and west toward India not held by a Christian prince on Christmas Day, 1492, beyond a line drawn one hundred leagues west of the Azores and Cape Verde Islands.

1493, Sept. 25-1496, June 11. SECOND VOYAGE OF COLUMBUS. He left with 17 caravels and 1500 men to establish Spanish power. On this voyage he discovered Dominica, Puerto Rico, and other of the Antilles and Jamaica, explored the southern coast of Cuba, and circumnavigated Española, where he founded the town of Isabella. He left his brother Bartholomew in charge, who in 1496 transferred the settlement to the southern coast (Santo Domingo).

1494, June 7. TREATY OF TORDESILLAS, between Portugal and Spain. The line of demarcation was moved 270 leagues further west, Portugal to have exclusive rights to all lands to the east of it, and Spain of all lands to the west. The making of this treaty is not entirely clear, and it has often been used as an argument to prove that Portugal already knew of Brazil, which, by the treaty, was brought into the Portuguese sphere.

1498, May 30-1500, Nov. 25. THIRD VOYAGE OF COLUMBUS. Discovery of Trinidad Island (1498, July 31) and South America (Aug. 1) near the mouth of the Orinoco. He explored the coast westward as far as Margarita Island. He then went to Española, where a revolt broke out against him. He requested the crown to send out a judge. The government sent out to the Indies **Francisco de Bobadilla** (1499), who sent Columbus and his brother to Spain as prisoners. Columbus was released and treated with distinction, but, despite the earlier rights granted him, was never restored to his former authority or monopolistic grants. With Bobadilla direct royal control was established.

1502, May 11-1504, Nov. 7. FOURTH VOYAGE OF COLUMBUS. He reached the coast of Honduras and passed south to Panama, returning after having suffered shipwreck at Jamaica.

1506, May. 21. Columbus died in relative obscurity at Valladolid. It is reasonably clear that he believed to the end of his days that he had discovered outlying parts of Asia, despite the fact that ever since 1493 the conviction had spread among experts (e.g. **Peter Martyr**) that a New World had been discovered.

d. POST-COLUMBIAN DISCOVERIES

1497, May 2-Aug. 6. VOYAGE OF JOHN CABOT. Cabot was a wealthy Italian merchant (born in Genoa, resident in Venice) who had traveled in the east (Black Sea, Alexandria, Mecca) and who settled in England about 1490. For several years he sent out expeditions from Bristol to seek the island of Brazil, in the hope of securing the valuable Brazil wood used in dyeing. Columbus' supposed discovery of Asia in the west spurred him on.

Columbus discovering the island of Española

The expedition reached land (June 24) evidently on Cape Breton Island, whence it then cruised along the southern coast of Newfoundland. Cabot was convinced that he had discovered the country of the great khan and intended to return, passing south along the coast to the region of Brazil wood and spices.

1498, May. John and Sebastian Cabot sailed with six ships on a second voyage. They went north, coasted along the east coast of Greenland, thence passed to Labrador and went south by Newfoundland, Nova Scotia, and the New England coast, as far as perhaps Delaware. Thence they returned to England. The date of their arrival is not known. Having found no spices, their efforts evidently no longer interested the king or country. John Cabot is not heard of after March 1499.

1498. King João of Portugal sent out the famous captain, explorer, and scientist, **Duarte Pacheco Pereira,** to investigate the lands in the west. Duarte's account (written in 1505

but published only in 1892) indicates that he may have reached the South American coast. He speaks of a vast continent extending from 70° N.L. to 28° S.L.

1499, May-1500, June. Voyage of **Alonso de Ojeda** and **Amerigo Vespucci** in the service of Spain. They landed in French Guiana, discovered the mouth of the Amazon, and proceeded as far as Cape St. Roque, after which they returned north and west along the coast as far as the Magdalena River and reached home by way of Española. An earlier voyage (1497-1498) by Vespucci, of which he himself tells in the confused and probably spurious sources, has been generally rejected by scholars. Vespucci (1451-1512) was a Florentine resident in Sevilla, probably an agent of the Medici banking firm.

1499, Sept.-1500, Dec. Voyage of **Vicente Yañez Pinzón.** Pinzón made a landfall near Cape St. Roque (1500, Jan.) and thence followed the coast northwestward. At about the same time the Spaniard **Diego de Lepe** explored the Brazilian coast from Cape St. Roque to about 10° S.L.

1500, Apr. 21. The Portuguese commander **Pedro Cabral,** sailing to India with 13 caravels, and accompanied by such distinguished captains as Dias and Duarte Pacheco, landed in Brazil, coming from the Cape Verde Islands. The party stayed only about ten days, but took official possession of the country which Cabral named *Tierra de Vera Cruz.* The idea of Cabral having been the first to discover Brazil, like the idea that his landing there was accidental, has now been given up by some scholars, but the question remains open.

1500. The Portuguese **Gasper de Corte Real,** son of João Vaz, voyaged to the east coast of Greenland and to Labrador. In 1501 he set out on a second expedition, exploring Labrador and thence turning south. He himself was lost on this expedition, but his brother Michael carried out yet another voyage in 1502 to the Newfoundland coast. He too was lost at sea.

1501, May-1502, Sept. SECOND VOYAGE OF AMERIGO VESPUCCI, this time in the service of Portugal. The voyage took him south along the Brazilian coast to about 32° S.L. if not farther. It was from the published account of this voyage and from Vespucci's conviction that what had been found was a *New World* that the geographer **Martin Waldseemüller** was led to propose that this New World be called *America* (1507). The name was at first applied only to South America and the use of it spread slowly until its general adoption toward the end of the 16th century.

Further explorations need not be listed in detail. **Rodrigo de Bastidas** traced the coast from Panama to Port Manzanilla (1500–1502); **Vicente Pinzón** followed the mainland from the Bay of Honduras to beyond the easternmost point of Brazil (1508); **Florián de Ocampo** circumnavigated Cuba (1508), which was conquered by **Diego Velázquez** (1511); **Juan Ponce de Leon,** the governor of Puerto Rico, discovered Florida (1512).

1513, Sept. 25. VASCO NUÑEZ DE BALBOA crossed the Isthmus of Panama and discovered the **Pacific Ocean.**

1515-1516. Juan Diaz de Solis, chief pilot of Spain, searching for a strait to the Pacific, explored the coast of South America from near Rio de Janeiro to the Rio de la Plata, where he was slain.

1517. Francisco Hernández de Córdoba discovered Yucatan, finding traces of large cities and great wealth.

1518. Juan de Grijalva followed the coast north from Yucatan to the Panuco River.

1519. Alvárez Pineda completed exploration of the Gulf of Mexico by coasting from Florida to Vera Cruz and back. **Francisco de Gordillo** advanced up the Atlantic coast to South Carolina (1521), and **Pedro de Quexos** as far as 40° N.L. (1525). At the same time (1524–1525) **Esteban Gómez,** sailing from Spain, followed the coast from Nova Scotia in the north to Florida in the south.

1519-1522. CIRCUMNAVIGATION OF THE GLOBE BY FERDINAND MAGELLAN (Fernão de Magalhaẽs, 1480–1521). Magellan was sent out by the Spanish crown to find a strait to the Moluccas. He reached the Brazilian coast near Pernambuco, explored the estuary of the Rio de la Plata and, after wintering at Port St. Julian, passed through the strait which bears his name and entered the South Sea, to which the name *Mare Pacificum* was given. After following the coast to about 50° S.L. he turned northwest and after months of sailing reached the Ladrones and Philippines. In the latter place he was killed in a skirmish with the natives. One of his vessels, under **Juan Sebastian del Cano,** continued westward and reached Spain, thus completing the circumnavigation of the globe.

(Cont. p. 858)

Amerigo Vespucci during his second voyage, 1501–1502 (engraving c. 1585)

Circumnavigation of the globe by Ferdinand Magellan, 1519–1522 (engraving c. 1585)

IV.
The Early Modern Period

IV. The Early Modern Period

A. Europe and the Near East, 1500–1648

1. *England, Scotland, and Ireland, 1485–1649*

[*For a complete list of the kings of England see Appendix VI.*]

(From p. 293)

1485–1603. HOUSE OF TUDOR.
1485–1509. HENRY VII.   Henry's first act was to imprison the **earl of Warwick,** son of the duke of Clarence. His first parliament (1485) confirmed the crown to him and his heirs. Though the traditional medieval checks on the power of the crown were maintained in theory, in practice Henry went a long way toward developing royal absolutism—establishment of the administrative court later called the **Star Chamber** (1487), suppression of private feudal armies, development of an efficient, if arbitrary, royal financial system (Empson, Dudley, "Morton's Fork").
1487.   The pretended earl of Warwick (Simnel) landed in England, but was defeated at **Stoke** (June 16, 1487), and became one of the king's scullions.
1488–1499.   Attempts of **Perkin Warbeck,** a Fleming who personated the duke of York, to overthrow Henry. Disavowed by Charles VIII in the **peace of Etaples** (Nov. 9, 1492), which ended the war in which Henry had engaged on account of the annexation of Brittany by Charles VIII (1491), Warbeck found a warm reception in Flanders from the duchess of Burgundy, sister of Edward IV. Expelled from Flanders, he fled to Scotland, where his claim was recognized. Warbeck and James IV of Scotland invaded England in 1496. In 1497 a formidable insurrection broke out in Cornwall on occasion of an imposition of a tax by parliament. It was suppressed by the defeat at **Blackheath** (June 22, 1497), and the leaders executed (Flammock). **Peace with Scotland** (Sept. 1497). Warbeck was soon taken and imprisoned in the Tower, whence he escaped, but was recaptured. Plotting another escape with the earl of Warwick, both Perkin and Warwick were executed (1499).
1494. STATUTE OF DROGHEDA (*Poyning's law*): (1) No Irish parliament should be held without the consent of the king of England. (2) No bill could be brought forward in an Irish parliament without his consent.

(3) All recent laws enacted in the English parliament should hold in Ireland.
1496.   *Intercursus magnus,* commercial treaty with Netherlands, granted mutual privileges to English and Flemings and provided fixed duties.
1502.   Marriage of Henry's eldest daughter, Margaret, with James IV, king of Scotland.

Henry VII

James IV

Henry VIII, *by Hans Holbein*

Anne of Cleves (*detail*), *by Hans Holbein*

1509–1547. HENRY VIII. He was six times married: (1) **Catherine of Aragon,** widow of his brother Arthur, mother of Mary the Catholic (married June 3, 1509, divorced March 30, 1533). (2) **Anne Boleyn,** mother of Elizabeth I (married Jan. 25, 1533, beheaded May 19, 1536). (3) **Jane Seymour** (married May 20, 1536, died after the birth of her son Edward VI, Oct. 24, 1537). (4) **Anne of Cleves** (married Jan. 6, 1540, divorced June 24, 1540). (5) **Catherine Howard** (married Aug. 8, 1540, beheaded Feb. 12, 1542). (6) **Catherine Parr** (married July 10, 1543, outlived the king). Henry united in his person the claims of both Lancaster and York.

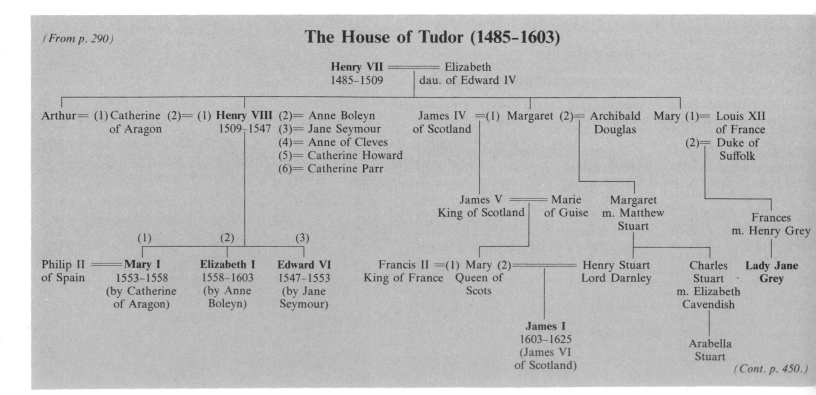

(From p. 290)

The House of Tudor (1485–1603)

Henry VII 1485–1509 ═══ Elizabeth dau. of Edward IV

Arthur ═ (1) Catherine of Aragon   (2)═ (1) **Henry VIII** 1509–1547   (2)═ Anne Boleyn (3)═ Jane Seymour (4)═ Anne of Cleves (5)═ Catherine Howard (6)═ Catherine Parr

James IV of Scotland ═(1) Margaret (2)═ Archibald Douglas   Mary (1)═ Louis XII of France (2)═ Duke of Suffolk

James V King of Scotland ═══ Marie of Guise   Margaret m. Matthew Stuart

Frances m. Henry Grey

(1)   (2)   (3)

Philip II of Spain ═══ **Mary I** 1553–1558 (by Catherine of Aragon)   **Elizabeth I** 1558–1603 (by Anne Boleyn)   **Edward VI** 1547–1553 (by Jane Seymour)

Francis II ═(1) Mary (2)═══ Henry Stuart King of France   Queen of Scots   Lord Darnley

Charles Stuart m. Elizabeth Cavendish   **Lady Jane Grey**

James I 1603–1625 (James VI of Scotland)

Arabella Stuart

(Cont. p. 450.)

Inca fortress Sacsuhuaman near Cuzco, Peru

Inca ruins of Machu Picchu, Peru (p.382)

Landing of Columbus (p.384) by N. C. Wyeth

Thomas Cromwell

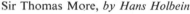

Sir Thomas More, *by Hans Holbein*

Cardinal Wolsey

1511. Henry a member of the **Holy League** *(pp. 403, 408).* Having laid claim to the French crown, he sent troops to Spain, which were unsuccessful (1512). In 1513 the king went to France in person and with Emperor Maximilian won the bloodless victory of

1513, Aug. 17. Guinegate, the battle of the Spurs.

1513, Sept. 9. Battle of Flodden Field. Defeat and death of James IV of Scotland, who was allied with France.

1514, Aug. Peace with France (Tournay ceded to England, afterward [1518] bought by France for 600,000 crowns) and with Scotland.

1515. Thomas Wolsey (1475?–1530), the king's favorite, cardinal and chancellor, papal legate.

1520, June 7. Meeting of Henry VIII and Francis I of France near Calais (Field of the Cloth of Gold).

1521. Execution of the **duke of Buckingham** on a charge of high treason. Buckingham was descended from Edward III.

1521. Henry wrote the *Assertion of the Seven Sacraments* in reply to Luther, and received the title of *Defender of the Faith* from Pope Leo X.

After the **battle of Pavia** *(p. 409),* the relations between Henry and the emperor, which had been weakened by the double failure of the emperor to secure the promised election of Wolsey as pope, became so strained that war seemed inevitable, and a forced loan was assessed on the kingdom, which brought in but little. In 1523 an attempt to force a grant from parliament met with no success, but a rebellion was provoked which was suppressed only by abandoning the demand.

1527. Henry, desiring to divorce his wife in order to marry **Anne Boleyn,** alleged the invalidity of marriage with a deceased brother's wife, and appealed to Rome. The delays of the pope and the scruples of Wolsey enraged the king, who in 1529 deprived the latter of the great seal and gave it to **Sir Thomas More** (1478–1535). Sentence and pardon of Wolsey, who, however, died in disgrace (1530). At the suggestion of **Thomas Cranmer** (1489–1556) the question was referred to the universities of England and Europe, and, a number deciding in the king's favor, Henry married Anne Boleyn. Henry also broke with the Church of Rome. Confiscation of the annates, followed by the resignation of Sir Thomas More (1532).

The **pope excommunicated Henry** and annulled his divorce from Catherine, which Cranmer, now archbishop of Canterbury, had pronounced. After the birth of **Elizabeth,** parliament confirmed the divorce, recognized Elizabeth as heir to the throne (1534), and secured the succession to other children of Anne in case of the death of the princess.

1534. ACT OF SUPREMACY, appointing the king and his successors *Protector and only Supreme Head of the Church and Clergy of England.* This may be taken as the decisive beginning of the **English Reformation.** The break with Rome had political and personal origins; at first there were no real differences in dogma and liturgy. Refusal to take the oath of supremacy was made high treason, under which vote Sir Thomas More was condemned and beheaded (1535).

Thomas Cromwell (1485?–1540), a former servant of Wolsey and his successor in the favor of the king, now vicegerent in matters relating to the Church in England, issued a commission for the inspection of monasteries which resulted in the suppression of the smaller ones in 1536 and the larger ones in 1539, and the confiscation of their property. Abbots now ceased to sit in parliament.

1536. Execution of Anne Boleyn on a charge of adultery. Princess Elizabeth proclaimed illegitimate by parliament. The crown was secured to any subsequent issue of the king, or should that fail, was left to his disposal.

1536. Publication of **Tyndale's translation of the Bible,** by Coverdale, under authority from the king.

1536. Suppression of the Catholic rebellion of **Robert Aske,** aided by **Reginald Pole,** son of Margaret, countess of Salisbury.

Edward VI

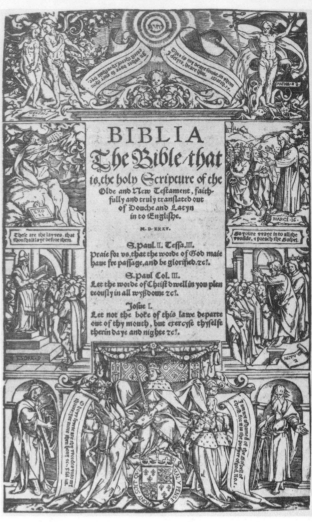

Title page of the first printed English Bible

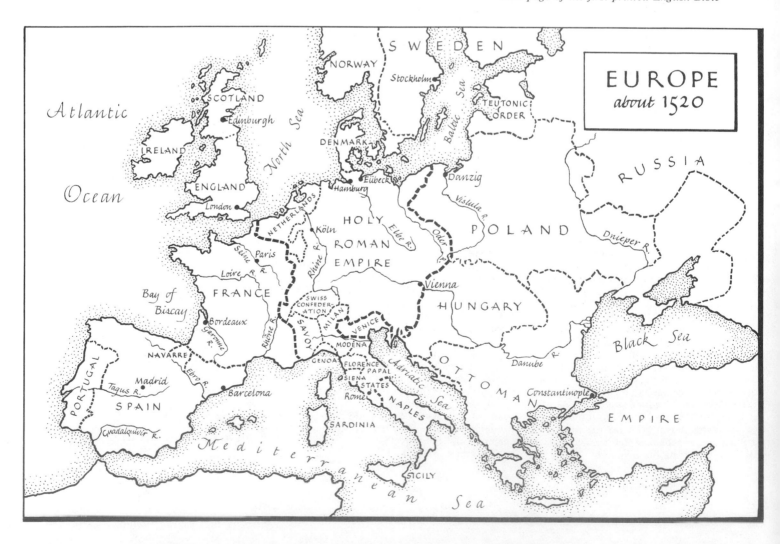

Mary Tudor (*1553–1558*), *by Antonio Moro*

Nicholas Ridley

1539. STATUTE OF THE SIX ARTICLES, defining heresy; denial of any of these positions constituted heresy: (1) transubstantiation; (2) communion in one kind for laymen; (3) celibacy of the priesthood; (4) inviolability of vows of chastity; (5) necessity of private masses; (6) necessity of auricular confession.

1540. Execution of Cromwell, on a charge of treason. Cromwell had fallen under Henry's displeasure by his advocacy of the king's marriage with **Anne of Cleves,** with whom the king was ill-pleased.

1542. IRELAND MADE A KINGDOM.

1542. War with Scotland. James V defeated at the **battle of Solway Moss** (Nov. 25). James V died shortly afterward. Henry proposed a marriage between his son, Edward, and James's infant daughter, Mary, but the Scottish court preferred an alliance with France, whereupon Henry concluded an alliance with the emperor.

1544. Parliament recognized **Mary and Elizabeth** as heirs to the crown in the event of the death of Edward without issue.

1547. Execution of the **earl of Surrey,** on charge of high treason.

Henry VIII died Jan. 28, 1547, leaving a will, wherein the crown was left to the heirs of his sister, **Mary, duchess of Suffolk,** in the event of failure of issue by all of his children.

1547–1553. EDWARD VI, ten years of age; his uncle, earl of Hertford, was appointed lord protector and **duke of Somerset,** and assumed the government. **Repeal of the Six Articles** (1547). Introduction of Protestant doctrines

(1549). Execution of Seymour, brother of the duke of Somerset, who wished to marry the Princess Elizabeth. Establishment of uniformity of service by act of parliament; introduction of Edward VI's *Book of Common Prayer* (1549) (second, 1552).

1550. Fall of the protector, Somerset, who was superseded by Lord Warwick, afterward **duke of Northumberland.** Execution of Somerset (1552).

1551. Forty-two articles of religion published by Cranmer. These were essentially the basis of Anglican Protestantism, though their form was not final until the thirty-nine articles of Elizabeth's reign.

1553. Edward assigned the crown to **Lady Jane Grey,** daughter of his cousin, Frances Grey, eldest daughter of Mary, daughter of Henry VII, to the exclusion of Mary and Elizabeth, daughters of Henry VIII. Lady Jane was married to the son of the duke of Northumberland. **Death of Edward VI** (July 6).

1553–1558. MARY, who had been brought up a Catholic.

The proclamation of **Lady Jane Grey** as queen by Northumberland meeting with no response, Northumberland, Lady Jane, and others were arrested. **Execution of Northumberland** (Aug. 22, 1553). Restoration of Catholic bishops. **Stephen Gardiner,** bishop of Winchester, author of the Six Articles, lord chancellor.

1553. Marriage treaty between Mary and **Philip of Spain,** son of Charles V, afterward

Philip II. Philip was to have the title of *King of England,* but no hand in the government, and in case of Mary's death could not succeed her. This transaction being unpopular, an insurrection broke out, headed by Sir Thomas Carew, the duke of Suffolk, and Sir Thomas Wyatt. The suppression of the rebellion was followed by the **execution of Lady Jane Grey** (Feb. 12, 1554) and her husband. Lady Jane was an accomplished scholar (pupil of **Roger Ascham**) and had no desire for the crown. Imprisonment of Elizabeth, who was soon released on the intercession of the emperor.

1554, July 25. Marriage of Mary and Philip.

1555. Return to Catholicism and persecution of the Protestants (**Bonner,** bishop of London). Oct. 16, **Ridley** and **Latimer;** March 21, 1556, **Cranmer** burnt at the stake. About 300 are said to have been burnt during this persecution. **Cardinal Pole,** archbishop of Canterbury and papal legate (1556).

1557. England drawn into the Spanish war with France. Defeat of the French at the **battle of St. Quentin** (Aug. 10, 1557).

1558, Jan. 7. Loss of Calais, which was captured by the duke of Guise.

1558–1603. ELIZABETH I, brought up a Protestant. **Sir William Cecil** (Baron Burleigh, 1571), secretary of state. **Sir Nicholas Bacon,** lord privy seal. Repeal of the Catholic legislation of Mary; re-enactment of the laws of Henry VIII relating to the Church; **act of Supremacy, act of Uniformity.** Revision of the prayer-book.

1559, Apr. 3. Treaty of Cateau-Cambrésis with France. Calais to be ceded to England in eight years.

On the accession of Francis II, king of France, Mary Stuart, his wife, assumed the title of *Queen of England and Scotland.* Conformity exacted in Scotland. **Treaty of Berwick** (Jan. 1560), between Elizabeth and the Scottish reformers. French troops besieged at Leith. **Treaty of Edinburgh** between England, France, and Scotland (1560, July 6). French interference in Scotland withdrawn. Adoption of a **Confession of Faith** by the Scotch estates. Mary returned to Scotland (1561) after Francis II died and was at once involved in conflict with the Calvinists **(John Knox).**

1563. Adoption of the **Thirty-Nine Articles,** in place of the forty-two published by Cranmer. Completion of the **establishment of the Anglican church** (Church of England, Episcopal Church). A compromise Church, largely Protestant in dogma (though many of the thirty-nine articles are ambiguous), but with a hierarchical organization similar to the Catholic, and a liturgy reminiscent of the Roman Catholic. Numerous **dissenters** or **nonconformists: Puritans**—even then a broad, inexact term, covering various groups which wished to "purify" the Church; to substitute a simple early-Christian ritual for the existing ritual, to make the Church more "Protestant"; **Separatists,** Puritans who left the Anglican church entirely to organize their own churches; **Presbyterians,** Puritans who sought to substitute organization by presbyters and synods for organization by bishops within the Anglican church: **Brownists,** extreme leftist Puritans religiously, the nucleus of the later **Independents** or **Congregationalists;** Brownists and Catholics alone of the Elizabethan religious groups could not be brought under the queen's policy of toleration within the Anglican church. Elizabeth therefore did not "tolerate" and did "persecute" Catholics, Brownists, and, of course, Unitarians (who denied the doctrine of the Trinity).

1564. Peace of Troyes with France. English claims to Calais renounced for 222,000 crowns.

Elizabeth I, 1558–1603

Sir Francis Drake, 1586

In Scotland Mary married her cousin Henry Stuart, **Lord Darnley,** who caused her favorite, David Rizzio, to be murdered (1566) and was himself murdered (Feb. 10, 1567) by Earl Bothwell. The exact part played by Mary in these intrigues is still debated by historians. **Marriage of Mary and Bothwell** (May 15, 1567). The nobles under Earl Moray, Mary's natural brother, revolted, defeated Mary at **Carbury Hill,** near Edinburgh, and imprisoned her at Lochleven Castle. **Abdication of Mary** in favor of her son, by Darnley, **James VI** (July 24, 1567). **Moray** (Murray), regent. In May 1568 Mary escaped from captivity; defeated at **Langside,** May 13, she took refuge in England, where, after some delay, she was placed in confinement (1568).

1577. Alliance of Elizabeth and the Netherlands.

1583–1584. Plots against the queen (Arden, Parry); Spanish plot of Throgmorton; execution of the **earl of Arundel** for corresponding with Mary. **Bond of Association.**

1585. Troops sent to the aid of the Dutch Republic under the **earl of Leicester. Victory of Zutphen** (Sept. 22, 1586), death of **Sir Philip Sidney.**

1586. Expedition of **Sir Francis Drake** to the West Indies, sack of Santo Domingo and Carthagena; rescue of the Virginia colony.

1586. Conspiracy of **Savage, Ballard, Babington,** etc., discovered by the secretary of state, **Sir Francis Walsingham;** execution of the conspirators. The government involved Mary, queen of Scots, in the plot. She was tried at Fotheringay Castle (Oct.), and convicted on the presentation of letters which she alleged to be forged. She was convicted Oct. 25 and executed Feb. 8, 1587.

1587. WAR WITH SPAIN. Construction of an English fleet of war. The Spanish fleet, called the *Invincible Armada* (132 vessels, 3165 cannon), was defeated in the Channel by the English fleet **(Howard, Drake, Hawkins),** July 31–August 8, 1588, and destroyed by a storm off the Hebrides.

1597. Rebellion of the Irish under **Hugh O'Neill, earl of Tyrone;** the failure of the earl of Essex to cope with the insurrection led to his recall, and his successor Lord Mountjoy quickly subjugated the country (1601). Capture of Tyrone, flight of the **earl of Desmond.** A rebellion of **Essex** in London was followed by his execution (1601).

1600. Charter of the East India Company.

1601. Elizabethan Poor Law, preceded by various measures regulating apprenticeship (1563), vagrancy, etc. This famous law charged the parishes with providing for the needy.

1603–1649 (1714). THE HOUSE OF STUART. Personal Union of England and Scotland.

1603–1625. JAMES I (as king of Scotland **James VI**), son of **Mary Stuart.** The Scots had brought him up in the Protestant faith. He was rather pedantic, and not popular with a people used to the hearty Tudors. Divine right of kingship, divine right of the bishops (*no bishop, no king*). In this century the after-effects of the Reformation made themselves felt in England as on the Continent, and in both places resulted in war. In England, however, owing to the peculiar circumstances of the Reformation, these effects were peculiarly conditioned; the religious questions were confused and overshadowed by political and constitutional questions. Under stress of their quarrel, both the first two Stuarts and the parliamentarians sought to bend the medieval English constitution, the Stuarts toward royal absolutism, the parliamentarians toward government by an oligarchy of great nobles and city merchants. Only at the end of the struggle, in the 1640's, did advanced democratic ideas, coupled usually with extreme religious doctrines, appear in minority groups (**Levelers, Fifth Monarchy Men**).

1603, Mar. 24. James I was proclaimed king; he entered London on the 7th of May, and was crowned July 25. Presentation of the **millenary petition** immediately after James's arrival in London, signed by 1000 (800) ministers, asking for the reform of abuses.

The Main and the Bye. The Main was a plot to dethrone James in favor of **Arabella Stuart** (see genealogical table), concocted by Lords Cobham, Grey, and others. **Sir Walter Raleigh** was also implicated and was imprisoned till 1616 (*History of the World* written in prison). The Bye or the *surprising treason* was a plot to imprison the king. **Alliance with France,** negotiated by Sully.

1604, Jan. Hampton Court Conference, between the bishops and the Puritans, James presiding. The Puritans failed to secure any relaxation of the rules of the Church. James issued a proclamation enforcing the **act of Uniformity,** and another banishing Jesuits and seminary priests. Friction between the king

Execution of Mary, Queen of Scots, 1586

The defeat of the Spanish Armada, 1588

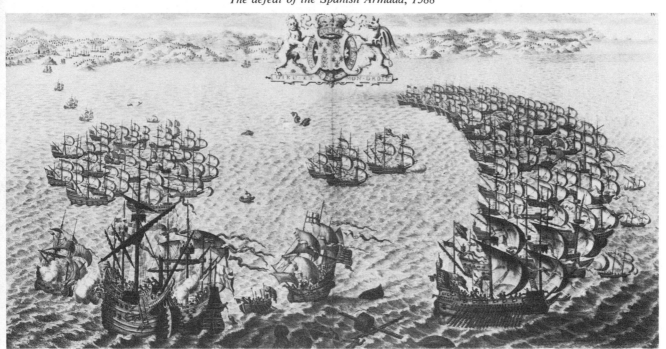

James I (*1603–1625*), *by Daniel Mytens*

and parliament over a disputed election in Bucks (**Goodwin** and **Fortescue**).

1604, Mar. 19–1611, Feb. 9. First parliament of James I. The king's scheme of a real union of England and Scotland unfavorably received. Appointment of a commission to investigate the matter.

Convocation (ecclesiastical court and legislature, at first established [Edward I] as an instrument for ecclesiastical taxation; afterward convened by archbishops for the settlement of church questions; since Henry VIII, convened only by writ from the king, and sitting and enacting [canons] only be permission of the king) adopted some new canons which bore so hard upon the Puritans that 300 clergymen left their livings rather than conform.

1604. Peace with Spain. James proclaimed *King of Great Britain, France, and Ireland* (Oct. 24). Punishment of many recusants (under the recusancy laws of Elizabeth, whereby refusing to go to church, saying Mass, or assisting at Mass was severely punished).

1605, Nov. 5. GUNPOWDER PLOT, originating in 1604 with **Robert Catesby,** after the edict banishing the priests. Preparations for blowing up the houses of parliament with thirty-six barrels of gunpowder. Disclosure of the plot through an anonymous letter. Arrest of **Guy Fawkes** in the vaults on Nov. 4, the day before the meeting of parliament. Trial and execution of the conspirators.

1606. Penal laws against papists. Plague in London. **Episcopacy restored in Scotland.** James urged the union anew, but in vain.

Impositions. The grant of customs duties made at the beginning of every reign (*tonnage* and *poundage,* established by Edward III) proving insufficient to meet James's expenditure, he had recourse to impositions without parliamentary grant, which Mary and Elizabeth had used to only a small extent. Trial of Bates for refusing to pay an imposition on currants. The court of exchequer decided in favor of the king.

1610. The Great Contract; in return for the surrender of some feudal privileges, the king was to receive a yearly income of £200,000. The agreement was frustrated by a dispute over the impositions. Dissolution of parliament (Feb. 9, 1611).

1611. Plantation of Ulster, which was forfeited to the crown by the rebellion of Tyrone.

1611. Completion of the **translation of the Bible,** which was authorized by the king and had occupied 47 ministers since 1604.

1613. Robert Carr, the king's favorite (Viscount Rochester in 1611), created duke of Somerset and lord treasurer, on the death of the earl of Salisbury (Robert Cecil). Death of Henry, prince of Wales (Nov. 1612).

1614, Apr. 5–June 7. Second parliament of James I. Three hundred new members, among whom were **John Pym** (Somersetshire), **Thomas Wentworth** (Yorkshire), **John Eliot** (St. Germains). The whole session was spent in quarreling with the king over the impositions, and parliament was dissolved without making an enactment, whence it is called the *Addled Parliament.*

1615. Renewal of the negotiation for the marriage of James's son to a Spanish princess (opened in 1611). Imposition of a benevolence, which was resisted by Oliver St. John and condemned by the chief justice, **Sir Edward Coke,** who was afterward dismissed from

Peace treaty with Spain, 1604 (English negotiators seated at right, Spanish and Austrians at left)

Flight of the townspeople to escape the plague, 1606

office. **Rise of George Villiers** in the king's favor; Viscount Villiers, earl, marquis, **duke of Buckingham.**

1617. Sir Walter Raleigh, released from the Tower, allowed to sail for the Orinoco, where he hoped to discover a gold mine. Failing in this he attacked the Spanish towns on the Orinoco. On his return to England in the following year, he was executed under the old sentence, as reparation to Spain.

1621, Jan. 30–1622, Feb. 8. Third parliament of James I. The parliament granted a supply for the prosecution of the war in the Palatinate *(p. 426)*, in which James was half-hearted, and then took up the subject of grievances. Impeachment of Mompesson and Mitchell, who had bought monopolies of inn-licensing and the manufacture of gold and silver thread; they were degraded, fined, and banished. **Impeachment of Francis Bacon** (1561–1626), famous essayist and writer on scientific method, lord chancellor since 1618. Bacon admitted that he had received presents from parties in suits, but denied that they had affected his judgment. He was fined £40,000 (which was remitted) and declared incapable of holding office in the future. Petition of the commons against popery and the Spanish marriage. The angry rebuke of the king for meddling in affairs of state (*"bring stools for the ambassadors"*) drew from the parliament

1621, Dec. 18. The **GREAT PROTESTATION:** "That the liberties, franchises, privileges, and jurisdictions of parliament are the ancient and undoubted birthright and inheritance of the subjects of England, and that the arduous and urgent affairs concerning the king, state, and defense of the realm . . . are proper subjects and matter of council and debate in parliament." The king tore the page containing the protestation from the journal of the commons, dissolved parliament (Feb. 8, 1622), and imprisoned **Southampton, Coke, Pym,** and **Selden.**

1623. Charles, prince of Wales, and the **duke of Buckingham** went to Spain and negotiated a marriage treaty, the provisions of which were so favorable to the Catholics as to excite great dissatisfaction in England; finally, being unable to secure any help from Spain in regard to the Palatinate, Charles and Buckingham returned in anger.

1624, Feb. 12–1625, Mar. 27. Fourth parliament of James I. The Spanish marriage was broken off, but even the anger of Buckingham could not drive the parliament into a declaration of war with Spain. Supplies voted for defense. Mansfeld raised 1200 men in England who reached Holland, but nearly all perished there from lack of proper provisions. This was, in fact, a breach with Spain. Marriage treaty with France for the marriage of Prince Charles with **Henriette Marie,** sister of Louis XIII.

1625–1649. CHARLES I.

1625, May 11. Marriage of Charles I and Henriette Marie. Ships sent to Louis XIII secretly engaged not to fight against the Huguenots.

1625. First parliament of Charles I. (Assembled June 18; adjourned to Oxford July 11; dissolved August 12). Grant of tonnage and poundage for one year only, and of £140,000 for the war with Spain. Proceedings against Montague. Unsuccessful expedition of Wimbledon against Cadiz.

1626, Feb. 6–June 15. Second parliament of Charles I. Charles had hoped for a more pliable parliament, as he had appointed several of the leaders of the first parliament sheriffs, and so kept them out of the second. But this parliament, under the lead of **Sir John Eliot,** was more intractable than the last. Lord Bristol, to whom no writ had been sent by order of the king, received one on the interference of the lords, but was requested not to appear. He took his seat and brought **charges against Buckingham,** on which that lord was impeached (May). Imprisonment of Sir John Eliot and Sir Dudley Digges, who were set at liberty only upon the refusal of parliament to proceed to business without them.

1626–1630. War against France. Inglorious expedition of Buckingham to the relief of Rochelle (1627).

Exaction of a **forced loan** to raise money for the French war, and for the subsidy which Charles had agreed to supply to Christian IV of Denmark.

1628, Mar. 17–1629, Mar. 10. Third parliament of Charles I. (May): Passage of the **PETITION OF RIGHT:** (1) Prohibition of benevolences, and all forms of taxation, without consent of parliament. (2) Soldiers should not be billeted in private houses. (3) No commission should

Sir Walter Raleigh and his son, 1602

be given to military officers to execute martial law in time of peace. (4) No one should be imprisoned unless upon a specified charge. Assent of the king (June 7). Grant of five subsidies.

Charles having, after the first year of his reign, continued to levy tonnage and poundage, the commons drew up a remonstrance

Massacre of Protestants in Ulster, 1641

against that practice. **Prorogation of parliament** (June 26). Seizure of goods of merchants who refused to pay tonnage and poundage.

Assassination of Buckingham (Aug. 23), by Felton.

1629, Jan. New session of parliament. The Commons at once took up the question of **tonnage and poundage;** claim of privilege in the case of Rolle, one of the merchants, whose goods had been seized, and who was a member of parliament. Turbulent scene in the house of commons; the speaker held in the chair while the **resolutions of Eliot** were read: Whoever introduced innovations in religion, or opinions disagreeing with those of the true Church; whoever advised the levy of tonnage and poundage without grant of parliament; whoever voluntarily paid such duties, was an enemy of the kingdom.

1629. Eliot and eight other members were arrested (Mar. 5); Eliot died in the Tower in Nov. 1632 and the others made submission. **Parliament dissolved** (Mar. 10). For eleven years (1629–1640) Charles governed without a parliament, raising money by hand-to-mouth expedients, reviving old taxes, old feudal privileges of the crown, selling monopolies. These were rarely wholly illegal, but seemed to parliamentarians contrary to recent constitutional developments. **Charles's advisers: William Laud** (1573–1645), bishop of London, 1628, archbishop of Canterbury, 1633; **Thomas Wentworth** (1593–1641), earl of Strafford and lord lieutenant of Ireland, 1639. Both were extremists. Strafford's policy of *thorough* further embittered Ireland. **Peace was made with France** (Apr. 1630) **and with Spain** (Nov. 1630). Conformity was enforced, and the communion table inrailed.

1634. The tax which focused hatred on Charles was **ship-money,** by which a writ issued in 1635

extended to the whole country a tax hitherto levied only on seaboard towns. **John Hampden,** a Buckinghamshire country gentleman, defying the tax, was tried, 1637–1638, and lost his case in court but won it with the public.

1637. An attempt to read the English liturgy in Edinburgh, ordered by Charles, produced a **riot at St. Giles'** (June 23). This was followed by the organization of the Scottish Presbyterians to resist episcopacy. On February 28, 1638 was signed the **Solemn League and Covenant** (whence *Covenanters*) for the defense of the reformed religion. In November a general assembly at Glasgow abolished episcopacy, settled liturgy and canons, and gave final form to the **Scottish Kirk.**

1639. The First Bishops' War. The Scots seized Edinburgh Castle and raised an army. Charles marched to meet them near Berwick, but concluded with them, without battle, the **pacification of Dunse** (June 18). After the armies had been disbanded, the questions were to be referred to a new general assembly and a new (Scottish) parliament. At the Edinburgh assembly the work of the Glasgow assembly was confirmed, and parliament proved intractable.

1640. Charles, in trouble in Scotland and financially distressed in England, now called his **fourth parliament,** the *Short Parliament* at Westminster (Apr. 13–May 5). This parliament, refusing to vote money until grievances were settled, was immediately dissolved. Riots, attacks on Laud's palace. The Scottish trouble broke out in the **Second Bishops' War,** and the royalists were beaten in a skirmish at **Newburn on the Tyne** (Aug. 28). By the **treaty of Ripon** (Oct. 26) Charles agreed to pay the Scottish army £850 a day until a permanent settlement could be made. These obligations made the calling of a parliament inevitable.

1640. The **LONG PARLIAMENT, the fifth parliament of Charles I** (Nov. 3, 1640–Mar. 16, 1660). First session until September 8, 1641.

The fact that the Scottish army was not to be disbanded until paid gave the commons an unusual hold over Charles. On November 11, **Strafford was impeached,** followed by **Laud,** and both were sent to the Tower. At the trial of Strafford in the following March, the result of impeachment being uncertain, it was dropped, and a bill of attainder introduced, which passed both commons and lords in April. Strafford was executed on May 12. Meanwhile, parliament passed the revolutionary **Triennial Act,** requiring the summoning of parliament every three years even without the initiative of the crown (May 15, 1641). This was followed in May by a bill to prevent the dissolution or proroguing of the present parliament without its own consent, which Charles reluctantly signed, along with Strafford's attainder. The culmination of radicalism was the introduction of a bill for the abolition of bishops. This was the **Root and Branch Bill,** on which the moderate Puritans split with the more radical Presbyterians.

1641, July. Abolition of the courts of Star Chamber and **High Commission.** These courts were a part of the constitution of England, and their abolition shows that parliament was determined to effect a revolution. In August a **treaty of pacification with Scotland** was made, and Scottish and English armies were paid with the proceedings of a special poll-tax granted by parliament. Charles took refuge with the

Scots. On the proroguing of parliament in September, each house appointed a committee to sit in the vacation (**Pym,** chairman of the commons' committee). Charles attempted to conciliate the moderate parliamentarians by giving office to their leader, Lucius Cary, Lord Falkland.

In Scotland, the **marquis of Montrose** plotted the seizure of the **earl of Argyll,** Presbyterian leader. The discovery of the plot seemed to involve Charles himself, who was thus thrown into the hands of Argyll. Charles practically surrendered all control over Scotland to Argyll and the Presbyterians, receiving from the latter only a promise not to interfere in English religious affairs (Oct. 1641).

1641, Oct. 21. Parliament assembled and heard the news of the **massacre of Protestants in Ulster** (30,000 killed). Still unwilling to entrust Charles with an army, it presented him with the **Grand Remonstrance** (Dec. 1) passed in the Commons in November by eleven votes, a summary of all the grievances of his reign. It was ordered printed by parliament on December 14.

1642, Jan. 3. Charles ordered the impeachment of Lord Kimbolton, and of **Pym, Hampden, Haselrig, Holles, Strode,** of the commons, for treasonable correspondence with the Scots in the recent troubles. The commons refusing to order the arrest, Charles with a few hundred soldiers went to the house and attempted to seize the five members (Jan. 4). Failing to find them, he withdrew. The five members had taken refuge in London, where the commons followed them, and formed a committee at the Guildhall under the protection of the citizens of London. Charles left London on January 10 and the five members returned. The victorious commons, emboldened, put before the king bills excluding bishops from the lords and giving command of the militia to parliament. From York he refused to sign the latter (March) and there he was joined by 32 peers and 65 members of the commons. He also had the great seal. The parliament at Westminster now was obliged to pass ordinances which were not submitted to the king and did not appear under the great seal.

June 2. Parliament made a final approach to Charles, submitting the **nineteen propositions:** that the king should give his assent to the militia bill; that all fortified places should be entrusted to officers appointed by parliament; that the liturgy and church government should be reformed in accordance with the wishes of parliament; that parliament should appoint and dismiss all royal ministers, appoint guardians for the king's children, and have the power of excluding from the upper house at will all peers created after that date. The propositions were rejected.

July. Parliament appointed a **committee of public safety,** and put Essex in charge of an army of 20,000 foot and 4000 cavalry. When on August 22 Charles raised the royal standard at Nottingham, the military phase of the **Great Rebellion** began.

1642–1646. THE CIVIL WAR. Roughly, northern and west-central England stood by the king; East Anglia, London, and the south with parliament. Socially, the gentry, the Anglican clergy, and the peasantry were royalist; the middle classes, the great merchants, and many great nobles were parliamentarians. But neither *Roundhead* (parliamentarian, Puritan) nor *Cavalier* (royalist) describes completely an economic or social class. Armies were small. Until Cromwell's *Ironsides* the royalist cavalry was superior. The war was relatively free from excesses.

1642. After the drawn **battle of Edgehill** (Oct. 23), where **Prince Rupert** (royalist cavalry leader, son of the Elector Palatine and Elizabeth of England) distinguished himself, the king marched on London, but turned back at Brentford when confronted by Essex (Nov. 12).

The associated counties of Norfolk, Suffolk, Essex, Cambridge, Hertford, and Huntingdon raised a force entrusted to **Oliver Cromwell** (1599–1658), which as the *Ironsides* finally became the best troops in the war. Meantime, the war was a series of raids and indecisive battles. **Capture of Reading** by Essex (Apr. 27, 1643); skirmish at **Chalgrove Field** in which Hampden was mortally wounded (June 18). **Capture of Bristol** by Rupert (July 25), counterbalanced by Essex's **relief of Gloucester** (Sept.), gallantly defended by Massey. **First battle of Newbury** (Sept. 20).

1643, July 1. Through all this the **Westminster Assembly,** which sat until 1649, debated religious and theological problems.

Sept. 25. The **SOLEMN LEAGUE AND COVENANT,** signed by 25 peers and 288 members of the commons, agreeing to make the religions of England, Ireland, and Scotland as nearly uniform as possible and to reform religion *"according to the word of God, and the examples of the best reformed churches."* All civil and military officials were required to sign the covenant (nearly 2000 clergymen refused and lost their livings). The Scots now consented to help the English parliamentarians; a Scottish army crossed the Tweed (Jan. 1644). Charles rashly enlisted Irish Catholic insurgents with whom he concluded peace, thus alienating many Englishmen.

1644, Jan. Charles convened a **royalist parliament at Oxford.** His opponents established (Feb. 15) a joint committee of the two kingdoms of Scotland and England. At the **battle of Nantwich** (Jan. 25) the royalist Irish were beaten by **Sir Thomas Fairfax,** who, in junction with the Scots, besieged York while Essex and Waller besieged Oxford.

July 2. BATTLE OF MARSTON MOOR. Prince Rupert, after defeating the Scots, was decisively beaten by Cromwell and his Ironsides. This was the crucial battle of the war, and gave the north to parliament. York surrendered (July 16); Newcastle (Oct. 16). In the south Waller was beaten at **Cropredy Bridge** (June 29) and Essex's infantry surrendered to Charles in Cornwall. The indecisive **second battle of Newbury** (Oct. 27), in which Charles was pitted against Essex, Waller, and Manchester, prefaced the so-called **treaty of Uxbridge,** a truce in January and February 1645, during which parliament's proposals were rejected by Charles, who had hitherto had the best of the war in south and southwest.

In Scotland, **Montrose,** after slipping into the country in disguise (Aug. 1644), raised highland clans for Charles and gained several victories over the Covenanters (**Tippamuir,** Sept. 1; **Inverlochy,** Feb. 2, 1645; **Auldcarn,** May 1; **Alford,** July 2). At one time he held most of Scotland, but his armies melted away

when the parliament sent General Leslie into Scotland after Naseby, and at **Philiphaugh** (Sept. 13, 1645) the Stuart partisans were decisively beaten. Montrose fled to the Continent.

1645, Jan. Laud, tried in March 1644, was attainted and executed. England was fast moving toward extreme Protestantism. With Cromwell, the **Independents** rose to leadership. **Presbyterianism,** with some reservations for the Independents, became the established Church. The **Self-Denying Ordinance** (April 3) having excluded members of either house from military command, Fairfax superseded Essex as captain-general, and Cromwell, with the ordinance suspended in his case, became lieutenant-general. The army was reformed into the *New Model* on the lines of the Ironsides.

1645, June 14. BATTLE OF NASEBY, decisive defeat of the king, ruin of his cause. Royalist towns and houses surrendered rapidly: Leicester (June 18), Bridgewater (July 23), Bristol (Sept. 11), Carlisle, Winchester, Basing House (Oct.), Latham House (Dec.). At **Stowe-on-the-Wold** (Mar. 26, 1646) Lord Ashley was beaten and captured in the final battle of the war. Charles surrendered himself to the Scots (May 5).

1646, July. Parliament submitted to the captive Charles the **Newcastle proposals:** that parliament control the militia for twenty years; that Charles take the Covenant; that he support the Presbyterian establishment. Hoping to profit by the obviously impending breach between the Presbyterians in parliament and the Independents in the army, Charles rejected the propositions.

1647, Jan. 30. The **Scots surrendered Charles to parliament** in return for their back pay (£400,000). He was brought to Holmby House in Northamptonshire. **Army and parliament in open conflict.** Parliament reappointed Fairfax commander-in-chief, re-enacted the self-denying ordinance, and voted the disband-

ment of all soldiers not needed for garrisons or for service in Ireland. This the army refused to accept, claiming full payment for arrears in salary. A detachment headed by Cornet Joyce seized Charles at Holmby House (June 4), and carried him prisoner to the army, thus forestalling an agreement between king and Presbyterians.

June 4. On the same day Cromwell fled from parliament to the army at **Triptow Heath,** where it had taken an oath not to disband until freedom of conscience was secured, and had erected a council of adjudicators. From St. Albans the army addressed to parliament a *humble representation* (June 10) and demanded the exclusion of eleven members, among them Holles, obnoxious to it. The two speakers, fourteen lords, and about one hundred of the commons fled to the army (July). Proposals were presented to the king by the army: that worship be free for all; that parliament control army and navy for ten years and appoint officers of state; that parliament serve for three years (**triennial parliaments**). The king rejected them, and moved to take refuge with the Presbyterian members of parliament; but the army entered London (Aug. 6) and forced parliament to take back the members who had fled to the army. Charles removed to Hampton Court, where he rejected a modified form of the previous proposals and fled to the Isle of Wight, where he was detained by the governor of Carisbrooke Castle (Nov. 11).

Dec. 24. The **Four Bills** presented to the king by parliament: (1) parliament to command the army for twenty years; (2) all declarations and proclamations against the parliament to be recalled; (3) all peers created since the great seal was sent to Charles to be incapable of sitting in the house; (4) the two houses should adjourn at pleasure. Charles, who was only playing with the parliament in the hope of securing aid from Scotland, rejected the four bills (Dec. 28), after he had already signed a **secret treaty with the Scots** (Dec. 26). Charles agreed to abolish Episcopacy and restore Presbyterianism; the Scots, who looked with horror on the rising tide of toleration in England, agreed to restore him by force of arms.

1648, Jan. 15. Parliament renounced allegiance to the king, and voted to have no more communication with him.

1648. SECOND CIVIL WAR. At once a war between Scotland and England, a war between the royalists and the Roundheads, and a war between the Presbyterians and the Independents.

Mar. At a meeting of army officers at Windsor it was decided to bring the king to trial. Parliament having reassembled with 306 members and the Presbyterians again in control, repealed the non-communication resolution and attempted to reopen negotiations with the king (July).

Aug. 17–20. Battle of Preston. Under the duke of Hamilton, a Scottish army invaded England, but was beaten by Cromwell. This ended the second civil war. The so-called **treaty of Newport,** between king and parliament, had no result, as Charles was seized by the army (Dec. 1) and, parliament having again attempted to treat with the king, **Colonel Thomas Pride,** by order of the council of affairs, forcibly excluded 96 Presbyterian mem-

Sir Thomas Fairfax, 1644

Richard Hooker, 1543–1600

Thomas Hobbes, 1588–1678

Benjamin Johnson, 1572–1637

William Shakespeare, 1564–1616

bers from the parliament (*Pride's Purge*, Dec. 6, 7), which is henceforth known as the *Rump Parliament* (some 60 members).

Dec. 13. The **Rump** repealed the vote to continue negotiations with Charles, and voted that Charles be brought to trial. Appointment of a high court of justice of 135 members to try the king was rejected by the lords (1649, Jan. 2) whereupon the commons resolved that the legislative power resided solely with the commons (Jan. 4; passed Jan. 6 without concurrence of the lords).

1649, Jan. 20. The army council drew up a temporary *Instrument of Government.* Charles was tried before the high court (67 members present, Bradshaw presiding) whose jurisdiction he simply denied (Jan. 20–27). **The king was sentenced to death and beheaded at Whitehall** (Jan. 30). *(Cont. p. 448.)*

BRITISH CULTURE

(1) Architecture

Inigo Jones (1573–1652) built Lincoln's Inn Chapel, the Banqueting-Hall at Whitehall, the Queen's House at Greenwich.

(2) Education

University of Glasgow (1452); University of Aberdeen (1494); St. Paul's School, London (1510); Rugby (1567); Harrow (1571); Trinity College, Dublin (1591).

(3) Literature

Prose: Archbishop Cranmer, *Book of Common Prayer;* **Thomas More** (1478–1535), *Utopia,* 1516; **Roger Ascham** (1515–1568), *The School-*master; **Raphael Holinshed** (d. 1580), *Chronicles of England, Scotland, and Ireland;* **Richard Hakluyt** (1553–1616) *Principall Navigations, Voyages and Discoveries of the English Nation,* 1589; **Richard Hooker** (1554–1600), *Laws of Ecclesiastical Polity;* **Sir Philip Sidney** (1554–1586), poet and critic, *Defense of Poesie;* **Sir Walter Raleigh** (1552–1618), *The History of the World;* **John Lyly** (1554–1606), *Euphues; The Anatomy of Wit;* the essayist **Francis Bacon** (1561–1626), *Essays, New Atlantis,* 1621; the dramatists **Thomas Nashe** (1567–1601); **Thomas Dekker** (1570–1641); **Robert Burton** (1577–1640), *Anatomy of Melancholy;* the political philosophers **Thomas Hobbes** (1588–1679), *Leviathan,* 1651; and **James Harrington** (1611–1677), *Oceana,* 1656; **Izaak Walton** (1593–1683), *The Compleat Angler,* 1653; **Sir Thomas Browne** (1605–1682), *Religio Medici.*

Poets: **John Skelton** (1460–1529); **Sir Thomas Wyatt** (c. 1503–1542); **Edmund Spenser** (c. 1552–1599), *Faerie Queene;* **Sir Walter Raleigh; Sir Philip Sidney; Michael Drayton** (1563–1631); **Ben Jonson** (1573–1637); **John Donne** (1573–1631); **Sir John Suckling** (1609–1642); **Thomas Carew** (1605–1639); **Richard Lovelace** (1618–1658). **Thomas Campion** (1567–1620) was composer and poet. Other composers: **Thomas Tallis** (c. 1505–1585); **William Byrd** (1540–1623); **Orlando Gibbons** (1583–1625).

Dramatists: Miracle plays ceased after the Reformation, but dramas in a popular vein were written by **John Lyly** (see above) and **Thomas Kyd** (*The Spanish Tragedy,* 1585). **Christopher Marlowe's** use of blank verse in his morality plays (*Dr. Faustus,* 1588; *The Jew of Malta,* 1589) established its use in the English theater.

William Shakespeare (1564–1616) was the greatest dramatist of the Elizabethan or any other age. The force of his dramas is dependent on his careful development of individual characters, his forceful and precise vocabulary, the universal and enduring appeal of his plots to other ages and other cultures. Many of his plays, especially the tragedies, relied on actual history for their stories (*Julius Caesar, King Lear, Henry IV, Henry V, Henry VI*); among the comedies are *A Midsummer Night's Dream* (1595–1596), *As You Like It, Twelfth Night.* Shakespeare also wrote some of the best sonnets in the English language, using a rhyme scheme of his own devising; also lyrics, often incorporated in the plays and the narrative poems *Venus and Adonis* and *The Rape of Lucrece.*

Shakespeare established the drama as a respected literary medium. The comedies of his contemporary, the poet **Ben Jonson,** dared to criticize the foibles of the age (*Volpone,* 1605). The collaborators **Francis Beaumont** (1579–1625) and **John Fletcher** (1584–1616) dared to poke fun at their society (*The Knight of the Burning Pestle,* 1607).

John Milton (1608–1674), the blind poet of the Puritan Revolution, composed sonnets and lyric poems (*L'Allegro, Il Penseroso, Lycidas*) in his youth; published his three major poems after the Restoration (*Paradise Lost,* 1667; *Paradise Regained,* 1671; *Samson Agonistes,* 1671), and a *History of Britain to the Conquest* (1670). During the twenty years of political unrest he wrote prose tracts in support of liberty—in religion, education, and in the press (*Areopagitica,* 1644).

2. The Netherlands, to 1648

The provinces of the **Low Countries,** originally inhabited by Batavians and other Germanic tribes, had formed a part of the empire of Charlemagne and, after the **treaty of Mersen** (870), belonged in large part to Germany, forming a dependency of the kingdom of Lotharingia. The decline of the ducal power favored the growth of powerful counties and duchies, such as Brabant, Flanders, Gelders, Holland, Zeeland, Hainault, and the bishopric of Utrecht. After 1384 the provinces were brought under the control of the dukes of Burgundy in the following manner: **Philip II** (the Bold), fourth son of **John II** of France, became the duke of Burgundy in 1363. He acquired Flanders and Artois (1384) through marriage with Margaret, heiress of Count Louis II. Their son was **John the Fearless,** duke of Burgundy (1404–1419), who was succeeded by his son, **Philip the Good** (1419–1467). Philip acquired Namur by purchase (1425). Brabant and Limburg came to him by bequest (Joanna, daughter of John III, duke of Brabant, left them to her great-nephew, Antoine, brother of John the Fearless). In 1433 he acquired Holland, Hainault, and Zeeland by cession from Jacqueline, countess of Holland; and in 1443, Luxemburg, by cession from Elizabeth of Luxemburg. He also added Antwerp and Mechlin. His son, **Charles the Bold** (duke of Burgundy 1467–1477), acquired Gelderland and Zutphen by bequest from Duke Arnold (1472).

Mary, the daughter and heiress of Charles the Bold, married **Maximilian,** archduke of Austria and later emperor *(p. 323).* Their son, **Philip the Handsome** (duke of Burgundy), married **Joanna,** the daughter of Ferdinand of Aragon and Isabella of Castile, and thus the Netherland provinces passed ultimately into the hands of Philip's son, **Charles I** (Charles V as emperor).
1548. Charles annexed the seventeen provinces (Brabant, Limburg, Luxemburg, Gelderland, Flanders, Artois, Hainault, Holland, Zeeland, Namur, Zutphen, East Friesland, West Friesland. Mechlin, Utrecht, Overyssel, Groningen) to the Burgundian circle of the empire.
1556. Abdication of Charles. The Netherlands, like Spain, passed to his son,
1556–1598. PHILIP II.
1568–1648. REVOLT OF THE NETHERLANDS. The provinces had long enjoyed ancient and important privileges. The estates (*staaten, états*) granted taxes and troops. **Calvinism** had taken firm root in the northern provinces (commonly called Holland), but the southern provinces (now Belgium) remained Catholic. The Spanish garrison, the penal edicts against heretics, the dread of the introduction of the Spanish Inquisition, all these factors led (during the rule [1559–1567] of **Margaret of Parma,** the natural sister of Philip II, and her adviser, **Cardinal Granvelle**) to the formation of a **league of nobles** (*Compromise of Breda*), headed by Philip Marnix

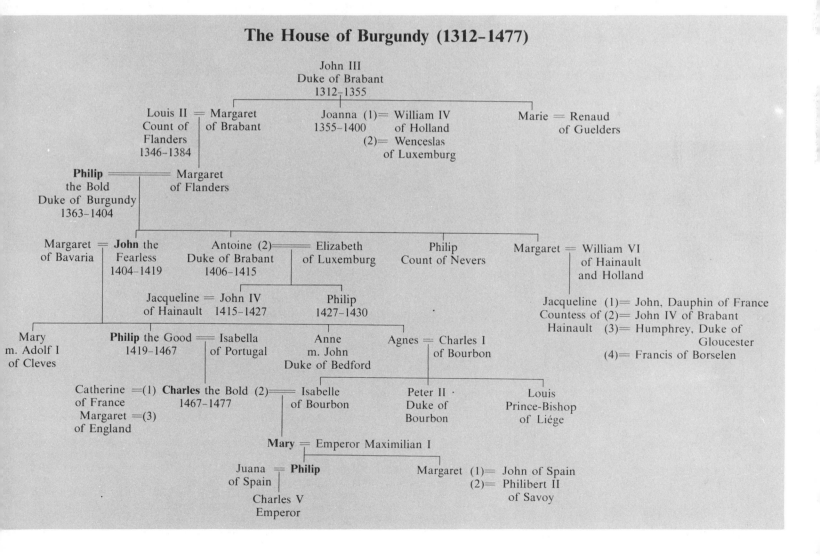

The House of Burgundy (1312–1477)

John III
Duke of Brabant
1312–1355

Louis II = Margaret
Count of   of Brabant
Flanders
1346–1384

Joanna (1)= William IV
1355–1400   of Holland
(2)= Wenceslas
of Luxemburg

Marie = Renaud
of Guelders

Philip ======= Margaret
the Bold   of Flanders
Duke of Burgundy
1363–1404

Margaret = John the   Antoine (2)======= Elizabeth   Philip   Margaret = William VI
of Bavaria   Fearless   Duke of Brabant   of Luxemburg   Count of Nevers   of Hainault
              1404–1419   1406–1415   and Holland

Jacqueline = John IV   Philip
of Hainault 1415–1427   1427–1430

Jacqueline (1)= John, Dauphin of France
Countess of (2)= John IV of Brabant
Hainault   (3)= Humphrey, Duke of
                                Gloucester
           (4)= Francis of Borselen

Mary
m. Adolf I
of Cleves

Philip the Good = Isabella   Anne   Agnes = Charles I
1419–1467   of Portugal   m. John   of Bourbon
                                   Duke of Bedford

Catherine =(1) Charles the Bold (2)====== Isabelle   Peter II ·   Louis
of France   1467–1477   of Bourbon   Duke of   Prince-Bishop
Margaret =(3)   Bourbon   of Liége
of England

Mary = Emperor Maximilian I

Juana = Philip   Margaret (1)= John of Spain
of Spain   (2)= Philibert II
                                            of Savoy
Charles V
Emperor

of St. Aldegonde. Presentation of a petition by 300 nobles (*Gueux = Beggars,* a party name, originating in the contemptuous remark of the count of Barlaimont: *"Ce n'est qu'un tas de gueux"*). Insurrection of the lower classes. Destruction of images and sack of the churches. These disturbances were opposed by **Lamoral, count Egmont** (1522–1568) and **William of Nassau,** prince of Orange (**William the Silent,** 1533–1584), the leaders of the higher nobility, who, however, soon lost control of the movement. Protestant and Catholic parties soon emerged.

1567. Philip sent to the Netherlands the **duke of Alva** (1508–1582) with an army of 20,000 Spaniards. William of Orange and many thousands of Netherlanders left their native land. Margaret resigned her regency and also departed. Creation of the Council of Blood. Ruthless suppression of opposition. **Execution of Egmont, Hoorn,** and many other prominent figures. The estates of those who failed to appear before the tribunal were confiscated, including those of William of Orange. The latter, with his brother Louis, thereupon invaded the Netherlands, but was repulsed by Alva.

The arbitrary taxes imposed by Alva (the tenth pfennig from the price of every article sold, the hundredth part of every income) produced a new revolt.

1572. Capture of Brill, by the "Water Beggars." The insurrection spread rapidly, especially throughout the north.

1573. Alva was recalled at his own request. His successor, **Luis de Requesens y Zuñiga,** gained a

1574. Victory at Mookerheide, where two brothers of the prince of Orange fell. But the

William of Nassau, 1533–1584

The Haywagon, *by Hieronymus Bosch, 1460–1516*

Spaniards could not suppress the revolt. Requesens died (1576). **Capture and sack of Antwerp, Maestricht, Ghent,** and other towns by the Spaniards led to the

1576. PACIFICATION OF GHENT, a treaty among all the provinces by which they united, without regard to national or religious differences, to drive out the Spaniards. The new governor, **Don John of Austria,** was unable to quiet the country, despite disputes between the various parties. He died in 1578, and was succeeded by

1578–1592. Alexander Farnese (duke of Parma), a shrewd statesman and an excellent general. Parma ultimately subdued the southern provinces, on the promise that their old political freedom should be restored. The seven northern provinces (Holland, Zeeland, Utrecht, Gelderland, Groningen, Friesland, Overyssel), thereupon concluded

1579. The **UNION OF UTRECHT,** followed by a proclamation of **independence from Spain** (1581). The hereditary *statthaltership* was settled on **William of Orange.** After his murder at Delft (1584, July 10), he was succeeded by his son

1584. Maurice of Nassau, only seventeen years old. Parma continued his victorious campaigns and managed to capture Antwerp. Thereupon the English came to the aid of the insurgents.

1588. Philip II, hoping to put an end to the Anglo-Dutch combination, organized the **Great Armada,** which was defeated by the English and destroyed in a terrible storm *(p. 394).*

1609. The **Twelve Years' Truce** put an end to sporadic and inconclusive fighting and virtually established the independence of the northern provinces. After its expiration the war was resumed by the Spaniards. The Hollanders, who had grown rich and powerful at sea in the course of the struggle, were well able to hold their own, and finally

1648. The **TREATY OF WESTPHALIA** recognized the independence of the Republic of the United Provinces. *(Cont. p. 463.)*

CULTURAL DEVELOPMENTS

Josquin Des Près (c. 1445–1521) composed sacred songs in the polyphonic style of the Flemish school which dominated 16th-century Renaissance music: for example, the madrigals of **Adrian Willaert** (1480–1563), the sacred and secular songs of the greatest Flemish composer, **Orlando di Lasso** (1532–1594). The religious tradition in painting carried over from the **Van Eycks, Hans Memling** (1435–1495), and **Hieronymus Bosch** (1460–1516), to the engravings of **Lucas Van Leyden** (1494–1533), and the paintings of **Quentin Massys** (c. 1466–1530). **Pieter Breughel** (1525–1569) painted both religious and everyday subjects, with the addition of humorous, earthy touches.

The golden age of painting came in the first half of the 17th century, especially with the portraits and religious paintings of **Peter Paul Rubens** (1577–1640); the portraits of **Anthony Van Dyck** (1599–1641), court painter to Charles I of England, and **Franz Hals** (1580–1666); the landscapes of **Meyndaert Hobbema** (1638–1709) and **Jacob Ruysdael** (1628–1682); the genre works of **Jan Vermeer** (1632–1675); and culminating in the work of **Rembrandt van Rijn** (1606–1669): his numerous paintings of himself and of Saskia (1633–1641), *The Anatomy Lesson* (1632), *The Night Watch* (1642), his etchings, and his religious paintings.

Hugo Grotius (1583–1645) laid the bases of international law in his *Mare liberum* (1609) and *De jure belli ac pacis* (1625).

(Cont. p. 463.)

3. *France, 1483–1641*

(From p. 301)

[*For a complete list of the kings of France see Appendix VII.*]

1483–1498. CHARLES VIII. Death of the duke of Brittany (1488) called forth a coalition of the empire, Spain and England to preserve the independence of the duchy, but this proved futile. Charles married Anne, the heiress, in 1491, and concluded the **treaties of Senlis** (with the emperor) and **Étaples** (with England). Spain was bought off by the cession of Roussillon and Cerdagne.

1495–1496. Charles's expedition to Italy to claim the inheritance of Naples (through his father from Charles, duke of Maine and Provence; see genealogical table). Charles marched victoriously through Italy and conquered Naples, but was soon obliged to withdraw in the face of the **Holy League** (Emperor Maximilian, Pope Alexander VI, Spain, Venice, Milan, and ultimately England), formed to protect Italy from foreign domination. Importance of the expedition in furthering the introduction of the Renaissance into France.

1498–1589. HOUSES OF ORLÉANS AND ANGOULÊME. Branch lines of the house of Valois (since 1328) whose relation to the main line is shown *on page 404.*

1498–1515. LOUIS XII obtained a divorce from Jeanne, daughter of Louis XI, and married **Anne of Brittany,** widow of Charles VIII, in order to keep this duchy for the crown; as grandson of Valentina Visconti he laid claim to Milan, drove out Ludovico Moro, who was imprisoned when he tried to return (1500).

1501. Louis, in alliance with Ferdinand the Catholic, king of Aragon, conquered the kingdom of Naples. The Spaniards and French soon falling out, the latter were defeated by the Spanish general Gonzalvo de Córdoba on the Garigliano (1503). Louis XII gave up his claims to Naples.

1508. Louis a party to the **league of Cambrai** *(p. 420)*. In 1511 the pope, Ferdinand the Catholic, and Venice renewed the **Holy League,** with the object of driving the French out of Italy. The latter, under the young **Gaston de Foix,** duke of Nemours, nephew of Louis XII. were at first successful in the war, taking Brescia (1512) by storm (**Seigneur de Bayard,** *sans peur et sans reproche,* 1476–1524), and defeating the united Spanish and papal armies at **Ravenna,** with the aid of 5000 German mercenaries, in the same year; they were, however, compelled by the Swiss to evacuate Milan. In 1513 the French formed a new alliance with Venice, but were defeated by the Swiss at **Novara** and withdrew from Italy. **Henry VIII of England,** who had joined the Holy League in 1512, and the **Emperor Maximilian,** who had joined in 1513, invaded France, and defeated the French at

1513, Aug. 17. Guinegate, called the *battle of the Spurs* from the hasty flight of the French.

France concluded peace with the pope, with Spain (1511), with the emperor, and with Henry VIII (1514). Anne of Brittany having died, Louis took as his third wife Mary, the sister of Henry VIII. He died soon after the marriage (1515) and was succeeded by his cousin and son-in-law, the count of Angoulême, who had married Claude, heiress of Brittany, which, however, was not actually incorporated with France until later.

1515–1547. FRANCIS I.

1515, Sept. 13–14. Francis reconquered Milan by the brilliant **victory of Marignano** over the Swiss. Peace and alliance between France and Switzerland. **Treaty of Geneva** (Nov. 7, 1515); **treaty of Fribourg** (Nov. 29, 1516). The latter (*la paix perpétuelle*) endured till the French Revolution.

1516. Increase of the royal power by the **concordat of Bologna** with the pope, which rescinded the Pragmatic Sanction of 1438 and placed the choice of bishops and abbots in the hands of the king; the pope on the other hand received the annates, or the first year's revenue of every ecclesiastical domain where the king's

Louis XII, 1498–1515

right of presentation was exercised. Francis also abandoned the principle of the council of Basel, that the pope was subordinate to an ecumenical council.

1520. Meeting of Francis and Henry VIII of England in the neighborhood of Calais (*Field of the Cloth of Gold*). The wars of Francis with Charles V *(pp. 409 ff.)* occupied the rest of the reign. Restrictions upon the political rights of the *parlements*. Beginnings of French Protestantism. Reformers of Meaux, **Lefebvre d'Étaples** (1455–1537). King and *parlements* condemned the movement.

1547–1559. HENRY II, son of Francis. Growing power of the **house of Guise (Francis,** duke of Guise, and **Charles,** cardinal of Lorraine).

Henry's mistress, **Diane of Poitiers,** duchess of Valentinois, ruled him almost absolutely. **Montmorency,** constable. Persecution of the Protestants in France; assistance to German Protestants.

1547. Final union of Brittany with the French crown.

1552. War with Charles V. Seizure of the three bishoprics (Toul, Metz, and Verdun) by the French.

1556–1559. War with Spain. The French were defeated by the Spaniards, supported by the

Francis I, *(1515–1547), by Jean Clouet (detail)*

1559–1560. **FRANCIS II**, the first husband of Mary Stuart of Scotland, who was a niece of the Guises. Measures against the Protestants (*chambres ardentes*). The king's mother, **Catherine de' Medici** (1519–1589), struggled for power and influence against the Bourbon princes: **Anthony** (king of Navarre); and **Louis de Condé**, who were descended from Louis IX. The **Guises**, at first rivals of the queen-mother and then in alliance with her, conducted all the affairs of state and surpassed in influence their opponents, the Catholic constable, **Montmorency**, and his nephews, the three Châtillon brothers: **Gaspard, Admiral de Coligny; François d'Andelot**, and **Cardinal Châtillon**, later leaders of the Huguenots. **Conspiracy of Amboise** against the Guises. This was defeated (1560). Death of Francis II.

1560–1574. **CHARLES IX** (ten years old), the brother of Francis. He was wholly under the influence of his mother.

1562–1598. **THE RELIGIOUS WARS.** Persecution compelled the **Huguenots** (as the French Protestants were called—derivation uncertain) to take up arms. At the same time they formed a political party. The ensuing struggles, therefore, did not constitute a purely religious war, but also a political, civil war, in which the leaders of both parties endeavored to exploit the weakness of the crown and get control of the government. The Huguenots were recruited primarily from the nobility (between two-fifths and one-half of the French nobility were at one time Protestant) and from the new capitalist-artisan class. Save in the southwest very few peasants became Protestants. Paris and the northeast in general remained Catholic throughout.

The **first three wars** form properly one war, interrupted by truces called peaces (**Amboise**, 1563; **Longjumeau**, 1568; **St. Germain**, 1570),

which bore no fruit. Battles, in which the Huguenots were worsted, were fought at **Dreux** (1562); **Jarnac** (1569); and **Moncontour** (1569). Huguenot cavalry, recruited from the nobility, was excellent; the infantry was generally weak.

The issue of the first period was that the Huguenots, despite defeat, were given conditional freedom of worship, which was guaranteed them by the surrender, for two years, of four strongholds (La Rochelle, Cognac, Montauban, La Charité).

1572, Aug. 23–24. **MASSACRE OF ST. BARTHOLOMEW.** Murder of Coligny and general massacre of Protestants in Paris and in the provinces, on the occasion of the marriage of **Henry of Bourbon**, king of Navarre, with the sister of Charles IX, **Margaret of Valois**. Henry of Navarre saved his life by a pretended conversion to Catholicism. The massacre led to the

1572–1573. **Fourth War. La Rochelle,** besieged by Henry, brother of Charles IX, made a brave defense. The election of the duke of Anjou to the crown of Poland brought about a compromise. **Edict of Boulogne** (July 8, 1573) ended the war favorably to the Huguenots.

Charles IX died May 30, 1574. His brother, who fled from Poland, became king.

1574–1589. **HENRY III.**

1574–1576. The **Fifth War**, during which **Henry of Navarre** reassumed the Protestant faith, was concluded by conditions more favorable to the Huguenots than those of any previous peace. **Peace of Chastenoy** (*Paix de Monsieur*, after the duke of Alencon) May 6, 1576. Hence dissatisfaction among the Catholics. Origin of the **Holy League** (1576), which, in alliance with Philip II of Spain, purposed the annihilation of the reformed party, and the elevation of the Guises to the throne. The king, out of fear of the league, proclaimed himself its head and

English, in the **battle of St. Quentin** (1557), and by Egmont at **Gravelines** (1558).

1558. **Calais,** the last English possession in France, was captured by the duke of Guise.

1559, Apr. 3. **PEACE OF CATEAU-CAMBRESIS,** which ended the Hapsburg-Valois wars. The French restored all their conquests except Calais and the three bishoprics. Henry II, who died of a wound received in a tournament, was succeeded by his son

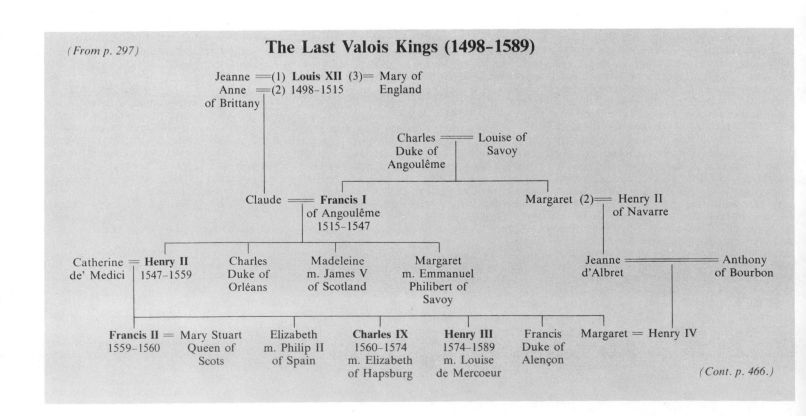

(From p. 297)

The Last Valois Kings (1498–1589)

(Cont. p. 466.)

forbade the exercise of the Protestant religion throughout France. The Protestants and moderate Catholics had joined forces in 1575 by the **confederation of Milhaud.**

1577. Sixth War, wherein the Huguenots were defeated, but obtained favorable terms at the **peace of Bergerac** or **Poitiers** (Sept. 17), as the king was unwilling to let the league become too powerful. In spite of the renewal of the treaty of peace, not one of its articles was executed. This caused the

1580. Seventh War, which was ended in the same year by the **treaty of Fleix** (Nov. 26), in which the conditions granted the Huguenots in former treaties were confirmed.

1584. The death of Francis, duke of Alençon (since the accession of Henry III, duke of Anjou), the younger brother of the king, rendered the extinction of the house of Valois certain. As it was the intention of the league to exclude from the throne Henry of Navarre, who belonged to the reformed religion, and to give the crown to the latter's uncle, the **cardinal of Bourbon,** and as the league meantime had induced the king to revoke the concessions granted to the Huguenots, there broke out the

1585-1589. Eighth War, called the *War of the Three Henrys* (Henry III of Valois, Henry of Navarre, Henry of Guise). The Catholic party triumphed in spite of the **victory of Coutras** (Oct. 20, 1587), gained by Henry of Navarre. Formation of the **league of Sixteen** at Paris, which purposed the deposition of the weak king. Guise entered Paris, was received with acclamation (*King of Paris*); the timid resistance of the king was broken by a popular insurrection (*Day of the Barricades,* May 12, 1588). Henry III fled to Blois, where he summoned the estates-general of the kingdom. Finding no support among them against the league, he caused Henry, duke of Guise, and

his brother, Louis the Cardinal, to be murdered (Dec. 23, 1588). At this news, a revolt of the Catholic party broke out, headed by the brother of the murdered men, the **duke of Mayenne.** Henry III fled to Henry of Navarre in the Huguenot camp, where he was murdered before Paris, at St. Cloud, by the monk **Jacques Clément** (July 31).

1589-1792. HOUSE OF BOURBON, descended from Louis IX's younger son Robert, count of Clermont, husband of Beatrice of Bourbon.

1589-1610. HENRY IV. The Catholic party refused to recognize Henry and made the old cardinal of Bourbon king under the name of **Charles X** (1590). Some wished the duke of Mayenne to be his successor, while others joined themselves to Philip II of Spain, who laid claim to the throne of France on behalf of his daughter by his third marriage with Elizabeth of Valois, sister of Henry III. Victory of Henry IV over the duke of Mayenne at **Arques** (1589) and at the

1590, Mar. 14. Battle of Ivry, crucial battle of these wars. Henry besieged Paris, which was relieved by Mayenne and the Spanish duke of Parma. Henry's ultimate success was made possible by the *politiques,* usually moderate Catholics, but above all French patriots who wished a strong national monarchy. **Michel de L'Hôpital** (1505-1573) their precursor and founder. Henry abjured the reformed religion at St. Denis (1593) and was crowned at Chartres (1594). Brissac having thereupon surrendered Paris to him, the power of the league was broken. Not, however, until Henry, after public penance by his ambassadors at Rome, had been freed from the papal ban, was he generally recognized (by Mayenne too). The civil wars of religion were ended by the

1598, Apr. 15. EDICT OF NANTES, which

Charles IX, 1560–1574

gave the Huguenots equal political rights with the Catholics, but by no means secured them entire freedom of religious worship. The edict granted the exercise of the reformed religion to nobles having the right of criminal jurisdiction (*seigneurs hauts justiciers*), and to the citizens of a certain number of cities and towns, but prohibited it in all episcopal and archiepiscopal cities, at the court of the king, and in Paris, as well as within a circle of twenty miles

Henry II, 1547–1559, jousting at the tournament in which he was mortally wounded

Henry IV, 1553–1610, enters Paris

of many projects for organizing Europe and ending war. Question of Cleves-Jülich succession. Henry IV supported the claims of Brandenburg. In the midst of great preparations for war, **Henry was assassinated** at Paris, 1610 (May 14) by the fanatic **François Ravaillac.**

1610–1643. LOUIS XIII, his son, nine years old. Regency of his mother, **Marie de' Medici** (1573–1642). Sully removed from office; the Italian **Concini** was placed in control of affairs. Louis XIII, declared of age in 1614, was in fact all his life under the guidance of others. **Summons of the estates-general,** 1614, being the last before the Revolution of 1789. Arrest and murder of Concini; the queen-mother banished to Blois (1617). The king under the influence of his favorite, the duke of Luynes. By the mediation of Armand-Jean du Plessis (1585–1642), **cardinal-duke of Richelieu,** a treaty was concluded between Luynes and the queen-mother (1619). New **civil war.** Contest of the crown with the nobility and the Huguenots. After the death of Luynes (1621) Marie de' Medici and her favorite, Richelieu, obtained control of affairs. The influence of the latter soon became supreme, and the queen-dowager quarreled with him.

1624–1642. Administration of Richelieu, whose influence over the king was henceforward unbroken. Numerous conspiracies against him instigated by Gaston of Orléans, the king's brother.

1625. Revolt of the Huguenots under the dukes of Rohan and Soubise.

1627–1628. Siege of La Rochelle, under the personal supervision of Richelieu. In spite of the dispatch of three fleets from England to the aid of the Huguenots, the city surrendered October 28, 1628, after an heroic resistance of fourteen months. Defeat of the duke of Rohan, and complete subjugation of the Huguenots, who thereafter were no longer an armed political party, but only a tolerated sect.

War in Italy with Spain; subjugation of Savoy, Richelieu at the head of the army.

around the capital. Public offices were opened to the Huguenots and **mixed chambers** were established in four *parlements* (Paris, Toulouse, Grenoble, Bordeaux). The Huguenots obtained some fortified towns, and were recognized, to a certain extent, as an armed political party. The edict of Nantes was registered by the *parlement* only after a long delay. Though it established nothing like a "free church in a free state," it did give legal status to a kind of toleration not yet formally recognized elsewhere. **Treaty of Vervins** (May 2, 1598) with Spain; restoration of all conquests to France.

Adoption of measures looking to the improvement of the finances and the general prosperity, which had gone to decay, especially by Rosny, afterward **duke of Sully** (1560–1641). *Grand Design,* attributed to Henry IV by Sully in his *Mémoires,* for the ensurance of perpetual peace through organization of a Christian Republic with the Holy Roman Emperor as first magistrate and a general council of Europe to discuss affairs of common interest and if possible settle disputes. Intended primarily to limit the Hapsburg power, this plan is nevertheless interesting as the first

Louis XIII, 1610–1643

Marie de' Medici, 1573–1642

The Inquisition (p.401) by Francisco Goya

The Council of Trent (p.409), 16th century Venetian School

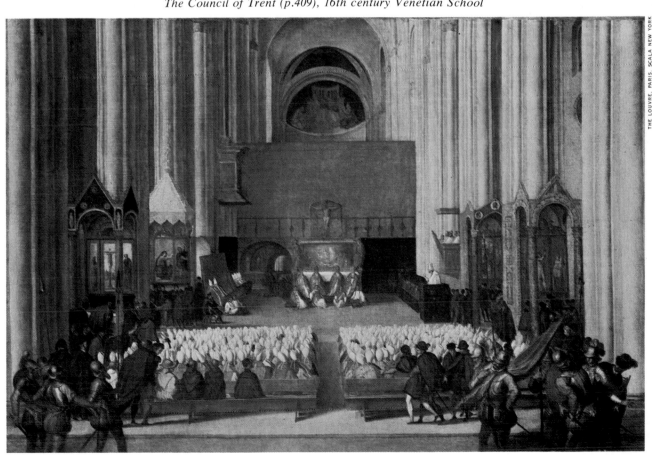

The Battle of Lepanto (p.410), Venetian School

Mary Tudor, Queen of England (p.390) by Antonio Moro

Pope Leo X (p.416) and Cardinals
by Raphael (portion)

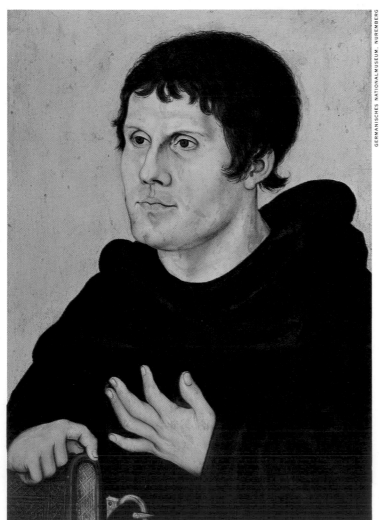

Martin Luther (p.420) by Lucas Cranach

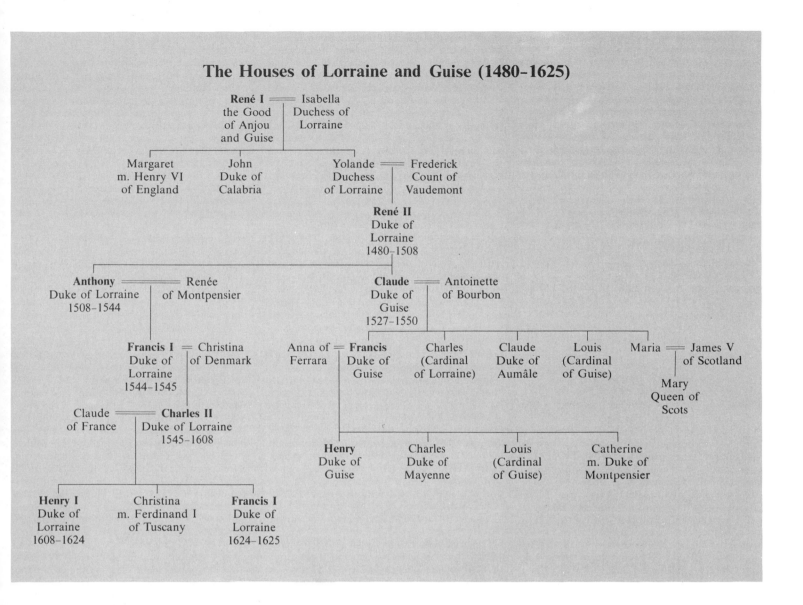

The Houses of Lorraine and Guise (1480–1625)

René I ═══ Isabella
the Good / Duchess of
of Anjou / Lorraine
and Guise

Margaret / John / Yolande ═══ Frederick
m. Henry VI / Duke of / Duchess / Count of
of England / Calabria / of Lorraine / Vaudemont

René II
Duke of
Lorraine
1480–1508

Anthony ═══ Renée / **Claude** ═══ Antoinette
Duke of Lorraine / of Montpensier / Duke of / of Bourbon
1508–1544 / Guise
1527–1550

Francis I ═ Christina / Anna of ═ **Francis** / Charles / Claude / Louis / Maria ═══ James V
Duke of / of Denmark / Ferrara / Duke of / (Cardinal / Duke of / (Cardinal / of Scotland
Lorraine / Guise / of Lorraine) / Aumâle / of Guise)
1544–1545

Mary
Queen of
Scots

Claude ═══ **Charles II**
of France / Duke of Lorraine
1545–1608

Henry / Charles / Louis / Catherine
Duke of / Duke of / (Cardinal / m. Duke of
Guise / Mayenne / of Guise) / Montpensier

Henry I / Christina / **Francis I**
Duke of / m. Ferdinand I / Duke of
Lorraine / of Tuscany / Lorraine
1608–1624 / 1624–1625

Cardinal-duke of Richelieu at the siege of La Rochelle, 1627–28

1631. Treaty of Cherasco. France renounced all conquests in Italy, but by a secret treaty with Victor Amadeus, duke of Savoy, Pignerol was surrendered to France (negotiators of these treaties, Richelieu's confidant, **Father Joseph,** and the pope's agent, **Mazarin**).

A final attempt of Marie de' Medici to overthrow the cardinal failed ignominiously (Nov. 11, 1630, the *Day of Dupes*).

1632, Oct. 30. Defeat of the conspiracy of Gaston and the duke of Montmorency. Execution of Montmorency.

1631–1648. FRENCH PARTICIPATION IN THE THIRTY YEARS' WAR *(pp. 428-430)*.

1641. Conspiracy of Henry d'Effiat, marquis of Cinq-Mars (*Monsieur le Grand*). His secret treaty with Spain. The plot was discovered by Richelieu.

Richelieu, though not a good financial administrator, helped somewhat to further the power of the royal bureaucracy (*intendants*) at the expense of the nobles, the Huguenots, and the *parlements.* His true greatness, however, lay in the field of foreign affairs. He restored French influence in Italy, in the Netherlands, and in Germany, and established it also in Sweden. It was his work that laid the foundation for the power of Louis XIV, and became the traditional basis of French foreign policy. *(Cont. p. 465.)*

CULTURAL DEVELOPMENTS

The literature of the French Renaissance bore the stamp of Italy. **François Rabelais** (1494–1553), a former monk, satirized the foibles of his society in *Pantagruel* (1532) and *Gargantua* (1534). His books also bear testimony to the importance the Renaissance placed on humanistic education. The reformer **John Calvin** (1509–1564) was his contemporary and complete antithesis. The poets **Pierre de Ronsard** (1524–1585) and **Joachim du Bellay** (1522–1560) were the leaders of **La Pléiade**, a group of young poets who urged the use of the French language in literature, at the same time reverting to a classical style. **Michel Eyquem de Montaigne** (1533–1592) introduced a question-and-answer technique in his *Essais* (1580–1595); his influence on the philosophy, style, and form of later writers such as Rousseau and the essayist Charles Lamb was marked.

In the 16th century several of the chateaux in the Loire valley were built. The sculptors **Michel Colombe** (1430–1512), **Jean Goujon** (1515–1560), and **Germain Pillon** (1535–1590) were active; and **François Clouet** (1516–1572) painted royal portraits.

In the field of political theory **Jean Bodin's** (1530–1596) *Six livres de la République* (1576) was outstanding.

4. *The Iberian Peninsula*

(From p. 304)

a. SPAIN, 1479–1659

1479–1516. REIGN OF FERDINAND of Aragon and his wife, **ISABELLA,** queen of Castile (1474–1504). During this period much progress was made, notably in Castile, toward the suppression of the fractious aristocracy and the regulation of the Church. Aragon, on the other hand, retained most of its privileges. The **conquest of Granada** (1492) ended Moorish power in the peninsula, while the **discovery of America** in the same year opened up endless possibilities of overseas empire. In matters of foreign policy, Ferdinand devoted his efforts to the conclusion of profitable marriage alliances and to the furtherance of his designs in Italy, which brought him into conflict with France and other Italian powers.

1493, Jan. 19. Treaty of Narbonne with Charles VIII of France. The latter, about to invade Italy, ceded to Ferdinand Roussillon and Cerdagne, in the hope of securing support. Ferdinand, with his usual duplicity, joined the pope, the Emperor Maximilian, Milan, and Venice, and helped to frustrate Charles's plans.

1494. Foundation of the *Consulado* for foreign trade at Burgos. This chamber, and the *Casa de Contratación* at Seville (1503) undertook to regulate Spanish trade and had much to do with the commercial expansion of the 16th century.

1500. By the **treaty of Granada,** France and Spain again engaged to co-operate in Italian affairs, but friction over Naples soon led to hostilities. Victories of the great Spanish commander, **Gonzalvo de Córdoba** (especially at **Garigliano,** 1503). Aragon retained Naples. By the **treaty of Blois** (1505), Louis XII of France ceded his rights to Naples to his niece, Germaine de Foix, whom Ferdinand, a widower since 1504, married.

1504. The **death of Isabella** made **Joanna** (wife of Philip, archduke of Austria) legal heiress to Castile. Ferdinand, who had long planned the union of Castile and Aragon, in Joanna's absence secured from the cortes authority to carry on the government in his daughter's behalf. In 1506 Philip and Joanna came to claim their inheritance. **Treaty of Villafavila** between Philip and Ferdinand, the former securing the regency. Philip's death in the same year and the **insanity of Joanna** (kept in confinement for 49 years, d. 1555) allowed Ferdinand to resume control.

1509–1511. African campaigns, organized, financed, and led by **Cardinal Jiménez de Cisneros** (1436–1517), aided by **Pedro Navarro.** Cisneros was one of the ablest statesmen of his time who, having reformed the Spanish church, now devoted himself to the crusade. The Spanish forces took Oran, Bougie, and Tripoli and forced the Moslem rulers to pay tribute.

1511. The **Holy League** (the pope, Ferdinand, and Venice) against France and the Empire. **Victory of the League at Novara** (1513). At the same time (1512) the Spaniards conquered **Navarre,** which was annexed to the Castilian crown, though it retained its own government (1515).

1516. Death of Ferdinand. **Regency of Cardinal Cisneros,** who vigorously repressed incipient disturbances by the nobles. The crowns now passed to the son of Philip and Joanna, Charles of Ghent, who became

1516–1556. CHARLES I of Spain, founder of the **Hapsburg dynasty.** Charles, who had been educated in Flanders, arrived (1517) with a large Flemish following, which regarded the Spaniards with disdain. Dissatisfaction of the Spaniards with Charles's election to the imperial throne (1519) led to widespread opposition to his leaving the country and using Spanish money and men for his imperial purposes.

1520–1521. UPRISING OF THE *COMUNEROS*. A group of cities (led by Toledo and by the Toledan **Juan de Padilla**) took issue with the government and organized a **Holy League** (*Santa Junta*) at Avila (July 1520). Though this was originally as much an aristocratic as a bourgeois movement, radical tendencies soon appeared and the upper elements

Joanna of Castile, 1462–1530

Isabella of Portugal, 1503–1539

withdrew. After the **defeat of the *comuneros* at Villalar** (Apr. 23, 1521) the leaders were executed and government authority re-established. But in future Charles avoided as much as possible any infringement of traditional rights.

1521-1529. **War between France and Spain,** the result of French support of the *comuneros* and French designs on Navarre. The French took Pampeluna and Fontarabia, but Charles, supported by the pope, Florence, and Mantua, expelled the French from Milan (1522). In 1524 the Spanish commanders, the **Constable de Bourbon** and the **Marqués de Pescara,** invaded Provence and advanced to Marseilles. Francis I was decisively defeated and captured at the **battle of Pavia** (Feb. 24, 1525) and in captivity at Madrid was obliged to sign the **treaty of Madrid,** by which he abandoned his Italian claims and ceded Burgundy. On his release he violated his promises and the war was resumed. By the **treaty of Cambrai** (1529), Charles was obliged to renounce Burgundy, while Francis once more abandoned his claims to Naples.

1535. The expedition of Charles to Tunis *(p. 440),* part of a great duel between Spain and the formidable Turkish power.

1535-1538. Another war with France, arising from the succession to Milan *(p. 418),* led to another invasion of Provence (1536) and to the inconclusive **treaty of Nice** (1538).

1541. Reverse of the Spaniards at Algiers.

1542-1544. Further hostilities with France.

1551-1559. The last war between Charles and the French kings, ending in the **treaty of Cateau-Cambrésis** (Apr. 3, 1559). (See below.)

Charles I (Charles V as emperor) gave Spain efficient government, continuing the work of Ferdinand and Isabella. On the other hand, his imperial position resulted in the involvement of Spain in all general European problems and in the expenditure of much blood and money, a drain not so noticeable at the time because of the great influx of gold from the New World. Culturally speaking, the whole 16th century and the first half of the

Charles I, 1516–1556 (engraving 1531)

Luis Vives, 1492–1540

Miguel de Cervantes Saavedra, 1547–1616

17th century was Spain's golden age, a period of humanism: **Luis Vives** (1492-1540), for a time professor at Oxford; **Elio Antonio de Nebrija** (or Lebrija), the leading humanist (1444-1532); **Juan del Encina** (c. 1469-1529), popular dramatist; poets **Garcilaso de la Vega** (1503-1536) and **Juan Boscán Almogáver** (d. 1542); and Spain's great mystical poet **Juan de la Cruz** (1542-1591); **Luis de León** (b. 1528), theologian, poet, and one of those who made Castillian a great literary language. To this period belong the first printings of the chivalrous romance *Amadis de Gaul* (1508), the first realistic novel *Celestina* (c. 1499), and the first important picaresque novel *Lazarillo de Tormes* (anon., 1554). It was also a time of **religious leadership** in the cause of Roman Catholicism: **Arias Montano** (1527-1598) was one of the outstanding scholars at the **council of Trent; Luis de Granada** (1504-1588) was one of the greatest preachers of the century and a religious writer whose books were translated into all leading languages; **Francisco Suarez** (1548-1617), a Jesuit, was a neo-scholastic and an outstanding jurist (*De Legibus ac Deo Legislatore,* 1612); while **Francisco de Vitoria** (1486-1546) wrote extensively on the government of the colonies and became a pioneer of international law (*De Indis et de iure belli relectiones,* 1532). In political theory **Juan Marquez** (1564-1621), *El Gobernador cristiano* (1612) and **Diego Saavedra Fajardo** (1584-1648), *Idea de un Principe político cristiano* (1640). At the same time the Spaniards took the lead in the work of the Catholic Reformation. **Ignatius de Loyola** (1491-1556), after receiving a serious wound in war, made a pilgrimage to Jerusalem (1523-1524) and then studied at Paris (1528-1535). In 1540 he founded the **Society of Jesus** at Rome, the Jesuit organization from the beginning being placed on a military basis, and engaging in widespread missionary and teaching activity. At the same time **Sta. Teresa de Jesús** (1515-

1582) undertook the reorganization of the Carmelite nunneries and, in her autobiography and her *Castillo interior,* made outstanding contributions to mystical literature. **San Juan de la Cruz** (1542-1591), her disciple, effected similar reforms of the monasteries.

The period was one of equal greatness in the realm of literature and art. **Juan de Mariana** (1536-1624) wrote a popular history of Spain, and an important work on political theory, *De Rege et Regis Institutione* (1599), while **Bartolomé de Las Casas** (1474-1566), **Fernandez de Oviedo,** and **Lopez de Gómara** distinguished themselves in treatment of the New World. **Felix Lope de Vega** (1562-1635), who produced over 2000 plays, poems, and stories, was one of the great literary figures of all time and a founder of the modern drama; **Tirso de Molina** (c. 1571-1648) and **Pedro Calderón** (1600-1681) continued the drama on a high plane; **Miguel de Cervantes Saavedra** (1547-1616) in his *Don Quijote* (1605) produced an incomparable picture of the Spain of his day and at the same time one of the world's most popular masterpieces. In the same year, **Mateo Alemán** (1547-1610) published the second part of *Guzmán de Alfarache,* a picaresque novel with a moral for each adventure.

In the field of **art** the Italian influence was very strong, though the **Escorial** (begun in 1563 and built by **Juan de Herrera**) had a severe style of its own. Prominent sculptors of the age were **Gregorio Fernández** (d. 1636); **Alonso Cano;** and **Martínez Montañés** (d. 1649), but the achievements of painting overshadowed those of the other arts. **El Greco** (1541-1614; really a Greek [Kyriakos Theotokopoulos] from Crete, trained in Italy) came to Spain in 1575 and lived at Toledo until his death in 1614. One of the greatest painters of the Renaissance, he was the first of a number of world-famous artists: **José Ribera,** called Spagnaletto (1588-1652); **Francisco de Zurbarán** (1598-1664); **Bartolomé Murillo** (1617-

1682); **Juan de Valdés Leal** (1630–1691) and above all the incomparable **Diego Rodríguez de Silva y Velásquez** (1599–1660). In music **Tomás Luis de Vitoria** was a worthy contemporary of Palestrina.

On the abdication of Charles I, Spain and the colonies, as well as the Netherlands, Franche-Comté, Naples, and Milan passed to his son

1556–1598. PHILIP II (b. at Valladolid in 1527), the most Spanish of the Hapsburg rulers and a monarch who spent most of his reign in Spain. Affable, yet dignified and serious, Philip was a very hard-working bureaucrat as well as an autocrat, and at the same time a hard-hearted and vindictive religious fanatic. His entire policy centered about his determination to defend the faith and to stamp out Protestantism, and further to stand by the Hapsburg interests, outside as well as inside Spain. This involved constant intervention in general European affairs and many costly wars that drained the country. During this period the Spanish infantry (largely volunteer and with a considerable noble element) reached the pinnacle of its prestige.

Philip married four times: (1) **Mary of Portugal,** mother of Don Carlos; (2) **Mary the Catholic,** queen of England; (3) **Elizabeth of Valois;** (4) **Anne of Austria,** daughter of Maximilian II.

1556–1559. Continuance of the **war with France.** Victories of the Spaniards under the **duke of Alva,** at **St. Quentin** (Aug. 10, 1557) and at **Gravelines** (July 13, 1558), led to

1559, Apr. 3. The **treaty of Cateau-Cambrésis,**

Philip II, 1556–1598

which reaffirmed the Spanish possession of Franche-Comté and the Italian states. Philip married Elizabeth, the daughter of Henry II.

1560. The capital was definitively established at **Madrid.** In 1563 the construction of the Escorial Palace was begun.

1567. Beginning of the prolonged **struggle for independence in the Netherlands** *(p. 401).*

1568. **Death of Don Carlos,** the son of the king, whom Philip is sometimes accused of having put away. Don Carlos appears to have been deranged and unmanageable, for which reason he was kept in confinement. There is no evidence of unnatural death.

1569–1571. **Revolt of the Moriscos** (converted Moslems suspected of secretly retaining their original faith). The rising was put down with great severity and ultimately (1609) the Moriscos were expelled from Spain.

1571, Oct. 7. **Battle of Lepanto,** the outstanding event in the long naval duel between the Spaniards and the Turks. **Don John of Austria** (natural brother of Philip), with the aid of a papal and a Venetian fleet, inflicted a tremendous defeat on the Turks *(p. 441).*

1574. The Spaniards lost Tunis.

1580. Philip succeeded to the **Portuguese throne** *(p. 412).*

1587. **Sir Francis Drake** destroyed the Spanish fleet at Cadiz. England had for some time been incurring the displeasure of Philip, partly because of the succession of Elizabeth and the progress of Protestantism, partly because of the aid given the Dutch rebels, and partly because of the piratical raids on the Spanish treasure ships. The **execution of Mary Stuart** (1587) brought matters to a crisis, and Philip sent against England

1588. The **GREAT ARMADA,** which met with complete disaster *(p. 394).* The war with England continued in a desultory way until 1603.

1589–1598. War with France, arising from Philip's intervention against Henry IV. The Spaniards played an important rôle in this last phase of the religious wars in France,

Infanta Margarita, *by Diego Rodriguez Silva y Velasquez, 1599–1660*

Philip III, 1598–1621

Philip IV, 1621–1665

Manoel I, 1495–1521

but failed to attain their objectives. The war ended with the **treaty of Vervins** *(p. 406)*.

1598-1621. PHILIP III, the son of Philip II by his last marriage. A melancholy, retiring, and deeply religious man, the king devoted himself to the interests of the Church (9000 monasteries in this period, and one-third of the population in the church service). Philip left the government to his favorite (*privado*), the **duke of Lerma,** who initiated the system of court intrigue and corruption. Formation of a court nobility; growth of huge estates; marked decline in agriculture (depopulation through wars and emigration to the colonies). Spain became to a large extent a wool-raising country. Industry and trade, so flourishing in the 16th century, suffered a marked decline.

1609. Expulsion of the Moriscos *(see p. 410)*.

1618. Beginning of the Thirty Years' War *(p. 424)*, into which Spain was drawn by Hapsburg interests and by religious considerations.

1621-1665. PHILIP IV, an amiable prince, not interested in politics and therefore quite content to leave the conduct of affairs to his *privado,* the **Count-Duke Olivares** (1587-1645; count of Olivares, duke of Sanlúcar), an able and patriotic administrator who, until his fall in 1643, made valiant efforts to modernize the governmental system by means of greater centralization and increase of the royal power.

1622. The occupation of the **Valtelline Pass** (between Milan and the Austrian lands) by the Spanish led to war with France, which, in a sense, was merely one aspect of the Thirty Years' War. France, under the able leadership of Richelieu, gradually established her ascendancy over Spain.

1640-1659. The great **REVOLT IN CATALONIA,** a direct result of the policy of Olivares. The king's failure to summon the Catalan cortes, the imposition of new taxes, the demands for aid for the foreign wars, the quartering of troops in the country, and in general the centralizing tendencies of the count-duke precipitated the conflict. The movement was supported by France, which

even recognized a **Catalan republic.** After the struggle had gone on for twelve years, Barcelona was finally obliged to submit (1652, Oct.). In the final settlement (1659) the Catalans retained most of their former rights and privileges.

1642. The French occupied Roussillon.

1643, May 19. The battle of Rocroi. Defeat of the Spaniards. This battle is generally taken as marking the end of the supremacy of the Spanish forces.

1647. Revolt of Naples, under **Masaniello** *(p. 419)*.

1648. The peace of Westphalia *(p. 429)*. This did not apply to the war between France and Spain, which continued for another eleven years.

1658, June 14. Battle of the Dunes; decisive defeat of the Spaniards.

1659, Nov. 7. TREATY OF THE PYRENEES (signed on the Isle of Pheasants, in the Bidassoa River). Spain was obliged to cede to France the frontier fortresses in Flanders and Artois, and also Roussillon and Cerdagne. Louis XIV married Maria Teresa, daughter of Philip IV. *(Cont. p. 472.)*

b. PORTUGAL, 1495-1640

(From p. 305)

1495-1521. MANOEL I (the Great, the Fortunate), brother-in-law of John II. His reign and that of his successor mark the apogee of Portuguese power and empire, following the great discoveries (**Vasco de Gama's** voyage to India, 1497-1498; **Pedro Alvares Cabral's** discovery of Brazil, 1500; **Magellan's** circumnavigation of the globe, 1519-1522, *p. 386*). The new empire was at first ruled by men of exceptional ability and courage (**Francisco de Almeida,** first viceroy of the Indies, 1505; **Afonso de Albuquerque,** viceroy, 1507-1511) and brought in large returns. Lisbon very soon displaced Venice as the entrepôt for Asiatic goods, and became a center of wealth and lux-

ury. Colonial trade was a royal monopoly, and the court became a mecca for concession-seekers. The old agrarian system became undermined by the introduction of black slavery, while the aristocracy to a certain extent abandoned itself to imperial war, to corruption at home, and to exploitation abroad. In short, the 16th century, outwardly brilliant, was already the beginning of decadence.

1497. Expulsion of the Jews from Portugal. This step was taken chiefly to please Ferdinand and Isabella of Spain, whose daughter, Isabella, Manoel married (1497; she died in the next year). Persecution and massacre followed the expulsion order, which deprived Portugal of many of its most educated and wealthiest inhabitants.

1521-1557. JOHN (João) III (the Pious), during whose reign

1536. The **Inquisition** was established in Portugal and the **Jesuit Order** invited in. The consequences were much like those in Spain.

1557-1578. SEBASTIAN I, the grandson of John, succeeded. Regency of his mother, Joanna of Austria, a daughter of Charles V, until 1562, followed by the regency of **Cardinal Henry** (Enrique), brother of John III and grand inquisitor. Sebastian himself was educated by the Jesuits and was consumed with the idea of a crusade against the infidel, which he undertook despite the contrary advice of Philip II of Spain and of the pope.

1578, Aug. 4. The **BATTLE OF AL KASR AL-KABIR** (Alcazar-Qivir), in which the Portuguese and their mercenary troops were completely defeated by the Moors. Sebastian, the king of Fez, and the Moorish pretender all lost their lives (*battle of the three kings*).

1578-1580. CARDINAL HENRY, king.

1580. Death of **Luis de Camões,** (b. 1524), greatest of Portuguese poets (*The Lusiads,* published 1572), whose work not only brought to culmination the literary flowering of the 16th century (dramas of **Gil Vicente**), but served as a profound commentary on Portuguese national life and imperial enterprise.

1580. A **regency of five** was established to govern the country on the death of Cardinal Henry. There were no less than seven claimants to the throne, of whom the most powerful was **Philip II of Spain** (son of Isabella, the daughter of Manoel I) and the most popular was **Antonio,** the prior of Crato (illegitimate son of Luis, the brother of John III). Philip's candidacy was supported by the high clergy and by part of the nobility. Antonio enjoyed the support of the townsmen and of the peasants, and was backed by France.

Aug. 25. The Spaniards, under the duke of Alva, invaded Portugal and defeated their opponents in the **battle of Alcántara,** near Lisbon.

1580–1598. PHILIP I (Philip II of Spain), who was accepted by the cortes. Philip promised to respect the rights of the country and to rule only through Portuguese. He himself generally observed this obligation, but under his successors it was more and more ignored. First Portugal itself, then the Portuguese Empire, was turned over to Spanish officials. The result was growing discontent in Portugal and increasing weakness abroad. After the defeat of the Spanish armada (1588), the British and the Dutch began to attack the Portuguese possessions, many of which were conquered before 1640.

1583. Antonio of Crato, with a French fleet, established himself in the Azores and prepared to reconquer the throne, but the French-Portuguese fleet was defeated by a Spanish fleet off the island of St. Miguel.

1589. Antonio, now supported by the British, made a landing in Portugal and marched on Lisbon, but was defeated by the Spaniards. He died at Paris in 1595.

Monastery of Geronimos, Lisbon, best-preserved example of Manoeline architecture

This marked the beginning of Dutch enterprise in the east and of the gradual conquest of Portuguese possessions.

1640, Dec. 1. REVOLT OF THE PORTUGUESE, inspired and organized by **João Ribeiro,** a professor at the University of Coimbra, and supported by the nobility and clergy.

1598. Dutch trade with Lisbon was prohibited.

The insurgents, all disillusioned about Spanish rule, took advantage of the revolt in Catalonia. Like the Catalonians they were supported by France, which was at war with Spain. The Spanish government, unable to devote much attention to Portugal, could not prevent the **election of John of Braganza** to the throne.

(Cont. p. 475.)

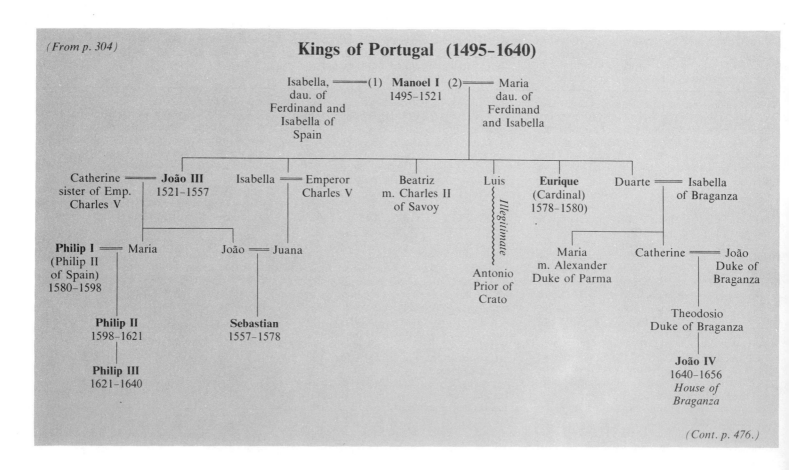

(From p. 304)

Kings of Portugal (1495–1640)

Isabella, dau. of Ferdinand and Isabella of Spain ═══(1)═══ **Manoel I** 1495–1521 ═══(2)═══ Maria dau. of Ferdinand and Isabella

Catherine sister of Emp. Charles V ═══ **João III** 1521–1557

Isabella ═══ Emperor Charles V

Beatriz m. Charles II of Savoy

Luis — *Illegitimate* — Antonio Prior of Crato

Eurique (Cardinal) 1578–1580)

Duarte ═══ Isabella of Braganza

Philip I (Philip II of Spain) 1580–1598 ═══ Maria

João ═══ Juana

Maria m. Alexander Duke of Parma

Catherine ═══ João Duke of Braganza

Philip II 1598–1621

Sebastian 1557–1578

Philip III 1621–1640

Theodosio Duke of Braganza

João IV 1640–1656 *House of Braganza*

(Cont. p. 476.)

5. *Italy*

(From p. 318)

a. THE ITALIAN WARS, 1494-1559

The period from about 1450 to 1550 not only marked the apogee of the Renaissance, but also the intellectual and artistic primacy of Italy. In the field of history and political science, **Francesco Guicciardini** (1483–1540; *Istoria d' Italia* published only in 1561) and **Niccolò Machiavelli** (1469–1527; *Il Principe,* 1513) were outstanding. **Pietro Aretino** (1492–1552) was a famous publicist of the time, while **Baldassare Castiglione** (*Il Cortegiano,* 1528) produced a famous handbook of the courtier. **Ludovico Ariosto** (1474–1533; *Orlando Furioso,* 1516) was one of the greatest epic poets of all time. In the field of music **Giovanni da Palestrina** (1525–1594; at St. Peter's after 1551) and **Orlando di Lasso** were men of the first rank. Architects and painters of eminence were too numerous to be listed, and it will suffice to recall names like **Leonardo da Vinci** (1452–1519); **Raffael Santi** (1483–1520; *Sistine Madonna,* 1516); **Michelangelo Buonarroti** (1475–1564; Sistine Chapel paintings, 1508–1512, 1534–1541; dome of St. Peter's, 1547); **Andrea del Sarto** (1486–1530); **Giorgione da Castelfranco** (1477–1510); **Titian** (Tiziano Vecelli, 1477–1576); **Gentile Bellini** (1429–1507); **Tintoretto** (Jacopo Robusti, 1512–1594); **Paolo Veronese** (1528 1588); **Andrea Mantegna, Allegri da Correggio, Benvenuto Cellini,** etc.

Politically, however, Italy was divided and soon became the "cockpit" of Europe, the victim of the rivalries of the strong monarchies which were arising in the west and all of which coveted the wealth of the peninsula. There were, at the time, five major states: **Venice,** the strongest of all, deriving her wealth and influence from the extensive eastern trade, from her possessions in the Adriatic, Ionian, and Aegean Seas, and from domination of the neighboring mainland; **Milan,** ruled by Ludovico Sforza and commanding the rich valley of the Po; **Florence,** long one of the most progressive of Italian communities, having attained to great splendor under Lorenzo the Magnificent; the **Papal States,** carved from the central part of the peninsula and in process of expansion under the political popes of the late 15th century; the **kingdom of Naples,** deeply involved in the Near East, ruled by a branch of the Aragonese house. These states maintained a precarious balance among themselves, but were almost all so imperialistic that they were constantly endeavoring to victimize each other and ultimately reached the point of calling in the foreigner, with the result that Italy became the prey of French, German, and Spanish ambitions.

1492. Formation of a secret alliance between Florence and Naples for the spoliation of Milan. This led to Ludovico Sforza's appealing to Charles VIII of France to make good the Anjou claims on Naples.

1494-1495. THE FRENCH INVASION OF ITALY. Charles arrived in September and met with no real resistance. Florence submitted, but then drove out **Piero de' Medici**

Mona Lisa, *by Leonardo da Vinci, 1425–1519*

(Nov.) and abandoned the French connection. Thereupon Charles attacked and took Florence, which was obliged to give up Pisa and other towns. Charles advanced on Rome (Jan. 1495) and thence into Naples. Alfonso fled to Sicily, leaving Naples to his son Ferrante, who was driven out by a revolt. The French entered Naples (Feb. 22, 1495), but their very success led to the formation of a coalition directed against them: Milan, Venice, Emperor Maximilian, Pope Alexander VI, and Ferdinand of Aragon leagued together against Charles, forcing his retreat to the north. Ferrante and the Spaniards (Gonzalvo de Córdoba) soon reconquered Naples. This first French invasion of Italy was poorly planned and carelessly executed, but had much importance in opening up the international side of the Italian problem as well as in disseminating the learning and art of Italy throughout western Europe.

1499, Feb. **Venice** agreed to support the claims of Louis XII of France to Milan, in return for a promise of Cremona. The French thereupon invaded Italy a second time (Aug.) and forced **Ludovico Sforza** to flee from Milan to Germany. Milan surrendered (Sept. 14). The next year Sforza returned with an army of German mercenaries and obliged the French to evacuate. Before long the German forces began to disintegrate and the French returned to Milan. Ludovico was captured and died (1508) in a French prison. Milan thus became French.

1500, Nov. 11. By the **treaty of Granada,** Ferdinand of Aragon agreed to support Louis's claim to Naples, which was to be divided between France and Spain. In 1501 (June) the French army, marching south, entered Rome, whereupon the pope declared Federigo of Naples deposed and invested Louis and Ferdinand with the kingdom. The French took Capua (July), while the Spanish fleet seized Taranto (Mar. 1502). So much having been gained, the two allies fell to quarreling over the division of the spoils, and war resulted (July). The Spaniards at first suffered reverses, but in 1503 defeated a French fleet and won a decisive victory at **Cerignola** (Apr. 28). They took Naples (May 13), and, after another victory at **Garigliano** (Dec. 28), forced the French to surrender at **Gaeta** (Jan. 1, 1504). This completed the Spanish conquest of Naples, which, with Sicily, gave them control of southern Italy, as the French had control of Milan in the north.

1508, Dec. 10. The **LEAGUE OF CAMBRAI,** organized to despoil Venice of her possessions on the mainland and in Apulia. Emperor Maximilian promised Louis XII the investiture of Milan in return for support. Ferdinand of Aragon and Pope Julius II joined the coalition. The French attacked and defeated the Venetians at **Agnadello** (May 14, 1509). Surrender of Verona, Vicenza, and Padua, which were handed over to Maximilian, while the pope occupied Ravenna, Rimini, Faenza, and other Venetian possessions in the Romagna. The Apulian towns, Brindisi, Otranto, etc., fell to Ferdinand. But the Venetians soon rallied and retook Padua (July 17), which was besieged in vain by Maximilian. Vicenza too rose against the emperor and recalled the Venetians. In 1510 the pope, fearful of the power of the Germans, deserted the league and joined Venice, while Ferdinand, having secured his share of the spoils, turned neutral. The papal forces took Modena and Mirandola (Jan. 1511), but the French conquered Bologna (May 13). In October Ferdinand completed a *volte face* and joined Venice and the pope, while Henry VIII of England also adhered. After a French victory at **Ravenna** (Easter, 1512), even the emperor and the Swiss cantons joined the coalition against the French, who were driven out of Milan (May). In a **congress of the league at Mantua** (Aug.) the Spaniards forced the Florentines to take back the Medici and join the league. Milan was given to Maximilian Sforza (son of Ludovico). The war continued until the French were badly defeated at **Novara** (June 6, 1513), after which the pope, Ferdinand, and Henry of England all made peace.

1515. The new French king, **Francis I,** as deeply interested in Italy as his two predeces-

The submission of Venice to Louis XII, 1499

sors, and quite as adventurous, concluded an alliance with Henry VIII and Venice against the Emperor Maximilian, the pope, Ferdinand, Milan, Florence, and the Swiss. The French won a great victory at **Marignano** (Sept. 13) by which they recovered Milan. Thereupon the pope came to terms, surrendered Parma and Piacenza, and in return secured the **concordat of Bologna** *(p. 403)*. After the death of Ferdinand (Jan. 1516), his successor, Charles I (later Emperor Charles V), confronted with serious problems in Spain and Germany and eager to secure European co-operation against the advance of the Turks, concluded with Francis the **treaty of Noyon** (Aug. 13, 1516), by which the French retained Milan, but gave up their claims to Naples. Maximilian returned Brescia and Verona to Venice in consideration of a money payment.

1522–1523. First of the **Hapsburg-Valois wars,** for many of which Italy became a battlefield.

The pope and England supported Charles V against Francis. Having been driven out of Milan, Parma, and Piacenza, the French were defeated at **Bicocca** (Apr. 27, 1522) and retained only the citadel of Milan. In May they were even driven from Genoa, their all-important sea-base. But in October 1524 the French invaded Italy with a large army. They retook Milan (Oct. 29). The pope changed sides and joined the French.

1525, Feb. 24. The **BATTLE OF PAVIA,** the most important engagement of the long Italian wars. The Spanish commanders, **Constable de Bourbon** (prominent French noble and opponent of Francis), and **Marquís de Pescara,** completely defeated the French. Francis himself was captured and sent to Madrid. There he concluded the **treaty of Madrid** (Jan. 14, 1526), by which he promised to surrender his Italian claims, give up Burgundy, and abandon his suzerainty over Artois and Flanders.

These engagements he never meant to observe, and they were repudiated by him as soon as he was liberated.

1526, May 22. The **LEAGUE OF COGNAC,** a coalition of Francis I, the pope, Sforza, Venice, and Florence against Charles and the Spaniards. The league was the natural result of the too great success of the Spaniards in Italy and the objective was to restore the *status quo* of 1522. But the Spaniards forced Sforza out of Milan (July 24) and before long attacked Rome (Sept. 21). The pope was helpless and could not prevent

1527, May 6. The **SACK OF ROME** by the Spanish and German mercenaries of Charles. The sack was horrible even when judged by the customs of the day, and ended Rome's pre-eminence in the Renaissance. The pope himself was captured.

May 17. Florence rose against the Medici, who were again driven out and replaced by a republic (under **Niccolò Capponi**). **Genoa also revolted,** under **Andrea Doria** (formerly in French service). The French were expelled and a republican constitution established. The French, however, having overrun Lombardy (Oct.), began to march south. Meanwhile the pope, who had fled to Orvieto (Dec.), made his peace with Charles (**treaty of Barcelona,** June 29, 1529—the Papal States to be restored and the Medici returned to Florence). The war was ended by

1529, Aug. 3. The **treaty of Cambrai** (*Paix des dames,* because negotiated by Charles's aunt, Margaret, and by Francis' mother, Louise of Savoy). Francis once more renounced his Italian claims and the overlordship of Artois and Flanders. Venice was obliged to disgorge her conquests (Apulian towns, Ravenna, etc.). The duchy of Milan was given to Francesco Maria Sforza, Charles V retaining the citadel. Florence was forced, after an eight months' siege, to take back Alessandro de' Medici as duke. On Feb. 23, 1530, Charles was crowned by the pope as emperor and king of Italy.

1535. The **death of Francesco Sforza** opened the question of the Milanese succession.

Pope Alexander VI, 1492–1503

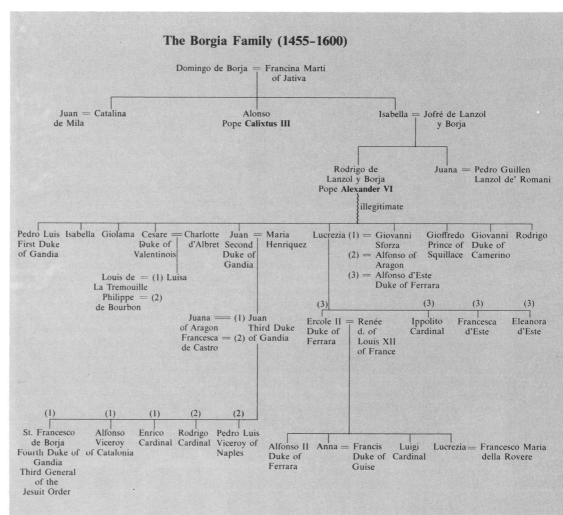

The Borgia Family (1455–1600)

Charles V claimed it as suzerain, but the French invaded Italy and took Turin (Apr. 1536). After an invasion of Provence by the imperialists, the **truce of Nice** was concluded for ten years (June 18, 1538). It reaffirmed the treaty of Cambrai, but the French remained in occupation of two-thirds of Piedmont and the emperor retained the rest.

1542–1544. The **war between Francis I and Charles V,** though fought out in the Netherlands and in Roussillon, had repercussions in Italy. The **treaty of Crespy** (Sept. 18, 1544) involved abandonment of French claims to Naples, but provided that the duke of Orléans should marry either Charles's daughter, with the Netherlands and Franche-Comté as a dowry, or else Charles's niece, who would bring Milan. The plan failed through the death of Orléans (1545). Piedmont and Savoy were to be restored to the legitimate ruler.

1556. Alliance of Pope Paul IV and Henry II of France to get Naples. The French, under the **duke of Guise,** invaded Italy, but were obliged to withdraw after their defeat at **St. Quentin** (1557). This practically ended the French struggle for Italy. The **treaty of Cateau-Cambrésis** (Apr. 3, 1559) involved the abandonment of French possessions, except Turin, Saluzzo, and Pignerol. Margaret, sister of Henry II, was to marry Emmanuel Philibert of Savoy.

b. THE PAPACY, 1484–1644

[For a complete list of the Roman popes see Appendix IV.]

(From p. 310)

The earlier part of this period marked the nadir of the Papacy viewed from the moral standpoint. Most of the popes were typical products of the Renaissance, patronizing the arts, living in splendor and luxury, using their position either to aggrandize their families or to strengthen the temporal position of the Church. Of religious leadership there was almost none, yet politically speaking the period was one of the utmost importance.

1484–1492. INNOCENT VIII (Giovanni Cibo), an indolent and altogether corrupt pontiff, who was entirely under the influence of Cardinal Giuliano della Rovere. A long-drawn conflict with Naples ended in marriage alliances of the pope's family with the Aragonese house and with the Medici.

1492–1503. ALEXANDER VI (Rodrigo Lanzol y Borgia), a stately, energetic, ruthless, and thoroughly immoral pope, whose life was a scandal even in the Italy of his time. The main objective of his policy was to establish the rule of his family in central Italy. He broke the power of the great Roman families (Orsini, Colonna), and, through his son, **Caesar Borgia**

(1475–1507), a former cardinal and the hero of Machiavelli's *Prince*, undertook the conquest of the Romagna. Caesar reduced most of the principalities (1499–1501) and became duke of the Romagna. In 1501 the Borgias joined France in the attack on Naples, and the French aided Caesar in putting down a revolt of his captains at Sinigaglia (Dec. 1502). But the death of the pope and the hostility of the new pontiff, Julius II, frustrated Caesar's schemes. Forced to disgorge his conquests, he turned to Spain for aid. In 1506 he was arrested at Naples and sent to Spain, where he died (1507).

1503. PIUS III (Francesco Piccolomini, a nephew of Pius II), died within 26 days of his election.

1503–1513. JULIUS II (Giuliano della Rovere), one of the greatest of the popes and the real founder of the Papal States, a man of great intelligence and boundless energy, more a statesman than a priest. He not only regained the Romagna, but took the lead in the effort to expel the foreigner from Italy. In 1508 he was in the forefront of the **league of Cambrai**, through which he hoped to acquire the Venetian possessions in the Romagna. Having humbled Venice, he turned on the French. In reply Louis XII summoned a church council at Pisa (1511), which obliged the pope to convoke a rival **council at the Lateran** (1512). This remained in session for several years, and first undertook reform of abuses in the Church.

1513–1521. LEO X (Giovanni de' Medici, son of Lorenzo the Magnificent), a noteworthy patron of art, but an easy-going churchman, whose pontificate was noted chiefly for the **beginning of the Reformation** in Germany (1517, *see p. 420*). There is no evidence that the pope realized the gravity of the situation and the only solution he could offer was to ban Luther (1521).

1522–1523. ADRIAN VI (of Utrecht), the last non-Italian pope. Adrian was, at the time of his election, regent of Spain for Charles V. An upright and austere man, he attempted to purge the Papacy of abuses and tried to reconcile Charles V and Francis I in order to unite Christendom in a crusade against the Turks. His efforts brought him great unpopularity in Italy and conflict, even with Charles V, but he died before accomplishing much.

1523–1534. CLEMENT VII (Giulio de' Medici), a hard-working but undecided pontiff. He failed entirely to cope with the religious revolt in Germany, and failed also to maintain a safe position in the conflict between the French and the Spaniards for domination of Italy. Hence the terrible **sack of Rome** (May 6, 1527, see above), which may be said to have brought to a close the greatness of Rome in the Renaissance.

1534–1549. PAUL III (Alessandro Farnese), another worldly pope, whose greatest concern was for his family. On the other hand, he recognized clearly the urgency of reform in the Church. He completely changed the direc-

torate of the church by naming devout scholars to the cardinalate. In 1536 he established a **reform commission** of nine, and on September 27, 1540, officially recognized the **Society of Jesus.** The **Universal Inquisition** was established at Rome (July 21, 1542). Finally the pope yielded to the demand of years, and in 1545 opened the **council of Trent,** which undertook the reform of the Church, under Jesuit guidance. The work of the council was several times interrupted and therefore divides into three periods: 1545–1547; 1551–1552; 1562–1563. The first period was perhaps the most important, both for organizational and doctrinal reform.

1550–1555. JULIUS III (Giovanni Maria del Monte), an elegant pope whose reign marked a short return to the Papacy of the Renaissance.

1555. Marcellus II (Marcello Cervini), whose election marked the victory of the strict reform party. The pope died within 22 days, and was succeeded by

1555–1559. PAUL IV (Gian Pietro Caraffa), a sincere and vigorous reformer and one of the chief inspirers of the **Counter-Reformation.** The powers and activities of the Inquisition were extended and the **first index of forbidden books** was drawn up (1559). As a Neapolitan the pope detested the Spanish rule and was soon in conflict with the Hapsburgs. He allied himself with France, but was defeated by the duke of Alba.

1559–1565. PIUS IV (Giovanni Medici, not

Pope Paul III (*1534–1549*), *by Titian*

St. Pius V, 1566–1572 (*contemporary painting*)

Rome at the time of the coronation of Pope Sixtus V, 1585–1590

related to the famous Florentine family), an amiable pontiff who followed the guidance of his high-minded and able nephew, **Carlo Bor-romeo,** archbishop of Milan. He made peace with the Hapsburgs and concluded the council of Trent (*Professio Fidei Tridentina*, 1564).

1566–1572. ST. PIUS V (Antonio Michele Ghislieri). Pius was an exceedingly devout and ascetic priest, whose attitude was well reflected in the **anathematization of Queen Elizabeth I** (1570) and in the financing of the naval crusade against the Turks which culminated in the great **victory of Lepanto** (Oct. 7, 1571, *see p. 441*). Under Pius's direction the decisions of the council of Trent were further embodied in the *Catechismus Romanus* (1566), the *Breviarium Romanum* (1568), and the *Missale Romanum* (1570).

1572–1585. GREGORY XIII (Ugo Buoncam-pagni), who continued the policy of his prede-cessor and did much to encourage the Jesuit colleges. He is remembered chiefly for his **reform of the calendar** (1582), which involved the dropping of ten days, and, for the future, the striking out of leap year at the close of each century, excepting every fourth century. This reform was not accepted by Protestant countries until long afterward (in Russia not until 1918).

1585–1590. SIXTUS V (Felice Peretti), one of the really great popes, who, after suppressing the powerful nobility of the Papal States and purging the territory of bandits, reorganized the government, re-established the finances on a sound basis, and encouraged industry (silk culture). In the same way he remade the papal curia (college of cardinals fixed at 70; estab-lishment of 15 congregations or commissions of cardinals to deal with particular aspects of church affairs). New edition of the Vulgate Bible. Beautification of Rome, which now took on its characteristic baroque appearance (con-struction of the Vatican Palace and Library, the Lateran Palace, the Santa Scala; comple-tion of the dome of St. Peter's according to Michelangelo's plans). There followed the three brief pontificates of

1590. Urban VII, who died in 14 days,

1590–1591. Gregory XIV, and

1591. Innocent IX, who died in two months.

1592–1605. CLEMENT VIII (Ippolito Aldo-brandini), a pious, serious pope, who sup-ported the Catholic cause in France and ulti-mately mediated the peace between France and Spain (1598). His reign was distinguished by the great cardinals, **Robert Bellarmine** (1542–1621), eminent theologian and defender of the papal right to interfere in temporal affairs (*De potestate summi pontificis in rebus temporalibus*, 1610; *De officio principis chris-*

Pope Paul V, 1605–1621

Pope Gregory XV, 1621–1623

Andrea Doria, 1468–1560

tiani, 1619), and **Caesar Baronius** (1538–1607), the great historian of the Catholic Church (*Annales ecclesiastici,* 1588–1607). During this pontificate Ferrara was added to the Papal States by reversion (1597).

1605. **Leo XI** lived only 25 days, and was succeeded by

1605–1621. **PAUL V** (Camillo Borghese), whose high idea of the papal power brought him into conflict with Venice and led to a compromise. On the outbreak of the Thirty Years' War the pope gave financial support to the Hapsburgs.

1621–1623. **GREGORY XV** (Alessandro Ludovisi), a weak old man who was guided by his able nephew, **Ludoviso Ludovisi.** He regulated the papal elections and organized the *Congregatio de propaganda fide* (1622), which united all missionary activity of the Church.

1623–1644. **URBAN VIII** (Maffeo Barberini). He secured Urbino by reversion (1631), thus completing the dominions of the Papal States. In the Thirty Years' War he attempted to maintain a neutrality which brought him much criticism from the imperialist side. His main concern appears to have been for the States of the Church, which he carefully fortified.

(Cont. p. 477.)

c. VENICE, 1500–1573

(From p. 317)

The discovery of the new route to the Indies struck at the old traditional trade through the Levant and at once began to undermine the prosperity of Venice. At the same time the steady advance of the Turks left the Venetians the choice between active opposition or accommodation. In general the latter policy was followed (much to the disgust of other European states), but nevertheless Venice became involved in a number of disastrous conflicts, which cost her most of her outposts in the east. The assault upon the possessions of Venice in Italy (**league of Cambrai,** *see p. 420)* proved less successful than the powers had expected, but thenceforth Venice was obliged to remain on the defensive and to observe, as well as might be, a neutral attitude as between France and Spain and later between France and Austria.

1570. The **Turks attacked Cyprus,** the largest and most important base of Venetian power in the east. In the course of the ensuing war, the allied Spaniards and Venetians, supported by the papal fleet, won the great

1571, Oct. 7. **Battle of Lepanto,** which, however, was not effectively followed up. The Venetians took the earliest opportunity to make peace, and

1573. Venice abandoned Cyprus and agreed to pay a heavy indemnity. Thenceforth only Candia (Crete), Paros, and the Ionian Islands remained in Venetian hands. *(Cont. p. 478.)*

d. OTHER ITALIAN STATES, 1525–1675

(From p. 317)

After the treaty of Cateau-Cambrésis (1559, *See p. 404)* all the Italian states, with the possible exception of Venice, were more or less directly under Spanish influence. The Counter-Reformation was soon in full swing, and by the end of the 16th century Italy was already losing the intellectual and cultural primacy which she held during the Renaissance.

MILAN declined rapidly in economic and political importance after 1525. The death of the last Sforza (**Francesco II**) in 1535 brought Milan under direct Spanish rule. In 1556 the duchy of Milan became an appanage of the Spanish crown, though held as a fief of the empire.

GENOA had been, in the later 15th century, a bone of contention between France and Milan. Torn by internal struggles of rival families (**Adorno** and **Fregoso),** it had lost its great commercial power and was important chiefly as a base of operations for France. In 1528 (Sept. 9), however, the great Genoese admiral, **Andrea Doria,** having left the French service, seized the town and re-established the republic, with a pronouncedly aristocratic constitution. Efforts of the French to recapture it failed. **Gian Luigi Fieschi** (Fiesco) in 1547 staged a spectacular conspiracy that was supported by France. Gianettino Doria, nephew of Andrea, was murdered and Andrea himself forced to flee. The conspirators secured most of the town, but then Fieschi was accidentally drowned and the movement collapsed. **Andrea Doria** returned as doge and the constitution was restored. On Andrea's death (1560) he was succeeded by **Gian Andrea Doria.** The **loss of Chios** to the Turks (1566) marked the end of Genoese power in the east.

SAVOY was an independent state, the rulers of which governed also Piedmont. Lying astride the Alps and commanding the passes from France into Italy, the state was one of considerable importance, but the feudal organization resulted in such weakness that for long the dukes were unable to pursue an independent policy. In the early 16th century Savoy was decidedly under French influence, and when, in 1536, the duke departed from the traditional policy, his dominions were overrun and for the larger part occupied by the French. **Emmanuel Philibert** (1553–1580) was the first really outstanding ruler. By following the Spanish lead he secured his dominions again in 1559, and in the course of his reign acquired Asti and other territories by negotiation. He made much progress in breaking the power of the nobility and in organizing a central government and an effective army. His successor, **Charles Emmanuel I** (1580–1630), squandered much of his father's achievement, waging war and neglecting the economic development of the country. **Victor Amadeus I** (1630–1637) was a wise and just ruler, but his short reign was followed by a civil war, and when finally **Charles Emmanuel II** (1638–1675) ascended the throne, his mother **Christina** (daughter of Henry IV of France) dominated the situation as regent.

MANTUA played a fleeting rôle on the international stage in the years 1627–1631, when the death of **Vincenzo II** (Gonzaga) without heirs provoked the **war of the Mantuan succession.** The best claim was that of **Charles of Nevers,** of the French branch of the Gonzaga line, but the emperor, at Spain's suggestion, sequestered the territory in order to keep the French out. The Spaniards overran the duchy, but the pope and Venice championed Nevers, appealing to France for aid. During 1629 the French fought the Spaniards in the duchy, but both sides were diverted by the larger obligations of the Thirty Years' War. The invasion of Germany by Gustavus Adolphus finally turned the scales in France's favor and by the **treaty of Cherasco** (Apr. 26, 1631), Nevers was invested with the duchy.

FLORENCE, like Milan, sank rapidly in importance during the 16th century. The Medici, restored in 1512, were expelled for a second time in 1527, when the republic was re-established. But in 1530 Charles V appointed Ales-

sandro de' Medici hereditary ruler. **Cosimo de' Medici** became duke in 1537 and ruled until 1574. During this period Siena was incorporated with Florence (1555) and Florence became the **grand duchy of Tuscany** (1569).

NAPLES, conquered by the Spaniards in 1504, became an appanage of the Spanish crown and was, throughout this period, the headquar-

ters of Spanish power in Italy. Though unpopular, the Spaniards were not threatened in their position excepting by the **revolt of Masaniello** (Tommaso Aniello, a fisherman), in July 1647. The insurrection, at first completely successful, led to extremism and confusion, in the midst of which Masaniello was murdered.

(Cont. p. 478.)

6. *Germany, 1493–1648*

[*For a complete list of the Holy Roman emperors see Appendix V.*]

(From p. 323)

a. GERMANY, 1493–1618

1493–1519. MAXIMILIAN I, who first took the title of *Roman Emperor elect.*

1495. The diet of Worms. Constitutional reform. Attempted "modernization" of the medieval empire. Perpetual public peace. Imperial chamber (*Reichskammergericht*), first at Frankfurt, then at Speier, and finally at Wetzlar (1689). At the **diet of Köln** (1512) the reorganization of the empire was carried further: establishment of ten circles for the better maintenance of public peace (*Landfriedenskreise*): (1) Austria; (2) Bavaria; (3) Swabia; (4) Franconia; (5) Upper Rhine; (6) Lower Rhine; (7) Burgundy (ceded to the Spanish line of the Hapsburgs, 1556); (8) Westphalia; (9) Lower Saxony; (10) Upper Saxony. In all there were 240 states in the empire, exclusive of the imperial knights. Bohemia and the neighboring states (Moravia, Silesia, Lusatia) with Prussia and Switzerland (which was

(From pp. 302, 320)

The House of Hapsburg (1493–1780)

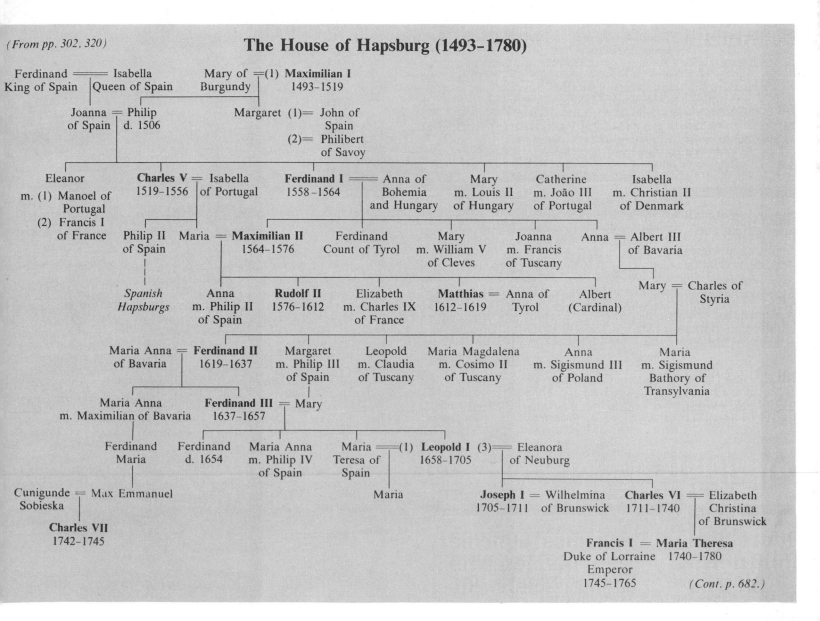

(Cont. p. 682.)

already completely independent in fact) were not included in the circles. Establishment of the **Aulic Council,** a court more under the control of the emperor than the imperial chamber, and to which a large part of the work of the latter was gradually diverted.

1508. The **league of Cambrai,** between Maximilian, Louis XII, Pope Julius II, and Ferdinand the Catholic. The purpose of the league was to break the power of Venice. Maximilian took possession of a part of the republic's territory, but he besieged Padua in vain (1509). The pope withdrew from the league, and concluded with Venice and Ferdinand the

1511. Holy League, directed against France. Maximilian finally (1513) joined in this.

The genealogical table shows the **claim of the Hapsburgs to Spain,** and division of the house into Spanish and German lines. Through these marriages the central European lands of the Hapsburgs, the Burgundian lands in what are now France and Belgium, and the united lands of the crowns of Castile and Aragon (Spain, Naples, and the Americas) all came by birth to **Charles I of Spain** (eldest son of Philip and Joanna). He acquired the empire and his better known title of **Charles V** by election in 1519.

1517. BEGINNING OF THE REFORMATION. Background: Wiclifite (Lollard), Hussite, and other preceding rebellions against the Roman Church; the Babylonian Captivity and the Great Schism, which weakened the prestige of Rome; corruption and worldliness of the Church during the Renaissance; the development of critical scholarship, as represented by **Desiderius Erasmus** of Rotterdam, whose editions of the Church Fathers and whose Greek text of the New Testament (1516) revealed the shortcomings of basic ecclesiastical writings; rise of national feeling and dislike of foreigners, especially in Germany and England; growth of a middle class and a capitalist economy, which felt Roman Catholicism as a restraint (economic interpretation of the Reformation in modern writings of Max Weber and R. H. Tawney); great landed wealth of the Church available for confiscation by ambitious and unscrupulous princes.

Martin Luther (1483–1546), born at Eisleben, the son of a miner; monk in the Augustine monastery at Erfurt; priest (1507); professor at Wittenberg (1508); visit to Rome (1511).

1517, Oct. 31. Luther nailed on the door of the court church at Wittenberg his **95 theses** against the misuse of absolution or indulgences (especially by the Dominican monk **Johann Tetzel**). In the following year another reformatory movement was begun in Switzerland by **Ulrich Zwingli** (1484–1531).

1518. Summoned to Augsburg by Cardinal de Vio of Gaëta (Cajetanus), Luther refused to abjure, but appealed to the pope. Mediation of the papal chamberlain, Karl von Miltitz.

1519. Discussion at Leipzig between **Andreas Bodenstein** (called Karlstadt) and **Johann Eck.** The latter secured a papal bull against 41 articles in Luther's writings. Luther burned the papal bull and the canon law (1520). Thereupon he was excommunicated.

Basic Lutheran doctrine: justification by faith alone, which makes priestly offices of the Catholics an unnecessary intermediary between the individual and God.

In the meantime the German electors, de-

Maximilian I (*1493–1519*), *by Albrecht Dürer*

spite the claims of Francis I of France, had chosen as emperor the grandson of Maximilian, King Charles I of Spain, who as emperor became

1519–1556. CHARLES V. He came to Germany for the first time in 1520, to preside at a grand **diet at Worms** (1521). There Luther defended his doctrines, coming under a safe-conduct. The ban of the empire having been pronounced against him, he was taken to the Wartburg by Frederick the Wise of Saxony, and there enjoyed protection. The **edict of Worms** prohibited all new doctrines. Luther's **translation of the Bible.**

1521–1526. First war of Charles V against Francis I of France. Charles advanced claims to Milan and the duchy of Burgundy. Francis claimed Spanish Navarre and Naples. The French, under Lautrec, were driven from Milan, which was turned over to **Francesco Sforza** (1522). The French constable, **Charles de Bourbon,** transferred his allegiance to Charles V. Unfortunate invasion of Italy

by the French, under Bonnivert (1523–1524). Imperial forces thereupon invaded southern France. Francis I crossed the Mt. Cenis Pass and recaptured Milan.

1522. Progress of the Reformation. Luther, hearing of Karlstadt's misdoings, returned to Wittenberg and introduced public worship, with the liturgy in German and communion in both kinds in Electoral Saxony and in Hesse. The spread of the Reformation was favored by the fact that the emperor was deeply engrossed in the war with France.

1522. The Knights' War. Franz von Sickingen and **Ulrich von Hutten** advocated the Reformation. Sickingen stood at the head of a league of nobles directed against the spiritual principalities. He laid siege to Trier (1522), but in vain. He was then himself besieged in Landstuhl and fell in battle. Hutten fled the country and died on the island of Ufnau in the Lake of Zurich (1523).

1524–1525. The **PEASANTS' WAR,** in Swabia and Franconia. The peasants took the occasion of the disorders attendant on Luther's revolt (inspiration of his passionate attacks on the constituted authorities) to rise against the social and economic inequalities of German feudalism. They incorporated their demands in the revolutionary **Twelve Articles.** Luther himself repudiated the peasants. They were defeated at **Königshofen** on the Tauber and cruelly punished. Another religious-social revolt was that of the **Anabaptists** in Thuringia, who denied the efficacy of infant baptism and put forward a program strongly colored with communism. Their leader, **Thomas Münzer,** was captured and executed.

1524. Ferdinand of Austria, younger brother of Charles V, to whom the emperor had entrusted the government of Germany in 1522, at the instigation of the papal legate, **Lorenzo Campeggio,** formed an alliance with the two dukes of Bavaria and the bishop of southern Germany, in the hope of checking the religious changes.

1525. The **BATTLE OF PAVIA** *(p. 414).* Francis was completely defeated and captured by the imperial forces. In the **peace of Madrid** (1526) he renounced all claim to Milan, Genoa, and Naples, as well as the overlordship of Flanders and Artois; he also assented to the cession of the duchy of Burgundy, and gave his sons as hostages.

1526. The **league of Torgau** formed by the Protestant princes (John of Saxony, Philip of Hesse, Lüneburg, Magdeburg, Prussia, etc.) to oppose Ferdinand and his Bavarian allies. The league procured the enactment of the **diet of Speier,** favorable to the new doctrine.

1526–1532. War with the Turks *(p. 440).*

1527–1529. Second war between Charles V and Francis I, who had declared that the conditions of the peace of Madrid were extorted by force, and hence void. **Alliance of Cognac** between Francis, the pope, Venice, and Francesco Sforza against the emperor. The im-

The Peasants' War, 1524–1525

Luther defending his doctrine at the Diet of Worms, 1521

perial army, unpaid and mutinous, took Rome by storm under the Constable de Bourbon, who fell in the assault; the pope besieged in the Castle of St. Angelo (1527). The French general, **Lautrec,** invaded Naples, but the revolt of Genoa (Doria), whose independence Charles V promised to recognize, and the epidemic of plague, of which Lautrec himself died, compelled the French to raise the siege of the capital and to retire to France.

1529, Aug. 3. Treaty of Cambrai (*Paix des dames*). So called from the fact that it was negotiated by Margaret of Austria, Charles's aunt, and Louise of Savoy, duchess of Angoulême, mother of Francis. Francis paid two million crowns and renounced his claims upon Italy, Flanders, and Artois; Charles promised not to press his claims upon Burgundy *for the present,* and released the French princes.

1529. Second diet at Speier, where, in consequence of the victorious position of the emperor, Ferdinand and the Catholic party took a more decided position. The strict execution of the decree of Worms was resolved upon. The evangelical states protested against this resolution, whence they were called **Protestants.**

1530. Charles crowned emperor at Bologna by the pope. This was the last coronation of a German emperor by the pope.

1530. Brilliant **diet at Augsburg,** the emperor presiding in person. Presentation of the **confession of Augsburg** by **Melanchthon** (Philipp Schwarzert). The enactment of the diet commanded the abolition of all innovations.

1531, Feb. 6. Schmalkaldic League, agreed upon in 1530, between the majority of Protestant princes and imperial cities.

Charles caused his brother, Ferdinand, to be elected king of Rome, and crowned at Aachen. The elector of Saxony protested against this proceeding in the name of the evangelicals. In consequence of the new danger which threatened from the Turks, Ferdinand concluded the

1532. Religious peace of Nürnberg. The Augsburg edict was revoked, and free exercise of their religion permitted the Protestants until the meeting of a new council to be called within a year.

1534–1535. The Anabaptists in Münster (**Johann Bockelsohn** of Leyden). Extreme anarchistic (*Antinomian*) consequences of Luther's doctrine of justification by faith alone.

1534. Philip, landgrave of Hesse, restored the Lutheran duke, Ulrich of Württemberg, who had been driven out (1519) by the Swabian league of cities. The emperor had invested his brother Ferdinand with the duchy, but the latter was obliged to agree to a compact, whereby he was to renounce Württemberg and in turn be recognized as king of Rome by the Evangelical party.

1534. FOUNDATION OF THE JESUIT ORDER. Ignatius de Loyola (Iñigo Lopez de Recalde, 1491–1556) with five associates founded the *Society of Jesus,* commonly known as the Jesuit Order. It was approved by Pope Paul III, in 1540. The Jesuits, organized with military strictness, under direct papal control, were the chief agents in spreading the Catholic (or Counter) Reformation.

1535. Charles's successful expedition against Tunis *(p. 440).*

1536–1538. Third war of Charles against Fran-

cis I of France. The latter, having renewed his claims to Milan after the death of Francesco Sforza II, without issue, Charles invaded Provence anew, but fruitlessly. Francis made an inroad into Savoy and Piedmont, and besought the alliance of **Suleiman,** who thereupon pressed his advance on Hungary and sent his fleets to ravage the coasts of Italy. The war was ended by

1538, June 18. The **truce of Nice,** which was concluded on the basis of possession, and for ten years.

1541. JOHN CALVIN (1509–1564) introduced the Reformation into Geneva. Calvin was born at Noyon, France, and published the *Christianae Religionis Institutio* in 1536. He was head of the state in Geneva, save for a short exile to Strassburg (1538–1541), until the time of his death. He systematized Luther's rather emotional revolt, adapting from St. Augustine the rigorous **doctrine of predestination.** Calvinist churches had a strict moral code, and, unlike Lutheran, maintained independence of the Church from the lay authority. In Geneva, in Scotland (**John Knox,** 1505–1572), and briefly in England and even in the New World (at Boston), the Calvinists erected theocratic states. In France and Hungary they became an important minority. In Holland and parts of Germany they were soon the dominant Protestant group.

1541. Charles's unsuccessful expedition against Algiers.

1542–1544. Fourth war between Charles and Francis, occasioned by the investiture of Charles's son, Philip, with Milan. The fact that two secret agents whom Francis had sent to Suleiman were captured in Milan and put to death served Francis as a pretext. Francis in **alliance with Suleiman** and the duke of Cleve. The allied Turkish and French fleets bombarded and plundered Nice. Charles, in alliance with Henry VIII of England, defeated the duke of Cleve, and advanced as far as Soissons. Suleiman invaded Hungary and Austria.

1544, Sept. 18. Treaty of Crespy. Francis' second son, the duke of Orléans, was to marry a princess of the imperial family and receive

Milan. He died in 1545, however; Milan continued in the possession of the emperor. Francis gave up his claims to Naples, and the overlordship of Flanders and Artois; Charles renounced his claims to Burgundy.

1545–1563. COUNCIL OF TRENT (not attended by the Protestants). The **Tridentine Decrees** effected a genuine internal reform in the Roman Catholic Church, and reaffirmed the supremacy of the pope as against conciliar claims. Under Jesuit guidance the doctrine of the church was rigidly formulated in direct opposition to Protestant teaching.

1546–1547. SCHMALKALDIC WAR. Charles V sought to crush the independence of the states of the empire in Germany, and to restore the unity of the Church, to which he was urged by the pope, who concluded an alliance with him, and promised money and troops. The leaders of the league of Schmalkalden, John Frederick, elector of Saxony, and Philip, landgrave of Hesse, placed under the ban. Duke Maurice of Saxony concluded a secret alliance with the emperor. Irresolute conduct of the war by the allies in upper Germany. They could not be induced to make a decisive attack, and finally retired, each to his own land. John Frederick reconquered his electorate, which Maurice had occupied. Charles V first reduced the members of the league in southern Germany, then went to Saxony, forced the passage of the Elbe, and defeated in the

1547, April 24. Battle of Mühlberg, the elector of Saxony, captured him, and besieged his capital, Wittenberg. Treaty mediated by Joachim II of Brandenburg. The electoral dignity and lands given to the **Albertine line** (Duke Maurice). The **Ernestine line** retained Weimar, Jena, Eisenach, Gotha, etc. The elector was kept in captivity. Philip of Hesse surrendered, and was detained in captivity **Interim of Augsburg** (1548), not generally accepted by the Protestants. The city of Magdeburg, the center of the opposition, placed under the ban. **Maurice of Saxony,** entrusted with the execution of the decree, armed himself in secret against Charles V and

1552. Surprised the emperor, after the conclusion of the **treaty of Friedewalde** (1551)

Ignatius de Loyola

John Knox

Council of Trent, 1545–1563

with Henry II of France, and forced him to liberate his father-in-law, Philip of Hesse, and to conclude the **convention of Passau:** Free exercise of religion for the adherents of the confession of Augsburg until the next Diet.

1552–1556. War between **Charles V** and **Henry II,** who, as the ally of Maurice, had seized Metz, Toul, and Verdun. Charles besieged Metz, which was successfully defended by Francis of Guise. The **truce of Vaucelles** left France, provisionally, in possession of the cities which had been occupied.

1553. Maurice defeated Albert, margrave of

Ferdinand I, 1558–1564

Brandenburg-Culmbach, at **Sievershausen,** but was mortally wounded.

1555, Sept. 25. RELIGIOUS PEACE OF AUGSBURG. The territorial princes and the free cities, who, at this date, acknowledged the confession of Augsburg, received freedom of worship, the right to introduce the Reformation within their territories (*jus reformandi*), and equal rights with the Catholic states. No agreement reached as regarded the **ecclesiastical reservation** that bishops and abbots who became Protestant should lose their offices and incomes; but this provision was inserted by imperial decree. This peace secured no privileges for the reformed (Calvinist) religion.

1556. ABDICATION OF CHARLES V at Brussels (effective 1558).

The crown of Spain with the colonies, Naples, Milan, Franche-Comté, and the Netherlands, went to his son **Philip;** the imperial office and the Hapsburg lands to his brother **Ferdinand I.** Charles lived in the monastery of Yuste as a private individual, but not as a monk, and died there in 1558.

1558–1564. FERDINAND I, husband of Anna, sister of Louis II, king of Bohemia and Hungary, after whose death he was elected king of these countries by their estates. Constant warfare over the latter country, which he was obliged to abandon, in great part, to the Turks (*p. 440*).

1564–1576. MAXIMILIAN II, son of Ferdinand, was of a mild disposition and favorably inclined to the Protestants, whom he left undisturbed in the free exercise of their religion. War with John Zápolya, prince of Transylvania, and the Turks. Sultan **Suleiman I** died in camp before Szigeth, which was defended by the heroic Nicholas Zrinyi. By the **truce**

with Selim II (1566) each party retained its possessions (*p. 441*).

REACTION AGAINST PROTESTANTISM: Catholic, or Counter, Reformation.

1576–1612. RUDOLF II, son of the Emperor Maximilian II, a learned man, an astrologer and astronomer, but incapable of governing. New quarrels over the ecclesiastical reservation. The imperial city of Donauwörth, placed under the ban by the emperor because a mob had disturbed a Catholic procession, was, in spite of the prohibition of the emperor, retained by Maximilian of Bavaria, who had executed the ban (1607). These troubles led to the formation of a

1608. Protestant Union (leader, **Frederick IV,** Elector Palatine), which was opposed by the

1609. Catholic League (leader, **Maximilian,** duke of Bavaria). Both princes were of the house of Wittelsbach.

Rudolf, from whom his brother, Matthias, had forced the cession of Hungary, Moravia, and Austria, hoping to conciliate the Bohemians gave them the

1609. Royal Charter (*Majestätsbrief*), which permitted a free exercise of religion to the three estates of lords, knights, and royal cities.

1609. Beginning of the quarrel about the **succession of Cleves-Jülich** on the death of John William, duke of Cleve. The elector of Brandenburg and the prince of Neuburg were the principal claimants.

Rudolf, toward the close of his life, was forced by Matthias to abdicate the government of Bohemia.

1612–1619. MATTHIAS, being childless, and having obtained the renunciation of his brothers, secured for his cousin Ferdinand, duke of Styria, Carinthia, and Carniola, who had

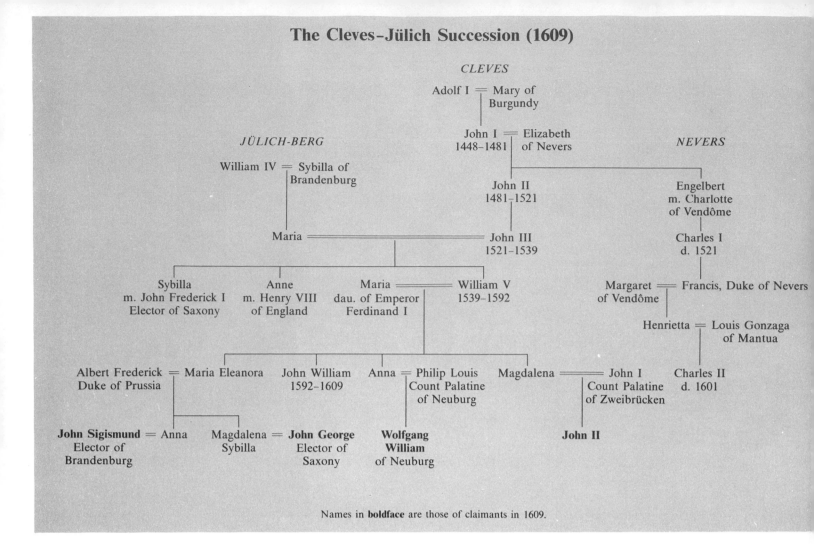

The Cleves-Jülich Succession (1609)

CLEVES

Adolf I = Mary of Burgundy

John I = Elizabeth
1448–1481 of Nevers

JÜLICH-BERG

William IV = Sybilla of Brandenburg

NEVERS

John II
1481–1521

Engelbert
m. Charlotte
of Vendôme

Maria ======== John III
1521–1539

Charles I
d. 1521

Sybilla
m. John Frederick I
Elector of Saxony

Anne
m. Henry VIII
of England

Maria ======= William V
dau. of Emperor 1539–1592
Ferdinand I

Margaret === Francis, Duke of Nevers
of Vendôme

Henrietta = Louis Gonzaga
of Mantua

Albert Frederick = Maria Eleanora
Duke of Prussia

John William
1592–1609

Anna = Philip Louis
Count Palatine
of Neuburg

Magdalena ======= John I
Count Palatine
of Zweibrücken

Charles II
d. 1601

John Sigismund = Anna
Elector of
Brandenburg

Magdalena = **John George**
Sybilla Elector of
Saxony

**Wolfgang
William**
of Neuburg

John II

Names in **boldface** are those of claimants in 1609.

---

been educated by the Jesuits in strict Catholicism, the succession in Bohemia and Hungary, in spite of the objections of the Protestant states.

LITERATURE AND ART

The greatest of the *Meistersinger* was **Hans Sachs** (1494–1576), composer also of numerous *Fastnachtspiele,* the popular plays which emerged as drama became more secular. Satire appeared in prose and poetry, in fable and in *Schwank,* or comic anecdote (**Sebastian Brant,** *Narrenschiff,* 1494); in the writings of **Thomas Murner** (1475–1537) and **Johann Fischart** (c. 1550–c. 1591); most particularly in the writings of the humanist scholar, the great Reformation author **Desiderius Erasmus** (b. Rotterdam c. 1466, d. 1536). His *Encomium Moriae* (*Praise of Folly,* 1509) satirized the foibles of individuals and of institutions, especially the Church; his *Colloquia* likewise contain criticisms of contemporary usage. The *Volkslied* remained a popular vehicle for lyric poetry, gradually having expanded to a polyphonic *Lied* in style.

The drama was further popularized by touring English players late in the 16th century. *Dr. Faustus,* first published anonymously in 1587 as a "chap-book," was immediately popular and translated into English.

Pre-Reformation artists continued to be concerned with church decoration: the sculptors **Tilman Riemenschneider** (1468–1531) and the two **Peter Vischers;** the artist **Matthias Grünewald** (1460–1527; *Isenheimer Altar*). The influence of the Reformation and a trend toward secularism are evident in the works of **Albrecht Dürer** (1471–1528), whose careful studies and theoretical treatises exerted tremendous influence on the development of techniques in the graphic arts. The paintings of **Lucas Cranach** (1472–1553) and **Hans Holbein the Younger** (1497–1543), court painter to Henry VIII of England, reflect the growing secularism in art.

b. THE THIRTY YEARS' WAR

1618–1648. The **Thirty Years' War** is generally divided into four periods, which were properly as many different wars. The first two, the Bohemian and the Danish, had a predominantly religious character; they developed from a revolt in Bohemia into a general conflict of Catholic Europe with Protestant Europe. The two latter, the Swedish and the French-Swedish, were primarily political struggles, wars directed against the power of the Hapsburg house and wars of conquest by Sweden and France, fought upon German soil.

(1) The Bohemian Period, 1618–1625

Origin of the war: closing of a (Protestant) Utraquist church in the territory of the abbot of Braunau, and destruction of another in a city of the archbishop of Prague. The irritation of the Bohemian Protestants was increased by the transference of the administration to ten governors, seven of whom were Catholics. Meeting of the defensors, and revolt in Prague, headed by **Count Matthias von Thurn.**

1618, May 23. Defenestration of Prague. The governors, Martinitz and Slawata, were thrown from a window in the palace of Prague. They fell fifty feet into a ditch, but escaped with their lives. The rebels then appointed thirty directors. The Protestant Union sent Count Peter Ernst Mansfeld to their aid, and from Silesia and Lusatia came troops under Margrave John George of Jägerndorf. The imperial forces were defeated by Mansfeld and Thurn.

1619–1637. FERDINAND II. Thurn marched upon Vienna. The Austrian estates, for the most part Protestant, threatened to join the Bohemians, and made rough demands upon Ferdinand, who, by his courage and the arrival of a few troops, was rescued from a dangerous situation. Thurn, who arrived before

Three Noble Ladies, *by Lucas Cranach, 1472–1553*

Desiderius Erasmus (*1466–1536*), *by Hans Holbein the Younger*

Self-portrait, *by Albrecht Dürer, 1471–1528*

The Defenestration of Prague, May 23, 1618

Vienna shortly afterward, was soon obliged to retire by an unfavorable turn of the war in Bohemia. Ferdinand went to Frankfurt, where he was elected emperor by the other six electors.

Meantime the Bohemians had deposed him from the throne of Bohemia and elected the young **Frederick V** (*The Winter King*) elector palatine, the head of the Union and of the German Calvinists, son-in-law of James I, king of England.

Thurn, for the second time before Vienna, allied with **Bethlen Gabor** (i.e. Gabriel Bethlen), prince of Transylvania (Nov. 1619). Cold, want, and the inroad of an imperial partisan in Hungary, caused a retreat.

Ferdinand leagued himself with (1) **Maximilian,** duke of Bavaria, head of the Catholic League, the friend of his youth, who helped him subdue the Austrian estates; with (2) Spain (Spinola invaded the County Palatine; **treaty of Ulm,** July 3, 1620; neutrality of the Protestant Union secured); and with (3) the Lutheran elector of Saxony, who resubjugated Lusatia and Silesia. Maximilian of Bavaria, with the army of the league commanded by **Tilly** (Jan Tserkales, baron von Tilly, in Brabant, 1559–1632), marched to Bohemia and joined the imperial general Buquoy. They were victorious in the

1620, Nov. 8. BATTLE OF THE WHITE MOUNTAIN, over the troops of Frederick V, under the command of **Christian of Anhalt.** Frederick was put under the ban, and his lands confiscated; he himself fled to Holland. Christian of Anhalt and John George of Brandenburg-Jägerndorf also put under the ban. Subjugation of the Bohemians, destruction of the royal charter, execution of the leading rebels, extirpation of Protestantism in Bohemia. Afterward, violent counter-reformation in Austria, and, with less violence, in Silesia.

Dissolution of the Protestant Union and transfer of the seat of war to the Palatinate, which was conquered in execution of the imperial ban by Maximilian's general, Tilly, aided by Spanish troops under Spinola.

1622, Apr. Battle of Wiesloch; defeat of Tilly by Mansfeld.

May. Battle of Wimpfen; victory of Tilly over the margrave of Baden-Durlach.

June. Battle of Höchst; victory of Tilly over Christian of Brunswick, brother of the reigning duke and administrator of the bishopric of Halberstadt.

1623. Maximilian received the electoral vote belonging to Frederick V and the Upper Palatinate; Saxony obtained Lusatia in pledge for the time being.

(2) The Danish Period, 1625–1629

Christian IV, king of Denmark and duke of Holstein, was the head of the Lower Saxon circle of the empire, and leader of the Protestants.

Albert (Albrecht) von Wallenstein (1583–1634), born in Bohemia of an Utraquist family, but educated in the Catholic faith, made duke of Friedland in 1624, became the commander of an imperial army recruited by himself and provisioned by a system of robbery.

1626. Wallenstein defeated Mansfeld at the **Bridge of Dessau,** and pursued him through Silesia to Hungary, where Mansfeld joined Bethlen Gabor. Death of Mansfeld and of Christian of Brunswick (1626).

Aug. Tilly defeated Christian IV at **Lutter am Barenberge,** in Brunswick.

1627. Tilly and Wallenstein conquered Holstein. Wallenstein alone subdued Schleswig and Jutland, drove the dukes of Mecklenburg from their country, and forced the duke of Pomerania into submission.

1628. Wallenstein besieged **Stralsund.** Heroic

defense of the citizens for ten weeks obliged Wallenstein to raise the siege.

1629, Mar. 29. EDICT OF RESTITUTION: (1) Agreeably to the ecclesiastical reservation, all ecclesiastical estates that had been confiscated since the convention of Passau (1552) should be restored. This affected two archbishoprics: Magdeburg and Bremen; twelve bishoprics: Minden, Verden, Halberstadt, Lübeck, Ratzeburg, Meissen, Merseburg, Naumburg (the latter three were, however, left in the possession of the elector of Saxony), Brandenburg, Havelberg, Lebus, and Camin, besides very many (about 120) monasteries and foundations. (2) Only the adherents of the Augsburg Confession were to have free exercise of religion; all other "sects" were to be broken up. Beginning of a merciless execution of the edict by Wallenstein's troops and those of the League.

1629, May 22. TREATY OF LÜBECK, between the emperor and Christian IV. The latter received his lands back, but promised not to interfere in German affairs, and abandoned his allies. The dukes of Mecklenburg put under the ban. Wallenstein invested with their lands.

1630. Electoral Assembly at Regensburg. The party of Bavaria and the League was hostile to Wallenstein and took up a position of determined opposition to the too powerful general. An excuse was found in the well-grounded complaints of all states of the empire, particularly the Catholics, of the terrible extortion and cruelty practiced by Wallenstein's army. The emperor consented to decree the dismissal of the general and a large part of the army.

(3) The Swedish Period, 1630–1635

1630, July. GUSTAVUS II ADOLPHUS (1594–1632), king of Sweden, landed on the coast of Pomerania.

Object and grounds of his interference: protection of the oppressed Protestants; restoration of the dukes of Mecklenburg, his relatives; rejection of his mediation at the **treaty of Lübeck;** anxiety in regard to the maritime plans of the emperor.

Political position of Sweden: Finland, Ingermannland, Estonia, Livonia, belonged to the kingdom of Gustavus; Courland was under Swedish influence; the acquisition of Prussia and Pomerania would have made the Baltic almost a Swedish sea. Gustavus concluded a subsidy treaty with France **(Richelieu);** drove the imperial forces from Pomerania and captured Frankfurt-on-the-Oder. Negotiations with his brother-in-law, George William, elector of Brandenburg (1619–1640), who was under the influence of Schwarzenberg. Spandau was at last surrendered to him. Negotiations in regard to the surrender of Wittenberg. Saxony, which endeavored to maintain the position of a third, mediatory party in the empire, a sort of armed neutrality (**diet of princes of Leipzig,** 1631), was with difficulty brought to form an alliance with an enemy of the empire. Meanwhile

1631, May 20. Capture of Magdeburg by Tilly. The storm was conducted by Count Gottfried Pappenheim. Terrible massacre and sack of the city by the unbridled soldiery of Tilly, who did what he could to check the outrages. Fire broke out suddenly in many places far removed from one another, and the whole city with the exception of the cathedral was consumed (*not* by Tilly's command).

Tilly took possession of Halle, Eisleben, Merseburg, and other cities, and burned them. John George, elector of Saxony, formed an alliance with Gustavus Adolphus, who crossed the Elbe at Wittenberg. Leipzig occupied by Tilly. The imperial army and that of the Swedes and Saxons, each about 40,000 strong, were face to face.

1631, Sept. 17. BATTLE OF LEIPZIG or BREITENFELD. The Saxons were at first put to rout by Tilly, but after a bloody fight Gustavus Adolphus won a brilliant victory.

The Saxons entered Bohemia. Gustavus crossed Thuringia and Franconia to the Rhine, and occupied Mainz.

Meantime Prague was captured by the Saxons under Arnim (Boytzenburg), a former subordinate of Wallenstein. The emperor held fruitless negotiations with the Saxons.

At the urgent request of Ferdinand, Wallenstein collected an army, over which he received unrestricted command. He recaptured Prague, and drove the Saxons from Bohemia. Their eagerness for the war and the Swedish alliance was already chilled.

1632. Gustavus advanced to the Danube by way of Nürnberg to meet Tilly. Conflict at **Rain,** near the confluence of the Lenz and the Danube. Tilly, mortally wounded, died at Ingolstadt.

Gustavus went to Augsburg, vainly besieged Maximilian in Ingolstadt, but forced Munich to surrender. Wallenstein summoned to the assistance of Maximilian.

1632, July–Sept. Fortified camp near Nürnberg. Gustavus and Wallenstein face to face for eleven weeks. Wallenstein declined battle. Reinforced by Bernhard of Saxe-Weimar, the Swedes attacked Wallenstein's entrenchments, but were repulsed with heavy loss. Gustavus advanced to the Danube. Wallenstein turned upon Saxony, now defenseless, Arnim having marched through Lusatia to Silesia with the Saxon and Brandenburg troops. Terrible ravages committed by the bands of Wallenstein. At the call of the elector of Saxony, Gustavus hastened back by way of Kitzingen and Schweinfurt, joined Bernhard of Saxe-Weimar at Arnstadt, marched upon Naumburg and, hearing that Wallenstein had dispatched Pappenheim from Leipzig to the Rhine, attacked the imperial forces (18,000 against 20,000 Swedes) in the

1632, Nov. 16. BATTLE OF LÜTZEN. Death of Gustavus Adolphus. Pappenheim, recalled in haste, took part in the battle with his cavalry, after three o'clock; he was mortally wounded. The victory of the Swedes was completed by **Bernhard von Saxe-Weimar.**

Bernhard, Gustavus Horn, and Johann Baner took command of the Swedish forces. The conduct of foreign affairs was assumed by the Swedish chancellor, **Axel Oxenstierna** (1583–1654). **League of Heilbronn** between the circles of Swabia, Franconia, Upper and Lower Rhine, on the one part, and Sweden on the other.

1633. Expedition of Bernhard to Franconia. He took Bamberg and Hochstädt, drove back the Bavarians under Aldringer, and joined Horn. Bernhard received from the chancellor the investiture, with the bishoprics of Würzburg and Bamberg, under the name of the duchy

Gustavus II Adolphus, 1594–1632

of Franconia, and occupied the upper Palatinate.

Feb. After Wallenstein had tried and punished with death many of his officers in Prague, and had filled their places with new recruits, he marched to Silesia, fought with the Saxon, Brandenburg, and Swedish troops, and negotiated frequently with Arnim. Negotiations with Oxenstierna.

Tilly's siege of Magdeburg, 1631 (engraving 1637)

Assassination of Wallenstein, February 25, 1633 (contemporary engraving)

Nov. **Regensburg captured** by Bernhard von Saxe-Weimar. Wallenstein found himself unable to go to the assistance of the elector of Bavaria, as the emperor urged, and went into winter quarters in Bohemia.

Growing **estrangement between Wallenstein and the imperial court.** The Spanish party and the League wished him removed from his command. Wallenstein conducted secret negotiations with the Saxons, the Swedes, the French. He intended to create, with the help of the army, an independent position for himself, whence he could, with the aid of the two North German electors, liberate the emperor from the control of the Spanish party, and, if necessary, *compel* him to make peace and reorganize the internal affairs of the empire. He had resolved upon open revolt if the hostile party continued in power. Whether he harbored a wish for the crown of Bohemia, along with other fantastic plans, it is hard to decide. The court of Vienna succeeded in detaching the principal generals (Piccolomini, Gallas,

Aldringer, Marradas, Colloredo) from his cause. Ilow, Trzka, Kinski, remained faithful.

1634, Jan. 24. **Imperial proclamation:** *"Friedland was concerned in a conspiracy to rob the emperor of his crown."* The chief officers of the army commanded to obey him no longer.

Feb. 18. **Second proclamation,** formally deposing Wallenstein. On the 24th Wallenstein went to Eger, where he was to be met by Bernhard von Saxe-Weimar and Arnim. There occurred the

Feb. 25. **Assassination of Wallenstein** by Captain Devereux, at the instigation of the Irish general, Butler, after his intimate friends had been treacherously massacred. The emperor had not commanded the murder, nor had he definitely desired it; but he had given rein to the party which he knew wished "to bring in Wallenstein, alive or dead," and, after the deed was done, he rewarded the murderers with honor and riches.

1634. Victory of the imperialists under Ferdinand, the emperor's son, and Gallas and the

Bavarians (Johann von Werth), over the Swedes at **Nördlingen.**

1635, May 30. **TREATY OF PRAGUE,** between the emperor and the elector of Saxony. (1) The elector received Lusatia permanently, and the archbishopric of Magdeburg for his second son, August, for life. (2) Those ecclesiastical lands, not held immediately of the emperor, which had been confiscated before the convention of Passau, should remain to the possessor forever; all others should remain for forty years (from 1627), and in case no further understanding was reached before the expiration of that period, forever, in the condition in which they were on November 12, 1627. (3) Amnesty, except for participants in the disturbances in Bohemia and the Palatinate; common cause to be made against Sweden. The Lutherans alone to be allowed freedom of worship. Brandenburg and most of the other Protestant states accepted the peace.

(4) The Swedish-French Period, 1635–1648

The policy of Sweden was determined by **Oxenstierna,** that of France by **Richelieu,** and afterward by **Mazarin.** France fought at first in the person of Bernhard of Saxe-Weimar only, with whom subsidy treaties had been concluded, and who was trying to conquer for himself a new state in Alsace, in place of the duchy of Franconia, which he had lost by the **battle of Nördlingen. Capture of Breisach** (1638). After his death (1639) France took control of his army.

1636. Victory of the Swedes under Baner at **Wittstock** over the imperialists and the Saxons. Death of Ferdinand II (1637).

1637-1657. **FERDINAND III,** his son, was desirous of peace. After the death of Baner (1641) **Count Lennart Torstenson** became commander-in-chief of the Swedes.

1640. **Death of George William. Frederick William,** elector of Brandenburg (the **Great Elector,** 1640–1688).

1641. Discussion of the preliminaries of peace in Hamburg. A congress agreed upon.

1642. **Second battle of Leipzig** (Breitenfeld). Torstenson defeated the imperialists under Piccolomini. He then threatened the hereditary states of the emperor. These Swedish successes aroused the envy of Christian IV of Denmark. Hence

1643-1645. War between Denmark and Sweden.

1643, Sept. Torstenson hastened by forced marches to the north, conquered Holstein and Schleswig, and invaded Jutland.

Meanwhile the French in South Germany, under Marshal Guébriant, had penetrated to Rottweil. Guébriant fell in battle. Shortly afterward the French, under Josias von Rantzau, were surprised at **Tuttlingen** by an Austro-Bavarian army under Franz von Mercy and Johann von Werth, and totally defeated.

1643. Opening of the negotiations for peace in Osnabrück with the Swedes; 1644 in Münster with the French.

Marshal Turenne and the twenty-one-year-old prince of Bourbon, duke of Enghien, afterward **prince of Condé,** appointed commanders-in-chief of the French troops.

1644. The French forced the Bavarians under Mercy to retreat. Condé captured Mannheim, Speier, and Philippsburg. Turenne took Worms, Oppenheim, Mainz, and Landau.

Meanwhile an imperial army, under Count

The Peace of Westphalia, 1648 (contemporary engraving)

Matthias Gallas, had been sent to the aid of the Danes, who were hard pressed, both by land and by sea, by the Swedish admiral, Gustavus Wrangel.

1645, Jan. The imperial force was repulsed by Torstenson and Königsmark, pursued into Germany, and almost annihilated at Magdeburg.

Mar. Brilliant victory of Torstenson over the imperialists at **Jankau** in Bohemia, whereupon, in union with the prince of Transylvania, George Rákóczi, he conquered the whole of Moravia, and advanced hard upon Vienna.

May. Turenne defeated by Werth at **Mergentheim** in Franconia.

Aug. Turenne, at the head of the French and Hessians, defeated the Bavarians at **Allersheim.**

Peace between Sweden and Denmark at **Brömsebro.**

After a futile siege of Brünn, the plague having broken out in his army, Torstenson returned to Bohemia. He resigned his command on account of illness, and was succeeded by Wrangel.

1646. Wrangel left Bohemia, united to his own force the Swedish troops under Königsmark in Westphalia, and joined Turenne at Giessen. Swedes and French invaded Bavaria and forced the Elector Maximilian to conclude the

1647. Truce of Ulm, and to renounce his alliance with the emperor. After Turenne had been recalled, from envy at the Swedish successes, and Wrangel had gone to Bohemia, Maximilian broke the truce and joined the imperialists again.

1648. Second invasion of Bavaria by the French and Swedes; terrible ravages. A flood on the Inn prevented the further advance of the allies, who returned to the Upper Palatinate.

Terrible condition of Germany. Irreparable losses of men and wealth. Destruction of towns and trade. Reduction of population; increase of poverty; retrogradation in all ranks.

1648, Oct. 24. TREATIES OF WESTPHALIA. Negotiations from 1643 to 1648. Impe-

rial ambassadors, Count Maximilian Trautmannsdorf and Dr. Volmar. French, Count d'Avaux and Count Servien. Swedish, Count Oxenstierna, son of the chancellor, and Baron Salvius. France and Sweden, against the will of the emperor, secured the participation of the states of the empire in the negotiations.

Terms of the treaties: (A) Indemnifications: (1) Sweden received as fief of the empire the whole of Hither Pomerania and Rügen, with a part of Farther Pomerania, the city of Wismar (formerly a possession of Mecklenburg), and the bishoprics of Bremen (not the city) and Verden as secular duchies. Indemnity of five million rix dollars. Sweden became a member of the German diet with three votes. **(2) France** received absolute sovereignty over the bishoprics and cities of Metz, Toul, and Verdun (in French hands since 1552); also Pignerol, the city of Breisach, the landgravate of Upper and Lower Alsace (which belonged to a branch of the Austrian Hapsburgs), and the government of ten imperial cities in Alsace.

Ulrich Zwingli, 1484–1531

These cities and the other imperial states of Alsace (particularly Strassburg) retained their membership in the empire. France received also the right to garrison Philippsburg. (3) **Hesse-Cassel** received the abbey of Hersfeld and part of the county of Schaumburg. (4) **Brandenburg** received, as indemnification for Pomerania (all of which had belonged to Brandenburg by right of inheritance, though only the larger part of Farther Pomerania had been taken over), the bishoprics of Halberstadt, Minden, and Kammin as secular principalities; the archbishopric of Magdeburg as a duchy, with the reservation that it should remain in possession of the administrator, August of Saxony, during his life (d. 1680). (5) **Mecklenburg** received the bishoprics of Schwerin and Ratzeburg, as principalities. (6) **Brunswick** was given the alternate presentation to the bishopric of Osnabrück, where a Catholic and an Evangelical bishop alternated until 1803.

(B) **Secular affairs of the empire:** (1) General amnesty and return to the condition of things in 1618. (2) The electoral dignity and the possession of Upper Palatinate were left to the Wilhelmian (Bavarian) line of the house of Wittelsbach, while a new electorate (the eighth) was created for the Rudolfian (Palatinate) line. (3) The territorial sovereignty (*Landeshoheit*) of all the states of the empire, as regarded their relation to the emperor, was recognized. This involved the right of concluding alliances with one another and with foreign powers, provided they were not directed against the empire or the emperor. (4) The republics of the United Netherlands and of Switzerland were recognized as independent of the empire.

(C) **Ecclesiastical affairs:** (1) The convention of Passau and the peace of Augsburg were approved and extended to include the Calvinists. (2) Catholic and Protestant states were to be on complete equality in all affairs of the empire. (3) January 1, 1624, was adopted as the norm (*annus normalis*) by which ques-

tions of ownership of ecclesiastical states and the exercise of religion should be determined. As things were on that date, so they were to remain forever, i.e. the ecclesiastical reservation was acknowledged to be binding for the future. The subjugated Protestants of Austria and Bohemia obtained no rights by the treaties, but those Evangelical states which had been won to the Counter-Reformation during the war (i.e. the Lower Palatinate, Württemberg, Baden, etc.) were allowed to resume the exercise of that religion which had been theirs in 1618. The *jus reformandi*, the privilege of deciding by fiat the religion of those subjects to whom the year 1628 did not secure free exercise of religion, was retained for the future by the territorial lords. The right of emigration was, however, reserved to the subjects in such cases. The imperial court (*Reichskammergericht*) was restored and its members were equally divided between Protestants and Catholics.

The treaties of Westphalia were guaranteed by France and Sweden. *(Cont. p. 481.)*

Literary output during the Thirty Years' War was sparse: hymns of **Paul Gerhardt** (1607–1676); mystical poems of **Angelus Silesius** (1624–1677), who was indebted to **Jakob Böhme** (1575–1624); poems and plays of another Silesian, **Andreas Gryphius** (1616–1664), especially his satiric comedy *Horribilicribrifax* (c. 1650); the acknowledged "prose classic of the century," *Simplicissimus* (1669), a vivid picture of contemporary life and manners by **Hans Jakob von Grimmelshausen** (c. 1625–1676). Another Silesian, **Martin Opitz** (1597–1639), won recognition as purifier of the language by his insistence on proper form in *Das Buch von der deutschen Poeterey* (1624).

Music in the period was chiefly for church use: **Heinrich Schütz** (1585–1672) composed vocal and instrumental music in various forms; his influence was apparent on Buxtehude and J. S. Bach.

c. THE SWISS CONFEDERATION, 1503–1648

(From p. 326)

The confederation, at the beginning of the 16th century, was still a loose union of practically independent cantons, each sending two representatives to a federal diet. There were, after 1513, thirteen cantons, of which six (Schwyz, Uri, Zug, Unterwalden, Glarus, and Appenzell) were rural, and seven (Lucerne, Zürich, Bern, Solothurn, Fribourg, Basel, and Schaffhausen) were urban. The Aargau, Thurgau, Ticino, and parts of Vaud were governed by the confederation or one or more of its members. Franche-Comté was under Swiss protectorate. In addition there was a number of states allied with the confederation (St. Gall, Upper Valais, Neuchâtel, Rothweil, Mülhausen, Geneva, etc).

Swiss military prestige had reached its zenith in the latter part of the 15th century. Swiss mercenaries took an important part in the Italian expedition of Charles VIII and continued to form a crucial part of the French and Italian armies.

1503. The Forest Cantons seized Bellinzona after the French conquest of Milan.

1510. The Swiss joined in the **Holy League** against France. In partnership with the Venetians they restored the Sforza to the Milanese

duchy (1512), taking for themselves Locarno, Lugano, and Ossola. Great victory of the Swiss over the French in the **battle of Novara** (June 6, 1513).

1515, Sept. 13–14. In the **battle of Marignano** *(p. 403)* the French won a decisive victory over the Swiss and Venetians. This led to the conclusion of peace (Nov. 12, 1515): the Swiss retained most of the Alpine passes and received a French subsidy in return for the right for the French to enlist mercenaries.

1519, Jan. 1. Beginning of the **REFORMATION IN SWITZERLAND,** under the leadership of **Ulrich Zwingli** (b. 1484; educated at Basel and Bern; priest at Glarus, 1506; after taking part in the Italian campaigns, became priest at Einsiedeln, 1516; preacher at Zürich, 1518). Zwingli denounced indulgences and other abuses in the Church and made a great impression in Zürich. In 1521 he denounced the hiring of mercenaries, and in 1522 condemned fasts and celibacy (he himself married in 1524). The town, following his teaching, abolished confession (1524) and closed the monasteries. Zwingli acted independently of Luther, from whom he was separated chiefly by difference of opinion on transubstantiation.

1524. Five cantons (Lucerne, Uri, Schwyz, Unterwalden, and Zug) banded together against Zürich and the Reformation movement.

1528. Bern and Basel accepted the Reformation, and were followed by three others. Fribourg and Solothurn remained Catholic and sided with the original five (rural) cantons.

1531. War of the Catholic cantons against Zürich. The Zürichers were defeated in the **battle of Kappel** (Oct. 11) and Zwingli was killed. Thus the division of the confederation was complete; the weakness resulting therefrom made impossible all effective action in the ensuing century.

1536. Geneva (allied with Bern) adopted the Reformation, largely through the efforts of William Farel. In the same year **John Calvin** (1509–1564) arrived in the city. His teaching made a deep impression, but also aroused

John Calvin, 1509–1564

much opposition. In 1538 he was banished and retired to Strassburg.

1536. Bern subdued Vaud, Chablais, Lausanne, and other territories of the duke of Savoy, thus laying the basis for a long-drawn duel between the two powers.

1541–1564. CALVIN, recalled to Geneva, organized the town as a theocratic state (*City of God*). A consistory of twelve laymen and six clericals controlled the council and the government. Drastic suppression of all godlessness (i.e. everything at variance with Calvinist doctrine).

1553. **Execution of Servetus** for denying the Trinity.

1555. Ruthless suppression of an anti-Calvinist uprising. Geneva a center for Protestant refugees from England and France and a radiating point for Calvinist doctrine. But the Protestant cantons of Switzerland remained predominantly Zwinglian.

1564. Bern was obliged, under pressure from the Spanish power in Italy, to retrocede Gex and Chablais to Savoy. The Savoyards, supported by Spain and also by the Catholic cantons, began a prolonged offensive against Geneva and Bern, which drove the Protestant cantons into the French fold.

1577. Opening of a Jesuit seminary at Lucerne, marking the most active phase of the **Counter-Reformation,** directed chiefly by Cardinal Carlo Borromeo of Milan.

1584. Alliance of Bern, Geneva, and Zürich against Savoy and the Catholic cantons, followed by an alliance of the latter with Spain (1587).

1602. Savoyard attack on Geneva. This was frustrated, but one important result was the renewal of the alliance between the whole confederation and France (the Catholic cantons, however, retained also their alliance with Spain).

1620–1639. Struggle for control of the **Valtelline Pass,** the most important link in the communications between Hapsburg Austria and the Spanish Hapsburg possessions in Italy. The pass was controlled by the **Grisons League,** but in 1620 was seized by the Spaniards, who enjoyed the support of the Catholic faction (under **Rudolf Planta**). Thereupon Bern and Zürich sent aid to the Protestant faction, led by the pastor **George Jenatsch** (1596–1639). The Protestants were at first successful, but in 1621 were expelled by the Austrians, Spain taking over control of the pass. In 1625 it was seized by a Swiss force in French pay. Governorship of the duke de Rohan. But in 1637 Jenatsch, having turned Catholic in the interest of patriotism, secured Austrian aid and once more drove out the foreigner. By **treaty with Spain** (Sept. 3, 1639) the passes were left open to the use of Spanish troops. The war had been conducted by both sides with the utmost cruelty, typical of the Thirty Years' War. In that great struggle the Swiss Confederation remained officially neutral, being paralyzed by the division between Catholic and Protestant cantons. Nevertheless, by

1648. The **treaties of Westphalia,** the confederation, owing to the efforts and diplomacy of **John Rudolf Wettstein,** burgomaster of Basel, was able to secure a European recognition of its independence of the German Empire.

(Cont. p. 480.)

7. *Scandinavia*

(From pp. 329, 330)

a. DENMARK AND NORWAY, 1513–1645

During this period the union of the three Scandinavian kingdoms became dissolved. The attempt of the Danish king,

1513–1523. CHRISTIAN II, to assert Danish supremacy in Sweden by invading the latter and executing the leaders of the national Swedish party (the **massacre of Stockholm,** 1520) led to a

1520. National revolt headed by **Gustavus Ericksson Vasa,** a young Swedish nobleman. The Danes were defeated, and

1523. Gustavus Vasa became first administrator of the kingdom, then king (see below, Sweden).

In his domestic policy Christian II, in alliance with the middle classes, tried to strengthen royal authority at the expense of the nobility and the Church. This caused a rebellion, led by the nobles and the bishops, who invited the duke of Holstein to rule over Denmark as

1523–1533. FREDERICK I. A civil war followed in which the middle classes sided with Christian II. Christian was defeated and deposed in 1532. After the death of Frederick in 1533, civil war broke out anew (the **Counts' War**). Order was restored with the accession of Frederick's son

1534–1559. CHRISTIAN III. During his reign the **Reformation** finally triumphed in Denmark. Church property was secularized and a national Protestant (Lutheran) church was established. Simultaneously there was a great strengthening of royal power. Christian III intervened in the religious struggle in Germany siding with the Protestant princes against the emperor.

1559–1588. **Frederick II.**

1588–1648. **CHRISTIAN IV.** At the same time rivalry with Sweden in the Baltic caused the

1611–1613. **War of Kalmar** with indecisive results, and

1625–1629. Denmark's participation in the **Thirty Years' War** *(p. 426).*

1643–1645. **A second war,** in which the Swedes were victorious. Denmark lost some territory on the farther side of the Sound. Upon the death of Christian IV an aristocratic reaction brought about a temporary weakening of the royal power.

Norway during this period remained under Danish domination: all the important posts in the administration were occupied by the Danes and the Danish language was predominant. However, Norway benefited from the activity of some of the Danish kings. Christian IV improved administration, developed national resources, founded **Christiania** (Oslo). Under the influence of Denmark, Norway also became Protestant (Lutheran).

(Cont. p. 491.)

b. SWEDEN, 1523–1654

1523–1654. The **HOUSE OF VASA,** under whom Sweden became the strongest power in the Baltic.

1523–1560. **GUSTAVUS I. War with Lübeck,** concluded by the **treaty of 1537,** put an end to the trade monopoly of the Hanseatic League in the Baltic region. In the internal life of Sweden the most important event was the progress of the **Reformation.** Olaus Petri successfully preached the Lutheran doctrine and translated the New Testament into Swedish (1526).

1527. By the decision of the **riksdag of Västeras,** bishops were made entirely dependent on the king, payment of the Peter's pence to the pope was discontinued, church estates were partially secularized.

1529. The ordinances of the **synod of Örebro** modified the church service in the Protestant sense. As the Swedish crown was made hereditary, Gustavus Vasa was succeeded by his son

1560–1568. **ERIC XIV.** Under him Baltic expansion continued and Sweden came into the possession of Reval (1561) and the adjoining territory. Toward the end of his life Eric became insane, and finally was deposed. Under his brother **John III** and John's son **Sigismund** (king of Poland since 1587), Sweden participated in the **Livonian War** *(p. 433)* in which she acquired all of Estonia with Narva, by the **treaty of Teusina** (1595).

1593. Sigismund's attempt to restore Catholicism was met by the reaffirmation of the Protestant faith, based on the **Confession of Augsburg,** at the **Convention of Uppsala,** while his absolutist tendencies provoked

1599. A rebellion which ended in his deposition. He was succeeded by the youngest son of Gustavus Vasa,

1604–1611. CHARLES IX (in virtual control of the government since 1599) under whom

(From p. 330)

Kings of Denmark and Norway (1448–1730)

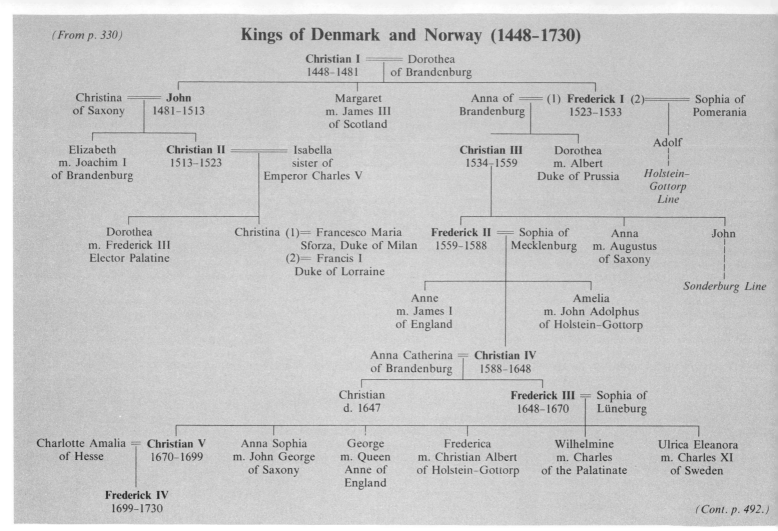

Christian I ══ Dorothea
1448–1481   of Brandenburg

Christina ══ **John** — Margaret — Anna of ══(1) **Frederick I** (2)══ Sophia of
of Saxony   **1481–1513** — m. James III — Brandenburg — **1523–1533** — Pomerania
of Scotland

Elizabeth — **Christian II** ══ Isabella — **Christian III** — Dorothea — Adolf
m. Joachim I — **1513–1523** — sister of — **1534–1559** — m. Albert
of Brandenburg — Emperor Charles V — Duke of Prussia — *Holstein-
Gottorp
Line*

Dorothea — Christina (1)═ Francesco Maria — **Frederick II** ══ Sophia of — Anna — John
m. Frederick III — Sforza, Duke of Milan — **1559–1588** — Mecklenburg — m. Augustus
Elector Palatine — (2)═ Francis I — of Saxony
Duke of Lorraine — *Sonderburg Line*

Anne — Amelia
m. James I — m. John Adolphus
of England — of Holstein-Gottorp

Anna Catherina ══ **Christian IV**
of Brandenburg — **1588–1648**

Christian — **Frederick III** ══ Sophia of
d. 1647 — **1648–1670** — Lüneburg

Charlotte Amalia ══ **Christian V** — Anna Sophia — George — Frederica — Wilhelmine — Ulrica Eleanora
of Hesse — **1670–1699** — m. John George — m. Queen — m. Christian Albert — m. Charles — m. Charles XI
of Saxony — Anne of — of Holstein-Gottorp — of the Palatinate — of Sweden
England

Frederick IV
1699–1730

(Cont. p. 492.)

The House of Vasa (1523–1818)

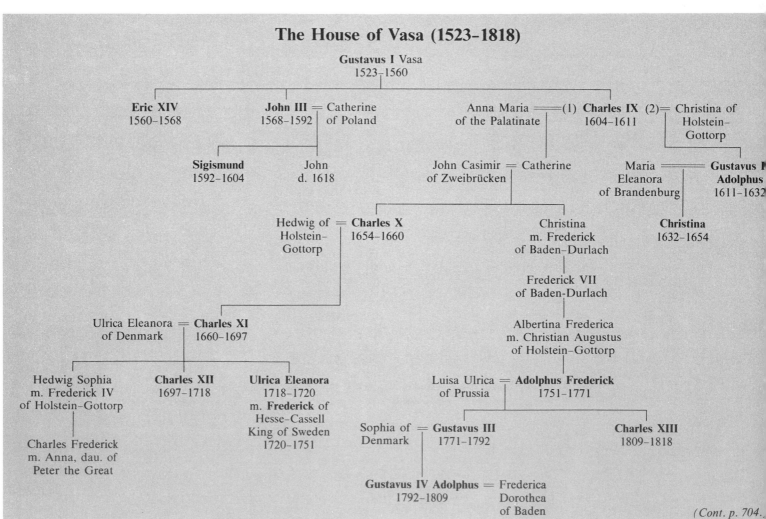

Gustavus I Vasa
1523–1560

Eric XIV — **John III** ══ Catherine — Anna Maria ══(1) **Charles IX** (2)═ Christina of
1560–1568 — **1568–1592** — of Poland — of the Palatinate — **1604–1611** — Holstein-
Gottorp

Sigismund — John — John Casimir ══ Catherine — Maria ══ **Gustavus**
1592–1604 — d. 1618 — of Zweibrücken — Eleanora — **Adolphus**
of Brandenburg — **1611–1632**

Hedwig of ══ **Charles X** — Christina — **Christina**
Holstein- — **1654–1660** — m. Frederick — **1632–1654**
Gottorp — of Baden-Durlach

Frederick VII
of Baden-Durlach

Ulrica Eleanora ══ **Charles XI** — Albertina Frederica
of Denmark — **1660–1697** — m. Christian Augustus
of Holstein-Gottorp

Hedwig Sophia — **Charles XII** — Ulrica Eleanora — Luisa Ulrica ══ **Adolphus Frederick**
m. Frederick IV — **1697–1718** — **1718–1720** — of Prussia — **1751–1771**
of Holstein-Gottorp — m. **Frederick** of
Hesse-Cassell
King of Sweden
1720–1751

Charles Frederick — Sophia of ══ **Gustavus III** — **Charles XIII**
m. Anna, dau. of — Denmark — **1771–1792** — **1809–1818**
Peter the Great

Gustavus IV Adolphus ══ Frederica
1792–1809 — Dorothea
of Baden

(Cont. p. 704.)

Sweden intervened in Russia during the **Time of Troubles** *(p. 436)*. Under his son and successor,

1611–1632. GUSTAVUS II ADOLPHUS, war with Russia was ended by the **treaty of Stolbovo** (1617): Sweden acquired eastern Carelia and Ingria, cutting Russia off from the Baltic Sea. This was followed by

1621–1629. A war with Poland, the result of dynastic competition, in the course of which Sweden occupied all of Livonia. For Swedish participation in the **Thirty Years' War** see *p. 426).*

Gustavus Adolphus' **domestic policy** was one of conciliation. A royal charter (1611) gave the council and the estates a voice in all questions of legislation, and a power of veto in matters of war and peace. Administration and courts were modernized, education promoted, commerce and industry sponsored, foreign immigration invited. The king's chief collaborator was his chancellor, **Axel Oxenstierna** (1583–1654), who became the actual ruler of Sweden under Gustavus Adolphus' daughter,

1632–1654. CHRISTINA. For Swedish acquisitions under the **treaties of Westphalia** see *p. 429.*

(Cont. p. 489.)

Queen Christina's accession to the throne

8. *Poland-Lithuania, 1492–1648*

(From p. 332)

The history of Poland in this period was marked by a constant growth of power on the part of the lesser nobility, so that Poland became transformed into a republic of the *szlachta* (*Rzeczpospolita*) with an elected king as the titular head. All efforts of the kings to strengthen the royal power, reform the government, and establish a modern standing army met with failure.

1492–1501. JOHN ALBERT, the son of Casimir IV, relied upon the gentry (szlachta) to reduce the power of the great magnates. The result was the

1496. Statute of Piotrkow (the Magna Carta of Poland) which gave the gentry extensive privileges at the expense of the burghers and peasants. The burghers were restricted from buying land and the peasants were practically deprived of freedom of movement.

1497–1498. A futile **invasion of Moldavia,** which was intended to secure a throne for the king's brother, resulted in a devastating invasion by the Turks.

1501–1506. ALEXANDER I, brother of John Albert and, since 1492, grand duke of Lithuania. His reign was important only for the **war with Ivan the Great** of Russia *(p. 337),* which resulted in the loss of the left bank of the Dnieper by Poland (1503), and for

1505. The **Constitution of Radom,** which definitely made the national diet, elected by the nobles at their provincial assemblies (the *dietines*), the supreme legislative organ. Henceforth no new laws were to be passed without the diet's consent.

1506–1548. SIGISMUND I, brother of John Albert and Alexander, during whose reign the diet (1511) passed laws finally establishing serfdom in Poland.

1512–1522. War with Russia over the White Russian region. The Russians made considerable gains and in 1514 took Smolensk, the key city.

1525. Secularization of Prussia and end of the rule of the Teutonic Knights. Prussia remained a fief of Poland.

1534–1536. Another war with Russia brought no success to the Poles. Smolensk remained in Russian hands.

1548–1572. SIGISMUND II (August). His reign was distinguished by the wide spread of the **Protestant Reformation,** which had taken root in 1518 and had gained ground, especially in the Baltic lands and in the towns, despite many edicts penalizing the adherents, who were known as **Dissidents.** Demands for a national church, marriage of the clergy, communion in both kinds, Slavonic liturgy, etc. **Calvinism** and **Antitrinitarianism** also established themselves. After the **council of Trent** *(p. 416)* the crown, backed by the recently formed Polish-Lithuanian chapter of the Jesuit Order (1565), succeeded in checking the movement and in restoring the supremacy of Roman Catholicism.

1557–1571. The **Livonian War,** arising from a disputed succession and from the conflicting claims of Poland, Russia, Sweden, and Denmark. The Russians invaded the country

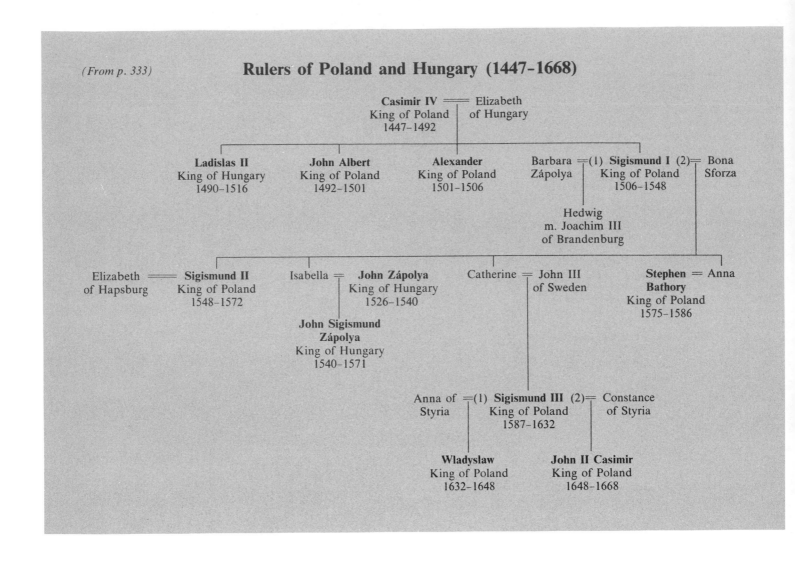

Rulers of Poland and Hungary (1447–1668)

(From p. 333)

Casimir IV == Elizabeth
King of Poland   of Hungary
1447–1492

Ladislas II
King of Hungary
1490–1516

John Albert
King of Poland
1492–1501

Alexander
King of Poland
1501–1506

Barbara ==(1) Sigismund I (2)== Bona
Zápolya   King of Poland   Sforza
                1506–1548

Hedwig
m. Joachim III
of Brandenburg

Elizabeth === Sigismund II
of Hapsburg   King of Poland
               1548–1572

Isabella = John Zápolya
          King of Hungary
          1526–1540

John Sigismund
Zápolya
King of Hungary
1540–1571

Catherine = John III
            of Sweden

Stephen = Anna
Bathory
King of Poland
1575–1586

Anna of ==(1) Sigismund III (2)== Constance
Styria   King of Poland   of Styria
              1587–1632

Wladyslaw
King of Poland
1632–1648

John II Casimir
King of Poland
1648–1668

(1557) and the Swedes took Estonia, while the Danes acquired part of Courland. In 1561 the Poles took over Livonia, but Ivan the Terrible of Russia conquered part of it in 1563.

1569, July 1. The UNION OF LUBLIN, which, despite opposition on the part of Lithuania, merged that country with the Polish kingdom. The two nations were to have a common sovereign, and a common diet, though Lithuania was to retain a separate administration and army.

With the death of Sigismund II the **Jagellon dynasty** came to an end and the Polish crown, already elective in theory, became so in fact. The result was a tremendous weakening of the royal power, constant embroilment in the rivalries of other nations, and a growing hopelessness of reform.

1573–1574. HENRY OF VALOIS was elected king on condition of signing the *Pacta Conventa*, formally recognizing the right of the nobility to elect kings and strictly limiting the royal power. The diet was to meet at least once every two years. Henry paid richly for his election and for the alliance of Poland with France, but, on the death of his brother, Charles IX, he slipped away and returned to France. There followed a period of confusion, during which the Hapsburgs made great efforts to secure the crown. The Poles ultimately elected

1575–1586. STEPHEN BATHORY, husband of Anna, the last Jagellon. Stephen was a strong ruler, but was unable to make much progress against the powerful nobility. His great success was in the field of foreign affairs and war. Plan for a union of eastern Europe under his leadership, preparatory to a united attack upon the Turk. This came to nothing, but Stephen, with a new army of peasant infantry, raised on the royal estates, was able, in the last phase of the Livonian War (1579–1582) to retake Polotsk and to put an end to the steady encroachment of Russia upon the White Russian regions.

1587–1632. SIGISMUND III (Vasa), son of King John of Sweden. He had been educated by the Jesuits and threw his entire influence on the side of the Counter-Reformation. For the rest he demonstrated little statesmanship and involved Poland in endless wars with Sweden because of his claims to the Swedish throne.

1595–1596. Attempts to reunite the Greek Orthodox Church in Poland with Rome foundered on the obstinacy of the Jesuits. However, part of the Orthodox formed the so-called **Uniate Church,** retaining Eastern rites but recognizing papal authority. The result was the **confederation of Vilna** (1599), an alliance between the Orthodox and the Dissidents against the power of the Roman church.

1609–1618. Polish intervention in Russia during the **Time of Troubles** *(p. 436)*. An attempt to put Sigismund's son, Wladyslaw, on the Russian throne ended in the expulsion of the Poles from Moscow.

1629. The **treaty of Altmark,** a truce in the long conflict with Sweden, signalized the defeat of the Poles and confirmed the loss of Livonia.

1632–1648. WLADYSLAW, the son of Sigismund. He was elected without opposition and pursued a policy diametrically opposed to that of his father. But his efforts to restrict the powers of the Jesuits were vain.

1632–1634. War with Russia, which was ended by the **treaty of Polianov** (1634): Wladyslaw renounced his claims to the Russian throne, but regained the Smolensk region for Poland.
(Cont. p. 492.)

Literature: *Aesop's Fables* were paraphrased and a life written by **Bernard of Lublin** (c. 1515). The spread of Renaissance culture and of the Reformation culminated in a "golden age" of prose and poetry: poets **Nicholas Rej of Naglowice** (1505–1569) and **Jan Kochanowski** (1530–1584). Prose writers **Lucas Gornicki** and **Peter Skarga** (1536–1612). Foremost poet of the 17th century: **Waclaw Potocki** (1625–1696).

9. *Russia, 1505–1645*

(From p. 334)

In Russia, as in many other countries, the period was one of conflict between the crown and the powerful landed nobility, accompanied by a decline in the influence of the townsmen and a gradual relapsing of the peasantry into serfdom. In Russia the latter problem was closely connected with defense and territorial expansion. Since 1454 the grand dukes of Moscow granted non-hereditary military fiefs (*pomestye*) to secure a supply of fighting men for use in the struggle against the Tatars. The corollary was a steady debasement in the position of the peasants, who consequently tended to run off to newly conquered territories in the southeast. Depopulation in the center resulted in ever more drastic measures to hold the cultivator on the land. At the same time there grew up on the borders the Cossack colonies, wild, free communities which were to play a great rôle in this period.

1505–1533. BASIL III, the son of Ivan the Great and Sophia. The reign was a fairly quiet one, during which the work of consolidation was continued by the reduction of Pskov (1510), Smolensk (1514), and Riazan (1517).

1533–1584. IVAN IV (the Terrible), the son of Basil. He ascended the throne at the age of three. The regency was in the hands of his mother, **Helen Glinski** (of Lithuanian family), until 1538, and thereupon fell into the hands of powerful noble (*boyar*) families, notably the **Shuiskys** and **Belskys,** whose oligarchic policy presented the young ruler with an almost insuperable problem.

1547. Ivan assumed power and had himself crowned *tsar*, the first Russian ruler to assume the title formally. At the same time he established a *chosen council*, composed of personally selected advisers, which he hoped to make a counterweight to the power of the **council of boyars** (*duma*). This was followed in 1549 with the convocation of the first national assembly or *zemski sobor*, also meant to broaden the support of the crown. In these early years Ivan made considerable progress in breaking down the power of the provincial governors and in establishing a measure of local government.

1552–1556. The **conquest of Kazan and Astrakhan** from the Tatars gave Russia control of the entire course of the Volga and opened the way for expansion to the east and southeast. Already in the last years of Ivan's reign (1581–1583) Russian traders (the Stroganov family) established themselves east of the Urals and Cossack pioneers, under **Yermak,** began the conquest of Siberia.

1553. The British, under Richard Chancellor, reached Moscow by way of the White Sea and Archangel. They were given trade rights in 1555 and formed an important link in Russian communications with the west, which were otherwise cut off by Poland-Lithuania and Sweden.

1557–1582. The **LIVONIAN WAR,** arising from the disputed succession to the Baltic territories ruled by the Teutonic Knights. Ivan appreciated to the full the importance of an outlet to the Baltic, and seized Narva and Dorpat. In 1563 he conquered part of Livonia, which had been taken over by the Poles.

1564. Conflict of Ivan with the powerful bo-

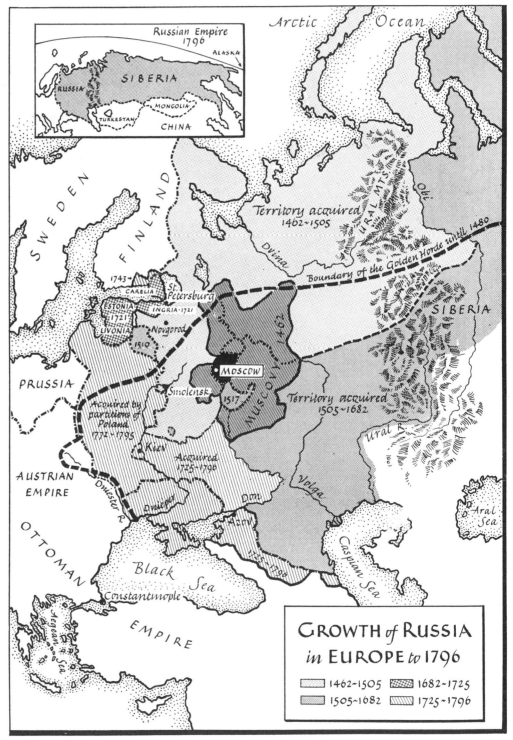

GROWTH *of* RUSSIA
in EUROPE *to* 1796

1462–1505
1505–1682
1682–1725
1725–1796

Muscovite warriors (1557 woodcut)

yars, led by **Prince Andrei Kurbski.** Ivan eventually withdrew from Moscow and issued an appeal to the people, who, through the metropolitan, urged him to return. He took a terrible revenge on his opponents and began a reign of terror marked by incredible excesses and fantastic self-debasement. At the same time Ivan set aside about half of the realm as his personal domain (*oprichnina*), in which he established a new administration and a separate royal army.

1570. Ivan ravaged Novgorod and massacred many of the inhabitants, whom he suspected of sympathy for the Poles.

1571. The **Crimean Tatars** attacked and sacked Moscow.

1578. Defeat of the Russians by the Swedes at Wenden, in the course of the struggle for the Baltic lands. Polotsk was lost in the following year.

1581. Stephen Bathory, king of Poland, invaded Russia and advanced victoriously to Pskov.

1582. Peace between Russia on the one hand and Poland and Sweden on the other, mediated by the Jesuit **Antonio Possevino,** who had been sent by the pope in the hope of effecting a union of the Orthodox and Roman churches. Ivan was obliged to accept most of his recent losses.

1584–1598. THEODORE (FEDOR) I, the son of Ivan, a feeble and utterly weak ruler. The actual government fell again into the hands of the boyars, notably Nikita Romanov (related to Ivan IV's first wife) and Boris Godunov, brother-in-law of Theodore.

1589. Establishment of the Russian patriarchate as separate from that of Constantinople. The Russian church thus became entirely independent. Theodore dying without issue, a national assembly elected to the throne

1598–1605. BORIS GODUNOV, an intelligent but none too courageous ruler, faced with the jealousy of other boyar families. Against these he acted by intrigue and persecution.

1604–1613. The **TIME OF TROUBLES,** which began with the appearance of a **false Dmitri,** i.e. a pretender who claimed to be the supposedly murdered son of Ivan IV. Dmitri was an able and forceful person who soon found extensive support among the Poles and the Cossacks. Boris' death at this crucial time initiated a period of utmost confusion during which boyar families struggled for supremacy while their position was challenged by the lower classes (led by the Cossacks), and while foreigners (Poles and Swedes) took full advantage of the situation to further their own interests.

1605. Theodore II, the son of Boris, succeeded to the throne. He was soon deposed and murdered by the boyars, many of whom accepted Dmitri. The latter advanced to Moscow and established himself on the throne.

1606. Basil Shuisky and a faction of the boyars succeeded in driving out the pretender and murdering him. Shuisky thereupon became tsar. But new pretenders soon appeared, and the situation became desperate when the Cossacks and peasants in the south and east rose in revolt.

1608. The new Dmitri defeated Basil and advanced to Tushino, outside Moscow. In urgent need, Basil ceded Carelia to the Swedes in return for aid.

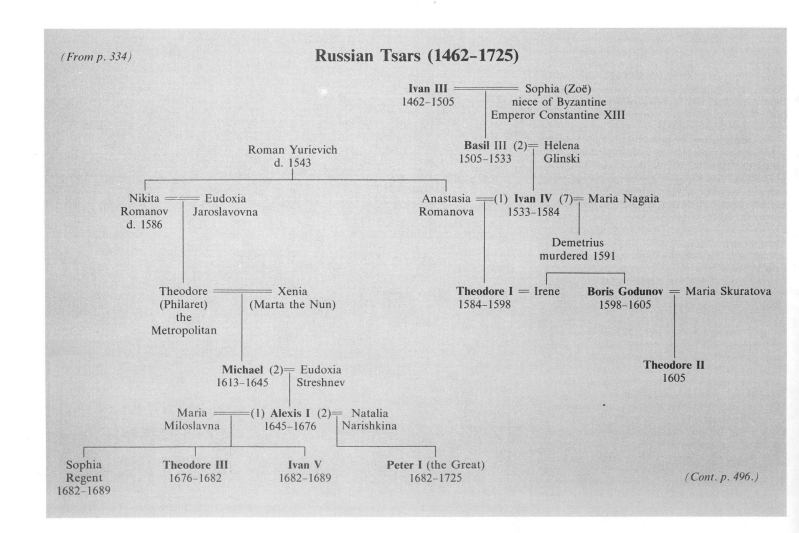

(From p. 334)

Russian Tsars (1462–1725)

Ivan III 1462–1505 ═══════ **Sophia (Zoë)** niece of Byzantine Emperor Constantine XIII

Roman Yurievich d. 1543

Basil III (2)═ Helena 1505–1533 Glinski

Nikita Romanov d. 1586 ═══════ Eudoxia Jaroslavovna

Anastasia Romanova ═(1) **Ivan IV** (7)═ Maria Nagaia 1533–1584

Demetrius murdered 1591

Theodore (Philaret) the Metropolitan ═══════ Xenia (Marta the Nun)

Theodore I = Irene 1584–1598

Boris Godunov = Maria Skuratova 1598–1605

Michael (2)═ Eudoxia 1613–1645 Streshnev

Theodore II 1605

Maria Miloslavna ═══(1) **Alexis I** (2)═ Natalia Narishkina 1645–1676

Sophia Regent 1682–1689

Theodore III 1676–1682

Ivan V 1682–1689

Peter I (the Great) 1682–1725

(Cont. p. 496.)

1609. **Sigismund of Poland** advanced to Smolensk and made extensive promises to the Russian boyars in the hope of acquiring the crown.

1610. **Skopin-Shuisky,** nephew of Basil, with a Swedish force under De La Gardie, relieved Moscow, but the Poles continued their advance. The Russians then deposed Basil and a boyar faction offered the throne to Wladyslaw son of Sigismund. The latter, jealous of his son and anxious to secure the throne himself, evaded the offer and advanced to Moscow.

1611. The turn of the tide was marked by the death of the pretender and by a powerful reaction against the Poles, especially in the northern and eastern provinces. A national militia was formed under **Pozharsky** and this in

1612. Relieved Moscow and drove out the Poles.

1613, Feb. 21. A **national assembly** (*zemski sobor*) elected to the throne

1613–1645. **MICHAEL ROMANOV,** grandnephew of Ivan IV and son of the patriotic leader, **Philaret.** Michael was crowned on July 11 and therewith began the **Romanov dynasty,** which ruled until 1917. Michael himself was a man of no ability, who was guided by his father and later fell under the influence of favorites. The reign saw the gradual restoration of order, but also the firmer establishment of serfdom and the gradual disappearance of local self-government. The national assembly, which was frequently summoned, failed to establish a regular organization or to develop beyond the status of a consultative body.

1617. **Treaty of Stolbovo,** with Sweden. The Swedes restored Novgorod, which they had occupied, but Russia was obliged to abandon the few towns that had still been held on the Gulf of Finland.

1634. **Treaty of Polianov,** with Poland, bringing to a temporary end a long period of conflict. In return for recognition of his title, Michael was obliged to give up many of the frontier towns (including Smolensk) which had been taken by the Poles.

1637. **Russian pioneers** reached the coast of the

Plan of the Kremlin in the reign of Boris Godunov, 1598–1605

Pacific, after a phenomenally rapid advance over the whole of Siberia.

1637. The **Cossacks** managed to take the important fortress of **Azov** from the Crimean Tatars. They offered it to Michael, who refused it (1642) in order to avoid conflict with the Turks. The fortress was thereupon returned.

(Cont. p. 494.)

10. *Bohemia, 1471–1627*

(From p. 325)

1471–1516. **LADISLAS II,** son of the king of Poland, first ruler of the **Jagiello family,** a boy of sixteen at his accession. Ladislas proved himself a gentle but weak and undecided ruler, wholly unsuited to the position. He continued the persecution of the Bohemian Brotherhood, but made no progress toward unifying the country. As king of Hungary also, he spent most of his time at Pressburg, leaving open the way for the domination of Bohemia by powerful nobles. During the entire later 15th century the aristocracy extended its possessions and power at the expense of the crown and Church. The towns declined in power and the peasantry sank back into serfdom or a status close to it. Great influx of German peasants in the west and north, and also in the towns.

1516–1526. **LOUIS,** son of Ladislas, who ascended the throne of Bohemia and Hungary at the age of ten. Conditions continued as under Ladislas, further complicated by the spread and persecution of Lutheranism.

1526. **Louis was defeated and killed** by the Turks at the **battle of Mohács. Ferdinand,** brother of Emperor Charles V and brother-in-law of Louis, was elected king, opening a long period of Hapsburg rule.

1547. The Bohemian crown was proclaimed hereditary in the house of Hapsburg. Constant growth of the royal prerogative at the expense of the diet and of town government.

1618. **Defenestration of Prague** and beginning of the Thirty Years' War *(p. 424).* Ferdinand II was declared deposed and the Protestant Frederick of the Palatinate was elected king (*the Winter King*).

1620, Nov. 8. BATTLE OF THE WHITE MOUNTAIN; defeat of Frederick and the Bohemians. Bohemia was virtually deprived of independence and a wholesale confiscation of the lands of the native nobility took place.

1627. A **new constitution** confirmed the hereditary rule of the Hapsburgs and strengthened royal power. The incorporation of Bohemia with the Hapsburg Empire was completed in the 18th century with the extension of the imperial administration under Joseph I (1705–1711) and with the **Pragmatic Sanction of 1720** (*p. 482*).

II. *Hungary, 1490–1648*

(*From p. 335*)

1490–1516. LADISLAS II, king of Bohemia, was elected king of Hungary by the nobles. A weak and ineffectual ruler, he allowed the work of Matthias Corvinus to be undone within a few years. In order to secure recognition from the Hapsburgs, he gave up Matthias' conquests and arranged dynastic marriages with the Hapsburgs (his infant son Louis was married to Mary, granddaughter of Maximilian; his own daughter, Anne, was married to Maximilian's grandson Ferdinand). This policy led to the formation of a national party among the Hungarian nobility, which was led by Stephen Zápolya (Szapolyai), the vaivode (prince) of Transylvania. The nobles refused Ladislas all effective financial support, so that he was unable to maintain an army and was soon at the mercy of the feudal elements.

1514. A great **revolt of the peasants,** led by George Dózsa, was directed against the ruthless exploitation by the aristocrats. It was suppressed in a sea of blood by John Zápolya, leader of the nobility.

1514. The *Tripartitum,* a constitution worked out by Stephen Verböczy, was passed by the diet. It established the equality of all nobles and at the same time fixed the system of serfdom on the peasantry.

1516–1526. LOUIS II, the son of Ladislas, succeeded his father at the age of ten. A dissolute youngster, devoted to pleasure, he did nothing to stop the disintegration of the royal power. His reign was marked chiefly by the spread of the **Protestant Reformation.** The movement first took root in the German areas and in the towns, and was vigorously opposed by the nobles. In 1523 it was declared punishable by death and confiscation of property, but despite all edicts it took firm hold of the country.

1521. The Turks took Belgrade, beginning their victorious advance into Hungary.

1526, Aug. 29–30. BATTLE OF MOHÁCS. Defeat and death of Louis when the Turks completely overwhelmed his disorganized feudal army of 20,000.

1526–1528. Louis's death was followed by a hot contest over the succession. Part of the nobility, hoping for German aid against the

George Rákóczi I, 1630–1648

Royal Palace, Budapest, 1541

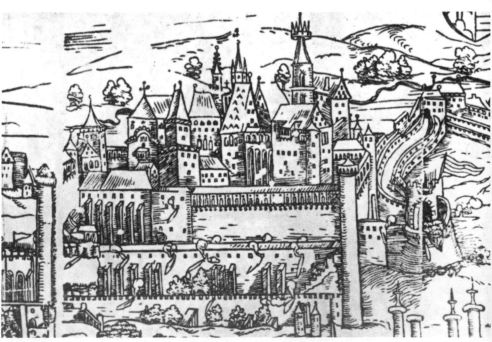

Turks, elected **Ferdinand of Hapsburg,** brother of Emperor Charles V. The national party, on the other hand, elected **John Zápolya** as king. After a civil war lasting two years, Zápolya was defeated. He appealed to the Turks, who supported him vigorously. By the **peace of Nagyvarad** the two kings recognized each other, each ruling part of the territory. Zápolya became a vassal of the Turks, but Ferdinand continued the war against them which was interrupted only by occasional truces *(p. 440)*.

1540. Death of John Zápolya. The Turks recognized his infant son, **John II** (Sigismund) **Zápolya** (1540–1571). This led to a new clash with Ferdinand, who began the invasion of eastern Hungary. The Turks again invaded and took Buda. They now took over the entire central part of Hungary (the great plain), which was organized in four *pashaliks.* There was no settlement by the Turks, but the territory was granted in military fiefs and subjected to heavy taxation. Religious tolerance of the Turks. Transylvania, under Zápolya, was a vassal state of the Turks, but was left almost entirely free. Under **Cardinal Martinuzzi** it was organized as a state (three nations: Magyars, Szeklers, and Germans, meeting in a *Landtag,* elected the king and passed laws).

The Transylvanians (even the nobility) soon accepted **Calvinism,** so that during the later 16th century the larger part of Hungary was either Lutheran or Calvinist. In 1560 religious toleration was established in Transylvania. The **Hapsburgs,** on the other hand, held only a narrow strip of western and northern Hungary, and even for this they long paid tribute to the Turks. Warfare was incessant on this frontier (blockhouses and constant raids). The Hapsburgs employed Italian and Spanish mercenaries to defend their possessions, and these ravaged the country as much as the Turkish territory. Ferdinand and his successors governed from Vienna or Prague and with little reference to the traditional rights of the Hungarian nobility. This led to growing friction and later to serious conflict.

1581–1602. Sigismund Bathory, prince of Transylvania. His efforts to unite with the Hapsburgs for a grand assault on the declining Turk power met with vigorous opposition on the part of the Transylvanian nobility.

1604. Beginning of the Counter-Reformation, under Hapsburg auspices. This resulted in a revolt of the Hungarians, who were supported by the Transylvanians.

1604–1606. STEPHEN BOCSKAY became prince of Transylvania and, after defeating the Hapsburgs, secured the **treaty of Vienna,** by which Protestantism was given equal status with Catholicism. Nevertheless, the Counter-Reformation made great strides, especially among the nobility, due to the efforts of Cardinal Pazmany and the Jesuits.

1613–1629. BETHLEN GABOR (Gabriel Bethlen), prince of Transylvania. He was one of the greatest rulers of the country and made his state the center of Hungarian culture and national feeling. On the outbreak of the **Thirty Years' War,** he openly sided with the enemies of the Hapsburgs and made Transylvania a vital factor in European politics.

1630–1648. GEORGE RÁKÓCZI I, another eminent prince of Transylvania. He continued the policy of his predecessor and managed to guide the country through the storms of the European crisis. At the same time he took full advantage of the growing weakness of the Turks, making Transylvania virtually an independent state, which played a part of some importance in international affairs.

Literary efforts of the 16th and early 17th centuries centered on Scripture translations, along with the poetry of **Valentine Balassa, John Rimay,** and **Nicholas Zrinyi** (1620–1664).

12. *The Ottoman Empire, 1481–1656*

(From p. 346)

1481–1512. BAYAZID II, a man of intellectual tastes, but the least significant of the first ten sultans. He was raised to the throne with the support of the Janissaries, but his position was challenged by his younger brother, Jem **(Djem),** who had himself proclaimed sultan at Bursa, and then proposed a division of the empire. Jem was defeated by Bayazid's forces at Yeni-Shehr and fled, first to Egypt, then to Rhodes. The Knights of St. John sent him to France and extracted from Bayazid a treaty of peace. As a valuable hostage many of the European powers tried to get control of Jem, but he was finally (1489) turned over to the pope, who tried to use him to extract money and support from Bayazid against Charles VIII of France. During the latter's invasion of Italy, Jem fell into his hands. He died under suspicious circumstances at Naples (1495).

1485–1491. War with Egypt for control of Cilicia. Six inconclusive campaigns.

1489. The Venetians acquired Cyprus from the Christian ruler by bequest, and tried to take advantage of Bayazid's weakness to strengthen their position in the Aegean.

1499–1503. Venetian-Turkish War, joined by Hungary in 1500. The Turkish fleet, under **Kemal Re'is** (possibly a Greek) defeated the Venetians and took Modon, Koron, and Lepanto. Turk cavalry raided as far as Vicenza. The peace deprived Venice of the lost stations, but left it Nauplion and some of the Ionian islands.

1511. Ismail, shah of Persia, incited an uprising of the Turkish nomads of the Taurus Mountains.

1512–1520. Selim I (the Grim). He forced his father to abdicate after a civil war between Bayazid's three sons, Ahmed, Corcud, and Selim.

1513. Selim defeated his brother Ahmed in Anatolia and had him executed.

1514. War against Shah Ismail of Persia, who had supported Ahmed. The struggle was accentuated by religious differences, the Kizilbashes in Anatolia being Shi'ites and wholly in sympathy with the Persians. Selim, a fanatic Sunnite, is said to have slaughtered 40,000 of his own heretic subjects before proceeding against the Persians.

1514, Aug. 23. Selim completely defeated the Persians at **Chaldiran,** east of the Euphrates. He took and plundered Tabriz, but was obliged to fall back because of the objections of the Janissaries to further advance.

1515. Conquest of eastern Anatolia and Kurdistan by the Turks.

1516. Selim embarked on a second campaign against Persia, but was diverted by the Mameluke sultan of Egypt, Kansu al-Gauri, who was allied with Persia and appeared at Aleppo with an army.

1516, Aug. 24. BATTLE OF MARJDABIK, north of Aleppo. Selim, with the use of artillery, completely defeated Kansu, who was killed. Aleppo and Damascus at once surrendered to the Turks. Selim, anxious to proceed against Persia, offered peace to the new sultan, Tuman Bey, on condition that he accept Turkish suzerainty. This was refused.

1517, Jan. 22. The Turks took Cairo, and sacked it. The **sherif of Mecca** surrendered voluntarily. The caliph **Mutawakkil** was sent to Constantinople, but after Selim's death returned to Egypt (legend of his having transferred his authority as caliph to Selim). The important thing was that Selim secured control of the Holy Places in Arabia. Tuman Bey was

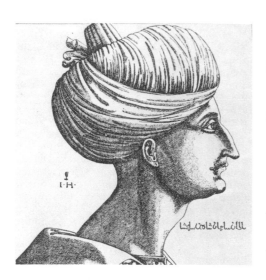

Suleiman I, 1520–1566

executed, but Egypt left under the rule of the Mameluke beys, under a Turkish governor-general. Legend of the Turks cutting the routes of oriental trade: these had really been cut by the Portuguese, operating at the entrance of the Red Sea.

1520–1566. SULEIMAN I (the Magnificent), only son of Selim, a highly cultivated but proud and ambitious ruler, generally rated as the greatest of the sultans. In reality he left affairs largely to his famous viziers. **Ibrahim Pasha,** son of a Greek of Parga, practically ruled the empire from 1523 to 1536. In 1524, after an attempt of the Turkish governor of Egypt to set himself up as sultan, Ibrahim completely reorganized the government with more effective control by the Turks.

1521. Capture of Belgrade, after several assaults. In the succeeding years the Turks raided regularly in Hungary and Austria, creating a panic throughout central Europe.

1522. Capture of Rhodes, which had become the headquarters for Catalan and Maltese pirates who threatened Turkish communications with Egypt. The Knights of St. John put up a valiant defense, but the help expected from the West did not materialize. They thereupon capitulated. In 1530 they were established at Malta by Charles V.

1526, Aug. 29-30. BATTLE OF MOHÁCS. Defeat of King Louis of Hungary and his 20,000 ill-disciplined knights and peasants. Louis was killed and the Turks advanced and took Ofen. Disputed succession in Hungary: John Zápolya elected in Transylvania, Ferdinand of Hapsburg at Pressburg. After two years of civil war Zápolya was defeated. He appealed to Suleiman.

1528. Second campaign in Hungary. Ofen retaken by the Turks.

1529, Sept. FIRST SIEGE OF VIENNA. After several assaults the Turks withdrew (Oct. 16), partly because of valiant resistance of the garrison, partly because of wretched weather and inability to bring up the heavy artillery. But Suleiman rejected repeated offers of Ferdinand to pay tribute for Hungary in return for recognition.

1529. Khaireddin Pasha, famous Turkish admiral and corsair (originally a Greek of Myti-

lene in the service of the bey of Tunis, 1512; entered Turkish service in 1516), took the Peñon of Algiers.

1532. Turkish campaign in Hungary. The Turks took Güns, after a valiant resistance. Suleiman then retired, because of the threat from Persia.

1533. Peace between Suleiman and Ferdinand. The latter retained that part of Hungary that he still held; Zápolya remained king of the rest; both paid tribute to the Turks. No peace made with Charles V, so that the naval war in the Mediterranean (Khaireddin and Andrea Doria) continued. Khaireddin evacuated thousands of Moors expelled from Spain.

1534. Khaireddin drove out the bey of Tunis and ravaged the coasts of Sicily and southern Italy.

1534. War against Shah Tahmasp of Persia, who had been negotiating with Charles V. The Turks marched to Tabriz, and conquered Baghdad and Mesopotamia.

1535, June-July. Great **expedition of Charles V to Tunis,** the fleet commanded by Andrea Doria. The town was taken after Khaireddin had been defeated off the coast. Horrible sack of three days. The bey, Mulai Hassan, was reinstated.

1536, Mar. Formal **alliance between Suleiman and Francis I** of France, against the Hapsburgs. This had been under discussion since 1525 and had led to some measure of co-operation.

1537-1540. War with Venice, forced by the Turkish threat to close the Straits of Otranto. The sultan and Khaireddin besieged Corfu, with French aid, but were obliged to give up the project.

1538. Holy League against the Turks (Charles V, the pope, and Venice). Abortive efforts of Charles V to buy off Khaireddin. After a defeat at sea **(battle of Prevesa)** the Venetians made peace (1540), losing Nauplion, their last station in the Morea, and paying a large indemnity.

1538. Turkish naval expedition through the Red Sea to the northwest coast of India. The entire east coast of the Red Sea (Yemen, Aden) was taken over.

1540. Death of John Zápolya, leaving an infant son as his successor, whom Suleiman recognized. Invasion of Hungary by Ferdinand, who tried to make good his claim to the whole country.

1541. Suleiman's campaign in Hungary. He marched to Buda and took over control during the minority of John Sigismund Zápolya. Direct Turkish administrative control established.

1547. Five years' truce between Suleiman and Ferdinand; the Turks retained the larger part of Hungary and Ferdinand paid tribute for the small strip remaining to him.

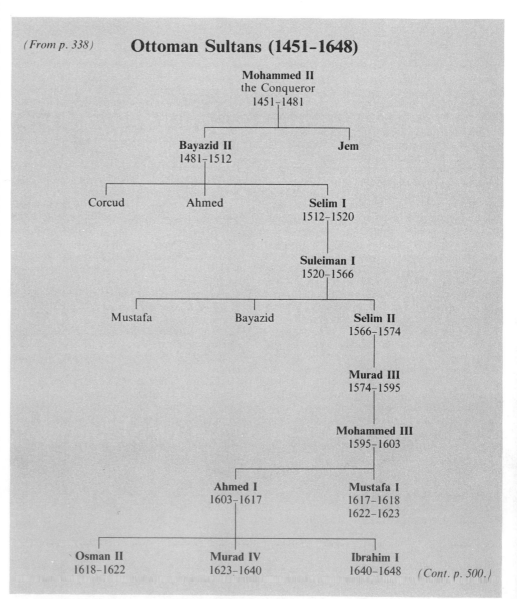

(From p. 338)

Ottoman Sultans (1451-1648)

Mohammed II
the Conqueror
1451–1481

Bayazid II
1481–1512

Jem

Corcud

Ahmed

Selim I
1512–1520

Suleiman I
1520–1566

Mustafa

Bayazid

Selim II
1566–1574

Murad III
1574–1595

Mohammed III
1595–1603

Ahmed I
1603–1617

Mustafa I
1617–1618
1622–1623

Osman II
1618–1622

Murad IV
1623–1640

Ibrahim I
1640–1648

(Cont. p. 500.)

Siege of Vienna, 1529

1548. Second expedition against Persia. Tabriz again occupied.

1551–1562. Renewal of war with Ferdinand. This was carried on in desultory fashion and consisted chiefly of sieges. After Ferdinand's succession to the imperial throne peace was made, Zápolya receiving Transylvania, the Turks retaining Hungary proper, and Ferdinand paying tribute for the western section.

1552. The Persians took the offensive and captured Erzerum.

1553. Suleiman proceeded against the Persians and ravaged the western part of the country. Peace was made in 1555, Suleiman retaining his conquests in Mesopotamia.

1554. Dragut, successor of Khaireddin (d. 1546), took Mehedia, a stong base on the Tunisian coast, from the Spaniards. The **conquest of the North African coast** was completed in the following two years.

1565. **Turkish siege of Malta,** the headquarters of the Spanish corsairs. After taking one of the three main forts the Turks were obliged to withdraw.

1566. Renewal of war in Hungary, the result of continued raids ordered by the Emperor Maximilian.

1566, Sept. 5. **Death of Suleiman,** at the siege of Szigeth. His last years had been embittered by family troubles. His wife, **Roxelana** (probably a Russian captive), and her son-in-law, the grand vizir **Rustem Pasha,** so poisoned his mind against his eldest son, Mustafa, that he had him strangled in 1553. There ensued a conflict between the sons of Roxelana, Selim

and Bayazid. The latter took up arms in 1559, but was defeated at Konia. He fled to Persia, where he and his sons were executed in return for a high money payment by Suleiman. But Suleiman left the empire the greatest in Europe and the best organized, an easy match for the European powers, rent by dynastic and religious antagonisms.

1566–1574. **SELIM II** (the Sot), an intelligent but indolent ruler, much given to drink. Divided counsels of **Mehmed Sökullu** (grand

Selim II, 1566–1574

vizir, 1560–1579), who favored close relations with Venice and continuance of the war against Spain (peace made with Maximilian in 1568), and the friend of Selim, **Don Joseph Nasi,** most prominent of the thousands of Spanish Jews who settled in Constantinople, Saloniki, Adrianople, and other towns of the empire after the expulsions from Spain and Italy. Nasi had come to Constantinople in 1553 and had financed Selim in the struggle with Bayazid. In return Selim had induced Suleiman to grant Nasi the region about Lake Tiberias, where Nasi undertook to settle Jewish refugees from Italy. In 1566 Selim made him duke of Naxos and other Aegean islands. Nasi was very hostile to France and Venice, for personal reasons.

1570. Nasi persuaded the sultan to declare **war on Venice,** after the latter had refused to cede Cyprus, which Nasi may have intended to make a refuge for Jews. Spain joined Venice in the war, but the two allies were unable to co-operate successfully and their fleets delayed the relief of Cyprus until too late.

1571, May 20. **Pope Pius V** finally succeeded in organizing a **Holy League** against the Turks. A great armada, under **Don John of Austria,** assembled at Messina.

Aug. 3. The Turks took Famagusta, after a siege of eleven months and six assaults.

Oct. 7. **BATTLE OF LEPANTO,** between the allied fleets (208 galleys, including 6 immense galleasses) and the Turks (230 galleys) under supreme command of **Ali Pasha.** After a ferocious fight of three hours, 80 Turkish

Battle of Lepanto, *1571, painting by Georgio Vasari*

galleys were sunk and 130 captured; 40 escaped from the wing. Greatest naval battle since Actium. Tremendous joy throughout Europe. But the advantages of the victory were lost through continued dissension between the Spaniards and the Venetians, the former insisting on the reconquest of North Africa, the latter desiring to reconquer Cyprus. The Turks rebuilt their fleet with astounding rapidity, and Don John refused to attack it in the Adriatic in 1572.

1573. Don John took Tunis, which had been captured by the Turks in 1569.

Mar. The Venetians deserted the Span-

iards and made peace, abandoning Cyprus and paying an indemnity of 300,000 ducats.

1574. The Turks drove the Spaniards out of Tunis again. Despite the Lepanto disaster, the Turks continued to ravage the coasts of the western Mediterranean during the rest of the century.

1574–1595. MURAD III.

1581. Peace between Spain and the Turks (definitive 1585) based on the *status quo*.

1585. Beginning of the phenomenal **decline of the empire,** due to the degeneracy of the sultans, the abandonment of the government to vizirs (mostly favorites), the growth of corrup-

tion and harem influence, the emergence of governing cliques (Jews, Greeks, etc.) and the inevitable decline of the military organization, especially the Janissary corps, to which Turks were gradually admitted. As the empire had advanced to the frontier of strong European states, conquests became more difficult and military grants fewer. The soldiers had to be kept quiet with presents and favors. Before long the Janissaries became a veritable praetorian guard, making and unmaking sultans, most of whom were mere puppets in their hands. The period was marked by rising taxation in the empire and general decline in the treasury. On the other hand, the Dutch, English, and French began to develop an extensive trade in the Levant.

1590. Peace between the Turks and Persia, after a long and desultory war that had begun in 1577. The Turks acquired Georgia, Azerbaijan, and Shirwan, thus extending their frontiers to the Caucasus and Caspian.

1593–1606. War between Austria and the Turks, in which **Sigismund Bathory,** prince of Transylvania, took the side of the emperor.

1596. Turkish victory at Keresztes (near Erlau in northern Hungary). The campaigning, however, remained desultory, due to the preoccupation of the emperor with Transylvania, which he took successively from Bathory and from Michael the Brave of Moldavia. The Turks thereupon supported **Stephen Bocskay** and helped him drive out the Austrians (1605). But the Turks, in turn, were diverted by troubles with Persia.

1602–1618. War with the Persians **(Abbas the Great),** who had completely reorganized their forces (with the help of **Sir Anthony** and **Sir Robert Shirley;** mission of Sir Anthony to Europe to secure co-operation).

1603. Abbas retook Tabriz, and then Erivan, Shirwan, and Kars. After a great victory at Lake Urmia, Abbas took Baghdad, Mosul, and Diarbekr. Peace was made in 1612, but the war was renewed in 1616. By the **treaty of 1618** the Turks abandoned Azerbaijan and Georgia.

1606. Treaty of Zsitva-Török (first peace treaty signed by the Turks outside Constantinople) between the Turks and Austrians. The Austrians abandoned Transylvania to Bocskay, but were recognized by the Turks as equals and ceased paying tribute for their part of Hungary.

1623–1640. MURAD IV, a boy of fourteen, who found the empire wracked by revolts and at the mercy of insubordinate Janissaries. By savage ruthlessness Murad asserted his authority.

1625. Murad's efforts to retake Baghdad were foiled by new uprisings, which he again suppressed with great ferocity.

1630. Murad took Hamadan from the Persians.

1635. The Turks reconquered Erivan and Tabriz.

1638. Murad retook Baghdad. By the **treaty of Kasr-i Shīrīm** (1639) a permanent border was finally established, the Persians keeping Erivan, the Turks Baghdad.

1638. Murad abolished the tribute in Christian children, reorganized the system of military fiefs, reduced the Janissary corps, and began the organization of a new military system. This first effort at reform was ended with his death in 1640.

1645–1664. Long **WAR WITH VENICE,** occasioned by Turkish designs on Candia (Crete). The Venetians showed themselves far stronger than the Turks and sent their fleets into the Straits. The Janissaries thereupon revolted, deposed **Ibrahim I** (1640–1648) and put on the throne

1648–1687. MOHAMMED IV, a boy of ten. There followed another period of anarchy, brought to an end in 1656 by a great Venetian victory off the Dardanelles.

1656. Mohammed Kiuprili, made grand vizier. He was a simple Albanian pasha, noted for his energy and firmness.

(Cont. p. 499.)

B.   Science and Learning, 1450–1700

1. *Science*

1469. Publication of Pliny's *Historia naturalis,* the first scientific book to be printed.

1500. Hieronymus Brunschwig (1450–c. 1512) published *Das Buch der rechten kunst zu distillieren;* its bold woodcuts were the first illustrations to depict chemical apparatus and operations.

1527–1541. Philippus Paracelsus [Theophrastus von Hohenheim] (1493–1541) crusaded for the use of chemicals in the treatment of disease. He introduced the system of salt, sulphur, and mercury as the three prime "elements," from which all things are made.

1537. Niccolò Tartaglia (?1500–1557), in *Nova scientia,* discussed the motion of heavy bodies and the shape of the trajectory of projectiles.

1540. Posthumous publication of *De la pirotechnica,* a handbook of metallurgy containing information about smelting and ore reduction compiled by **Vannoccio Biringuccio** (1480–1539).

1542. Leonhart Fuchs (1501–1566) used the botanical work of his contemporaries, **Otto Brunsfels** (1488–1534), **Jerome Bock** (1498–1554), and **Conrad Gesner** (1516–1565) to prepare a great herbal, describing some four hundred plants, illustrated by realistic woodcuts.

1543. NICOLAUS COPERNICUS [Niklas Kopernik] (1473–1543) published *De revolutionibus orbium coelestium,* which asserted that the planets, including the earth, circle around a stationary sun. He believed this theory represented the true structure of the world.

1543. ANDREAS VESALIUS (1514–1564) produced *De fabrica corporis humani,* an illustrated, systematic study of the human body. This work is a union of Renaissance artistic endeavor and of a revived interest in the empirical study of **human anatomy.**

1545. Jerome Cardan (1501–1576) published the solution of the **cubic equation** in *Ars Magna.* This solution, the first major advance in mathematics in the European Renaissance, was due to **Niccolò Tartaglia** (?1500–1557), and was used without his permission.

Nicolaus Copernicus, 1473–1543

Johannes Kepler, 1571–1630

Galileo Galilei, 1564–1642

1545–1573. Ambroise Paré (1510–1590) encouraged a **pragmatic approach to surgery.** He promoted the dressing of gunshot wounds rather than the traditional practice of cauterizing them with boiling oil.

1546. Georgius Agricola [Georg Bauer] (1494–1555) applied observation rather than mere speculation to the study of rocks, publishing *De natura fossilium,* an early handbook of mineralogy, and *De re metallica* (1556), which dealt with mining and metallurgy.

1546. Girolamo Fracastoro (?1483–1553) developed the theory that **contagion** (infectious disease) is caused by a living agent transmitted from person to person.

1551. Erasmus Reinhold (1511–1553) issued the *Prutenic Tables (Tabulae Prudenticae),* astronomical tables based on numerical values provided by Copernicus. These were an im-

provement on the *Alfonsine Tables* then widely in use.

1551–1555. Pierre Belon (1517–1564) and **Guillaume Rondolet** (1507–1566) initiated the study of **comparative anatomy** with their studies of fishes.

1551–1587. Conrad Gesner (1516–1565) amassed in the first great Renaissance encyclopedia, *Historia animalium,* ancient and contemporary knowledge of the animal kingdom.

1554. Jean Fernel (1497–1558) codified the practical and theoretical medicine of the Renaissance, rejecting magic and astrology but emphasizing the functions of organs.

1572. TYCHO BRAHE (1546–1601) observed a bright new star, a *super nova,* and determined that it was beyond the moon, thereby destroying the prevailing Aristotelian notion that no change occurred in celestial regions. Through systematic observation, using instruments designed by himself, Tycho accumulated very accurate data on planetary and lunar positions and produced the **first modern star catalog.**

1572. Volcher Coiter (1543–1576) revived interest in **descriptive embryology.**

1582. Pope Gregory XIII (1502–1585) introduced, into the Catholic nations, the **Gregorian** or **New Style calendar.** This reformed calendar utilized astronomical data compiled during the 16th century.

1583. Andrea Cesalpino (1519–1603) compiled the first modern **classification of plants** based on a comparative study of forms.

1585. Simon Stevin (1548–1620) published *La disme,* introducing decimal fractions into arithmetic. A year later he published treatises on **statics and hydrostatics.** The work on statics gave a mathematical proof of the law of the lever, elegantly proved the law of the inclined plane, and showed that two unequal weights fell through the same distance in the same time.

1591. François Viète [Vieta] (1540–1603) in-

troduced **literal notation** in algebra, i.e., the systematic use of letters to represent both coefficients and unknown quantities in algebraic equations.

c. 1600. Dutch lens-grinders in Middleburg are thought to have constructed the **first refracting telescope** and the **compound microscope.**

1600. William Gilbert (1540–1603) provided in *De magnete* a methodical experimental study of the **electric and magnetic properties of bodies,** and established that the earth itself is a magnet.

1603. Johann Bayer (1572–1625) produced a **celestial atlas** which introduced the use of Greek letters to indicate the brightest stars in every constellation.

1603. Foundation of the **Accademia dei Lincei,** one of the earliest learned societies, at Rome.

1609. JOHANNES KEPLER (1571–1630) announced in *Astronomia nova* his first two **laws of planetary motion:** planets move in ellipses with the sun in one focus; the radius vector from the sun to a planet sweeps out equal areas in equal times. In *Harmonices mundi* (1619) he added his third law: the squares of the periods of revolution of all planets are proportional to the cubes of their mean distances from the sun.

1610. GALILEO GALILEI (1564–1642), in *Sidereus nuncius,* revealed the results of the first telescopic observations of celestial phenomena. He used these observations to destroy the Aristotelian-Ptolemaic cosmology and to argue for the plausibility of the Copernican system.

1614. John Napier (1550–1617) introduced **logarithms** as a computational tool.

1627. Kepler, on the basis of Tycho Brahe's observations and his own theories, compiled the *Rudolphine Tables (Tabulae Rudolfinae)* which made possible the calculation of future planetary positions and other astronomical events; they were standard for over a century.

René Descartes, 1596–1650

Blaise Pascal, 1623–1662

1628. WILLIAM HARVEY (1578–1657) in his classic *Exercitatio anatomica de motu cordis et sanguinis in animalibus* blended reason, comparative observation, and experimentation to demonstrate the **circulation of the blood.**

1632. Galileo fashioned in *Dialogo sopra i due massimi sistemi del mondo Tolemaico e Copernicano* a brilliant polemical masterpiece, which clearly showed the superiority of the Copernican system over the Ptolemaic system of the world. This work led to **Galileo's trial and recantation** before the Roman Inquisition of the Catholic Church.

1637. RENÉ DESCARTES (1596–1650) published *Discours de la méthode,* an introduction to his philosophy, which served as a preface to his works on dioptrics, meteorology, and geometry. In the same year he published *La géometrie,* setting forth an **analytic geometry,** i.e., representation of geometric figures by algebraic equations and algebraic equations by geometric figures. **Pierre de Fermat** (?1608–1665) simultaneously and independently developed an analytic geometry. Both Descartes and Fermat applied analytic geometry to the finding of tangents to curves; Fermat also devised a general method for finding maxima and minima.

1638. Galileo in *Discorsi e demonstrazione matematiche intorno à due nuove scienze* established the basic principles of a mathematical description of falling bodies and projectile motion.

1642–1671. Blaise Pascal (1623–1662) constructed the first **adding machine** that could perform the operation of carrying. Some thirty years later, **Gottfried Wilhelm Leibniz** (1646–1716) invented a more complex calculating machine which would multiply rapidly by repeated additions.

1644. Descartes in his *Principia philosophiae* provided mechanistic explanations in terms of matter and motion of a wide variety of physical, chemical, and biological phenomena, and presented his **vortex theory of planetary motion.**

1648. Jan Baptist van Helmont (1577–1644), in his posthumously published collected works, *Ortus medicinae,* assigned the name "gas" to the "wild spirits" which were produced in various chemical processes and argued that acid fermentation, not "innate heat," was the operative agent of digestion.

1654. Correspondence between Pascal and Fermat on mathematical treatment of games of chance resulted in the beginning of **probability theory.**

1655. John Wallis (1616–1703) published *Arithmetica infinitorum,* which studied infinite series, infinite products, solved problems of quadratures, and found tangents by use of infinitesimals.

1657. The foundation of the **Accademia del Cimento** of Florence, the first organized scientific academy and a center for the new experimental science which stemmed from the work of Galileo.

1659. Christiaan Huygens (1629–1695) revealed, in *Systema Saturnium,* that Saturn is surrounded by a thin, flat ring.

1660–1674. ROBERT BOYLE (1627–1691) described his first **pneumatic pump,** an improvement on that invented by **Otto von Guericke** (1602–1686), in *New Experiments Physicomechanical, Touching the Spring of the Air.* In

the second edition (1662) Boyle noted the relation between pressure and volume now called **Boyle's Law.** With this pump Boyle showed that animals die from a lack of air, not from the accumulation of noxious vapors. So began an era in respiration studies that included the elucidation of lung structure (1661) by **Marcello Malpighi** (1628–1694), the proof that fresh air is necessary for respiration (1667) by **Robert Hooke** (1635–1703), the observation that blood changes color when in contact with air (1667–1669) by **Richard Lower** (1631–1691), and the demonstration that the volume of air is reduced in respiration (1674) by **John Mayow** (1640–1679).

1661. Boyle published his *Sceptical Chymist,* which contained a vigorous criticism of the Aristotelian theory of elements and the Paracelsian theory of principles.

1662. Charles II of England chartered **The Royal Society of London,** an independent organization that became the major center of English scientific activity during the 17th and 18th centuries.

1662. Jeremiah Horrocks (1619–1641) predicted and was the first man to observe (1639) a **transit of Venus** across the disk of the sun. His work was posthumously published in *Venus in sole visa* (1662).

1664. Publication of Descartes' posthumous work *L'homme,* expounding a mechanistic interpretation of the animal body. **Giovanni Borelli** (1608–1679), in *De motu animalium* (1680), linked Galilean mechanics to Cartesian mechanistic biology.

1663. Pascal reported his principles and experiments on hydrostatics and pneumatics.

1664–1668. Isaac Barrow (1630–1677), the teacher of **Isaac Newton,** showed, in his mathematical lectures at Cambridge University, that the method of finding tangents and the method of finding areas were inverse processes.

1665. The Royal Society of London published the first issue of its *Philosophical Transactions* (March 1665), the first scientific journal in the English-speaking world.

1665. Robert Hooke published *Micrographia,* containing descriptions of his microscopic observations. He first used the word *cells* to describe the lacework of rigid walls seen in cork. The observations of Hooke and other classical microscopists—**Marcello Malpighi, Nehemiah Grew** (1641–1712), **Jan Swammerdam** (1637–1680), **Antony van Leeuwenhoek** (1632–1723)—revealed the complex minute structure of living matter and the existence of micro-organisms.

1666. Louis XIV of France founded the **Académie Royale des Sciences,** a government-controlled and financed organization dedicated to experimental science. The activity of the Académie was regularly recorded in the *Journal des Savants,* one of the earliest scientific periodicals. In 1667 the king founded the **Observatoire de Paris** and named the Italian astronomer **Giovanni Domenico Cassini** (1625–1712) as its first director (1669).

1669. Erasmus Bartholin (1625–1698) published his observations on double refraction in crystals of Iceland spar.

1669. ISAAC NEWTON (1642–1727) announced his **calculus,** in *De analysi per aequationes numero terminorum infinitas,* which circulated in manuscript but was first published

Gottfried Wilhelm von Leibniz

Antony van Leeuwenhoek, 1632–1723

in 1711. He further developed the calculus in *Methodus fluxionum et serierum infinitarum* (1671, published 1736), using as fundamental notions "fluxions" (time derivatives) and "fluents" (inverse of fluxions), fluents being interpreted as areas.

1669. Nicolaus Steno [Niels Stensen] (?1631–1687?) established the fundamental concept of the superposition of strata settling from water, and also observed the constancy of interfacial angles in quartz crystals, basic to mineralogy.

1669. Jan Swammerdam, by his study of insect metamorphosis, provided the apparent proof which entrenched for the next century the **doctrine of preformation.** Preformation held that the foetus exists before fertilization as a complete miniature in either the egg or the sperm.

1669. Johann Joachim Becher (1635–1682) as-

Isaac Newton, 1642–1727

serted that all bodies are composed of air, water, and three earths: *terra lapida, terra mercurialis,* and *terra pinguis.* In combustion the "fatty earth" (*terra pinguis*) burns away, and in calcination it is driven off by the action of fire. This was a forerunner of the phlogiston theory (1723).

1671–1684. Cassini discovered four new **satellites of Saturn** and observed a dark marking in Saturn's ring.

1671–1673. Jean Richer (1630–1696), on a scientific expedition to Cayenne (latitude 5°N), found the **intensity of gravity** was less near the equator than in higher latitudes.

1672. Newton presented to the Royal Society a **reflecting telescope** which he constructed on principles learned in his optical studies. Newton also published his "New Theory about Light and Colors" showing notably that white light is composed of the various spectral colors, each of which has a different index of refraction.

1673. Christiaan Huygens announced in *Horologium oscillatorium* the invention and theory of the **pendulum clock.** This work included theorems on centrifugal force in circular motion.

1674. John Mayow asserted in his *Tractatus quinque medico-physici* that the air contains "nitro-aërial particles," which he thought necessary to support combustion and respiration.

1675. Olaus Roemer (1644–1710), by studying the eclipses of Jupiter's moons, determined that light is transmitted with a finite, though very great, speed.

1675. Charles II of England established the **Royal Observatory, Greenwich** and designated **John Flamsteed** (1646–1719) as the first Astronomer Royal.

1676. Thomas Sydenham (1624–1689) rejected the view that the diseased state was an exception to natural law. He emphasized the importance of clinical observation, experience, and common sense in therapy.

1678. Robert Hooke provided an account of the law of elastic force, *ut tensio, sic vis* (stress is proportional to strain), which is now known by his name.

1679. Edmé Mariotte (?1620–1684) announced his discovery of the constant **relation between the pressure and volume** of an enclosed quantity of air (discovered independently of Robert Boyle).

1681. Thomas Burnet (1635–1715) published *Telluris theoria sacra,* the most popular of several religiously orthodox cosmogonical treatises of the late 17th century, focusing on Noah's flood as the central fact of earth history.

1684. LEIBNIZ first published his **differential calculus,** based on work done independently of Newton during the period 1673–1676. Leibniz based his calculus on the finding of differentials, which he understood as infinitesimal differences, and defined the integral as an infinite sum of infinitesimals; the operations of summing and of finding the differences were mutually inverse. His vision of a universal symbolic language led him to devise notation of great heuristic power, such as d for differential and $\int$ for integral.

1686–1704. John Ray (1627–1705) in the three volumes of *Historia generalis plantarum* provided an able account of the structure, physiology, and distribution of plants and laid the foundations of modern **systematic classification.**

1687. NEWTON in his *Philosophiae naturalis principia mathematica* founded mechanics, both celestial and terrestrial, on his three axioms or **laws of motion.** He demonstrated that the sun attracts the planets and the earth attracts the moon with a force inversely proportional to the square of the distance between them. In his **principle of universal gravitation** he states that any two bodies attract each other with a force proportional to the product of their masses and inversely proportional to the square of the distance between them.

1688. Francesco Redi (1621–1697) challenged the ancient belief in spontaneous generation and began a two-century-long debate on the subject by his controlled experimentation on the production of maggots.

1690. Christiaan Huygens developed in his *Traité de la lumière* a mechanistic theory which presents light as a propagation of impulses in a subtle aether. He used this theory to explain reflection, refraction, and double refraction.

1696. Guillaume de L'Hôpital (1661–1704) published the first textbook of the **infinitesimal calculus,** *Analyse des infiniment petits,* based on the lectures of his teacher, **Johann Bernoulli** (1667–1748).

1697. Bernoulli showed that the curve of quickest descent was the cycloid, thereby solving the first problem of the **calculus of variations.**

(Cont. p. 502.)

2. *Mechanical Inventions and Technological Achievements*

c. 1450. Printing with moveable type introduced into Europe by **JOHANNES GUTENBURG** (?1400–1468). **Laurens Coster** (fl. 1440), cheapened and widened the diffusion of knowledge. This development accompanied an increased use of wood-block illustrations.

1485. Publication of **Leon Battista Alberti's** (1404–1472) *De re aedificora* exemplifies the extended interests of Renaissance architects and artists in the realm of applied science. A more famous example is **Leonardo da Vinci** (1452–1519), who was a military engineer and speculated on various types of machines. Structural theory did not advance until the work of **Galileo Galilei** (*Dialogues concerning Two New Sciences,* 1638), **Christopher Wren,** and **Robert Hooke.** The revival of interest in classical architecture, sparked by the rediscovery of the works of Vitruvius, led architects to develop new techniques, flat ceiling, and the dome. Some architects of the period were **Filippo Brunelleschi** (?1377–1446), **François Mansard** (1598–1666), **Claude Perrault** (1613–1688), **François Blondel** (1617–1686), **Inigo Jones** (1573–1652), and **Christopher Wren** (1632–1723).

1500. The expansion of trade brought a **development in ship construction.** Galleys were in use until the 17th century but the fully rigged ship with stern-post rudder developed during the 15th century, and by 1700 the four-masted galleon had evolved.

c. 1510. First of the handbooks on metallurgy appeared, *Probierbergbüchlein* on assaying, *Bergbüchlein* on mining. In 1540 **Vannocio Biringuccio's** (1480–1539) *Pyrotechnica* published, the first practical, comprehensive metallurgy text by a professional metallurgist. Included were descriptions of alloying and cannon-molding processes. In 1556 *De re metallica* of Agricola (Georg Bauer), a physician in the mining area of Saxony, ap-

Façade of St. Paul's Cathedral, London, by Christopher Wren, 1632–1723

peared. It covered all aspects of mining from the survey of the site through the equipment and methods of mining to assaying, blast and glass furnace descriptions as well as the treatment of iron, copper, and glass. Agricola was concerned with miners' health, and described the diseases to which they are prone.

1520. **Wheel lock** invented, probably in Italy, one of the steps to a single-handed pistol. **Rifling** of the gun barrel was a known technique, 1525, and by 1697 **iron cannon** were cast directly from the blast furnace.

1533. The principle of **triangulation** in surveying discovered by **Gemma Frisius,** a German.

More technical maps began to appear to replace the earlier Portalan maps (first **road map of Europe** appeared in Germany, 1511). **Maritime charts** were improved; in 1536 **Pedro Nuñez** (1492–1577) wrote on the errors in the plain charts used at sea. In 1569 **Gerhard Mercator** [Kremer] (1512–1594) devised the mercator chart; in 1600 the first seaman's calendar appeared. The **telescope,** invented c. 1590, and the back-staff (1595) of **John Davis** (?1550–1605), superseded the older navigational instruments, the astrolabe and crossstaff.

c. 1589. **William Lee** (d. 1610) invented the

first frame **knitting machine,** slowly accepted during the 17th century.

1560–1660. Increased **use of coal,** especially in England, as a power source. The output of coal in Newcastle rose from 32,951 tons in 1563–1564 to 529,032 tons in 1658–1659. The use of coal was dictated by serious deforestation both in England and on the Continent. By 1615 wood-fired glass furnaces were illegal in England; thus technology was stimulated by the necessity of using coal.

1575–1680. The evolution of the **glass-maker's "chair."** Many new techniques were introduced into glass-making, including those of producing ruby glass (before 1620), lead and white glass (1679).

1603. Cannon were bored in Spain. By 1650 lead shot was molded by means of a split mold.

1698. Thomas Savery's (?1610–1715) steam engine. The steam mill of **Giovanni Branca,** 1629, was ill conceived, and the engine of **Denis Papin,** 1688, was not developed and had no effect on the Industrial Revolution.

1700. By this date many **foods and crops** were exchanged between Europe, Asia, and the Americas. From the New World came the **potato** (in Spain c. 1570), maize, tea, chocolate, **tobacco. Coffee** grew wild in Ethiopia (known c. 1450) and was introduced into Europe (in England by 1650). By this date **sugar** was a common, cheap commodity in England; cane was shipped to America to form the basis of the industry in the Caribbean in the 18th century. **Cotton** was exported to America where it became an important crop.

(Cont. p. 506.)

C. Europe and the Near East, 1648–1812

1. *England, Scotland, and Ireland, 1648–1812*

[*For a complete list of the kings of England see Appendix VI.*]

(From p. 400)

1649–1660. The **COMMONWEALTH,** a republican form of government. Power in the army and its leader **Oliver Cromwell.** Theoretically legislative power still in the Rump (some 50 Independent members of the Long Parliament), executive power in a council of state of 41 (three judges, three officers of the army, five peers, 30 members of the commons). Title and office of king abolished, as was the house of lords.

1649, Feb. 5. The Scots proclaimed **Charles II** in Edinburgh and the Irish rose in his favor under Ormonde. Cromwell went to Ireland himself and quickly suppressed the rebellion at the **storming of Drogheda** (Sept. 12) and **Wexford.** Massacres of both garrisons. Cromwell returned to London (May) leaving Ireton to complete his work. By 1652 the Cromwellian settlement had been achieved. Catholic landholders were dispossessed in favor of Protestants; many Catholics killed. The Irish question took on a new bitterness.

1650. Montrose came again to Scotland, was beaten at **Corbiesdale** (April 27), captured and executed at Edinburgh (May 21).

June 24. Charles II landed in Scotland, took the covenant, and was proclaimed king. At the **battle of Dunbar** (Sept. 3) the Scots under Leslie were totally defeated by Cromwell. Charles II, however, was crowned at Scone and marched on into England while Cromwell took Perth (Aug. 2, 1651). Cromwell then turned and pursued the king, completely defeated the royal army at the **battle of Worcester** (Sept. 3). Charles in disguise escaped to France, after romantic adventures.

1651, Oct. 9. First Navigation Act passed for-

The House of Commons as shown on the reverse of the Great Seal of England, 1651

bidding the importation of goods into England except in English vessels or in vessels of the country producing the goods. This typical measure of mercantile economy helped the British merchant marine to gain supremacy over the Dutch.

1652, July 8. War with the Dutch broke out because of this act. It was almost wholly naval. English commanders, Blake, Monk; Dutch, Tromp, Ruyter. The English won off the **Downs** (May, before the declaration of war); defeated Tromp off **Portland** (Feb. 18, 1653) and off the **North Foreland** (June 2–3). Monk won an important victory of the **Texel** (July 31) where Tromp died. **Peace with the Dutch** (April 5, 1654).

Trouble had long been brewing between the Rump and the army. Negotiations for the return of confiscated royalist estates led to charges of bribery of members. After an **Act of Indemnity and Oblivion** (Feb. 1652) and an **Act of Settlement for Ireland** (Aug.) had been passed,

1653, Apr. 20. Cromwell turned out the Rump and dissolved the council of state. He set up a new council and a nominated parliament of 140 members, called **Barebones'** or the **Little Parliament** (July 4). The Cromwellians in parliament resigned their powers to Cromwell (Dec. 12), who set up the **Protectorate** (Dec. 16).

1653, Dec. 16–1658, Sept. 3. CROMWELL, LORD PROTECTOR OF THE COMMONWEALTH OF ENGLAND, SCOTLAND, AND IRELAND. The *Instrument of Government*, a written constitution. The executive (lord protector) had a co-operative council of 21; there was a standing army of 30,000; parliament was to be triennial, and composed of 460 members; once summoned, it could not be dissolved within five months. The protector and council could issue ordinances between sessions, but parliament alone could grant supplies and levy taxes.

1654, Sept. 3. The **new parliament** quarreled with the protector, who ordered an exclusion of members (Sept. 12). After voting that the office of protector should be elective instead of hereditary, the parliament was dissolved (Jan. 22, 1655).

1655, Mar.–May. The **rising of Penruddock** at Salisbury was suppressed and Penruddock executed. England was divided into 12 military districts, each with a force supported by a tax of 10 per cent on royalist estates. Anglican clergy were forbidden to teach or preach. Catholic priests ordered out of the kingdom. Censorship of the press. Rigid "puritanical" rule in arts and morals.

Oct. Pacification of Pinerolo, with France: the duke of Savoy stopped the persecution of the Vaudois and Charles II was to be expelled from France.

1656–1659. War with Spain. An English raid under Penn and Venables which had captured Jamaica in the West Indies (May) brought on the war. Capture of Spanish treasure ships off **Cadiz** (Sept. 9, 1656). Victory of Blake off **Santa Cruz** (April 20, 1657).

1656, Sept. 17–1658, Feb. 4. Cromwell's third parliament witnessed another exclusion of members, and the **Humble Petition and Advice** (March–May, 1657) altering the constitution. Establishment of a second house; reduction of the power of the council of the state; the pro-

Oliver Cromwell, 1599–1658

tector deprived of the power of excluding members; fixed supply for army and navy; toleration for all trinitarian Christians except Episcopalians and Catholics. Cromwell rejected the title of king (May 8).

1658. Dunkirk besieged by the English and French. A Spanish relieving force was beaten in the **battle of Dunes** (June 4). Dunkirk surrendered to the English, who retained it at the **peace of the Pyrenees** *(p. 465)*.

1658, Sept. 3. Death of Oliver Cromwell.

1658, Sept. 3–1659, May 25. Richard Cromwell, Oliver's son, lord protector. A new parliament met (Jan. 27, 1659) and was soon involved in a dispute with the army, which induced Richard to dissolve parliament (Apr. 22). The Rump Parliament came together under Lenthall as speaker (May 7) and Richard was induced to resign as lord protector. After the futile insurrection of Booth (Aug.) the army, under Lambert, expelled the Rump and appointed a military committee of safety (Oct.). There was a reaction against military *coups d'état*, and the Rump was restored (Dec. 26).

1660, Feb. 3. General George Monk led his army from Scotland to London, assumed control as captain-general, and re-established the Long Parliament with the still living members excluded by Pride's Purge restored (Feb. 21). Final dissolution (Mar. 16).

1660, Apr. 14. Charles issued his **declaration of Breda,** proclaiming amnesty to all not especially excepted by parliament, promising liberty of conscience and the confirmation of confiscated estates in the hands of the actual holders. A **Convention Parliament,** 556 mem-

bers chosen without restrictions (Apr.), returned a favorable answer to Charles (May 1) and proclaimed him king (May 8); on May 29 he entered London.

1660–1685. CHARLES II. The king's brother, James, duke of York, appointed lord high admiral and warden of the Cinque Ports; Monk (later duke of Albemarle), captain-general; Sir Edward Hyde (later earl of Clarendon), chancellor and prime minister. Abolition of the rights of knight service, worship, and purveyance in consideration of a yearly income for the king of £1,200,000. Restoration of the bishops to their sees and to the house of lords. Acts of indemnity for all political offenses committed between January 1, 1637, and June 24, 1660 (the regicide judges were excepted from this act). All acts of the Long Parliament to which Charles I had assented were declared in force. This meant that the Restoration was by no means a restoration of "divine right" monarchy, but rather a restoration of the moderate parliamentarian régime aimed at by Pym and Hampden. The army was disbanded (Oct. 2) except some 5000 men. The Cromwellian settlement of Ireland was reaffirmed.

1660, Dec. 29. Dissolution of the Convention Parliament. Rising of Fifth Monarchy men in London put down (Jan. 1661). Bodies of Cromwell, Ireton, Bradshaw disinterred and scattered. Royalist parliament in Scotland **abolished the covenant** and repealed all preceding parliamentary enactments for the last twenty-eight years.

1661, May 8–1679, Jan. 24. First parliament of Charles II. The **Cavalier Parliament,** over-

Charles II, 1630–1685

whelmingly royalist. Social reaction against puritanism; revival of games, dancing, the theater. Parliament enacted a series of repressive measures since known as the **Clarendon Code** (Clarendon himself was opposed to many of these measures). They were: (1) The **Corporation Act** (Nov. 20, 1661), by which all magistrates were obliged to take the sacrament according to the Church of England, to abjure the covenant, and to take an oath declaring it illegal to bear arms against the king.   (2) The **Act of Uniformity** (Aug. 24, 1662), which required clergymen, college fellows, and schoolmasters to accept everything in the Book of Common Prayer (those who refused were the *Nonconformists*).   (3) The **Conventicle Act** (May 1664), which forbade nonconformist (dissenting) religious meetings of more than five persons, except in a private household.   (4) The **Five-Mile Act** (Oct. 1665), which required all who had not subscribed to the Act of Uniformity to take an oath of nonresistance, swearing never to attempt any change in church or state; and which prohibited all who refused to do this from coming within five miles of any incorporated town, or of any place where they had been ministers. The code, and especially this last act, was impossible of strict enforcement.

1662, May 20. Charles married Catherine of Braganza, daughter of John IV of Portugal. Dunkirk was sold to France for £400,000.

1665–1667. War with Holland, marked by the defeat of the Dutch by the English fleet off **Lowestoft** (June 3, 1665). France entered the war against England (Jan. 1666). Albemarle beaten by de Ruyter and De Witt off the North Foreland. Defeat of the Dutch in another naval fight (July 25). The Dutch rallied, burnt Sheerness, entered the Medway (June 1667); low point of English naval power.

1665–1666. Two great domestic disasters: the **great plague** in London (April 1665); the **great London fire** (Sept. 2–9, 1666), burning 450 acres. St. Paul's Cathedral rebuilt by Wren.

1666. The **Scottish Covenanters revolted** against restrictions laid on them by the triumphant Episcopalians, and were crushed by Dalziel in the **battle of Pentland Hills** (Nov. 28).

1667, July 21. Treaties of Breda between England, Holland, France, Denmark. England received from France Antigua, Montserrat, St. Kitts; France received Acadia; England and Holland adopted the *status quo* of May 21, 1667, England retaining New Amsterdam and Holland, Surinam. The navigation acts were modified to permit the bringing to England in Dutch vessels of goods brought down the Rhine.

1667. Clarendon, who had had to bear the burden of unpopularity for much of the work of the Cavalier Parliament, was forced to resign, and was impeached and exiled. The chief officers of state now began to be looked on as a distinct (if perhaps unconstitutional) council, the nucleus of the future cabinet system. This was emphasized by the accession to power of the so-called **Cabal** (Clifford, Arlington, Buckingham, Ashley, Lauderdale). There was no cabinet solidarity, and no clear party system. The court and the country factions did, however, foreshadow the later **Tories and Whigs.** The court (Tory) party were supporters of the royal prerogative, and in a sense heirs of the Cavaliers; the country (Whig) party, supporters of the power of parliament and heirs of the majority group in the Long Parliament, but *not* democrats or radicals. Both *Whig* and *Tory* were originally terms of reproach, the first Scottish, the second Irish in origin.

1668, Jan. 23. The **Triple Alliance** between England, Holland, and Sweden negotiated by Sir William Temple and John De Witt as a

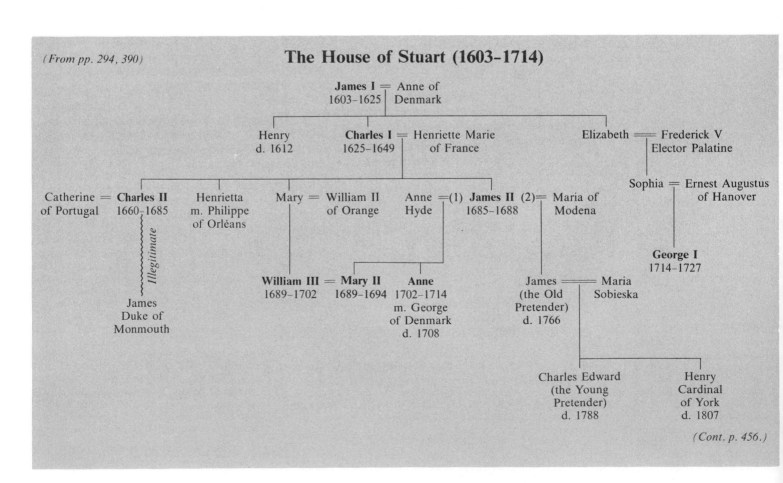

(From pp. 294, 390)

The House of Stuart (1603–1714)

James I = Anne of
1603–1625 | Denmark

Henry
d. 1612

Charles I = Henriette Marie
1625–1649 | of France

Elizabeth === Frederick V
Elector Palatine

Catherine = **Charles II**
of Portugal | 1660–1685

Henrietta
m. Philippe
of Orléans

Mary = William II
of Orange

Anne =(1) **James II** (2)= Maria of
Hyde | 1685–1688 | Modena

Sophia = Ernest Augustus
of Hanover

Illegitimate

James
Duke of
Monmouth

William III = **Mary II**
1689–1702 | 1689–1694

Anne
1702–1714
m. George
of Denmark
d. 1708

James === Maria
(the Old | Sobieska
Pretender)
d. 1766

George I
1714–1727

Charles Edward
(the Young
Pretender)
d. 1788

Henry
Cardinal
of York
d. 1807

(Cont. p. 456.)

check on Louis XIV. Charles II went behind parliament and signed with Louis the **treaty of Dover** (May, 1670) in secret provisions of which he agreed that he and his brother James would openly join the Church of Rome as soon as expedient, and that he would support Louis in his wars with Spain and Holland. Louis promised Charles £200,000 a year while the war lasted and the assistance of 6000 men in case of an insurrection. James, duke of York, at once professed his belief in Roman Catholicism.

1672, Mar. Charles issued a **Declaration of Indulgence,** which aimed to free both nonconformist Protestants and Catholics from restrictions. Parliament, insisting that the royal power of dispensing from statutory obligations could be applied only to particular, never to generalized, cases, forced him to withdraw the indulgence (1673).

1672, Mar. 17–1674, Feb. 9. WAR WITH HOLLAND, pursuant to the policy of the treaty of Dover. English naval victory at **Southwold Bay** (May 28, 1672). **William of Orange,** Dutch stadholder. Marriage of the duke of York with the Catholic Maria d'Este of Modena (Nov. 21, 1673). The war was concluded by the **treaty of Westminster** (Feb. 9, 1674).

1673. The **Test Act,** an attempt to salvage something from the Clarendon Code, and to attack the duke of York and his supporters. All persons holding office were compelled to take oaths of allegiance and of supremacy, to adjure transubstantiation, and to take the sacrament of the Church of England. This act was not repealed until 1828, but it was nullified after 1689 by the typically English practice of passing bills of indemnity to legalize the acts of magistrates who had not conformed—i.e. taken communion in the Established Church—while in office. Such officials were commonly dissenters rather than Roman Catholics.

1673. Shift in the ministry; the duke of York, Shaftesbury, Clifford resigned, being superseded by Prince Rupert, Sir Thomas Osborne (later earl of Danby), Sir Heneage Finch (later earl of Nottingham). Buckingham out of office.

1677, Nov. 4. Marriage of Mary, daughter of the duke of York, with **William of Orange** (later William III).

1678, Sept. The Popish plot. Titus Oates began the scare by alleging that Don John of Austria and Père La Chaise had plotted to murder Charles and establish Roman Catholicism in England. In the ensuing wave of frenzy against the "papists," five Catholic lords (Powys, Bellassis, Stafford, Petre, Arundel) were sent to the Tower. Coleman, confessor of the duchess of York, convicted and executed. Passage of the **Papists' Disabling Act,** excluding Roman Catholics from parliament (repealed 1829).

1679, Jan. 24. Dissolution of the Cavalier parliament. Danby, who had been impeached (Dec. 1678) on a charge of criminal correspondence with France, was dismissed from the office of lord high treasurer. The duke of York left the kingdom.

1679, Mar. 6–1680, May 27. Third parliament of Charles II. Danby's impeachment resumed, but not carried; he remained in the Tower until 1685. A new cabinet council

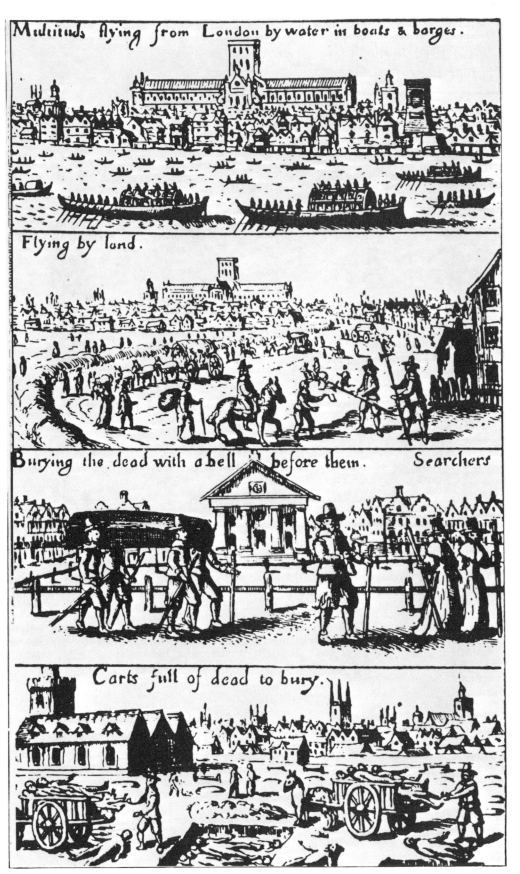

The Great Plague of London, 1665 (contemporary English broadside)

composed of Sir William Temple, Viscount Halifax, the earl of Essex, the earl of Sunderland, and Shaftesbury (afterward in opposition). Introduction of a bill to prevent the duke of York, as a Catholic, succeeding to the throne. Charles fought various exclusion bills, which were backed by Shaftesbury, until he had secured his brother's succession.

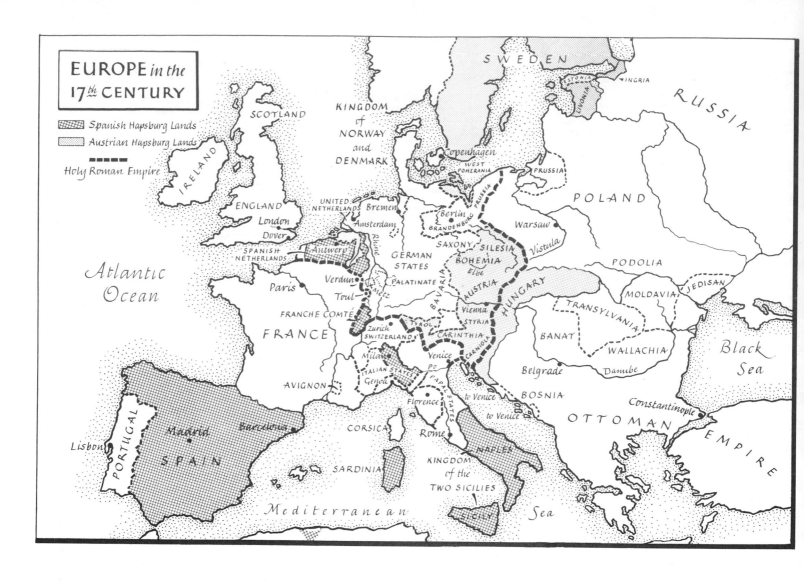

EUROPE in the 17th CENTURY

- Spanish Hapsburg Lands
- Austrian Hapsburg Lands
- ----- Holy Roman Empire

1679, May. The Habeas Corpus Act. Judges were obliged on application to issue to any prisoner a writ of *habeas corpus,* directing the jailer to produce the body of the prisoner, and show cause for his imprisonment; prisoners should be indicted in the first term of their commitment, and tried not later than the second; no person once set free by order of the court could be again imprisoned for the same offense.

1679. The **Covenanters** again rose in Scotland against the repressive measures of Lauderdale. Murder of Archbishop Sharpe (May 3). Defeat of Claverhouse by the Covenanters under Balfour at **Drumclog** (June 1). Defeat of the Covenanters by the duke of Monmouth at **Bothwell Brigg** (June 22). Covenanters, Conventiclers, Cameronians—all shades of Presbyterians repressed, but not successfully. Passage of a **Test Act** against the Presbyterians (1681) caused some eighty Episcopalian bishops to resign. Trial and condemnation of Argyle (Dec. 1681), who fled the kingdom.

1679, Oct. 7. Charles, without advice of the cabinet, prorogued his third parliament before it had done any business. Temple, Essex, and Halifax resigned, and were succeeded by the earl of Godolphin and Laurence Hyde, earl of Rochester. Another alleged papist conspiracy **(meal-tub plot)** disclosed by Dangerfield. Petition that parliament be called; whence **petitioners** (country party, Whigs) and those who expressed their abhorrence at this interference with the prerogative, **abhorrers** (court party, Tories).

1680, Oct. 21-1681, Jan. 18. Fourth parliament of Charles II. The exclusion bill passed the commons, but lost in the lords (Halifax).

1681, Mar. 21-28. Fifth parliament called at Oxford, and immediately dissolved when the exclusion bill was introduced.

1683, June. Judgment given against the city of London on a *quo warranto;* forfeiture of the charter, which was ransomed. The process repeated for other corporations. Confederacy of leaders of the country party against the policy of Charles, which seemed to them a repetition of earlier Stuart attempts to extend the power of the crown (Essex, Russell, Grey, Howard, Sidney, Hampden, Monmouth). This was supplemented by, and at the same time confused with, the **Rye House plot,** a plan concerted by quite different persons to assassinate the king. Both plots were revealed. Essex committed suicide; Russell and Sidney were executed, becoming republican martyrs for later generations; Monmouth (natural son of Charles and Lucy Walters) was pardoned, and retired to Holland. The duke of York was reinstated in office (Sept.) and Oates, now known to be a liar, was fined.

1685, Feb. 6. Charles died knowing that his brother would succeed and that the Whigs were at the moment worsted.

1685-1688. JAMES II, a Roman Catholic, whose tactless attempt to secure freedom of worship for his co-religionists united against him Whigs and Tories in defense of the Anglican Church (*not,* as far as the Tories were concerned, in defense of parliamentary supremacy).

1685, May 19-1687, July 2. Parliament of James II. Halifax, president of the council; Sunderland, secretary of state; Godolphin, chamberlain; Clarendon, lord privy seal; Rochester, treasurer. Trial and condemnation of Baxter, a dissenting clergyman. Danby and the five Catholic lords were liberated. Oates and Dangerfield were tried, condemned, and sentenced to whipping, from which Dangerfield died (May 1685).

1685. Rebellion of Monmouth and Argyll. Argyll landed in Scotland, but could not arouse the Covenanters. He was captured and executed (June 30). Monmouth landed in Dorsetshire and proclaimed himself king, but his motley followers were easily beaten at the **battle of Sedgemoor** (July 6)—the last formal warfare in England until German naval attacks and Zeppelin raids in 1914-1918. **Monmouth was executed,** and **Jeffreys** sent on a circuit in the west to try the rebels (*the Bloody Assizes*). Jeffreys became lord chancellor;

Halifax was dismissed; Sunderland, converted to Catholicism, took his place.

1686. James set out to test the **anti-papal laws.** By dispensation, he appointed a Catholic, Sir Edward Hales, to office. In a test suit, decision was rendered in favor of the king by judges he had appointed. Compton, bishop of London, refused to remove the rector of St. Giles', who had disobeyed a royal order against violent doctrinal sermons. He was tried before a new court of ecclesiastical commission (July) and suspended. The fellows of Magdalen College, Oxford, having refused to accept Farmer, a Catholic, whom James had appointed their president, were expelled from the college (1687). These and other specific cases were rapidly rousing opinion against the king.

1687. James generalized his action; he issued the first **Declaration of Liberty of Conscience,** granted liberty to all denominations in England and Scotland (Apr.).

1688, Apr. A **second Declaration of Liberty of Conscience** was ordered to be read in all churches. Sancroft, archbishop of Canterbury, and six other bishops were committed to the Tower for having petitioned the king not to insist on their reading what they held to be an illegal order.

June 10. **Birth of a son to James,** said by

James II, 1685–1688

Whigs at the time to have been introduced in a warming-pan. The knowledge that James's policies might be continued by a son to be brought up as Catholic turned against him many Tories hitherto loyal.

June 29, 30. **Trial of the bishops for seditious libel.** The bishops were acquitted. Great popular enthusiasm. An invitation was dispatched to William of Orange to save England from Catholic tyranny: it was signed by the *seven eminent persons* (Devonshire, Shrewsbury, Danby, Compton, Henry Sidney, Lord Lumley, Admiral Russell).

Sept. 30. **Declaration of William** accepting the invitation. William's real purpose in accepting was to bring England into the struggle against Louis XIV, begun by the **League of Augsburg.** His success reversed the policy of Charles II and James II, which had been broadly pro-French, and re-established English foreign policy along lines which were later considered "traditional"—opposition to any overwhelmingly powerful continental state, especially if that power threatened the Low Countries.

James, frightened by the declaration, dismissed Sunderland and tried to retrace his steps. William left Helvoetsluys with 14,000 men (Oct. 19), but was driven back by a gale.

Nov. 5. **William succeeded in landing** at Torbay. Risings in various sections of England. **Grafton** and **Churchill** (later **duke of Marlborough**) went over to William (Nov. 22). James issued writs for a new parliament and endeavored to treat with William. The queen and the baby prince were sent to France (Dec. 10) and James, throwing the great seal into the Thames, fled on Dec. 11. **Interregnum,** rioting in London, seizure of Jeffreys.

Dec. 12. The peers set up a **provisional government** in London. James, stopped at Sheerness, was brought back to London, but succeeded in escaping to France (Dec. 22), after William had entered London (Dec. 19). Louis XIV set up the exiled Stuarts at the Court of St. Germain.

1689, Jan. 22–1690, Jan. 27. Convention Parliament, summoned by advice of the peers. On Jan. 28 the commons declared: "That King James II, having endeavored to subvert the constitution of the kingdom by breaking the original contract between king and people, and by the advice of Jesuits and other

Battle of Sedgemoor, July 6, 1685

The seven bishops are brought to the Tower, April 1688

wicked persons having violated the fundamental laws, and having withdrawn himself out of the kingdom, has abdicated the government, and that the throne is vacant." Also: "That it hath been found by experience to be inconsistent with the safety and welfare of this Protestant kingdom to be governed by a popish prince." The lords objected to the use of the word "abdicated," and to the declaration of the "vacancy" of the throne, but an agreement being reached in a conference of the two houses, the crown was offered to Mary and the regency to William; this being refused, parliament offered the crown to William and Mary jointly.

1689, Feb. 13. The offer was accompanied by the **Declaration of Rights,** asserting the "true, ancient, and indubitable rights of the people of this realm": (1) that the making or suspending law without consent of parliament is illegal; (2) that the exercise of the dispensing power is illegal; (3) that the ecclesiastical commission court and other such like courts are illegal; (4) that levying money without consent of parliament is illegal; (5) that it is lawful to petition the sovereign; (6) that the maintenance of a standing army without the consent of parliament is illegal; (7) that it is lawful to keep arms; (8) that elections of members of parliament must be free; (9) that there must be freedom of debate in parliament; (10) that excessive bail should never be demanded; (11) that juries should be empaneled and returned in every trial; (12) that grants of estates as forfeited before conviction of the offender are illegal; (13) that parliament should be held frequently. William and Mary were declared king and queen of England for life, the chief administration resting with William; the crown was next settled on William's children by Mary; in default of such issue, on the Princess Anne of Denmark and her children; and in default of these, on the children of William by any other wife. The crown was accepted by William and Mary, who were on the same day proclaimed king and queen of Great Britain, Ireland, and France.

1689–1702. WILLIAM III AND MARY II (until 1694). Privy councillors: earl of Danby (marquis of Carmarthen), president; Nottingham, Shrewsbury, secretaries of state; marquis of Halifax, privy seal; Schomberg (duke of Schomberg), master-general of ordnance; Bentinck (earl of Portland), privy purse.

1689, Feb. 22. The **Convention Parliament** was transformed by its own act into a regular parliament. **Oaths of allegiance and supremacy** were taken by the houses, the clergy, etc. Six bishops and about 400 clergymen refused them, and were deprived of their benefices (1691). These **non-jurors** ordained their own bishops, and maintained their own private Church of England until the 19th century.

Mar. 14. James landed in Ireland with a few followers, was joined by **Tyrconnel,** and entered Dublin (Mar. 24) amid popular enthusiasm. Irish parliament (May 7). James besieged the Protestant town of Londonderry (April 20–July 30), which was finally relieved by Kirke.

The first **Mutiny Act,** to punish defection in the army, made necessary by the **Declaration of Rights** (Mar.), passed henceforth annually. The Protestant dissenters who had disdained

William III and Mary, 1689–1702

James's gift of freedom were rewarded by the **Toleration Act** (May 24) which exempted dissenters who had taken the oaths of allegiance and supremacy from penalties for non-attendance at the services of the Church of England.

1689, May 7. WAR BROKE OUT WITH FRANCE. In Scotland Claverhouse (Viscount Dundee) raised his standard for James among the Highlanders, after episcopacy had been abolished by law. At the **battle of Killiecrankie** (July 17) he defeated the Whig general, Mackay, but fell on the field. The revolt gradually petered out.

1689–1690. A series of measures made the constitutional adjustments necessitated by the **Glorious Revolution.** The system of requiring estimate and accounts for supplies, and of specific appropriations—i.e. the nucleus of modern budgetary systems—now became fixed. The **Bill of Rights** (Dec. 16, 1689) was a parliamentary enactment of the **Declaration of Rights,** repeating the provisions of that paper, settling the succession, and enacting that no Roman Catholic could wear the crown. William's **second parliament** (Mar. 20, 1690–May 3, 1695) by an act of recognition further legalized the already legal acts of the Convention Parliament, settled William's civil list (at a smaller figure than James's or Charles's) and by the **Act of Grace** (May 20, 1690) gave indemnity to all supporters of James II except those in treasonable correspondence with him. Shrewsbury and Halifax resigned.

1690. William went to Ireland, and defeated James at the crucial **battle of the Boyne** (July 1). James fled to France. Dublin and Waterford fell quickly. Limerick resisted successfully under Sarsfield (Aug). In the open field Ginkel defeated Sarsfield and the French St. Ruth at the **battle of Aughrim** (July 12, 1691). Limerick, besieged a second time, surrendered (Oct. 3) under the conditions known as the **pacification of Limerick:** free transportation to France of all Irish officers and soldiers so desiring. (The Irish Brigade in the French armies had a long and distinguished history.) All Irish Catholics to have the religious liberty they had had under Charles II, carry arms, exercise their professions, and receive full amnesty. The English parliament confirmed the treaty, but the Irish parliament, consisting wholly of Protestants, refused to ratify it (1695) and enacted severe anti-Catholic legislation contrary to the pacification terms.

1690, June 30. Defeat of the English fleet by the French at the **battle of Beachy Head.** Lord Torrington, the English admiral, was tried by court martial and acquitted, but dismissed from the service. This defeat was redeemed by the **English naval victory** under Russell over the French under Tourville at **Cap de La Hogue** (May 19, 1692).

1692, Feb. 13. Massacre of Glencoe. The Highlanders, incompletely pacified after Dundee's rising, had been given until December 31, 1691 to take oath to William. This had been done by all the chieftains save MacIan of the MacDonalds of Glencoe. He took the oath on January 6, 1692, but this fact was suppressed by William's agent, the Master of Stair. A company of soldiers commanded by a Campbell (hereditary foes of the MacDonalds), quartered peacefully at Glencoe, turned suddenly on the Highlanders, killed MacIan and some forty others. The incident was of great political use to William's enemies.

William's land campaigns were unsuccessful; he was defeated by the French at **Steinkirk** (July 24, 1692) and at **Neerwinden** (July 29, 1693) (p. 480). At home he was obliged to turn for support to the **Whig Junto**—Somers, lord keeper; Russell, Shrewsbury, Thomas Wharton, secretaries of state; Montague, chancellor of the exchequer. **Marlborough** had been detected in correspondence with James (Jan. 1692) and disgraced. Sunderland returned to parliament.

1693, Jan. Beginning of the national debt. £1,000,000 borrowed on annuities at 10 per cent.

1694, July, 27. Charter of the Governor and Company of the **Bank of England,** a company of merchants who, in return for certain privileges, lent the government £1,200,000. Bill for preventing officers of the crown from sitting in the house of commons **(Place Bill).** Unsuccessful **attack on Brest.**

1694, Dec. 22. The **Triennial Bill** became law; **Queen Mary died** (Dec. 28); the **Licensing Act** ran out, and was not renewed for the next year, thus abolishing censorship of the press.

1695, Nov. 22–1698, July 5. Third parliament of William III (first triennial parliament). Whigs in majority. **Recoinage Act.** Isaac Newton, master of the mint. **Trials for Treason Act** (1696); two witnesses required to prove an act of treason. Plot to assassinate William discovered, and conspirators executed; one of them, Fenwick, was the last person to be condemned by a bill of attainder and executed (1696). Formation of a loyal association. Suspension of the Habeas Corpus Act.

1697, Sept. 20. TREATY OF RYSWICK *(p. 467).*

1698, Dec. 6–1700, Apr. 11. Fourth parliament of William III. London Stock Exchange, the first true stock exchange, formed (1698). **Disbanding Act,** reducing the army to 7000 men (Feb. 1699). Act for the resumption of forfeited estates, aimed at William's Dutch favorites. Further anti-papal measures: Catholic teachers and priests liable to life imprisonment (repealed 1778).

1701, Feb. 6–June 24. Fifth parliament of William III. Tories in a majority. Harley (later earl of Oxford) speaker. Portland, Somers, Orford (Russell). Halifax impeached (Apr.-June).

June 12. ACT OF SETTLEMENT. The

The Defense of Cadiz (p.410) by Francisco Zurbaràn

The Surrender of Breda (p.450) by Diego Velásquez

*The Fleet of Charles II
of England at Dordrecht
(p.450) by Adriaen van de Velde*

crown was settled on **Sophia,** princess of Hanover, granddaughter of James I, and her issue. The sovereigns of Great Britain were to be Protestant and not leave the kingdom without consent of parliament; the country should not be involved in war for the defense of the foreign possessions of the sovereigns; no foreigner should receive a grant from the crown, or hold office, civil or military; ministers should be responsible for the acts of their sovereigns; judges should hold office for life unless guilty of misconduct.

Sept. 16. Death of James II. His son **James Edward** (the **Old Pretender**) proclaimed king of Great Britain and Ireland by Louis XIV.

1701, Dec. 30–1702, July 2. Sixth parliament of William III. Attainder of James Edward, "pretended" prince of Wales. Oath of abjuration reimposed.

1702, Mar. 8. Death of William III.

1702–1714. ANNE, second daughter of James II, wife of Prince George of Denmark. In the first part of her reign Anne was under the influence of her favorite, **Sarah, duchess of Marlborough,** and her husband, the duke.

1702, May 4. War declared upon France by the Grand Alliance; for this **War of the Spanish Succession,** *see p. 467.* **Marlborough** was captain-general of the land forces. Godolphin, lord high treasurer; Nottingham, secretary of state. Halifax and Somers not in the privy council.

1702. The campaign: **capture of Venloo and Liège** by the allies, loss of the lower Rhine to France. Sir George Rooke failed to take Cadiz, but seized part of the Spanish treasure fleet at Vigo Bay (Oct.).

1702, Oct. 20–1705, Mar. 14. First parliament of Anne. Harley, speaker.

1703, Nov. Establishment of **Queen Anne's Bounty,** a grant of the first fruits and tithes that Henry VIII had confiscated for the crown, in trust for increasing the incomes of small benefices.

Dec. 27. Treaty between England and Portugal, known from its English negotiator as the **Methuen Treaty.** England admitted Portuguese wines at duties one-third less than those paid by French wines, while Portugal agreed to import all her woolens from England.

1703–1706. Progress of the war: Marlborough took Bonn, Huy, Limburg, and Guelders (1703). Rooke took **Gibraltar** (July 24, 1704). Marlborough's great victory at **Blenheim** (Aug. 13, 1704). Capture of Barcelona by Lord Peterborough (Oct. 4, 1705). **Battle of Ramillies** (May 23, 1706) won by Marlborough.

1707, May 1. UNION OF ENGLAND AND SCOTLAND under the name of **Great Britain.** This measure, which was made necessary by the omission of Scotland from the Act of Settlement, provided that: (1) Sophia, princess of Hanover, and her Protestant heirs should succeed to the crown of the united kingdom; (2) there should be one parliament, to which Scotland should send sixteen elective peers and forty-five members of the commons. No more peers of Scotland to be created. Scottish law and legal administration to be unchanged; the Episcopal Church in England and Presbyterian in Scotland to be unchanged. **Adoption of the Union Jack** (Crosses of St. George and St. Andrew) as the national flag of Great Britain.

Oct. 23. Second parliament of Anne. First parliament of Great Britain. The influence of Marlborough and his wife had been gradually weakened by Harley and by the influence of the queen's new favorite, Abigail Hill, now Mrs. Masham. Marlborough, however, was still so strong that a hint at resignation secured the dismissal of Harley and St. John from the cabinet, and the substitution of Boyle and Robert Walpole (secretary-at-war). Last royal veto.

1708, Mar. James Edward landed in Scotland; the French fleet sent to help him was beaten by Admiral Byng. The pretender soon returned to France.

1708, Nov. 16–1710, Apr. 5. Third parliament of Anne. Whig majority. Somers, president of the council. Leaders of the Whigs (*Junto*): Somers, Halifax, Wharton, Orford, Sunderland.

1708–1709. The progress of the war: Marlborough won at **Oudenarde** (July 17, 1708) and again after a bloody battle, at **Malplaquet** (Sept. 11, 1709). Marlborough called by his Tory enemies "the butcher."

1710, Feb.–Mar. Trial of Dr. Henry Sacheverell for preaching sermons of an ultra-Tory cast. His conviction further endeared him to the people, and helped the Tory cause.

1710, Nov. 25–1713, July 16. Fourth parliament of Anne. Tory majority clear in the commons. In the lords it was made certain in 1712 by the creation of twelve Tory peers for the purpose. Complete change in ministry. This election was the first clean-cut peaceful transfer of power under the modern party sys-

Queen Anne, 1702–1714

tem in England. Harley (earl of Oxford in 1711), lord high treasurer. St. John (Viscount Bolingbroke in 1712), secretary of state. Godolphin dismissed. Mrs. Masham had a large part in this transfer of power. The duke of Marlborough was accused of peculation (Nov. 1711), dismissed from his offices, and supplanted as commander-in-chief by the duke of Ormonde. British participation in the war reduced by Tory policy to a negligible point. Complicated peace negotiations begun with France.

1711. South Sea Company incorporated by vote of parliament in a bill dated 1710. Passage of the **Occasional Conformity Bill,** directed against dissenters who technically satisfied the Test Act by one communion in an Anglican Church, and then attended a nonconformist "chapel" regularly. **Landed Property Qualification Act,** an attempt by landed proprietors to exclude merchants, financiers, and industrialists from parliament (repealed

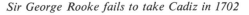

Sir George Rooke fails to take Cadiz in 1702

1866). Neither of these Tory measures were long successfully enforced.

1713, Apr. 11. TREATY OF UTRECHT. Articles affecting **Great Britain:** renunciation of the pretender by Louis XIV, who recognized the Protestant succession in Great Britain; crowns of France and Spain *not* to be united under one head; fortifications of Dunkirk to be razed and its harbor filled up; cession by France of Hudson's Bay and Acadia, Newfoundland and St. Kitts to Great Britain. **Great Britain and Spain:** cession of Gibraltar and Minorca to Britain; grant of the Asiento (*el pacto del asiento de negros*), or contract for supplying slaves to Spanish America, to the subjects of Great Britain for thirty years (Royal African Company).

1714, Feb. 16–Aug. 25. Fifth parliament of Anne. Death of Sophia of Hanover (May 28). **Schism Act.** Oxford dismissed (July 27) and succeeded as lord high treasurer by the earl of Shrewsbury. Many leading Tories, who foresaw that the Hanoverian succession would mean a Whig monopoly of power, attempted negotiations with the pretender.

   Aug. 1. Death of Anne.

1714. HOUSE OF HANOVER or **BRUNSWICK,** changed (1917) to house of Windsor. None of Anne's seventeen children having survived her, the crown, according to the Act of Settlement, descended to the Protestant house of Hanover, the Catholic line of the Stuarts being excluded.

George I, 1714–1727

1714–1727. GEORGE I.
1714, Sept. 18. The king landed in England. George I favored the Whigs in the formation of the first government; Lord Townshend, secretary of state; Shrewsbury resigned, and Halifax was made first lord of the treasury (Shrewsbury was the last lord high treasurer); Sunderland, lord lieutenant of Ireland; Lord Cowper, chancellor; earl of Nottingham, president of the council; Marlborough, commander-in-chief.

1715, Mar. 17–1722, Mar. 7. First parliament of George I. Impeachment of Bolingbroke, Ormonde, Oxford. Flight of Bolingbroke and Ormonde. Oxford in the Tower. Jacobite riots in England.
1715–1716, Sept. "The Fifteen," Jacobite rising in Scotland under the earl of Mar. **Battles of Sheriffmuir** and **Preston.** Arrival of the pretender ("James III") from France (Dec. 1715). The duke of Argyll (John Campbell) dispersed the Jacobite troops without a battle, and the pretender fled (Feb. 5, 1716). Impeachment of Jacobite leaders, execution of Derwentwater and Kenmure (Feb. 24).
1716. Partly because of this Jacobite scare, parliament passed the **Septennial Act,** prolonging its own life to seven years, and making that the full legal term for future parliaments.
1717, Jan. 4. Triple alliance between Britain, France, and Holland because of the intrigues of the pretender, Charles XII, and Alberoni; the Empire joined these in the **quadruple alliance** (Aug. 2, 1718). War between Great Britain and Spain *(see p. 473).*
1718, Jan. Repeal of the Occasional Conformity Act and the Schism Act.
1719. Abortive Spanish expedition to Scotland to help the pretender. **Treaty of Stockholm** (Nov. 20, 1719): Sweden ceded Bremen and Verden to George I (as elector of Hanover) for 1,000,000 rix dollars.
1720, Jan. Spain joined the quadruple alliance, making peace with Great Britain.

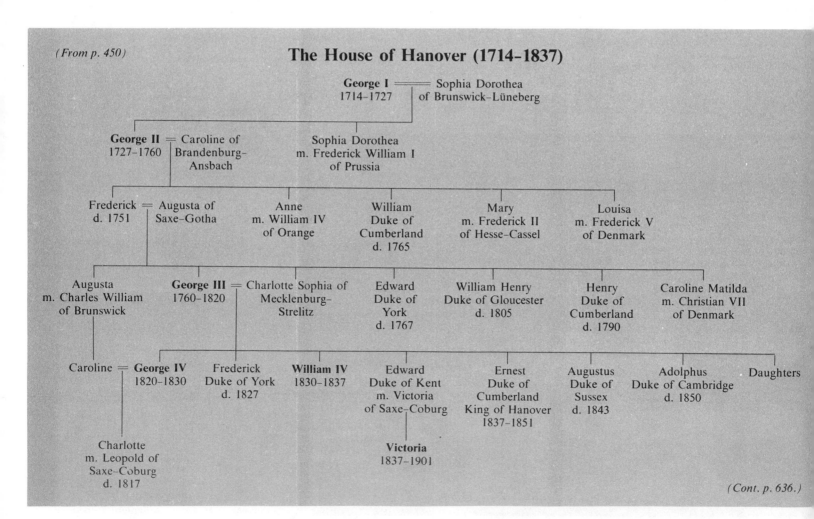

(From p. 450)

The House of Hanover (1714–1837)

George I = Sophia Dorothea
1714–1727   of Brunswick-Lüneberg

George II = Caroline of   Sophia Dorothea
1727–1760   Brandenburg-   m. Frederick William I
            Ansbach   of Prussia

Frederick = Augusta of   Anne   William   Mary   Louisa
d. 1751   Saxe-Gotha   m. William IV   Duke of   m. Frederick II   m. Frederick V
                          of Orange   Cumberland   of Hesse-Cassel   of Denmark
                                          d. 1765

Augusta   George III = Charlotte Sophia of   Edward   William Henry   Henry   Caroline Matilda
m. Charles William 1760–1820 Mecklenburg-   Duke of   Duke of Gloucester Duke of   m. Christian VII
of Brunswick   Strelitz   York   d. 1805   Cumberland   of Denmark
                                                     d. 1767   d. 1790

Caroline = George IV   Frederick   William IV   Edward   Ernest   Augustus   Adolphus   Daughters
           1820–1830   Duke of York   1830–1837   Duke of Kent   Duke of   Duke of   Duke of Cambridge
                        d. 1827   m. Victoria   Cumberland   Sussex   d. 1850
                                                     of Saxe-Coburg   King of Hanover   d. 1843
                                                                      1837–1851

Charlotte   Victoria
m. Leopold of   1837–1901
Saxe-Coburg
d. 1817

(Cont. p. 636.)

1720, Jan. Bursting of the **South Sea Bubble:** disastrous financial panic influenced by the earlier bursting of Law's **Mississippi Bubble** in France *(p. 470)*.

1721-1742. **Administration of Sir Robert Walpole.** The cabinet system and the party system now took the form they held until 1832. Parallel administration of Fleury in France (1726-1742). Both ministers were cautious and peace-loving, anxious to restore prosperity after the ravages of the "first World War." Period of stability, of common sense, the **Augustan Age** of European letters, great advances in commerce and industry.

1722, Oct. 9–1727, July 17. **Second parliament of George I.** **Treaty of Hanover** between Britain, France, and Prussia (Sept. 3, 1725).

1727-1760. GEORGE II. Walpole continued in office. The king was much influenced by his wife, the capable Caroline of Ansbach, who remained loyal to Walpole.

1728, Jan. 23–1734, Apr. 16. **First parliament of George II.**

1729, Nov. 9. **Treaty of Seville** with Spain: restoration of conquests; Britain retained Gibraltar; the *asiento* confirmed.

1731, Mar. 16. **Treaty of Vienna** with the Empire; dissolution of the Ostend East India Company, which had been formed as rival to the English India Company, by the emperor.

1735, Jan. 14–1741, Apr. 25. **Second parliament of George II.**

1736. John Wesley and his brother **Charles** returned from Georgia, set up the little groups of evangelical Christians out of which came the **Wesleyan societies,** and, after the death of John Wesley (1791), the various independent **Methodist churches.** **George Whitefield** was ordained in 1736. The Methodists were emotional and revivalistic, but politically conservative.

1739-1748. **WAR WITH SPAIN** (War of Jenkins' Ear). Capture of Porto Bello in Darien by Vernon (Nov. 22, 1739). Futile attack upon Cartagena by Vernon and Wentworth (1740). Voyage of Commodore Anson to Chile and Peru and around the world (Sept. 1740–June, 1744).

1741, Dec. 1–1747, June 17. **Third parliament of George II.** Fall of Walpole (Feb. 1742). Interim administration of the earl of Wilmington, followed (1743–1754) by that of **Henry Pelham,** first lord of the treasury. The Whig party tended to disintegrate into rival groups, held together loosely by place and privilege, and by the "interest" of the duke of Newcastle. **Broadbottom ministry.** Pelham, Pitt, Newcastle, Harrington (later Earl Stanhope), Bedford.

1740-1748. **WAR OF THE AUSTRIAN SUCCESSION.** Britain took part on the side of Austria. For further details *see p. 483.*

1745, May 11. **Battle of Fontenoy,** victory of the French under Saxe over the allies under Cumberland.

1745-1746. **SECOND JACOBITE REBEL-**

George II, 1727–1760

LION (The Forty-five). The Young Pretender, **Charles Edward,** landed in Scotland (July 25) and proclaimed his father as **James VIII** of

The South Sea Bubble: A Scene in Change Alley in 1720, *painting by E. M. Ward*

William Pitt the Elder, 1708–1778

George III, 1760–1820

Lord North (1732–1792) in 1770

Scotland and III of England. The Jacobites entered Edinburgh with some 2000 men (Sept. 11), won the **battle of Prestonpans** (Sept. 21), and under Charles Edward himself marched down into England, where they reached Derby, his farthest point, on December 4. Jacobite victories at **Penrith** (Dec. 18) and at **Falkirk Moor** (Jan. 17, 1746). But only in the Highlands was the Jacobite cause strong, and here they were beaten decisively at **Culloden** (Apr. 16). The pretender escaped to France (Sept. 20). This was the last Stuart effort.

1747, Nov. 10–1754, Apr. 6. Fourth parliament of George II.

1748. Treaty of Aix-la-Chapelle, p. 503. Britain emerged from this war a defeated nation, except in North America. The divisions of the Whigs continued, and their ablest man, **William Pitt** (earl of Chatham in 1766), was not trusted with power save at the crisis of the **Seven Years' War** (1757).

1752. The **Gregorian calendar** adopted in Britain and the colonies. The eleven days between September 2 and 14 were omitted. ("Give us back our eleven days!")

1753. Foundation of the **British Museum** by government purchase of the collection of Sir Hans Sloane.

1754. On the death of Pelham (Mar.) he was succeeded as prime minister by his brother, the duke of Newcastle. Henry Fox, secretary of state.

1754, May 31–1761, Mar. 19. Fifth parliament of George II.

1756-1763. Land and Naval **WAR BETWEEN BRITAIN AND FRANCE.** (Seven Years' War) originating in boundary disputes in North America, carried on by land in America (and Germany), by sea in all parts of the world. The British had the ultimate advantage of the French almost everywhere. (War in America, *p. 534;* in India,. *p. 552).*

1757-1761. Coalition ministry of Newcastle, first lord of the treasury, and the elder **Pitt,** secretary of state, to centralize war policy and

administration. Pitt was the real leader, and helped make possible Britain's victory in the duel with France.

1759, Sept. 13. Battle of Quebec, death of **Wolfe** and **Montcalm.** Naval **battle of Quiberon Bay** (Nov. 20); defeat of the French by Sir Edward Hawke.

1760-1820. GEORGE III.

1761, Aug. 15. Bourbon family compact between France and Spain, with the assumption of the accession of Naples and Parma, for reciprocal guarantee of all possessions and an offensive and defensive alliance.

Oct. 5. Pitt, insisting that war be declared against Spain, resigned. **Lord Bute,** adviser to the king. George attempted to exercise influence and authority, but in a way thoroughly consonant with the organization of politics in 18th century England. He built up in parliament, with Tory aid and by the usual means of patronage and bribery, a party of **king's friends,** and thus brought the Tories into power for the first time since 1714. Newcastle continued prime minister in the new cabinet (Oct. 5, 1761). Egremont and Bute, secretaries of state, George Grenville, leader of the commons.

1761, Nov. 3–1768, Mar. 10. First parliament of George III. War declared against Spain (Jan. 1762). Bute became prime minister (May 29, 1762), Grenville, secretary of state.

1763, Feb. 10. TREATY OF PARIS between Great Britain, France, and Spain. (1) France ceded to Britain: in North America, Canada, and Cape Breton Island; the Mississippi was recognized as the boundary between Louisiana and the British colonies; in the West Indies, Grenada; in Africa, the French possessions on the Senegal. Britain restored to France Goree in Africa, and Pondichéry and Chandernagor in India. (2) Spain ceded to Britain Florida, as indemnification for which France had already ceded Louisiana to Spain; Spain received from Britain all conquests in Cuba including Havana. In consequence of this peace and her acquisitions in India, Great Britain approached the apogee of her extent and

power; the North American colonies had gradually developed into virtually self-governing states.

1763, Apr. 1–1765, July; Ministry of George Grenville; Halifax and Egremont, secretaries of state; Fox created Lord Holland.

1763-1764. No. 45 of the *North Briton* (Apr. 23, 1763), containing insulting remarks concerning the king by **John Wilkes;** general warrants for the apprehension of the authors, printers, and publishers, were issued. Wilkes was arrested and expelled from the commons (Jan. 19, 1764). General warrants declared illegal by the chief justice. Wilkes outlawed.

1765, July–1766, July. Ministry of the marquis of Rockingham; Conway, leader of the commons. This was succeeded by a ministry headed by **Chatham** (Aug. 1766–Dec. 1767) and then by the ministry of the **duke of Grafton** (Dec. 1767–Jan. 1770); Townshend, chancellor of the exchequer; Conway, Shelburne, secretaries of state; the earl of Chatham, lord privy seal. Lord Hillsborough the first colonial secretary.

1768, May 10–1774, June 22. Second parliament of George III. Wilkes returned and was elected to the commons from Middlesex. He was expelled from the house by votes of the "king's friends," but was thrice elected and thrice rejected; at the last election his opponent, Colonel Luttrell, who received a small minority of votes, was declared elected. This was a Pyrrhic victory for George. The affair of the **Middlesex election** stirred up animosities against him, and resulted finally in establishing freedom of election of the house of commons.

1769-1772. *Letters of Junius,* containing bitter attacks on the duke of Grafton, Lord Mansfield, and other members of the government appeared in the *Daily Advertiser.* The author is still unknown, but the weight of evidence favors **Sir Philip Francis.**

1770, Jan.–1782, Mar. Ministry of Lord North, first lord of the treasury and chancellor of the exchequer, and George's favorite. Full Tory government. Under North, third parliament of George III (Nov. 29, 1774–July 8, 1780) and fourth parliament (Oct. 31, 1780–Mar. 24, 1784).

Constitutional developments: Establishment of publication of speeches in the commons, in spite of their protests (1771). Wilkes made lord mayor of London and member for Middlesex. The sixth motion to expunge the resolution rejecting him, as "subversive of the rights of electors," carried (May 3, 1782). Repeal of some of the penal laws against Roman Catholics (1778) helped bring on the **Lord George Gordon riots** in London (June 1780), originating as a protest against further Catholic emancipation, but degenerating into drunken orgies and brawls. London in the hands of the mob for three days.

The failure of North to subdue the American colonies resulted in a series of motions hostile to him, culminating in that of Sir J. Rous (Mar. 15, 1782) "that the House could no longer repose confidence in the present ministers" (lost by only nine votes). On threat of renewal of the motion, **North resigned,** thus setting a further precedent in parliamentary government.

1775–1783. WAR OF AMERICAN INDEPENDENCE *(see p. 535).* The war widened in 1778 with the entrance of France against Great Britain, in 1779 with the entrance of Spain against her. Gibraltar, defended by Elliott, besieged by French and Spanish in vain

(1779–1782). Holland entered the war against Great Britain (Dec. 30, 1780). In 1781 the British lost Pensacola, Tobago, St. Eustace, Demerara, St. Kitts, Nevis, Monserrat; Cornwallis surrendered at **Yorktown** (Oct. 19, 1781). Minorca lost (1782). A British naval victory near Guadeloupe, Rodney and Hood over De Grasse (Apr. 12, 1782) helped restore the balance. But England was sick of the war, and the new government had, without a formal election, a mandate to make peace.

1782, Mar. 20–July 1. Ministry of Rockingham: Shelburne and **Charles James Fox** (1749–1806), secretaries of state; Thurlow, lord chancellor; **Edmund Burke** (1729–1797), paymaster of the forces; **Richard Sheridan** (1751–1816), undersecretary of state. With Chatham, Fox, Burke, Sheridan, the golden age of English oratory. On Rockingham's death (July 1), Lord Shelburne became prime minister in a cabinet (July 1, 1782–Feb. 24, 1783) from which Fox, Burke, and Sheridan were excluded, and **William Pitt** (1759–1806) included as chancellor of the exchequer.

1782, Nov. 30. PRELIMINARY TREATY OF PARIS with the United States *(p. 542)* followed by the general **treaty of Paris** (Jan. 20, 1783–Sept. 3) between the United States, Great Britain, France, Spain, and Holland. (1) Recognition of the independence of the thirteen United States. (2) Britain surrendered Tobago and Senegal to France. (3) Spain retained Minorca and Florida. (4) Holland, badly

worsted (separate peace, May 20, 1784), gave Negapatam and the right of free navigation in the Moluccas to Britain.

1783, Apr. 2–Dec. 13. Coalition ministry of North and Fox, nominally headed by the duke of Portland; Cavendish, chancellor of the exchequer; North and Fox, secretaries of state; Burke, paymaster. The alliance of two such bitter opponents as North and Fox shocked public opinion and paved the way for the ministry of the younger Pitt.

1783, Dec. 26–1801, Mar. 17. First ministry of William Pitt the Younger, formed after Fox's bill to reform the government of India was lost in the lords. Pitt's bill was also rejected, whereupon parliament was dissolved (1784, Mar. 25) and new elections held.

1784, May 18–1795. Fifth parliament of George III.

Aug. 13. Pitt's India bill became law *(p. 553).*

1788. Temporary insanity of George III. In the course of discussion regarding the regency, the king recovered.

1793, Feb. 1. The **French Republic declared war on Great Britain** *(p. 611).* The government at once took measures against revolutionary agitation (Traitorous Correspondence Bill; suspension of the Habeas Corpus Act, [1794] renewed annually until 1801).

1794, May. Trial of Hardy, Horne Tooke, and Thelwall, on charge of high treason, all of whom were eventually acquitted (Dec.).

The House of Commons discussing the Traitorous Correspondence Bill

Press gangs, English satirical engraving of 1797

Nov. **Jay's treaty** between the United States and Great Britain *(p. 751).*

1796, Sept. 17. The sixth parliament of George III convened.

1797, Apr. 15. The mutiny at Spithead. The sailors' demands for better treatment were reasonable and were met by the government (May 17), but immediately afterward a more serious outbreak occurred at the **Nore,** which had to be suppressed by force (June 30).

1799. Supression of the **insurrection of the United Irishmen.** This organization had been formed in 1791 to secure the complete separation of Ireland from England. The French had sent several expeditions to aid them (notably that of Hoche, which was scattered by a storm, Dec. 1796), but the United Irishmen were defeated at **Vinegar Hill** (June 21, 1798) and the insurrection stamped out. As a result

1801, Jan. 1. The **LEGISLATIVE UNION OF GREAT BRITAIN AND IRELAND,** under the name of the *United Kingdom,* was brought about. The Act of Union provided that there should be one parliament, to which Ireland should send four spiritual lords, sitting by rotation of sessions; 28 temporal peers, elected for life by the Irish peerage; and 100 members of the commons. The churches of the two countries were to be united into one Protestant Episcopal church. Pitt proposed to make some concessions to the Roman Catholics, but the king was persuaded that this would involve a breach of his coronation oath. Thereupon

Feb. 3. Pitt resigned.

Mar. 14. His friend **Henry Addington** then headed the cabinet, with Pitt advising, and concluded peace with France, embodied (Mar. 27, 1802) in the **treaty of Amiens.**

The passage of the **Health and Morals of Apprentices Act** in this year marks a step toward government supervision of labor conditions. The act forbade the hiring out of pauper children for work in the cotton mills until they were nine years of age, restricted their working day to 12 hours, and prohibited their employment at night work.

1803, May 16. The war between Britain and France was renewed. (See *p. 619*).

William Pitt the Younger, 1759–1806

Samuel Pepys, 1633–1703

Alexander Pope, 1688–1744

1804, May 10. Pitt returned to office and helped to organize the **Third Coalition** against France. He was stricken by the news of Napoleon's victory at Austerlitz and died on Jan. 23, 1806.

1806. Pitt's place was taken by **Lord William Grenville,** with **Charles James Fox** as foreign secretary until the latter's death, Sept. 13.

1807. Abolition of slavery decreed in the British dominions. The **duke of Portland** formed his second ministry (March) and held office until May 1809, when **Spencer Perceval** replaced him, to be followed (June 1812) by the **earl of Liverpool,** whose unusually long ministry lasted until April 1827. *(Cont. p. 630.)*

BRITISH ART AND LITERATURE, 17th AND 18th CENTURIES

(1) Architecture

Christopher Wren (1632–1723): chief architect of the Greenwich Observatory (1676) and Royal Hospital (1696–1705), St. Paul's Cathedral (1710). **James Gibbs** (1682–1752): churches in London, buildings at Oxford and Cambridge Universities. The brothers **Adam** (James, John, Robert, William) designed many buildings in the West End of London; Robert (1728–1792) set the fashion in his design of furniture and interiors.

(2) Literature, Late 17th Century

Prose: John Dryden (1631–1700) was the foremost prose writer of the latter part of the 17th century and his style established a pattern for later writers (*Essay of Dramatic Poesy,* 1668, rev. 1684; preface to *Fables,* 1700); he also wrote poetry and plays (*Conquest of Granada,* 1672).

Diaries: Samuel Pepys (1633–1703); **John Evelyn** (1620–1706).

Philosophy: John Locke (1632–1704) founded the empirical school (*Essays Concerning the Human Understanding,* 1690) and laid the basis for political liberalism.

History and biography: Anthony à Wood, with John Aubrey, *Athenae Oxoniensis* (1691–1692); William Dugdale, with Roger Dodsworth,

Monasticon Anglicanum (1655–1673); Edward Hyde, first **earl of Clarendon** (1609–1674), *History of the Rebellion* (1702–1704).

A dictionary was compiled by Edward Phillips: *New World of English Words* (1658).

John Bunyan (1628–1688), an itinerant preacher jailed after the restoration of Charles II, wrote *The Pilgrim's Progress* (1678) during his imprisonment; written in everyday language and hence immensely popular among the poor classes; an allegory full of simple but colorful prose.

Drama: In addition to Dryden (see above), **William Congreve** (1670–1729; *Love for Love,* 1695; *Way of the World,* 1700) created outstanding dialogue; comedies of manners also written by **William Wycherley** (*The Country Wife,* 1675) and **Sir George Etherege** (*The Man of Mode,* 1676).

Poets: John Dryden (*Absalom and Achitophel,* 1601) and **Samuel Butler** (*Hudibras,* 1663–1664); also **Robert Herrick** (1591–1674), **George Wither** (1588–1667), **Abraham Cowley** (1618–1667), **Andrew Marvell** (1621–1678), **Henry Vaughan** (1622–1695).

Music: John Blow (1647–1708), composer of the first English opera (*Venus and Adonis,* c. 1685); **Henry Purcell** (c. 1658–1695), composer of opera (*Dido and Aeneas,* c. 1689), songs, church and chamber music.

(3) Literature and Art, 18th Century

In general, literature showed a reaction to the puritanism of the Commonwealth and the laxity of the Restoration; discussion of mores and ideas became more generally accepted; new impetus was given the newspapers by the failure to renew the Licensing Act with its censorship provisions. The essay was a popular literary vehicle; *The Tatler* (1709–1711) and the *Spectator Papers* (1711–1712), under the editorship of **Joseph Addison** (1672–1719) and **Richard Steele** (1672–1729), offered all kinds of social criticism.

The prose novel, often a satire, was a popular form: **Daniel Defoe** (1660–1731; *Robinson Crusoe,* 1719; *Moll Flanders,* 1722); **Jonathan Swift** (1667–1745; *Gulliver's Travels,* 1726);

Samuel Richardson (1689–1761; *Pamela,* 1750; *Clarissa,* 1747–1748); **Henry Fielding** (1707–1754; *Joseph Andrews,* 1752; *Tom Jones,* 1749); **Tobias Smollett** (1721–1771; *Roderick Random,* 1748, suggested by *Gil Blas*); **Laurence Sterne** (1713–1768; *Tristram Shandy,* 1759–1767). The Gothic horror novels began to appear with **Horace Walpole,** *Castle of Otranto* (1764).

Biography and literary criticism: Samuel Johnson (1709–1784), in his *Lives of the English Poets* (1779–1781), gave sound reasons for his critical observations; his *Dictionary of the English Language* (1755) established the pattern for later models. **Anthony Ashley,** earl of Shaftesbury (1673–1711), *Characteristics of Men, Manners, Opinions, Times* (1711); **James Boswell** (1740–1795), *Life of Samuel Johnson* (1785).

Poetry: Alexander Pope (1688–1744) translated the *Iliad* and portions of the *Odyssey;* wrote *The Rape of the Lock* (1711). Lyric poetry of **William Blake** (1757–1827), mystic, who cre-

John Locke, 1632–1704

John Bunyan, 1628–1688

Henry Purcell, c. 1658–1695

Jonathan Swift, 1667–1745

The Honourable Frances Dunscombe, *by Thomas Gainsborough, 1727–1788*

ated engraved illustrations for many of his poems; the Scot **Robert Burns** (1759–1796). Also: **James Thomson** (1700–1748), **Thomas Gray** (1716–1771), **William Cowper** (1731–1800), **William Collins** (1721–1759).

Drama: Richard Brinsley Sheridan (1751–1816) satirized his age in *The Rivals* (1775) and *The School for Scandal* (1777).

Music: George Frederick Handel (1685–1759), German-born composer of oratorio and orchestral works, spent much of his life in England, becoming a naturalized British subject in 1726. **John Gay** (1685–1732) and **John Christopher Pepusch** (1667–1752) collaborated on the comic *Beggar's Opera* (1728).

Painting: William Hogarth (1697–1764) was the artist-critic of his society (*A Rake's Progress,* 1735; *Marriage à la Mode,* 1744). The favorite technique of the 18th century was the portrait: **Sir Joshua Reynolds** (1723–1792); **Thomas Gainsborough** (1727–1788); **George Romney** (1734–1802); **Sir Henry Raeburn** (1756–1823); **John Hoppner** (1758–1810). Also landscapes by **Gainsborough** and by **Richard Wilson** (1714–1782). The **Royal Academy of Art** in London was founded in 1768.

2. The Dutch Republic, 1602–1810

(From p. 403)

The first half of the 17th century, during which the Dutch provinces were still at war with Spain to secure their independence, was nevertheless the golden age of the Netherlands, a period of unexampled flowering in art *(p. 403)*. This was probably due primarily to the unprecedented expansion of Dutch commerce, which resulted from the closing of Lisbon to Dutch trade after the annexation of Portugal to Spain. The Dutch were obliged to find their own way to the east and within a remarkably short time they were disputing the command of the Indies with the Portuguese, whom they soon displaced. The **Dutch East India Company** (founded 1602), was given extensive political and military authority and became one of the chief organs of Dutch imperialism. In the east, Batavia was founded in 1619. The Portuguese were expelled from Ceylon (1638–1658), and Malacca taken from them (1641). In 1652 the Dutch established themselves at the Cape of Good Hope and in 1667 they took Sumatra. The **Dutch West India Company** (founded 1621) had the same extensive control over the American and African coast trade. In 1623 the Dutch seized Pernambuco and began extensive conquests in Brazil (till 1661). They took the islands of St. Eustace and Curaçao (1634–1635), Saba (1640), and St. Martin (1648). With this far-flung colonial empire, the Dutch provinces became the commercial center of Europe, Amsterdam easily holding the lead as a financial center.

The provinces, however, were politically connected only in the loosest fashion. Despite the stadholdership of the house of Orange, there continued to be (especially in Holland, the chief province) strong suspicion of all centralizing tendencies and an almost fanatical attachment to state rights.

1647–1650. WILLIAM II, a young man of 23, succeeded his father, Frederick Henry, in the stadholdership. Able, ambitious, and restless, William disapproved of the **treaty of Münster** (1648), which recognized the independence of the provinces, and would have preferred to continue the war. He soon became involved in conflict with the states-general and, by arresting some of the leaders of Holland and attacking Amsterdam itself (1650), he forced the submission of the state-rights group.

1650, Nov. 6. William's early death gave the decentralizing party a golden opportunity, for William's son was born posthumously and there was no one to dispute the taking over of control by the states-general. In 1653 **John De Witt** became grand pensionary of Holland, and thereby controlled general policy. An able statesman and adroit diplomat, he easily maintained Dutch prestige and greatness.

1652–1654. The **FIRST ANGLO-DUTCH WAR,** the direct outgrowth of the **English Navigation Act** (1651) and the steadily growing competition of English and Dutch, especially in the east. The English and the Dutch, led by outstanding commanders like Blake, Monk, Tromp, de Ruyter, and De Witt, fought no less than twelve naval engagements, most of them indecisive. By the **treaty of Westminster** (Apr. 5, 1654) the Dutch agreed to enter a defensive league with England and to pay indemnity. The province of Holland secretly agreed to exclude all members of the house of Orange from the stadholdership (this was due to Cromwell's uneasiness about the relationship of the Stuarts and Oranges—William II having married the daughter of Charles I).

1657–1660. The Dutch interfered successfully in the Swedish-Danish War in order to prevent the entrance of the Baltic from falling into exclusively Swedish control.

1657–1661. War with Portugal, over conflicting interests in Brazil.

1660. On the restoration of the Stuarts in England, the Dutch states-general at once rescinded the exclusion of the house of Orange from the stadholdership.

1662. The Dutch allied themselves to the

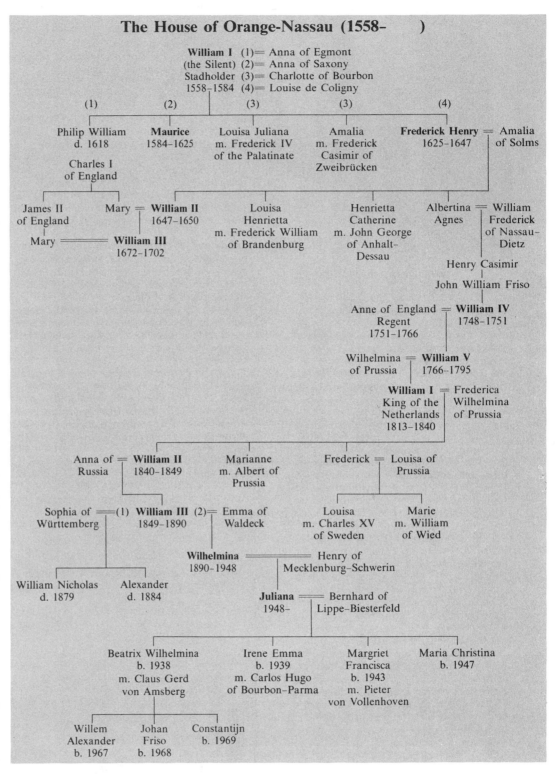

The House of Orange-Nassau (1558–   )

William I (the Silent) Stadholder 1558–1584
- (1)= Anna of Egmont
- (2)= Anna of Saxony
- (3)= Charlotte of Bourbon
- (4)= Louise de Coligny

(1) Philip William d. 1618 — Charles I of England

(2) **Maurice** 1584–1625

(3) Louisa Juliana m. Frederick IV of the Palatinate

(3) Amalia m. Frederick Casimir of Zweibrücken

(4) **Frederick Henry** 1625–1647 = Amalia of Solms

James II of England — Mary = **William II** 1647–1650

Louisa Henrietta m. Frederick William of Brandenburg

Henrietta Catherine m. John George of Anhalt-Dessau

Albertina Agnes = William Frederick of Nassau-Dietz

Mary === **William III** 1672–1702

Henry Casimir

John William Friso

Anne of England Regent 1751–1766 = **William IV** 1748–1751

Wilhelmina of Prussia = **William V** 1766–1795

William I King of the Netherlands 1813–1840 = Frederica Wilhelmina of Prussia

Anna of Russia = **William II** 1840–1849

Marianne m. Albert of Prussia

Frederick = Louisa of Prussia

Sophia of Württemberg =(1) **William III** 1849–1890 (2)= Emma of Waldeck

Louisa m. Charles XV of Sweden

Marie m. William of Wied

William Nicholas d. 1879

Alexander d. 1884

Wilhelmina 1890–1948 === Henry of Mecklenburg-Schwerin

Juliana 1948– === Bernhard of Lippe-Biesterfeld

Beatrix Wilhelmina b. 1938 m. Claus Gerd von Amsberg

Irene Emma b. 1939 m. Carlos Hugo of Bourbon-Parma

Margriet Francisca b. 1943 m. Pieter von Vollenhoven

Maria Christina b. 1947

Willem Alexander b. 1967

Johan Friso b. 1968

Constantijn b. 1969

William III, 1672–1702

French to provide against the danger of attack by the British.

1664. The **British seized New Amsterdam** (New York) and appropriated various Dutch stations on the African coast.

1665–1667. SECOND ANGLO-DUTCH WAR. France and Denmark supported the Dutch, who, on the whole, maintained the upper hand at sea (attack on the English fleet in the Medway, etc., but by the **treaty of Breda** (July 21, 1667) they abandoned claims to New Amsterdam in return for Surinam.

1668, Jan. 23. Triple Alliance of England, Holland, and Sweden to check the aggression of Louis XIV in the Spanish Netherlands. Louis soon managed to buy off the English and the Swedes and thereafter concentrated his hatred upon the Dutch.

1672–1678. WAR WITH FRANCE AND ENGLAND *(p. 465)*. The Dutch were quite unprepared for a land war and consequently the French were able to overrun much of the country. The result was much agitation against **John De Witt,** who, with his brother Cornelius, was brutally murdered by a mob (Aug. 27, 1672).

1672–1702. WILLIAM III (son of William II), stadholder. With the aid of the emperor and of Brandenburg he was able to hold his own against the French and indeed to force their retirement. The British abandoned the war (1674) and by the **treaty of Nijmwegen** (Nimwegen, Nimeguen) of 1678, the Dutch came off without losses.

1688, Nov. 5. William III (married in 1677 to **Mary,** the daughter of James II of England) landed in England in response to an appeal from the opponents of James II. In 1689 he was proclaimed king and joint ruler with Mary *(p. 454)*.

1689–1697. WAR OF THE LEAGUE OF AUGSBURG against Louis XIV *(p. 466)*. William was very decidedly the leader in the coalition and threw the whole weight of England as well as of the Netherlands into the struggle. Though rarely successful in the field, William's perseverance and able management

saved him from disaster. By the **treaty of Ryswick** (1697), France and the Netherlands returned to the *status quo ante.*

1702, Mar. 8. The **death of William III,** without children, brought to an end the direct line of the house of Orange, which, however, was continued by the related house of Nassau. For the time being, however, the states-general resumed control of affairs, which were ably conducted by **Antonius Heinsius,** since 1688 grand pensionary of Holland and close collaborator of William III. Heinsius remained in power until his death in 1720.

1702–1713. The **WAR OF THE SPANISH SUCCESSION** *(p. 467)*, in which the Dutch again played their part in conjunction with England. These wars, costly in men and money, reacted most unfavorably on the Dutch position. After 1715 there was a marked and steady economic decline. The republic was soon overshadowed by Britain and became more and more an adjunct of the British system.

1715, Nov. 15. By the **Barrier Treaty,** the Empire ceded to the Dutch a number of strong places on the French frontier of the (since 1713) Austrian Netherlands, as protection against attack by France.

1731. The Dutch signed the **Pragmatic Sanction** of Emperor Charles VI in return for abolition of the Ostend Company, which had been set up as a rival to the Dutch East India Company.

1734. The prince of Orange-Nassau married Anne, the daughter of George II.

1743. The Dutch Republic joined Britain in the alliance with Maria Theresa against Prussia and France. The French conquests in the Austrian Netherlands constituted a direct danger to the republic.

1748–1751. WILLIAM IV of Orange-Nassau (grandson of William III's cousin) proclaimed stadholder, a dignity which now became hereditary in the family.

1751. On the death of William IV, his widow, Anne, acted as regent for the three-year-old heir.

1766–1795. WILLIAM V assumed the position of stadholder. He proved himself a weak and ineffectual ruler.

1780–1784. The Dutch went to war with Britain over the question of the right to search ships at sea. As a result the Dutch lost some of their possessions in both the East and the West Indies.

1785. Beginning of serious conflict between William and the states-general, due to the emergence of the **Patriot Party** (representing the French influence). William ultimately had to call in Prussian troops (1787) to restore his authority.

1793. France declared war on the Dutch Republic as well as on Britain (friction over the opening of the Scheldt by the French in 1792).

1794–1795. The French general, Pichegru, overran the country, capturing the Dutch fleet while it was frozen in the ice in the Texel. William V fled to England.

1795–1806. The **BATAVIAN REPUBLIC,** modeled on France and governed by the Patriots under more or less direct French influence. In the interval the British, still at war with France, seized the Dutch colonies.

1806–1810. LOUIS, the brother of Napoleon, king of Holland. His policy, aimed at the good of his adopted kingdom, brought him into conflict with his brother.

1810. The **KINGDOM OF HOLLAND** was incorporated with France as an integral part of the empire. *(Cont. p. 645.)*

French troops enter the territory of the Dutch republic, January 21, 1795

3. France, 1643–1788

[*For a complete list of the kings of France see Appendix VII.*]

(From p. 408)

1643-1715. LOUIS XIV, who ascended the throne at the age of five. His mother, **Anna of Austria** (daughter of Philip III of Spain) acted as guardian. The government, even after Louis's arrival at majority, was conducted by **Cardinal Mazarin.**

1648-1653. Disturbances of the **Fronde (Cardinal Retz; Prince of Condé;** resistance of the *parlement* of Paris), the last attempt of the French nobility to oppose the court by armed resistance. The parlementary, as contrasted with the noble, Fronde, was, however, an attempt to substitute government by law for government by royal or any other irresponsible will. Condé, at first loyal, afterward engaged against the court, fought a battle with the royal troops under Henri de la Tour d'Auvergne, Vicomte de **Turenne,** in the Faubourg Saint Antoine, and took refuge in Spain. The first conspiracy, the old Fronde, ended in 1649, with the second **treaty of Rueil;** the second conspiracy, the new Fronde, which involved treasonable correspondence with Spain, failed in 1650. A union of the two was crushed in 1653. (Gaston of Orléans, and his daughter "Mademoiselle.")

1648. Acquisitions of France in the **treaties of Westphalia,** *p. 429.*

The war with Spain, which sprang up during the Thirty Years' War (victory of Condé at **Rocroi,** May 19, 1643; alliance with England, 1657; Cromwell sent 8000 men of his army to the assistance of Turenne) was continued till the

1659. TREATY OF THE PYRENEES: (1) France received a part of Roussillon, Conflans, Cerdagne, and several towns in Artois and Flanders, Hainault and Luxemburg; (2) the duke of Lorraine, the ally of Spain, was partially reinstated (France received Bar, Clermont, etc., and right of passage for troops); the prince of Condé entirely reinstated; (3) marriage between Louis XIV and the infanta **Maria Teresa,** eldest daughter of Philip IV of Spain, who, however, renounced her claims upon her inheritance for herself and her issue by Louis forever, in consideration of the payment of a dowry of 500,000 crowns by Spain.

1661. Death of Mazarin. Personal government of Louis XIV (1661-1715), absolute, at least in the theory of certain royalist pamphleteers, and perhaps of Louis himself, without estates-general, without regard to the remonstrances of the parlement of Paris (*L'état, c'est moi*). Louis was in practice, however, limited by his inability to do everything himself. The French bureaucracy was a privileged group, often owning their offices (*vénalité des offices; Paulette,* a tax to the crown paid by office owners). Three constitutional limitations on the crown: king must be a Catholic; no woman may occupy the throne **(Salic law);** king may not alienate his lands by *appanage* system. **Jean Baptiste Colbert,** controller general of the finances from 1662-1683. **Reform of the finances;** mercantile system. Construction of a fleet of war. François Michel Le Tellier **(Marquis de Louvois),** minister of war, 1666-1691. Quarrel for precedence in rank with Spain. Negotiations with the pope concerning the privileges of French ambassadors at Rome. The ambition of Louis for fame and his desire for increase of territory were some of the causes of the following wars, in which these generals took part: Turenne, Condé, Luxembourg, Catinat, Villars, Vendôme, Vauban (inventor of the modern system of military fortification).

1667-1668. FIRST WAR (War of Devolution) on account of the Spanish Netherlands.

Cause: After the death of his father-in-law, Philip IV of Spain, Louis laid claim to the Spanish possessions in the Belgian provinces (Brabant, Flanders, etc.), on the ground that, being the personal estates of the royal family of Spain, their descent ought to be regulated by the local *droit de dévolution,* a principle in private law, whereby in the event of a dissolution of a marriage by death, the survivor enjoyed the usufruct only of the property, the ownership being vested in the children, whence it followed that daughters of a first marriage inherited before sons of a second marriage. The renunciation of her heritage which his wife had made was, Louis claimed, invalid, since the stipulated dowry had never been paid.

1667. Turenne conquered a part of Flanders and Hainault. By the exertions of John De Witt, pensioner of Holland, and Sir William Temple, England, Holland, and Sweden concluded the **Triple Alliance** (1668, Jan. 23) which induced Louis, after Condé had, with great rapidity, occupied the defenseless free county of Burgundy (Franche-Comté), to sign the

1668, May 2. Treaty of Aix-la-Chapelle: Louis restored Franche-Comté (the fortresses having been dismantled) to Spain, in return for which he received twelve fortified towns on the border of the Spanish Netherlands, among others Lille, Tournay, and Oudenarde. The question of the succession was not settled, but deferred.

1672-1678. SECOND WAR (against Holland). The course of Holland in these transactions had inflamed the hatred of Louis against her, a hatred made still stronger by the refuge given by the provinces to political writers who annoyed him with their abusive publications. To gain his purpose, the destruction or the humiliation of Holland, Louis secured the disruption of the Triple Alliance by a private

Louis XIV, 1643–1715

treaty with Charles II of England (the **treaty of Dover,** 1670, *p. 451),* and between France and Sweden (*p. 451).* Subsidy treaties with Köln and Münster; 20,000 Germans fought for Louis in the following war.

1672. Passage of the Rhine. Rapid and easy conquest of southern Holland by Turenne, Condé, and the king, at the head of 100,000 men. The brothers De Witt, the leaders of the aristocratic republican party in Holland, were killed during a popular outbreak (Aug. 27), and **William III of Orange** was placed at the head of the state. The opening of the sluices saved the province of Holland, and the city of Amsterdam. Alliance of Holland with Frederick William, elector of Brandenburg (1640-1688), afterward joined by the emperor and by Spain.

1673. Frederick William concluded the separate **peace of Vossem,** in which he retained his possessions in Cleves, except Wesel and Rees.

1674. Declaration of war by the Empire. Peace between England and Holland. Louis conquered Franche-Comté in person; Condé fought against Orange (drawn **battle at Senef)** in the Netherlands. Brilliant campaign of **Turenne** on the upper Rhine (first ravaging of the Palatinate) against Montecucculi, the imperial general, and the elector of Brandenburg. The latter, recalled by the inroad of the Swedish allies of Louis XIV into his lands, defeated the Swedes in the

1675, June 28. Battle of Fehrbellin. Turenne fell at Sasbach, in Baden (July 27). The French retreated across the Rhine.

1676. Naval successes in the Mediterranean against the Dutch and Spanish. Death of de Ruyter.

1678. Surprise and capture of Ghent and Ypres by the French. Negotiations with each combatant, which had been for some time in progress, resulted in the

1678-1679. TREATIES OF NIMWEGEN (Nijmwegen, Nimeguen). **Holland** and **France** (Aug. 10, 1678); **Spain** and **France** (Sept. 17, 1678); the **emperor,** with **France** and **Sweden** (Feb. 6, 1679); **Holland** with **Sweden** (Oct. 12,

(From p. 404)

The French Bourbons (1589–1883)

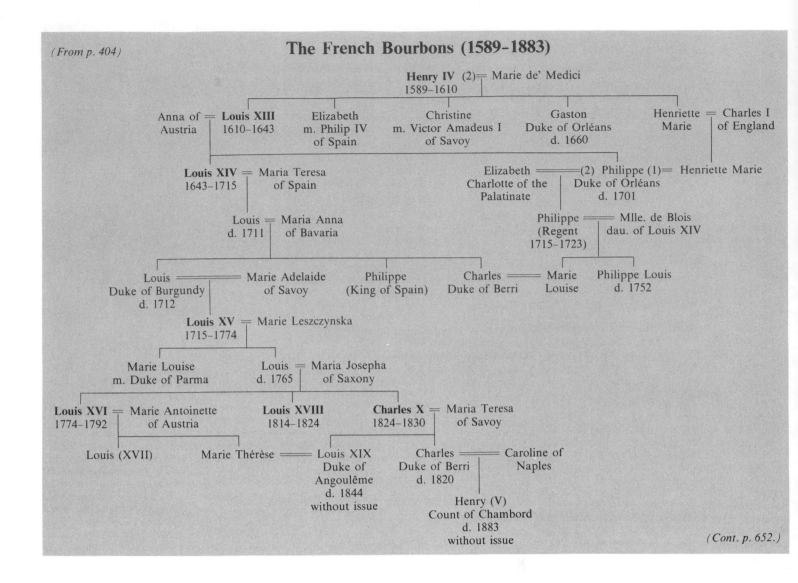

Henry IV (2)= Marie de' Medici
1589–1610

Anna of = **Louis XIII** | Elizabeth m. Philip IV of Spain | Christine m. Victor Amadeus I of Savoy | Gaston Duke of Orléans d. 1660 | Henriette = Charles I Marie of England
Austria 1610–1643

Louis XIV = Maria Teresa
1643–1715 of Spain

Elizabeth ======(2) Philippe (1)= Henriette Marie
Charlotte of the Duke of Orléans
Palatinate d. 1701

Louis = Maria Anna
d. 1711 of Bavaria

Philippe ===== Mlle. de Blois
(Regent dau. of Louis XIV
1715–1723)

Louis ======== Marie Adelaide | Philippe (King of Spain) | Charles ===== Marie | Philippe Louis
Duke of Burgundy of Savoy Duke of Berri Louise d. 1752
d. 1712

Louis XV = Marie Leszczynska
1715–1774

Marie Louise m. Duke of Parma | Louis = Maria Josepha d. 1765 of Saxony

Louis XVI = Marie Antoinette | **Louis XVIII** | **Charles X** = Maria Teresa
1774–1792 of Austria 1814–1824 1824–1830 of Savoy

Louis (XVII) | Marie Thérèse ===== Louis XIX Duke of Angoulême d. 1844 without issue | Charles ===== Caroline of Duke of Berri Naples d. 1820

Henry (V) Count of Chambord d. 1883 without issue

(Cont. p. 652.)

1679). At Fontainebleau, **France** and **Denmark** (Sept. 2, 1679). At Lund, **Denmark** and **Sweden** (Sept. 26, 1679).

(1) Holland received its whole territory back, upon condition of preserving neutrality. (2) Spain ceded to France: Franche-Comté, and on the northwest frontier, Valenciennes, Cambray, and the Cambrésis, Aire, Poperingen, St. Omer, Ypres, Condé, Bouchain, Maubeuge, and other towns; France ceded to Spain: Charleroi, Binche, Oudenarde, Ath, Courtray, Limburg, Ghent, Waes, etc.; and in Catalonia, Puycerda. (3) The emperor ceded to France: Freiburg in the Breisgau; France gave up the right of garrison in Philippsburg; the duke of Lorraine was to be restored to his duchy, but on such conditions that he refused to accept them.

Louis XIV forced the elector of Brandenburg to conclude the

1679, June 29. Peace of St. Germain-en-Laye, whereby the elector surrendered to Sweden nearly all of his conquests in Pomerania, in return for which he received only the reversion of the principality of East Friesland, which became Prussian in 1744, and a small indemnification.

Louis was now at the height of his power. Stimulated by the weakness of the Empire, he established the

1680–1683. Chambers of Reunion at Metz, Breisach, Besançon, and Tournay. These were French courts of claims with power to investigate and decide what dependencies had at any time belonged to the territories and towns which had been ceded to France by the last four treaties of peace. The king executed with his troops the decisions of his tribunals. Saarbrücken, Luxemburg, Zweibrücken, Strassburg (1681), and many other towns were thus annexed to France.

1683. Invasions of the Spanish Netherlands, occupation of Luxemburg, and seizure of Trier (1684). Lorraine permanently occupied by France. To the weakness of the Empire, the wars with the Turks, and the general confusion of European relations since the peace of Nimwegen, is to be attributed the fact that these aggressions were met by nothing more than empty protests, and that

1684. A truce for twenty years was concluded at Regensburg between Louis and the emperor and the Empire, whereby he retained everything he had obtained by reunion up to August 1, 1681, including Strassburg.

Louis's mistresses: Louise de la Vallière; Madame de Montespan; Madame de Maintenon, a devout Catholic whose influence over the king was boundless. Maria Teresa died 1683. Louis privately married to Madame de Maintenon. **War upon heresy.** The dragonnades in Languedoc. Wholesale conversions of Calvinists.

1685, Oct. 18. REVOCATION OF THE EDICT OF NANTES. The exercise of the reformed religion in France was forbidden, children were to be educated in the Catholic faith, emigration was prohibited. In spite of this more than 50,000 families, including military leaders (Schomberg), men of letters, and a large part of the artisans of France, made their way to foreign countries. Their loss was a blow to the industry of the country that perhaps hastened the approach of the revolution. The exiles found welcome in Holland, England (Spitalfields), Brandenburg, English North America, and South Africa. The Protestants of Alsace retained the freedom of worship that had been secured to them.

1688–1697. THIRD WAR. (War of the League of Augsburg).

Cause: After the extinction of the male line of the electors palatine in the person of the **Elector Charles** (d. 1685), whose sister was the wife of Louis XIV's brother, the duke of Orléans, the king laid claim to the allodial lands of the family, a claim he soon extended to the greater portion of the country. Another ground for war was found in the quarrel over the election of the archbishop of Köln, which

Louis was resolved to secure for Von Fürstenberg, bishop of Strassburg, in place of Prince Clement of Bavaria (1688).

Meantime the unfavorable impression produced throughout Protestant Europe by the revocation of the edict of Nantes had contributed to the success of the plans of William of Orange, and on July 9, 1686, the **League of Augsburg,** directed against France, was signed by the emperor, the kings of Sweden and Spain, the electors of Bavaria, of Saxony, and the Palatinate. In 1688 occurred the revolution in England that placed William of Orange on the throne of that country, and added a powerful kingdom to the new foes of Louis. The exiled James II took refuge with the French monarch (court at St. Germain).

1688, Oct. Invasion and devastation of the Palatinate, by order of Louvois. The military successes of the French on the Rhine were unimportant, especially after 1693, when **Prince Louis of Bavaria** assumed the chief command against them.

1689, May 12. The Grand Alliance, between the powers who had joined the League of Augsburg and England and Holland (Savoy had joined the league in 1687). The principal scene of war was in the Netherlands.

1690, June 30. Battle of Fleurus, defeat of the prince of Waldeck by Louis's general, Marshal **Luxembourg.** The French expedition to Ireland in aid of James had but a temporary success, and ended in defeat, 1690. French successes in Piedmont; Catinat reduced Savoy; defeat of Victor Amadeus at Staffarda.

1692, May. Defeat of the French fleet under Tourville by the English and Dutch at **Cap La Hogue.** The mastery of the sea passed from the French to the English. Death of Louvois.

July 24. Battle of Steinkirk (Steenkerken). Victory of Luxembourg over William III.

1693, June 30. Battle of Lagos; defeat of the British fleet by the French under Tourville.

July 29. Battle of Neerwinden. Victory of Luxembourg over William III, who in spite of his many defeats still kept the field.

In Italy Marshal Catinat defeated the duke of Savoy at **Marsaglia.** Rise of **Prince Eugene of Savoy** (1663–1736).

1695. Death of Luxembourg, who was succeeded by the incapable Villeroy.

1695, Sept. Recapture of **Namur** by William III.

1696, May 30. Separate peace with Savoy at Turin. All conquests were restored to the duke (Pignerol and Casale), and his daughter married Louis's grandson, the duke of Burgundy. Savoy promised to remain neutral.

1697, Sept. 30. TREATY OF RYSWICK between France, England, Spain, and Holland. (1) Confirmation of the separate peace with Savoy. (2) Restoration of conquests between France and England and Holland; William III acknowledged as king of England, and Anne as his successor, Louis promising not to help his enemies. (3) It was agreed that the chief fortresses in the Spanish Netherlands should be garrisoned with Dutch troops as a barrier between France and Holland. (4) France restored to Spain all places which had been "reunited" since the treaty of Nimwegen, with the exception of 82 places, and all conquests. (5) Holland restored Pondichéry in India to the French East India Company and received commercial privileges in return.

Oct. 30. Treaty between France and the emperor (and Empire). (1) France ceded all the "reunions" except Alsace, which henceforward was lost to the Empire. (2) Strassburg was ceded to France. (3) France ceded Freiburg and Breisach to the emperor, and Phillipsburg to the Empire. (4) The duchy of Zweibrücken was restored to the king of Sweden, as count palatine of the Rhine. (5) Lorraine was restored to Duke Leopold (excepting Saarlouis). (6) The claims of Cardinal Fürstenberg to the archbishopric of Köln were disavowed. (7) The Rhine was made free.

1701–1714. WAR OF THE SPANISH SUCCESSION. The family relations that led to the war will be made clear by the genealogical table.

Leopold I had, besides his daughter **Maria Antonia,** two sons by his third marriage, **Joseph I,** emperor from 1705 to 1711 and **Charles VI,** emperor from 1711 to 1740.

Charles II, king of Spain, was childless; the extinction of the Spanish house of Hapsburg in the near future was certain; hence the question of the Spanish succession formed the chief occupation of all the European cabinets after the **treaty of Ryswick.** The question had two aspects: (a) The *legal,* according to which there were three claimants: (1) **Louis XIV,** at once as son of the elder daughter of Philip III and husband of the elder daughter of Philip IV. The solemn renunciations of both princesses were declared null and void by the parlement of Paris. (2) **Leopold I,** the representative of the German line of Hapsburg, as son of the younger daughter of Philip III, and husband of the younger daughter of Philip IV. Both princesses had expressly reserved their right of inheritance. (3) The **electoral prince of Bavaria,** as great-grandson of Philip IV, and grandson of the younger sister of the present possessor, Charles II. (b) The *political* aspect with regard to the balance of power in Europe, in consideration of which the naval powers, England and Holland, would not permit the crown of the great Spanish monarchy to be united with the French, or to be worn by the ruler of the Austrian lands. On this account Leopold I claimed the Spanish inheritance for his second son Charles only, while Louis XIV's claim was urged in the name of his second grandson, Philip of Anjou.

1698, Oct. 11. First Treaty of Partition. Spain, Indies, and the Netherlands to the electoral prince of Bavaria; Naples and Sicily, seaports in Tuscany, and the province of Guipuzcoa, to the dauphin; the duchy of Milan, to Archduke Charles. The negotiations of the powers in regard to the succession, and the conclusion of a treaty of partition without the participation of Charles II, provoked that monarch. In order to preserve the unity of the monarchy, he made the prince elector of Bavaria, then seven years old, sole heir of the whole inheritance; a settlement to which the naval powers agreed.

1699, Feb. 6. Sudden death of the prince elector. New intrigues of France (Harcourt ambassador, Cardinal Portocarrero) and Austria at Madrid, while both parties were negotiating a new treaty of partition with the naval powers.

1700, Mar. 13. Second Treaty of Partition. Spain and the Indies to Archduke Charles;

The Battle of Cap La Hogue, May 1692

Naples and Sicily and the duchy of Lorraine to the dauphin; Milan to the duke of Lorraine in exchange. Finally Charles II, although originally more inclined to the Austrian succession, signed a new will, making Louis's grandson, Philip of Anjou, heir. Immediately afterward

1700, Nov. 1. Charles II died. Louis XIV soon decided to follow the will rather than the treaty with England. The duke of Anjou was proclaimed as **Philip V,** and started for his new kingdom. (*Il n'y a plus de Pyrénées.*)

1701, Sept. 7. Grand Alliance of the naval powers with the Emperor Leopold I, for the purpose, at first, of securing the Spanish possessions in the Netherlands and in Italy for the Austrian house, while France allied herself with the dukes of Savoy and Mantua, the electors of Bavaria and Köln. The other states of the Empire, especially Prussia, joined the emperor. Portugal afterward joined the Grand Alliance, and in 1703 Savoy did likewise, deserting France. Three men were at the head of the Grand Alliance against France: **Eugene, prince of Savoy,** imperial general; **Marlborough,** English general, formerly John Churchill; **Antonius Heinsius,** after the death of William III, 1702, pensionary of Holland. Spain, the real object of the war, had but little importance in the campaigns, the chief seats of war being Italy, the Netherlands, and Germany. Philip of Anjou was recognized in Spain as **King Philip V.** His strongest support was in Castile.

1701. Commencement of the war by Eugene's **invasion of Italy.** Victory over Catinat at Carpi, over Villeroy at **Chiara;** the latter was captured at Cremona (1702).

1702. Eugene and Vendôme fought a drawn **battle at Luzzara,** after which the French had the advantage in Italy until 1706.

1703. The **Bavarians invaded Tyrol,** but were repulsed. Eugene went to Germany along the Rhine. Marlborough invaded the Spanish Netherlands. The Archduke Charles landed in Spain, and invaded Catalonia, where he established himself as Charles III. **The English captured Gibraltar** (1704).

1704, Aug. 13. BATTLE OF HÖCHSTÄDT AND BLENHEIM (BLINDHEIM), (between Ulm and Donauwörth), Bavarians and French (Tallard) defeated by Eugene and Marlborough.

1706. Charles conquered Madrid but held it for a short time only.

May 23. VICTORY OF MARLBOROUGH AT RAMILLIES over Villeroy. Submission of Brussels, Antwerp, Ghent, Ostend, etc.

Sept. 7. VICTORY OF EUGENE AT TURIN, over Marsin and the duke of Orléans with the help of the Prussians under Leopold of Dessau. Submission of all Lombardy. Charles III proclaimed at Milan. **The French excluded from Italy.**

1708, July 11. VICTORY OF MARLBOROUGH AND EUGENE AT OUDENARDE over Vendôme and the duke of Burgundy. Siege and surrender of Lille.

Negotiations for peace. Demands of the allies: surrender of the Spanish monarchy to Charles of Austria, and of the border fortresses of the Netherlands to the Hollanders; restoration of all matters relating to the Empire and the emperor to the state prescribed in the peace of Westphalia, i.e. the cession of Strassburg, Breisach, etc. Britain insisted on the recognition of Anne and the Protestant succession and the banishment of the Pretender. These terms Louis was willing to accept, but when the demand was added that he should drive his grandson from Spain with French weapons, it was too much. The negotiations were broken off, Louis made a successful appeal to the people of France, and the war was continued.

1709, Sept. 11. BATTLE OF MALPLAQUET. The French were again beaten by Eugene and Marlborough, but, by no means broken, retired in good order. The bloodiest battle of the war. The argument of "butchery" helped overthrow the Whigs in England. The allies lost 20,000 men. New approaches on the part of Louis. Capture of Douai, Mons, etc. (1710). In Spain Philip, by the aid of Vendôme, had the advantage of Charles. The Spanish people favored Philip. Renewal of the negotiations at Gertruydenburg. Louis offered to pay subsidized troops against his grandson. The allies demanded that he should send his armies against Philip. Renewal of the war. Victories of Vendôme over the British (**Brihuega,** 1710) and the imperialists (**Villaviciosa,** in Spain).

1710, Aug. Fall of the Whig ministry in England, and accession of the enemies of Marlborough.

1711. Death of the Emperor Joseph, whereby Charles became heir of all the Austrian possessions, so that the monarchy of Charles V would have been restored had the Spanish inheritance also devolved upon him. These events completely altered all political relations, in favor of Louis XIV. **Marlborough** removed from command, the Grand Alliance dissolved, preliminaries of peace between Britain and France. Death of the dauphin, of Adelaide of Savoy, her husband, and their son, the duke of Brittany.

1712. Victory of the French commander Villars at **Denain** over Lord Albemarle. Recapture of Douai, Le Quesnoy, and Bouchain. Opening of the **congress at Utrecht.** Each of the allies presented his demands separately.

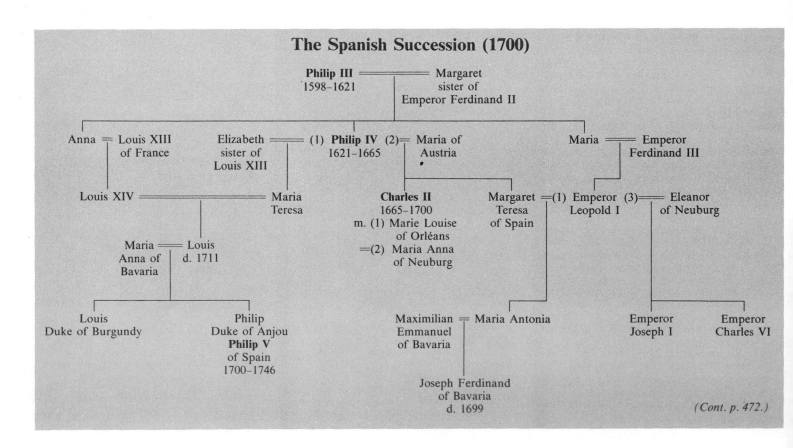

The Spanish Succession (1700)

(Cont. p. 472.)

The Battle of Malplaquet, September 11, 1709

Dissensions between the allies caused the conclusion of separate treaties of peace, which are comprehended under the name of the

1713, Apr. 11. TREATY OF UTRECHT.

(1) **Britain:** Recognition of the Protestant succession in England; confirmation of the permanent separation of the crowns of France and Spain. France ceded to Britain Newfoundland, Nova Scotia (Acadia), and Hudson Bay territory, but retained New France (Quebec); Spain ceded to Britain Gibraltar, the island of Minorca, and the *asiento,* or contract for supplying the Spanish colonies with African slaves.

(2) **Holland:** Surrender of the Spanish Netherlands to the Republic of Holland, in order that they should be delivered to the Austrians, after the conclusion of a barrier treaty, in regard to the fortresses along the French border from Furnes to Namur, which were to be garrisoned by the Dutch. Lille restored to France. Demolition of the fortifications of Dunkirk.

(3) **Savoy** received the island of Sicily as a kingdom, and an advantageous change of boundary in upper Italy, renounced its claims upon Spain, reserving, however, its right of

inheritance in case the house of Bourbon should become extinct.

(4) **Prussia** received recognition of the royal title, and possession of Neuchâtel and the upper quarter of Guelders. Prussia's claim upon the principality of Orange, on the Rhône, was transferred to France.

(5) **Portugal** obtained a correction of boundaries in South America.

Philip V (founder of the Spanish branch of the Bourbons) was recognized as king of Spain and the colonies.

Reservations in the peace: (1) for the emperor, the possession of the appanages of the Spanish monarchy, the Netherlands, Milan, Náples, Sardinia, but *not* Sicily; (2) for the Empire the *status quo* of the treaty of Ryswick, only.

1713. The emperor and the Empire continued the war. Unsuccessful campaign of Eugene, who was wretchedly supported. Landau and Freiburg taken by Villars. After these losses the emperor concluded peace with France, in his own name at Rastatt, in that of the Empire at Baden (in Switzerland).

1714, Mar.-Sept. TREATY OF RASTATT AND BADEN. Austria took possession of the

Spanish Netherlands, after the barrier for Holland had been agreed upon, and retained Naples, Sardinia, and Milan, which she had already occupied. For the Empire: ratification of the treaty of Ryswick; the electors of Bavaria and Köln, who had been placed under the ban of the Empire, were reinstated in their lands and dignities. Landau was left in the hands of France. No peace between Spain and the emperor, who did not recognize the Bourbons in Spain.

FRENCH LITERATURE AND ART, 17TH CENTURY

The 17th century was the **golden age of French literature,** with the baroque giving way to classicism, new status given to intellectual matters, the establishment of the *Académie française* (1635). The poet **François de Malherbe** (1555–1628) was critical of his baroque predecessors; the philosopher **Blaise Pascal** (1623–1662) wrote his *Pensées sur la religion* (1669) under the influence of Cornelius Jansen (1585–1638). The drama was the most important literary medium of the period. **Pierre Corneille** (1606–1684) violated the classical dramatic unities of time, place, and action in *Le Cid* (1636), thereby creating a great controversy as to their observance; the classical tradition, upheld by the Royal Academy, eventually won, and Corneille conformed to its dictates as did the other great tragedian, **Jean Racine** (1639–1699; *Phèdre,* 1677; *Bérénice,* 1670). **Molière** (Jean Baptiste Poquelin, 1622–1673) raised the standards of French comedy to a new level with his comedies of manners (*Les précieuses ridicules,* 1659; *Le misanthrope,* 1666; *Tartuffe,* 1669). This was also an age of fable, with the verse *Fables* of **Jean de La Fontaine** (1621–1695) and the *Contes de ma mère l'oye* of **Charles Perrault** (1628–1703); and an age of essays and letters (**Nicolas Boileau-Déspreaux,** 1636–1711; **Madame de Sévigné,** 1626–1696). In the field of history **Jean Mabillon** (1632–1707) *De re diplomatica* (1681); **Jacques Bossuet** (1627–1704) *Discours sur l'histoire universelle* (1681); **Pierre Bayle** (1647–1706) *Dictionnaire historique et critique* (1695–1697), a criticism of existing beliefs and

François de Malherbe, 1555–1628

Louis XV, 1715–1774

Marquise de Pompadour (1745–1764), by François Boucher

institutions, commonly regarded as the first important work of the Enlightenment.

The classical style prevailed in the paintings of **Nicolas Poussin** (1594–1665), **Claude Lorrain** (1600–1682), and **Charles LeBrun** (1619–1690). The tradition carried over too into the music of **Robert Cambert,** whose *Pastorale,* performed at the **Académie royal de musique** in Paris (1659), was the first opera in French, and to the operas of **Jean-Baptiste Lully** (1632–1687), who introduced ballets into his operas and collaborated with Molière to write *Le bourgeois gentilhomme* (1670).

The second half of the 17th century also marked the beginning of construction of many outstanding royal buildings in and about Paris (Versailles, Louvre, Hôtel des Invalides).

1715–1774. LOUIS XV, five years old, greatgrandson of Louis XIV. **Philip, duke of Orléans,** became regent during the minority of Louis XV (1715–1723), thus setting aside the will of Louis XIV. An attempt was made to use the higher nobility in government by means of councils, but this failed. Under the regent's favorite, **Cardinal Dubois,** a man of low birth who had risen through political skill, the foreign policy of Louis XIV was reversed. **Alliance with Britain and Holland.**

1718–1720. War with Spain *(p. 473).* By the **treaty of The Hague** (Feb. 17, 1720) the emperor received Sicily, and Savoy received Sardinia in exchange. In domestic policy, increased religious toleration of Protestants and Jansenists.

1718–1720. Law's Mississippi scheme. In his financial distress the regent grasped at the dazzling plans of the Scotsman **John Law.** Royal bank, Company of the West, grant of Louisiana. Characteristic boom phenomena—rise in value of stock of the Mississippi Company, inflation (made worse by paper). Sudden collapse of the company bringing widespread disaster (1720). Law's boom, like most such speculative manias, left behind it some definite achievements—increased shipping, some colonization in Louisiana, private fortunes for

those who had sold out in time. With the contemporary English **South Sea Bubble,** Law's scheme forms an introduction to modern speculative finance.

1723–1726. Administration of the duke of Bourbon. Louis XV married (1725) the daughter of the deposed king of Poland, **Stanislas Leszczynski,** having broken off a projected marriage with the infanta of Spain and sent her back, to the great indignation of Philip V. Louis was under the influence of his tutor, **Cardinal Fleury,** who replaced Bourbon and his favorite Prie, and banished them from court.

1726–1743. Administration of Fleury, generally peaceful, and marked by economic growth. Quarrels over the papal bull *Unigenitus,* marked by the government's abandonment of the Jansenists and their defense by the courts (*parlements*). Wave of religious revivalism, similar to Methodism in England (*convulsionnaires,* Archdeacon Pâris). Growth of deism among the literate classes.

1773–1738. France, with Spain and Sardinia, took part in the **War of the Polish Succession** *(p. 483)* and occupied Lorraine (1733).

1740–1748. War of the Austrian Succession (p. 501). France supported the claims of the Bavarian elector and allied with Frederick the Great against Maria Theresa (1741). This involved France in conflict with Britain, especially in North America and India *(pp. 532, 552).*

1756–1763. The **Seven Years' War** *(p. 485)* in which France played a leading rôle, but this time on the Austrian side, against Prussia. The war overseas led to the loss of most of the French colonial empire.

After the **death of Fleury,** a series of administrations influenced by the royal mistresses, especially the **marquise de Pompadour** (1745–1764), who helped make possible the Austrian alliance of 1756 (*The Diplomatic Revolution, p. 486*). Heavy expenditures, growth of luxury. The king, once *Louis le bien-aimé,* now hated. **Damiens,** who attempted to assassinate the king (Jan. 5, 1757), was tortured and killed.

In spite of general failure in war, France added in this reign Lorraine (1766) and Corsica (1768). In his old age, Louis came under the influence of the politically least able of his mistresses, the plebeian Jeanne Vaubernier, by marriage with a superannuated courtier, **Comtesse du Barry.**

Throughout the reign, quarrels with the parlements, especially that of Paris, which asserted a claim to something like a power of judicial review over the royal decrees. The parlements were abolished in 1771 by the chancellor, Maupéou, and a more simple and efficient system of courts set up, but the reform was very unpopular, and Louis XVI restored the parlements as one of the first acts of his reign. The crown was made still more unpopular by the affair of the *pacte de famine,* an attempted corner in the grain trade in which the king himself was implicated. Steady growth of a literature of attack on the government.

1774–1792. LOUIS XVI, grandson of Louis XV. The new king's personal morality and good will were neutralized by a lack of energy and understanding. As dauphin he had (1770) married **Marie Antoinette,** daughter of the Empress Maria Theresa. The queen, always unpopular with the anti-Austrians at court, was a proud and tactless woman, fond of dances, theaters, parties, and was easily made unpopular with the masses by the propaganda of the *philosophes* and their friends. (*"Let 'em eat cake."*) The scandal of the **diamond necklace** (1785) was especially disastrous to her reputation. She did much, by purely personal choices of favorites, to prevent any consistent or thoroughgoing reforms in French administration.

Yet the early years of the reign were marked by an effort, in keeping with the spirit of "Enlightened Despotism," to achieve reforms. **Robert Turgot,** minister of marine and finance (1774–1776), by the **Six Edicts** made reforms in taxation, dissolved the old trade guilds, and tried to carry out the *laissez-faire* economics of the **physiocrats,** of whom he was one of the leading thinkers. He was dismissed, partly by

Louis XVI, 1774–1792

Marie Antoinette, 1755–1793

istically rococo in spirit: **Antoine Watteau** (1684–1721), **François Boucher** (1703–1770), **Jean-Honoré Fragonard** (1732–1806). Most prominent sculptor was **Jean-Antoine Houdon** (1741–1828), whose subjects were the leading literary and political figures of the day.

The composers **François Couperin** (1668–1733) and **Jean-Philippe Rameau** (1683–1764) carried on the operatic tradition of Lully. **Jean Marie Leclair** (1697–1764) founded a French school of violin playing.

Voltaire, 1694–1778

Jean-Jacques Rousseau, 1712–1778

court intrigue, partly by the opposition of the guilds, and his work largely undone. **Jacques Necker,** a Swiss banker, was minister of finances (1777–1781) and effected piecemeal reforms. The greatest achievements of Louis's reforming ministers were those of the **comte de St. Germain** at the war office. The standing army was improved, especially in the artillery. St. Germain and his aids, **Guibert** and **Gribeauval,** did much to make the victories of the armies of 1792–1794 possible. **Maurepas** was the head of the ministry, 1774–1781, and on his death was succeeded by the **comte de Vergennes** (1781).

1778–1783. France intervened in the **War of American Independence** on the side of the colonists *(p. 541).* Her expenses in this war added disastrously to her financial deficit.

1781. Necker, dismissed from office, published a somewhat disingenuous *compte rendu* of the finances, the effect of which was to bring the deficit dramatically before the public. The next seven years were filled with the desperate expedients of a series of ministers to solve the financial problem. A solution was probably impossible without taxing heavily the *privilégiés* (nobles, state officials, clergy, and even certain commoners). These resisted the efforts of the government, no matter how well intentioned.

1783–1787. Calonne (minister of finances), a facile courtier, contracted an immense debt, but came in the end to the sensible decision to reform the land-tax thoroughly. He encountered resistance, and was forced out in favor of **Loménie de Brienne.** Meanwhile

1787, Feb. 22. An **assembly of notables,** a purely consultative body, with not very clear constitutional precedents, called to Versailles, was dissolved (May 25) without having achieved any real reform. Loménie de Brienne attempted to issue reform edicts on lines Calonne had worked out, but the parlements, headed by the parlement of Paris, refused to register them. The parlement of Paris was banished to Troyes (Aug. 14). Public opinion was in favor of the parlement, and its president,

d'Espréménil, became a hero, largely because he had defied the government. The parlement was recalled (Sept. 24), but continued its resistance when Brienne proposed new loans. In January 1788 it presented a list of grievances, and was abolished in favor of a *cour plénière* (May 8). Louis and his advisers now decided to give in to many pressures, and summon the old medieval legislative body of the realm, the **estates-general,** which had last met in 1614. In August 1788 Brienne resigned and amid popular rejoicing **Necker was recalled** to arrange for the estates. *(Cont. p. 608.)*

FRENCH LITERATURE AND ART, 18TH CENTURY

The 18th century was the **"Age of Enlightenment"** and its best authors wrote mostly prose. Charles-Louis de Secondat, **Baron de Montesquieu** (1689–1755) wrote letters and essays (*Lettres persanes,* 1721) and *L'Esprit des lois* (1748) which played a considerable part in establishing the ideas that culminated in the French Revolution. **Denis Diderot** (1713–1784) edited a 34-volume *Encyclopédie, ou dictionnaire raisonné des sciences, des arts et des métiers* to which the great contemporary writers contributed, using it as the medium for airing their views on individual liberty. The novel flourished: **Alain Lesage** (1668–1747), *Gil Blas* (1715) a picaresque novel; **L'Abbé Prévost** (1696–1763), *Manon Lescaut* (1731); and finally **Jean-Jacques Rousseau** (1712–1778; *Julie ou la nouvelle Héloïse,* 1761; *Émile,* 1762). It was in his essays (*Discourses,* 1750, 1755; *Le contrat social,* 1762) that Rousseau expounded his views of the "noble savage," of the "inalienable right" of the individual to equality before the law.

The political writings of **Voltaire** (François-Marie Arouet, le jeune, 1694–1778) were so critical of French institutions that he was forced to flee from France. He also wrote drama, poetry, histories (*Siècle de Louis XIV,* 1751; *Essai sur les moeurs,* 1756), literary criticism, letters, and message novels (*Candide,* 1759).

The paintings of the period were character-

4. *The Iberian Peninsula*

(From p. 411)

a. SPAIN, 1659–1807

The **peace of the Pyrenees** (1659) marked the end of the Spanish ascendancy in Europe, which now passed to France. Thenceforth Spain came to be looked upon increasingly as suitable spoil for the stronger states.

1665–1700. CHARLES II, the four-year-old son of Philip IV and the last of the Spanish Hapsburgs. Until 1676 his mother, **Maria Anna of Austria,** headed the council of regency. She, in turn, was wholly under the influence of her Jesuit advisers (**Everard Nitard,** *et al.*). The general laxity and incompetence of the government, as well as the queen-mother's preference for foreigners, aroused much opposition, led by **John Joseph of Austria** and some of the nobles. These ultimately effected the downfall of Nitard and even the departure of the queen-mother. Thereafter John Joseph controlled the king until the former's death in 1679.

1667–1668. The **War of Devolution** *(p. 465),* representing an attack by Louis XIV on the Spanish possessions in the Netherlands. He was forced, by the combined action of Eng-land, Holland, and Sweden, to restore most of his conquests, but by the **treaty of Aix-la-Chapelle** (May 2, 1668) Louis retained twelve fortified places in Flanders.

1674. Spain joined the coalition against France occasioned by Louis's attack on Holland. By the **treaty of Nimwegen** (Sept. 17, 1678) Spain, as the ally of Holland, lost to France Franche-Comté, Artois, and sixteen fortified places in Flanders *(p. 465).*

1680. Charles II married Marie Louise of Or-léans. On her death he

1689. Married Maria Anna, daughter of the elector palatine.

1690. Spain joined the League of Augsburg *(p. 467)* against Louis XIV. By the **treaty of Ryswick** (1697), which concluded the war, Spain was obliged to cede Haiti to France.

1698, Oct. 11. First partition treaty between England, Holland, and France, regarding the succession to Spain and the Spanish Empire. Charles, naturally irritated by this cavalier treatment,

1700, Oct. 3. Named **Philip of Anjou,** grandson of Louis XIV, heir to his dominions. The king, long ill, died on November 1.

1700–1746. PHILIP V, the first Bourbon king, 17-years-old at the time of his accession: a mediocre, irresolute, but pious ruler.

1701–1715. WAR OF THE SPANISH SUCCESSION *(p. 467).*

1703. The powers of the Grand Alliance against France proclaimed Archduke **Charles of Austria** as king of Spain.

1704, Aug. 4. The **English took Gibraltar,** which they have held ever since.

1705. Charles landed in Catalonia and took Barcelona (Oct. 14). Catalonia and Valencia, ever strongholds of anti-French sentiment, accepted Charles and supported him.

1706, June. The **Portuguese,** acting with the Grand Alliance, invaded Spain and occupied Madrid, but were driven out by Philip in October.

1707, Apr. The forces of the allies were defeated at **Almanza** by the duke of Berwick, in Spanish service.

1709. The British seized **Minorca.** Philip was defeated by the Austrians at **Almenara** and **Saragossa,** and

1710, Sept. 28. Charles took Madrid. Before long, however, Philip and the French won

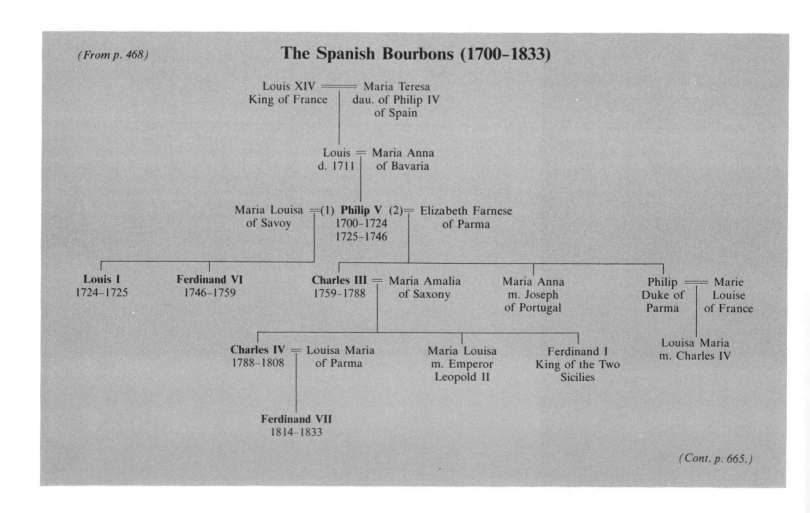

(From p. 468)

The Spanish Bourbons (1700–1833)

Louis XIV === Maria Teresa
King of France | dau. of Philip IV
of Spain

Louis === Maria Anna
d. 1711 | of Bavaria

Maria Louisa ===(1) **Philip V** (2)=== Elizabeth Farnese
of Savoy | 1700–1724 | of Parma
1725–1746

Louis I — **Ferdinand VI** — **Charles III** === Maria Amalia — Maria Anna — Philip === Marie
1724–1725 | 1746–1759 | 1759–1788 | of Saxony | m. Joseph | Duke of | Louise
of Portugal | Parma | of France

Charles IV === Louisa Maria — Maria Louisa — Ferdinand I — Louisa Maria
1788–1808 | of Parma | m. Emperor | King of the Two | m. Charles IV
Leopold II | Sicilies

Ferdinand VII
1814–1833

(Cont. p. 665.)

victories at **Brihuega** and **Villaviciosa** (Dec. 10) and Charles was obliged to abandon Madrid again.

1713, Apr. 11. The **treaty of Utrecht** (p. 483). Philip was recognized as king of Spain by Britain and Holland, on condition that the French and Spanish crowns should never be united. At the same time he ceded to his father-in-law, Victor Amadeus of Savoy, the island of Sicily. The British retained Gibraltar and Minorca and secured the *asiento,* a contract allowing them to import into the Spanish colonies 4,000 Negroes a year and to keep one ship stationed at Porto Bello.

1713, May. The **Salic law** was introduced in Spain to govern the succession to the throne.

1714, Mar. 6. **Treaty of Rastatt,** ending the war with Austria. Spain gave up her possessions in Flanders (henceforth the Austrian Netherlands), Luxemburg, and Italy.

Sept. 11. **Barcelona** finally capitulated to Berwick. The privileges of Catalonia and Valencia had already been declared abolished (1707). The provinces were now put under Castilian law and the use of the Catalan language was forbidden in the courts.

With the end of the War of Succession the **Bourbon rule in Spain** may be said to have begun, properly speaking. The rulers of the line soon proved themselves to be no more efficient than the later Hapsburgs and the court continued to be a hotbed of intrigue, dynastic and personal. On the other hand, the Bourbon kings regarded themselves as absolute rulers and did their utmost to reduce the old feudal privileges. They reorganized the administration (central secretariats in the place of the old commissions) and established a bureaucracy (intendants, corregidores). An impressive number of **reforming ministers** succeeded each other through the century, of whom may be mentioned Patiño, Ensenada, Aranda, Floridablanca, Campomanes, Jovellaños, and Godoy. They succeeded in putting the finances on a sounder basis, in rebuilding the army and navy (introduction of conscription—every fifth man), and above all devoted themselves to economic development—road- and bridge-building, encouragement of industry and trade, establishment of technical schools, agricultural improvements, etc.

1714. **Philip married Elizabeth Farnese** of Parma, on the death of his first wife, Maria Louisa of Savoy. Elizabeth was a handsome, alert, and very ambitious woman, who soon had the king wholly under her influence. With the aid of her adviser, Abbé (later Cardinal) **Giulio Alberoni,** an Italian of humble extraction, she devoted herself to the problem of supplanting the Austrian power in Italy and providing Italian thrones for her children. Philip, on the other hand, appears to have hoped for many years to succeed to the French throne and did his utmost to undermine the position of the French regent, the duke of Orléans. Thus Spain antagonized both France and Austria at the same time.

1717. Philip secretly sent an expeditionary force which seized Sardinia, and, later (July 1718), Sicily also.

1718, Aug. 2. Conclusion of the **Quadruple Alliance** (Britain, France, Holland, and Austria) to counteract the attempts of Philip to overturn the peace settlements. The British fleet landed an Austrian force in Sicily, while

Charles IV and His Family, *by Francisco Goya, 1746–1828*

the French invaded the Basque country and Catalonia. The war was concluded by

1720, Feb. 17. The **treaty of The Hague,** by which Philip abandoned his Italian claims in return for an Austrian promise of the succession to Parma, Piacenza, and Tuscany for Charles, the eldest son of Philip and Elizabeth Farnese. At the same time the emperor gave up his claims to Spain. Savoy was given Sardinia in place of Sicily, which was turned over to Austria.

1721, June. Spain joined the alliance of Britain and France. Louis, son of Philip by his first wife, married Louise Elizabeth of Orléans (1722), while Louis XV of France was betrothed to a daughter of Philip and Elizabeth, who was then only five years old.

1724. **Abdication of Philip,** for reasons not clear. He was succeeded by his son

1724. **LOUIS I,** who, however, died in the same year. Philip then resumed the crown.

1725. The **duke of Bourbon,** chief minister of Louis XV of France, eager for an heir to the throne, cancelled the engagement of the king to the girl-princess of Spain. In reply Philip allied himself with Austria (work of the adventurer, Baron de Ripperdá) by the **treaty of Vienna** (Apr. 30, 1725). This alliance, in turn, provoked the **treaty of Hanover** (Sept. 3) between Britain, France, Prussia, and Holland.

1727–1729. **War with Britain and France.** By the **treaty of Seville** (Nov. 1729), Britain and France agreed to the Spanish succession in the Italian duchies.

1731. **Charles,** the son of Philip and Elizabeth, on the extinction of the Farnese family, succeeded to the Italian duchies. At the same

time Spain recognized the **Pragmatic Sanction** of Charles VI *(p. 482)*.

1733. First *pacte de famille* between France and Spain. Spain thereupon joined France in

1733–1735. The **War of the Polish Succession** *(p. 483)* against Austria. A Spanish force was sent to invade Lombardy, while another seized Naples and Sicily (1734). By the **treaty of Vienna** (Nov. 13, 1738) Austria gave up Naples and Sicily *(p. 483)* and received Parma and Piacenza.

1739–1741. **War of Jenkins' Ear,** with Great Britain *(p. 457)*.

1740–1748. **War of the Austrian Succession** *(p. 483)*. Spain took part in the war as the ally of France against Austria. By the **treaty of Aix-la-Chapelle** (1748), Philip, the second son of Philip V and Elizabeth, was given the duchies of Parma, Piacenza, and Guastalla, while his brother Charles retained Naples and Sicily. Thus the dynastic aspirations of their mother were realized.

1746–1759. **FERDINAND VI,** the second son of Philip V by his first wife. Ferdinand was a good but timid ruler, who did but little to impress his age or his people.

1754. **Concordat with the Vatican.** Thereby the Spanish church became practically independent of Rome and was placed under the control of the government.

1756–1763. The **Seven Years' War** *(p. 485)*. Spain at first remained neutral, though Spanish troops recovered **Minorca** (1756).

1759–1788. **CHARLES III,** son of Elizabeth Farnese and thitherto king of the Two Sicilies, which he now passed on to his son Ferdinand. Charles has been classified as one of the enlightened despots and he did, in fact, give considerable impetus to administrative and economic reform.

1761, Aug. 15. Second *pacte de famille* with France, against Britain. In this generally defensive arrangement the Bourbon states of Italy were included.

Joseph Bonaparte, King of Spain, 1807

1762. Spain joined in the war against Britain. The British seized Cuba and the Philippines. By the **treaty of Paris** (Feb. 10, 1763) Spain recovered these possessions, but lost Minorca and Florida. In return for the loss of Florida, France ceded Louisiana to Spain.

1767, Mar. 1. Without warning or trial the king secretly expelled the **Jesuits** from Spain. Some 10,000 of them were deported to the Papal States.

1779, June. Spain joined France in the **War of American Independence** against Britain. The Spaniards seized Florida and Honduras and Minorca (1782), but failed to retake Gibraltar (1779–1783). By the **treaty of Versailles** (Sept. 3, 1783), Spain retained both Minorca and Florida.

1788–1808. CHARLES IV, the son of Charles III, a well-intentioned but weak and undecided ruler. A portrait of his family was painted (1800) by the great Spanish artist **Francisco Goya** (1746–1828). His ministers, **Conde de Floridablanca** and **Conde de Aranda,** made great efforts to shut out the teaching and influence of the French Revolution, and the Spanish court did its utmost to save the life of Louis XVI, but the queen effected the overthrow of Aranda and brought into power her favorite, **Manuel Godoy.**

1793, Mar. 7. FRANCE DECLARED WAR ON SPAIN. Spain made an alliance with Great Britain (Mar. 13) and the Spaniards invaded Roussillon and Navarre. But in 1794–1795 the French took the offensive, invading

Catalonia and Guipúzcoa. By the **treaty of Basel** (June 22, 1795), the French returned their conquests and secured in return Santo Domingo. Godoy was given the title *Prince of the Peace.*

1796, Aug. 19. Treaty of San Ildefonso. Spain joined France in the war against Britain. Defeat of the Franco-Spanish fleet at **Cape St. Vincent** (Feb. 14, 1797). The British seized Trinidad.

1800, Oct. 1. Second treaty of San Ildefonso. France secured Louisiana in return for a promise to enlarge Parma. By agreement of January 20, 1801, Spain promised to detach Portugal from Britain, by force if necessary. This latter provision resulted in the **War of the Oranges,** between Spain and Portugal.

1802, Mar. Treaty of Amiens, between Great Britain, France, and Spain. The Spaniards secured Minorca but abandoned Trinidad.

1805, Jan. 4. Spain entered the **War of the Third Coalition** on the side of France. Defeat of the Franco-Spanish fleet at **Trafalgar** (Oct. 21, 1805). Growing opposition of the Spanish people to the disastrous Francophile policy of Godoy. Ferdinand, the heir to the throne, soon emerged as the leader of the opposition.

1807, Oct. 27. Treaty of Fontainebleau, between Napoleon and Spain. Portugal was to be divided between Charles IV and Godoy (who was to become prince of the Algarves, under Spanish suzerainty). The French were to aid in the conquest, and a French army, under **Junot,** soon arrived in Spain. Invasion

Horatio Nelson receiving the surrender of the Spanish admiral at Cape St. Vincent, February 14, 1797

Proclamation of the Peace of Amiens at the Royal Exchange, London, 1802

of Portugal and capture of Lisbon (Nov. 30, 1807).

1807, Mar. 17.   Popular uprising against Godoy at Aranjuez.   Charles thereupon abdicated (Mar. 19), but **Murat,** who arrived soon afterward at Madrid, induced the king to retract his abdication and persuaded both Charles and Ferdinand to meet Napoleon.

Apr. 30.   The Bayonne Conference.   Napoleon told Ferdinand to abdicate the throne he had just assumed.   Then Charles was forced to abdicate in Napoleon's favor (May 10). Both princes were given estates in France and handsome pensions.

June 6.   JOSEPH, Napoleon's brother, became king of Spain.

In the early 18th century encouragement was afforded Spanish culture with the founding of the National Library (1712), the Royal Spanish Academy (1714), and the Academy of History (1735); but there was little significant literary production in the period (a novel, *Fray Gerundio* [1758], by **José Francisco de Isla y Rojo,** 1703–1781). *(Cont. pp. 622, 664.)*

b. PORTUGAL, 1640–1807

(From p. 412)

The story of Portugal in this period parallels that of Spain.   The period was one of growing weakness, economically and socially, accompanied by a growth of the royal power.   The last cortes was called in 1697.   The nobility became more and more a court group, dependent on royal favor.   The Church, too, was subjected to the state, though within the country the Church possessed great wealth and exercised immense influence.

1640–1656.   JOHN (João) IV, first king of the house of Braganza.   He was recognized almost at once by France and Holland, but Spain fostered a plot of Portuguese nobles against him. This was discovered and the leaders executed. Hostilities with Spain continued in desultory fashion.   In 1644 the Portuguese, supported by England and France, took the offensive and invaded Spain **(victory of Montijo).**   This brought a suspension of operations for some years.

1654.   The **Dutch** were finally driven from Brazil, where they had established themselves during the Spanish period.

1656–1667.   AFONSO VI, a frivolous, profligate, and vicious young man, during the first period of whose reign his mother, **Luisa María de Guzmán,** served as regent.   In these years hostilities with Spain were reopened. The Spaniards were defeated at **Elvas** (Jan. 14, 1659), and, when they attempted to invade Portugal (1662) were again overwhelmed **(battle of Ameixal,** June 8, 1663) in a series of Portuguese victories in 1664–1665.

1662.   Charles II of England married Catherine, the daughter of John IV, thus preparing the way for ever closer relations between England and Portugal.

1667.   Peter (Pedro), the brother of Afonso, led the opposition to the outrageous conduct of the king.   He set himself up as regent and exiled Afonso to the Azores (d. 1683).   Peter's rule was more respectable and enjoyed wide popular support.

1668, Feb. 13.   Conclusion of **peace with Spain,** through the mediation of Charles II of England.   Spain at last recognized Portuguese independence.

1683–1706.   PETER II ruled as king after the death of Afonso.   His reign was memorable for the conclusion of the

1703, Dec. 27.   Methuen-Alegrete agreement, by which British wool and woolens were to be admitted into Portugal duty-free, and Portuguese wine to be admitted into England at a greatly reduced rate.   The agreement resulted in great gains in the Portuguese trade for the British, at French and Spanish expense.

1704.   Invasion of Portugal by a French-Spanish force, as a result of Portuguese participation in the War of the Spanish Succession. The British landed a force at Lisbon and joined the Portuguese in driving out the enemy.

1706.   Anglo-Portuguese invasion of Spain and brief **occupation of Madrid** (June).

1706–1750.   JOHN V, the son of Peter II, a profligate, extravagant, and bigoted ruler, during whose reign the court became another Versailles (construction of the **Mafra palace**), filled with mistresses and favorites.

1707, Apr. 25.   Battle of Almanza.   Defeat of the Anglo-Portuguese army by the French forces under Marshal Berwick.   Thereafter Portugal played no further part in the war.

1750–1777.   JOSEPH I, during whose entire reign the government of the country was in the hands of the **marquis de Pombal** (Sebastião José de Carvalho e Mello, who became marquis de Pombal only in 1770), the most remarkable statesman of modern Portuguese history.   Pombal was a ruthless and heartless

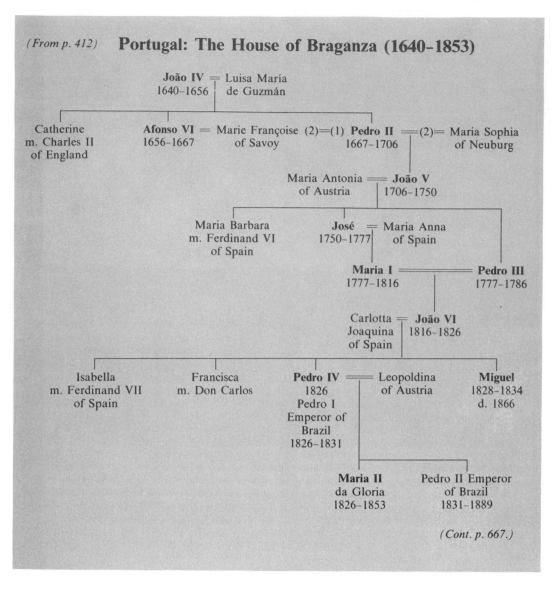

Portugal: The House of Braganza (1640–1853)

(From p. 412)

João IV = Luisa María
1640–1656   de Guzmán

Catherine
m. Charles II
of England

Afonso VI = Marie Françoise (2)=(1) **Pedro II** =(2) Maria Sophia
1656–1667   of Savoy   1667–1706   of Neuburg

Maria Antonia == **João V**
of Austria   1706–1750

Maria Barbara   **José** = Maria Anna
m. Ferdinand VI   1750–1777   of Spain
of Spain

Maria I =========== **Pedro III**
1777–1816   1777–1786

Carlotta = **João VI**
Joaquina   1816–1826
of Spain

Isabella   Francisca   **Pedro IV** == Leopoldina   **Miguel**
m. Ferdinand VII   m. Don Carlos   1826   of Austria   1828–1834
of Spain   Pedro I   d. 1866
                                      Emperor of
                                      Brazil
                                      1826–1831

Maria II   Pedro II Emperor
da Gloria   of Brazil
1826–1853   1831–1889

(Cont. p. 667.)

dictator, but at the same time a man affected by the French philosophy of the enlightenment. He devoted himself to breaking the power of the privileged nobility and even more of the Church. On the other hand, he reformed the finances and the army, encouraged industry and trade (establishment of trade companies with monopolistic powers), tried to revive agriculture (silk-raising), and did much to develop primary and technical education.

1755, Nov. 1. The **GREAT EARTHQUAKE AT LISBON,** which was accompanied by fire and by flood of the Tagus. Tens of thousands lost their lives in the disaster. Lisbon was destroyed, with many of its treasures. The city was rebuilt under Pombal's energetic direction.

1758, Sept. Conspiracy of the Tavoras, a plot by a group of nobles against the king and more especially against Pombal. The leaders, among them members of the highest aristocracy, were tortured and executed.

1759, Sept. 3. Expulsion of the Jesuits, who were deported to the Papal States. This was a direct result of the Tavora conspiracy, in which some Jesuits were involved. Pombal thus set the example for Spain and other states and in fact took a leading part in inducing the pope to abolish the Society of Jesus (1773).

1761. During the Seven Years' War, the Portuguese stood by Great Britain. The result was an invasion by Spanish and French forces, repulsed with British aid (Dec. 1762).

1774. Insanity of Joseph I, and regency of his wife, **Maria Anna.** She began gradually to reduce the power of Pombal.

1777–1816. MARIA I, the daughter of Joseph I, queen. She married her uncle, Peter, who assumed the title of king as **Peter III,** but who died in 1786. Under Maria the nobility began to recover its position. Pombal was exiled (d. 1782), but his reform policies were continued at a reduced pace.

The great earthquake at Lisbon, November 1, 1755

1792. Insanity of Maria and regency of her son John. John, ardently supported by the clergy, undertook a drastic repression of all revolutionary agitation and thought.

1801, Feb.-Sept. War of the Oranges, with Spain, resulting from the bargain made between Spain and France. After a Spanish invasion the Portuguese made peace. By the **treaty of Madrid** (Sept. 29) Portugal paid a heavy indemnity and renounced the treaties with Britain.

1807, Oct. 27. Treaty of Fontainebleau between France and Spain, envisaging the **partition of Portugal.** The provinces of Entre-Douro and Minho (with Oporto) were to go to Louis, king of Etruria, who was to become king of Northern Lusitania. Alentejo and Algarve were to go to Godoy as prince of the Algarves; Beira, Tras-ós-Montes, and Estramadura were to be disposed of later.

Nov. 30. Lisbon was taken by a French army under Junot, assisted by the Spanish. The Portuguese royal family thereupon fled to Brazil. *(Cont. pp. 622, 666.)*

5. *Italy and the Papacy*

(From p. 419)

a. ITALY (GENERAL), 1600-1800

Italy remained, during the late 17th and in the 18th centuries, a mere geographical expression, politically divded and for the most part under foreign rule. But the cultural decadence of the 17th century gave way in the 18th to a remarkable flowering which again made Italy an important factor in European art and thought and contributed much to the general European enlightenment. In music Italy was outstanding. **Niccolò Amati** (1596-1684) and **Antonio Stradivari** (1644-1737) built the finest stringed instruments; the **opera** (dating from 1600) was brought to a high stage of development by **Claudio Monteverdi** (1567-1643), **Giovanni Pergolesi** (1710-1736), **Domenico Cimarosa** (1749-1801), and **Giovanni Paisiello** (1741-1816). **Girolamo Frescobaldi** (1583-1643), composer of organ music; **Arcangelo Corelli** (1653-1713), eminent violinist and composer of sonatas and concerti grossi; **Alessandro Scarlatti** (1659-1725), of operas; and **Antonio Vivaldi** (c. 1678-1741), of chamber music. Two great schools of music at Venice and Naples.

Lorenzo Bernini (1598-1680), architect and sculptor, was one of the leading artists of the baroque period, which preceded the rococo of the 18th century and the classical revival represented by **Antonio Canova** (1757-1822). **Bernini** designed and built the Vatican Palace and St. Peter's Square, while **Francesco Borromini** (1599-1667) reconstructed St. John Lateran and built other Roman churches.

In painting, **Giambattista Tiepolo** (1696-1770) for a time brought Venice a final burst of glory. Other artists: the painter Antonio Canale (**Canaletto,** 1697-1768); the engraver **Giovanni Battista Piranesi** (1720-1778), whose etchings of Rome appeared in *Le antichità romane;* the sculptor **Antonio Canova.**

The **Academy of Arcadia** (1692) started a widespread vogue of the conventional and artificial in literature, which, however, was counterbalanced by the comedies of **Carlo Goldoni** (1707-1793) and the serious patriotic dramas of **Vittorio Alfieri** (1749-1803). A return to classicism was apparent in the dramas of Goldoni as well as in the work of Alfieri and the poetry of **Giacomo Leopardi** (1798-1837). **Alessandro Manzoni** (1785-1873), lyric poet and dramatist, wrote the one great historical novel of Italy, *I promessi sposi* (*The Betrothed,* 1826).

But Italy was pre-eminent also in the fields of social and physical science. **Pietro Giannone** (1676-1748) created a profound stir with his anti-clerical *Istoria civile del regno di Napoli* (1723); **Antonio Genovesi** (1712-1769) was an outstanding physiocrat; another distinguished economist was **Pietro Verri** (1728-1797); **Giambattista Vico** (1668-1744), with his *Scienza nuova* (1725), laid the basis of the modern philosophy of history; while **Cesare Beccaria** (1738-1794) in his *Dei delitti e delle pene* (1764) founded the modern science of penology. In the natural sciences **Lazzaro Spallanzani** (1729-1799) made fundamental contributions to the study of digestion, while **Luigi Galvani** (1737-1798) and **Alessandro Volta** (1745-1827) were in the front rank among the pioneers of electricity.

b. THE PAPACY, 1644-1799

[For a complete list of the Roman popes see Appendix IV.]

(From p. 418)

Most of the popes of the later 17th and 18th centuries were altogether worthy men, but the currents of the time were against the Papacy. By attempting to remain neutral in the great conflicts between the Bourbons and the Hapsburgs, the popes sacrificed the support of both. Furthermore, the Church before long became divided on the question of **Jansenism** (from **Cornelius Jansenius,** bishop of Ypres, who died in 1638, leaving a famous book, *Augustinus,* published in 1640. In this he emphasized inner regeneration rather than external reorganization of the Church, as represented by the Jesuits). Jansenism and Jesuitism soon came into conflict and the Papacy was sapped in the process. The enlightenment of the 18th century completed the development and by the time of the French Revolution the Papacy appeared as an ineffectual and outworn, as well as superfluous institution.

1644-1655. INNOCENT X (Giambattista Pamfili), a pope who was entirely under the control of his sister-in-law, **Olympia Maidalchini,** whose machinations brought about almost complete financial collapse. The pope denounced the **treaty of Westphalia** because of the abolition of bishoprics, etc., but the protest was of no effect. By the bull *Cum occasione impressionis libri* (May 31, 1653) the pope condemned five propositions in the work of Jansenius, thus initiating the **Jansenist controversy.**

1655-1667. ALEXANDER VII (Fabio Chigi), an honest and cultured, but apathetic pontiff, who left the conduct of affairs to his nephew, **Flavio Chigi.** Beginning of friction with Louis XIV over the prerogatives of the Church.

1667-1669. CLEMENT IX (Giulio Rospigliosi), elected by French influence. He attempted to mediate between Jesuits and Jansenists, but died before much could be achieved.

1670-1676. CLEMENT X (Cardinal Altieri), regarded as pro-Spanish. He disapproved of the French alliance with the Turks and did what he could to support the war of the Hapsburgs against the enemy.

1676-1689. INNOCENT XI (Benedetto Odescalchi), one of the outstanding popes of the period. He undertook a much-needed financial reorganization of the Papacy, refused to practice nepotism, enforced regulations to improve the morality of the clergy. At the same time he financed the Austrians in their campaigns against the Turks. The **conflict with Louis XIV** came to a head when the French ruler called a church assembly at St. Germain (1682) which adopted the **four articles:** (1) sovereigns are not subject to the pope in temporal matters; (2) a general council is superior to a pope; (3) the power of the pope is subject to the regulations of a council and a pope cannot decide contrary to the rules of the Gallican Church; (4) decisions of the Papacy are not irrevocable. In reply to these articles the pope refused to invest as bishops any French clerics who had taken part in the assembly. Ultimately 35 French bishoprics were vacant. Further friction developed. The pope protested against the suppression and expulsion of the Huguenots and actually approved the expedition of William III to England, as part of an anti-French policy.

1689-1691. Alexander VIII (Pietro Ottoboni).

1691-1700. INNOCENT XII (Antonio Pignatelli), another able pope. By the bull *Romanum decet pontificem* (1692) he definitely limited the number of offices that could be held by relatives of the pope, thus putting an end to nepotism in its worst form. He also checked the sale of offices. In 1697 he made peace with France, winning a substantial victory. **Louis XIV abrogated the four articles** of 1682, probably in order to win support in the matter of the Spanish succession.

1700-1721. CLEMENT XI (Gian Francesco Albani), an upright priest, who, though he inclined toward France, attempted to maintain neutrality in the Bourbon-Hapsburg struggle. The Austrians therefore ignored papal claims. In the course of the war they occupied Parma and Piacenza, marched through the Papal States and conquered Naples. In 1709 the pope was obliged to recognize Charles as king of Spain. But Clement's pontificate was noteworthy chiefly for the renewed **condemnation of Jansenism,** which had made extraordinary progress in France. The bull *Unigenitus* (Sept. 8, 1713) was a landmark in the controversy.

1721-1724. Innocent XIII (Michelangelo dei Conti), a kind but ineffectual pope, who was followed by two other unimportant pontiffs,

1724-1730. Benedict XIII (Pietro Francesco Orsini), and

1730-1740. Clement XII (Lorenzo Corsini).

1740-1758. BENEDICT XIV (Prospero Lambertini), a charming, learned, and seriousminded pope. He was much influenced by the enlightenment in Europe, was a friend of Voltaire and Montesquieu, did much to encourage agriculture and trade. His policy was to seek a compromise with the absolute rulers, whose efforts to establish national churches had so much weakened the Papacy. Conclusion of **concordats with Naples** (1741) and **Spain** (1753) were important steps in this direction, though they cost the Papacy far-reaching concessions.

1758-1769. CLEMENT XIII (Carlo Rezzonico), a pope elected through the efforts of the Jesuits (*Zelanti*), but who proved too weak and mild to save them. The Jesuits had become unpopular as a result of Jansenist attacks, and because of their interference in politics, their engagement in commercial and industrial enterprise, etc. Their expulsion from Portugal (1759) and France (1762) set the ball rolling, and the next pope,

1769-1774. CLEMENT XIV (Lorenzo Ganganelli), was unable to resist the pressure of the Bourbon governments. By the breve *Dominus ac redemptor noster* (July 21, 1773) the **Society of Jesus was ordered dissolved.**

1775-1799. PIUS VI, during whose pontificate the Papacy felt the full force of the revolutionary doctrine. The pope tried to deter Emperor Joseph II from his anti-clerical policy, but was soon confronted with the radical anticlericalism of the French Revolution. As a result the French armies invaded papal territory (1796) and, after a short truce, intervened in Rome to set up the revolutionary **Roman Republic** (1798). The pope was taken off to southern France (Valence), where he died in the next year. *(Cont. pp. 618, 624, 675.)*

c. SAVOY (SARDINIA), 1638-1796

(From p. 418)

The beginning of the period was one of almost complete eclipse for Savoy, where the **regency of Duchess Christine** for her son, Charles Emmanuel II, formed a long interlude of conflict between the French and Spanish factions and brought on a decisive weakening of the ducal power. In the 18th century, however,

Savoy re-emerged as a strong military state (the Prussia of Italy).

1638-1675. CHARLES EMMANUEL II, who came of age in 1648, submitted to the domination of his mother until her death in 1663. His reign was scarred by the horrible **massacres of the Waldenses** (1655) which stirred the indignation of Europe.

1675-1730. VICTOR AMADEUS II. His mother, **Jeanne de Nemours,** acted as regent not only until the young duke attained his majority, but until 1684. She continued the Francophile orientation of Savoyard policy. In 1681 Louis XIV appropriated Casale as part of his reunion plan.

1685. Further persecution of the heretics, at the behest of Louis XIV.

1690. The duke at last made a break in the pro-French policy and joined the League of Augsburg against the French. But in 1696, hoping to make better terms with Louis, he reversed himself and received Pinerolo in return. The French and Savoyard forces obliged the powers of the league to evacuate Italy and agree to its neutralization for the duration of the war.

1701, Apr. War of the Spanish Succession *(p. 467)*. Victor Amadeus stuck by the French connection and allowed the French to occupy Milan and Mantua. But once again the duke changed sides, joining the Grand Alliance in 1703. As a result the French, under Vendôme, overran Savoy in 1704, but the Austrians, under **Prince Eugene of Savoy,** relieved the situation in 1705. During the following year the French again invaded and besieged Turin until, in September, they were again driven out by Prince Eugene. Occupation of Milan by the Austrians and Savoyards (Sept. 24). This practically ended the war in Italy.

1713. By the **treaty of Utrecht,** Victor Amadeus was awarded Sicily as his share of the Spanish spoils. At the same time he assumed the royal title.

1717. A Spanish raid on Sicily resulted in war *(p. 473)* and a new peace settlement, by which

1720. Victor Amadeus gave up Sicily to Austria and received in exchange the island of Sardinia. Henceforth he was king of Sardinia.

1730-1773. CHARLES EMMANUEL III, king. He joined France and Spain in the War of the Polish Succession, in the hope of driving the Austrians out of Italy. By the **treaty of Vienna** (Oct. 3, 1735), however, his possessions remained unchanged.

1742-1747. Savoy sided with Austria in the War of the Austrian Succession, and by the **treaty of Aix-la-Chapelle** (1748) was rewarded with that part of the duchy of Milan which lay west of the Ticino.

Savoy-Piedmont had relatively little share in the intellectual and artistic life of Italy, being essentially a military state. The army, however, was not nearly strong enough to resist the storms of the French Revolution.

1773-1796. VICTOR AMADEUS III. Strongly anti-revolutionary by temperament and policy, the king in 1792 joined Austria in the war against France, rejecting French offers of Lombardy. His territories were soon overrun by the French and

1796. Napoleon's appearance in Italy sealed the fate of the kingdom. The armies of the king were quickly defeated and, by the **armistice of Cherasco** (Apr. 28) the king was

obliged to abandon the Austrian alliance. Napoleon's defeat of the Austrians led to a fundamental remaking of the whole Italian situation *(p. 614)*. *(Cont. pp. 614, 668.)*

d. NAPLES, 1707-1825

(From p. 419)

The Spanish rule continued in Naples until the War of the Spanish Succession (p. 481). During this conflict

1707. The Austrians occupied Naples, and

1713. By the **treaty of Utrecht,** Spain ceded to Austria Sardinia and Naples, while Sicily passed to Savoy. In 1720 Austria exchanged Sardinia for Sicily, but, after the War of the Polish Succession

1735. Austria ceded Naples and Sicily to the Spanish Bourbons, on condition that they should never be united with Spain as one crown.

1735-1759. CHARLES III (son of Philip V of Spain), king of Naples and Sicily. His reign was one of reform and enlightenment, guided by **Bernardo Tanucci.** Restriction of feudal privilege, reform of finance and taxation, reorganization of prisons, reduction of church wealth and power (**concordat of 1741**). Naples the musical and intellectual center of Italy. Excavation of Herculaneum (1738) and discovery of the temples at Paestum (1752) paved the way for neo-classicism in art (Winckelmann, etc.).

1759-1825. FERDINAND I, the third son of Charles, succeeded to the throne when his father was called to assume the Spanish crown. Ferdinand was only nine years old, and continued under the influence of Tanucci until the latter's fall in 1771. By that time his wife, **Maria Carolina** (daughter of Maria Theresa) already dominated him. She, in turn, followed the lead of an English adventurer, **Sir John Acton,** who was busily engaged in rebuilding the Neapolitan army and navy. The result of Maria Carolina's policy was to break down the Spanish influence and to direct the king toward the Austrian connection.

(Cont. pp. 629, 668.)

e. OTHER STATES, 1645-1790

(From p. 419)

VENICE continued to fall into ever deeper decline, the old aristocratic rule becoming ever more unsuited to the demands of the European world. In international affairs Venice became entirely devoted to peace and neutrality, and only in the wars with the Turks was there some reflection of earlier glory.

1645-1669. The **Candian War** *(p. 443)*, during the earlier part of which the Venetians won resounding naval victories at the Dardanelles (under Grimani and Mocenigo). The war ultimately centered on the siege of Candia (1658-1669). France came to the aid of Venice and the Venetians themselves put up a stout defense, under **Francesco Morosini.** Finally, however, the Venetians were obliged to yield. By the peace settlement they lost Candia (Crete).

1684. Venice joined with Austria and Poland in the war against the Turks *(p. 499)*. In 1685 Morosini began the **conquest of the Morea,**

which was completed in 1687. The Venetians even captured Athens (explosion of the ammunition stores in the Parthenon). By the **treaty of Karlowitz** *(p. 499)*, the Venetians retained the Morea.

1718. By the **treaty of Passarowitz** *(p. 500)*, the Venetians, who had joined in the Turkish War at the side of the Austrians, lost the Morea. Thenceforth Venice retained only the Ionian Islands and the Dalmatian coast. Politically Venice stagnated, while artistically it remained one of the most active centers in Europe.

MILAN remained under Spanish rule until, by

1713. The **treaty of Utrecht** it passed to Austria. Mantua was incorporated with the duchy of Milan, after the last Gonzaga had, in 1701, sold it to Louis XIV.

Parma and Piacenza changed hands several times during the 18th century.

1731. On the extinction of the Farnese family, the duchies were given to Charles, the son of Philip V of Spain and his second wife, Elizabeth Farnese. In 1733 (War of the Polish Succession) Charles conquered Naples and Sicily, and these territories were awarded him in the peace settlement. In return he abandoned Parma and Piacenza to Austria.

1748. As a result of the **War of the Austrian Succession,** Maria Theresa ceded Parma and

Pasquale Paoli (1730)

Piacenza to **Philip,** the younger brother of Charles of Naples. Philip ruled until 1765 and was succeeded by his son **Ferdinand,** who married a daughter of Maria Theresa and generally followed the lead of the Vienna government.

The **GENOESE REPUBLIC,** like the Venetian, remained independent, though constantly exposed to encroachment by Savoy, France, and Austria.

1730. Revolt of Corsica against Genoese rule. After a long and variable struggle, during which a German adventurer, Baron Neuhof of Westphalia, appeared for a time as **King Theodore I** (1736), the Genoese called upon the French for assistance. After many engagements (especially against **Pasquale Paoli,** the Corsican leader), the French subjugated the island, which the Genoese ceded to them (1768).

TUSCANY (Florence) continued under the decadent and unedifying rule of the Medici (**Cosimo III,** 1670–1723; **Gian Gastone,** 1723–1737) until the extinction of the line in 1737.

1737–1745. Francis of Lorraine, grand duke of Tuscany. He became the husband of Maria Theresa and, after his election as German emperor (Francis II, 1745), turned over Tuscany to a regency, and eventually to his son,

1745–1790. Leopold I, who devoted himself to the thoroughgoing reform of his dominion. The administration was remade, serfdom abolished, trade and industry encouraged. Tuscany became perhaps the best ruled and most progressive region of Italy. In 1790 Leopold was elected Roman Emperor as Leopold II.
(Cont. p. 668.)

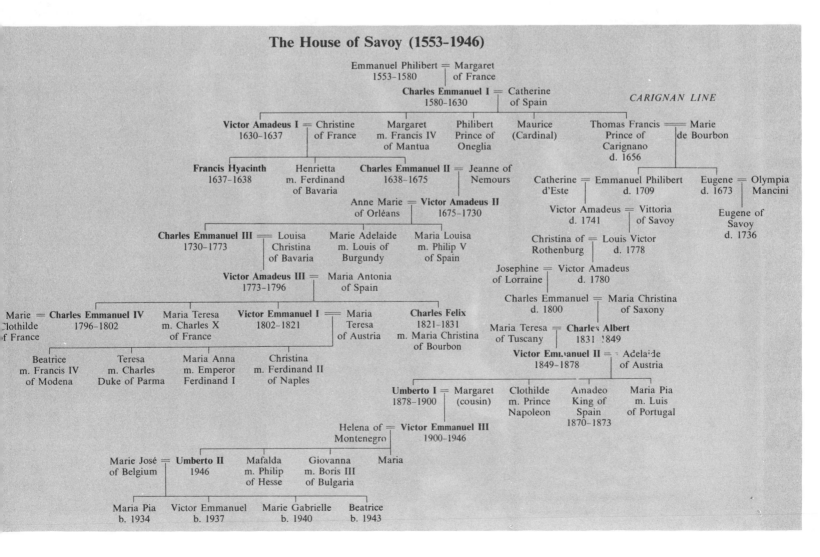

The House of Savoy (1553–1946)

6. *The Swiss Confederation, 1650–1798*

(From p. 431)

The century from 1650 to 1750 was one of stagnation and decline in Switzerland. The confederation continued to be the loosest kind of union, the cantons divided against each other by religious issues. Within the cantons patrician oligarchies became dominant and ruled in a reactionary fashion. The main occupation of the Swiss continued to be fighting, and mercenaries were engaged by foreign states (especially France) by the tens of thousands. Only after 1750 was there a renaissance, which brought Switzerland to the threshold of the French Revolution.

1653. A **peasant revolt,** led by Nicholas Leuenberg, brought the insurgents to the very gates of Bern, but was suppressed with the aid of other cantons.

1655. Proposals for the establishment of a more centralized state, put forward by Zürich, were defeated by the Catholic cantons.

1656. The **FIRST VILLMERGEN WAR,** in which Bern and Zürich were pitted against the Catholic cantons. The Protestants were defeated at Villmergen (Jan. 24) and complete control of religious affairs had to be left to the individual members of the confederation.

1663. Renewal of the **alliance with France,** enabling Louis XIV to draw as many mercenaries as he chose from the cantons. The alliance was opposed by Zürich and some of the Protestant cantons, and in the ensuing period there was much friction between France and Switzerland over the question of service with France against Protestant states, over the reception of Huguenots expelled from France, etc.

1663–1776. During more than a century there was no meeting of the federal diet, indicating the almost complete collapse of the federal connection.

1678. **Franche-Comté,** hitherto under federal protection, was annexed to France.

Pestalozzi, the Children's Friend, *by Konrad Grobb*

1693. The Protestant cantons, incensed by French use of mercenaries against the Dutch, agreed to supply soldiers to the Dutch, and later to the English. Thereupon the Catholic cantons made an agreement to supply men to the Spaniards. In the War of the Spanish Succession the Swiss fought by the thousands on both sides.

1707. A popular insurrection at Geneva, led by **Peter Fatio,** was suppressed with the aid of the Bern and Zürich oligarchies.

1708. The **house of Hohenzollern** succeeded to the principality of Neuchâtel. Louis XIV was prevented by the war from pressing the claims of the prince of Conti.

1712. The **SECOND VILLMERGEN WAR,** another conflict between Catholics and Protestants. This time the Bernese won a decisive victory, again at Villmergen (July 25), after which the dominance of the Protestant cantons was firmly established.

1723. **Revolt of Abraham Davel** in the Vaud, against the oppressive rule of Bern. The whole affair was a harebrained undertaking, inspired by noble motives. After taking Lausanne, Davel was easily outmaneuvered, captured, and executed.

1725. Renewal of the treaty with France, but this time with the abstention of the Protestant cantons.

1734, 1737. Further uprisings in Geneva led to some constitutional revision in the popular direction.

With the middle of the century there came a distinct economic improvement in Switzerland, marked by the expansion of industry. This brought with it a falling-off of the mercenary system, but also a rise of the middle class and an intellectual renaissance: Zürich (with **Johannes J. Bodmer,** 1698–1783, **Albrecht von Haller,** 1708–1777, and **Johannes C. Lavater,** 1741–1801) became an important center of German literature and thought; Geneva (with **Rousseau,** 1712–1778, **Voltaire,** resident in the vicinity after 1755, etc.) became a refuge for advanced thinkers of the French school. The **Helvetic Society** (founded 1762) was an exuberant organization devoted to the new ideas. The educational reformer **Johann Heinrich Pestalozzi** (1746–1827) was strongly influenced by Lavater. After publication of *How Gertrude Teaches her Children* (1801) his influence became international.

1776. The whole confederation once more allied itself with France, but Swiss mercenaries in French service fell to less than 10,000.

1789–1792. In the first years of the **French Revolution** the Swiss oligarchies were strongly hostile and seriously considered intervention by the side of Austria and Prussia. In the end they determined on neutrality, though pursuing at home a repressive policy (crushing of unrest in the Vaud by the Bern government).

1792, Dec. 5. A revolutionary **coup at Geneva** put the government in the hands of the popular party. Thenceforth the developments in France were faithfully mirrored in Geneva.

1793. The French Republic annexed the bishopric (not the town) of Basel.

1797, Oct. **Napoleon,** following his successes in Italy, annexed the Valtelline and Chiavenna to the Cisalpine Republic.

Dec. Revolutionists seized the town of Basel.

1798, Jan. 23. The French declared the Vaud free from Bernese rule and organized it as the **Lemanic Republic.**

Feb. 9. France decreed the establishment of a **Helvetic Republic.** The move was inspired by the Helvetic Committee in Paris, a revolutionary group headed by **Frédéric-César de La Harpe,** 1754–1838, a Vaudois whose great aim was the liberation of his homeland from the hated Bernese aristocracy, and by **Peter Ochs,** a less high-minded radical. The new republic was to be organized along French lines; excepting for territory annexed to France, all the cantons, together with the subject territories, were to be made into 23 cantons, bound together by a centralized government consisting of an elected chamber of deputies (eight members from each canton), and a senate (four from each canton). At the head was to be a directory of five.

The French move finally convinced the Swiss oligarchies of the danger. Bern declared war and the Bernese defeated the French army under Brune at **Laupen** (Mar. 5). But another Bernese force was vanquished on the same day by Schauenberg. Bern surrendered and was sacked. Indemnity of 17 million francs.

Apr. **Five Forest** (Catholic) **Cantons** revolted against the French under Aloys von Reding. They won some successes, but then made peace, accepting the Helvetic constitution on condition that the French should not interfere or occupy territory of the five cantons.

Apr. 26. **Geneva was annexed to France.**

(Cont. pp. 616, 678.)

7. *Germany, 1658–1792*

[For a complete list of the Holy Roman emperors see Appendix V.]

(From p. 430)

1658–1705. **LEOPOLD I,** the son of Ferdinand III. After 1663 a permanent **diet at Regensburg,** consisting of representatives of the 8 electors, the 69 secular princes, and the imperial cities; an ineffectual legislature, often degenerating into a squabble for precedence ("a bladeless knife without a handle"). *Corpus Catholicorum* and *Corpus Evangelicorum,* the corporate organizations of the Catholic and Protestant states, the latter being the most important. This organization of the Protestant states had existed, in fact, since the latter half of the 16th century, but it was legally recognized in the treaty of Westphalia, which decreed that in the diet matters relating to religion and the Church should not be decided by a majority, but should be settled by conference and agreement between the Catholic and Protestant states, as organized corporations.

1661–1664. War against the Turks *(p. 499).*

1666. Settlement of the contested **succession** in **Cleve-Jülich:** Cleve, Mark, and Ravenstein, as well as half of Ravensberg, were given to Brandenburg; afterward the whole of Ravensberg in place of Ravenstein.

1668. The Empire joined in the **War of Devolution,** against Louis XIV of France *(p. 465),* and likewise in

1674. The **Dutch War,** siding with the Dutch against the ambitious aggression of Louis XIV.

1682–1699. The **LIBERATION OF HUNGARY** as a result of a prolonged war against the Turks. Hungary had undergone a marked decline in the mid-century. The greatness of Transylvania came to an end with **George Rákóczi II** (1648–1660) whose ambitious dynastic policy (alliance with Sweden; attempt to secure the Polish crown) had led to trouble with the Turks, who finally drove him from the throne. In that part of Hungary ruled by the Hapsburgs there continued to be persecution of the Protestants and, under Leopold I, extension of the royal power, confiscation of estates of opponents, etc. This led to much unrest (insurrection of **Imre Tökölli**), but the reconquest of the country entirely transformed the situation.

For details of the **war against the Turks** see *p. 499.* After the siege of Vienna (1683), the imperial generals, Charles of Lorraine and Louis of Baden, advanced into Hungary. Buda was taken (1686) and, after the **victory at Mohács** (1687) the Turks were driven beyond the Danube. Eugene of Savoy's great **victory at Zenta** (1697) brought the war to a close. By the **treaty of Karlowitz** (Jan. 26, 1699) the Hapsburgs secured all Hungary excepting the Banat of Temesvar. Meanwhile the Hungarian diet had (1687) fixed the succession to the throne in the male line of the Hapsburgs. In view of the general devastation and depopulation the government began an extensive policy of colonization (1690: Serbs in southern Hungary; 1720–1800: large-scale settlement of Germans). The reconquered territories were awarded in large part to German commanders and soldiers and during the whole century following the reconquest there was a steady increase of royal power and an ever greater concentration of authority in the Vienna government bureaus. The ancient constitution of Hungary subsisted, but it fell more and more into neglect. The higher aristocracy tended to devote itself to the pleasures of the Vienna court, and the opposition of the gentry (concentrated in the local assemblies or comitats) was not sufficient to stem the tide of absolutism.

1688–1697. War of the League of Augsburg, against Louis XIV *(p. 467)*. This war distracted the empire to such an extent that the reconquest of Hungary was delayed for a decade.

During this period several of the German princes were elevated in rank:

1692. Hanover became an electorate (the ninth).

1697. Augustus II, elector of Saxony, was elected king of Poland on the death of John Sobieski. He thereupon adopted the Catholic faith.

1701, Jan. 18. FREDERICK III, elector of Brandenburg (1688–1713), with the consent of the emperor, assumed the title of *king in Prussia* (*König in Preussen*) (Frederick I) and crowned himself at Königsberg.

1701–1714. War of the Spanish Succession (p. 481). The emperor, though he and his allies failed to prevent the succession of the Bourbon house in Spain, nevertheless effected the breakup of the Spanish dominions in Europe. By the final settlement Austrian power and influence replaced that of Spain in Italy, and Austria also succeeded to the Spanish Netherlands (henceforth the Austrian Netherlands).

1703–1711. Revolt of the Hungarians under **Francis II Rákóczi.** This was the result of widespread discontent with the policy of the Vienna government. Ultimately the movement became a real social upheaval. Rákóczi soon controlled most of Hungary and even began to threaten Vienna. But his followers accepted the **peace of Szatmar** (May 1, 1711), by which the emperor promised respect for the Hungarian constitution and redress of grievances. Rákóczi himself refused these terms and took refuge in Turkey (d. 1735).

1705–1711. JOSEPH I, son of Leopold. He was succeeded by his brother,

1711–1740. CHARLES VI.

1713–1740. FREDERICK WILLIAM I, son of Frederick I, king of Prussia, by wise economy, military severity, and the establishment of a formidable army, laid the foundation of the future power of Prussia. Maintenance of a standing army of 83,000 men, with a population of two and a half million inhabitants.

Prince Leopold of Anhalt-Dessau (*der alte Dessauer*).

1714–1718. War of the Turks with Venice, and after 1716 with the emperor *(p. 500)*. The seizure of Sardinia (1717) and Sicily (1718) by Spain, where Elizabeth of Parma, the second wife of Philip V, and her favorite, the minister and cardinal **Alberoni,** were planning to regain the Spanish appanages lost by the **treaty of Utrecht,** brought about the

1718, Aug. 2. Quadruple Alliance for the maintenance of the **treaty of Utrecht,** between France, Britain, the emperor, and (1719) the Republic of Holland. After a short war and the fall of Alberoni, who went to Rome (d. 1752), the agreements of the Quadruple Alliance were executed in 1720: (1) **Spain** evacuated Sicily and Sardinia, and made a renunciation of the appanages forever, in return for which the emperor recognized the Spanish Bourbons; (2) **Savoy** was obliged to exchange Sicily for Sardinia. After this time the **dukes of Savoy** called themselves **kings of Sardinia.**

The Emperor Charles VI was without male offspring. His principal endeavor throughout his reign was to secure the various lands which were united under the scepter of Austria against division after his death. Hence he established an order of succession under the name of the **Pragmatic Sanction,** which decreed that: (1) the lands belonging to the Austrian Empire should be indivisible; (2) that

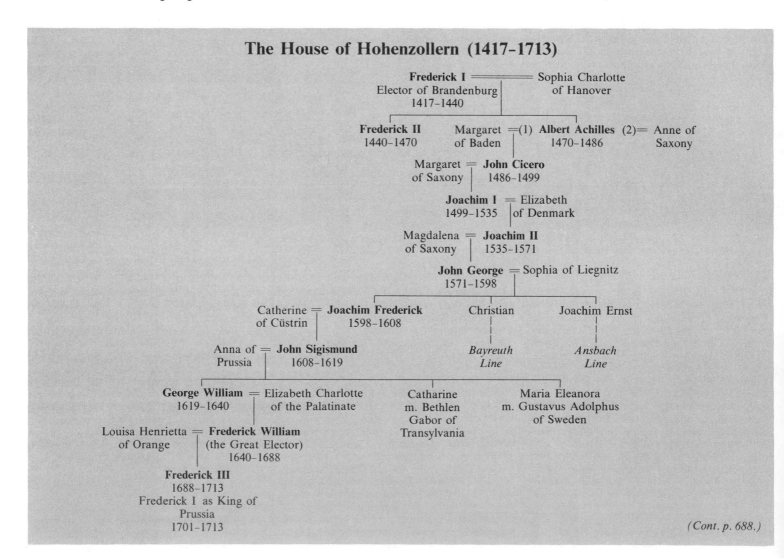

The House of Hohenzollern (1417–1713)

Frederick I ══════ Sophia Charlotte
Elector of Brandenburg — of Hanover
1417–1440

Frederick II — Margaret ═(1) **Albert Achilles** (2)═ Anne of
1440–1470 — of Baden — 1470–1486 — Saxony

Margaret ═ **John Cicero**
of Saxony — 1486–1499

Joachim I ═ Elizabeth
1499–1535 — of Denmark

Magdalena ═ **Joachim II**
of Saxony — 1535–1571

John George ═ Sophia of Liegnitz
1571–1598

Catherine ═ **Joachim Frederick** — Christian — Joachim Ernst
of Cüstrin — 1598–1608

Anna of ═ **John Sigismund** — *Bayreuth* — *Ansbach*
Prussia — 1608–1619 — *Line* — *Line*

George William ═ Elizabeth Charlotte — Catharine — Maria Eleanora
1619–1640 — of the Palatinate — m. Bethlen — m. Gustavus Adolphus
— Gabor of — of Sweden
— Transylvania

Louisa Henrietta ═ **Frederick William**
of Orange — (the Great Elector)
— 1640–1688

Frederick III
1688–1713
Frederick I as King of
Prussia
1701–1713

(Cont. p. 688.)

Frederick II (1740–1786), informing himself on the cultivation of potatoes

in case male heirs should fail, they should devolve upon Charles' daughters, the eldest of whom was **Maria Theresa,** and their heirs according to the law of primogeniture; (3) in case of the extinction of this line the daughters of Joseph I and their descendants were to inherit.

To secure the assent of the various powers to the Pragmatic Sanction was the object of numerous diplomatic negotiations. The Hungarian diet accepted it in 1723. A special agreement between Austria and Spain (1725), in regard to this measure, produced the **alliance of Herrenhausen,** in the same year, between Britain, France, and Prussia in opposition. Prussia soon withdrew from the alliance and joined Austria by the **treaty of Wusterhausen.** The alliance between Austria and Spain was also of short duration.

1733-1735. WAR OF THE POLISH SUCCESSION, after the death of Augustus II.

Cause: The majority of the Polish nobles, under the influence of France, elected **Stanislas Leszczynski,** who had become the father-in-law of Louis XV, king, a second time. Russia and Austria induced a minority to choose **Augustus III,** elector of Saxony (son of Augustus II), and supported the election by the presence of troops in Poland. France, Spain, and Sardinia took up arms for Stanislas.

The seat of war was at first in Italy, where Milan, Naples, and Sicily were conquered, and the Austrians lost everything except Milan; and afterward on the upper Rhine, where the old **Prince Eugene** fought unsuccessfully, and Francis Stephen, duke of Lorraine, the future husband of **Maria Theresa,** alone upheld the

honor of the imperial arms. Lorraine occupied by the French. Kehl captured. Preliminaries of peace (1735), and, after long negotiations, **1738, Nov. 18. TREATY OF VIENNA:** (1) **Stanislas Leszczynski** made a renunciation of the Polish throne, receiving as compensation the duchies of Lorraine and Bar, which at his death were to devolve upon France. Stanislas died 1766. (2) The duke of Lorraine, **Francis**

Maria Theresa, 1740–1780

Stephen, received an indemnification in Tuscany, whose ducal throne had become vacant by the extinction of the family of Medici, 1737. (3) **Austria** ceded Naples and Sicily, the island of Elba and the Stati degli Presidi to Spain as a *secundogeniture* for Don Carlos, so that these lands could never be united with the crown of Spain, receiving in exchange Parma and Piacenza, which Don Carlos had inherited in 1731 upon the death of the last Farnese, his great-uncle. (4) **France** guaranteed the Pragmatic Sanction.

1736-1739. Unsuccessful war with the **Turks** *(p. 500).*

1740, May. Death of Frederick William I of Prussia.

1740-1786. FREDERICK II, THE GREAT of Prussia.

1740, Oct. With the **death of Charles VI,** the male line of the Hapsburgs was extinct.

1740-1780. MARIA THERESA, queen of Bohemia and Hungary, archduchess of Austria, etc., married **Francis Stephen** of the house of Lorraine, grand duke of Tuscany (co-regent).

1740-1748. WAR OF THE AUSTRIAN SUCCESSION:

Cause: The following claimants for the Austrian inheritance appeared: (1) **Charles Albert,** elector of Bavaria, who had never recognized the Pragmatic Sanction, a descendant of Anna, the eldest daughter of Ferdinand I. He based his claim upon the marriage contract of Anna, and upon the will of Ferdinand I, whereby the Austrian inheritance was (he claimed) secured to the descendants of Anna, in case the *male* descendants of her brother should become extinct. (The *original* will, however, read, in

Maria Theresa with the infant Joseph before the Diet of Pressburg, 1741

Joachim II had made an hereditary alliance in 1537 with the duke of Liegnitz, Brieg, and Wohlau, which Ferdinand I had forbidden as king of Bohemia and feudal superior of the duke. After the extinction of the ducal house (1675) Austria took possession of the inheritance.

In 1686, Frederick William, the great elector, of Brandenburg, renounced his claims to the Silesian duchies in return for the cession of one of them, viz. Schwiebus. His son Frederick, however, in an agreement concealed from his father, undertook to retrocede to Austria the Schwiebus district. This was done (1695) after Frederick had succeeded to the electorate.

1740. Occupation of Silesia by Frederick's troops. Capture of Glogau.

1741, Apr. 10. Prussian victory at **Mollwitz.**

May. Secret **alliance of Nymphenburg** against Austria concluded by France, Bavaria, and Spain, afterward joined by Saxony, and lastly by Prussia. The allied French (Belle-Isle) and Bavarian army invaded Austria and Bohemia. Prague taken in alliance with the Saxons. Charles Albert caused himself to be proclaimed archduke in Linz, while Frederick II received homage in Silesia. Charles Albert was elected emperor in Frankfurt as

1742-1745. CHARLES VII. Meantime **Maria Theresa** had gone to Hungary. **Diet at Pressburg** (1741); enthusiasm of the Hungarian nobility which was guaranteed immunity from taxation; two armies raised; alliance concluded with Britain. An Austrian army conquered Bavaria, where Maria Theresa received the homage of Munich; a second besieged the French in Prague.

1742, May 17. The victory of Frederick at **Czaslau** and **Chotusitz,** and Maria Theresa's desire to rid herself of a dangerous enemy led to the separate

June and July. Treaty of **Breslau and Berlin** between Austria and Prussia: (1) **Frederick** withdrew from the alliance against Maria Theresa. (2) **Austria** ceded to Prussia upper and lower Silesia and the county of Glatz, retaining only the principality of Teschen, and the southwestern part of the principalities of Neisse, Troppau, and Jägerndorf, the Oppa forming the boundary. (3) **Prussia** assumed the debt upon Silesia held by English and Dutch creditors, to the amount of 1,700,000 rix dollars.

Austria prosecuted the war against the allies with success, driving them entirely out of Bohemia (1742) and Bavaria (1743); the Pragmatic army (British, Hanoverians, Hessians), under King George II, defeated the French in the

1743, June 27. Battle of Dettingen. The Emperor Charles VII was a refugee in Frankfurt.

These Austrian successes and the treaties with Sardinia and Saxony (1743) made the king of Prussia anxious about his new acquisitions. He concluded a second alliance with Charles VII and France, and began the

1744-1745. SECOND SILESIAN WAR, by forcing his way through Saxony with 80,000 men and invading Bohemia. He took Prague, but, deserted by the French, was soon driven back into Saxony (1744).

1744. East Friesland, upon the extinction of the reigning house, fell to Prussia.

1745, Jan. Alliance between Austria, Sax-

case the *legitimate* descendants of her brother became extinct.) (2) **Philip V,** king of Spain, relying on a treaty between Charles V and his brother Ferdinand, on occasion of the cession of the German lands, and upon a reservation made by Philip III in his renunciation of the German lands. (3) **Augustus III** of Saxony, the husband of the *eldest* daughter of Joseph I.

The claims advanced by **Frederick II** to a part of Silesia, and his desire to annex the whole of Silesia to his kingdom, the rejection of the offer which he made at Vienna to take the field in favor of Austria if his claims were recognized, brought about, before the com-

mencement of hostilities by the other claimants, the

1740-1742. FIRST SILESIAN WAR. Legal claims of Prussia to a portion of Silesia: (1) The principality of Jägerndorf was purchased in 1523 by a younger branch of the electoral line of Hohenzollern, and the future acquisition of Ratibor and Oppeln secured at the same time, by an hereditary alliance. In 1623 Duke John George was placed under the ban by the Emperor Ferdinand II, as an adherent of Frederick V, the elector palatine, and in spite of the peace of Westphalia, neither he nor his heirs had been reinstated. (2) The elector

ony, Britain, and Holland against Prussia. The French and Bavarians took Munich. Charles VII died (1745, Jan.). His son **Maximilian Joseph** concluded the

Apr. Separate **treaty of Füssen**, with Austria. (1) **Austria** restored all conquests to Bavaria. (2) The **elector of Bavaria** surrendered his pretensions to Austria and promised Francis Stephen, the husband of Maria Theresa, his vote at the imperial election.

The French under Marshall **Maurice of Saxony** (*Maréchal de Saxe*, son of Augustus II and the Countess Aurora of Königsmark) defeated the Pragmatic army in the

May 11. BATTLE OF FONTENOY (Irish Brigade), and began the conquest of the Austrian Netherlands.

Frederick the Great defeated the Austrians and Saxons under Charles of Lorraine in the

June 4. Battle of Hohenfriedberg, in Silesia, and the Austrians alone in the

Sept. 30. Battle of Soor, in northeastern Bohemia.

By the election of the husband of Maria Theresa as emperor, the

1745-1806. HOUSE OF LORRAINE-TUSCANY acceded to the imperial throne in the person of the emperor,

1745-1765. FRANCIS I.

After a victory of the Prussian general, Leopold von Dessau, over the Saxons at **Kesseldorf,** December 15, the

1745, Dec. 25 TREATY OF DRESDEN was concluded between Prussia and Austria (Saxony). (1) Ratification of the **treaty of Breslau and Berlin** in regard to the possession of Silesia. (2) **Frederick II** recognized Francis I as emperor. (3) **Saxony** paid Prussia one million rix dollars.

After the flower of the British army had been recalled to England, where it was needed in the contest with the "young pretender" *(p. 457)*. **Marshal Saxe** obtained at **Raucoux** (1746) a second victory over the allies of Austria and completed the conquest of the Austrian Netherlands.

At the same time, the naval war between France and Great Britain, and the war in Italy between Spain, France, and Austria, were carried on with varying fortune. Sardinia had

Battle of Fontenoy, May 11, 1745

Commemorative medal (reverse) of the Battle of Dettingen, June 27, 1743

concluded peace with Austria as early as 1743. At last the empress of Russia, **Elizabeth** (p. *497)*, joined the combatants as the ally of Austria and sent an army to the Rhine. Congress, and finally,

1748, Oct. TREATY OF AIX-LA-CHAPELLE. (1) Reciprocal restoration of all conquests. (2) Cessions of Parma, Piacenza, and Guastalla to the Spanish infant, Don Philip, making the second *secundogeniture* of the Spanish Bourbons in Italy. The following guaranties were given: that Silesia should belong to Prussia; that the Pragmatic Sanction should be sustained in Austria; that the house of Hanover should retain the succession in its German states and in Great Britain.

Change in the relations of European states induced by the rise of Prussia to the rank of a great power. Envy between Prussia and Austria; the latter seeing a disgrace in the loss of Silesia to a smaller power, and intriguing for the recovery of the lost province. Thus began the

1756-1763. THIRD SILESIAN, or **SEVEN YEARS' WAR.**

Cause: Before the treaty of Aix-la-Chapelle Maria Theresa had concluded a **defensive alliance** with Frederick's personal enemy, Elizabeth, empress of Russia (May 1746). Secret articles of this treaty provided for the reunion of Silesia with Austria under certain specified conditions. In September 1750, George II of Great Britain, moved by anxiety for his principality of Hanover, signed the main treaty, the secret articles being excepted. Saxony (minister, Count Brühl) signed the treaty unconditionally. **Count** (Prince in 1764) **Wenzel von Kaunitz** (until 1753 Austrian ambassador in France, then chancellor of the Empire in Vienna) succeeded in promoting a reconciliation between the cabinets of Versailles and Vienna, and securing the marquise de Pompadour in favor of an Austrian alliance. Formation of a party inimical to the Prussian alliance at the French court.

Maria Theresa and Kaunitz induced Britain to conclude a new subsidy treaty with Russia in 1755. In June of the same year, however, hostilities broke out between Britain and France in North America without any declaration of war. Dreading a French attack upon Hanover, George II concluded, in January 1756, a treaty of neutrality with Frederick at Westminster, which caused a rupture between Britain and Russia. Kaunitz made skillful use of the indignation at Versailles over the **treaty of Westminster.** In May 1756 conclusion of a defensive alliance between France and Austria. In June 1756 war broke out between France and Britain in Europe.

Frederick, well informed concerning the alliances of the powers, and knowing that Russia and France were not in condition to take the offensive against him in 1756, decided to take his enemies by surprise.

1756, Aug. He invaded Saxony with 67,000 men and took Dresden (Sept. 2). On October 1 he defeated the Austrians at **Lobositz,** and on October 15 the Saxons (18,000) surrendered at **Pirna.**

1757, Jan. 10. War was declared on Frederick in the name of the Empire. Hanover, Hesse, Brunswick, and Gotha, however, continued in alliance with Prussia. Conclusion of an agreement between Austria and Russia (Jan.) con-

Battle of Rossbach, November 5, 1757

cerning the partition of the Prussian monarchy. Offensive treaty between Austria and France (May 1).

Frederick invaded Bohemia in four columns, and won a

May 6. Victory over the Austrians at **Prague.** Death of Schwerin. Frederick besieged Prague and attacked the army of Count Daun, who attempted to relieve the city. But Frederick was defeated in the

June 18. Battle of Kolin, as a result of which he had to evacuate Bohemia.

July 26. Victory of the French over the British at **Hastenbeck,** which led to the capitulation of the British army (duke of Cumberland) at **Kloster-Zeven** (Sept. 8). The French occupied Hanover, though the treaty was rejected by the British government.

July 30. Battle of Grossjägerndorf, in which the Russians, under Apraxin, after invading East Prussia with a large force, defeated the Prussians under Lehwald. Nevertheless the Russians withdrew from East Prussia and did not exploit their success. But the Swedes in the meanwhile began to occupy Pomerania, promised them in return for participation in the war.

Nov. 5. BATTLE OF ROSSBACH, one of the most spectacular victories of Frederick. The French, under Soubise, had joined the imperial army, under Duke Frederick William, for the purpose of liberating Saxony. But Frederick surprised them on the march and completely overwhelmed them. He then led his victorious army into Silesia, where the Austrians had just won a victory over the duke of Brunswick-Bevern at Breslau (Nov. 22).

Dec. 5. Battle of Leuthen. Frederick completely defeated the Austrians under Charles of Lorraine and Daun.

1758. Frederick campaigned in Moravia, but failed to take Olmütz. In the west, Ferdinand of Brunswick drove the French back over the Rhine and defeated them in the

June 23. Battle of Crefeld. But the greatest Prussian victory of the year was Frederick's defeat of another invading Russian army in the

Siege of Schweidnitz, 1761

Charles II of Spain (p.472)
by Juan Carreno de Miranda (portion)

Charles IV of Spain (p.474) by Francisco Goya

Maria Anna of Austria (p.472) by Diego Velásquez

Tomb of Pope Alexander VII (p.477) in St. Peter's Cathedral, Rome

Charles of Bourbon Visiting Benedict XIV (p.478) by Pannini (portion)

Aug. 25. Battle of Zorndorf. But this was counterbalanced by the

Oct. 14. Battle of Hochkirch. The Austrians had invaded Lusatia and Frederick had hurried to the relief of his brother Henry. Daun defeated the Prussians at Hochkirch, but was not able to drive Frederick out of Saxony and Silesia.

1759. The French resumed the offensive in the west and, under the duke of Broglie, defeated Ferdinand of Brunswick at **Bergen,** near Frankfurt (Apr. 13). Later in the year Ferdinand made good this defeat by his victory over the French in the

Aug. 1. Battle of Minden. The Russians once again advanced into Germany and defeated the Prussian general, Wedell, at **Kay** (July 23). Frederick was unable to prevent their union with the Austrians under Laudon and suffered a major reverse in the

Aug. 12. BATTLE OF KUNERSDORF. The Austrians thereupon captured Dresden. On November 20 Daun surrounded and captured 13,000 Prussians under Finck at **Maxen.**

1760, June 23. The Prussians, under Fouqué, were defeated and captured by the Austrians in the battle of **Landshut,** but

Aug. 15. Frederick's victory over Laudon in the battle of **Liegnitz** (Pfaffendorf) enabled him to prevent the union of the Austrians and Russians. The latter, under Tottleben, nevertheless

Oct. 9-12. Surprised and burned **Berlin,** retreating only as Frederick hurried to the relief.

Nov. 3. Victory of Frederick over Daun at **Torgau.**

1761. Frederick established a defensive position opposite the united Austrians and Russians near Bunzelwitz. But on October 1 the Austrians took Schweidnitz and the Russians occupied Kolberg before the year was out (Dec. 16). By this time Frederick, deprived of the British subsidies by the accession of George III (1760), was in great distress. His position was saved by

1762, Jan. 5. The **death of Elizabeth** of Russia. Her successor, **Peter III,** was an admirer of Frederick and very soon concluded the

Mar. 16. Truce of Stargard, which was followed by the

May 5. Treaty of St. Petersburg. Russia restored all conquests and both parties renounced all hostile alliances. The defection of Russia brought with it also the

May 22. Treaty of Hamburg between Sweden and Prussia, which restored the *status quo ante bellum.* The alliance between Prussia and Russia was soon broken off by the deposition of Peter III (July 9). His successor, **Catherine II,** recalled her troops from Frederick's army; nevertheless their inactivity upon the field contributed to the

July 21. Victory of Frederick at Burkersdorf (Reichenbach) over the Austrians (Daun). After Prince Henry in the

Oct. 29. Battle of Freiburg had defeated the Austrians and the imperial forces, and the preliminaries of the **treaty of Fontainebleau** between England and France had made it certain that the French armies would be withdrawn from Germany, Austria and Prussia concluded the

1763, Feb. 15. TREATY OF HUBERT(U)S-BURG: (1) Ratification of the treaties of Breslau and Berlin, and of Dresden, i.e. Prussia retained Silesia. (2) Prussia promised her vote for the Archduke Joseph at the election of the king of Rome. Saxony (restoration to the *status quo*) and the Empire were included in the peace.

Frederick's endeavors to heal the wounds inflicted by the war upon his kingdom; distribution of the magazine stores; remission of taxes for several provinces; establishment of district banks, of the Bank (1765) and the Maritime Company (1772) at Berlin. Afterward, however, introduction of an oppressive financial administration; tobacco and coffee were made government monopolies. Drainage of the marshes along the Oder, Werthe, and Netze. Canal of Plauen, Finow, and Bromberg. Reform of the jurisdiction. Codification of the common law by grand chancellor von Carmer, a part of which was published in 1782.

1765-1790. JOSEPH II, emperor, for the Austrian lands co-regent only with his mother, **Maria Theresa,** until 1780, and without much influence.

1778-1779. WAR OF THE BAVARIAN SUCCESSION. Cause: Extinction of the electoral house of Bavaria with Maximilian Joseph (1777). **Charles Theodore,** elector palatine, the legal heir of the Bavarian lands, as head of the house of Wittelsbach, and in consequence of various treaties, was persuaded by Joseph II to recognize certain old claims of Austria to Lower Bavaria, and a part of the Upper Palatinate. **Treaty of Vienna** (1778, Jan.): occupation of Lower Bavaria by Austrian troops. Charles Theodore was childless; his heir presumptive was Charles Augustus Christian, duke of the palatinate of Zweibrücken (Deux-Ponts). **Frederick II** opened secret negotiations with this wavering and irresolute prince through Count Eustachius von Görz and encouraged him, under promise of assistance, to make a formal declaration of his rights against the Austrian claims. Saxony and Mecklenburg, also incited by Frederick, protested as heirs presumptive of a part of the Bavarian inheritance. As direct negotiations between Austria and Prussia were without result, Joseph and Frederick joined their armies, which were already drawn up face to face on the boundary of Bohemia and Silesia.

Saxony allied with Prussia. No battle in this short war. Frederick and Prince Henry invaded Bohemia (July 1778). Impossibility of forcing Joseph from his strong position along the upper Elbe, or of getting around it. The armies maintained their positions of observation so long that want began to make itself felt. In the autumn Prince Henry retired to Saxony, Frederick to Silesia. Unimportant skirmishes along the frontier. A personal correspondence between **Maria Theresa** and **Frederick,** commenced by the former, led in the following spring, with the help of Russian and French mediation, to a truce and a congress, and soon after to the

1779, May 13. TREATY OF TESCHEN. (1) The treaty of Vienna with Charles Theodore was abrogated. Austria retained only the district of the Inn, in Bavaria, i.e. the part of Lower Bavaria between the Inn, Salzach, and Danube. (2) Austria agreed to the future union of the margravates of Ansbach and Baireuth with the Prussian monarchy. (3)

Saxony obtained some hitherto disputed rights of sovereignty and nine million rix dollars; Mecklenburg the *privilegium de non appellando.*

1780-1790. JOSEPH II. Period of his reign alone and of his attempts at reform. The prudent government of Maria Theresa (d. 1780), with its carefully matured scheme of reform, was succeeded by the essentially revolutionary reign of Joseph II, whereby the ancient forms were shaken to their foundations, and their substance, reluctant and stiff from lack of change, forcibly subjected to experiments made in sympathy with the enlightenment of the century. Joseph II is the best representative of the contradictions of the 18th century, and of its philanthropy and its devotion to right, and again of its severity and lack of consideration, where there was question of executing some favorite theory. Filled with dislike of the clergy and the nobility, and entertaining the ideal of a strong, centralized, united state, Joseph pursued his reforms with

Joseph II, 1780–1790

the purpose of breaking the power of the privileged classes mentioned above, of destroying all provincial independence, and of establishing unity in the administration (centralization). Despite all his failures, despite the fact that, with few exceptions his reforms did not outlive him, Joseph's reign regenerated the Austrian monarchy, lending it mobility and vitality.

1781, Oct. 13. Edict of tolerance. Within eight years 700 monasteries were closed and 36,000 members of orders released. There still remained, however, 1324 monasteries with 27,000 monks and nuns. For those which remained a new organization was prescribed. The connection of the ecclesiastical order with Rome was weakened, schools were established with the property of the churches, innovations in the form of worship were introduced, nor did the interior organization of the Church escape alteration. Futile journey of Pope

Gotthold Ephraim Lessing, 1729–1781

Johann Wolfgang von Goethe, 1749–1832

Pius VI to Vienna (1782), undertaken to prevent these changes. Reform of jurisdiction. The feudal burdens were reduced to fixed norms, and attempts were made to abolish completely personal servitude among the peasants.

1781. Disputes between Joseph and the Dutch; the emperor arbitrarily annulled the **Barrier Treaties** *(p. 464)*. He demanded that the Scheldt, which had been closed by the treaty of Westphalia to the Spanish Netherlands, in favor of the Dutch, should be opened. Finally, after four years of quarreling, French mediation brought about the **treaty of Versailles** (1785). Joseph withdrew his demands in consideration of ten million florins.

Joseph attempted to improve the legal system of the Empire. His encroachments in the Empire. Violent proceedings in the case of the **bishop of Passau** (1783).

1783. The endeavors of Frederick the Great to conclude a union of German princes (1783), which should resist the encroachments of the emperor, and to strengthen Prussia in her political isolation by a "combination within the Empire," were at first but coldly supported by his own ministers and the German princes. Frederick's plan was not taken into favor until news was received of

1785. Joseph II's plan of an exchange of territory, according to which Charles Theodore was to cede the whole of Bavaria to Austria, and accept in exchange the Austrian Netherlands (Belgium), excepting Luxemburg and Namur, as the kingdom of Burgundy. France maintained an attitude of indifference. Russia supported the project and endeavored by persuasion and threats to induce the heir of Bavaria, the count palatine of Zweibrücken, to consent to the scheme. The latter sought help from Frederick the Great, who, a year before his death (d. 1786, Aug. 17), succeeded in forming the

1785, July. League of the German Princes between Prussia, Electoral Saxony, and Hanover, which was afterward joined by Brunswick, Mainz, Hesse-Cassel, Baden, Mecklenburg, Anhalt, and the Thuringian lands, directed against Joseph's scheme.

Opposition to Joseph's reforms in the Austrian Netherlands and in Hungary. The removal of the crown of Hungary to Vienna produced so great a disturbance that the emperor yielded and permitted its return. The revocation of the constitution of Brabant caused a revolt in the Belgian provinces (1789). War with the Turks *(p. 501)*. **Death of Joseph II** (1790). His brother became

1790–1792. LEOPOLD II, emperor. He suppressed the Belgian insurrection, but restored the old constitution and the old privileges. A **conference at Reichenbach** prevented a war with Prussia, which (Jan. 31, 1790) had concluded a treaty with the Turks, in order to procure more favorable conditions for the latter from Austria and Russia *(p. 501)*.

(Cont. pp. 610, 679.)

CULTURAL DEVELOPMENTS

German literature began to revive after the appearance of **Johann Christoph Gottsched's** *Kritische Dichtkunst* (1730), which was answered by the Swiss **Johann J. Breitinger's** treatise (1739) of the same name, pleading for greater freedom of inspiration and imagination in literature. The first poet of this modern period was **Friedrich Gottlieb Klopstock** (1724–1803), whose epic *Messias* appeared in twenty cantos. **Gotthold Ephraim Lessing** (1729–1781) was the first great German critic of literature and of art (*Laokoon,* 1766) and a classical dramatist whose plays gave new stature to German drama (*Minna von Barnhelm,* 1767; *Nathan der Weise,* 1779). The later German novel owed much to **Christoph Martin Wieland's** *Agathon* (1766–1767), a pyschological study.

The **Sturm und Drang** movement, reflecting much of Rousseau's emphasis on the return to naturalism and individual liberties, was in part founded by **Johann Gottfried Herder** (1744–1803); he stressed the national quality in the folk-songs he collected; stated in four volumes his *Ideen zu einer Philosophie der Geschichte der Menschheit* (1784–1791); had considerable influence on the young **Johann Wolfgang von Goethe** (1749–1832), the foremost poet of the

Johann Sebastian Bach, 1685–1750

Mozart (1732–1809) as a child at the piano

Ludwig van Beethoven, 1770–1827

Sturm und Drang period, author of the first important drama of the movement (*Götz von Berlichingen*, 1773) and of the first novel (*Werthers Leiden*, 1774).

Goethe soon came under the influence of **Johann J. Winckelmann** (1717–1768), the great historian of classical art; his plays (*Iphigenie auf Tauris*, 1787; *Torquato Tasso*, 1790) conformed to the classical ideal. *Faust*, the first part of which was begun in the Sturm and Drang period, is highly classical in its second part.

Goethe's contemporary and great friend, **Friedrich von Schiller** (1759–1805), also bridges the gap from the excessive demands of the Sturm und Drang period (*Die Räuber*, 1781) to purely classical dramas (the trilogy *Wallenstein*, 1798–1799; *Die Jungfrau von Orleans*, 1801).

These were the two great authors of Germany's classical period of literature.

Music: Influence of sacred music of **Dietrich Buxtehude** (1637–1707) on **Johann Sebastian Bach** (1685–1750). Baroque music of **George Frederick Handel** (1685–1759) followed by operas of **Christoph Willibald Gluck** (1714–1787), symphonies and chamber music of **Joseph Haydn** (1732–1809) and of **Wolfgang Amadeus Mozart** (1756–1791), who also composed several operas in the rococo style (*Marriage of Figaro*, 1786; *Don Giovanni*, 1787; *Così fan tutte*, 1790). Greatest composer of classical symphonies was **Ludwig van Beethoven** (1770–1827); also chamber music, oratorio, opera, and piano music.

8. *Scandinavia*

a. SWEDEN, 1654–1792

(From p. 433)

Gustavus Adolphus and his able lieutenants and successors took advantage of the Thirty Years' War to raise Sweden to the rank of a first-class power, with dominance over the whole Baltic area. But the greatness of Sweden was to be short-lived. During the later 17th century the royal power was greatly strengthened, but nevertheless Sweden lacked the resources to compete with the neighboring powers, like Prussia and Russia. The attempts of the Swedish kings to establish control in Poland and the extravagant schemes of Charles XII soon reduced Sweden to the position of a second-class power.

1654. Queen Christina, the daughter of Gustavus Adolphus, abdicated the throne and spent the rest of her life as a converted Catholic, devoted to religion and art. She left the throne to her cousin, Charles Gustavus of Pfalz-Zweibrücken, son of a sister of Gustavus Adolphus, who became

1654–1660. CHARLES X GUSTAVUS. His reign was pre-eminently one of military activity, devoted to

1655–1660. The First Northern War. Charles declared war on Poland on the pretext that John Casimir (of the house of Vasa) refused to acknowledge him. Actually Charles' purpose was to extend the Swedish possessions on the southern Baltic coast.

1656. The Swedes, allied with the elector of Brandenburg **(treaties of Königsberg and Marienburg)** invaded Poland and won a great **battle at Warsaw.** Thereupon Russia, Denmark, and the Empire declared war on the Swedes, and Brandenburg soon deserted the Swedish cause to join the coalition (Poland recognized the elector's sovereignty over East Prussia).

1657. The Swedes were driven out of Poland, but

1658. Charles twice invaded Denmark. The valiant defense of Copenhagen saved the Danish monarchy from annihilation and the death of Charles facilitated the

1660, May 3. Treaty of Oliva: John Casimir of Poland abandoned his claims to the Swedish throne and ceded Livonia to Sweden. By the

Charles X Gustavus, 1654–1660 (center), *at the Battle of Warsaw, 1656*

Charles XII, 1697–1718

treaty of Copenhagen Denmark surrendered to Sweden the southern part of the Scandinavian Peninsula, but retained Bornholm and Trondheim. The **treaty of Kardis** (1661) between Sweden and Russia re-established the *status quo ante bellum*.

1660–1697. CHARLES XI.

1672–1679. Sweden took part in the Dutch War as an ally of France, but the Swedes achieved little. The invasion of Brandenburg resulted in the

1675, June 28. Battle of Fehrbellin, in which the Swedes were defeated by the forces of the Great Elector. A severe blow to Swedish military prestige. The elector then invaded Swedish Pomerania, took Stettin, Stralsund, and Greifswald; but, by the **treaty of St. Germain-en-Laye** (1679), Sweden, through her French ally, was able to recover all that had been lost.

In the internal history of Sweden this reign was marked by the establishment of an **absolutist government.** The council was reduced to impotence, and the estates were kept in submission.

1680. Under the pressure of the king the estates passed a law by the terms of which all earldoms, baronies, and other large fiefs should revert to the crown. This wholesale confiscation of properties dealt a severe blow to Swedish aristocracy.

1697–1718. CHARLES XII. He ascended the throne at the age of 15, but was soon to prove himself one of the military geniuses of modern times. His reign was taken up almost entirely by the

1700–1721. GREAT NORTHERN WAR, which, in a sense, was one aspect of the general war in Europe during the first fifteen years of the century.

The **Northern War** was caused by the common opposition of Russia, Poland, and Denmark to the Swedish supremacy in the Baltic region. **Peter of Russia** was firmly determined to make his country a naval power, and to get possession of harbors on the Baltic; **Augustus II,** elector of Saxony and king of Poland, had a scheme for the reunion of Livonia with

Poland; the **king of Denmark,** besides desiring the general weakening of Sweden, resented Swedish support of the duke of Holstein-Gottorp in his struggle with Denmark. A secret alliance between the three sovereigns was concluded in the fall of 1699, and next year the war opened with an invasion of Schleswig by the Danes, and of Livonia by Augustus' Saxon troops. Unexpected landing of Charles XII of Sweden in Zeeland; he threatened Copenhagen and extorted from the Danes the

1700, Aug. 18. Treaty of Travendal: (1) Indemnification of the duke of Holstein. (2) Denmark promised to abstain from hostilities against Sweden for the future.

Meantime the Saxons were besieging Riga (in Livonia), and the Russians Narva (in Ingermanland).

Nov. 30. Landing of Charles XII with 8000 men and decisive **victory of Narva** over the Russians. Instead of pursuing the Russians, Charles turned west, relieved Riga (1701, June 17) and then invaded Poland.

The following six years were spent by Charles in an effort to defeat Augustus II. After a series of victories over the Poles and Saxons, Charles invaded Saxony and compelled Augustus to sign the

1706, Sept. 24. Treaty of Altranstädt: (1) Augustus abdicated the Polish crown and recognized the previously elected **Stanislas Leszczynski** (the candidate of the pro-Swedish party) as king of Poland. (2) Augustus broke his alliance with the Russian tsar.

1707, Sept. After this, Charles took the field against Peter, who had employed the interval in making conquests and establishing his power in the Baltic (St. Petersburg founded at the mouth of the Neva in 1703, Narva captured in 1704), and in forming a trained and well-supplied army.

1708. Charles advanced in the general direction of Moscow, and then suddenly turned south into the Ukraine where his secret ally,

the Cossack hetman, **Mazeppa,** had promised him a general anti-Russian uprising. The uprising failed to materialize, and the Swedish army found itself in a difficult situation. Meanwhile the Russians had intercepted and defeated an auxiliary Swedish corps, under Loewenhaupt, which was moving south from Livonia with supplies for Charles' army. In an attempt to seize the city of Voronezh, Charles besieged the fortress of Poltava which lay on his way there, and Peter led his main army to the rescue of the stronghold.

1709, July 8. BATTLE OF POLTAVA. The Russian army, superior in numbers and equipment, completely defeated the Swedes, who were exhausted by long marches and lack of food. The Swedish army was broken up, and a large part of it captured. Charles, accompanied by Mazeppa, found refuge in Turkey. Two years later he induced the Porte to declare war against Peter.

1711. Peter, allied with the rulers of Moldavia and Wallachia, moved to the river Pruth, but was surrounded by a much larger Turkish army and was obliged to conclude the **treaty of the Pruth:** (1) Azov given back to the Porte. (2) Charles allowed to return to Sweden.

Charles XII, indignant at this treaty, refused to depart, and remained in Turkey for three more years. Meanwhile (1709) Augustus II drove King Stanislas from Poland. Peter occupied all of Livonia, Estonia, Ingermanland, Karelia, Finland. The Danes took Schleswig from the duke of Holstein-Gottorp, conquered the Swedish duchies of Bremen and Verden, which they afterward sold to Hanover upon condition that that state should take part in the war against Sweden, and jointly with the Poles invaded Pomerania. The Prussians occupied Stettin.

1714. Charles XII at last returned to his kingdom through Hungary and Germany. After this the war dragged on for several years with

Battle of Hangö in the Baltic Sea, June 27, 1714, between Russian and Swedish fleets

Russia, Saxony, Poland, Denmark, Prussia, Hanover allied against Sweden.

1718, Dec. 11. **Charles XII was shot** near Fredrikshald during a military expedition to Norway. He was succeeded by his sister

1718-1720. ULRICA ELEANORA, who was accepted on condition that the riksdag should be allowed to draw up a constitution. The **new constitution** provided for joint rule of the monarch and the council when the riksdag was not in session. While the riksdag was sitting, the principal decisions were to be made by a secret committee composed of members of the three higher estates (nobility, clergy, and burghers). The peasants were, however, to be heard in matters of taxation. This new system involved the re-establishment of the political power of the nobility and clergy and continued until 1771. But the ruling class was divided in the 18th century, between the party of the *Caps*, who favored a prudent foreign policy, and that of the *Hats*, who were eager to regain Sweden's supremacy in the Baltic.

1720-1751. FREDERICK I (of Hesse-Cassel), the husband of Ulrica Eleanora, to whom she turned over the government. Cautious policy of the minister, **Count Arvid Horn,** a Swedish Fleury, who allowed the dangerous connection with France to lapse, and sought better relations with Great Britain and Russia. In 1738 he was overthrown by **Count Gyllenborg,** leader of the Hats and wholly under the French influence (alliance of 1738). This brought Sweden before long into conflict with Russia. The Hats remained in power until 1766.

1720-1721. Conclusion of the Northern War. By the **treaties of Stockholm:** (1) The *status quo ante bellum* was restored as between Sweden, Saxony, and Poland. (2) Hanover was allowed to retain Verden, but paid Sweden 1,000,000 thalers. (3) Prussia received Stettin, western Pomerania as far as the Peene, the islands of Wollin and Usedom, but paid Sweden 2,000,000 thalers. (4) Denmark restored all conquests, in return for which Sweden paid 600,000 rix dollars, gave up its freedom from customs duties in the Sound, and abandoned the duke of Holstein-Gottorp, whom Denmark deprived of his share of Schleswig.

1721, Aug. 30. Treaty of Nystadt, between Sweden and Russia: Sweden ceded to Russia: Livonia, Estonia, Ingermanland, part of Karelia, and a number of islands, among others Oesel and Dagö. Russia restored Finland and paid 2,000,000 rix dollars.

The main results of the great war were the destruction of Sweden's preponderance in the Baltic and the emergence of Russia as a great European power.

1741-1743. War against Russia, provoked by the Hats, who were under French influence and were thirsting for revenge. By the **treaty of Åbo** (Aug. 7, 1743), Sweden ceded to Russia more territory in Finland.

1751-1771. ADOLPHUS FREDERICK of Oldenburg-Holstein-Gottorp, king, introducing a collateral line.

1771-1792. GUSTAVUS III, the son of Adolphus Frederick. Gustavus, fearful lest Sweden should be victimized by Russia and Prussia, restored absolute government by means of a military *coup d'état* (Aug. 19, 1772). The power of the council was ended and the king again acquired full authority over the admin-

John Frederick Struensee arrested, 1772, and condemned to death

istration. The riksdag lost its initiative in legislation. Gustavus tried to be an "enlightened despot." He abolished torture, improved the poor laws, proclaimed religious toleration and liberty of the press, and encouraged trade. But with the outbreak of the French Revolution his policies became more reactionary.

1788-1790. War with Russia. Gustavus invaded Russian Finland and achieved several victories, but was attacked by the Danes and in the end was obliged to conclude the **treaty of Wereloe,** which left Finland and Karelia in Russian hands.

1789, Feb. By the **Act of Unity and Security,** Gustavus, taking advantage of his victory over the Danes, effected another *coup* and established his despotic power in Sweden.

1792, Mar. Gustavus III was murdered by Jacob Johan Ankarström, a Swedish aristocrat.

(Cont. pp. 624, 703.)

b. DENMARK AND NORWAY, 1648-1788

(From p. 431)

1648-1670. FREDERICK III. A few months after the conclusion of peace with Sweden (1660), a monarchical *coup d'état,* supported by the clergy and the burghers, transformed the king into an hereditary and virtually absolute ruler, with the council relegated to the position of a mere advisory body. A treatise

expressing absolutist ideas was composed for the king by **Peter Schumacher** (afterwards **Count Griffenfeld**). Published under the title of *Kongelov* (*King's Law*), it guided Griffenfeld's administration during the early years of

1670-1699. CHRISTIAN V's reign.

1699-1730. Under **FREDERICK IV,** Denmark took part in the **Northern War** *(p. 490).* As a result of the war a certain balance between Denmark and Sweden was established in the Baltic region: Denmark was no longer afraid of a Swedish invasion, and on her part gave up ideas of reconquering her lost possessions in the south of the Scandinavian Peninsula. In his domestic policies, Frederick IV perfected the machinery of royal absolutism.

These gains, however, were partially lost during the reigns of his feeble successors (**Christian VI,** 1730–1746; **Frederick V,** 1746–1766) characterized by the rule of royal favorites mostly of German origin. Under the mentally unbalanced

1766-1808. CHRISTIAN VII an attempt at radical internal reform was made during the administration (1770–1771) of the German, **John Frederick Struensee,** an exponent of "enlightened despotism": Struensee tried to make the royal power independent of the nobility by suppressing the council, attacked aristocratic privileges, reorganized the administration, abolished torture and censorship of the press.

1772. Struensee was overthrown by a palace

The Danish Royal House (1699–

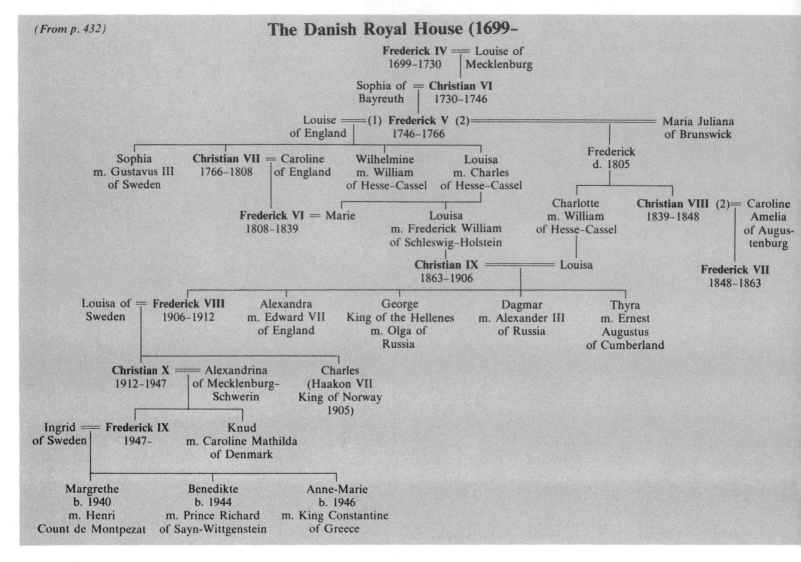

Frederick IV ══ Louise of
1699–1730 │ Mecklenburg

Sophia of ══ Christian VI
Bayreuth │ 1730–1746

Louise ══(1) Frederick V (2)══════════════ Maria Juliana
of England │ 1746–1766 │ of Brunswick

Sophia   Christian VII ══ Caroline   Wilhelmine   Louisa   Frederick
m. Gustavus III   1766–1808 │ of England   m. William   m. Charles   d. 1805
of Sweden   of Hesse-Cassel   of Hesse-Cassel

Frederick VI ══ Marie   Louisa   Charlotte   Christian VIII (2)══ Caroline
1808–1839   m. Frederick William   m. William   1839–1848   Amelia
                          of Schleswig-Holstein   of Hesse-Cassel   of Augus-
                                                                                  tenburg

                                                                                  Frederick VII
                                                                                  1848–1863

                          Christian IX ══════════ Louisa
                          1863–1906

Louisa of ══ Frederick VIII   Alexandra   George   Dagmar   Thyra
Sweden   1906–1912   m. Edward VII   King of the Hellenes   m. Alexander III   m. Ernest
                           of England   m. Olga of   of Russia   Augustus
                                           Russia   of Cumberland

Christian X ═══ Alexandrina   Charles
1912–1947   │ of Mecklenburg-   (Haakon VII
             │   Schwerin   King of Norway
             │   1905)

Ingrid ══ Frederick IX   Knud
of Sweden   1947–   m. Caroline Mathilda
                          of Denmark

Margrethe   Benedikte   Anne-Marie
b. 1940   b. 1944   b. 1946
m. Henri   m. Prince Richard   m. King Constantine
Count de Montpezat of Sayn-Wittgenstein   of Greece

revolution and subsequently executed. This was followed by the rule of a reactionary aristocratic group, headed by **Guldberg,** and after his fall (1784) by the
1784–1788. Administration of an able and enlightened statesman, **Count Andreas Peter Bernstorff,** who began by regulating relations between the landlords and their peasant tenants, and then passed a series of measures (1787–1788) virtually abolishing serfdom in Denmark.

In **NORWAY,** which remained under Danish domination, this period saw the vigorous growth of a national cultural movement: literary activity of **Ludwig Holberg** (1684–1754), formation of the **Norwegian Society** among the university students in Copenhagen (1772).

(Cont. pp. 622, 702.)

9. *Poland, 1648–1795*

(From p. 434)

1648–1668. JOHN II CASIMIR. His reign was marked by grave internal disturbances and unsuccessful foreign wars against the Swedes, Russians, and Turks. Frequent uprisings of the serfs and of the Ukrainian Cossacks.
1654. The hetman of the Cossacks, **Bogdan Khmelnitsky,** placed himself under the protection of Russia, thus precipitating a prolonged conflict between Russia and Poland for possession of the Ukraine.
1655–1660. War between Sweden and Poland

(p. 489). Invasion of the Swedes. By the **treaty of Oliva** (May 3, 1660), Poland lost to Sweden her last Baltic territories.
1667, Jan. 20. Treaty of Andrussovo, ending the conflict with Russia. Poland ceded to Russia the eastern Ukraine and Smolensk.
1668. John Casimir abdicated and there followed a period of ardent struggle for the throne. The Poles finally elected a national candidate,
1669–1673. MICHAEL WISNIOWIECKI,

during whose short reign the Cossacks again rose in revolt and appealed to the Turks for aid.
1672–1676. War with Turkey. The Turks, having taken Kameniec, secured from the disheartened Polish king the **treaty of Buczacz** (1772), by which Poland lost Podolia and recognized the western Ukraine as independent under Turkish protectorate. The Polish diet refused to ratify the treaty and the Poles resumed the struggle under the lead of **John**

Sobieski, an able commander who gradually drove the Turks back.

1674–1696. JOHN III SOBIESKI, king after the death of Michael. After a victory over the Turks at Lemberg (1675), he concluded with them the

1676, Oct. Treaty of Zuravno, by which the Turks retained only part of the Ukraine.

1683, Mar. 31. John Sobieski made an **alliance with Austria** in order to present a united front to the Turkish advance on Vienna. The Poles then played an important rôle in the relief of Vienna from the famous second siege *(p. 499)*. Sobieski continued to participate in the reconquest of Hungary until 1685.

These military successes, however, were not enough to arrest the process of decline which resulted from the basic defects of the Polish political organization, viz. the absence of real unity, the lack of strong central authority, the impotence of the national diet (repeatedly paralyzed by the use of the *liberum veto* or right of each individual member of the diet to defeat a resolution by his protest, and thus to break up the session).

1697–1733. AUGUSTUS II (elector of Saxony), king of Poland. He attempted to strengthen the royal power, but without much success.

1699, Jan. 26. Treaty of Karlowitz, ending the long war against Turkey *(p. 499)*. By this settlement the Poles regained Podolia and the Turkish part of the Ukraine.

1700–1721. The **Great Northern War** *(p. 490)*, which was fought largely on Polish soil. The Poles had made an agreement with Russia to despoil Charles XII of Sweden. They invaded Livonia (1700), but in 1701–1702 Charles invaded Poland, taking Warsaw and Cracow (1702). The Polish magnates then dethroned Augustus, and elected

1704–1709. STANISLAS LESZCZYNSKI as king. By the **treaty of Altranstädt,** with Sweden (1706), Augustus gave up his claims. The Empire, Brandenburg, England, and Holland all recognized Stanislas. But after the defeat of Charles at Poltava (1709), Augustus returned and drove out his rival. Poland suffered tremendously from the Swedish invasion and the civil war, yet gained nothing whatever from the defeat of Charles.

1715–1717. Further disorders, resulting from a rising of the nobles against the absolutist policies of Augustus. This offered an opportunity for Russian intervention and initiated the gradual subordination of Poland to Russia.

1733–1735. WAR OF THE POLISH SUCCESSION. The Poles, supported by France, elected Stanislas Leszczynski, who had become the father-in-law of Louis XV. The Russians and Austrians insisted on the election of Augustus of Saxony, son of Augustus II. A huge Russian army invaded the country and drove out Stanislas, who withdrew to Danzig. France, supported by Spain and Sardinia, declared war on the Empire. French expedition to the Baltic to relieve Danzig (besieged by the Russians from October 1733 onward).

1734, June 2. Capitulation of Danzig; Stanislas fled to Prussia. Meanwhile the main fighting was done in Italy (French and Spanish victories, *p. 483*) and on the Rhine (indecisive). The war was finally ended by the **treaty of Vienna** (Oct. 5, 1735, ratified 1738), which wrought profound changes in Italy and assured

John III Sobieski, 1674–1696

the victory of the Russian-Austrian policy in Poland.

1734–1763. AUGUSTUS III, king. He spent but little time in Poland, and did little to prevent Russian encroachment, especially during the Seven Years' War. Growing agitation for reform in Poland after 1740: two parties, led by the **Potocki** and **Czartoryski** families. The former looked to France for support and aimed at the establishment of an aristocratic constitution; the latter, relying on Russian support, envisaged strengthening of the royal power, abolition of the *liberum veto,* etc.

1764–1795. STANISLAS PONIATOWSKI, king. He was a nephew of Prince Czartoryski and was the favorite of Catherine II of Russia. By agreement of April 11, 1764, Russia and Prussia had arranged for co-operation in Polish affairs. Poniatowski and the reformers attempted to introduce changes, but Russia soon showed herself lukewarm on the subject.

1766–1768. Question of the Dissidents (Greek Orthodox Catholics and Protestants), who were granted equal rights with Roman Catholics, at the insistence of Russia and Prussia. This raised a storm of protest in Poland and led (1768) to the formation of the **Confederation of Bar,** an anti-Russian association which soon enjoyed the active support of France. Civil war of the most violent type broke out in Poland; invasion and campaigns of the Russians

against the Confederates. Ultimately the Turks, encouraged by the French, declared war on Russia, in support of Polish "liberties."

1772, Aug. 5. THE FIRST PARTITION OF POLAND. This resulted directly from the Russian victories against the Turks, which so alarmed the Austrians that they came to the point of making war on Russia. Frederick the Great, fearing involvement in a general European conflict, engineered the partition of Poland, by which Russia might make gains unobjectionable to Austria, while Prussia and Austria might participate in the spoils. By the first partition **Russia** acquired White Russia and all territory to the Dvina and Dnieper, about 1,800,000 inhabitants (mostly Greek Orthodox); **Austria** took Red Russia, Galicia, and western Podolia, with Lemberg and part of Cracow (2,700,000 inhabitants); **Prussia** took Polish Prussia, except Danzig and Thorn (416,000 inhabitants). In all Poland lost about one-third of its territory and about one-half of its inhabitants.

1773. The **Polish diet,** forced to accept the partition, began to effect reforms (council of state, divided into five ministries, to govern when the diet was not in session). Intellectual awakening under the influence of French ideas, educational reforms, etc.

1788–1792. The **Four Years' Diet,** dominated by the progressive patriotic party, while Prus-

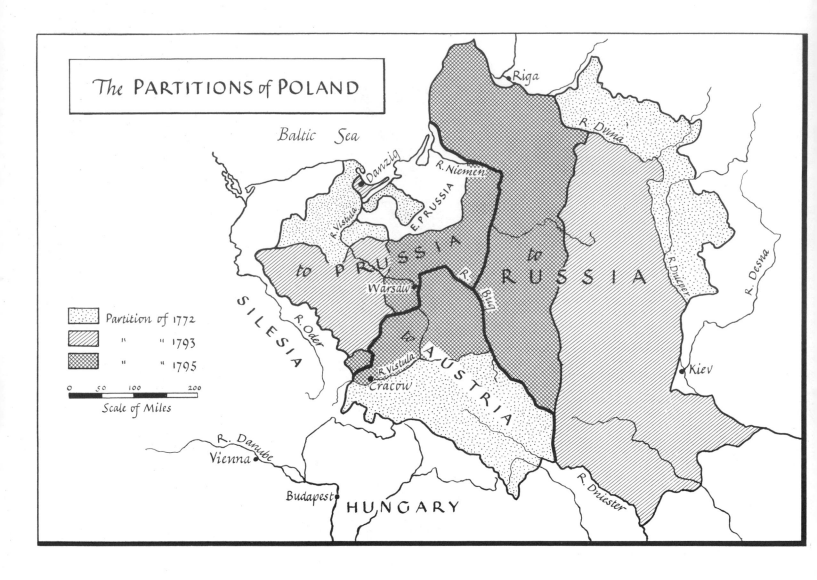

The PARTITIONS of POLAND

Baltic Sea

Riga

R. Dvina

Danzig

R. Niemen

R. Vistula

E. PRUSSIA

to P R U S S I A

R. Dnieper

R. Desna

Warsaw

to   R U S S I A

R. Bug

SILESIA

R. Oder

Kiev

to   A U S T R I A

R. Vistula

Cracow

Partition of 1772

"   " 1793

"   " 1795

0   50   100   200

Scale of Miles

R. Danube

Vienna

Budapest **HUNGARY**

R. Dniester

---

sia, Austria and Russia were at war with the Turks. The Prussian minister **Hertzberg** hoped to secure Danzig and Thorn by agreement with a reformed Poland. Developments in France led to an agreement between Prussia and Austria and to postponement of the scheme.

1791, May 3. The Polish patriots put through a **new constitution** which (1) converted the elective monarchy into an hereditary monarchy (the elector of Saxony to succeed Poniatowski and to establish a Saxon dynasty); (2) conferred the executive power upon the king and council of state; (3) vested the legislative power in a diet of two chambers; (4) abolished the *liberum veto*. Prussia and Austria accepted this change, but the Russians organized

1792, May 14. The **Confederation of Targowicz,** in defense of the old constitution. Russian invasion was followed by similar action on the part of the Prussians, and finally led to a bargain between the two powers in the

1793, Jan. 23. SECOND PARTITION OF POLAND. Russia took most of Lithuania and most of the western Ukraine, including Podolia (3,000,000 inhabitants); **Prussia** took Danzig and Thorn, as well as Great Poland (1,100,000 inhabitants). In addition, Russia forced Poland to accept a **treaty of alliance,**

Thaddeus Kosciuszko, 1746–1817

whereby Russia was given free entry for her troops in Poland and the right to control Poland's relations with other powers.

1794, Mar. 24. NATIONAL UPRISING in Poland, led by **Thaddeus Kosciuszko.** After an unequal struggle against the forces of Russia and Prussia, the Poles were defeated (capture of Kosciuszko, surrender of Warsaw to Suvorov), and Austria joined Russia and Prussia in the

1795, Oct. 24. THIRD PARTITION OF POLAND. **Russia** took what remained of Lithuania and the Ukraine (1,200,000 inhabitants); **Prussia** secured Mazovia with Warsaw (1,000,000 inhabitants), while **Austria** obtained the remainder of the Cracow region (1,000,000 inhabitants). Courland, long under the suzerainty of Poland, but since 1737 practically under Russian influence (Biron, duke of Courland), was incorporated with Russia.

The "Age of Enlightenment" produced much satirical writing: **Ignatius Krasicki** (1735–1801), poet, novelist, author of satires and fables. With the establishing of the first public theater in 1765 in Warsaw, new dramatists emerged: **Francis Zoblocki** (1754–1821) and **Julian Ursyn Niemcewicz** (1757–1841), also translator of English poems, author of novels, memoirs, *Collection of Historical Songs* (*Spiewy historyczne*).

10. *Russia, 1645–1801*

(From p. 437)

1645–1676. ALEXIS, the son of Michael Romanov, who ascended the throne at the age of sixteen. His reign was marked by much internal unrest (serious revolt in Moscow, 1647) and by the adoption by a national assembly (1649) of a new code of law (in force until 1832) designed to improve the administration and to eliminate various abuses. In some of its provisions, however, it involved the final establishment of peasant serfdom in Russia.

1654–1667. War with Poland for the possession of the Ukraine, after the Cossack hetman, **Bogdan Khmelnitsky,** had placed himself under Russian protection. By the **treaty of Andrussovo** (Jan. 20, 1667) Russia obtained the Smolensk region and the eastern Ukraine, with Kiev. The outcome of the war was of great importance, since the Russian gains first brought them in contact with the Turks in the Balkans.

1667. Revision of the Russian church ritual and liturgical books in accordance with Greek practice. This reform, undertaken by the patriarch, **Nikon,** resulted in secession from the Church of the so-called **Old Believers,** who were condemned by a church council as schismatics. Epistles of **Archpriest Avvakum** (c. 1620–1681) denouncing the reforms.

1670–1671. A great **peasant revolt** in the southeast, led by the Don Cossacks, under **Stephen Razin,** was suppressed with great difficulty.

By the end of the reign of Alexis the government had established more effective control and the crisis of the early 17th century was definitely overcome. The tsar, indeed, felt strong enough to discontinue calling the national assembly. At the same time there was a rapid infiltration of western influences, which foreshadowed the westernizing reforms of Peter the Great.

1676–1682. THEODORE III, the son of Alexis, during whose short reign Russia fought the first of many wars against the Ottoman Turks. By the **treaty of Radzin** (1681) the Turks abandoned most of the Turkish Ukraine to Russia.

1682–1689. IVAN V (son of Alexis' first wife), with whom was associated **Peter I** (son of Alexis' second wife) as co-tsar. **Sophia,** the daughter of Alexis, acted as regent. In 1689 the partisans of Peter overthrew Sophia and

1689–1725. PETER I (the Great) was effectively the sole ruler, though Ivan V lived until 1696. Peter, an intelligent but ruthless and headstrong ruler (b. 1672), spent the first years of his reign in a process of self-education (chiefly technical and military). He established close relations with members of foreign colonies in Moscow and prepared for his later campaigns through his military and naval "games."

1689. Conflict with China, resulting from the penetration of Russian pioneers into the Amur region. By the **treaty of Nerchinsk** (1689)—the first Russian treaty with China—the Russians were obliged to withdraw from the occupied territory.

1695–1696. Peter's **expeditions against Azov,** the fortress commanding the Sea of Azov and the entrance to the Black Sea. The first expedition, by land, was unsuccessful, but the second, supported by a naval force, resulted in the capture of the stronghold (July 28, 1696).

1697–1698. Peter's **European journey,** which he undertook *incognito* as part of a grand embassy sent to secure allies in western Europe for a crusade against the Turks. Peter was the first Russian sovereign to go abroad and his travels in France, England, and Holland

Peter I (1689–1725) strikes one of the Strelitzy in the face

strengthened him in the determination to "westernize" Russia. He returned to Moscow to suppress a **revolt of the streltsy** (soldiers of the Moscow garrison, among whom there were many Old Believers), and then embarked upon his first reforms. At the same time he prepared for war with Sweden for possession of the Baltic coast, having failed to induce the western powers to continue the Turkish war beyond the year 1699 (**treaty of Karlowitz**, *p. 499*). Peace was concluded with the Turks in 1700, Russia retaining Azov.

1700–1721. The GREAT NORTHERN WAR *(p. 490)*. Peter was at first no match for Charles XII, who defeated him at **Narva** (Nov. 30, 1700). But Charles spent the next years campaigning in Poland, thus giving Peter an opportunity to reorganize his army on European lines and to construct a fleet in the Baltic. The capital was moved to the newly founded city of **St. Petersburg** (modern Petrograd and Leningrad) in 1703.

1709, July 8. The BATTLE OF POLTAVA, a decisive battle in Russian history. Charles XII, having allied himself with **Mazeppa,** the Cossack hetman, began to march on Moscow, but then turned off south. At Poltava Peter won a resounding victory which broke the power of Charles and marked the emergence of Russia in place of Sweden as the dominant power in the north.

1710–1711. War with Turkey, due to pressure from Charles XII (a refugee in Turkey) and France *(p. 500)*. The Russians were surrounded by the Turks on the Pruth River and Peter had to buy himself off. By the **treaty of the Pruth** (July 21, 1711), he was obliged to return Azov to the Turks.

1721, Aug. 30. Treaty of Nystadt, between Russia and Sweden, concluding the Northern War. Russia acquired Livonia, Estonia, Ingermanland, part of Karelia and a number of Baltic islands. Thus Peter had achieved his great purpose of acquiring a "window" on the Baltic which would open up connections with the west. Russia now definitely took her place as a European power.

INTERNAL REFORMS: centralization of the administration. The old council of the boyars was abolished and was replaced by a governing *senate* (1711), consisting of nine members appointed by the tsar. New government bureaus were set up (1718) under the name of *colleges*. The nobility was made to serve the state (establishment of a hierarchy of offices) and Peter did much to encourage trade, industry, and education (Academy of Science opened the year after Peter's death). In order to sub-

ordinate the Church to state control, Peter abolished the patriarchate and in its place established (1721) a synod composed of bishops, but presided over by a layman (procurator of the Holy Synod). Many of Peter's reforms were incomplete and even more of them were hasty and premature, but his drastic innovations no doubt did much to arouse Russia from the stagnation of the preceding period.

Alexis, the son of Peter I, who had become the center of opposition to Peter's policies, died in prison of torture in 1718. In 1722 Peter issued a law that empowered the reigning sovereign to appoint his own successor. He himself died without making use of this right. Upon his death the officers of the palace guard elevated to the throne his second wife,

1725–1727. CATHERINE I, a woman of lowly birth, but intelligent and energetic. During her short reign the most influential member of the government was **Prince Alexander Menshikov,** one of Peter's closest collaborators. Catherine named as her successor

1727–1730. PETER II, the son of Alexis and grandson of Peter I, a boy of 12. There ensued a struggle between the Menshikov and the Dolgoruki families, which ended in the exile of the former. Peter II died young and was succeeded by

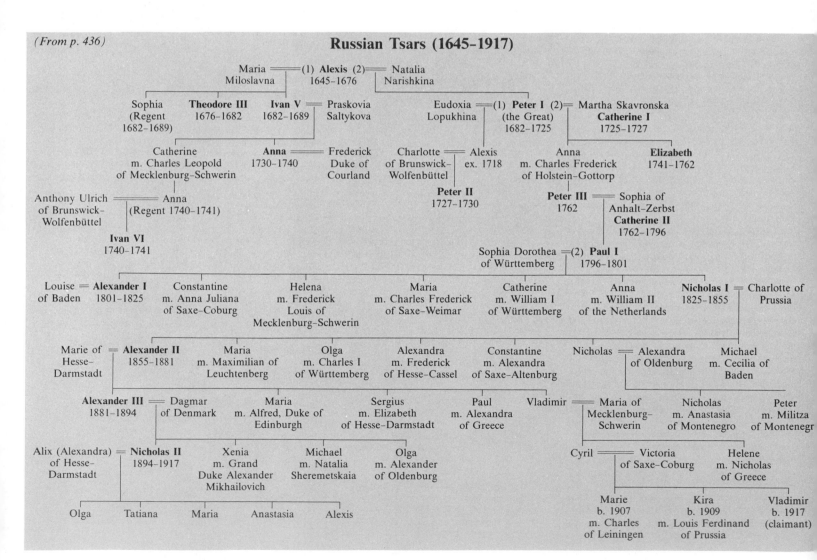

(From p. 436)

Russian Tsars (1645–1917)

1730-1740. ANNA, daughter of Ivan V, who was married to Frederick, duke of Courland. Anna was an ineffectual person, dominated by her favorite, **Ernst Johann Biron** (properly Bühren). The government began to fall almost entirely into the hands of Germans, many of them adventurers, but many of them extremely able. Foreign affairs were competently handled by **Count Andrei Ostermann,** while the army, under **Count Burkhard von Münnich,** scored great successes in its campaigns.

1733-1735. War of the Polish Succession (*p. 483*). As a result of the internal weakness of Poland, the Russians were able to establish on a firm basis their control over Polish affairs and to prepare the way for the final partitions.

1736-1739. War against the Turks (*p. 500*), in alliance with Austria. The war was the result of Russian action in Poland. The Russians recaptured Azov and, after some reverses in 1737, Münnich advanced victoriously into Moldavia. French mediation deprived Russia of gains she might have made. By the **treaty of Belgrade** (Sept. 18, 1739) the Russians retained Azov, but agreed to raze the fortifications and not to build a fleet on the Black Sea.

1740-1741. IVAN VI, the grandson of Anna's sister Catherine. Ivan's mother conducted the government for a short time after the fall of Biron (effected by Münnich), but a military revolt soon placed on the throne

1741-1762. ELIZABETH, the youngest daughter of Peter the Great, a thoroughly Russian character, politically keen, but dissolute and easy-going. Nationalist reaction against German favorites. Elizabeth set up a brilliant if somewhat uncouth court and gave wide rein to the court nobility. **Golden age of the aristocracy,** which began to emancipate itself from onerous obligations of service to the state, while gradually increasing its privileges. Development of learning and science: **first Russian university** founded at Moscow (1755); activity of the Academy of Sciences (**Mikhail Lomonosov,** 1711-1765, the first outstanding native scientist. Also poet, founder of modern Russian literature, literary stylist). **Bartolomeo Restrelli** (1700-1771) built palaces in St. Petersburg (Winter Palace) and Peterhof, as well as a castle and monastery in Zarskoye Selo and a cathedral in Kiev.

Foreign policy was, during most of the reign, directed by **Count Alexis Bestuzhev-Riumin,** and was based on the alliance with Austria and Great Britain as against Prussia and France. The great objectives of Russia continued to be expansion at the expense of Swe-

Mikhail Lomonosov, 1711–1765

den, domination of Poland, and conquest at the expense of the Turk.

1741-1743. War with Sweden, provoked by the pro-French party in Sweden. After some

Coronation of Elizabeth (1741–1762) in St. Petersburg (contemporary print)

fighting, the Swedes, by the **treaty of Abö** (1743, Aug. 7) were obliged to cede to Russia further territory in Finland.

1746, June 2. By treaty with Austria, Russia finally joined in the **War of the Austrian Succession** *(p. 483)*, in which, however, the Russians played an insignificant rôle.

1756–1763. The **SEVEN YEARS' WAR,** in which Russia took an active and important part. The "diplomatic revolution" of 1756, which brought Austria and France together, led to the estrangement of Russia and Britain, and to the downfall of Bestuzhev. Russia fought on the side of Austria and France against Frederick the Great, but made no direct gains as a result of the war.

Elizabeth named as her successor **Peter,** duke of Holstein-Gottorp, her sister's son, who in 1744 married Sophia-Augusta of Anhalt-Zerbst. Sophia took the name Catherine on conversion to the Orthodox faith.

1762. PETER III, a weak and incompetent

Paul I, 1796–1801

ruler. As an intense admirer of Frederick the Great, he effected Russia's withdrawal from the war, thereby causing much resentment among the officers and the aristocracy (despite the fact that he proclaimed the freedom of the nobility from obligatory state service). After a six months' reign, Peter was deposed (July) by a military revolution led by the **Orlov brothers.** A few days later he was killed while in captivity. Peter was succeeded by his wife

1762–1796. CATHERINE II (the Great), an exceptionally astute and energetic ruler, who completed the work initiated by Peter the Great. In domestic affairs Catherine was guided by the teachings of the French Enlightenment (especially Voltaire) and tried to establish a benevolent despotism. On the other hand, she was obliged to cultivate the good will of the nobility, to which she owed her power. In order to codify the Russian law and also in order to learn the needs of the country, she convoked at Moscow a **legislative commission** (1767–1768), consisting of representatives of all classes excepting the serfs. Although no law code was produced, Catherine made good use of the commission's findings in planning her later legislation.

1766–1768. Drastic interference of Catherine in the **affairs of Poland,** where one of her favorites, Stanislas Poniatowski, had been placed on the throne *(p. 493)*. The Russian advance in Poland led to

1768–1772. WAR WITH THE TURKS (p. *500)*, in which the Russians won unprecedented victories. The prospective gains of Russia so excited the Austrians (thitherto the partners of the Russians in the advance against the Turks) that the two powers came to the very verge of war. In order to prevent a general conflagration, Frederick the Great engineered the

1772, Aug. 5. FIRST PARTITION OF POLAND *(p. 493)*. The Russian operations against Turkey were hampered further by

1773–1775. Pugachev's revolt, a formidable insurrection of the peasants and Cossacks of southeastern Russia, which was suppressed only with great difficulty.

1774, July 21. The **treaty of Kuchuk Kainarji**

ended the war against Turkey. Russia acquired Kinburn, Yenikale, and Kertch in the Crimea and secured the right of free navigation for commercial ships in Turkish waters. The Tatars of the Crimea were recognized as "independent" and Russia was given important rights of intervention in Moldavia and Wallachia and in behalf of Christians in the Ottoman Empire (for details *see p. 500).*

1775. The statute of **provincial administration** was a direct result of Pugachev's revolt, which convinced Catherine of the need for reform. It completely reorganized local government (small administrative units, better division of functions among the branches of government, some measure of self-government, more particularly for the nobility). Catherine did not dare, however, to touch the evil of serfdom. On the contrary, this institution reached its fullest development in her reign. Catherine's encouragement of education, art, and letters contributed to the growth of a liberal public opinion on the social problem. After the outbreak of the French Revolution, Catherine became decidedly hostile to this movement. **Alexander Radishchev** (1749–1802) was arrested and exiled to Siberia (1790) for having published his *Journey from St. Petersburg to Moscow,* which contained a vigorous protest against serfdom.

1780. Armed neutrality at sea, an idea advanced by Russia during the War of American Independence, as a method of protecting commerce. The idea was supported by Denmark and Sweden (1780) and later by Prussia, Austria (1782), and Portugal (1783); France and Spain recognized the principle, but Britain prevented Holland from joining the league by declaring war on the Dutch. The demands of the **League of Armed Neutrality** were: (1) free passage of neutral ships from port to port and along the coasts to combatants; (2) freedom of enemy goods in neutral ships (*le pavillon couvre la marchandise*), excepting for contraband; (3) definition of blockade (nominal, "paper" blockade not sufficient; a blockade, to be legal, must be effective).

1780. Visit of the Emperor Joseph II to Catherine and conclusion (1781) of an **Austro-**

Emelyan I. Pugachev

Catherine II, 1762–1796

Alexander Radishchev, 1749–1802

Russian treaty. Catherine's **Greek Scheme** for the disruption of the Ottoman Empire and division of the Balkans between Russia and Austria *(p. 501)*. In keeping with her Near-Eastern plans, Catherine carried through

1783. The **annexation of the Crimea,** on the plea of restoring order. The Turks were with difficulty dissuaded by Britain and Austria from declaring war on Russia.

1785. **Charter to the nobility,** recognizing their corporate rights. A similar charter was issued for the towns, but not for the peasantry.

1787-1792. **Second war of Catherine against the Turks** *(p. 501)*. Austria joined in the war. The Russians advanced to the Danube, but were badly distracted by

1788-1790. **War with Sweden,** and the Swedish invasion of Finland *(p. 491)*. Under Prussian pressure, the Austrians finally backed out of the Turkish war, and Russia concluded the **treaty of Jassy** (1792, Jan. 9), by which she secured Oczakov and the boundary of the Dniester River.

1793, Jan. 23. The **second partition of Poland,** between Russia and Prussia *(p. 493)*. Catherine, though very hostile to the French Revolution, took care not to become involved. Instead, she furthered her own designs in Poland, and, by

1795, Oct. 24. The **third partition of Poland** *(p. 493)* helped to extinguish the kingdom. By her immense gains in Poland, Russia advanced far into central Europe and became an ever more important factor in European affairs. Catherine was succeeded by her son

1796-1801. **PAUL I,** a tyrannical and mentally unbalanced ruler. Nevertheless, he was the first Russian ruler who tried to put certain limits to the spread of serfdom (1797, manifesto limiting the peasants' work for the landlord to three days a week).

1797. Paul repealed the law of succession of Peter the Great and decreed that succession should be by genealogical seniority.

1799-1801. Russia participated in the **War of the Second Coalition** against France *(p. 617)*.

1801, Mar. 24. **Paul was assassinated** in the course of a palace revolution, and was succeeded by his son

1801-1825. ALEXANDER I.

(Cont. pp. 617, 705.)

II. *The Ottoman Empire, 1656–1792*

(From p. 443)

1656-1661. **Mohammed Kiuprili,** grand vizir. Through unlimited ruthlessness he tamed the restless Janissaries, executed incapable commanders, purged the court, raised the finances (taxes and confiscations). The war with Venice was vigorously pressed and Lemnos and Tenedos retaken (1657). **George II Rákóczi** of Transylvania was defeated and deposed.

1661-1678. **Ahmed Kiuprili** (son of Mohammed), grand vizir. Order having been restored, he ruled with a lenient hand, humoring the sultan and outwitting his enemies. The war with Venice he tried, in vain, to bring to an end by compromise.

1663-1664. **War with Austria.** After the treaty of Westphalia, Austria was able to devote attention to the Near East once more.

1664, Aug. 1. **Battle of St. Gotthard,** a victory of the imperial general, Montecuccoli, over the Turks. A 20-year truce concluded at Vasvar, the Turks losing no territory, but recognizing the election of the prince of Transylvania by the local estates.

1669. **Fall of Candia,** after a long siege. In the peace with Venice (1670) the latter retained only three fortified posts on the island.

1672-1676. **War with Poland,** the result of countless border raids (Tatars and Cossacks) and rivalry for control of the Ukraine. The Turks raided as far as Lemberg, but were twice defeated by King John Sobieski. In the **treaty of Zuravno** (Oct. 16, 1676) the Turks acquired most of Podolia and the Polish Ukraine, thus coming in contact with Russia.

1677-1681. **First war with Russia,** following Cossack raids. By the **treaty of Radzin** (1681) the Turks were obliged to give up most of the Ukraine and accord the Cossacks trading rights on the Black Sea.

1678. **Kara Mustafa** (brother-in-law of Ahmed Kiuprili), grand vizir. He was an incompetent but ambitious man, who at once supported Imre Tökölli as king of Hungary against the Emperor Leopold I.

1682-1699. **War with Austria,** which was allied to Poland.

1683, July 17-Sept. 12. **SIEGE OF VIENNA** by Kara Mustafa. Violent assaults on the walls; extensive mining operations; valiant defense by the garrison under **Rüdiger von Stahremberg.** Successful relief of the city by a united German and Polish army under **Charles of Lorraine** and **John Sobieski.**

1684. Venice joined Austria and Poland in a **Holy League,** sponsored by the pope. The Poles, however, soon withdrew, influenced thereto by Louis XIV of France. The Austrians advanced rapidly to Budapest (1686), while the Venetians took most of the fortresses in the Morea and the Russians laid siege to Azov (1687, 1689).

1687, Aug. 12. **Second battle of Mohács.**

Kara Mustafa (1678)

Ahmed Kiuprili, 1661-1678

Charles of Lorraine defeated the Turks and the diet of Pressburg conferred hereditary succession to the Hungarian throne upon the male line of Austria. Panic in Constantinople; **deposition of Mohammed IV,** who was succeeded by **Suleiman III** (1687-1691).

1688. The Austrians took Belgrade and then (1689) Vidin.

1689. **Mustafa Kiuprili** (brother of Ahmed), grand vizir.

1690. The Turks drove the Austrians out of Bulgaria, Serbia, and Transylvania and retook Belgrade (flight of the Serbs into southern Hungary).

1691, Aug. 19. The Turks defeated by Louis of Baden in the **battle of Slankamen;** Mustafa killed. The war continued, but was not pressed by Austria, which had become involved in war with France (**War of the League of Augsburg,** 1688-1697).

1696, July 28. **Peter the Great** finally took Azov from the Turks.

1697, Sept. 11. **Battle of Zenta,** a great victory of **Eugene of Savoy** over the Turks.

1699, Jan. 26. **TREATY OF KARLOWITZ,**

concluded for 25 years: **Austria** received all of Hungary (except the Banat of Temesvar), Transylvania, Croatia and Slavonia; **Venice** received the Morea and most of Dalmatia; Poland obtained Podolia. **Russia** continued the war until 1700, when the peace treaty recognized the Russian conquest of Azov. Peter was obliged to postpone his far-reaching plans to liberate his coreligionists in the Balkans.

1710-1711. War with Russia, instigated by France and by Charles XII of Sweden, who had fled to Turkey after his defeat by the Russians at Poltava (1709). Peter posed as the champion of the Balkan Christians and made efforts to stir up revolts. But in 1711 he was surrounded on the Pruth River by a vastly superior Turkish army and had to buy himself off. By the **treaty of the Pruth** (1711, July 21) Russia was obliged to give up Azov again.

1714-1718. War with Venice. Corinth and the Venetian stations in Candia were taken, but Austria entered the war and pressed the campaign in Hungary.

1716, Aug. 5. Eugene of Savoy won a victory at **Peterwardein** and captured Belgrade (1717),

1718, July 21. TREATY OF PASSAROWITZ: The Turks lost the Banat of Temesvar, northern Serbia, and Little Wallachia, but they retained the Morea.

1725-1727. The Turks, by agreement with Russia, secured the western part of Transcaucasia.

This led to war with Persia **(Nadir Shah),** who drove the Turks out (1730).

1736-1739. War with Austria and Russia, partly the result of Turkish protests against Russian action in Poland, partly of French pressure. The Russians retook Azov and raided the Crimea, but in the campaigns of 1737 the Turks were successful against both Russians and Austrians.

1739. Spectacular advance of the Russian general, Münnich, to Jassy. Austria, alarmed by the successes of Russia, accepted French mediation.

1739, Sept. 18. TREATY OF BELGRADE. Austria gave up northern Serbia and Belgrade. The Russians, deserted by Austria, joined in the peace, agreeing to raze the fortifications of Azov and not to build a fleet on the Black Sea.

1743-1746. An indecisive **war with Persia,** marking, in a general way, the end of a long duel. The mid-century was, on the whole, a period of peace (European powers involved in the War of the Austrian Succession and the Seven Years' War) and cultural progress **(Raghib Pasha,** grand vizir, 1757–1763). But the unaggressiveness of the central government soon led to the rise of the **Derebeys** (lords of the valley), who established themselves in many parts of Anatolia and set themselves up as semi-independent potentates.

1768-1774. First war of Catherine the Great

against the Turks. This arose from the Russian policy in Poland, the rising of the Poles, and their subsequent flight into Turkey, whither they were pursued by Russian troops. The Turks, instigated by France, declared war. Catherine, though she did not want the war, threw herself into it energetically. Her generals overran Moldavia and Wallachia and sent agents to Greece to raise a revolt, which was officered by Russians.

1770, July 6. Battle of Chesmé, in which a Russian fleet, officered by British, having come from the Baltic to the Anatolian coast, defeated the Turkish fleet.

1771. The Russians conquered the Crimea. Frederick the Great, alarmed by the Russian successes, offered mediation and arranged the first partition of Poland *(p. 493),* but the war went on until the Russians were diverted by the great revolt of Pugachev (1773).

1774, July 21. TREATY OF KUCHUK KAINARJI (a village near Silistria on the Danube); Russia received Kinburn, Yenikale, and Kertch in the Crimea and obtained the right of free navigation for trading vessels in Turkish waters; the Tatars of the Crimea were recognized as "independent" on condition that they accept the sultan as caliph (first move of the sultan to exploit his claim to religious leadership of Islam); Moldavia and Wallachia were returned to Turkey on condition that they be leniently ruled (Russia reserved the

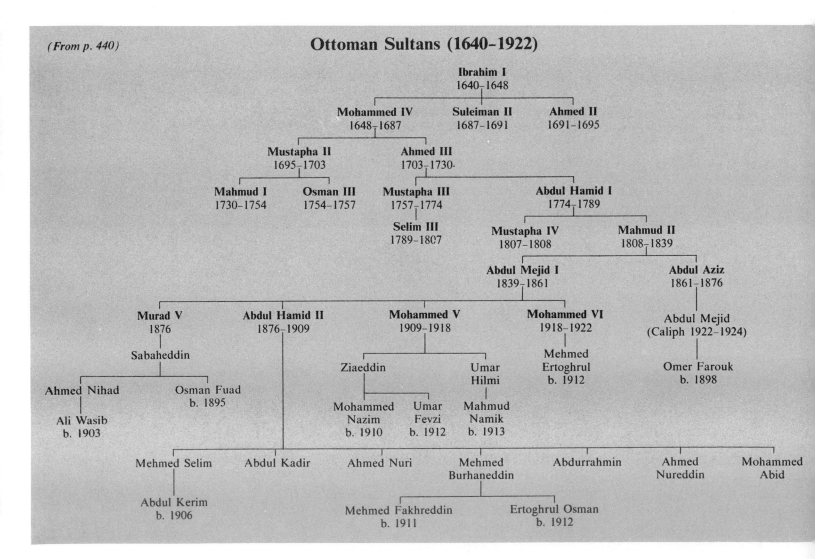

(From p. 440) **Ottoman Sultans (1640–1922)**

right to intervene on their behalf); Russia was given the right to build a Greek church in Galata (foreign quarter of Constantinople); the Turks promised protection to the Christian churches and recognized the right of Russia to make representations in behalf of the church to be built in Galata. These provisions were to become the basis of much Russian interference later.

1781. **Austro-Russian Treaty,** following a famous meeting of Catherine and Joseph II (1780). Catherine's **Greek Scheme** to drive the Turks out of Europe and restore the Greek Empire, with her grandson Constantine (born 1779) as emperor. The Austrians were to receive the whole western half of the Balkans.

1783. The Russians incorporated the Crimea, on the plea of restoring order. Britain and Austria persuaded the outraged Turks to accept the inevitable.

1787–1792. **Second War of Catherine** against the Turks, resulting from Turkish intrigues with the Crimean Tatars and from Russian designs on Georgia. Austria joined Russia (1788) under the terms of the alliance treaty of 1781.

1788. The campaign was indecisive, the Russians being unprepared and the Turks having difficulty in getting troop contingents from the derebeys.

1789–1807. **SELIM III,** an intelligent ruler, bent on victory and reform of the empire.

1789. The Austrians took Belgrade and the Russians, under Prince Gregory Potemkin and Count Alexander Suvorov, advanced to the Danube.

1791, Aug. 4. The Austrians, under Prussian pressure, made the separate **treaty of Sistova,** giving back Belgrade in return for a strip of northern Bosnia.

1792, Jan. 9. **TREATY OF JASSY,** between Turkey and Russia, which, worried by Prussian activity in Poland and deserted by Austria, decided to end the war: Russia obtained Oczakov and a boundary along the Dniester River, but returned Moldavia and Bessarabia.

(Cont. p. 722.)

D. Science and Society, 1700–1800

1. *Philosophical, Religious, and Social Thought*

THE 18TH CENTURY is commonly referred to as the **Age of Enlightenment,** during which European thinkers, strongly influenced by the advances in scientific knowledge, reviewed the institutions of human society in the light of pure reason. As a result almost all accepted ideas were called in question. It was an age of destructive criticism, but also one of healthy skepticism and broad humanitarianism.

1697. **Pierre Bayle** (1647–1706) brought out his *Dictionnaire historique et critique*, which set the tone for 18th-century thought.

1710. **Bishop George Berkeley** (1685–1753), in his *Treatise concerning the Principles of Human Knowledge*, inaugurated the empiricist school of philosophy.

1721. **Louis, Baron de Montesquieu** (1689–1755), in his *Lettres persanes*, viewed European society through the eyes of two imaginary Persians.

1725. **Giambattista Vico's** (1668–1744) *Principi di una scienza nuova intorno alla commune natura delle nazione* combated the intellectualism prevalent in his day and attempted to set up a philosophy of history based on the notion of cyclical change.

1734. The *Lettres anglaises ou philosophiques* of **Voltaire** (Francois-Marie Arouet, 1694–1778) glorified the English constitution, with particular reference to representative government.

1739. **David Hume** (1711–1776), in his *Treatise on Human Nature* and later in his *Philosophical Essays* (1748), developed the empiricist philosophy and advanced a doctrine of extreme

skepticism with respect to the possibilities of human knowledge.

1748. **Montesquieu's** *L'Esprit des lois*, one of the greatest and most influential of all works on political theory.

1751. In his *Le siècle de Louis XIV*, followed by his *Essai sur les moeurs* (1756), **Voltaire** established the new genre of cultural history.

1751–1772. Publication of the *Encyclopédie, ou dictionnaire raisonné des sciences, des arts et des métiers*, in 28 volumes, followed by a six-volume supplement (1776–1777). Edited by **Denis Diderot** (1713–1784) and **Jean d'Alembert** (?1717–1783), it numbered among its contributors Rousseau, Voltaire, Buffon, Holbach, Turgot, Quesnay, Mirabeau, and Montesquieu. Building on the critical analysis of Bayle, the *Encyclopédie* stands as a monumental digest of 18th-century rationalism.

1755. Posthumous publication of **Richard Cantillon's** (d. 1734) *Essai sur la nature du commerce en général*, the earliest systematic analysis of wealth and economic process. Cantillon's book influenced the **Physiocratic School,** a group of economists who stressed agriculture as the source of wealth and attempted to establish the working of natural law in economic life. Pre-eminent in this group were **François Quesnay** (1694–1774), author of *Tableau économique* (1758); **Pierre Dupont de Nemours** (1739–1817: *La physiocratie*, 1768); **A. R. J. Turgot** (1727–1781: *Réflexions sur la formation . . . des richesses*, 1766).

1758. **Emanuel Swedenborg** (1688–1772), emi-

nent Swedish naturalist and scientist, published *De nova Hierosolyma*, one of his many religious treatises and revelations which served as the foundation of the **Church of the New Jerusalem.**

1761. **Johann P. Süssmilch** (1707–1767) pio-

Emanuel Swedenborg, 1688–1772

neered the study of statistics and demography in his fundamental work *Die göttliche Ordnung in den Veränderungen des menschlichen Geschlechts aus der Geburt, dem Tode, und der Fortpflanzung desselben erwiesen.*

1762. **Jean-Jacques Rousseau's** (1712–1778) *Le contrat social* and his *Émile, ou traité de l'éducation,* setting forth the political theory of democracy and the doctrine of rational elementary education.

1764. **Cesare Beccaria** (1738–?1794) established the science of modern penology in his classic *Tratto dei delitti e delle pene.*

1765–1769. The *Commentaries on the Laws of England* by **William Blackstone** (1723–1780), a landmark in the history of the common law.

1776. *An Inquiry into the Nature and Causes of the Wealth of Nations* by **Adam Smith** (1723–1790), an epoch-making treatise on economics, formulating the doctrine of economic liberal-

Immanuel Kant, 1723–1804

ism and inaugurating the classical school of political economy.

1776–1788. **Edward Gibbon's** (1737–1794) *The History of the Decline and Fall of the Roman Empire,* an immortal masterpiece of rationalist historiography, based on wide as well as intensive study of the sources.

1781. **Immanuel Kant** published his *Die Kritik der reinen Vernunft,* to be followed by his *Kritik der praktischen Vernunft* (1788) and his *Kritik der Urteilskraft* (1790). These basic works of the greatest of modern philosophers examined the limitations of the human understanding and established the rationalism of pure experience.

1784–1791. **Johann Gottfried Herder** (1744–1803) published his four-volume *Ideen zur Philosophie der Geschichte der Menschheit* in which, drawing on his earlier researches in primitive literatures, he argued that institutions reflect the soul of a people (*Volksgeist*), in constant process of development. The book provided the foundation for the doctrine of cultural nationalism.

1789. The *Introduction to the Principles of Morals and Legislation,* by **Jeremy Bentham** (1748–1832) set forth a comprehensive system of rational legislation and expounded the philosophy of utilitarianism.

1790. **Edmund Burke** (1729–1797), in his *Reflections on the Revolution in France,* criticized vigorously the political theories of liberalism and inaugurated modern traditionalist doctrine.

1791–1792. *The Rights of Man,* by **Thomas Paine** (1737–1809), an eloquent defense of the French Revolution, its aims and achievements.

1792. Mary Wollstonecraft's (1759–1797) *Vindication of the Rights of Women,* the basic text of the modern feminist movement.

1793. **William Godwin's** (1756–1836) *Enquiry concerning Political Justice,* a restatement of the political tenets of the Enlightenment, eventuating in a system of philosophical anarchism.

1794. Elaborating the Kantian philosophy, **Johann Gottlieb Fichte** (1762–1814) expounded a philosophy of transcendental idealism: *Grundlage der gesamten Wissenschaftslehre* (1794); *Grundlage des Naturrechts* (1796–1797); *System der Sittenlehre* (1798); *Ueber die Bestimmung des Menschen* (1800).

William Blackstone, 1723–1780

1795. **Marie-Jean Condorcet** (1743–1794) in his *Tableau historique des progrès de l'esprit humain* provided a classic exposition of the idea of human progress and of the ultimate perfectibility of mankind.

1797. **Friedrich von Schelling** (1775–1854), deriving from the teaching of Kant, developed a pantheistic philosophy of nature which was highly influential in the Romantic Age: *Ideen zu einer Philosophie der Natur* (1797); *Von der Weltseele* (1798); *System des transcendentalen Idealismus* (1800).

1798. First edition of **Thomas Malthus'** (1766–1834) *Essay on the Principle of Population,* the most influential of all treatises on demography. The second, greatly enlarged edition, appeared in 1803.

1799. Friedrich Schleiermacher (1768–1834), in his *Reden über die Religion,* initiated the attempt to reconcile religion with modern science and learning. *(Cont. p. 571.)*

2. *Scientific Thought*

(From p. 446)

1700. **Gottfried Wilhelm Leibniz** (1646–1716) was instrumental in the foundation of the **Berlin Academy,** Germany's first stable scientific organization.

1701–1713. **Jakob (Jacques) Bernoulli** (1654–1705) worked on problems (1701) which later became the calculus of variations. His *Ars conjectandi,* posthumously published in 1713,

on probability theory, permutations and combinations, and binomial distribution.

1704. **Isaac Newton** (1642–1727), reporting on the optical researches he had undertaken since the 1660's, published his *Opticks.* He treated experimentally of the reflection, refraction, diffraction, and spectra of light.

He investigated the dispersion and composi-

tion of white light, showing that it is not homogeneous, as was traditionally thought, but decomposable into simple colors. The *Opticks* concluded with a group of "Queries," which in later editions developed Newton's speculations and conjectures concerning heat, chemical affinity, pneumatics, physiology, atomism, the nature of gravitation and the

Newton (1642–1727) analyzing a ray of light

Benjamin Franklin, 1706–1790

aether, the relation of the world of nature to God, and the proper manner of scientific inquiry. These speculations determined much of the experimental science of the 18th century.

1705. **Edmund Halley** (1656–1742) noted the resemblance in the paths of the comets of 1531, 1607, and 1682, and conjectured that these were different appearances of the same comet, now called *Halley's Comet*. He correctly predicted the return of this comet in 1758.

1708. **Hermann Boerhaave** (1668–1738) systematized physiology in the mechanistic terms of chemistry. As teacher of theoretical medicine at Leyden he influenced a whole generation of physicians.

1713. Publication of the second edition of Newton's *Principia,* to which was added the famous *General Scholium* containing the phrase "Hypotheses non fingo" (I feign no hypotheses).

1715. **Brook Taylor** (1685–1731) published *Methodus incrementorum directa et inversa,* the first treatise on finite differences and the source of *Taylor's series.* The series took on great importance in the work of **Leonhard Euler** (1707–1783) and **Joseph-Louis Lagrange** (1736–1813).

1717. **Gabriel D. Fahrenheit** (1686–1736) proposed the *Fahrenheit System* and a mode of calibrating thermometers.

1718. **Etienne F. Geoffroy** (1672–1731) published the first table of *chemical affinities,* a chart designed to indicate the reactivity of individual chemicals toward each other.

1723. **Georg E. Stahl** (1660–1734) popularized the views of **Johann Becher** (1669). Stahl renamed *terra pinguis, phlogiston,* which he thought to be an inflammable principle given off into the air by combustible bodies in burning.

1725. **Peter the Great** founded the **Academy of Sciences** at St. Petersburg. The original resident membership of sixteen included thirteen Germans, two Swiss, and one Frenchman.

1725. **John Flamsteed** (1646–1720) published *Historia coelestis britannica,* a catalog of the positions of nearly 3,000 stars. This work replaced the catalog of **Tycho Brahe** as the standard reference source.

1727–1733. **Stephen Hales** (1677–1761) in *Vegetable Staticks* (1727) and *Haemastaticks* (1733) recorded a series of experiments in plant and animal physiology and demonstrated that biological phenomena, such as blood pressure, could be investigated on a quantitative basis. He also invented a pneumatic trough, an indispensible apparatus for collecting gases.

1728. **James Bradley** (1693–1762) explained an anomalous motion of the fixed stars by his discovery of the aberration of light.

1732. **Boerhaave** published *Elementa chemiae,* a standard chemistry textbook influential until the end of the 18th century.

1733. **Abraham de Moivre** (1667–1754) published the discovery of the normal curve of error.

1734–1742. **Berkeley,** in *The Analyst* (1734), attacked the calculus as based on unclear and fallacious premises. This attack stimulated **Colin Maclaurin** (1698–1746) to write *A Treatise on Fluxions* (1742) in which he tried to provide a rigorous foundation for the calculus on the basis of Greek geometry and first applied the calculus to dynamics.

1736. **Leonhard Euler** published *Mechanica sive motus analytice exposita,* generally considered to be the first systematic textbook of mechanics. During his life, Euler made fundamental contributions in many areas of analytical mechanics, e.g., the theory of the motion of rigid bodies, hydrodynamics, the application of variational principles in mechanics, and celestial mechanics.

1738. **Pierre de Maupertuis** (1698–1759) published *Sur la figure de la terre,* a report of a scientific expedition to Lapland which confirmed Newton's view that the earth is a spheroid flattened near the poles with a bulge near the equator.

1738. **Daniel Bernoulli** (1700–1782), in *Hydrodynamica,* presented investigations of the forces exerted by fluids, and presented an early version of the **kinetic theory of gases.**

1743. **Jean d'Alembert** (1717–1783) published *Traité de dynamique,* which formulated *d'Alembert's principle,* and successfully applied it to the solution of many difficult problems in mechanics.

1743. **Alexis Clairaut** (1713–1765) presented his *Théorie de la figure de la terre,* a mathematical investigation on hydrostatic principles of the shape of the earth.

1743–1744. **Benjamin Franklin** (1706–1790) was instrumental in the establishment of the **American Philosophical Society** at Philadelphia, America's first scientific society, devoted to "the promotion of useful knowledge."

1744. **César Cassini** (1714–1784) directed the triangulation of France, the first national survey, which was completed during the French Revolution.

1748. **James Bradley** reported his discovery, made earlier, of the **mutation of the earth's axis.**

1748. **Euler** published *Introductio in analysin infinitorum,* systematizing the calculus and emphasizing the study of functions, classifying differential equations, and treating trigonometric functions and equations of curves without reference to diagrams. He gave an elegant and highly influential exposition of the Leibnizian calculus, together with many new results of his own, in his *Institutiones calculi differentialis* (1755) and *Institutiones calculi integralis* (1768–1770).

1748. **John Tuberville Needham** (1713–1781), in *Observations upon the Generation, Composition, and Decomposition of Animal and Vegetable Substances,* reported that boiled, sealed flasks of broth teemed with "little animals" when opened. His rival **Lazzaro Spallanzani** (1729–1799) devised controlled experiments to test such factors as the amount of heating necessary to kill micro-organisms.

1749. **George Leclerc, Comte de Buffon** (1707–1788), in the fifty-four volumes of his celebrated treatise *Histoire naturelle,* posed a ma-

Gottfried Wilhelm Leibniz, 1646–1716

jority of the problems dominating evolutionary biology for the next 150 years: geographical distribution, progressive development, isolation, transmutation, correlation, and variation.

1750. **Thomas Wright** (1711–1786) suggested that the appearance of the Milky Way from the earth is due to the distribution of the visible stars in a disc.

1751. **Robert Whytt** (1714–1764) explicitly distinguished voluntary from involuntary motions, recognized that only a segment of the spinal cord is necessary for reflex action, and established the **study of reflexes** as a distinct branch of physiology.

1751–1754. **Franklin** published *Experiments and Observations on Electricity,* in which he explained his theory that electricity is a single fluid and used it to account for the properties of the Leyden jar and other known electrical phenomena. He deduced the principle of the **conservation of electric charge** from his theory, and established that lightning is identical with electricity produced by friction.

1752. **Jean Guittard** (1715–1786) noted the existence of extinct volcanoes in the Auvergne region, thereby beginning an extended controversy over the origin of certain kinds of rocks.

1755. **Mikhail Lomonosov** (1711–1765) played a leading role in the founding of **Moscow University.** Known for his work in chemistry, electricity, mechanics, and history, his major contribution was the establishment of the scientific tradition in Russia.

1756–1762. **Joseph Black** (1728–1799), in *Experiments upon Magnesia Alba* (1756), announced the isolation of a new gas, "fixed air" (carbon dioxide). In researches conducted between 1759 and 1762, but published posthumously (1803) in his *Lectures on the Elements of Chemistry,* he distinguished between temperature and quantity of heat, and introduced the terms and concepts *latent heat, heat of fusion, thermal capacity,* and *caloric.*

1756. **Johann Lehmann** (d. 1767) contributed to knowledge of geological succession by classifying orders of strata. Similar work was carried on by **Giovanni Arduino** (1713–1795),

who gave the names *primitive, secondary,* and *tertiary* to lithologically distinct sequences of strata; and earlier by **John Strachey** (1671–1743), whose "Observations on the Strata in the Somersetshire Coal Fields" (1719) established stratigraphical divisions and offered an early attempt at a structure section.

1758. **Carl Linnaeus** (1707–1778) in the tenth edition of his *Systema naturae* catalogued all known flora and fauna, (including man), and laid the basis for modern taxonomy by his consistent use of a **binomial nomenclature.**

1759–1766. **Albrecht von Haller** (1708–1777) delineated the phenomena of "irritability" and "sensibility" in animal tissues and searched for the problems and laws peculiar to physiology.

1760–1761. **Joseph-Louis Lagrange** presented a complete *calculus of variations,* incorporating both old and new results in an elegant and systematic treatment.

1761. **Giovanni Morgagni** (1682–1771) presented in *De sedibus et causis morborum* a correlation of clinical symptoms and anatomic lesions challenging the notion of disease as an imbalance of humors.

1761–1769. **Transits of Venus** across the face of the sun were observed by astronomical expeditions sent out by France, Britain, Germany, Russia, and the American colonies: an early example of international scientific cooperation.

1765–1780. The creation of provincial English scientific societies—**Lunar Society of Birmingham; Manchester Literary and Philosophical Society**—marked the decline of the **Royal Society of London** and a new alliance between science and industry.

1768–1779. **Captain James Cook** (1728–1779), an English naval officer, led three expeditions opening the Pacific to scientific explorers and collectors *(p. 603).*

1770–1771. **Lagrange** published *Réflexions sur la résolution algébrique des équations,* considering the question of why the methods which solve equations of degrees less than 5 do not work for the quintic. He considered the rational functions of the roots and their behavior

on permutation of the roots, leading **Evariste Galois** (1811–1832) and **Niels Henrik Abel** (1802–1829) to their results on solvability.

1771. **Charles Messier** (1730–1817) published the first installment of a star catalog which eventually recorded 103 nebulae and clusters.

1771–1794. **John Hunter** (1728–1793) raised surgery from a technical trade to the ranks of a science by connecting morphology with physiology and emphasizing the natural healing powers of the body.

1773–1784. **Pierre Laplace** (1749–1827) and **Lagrange** in a long series of papers finally solved the "long-term inequality" of Jupiter and Saturn, thus giving important evidence for the stability of the solar system.

1774–1817. **Abraham Werner** (1749/50–1817) propagated his view that features of the earth's crust are of aqueous origin (neptunism). Werner's methodical systematization of rocks and their formations helped found mineralogy as a science.

1774. **Nicholas Desmarest** (1725–1815) established the igneous origin of basalt in a study of the Auvergne volcanoes, thereby challenging neptunism.

1774–1786. **Joseph Priestley** (1733–1804) in his *Experiments and Observations on Different Kinds of Air* reported his studies on gases and announced the discovery of a number of water soluble gases, including ammonia, sulfur dioxide, and hydrogen chloride. In 1775 Priestley isolated **oxygen,** which he called "dephlogisticated air," in experiments with red calx of mercury.

1777. **Carl Scheele** (1742–1786) published his *Chemische Abhandlung von der Luft und dem Feuer.* He reported on his production of hydrogen in 1770 ("inflammable air"), his isolation of oxygen in 1773 ("fire air"), and his discoveries of many new and important substances, both organic and inorganic.

1778. **Buffon** argued in *Epoques de la nature* that the earth is far older than the 6000 years allowed by contemporary theological doctrine.

1779. **Jan Ingenhousz** (1730–1799) showed that plants make the atmosphere fit for breathing by producing oxygen during the day, that

Carl Linnaeus, 1707–1778

George Leclerc, 1707–1788

Joseph Priestley 1733–1804

The Cow-Pock, *1802, caricature on the finding by Edward Jenner (1749–1823) of a vaccine against smallpox*

green leaves and stalks are the functional parts in this process, and that plants carry out respiration concomitantly with photosynthesis.

1780–1781. Claude Berthollet (1748–1822) and Antoine Lavoisier (1743–1794), using the new chemical techniques of pneumatic and combustion analysis, isolated carbon, oxygen, and hydrogen as the elements of organic substances. Their work opened a new era in elementary organic analysis and physiological chemistry.

1781. William Herschel (1738–1822) discovered by telescopic observation the planet **Uranus,** the first planet to be discovered in recorded history.

1783. John Goodricke (1764–1786) observed regular variations in the brightness of the star Algol and demonstrated that Algol was an eclipsing binary.

1784. René-Just Haüy (1743–1821/22) gave an exposition of the laws of crystal form in *Essai d'une théorie sur la structure des crystaux.*

1784. Henry Cavendish (1731–1810) published *Experiments on Air*, in which he showed from experimental results obtained in 1781 that the explosion of a mixture of two volumes of "inflammable air" (hydrogen) with one volume of "dephlogisticated air" (oxygen) produced water.

1784. Lavoisier and Laplace measured the amount of oxygen consumed and of carbon dioxide and heat produced in respiration and combustion.

1785–1789. Charles Augustin de Coulomb (1736–1806) published *Mémoires sur l'électricité et le magnétisme*, in which, by using a torsion balance, he measured the force of electric and magnetic attraction and repulsion and found it inversely proportional to the square of the distance between point charges or magnetic poles.

1788. Lagrange published *Méchanique analitique*, a strictly analytical treatment of mechanics. Here statics is founded on the principle of virtual velocities and dynamics on d'Alembert's principle.

1788. Tobern Bergman (1735–1784) published his *Traité des affinités chymiques, ou attractions electives*, which included lengthy affinity tables summarizing the results of extensive investigations of displacement reactions.

1789. Lavoisier published his *Traité élémentaire de chimie* rejecting the phlogiston theory. He championed his new **theory of combustion** which maintained that oxygen supports combustion and respiration, and combines with metals to form a calx. He also presented a new and empirically determined list of chemical elements. Two years earlier, in collaboration with **Guyton de Morveau** (1737–1816), **Claude-Louis Berthollet** (1748–1822), and **Antoine Fourcroy** (1757–1809), he published a treatise outlining a new method of chemical nomenclature, essentially the one used today.

1790–1801. The revolutionary government of France decreed the adoption of a **decimal system** of weights, measures, and coinage (the **metric system**).

1791. *The Ordnance Survey of Great Britain* was instituted; during the next several decades the entire island was mapped.

1791. Luigi Galvani (1737–1798) in a series of experiments reported in *De viribus electricitatis in motu musculari animalium*, postulated the existence of "animal electricity."

1793. The **Académie Royale des Sciences** was first suppressed by the revolutionary government and then reopened as a section of the **Institut de France.** Motivated by a new concern for applied science, the government established the **École Polytechnique** (1794), providing training and posts for eminent French scientists.

1795. James Hutton (1726–1797) published his *Theory of the Earth*, setting forth the uniformitarian principle that geological change is produced by continuous natural forces.

1797. Lagrange published his *Théorie des fonctions analytiques*, studying real valued functions by means of their Taylor series expansions, and giving the first form for the remainder term as an estimate of error in the Taylor series.

1798. Edward Jenner (1749–1823) described his success at using the scrapings from cowpox as a "vaccination" against smallpox.

1798. Benjamin Thompson (Count Rumford) (1753–1814), in "Inquiry Concerning the Heat which is Caused by Friction," explained, on the basis of experiments in the boring of a cannon's barrel, that the caloric or fluid substance theory of heat was untenable, and suggested that heat of a body was identical with the motions of a body's particles.

1799. Carl Friedrich Gauss (1777–1855) gave the first rigorous proof of the fundamental theorem of algebra, that an nth degree algebraic equation with real coefficients has n roots.

1799. Joseph Louis Proust (1754–1826) announced the **law of definite proportions,** according to which the same chemical compound, however it is prepared, always contains the same elements combined in the same proportions by weight.

1800. Alessandro Volta (1745–1827), in his essay "On the Electricity Excited by the mere Contact of Conducting Substances of Different Kinds," disagreeing with **Luigi Galvani** (1791), showed that the electrically produced effects in muscular contraction arise not from innate animal electricity, but from the moist contact of different metals. This observation led him to construct the **voltaic pile,** the forerunner of the modern battery and the first source of a continuous electric current.

(Cont. p. 576.)

3. *Technological Achievements*

(From p. 448)

Technical achievements of this century in agriculture, mining, metallurgy, and machinery (prime movers, textiles, and machine tools) laid the groundwork for the Industrial Revolution, commencing about the mid-century, which was markedly to change the nature of society and civilization. Industrialization, commencing first in England and first in the textile industry, was to urbanize society, transform the international power structure, and put its mark upon every aspect of modern life.

c. 1700. Christopher Polhem (1661–1751), the "Father of Swedish Technology," developed an improved **rolling mill** and utilized water power for primitive mass production.

1709–1717. Abraham Darby (1677–1717) produced iron from a **coke-fired blast furnace** at Coalbrookdale; despite shortage of charcoal, it took 50 years and improvements made in the method by his son Abraham Darby II before coke was regularly used for this purpose.

1712. Low pressure **steam pump** ("atmospheric engine") of **Thomas Newcomen** (1663–1729) used to pump water from mines. Newcomen utilized some features of **Denis Papin's** (1647–1714) atmospheric engine of 1695, but his invention was quite independent of **Thomas Savery's** (?1650–1715) first useful "fire-engine" of 1698. **John Smeaton** (1724–1792) made many empirical improvements of the Newcomen engine; he also designed bridges, harbors, canals, and the Eddystone Lighthouse (1759), and lowered the price of iron by his water-powered bellows (1761).

1716. Corps des Ponts et Chaussées established in France for civil engineering works; clear distinction made between civil engineer and architect. First improvements in **road-making** since Roman times with work of **P. M. J. Trésaguet** (1716–1794) in France, and **John L. McAdam** (1756–1836) ("metalled" or "macadamized" roads) and **Thomas Telford** (1757–1834) in England. Trésaguet and Telford emphasized a road foundation of large stones, with smaller stones for top layer; McAdam stressed a roadtop impervious to water.

1722. First technical treatise on iron, *L'Art de convertir le fer forgé en acier et l'art d'adoucir le fer fondu,* by **René A. F. de Réaumur** (1683–1757). **Metallurgical techniques** developed during this century included **Benjamin Huntsman's** (1704–1776) crucible process for casting steel (1751), utilized for cutlery and instruments but not commercially successful until 1770; **Henry Cort's** (1740–1800) puddling process to produce wrought (bar) iron from cast iron in a reverberatory furnace (1784); and Cort's perfected rolling mill with grooved rollers (1784).

1732. Publication of **Jethro Tull's** (1674–1741) *New Horse Hoeing Husbandry* in which he described his innovations in **scientific cultivation:** seed drill (1701) to plant seed in rows rather than the older, casual method of tossing seeds; the horse-hoe (introduced by Tull from France in 1714); and the technique of soil pulverization. **Robert Bakewell** (1725–1795) introduced selective breeding of livestock, and **Charles Townshend** (1674–1738) introduced useful new crops, turnips and clover, for winter fodder. The work of these pioneers in scientific cultivation, publicized by **Arthur Young** (1741–1820), helped to produce the **Agricultural Revolution,** which effected radical transformations in agricultural crops and techniques and a large increase in the production of foodstuffs and animal materials (wool, hides).

1733. John Kay (d. 1764?) patented the **flying shuttle,** the first of a series of inventions which were to transform the manufacture of textiles, substitute the factory system for the older method of domestic production, introduce power-driven machinery into manufacuring processes, and mark the first steps in the Industrial Revolution. Other landmarks in the

The cotton gin of Eli Whitney, 1765–1825 (1869 engraving for an American newspaper)

industrialization of textile production were the **spinning jenny** invented (1764) by **James Hargreaves** (d. 1778); the spinning machine **(water-frame)** developed (1769) by **Richard Arkwright** (1732–1792), perhaps based on earlier machines for roller spinning (especially that devised by Lewis Paul in 1733 with some assistance from John Wyatt), and which made Arkwright Lancashire's largest cotton-manufacturer and one of England's richest men; the **spinning "mule"** (1784) of **Samuel Crompton** (1753–1827); the power-loom (1785) of **Edmund Cartwright** (1743–1823), and the cotton gin (1793) of **Eli Whitney** (1765–1825).

1753. Publication by **Johann Heinrich Pott** of the *Lithogeoginoise pyrotechnique* on the **ceramic arts,** which developed during this period as Europeans sought to reproduce the much admired Chinese porcelain introduced to Europe in the later 17th century. First to produce quality china were the **Meissen** works in Saxony (Dresden China), followed by the French state manufactory at **Sèvres** (1768). The English developed bone-china (utilizing bone-ash as an ingredient). **Josiah Wedgwood** (1730–1795) was appointed royal potter (1762) and established his **Etruria** works in 1769. By the 1750's The Potteries, a series of towns in Staffordshire, had become the center of world production of inexpensive earthenware.

1754. Society for the Encouragement of Arts, Manufactures and Commerce (later, **The Royal Society of Arts**) established, inspiring the organization of similar societies in France, Netherlands, and Russia. The first exhibition of the industrial arts was held in Paris (1763). The French *Encyclopédie* (1751–1772) provided a comprehensive treatise, with illustrations, of contemporary technology.

1770. Completion of the English **Grand Trunk Canal** linking the Trent and the Mersey Rivers, giving the industrial towns of the Midlands a direct water route for exports and initiating a **canal-building** fever in England, which reached America and France in the early 19th century. Principal English canal engineers were **James Brindley** (1716–1772), **John Rennie** (1761–1821), and **Thomas Telford** (1757–1834).

1774. **John Wilkinson** (1728–1808) invented the **boring-mill.** Originally designed to bore cannon, this machine was to find its most important use in the boring of cylinders for

1776. The steam engine of **James Watt** (1736–1819). Based upon the older Newcomen engine, the first working model (1768, patented 1769) contained the separate steam condenser. Put into practical use in 1776, Watt's engine was not a commercial success until 1785, when Watt went into partnership with the entrepreneur **Matthew Boulton** (1728–1809) and only after further improvements had been made: the epicyclic (sun-and-planet) gear (1781) producing rotary motion by the reciprocal piston action, and the double-acting expansive engine (1782). (The "steam engine," actually a two-cylinder atmospheric pressure engine, of the Russian Polzunov [1729–1766] operated only for a short time [1767] and had no influence on subsequent engine development.)

1783. First balloon ascent by **Montgolfier brothers** in France, using a paper balloon lifted by hot air. (Balloons a Chinese invention.) Later ascents (1784) by the **Roberts brothers** utilized hydrogen for lifting power. First military use for observation at battle of Fleurus (1794).

Ballooning, *French copper engraving, c. 1784, dedicated to the Roberts brothers*

1785. Introduction of **chemical bleaching** with chlorine (*eau de Javel*) by the French chemist **C. L. Berthollet** (1748–1822).

1789. The **Leblanc process** for obtaining soda from common salt invented by **Nicolas Leblanc** (1742–1806) in France, but first exploited in England.

1793. Claude Chappe (1763–1805) developed the **semaphore** (visual telegraph); rapid spread after success of first line from Paris-Lille.

1794. Establishment of **École Polytechnique,** premier institution of higher technological education in France; emphasis upon mathematics and applied science.

1797. Henry Maudslay (1771–1831) designed a **screw-cutting lathe,** made entirely of metal and utilizing a slide-rest. This tool was the

culmination of much previous precision tool development, including the drill and lathe (1768–1780) of **Jacques de Vaucanson** (1709–1782), the screw-cutting lathe (1770) of **Jesse Ramsden** (1735–1800); the marine chronometer (1759) of **John Harrison** (1693–1776); the spring-winding machine of **Joseph Bramah** (1748–1814), who also invented the modern water closet (1778) and a hydraulic press (1796).

1798. P. L. Guinand (1748–1824), a Swiss, patented a stirring process for making optical glass which became the foundation of the great German **optical industry** of the 19th century.

1798. Aloys Senefelder (1771–1834) of Prague invented **lithography.**

(Cont. p. 583.)

E. Latin America, 1500–1803

1. *Nature of the Conquest*

IN THE BROADER SENSE the conquest and colonization of Spanish America progressed logically outward from the earliest colony in Santo Domingo until by 1600 the territory from New Mexico and Florida on the north to Chile and the Río de la Plata on the south was, with the exception of Brazil, effectively under the rule of the crown of Castile.

The motives which inspired the Castilian sovereigns to create a vast empire in the Americas were the desire to achieve more extensive realms, propagate Christianity, and obtain increased revenues. The early *conquistadores* were impelled by several motives which varied in intensity with regard to individuals, time, and place: desire to gain wealth and position, desire to add to the glory of the Castilian crown, zeal to propagate Christianity, and love of adventure. The most important of the early conquests were achieved at no direct cost to the crown. Individual leaders by their own initiative, in the name of the sovereign or by virtue of royal patents, conquered territory at their own expense, hoping to receive or to be assigned authority and revenues in the lands subjugated. In this manner Cortés conquered Mexico, Alvarado Guatemala, Pizarro Peru, Jiménez de Quesada New Granada, and Montejo Yucatan. The crown of Castile soon established direct and absolute control and evolved complex machinery of government to rule its vast colonial empire. The Church, over which the crown exercised patronage, achieved complete organization and exercised vast influence. The military triumphs of the Spaniards over incredible numerical odds were the triumph of indomitable representatives of a more highly developed society over those of a lesser. The conquest was accompanied by great cruelty, but it was no greater than that of contemporary conquest elsewhere. Ruthless exploitation of the natives followed colonization, but such was the common lot of subject peoples during the period. The intent of the Castilian crown toward the Indian masses, if not the actual practice, was beneficent. While the production of gold and silver was the chief source of crown revenues in the Indies and became the basis of much private wealth, agriculture, grazing, and commerce were soon highly developed and local industries of various types came into existence. Certain colonies like Chile, Yucatan, and the Río de la Plata were almost exclusively agricultural and pastoral. A relatively large measure of intellectual activity came into being in the larger cities and within the Church. The existence of a large Indian population, many groups of which possessed high cultures of long standing and the impact of European culture and Christianity on the New World civilizations led to fundamentally important social, cultural, and racial developments.

2. *The West Indies and the Isthmus, 1501–1531*

Santo Domingo became the first seat of Spanish government in the Indies. Immigration to Española, although not heavy, increased and mining and agriculture were developed.

1501. **Negro slavery** was introduced. The Indian population rapidly diminished as a result of warfare, enslavement, and disease.

1508-1511. **Puerto Rico** was conquered, San Juan being founded, and **Jamaica** was settled.

1511-1515. **Diego Velázquez,** as lieutenant of the viceroy, Diego Columbus, conquered Cuba and founded Santiago and San Cristóbal de la Habana.

1509-1513. Under royal patents **Alonso de Ojeda** founded a colony on the coast of South America east of the Isthmus of Panama and **Diego de Nicuesa** founded Nombre de Dios on the Isthmus. The settlement founded by Ojeda was transferred to the Isthmus at the suggestion of Vasco Nuñez de Balboa (1474-1519). There the colonists united with those of Nicuesa.

1513. **Balboa** became governor of the colony and as such he discovered the South Sea (Pacific Ocean) and took possession for the crown of Castile.

1513-1514. A jurisdiction independent of Española, **Castilla del Oro** (Darien); was created in the region of the Isthmus and **Pedro Arias de Ávila** (1442-1531) was appointed royal governor, bringing some 1500 colonists from Spain.

1514-1519. Ávila dispatched expeditions by land and sea to adjacent areas, including the Gulf of Nicoya, Zenú, and the Gulf of San Miguel, founded **Panama** as the seat of government, refounded Nombre de Dios, and established a route across the Isthmus. Balboa, as *adelantado* of the South Sea and subordinate to Ávila, continued explorations on the Pacific coast, but as a result of quarrels with the governor, was executed by him (1519).

1522-1523. Under authority independent of Ávila, **Gil González Dávila** and Alonso Niño led a combined land and sea expedition westward from the Isthmus. Dávila conquered the area about the Gulf of Nicoya and Lake Nicaragua and Niño sailed to Fonseca Bay. Ávila then dispatched **Francisco Hernández de Córdoba** to conquer Nicaragua for himself.

1523-1531. Dávila, returning to Española, secured license to continue exploration and conquest, and returned to Central America by way of Honduras. Hernández de Córdoba, after establishing a short-lived colony on the Gulf of Nicoya, entered Nicaragua and founded León and Granada. Forces sent northward by him were defeated by Dávila, who in turn was overcome by Cristóbal de Olid. Hernández de Córdoba rebelled against Ávila and was executed, after which Ávila became governor of Nicaragua. In this capacity he dispatched an expedition along the San Juan River to the sea, exploration which was continued after his death (1531).

(Cont. p. 515.)

3. Venezuela and New Granada, 1521–1549

Early efforts to colonize the eastern portion of the north coast of South America failed.

1521. An attempt made by **Bartolomé de Las Casas** (1474–1566) to found a colony at Cumaná in accord with his theories of peaceful reduction failed.

1530. **Antonio de Sedeño** achieved but little success in an effort to occupy Trinidad Island.

1531–1535. The efforts of **Diego de Ordaz** to explore the region of the Orinoco led to no result. Ordaz lost his life. In the western areas permanent colonization was established at an early date.

1527. **Juan de Ampués,** commissioned by the *audiencia* of Santo Domingo, founded Santa Ana de Coro. This territory was granted by the Emperor Charles V to the **Welsers,** the great Augsburg banking firm to which he was heavily indebted.

1529. The Welsers at once sent out colonists and established an administration. Exploration was carried on through the valley of the Orinoco and into the Andes. The government of the Welsers was marked by ruthless enslavement and maltreatment of the Indians. On that account and because of protests in Spain against grant of lands in the New World to foreigners, their concession was ultimately revoked (1546–1556). The conquest and colonization of Venezuela was then undertaken by the Spaniards. Caracas was founded by Diego de Losada in 1567.

1525. **Rodrigo de Bastidas** founded Santa Marta, the first permanent settlement in what was to become New Granada. **Cartagena** was founded in 1533 by Pedro de Heredia, acting directly under royal authority.

1536–1538. **Gonzalo Jiménez de Quesada** (1495–1576), under commission from the governor of Santa Marta, moved up the Magdalena River, reached the plateau of Bogotá, reduced the Chibchas *(p. 381),* and founded **Santa Fé de Bogotá.**

1539. **Nikolaus Federmann,** an agent of the Welsers, arrived at Bogotá after three years of wandering in the lowlands. Very soon afterward there appeared from the west coast **Sebastian de Belalcázar,** one of Pizarro's lieutenants. A dispute arose regarding jurisdiction. Finally the three captains went to Spain to lay the controversy before the crown. Federmann died. Belalcázar was confirmed in the governorship of Popayán, but Quesada's claims were rejected in favor of those of the son of the deceased governor of Santa Marta.

1549. The *audiencia* of **New Granada** was created. It included Santa Marta, Cartagena, Popayán, and Santa Fé (Bogotá), the latter town being the seat of government over this large area. *(Cont. p. 515.)*

The earliest known European print, a German woodcut (c. 1505) of the mainland and natives of South America

4. Peru and the West Coast, 1522–1581

1522. Continuing exploration southward from Panama, **Pascual de Andagoya** (c. 1495–1548) reached a point south of the Gulf of San Miguel and advanced into **Biru (Peru),** where he learned of the rich and powerful **Inca Empire** *(p. 382)*. Andagoya planned the conquest of the lands reported, but was forced to relinquish the project by ill health.

1524–1528. **Francisco Pizarro** (1470–1541), under authority of Ávila, in association with Diego de Almagro (1475–1538) and Hernando de Luque, a priest, determined upon the conquest of Peru. An initial expedition reached the San Juan River and a second the Gulf of Guayaquil and Túmbez, where evidence of the high civilization and great wealth of the Inca was encountered.

1528–1529. Pizarro went to Spain and concluded a capitulation with the crown by which he was granted the right of discovery and conquest in Peru for a distance of 200 leagues south of the Gulf of Guayaquil with the offices of *adelantado,* governor, and captain general. Almagro was assigned command of the fortress of Túmbez, and Luque was named bishop of Túmbez.

1531. Returning to Panama, accompanied by his brothers, Gonzalo (c. 1505–1548) and Hernando, and a small group of recruits, Pizarro organized an expedition of 180 men, with 27 horses and two pieces of artillery, and sailed for the conquest. Pizarro consolidated his position at Túmbez and founded San Miguel. After having been joined by further recruits, Pizarro moved into the interior with 62 horse and 102 foot, invited by the Inca **Atahualpa,** and reached Cajamarca on the central plateau, near which the Indian monarch was encamped with a large army.

1532, Nov. 16. When Atahualpa visited the Spanish camp, Pizarro seized him. This bold stroke produced great moral effect among the Inca and paralyzed the machinery of government. While a prisoner, Atahualpa caused his rival, his half-brother Huascar, to be murdered.

1533. The Inca paid an enormous ransom in gold and silver, but for political reasons was executed by the Spaniards. Having been joined by Almagro, Pizarro occupied **Cuzco,** the Inca capital, and set up **Manco,** brother of Huascar, as Inca.

1535. Pizarro, having left Cuzco, founded **Lima,** which became the capital of the later viceroyalty of Peru. In Pizarro's absence the natives revolted under Manco and conducted a lengthy but unsuccessful **siege of Cuzco.** This was the only serious attempt of the Incas to expel the Spaniards (1535–1536).

In the following years the area of Spanish dominion was greatly extended. In the south the region about Lake Titicaca was reduced and Chuquisaca founded (1536–1539). The rich silver mines of **Potosí** were opened in 1545. To the north the region of Quito, where lieutenants of Atahualpa had established control after his seizure, was reduced in 1534 by Pizarro's subordinate, Belalcázar (1495–1550). **Pedro de Alvarado,** governor of Guatemala, having heard of rich lands in Peru, led an expedition of some 500 men from Central America and sought to secure control of Quito in 1534–1535. Alvarado was ultimately

Inca ruins near Cuzco, Peru

induced to relinquish his claims in return for monetary compensation. Belalcázar founded Cali and Popayán (1535–1536) and advanced to the Bogotá plateau, where in 1539 he encountered Quesada. In the same year Gonzalo Pizarro, governor of Quito, led an expedition across the Andes and reached the upper Amazon. One of his lieutenants, **Francisco de Orellana,** seeking to gain territory for himself, continued down the Amazon and reached the sea (1541). He went to Spain and secured authority to conquer the Amazonian area, but died on the return to the New World. His followers accomplished nothing.

1537. After a dispute with Pizarro regarding jurisdiction over the city of Cuzco, Almagro occupied the city, thus beginning a series of **civil wars** between the Spaniards. Almagro was defeated and executed (1538).

1541. Dissension continued. Partisans of Almagro assassinated Pizarro and set up Almagro's son as governor, but the younger Almagro was, in turn, overthrown by the royal governor Vaca de Castro (1542).

Meanwhile the Spaniards had begun **expansion into Chile.**

1535–1537. Almagro the elder had advanced as far as the Maule River.

1540–1553. **Pedro de Valdivia** (c. 1498–1553) penetrated the fertile valley and founded **Santiago** (1541). A series of wars ensued with the **Araucanian Indians,** most warlike of the tribes.

Valdivia having lost his life in the wars (1553), the conquest was continued by **García Hurtado de Mendoza** (1557–1561) whose forces advanced to the Straits of Magellan. The conquest was extended into Cuyo and the town of Mendoza founded.

With the creation of the viceroyalty and *audiencia* of Peru (1542), **Blasco Núñez Vela,** the first viceroy, proclaimed the **New Laws,** with provision for eventual abolition of *encomiendas* (1544). This aroused much opposition, culminating in open revolt under the leadership of **Gonzalo Pizarro.** Vela was deposed and Pizarro assumed the position of governor (1544). The viceroy sought to quell the revolt, but was defeated and killed (1546).

1546–1550. The emperor, fearing a separatist movement, appointed **Pedro de la Gasca,** a churchman with high qualities of statesmanship, his representative and endowed him with virtually unlimited powers. Gasca, adopting a conciliatory policy and promising remedy of the causes of complaint, won over many of the opposing party, defeated Pizarro in the **battle of Xaquixaguana** (1548), and restored direct royal authority. Gonzalo Pizarro was executed.

1550–1551. **Antonio de Mendoza** was named viceroy of Peru, but died after a short period in office. The *audiencia* exercised interim authority, crushing a revolt of yet dissatisfied elements led by Francisco Girón, until the arrival of Andrés Hurtado de Mendoza (1557).

1569–1581. **Francisco Alvarez de Toledo,** a proved soldier and diplomat, and one of the greatest of the magistrates of the colonial period, as viceroy of Peru systematized the administration. Codes were promulgated, mining was stimulated and regulated, *corregimientos* on the Castilian model were erected for both Spanish and Indian districts, the tribute of the natives was regularized, the *mita,* or system of enforced labor of the Indians in the mines, on the *haciendas,* and for public

Francisco Pizarro, 1470–1541

works was established, the natives were concentrated in towns to facilitate administration and indoctrination, and public works were constructed. **Francis Drake** raided the coast of Peru during the incumbency of Toledo.

(Cont. p. 515.)

5. *The Rio de la Plata, 1526–1580*

1526–1532. **Sebastian Cabot,** in the service of a group of merchants of Seville, set out with an expedition to reach the Moluccas, but diverted it to the **Río de la Plata** in search for a passage to the east. The expedition passed up the Paraná and Paraguay Rivers and founded a short-lived settlement on the lower Paraná.

1535. Permanent colonization of the La Plata was undertaken by the expedition of **Pedro de Mendoza,** to whom the conquest of the area was assigned.

1536. Mendoza founded **Buenos Aires** (Santa María de Buenos Aires) on the estuary of the La Plata. Expeditions were sent to explore the Paraná and Paraguay and search for a

route to Peru. A fort was established at Asunción (1537) to which the colony at Buenos Aires was soon transferred. Mendoza died (1537) on a voyage to Spain, and Domingo Martínez de Irala was elected governor.

1542–1544. **Alvar Núñez Cabeza de Vaca,** named by the crown to replace Mendoza, reached Asunción with more colonists, having traveled overland from southern Brazil. He was opposed by Irala, who again became governor and was at length confirmed by the crown.

1573. **Juan de Garay,** with colonists from Asunción, founded Santa Fé and a few years later refounded Buenos Aires (1580).

(Cont. p. 515.)

Sebastian Cabot, 1476–1557

TEXAS

Colonial
LATIN AMERICA

Zacatecas
Guadalajara
Mexico
Tlaxcala
Vera Cruz
Oaxaca
YUCATAN
Tehuantepec
GUATEMALA
GUATEMALA
HONDURAS
COSTA RICA
Havana
CUBA
Campeche
Santiago
ESPAÑOLA
PUERTO RICO

Viceroyalty of New Spain

Porto Bello
Nombre de Dios
Cartagena
Sta. Marta
1567
Caracas Cumaná
Trinidad
Panama 1519
Darien
VENEZUELA
GUIANAS
Cali
Bogotá 1538
Popayán
Orinoco R.

Equator

Quito 1587

Viceroyalty of NEW GRANADA

Amazon River

Belém (Para)
São Luiz de Maranhão
Natal
Paraiba
Recife (Pernambuco) 1536

Guayaquil
Túmbez
Cajamarca

B R A Z I L

São Francisco

Salvador (Baía) 1549
MINAS GERAIS
Porto Seguro, 1537

Lima 1535
Cuzco
L. Titicaca
Potosí
Charcas 1558

Viceroyalty of PERU

São Paulo
Asunción
Rio de Janeiro
Santos 1532

BANDA ORIENTAL
Córdoba
Rio Grande do Sul, 1736

Valparaiso
Santiago
Mendoza
Buenos Aires 1580
Montevideo 1723
Rio de la Plata

Viceroyalty of LA PLATA

Pacific Ocean

Atlantic Ocean

Cg. of Chile

Str. of Magellan

Cape Horn

Moctezuma, 1480?–1520

zuma), ruler of the Aztecs *(p. 379)*, and after winning the support of the **Totonac,** a people subject to the Aztec, Cortés moved into the interior, overcame Tlaxcala, and formed an alliance with the republic. Moving on the Aztec capital, Cortés thwarted a treacherous attempt to destroy his force at Cholula and entered **Tenochtitlán** (1519, Nov. 8), where he was amicably received by Moctezuma. To safeguard his position, Cortés soon made the native ruler a prisoner, and the latter and his chiefs swore fealty to the Castilian sovereign.

1520. Meanwhile Velázquez, named royal *adelantado* of the lands discovered by Hernández de Córdoba and Grijalva, sent an expedition under **Pánfilo de Narváez** to reduce Cortés to obedience. Cortés, placing Pedro de Alvarado (1485–1541) in command at Tenochtitlán, went to the coast and by combined subterfuge and vigorous action won over the majority of the force of Narváez, thereupon returning to the Aztec capital. Harsh rule by Alvarado aroused the Aztecs to revolt against the Spaniards and Moctezuma, and Cortés was forced to evacuate Tenochtitlán with heavy losses (1520, June 30). Moctezuma, who had been injured by his own subjects, died or was killed by the Spaniards at the time of the evacuation. Cortés retreated around the northern end of Lake Tezcuco, overcame an overwhelming Aztec army at **Otumba** (1520, July 7), and reached Tlaxcala, which remained loyal. At Tlaxcala Cortés reorganized his forces. He then conquered the province of Tepeaca, founding Segura de la Frontera. An expedition was sent into southern Vera Cruz, and two outposts were established. Having received reinforcements, among them the members of the Garay expedition to Pánuco, Cortés established his base at Tezcuco and undertook the investment of Tenochtitlán by land and water.

1521, May 26–Aug. 13. After a prolonged and desperate siege the Spaniards, aided by a horde of native allies, captured the Aztec capital, making prisoner **Cuauhtémoc,** who had become emperor and had organized resistance. Spanish control was firmly established over

6. *New Spain, 1518–1574*

a. THE CONQUEST OF MEXICO, 1518–1522

1518–1519. To continue the discoveries of Hernández de Córdoba and Grijalva *(p. 386)*, Diego Velázquez and **Hernándo Cortés** (1485–1547) organized an expedition of some 600 men, with 17 horses and 10 cannon. Cortés was put in command. Sailing from Cuba despite Velázquez's orders, he followed the coast of Yucatan, subjugated Tabasco and reached San Juan de Ulloa. There he renounced the authority of Velázquez and, acting as a direct agent of the crown, founded **Villa Rica de la Vera Cruz.** Cortés was elected chief magistrate by the soldiers and sent representatives to Spain to secure confirmation.

After negotiations with **Moctezuma** (Monte-

the immediate vicinity and the conquest was rapidly extended. Tenochtitlán was razed and **Mexico City,** which became the seat of government of the later viceroyalty of New Spain, was erected. A bitter suit between Cortés and Velázquez, carried on before the crown during the period of the conquest, terminated in favor of Cortés and the emperor named him *governor* and *captain-general of New Spain* (1522, Oct. 15).

b. EXPANSION TO THE SOUTH, 1522–1546

1522–1524. Cristóbal de Olid subdued Colima and part of Jalisco. Another settlement was made in Michoacan, the territory of the independent and civilized Tarascans, whose ruler had given allegiance to Cortés. Farther south Oaxaca and Tehuántepec were reduced, the latter by Alvarado.

1523–1525. Embassies from certain towns of Guatemala having made submission, Cortés sent Alvarado to that region. Alvarado conquered the civilized Quiché and Cakchiquel and founded the city of Guatemala. The conquest was then extended into **Salvador,** and Alvarado became governor of the general district of Guatemala. Chiapas was reduced by expeditions from New Spain (1523–1528).

1524–1526. Cortés then sent Olid to conquer and settle **Honduras.** Olid sought to free himself from the authority of Cortés and overcame Gil González Dávila, but was defeated and later killed by a lieutenant of Cortés. Trujillo was founded during this period (1523–1526). Cortés led an expedition overland to Honduras by way of Tabasco and Petén, and established his authority, thereupon returning to Mexico (1524–1526).

1526–1536. Almost complete anarchy continued in Honduras, despite appointment of royal governors. The acting governor, **Andrés de Cerezeda,** established the majority of the colonists in the area of the Río de Ulúa (Higueras), and soon summoned Alvarado to preserve the colony (1534–1536). Alvarado as governor founded **San Pedro** and dispatched an expedition to found Gracias a Dios, but departed for Spain without definitely reducing the area (1536).

1527–1535. The **conquest of Yucatan** was assigned to **Francisco de Montejo** (c. 1473–1553) as *adelantado.* The first attempt of Montejo to conquer the Maya failed after eight years of effort, and he was diverted to Honduras

upon appointment as governor. The final conquest and colonization of Yucatan were achieved by the son and nephew of Montejo under his general direction. Campeche, Mérida, Valladolid, and Salamanca (Bacalar) were founded (1539–1545).

1537–1539. Francisco de Montejo, as royal governor, conclusively subjugated Higueras, founding Comayagua. Alvarado, upon returning, again became governor, but after his death (1541) governmental affairs fell into confusion. Stability was created with the establishment of the ***audiencia* of Confines** (1542–1544).

1546. A serious **revolt of the Maya** was crushed.

Tabasco, which had been colonized at an early date but was in danger of abandonment, was assigned to the jurisdiction of Montejo and was pacified by him and his son (1529–1540). The area of Petén was not conquered until the close of the 17th century.

c. EXPANSION TO THE NORTH, 1522–1795

1522–1527. The initial efforts of Garay to colonize Amichel having failed, Cortés subdued the region of the Panuco River and founded a

Cuauhtémoc brought captive before Cortés, 1521

Juan Ponce de León, 1460?–1521

Hernando De Soto, 1499–1542

Pedro Menéndez de Avilés, 1519–1574

town. Further efforts by Garay were forestalled, and a revolt of the natives was put down by one of Cortés' lieutenants (1523). The Pánuco district became a special jurisdiction under the crown, with Nuño de Guzmán as governor (1527).

1531–1550. In the interior Spanish expansion was slower. **Querétaro** was reduced and the town of that name was founded. The Zacatecas and Guanajuato **silver mines** were opened, the former proving to be the richest in New Spain. **San Luis de Potosí,** in which mining was soon developed, was conquered by Francisco de Urdiñola, whose son continued the work of colonization.

1539. Reports brought by Cabeza de Vaca and the legend of the *Seven Cities of Cíbola* caused the viceroy, Mendoza, to send the Franciscan **Fray Marcos de Niza** northward. Having reached the Zuñi pueblos of New Mexico, the friar returned with exaggerated accounts.

1540–1542. Francisco Vásquez de Coronado, governor of New Galicia, with the authority of the viceroy, led an expedition overland to the new lands, while **Hernando de Alarcón** proceeded by sea along the west coast. Coronado reached the Zuñis and his lieutenants reached the Moqui pueblos and the **Grand Cañon** of the Colorado. In search of Gran Quivira, Coronado traversed northern Texas, Oklahoma, and eastern Kansas before his return.

1562–1570. Francisco de Ibarra, governor and captain-general, conquered New Vizcaya and founded **Durango.**

1598–1608. Under royal patent, **Juan de Oñate** secured the submission of New Mexico and sent out expeditions which explored the region from Kansas to the Gulf of California. **Santa Fé** was founded soon after the resignation of Oñate.

Meanwhile the Spaniards had extended their conquests far up the Pacific Coast.

1529–1531. Nuño de Guzmán, president of the first *audiencia* of New Spain, subjugated a considerable area to the north and west of Mexico City, including Jalisco and Sinaloa. This region was called *New Galicia,* of which Campostela became the capital.

1532–1533. In search of a strait and of new lands, Cortés dispatched expeditions which reached northern Sinaloa and Lower California.

1535. Cortés himself attempted, though without success, to found a colony in Lower California, but **Francisco de Ulloa,** in command of an expedition organized by Cortés, reached the head of the **Gulf of California** (1539). Alarcón, co-operating by sea with Coronado's expedition to New Mexico, reached the same district and passed up the **Colorado River** (1540).

1541. In the absence of Coronado, the natives of New Galicia rose in revolt, but were finally subdued by the viceroy, Antonio de Mendoza.

1542–1543. As part of his project for South Sea discovery, Mendoza sent **Juan Rodríguez de Cabrillo** to search for a northern strait. Cabrillo, and, after his death, the pilot Bartolomé Ferrelo, explored the Pacific coast as far as **Oregon,** but failed to discover the Bays of Monterey and San Francisco.

1548. An *audiencia* was created to govern New Galicia, **Guadalajara** becoming the political and ecclesiastical capital.

1602. The occupation of the Philippines *(p. 560),* the development of trade, and the need for protection against English, French, and Dutch aroused renewed interest in the California coast and the possibility of a northern strait. The Madrid government having ordered the exploration of the coast, **Sebastian Vizcaino** proceeded to a point above San Francisco Bay, which, however, he did not discover. Plans to colonize the Monterey Bay region did not materialize.

1680. The Spaniards, driven from New Mexico by a revolt of the natives, reconquered the area somewhat later (1696).

1720–1722. Fearing loss of territory to France, the Spaniards permanently occupied **Texas,** mainly through the efforts of the marquis of Aguayo, governor of Coahuila.

1769–1786. Under Gálvez's direction Upper California was occupied. San Diego (1769), Monterey (1770), Los Angeles (1781), and San Francisco (1776), were founded and a system of *presidios* and missions, the latter under the Franciscan order, was established.

1774–1776. Juan Pérez, Bruno de Heçeta, Bodega y Quadra, and other Spanish explorers were sent north along the coast to counter British and Russian activity. They discovered the mouth of the **Columbia River** and advanced as far as 60° N.L.

1776. José de Gálvez, minister of the Indies, erected New Vizcaya, Sinaloa, Sonora, the Californias, Coahuila, New Mexico, and Texas into the *Provincias Internas* under the governorship of a commandant-general responsible directly to the crown.

1789–1795. Attempts were made to colonize the region north of California. Settlements were made on Vancouver Island and at Cape Flattery, but without permanent results.

d. THE GULF COAST, FLORIDA, AND THE CAROLINAS, 1521–1574

1521. Juan Ponce de León, under royal patent, tried unsuccessfully to colonize Florida.

1526–1528. A colony, **San Miguel de Gualdape,** was established in the Carolinas by **Lucas Vásquez de Ayllón,** but was abandoned on his death.

1528. Pánfilo de Narváez, having secured authority to colonize the territory assigned to Garay on the Gulf coast and to Ponce de León in Florida, landed in Florida with colonists from Spain. After exploration he tried to reach the area of the Pánuco River. The expedition was wrecked on the coast of Texas and most of the colonists died of hunger and disease, or at the hands of the Indians.

1536. Alvar Núñez Cabeza de Vaca and three companions, after six years of captivity, escaped and traversed Texas and northern Mexico, reaching Culiacán.

1539–1543. Hernando De Soto (1499–1542), granted a patent for the colonization of the Gulf coast (Florida), headed an expedition from Spain, landed in Florida, explored the southeastern portion of the United States, **discovered the Mississippi River** (1541), traversed Arkansas and Oklahoma to the Arkansas River, and followed the latter river to the Mississippi. While moving down the Mississippi, De Soto died (1542) and the expedition, under Luìs de Moscoso, continued on to the area of the Pánuco (1543). Luis De Cancer, a Dominican, and certain companions sought to bring the nations of Florida to obedience by peaceful means, in accord with theories of Las Casas, but De Cancer was killed, and the attempt was abandoned (1549).

1559-1561. Under directions from the crown, the viceroy, Velasco, dispatched a large expedition under **Tristán de Luna** to colonize the region of the Carolinas (Santa Elena). Luna established a garrison at Pensacola, moved inland, and founded a settlement. The colonists were soon transferred to Pensacola. Villafañe replaced Luna as governor and sought without success to colonize the Carolinas. The garrison left at Pensacola was soon withdrawn. In view of constant failure, Philip II ordered that no further attempt be made to colonize Florida (1561), but need for protection of the Bahama Channel (the route for the return to Spain of plate and merchant fleets) and French attempts to occupy the region led to a reversal of this policy.

1562. **Jean Ribaut** failed in an attempt to establish a French Huguenot settlement at Port Royal (in South Carolina), but shortly afterward **Laudonnière** founded Fort Caroline, on the St. John's River (1564). Ribaut arrived with a third expedition, with instructions to establish a fortified place to command the route of the Spanish plate fleets. As a result of these activities Philip II determined upon the expulsion of the French and the permanent colonization of Florida.

1565. As *adelantado* of Florida **Pedro Menéndez de Avilés founded St. Augustine,** captured Fort Caroline, and slew the garrison. Thus danger of French occupation was removed.

1565-1574. Menéndez de Avilés established *presidios* and posts throughout a wide area and explored and sought to colonize the area north of the peninsula. **Jesuits,** and later **Franciscans,** supported by the *adelantado*, established missions as far north as Virginia. The peninsula of Florida was secured for Spain by Menéndez de Avilés, but the attempts to achieve permanent possession of the territory to the north failed. *(Cont. below.)*

7. *Foreign Encroachments and Territorial Changes, 1580–1800*

The commercial and territorial monopoly of Spain in the Indies, international war, and religious conflict caused England, France, and the Netherlands to attack Spanish shipping and coastal towns in the colonies and to colonize within areas controlled by Spain.

16th cent. French corsairs early attacked Spanish vessels off the coasts of Europe and at the Azores and Canaries and soon extended their activities into the Caribbean, where they attacked towns as well as commerce. In the latter half of the 16th century English freebooters, with the tacit approval of the crown, became active in the Atlantic, Caribbean, and Pacific. The raiding of the Pacific coast by **Drake** during his voyage around the world (1577–1580) is the most outstanding example of English activity in the Pacific during this period. The activities of English freebooters became official after the outbreak of war between Spain and England. Spanish commerce suffered greatly, and many towns were held for ransom or sacked, among them Nombre de Dios, Cartagena, Santo Domingo, and Valparaiso. **Drake, Hawkins, Oxenham,** and **Cavendish** were the most important of the English mariners, and two of the expeditions commanded by Drake constituted formidable armaments. Coincident with the struggle for independence in the Netherlands, Dutch mariners became active.

17th cent. With the decline of Spanish power, official **colonization of the Lesser Antilles,** neglected by Spain, was undertaken by England, France, and Holland. Settlements were established by these powers in the Guianas. England colonized Bermuda and the Bahamas, the Netherlands unsuccessfully sought to colonize the Pacific coast of South America, and France and Holland sought to gain possession of portions of Brazil. Powerful Dutch armaments were dispatched to American waters, one of which, under Piet Heyn, captured a plate fleet from New Spain (1628). An expedition sent against Spanish possessions by Cromwell captured Jamaica (1655), of which England remained in permanent possession. Western Española, in which French buccaneers had secured a foothold and official colonization had later been undertaken, was ceded to France by the **treaty of Ryswick** (1697). The activity of English, French, and Dutch freebooters in the Caribbean reached its height during the 17th century, and played an important part in the decline of Spanish commerce. The Englishman **Henry Morgan** was the most important of these freebooters, who during his career captured numerous cities and towns, including Porto Bello and Panama (1655–1671).

18th cent. The European wars in which Spain was involved in the 18th century and the early part of the 19th had important consequences in the Americas. Control of the seas by Great Britain rendered protection of the colonies increasingly difficult. The Spanish commercial monopoly was, moreover, incapable of enforcement, and extensive illicit commerce participated in by British, French, and Dutch merchants developed.

1701-1713. During the **War of the Spanish Succession** there was considerable fighting between the allied Spaniards and French in the West Indies and Florida. By the **treaty of Utrecht** (1713) Great Britain was granted the

Henry Morgan, 1635?–1688   *Sir Francis Drake, 1540?–1596*

asiento, or monopoly of the slave trade with the Spanish possessions and the right to send one ship each year to trade with Atlantic ports of the Spanish colonies.

1718-1720. Incident to war between France and Spain, military operations took place in Florida and Texas, as a result of which Spanish possession of Texas was assured, although the boundary remained disputed.

1739-1748. In the **"War of Jenkins' Ear,"** which merged into the **War of the Austrian Succession,** Spain, as a result of reforms introduced by the Bourbons, maintained a successful defense of her possessions. Inconclusive operations took place in Florida and on the frontier of Georgia, and a powerful British expedition under Admiral Vernon was repulsed at Cartagena, which had been heavily fortified as a principal bulwark of colonial defense (1741). The **treaty of Aix-la-Chapelle** (1748) provided for no important territorial changes.

1762. When Spain entered the **Seven Years' War** as an ally of France, British expeditions captured Havana and Manila (1762). By the **treaty of Paris** (1763) Spain ceded Florida to Great Britain and received Havana, Manila being restored later. France ceded Louisiana to Spain, although Spanish authority was not established in the latter without opposition from the French colonists.

With the temporary elimination of France by the Seven Years' War, Great Britain and Spain became the great colonial powers, and **Charles III** (1759-1788), convinced that Great Britain would seek to possess itself of the Spanish colonies, believed a decisive conflict inevitable. Internal and colonial reforms introduced by Charles III raised Spain to the highest position of power and influence enjoyed since the 16th century, and she was comparatively well prepared for an eventual conflict.

1771. A dispute between Spain and Great Britain concerning possession of the **Falkland Islands** brought the two nations to the verge of war, but France refused to afford the support anticipated under the **Family Compact** *(p. 473)* and Spain was obliged to accept an accommodation.

1775-1783. The **American War of Independence,** becoming a European war after the alliance between France and the colonies, afforded Spain a desired opportunity to check British expansion, and she entered the conflict (1779). Spanish forces captured Mobile and Pensacola, overran the Bahamas, and blocked

Charles III, 1759-1788

British attempts to gain control of the Mississippi (1779-1783). By the **treaty of Versailles** (1783) Spain regained Florida, but relinquished the Bahamas.

1789. Controversy between Great Britain and Spain arose over the seizure of British ships at Nootka. Considering sovereignty involved, Spain invoked the **Family Compact** and prepared for war. The French revolutionary government failed fully to support Spain and she yielded. Great Britain and Spain adjusted the incident by treaty (1790-1794).

1795. By the **treaty of Basel** Spain relinquished the eastern two-thirds of Española to France. This territory was returned to Spain by the **treaty of Paris** (1814). Trinidad was forced to capitulate (1797) and was ceded to the British by the treaty of Amiens (1802). Great Britain during the 18th century gained permanent control of Belize and established a protectorate over the Mosquito Indians of Honduras and Nicaragua.

Controversy arose with the **United States** concerning the navigation of the Mississippi, the mouth of which Spain controlled through the acquisition of Louisiana.

1800. France under the consulate forced Spain to return **Louisiana,** guaranteeing that the territory would not be transferred to any power other than Spain.

1803. France, notwithstanding, soon sold Louisiana to the United States. As a result of

increasing pressure from the United States, Spain sold **Florida** to that nation (1819-1821).

The establishment of territorial jurisdiction in South America in accord with the **Line of Demarcation** *(p. 385)* created much friction between Spain and Portugal. **Colonia** was established on the left bank of the estuary of the Río de la Plata by the Portuguese (1680-1683) and Montevideo was founded some years later by the Spaniards to prevent Portuguese expansion (1723). Colonia soon became a base for illicit British and Portuguese trade with the province of the Río de la Plata. The **treaty of Madrid** (1750), an attempted settlement, provided that Colonia should be given to Spain in return for seven Jesuit *reductions* on the east bank of the Uruguay; that Portuguese claims to the basins of the Amazon and Paraná and Spanish claims to the Philippines be recognized, and that boundaries be surveyed. The Guaraní of the seven *reductions,* incited by the Jesuits, rebelled against transfer, and it became necessary for the Portuguese to subdue them by force, the **War of the Seven** *Reductions* (1752-1756). Portugal, notwithstanding, retained Colonia, and Charles III annulled the treaty of Madrid (1761). Spanish forces captured Colonia (1762) and invaded Río Grande do Sul (1762), but these territories were returned by the **treaty of Paris** (1763). Pombal (p. 491) desired to expand Portuguese territory, and, relying on British support, encroached upon Spanish territory. Rivalry between Spain and Portugal continued, and when Great Britain, because of developments in Europe and North America, failed effectively to support Portugal, Charles III dispatched a strong force which captured Colonia and moved against other Portuguese territories (1776-1777). With the dismissal of Pombal (1777) hostilities were suspended and the **treaty of San Ildefonso** was concluded (1777), by which Colonia and disputed Paraguayan territory were assigned to Spain, and Portuguese claims to the interior were recognized. Meanwhile the **Viceroyalty of La Plata** had been created as a defensive as well as an administrative measure (1776). The Portuguese later occupied the disputed missions territory incidental to European hostilities (1801), but by posterior settlements Spain received Colonia and Uruguay while Portugal secured Río Grande do Sul. Attempts of Great Britain to secure territory in the region of the Río de la Plata failed completely (1806-1807). *(Cont. p. 788.)*

(Cont. p. 788.)

8. *The Spanish Colonial System*

a. POPULATION

Emigration to the Indies was rigidly controlled by the crown and the *Casa de Contratación.* Heretics, Moors, Jews, and their descendants were excluded. The vast majority of immigrants were from the realms of the crown

of Castile. In the early 16th century the crown adopted active measures to encourage immigration. Negro slavery, introduced at the opening of the century, was extensive only in the West Indies and northern South America. Intermixture between male Spaniards and native women produced a large mixed group (*mestizos*). In

1574 the Spanish population was estimated at some 160,000, and at the close of the colonial period the estimated population was 3,276,000 whites, 5,328,000 *mestizos,* 7,530,000 Indians, and 776,000 Negroes (New Spain, 1,230,000 whites, 1,860,000 *mestizos,* 3,700,000 Indians; Guatemala, 280,000 whites, 420,000 *mestizos,* 880,000

Indians; Peru and Chile, 465,000 whites, 853,000 *mestizos*, 1,030,000 Indians; Colombia and Venezuela, 642,000 whites, 1,256,000 *mestizos*, 720,000 Indians; Río de la Plata, 320,000 whites, 742,000 *mestizos*, 1,200,000 Indians; Cuba and Puerto Rico, 339,000 whites, 197,000 mixed, 389,000 Negroes). Negroes in all colonies except Cuba and Puerto Rico numbered 387,000.

Social composition. There existed six relatively distinct groups in the population of the colonies: Spanish colonial officials; upper grade creoles (those of Spanish blood born in the Indies) and socially superior Spanish immigrants; lower grade creoles and Spanish immigrants, high rank *mestizos* and Indian nobility; *mestizos* (mixed white and Indian), mulattoes, *zambos* (mixed Negro and Indian), and certain Indians; Indians, who constituted the largest group numerically; Negro slaves. The two upper classes possessed virtually all the wealth of the colonies.

b. ADMINISTRATION

The discovery of America was accomplished under commission of the sovereign of Castile and the new lands consequently became realms of the Castilian crown, from which all authority emanated. In accord with the theory of royal absolutism the crown abrogated governmental authority granted Columbus and the early conquistadores and established direct royal control. The machinery of royal government was fully formed by the third quarter of the 16th century.

After appointment to supervise preparations for the second voyage of Columbus (1493) **Juan Rodríguez de Fonseca** became virtual minister of the Indies, and as such laid the foundation for the expansion of the machinery of royal government. With the development of trade the *Casa de Contratación* was established at Seville to control colonial commerce and maritime enterprise (1503). The nucleus of a council to administer the Indies was evolved and this body, under the presidency of Rodríguez de Fonseca, rapidly developed into a formal **Council of the Indies** (*Consejo de Indias*). Upon the death of Rodríguez de Fonseca the *Consejo de Indias* was reorganized (1524) and by the close of the reign of Charles V its organization and functions were fully developed. The *Consejo de Indias* exercised supreme administrative, judicial, and ecclesiastical authority over the Indies and possessed supervisory authority over the *Casa de Contratación*. The legislation for the Indies promulgated by the crown and Consejo de Indias was codified in the *Recopilación de Leyes . . . de las Indias*, one of the greatest of colonial codes (1680). At the opening of the 17th century a *Junta de Guerra y Armadas de Indias*, to administer the armed forces and the dispatch of fleets to the Indies, and a *Cámara de Indias*, to control ecclesiastical affairs and appointments, were created as adjuncts to the *Consejo de Indias*. Early in the Bourbon period the office of *Minister of the Indies* was created with the establishment of a *Secretaría de Guerra, Marina e Indias* (1714). This secretariat underwent numerous changes and before the close of the century a separate **secretariat of the Indies** was formed. With the creation of these institutions the *Consejo de Indias* declined in importance.

Direct royal government in the Indies was instituted with the appointment of **Francisco de Bobadilla** as judge and governor of Española and the removal of Columbus (1499–1500). Bobadilla was succeeded by Nicolás de Ovando (1502), and he by Diego Columbus, son of the admiral, named governor at the will of the crown (1509). A tribunal of three royal judges was created in Santo Domingo as a check on the governor (1511), and this body was later established in a fully developed form as the *audiencia of Santo Domingo* and given governmental authority over the West Indies (1526).

On the mainland government was at first permitted to rest with those who had conquered the several areas under royal patent or with crown recognition and who governed with the titles of *adelantado*, governor, or captain-general. The threat to royal absolutism inherent in government by powerful vassals with privileged positions caused early extension of direct government to the mainland.

The institution of the *adelantado* was of great importance during the period of conquest. By capitulation with the crown the *adelantado* undertook the conquest of a specified area at his own cost and in return was assigned governmental authority and hereditary privileges. The institution was of value in bringing new lands under Spanish dominion, but its character threatened royal authority and the powers granted were revoked after achievement of the royal purpose.

An *audiencia* was created to govern New Spain (1527), but proved weak in its executive aspects and shortly after a viceroy, Antonio de Mendoza, was appointed (1529), although he did not take office for some years (1535). The **viceroyalty of Peru** was created by the New Laws (1542), which also established an *audiencia* at Lima. The **viceroyalty** (or *Reino*) **of New Spain,** with its capital Mexico City, came to include all Spanish territory north of Panama, the West Indies, Venezuela, and the Philippine Islands. That of Peru, with its capital Lima, included Panama and all Spanish territory in South America except Venezuela.

Audiencias, each with its definite area, were created for Guatemala (1542), New Galicia (1548), New Granada (1549), Charcas, or Upper Peru (1556), Quito (1563), and the Philippine Islands (1583–1593).

The viceroys, as direct representatives of the sovereign, possessed wide civil and military authority, and certain ecclesiastical powers. They were presidents of the *audiencias* of their capitals. The *audiencias*, composed of a president, *oidores*, a *fiscal* (crown prosecutor), and lesser officials, exercised supreme judicial authority within their districts, and the *audiencias* not directly under viceroys exercised governmental authority. The viceregal *audiencia* acted as an advisory council to the viceroy and in this function evolved legislative power. The *audiencias* were co-ordinate in judicial affairs, appeals going directly before the *Consejo de Indias*, and they were empowered to correspond directly with the crown. The *audiencias* varied in status according to the rank of the presiding officer, i.e., viceroy, president and captain-general, or president. The presidents of the *audiencias* of Santo Domingo, Guatemala, and New Granada were early accorded military authority and became presidents and captains-general. As such they became practically independent of the viceroys. Guadalajara, Quito, and Charcas remained presidencies. In the absence of the viceroy or president and captain-general the *audiencia* assumed the government. During the Bourbon period New Granada, Panama, Venezuela, and Quito were erected into the **viceroyalty of New Granada** (1717–1739), the **viceroyalty of La Plata** was established (1776), the captaincies-general of Venezuela (1773), Cuba (1777), and Chile (1778) were created, and *audiencias* were established in Buenos Aires (1783), Caracas (1786), and Cuzco (1789).

Major administrative areas were divided into *gobiernos, corregimientos,* and *alcaldías mayores,* of which the *gobiernos* were, in general, the more important and frequently consisted of more than one province. This organization persisted until the reign of Charles III, when a system of intendants was established throughout the Indies (1769–1790). The intendants possessed administrative, judicial, financial, and military authority, and in fiscal and economic matters were directly responsible to the crown.

In accord with medieval Castilian traditions the **municipalities** at first enjoyed a large measure of self-government under their *cabildos*, composed of *regidores* (councilmen) and *alcades* (mayors), the former elected by the householders and the latter by the *regidores*. Before the close of the 16th century the election of *regidores* gave way to royal appointment, hereditary tenure, and venality of office. *Cabildos abiertos* of all citizens were at times held to discuss important matters. The municipal government exercised executive, legislative, and judicial authority within its district, although frequently under control of royal officials.

Fiscal administration was from the first directly under the crown through the *Casa de Contratación* and *contadores, factors, tesoreros,* and *veedores* in the New World jurisdictional areas. With the establishment of the intendants those officials assumed administration of fiscal affairs.

The Castilian institutions of the *residencia, visita,* and *pesquisa* were early instituted in the New World.

The principal sources of **crown revenues** were the *quinto*, or one-fifth of the products of the subsoil (gold, silver, precious stones) under the theory of crown ownership of the subsoil; the *almojarifzgo* (customs imposts); the *alcabala* (sales tax); the tributes of the natives; the *media anata* of civil and ecclesiastical offices; and the sale of the *Crusada*. Although revenues from the Americas were great, they at no time during the period of Spanish greatness exceeded 25 per cent of the total income of the crown.

The presence of a great **Indian population** created extraordinary administrative problems. Municipal governments on the Castilian model were established in the Indian towns. Local Spanish officials had jurisdiction over the native towns in their districts. Protectors of the Indians were created for general and local districts to guard their interests. The *repartimiento-encomienda*, which early developed, was an institution of great political, social, and economic importance. In the earlier period this institution involved the assignment of specified towns to *conquistadores* and colonists, the Indians of which gave tribute, labor, and service to the *encomendero*, who was obligated to afford protection, indoctrination in Christianity, and instruction. Abuses caused the crown to regulate the system. Fixed quotas of tribute were established and labor and service were eliminated about the middle of the 16th century. Before the close of the century the *encomienda* was virtually reduced to the right to enjoy the revenues from specified towns. The crown after the publication of the **New Laws** (1542–1543) assumed control of many towns, and grants of *encomiendas* were brought under control of higher authorities. Attempts were made to abolish the system, notably in the New Laws, but it was not until the first part of the 18th century that abolition was definitely decreed. In certain areas the institution persisted almost until the close of the colonial period. The *mita*, forced labor of the natives in the mines, on the *haciendas*, and for public works, was established late in the 16th century. Indians not within the *encomienda* system were required to pay an annual tribute and after the abolition of the *encomienda* this was required of all.

Extensive **enslavement of Indians** took place during the period of conquest under the law of just war, but this was prohibited by the New Laws. The natives were regarded as wards of the crown and throughout the colonial period legislation was promulgated for their welfare and protection, notable examples of such legislation being the Laws of Burgos (1512), and the New Laws. A section of the Laws of the Indies was devoted to Indian legislation (1680). The beneficent intent of the crown was to a large degree rendered nugatory by the difficulties of administration and the conflict of theory and practice. Many Spaniards acted as advocates of the Indians, the greatest of whom was **Bartolomé de Las Casas** (1474–1566).

c. THE CHURCH AND THE MISSIONS

The union of State and Church in the Spanish Americas was exceedingly close. The crown early secured almost complete control of ecclesiastical affairs through the patronage of the Indies (*real patronato de Indias*) granted by Alexander VI in the bulls *Inter caetera* (1493, May 4) which assigned dominion over the Indies and exclusive authority to convert the natives, and *Eximiae devotionis* (1501, Nov. 16), which granted the titles and first fruits of the Church in the Indies, and by Julius II in the bull *Universalis ecclesiae* (1508, July 28), which conceded universal patronage. The extent and nature of the patronage was further defined by bulls issued at intervals throughout the colonial period. The crown exercised ecclesiastical control through the *Consejo de Indias* and later through that body and the *Cámara de Indias*. Papal bulls were not permitted to be placed in effect without the approval of the crown.

The full **organization of the Church** in the Indies followed closely upon the conquest and colonization, and at the close of the colonial period there existed seven archbishoprics and some 35 dioceses. The Church possessed its own courts, with jurisdiction over all cases touching the clergy and spiritual affairs. The **Spanish Inquisition** was introduced (1569), and tribunals were established in Mexico City and Lima (1570–1571). This institution rapidly achieved great religious and political influence. Indians, considered incapable of rational judgment, were exempt from the Inquisition.

The Church played an important part in the Indies through conversion of the natives, aid in the maintenance of Spanish political authority, transmission of culture, and education. It achieved vast wealth and a privileged position, and at the close of the colonial period is estimated to have controlled half of the productive real estate in the Indies.

The **religious orders,** Franciscan, Dominican, Jesuit, Augustinian, Capuchin, and others, early achieved complete organization and carried on an exceedingly important work in converting the natives and instructing them in the rudiments of European civilization. The task of preserving and extending Spanish control in outlying areas was assigned to the religious orders, especially the Franciscan, Dominican, Capuchin, and Jesuit, as official agencies of the crown. Missionaries, accompanied by small groups of soldiers, and frequently by colonists, established missions and instructed the natives in Christianity. They developed agriculture, grazing, and simple industry. *Presidios* were established to protect the missions. Civilian colonists occupied the territory and secularization followed. Carrying forward on the northern frontier of New Spain, toward the close of the 17th century, Jesuits under the leadership of **Eusebio Kino** began the establishment of missions in Pimeria Alta (Arizona) and under **Juan María Salvatierra** in Lower California, over which the order was granted complete authority. A wide area was eventually brought under Spanish control. Early in the 18th century a system of missions and *presidios* was established in Texas and late in the century in California. Dominicans and Franciscans were active in Guatemala, Capuchins in the area of the lower Orinoco—to check French, English, and Dutch encroachments— and Jesuits in the territory of the Araucanians and Paraguay. The mission system in Paraguay was one of the most important in the New World. Granted complete authority to convert and organize the Guaraní east of Asunción, the Jesuits established missions (*reductions*) along the upper Paraná. The natives were later transferred farther south because of Portuguese slave raids. A complete governmental organization was established, controlled by a father superior at Candelaria, the natives were instructed in Christianity, and the rudiments of European civilization, and agriculture and industry were extensively developed. By the **treaty of Madrid** (1750) seven *reductions* were transferred to Portugal. The Guaraní, incited by the Jesuits, rose in revolt to resist transfer, but were defeated. By later adjustments the territory remained in Spanish possession. With the expulsion of the Jesuits (1767) the Paraguayan *reductions* were given to Franciscans, but failed to prosper.

d. ECONOMIC CONDITIONS AND POLICIES

Mining of gold and silver, fostered by the crown, rapidly became the most important industry in the Spanish colonies. Rich silver deposits were early discovered throughout central Mexico, especially in the districts of Zaca-

The religious orders were responsible for the conversion of the natives

Moctezuma Being Arrested by Cortés (p.512)

*Zapotec ruins at Mitla, above, and
Memory Stones at Monte Albán, at left,
both near Oaxaca, Mexico (p.513)*

tecas, Guanajuato, Pachuca, Taxco, and San Luis Potosí, and at Potosí in Upper Peru (1530–1600). Gold deposits were worked throughout the Indies. Silver production came to surpass that of gold, and after the third quarter of the 16th century Peru produced about two-thirds of the total output of precious metals.

Agricultural and pastoral pursuits were highly developed. All plants and animals of Spain were introduced into the Indies and native plants, especially maize, potatoes, cotton, tobacco, and cacao were cultivated.

Local textile, iron, pottery, shipbuilding, gold and silver working, and sugar (West Indies) industries developed.

The **principal imports** into the colonies were manufactured goods, and **exports** consisted almost exclusively of precious metals, raw materials and agricultural products.

The **economic policy of Spain** was based upon mercantilist theory. Trade was a monopoly of the metropolis under direct crown control and economic activity in the colonies which competed with that of Spain was prohibited or restricted.

The economic privileges of Columbus were almost immediately rendered inoperative and the crown assumed direct control over all phases of economic activity. In the earliest period Juan Rodríguez de Fonseca as *de facto* minister of the Indies controlled commerce (1493–1503), and trade under license was authorized by the crown (1495–1501). The *Casa de Contratación*, "a board of trade, a commercial court, and a

Spanish Colonial Church of San Augustine at Arequipa, Peru

Indians beaten into slavery by Spanish mercenaries

clearing-house for the American traffic," was established at Seville (1503). This body came under the supervisory authority of the *Consejo de Indias.* Seville was accorded a monopoly of the American trade. In the New World, Vera Cruz, Cartagena, and Porto Bello alone were permitted direct trade with Spain. General intercolonial commerce was early prohibited, and before the close of the 16th century commerce with the Philippines was restricted to Acapulco. Trade between Manila and China was confined to Chinese.

Naval warfare, attacks by corsairs, and the necessity of protection for gold and silver shipments caused the establishment of a system of **convoyed fleets,** one each year for New Spain (the *flota*) and one for Peru (the *galeones*) (1543–1561). On the return the fleets united at Havana and sailed for Spain together. Fairs for the exchange of goods were held annually at Porto Bello and Jalapa (Mexico). Trade between Acapulco and the Philippines (Manila) was restricted to one vessel a year each way. With the period of Spanish decadence trade declined greatly.

Under the Bourbons many reforms were introduced. By the treaty of Utrecht (1713) Great Britain was conceded the monopoly of the slave trade with the colonies (*asiento*) and the privilege of sending one vessel each year to Porto Bello to trade. With the establishment of the office of the minister of the Indies early in the 18th century (1714) the *Casa de Contratación* tended to decline in importance. The *Casa de Contratación* and trade monopoly were transferred to Cadiz (1717–1718). To develop trade the monopolistic **chartered companies** of

Honduras (1714), Guipúzcoa, or Caracas (1728), Havana (1740), and Santo Domingo (1757) were formed. With the decline in trade the sailings of the fleets became irregular. Supplies were increasingly carried to the Indies in registered vessels and by the chartered companies and in the middle of the 18th century the fleet system was abolished (1748). Charles III promulgated a series of reform measures authorizing trade between more than twenty Spanish ports besides Seville and Cadiz and a large number of ports throughout the Indies, and permitting direct intercolonial trade between New Spain and Peru and Guatemala and New Granada (1764–1782). A great increase in trade resulted. Royal secretaries having increasingly assumed its functions, the *Casa de Contratación* was abolished (1790). During the wars of the French Revolution neutral vessels were permitted to engage in the carrying trade with the colonies (1797).

e. EDUCATION, LEARNING, AND FINE ARTS

Education in Spanish America, with the exception of the rudimentary instruction afforded the Indians by the Church, was largely confined to the upper classes. The earliest universities were those of **Mexico** (1551), **San Marcos de Lima** (1551), and **St. Thomas Aquinas** of Santo Domingo (1558), founded by royal decree. They were modeled after the University of Salamanca. A school of mines was established in Mexico by Charles III (1783).

A vast body of **historical writing**, much of it of high quality, was produced during the colonial period, and important anthropological and linguistic studies were made. In the sciences the most important figures were **Carlos Sigüenza y Góngora** (1645–1700) and **Pedro de Peralta Barnuevo Rocha y Benavides** (1663–1743).

Juan Rúz de Alarcón (d. 1639), a Mexican creole, achieved a high place in the Spanish drama and **Sor Juana Inés de la Cruz** (b. 1651), also a Mexican creole, attained recognition for her poetry.

The first **printing press** was introduced into Mexico by the Viceroy Mendoza (1535). At the close of the colonial period there were a number of presses in operation in the larger cities. Newssheets and scientific and literary publications appeared in Lima and Mexico City toward the close of the 18th century.

Intellectual activity was, in general, seriously hampered by the Inquisition.

In **art and architecture** Spanish models were followed. Local schools of painting developed in Mexico and Quito. Charles III founded the **San Cárlos Academy of Fine Arts** in the former city (1778). An outstanding architectural achievement was the **Cathedral of Mexico,** begun late in the 16th century and completed in the first part of the 19th.   *(Cont. p. 788.)*

9. *Portuguese America, 1500–1821*

1500–1521. Absorbed by interests in the Orient, **Manuel the Fortunate** (1495–1521) made no effective effort to colonize the territory claimed by Portugal in South America, although certain royal expeditions were dispatched and trading posts were established through private enterprise.

1521–1530. French activities having menaced Portuguese possession, **John III** (1521–1557) undertook systematic colonization.

1530–1532. **Martin Afonso de Souza,** as captain-major and leader of a colonizing and exploratory expedition, founded São Vicente and actively furthered colonization, introducing cattle and European grains and fruits and laying the foundations of a sugar industry.

1532–1536. A system of feudal **hereditary captaincies** under *donatarios* with virtually sovereign authority was established by the crown, but proved unsuccessful and a more centralized administration with a directly responsible governor-general at its head was created.

1549. **Thomé de Souza,** the first governor-general, founded **São Salvador** (Bahia), which was made the seat of government. Souza firmly established the administration and effectively furthered colonization. This task was ably continued by **Mem de Sá** (1558–1572). **São Paulo** was founded shortly after the middle of the century.

1549. **Jesuits,** headed by Manuel de Nobrega and José de Anchieta, undertook the conversion of the natives and established missions, playing an important part in colonization.

1551. The fundamental relationship between Church and State was established by a bull of Julius III which conceded to the crown complete spiritual jurisdiction over conquests and the right to nominate bishops, collect tithes, dispense church revenues, and receive appeals from ecclesiastical tribunals. The bishopric of Bahia, suffragan to the archbishop of Lisbon, was erected (1551).

France, Holland, and England did not permit Portugal to remain in possession of Brazil unchallenged. French efforts to establish an empire in South America passed through two distinct phases.

1555. With the intention of creating an "Antarctic France," a colony was founded on the Bay of Rio de Janeiro under **Nicolas Durand de Villegagnon.**

1565–1567. The Portuguese under leadership of Mem de Sá destroyed the colony and founded the city of **Rio de Janeiro,** ending French attempts in that area. Henry IV projected the establishment of an "Equinoctial France."

1612. After his death, although without direct royal aid, a town was founded on the island of **Maranhão** and exploration was conducted on the mainland with the purpose of occupying the area of the mouths of the Amazon. The state of Maranhão was created (1621), directly subordinate to the home government. The Jesuits established missions along the Amazon and gave France control of the vast river basin. Maranhão was independent of Brazil until 1777.

1615. The Portuguese forced the surrender of the colony, and shortly thereafter founded Belem, ending French efforts to establish an extensive empire in South America.

The personal union of the crowns of Spain and Portugal *(p. 412)* carried important consequences for Brazil. **English attacks** on coastal towns occurred in the final decades of the 16th century, Santos being sacked.

1624–1625. Dutch activities were far more serious. Shortly after the organization of the Dutch West India Company *(p. 463)*, the Dutch captured Bahia (1624), but were forced to capitulate to a Spanish fleet (1625).

1630. Continuing the effort, a powerful Dutch armament captured Recife and Olinda. The conquest was extended over a wide area.

1637. The West India Company named **Prince Maurice of Nassau-Siegen** governor, and under his able administration Dutch control was established over an area extending from the São Francisco River to Maranhão.

1644. As the West India Company displayed greater interest in profit than in colonization, Prince Maurice returned to Holland.

1645. Immediately thereafter, in a truly popular movement, the Portuguese rebelled and within a decade forced the Dutch to capitulate (1654). These events ended Dutch occupation of Brazilian territory, a situation later recognized by treaty (1661, Aug. 6).

Slave-raiding parties began to penetrate into the interior from São Paulo (1629) and by the middle of the century these Paulistas had explored an extensive area of southern Brazil. They attacked the Spanish Jesuit *reductions* on the upper Paraná, forced their transfer to a more southern area, and made possible Portuguese possession of the region. Simultaneously Portuguese Jesuits established missions in the south, coming into conflict with the Paulistas in their efforts to protect the Indians, in which they received royal support.

1680–1683. Seeking to gain possession of the left bank of the Río de la Plata (*Banda Oriental*), the Portuguese founded **Colonia.** Spain and Portugal immediately came into conflict over this area; **Montevideo** being founded by the Spaniards (1726). The territory changed hands frequently during the remainder of the colonial period.

Modern Rio de Janeiro (Copacabana section)

nized Portuguese claims to extensive areas in the basins of the Amazon and Paraná, and although this treaty was abrogated, the bases of settlement were reaffirmed by the **treaty of San Ildefonso** (1777). While the limits were not definitely surveyed, Portuguese claims to territory vastly greater than that assigned under the **treaty of Tordesillas** *(p. 385)* were permanently established.

1750–1777. **Pombal** as minister of Joseph I *(p. 475)* introduced far-reaching colonial reforms. Administration was unified, the capital being transferred from Bahia to Rio de Janeiro and Maranhão being incorporated with Brazil (1777). Commerce between Portugal and Brazil was encouraged, certain restrictions and taxes were removed, and trading companies were organized. Native Brazilians were appointed to important governmental posts, racial equality was advocated, and defenses were improved. Pombal strongly pressed Portuguese territorial claims. The **Jesuits were expelled** from Portugal and its possessions during his ministry (1759).

1789. **The Conspiracy of Minas.** Maladministration, heavy taxes, and reactionary government led to an abortive attempt at revolution in Minas Gerães, led by **Joaquim José de Silva Xavier** (*Tiradentes*).

1807. The determination of Napoleon to force Portuguese adherence to the Continental Sys-

Colonial Church of San Marcello, Lima, Peru

1693. Decreasing profits from slaving operations and increasingly effective protection afforded the Indians by the Jesuits caused the Paulistas to direct their efforts to a search for gold, and toward the end of the 17th century extensive deposits were discovered in **Minas Gerães.** An influx of gold-seekers ensued, among them many newly arrived Portuguese.

1701–1713. The alliance of Portugal with England during the War of the Spanish Succession led to French attacks on Brazilian ports, **Rio de Janeiro** being sacked and held for ransom by Duguay-Trouin (1711).

1708–1709. Efforts of the Portuguese to displace the Paulistas resulted in open warfare, the **War of the Emboabas,** in which the former were successful. Through the efforts of the Paulistas, Matto Grosso and Goyaz, far to the west of the Line of Demarcation, were gained for Portugal.

1709. With the colonization of the interior the crown created the captaincy of **São Paulo and Minas Gerães,** with a captain-general directly responsible to the sovereign, erected Minas Gerães into a separate jurisdiction (1720), and established the captaincies of Matto Grosso (1744) and Goyaz (1748).

1710–1711. **The War of the Mascates.** Rivalry between the native Brazilians of Olinda, the political capital of Pernambuco, and the Portuguese of the commercial town of Recife, concerning the elevation of the latter to *villa* status, led to armed conflict. Recife, notwithstanding, was accorded municipal privileges and eventually superseded Olinda as the seat of government.

The **Line of Demarcation** never having been surveyed, as Portuguese expansion progressed, efforts were made to establish limits.

1750. In the **treaty of Madrid** Spain recog-

tem and his plan to partition Portugal exercised a decisive influence on Portuguese and Brazilian history.

1807-1808. Apprised of the designs of the emperor, upon the approach of a French army, **Prince John,** regent after 1792 because of the insanity of Maria I, created a regency in Portugal, fled to Brazil, and established his government at Rio de Janeiro.

1808-1816. The regent adopted many reforms advantageous to Brazil. Decrees were issued establishing free trade, removing restrictions on industry, promoting agriculture and communications, establishing a royal press, founding the Bank of Brazil, and encouraging the arts and sciences. Brazil was erected into a coordinate member of the **United Kingdom of Portugal, Brazil, and Algarves** (1815, Dec. 16). The regent became **John VI** upon the death of Maria I (1816, Mar. 1).

1808. Prince John declared war on France and dispatched an expedition which occupied **French Guiana.** This territory was returned by the **treaty of Paris** (1814). The regent sought also to annex the *Banda Oriental* and supported the designs of his wife, Carlotta Joaquina, sister of Ferdinand VII of Spain, to establish her rule over the provinces of the **Río de la Plata.**

1812. The opposition of the viceroy and the revolutionary *junta* of Buenos Aires and British influence caused the regent temporarily to renounce intervention in the area of the Río de la Plata.

1816-1821. After becoming king, John took advantage of the situation arising from the struggle for independence in the *Banda Oriental* and the violation of Brazilian territory by the leader of the movement, **José Artigas** *(p. 790).* He then intervened again in the *Banda Oriental.* Portuguese troops occupied Montevideo and defeated Artigas, and the territory was incorporated into Brazil as the **Cisplatine Province** (1821). Projects against other provinces of the Río de la Plata were renounced under threat from Ferdinand VII and in face of a potentially united Argentina.

10. *The Portuguese Colonial System*

Population and Race. A complex racial situation developed in Brazil. Intermixture between Portuguese males and Indian women gave rise to a large group of *mestizos.* From the middle of the 16th century onward Negro slaves were introduced in large numbers to meet labor requirements and extensive intermixture of Negro and white blood occurred. There was also intermixture between Negroes and natives. In 1583 the population was estimated at 25,000 whites, 18,000 civilized Indians, and 14,000 Negro slaves. In the mid-17th century, considerable immigration having taken place, the population was estimated at 150,000 to 200,000, three-fourths of whom were Indians, Negroes, and mixed. At the close of the 18th century at 3,000,000, a population already greater than that of Portugal. In 1818 the population was estimated at 843,000 whites, 1,887,500 Negroes, 628,000 mixed, and 259,400 civilized Indians. The bulk of the population was concentrated in São Paulo, Minas Gerães, Pernambuco, and Bahia. Originally the crown permitted any person of Catholic faith to enter Brazil, but after 1591 aliens were excluded.

Portuguese **colonial administration** was not clearly differentiated from that of the metropolis prior to the union of the crowns of Portugal and Spain. For general purposes there existed an inspector of finances and a *Casa da India.* The *Mesa da Consiencia e Ordems,* with ecclesiastical and financial powers, was created in 1532. Upon the establishment of a more centralized government in Brazil, a commissioner of finances and a chief justice were appointed for the colony (1548). For local administration there were *corregedores,* with judicial and military functions. Municipal organization was patterned on that of Portugal. The fundamental code was the *Ordenanças Manuelinas* (1521).

During the period of the union of the thrones of Spain and Portugal (1580/1581-1640) Spanish administrative forms were introduced. The inspector of finance was replaced by a council, the *Conselho da Fazenda.* A Council of the Indies (*Conselho da India*) was created (1604), a supreme court was established in Bahia (1609), and the title of *viceroy* was introduced (1640). Under Philip III (1598-1621), the *Ordenanças Philippinas,* which permitted greater local autonomy, superseded the *Ordenanças Manuelinas.* Most of these innovations were permanent.

By the close of the 18th century the structure of royal government was fully formed. The **Transmarine Council** (*Conselho do Ultramar*), formerly the Council of the Indies, exercised general religious and military authority over Brazil. Pará, Maranhão, Pernambuco, Bahia, São Paulo, Minas Gerães, Goyaz, Matto Grosso, and Rio de Janeiro were captaincies-general, provinces of the first rank, under captains-general usually appointed by the crown. The viceroy, who was also captain-general of Rio de Janeiro, possessed legal authority over the captains-general in certain matters, but the latter frequently received instructions from the crown, with which they could correspond directly. A tendency toward local autonomy existed. There were a number of districts of inferior status, captaincies, subordinate to the captaincies-general. Two superior judicial districts existed, with high tribunals at Bahia and Rio de Janeiro (founded 1757) respectively. Appeals from these courts went directly to Lisbon. The municipalities, with their councils (*senados da camera*), enjoyed a certain degree of self-government.

Portuguese **economic policy** was founded upon mercantilist theory. Commerce was a monopoly of Portugal until 1808 and trade was restricted to Lisbon and Oporto. In 1649 a monopolistic **Commercial Company of Brazil** was organized and greatly developed commerce. The **Maranhão Company,** also monopolistic, was formed in 1682. Both companies aroused opposition and were abolished in the first part of the 18th century. To foster commerce two chartered companies, one with a monopoly of the trade of Pará and Maranhão and the other with a monopoly of that of Pernambuco and Parahyba, were formed during the period of Pombal, but were abolished after his fall. Between 1548 and the formation of the Commercial Company of Brazil commerce was carried on through convoyed fleets. Discontinued during the existence of the company, the system was re-established upon its abolition and continued until finally abolished by Pombal.

Restrictions were placed upon **industry and agriculture** which competed with that of Portugal, and a government monopoly, which produced important crown revenues, existed for the exploitation of Brazil wood, mining of diamonds, and other activities. Customs duties were levied, and a royal fifth (*quinto*) of the product of mining activity was required. Agriculture and pastoral pursuits were highly developed. Cotton and sugar cane were the principal agricultural products. The cultivation of coffee was introduced. The mining of gold and diamonds (rich deposits of the latter were discovered in 1721), the gathering of Brazil wood, and the production of sugar and hides were the chief industries. Brazilian sugar production became the greatest in the world and was the basis of the wealth of the colony.

The Church and education. In 1676 Innocent XI created the **archbishopric of Brazil,** with Bahia as the metropolitan see, at the same time erecting the suffragan bishoprics of Rio de Janeiro and Pernambuco. At the close of the 18th century there were nine bishoprics, two of which were suffragan to the archbishop of Lisbon. The **Inquisition** was not introduced into Brazil. The **Jesuits,** until their expulsion, (1759) played an important rôle through conversion of the natives, extension of Portuguese influence, and establishment of schools and colleges, the earliest being that of São Paulo (1554). No institution of university status was created in Brazil during the colonial period, but seminaries and academies were established, among them the seminaries of São Pedro and São José at Rio de Janeiro (founded 1736).

(Cont. p. 788.)

F. North America, 1500–1788

1. *Exploration and Settlement*

a. THE FRENCH IN NORTH AMERICA, 1500–1719

Norman and Breton fishermen visited Newfoundland coasts perhaps as early as 1500. There are unconfirmed reports of attempts to explore the Gulf of St. Lawrence in 1506 and 1508, and of an unsuccessful colony on Sable Island in 1518.

1524. **Giovanni de Verrazzano,** sent out by Francis I, probably explored the coast from Cape Fear to Newfoundland.

1534–1541. Voyages of **Jacques Cartier.** On the first voyage he sighted the Labrador coast, passed through the Straits of Belle Isle and explored the Gulf of St. Lawrence. On the second (1535–1536) he sailed up the St. Lawrence, stopped at the site of Quebec, proceeded to the La Chine Rapids and to the site of Montreal. On the third (1541) he was accompanied by M. de Roberval, a Picard nobleman, whom Francis I had made viceroy of Canada, Newfoundland, and Labrador. Unsuccessful attempts were made to establish a settlement at Quebec, and therewith the French efforts to colonize the St. Lawrence Valley came to an end until the 17th century.

In the south the activities of the French necessarily led to conflict with the Spaniards.

1562. Admiral Coligny, as part of his plan to attack Spain, sent **Jean Ribaut** to establish a colony in Florida. A colony on Port Royal Sound failed, but in 1564 Ribaut and **René de Laudonnière** established **Fort Caroline** on St. John's River. In the very next year the Spaniards, led by Menéndez de Avilés, massacred the French colonists and took the fort. Commanded by the Chevalier de Gourgues, the French (1567) avenged themselves by attacking the Spanish fort on the St. John's and putting the garrison to death.

1598. **Marquis de La Roche** attempted to found a colony on Sable Island. The survivors were rescued five years later.

1600. **Pontgravé, Chauvin,** and **De Monts,** with a grant of the fur-trade monopoly, made another unsuccessful attempt to colonize, this time at **Tadoussac** on the lower St. Lawrence.

1603. Pontgravé, accompanied by **Samuel de Champlain,** explored the St. Lawrence as far as La Chine Rapids. Champlain also explored the Acadian coast. In the next three years De Monts and Champlain organized a settlement on St. Croix Island, but moved later to **Port Royal.** Champlain followed the New England coast as far as Cape Cod, and returned to France in 1607.

1608, July 3. Champlain, acting as lieutenant for De Monts, founded the settlement of **Quebec.** In the following year, accompanied by a party of Algonquin and Huron Indians, he ascended the Richelieu River to the lake that now bears his name.

1610. Poutrincourt re-established Port Royal.

1613. Champlain explored the Ottawa River to about 100 miles above the present city of Ottawa. In 1615 he went up the river to Lake Nipissing and thence to Georgian Bay, being the first white man to blaze the fur-trader's route into the interior.

1615. Four **Recollet friars** arrived at Quebec, marking the beginning of French missionary activity. In 1625 five **Jesuits** arrived, beginning the work of that order.

1625–1664. **French settlements in the West Indies.** The first was St. Christopher (1625). The **Company of St. Christopher** was formed in 1626, to extend the settlement. This was superseded in 1635 by the **Company of Isles of America.** Guadeloupe, Martinique, and Tortuga were occupied, and between 1648 and 1656 settlements were made on St. Martin, St. Bartholomew, St. Croix, The Saints, Maria Galante, St. Lucia, and Grenada.

1627. Richelieu organized the **Company of the Hundred Associates** to colonize New France. The company was given all lands between Florida and the Arctic Circle, with a monopoly of trade, except in cod and whale fisheries.

1628. Acadia and Quebec captured by the English, but restored in 1632.

1634. Champlain, hearing of a great waterway in the west and believing it might be a passage to China, sent **Jean Nicolet** on an exploring expedition. Nicolet reached Sault Ste. Marie, explored the south shore of the upper peninsula of Michigan, and reached the southern extremity of Green Bay.

1642. **Paul de Maisonneuve founded Montreal.**

1658–1659. Radisson and Groseillers traded and explored in the country at the western end of Lake Superior.

1665. **Father Allouez** established the La Pointe Mission near the west end of Lake Superior.

1673. **Father JACQUES MARQUETTE** and **LOUIS JOLIET,** a trader, followed the Fox and Wisconsin Rivers to the Mississippi, which they descended to the confluence of the Arkansas. In the same year **Count Louis de Frontenac,** governor of New France, founded Fort Frontenac on Lake Ontario.

1679–1683. **Explorations of Robert de La Salle,** along the shores of Lake Michigan and in the Illinois country. He erected **Fort Crèvecoeur** near present Peoria (1679) and sent Hennepin to explore the upper Mississippi while he himself returned to Fort Frontenac.

Champlain (center) *fighting the Iroquois, 1609*

Capture of Quebec by the English, 1629

La Salle's landing at Matagorda Bay, 1685

In 1682 La Salle reached the mouth of the Mississippi and took possession of the whole valley in the name of the king of France.

1683-1689. Attempts of La Salle to establish a French colony at the mouth of the Mississippi, in order to control the fur trade and to provide a base for attack upon Spain in America. He left France with some 400 men in 1684 and reached the West Indies. Continuing his voyage he missed the mouth of the Mississippi and landed at Matagorda Bay, on the coast of Texas. In the meanwhile, **Tonty** had descended the Mississippi, but had failed to find La Salle (1686). La Salle conducted four expeditions to the northeast in the hope of finding the Mississippi. On the fourth of these (1687) he was murdered by his companions. His colony was completely wiped out by an Indian attack (1689).

1699-1702. To check the Spanish advance, to control the Gulf coast and to forestall possible English occupation of the lower Mississippi, French forces under **Pierre de Iberville** established posts at Biloxi and started the French colony in **Louisiana** (1699). The post was moved to Mobile Bay in 1702 and named St. Louis. **Mobile** was founded in 1710 and **New Orleans** in 1718.

1699. A Sulpician mission was set up at Cahokia in the Illinois country. In 1700 Jesuits moved down the Illinois River to Kaskaskia.

1701. Detroit founded by Antoine de Cadillac, to control the entrance from Lake Erie to Lake Huron and to control the trade with the Illinois country.

1712. Antoine Crozat was granted a monopoly of the trade in the territory from Illinois to the coast. Crozat surrendered his patent (1717) and Louisiana was in the same year taken over by the **Compagnie d'Occident,** which became the **Compagnie des Indes Orientales** (1719). *(Cont. p. 532.)*

b. THE ENGLISH IN NORTH AMERICA, 1562-1640

(1) Exploration

Following the voyages of the **Cabots** (see *p. 385)* the English showed little interest in the New World until the second half of the 16th century.

1562. John Hawkins, having taken a cargo of slaves in Africa, disposed of them in Española. The Spaniards made efforts to stop a second slave-trading voyage (1564-1565), and on his third voyage (1567-1568) Hawkins was driven by a storm into the harbor of Vera Cruz, where his fleet was largely destroyed.

1572-1580. Francis Drake, nephew of Hawkins, carried out reprisals on Spanish commerce. Sailing in 1577 he passed through the Straits of Magellan, up the west coast of South America, and north to Drake's Bay, California. He named the region **New Albion** and took possession for England. He then sailed to the East Indies, across the Indian Ocean, around the Cape of Good Hope, and thence home to England, being the first Eng-lishman to circumnavigate the globe.

1576-1578. After unsuccessful efforts by explorers of the **Muscovy Company** to find a northeast passage to China, English efforts became concentrated on the search for a northwest passage. **Martin Frobisher** sailed from England in June 1576, explored the Labrador coast, crossed Hudson Strait, coasted along Baffin Land, and entered the inlet known as **Frobisher Bay.** In 1577-1578 he made a second voyage *(p. 596).*

1583. Sir Humphrey Gilbert took possession of Newfoundland in the name of Elizabeth, but lost his life on the return voyage.

1585. John Davis explored Davis Strait, but failed to find a northwest passage. A second attempt (1586) was equally unsuccessful *(p. 597).*

1586-1588. Thomas Cavendish, following Drake's course, plundered Spanish commerce and circumnavigated the globe.

(2) Virginia

1584. Sir Walter Raleigh, under patent, sent out Philip Amadas and Arthur Barlow to establish a colony. They landed on Roanoke Island and named the country **Virginia.** Supply ships were sent out in 1586, but they found the colony deserted, the colonists having been taken back to England by Drake.

1587. Another party of colonists was sent out, under Governor **John White.** Upon his return in 1591, White found only the ruins of the colony.

1602-1606. A number of voyages were made to America, the most important having been that of **George Weymouth** in 1604. Weymouth visited the New England coast and his favorable report did much to stimulate the desire to establish further colonies.

1606, Apr. A group of London men was given a charter to organize the **London Company,** with the object of colonizing the region between 34° and 41° N.L. Another group, composed of Plymouth, Bristol, and Exeter men, was chartered as the **Plymouth Company,** to operate between 38° and 45° N.L. The London Company at once sent out (Dec. 1606) three ships with 120 colonists, under command of Captain **Christopher Newport.**

1607, May. FOUNDING OF JAMESTOWN COLONY at the mouth of the James River. The colony was held together largely through the efforts of Captain **John Smith.**

1609. The London Company was enlarged and given a new charter which vested the government in a council with power to appoint its own officers.

1610, May. Captain Newport arrived with 400 more colonists and with **Lord Delaware,** the new governor. Delaware left again in 1611, but remained governor until his death in 1618. **Sir Thomas Dale** was left in command of the colony and ruled with an iron hand.

1612. Beginning of the **cultivation of tobacco,** which was to play a vital part in the economic and social life of the colony.

1612. Third charter of the London Company. The Bermuda Islands were included in its jurisdiction.

1618. Sir Edwin Sandys became the dominant figure in the colony. He assigned 50 acres of land to every person who would transport one more settler to the colony.

1619. Arrival of the first **Negro slaves** in the colony.

1619. Sir Thomas Yeardley arrived as governor, bringing instructions for each plantation to elect two burgesses to a general assembly. The assembly met at Jamestown on July 30 and was the **first representative assembly** in America.

1621. Sir Francis Wyatt, the governor, brought over new regulations providing for government through a governor, council of state, and assembly, the latter consisting of two burgesses each elected from every plantation and town.

1624. Revocation of the charter. This step was taken as a result of dissension within the company and because of the king's disapproval of popular government and of the raising of tobacco, as well as because of his desire to please the Spanish, who had protested against

Sir Walter Raleigh

Captain John Smith's adventures in Virginia, as illustrated in 1624

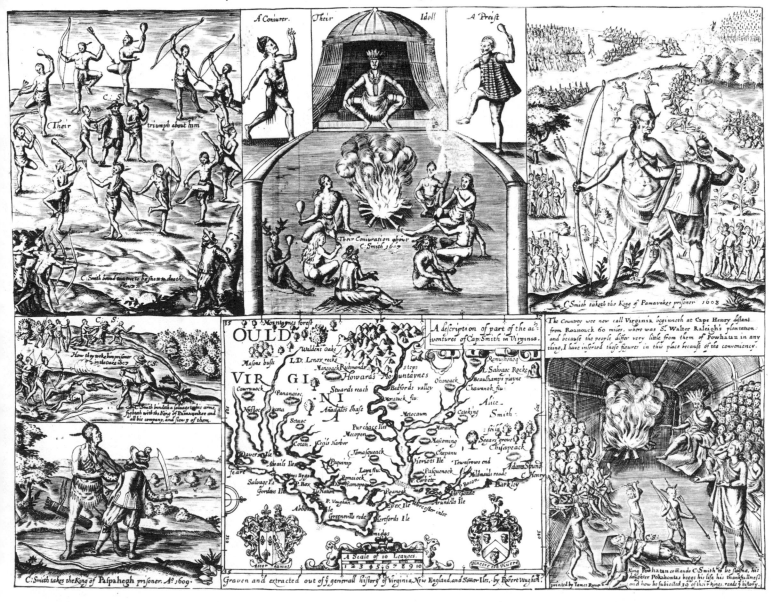

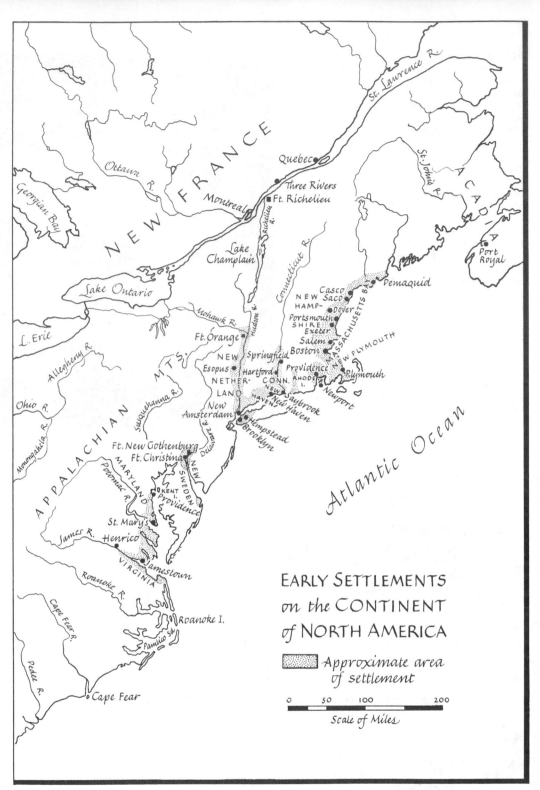

EARLY SETTLEMENTS on the CONTINENT of NORTH AMERICA

Approximate area of settlement

0   50   100   200
Scale of Miles

separatists who had migrated from Scrooby to Amsterdam and thence to Leyden in Holland. In 1617 they decided to seek a new home in order to preserve their English identity. They obtained a patent from the London Company and **John Carver** was made their governor. They left England in the *Mayflower* and reached Cape Cod, which they found to be outside the jurisdiction of the London Company. They therefore drew up the **Mayflower Compact,** by which they formed themselves into a body politic and agreed to enact laws for the welfare of the colony. The basis of government, then, was the will of the colonists rather than that of the crown. **Plymouth** was selected as the site of the settlement.

1621. William Bradford became governor on the death of Carver.

1623. Settlements at Portsmouth and Dover (New Hampshire) and at **Casco Bay** and **Saco Bay** (Maine) were made under the auspices of the Council for New England. A group of Dorchester merchants settled on Cape Ann (1624).

1628, Sept. John Endicott and some 50 colonists arrived at Salem, acting under a patent obtained by Rev. **John White** of Dorchester from the Council for New England. This patent ran for lands between the parallel three miles north of the source of the Merrimac River and that three miles south of the Charles River.

1629, Mar. ROYAL CHARTER issued confirming the grant to Endicott and his associates, which members of the Gorges family had protested. The new corporation was known as the **Governor and Company of Massachusetts Bay** in New England.

   June 27. Five ships, with some 400 settlers, arrived at Salem. **John Winthrop** and other prominent men meeting at Cambridge (England) agreed to emigrate to Massachusetts Bay, provided the charter and government might be legally transferred to America. The company decided to make the transfer and Winthrop was named governor.

1630. Seventeen ships brought about 1000 persons to the colony. By the end of the year settlements had been made at Dorchester, Boston, Watertown, Roxbury, Mystic, and Lynn. The first **general court** of the colony was held at Boston (Oct. 19). From then on no person was to be admitted as a freeman of the corporation unless a member of some

the founding of the colony. Virginia became a royal colony, with a governor and council appointed by the crown.

(3) New England

(a) Massachusetts

1606. Granting of the charter to the **Plymouth Company.** In this very year two unsuccessful attempts were made to found colonies. In 1607 settlers were landed at the mouth of the **Kennebec River,** but the enterprise was abandoned the next spring.

1614. Captain John Smith, of the Virginia settlement, explored the coast of New England

and mapped it. He was made *Admiral of New England* by the Plymouth Company (1615) and made an abortive effort to start a colony. Several fishing and trading voyages were made to the New England coast between 1615 and 1620 under the direction of **Sir Ferdinando Gorges,** a member of the Plymouth Company.

1620, Nov. 13. The Council for New England. The Plymouth Company having failed to found a colony, Gorges and others secured the incorporation of the council, which was given jurisdiction between 40° and 48° N.L.

1620, Nov. ARRIVAL OF THE PILGRIMS at Cape Cod. The Pilgrims were a group of

First Colonial Assembly in Virginia, 1619

The Mayflower

The Pilgrims signing the Mayflower Compact aboard ship

church within the colony. In 1634 a representative system was introduced into the general court, because the growth of the colony prevented attendance of all freemen.

1630-1642. The **Great Migration** to Massachusetts Bay Colony. During these years some 16,000 settlers arrived from England.

1635. The coast of New England was reapportioned. **Gorges** received the land in Maine between the Penobscot and Piscataqua Rivers; **John Mason** received New Hampshire and northern Massachusetts as far as Cape Ann; **Edward Gorges** from Cape Ann to Narragansett Bay. In this same year the Council for New England gave up its charter and the king demanded also the charter of the Massachusetts Bay Colony, because of Archbishop Laud's dislike of the Puritan Commonwealth. The king was unsuccessful.

1636. The general court voted £400 toward the founding of a college. In 1638 **John Harvard** bequeathed to the college £780 and 260 books. The institution was named **Harvard College** in 1639.

(b) Connecticut and Rhode Island

1631. The **earl of Warwick,** to whom the Council for New England had granted much of the Connecticut River Valley, transferred his rights to William Fiennes, **Lord Saye and Sele.**

1633. The **Dutch,** who had explored the coast, erected a fort on the river near the present **Hartford.**

1635. Lord Saye, with his associates, sent out settlers under John Winthrop, Jr., who established **Fort Saybrook,** at the mouth of the river. In the same year settlers from Dorchester (Massachusetts), seeking better land, established themselves at Windsor. In 1636 Rev. **Thomas Hooker** led Cambridge settlers to Hartford, while other colonists from Watertown settled at **Wethersfield.**

1638. Rev. **John Davenport** and **Theophilus Eaton** founded a theocratic colony at **New Haven.**

1639. Hartford, Windsor, and Wethersfield drew up **Fundamental Orders,** which provided that the governor and assistants, with four representatives from each town, should constitute the general court. These three settlements were commonly referred to as **Connecticut.**

Meanwhile **Roger Williams** had arrived at Boston, from England (1631). After spending some time at Salem, he repaired to Plymouth, where he concluded that the land rightfully belonged to the Indians and that the king had no right to grant it. He returned to Salem, where he argued that the Church and the State should be separated. He denied the right of the magistrate to control the churches, and objected to enforced oaths, since they obliged wicked men to perform a religious act, thereby destroying the freedom of the soul. In October 1635 he was banished from Salem.

1636, June. ROGER WILLIAMS SETTLED AT PROVIDENCE, where he organized a gov-

Rev. Hooker en route to Hartford, 1636

Harvard College as it looked in 1725

Roger Williams and Narragansett Indians, 1636

The purchase of Manhattan Island, 1626

ernment democratic in character, with separation of Church and State.

1638. Mrs. Anne Hutchinson, the center of a controversy which shook Massachusetts Bay Colony to its foundations, was banished and took refuge on the island of Aquidneck, later called **Rhode Island,** where she and a small group of associates founded the settlement of **Portsmouth.** The following year another settlement was made at **Newport.**

(4) Maryland

George Calvert (later Lord Baltimore) had bought the southeastern peninsula of Newfoundland from **Sir William Vaughan** (1620) and had secured a charter (1623) for a colony, which he called **Avalon.** He visited Newfoundland in 1627 and resolved to abandon the colony because of the unfavorable climate. He then asked for a grant in Virginia, which was made in 1632, despite opposition from the Virginians.

1632, Apr. The charter of the new colony was drawn up in the name of Cecilius Calvert, George Calvert having died. The province was named **Maryland,** and Calvert, as proprietor, was given the right to collect taxes, make grants of land, create manors, appoint ministers, and found churches according to the laws of England. As the charter did not forbid the establishment of other churches than the Protestant, Baltimore (Calvert) made use of it to help his co-religionists, the Catholics.

1633, Oct. Baltimore dispatched to Maryland two vessels with some 20 gentlemen, mostly Catholics, and about 200 laborers, chiefly Protestants. Arriving at the mouth of the Potomac (1634, Mar.), they founded the settlement of **St. Mary's.**

(5) Island Settlements

1609. A Virginia supply ship, under command of **Sir George Somers,** was wrecked on one of the Bermuda Islands. On his return to England Somers interested a number of persons, mostly members of the Virginia Company, in the islands, with the result that the **Somers Islands Company** was formed (1612) for the colonization of Bermuda. The island had 600 settlers in 1614 and between 2000 and 3000 in 1625. It became an important producer of tobacco.

1625. St. Christopher was settled, and **Sir William Courten** established the first colony on Barbados. Nevis was occupied by the British in 1628, and settlements were made on Antigua and Montserrat in 1632. By 1640 the island possessions of England had a population of 20,000, devoted chiefly to the cultivation of sugar, which soon supplanted tobacco as the leading crop. *(Cont. p. 529.)*

New Amsterdam as it appeared in 1650

c. DUTCH AND SWEDISH SETTLEMENTS, 1602-1655

1602. The **United East India Company** was chartered by the states-general of Holland.

1609. The company employed **Henry Hudson,** an Englishman, to search for the northwest passage. He sighted land at Newfoundland, explored the New England coast, rounded Cape Cod, proceeded south to Virginia, probably entered Chesapeake Bay, entered Delaware Bay, and explored the **Hudson River** to Albany. Friendly relations with Iroquois Indians.

1612. Dutch merchants sent **Christianson and Block** to Manhattan Island to engage in fur trade. A post was established in 1613.

1614. Fort Nassau, later Fort Orange, built near present Albany. Exploration by Adrian Block of Long Island Sound, Connecticut coast, Narragansett Bay, and Cape Cod. As a result the **New Netherland Company** was formed and given monopoly of trade between the 40th and 45th parallels. Fur trade carried on and the coast explored.

1621. The **Dutch West India Company** was chartered and given a monopoly of trade in Africa and America.

1626. **Peter Minuit** became director-general of the company. He purchased **Manhattan Island** from the Indians for 24 dollars and founded the settlement of **New Amsterdam**. The company also made settlements in Con-

necticut, New Jersey, Delaware, and Pennsylvania. Men, known as *patroons*, were given large areas of land on condition that they bring over a stipulated number of settlers. The Dutch, under Governor Kieft of New Netherland, protested in vain against the founding of New Haven.

Meanwhile the attention of Gustavus Adolphus of Sweden was called to the Delaware country by **William Usselincx,** who had withdrawn from the Dutch West India Company. Usselincx received a charter for the **South**

Company which came to naught. In 1633 the **New South Company** was organized, but it too failed to achieve anything. In 1637 the **New Sweden Company** was organized, chiefly as a result of the encouragement of two Dutchmen, Samuel Blommaert and Peter Minuit.

1638. Two Swedish vessels arrived on the Delaware and **Fort Christina** was established. This intrusion of the Swedes angered **Peter Stuyvesant** of New Netherland, who urged the West India Company to occupy New Sweden, which was done in 1655.

2. *Colonial History*

a. NEW ENGLAND, 1641–1728

1641. The **Body of Liberties,** a code of 100 laws, was established by the general court of the Massachusetts Bay Colony.

1643, May 19. The **New England Confederation** was formed by Connecticut (Hartford, Windsor, and Wethersfield), New Haven, Plymouth, and Massachusetts Bay for purposes of defense.

1644. Union of Providence and the Rhode Island towns (Newport and Portsmouth) under a charter obtained by Roger Williams. Union of Saybrook and Connecticut under the latter name.

1646. In Massachusetts, **John Eliot** began his missionary work among the Indians, translating the Bible into Massachusetts dialect, 1661–1663.

1649. Incorporation in England of the **Society for Propagating the Gospel in New England.**

1653. Settlements in southern Maine accepted the jurisdiction of Massachusetts.

1662. **Charter of Connecticut** granted by the king. Assembly composed of the governor, deputy-governor, 12 assistants, and two deputies from each town.

1663. **Charter of Rhode Island and Providence Plantations,** kept throughout the colonial period and the constitution of the state until 1842.

1664. **Union of Connecticut and New Haven,** because of the latter's fear of annexation to New York.

1665. **Maine** was restored to the heirs of Sir Ferdinando Gorges.

Royal commissioners, after an unsuccessful attempt to hear complaints in New England, left the provinces.

1668. Massachusetts reassumed the government of Maine.

1675–1676. **KING PHILIP'S WAR** in New England. Although primarily due to the advance of the frontier of settlement upon the Indian hunting grounds, there were numerous minor infractions of the law. Christianizing of Cape Cod Indians by John Eliot aroused the suspicions of the Wampanoags, who saw in it an attempt to weaken their power. **Philip,** son of **Massasoit,** chief of the Wampanoags, formed a league comprising most of the Indi-

ans from Maine to Connecticut. Border attacks were followed by the white attack upon the stronghold of the Narragansetts near Kingston, Rhode Island, in December 1675, with heavy losses to the Indians. Deerfield was attacked by Indians and most of the houses were burned. During the war 500 white men were captured or killed and nearly 40 towns damaged, 20 being destroyed or abandoned. Chief Canonchet of the Narragansetts was shot (Apr. 1676) and the war came to a close with the death of Philip (Aug. 1676).

1677. The dispute between Massachusetts and the heirs of Sir Ferdinando Gorges regarding Maine having been decided in favor of the latter by the English courts, Massachusetts bought all of the province except that granted to the duke of York.

1680. **New Hampshire** was separated from Massachusetts by royal charter.

1684. **ANNULMENT OF THE MASSACHUSETTS CHARTER.** The independent course of Massachusetts had long irritated the crown. The heirs of Mason and Gorges charged that Massachusetts has usurped their rights. London merchants claimed the colony evaded the navigation acts by sending tobacco and sugar directly to Europe. Lack of respect for the king's authority and the exercise of powers not warranted by the charter were also charged. In 1679 **Edward Randolph** arrived in Boston as collector of the customs, bearing instructions for the colony to relinquish jurisdiction over New Hampshire and Maine, the latter of which was disregarded. Friction continued, as did Randolph's complaints against the colony, until legal action in 1684 resulted in the annulment of the charter.

1686. **DOMINION OF NEW ENGLAND** formed through consolidation of the New England colonies. **Sir Edmund Andros** was made governor. *Quo warranto* proceedings were instituted against Connecticut and Carolina. Andros arrived in Boston (Dec. 20) and assumed the government of Plymouth and Rhode Island. In 1687 he assumed the government of Connecticut and demanded the charter, which Captain William Wadsworth concealed in a hollow tree, the famous *Charter Oak.*

1689. Upon news of the flight of James II from

England, the people of Boston rose in revolt, imprisoned Andros and restored charter government. Similar action was taken in Rhode Island and Connecticut.

1691. **New charter for Massachusetts,** which included Plymouth, Maine, Nova Scotia, and all land north to the St. Lawrence. A governor, to be appointed by the crown, was vested with the power of calling and dissolving the general court, appointing military and judicial officers, and vetoing acts of legislature. The electoral franchise was extended and religious liberty secured to all except Catholics. **Sir William Phips** was made governor.

King Philip

Hanging of "witches" in Salem, 1692

William Penn's treaty with the Indians, 1683

1692. Salem witchcraft trials.

1701. Founding of Yale College, New Haven, Connecticut.

1728. William Burnet, governor of Massachusetts, became involved in a quarrel with the legislature over the question of a fixed salary for the governor, which the court refused to grant "because it is the undoubted right of all Englishmen, by Magna Carta, to raise and dispose of money for the public service, of their own accord, without compulsion."

Death of **Cotton Mather,** (b. 1663), prolific author of Puritan tracts. More liberal were the writings of a later divine, **Jonathan Edwards** (1703–1758).

b. NEW YORK, NEW JERSEY, PENNSYLVANIA, 1664–1735

1664. Grant of New Netherland, from the Connecticut to the Delaware, to the king's brother, **James, duke of York.** The grant included the eastern part of Maine and islands south and west of Cape Cod. The region between the Hudson and the Delaware was granted by the duke of York to **Lord Berkeley** and **Sir George Carteret.**

1664, Aug. 27. SURRENDER OF NEW AMSTERDAM to the English. Name of the colony changed to **New York.** On September 24 surrender of Fort Orange, whose name was changed to **Albany.**

1673. In the war between England and Holland, the **Dutch captured New York** and established temporary control over Albany and New Jersey. These places were restored when peace was made in 1674.

1676. Line of demarcation between East and West New Jersey. **Settlement of Quakers** in West New Jersey (1677–1681).

1681, Mar. 4. CHARTER OF PENNSYLVANIA signed, granting to **William Penn** the region between 40° and 43°, extending 5° west from the Delaware River. These limits brought the colony into conflict with New York on the north and Maryland on the south. The dispute with Maryland was finally ad-

justed when in 1767 two surveyors, **Mason and Dixon,** ran the present boundary between the two states. The form of government of the colony was to be determined by the proprietor. The first body of colonists arrived in 1681 and a frame of government was provided for the government of the colony.

1682–1683. Penn arrived in the colony and **Philadelphia** was laid out (1682). Penn entered into a treaty with the Indians (1683) which had the effect of keeping the colony free from Indian wars.

1683. In response to persistent demands of the people, the duke of York conceded a legislative assembly to New York. In October, 17 representatives drew up a **Charter of Franchises and Liberties,** which the duke signed, only to reject it when he became king.

1688. The **Lords of Trade** determined to bring New York and New Jersey under the government of Andros. In 1689 New York proclaimed William and Mary.

1702. New Jersey reunited as a royal province.

1715–1750. SETTLEMENT OF THE PIEDMONT, partly by newcomers and old settlers, who crossed the fall line into the areas, partly by Germans, Swiss, and Scotch-Irish entering at the port of Philadelphia and pushing southward through the valleys, especially the Shenandoah. **German immigration,** which began with the founding of Germantown, Pennsylvania (1683), increased greatly in volume after

Pages from John Peter Zenger's newspaper

THE
New-York Weekly JOURNAL

Containing the freſheſt Advices, Foreign, and Domeſtick.

MUNDAT November 12, 1733.

THE
New-York Weekly JOURNAL

Containing the freſheſt Advices, Foreign, and Domeſtick.

MUNDAT Auguſt 18th, 1735.

1710. Occupation of the piedmont resulted in the formation of a restless, aggressive frontier society which was to become increasingly important.

1720–1726. William Burnet, governor of New York, began efforts to counteract French attempts to hem in the English colonies in the west. He prohibited trade between the Iroquois and the French. In 1722 he established a trading post at **Oswego** and carried on negotiations at Albany with the Six Nations. A treaty with the Senecas, Cayugas, and Onondagas (1726) added their lands to those of the Mohawks and Oneidas, which were already under English protection.

1732. Benjamin Franklin (1706–1790), journalist as well as statesman, published *Poor Richard's Almanac.*

1735. Trial in New York of **John Peter Zenger,** printer of a paper, for libel. The court contended that it should decide the libelous nature of the statements made, and that the jury should determine the fact of publication. Zenger's lawyer, Andrew Hamilton, argued that the jury must decide whether or not the publication was libelous. He won his suit, thereby materially safeguarding the freedom of the press.

c. VIRGINIA, DELAWARE, AND MARYLAND, 1652–1716

1652. Parliament assumed control of Maryland and suspended the governor.

1659. Virginia proclaimed Charles II king of England, Scotland, and Ireland, and restored the royal governor, **Sir William Berkeley.**

1662. Lord Baltimore was confirmed in the government of Maryland.

1676. Bacon's Rebellion in Virginia. Led by Nathaniel Bacon, this revolt was largely the result of the indifference of Governor Berkeley to the problem of frontier defense against the Indians. Jamestown was burned, but the rebellion collapsed with the death of Bacon.

1689. Virginia and Maryland proclaimed William and Mary.

1693. College of William and Mary founded in Virginia.

1716. Governor Alexander Spotswood of Virginia led an expedition to the Blue Ridge, and into the Shenandoah Valley. He recommended the securing of the mountain passes and the establishment of settlements on Lake Erie.

d. THE SOUTHERN COLONIES, 1663–1737

1663. Grant of Carolina by the king to eight proprietors, including the earl of Clarendon. The grant included land between 31° and 36° N.L. After Raleigh's unsuccessful effort, the region between Virginia and the Spanish settlements in Florida had received little attention until the grant of the region to Sir Robert Heath (1629), which also came to naught.

1667. Grant of the Bahamas to the Carolina proprietors.

1669. Adoption of the Fundamental Constitutions, drawn up for Carolina by John Locke, which provided for an archaic feudal régime

William and Mary College, c. 1740

totally unsuited to the needs of a frontier colony.

1711. Tuscarora War in North Carolina. The Tuscaroras massacred some 200 settlers. Virginia and South Carolina sent aid and the Indians were defeated (1712). Remnants of the Tuscaroras moved to New York and were incorporated in the Iroquois as a sixth nation.

1715. Defeat of the Yamassees and allied Indian tribes in Carolina. They were driven across the Spanish border into Florida.

1719–1729. REORGANIZATION OF THE CAROLINAS. Economic differences between the northern and southern portions of Carolina had resulted in governmental differentiation. The governor was located at Charleston with a deputy governor in the north. In 1713 the proprietors appointed **Charles Eden** governor of North Carolina and from this time the provinces were virtually separate. Popular discontent with the proprietors because of their indifference to defense against Indians and pirates. The situation was aggravated by refusal of the proprietors to allow the distribution of the Yamassee lands. Meanwhile the proprietors had incurred the ill-will of the British government. Their incompetence in the Yamassee War was the last straw which convinced the Board of Trade that a change was necessary. It upheld the people against the proprietors and in 1729 an act of parliament established royal governments in both North and South Carolina.

1733. FOUNDING OF GEORGIA, the last of the 13 English colonies on the continent. In the triangle between the Carolinas, Florida, and Louisiana, British, French, and Spanish claims conflicted. The international boundaries had never been defined. In 1716 the Carolinians had established a fort on the Savannah River and from 1721 to 1727 had maintained **Fort George** on the Altamaha. In 1730 **Sir Alexander Cuming** was sent on a mission to the Cherokees which resulted in their acknowledgement of British supremacy. The need of a buffer colony on the southern boundary had long been realized by the British. In 1717 **Sir Robert Montgomery** had secured from the Carolina proprietors a grant of the land between the Savannah and Altamaha Rivers, known as the **margravate of Azilia.** Plans for its settlement proving unsuccessful, **James Oglethorpe** became interested in the settlement of the region. An advocate of a strong policy against the Spanish and a humanitarian interested in improving the condition of imprisoned debtors, he conceived the idea of a barrier colony. In 1732 he secured a charter, granting to him and his associates the region between the Savannah and the Altamaha from sea to sea. Proprietary government was to prevail for 21 years, when the colony was to become a royal province. Religious liberty was guaranteed to all except Catholics. Colonists left England in the autumn of 1732, arriving at Charleston in January 1733. The town of **Savannah** was immediately laid out; and in 1737 a fort was established at **Augusta.**

Savannah, Georgia in 1734

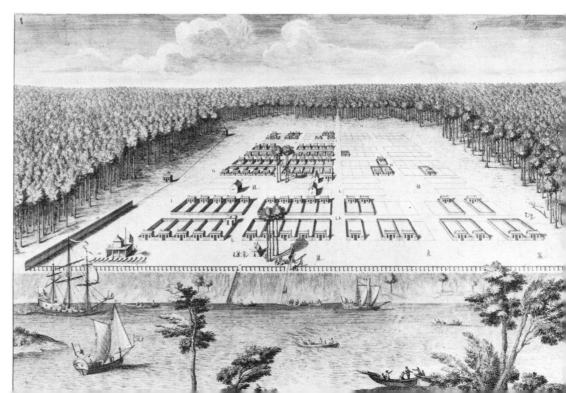

3. *Wars of England with France and Spain, 1651–1775*

1651–1673. The British Navigation Laws. These applied mercantilist doctrine to colonial trade. The **Act of 1651,** designed to strike a blow at Dutch shipping, required that colonial products be shipped to England in ships of Great Britian or the Plantations. This law was re-enacted in 1660, with the additional provision that certain enumerated articles of colonial production could be shipped only to England. The **Staple Act** of 1663 required that articles of European production destined for the colonies must be shipped first to England. The **Act of 1673** imposed intercolonial duties on sugar, tobacco, and other products.

1667. Treaty of Breda between England and France. Antigua, Montserrat, and the French port of St. Christopher surrendered to England.

1670. The **Hudson's Bay Company** incorporated and given a monopoly of the trade in Hudson's Bay Basin.

1689–1697. KING WILLIAM'S WAR, with France. This was the American phase of the general war against Louis XIV known as the **War of the League of Augsburg** *(see p. 466).* The French were aided by the Indians of Canada and Maine, while the Iroquois supported the English. In 1690 the French and Indians massacred colonists at Schenectady,

Proclamation forbidding trade in Indian corn

By His Excellency

Coll. *Benjamin Fletcher* Captain General and Governour in Chief of His Majesties Province of Neu-York, &c.

A PROCLAMATION

WHEREAS The *French* and *Indians* of *Canada* have lately Invaded the Country of the Indians of the Five Nations in Amity with the Subjects of the Crown of *England*, and have destroyed their Indian Corn. To the end that the said *Indians* that have so suffered the loss of their Corn, may be supplyed with what is necessary for their Maintenance for the Year ensuing, I have therefore, by and with the Advice and Consent of His Majesties Council for this Province, Prohibited the Transportation of Indian Corn and Peas from the County of *Albany, Ulster* and *Dutchess County,* to any other County or Place down the River, until the first day of *April* now next ensuing. And all Masters of Sloops, and other Vessels are hereby prohibited accordingly, as they will answer the contrary at their peril.

Given at Fort William Henry the Twelfth Day of September, in the Eighth Year of the Reign of our Soveraign Lord **WILLIAM** the Third, by the Grace of God, King of England, Scotland, France and Ireland, Defender of the Faith, &c. Annoq; Domini 1696.

Ben. Fletcher.

God Save the K I N G

Printed by William Bradford, *Printer to the Kings most Excellent Majesty, at the Bible in the City of* New-York, 1696.

Salmon Falls, and Casco Bay. An English force under **Sir William Phips** captured Port Royal (1690, May 11), but a Massachusetts expedition against Quebec, led by Phips, resulted in failure. The **treaty of Ryswick** restored all conquests (1697).

1696–1698. Renewed efforts of the English government to control colonial trade. A **Board of Commissioners for Trade and Plantations** was organized (1696) and a navigation act of the same year was designed to prevent further evasion of earlier regulations. Since the war with France had interrupted the usual trade, the New Englanders had taken up manufacturing. The **Woolens Act** (1698) forbade the colonists to ship wool or woolen products from one colony to another.

1702–1713. QUEEN ANNE'S WAR, the American phase of the **War of the Spanish Succession** *(see p. 467).* In 1702 the English plundered and burned St. Augustine in Florida, while in 1704 the French and Indians surprised Deerfield in the Connecticut Valley. Their attacks soon spread over much of the frontier and even to the outskirts of Boston. In 1707 the English organized an **expedition against Acadia.** Troops from New England laid siege to Port Royal, but failed to reduce it. The French province was, however, conquered in 1710, when 4000 colonists under **Francis Nicholson,** aided by British ships and a regiment of marines, attacked and captured Port Royal. Acadia then became the British province of **Nova Scotia** and the name of Port Royal was changed to **Annapolis Royal.** For the year 1711 a joint land and sea campaign against Canada was planned. Nicholson's colonials and Iroquois were to attack Montreal, while an expedition was to be led against Quebec by Admiral Sir Hovenden Walker and General Sir John Hill. Seven of Marlborough's best regiments were included. The force gathered at Boston, where it was reinforced by 1500 colonials. In August the fleet entered the St. Lawrence, but the destruction of ten ships compelled the abandonment of the attack. News of this reached Nicholson and induced him to give up the campaign against Montreal. By the **treaty of Utrecht** (1713) Great Britain secured recognition of its claims in the Hudson's Bay country and the possession of Newfoundland and Acadia. The claim of the British to the Iroquois country was also admitted, and St. Christopher was ceded to Britain. The French were excluded from fishing on the Acadian coast, but were allowed to retain Cape Breton Island. The *asiento* gave the English the exclusive right for 30 years of bringing Negroes into the Spanish possessions.

1733. The Molasses Act. The increased production of sugar in the French and Dutch West Indies after 1715, the disposition of the

English colonists on the mainland (especially the New Englanders) to take advantage of the low prices of sugar, molasses, and rum in the foreign islands, and their desire to avail themselves of the market afforded for their own products in the islands contributed to bring about a severe depression among the sugar planters of the British island possessions. In response to pleas from the West Indian planters, parliament enacted the Molasses Act, which placed prohibitive duties on sugar and molasses imported into the colonies from other than British possessions. In 1732 parliament had stopped the importation of hats from the colonies and had restricted their manufacture. This was in accord with the mercantilist policy of encouraging the production of raw materials (including furs) and of discouraging manufactures that would conflict with those of the mother country.

1739. WAR BETWEEN SPAIN AND ENGLAND (War of Jenkins' Ear, *see p. 457).* Dissatisfied with the provisions of the treaty of Utrecht with respect to trade with Spanish possessions, British merchants had resorted to extensive smuggling, which, in turn, had led to the seizure of British ships and the rough treatment of British sailors by the Spaniards. The loss of Jenkins' ear was merely one of many similar episodes. In the course of the ensuing war the British captured Porto Bello and demolished its fortifications (1739). In 1740 they bombarded Cartagena and captured Chagres, while Oglethorpe led an expedition of Georgia, Carolina, and Virginia troops into Florida and made an unsuccessful attack on St. Augustine. The British were likewise unsuccessful in an attack on Santiago (Cuba) in 1741. In the next year they planned, but then abandoned, an attack on Panama. The Spanish attacked Georgia (1742), but soon withdrew again to Florida. In 1743 Oglethorpe once more invaded Florida, but failed to take St. Augustine.

1743–1748. KING GEORGE'S WAR, the American phase of the **War of the Austrian Succession** in Europe *(see p. 483).* The outstanding event in the war in America was the **capture of Louisburg** (1745). The French had made the fortress one of the strongest in the New World. After an invasion of Nova Scotia by the French, Governor William Shirley of Massachusetts assembled volunteers from Massachusetts, New Hampshire, and Connecticut and placed them under the command of **William Pepperell.** Transports were supplied by the colonies, while warships were provided by the British navy. The expedition appeared before Louisburg on April 30 and the fortress capitulated after a siege (June 16). An attempt of the French to recover Cape Breton and Nova Scotia was made in 1746, but was doomed to failure when a storm destroyed the

The surrender of Louisburg, 1745

fleet off the coast. In the interior an abortive attempt of the northern colonies to conquer Canada spurred the French and Indians to attack the frontier as far south as New York (1746–1748). The New York and Pennsylvania frontiers were protected by **Sir William Johnson,** British superintendent of the Six Nations, who kept the Mohawks friendly, and by **Conrad Weiser,** whose support of the Iroquois land claims as against the Delawares kept the Six Nations on the English side. At sea the British twice defeated the French in the West Indies (1745, 1747) and in 1748 the British admiral, Sir Charles Knowles, captured Port Louis on the southern coast of Haiti, bombarded Santiago, and attacked the Spanish fleet off Havana.

1748. The **treaty of Aix-la-Chapelle,** based upon European rather than colonial considerations, restored all the conquests of the war. In America the treaty was merely a truce, for Nova Scotia, the Ohio Valley, and the Cherokee country continued to be areas of conflict. In order to strengthen the British hold on Nova Scotia, Lord Halifax sent out 2500 settlers in 1749 and founded the town of **Halifax.** In the Ohio Valley traders from Virginia and Pennsylvania pushed westward as far as the Indian villages on the Mississippi. Virginia frontiersmen made a settlement at **Draper's Meadow** on the Greenbrier River in 1748.

1749. The **Ohio Company,** organized by a group of Virginians and a number of prominent Englishmen. The company obtained a grant of 500,000 acres on the upper Ohio and sent out **Christopher Gist** (1750) to explore the

Sir William Johnson

region as far as the falls of the Ohio. His favorable report led to the erection of a trading house at **Wills's Creek,** the present Cumberland (Maryland), and to the blazing of a trail to the junction of Redstone Creek and the Monongahela River. This activity roused the French to action. In an effort to detach the Iroquois from the British they founded the mission at present-day **Ogdensburg** (1748). To divert trade from Oswego they established **Fort Rouillé** on the site of present-day **Toronto**

(1749). Another post was located at **Niagara** portage, **Detroit** was strengthened, and in 1749 the governor of Canada sent **Céloron de Blainville** to take possession of the Ohio Valley.

1753. **Marquis Duquesne** sent an expedition of 1500 men to occupy the Ohio country. **Fort Presqu'Isle** was erected and a road was cut to French Creek, where **Fort Le Boeuf** was built. It was planned to establish another fort at the forks of the Ohio. In the same year Governor Robert Dinwiddie of Virginia sent out **George Washington,** a young surveyor, to demand the withdrawal of the French. He proceeded to Fort Le Boeuf, but was told that Dinwiddie's letter would be forwarded to Duquesne. It was quite clear that the French would not leave the valley peacefully.

1754. Virginia troops dispatched to the Ohio, with Washington second in command. The French had, in the meanwhile, built **Fort Duquesne** at the forks of the Ohio. Washington pushed on to Great Meadows where he constructed **Fort Necessity.** He was attacked by the French and forced to surrender.

1754, June 19. The Albany Convention. The advance of the French had shown the need for a common plan of defense. Representatives of New York, Pennsylvania, Maryland, and the New England states met with the Six Nations. Upon the suggestion of **Benjamin Franklin,** the convention drew up a plan of union which was, however, rejected by the colonies. The plan called for union under a president appointed by the crown, with a grand council of delegates elected by the colonial assemblies, this body to have legislative

power subject to approval by the president and the crown.

1755–1763. The FRENCH AND INDIAN WAR, the American phase of the **Seven Years' War** in Europe *(see p. 485).* In 1755 the governors of Virginia, North Carolina, Pennsylvania, Maryland, New York, and Massachusetts met in conference at Alexandria (Virginia) with **General Edward Braddock,** the British commander, recently arrived. They planned a fourfold attack on the French: upon Fort Duquesne, Niagara, Crown Point, and Fort Beauséjour. Braddock led the expedition into the Ohio country, but was surrounded and defeated near **Fort Duquesne** (July 9). In the Crown Point campaign the French were defeated in the **battle of Lake George** (Sept. 8), but the British made no attempt to capture Crown Point itself. They built **Fort William Henry** at the southern end of Lake George, while the French fortified **Ticonderoga.** In 1756 war was formally declared between France and Great Britain. **Lord John Loudoun** was

named commander-in-chief of the British forces in America. The French were commanded by **Marquis Louis de Montcalm,** who took and destroyed Forts Oswego and George (Aug.) and in 1757 took Fort William Henry (Aug. 9). The garrison, whose retreat to Fort Edward had been guaranteed by Montcalm, was massacred by his Indian allies.

The resistance of the British was weakened by the friction between Loudoun and the Massachusetts general court over quartering of troops, and between the governor and assembly of Virginia over various matters of taxation. In 1758 (July 8) General James Abercromby was defeated before Ticonderoga, but General Jeffrey Amherst and General James Wolfe took Louisburg (July 26), Bradstreet took Fort Frontenac (Aug. 27) and Forbes took Fort Duquesne (Nov. 25).

For the year 1759 the English planned four campaigns: against Niagara, against settlements on Lake Erie, against Ticonderoga and Crown Point, and against Quebec. The **battle of the Plains of Abraham** (Quebec) was fought on September 13, both Wolfe and Montcalm losing their lives. Quebec surrendered to the British on September 18. On September 8, 1760 Montreal surrendered and all Canada passed into the hands of the British. In 1762 **Admiral George Rodney** forced the surrender of Martinique, Grenada, St. Lucia, St. Vincent, and the other French West Indies.

1763, Feb. 10. The **TREATY OF PARIS,** between Great Britain, France, Spain, and Portugal. France ceded to Britain all claim to Acadia, Canada, Cape Breton, and all that part of Louisiana situated east of the Mississippi except the Island of Orleans. France retained certain fishing rights on the Newfoundland Banks and was given the islands of St. Pierre and Miquelon. Britain restored

to France the islands of Guadeloupe, Martinique, Belle Isle, Maria Galante, and St. Lucia. Britain restored Havana to Spain, in return for which Spain ceded Florida to Britain. France, by a previous treaty (1762, Nov. 3) had ceded to Spain all French territory west of the Mississippi and the Island of Orleans, as compensation for the loss of Florida to Britain.

1763. The Conspiracy of Pontiac. This was an aftermath to the war. Indian tribes north of the Ohio, fearing eviction by the British, embittered by the arrogance and dishonesty of British traders, and disappointed by the economy of General Amherst in the matter of presents, were ready to revolt against British occupation of the posts recently held by the French. Pontiac, chief of the Ottawas, organized a rising of the Algonquins, of some of the Iroquois, and of tribes on the lower Mississippi. In a simultaneous attack all but three of the northwestern posts fell in May. By 1765, however, the British forces were in possession of the last of the French posts in the west.

1763, Oct. 7. Proclamation of 1763, issued by George III. It created four distinct provinces from the recent conquests: Quebec, East Florida, West Florida, and Grenada. It also temporarily closed to white settlement all lands west and north of the streams flowing into the Atlantic Ocean. Fur trade in this Indian reserve was opened to licensed subjects. In 1764 **Lord Hillsborough** drew up a plan for the management of the Indians and the fur trade. It continued the northern and southern departments for Indian affairs (created in 1755) and provided that in the north all trade must be conducted at regularly established posts and in the south at the Indian towns.

1763–1775. Expansion beyond the mountains.

The Battle of Lake George in the French and Indian War, 1755

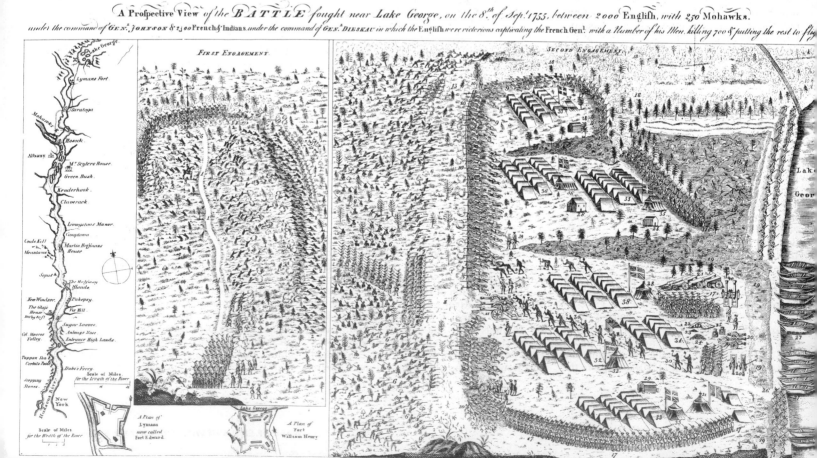

British troops assaulting Quebec in September, 1759

The death of General Wolfe

Numerous colonies had been planned by land companies before 1763. With these the Proclamation of 1763 interfered. In 1768, however, a plan for the gradual and controlled establishment of colonies in the west was worked out. In that year treaties with the Creeks, Cherokees, and Iroquois extinguished Indian rights to large areas. A group of Pennsylvanians, including Franklin, organized the **Vandalia Company** for the establishment of a colony in what is now West Virginia. Purchase of land was made in 1769 and by 1775 the proposed colony of Vandalia had been approved by the king and council. The outbreak of the Revolution rendered the plan abortive.

The **Watauga settlement** in eastern Tennessee was made in 1769 and was augmented by the arrival of Virginians and North Carolinians under **James Robertson** and **John Sevier** (1770–1771). Finding themselves beyond the pale of organized law, the settlers, proceeding on the compact theory, formed the **Watauga Association** (1772), organized as Washington County (North Carolina) in 1777.

Richard Henderson, of North Carolina, together with his associates, organized the **Transylvania Company,** purchased land from the Cherokees, and established the Transylvania settlement in Kentucky in 1775. **Daniel Boone** was Henderson's agent and cleared the wilderness road to Kentucky. The **settlement of Kentucky** (1775–1777) was facilitated by the peace forced on the Indians as a result of **Lord Dunmore's War** (1774).

Daniel Boone leading pioneers through the Cumberland Gap

4. *The American Revolution, 1763–1788*

1763–1775. The Preliminaries of the American Revolution. By 1761 the British government was thoroughly aroused by the systematic evasion of the **Molasses Act** of 1733 through colonial smuggling, and by the illicit trade which the colonies had carried on with the enemy during the War of the Austrian Succession and the Seven Years' War. British officials felt that the trade prolonged French resistance. To prevent smuggling, the British resorted to **writs of assistance,** general search warrants, which made possible the search of all premises where smuggled goods might be found. This aroused the opposition of merchants who alleged the writs were illegal. In 1761, when Boston customs officers applied for the writs, the merchants contested their use. **James Otis** argued cogently against their legality before the Massachusetts supreme court. Although the court decided they were legal, the argument of Otis did much to shape public opinion.

1763. The **Parsons' Cause,** argued in Virginia by **Patrick Henry,** still further aroused and

Patrick Henry

Death of the Stamp Act, 1766—a contemporary English cartoon

molded public opinion against British policy, in this instance the disallowance of a Virginia statute.

1763-1765. George Grenville in power in England. The acquisition of the vast territory from France in America necessitated increased revenues for defense and Indian administration. The ministry decided to enforce the navigation laws, tax the colonies directly, and use the revenue to maintain an army in America. Powers of the admiralty courts were enlarged, and colonial governors were instructed to enforce the trade laws.

1764. Enactment of the **Sugar Act,** with the avowed purpose of raising revenue in the colonies and reforming the old colonial system, both economically and administratively.

The **Colonial Currency Act** prevented colonies from paying their debts in England in depreciated currency and forbade issues of unsound money. This act created a shortage of money in the colonies at a time when the Sugar Act injured the West Indian trade of the colonies, which had previously supplied the necessary specie.

1765. Disregarding colonial protests against the two previous acts, Grenville pushed through parliament the **Stamp Act,** providing for stamps on commercial and legal documents, pamphlets, newspapers, almanacs, playing cards, and dice.

The **Quartering Act** was passed, providing that, in the event of insufficiency of barracks in the colonies, British troops might be quartered in public hostelries.

May 29. Patrick Henry introduced into the Virginia house of burgesses a series of resolutions boldly challenging the position of the British government.

June. The Massachusetts general court sent an invitation to colonial assemblies to send delegates to meet in New York and consider the Stamp Act. Meanwhile the arrival of the stamp officers led to riots in various cities, including Boston, where the house of

Lieut.-Gov. Thomas Hutchinson was sacked.

Oct. 7. Stamp Act Congress at New York. Twenty-eight delegates from nine colonies drew up memorials to the king and parliament and adopted a **Declaration of Rights and Liberties** (Oct. 19).

1766. Mar. Repeal of the Stamp Act, followed by the **Declaratory Act** (Mar. 18), declaring that the king, by and with consent of parliament, had authority to make laws to bind the colonies in all respects.

1767. Suspension of the New York Assembly because of its refusal fully to comply with the Quartering Act.

The **Townshend Acts** imposed duties on glass, lead, painters' colors, tea, and paper imported into the colonies. Out of these revenues fixed salaries were to be paid to royal officials in the colonies. A Boston town-meeting adopted a **non-importation agreement.**

1768. The Massachusetts general court drew up a petition to the king, sent letters to the ministry, and dispatched a circular letter to the other colonies.

June. The seizure of John Hancock's sloop *Liberty,* because of false entry, led to a riot.

Oct. British troops arrived in Boston and the town refused to provide quarters.

1769. Parliament advised the enforcement of a statute of Henry VIII, allowing the government

The landing of British troops in Boston, 1768

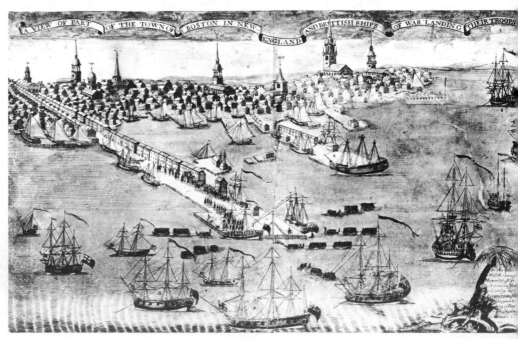

to bring to England for trial those alleged to have committed treason outside the realm. Resolutions of protest adopted by the Virginia house of burgesses.

1770. Mar. 5. The Boston Massacre. Popular hatred of the British troops in the city led to a brawl in which several citizens were killed or wounded. Preston, the commanding officer, was acquitted, being defended by John Adams and Josiah Quincy.

An **act repealing duties** on paper, glass, and painters' colors, but retaining that on tea. This gesture produced a conservative reaction in the colonies, in which the merchants worked for conciliation. This truce was broken by the arbitrary acts of crown officials and by the announcement in

1772. That salaries of governors and judges in Massachusetts were to be paid by the crown, thus rendering them independent of the assembly's control of the purse, and by

June 10. The **Gaspée Affair,** in which a revenue boat, whose commander's conduct had enraged public opinion in Rhode Island, was burned by a mob in Narragansett Bay.

1772, Nov. 2–1773, Jan. Formation of 80 town **committees of correspondence** in Massachusetts under the leadership of **Samuel Adams.**

1773, Mar. 12. The Virginia house of burgesses appointed a **Provincial Committee of Correspondence** to keep in touch with sister colonies. By February 1774 all the colonies except Pennsylvania had appointed such committees.

To provide relief for the East India Company the government allowed it a drawback of the tea duty in England, but the full duty was to be paid in the colonies. There was a protest to the landing of the tea in Charleston, Philadelphia, and New York, while in Boston there occurred

Dec. 16. The **Boston Tea Party** in which citizens, disguised as Indians, boarded the ships and dumped the tea into the harbor.

1774. The resistance to the landing of the tea provoked the ministry to the adoption of a punitive policy. The so-called **Coercive Acts** were passed, including: The **Boston Port Act,** closing the port after June 1; the **Massachusetts Government Act,** depriving the people of most of their chartered rights, and greatly enlarging the governor's powers; the **Administration of Justice Act,** providing that persons accused of a capital crime in aiding the government should be tried in England or a colony other than that in which the crime was committed; the **Quartering Act;** and the **Quebec Act,** extending the boundary of that province to the Ohio River, cutting athwart the claims of Massachusetts, New York, Connecticut, and Virginia. Although not designed as a punitive measure the Quebec Act was so regarded by the colonies.

County conventions in Massachusetts protested against the acts (Aug.–Sept.). The **Suffolk Convention** resolved that they should be "rejected as the attempts of a wicked administration to enslave America" **(The Suffolk Resolves).**

May 27. The Virginia house of burgesses adopted resolutions calling for a congress of the colonies. Copies sent to other assemblies.

Sept. 5. The **FIRST CONTINENTAL CONGRESS** assembled at Philadelphia. All colonies except Georgia represented. Mem-

The Boston Massacre, 1770

The Boston Tea Party, 1773

Opening prayer of First Continental Congress, September, 1774

The Battle of Lexington, April 9, 1775

bers divided into radicals led by **Samuel Adams** and conservatives led by **Joseph Galloway** of Pennsylvania. The radicals obtained approval of the Suffolk Resolves and defeated Galloway's proposed plan of union, designed to effect an adjustment of difficulties. **Declaration of Rights and Grievances** drawn up.

Oct. The delegates adopted the *Association* providing for non-importation of English goods after December 1. If redress had not been obtained by September 11, 1775, non-exportation was to go into effect.

1775, Feb. 1. **Lord Chatham** presented to parliament a plan of conciliation, based on mutual concessions, but it was rejected.

Feb. 20. **Lord North** made an unsuccessful effort toward conciliation.

1775-1783. WAR FOR INDEPENDENCE.

1775, Apr. 19. Battles of Lexington and Concord. British troops detailed to destroy stores at Concord became embroiled with provincials at Lexington. Proceeding to Concord, the troops destroyed the stores, but after the fight at the bridge were forced to retreat, first to Lexington, then to Boston.

May 10-12. **Ticonderoga** captured by **Ethan Allen** and **Crown Point** captured by **Seth Warner.**

May 10. The **Second Continental Congress** assembled at Philadelphia.

May 31. Troops before Boston were adopted as the **Continental Army** and on

June 15. George Washington (1732–1799) appointed commander-in-chief of the forces.

June 17. Battle of Bunker Hill, opposite Boston. Americans driven from entrenchments, but only after inflicting great losses on the British.

1775, July–Mar. 17, 1776. Siege of Boston.

1775. A letter by Congress to the people of Canada having failed to enlist their aid, a campaign against them was planned. One force, under **Richard Montgomery,** proceeded by Lake Champlain to Montreal, which was taken on November 12. Another force, under **Benedict Arnold,** advanced by the Kennebec with a view to meeting Montgomery at **Quebec.** Montgomery was killed before Quebec (Dec. 21). Arnold carried on the unsuccessful siege for the remainder of the winter.

Samuel Adams

Ethan Allen at the capture of Fort Ticonderoga, May 10, 1775

1776, Mar. 4. Occupation of **Dorchester Heights** by Washington.

Mar. 17. **Evacuation of Boston** by the British forces.

Meanwhile the unyielding attitude of the British government, the hiring of German mercenaries, the events on the Canadian frontier, and the burning of Norfolk inflamed public opinion. The appearance of **Thomas Paine's** *Common Sense* crystallized that opinion in favor of independence.

Most of the writing of the period was in the form of patriotic pamphlets and essays. Only two prominent literary figures emerged: the poet **Philip Freneau** (1752–1832) and the novelist **Charles Brockden Brown** (1771–1810).

America could now also claim some fine portrait painters: **John Singleton Copley** (1737–1815), **Benjamin West** (1738–1820) in whose studio in England **Charles Willson Peale** (1741–1827) and his son **Rembrandt Peale** (1778–1860), as well as **Gilbert Stuart** (1755–1828) received some training.

May 15. Congress announced that the authority of the British crown should be suppressed and power of government established under authority of the people of the colonies.

May 15. The **Virginia Convention,** called to form a new government, instructed Virginia delegates in Congress to propose independence.

June 7. Resolution of **Richard Henry Lee** in Congress, "That these United Colonies are and of right ought to be free and independent States." Congress appointed a committee of five to draft a declaration of independence.

The committee asked **Thomas Jefferson** to prepare the document.

1776, July 4. **DECLARATION OF INDEPENDENCE** adopted.

Following the British evacuation of Boston, Washington proceeded to New York. **General Sir William Howe** and **Admiral Lord Howe** prepared to attack, but the latter first proffered peace terms which were rejected.

Aug. 27. **Battle of Long Island,** with defeat of General Israel Putnam and retreat to New York.

Sept. 15. New York occupied by the British; Washington retreated to Harlem Heights.

Oct. 11–13. Arnold defeated in two naval engagements on **Lake Champlain.**

Oct. 28. Engagement between Howe and Washington at **White Plains,** followed by retirement of Washington to a line of heights back of his previous position on October 31.

Nov. 16. Surrender of **Fort Washington** to the British, followed by that of **Fort Lee** on November 20.

Nov. 28. Beginning of Washington's retreat across New Jersey into Pennsylvania.

Dec. 26. **Battle of Trenton.** Crossing the Delaware by night, Washington surprised and captured about a thousand Hessians at Trenton. This was followed by the defeat of the British at the

1777, Jan. 3. **Battle of Princeton.** The British plan of campaign for 1777 was to divide the states by the line of the Hudson. General John Burgoyne was to proceed from Canada by way of Lake Champlain, General Barry St. Leger was to co-operate with Burgoyne

Washington, painted by Charles Wilson Peale

General Washington at the Battle of Princeton

Song rejoicing American victory at Yorktown

Loyalist recruiting call for volunteers, 1777

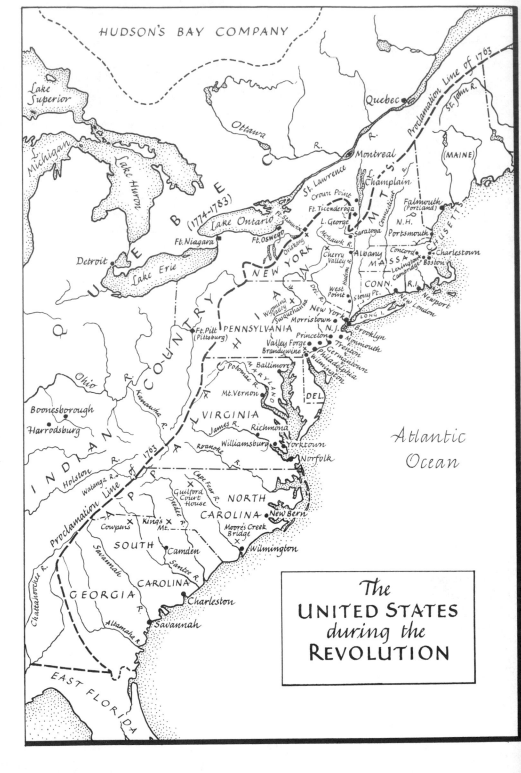

The UNITED STATES during the REVOLUTION

British attack on Philadelphia, September, 1776

John Paul Jones

from Lake Ontario, while Howe was to ascend the Hudson and join Burgoyne.

Aug. 16. Battle of Bennington, in which General John Stark defeated Colonel Baum, sent by Burgoyne to seize stores.

Sept. 19. First battle of Bemis Heights, in which Burgoyne held the field, although suffering heavy losses.

Oct. 7. Second battle of Bemis Heights, or **Saratoga.** Burgoyne was defeated and, finding himself surrounded, called a council of war at which it was decided to negotiate terms.

Oct. 17. Burgoyne surrendered his entire force to General Horatio Gates.

Howe's campaign. Instead of advancing up the Hudson, Howe, on August 25, disclosed his purpose of attacking **Philadelphia.** Washington offered battle, but in the

Sept. 11. Battle of Brandywine, the Americans, under General Nathanael Greene, were defeated.

Sept. 27. Howe occupied Philadelphia.

Oct. 4. Attempting to surprise the camp at Germantown, Washington was defeated in the **battle of Germantown.** With the capture of Fort Mifflin and Fort Mercer on November 16 and 20, British control of the Delaware was complete.

1777–1778. Winter suffering of Washington's army at **Valley Forge.** Unsuccessful attempt of the **Conway Cabal** to remove Washington from command.

1777, Nov. 15. ARTICLES OF CONFEDERATION and perpetual union agreed upon in Congress. These provided for a confederacy to be known as *The United States of America,* and were sent to the states for ratification.

Burgoyne's defeat and surrender stirred France to action in support of the United States. To re-establish French prestige in Europe, so greatly weakened in the Seven Years' War, was the aim of **Count Charles de Vergennes,** the French minister of foreign affairs. After supplying secret aid in money and supplies to the Americans for two years, France signed

1778, Feb. 6. Treaties of Commerce and Alliance with the United States. **Marquis Marie Joseph de Lafayette** and **Baron Johann de Kalb** had arrived the previous summer to offer their services. **Pierre de Beaumarchais,** French playwright, had drawn heavily on his personal resources to aid the Americans.

Feb. 17. Lord North presented to parliament his plan for conciliating the Americans, which included renunciation of the right of taxation. Commissioners sent to the United States with a peace offer, which was rejected by Congress (June 17). With the French alliance an assured fact, only independence would now satisfy the Americans.

June 18. Evacuation of Philadelphia by Sir Henry Clinton, who started to march across New Jersey, where on

June 28. Washington won the **battle of Monmouth.**

July 4. Wyoming massacre in Pennsylvania.

July 8. Arrival of **Count Jean Baptiste d'Estaing's** fleet off Delaware Capes. He and Washington planned a land and sea attack on the British in Newport. After a storm on August 9, which prevented a clash between the French and British fleets, d'Estaing sailed

to Boston for repairs, leaving General John Sullivan unsupported, who on August 29 gave up the siege of Newport.

Nov. 11. Massacre of Cherry Valley in New York.

1779, Feb. George Rogers Clark, with a force of Virginians, completed the conquest of the Old Northwest, capturing Hamilton, the British commander, at **Vincennes.**

June. **Spain entered the war** against Britain, on the promise of France that she would assist Spain to recover Gibraltar and the Floridas.

Sept. 23. Naval victory of **John Paul Jones** of the *Bonhomme Richard* over the *Serapis* and the *Countess of Scarborough.*

Meanwhile the British had decided to try, with the aid of loyalists, to overrun the southern states. In 1778 **Savannah** was captured and in 1780 Sir Henry Clinton laid siege to Charleston.

1780, May. Charleston surrendered.

July. Count Jean Baptiste de Rochambeau arrived at Newport with 6000 French troops.

Despite brave resistance of Thomas Sumter and Francis Marion, South Carolina was overrun by the British, and in the

Aug. 16. Battle of Camden, Gates was defeated by General Charles Cornwallis.

Aug. 18. Sumter's force was defeated by Tarleton, and Marion retreated to North Carolina.

Sept. 23. A plot of **Benedict Arnold** to surrender West Point to Sir Henry Clinton was revealed through capture of the British agent, **Major John André.** Arnold escaped, but on

Oct. 2. André was hanged as a spy.

Oct. 7. Battle of King's Mountain, in North Carolina, in which the British, under Major Ferguson, were defeated.

1781, Jan. 17. Battle of the Cowpens, in which the British cavalry under Sir Banastre Tarleton was defeated by General Daniel Morgan.

Mar. 15. Battle of Guilford; British victory and withdrawal.

Sept. 8. Battle of Eutaw; defeat of Greene, followed by retreat of British to Charleston.

Meanwhile British forces under Cornwallis were concentrating in Virginia, where they fortified themselves at **Yorktown.** While Cornwallis remained inactive, Washington, Lafayette, and Rochambeau closed in on him at Williamsburg, and Count François de Grasse, with the French fleet, entered Chesapeake Bay.

Sept. 30–Oct. 19. Siege of Yorktown. Finding himself bottled up,

Oct. 19. CORNWALLIS SURRENDERED with 7000 men.

In the peace negotiations, Vergennes was in the difficult position of trying to please both of his allies, Spain and the United States. This led to delay which aroused the impatience of the American commissioners, who, disregarding their instructions not to negotiate a

Surrender of Lord Cornwallis to General Washington

British political cartoon, 1782

separate peace with Great Britain, proceeded to do so. The British, eager to win American friendship and trade, thereby defeating the aspirations of the French, readily acceded to the American demand for the Mississippi as the western boundary and full rights in the fisheries off the Canadian coast.

1783, Sept. 3. DEFINITIVE TREATY OF PEACE between Great Britain and United States, signed at **Paris.** It recognized the independence of the United States. Provisions of the treaty with respect to the northeastern and northwestern boundaries led to later difficulties with Britain, while the southern boundary provision led to trouble with Spain. Full rights in the Newfoundland fisheries were guaranteed to the United States. Creditors of neither country were to encounter legal obstacles to collection of debts, while the Congress would recommend to the states the restoration of the confiscated estates of loyalists.

Navigation of the Mississippi was to be open to both Great Britain and the United States.

1783-1787. THE CRITICAL PERIOD OF AMERICAN HISTORY. The Articles of Confederation had gone into effect in 1781, and with the achievement of independence in 1783 the young nation found itself in a difficult economic situation, not due primarily to the particular forms of government then in operation. Treated as a foreign people by Britain as well as by other European countries, and denied participation of their ships in the trade of the British West Indies, so important in their economy before the Revolution, far-reaching economic dislocations resulted, producing a deep depression in 1784-1785, from which the country began to recover as early as 1787. While not fundamentally responsible for the unfortunate situation, the Articles of Confederation received the blame and were widely believed to be inadequate. The economic situation was aggravated by paper-money experiments of the states and by the inability of Congress to raise an adequate revenue. The weakness of the central government was dramatized by **Shays's Rebellion** (1786) in Massachusetts, in which the use of state troops was necessary to protect the federal arsenal at Springfield.

1785. The **Land Ordinance** enacted. The cession by the landed states of their claims to western lands, made necessary by Maryland's refusal to ratify the Articles of Confederation unless such cessions should be made, created the public domain of the United States, for the administration of which a land policy was necessary. (*See map on page 752.*) This ordinance established the rectangular system of survey, provided for survey in advance of sale, and laid down terms and conditions of sale.

1787. The **NORTHWEST ORDINANCE** enacted, providing for the government of the northwest. The region was to be divided into not less than three and not more than five districts, which, after passing through territorial or colonial stage, should be admitted to statehood. This **principle of co-ordinancy** or ultimate statehood became the basic and distinguishing feature of the American colonial system of the 19th century. Slavery and involuntary servitude were prohibited in the area.

1787, May. The **CONSTITUTIONAL CONVENTION** assembled at Philadelphia. The inability of Congress to raise revenue, the outbreaks of disorder, and the obstructions to commerce resulted in an increasing desire for a more perfect government. Commissioners from Virginia and Maryland met at **Mount Vernon** in 1785 to consider the possibility of a uniform commercial code. This conference made clear the need for wider co-operation, so Virginia invited all the states to send delegates to a convention at **Annapolis** (1786). This convention was attended by delegates from only five states, who proposed a convention to meet at Philadelphia in May 1787. Congress officially called such a convention to convene on May 5. All states except Rhode Island were represented. After four months of labor,

1787, Sept. 17. The **Constitution was signed** by the delegates present. The document was sent to the states for ratification, with the provision that it should become operative upon the acceptance of nine states.

1788, June. Ratification by New Hampshire, the ninth state, placed the constitution in operation. In several states the anti-Federalists exacted promises of amendments in return for unconditional ratification. *(Cont. p. 750.)*

George Washington presiding at the Constitutional Convention, 1787

G. Africa, 1517–1800

(From pp. 348, 379)

1517. **Conquest of Egypt** by Selim I *(p. 439)*. The country was put under a Turkish governor, but the Mamluk beys were left in effectual control, acting as a landholding oligarchy.

1517. Regular establishment of the **slave trade** through a concession granted by Charles I of Spain to a Flemish merchant.

1517. Defeat of the Songhoy ruler by the forces of the **Haussa Confederation,** which became the dominant power east of the Niger, under the leadership of Kebbi.

1520–1526. Mission of **Francisco Alvarez** to Ethiopia. He wrote the first detailed description of the country.

1527. **Ethiopia** was overrun by the Moslem Somali chief, Ahmed Gran, who used firearms. The negus thereupon called upon the Portuguese for aid.

1534. The Turks, under Khaireddin Barbarossa, took **Tunis** *(p. 440)*.

1535. **Spanish conquest of Tunis,** completing the conquest of the North African coast begun in 1494 with the acquisition of Melilla.

1541. Abortive expedition of Charles V to Algiers *(p. 440)*.

1541. Portuguese expedition to Ethiopia under **Christopher da Gama,** son of Vasco. The Portuguese succeeded in expelling Ahmed Gran.

1555–1633. **THE PORTUGUESE** (Jesuit) **MISSIONS IN ETHIOPIA.** Conversion of

John Hawkins

two successive rulers. Remarkable influence and work of **Pedro Paez.** The conversion led to repeated religious wars against the Portuguese faction. Ultimately the Portuguese were expelled and all Catholic missions prohibited.

1562–1568. **John Hawkins** initiated the British slave trade, making three voyages from West Africa to the New World with slave cargoes.

1571–1603. Apogee of the **EMPIRE OF KANEM** or **BORNU** (dating from the 13th century) under **Idris III.** It controlled most of the territory about Lake Chad.

1574. The Spaniards lost Goletta. End of the Spanish rule in Tunis, which became a Turkish regency, with an elected bey.

1574. The Portuguese began the settlement of Angola at **São Paulo de Loanda.**

1578. **Sebastian** of Portugal, called upon to intervene in the dynastic struggles in Morocco and determined to conquer the country for himself, was overwhelmingly defeated at **Kasr al-Kabir. Ahmed al Mansur** established the Sharifian dynasty.

1580. The Spaniards occupied **Ceuta,** which remained technically a possession of Portugal till 1688.

1581. The Moroccans took Tuat, beginning the penetration of the Sahara.

1591. A force of Spanish and Portuguese renegades in the service of the Moroccans crossed the desert and defeated the forces of **Songhoy** by use of firearms. Gao was destroyed and the Moroccans established themselves at **Timbuktu.** The entire Negro culture was destroyed and the country fell a prey to rival pashas. These made themselves independent of Morocco in 1612 and continued to rule at Timbuktu until 1780.

1595. First establishments of the **Dutch** on the **Guinea coast.**

1598. The Dutch took Mauritius (Isle de France).

1616. The Portuguese, **Gaspar Boccaro,** journeyed from the upper Zambezi to Kilwa on the coast, one of the first recorded explorations of the interior.

1618. Journey of the Frenchman, **Paul Imbert,** to Timbuktu.

1618–1619. **G. Thompson** ascended the Gambia River for about 400 miles.

1621. The Dutch took **Arguin and Goree** from the Portuguese.

1626. The French established themselves at St. Louis at the mouth of the Senegal.

1626. First French settlements on **Madagascar** (inhabited by various primitive tribes and by the **Hovas,** who had arrived from overseas about 1000 A.D.).

Turks under Selim I enter Cairo, 1517

An early Dutch settlement on Madagascar, 1623

Jan van Riebeeck

French bombardment of Algiers, 1684

1637. The Dutch took Elmina from the Portuguese and built numerous forts on the Gold Coast.

1637. The French, under de Rochefort, explored the Senegal for about 100 miles and established posts.

1645. Capuchin monks ascended the Congo River, possibly as far as Stanley Falls.

1650. **Ali Bey** made himself hereditary bey of Tunis.

1652, Apr. 7. CAPETOWN FOUNDED by the Dutch under **Jan van Riebeeck.**

1660. Rise of the **BAMBARA KINGDOMS** (Segu and Kaarta) on the upper Niger. They defeated and replaced the **Manding Empire** (1670) which thenceforth became a minor state.

1662. Portugal ceded **Tangier** to England.

1662. The British built a fort at James Island at the mouth of the Gambia.

1668. The Dutch advanced their South African settlement as far as Mossel Bay.

1672. Foundation of the **Royal African Company.**

1677. The French conquered the Dutch posts on the Senegal.

1683. The Prussians built the fort of **Grossfriedrichsburg** on the Guinea Coast (abandoned 1720).

1684. The British abandoned Tangier to the sultan of Morocco.

1684. French expeditions against the piratical deys of **Algiers.** Various coast towns were bombarded and the deys were obliged to surrender Christian slaves.

1686. Louis XIV proclaimed the annexation of **Madagascar.**

1697. The French, under **André de Brue,** completed the conquest of the Senegal region and advanced up the river to Mambuk (1715).

1698. The Portuguese were expelled from their posts on the east coast by Arabs from Oman. Mombasa was abandoned in 1730, but the Portuguese retained Mozambique.

1699. **C. Poncet,** an emissary of Louis XIV, traveled overland from Cairo to Gondar in Ethiopia.

1705. Hussein ibn Ali founded the **Husseinite dynasty** in Tunis and threw off Turkish authority.

1708. The Spaniards were expelled from Oran.

1713. The *Asiento treaty* (p. 468) gave Britain the right to import African slaves into the Spanish colonies in the New World, thus initiating the most active period of the British slave trade.

1714. **Ahmed Bey** made himself ruler of Tripoli, founding the Karamanli dynasty which lasted until 1835.

1715. The French took the island of Mauritius.

1723. **Bartholomew Stibbs,** for the African Company, took over the Gambia region as far as the Barrakonda Falls.

1732. The Spaniards retook Oran.

1757–1789. Reign of **Sidi Mohammed** in Morocco. He established law and order and abolished Christian slavery (1777).

1758. The British captured the French possessions on the Senegal.

1760. The Dutch, in South Africa, crossed the Orange River and began the penetration of Great Namaqualand.

1766. **Ali Bey** established himself as ruler of Egypt and proclaimed independence of the Turks. His successor, Mohammed Bey, recognized Turkish suzerainty again (1773).

1768–1773. **James Bruce** explored Ethiopia, traveling from Massawa to Gondar and thence to the Blue Nile. He returned by way of Egypt and reported the Ethiopian Empire in decline, restricted to the area north of the Blue Nile and wracked by rebellion.

1776. Rise of the Tukulor power in West Africa.

1778. The French recovered their possessions on the Senegal.

1778. Explorations of **W. Paterson** in the Kafir country.

1783. By the treaty of Paris the British secured the Senegal again. They held it until 1790.

1787. The British acquired **Sierra Leone** from the natives. In 1791 it was devoted to the settlement of freed slaves.

1788. **Sir Joseph Banks** founded the *African Association* for the furtherance of exploration and the development of trade.

1791. The Spanish abandoned Oran, retaining only Melilla and Ceuta and a few minor stations on the North African coast.

1792. **Denmark prohibited the slave trade,** the first country to take this step.

1801. Conquest of the Haussa power by **Usman dan Fodio,** a Tukulor chief, who converted this area to Islam and founded the **kingdom of Sokoto.** *(Cont. p. 808.)*

African natives enslaved by European captors

James Bruce exploring region of the Nile

1. *Persia, 1500–1794*

(From p. 349)

1502-1524. SHAH ISMAIL, founder of the **Safavid dynasty,** the first national dynasty in many centuries. Ismail traced his descent to **Safi al-Din** of Ardabil (1252–1334), a supposed descendant of Ali, the fourth caliph. Safi al-Din founded among the Turk tribes an order of dervishes devoted to mystic teachings and Shi'a doctrine. His influence and that of his successors spread over northwestern Persia and into eastern and southern Anatolia. Sheikh Joneid, head of the order from 1448–1460, attempted to extend his temporal power and ultimately secured the protection and alliance of **Uzun Hasan,** whose sister he married. His son, Haidar, married a daughter of Uzun Hasan and devoted himself to the reorganization of the order, which became a powerful military instrument (*Kizilbashes i.e.* red heads, from their headdress). Haidar was defeated and killed by Jaqub of the White Sheep, but left several sons, of whom Ismail was one. After years spent in hiding, Ismail was able to take advantage of the confusion following the death of Rustam Shah.

1501. Battle of Shurur, in which Ismail defeated Alwand of the White Sheep. He soon took Tabriz and had himself proclaimed shah. With his accession the Shi'a doctrine became officially established in Persia.

1507-1622. The Portuguese established themselves at Hormuz.

1510. Ismail defeated the Uzbeks and drove them out of Khorasan.

1514. BATTLE OF CHALDIRAN, following the invasion of Persia by the Turks under Selim I *(p. 439)*. Ismail was defeated and Tabriz taken, though later evacuated by the Turks. Beginning of a long duel between Turks and Persians, resulting largely from religious conflict.

1524-1576. SHAH TAHMASP I, the son of Ismail, who ascended the throne at ten. His reign was marked by continuous raids and campaigns against the Uzbeks of Transoxiana and by repeated incursions of the Turks, who conquered Mesopotamia and on several occasions took Tabriz, Sultanieh, and Isfahan. **Peace with the Turks** was finally concluded in 1555.

1561-1563. Anthony Jenkinson, of the English Muscovy Company, reached Persia overland through Russia and opened commercial relations which continued until 1581.

Shah Tahmasp I

Shah Abbas I

Robert Shirley

Anthony Shirley

1576-1578. ISMAIL II, fourth son of Tahmasp, who succeeded on the death by poison of his father. He killed off all his relatives and rivals, but himself died after a year of office.

1578-1587. MOHAMMED KHUDABANDA, the half-blind eldest son of Tahmasp, who had escaped his brother's vengeance. Renewal of the Turkish attack; which was less decisive than before.

1587-1629. SHAH ABBAS I (the Great), most highly esteemed of the Persian rulers. He was a man of broad outlook and strong will, though personally suspicious and cruel (he had one son murdered and two others blinded). In his early years Abbas was wholly under the domination of the Kizil-bash chiefs, but he later succeeded in counteracting their influence by organizing a new tribe of "friends of the shah," and by building up a new infantry and artillery force, modeled on the Turkish. In this he was greatly aided by **Anthony** and **Robert Shirley,** two brothers who came with 26 followers in 1598. Robert remained in Persian service during most of Abbas' reign.

1590. Abbas made peace with the Turks, aban-

The Safavid Dynasty

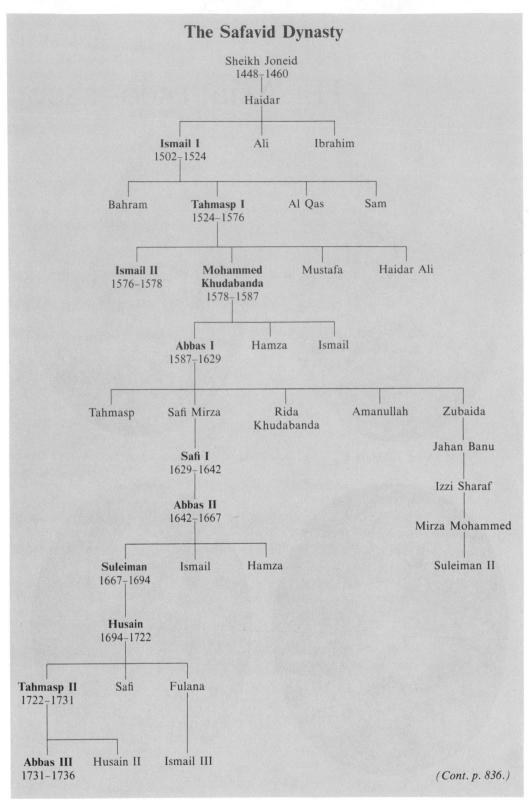

Sheikh Joneid
1448–1460

Haidar

Ismail I — Ali — Ibrahim
1502–1524

Bahram — **Tahmasp I** — Al Qas — Sam
1524–1576

Ismail II — **Mohammed Khudabanda** — Mustafa — Haidar Ali
1576–1578 / 1578–1587

Abbas I — Hamza — Ismail
1587–1629

Tahmasp — Safi Mirza — Rida Khudabanda — Amanullah — Zubaida

Safi I — Jahan Banu
1629–1642

Abbas II — Izzi Sharaf
1642–1667

Suleiman — Ismail — Hamza — Mirza Mohammed
1667–1694

Husain — Suleiman II
1694–1722

Tahmasp II — Safi — Fulana
1722–1731

Abbas III — Husain II — Ismail III
1731–1736

(Cont. p. 836.)

doning Tabriz, Shirvan, Georgia, and Luristan. This he did in order to be free to deal with the Uzbeks, who, under Abdullah II, had taken Herat, Meshed, and other towns of Khorasan.

1597. The Persians defeated the Uzbeks, whose invasions of Khorasan were stopped for many years.

1602–1627. Further **wars with the Turks** (mission of Sir Anthony Shirley to Europe to enlist the co-operation of the emperor and king of Spain). In 1603 Abbas managed to retake Tabriz, and then Erivan, Shirvan, and Kars. A great victory was won over the Turks at **Lake Urmia.** Thereafter Abbas conquered Baghdad, Mosul, and Diarbekr. Peace was made in 1612, but war broke out again in 1616. Efforts of the Turks to retake Baghdad (1625) failed.

1616. The **English East India Company** began trading with Persia from Surat. The activity of the English was resented by the Portuguese, who attacked them, but were defeated in the **battle of Jask** (1620).

1622. The English merchants, co-operating with a Persian army, took **Hormuz** from the Portuguese, receiving special privileges there.

1629–1642. SHAH SAFI, the grandson of Abbas. Beginning of harem rule and rapid decline, as in the Ottoman Empire fifty years before. Like his contemporary, Murad IV *(p. 443),* Shah Safi distinguished himself by wholesale executions.

1630. Murad IV took and sacked Hamadan, the first move in the campaign to retake the conquests of Abbas the Great.

1635. The Turks took Erivan and Tabriz.

1638. The Turks took **Baghdad** and forced the shah to make peace. Erivan was left to the Persians, while the Turks retained Baghdad.

1642–1667. SHAH ABBAS II, the son of Safi. He was only ten when he reached the throne and at no time showed any particular ability.

1664. First Russian mission to Isfahan. Beginning of Cossack raids on the Caucasus front. In the same year the French secured permission to trade in Persia.

1667–1694. SHAH SULEIMAN, the son of Abbas II, another dissolute ruler who did nothing to check the decline.

1694–1722. SHAH HUSSEIN, a devout ruler whose renewed emphasis on Shi'a doctrine gave his Sunnite neighbors an excuse for making trouble.

1709. Rising of the Afghans at Kandahar, led by **Mir Vais,** a Ghilzai chieftain and a Sunnite. Mir Vais succeeded in defeating the Persian armies sent against him (1711) and established the independence of the Afghan state.

1715–1717. Mir Abdullah, ruler of Kandahar in succession to Mir Vais. He was overthrown when he attempted to make peace on the basis of Persian suzerainty over Kandahar.

1717–1725. Mir Mahmud, ruler of Kandahar. In 1717 the Abdalis of Herat also revolted and established another Afghan state.

1722. Invasion of Persia by Mir Mahmud and an army of Afghans. The Persian court and army were completely demoralized and offered little real resistance. They were defeated at **Gulnabad,** after which Mahmud took Isfahan. Husain abdicated and

1722–1725. Mahmud became shah. Husain's son, **Tahmasp,** however, escaped to Mazandaran and tried to organize national resistance.

1722. Peter the Great, taking advantage of the confusion, took Derbent on the plea of supporting Tahmasp. In 1723 he added Resht and Baku, and Tahmasp agreed to cede all of Shirvan, Daghestan, Gilan, Mazandaran, and Astrabad in return for effective aid.

1723. The Turks, hoping for a share of the spoil, took Tiflis.

1724. Russia and Turkey made an agreement for the dismemberment of Persia, the Turks reserving for themselves Tabriz, Hamadan, and Kermanshah. These places they occupied in 1724–1725.

1724–1725. Reign of terror in Isfahan, where Mahmud, gone mad, ordered the massacre of the Persian nobility and of all available Safavid princes, to say nothing of large numbers of soldiers and inhabitants.

1725–1730. ASHRAF SHAH, in succession to Mahmud. He was more conciliatory, but from the outset failed to get much sympathy from the Persians, or much support from Kandahar.

1726. Ashraf defeated the Turks, who were

advancing on Isfahan. Peace was concluded in 1727, Ashraf securing recognition from the sultan in return for the cession of the conquered territories.

1726–1728. Tahmasp, supported by Nadir Kuli, a powerful chief of the Afshar tribe of Khorasan, conquered Meshed and Herat and, after defeating an Afghan army, retook Isfahan.

1730. Final defeat of the Afghans near Shiraz. Ashraf was murdered on his way to Kandahar and his followers fled from Persia as best they could.

1730–1731. SHAH TAHMASP II was hardly more than a figurehead, the real ruler being **Nadir Kuli,** who married Tahmasp's sister. Nadir, having defeated the Afghans, turned against the Turks, whom he forced to give up Hamadan, Kermanshah, and Tabriz. He then marched east to deal with the Abdalis, and Tahmasp, thinking to complete the victory over the Turks, met with disaster and lost all that Nadir had gained. He agreed to the terms submitted by the Turks, for which Nadir deposed him.

1731–1736. ABBAS III, the eight-months-old son of Tahmasp, was elevated to the throne as a mere puppet. He was the last of the Safavid dynasty.

1732. By the **treaty of Resht** the Russians gave up their claims to Mazandaran, Astrabad, and Gilan, which had never been effectively occupied.

1733. Nadir, having been seriously defeated by the Turks in the **battle of Kirkuk,** managed to retrieve his position and blockade Baghdad. But these operations were interrupted by the need for a further campaign in Transcaucasia (1734).

1735. Russia, by treaty, gave up the last Persian acquisitions of Peter the Great, Baku and Derbent, and joined in alliance with Nadir against the common enemy, the Turk. Nadir won a great victory over the Turks at **Baghavand,** and took Tiflis.

Nadir Shah

Karim Khan

1736–1747. NADIR SHAH became ruler on the death of Abbas III. He accepted the throne on condition that the Persians renounce the Shi'a heresy. He himself, being a Turk by race, was also a Sunnite. But he never succeeded in making orthodoxy acceptable to the Persians.

1737. Nadir and his generals reduced Baluchistan and Balkh.

1738. Capture of Kandahar. Nadir thereupon proceeded to invade India. Kabul, Peshawar, and Lahore were taken and in 1739 a huge army of the Mogul emperor was defeated at **Karnal,** near Delhi. **Delhi** was taken and a tremendous massacre followed. Nadir left the Mogul emperor on the throne, but levied an indemnity of almost half a billion dollars and took all the territory north and west of the Indus.

1740. Nadir subjected **Bokhara and Khwarezm** (Khiva). This marked the greatest extent of his dominion and at the same time marked a turning-point in his career. Nadir was a great soldier, but he lacked real statesmanship and administrative ability. His efforts to stamp out Shi'ism resulted in growing unrest, and the need for suppressing discontent made the shah ever more ruthless and cruel. In the end he ruined the country by his huge exactions and despotic exploitation.

1743–1747. Resumption of **war with the Turks,** the sultan having refused the Persian terms. In 1745 Nadir won a resounding victory near **Kars** and in 1747 was able to secure peace: he gave up his demand for recognition of a fifth (Persian) orthodox sect, but secured recognition for the frontier as it had been in the time of Murad IV.

1747. Nadir Shah was assassinated by one of his own tribesmen.

1747–1750. A period of anarchy, during which the succession was hotly disputed. **Ahmad Khan Durani** established himself at Kandahar, took Meshed and Herat, and annexed Sind, Kashmir, and parts of the Punjab, founding a powerful Afghan state.

1747–1748. Adil Shah, the nephew of Nadir, became shah, but was soon dethroned and executed.

1748–1751. Shah Rukh, grandson of Nadir, was elevated to the throne. He was defeated and blinded by a Shi'a rival, but ultimately established his rule in Khorasan (to 1796). The rest of Persia continued to be hotly disputed between competing chieftains, until

1750–1779. KARIM KHAN, of the **Zand dynasty,** succeeded in maintaining himself against the powerful Kajar leader. Karim Khan, whose strength was in the south (Shiraz the capital), was a just and benevolent ruler, during whose reign the country was enabled to recover.

1763. The British established a factory at

The Imperial Palace at Delhi

Bushire, and somewhat later (1770) at Basra.

1775–1776. Karim Khan sent an expedition against Basra. This important station was taken, but was voluntarily abandoned on the death of Karim.

1779–1782. Another period of anarchy, during which Karim's brothers disputed the succession and the Kajar chief, Aga Mohammed, again took the field.

1782–1785. Ali Murad Shah. He re-established the capital at Isfahan.

1785–1789. Jafar Shah. Continuation of the confusion, marked by cruelty and barbarity.

1789–1794. Lutf Ali Khan, last of the Zand dynasty; a brilliant and chivalrous, but arrogant ruler. Unable to get the better of his rivals, Lutf was finally defeated and killed.

1794. Aga Mohammed founded the Kajar dynasty.

(Cont. p. 835.)

2. *Afghanistan, to 1793*

(From p. 353)

Prior to the 18th century, Afghanistan was in part ruled by Persia, in part by India and in part by the central Asian khanate of Bokhara. In 1706 **Kandahar** made itself independent and there followed the Afghan conquest of Persia (1722, see *p. 546*). This remained but an episode, for in 1737 Nadir Shah, having driven the Afghans out of Persia, carried the offensive eastward and subjected all of Afghanistan and western India.

1747–1773. AHMAD SHAH, one of the Afghan generals of Nadir Shah, on the murder of the latter assumed control of the Afghan provinces. He was a member of the Durani (Sauzai) clan of the Abdali tribe and established the **Durani dynasty** and empire. Most of his reign was filled by his nine **expeditions to India,** where he successfully asserted his claim to the Indian provinces of Nadir's empire. The dying Mogul Empire was unable to offer effective resistance. Ahmad took Lahore (1752) and then Delhi, which he plundered (1755). In 1761 he won a resounding victory over the Marathas at **Panipat,** and in 1762 over the Sikhs near Lahore. On his death the Afghan Empire extended from eastern Persia (Meshed) over Afghanistan and Baluchistan and eastward over Kashmir, and the Punjab.

1773–1793. Timur Shah, the son of Ahmad, proved to be a weak and ineffectual ruler. He moved the capital from Kandahar to Kabul, but was unable to prevent the loss of some of the Indian territory or the gradual disintegration of his authority even in Afghanistan.

(Cont. p. 837.)

3. *India, 1498–1796*

(From p. 356)

1498. VASCO DA GAMA, having rounded the Cape of Good Hope, reached Malabar. The Portuguese, after constructing forts at Cochin (1506) and Socotra (1507), soon diverted the spice trade from the Red Sea route.

1504. Yusuf Adil Shah of Bijapur, having annexed Gulbarga, established the Shi'a form of Islam, despite protest from many Sunnites.

1509. The Portuguese, under **Francisco de Almeida,** at Diu destroyed an Egyptian-Indian fleet which had, in the previous year, defeated a Portuguese squadron at Chaul.

1510. The **Portuguese acquired Goa** as headquarters, in place of Cochin.

1512. Golconda became independent (till 1687).

1526–1537. Bahadur, the last active sultan, with the aid of Khandesh, captured Mandu and annexed Malwa (1531), after which he captured Chitor (1534).

1526–1761 (1857). The **MOGUL EMPIRE** in India was founded by **Babar** (1483–1530), descendant of Timur in the fifth generation, who had seized Kabul (1504) and Lahore (1524) as compensation for loss of Ferghana and Samarkand. Decisive victory at **Panipat** over Ibrahim Shah Lodi gave him Delhi and Agra, which he defended in the

1527. Battle of Khanua against Rana Sanga of Chitor, chief of a Rajput confederacy.

Vasco da Gama

Palace of the Emperor Akbar at Agra

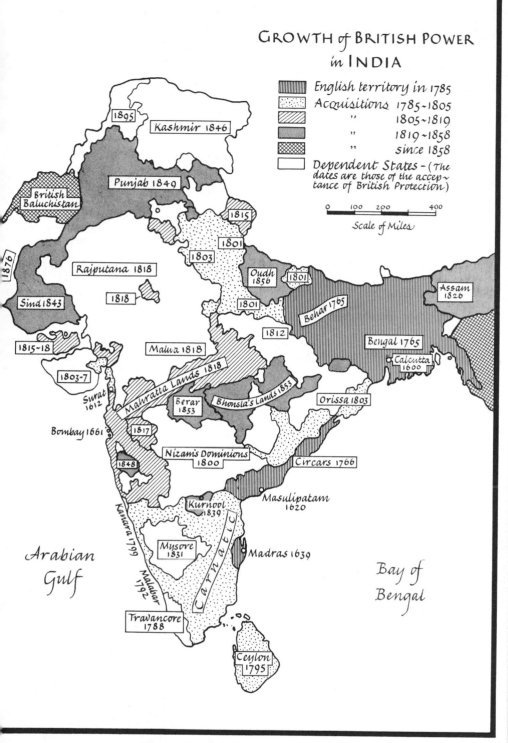

GROWTH of BRITISH POWER in INDIA

Legend:
- English territory in 1785
- Acquisitions 1785–1805
- " 1805–1819
- " 1819–1858
- " since 1858
- Dependent States – (The dates are those of the acceptance of British Protection)

Scale of Miles: 0 100 200 400

Map labels:
1805
Kashmir 1846
Punjab 1849
British Baluchistan
1876
Rajputana 1818
Sind 1843
1818
1815
1801
1803
Oudh 1856
1801
Assam 1826
Berar 1765
1815–18
Malwa 1818
1812
Bengal 1765
1803–7
Mawratta Lands 1818
Berar 1853
Bhonsla's Lands 1853
Orissa 1803
Calcutta 1600
Surat 1612
Bombay 1661
1817
Nizam's Dominions 1800
Circars 1766
1848
Kurnool 1839
Masulipatam 1620
Kanara 1799
Mysore 1831
Carnatic
Madras 1639
Arabian Gulf
Malabar 1792
Travancore 1788
Bay of Bengal
Ceylon 1795

1561. **Conquest of Malwa** was effected by the harem party (dominant 1560–1562).

1562. Akbar's marriage to a Rajput princess of Amber (mother of Jahangir) and abolition of the *jizya* tax on non-Moslems (1564) marked a new policy of impartiality and conciliation of subjects.

1564. The Gond Chandels (capital Chauragarh) were conquered. (Construction of the stone fort at Agra was begun.)

1565. A coalition of Ahmadnagar, Bijapur, Bidar, and Golconda decisively defeated Vijayanagar at **Talikota,** and led to the execution of the rajah. In 1574 Ahmadnagar annexed Berar, which had hindered the allied campaign.

1568. **Chitor** was taken by Akbar and about 30,000 Rajputs massacred.

1571. A new city at Fathpur Sikri, near Agra, was founded and magnificently built, but abandoned on Akbar's death.

1572–1573. **Conquest of Gujarat** gave Akbar access to the sea, new ideas, and revenues. To defend his conquest he rode with 3000 horsemen 450 miles in 11 days.

Reorganization of administration was begun by (1) resumption to the crown of all lands, hitherto held by officials as temporary assignments, but now to be administered and revenue collected directly; (2) establishment of

Page from Memoirs *of Emperor Babar*

---

529. **Victory on the Gogra,** where it meets the Ganges, completed conquest of the kingdom of Delhi to the frontier of Bengal.

Babar's acts, problems, and personality appear in his Turki *Memoirs.*

530–1556. **Humayun** drove Bahadur Shah of Gujarat to flight before Chitor and captured Mandu and Champanir (1535), but lost both through a year of inaction. The same fault and treachery of his brothers lost the empire to the

539–1555. **Sur dynasty** of the Afghan **Sher Shah** (1539–1545) who had consolidated his power in Bihar and drove Humayun to seek

refuge in Persia, whence he returned precariously to Delhi and Agra (1555).

1535. The Portuguese secured by treaty Bassein, and were allowed to fortify Diu, which they defended against an Ottoman fleet and a Gujarati army (1538).

1546. Efforts to expel the Portuguese failed miserably.

1556–1605. **AKBAR** (b. 1542, personal rule 1562) restored and consolidated the empire throughout northern India.

1556. Guided by **Bairam Khan,** his guardian (till 1560), he crushed the Afghans at Panipat.

1559. Constantine de Braganza seized Daman.

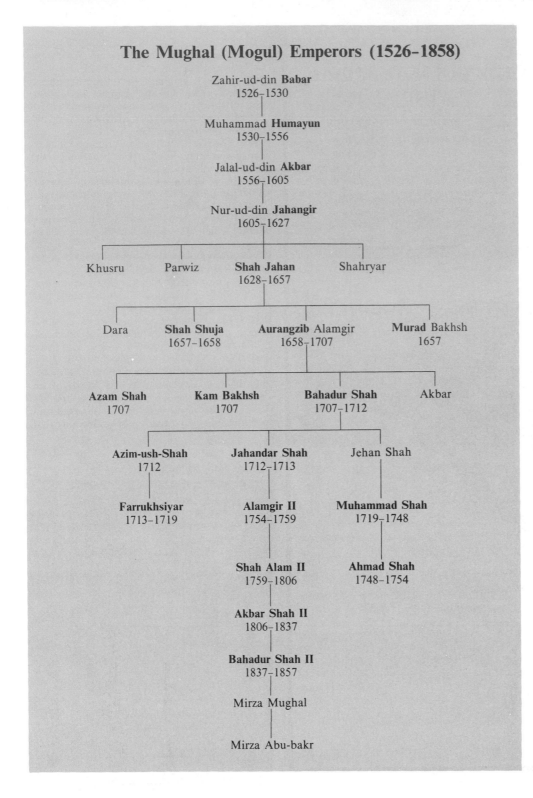

The Mughal (Mogul) Emperors (1526–1858)

Zahir-ud-din **Babar**
1526–1530

Muhammad **Humayun**
1530–1556

Jalal-ud-din **Akbar**
1556–1605

Nur-ud-din **Jahangir**
1605–1627

Khusru   Parwiz   **Shah Jahan** 1628–1657   Shahryar

Dara   **Shah Shuja** 1657–1658   **Aurangzib** Alamgir 1658–1707   **Murad** Bakhsh 1657

Azam Shah 1707   **Kam Bakhsh** 1707   **Bahadur Shah** 1707–1712   Akbar

Azim-ush-Shah 1712   **Jahandar Shah** 1712–1713   Jehan Shah

Farrukhsiyar 1713–1719   **Alamgir II** 1754–1759   **Muhammad Shah** 1719–1748

Shah Alam II 1759–1806   **Ahmad Shah** 1748–1754

Akbar Shah II 1806–1837

Bahadur Shah II 1837–1857

Mirza Mughal

Mirza Abu-bakr

1589–1591. Jamal Khan, minister of Ahmadnagar, an adherent of the Mahdavi heresy which anticipated the advent of the Mahdi (world savior) in A. H. 1000, persecuted both Sunnites and Shi'ites.

1601–1604. Prince Salim, later Jahangir, rebelled but was restored to favor.

1603. John Mildenhall, representative of the English East India Company (London Company, founded December 31, 1600) arrived at Agra, but secured no concession until 1608.

1605–1627. JAHANGIR maintained his father's empire in northern India but, himself given to drink, allowed power to pass to his wife Nur Jahan (1611).

1609–1611. William Hawkins failed to secure a treaty for James I, as did **Sir Thomas Roe** (1615–1619), but the English won trading rights at Surat after defeating a Portuguese fleet (1612).

1616. Bubonic plague, clearly identified for the first time, became epidemic.

1628–1657. SHAH JAHAN (d. 1666) ruled with even less regard for his subjects, but destroyed Ahmadnagar (1632) and defeated Golconda (1635) and Bijapur (1636).

1632–1653. The **Taj Mahal** was built as tomb for his wife, Mumtaz Mahal, for whom he had already built the splendid palace Khass Mahal on the fort at Agra.

1639. The site of **Madras** was granted to an Englishman.

1647. Aurangzib campaigned unsuccessfully in Badakhshan and Balkh, and

1649–1653. Failed to wrest Kandahar from the Persians.

1653–1657. Again governing the Deccan, he campaigned ambitiously and arrested the revival of Bijapur; but failed to check the Maratha raider Sivaji.

1658. Aurangzib rebelled, following the illness of Shah Jahan and competition for the succession among his four sons. He imprisoned Shah Jahan and became emperor.

1658–1707. AURANGZIB emperor. The Mo-

Shah Jahan

the **Mansabdari system,** a unified state service of officers arranged in a hierarchy of military (cavalry) rank, but performing civil (mainly financial) as well as military functions if required; (3) substitution of a single tax of one-third produce of the land for the traditional levy of one-sixth plus numerous cesses which were now declared abolished; (4) the branding of all horses maintained for government service, to prevent usual fraud.

1576. Bengal was definitely conquered from the Afghans.

1577. Khandesh was induced to submit as first step toward reconquest of the Deccan, actually accomplished only by Aurangzib (1659–1707).

1578. Public debates on religion, instituted for Moslems only in 1575, were thrown open to Hindus, Jains, Zoroastrians, Sabaeans, and Christians. Akbar showed new respect for animal life (Jain *ahimsa*), Zoroastrian reverence for the sun, and invited to court from Goa the Portuguese Jesuits Antonio Monserrate and Rodolfo Acquaviva (1579; arr. 1580). These, like later missions (1590, 1595), failed despite a friendly reception.

1582. In spite of revolt which followed a claim to infallibility under Moslem law (1579), the emperor decreed a new *Divine Faith* much influenced by Sufi practice. The limited support he won for it collapsed at his death.

The First Sermon Ashore (p.526) by J. L. G. Ferris

Pilgrim house in Plymouth, Mass. (p.526)

Landing of William Penn (p.530) by J. L. G. Ferris

Drafting the Declaration of Independence
(p.539) by J. L. G. Ferris

The Death of General Montgomery (p.538) by John Trumbull (portion)

The Taj Mahal

Aurangzib receiving his brother's head

The zealous political reformer Sivaji

gul dominion was undermined, in part by Aurangzib's sacrifice of political stability to religious zeal, and his failure to control his subordinates, of whom he was inordinately suspicious.

1659–1680. Sivaji reduced Bijapur (1659) and sacked Surat (1664 and 1670); the English factory escaped harm. In 1667 he won the title of *rajah* from Aurangzib and began to levy land taxes in Mogul territory (Khandesh, 1670); he successfully organized Maratha government on Hindu principles with the guidance of the poets Ramdas and Tukaram, and was enthroned as an independent ruler (1674).

1666. Chittagong was annexed for Aurangzib by the Bengal governor.

1669. In the first purely religious persecution since Akbar's accession, the **Hindu religion was prohibited** and Hindu temples destroyed, with great loss to Indian art, and the *jizya* reimposed on non-Moslems (1679). The period was marked by Jat rebellions (1669, 1681, 1688–1707), Hindu uprisings, and troubles with Afghan tribes and with the now militant and theocratic Sikhs (1675–1678).

1679. **Marwar** was annexed in war against the Rajputs; hostilities continued nearly thirty years.

1681. Prince Akbar revolted unsuccessfully against his father's misgovernment, and died in exile.

1681–1707. Assuming personal command in the Deccan, Aurangzib subjugated Bijapur (1686) and Golconda (1687) but failed to check the Marathas.

1685–1688. **Aurangzib seized Surat** (1685), intending to expel the English, whose unwise attempt to seize Chittagong lost them all their claims in Bengal (1688); their naval superiority menaced Mogul trade, however, and they were encouraged to return to Bengal (**Calcutta founded,** 1690).

Following the decline of the Portuguese power in India, that of the English had been increased by the acquisition of **Bombay** (1661) and the absorption of Dutch ambitions chiefly in the Spice Islands. Foundation of the French *Compagnie des Indes Orientales* (1664) under strict government control, and numerous settlements (Pondichéry, 1674), now opened the way for acute Anglo-French rivalry.

1689. Capture of Sivaji's successor, **Sambhaji,** failed to crush the Marathas and indecisive warfare continued until 1707.

The intellectual curiosity and luxurious tastes of the Mogul rulers, except Aurangzib, fostered brilliant cultural progress. Histories, annals, and memoirs, chiefly in Persian, a dictionary supported by Jahangir, and the unsurpassed poems of **Tulsi Das** (1532–1623), formed important literary contributions. Slavish imitation of Persian painting was modified by Hindu and even European influences; a height of keen observation and delicate rendering was attained under Shah Jahan. Under him also the building of palaces, mausoleums, and mosques in Indo-Persian style attained an exquisite elegance.

1707– Following Aurangzib's death the empire rapidly disintegrated; various provincial governors became virtually independent (1722 ff.), and wars of succession and foreign invasions culminated in anarchy.

c. 1708. The **Sikhs,** who had been founded in the 15th century as a strictly religious order, proclaiming Moslem and Hindu fellowship and monotheism, and opposing caste restrictions and priestcraft (except for the secular and religious authority vested in the Guru Hargovind, 1606), became a thoroughly militant order under the last Guru, **Govind Singh** (1666–1708); they menaced Mogul rights in the Deccan but their strength was broken by Bahadur Shah (1707–1712).

1717. The **English East India Company,** through gifts and medical service, secured from the Mogul emperor exemption from customs duties and other concessions.

The reorganized Maratha government gradually became pre-eminent in India, exacting taxes from the whole Deccan excepting Hyderabad, which became virtually independent of Delhi (1724) under its governor, the **Nizam-ul-Mulk** (d. 1748). The governors of Avadh (Oudh) (1724) and Bengal (1740) also became independent, but maintained the fiction of allegiance to the Mogul emperor.

1739. A pillaging invasion of Persians under **Nadir Shah** checked the Maratha expansion northward, defeated imperial troops, and withdrew, retaining possession of Afghanistan and the wealth of Delhi.

1746–1748. Following the outbreak of the **War of the Austrian Succession** in Europe, the French, strengthened by their participation in Indian intrigue under the guidance of **Joseph Dupleix,** captured Madras (1746) and defeated the protesting nawab of the Carnatic. The **treaty of Aix-la-Chapelle** (1748) restored Madras to Britain.

1748–1754. **Anglo-French rivalry** continued, each side supporting candidates for the positions of nizam of the Deccan and nawab of the Carnatic. French domination, at its height in 1751 when **Bussy** virtually ruled the Deccan

Robert Clive

and Dupleix the Carnatic, was checked by **Robert Clive's** (1727–1774) brilliant seizure of Arcot (Sept. 12, 1751). The recall of Dupleix (1754) left English prestige firmly established.

1756. The nawab **(Siraj-ud-Daulah)** of the Bengal region captured Calcutta (June 20) and imprisoned unescaped residents in a small storeroom in the fort (later called the "Black Hole"), where over a hundred perished from suffocation, wounds, and the heat.

1757. British forces under **Watson** and Clive retook Calcutta and, being again at war with France, seized Chandernagor (Mar. 23). Clive formed a conspiracy with Hindu bankers and the nawab's general, **Mir Jafar,** which enabled his forces to rout those remaining loyal to the nawab at **Plassey** (June 23). Mir Jafar, having executed Siraj-ud-Daulah, was

A representative of the English East India Company negotiates with the Mogul Emperor

Siraj-ud-Daulah

Haidar Ali greets a French delegation

Bombay in 1767

installed as nawab under a virtual English protectorate of Bengal.

1758-1760. Maratha occupation of the Punjab (1758) and renewed northern activity (1760) excited allied opposition of the Rohilla Afghans and **Ahmad Shah Abdali** (the Durani Afghan chief, who had invaded the Punjab almost annually between 1748 and 1759). The Marathas were crushingly defeated by this coalition in

1761. Jan. 14. The battle of Panipat. Subsequent mutiny caused Ahmad Shah's withdrawal, leaving India in dissension.

British supremacy in India's foreign relations was assured by their defeat of the Dutch (1759) and capture of **Pondichéry** from the French, who by the **treaty of Paris** (1763) retained only Pondichéry, Chandernagor, and other scattered stations, with limited numbers of troops. The *Compagnie des Indes Orientales* was dissolved in 1769.

1764, Oct. 22. Victory at Baksar over forces of the deposed nawab of Bengal, the nawab of Avadh, and the titular Mogul emperor gave the British uncontested control in Bengal and Bihar.

1765-1767. Clive administered Bengal affairs for the company: the powerless Mogul emperor was induced to grant it *diwani* (revenue control) in Bengal, Bihar, and part of Orissa, the company taking over the actual collection of revenue in 1771. Official perquisites were reduced among the company's servants, whose rapacity since 1757 Clive had encouraged by his own example.

The militarism of the Moguls and the predatory policy of the Marathas led to an emphasis on warfare and piracy as sources of prestige and wealth, and a gradual decline of industry, education, and cultural progress except as maintained by some Moslem and Hindu poets and scholars, notably the Delhi reformer **Shah Wali-Ullah** (1703-1760) and the Bengali poet **Bharatchandra** (1717-1760). General economic chaos ensued, with Europeans profiting greatly from gifts, forced sales, and usury. One exception was Indore (1765-1795) under the rule of the pious **Ahalya Bai.**

During dissension in the Maratha confederacy, **Haidar Ali** (1721-1782) gained power, usurped the throne of Mysore (1761), and

1769. Compelled the British at Madras, who became involved in war against him (1767), to sign a treaty of mutual assistance.

1769-1770. Disastrous famine in Bengal wiped out an estimated one-third of the population.

1772-1785. As governor of Bengal, **Warren Hastings** (1732-1818) initiated reforms, including simplification of the revenue system, improved coinage, government control of salt and opium manufacture, reduction of dacoity, and study of Moslem and Hindu law (Calcutta Madrasa, 1781). He was styled governor-general, with certain supervisory powers over the other two company presidencies (Bombay and Madras) under the

1773. REGULATING ACT, by which parliament also established a supreme court for British subjects in the company's territories, limited the rights of the company's directors, and prohibited officers' private trade and receipt of presents. Hastings' high-handed measures kept the company solvent and relatively secure in a turbulent period, but incurred the censure of jealous colleagues, notably Philip Francis, and led to his impeachment (after his retirement in 1785) with a trial (1788-1795) resulting in acquittal.

1775-1782. First Anglo-Maratha War, the result of the Bombay government's alliance with the would-be Maratha peshwa, **Raghoba.** Hastings sent an expedition across the peninsula from Calcutta to Surat (1778, arrived 1779), and broke the coalition between the Marathas, Haidar Ali, and the nizam. The **treaty of Salbai** (1782) obtained for Bombay twenty years' peace with the Marathas and the cession of Salsette and Elephanta.

1778. France and Britain being again at war, Hastings took Pondichéry and Mahé. Provoked by this action,

1780-1784. Haidar Ali, with French help, attacked the British in the Carnatic, but was defeated at **Porto Novo** (1781) and died (1782); the **Second Anglo-Mysore War,** continued by his son, **Tipu Sultan,** was terminated when

French aid was withdrawn.

1784. PITT'S INDIA ACT, in an endeavor to check territorial expansion, forbade interference in native affairs or declaration of war except in case of aggression, and made the company's directors answerable to a board of control appointed by the crown.

1786-1793. Lord Cornwallis (after a 20-month interregnum of Sir John MacPherson) became governor-general and commander-in-chief, with power to overrule his council. Under injunctions to preserve peace, he made administrative reforms: company officers given adequate fixed salaries and their private trade eliminated; separation of administrative from commercial branches of service.

1790-1792. Tipu attacked Travancore, opening the **Third Anglo-Mysore War;** Cornwallis

Warren Hastings

allied himself with the peshwa and the nizam, and Tipu was defeated and ceded half his territory, paying a large indemnity (Mar. 19, 1792).

1791. The Sanskrit College was established at Benares by Jonathan Duncan.

1793. **Cornwallis' Code** inaugurated substantial reforms. The *Permanent Settlement* stabilized the revenue system by fixing the assessment in Bengal, Bihar, and Orissa (and Benares Province, 1795) with collection through *zamindars,* but failed to check the latter's exploitation of the peasantry; it also effected ruthless sale of *zamindar* rights in case of default, and closed the way to later reassessments, thereby eventually causing great financial loss to the government. The **judicial system** was reshaped on the British model, but with a paucity of courts. **Indians were excluded from all higher posts.** *Zamindars* were left only revenue duties, their magisterial and police functions being transferred to European district judges and Indian police (*darogas*).

In the Madras presidency a careful survey along the lines of local practice led to a system of direct levy (periodically reassessed) from the *ryot* (peasant), later extended to Bombay presidency; in the Northwest and Central Provinces, somewhat later, the *mahalwari* system was introduced, collecting revenue through villages or estates.

Meanwhile the principal Maratha leader,

Sons of Tipu Sultan surrender to the British, 1792

Mahadaji Sindhia (d. 1794) assumed protection of the emperor, reclaimed Delhi, and extended his power in northern India.

1793. **Sir John Shore,** governor-general.

1796. **Ceylon** conquered from the Dutch, and administered jointly by the East India Company and the crown until 1802, the latter assuming full responsibility thereafter.

(Cont. p. 839.)

4. *China, 1520–1798*

The Portuguese colony of Macao, c.1598

(From p. 363)

AMACAO.

1520–1521. The **Portuguese,** who under Albuquerque had seized Malacca (1511), sent Thomé Pires to Peking. Piratical conduct of Simao d'Andrade and others led to their expulsion from China in 1522.

1522–1566. The **CHIA CHING REIGN** of Shih Tsung was filled with the effort to repel attacks (especially 1542 and 1550) of Altan Khan, prince of the Ordos; and of Japanese pirates (1523 and 1552), who even besieged Nanking (1555).

1557. A Portuguese settlement was permanently established at **Macao.**

1577. **So-nam gya-tso,** third successor of Tsong-kha-pa (1357–1419), who reformed **Tibetan Buddhism** by foundation of the yellow-capped "Virtuous" church, and himself an incarnation of Avalokitesvara, presided over a Mongol assembly beside Koko-nor. Altan Khan entitled him *Dalai Lama* (Lama of all within the seas), and formally accepted his spiritual authority for his people. The hold of the Tibetan church over Mongolia was cemented by recognition of two new divine incarnations: **Manjusri** in the Dongkur Hutuktu of the Ordos (1579) and **Maitreya** in the Jebdzun-damba Hutuktu of Urga (c. 1602).

1573–1620. The **WAN LI REIGN** of Shen Tsung is famous for cultural achievements.

1592–1593, 1597–1598. **Japanese invasions** of tributary Korea sent by Hideyoshi were repelled, the first from P'yong-yang (1593), the second from southern Korea.

1615. **Nurhachi** gave military organizations as eight banners to a group of Tungus tribes in eastern Manchuria.

1616. He adopted the title *Chin Khan* and the surname *Aisin Gioro,* "Golden Tribe," to identify his people as heirs of the Chin (1116–1234). They later (1652) called themselves *Manchus* (Man-chou, probably from the Bodhisattva of learning, Manjusri).

1621. He expelled the Ming from the Liao Basin and moved his capital to Liaoyang.

1636. The **MANCHUS** proclaimed an imperial Ta Ch'ing dynasty at Mukden, and set up a civilian administration copied closely from the Chinese.

1644. The **last Ming emperor** hanged himself when a bandit, Li Tzu-ch'eng, seized Peking.

MING THOUGHT was at first almost wholly dominated by authority of **Chu Hsi** and his school. The *Hsing Li Ta Ch'üan,* a digest of moral philosophy from the works of 120 of these scholars, was published under imperial authority in 1416. Opposition to the positive and authoritarian aspects of such teaching was most vigorously expressed by **Wang Shou-jen** (pen-name *Wang Yang-ming*) (1472–1528 or 1529), who insisted that moral judgments spring from the intuitive faculties within all men. Sages differ from common men in quantity, not quality, of true perceptions. Experience is for him the test of truth. Chu Hsi, through emphasis on objective study, had opened the door to scientific research. Wang, by insistence on subjectivity, did much to prevent it.

The early part of the dynasty saw a vigorous national reaction led by the **Academy of Let-**

ters (*Han Lin Yüan*) against all things foreign. Buddhism was now almost completely naturalized as Chinese, and Islam was too strongly entrenched in the north and southwest to be eradicated; but both Nestorian and Roman Christianity were suppressed. So too were various secret fraternities with obscure social and political objectives, like the **White Cloud** and the **White Lotus,** which had enjoyed official status under the Mongols.

Matteo Ricci (1552–1610, Macao, 1582) won toleration for the Jesuits and a salary at court (1601) by presenting clocks, etc., to the throne and preparing a huge map of the world. News in Peking (1606) of the arrival in Kansu of **Benedict de Goez,** who had come overland from India (1603–1605), first established for modern Europe identity of Marco Polo's **Cathay** with maritime China (*Thinai* in the *Periplus,* A.D. 80–89, from Sanskrit *Cina*). Rapid conversions and private church services at Nanking brought suspicion of secret aims like those of the White Lotus, and consequent deportation (1616) of the missionaries to Macao, whence they gradually returned. **Johann Schall von Bell** (1591–1666, Peking, 1622) was charged (1630) to reform the dynastic calendar (already begun by Jesuits, 1611 and 1629). He cast astronomical instruments; and (1636–1637) twenty 40-pound cannon, with camel-guns for use against the Manchus.

The **Academy of Letters** supervised an imposing series of official compilations. The *Yung Lo Ta Tien,* an encyclopedia into which numerous whole works were transcribed, was compiled in 10,000 manuscript volumes of folio size (1403–1409). The precedents of the T'ang, Sung, and Yüan were followed by issue, in numerous editions, of the dynastic legal and

administrative codes and a territorial survey of the empire. The practice was begun of gathering many small choice works by various authors into uniform collections. **Mao Chin** published from his private library the *Chi Ku Ko,* fine critical editions of the *Thirteen Classics with Commentaries,* the *Seventeen Standard Histories,* and many other works.

Ming painters, besides much imitation of Sung ink landscape, which was now reduced

Matteo Ricci, 1552–1610

to conventional formulae, revived a coloristic tradition of vivid blues and greens. **Tai Chin** (fl. c. 1446) especially developed a new style of free rapid composition in ink which was better adapted to representation of life and movement than the exquisite but somewhat static Sung technique. The potters of the Hung Wu and Yung Lo reigns achieved bold effects by application of "three-color" glazes (aubergine, turquoise, and yellow) with dark blue to monumental potiches. In the Hsüan Te period they learned to control copper oxide red for decoration of white paste under clear glaze, in addition to the cobalt "Mohammedan blue" of which the purest supply came intermittently from Turkestan. Decoration in overglaze enamels, often in combination with underglaze blue, was used brilliantly on rather bombastic vases in the Chia Ching and Wan Li periods. The imperial kilns at Ching-te-chen in Kiangsi were developed to supply immense quantities of porcelain to the palace.

1644–1912. The **CH'ING DYNASTY** entered Peking by surprise when the Manchu regent **Dorgun** (1643–1650) had helped the Ming general Wu San-kuei to drive off the bandit Li Tzu-ch'eng.

The last Ming emperor hangs himself, 1644

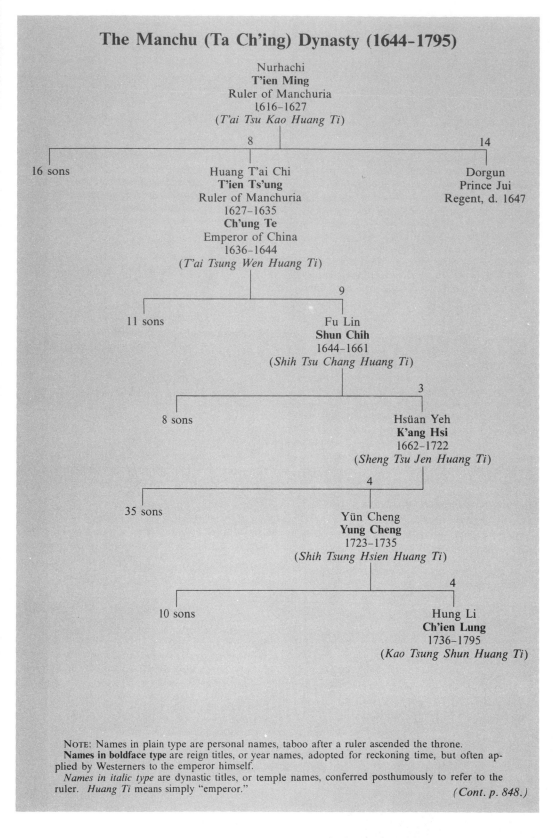

The Manchu (Ta Ch'ing) Dynasty (1644–1795)

Nurhachi
T'ien Ming
Ruler of Manchuria
1616–1627
(*T'ai Tsu Kao Huang Ti*)

8 — 14

16 sons

Huang T'ai Chi
T'ien Ts'ung
Ruler of Manchuria
1627–1635
Ch'ung Te
Emperor of China
1636–1644
(*T'ai Tsung Wen Huang Ti*)

Dorgun
Prince Jui
Regent, d. 1647

9

11 sons

Fu Lin
Shun Chih
1644–1661
(*Shih Tsu Chang Huang Ti*)

3

8 sons

Hsüan Yeh
K'ang Hsi
1662–1722
(*Sheng Tsu Jen Huang Ti*)

4

35 sons

Yün Cheng
Yung Cheng
1723–1735
(*Shih Tsung Hsien Huang Ti*)

4

10 sons

Hung Li
Ch'ien Lung
1736–1795
(*Kao Tsung Shun Huang Ti*)

NOTE: Names in plain type are personal names, taboo after a ruler ascended the throne.
Names in boldface type are reign titles, or year names, adopted for reckoning time, but often applied by Westerners to the emperor himself.
Names in italic type are dynastic titles, or temple names, conferred posthumously to refer to the ruler. *Huang Ti* means simply "emperor."

(*Cont. p. 848.*)

1644–1661. The **SHUN CHIH REIGN** of Shih Tsu was filled with military effort to destroy Ming resistance, which centered about Prince Fu at Nanking (1644–1645), Prince T'ang in Fukien (1645–1646), Prince Lu at Shaohsing, Amoy, Chusan (1645–1651), and Prince Kuei from Canton to Yünnan (1646–1659). Conquest was accompanied by imposition of the Manchu shaven head with queue. Foot-binding, at first forbidden (1638, 1645, 1662), was at length permitted to Chinese only (1668). Manchus were appointed as colleagues of Chinese in all principal posts of central administration, and garrisons from the eight Manchu banners were distributed among strategic provincial cities; but Chinese were appointed in the provinces both to civil posts and to command of Chinese auxiliary troops. Four Chinese were sent as viceroys to hold the south and southwest.

1645–1683. A pirate dynasty upheld the Ming. Chen Chih-lung (1645–1646, executed at Peking 1661) was succeeded by **Cheng Ch'eng-kung,** known to the Portuguese as *Koxinga* (1646–1662). Koxinga seized Amoy (1653), Ch'ung-ming Island (1656), attacked Nanking (1657), and by a long siege of Fort Zelandia (1661–1662) wrested Formosa from the Dutch. So formidable was his naval power that the Manchus decreed (1661) evacuation of the whole coastal population to a depth of ten miles from the sea.

1662–1722. The **K'ANG HSI REIGN** of Sheng Tsu (b. 1654, personal rule in form 1667, in fact 1669) opened a period of cultural achievement which surpassed the greatest of earlier dynasties. The fifteen provinces of the Ming were increased to eighteen by separate recognition of Anhuei (1662), Hunan (1664), and Kansu (1705).

The **Dutch** had founded Batavia (1619), a Formosan station (1624–1625), and captured Malacca (1641) from the Portuguese, who lost their commercial empire, but retained Macao. A mission of Pieter van Goyer and Jacob van Keyser (1656) secured nothing better than tributary status, only slightly improved (1667) by the mission of Pieter van Hoorn. Disgruntled by loss of Zelandia,

1663–1664. Balthasar Bort with a Dutch fleet helped a Chinese army drive Koxinga's son and successor, Cheng Chin (1662–1681), from the Fukien coast to Formosa.

1670. A Portuguese embassy under **Manoel de Saldanha,** like that of Bento Pereyra de Faria (1678–1679), won only confirmation of the status of Macao. The much later missions of A. M. de Souza y Menezas (1726) and F.-X. Assis Pacheco y Sampayo (1742) achieved no more.

1674–1681. Revolt of three viceroys followed imperial orders providing for their withdrawal (1673).

1674. Viceroy Wu San-kuei from Yünnan held Szechuan, Kueichou, Hunan, and Kwangsi for five years (1674–1679). Keng Ching-chung, grandson and heir of the Fukien viceroy, joined him and invaded Kiangsi.

1675. A revolt by Burni in Chahar was quickly suppressed. Cheng Chin's pirates resumed depredations in Chekiang and Fukien.

1676. Shang Chih-hsin forced his aged father, viceroy of Kwangtung, to surrender Canton to the rebels.

1681. Re-entrance of imperial armies to Yünnan City marked complete military triumph, supplemented by

1683. Surrender of Formosa by Cheng Chin's son Cheng K'o-shuang (1681–1683). Formosa was for the first time given imperial administration, as appendage of Fukien.

The Russian **Poyarkhov** explored the Amur (1643–1646) and Khabarov built a fort at Albazin (1651). A mission under Baikov (1656) proved futile, but Spatar Milescu (1676) performed the kotow (*k'ou t'ou*) with dignity on a reciprocal basis, and mapped Siberia.

1689. By the **treaty of Nerchinsk** the Russians adopted advice of the Jesuit negotiator Jean-François Gerbillon to abandon Albazin and military pressure for commercial penetration. L. V. Izmailov (1720–1721) established a trading agent and an Eastern Orthodox church in Peking.

1691. The emperor, at a great assembly of

Mongols at Dolon Nor, reorganized the four Khalkha states of central Mongolia which he had just defended (1690) against the provoked attack (1688) of Galdan, chief of the Olöt (West Mongol) Jungars.

1696. Galdan was crushed near Urga and took poison (1697).

1705. Forcible enthronement as dalai lama at Lhasa of an imperial candidate aroused Tibetan opposition and appeal to the Olöt (1714).

1712. Domestic peace since 1681 and vigilant administration with frugality not only paid for foreign wars, but led to a permanent settlement of land and poll-taxes on the basis of returns for 1711.

1717. Olöt **seizure of Lhasa** by direction of Galdan's nephew, Tsewang Rabdan (1697–1727), was learned in Peking too late to save a relief column from annihilation (1718). Well-prepared armies from Kansu and Szechwan.

1720. Enthroned a popular dalai lama and established imperial garrisons in Tibet.

1721. Revolt in Formosa led by Chu I-kuei was suppressed.

The **Jesuits** enjoyed toleration and favor in return for scientific services. **Johann Schall von Bell** prepared the dynastic calendar (1630–1664) until imprisoned on representations of jealous Moslem astronomers. **Ferdinand Verbiest** (1623–1688, arr. 1659) was reinstated in control of the almanac (1669), installed a new set of instruments on the observatory (1674), and promulgated a perpetual calendar (1678). **Fontaney** cured the emperor of fever with quinine (1693). **Régis** and eight others prepared the first maps of China to be based on astronomical observation, triangulation, and measurement (1708–1718). Benefits of an edict of toleration (1692) were ruined by a bitter quarrel over Jesuit acceptance of Chinese rites toward Heaven, Confucius, and ancestors. These rites were condemned (1693) by Mgr. Maigrot. Appeal to the emperor (1700) accentuated conflict of imperial and papal authority, which neither of two patriarchs, De Tournon (1705)

Rites honoring Confucius

The retinue of a viceroy when he appeared in public during the Shun Chih reign, 1644–1661

Johann Schall von Bell, 1622–1666

and Mezzabarba (1720), sent by Clement XI, could reconcile. Dabbling in intrigue for succession among the twenty adult sons of the emperor won only (1722) permanent hostility of the victor, the end of the active mission.

From his accession **Sheng Tsu** labored to win support of the scholar class by daily classical study, honors to Confucius and the Sung Neo-Confucianists (*Ju*), and patronage of scholarship. He founded (1677) the **College of Inscriptions** (*Nan San So*) affiliated to the Academy of Letters. Most important among many books compiled by his order, in addition to the several administrative and archival works prescribed by precedent, were the standard *Ming History* (53 scholars appointed, 1679), *Complete T'ang Poetry* (1707), the *P'ei Wen Chai Shu Hua P'u* repertory of works on painting (1708), the *Yüan Chien Lei Han* encyclopedia (1710), *P'ei Wen Yün Fu* thesaurus of literary phrases (1711), *K'ang Hsi* dictionary (1716), and the *T'u Shu Chi Ch'eng* encyclopedia (5020 volumes 1726). Private scholars were also active: **Huang Tsung-hsi** (1610–1695), the philosopher and critical historian of Sung, Yüan, and Ming philosophy; **Ku Yen-wu** (1613–1681), historical geographer and critic; **Chu I-tsun** (1629–1709), author of the critical bibliography of the classics *Ching I K'ao;* **Hsü Ch'ien-hsüeh** (1631–1694), who brought together 480 volumes of choice classical comment, *T'ung Chih T'ang Ching Chieh;* **Mei Wen-ting** (1633–1721), the mathematician; and many others.

The most brilliant epoch in the history of the imperial kilns at Ching-te-chen followed appointment of **Ts'ang Ying-hsüan** as supervisor (1682). The techniques of enameling on the biscuit, of composite monochrome glazing over colored glaze, of application of underglaze blue in powder form, and of decoration overglaze in transparent *famille verte* enamels were perfected. Progress of the minor arts followed establishment of 28 kinds of artisans within the palace precincts (1680).

1723–1735. The **YUNG CHENG REIGN** of Shih Tsung, although peaceful at home, was filled with inconclusive war against Mongols and western tribesmen.

1727. The **Kiakhta treaty** fixing the Russian frontier was concluded by Sava Vladislavich after a mission to Peking (1726–1727).

1729. Large-scale operations against the Jungars led to

1732. Establishment of an advisory military council (*Chün Chi Ch'u*) which gradually usurped the executive functions of the grand secretariat (*Nei Ko*).

1736–1795. The **CH'IEN LUNG REIGN** of Kao Tsung marks a new advance in population and wealth, which supported imposition of imperial control throughout Central Asia. Cultural activity continued to enjoy imperial patronage and leadership. Corruption of the civil service led by the venal Ho Shen (1750–1799) during the last twenty years of the reign provoked revolts which continued until the end of the dynasty.

1747–1749, 1755–1779. Campaigns of exceptional difficulty were waged to pacify the native tribes of the Tibetan border.

1750. Violence by and against the imperial residents at Lhasa led to the

1751. **INVASION OF TIBET** and establishment of control over the succession and the temporal acts of the dalai lama.

1755. **Amursana,** grandson of Tsewang Rabdan, after ten years' succession struggle, was enthroned by imperial troops as prince of the

Yung Cheng, 1723–1735

Jungars, but revolted. Suppression of the revolt, following a smallpox epidemic, depopulated the Ili Valley. The Jungars were annihilated or dispersed.

1757–1842. Restriction of foreign maritime trade to Canton was maintained despite efforts of the British interpreter Flint at Tientsin (1759), Capt. Skottowe at Canton (1761), and the earl of Macartney at Jehol and Peking (1793).

1758–1759. Kashgaria was conquered by Chaohui from the Turkish Khoja dynasty.

1765–1769. Invasion of Burma failed to reach Ava, but secured recognition of suzerainty.

1771. The Torgud, who had fled beyond the Volga to escape the Jungars, now dared accept an invitation by T'u-li-ch'en (1712), and migrated back to Ili.

1774. The first Chinese rebellion in nearly a century broke out in Shantung and was traced to the White Lotus Society.

1781, 1784. Revolts in Kansu by Moslems, including the Wahabis, were suppressed.

1784. The **United States** entered the profitable Canton trade.

1786–1787. Revolt in Formosa was suppressed.

1792. Invasion of Nepal under Fu-k'ang-an, provoked by attack on Tashilunpo, the seat of the panchan lama, resulted in defeat of the Gurkhas and their recognition of imperial suzerainty.

1795–1797. Revolt by the Miao tribes of Hunan and Kueichou was suppressed.

The best critical edition of the 24 *Standard Histories* was issued by imperial authority (1739–1746). Chief among many later imperial literary enterprises was the assemblage (1772–1781), by manuscript transcription, of a select library, *Ssu K'u Ch'üan Shu* or *Complete Work of the Four Treasuries,* embracing 3462 works in 36,300 volumes. Seven copies were eventually distributed. The printed critical *General Catalogue* in 92 volumes (1789) contains additional notices of 6734 works not included in the library. The emperor exploited the occasion of compilation to expurgate from Chinese literature all derogatory references to the Manchus and their northern predecessors. More than 2000 works were condemned to total destruction (1774–1782), most of them minor writings of the period 1616–1681. Contrary to precedent, two propagandist histories were compiled fraudulently to identify the Manchus as descendants of the Jürchen Chin. The technique of textual criticism was perfected and applied by numerous able scholars to the classics, especially by **Lu Wen-ch'ao** (1717–1795), **Chiang Sheng** (1721–1799), and **Tuan Yüts'ai** (1735–1815). **Wang Ming-sheng** (1722–1797) and **Ch'ien Ta-hsin** (1728–1804) distinguished themselves as commentators on the standard histories. **Pi Yüan** (1730–1797) compiled a supplement to the general history of Ssu-ma Kuang. The practice of gathering choice literature of diverse kinds into uniform collections was spurred by issue from the imperial Wu Ying Tien of a series of 138 works printed from movable wooden type in 800 volumes (1773–1783). **Pao T'ing-po** (1728–1814) published his *Chih Pu Tsu Chai Ts'ung Shu* in 240 volumes.

Under direction of **T'ang-Ying** (1736–1749) the imperial kilns at Ching-te-chen developed the elaborate *famille rose* palette of opaque overglaze enamels, which is distinguished by

The Dutch enter Batavia, May 28, 1619

mixed colors and replacement of ferric oxide red by carmine derived from gold.

1795. Kao Tsung abdicated, but continued to direct affairs until death (1798).

(Cont. p. 846.)

a. BURMA, 1519-1767

(From p. 363)

Following the arrival during the 15th century of a few European travelers (Nicolo di Conti, c. 1435), in

1519. The Portuguese by treaty secured trading privileges at Martaban, and an increasing portion of the foreign trade was conducted by Europeans.

1539. Tabin Shwehti, ruler of Toungoo (1531–1550), captured Pegu, was crowned king of Lower Burma (1542), and after extending his power northward to Pagan (1546) assumed the title of *King of all Burma.* With Portuguese mercenaries he attacked unsuccessfully both Arakan to the west and Siam to the east.

1555. His successor, **Bayin Naung** (ruled 1551–1581), took Ava, destroyed the Tai kingdom of Chiengmai (1557) in northern Siam, and subdued Ayuthia (1563) temporarily. Exhausted by these wars, the central power declined; in

1600. Pegu was destroyed and Burma broke up into a number of petty states.

1619. The Dutch and English East India Companies opened factories. They did not flourish and were closed later in the century.

1753. Alaungpaya reunited Burma, with assistance from the English East India Company and in opposition to the French. His second successor destroyed Ayuthia (1767) and subdued Siam for a time, retaining the Tenasserim coast in Burmese possession. *(Cont. p. 843.)*

b. SIAM, 1602-1782

(From p. 364)

Portuguese trading stations were established in the 16th century and about the beginning of the 17th century large numbers of Japanese were active in Siam, in war and trade.

1602. A Dutch trading post was established at Patani, where the English soon followed, until their withdrawal from Siam in 1623.

1664. By a commercial treaty, the Dutch gained a monopoly of Siamese foreign trade, which was, however, thwarted by French intrigue; a French embassy and military expedition (1685) in turn failed to secure the acceptance of Christianity and French influence, and led to

1688. A popular revolt which began a period of prolonged civil war.

1767. A **Burmese invasion** destroyed Ayuthia and compelled temporary acceptance of Burmese rule until

1782. Rama I founded a new Siamese dynasty, with its capital at Bangkok. *(Cont. p. 844.)*

c. MALAYSIA, 1511-1790

(From p. 365)

1511. The Portuguese, under **Albuquerque, captured Malacca,** center of the spice trade. They then sent envoys to open trade relations with native states and set up fortified posts to protect the trade.

1594. The Lisbon spice market was closed to Dutch and English traders, thus providing an incentive to direct trade with the Far East. The English and Dutch **East India Companies** (1600, 1602) presently destroyed the Portuguese forts in Malaysia.

1596. The Dutch set up a factory at **Palembang** (Sumatra).

1602. The English established themselves at **Bantam** (northwest Java).

1605. The Dutch seized Amboina, then settled in western Timor (1613) and in

1619. Built Batavia. It became the headquarters of the Dutch East India Company, which worked trade to the limit.

1623. Massacre of the English by the Dutch at **Amboina.** The English forced to abandon trade in Siam, Japan, and the East Indies.

1639. Expulsion of the Portuguese from Japan.

1641. Capture of Malacca by the Dutch, who thenceforth dominated the East Indies.

1666. The Dutch took Celebes from the Portuguese.

1685. The British set up a **factory at Bengkulen** (Sumatra).

During the 18th century the Dutch continued to hold the upper hand. Growing ruthlessness and corruption of the company. In order to control the trade, the company had to widen its control over northern Java.

1769. The **British East India Company** opened stations in northern Borneo, but the settlements (especially **Balambangan,** 1773) had to be given up under pressure from the natives (1775).

1781. The British conquered all the Dutch settlements on the west coast of **Sumatra,** Holland having joined the armed neutrality against Britain.

1783. By the **treaty of Paris** the British returned the Dutch colonies, but secured the right to trade throughout the Dutch island possessions.

1786. The British East India Company secured a grant of Penang (permanent cession 1790), which made a fourth Indian presidency (1805), but proved useless as a naval and commercial base. *(Cont. p. 845.)*

5. *The Philippines, 1521–1764*

1521, Mar. 15. The islands were discovered by **Magellan,** who was killed there (Apr. 25) in a fight with the natives.

1525-1527. In order to strengthen Castilian claims against Portugal, Charles V sent out an expedition under **García Jofre de Loyasa,** who died en route. The expedition visited Mindanao, but Portuguese opposition was encountered and no results were obtained.

1527. Under orders from home, **Cortés** (in Mexico) sent out **Alvaro Saavedra Ceron,** whose fleet was dispersed without accomplishing anything.

1529. Lack of success in these efforts induced Charles V to conclude with Portugal the **treaty of Saragossa,** by which the line of demarcation in the Far East was fixed 297.5 leagues east of the Moluccas, which remained Portuguese. The Philippines, though within Portuguese jurisdiction, were not occupied by Portugal.

1532. Charles V granted **Pedro de Alvarado** authority to conduct discovery and colonization in the Pacific. Alvarado abandoned the project in order to attempt the conquest of Quito.

1541. The viceroy of New Spain, **Antonio de Mendoza,** was given authority for the same purpose but was to share the results with Alvarado.

1542-1543. Mendoza sent out **Ruy Lopez de Villalobos,** who landed and named the islands, though he was then driven off by the natives and later captured by the Portuguese.

1565-1571. Under instructions from Philip II, the viceroy **Luis de Velasco** sent out an expedition under **Miguel Lopez de Legazpi,** who made the first settlement (San Miguel), sub-

Ferdinand Magellan is killed, April 25, 1521

jugated the natives, and founded **Manila** (May 19, 1571). An *audiencia* was established at Manila (1583) and the islands were subordinated to the government of New Spain.

1762, Sept. 22. A British fleet bombarded Manila and took the city (Oct. 5).

1764, Mar. 31. The British evacuated Manila on the conclusion of peace. *(Cont. p. 870.)*

6. *Korea, 1506–1800*

(From p. 365)

1506. A revolt against the cruel ruler, Yonsangun, brought to the throne

1507-1544. Chungjong, whose attempt to curb

the great families by means of the Confucian scholars led to the defeat of the latter.

c. 1570. The Confucian scholars gradually

established their control over the court, but, although only the orthodox Chu Hsi school of philosophy was tolerated, they broke up into bitterly antagonistic factions. Meanwhile the decline of the Ming brought a similar political and cultural decline in Korea.

1592-1598. Japanese invasions laid waste the land *(p. 564)*.

1623. Injo was put on the throne by the so-called western faction of Confucianists, which had triumphed over the big northern faction (one branch of the northern faction), which previously had superseded the western faction.

1627. The Manchus overran Korea.

1637. Korea became a vassal state of the Manchus (Ch'ing dynasty) after an invasion led by T'ai-tsung, but the court and people remained loyal to the Ming.

1675-1720. Under Sukchong the western fac-

tion of Confucianists returned to power and divided into the old and young factions, which fought bitterly with each other.

1725-1800. A period of great intellectual activity, for the most part limited to moral philosophy and to genealogical research or fabrication.

(Cont. p. 851.)

7. *Japan, 1542–1793*

(From p. 375)

1542 or 1543. Portuguese landed from a Chinese ship on the island of Tanegashima, off the southern coast of Kyūshū. These were the first Europeans to visit Japan. They introduced the musket, which soon modified Japanese warfare. Other Portuguese ships followed and entered into trade relations with the lords of western Japan.

1549-1551. ST. FRANCIS XAVIER (1506-1552), the famous Jesuit missionary, introduced Christianity into Japan, proselytizing in the feudal domains of the west and also in Kyōto, but with no great success. On the whole he was well received and in some cases the feudal lords even encouraged conversions in the hope of attracting Portuguese trade. But the dogmatic intolerance of the missionaries soon earned them the bitter enmity of the usually tolerant Buddhist clergy and led to proscriptions of the new religion in certain fiefs. Xavier left behind two Jesuits and the Japanese converts, who formed the nucleus of the new church.

1568. Oda Nobunaga (1534-1582) seized Kyōto and set up a puppet *shōgun*, Yoshiaki (1568-1573, d. 1597). Lord of the provinces of Owari, Mino, and Mikawa east of Kyōto, Nobunaga had acted in response to a secret appeal from the emperor. By this daring blow he became the virtual dictator of central Japan, and with this date commenced

1568-1600. The **PERIOD OF NATIONAL UNIFICATION** (usually called the *Azuchi-Momoyama Period*). The process of political disintegration of the nation had already run its course, and in these few decades, through the efforts of three great leaders, the nation was again united as the periphery was gradually subjugated by the military hegemons of the capital region. This was unquestionably one of the most dynamic epochs of Japanese history. The Japanese pirate traders were at their height and were active even in Siamese and Philippine waters. Excess national energy also expressed itself in a great **invasion of Korea.** Closer contacts with the Asiatic main-

Oda Nobunaga, 1534–1582

Nobunaga is killed, 1582

land and with Europeans resulted in an influx of new intellectual and artistic currents. Buddhism was in decline, and its monasteries were being deprived of their military power, but militant Christianity was at its height in Japan, and there was a revival of lay learning after the years of warfare. New skills and new products from the Occident profoundly affected the economy of the land, and in these years of relative peace the wealth and productivity of the nation expanded rapidly. The private customs barriers which had hampered trade were abolished, and the old monopolistic guilds (*za*) for the most part came to an end.

The artistic and intellectual spirit of the period was almost the antithesis of what it had been in Ashikaga times. It was an exuberant, expansive age. Refined simplicity had given way to ostentatious pomp and faddism. Architecture, which perhaps most clearly expressed the spirit of the age, showed a love of gorgeous decoration and majestic size. Castles and palaces rather than monasteries were the typical structures of the day.

1570. Nagasaki was opened to foreign trade by

Tokugawa Ieyasu, 1543–1616

the local lord, Ōmura (sometimes dated 1567 or 1568). A hitherto unimportant fishing village, it soon became Japan's greatest port for foreign commerce.

1571. **Nobunaga** destroyed the Enryakuji on Mt. Hiei, thus eliminating this, the most powerful of all the monasteries, as a military force. In these same years he also waged usually successful wars against other Buddhist groups, especially the militant groups of the True Pure Land sect (Ikkō sect), as in the siege of their central monastery, the Ishiyama-honganji in Ōsaka (1570–1580). Nobunaga's violent opposition to Buddhism as an organized political force finally broke the temporal power of the monasteries.

1576. Nobunaga commenced work on the **Azuchi castle** on the shores of Lake Biwa. This was the first great castle of Japan and heralded the beginning of several decades of widespread castle-building. Azuchi was destroyed at the time of Nobunaga's death.

1577–1582. **Toyotomi** (at this time Hashiba) **Hideyoshi** (1537–1598), the brilliant but basely born chief general of Nobunaga, conquered much of western Japan from the Mōri family in the name of Nobunaga.

1578. The death of **Uesugi Kenshin** (1530–1578), together with the earlier demise of his great enemy, **Takeda Shingen** (1521–1573), removed Nobunaga's two most formidable rivals in eastern Japan.

1578. The conversion of **Ōtomo Yoshishige** (Sōrin) (1530–1587), one of the greatest lords of Kyūshū, to Christianity gave the foreign religion a greater foothold in the island, where it had already become quite strong since the conversion of some lesser lords of the western littoral, such as Ōmura (1562) and Arima (1576). The Christians, who were for the most part confined to the fiefs with Christian lords, were estimated at 150,000 in 1582.

1582. **Nobunaga was killed** by a discontented general, Akechi Mitsuhide (1526–1582). Hideyoshi returned from his western campaigns and destroyed Mitsuhide. A contest for power with the remaining members of the Oda family, supported by **Tokugawa Ieyasu** (1543–1616), one of Nobunaga's vassal lords in eastern Japan, brought about the elimination of the Oda and an understanding with Ieyasu, resulting in

1584. The hegemony of Hideyoshi over central Japan. The preceding year he had already commenced the construction of the great Ōsaka castle as his home base.

1585. Hideyoshi was appointed civil dictator (*Kampaku*), and two years later he became prime minister (*Dajodaijin*) as well.

1585–1587. A greater stratification of the classes (1, gentlemen-warriors; 2, farmers; 3, artisans; 4, merchants) was brought about by legislation (1585, 1586) and by the disarming of the peasantry (1587).

1587. The subjugation of the Shimazu family of southern Kyūshū completed Hideyoshi's conquest of western Japan.

1587. Hideyoshi issued a decree banishing the

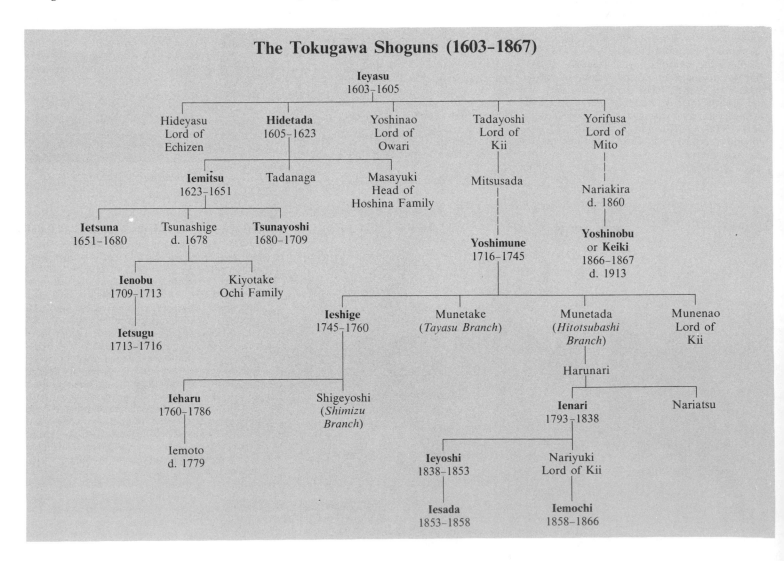

The Tokugawa Shoguns (1603–1867)

Ōsaka Castle in the late 16th century

Portuguese missionaries from Japan, but failed to enforce it for ten years. His motive for this sudden opposition to Christianity was probably fear of the growing political and military strength of the Christians.

1590. The capture of the stronghold of the Hōjō family at Odawara induced all eastern and northern Japan to accept Hideyoshi's rule and completed the political unification of the land. At this time Hideyoshi's prominent vassal, Tokugawa Ieyasu, moved his administrative and military base to Edo (the modern Tōkyō), a strategic spot for the domination of the great plain of eastern Japan.

1592. The **INVASION OF KOREA.** Possibly motivated by the fear of the excess of experienced warriors in Japan, the ambitious Hideyoshi planned the conquest of China. When Korea refused to grant the Japanese transit, he invaded the peninsula. Under the leadership of **Katō Kiyomasa** (1562–1611) and **Konishi Yukinaga** (d. 1600) the expeditionary force of some 200,000 overran almost the whole of Korea, but was forced by a large Chinese army to withdraw to the southern coast in 1593.

1597. The Korean campaign was resumed, but with no great success. After Hideyoshi's death (1598) all the Japanese soldiers returned to Japan. The lasting political results of the Korean venture were negligible, but a rapid development and expansion of the ceramic industry in Japan was brought about by many Korean potters who were taken back to Japan by the retreating captains.

1597. Hideyoshi, irritated by the bickerings between the Portuguese Jesuits and the Spanish Franciscans (who had come to Japan in 1593), and suspecting that Christian proselytizing was merely an opening wedge for the subsequent conquest of Japan by the Europeans, executed three Jesuits, six Franciscans, and seventeen Japanese Christians. The remaining missionaries were ordered to leave, but only a small number did so. Hideyoshi did not press the persecution further, because he did not wish to drive away the Portuguese traders, who were then especially welcome, since direct commercial intercourse with China had been stopped.

1598. **Hideyoshi's death** was soon followed by a contest for power among his former vassals, culminating in

1600. The **battle of Sekigahara,** where Ieyasu defeated a coalition of his rivals. This victory made Ieyasu the virtual ruler of the whole land, and although he was not appointed *shōgun* until 1603, from this time is usually dated

1600–1868. The **TOKUGAWA** (or Edo) **PERIOD.** Ieyasu established the military capital at Edo (Tōkyō), which grew phenomenally to become the economic and cultural as well as political capital of the nation. Because of the fate of the Oda and Toyotomi families, Ieyasu made the perpetuation of the rule in his family his major objective, and this colored the whole spirit as well as the political organization of the epoch, giving them strong conservative and even reactionary tendencies. The feudal lords were divided into the *Fudai* and *Tozama Daimyō.* The former, who were the vassals and allies of Ieyasu before Sekigahara, now occupied the central provinces. The latter, who had only submitted after Sekigahara, were located in more remote regions and were usually excluded from the central government. Both groups were compelled to leave hostages in Edo and to spend alternate periods there and in their fiefs. Important cities were ruled directly by Edo. The building and repairing of castles were strictly limited. The conduct of the warriors was closely regulated, and the emperor and his court, though financially generously treated, were strictly controlled.

The **administrative hierarchy,** which grew out of the Tokugawa family organization, consisted in order of rank of a *shōgun;* at times, and especially between 1638 and 1684, one or more prime ministers (*tairō*); four or five elders (*toshiyori* or *rōju*) as a council of state; a group of junior elders (*wakadoshiyori*), who controlled the direct petty vassals of Edo; a class of officials known as *metsuke,* who served as censors or intelligence officers; and a large group of civil administrators called *bugyō.* The laws lacked coherent organization, but were based on certain fundamental moral precepts, primarily that of loyalty. Criminal codes were severe and cruel. There was a stringent stratification of the classes. *Daimyō* were to a large extent autonomous rulers in their own domains, but Edo kept a watchful eye on them, and there was a strong tendency for the feudatories to adopt the laws and organization of Edo.

The peace and prosperity of the early Toku-

Revival of lay learning, 1600–1868 (a Japanese lecturer)

Toshogu Shinto shrine at Nikko

gawa period brought a gradual rise in the standard of living and an increase in population as well as in the national wealth. With the **growth of industry and commerce,** a powerful merchant class grew up in the larger cities, and a gradual transition from a rice economy to a money economy commenced. This transition, together with the rise in living standards and the increase in population, tended to make production inadequate and

brought about great economic ills during much of the period.

Political conservatism and **isolation** from the rest of the world made the Tokugawa period outwardly stagnant, but it was inwardly a time of great intellectual development. Buddhism was in decline, and Christianity was early stamped out, but there was a great **revival of lay learning,** the old feudal code of conduct received definite formulation under the name of

bushidō, Confucian philosophy enjoyed a protracted period of unparalleled growth and popularity, philosophers and teachers of ethics abounded, there was a revival of interest in Japanese antiquity, Shintō developed new life both as a nationalistic philosophy and as a popular religion, and the newly arisen merchant class contributed greatly to the intellectual and cultural growth of the land.

Literature and art in the Tokugawa period

were comparatively free from Chinese influences and were less aristocratic and more popular than in earlier periods because of the influence of the merchant class. A new poetic form, the *haiku,* which consists of only 17 syllables as opposed to the classic form of 31 syllables, was popularized at this time. The novel enjoyed a second great period of flowering. The refined *Nō* drama slowly gave way to more realistic, more exciting, and decidedly less restrained forms, the *Kabuki* and puppet plays, which both developed from long poetic recitations called *Jōruri.* Applied arts reached great heights of technical excellence, but architecture was an uninspired and often debased imitation of 16th-century styles. Painting was largely traditional, but there were able masters of design and an important new school of realism. The most interesting development in painting was the so-called *ukiyo-e* school, a school of popular artists who chose for their subject matter not Chinese scenes and historical events but the people, street scenes, and landscapes of contemporaneous Japan. The style was introduced in the 17th century and found its most popular expression in the prints of the great wood-block masters of the 18th and first half of the 19th centuries.

c. 1602. The arrival of **Spanish traders** in eastern Japan. Ieyasu befriended Spanish missionaries, hoping thereby to persuade Spanish traders to trade directly with eastern Japan, but, although a formal treaty was negotiated with the Spanish acting governor of the Philippines in 1610, few traders ever came.

1605–1623. HIDETADA as *shōgun* (d. 1632). This was the formative period of the Edo government, first under the direction of the retired *shōgun,* Ieyasu (d. 1616), and then under that of his uninspired but dependable son, Hidetada.

1608. Hayashi Razan (1583–1657), a Confucian scholar, was appointed attendant scholar (*jidoku*) to Ieyasu. This marked the beginning of a Tokugawa policy of using **Confucianism** as a stabilizing force in politics and society. Razan, who founded the Edo Confucian temple in 1623, represented the orthodox Sung Confucian school of Chu Hsi (Japanese *Shushi*), which was the orthodox school in Japan throughout the period. Other schools of Confucian philosophy were those of **Wang Yang-ming** (Japanese *Ōyomei*); of Ming China

(represented by Nakae Tōju [1608–1648] and Kumazawa Banzan [1619–1691]); and the **Ancient School** (*Kogakuha*), a reformed school which returned to pre-Sung Confucian commentators (represented by Itō Jinsai [1627–1705] and Ogyū Sorai [1666?–1728]). The Japanese Confucianists made many contributions in various fields of learning and some attacked the pressing economic problems of the time.

1609. The **Dutch** established a trading post at Hirado in western Japan after an invitation from Ieyasu in 1605. This invitation had been obtained by Will Adams (d. 1620), the English pilot of a Dutch vessel wrecked in Japan in 1600. Adams was forced to remain in Japan by Ieyasu, who made of him an honored adviser.

1612. A definite **persecution of Christianity** commenced after a series of anti-Christian edicts beginning in 1606. Ieyasu's mounting fears of the political menace from Christianity and his realization that trade with Europe could be maintained without the presence of Catholic missionaries as decoys had made him gradually abandon his at first friendly attitude toward the missionaries.

1613. Cocks established an English factory at Hirado.

1613. Date Masamune (1565–1636), a prominent lord of northern Japan, dispatched an embassy to Spain and to the pope.

1614–1615. The Siege of Ōsaka Castle. Hideyori (1593–1615), the son and heir of Hideyoshi, and the former's mother, **Yodogimi** (1577–1615), had remained in the Ōsaka Castle after the battle of Sekigahara, constituting a dangerous rallying-point for disaffected elements. Their ultimate destruction was deemed necessary by Ieyasu. In 1614 on a trumped-up charge he laid siege to the castle, and after a short truce captured and destroyed it and its inmates in 1615.

1615. The **Bukeshohatto,** a collection of general maxims for the warrior class, was issued.

1616. Death of Ieyasu.

1617. Hidetada, aroused by the mutual recriminations of the various European nationalities and religious associations in Japan, intensified the persecution of the Christians (estimated then at 300,000), and for the first time since 1597 European missionaries were executed. Jesuits, Franciscans, and native believers were

executed in increasing numbers in the following years (particularly 1622–1624). This marked the height of the Christian persecution. Catholic missionaries still continued to arrive, but eventually all were killed or forced to leave or to apostatize.

1623–1651. IEMITSU as *shōgun.* This was the period of consolidation of Tokugawa rule. As means of achieving this goal the **suppression of Christianity** was carried to a successful end and the policy of national isolation was adopted.

1623. The English voluntarily left Hirado because their trade with Japan had not proved profitable.

1624. All Spaniards were driven from Japan and all intercourse with the Philippines was stopped.

1636. Japanese were forbidden to go abroad, and those abroad were not allowed to return. Two years later the building of large ships was also proscribed.

1637–1638. The Shimabara uprising. The peasants of the peninsula of Shimabara and the island of Amakusa near Nagasaki, which had been a thoroughly Christianized region for decades, rose in desperation over economic and religious oppression. Some 37,000 of them defended themselves in the dilapidated Hara Castle on the coast of Shimabara for almost three months against vastly superior forces, aided by a Dutch vessel, until food and musket ammunition, on which they depended, failed them. They were killed almost to a man in the fall of the castle, and with this slaughter Christianity was virtually stamped out.

1638. The Portuguese traders were expelled because of suspicions as to their complicity in the Shimabara uprising. When they sent an embassy in 1640 to reopen trade, almost the whole party was summarily executed. This left the Dutch at Hirado and some Chinese traders at Nagasaki as Japan's sole means of contact with the outside world.

1641. The Dutch traders were moved from Hirado to the islet of Deshima in Nagasaki Harbor, where they were in virtual imprisonment and were subjected to many inconveniences and indignities.

1651–1680. IETSUNA as *shōgun.*

1651–1652. Two successive abortive *coups d'état* at Edo were the last revolutions the Tokugawa had to face until the 19th century.

1657. Tokugawa Mitsukuni (1628–1701), lord of Mito, commenced the compilation of a *History of Japan* (*Dainihonshi*) on the model of Chinese dynastic histories. Among the many scholars who aided him were Chinese *émigrés.* The original task was not officially completed until 1720, and supplementary work was continued until 1906. The school of Japanese historians that grew up around this enterprise was one of the important factors in the imperial revival movement.

1657. A great fire destroyed most of Edo and the Edo castle buildings.

1680–1709. TSUNAYOSHI as *shōgun.* Sakai Tadakiyo (1624–1681), prime minister at the time of Ietsuna's death, proposed to have an imperial prince succeed the heirless Ietsuna, but on the insistence of Hotta Masatoshi (1634?–1684) Ietsuna's brother, Tsunayoshi, was made *shōgun,* and presently Masatoshi succeeded Tadakiyo as prime minister. The

Scene from Momiji-Gari, *a Kabuki play based on a Nō drama of the same name*

The Lion Dancer, one of the best-known and best-loved of all Kabuki characters

Japanese 17th-century ship

early years of this period were characterized by vigorous administrative measures until

1684. The **assassination of Hotta Masatoshi** left Tsunayoshi with inferior counsellors who allowed him to ruin the Edo finances and to bring great hardships on the people by edicts inspired by Buddhism prohibiting the killing of any living creature and extending special protection and privileges to dogs.

1688–1704. The **Genroku year period** is regarded as the apogee of the vigorous culture of the merchant class of the Tokugawa period. Already by this time the warrior class was becoming mired in debt to the merchants, into whose hands the wealth of the nation was beginning to pass. Consequently, this was a time of ebullient and unsuppressed self-expression on the part of the merchant class. The gay and extravagant life of the cities centered in the puppet and *Kabuki* theaters and the licensed quarters, the famous Yoshiwara in the case of Edo. Among the great spirits of the age were **Matsuo Bashō** (1644–1694), who made of the *haiku* a great poetic medium; **Ibara Saikaku** (1642–1693), the author of *risqué* novels about courtesans; **Chikamatsu Monzaemon** (1653–1725), Japan's greatest playwright; and **Hishikawa Moronobu** (1638–1714), an early *ukiyo-e* master. Repressive measures and a gradual amalgamation of the merchant and warrior classes in time tempered the Genroku spirit.

1703. The **Chūshingura** (called the "Forty-Seven *Rōnin*") **Incident.** Kira Yoshinaka was killed by a group of former retainers of Asano Naganori, lord of Akō, whose execution in 1701 they felt to be Yoshinaka's fault. The deed thrilled the nation, for, although they had broken the laws of the land, they were but following Confucian ethics in avenging their lord's death. They were eventually ordered to commit suicide.

1703. A great earthquake and fire at Edo was followed in the next five years by several other catastrophes, including the last eruption of Mt. Fuji (1707).

1709–1713. **IENOBU**, as *shōgun*. With the aid of the orthodox Confucian scholar, **Arai Haku-seki** (1657–1725), this able and vigorous ruler carried out a series of much-needed financial reforms.

1713–1716. The infant **Ietsugu** as *shōgun*.

1715. The quantity of copper allowed exported by the Dutch was greatly reduced. Copper was the mainstay of the Dutch trade, but its export by them and by the Chinese was a drain on the metal resources of the land. This reduction was followed later by even greater reductions and resulted in the limitation of the number of Dutch vessels calling at Japan to two a year.

1716–1745. YOSHIMUNE as *shōgun* (d. 1751). Since Hidetada's line had come to an end the new *shōgun* was chosen from the Tokugawa house of Kii, which, with the houses of Owari and Mito, were made by Ieyasu the three Tokugawa cadet branches (*Gosanke*) from which *shōgun* were to be selected when needed. Perhaps next to Ieyasu the ablest and wisest of the Tokugawa rulers, Yoshimune attempted to revive the feudal regimentation and military virtues of Ieyasu's day and to carry through economic reforms. He also encouraged scholarship in all fields, and the Confucian scholar, **Muro Kyūsō** (1658–1734), was one of his chief advisers. Despite this able leadership, economic and social ills began to become acute in Yoshimune's time. The peasants were losing the ownership of their land, and the farm population began to decline because of infanticide and movements to the towns. The military class was badly indebted to the merchants, and to save them from ruin a long series of petty laws in favor of the debtor class was commenced at this time. These economic conditions led to a mingling of the classes, which began to efface the old rigid class barriers.

1720. Yoshimune removed the ban on the study of Europe and on the importation of European books, exclusive of those on religion. This broadminded move made possible the development of a small but vigorous group of students of Dutch and through this medium of occidental sciences, particularly medicine. A manuscript Dutch-Japanese dictionary was produced in 1745, and in 1774 **Sugita Gempaku** translated a text on anatomy. This early start in the occidental scientific method produced achievements in cartography and military science and proved of great value in Restoration days.

1732–1733. A great famine in western Japan was met with positive measures of relief by Yoshimune.

1742. The criminal law of the land was codified for the benefit of judges and administrators. This codification remained the basis of criminal law during the rest of the Tokugawa period.

1745–1760. IESHIGE as *shōgun* (d. 1761). An incompetent sensualist, Ieshige made no attempt to stem the rapid administrative and economic decline which set in after Yoshimune's death in 1751.

1758. Takenouchi Shikibu (1714?–1768), a scholar favoring an imperial restoration, and his noble disciples in Kyōto were punished by Edo.

1760–1786. IEHARU as *shōgun*. Though an able man, Ieharu was dominated by the tyrannical and avaricious **Tanuma Okitsugu** (often called Mototsugu) (1719–1788), and Tokugawa rule continued its downward course. During this period peasant uprisings became frequent and serious, and they continued to be so until the fall of the Tokugawa.

1783. A great **eruption of Mt. Asama** and a famine in the north came as a double climax to a series of disasters resulting in

1787. Rice riots in Edo.

1787–1793. Matsudaira Sadanobu (1759–1829) as head of the government for the child *shōgun,* **Ienari,** carried through a series of reforms. At this same time imperialist opposition to Edo became apparent in Kyōto and the military government became aware of the menace of the rapidly expanding European powers.

(Cont. p. 853.)

V. The Modern Period

V. The Modern Period

A. Science and Society, 1800–1960

1. *Philosophical, Religious, and Social Thought*

(From p. 502)

1802. The French author, **François René de Chateaubriand** (1768–1848), initiated the Catholic revival with his *Génie du christianisme,* stressing the aesthetic rather than the theological aspect of the faith.

1803. The *Traité d'économie politique* of **Jean-Baptiste Say** (1767–1832) was one of the most lucid and influential expositions of economic liberalism. Say followed it in 1828–1830 with a much more extensive *Cours complet d'économie politique pratique.*

1806. **Johann F. Herbart's** (1776–1841) *Allgemeine Pädogogik,* a landmark in the development of modern education based on psychology and ethics.

1807. The Hegelian philosophy of the absolute, the dominant philosophy of the early 19th century, was introduced by **Georg W. F. Hegel** (1770–1831) in his *Phänomenologie des Geistes,* followed by *Wissenschaft der Logik* (1812–1816) and *Grundlinien der Philosophie des Rechts* (1821).

1810. The political philosophy of conservatism was further elaborated in the brilliant writings of **Joseph de Maistre** (1754–1821), the *Essai sur le principe générateur des constitutions politiques* (1810) and especially *Du pape* (1819), with its emphasis on the importance of papal authority.

1813. **Robert Owen** (1771–1858), British industrialist and philanthropist, is generally regarded as the first of the **Utopian Socialists.** In his *New View of Society* (1813) he argued for co-operation in production and advocated the organization of new social units, many of which (notably **New Harmony,** Indiana, 1825–1828) were established in Europe and the United States. Subsequently the French reformer, **Charles Fourier** (1772–1837), proposed the setting up of *phalanstères* or co-operative communities in a rural setting; and **Étienne Cabet** (1788–1856) in his *Voyage en Icarie* (1840) pictured an imaginative, highly planned, and regulated community. **Louis Blanc** (1811–1882) in his *Organisation du travail* (1839) urged the foundation of state-financed producers' associations, while **Pierre-Joseph Proudhon** (1809–1865), the great French polemicist, demanded justice, equality, and anarchy as the only remedies for the corruption of society. In exile in Paris, the self-educated German tailor, **Wilhelm Weitling** (1808–1871), came under the influence of French socialist ideas. In his *Garantien der Harmonie und Freiheit* (1842) he presented a system not unlike those of Fourier and Cabet. **Johann Karl Rodbertus** (1805–1875) was also instrumental in introducing French ideas into Germany.

1815–1831. **Friedrich Karl von Savigny** (1779–1861) in his six-volume *Geschichte des römischen Rechts im Mittelalter* contributed greatly to the development of the historical school of jurisprudence.

Georg W. F. Hegel, 1770–1831

Robert Owen, 1771–1858

David Ricardo, 1772–1823

Count Henri de Saint-Simon, 1760–1825

Auguste Comte, 1798–1857

Arthur Schopenhauer, 1788–1860

thought but, on the basis of his late book *Le nouveau christianisme* (1825), organized a Saint-Simonian sect on communist principles. This was soon suppressed by the authorities. Meanwhile Saint-Simon's secretary, **Auguste Comte** (1798–1857), developed his scientific thought and founded the philosophy known as positivism (*Cours de philosophie positive*, six volumes, 1830–1842; *Système de politique positive*, four volumes, 1851–1854).

1817–1821. The Abbé **Felicité de Lamennais** (1782–1854) wrote an eloquent defense of papal and royal authority in his *Essai sur l'indifférence en matière de religion*, but after 1830 became converted to liberalism. With **Count Charles de Montalembert** (1810–1870) he launched the liberal Catholic movement, which was condemned by the papacy. Eventually Lamennais became identified with the socialist movement. His fervent booklet *Paroles d'un croyant* (1833) was at once translated into many languages and aroused much sympathy for the lower classes.

1819. Arthur **Schopenhauer's** (1788–1860) *Die Welt als Wille und Vorstellung* formulated a philosophy of pessimism which, though generally ignored for a generation, became highly influential in the later 19th century.

1819–1837. Jacob **Grimm's** (1785–1863) *Deutsche Grammatik* was a landmark in the development of modern philology. Jacob and his brother Wilhelm (1786–1859) collaborated in collecting folktales, myths, and laws, and in publishing a great dictionary of the German language (Vol. I, 1854).

1819. The Swiss historian **Simonde de Sismondi** (1773–1842) in his *Nouveaux principes d'économie politique* attacked the *laissez-faire* doctrines of the liberal school and was one of the first to call for state action in behalf of the helpless working classes.

1821–1822. *Der christliche Glaube nach den Grundsätzen der evangelischen Kirche*, one of the great theological treatises of the century, by **Friederich Schleiermacher** (1768–1834). The book emphasized the individual and

Jacob Grimm, 1785–1863

1816–1826. **Karl Ludwig von Haller** (1768–1854) published his six-volume *Restauration der Staatswissenschaften*, one of the most comprehensive as it was one of the last refutations of 18th-century political theory and restatements of the principles of absolutism and paternalism.

1817. The *Principles of Political Economy and Taxation* by the British banker **David Ricardo** (1772–1823) provided a classical formulation of economic doctrine. Ricardo set forth the law of "differential rent" and explained wages as tending to seek the minimum subsistence level. He also analyzed the conflicting interests of social classes, thereby foreshadowing the doctrine of the class struggle. His teaching was enthusiastically adopted by the rising manufacturing class and was further elaborated in England by the utilitarian **James Mill** (1773–1836), **John Ramsay McCulloch** (1789–

1864), and **Nassau William Senior** (1790–1864), and in France by **Pellegrino Rossi** (1787–1848), **Charles Dunoyer** (1786–1863), **Michel Chevalier** (1806–1879), and **Frédéric Bastiat** (1801–1850).

1817–1818. **Count Henri de Saint-Simon** (1760–1825), eccentric scion of the high French aristocracy, published his four-volume study of industry (*L'industrie, ou discussions politiques, morales et philosophiques*) followed by *Du système industriel* (1821) and *Le catéchisme des industriels* (1823). In these writings he called for a reorganization of society to accord with modern methods of production and to assure the greatest good of the greatest number. He dreamed of integrating the sciences in a new sociology and forecast modern technocracy. His disciples, **Prosper Enfantin** (1796–1864) and **Saint-Amand Bazard** (1791–1832) not only systematized and expounded his

emotional side of the Protestant religion and contended against dogmatism and rigidity.

1825. **Augustin Thierry's** (1795–1856) *Histoire de la conquête de l'Angleterre par les Normands* provided a highly colored, romantic narrative history and at the same time pictured the ruling aristocracies as brutal conquerors and exploiters of "the people." The French statesman, **François Guizot** (1787–1874), in his brilliant lectures *Histoire de la civilisation en Europe* (1828), likewise stressed the importance of the middle class and the rise of representative institutions.

1825. **James Mill's** (1773–1836) *Analysis of the Phenomena of the Human Mind* was a basic work of modern psychology.

1826. Beginning of the publication of the *Monumenta Germaniae Historica,* the first of many scholarly collections of historical sources and a landmark in the development of national history.

1833. Establishment of a historical seminar by **Leopold von Ranke** (1795–1886) as a center for advanced training in historical writing. Ranke's emphasis on criticism of sources and the utmost objectivity in presentation marked the beginning of modern professional history. His *Die römischen Päpste* (1834–1839) was only the first of various historical studies of the 16th and 17th centuries.

1834–1840. *La Démocratie en Amérique* by **Alexis de Tocqueville** (1805–1859), a most discerning analytical study of democracy, based largely on personal observation and study.

1835–1836. **David Friedrich Strauss** (1808–1874) published *Das Leben Jesu* (two volumes), a critical examination of the sources that led him to question the historicity of Jesus. Strauss's book marked the appearance of the **Young Hegelians,** a group that interpreted the Hegelian philosophy in a radical and destructive sense: **Bruno Bauer** (1809–1882): *Kritik der evangelischen Synoptiker* (1841); **Ludwig Feuerbach** (1804–1872): *Das Wesen des Christentums* (1841); **Max Stirner** (1806–1856): *Der einzige und sein Eigentum* (1845).

1841. **Friedrick List** (1789–1846) in his *Nationales System der politischen Ökonomie* stressed national welfare rather than individual gain and propounded a theory of relativity in economic policy: countries in the early stages of industrialization should protect their industries until free trade should become feasible.

1843–1845. In a series of brilliant writings (*Euten-Eller,* 1843; *Begrebet Angst,* 1844; *Stadier paa Livetsvej,* 1845) the Danish philosopher **Sören Kierkegaard** repudiated the Hegelian philosophy and preached a religion of acceptance and suffering on the part of the individual. His teaching presaged the philosophy of existentialism.

1848. **John Stuart Mill's** (1806–1873) *Principles of Political Economy* was the most logical and persuasive exposition of classical economics, with some concessions to state intervention where private initiative could not work.

1848. **Karl Marx** (1818–1883) and **Friedrich Engels** (1820–1895) issued the *Communist Manifesto,* a fiery appeal to the workers of all countries to unite in the struggle against capitalist exploitation, and at the same time a succinct presentation of "scientific" as contrasted with "utopian" socialism.

1851. **Herbert Spencer's** (1820–1903) *Social Statics,* the first work of the author of *Synthetic Philosophy* (*First Principles,* 1862), an attempt to organize the corpus of human knowledge and to establish the laws of social evolution.

1851. The *Ensayo sobre el Catolicismo, el Liberalismo y el Socialismo,* by **Juan Donoso Cortés** (1809–1853), the Spanish statesman who clearly reflected the fears inspired by the revolutions of 1848 and the ensuing disillusionment with liberalism and radicalism.

1853–1855. **Count Joseph de Gobineau's** (1816–1882) *Essai sur l'inégalité des races humaines,* the basis for much later writing on racial superiority.

1855. *Kraft und Stoff,* by **Ludwig Büchner** (1824–1899), a classic of modern materialism.

1857. Publication of the first volume of **Henry**

Herbert Spencer, 1820–1903

T. Buckle's (1821–1862) *History of Civilisation in England,* a valiant attempt to approach history scientifically.

1860. *Die Cultur der Renaissance in Italien,* by the Swiss historian **Jakob Burckhardt** (1818–1897), was a masterpiece of cultural history and a brilliant essay in interpretation. Likewise Burckhardt's posthumous *Weltgeschichtliche Betrachtungen* (1898) was a highly provocative critique of the materialistic, democratic culture in which he lived.

1861. **Johann J. Bachofen's** (1815–1887) study *Das Mutterrecht* explored the matriarchal institutions of primitive man and greatly stimulated anthropological investigations.

1863. **Ernest Renan's** (1823–1892) *Vie de Jésus* was the first of a series of studies of the origins of Christianity. Translated into all European languages, it was a classic of urbane

Alexis de Tocqueville, 1805–1859

Ludwig Feuerbach, 1804–1872

Karl Marx, 1818–1883

Ivan Petrovich Pavlov (1849–1936) performing (center *with white beard*) *a demonstration before students*

skepticism and rationalism. In his *Réforme intellectuelle et morale* (1871) he called in question the democratic system and envisaged government by an intellectual elite.

1864. The foundation of the **First International Workingmen's Association** by Karl Marx, with headquarters first in London, then in New York. Designed to unite the workers of all countries in support of Marxian socialism, it was eventually wrecked (1876) by the conflict between Marx and Bakunin, who advocated "direct action" to hasten the advent of anarchy. After Bakunin's death anarchist doctrine was

Friedrich von Nietzsche, 1844–1900

further elaborated by **Prince Peter Kropotkin** (1842–1921) and in the later 19th century gained many adherents, especially in the Latin countries, where a series of assassinations and other outrages were committed in the 1880's and 1890's.

1867, 1885, 1895. *Das Kapital* (three volumes) by Karl Marx, an elaborate analysis of economic and social history and at the same time the basic exposition of "scientific" socialism.

1879. Wilhelm Wundt (1832–1920) established the first psychological laboratory. **Ivan Petrovich Pavlov** (1849–1936) discovered the "conditioned reflex" and induced "experimental neurosis" in dogs.

1883–1888. The provocative and highly original works of cultural criticism of **Friedrich von Nietzsche** (1844–1900): *Also sprach Zarathustra* (1883); *Jenseits von Gut und Böse* (1886); *Zur Genealogie der Moral* (1887); *Der Wille zur Macht* (1888). Nietzsche denounced the morality of slaves and called for the utmost development of the individual, even at the cost of much suffering and sacrifice. Tremendous influence of his doctrine of the "superman" in the early 20th century.

1886–1890. The *Lehrbuch der Dogmengeschichte* of **Adolf von Harnack** (1851–1930) was only the most outstanding of that scholar's many studies of Christian dogma and of the influence of Greek thought and religion on the development of Christianity.

1889–1914. The **Second International Workingmen's Association,** which held periodic meetings of representatives of the various national Social Democratic parties. It never had any central authority and at all times suffered from divergence of interest among its constituents. It was finally discredited by the patriotic participation of the Socialist parties in the First World War.

1890. Gabriel Tarde (1843–1903) published his

Les lois d'imitation, a pioneer work in the field of social psychology. At the same time **Pierre Janet** (1859–1949) carried on studies of hypnosis and hysteria. In 1895 **Gustave Le Bon** (1841–1931) published his *Psychologie des foules.*

1890. William James (1842–1910), the American psychologist, published his *Principles of Psychology,* to be followed by *The Will to Believe* (1897), *The Varieties of Religious Experience* (1902), and *Pragmatism* (1907). James' "pragmatism" viewed thinking and knowledge as aspects of the struggle to live. This school of thought went back to the Amer-

William James, 1842–1910

ican logician **Charles Sanders Peirce** (1839–1914) and was espoused also by **John Dewey** (1859–1952): *How We Think* (1909); *Democracy and Education* (1916). In Europe the related "logical empiricists" included **Pierre Duhem** (1861–1916), **Ernst Mach** (1836–1916), and **Henri Poincaré** (1854–1912).

1893. *Appearance and Reality,* by **Francis H. Bradley** (1846–1924), rejected utilitarianism and attempted a return to absolute idealism.

1897–1922. The philosophical writings of **Henri Bergson** (1859–1941) stressing intuition and irrational forces: *Matière et mémoire* (1897); *Évolution créatrice* (1906); *Durée et simultanéité* (1922).

1899. The revisionist or reformist current in social democracy was established by **Eduard Bernstein** (1850–1932) in his *Die Voraussetzungen des Sozialismus und die Aufgaben der Sozialdemokratie,* in which he queried Marx's predictions and advocated evolutionary as distinguished from revolutionary socialism.

1900. *Traumdeutung,* by **Sigmund Freud** (1856–1939), may be taken to mark the beginning of **psychoanalysis.** Other important works: *Über Psychoanalyse* (1910); *Vorlesungen zur Einführung in die Psychoanalyse* (1917); *Das Ich und das Es* (1923); *Die Zukunft einer Illusion* (1927); *Das Unbehagen in der Kultur* (1930); *Neue Folge der Vorlesungen* (1932). Among Freud's earlier adherents were **Alfred Adler** (1870–1937) and **Carl G. Jung** (1875–1964), both of whom broke away and established schools of their own.

1902. **John A. Hobson** (1858–1940) published *Imperialism: A Study,* undoubtedly the most comprehensive critique of economic imperialism. Through the German theorists **Rosa Luxemburg** and **Rudolf Hilferding** his arguments found their way into Lenin's famous pamphlet: *Imperialism, the Highest Stage of Capitalism* (1916), which constitutes the official Communist view.

1904–1905. **Max Weber** (1864–1920), the eminent German economist-sociologist, published *Die protestantische Ethik und der Geist des Kapitalismus,* in which he concluded that the teachings of Luther and Calvin were among the main springs of the capitalist spirit. This thesis was further developed by **Richard H. Tawney** (1880–1962) *Religion and the Rise of Capitalism* (1926).

1908. **Georges Sorel's** (1847–1922) *Réflexions sur la violence* supplied a theoretical background for the syndicalist movement, an outgrowth of anarchism which aimed at destruction of the state through a general strike engineered by trade unions.

1910–1913. *Principia Mathematica,* by **Bertrand Russell** (1872–1970) and **Alfred North Whitehead** (1861–1947), setting forth the principles of mathematical logic which were to be applied to sociology, education, and politics.

1912. **Gestalt psychology** expounded by **Max Wertheimer** (1880–1943) and developed further by **Kurt Koffka** (1886–1941) and **Wolfgang Köhler** (1887–1967).

1916. **Vilfredo Pareto** (1848–1923), in his *Trattato di Sociologia Generale,* provided a comprehensive mathematical analysis of economic and sociological problems, based on the distinction between the fundamental motivations of human nature (*residues*) and their outward appearance or rationalization (*derivations*).

1918–1922. **Oswald Spengler** (1880–1936), in a learned and brilliantly written study, *Der Untergang des Abendlandes,* produced a cyclical interpretation of history and forecast the eclipse of western civilization as inevitable.

1934–1954. *A Study of History* (ten volumes) by **Arnold J. Toynbee** (1889–) constituted an exhaustive re-examination of human development in the light of an idealist philosophy of history.

1936. **John Maynard Keynes** (1883–1946), in his *General Theory of Employment, Interest and Money,* explained how and why an economy might fail to maintain a level of activity required for full employment. Though dealing primarily with short-run phenomena, the "Keynesian economics" became crucial in the development of theories of economic growth.

Bertrand Russell, 1872–1970

Oswald Spengler, 1880–1936

Ernst Mach, 1836–1916

Max Weber, 1864–1920

Sigmund Freud, 1856–1939

2. *Science and Learning*

(From p. 506)

a. MATHEMATICS, PHYSICS, ASTRONOMY

1799-1825. Pierre Laplace (1749-1827) published his *Traité de mécanique céleste,* in which he aimed at presenting analytically all of the developments in gravitational astronomy since the time of Newton.

1800. The **Royal Institution of Great Britain,** center for the diffusion of technical and scientific knowledge, was founded by the American **Benjamin Thompson (Count Rumford)** (1753-1814).

1801. Giuseppe Piazzi (1746-1826) discovered the first asteroid *Ceres;* its orbit was computed by Gauss.

1801. Carl Friedrich Gauss (1777-1855) published *Disquisitiones arithmeticae,* developing the theory of congruences, quadratic forms, and quadratic residues, using methods and concepts basic to the subsequent progress of number theory and algebra.

1802. Thomas Young (1773-1829) demonstrated in his paper "On the Theory of Light and Colours" that the properties of light, including interference phenomena, are satisfactorily explained by considering it as a periodic wave motion in an aether.

1803-1804. William Herschel (1738-1822) reported observations on six cases of double stars, and concluded that each was a binary or connected pair of stars in which each member influenced the motion of the other. This was the first observation of changes taking place under gravity beyond the solar system.

1809. Gauss expounded his new "least-squares" method of computing planetary orbits in *Theoria motus corporum coelestium.*

1815-1821. Augustin Fresnel (1788-1827), through a series of mathematical and experimental researches on interference, diffraction, polarization, and double refraction, was able to establish the **transverse wave theory of light.**

1817. Joseph von Fraunhofer (1787-1826), following the 1802 observations by **William Wollaston** (1766-1828) that the solar spectrum contains black lines, and using an improved spectroscope, charted these lines, naming the principal ones.

1820. Hans Oersted (1777-1851) showed that a magnetic needle placed near a current-carrying wire deviated from its position, and that the direction of deviation depended on the direction of current flow.

1820. André-Marie Ampère (1775-1836) repeated Oersted's experiments (1820), and reported his discovery that two current-carrying wires exercise a reciprocal action upon one another. He later established a mathematical theory of known electrical phenomena, and experimentally demonstrated the principles of the electrodynamics of adjacent current-carrying conductors.

1821-1859. Michael Faraday (1791-1867) demonstrated electromagnetic rotation (1821) and discovered electromagnetic induction (1831). He independently discovered self-induced currents (1834), found two years earlier by **Joseph Henry** (1797-1878). He found the laws of electrochemical decomposition and conduction, and established a general theory of electrolysis. He also introduced the concept of *field* into physics. These and other investigations were collected in his *Experimental Researches in Electricity* (1839-1855) and in his *Experimental Researches in Chemistry and Physics* (1859).

1821-1823. Augustin-Louis Cauchy (1789-1857), who successfully sought rigor in analysis, gave the first essentially correct definition of limit in *Cours d'analyse* (1821). This work also contained the first systematic study of convergence of series and general tests for it, and the first theory of functions of a complex variable. He defined the derivative and integral in terms of limit, and obtained the fundamental theorem of calculus (1823).

1822. Joseph Fourier (1768-1830) published *Théorie analytique de la chaleur,* giving a mathematical theory of heat conduction. He introduced trigonometric series, *Fourier series* of arbitrary, piecewise, continuous functions, thus extending the notion of function.

1824. Niels Abel (1802-1829) proved that the general quintic cannot be solved by radicals.

1824. Nicolas Sadi Carnot (1796-1832) published *Réflexions sur la puissance motrice du feu.* Here he showed that the transformation of heat into motive power depends on the quantity of heat ("caloric"), and the temperature difference between the source and sink of heat. He also introduced the reversible cycle of a heat engine—now called the *Carnot cycle.*

1827-1829. Niels Abel and **Karl Jacobi** (1804-1851) independently founded the theory of elliptic (doubly periodic) functions.

1827. Georg S. Ohm (1789-1854) found that the ratio of electromotive force to the current, in an electric circuit, is a constant (*Ohm's Law*) and called this constant the resistance of the circuit.

1829-1832. Nikolai Lobachevskii (1793-1856) and **János Bólyai** (1802-1860) independently developed the first **non-Euclidean geometries.**

1831. The foundation of the British Association for the Advancement of Science, dedicated to the promotion and professionalization of British science. The B.A.A.S. was based on a German model, **Gesellschaft deutscher Naturforscher,** and served as an example for the **American Association for the Advancement of Science** (1848).

1832. Evariste Galois (1811-1832) left posthumous papers using group theory to give necessary and sufficient conditions for the solution of equations by radicals. He emphasized the importance of the invariant or normal subgroup.

1833. Charles Babbage (1792-1871) conceived

Michael Faraday, 1791-1867

an "analytical engine" (a large-scale digital calculator). In 1822, he had made a working model of a smaller, "difference engine" to calculate tables of functions by finite difference methods.

1833. Gauss, in his *Intensitas vis magnetica terrestris,* presented a rigorous mathematical analysis of the earth's magnetic field, and proposed a system of absolute units for the measurement of terrestrial magnetism.

1834. Adolphe Quetelet (1796-1874) initiated the **London Statistical Society,** and later helped found several other such groups. He applied the theory of probability to the statistics of society, especially in *Sur l'homme* (1835).

1835. Cauchy published the first existence proof for the solution of a differential equation.

1838-1839. Friedrich Bessel (1784-1846), **Friedrich Struve** (1793-1864), and **Thomas Henderson** (1798-1844) measured *stellar parallax* for the first time.

1842. Julius von Mayer (1814-1878) stated that the total amount of energy in the universe is constant (a form of the **first law of thermodynamics**), and that in natural processes energy is never lost, but only transformed from one kind to another.

1843-1846. John Adams (1819-1892) and **Urbain LeVerrier** (1811-1877) independently predicted the existence of a new planet and constructed its orbit from a consideration of irregularities in the motion of Uranus. This planet, later named *Neptune,* was sighted in 1846 by **Johann Galle** (1812-1910)—a great triumph for gravitational astronomy.

1843. James Joule (1818-1889) sought the connection between electricity, heat, and mechanical energy in "The Calorific Effects of Magneto-Electricity, and the Mechanical Value of Heat," and determined by four different procedures the mechanical equivalent of heat. In 1847 he enunciated the principle of the **conservation of energy.**

1846. The **Smithsonian Institution** for the increase and diffusion of knowledge was estab-

Hermann Helmholtz, 1821–1894

William Crookes, 1832–1919

Wilhelm K. Röntgen, 1845–1923

lished by the United States Congress, utilizing the funds bequeathed by England's **James Smithson** (1765–1829).

1847. Hermann Helmholtz (1821–1894) announced the principle of the conservation of energy in *Über die Erhaltung der Kraft.* He discussed the principle in great theoretical detail and elucidated its meaning.

1848. William Thomson (Lord Kelvin) (1824–1907) established the absolute thermodynamic scale of temperature, which is named after him.

1849. Armand Fizeau (1819–1896) for the first time successfully measured the **speed of light** by observations which do not involve astronomical constants.

1849. Jean Bernard Foucault (1819–1868) measured the speed of light accurately in media other than air, and thereby determined that the speed of light in air is greater than in water. Later, in a famous pendulum experiment, he demonstrated that the earth rotates (1851).

1850. William Cranch Bond (1789–1859), using the Harvard College Observatory's 15-inch refractor, took the first photograph of a star.

1850. Rudolph Clausius (1822–1888) announced the **second law of thermodynamics:** heat cannot of itself pass from a colder to a warmer body. In *Über die bewegende Kraft der Wärme* (1865) he introduced the term *entropy,* stating that the entropy of the universe tends to increase.

1851. Bernhard Riemann (1826–1866) introduced topological considerations into analysis.

1853. The first **International Statistical Congress** was held at Brussels, organized and inspired by **Adolphe Quetelet.**

1854. Riemann established the mathematical importance of non-Euclidean geometries, discussing them in his general theory of manifolds. In the same year he gave the most comprehensive and general definition of the classical definite integral, since called the *Riemann integral.*

1854. George Boole (1815–1864) published *The Laws of Thought,* an expansion of his 1847 work, *The Mathematical Analysis of Logic,*

which marks the beginning of **symbolic logic,** i.e., the attempt to express the laws of thought in algebraic symbols.

1856. Karl Weierstrass (1815–1897) began to lecture at the University of Berlin. In these lectures, which spanned over thirty years, he gave the modern (delta-epsilon) definition of a limit, eliminated the remaining vagueness in the concepts of the calculus, introduced the notion of uniform convergence, and founded the theory of functions of a complex variable on power series.

1860–1877. James Clerk Maxwell (1831–1879) and **Ludwig Boltzmann** (1844–1906) developed statistical mechanics, a theory of the behavior of a gas considered as a collection of large numbers of molecules obeying the laws of classical mechanics.

1863. The United States Congress approved creation of the **National Academy of Sciences** as a scientific adviser to the federal government and promoter of scientific research.

1868. William Huggins (1824–1910), noting a slight shift toward the red in the spectrum of Sirius, calculated the radial velocity of a star for the first time.

1870–1883. Georg Cantor (1845–1918) published his major works, founding the **theory of sets** (1870) and the **theory of transfinite numbers** (1883).

1872–1882. Richard Dedekind (1831–1916) gave arithmetic definitions of irrational numbers (the *Dedekind cut*), constituting the first rigorous theory of irrationals.

1873. Johannes van der Waals (1837–1923) found an equation of state for imperfect gases.

1873. Maxwell published his *Treatise on Electricity and Magnetism* where he described the properties of the electromagnetic field in a series of equations (*Maxwell equations*) which entailed the electromagnetic theory of light.

1877. Giovanni Schiaparelli (1835–1910) observed long, narrow, straight, intersecting, dark lines on Mars, which he called *canali.*

1877–1893. Francis Galton (1822–1911) and **Karl Pearson** (1857–1936) developed the major statistical tools of present-day social science,

e.g. regression (Galton, 1877), correlation coefficients (Galton, 1888), moments and standard deviation (Pearson, 1893).

1878. William Crookes (1832–1919) showed that cathode rays proceed in straight lines, are capable of turning a small wheel, can be deflected by a magnet, excite fluorescence in certain substances, and heat and sometimes even melt some metals.

1884. Gottlob Frege (1848–1925) published *Grundlagen der Arithmetik,* in which arithmetical concepts were defined in logical terms.

1887. Heinrich Hertz (1857–1894) demonstrated the existence of electromagnetic waves in the space about a discharging Leyden jar, and found that electromagnetic waves were propagated with the velocity of light as Maxwell had predicted (1873). Hertz's work led to modern radio communications.

1887. Albert Michelson (1852–1931) and **Edward Morley** (1831–1923) announced that they were unable to detect any effect of the earth's motion through the aether in experiments with an extremely sensitive interferometer.

1895. Wilhelm K. Röntgen (1845–1923) announced the discovery of x-rays in *Eine neue Art von Strahlen.*

1895. John W. Strutt (Lord Rayleigh) (1842–1919) and **William Ramsay** (1852–1916) discovered the "inert" or "noble" gas *argon.* Ramsay later discovered the other noble gases: helium, krypton, neon, xenon, and radon.

1895. Henri Poincaré (1854–1912) founded **algebraic topology.** He first applied topology to celestial mechanics (1892–1899).

1896. Alfred B. Nobel (1833–1896) endowed prizes for outstanding achievements in physics, chemistry, medicine, and physiology. The first prizes were awarded in 1901, to **Wilhelm K. Röntgen** in physics, **Jacobus H. van't Hoff** (1852–1911) in chemistry, and **Emil A. von Behring** (1854–1917) in medicine and physiology.

1896. Antoine H. Becquerel (1852–1908) discovered radioactivity in uranium compounds.

1897. Joseph John Thomson (1856–1940) announced the discovery of the **electron,** the first

Max Planck, 1858–1947

Marie Sklodowska Curie, 1867–1934

Albert Einstein, 1879–1955

Niels Bohr, 1885–1962

sub-atomic particle, and determined experimentally the ratio of its mass to its charge.

1900. Max Planck (1858–1947) stated that energy is not emitted continuously from radiating bodies, but in discrete parcels, or **quanta.**

1902-1904. Henri Lebesgue (1875–1941) gave a theory of measure and the Lebesgue integral, extending the notions of integration and area to more general sets.

1904. Marie Sklodowska Curie (1867–1934) showed that pitchblende (uranium ore) contained two new radioactive elements: **radium** and **polonium.**

1904. Ernst Zermelo (1871–1953) published a proof that every set can be well ordered, which made possible the use of transfinite methods in mathematics.

1905. Albert Einstein (1879–1955) announced his **special theory of relativity,** which required a fundamental revision in the traditionally held Newtonian views of space and time, and introduced the celebrated equation $E = mc^2$.

1905. Einstein attributed to radiation itself a particle structure, and by supposing each particle of light **(photon)** to carry a quantum of energy, explained the photoelectric effect.

1910-1913. Bertrand Russell (1872–1970) and **Alfred North Whitehead** (1861–1947) published *Principia Mathematica,* carrying out the reduction of arithmetic to symbolic logic. This work is the foundation of the calculus of propositions and modern symbolic logic.

1911. Robert A. Millikan (1868–1953) established that electric charge always consists of an integral multiple of a unit charge, which he determined with great accuracy, in his oil-drop experiment.

1911. Ernest Rutherford (1871–1937) introduced the nuclear **model of the atom,** i.e., a small positively charged nucleus, containing most of the mass of the atom, surrounded by electrons.

1911-1913. Ejnar Hertzsprung (1873–1967) studied double stars and their colors, especially in the Pléiades, and with **Henry Norris Russell** (1877–1957) devised the Hertzsprung-Russell Diagram, a graphic way of grouping stars by the relation between their absolute magnitudes and spectral types.

1912. Max von Laue (1879–1960) discovered **X-ray diffraction,** a powerful technique for directly observing the atomic structure of crystals.

1913. Niels Bohr (1885–1962) devised a new model of the atom by applying quantum theory to Rutherford's nuclear atom. Although this model violated classical electromagnetic theory it successfully accounted for the spectrum of hydrogen.

1915. Einstein announced his **general theory of relativity,** which explained the advance of Mercury's perihelion, and predicted the subsequently observed bending of light rays near the sun.

1918. Harlow Shapley (1885–   ), from an extensive study of the distribution of globular clusters and cepheid variable stars, increased the estimated size of our galaxy about ten times. He envisioned the galaxy as a flattened lens-shaped system of stars in which the solar system occupied a position far from the center.

1919. Rutherford found that the collision of alpha particles with nitrogen atoms resulted in the disintegration of the nitrogen and the production of hydrogen nuclei (protons) and an isotope of oxygen. He was the first person to achieve artificial transmutation of an element.

1919. Arthur S. Eddington (1882–1944) and others, by studying data obtained during a total solar eclipse, verified Einstein's prediction of the bending of light rays by the gravitational field of large masses.

1919-1929. Edwin P. Hubble (1889–1953) detected cepheid variable stars in the Andromeda Nebula, a discovery that allowed him to determine the distances between galaxies.

1924. Louis-Victor de Broglie (1892–   ) determined from theoretical considerations that the electron, which had been considered a particle, should behave as a wave under certain circumstances. Experimental confirmation was obtained in 1927 by **Clinton Davisson** (1881–1958) and **Lester H. Germer** (1896–   ).

1925. Wolfgang Pauli (1900–1958) announced the **exclusion principle** (in any atom no two electrons have identical sets of quantum numbers). This principle was an important aid in determining the electron structure of the heavier elements.

1925-1926. Werner Karl Heisenberg (1901–   ) and **Erwin Schrödinger** (1887–1960) independently, and in different ways, laid the theoretical foundations of the new **quantum mechanics** which, though violating classical notions of causality, successfully predicts the behavior of atomic particles.

1927. George Lemaître (1894–   ), in order to explain the red shift in the spectra from distant galaxies, introduced the concept of the **expanding universe. Eddington** pursued research in this subject from 1930.

1928. Paul A. Dirac (1902–   ), by combining quantum mechanics and relativity theory, devised a relativistic **theory of the electron.**

1930. Vannevar Bush (1890–   ) and his associates placed into operation a "differential analyzer," the first modern analog computer.

1931. Ernest O. Lawrence (1901–1958) invented the **cyclotron,** a device for accelerating atomic particles, which has become the fundamental research tool in high-energy physics and has made possible the creation of transuranium elements.

1931. Kurt Gödel (1906–   ) published *Uber formal unentscheidbare Sätze der Principia Mathematica und verwandter Systeme,* showing that in any formal mathematical system in which elementary arithmetic can be done, there are theorems whose truth or falsity cannot be proved.

1932. Karl Jansky reported the reception of radio waves from cosmic sources, making **radio astronomy** possible.

1938-1939. Otto Hahn (1879–1968) and **Otto Strassmann** bombarded uranium with neutrons and found an isotope of barium in the product (1938). **Lise Meitner** (1878–1968) and **Otto Frisch** (1904–   ) explained this result by assuming the fission of the uranium nucleus (**nuclear fission**).

1939. Nicolas Bourbaki (pseudonym assumed by a group of mathematicians) published the first of a long series of expository works on modern mathematics.

1939. Hans A. Bethe (1906–   ) and **Carl von Weizsäcker** (1912–   ) independently proposed two sets of nuclear reactions to account for stellar energies: the carbon-nitrogen cycle and the proton-proton chain.

1939-1945. World War II research needs stimulated the formation of large groups or teams of research workers to concentrate effort on a single problem, e.g., radar and atomic bomb. Such group research has become a common feature of post-war science.

1940. Gödel in *The Consistency of the Axiom of Choice and of the Generalized Continuum Hypothesis with the Axioms of Set Theory,* proved that transfinite methods could not introduce inconsistencies into mathematics.

1942. Enrico Fermi (1901–1954) and associates built the first controlled self-sustaining **nuclear reactor.** Fermi was one of the chief architects of the theory of the atomic nucleus.

1944. Mark I, the Harvard-IBM Automatic Sequence Controlled Calculator was put into operation at Harvard University. This was the first large-scale digital calculating machine.

1945. Vannevar Bush issued the report *Science: The Endless Frontier,* recommending the creation of a United States foundation for the support and encouragement of basic research and education in science. In 1950 the United States Congress established the **National Science Foundation** to implement this recommendation.

1946. The foundation of the **United States Atomic Energy Commission** assured civilian control of United States developments in atomic energy.

1946. ENIAC (Electronic Numerical Integrator and Calculator) was put into operation at the University of Pennsylvania, the first electronic high speed digital calculating machine.

1951. Harold I. Ewen and **Edward M. Purcell** (1912–   ) detected the 21-centimeter hydrogen spectral line in galactic radiation, which had been predicted in 1944 by **Hendrik van de Hulst** (1918–   ). This discovery has

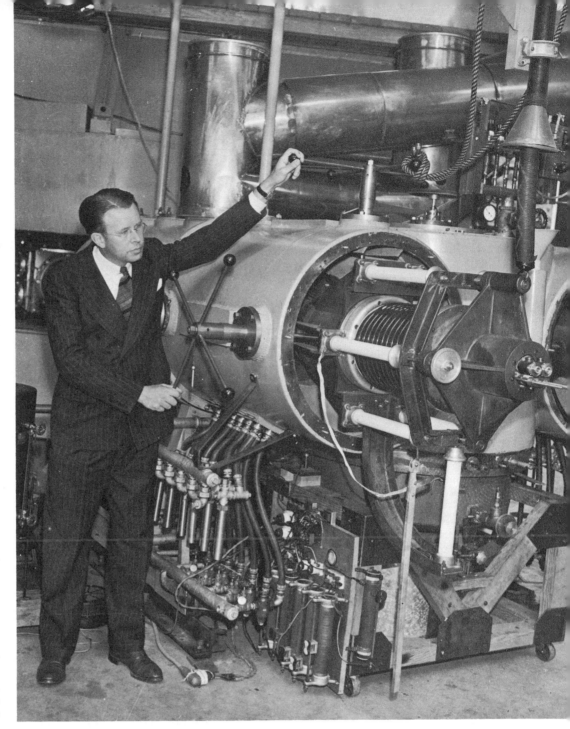

Ernest O. Lawrence (1901–1958) with his invention, the cyclotron

An artist's sketch of the first self-sustaining nuclear chain reactor, 1942

enabled astronomers to map the structure of the Milky Way.

1956. Tsung Dao Lee (1926–) and **Chen Ning Yang** (1922–) showed theoretically that a basic symmetry principle, previously thought to hold in all atomic interactions (conservation of parity), is invalid for weak interactions. **Chien-Shiung Wu** (1915–) in the same year experimentally demonstrated the violation of conservation of parity.

1962. Neil Bartlett announced that he had combined xenon with platinum and fluorine to form xenon-platinum hexafluoride; other compounds of xenon and radon were found, thus destroying the notion that the noble gases are all nonreacting.

b. CHEMISTRY, BIOLOGY, GEOLOGY

1799–1805. Georges Cuvier (1769–1832) founded **comparative anatomy** on functional grounds maintaining that the parts of the organism are correlated to the functioning whole.

1800–1802. Marie-François Bichat (1771–1802) stimulated the separate and systematic study of each anatomical structure and physiological function by his classification of the body into textures or *tissus* each with its particular vital property.

1801. Claude Berthollet (1748–1822) opposed the prevailing doctrine of elective affinities with his **law of mass action.**

1802. John Playfair (1748–1819), friend and disciple of **James Hutton** (1726–1797), produced *Illustrations of the Huttonian Theory of the Earth*, bringing a clear exposition of uniformitarianism to a wide audience and establishing this philosophy as the basis of modern geology.

1802–1804. Jean d'Aubuisson de Voisins (1769–1819) and **Leopold von Buch** (1774–1853), two of the most illustrious students of **Abraham Werner** (1749/50–1817), accepted the volcanic origin of basalt, signalling the defeat of Wernerian neptunism.

1804. Nicholas de Saussure (1767–1845) explained the process of photosynthesis in terms of the new chemistry of **Antoine Lavoisier** (1743–1794).

1807. Humphry Davy (1778–1829), using the new voltaic battery, isolated the metals potassium and sodium.

1807. Establishment of **United States Coast Survey,** the first United States scientific agency.

1807. Foundation of the **Geological Society of London,** which served as a center for research and discussion and as a model for similar societies in other countries.

1808. John Dalton (1766–1844) published his *New System of Chemical Philosophy,* which established the **quantitative atomic theory** in chemistry.

1808. Joseph Gay-Lussac (1778–1850) announced his discovery of the law of combining volumes for gases, i.e., the ratios of the volumes of reacting gases are small whole numbers.

1809. Jean-Baptiste Lamarck (1744–1829), in *Philosophie zoologique,* gave the most complete explanation of his **theory of evolution.** He argued that through a combination of unconscious striving, the physiological effects of use and disuse, and the influence of the environment, anatomical parts became modified.

Georges Cuvier, 1769–1832

Furthermore, he believed that by the "inheritance of acquired characteristics" living forms evolved in an ever-ascending scale of perfection.

1809. Lorenz Oken (1779–1815), one of the leaders of the German **Naturphilosophie** movement, published an anti-mechanist treatise which taught the superiority of intuitively derived concepts, expressed a belief in the archetypal polarities of nature, and championed a search for ideal types and a teleological unity in nature.

1809. Ephraim McDowell (1771–1830) performed a successful ovariotomy, thus showing that surgery of the abdominal cavity was not necessarily fatal.

1811. Amedeo Avogadro (1776–1856) concluded that equal volumes of all gases at the same temperature and pressure contain equal numbers of molecules; in effect he distinguished between atoms and molecules, but his ideas were neglected until 1858.

1811. Georges Cuvier (1769–1832), the founder of modern vertebrate paleontology, and **Alexandre Brongnïart** (1770–1847) brought out their *Essai sur la géographie minéralogique des environs de Paris* with a map, ordering important tertiary strata.

1812. Jöns Berzelius (1779–1848) developed a dualistic electrochemical theory to account for electrolysis and chemical combination.

1815. William Prout (1785–1850) published an anonymous paper in which he advanced the hypothesis that the atoms of all other elements were really aggregates of hydrogen atoms.

1815. William Smith (1769–1839) published his famous **geological map of England and Wales,** and established that specific strata can be identified by their fossil content, the principle upon which historical geology is founded. He also worked out the main divisions of the **Secondary** or **Mesozoic** strata.

1819. Pierre Dulong (1785–1838) and **Alexis Petit** (1791–1820) formulated the rule that the product of the relative atomic weight and the

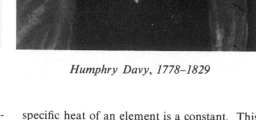

Humphry Davy, 1778–1829

specific heat of an element is a constant. This made possible the experimental determination of relative atomic weights.

1819. René Laënnec (1781–1826) invented the **stethoscope.**

1822. François Magendie (1783–1855) showed that the sensory and motor functions arise from different spinal roots. He was anticipated in 1811 by the more discursive work of **Charles Bell** (1774–1842).

1824. Justus von Liebig (1803–1873) obtained the chair of chemistry at Giessen, where he established the first truly effective laboratory for the teaching of chemistry. He greatly improved methods of organic analysis and, with his students, accurately analyzed a great number of organic compounds.

1826–1840. Johannes Müller (1801–1858) developed his doctrine of specific nerve energies. He taught some of the most productive men in German physiology.

1828. Friedrich Wöhler (1800–1882) announced the **synthesis of urea,** a typical product of animal metabolism. Urea synthesis and subsequent advances in organic synthesis crippled the vitalistic notion that a special force controls life processes.

1828. Karl von Baer (1792–1876) founded modern comparative embryology with the publication of *Über Entwickelungsgeschichte der Thiere.* Here he proclaimed that embryonic development is the history of increasing specificity.

1830–1833. Charles Lyell (1797–1875) published his *Principles of Geology,* a powerful synthesis expounding and extending Hutton's uniformitarian theory.

1831–1836. Charles Darwin (1809–1882), as naturalist aboard *H. M. S. Beagle,* studied South American flora and fauna, and gathered information he was later to use in his theory of evolution.

c. 1831–1852. Roderick Murchison (1792–1871) and **Adam Sedgwick** (1785–1873) described the succession of Paleozoic strata in

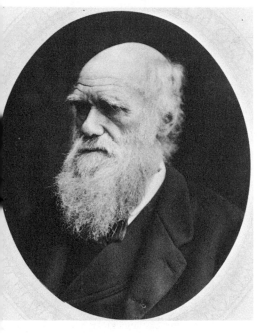

Charles Darwin, 1809–1882

Louis Pasteur, 1822–1895

Ivan M. Sechenov, 1829–1905

Wales, Murchison defining the *Silurian* system (1839) and Sedgwick defining the *Cambrian* system.

1838–1842. The **United States Exploring Expedition,** under the command of Lieut. **Charles Wilkes** (1798–1877), explored the Pacific Ocean, the first example of a United States government-sponsored scientific maritime venture.

1839. Theodor Schwann (1810–1882) extended the 1838 observations on plants cells of **Matthias Schleiden** (1804–1881) into the generalization that cells are the common structural and functional unit of all living organisms.

1840. Louis Agassiz (1807–1873) elucidated the role of glaciers in geological change and enunciated his **ice age theory.**

1841. Carlo Matteucci (1811–1868) demonstrated that a difference of electropotential exists between an excised nerve and damaged muscle. This stimulated **Emil du Bois-Reymond** (1818–1896) to work in electrophysiology and to champion the German school of physiologists who wished to reduce physiological phenomena to physical and chemical processes.

1842. Liebig published *Die Thierchemie,* which promoted the analysis of organic compounds and described all physical and mental actions of animals as the result of chemical reactions.

1846. William T. G. Morton (1819–1868) gave the first public demonstration of the use of **ether as an anaesthetic** in surgery.

1847. Carl Ludwig (1816–1895) perfected the **kymograph,** which became an invaluable measuring instrument for physiology.

1848. Louis Pasteur (1822–1895), in a series of brilliantly conceived and executed experiments, demonstrated the connection between the optical activity of organic molecules and crystaline structure, thus founding **stereochemistry.**

1848. Claude Bernard (1813–1878) demonstrated the ability of the liver to store sugar in the form of glycogen. His widely read

Introduction à l'étude de la médecine expérimentale (1865) influenced literary men as well as scientists.

1852. Edward Frankland (1825–1899) announced his **theory of valency,** i.e., each atom has a certain "valency," or capacity for combining with a definite number of other atoms.

1856–1864. Bernard evolved the concept of the *milieu interieur,* envisioning that cells were autonomous physiological units, yet were dependent upon and protected by the internal environment of the whole organism.

1856–1866. Hermann Helmholtz (1821–1894) extended the doctrine of specific nerve energies developed by **Johannes Müller** to vision and hearing, indicating the penetration of physics and physiology into psychology.

1857–1860. Louis Pasteur demonstrated that fermentation was a product of yeast cell activity. This challenged the view of Liebig that the ferment was merely an unstable chemical substance.

1858. Rudolph Virchow (1821–1902) in *Die Cellularpathologie* declared that disease reflects an impairment of cellular organization. Here, too, he stated his famous generalization *"omnis cellula e cellula"* (all cells arise from cells) and described the cell as the basic element of the life process.

1858. Friedrich A. Kekulé (1829–1896) published *Über die Konstitution und die Metamorphosen der chemischen Verbindungen und über die chemische Natur des Kohlenstoffs,* in which he recognized that carbon is quadrivalent, and that carbon atoms link together to form long chains that serve as skeletons for organic molecules.

1858. Stanislao Cannizzaro (1826–1910) showed that one could unambiguously determine atomic weights. He was thus able to provide a table giving the correct molecular formulas of many compounds.

1859. Gustav R. Kirchhoff (1824–1887) and **Robert W. Bunsen** (1811–1899) began researches that made **spectrum analysis** a power-

ful method for the investigation of matter. They showed that a chemical element was clearly characterized by its spectrum, and by spectrum analysis they were able to discover previously unknown elements.

1859. Darwin amassed twenty-five years of careful research in *The Origin of Species.* Inspired by the evidence in geology, paleontology, zoogeography, and domestic animal breeding, he declared that species evolved through variation and the natural selection of those individuals best suited to survive in given environmental conditions. A similar theory was developed independently by **Alfred R. Wallace** (1823–1913).

1860. Marcelin Berthelot (1827–1907) published *Chimie organique fondée sur la synthèse,* which showed that total synthesis of all classes of organic compounds from the elements carbon, hydrogen, oxygen, and nitrogen was possible.

1861. Alexander M. Butlerov (1828–1886) introduced the term "chemical structure" at a chemical meeting in Germany. Butlerov shares credit with **Kekulé** for the development of the theory of the structure of organic compounds.

1861. Pasteur, in a classic paper "Mémoire sur les corpuscles organisés qui existent dans l'atmosphère," described a series of experiments which confuted the doctrine of the spontaneous generation of micro-organisms.

1862–1877. Pasteur investigated several types of micro-organisms to advance the **germ theory of disease.** His evidence encouraged **Joseph Lister** (1827–1912) to initiate the practice of **antiseptic surgery** (1865).

1863. Ivan M. Sechenov (1829–1905) published *Reflexes of the Brain,* one of the earliest attempts to establish the physiological basis of psychic processes. His teaching and research was a decisive influence on the development of physiology in Russia.

1865. Gregor Mendel (1822–1884), an Augustinian monk, described cross-breeding experiments with peas which demonstrated the par-

Dmitrii I. Mendeleev, 1834–1907

ticulate nature of inheritance. He concluded that many traits segregated into dominant and recessive alternatives and that combined traits assorted independently. Little attention was paid to his results until 1900 when cytological work suggested such unit characters existed.

1869. **Dmitrii I. Mendeleev** (1834–1907), in *Principles of Chemistry,* devised his periodic table of the chemical elements, which arranged the elements in the order of increasing atomic weight, noted the periodic recurrence of similar properties in groups of elements, and successfully predicted the properties of elements yet to be discovered.

1872–1876. **H. M. S.** *Challenger* made an extended voyage of scientific investigation, led by **Wyville Thomson** (1830–1882). The information gathered and reported largely by **John Murray** (1841–1914) gave much impetus to the science of **oceanography.**

1874. **Jacobus van't Hoff** (1852–1911) and **Achille LeBel** (1847–1930) independently interpreted the 1848 results of **Pasteur** and developed the stereochemistry of carbon.

1878. **Josiah W. Gibbs** (1839–1903), in his rigorously mathematical thermodynamic study on the *Equilibrium of Heterogeneous Substances,* used the concept of chemical potential and introduced the phase rule.

1879. **Ivan P. Pavlov** (1849–1936) showed the production of gastric juices could be achieved without the introduction of food into the stomach. His work in the physiology of digestion led him to develop the concept of the acquired or *conditioned reflex.*

1879. The **United States Geological Survey** was founded, consolidating under one office the several surveys which had been gaining valuable information in western North America for over a decade. Under the directorship of **John W. Powell** (1834–1902) after 1881, the survey grew into a powerful agency for the progress of science in the United States.

1880. **John Milne** (1850–1913) developed the first accurate **seismograph,** permitting the care-ful study of earthquakes and opening the way to new knowledge of the earth's interior.

1882. **Robert Koch** (1843–1910) described the etiology of the **tubercle bacillus.** This discovery led him (1884) to state *Koch's postulates,* a method for isolating micro-organisms and proving that they are specific causes, not merely concomitants, of disease.

1883. **Ilia I. Mechnikov** (1845–1916) described the action of phagocytic cells in transparent starfish larvae. His discovery led to a general explanation of local inflammation.

1883. **Edouard van Beneden** (1845–1901) described how the chromosomes are derived in equal numbers from the conjugating germ cells. This led to the discovery of reduction division in the formation of the gametes.

1887. **Svante A. Arrhenius** (1859–1927) announced his theory of electrolytic dissociation, according to which most of the molecules of an electrolyte are immediately dissociated into two ions when dissolved.

1888–1891. **Wilhelm Roux** (1850–1924) destroyed half of the two-cell stage of a frog's embryo (1888). The remaining cell developed into half an embryo. In 1891 **Hans Driesch** (1867–1941) working with sea urchin embryos got results contradictory to Roux's. This drew attention to the relative rôles of the internal and external environment on the development of cells.

1890. **Emil von Behring** (1854–1917) and **Shíbasaburo Kitasato** (1856–1931) demonstrated that the serum of immunized rabbits neutralized the toxin of tetanus. This discovery opened the possibility that disease could be prevented through the stimulation of specific antibody production.

1892. **August Weismann** (1834–1914) described in *Das Keimplasma* his theory of the continuity of the germ plasm and a scheme for the unfolding of a particulate hereditary pattern in embryogenesis.

1893. **Theobald Smith** (1859–1934), in "Investigations into the Nature, Causation and Prevention of Southern Cattle Fever," demonstrated that parasites could act as vectors of disease.

1895. **Wilhelm K. Röntgen** (1845–1923) discovered x-rays and immediately realized that his discovery had a practical application in medicine.

1897. **Eduard Buchner** (1860–1917) discovered that *zymase,* a cell-free yeast extract, caused fermentation, thus resolving a long-standing controversy over "vital" and "inorganic" ferments.

1900. **Hugo de Vries** (1848–1935), **Carl Correns** (1864–1933), and **Erich Tschermak** (1871–1962) independently rediscovered the 1865 work of **Gregor Mendel** while searching the literature to confirm their own experimental results.

1903. **Walter S. Sutton** (1876–1916) pointed out that the Mendelian ratios could be explained by the cytological behavior of the chromosomes.

1906. **Charles Sherrington** (1861–1952) described in *The Integrative Action of the Nervous System* the properties of the synapse and the complex integration of reflexes in behavior.

1907. **Ross G. Harrison** (1870–1959) announced a technique for culturing tissue cells outside of the body.

1909. **Paul Ehrlich** (1854–1915) showed that the synthetic compound, *Salvarsan,* was an effective treatment for syphilis. This discovery was a tremendous stimulus to the field of chemotherapy. In 1935 **Gerhard Domagk**

Sir Alexander Fleming (1881–1955) demonstrating the ability of penicillin to diffuse

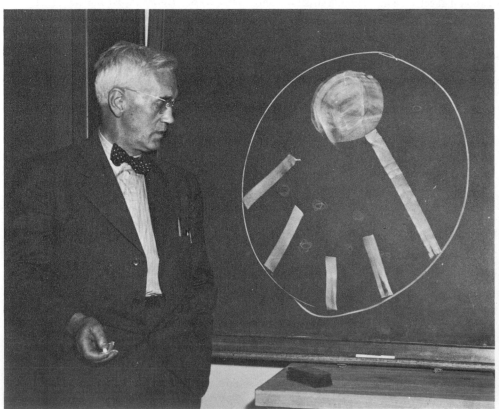

The Ship that Sank in Victory (Bonhomme Richard; *p.541) by J. L. G. Ferris*

The Battle of Bunker Hill (p.538) by Howard Pyle

The Surrender of Cornwallis at Yorktown (p.541) by John Trumbull

(1895–1964) made the fundamental discovery which led to the introduction and widespread use of **sulfa drugs.**

1911. Thomas H. Morgan (1866–1945) claimed that certain traits were genetically linked on the chromosome, thus visualizing a linear arrangement of genes and stimulating the construction of genetic maps.

1915. Alfred Wegener (1880–1930) gave the classic expression of the controversial theory of continental drift in *Die Entstehung der Kontinente und Ozeane.*

1921. Hans Spemann (1869–1941) postulated an organizer principle which was responsible for the formative interaction between neighboring embryonic regions. He stimulated contemporary embryologists to search for the inductive chemical molecule.

1927. Hermann J. Muller (1890–1967) announced that he had successfully induced mutations in fruit flies with x-rays. This provided a useful experimental tool, yet in retrospect gave warning to the generations of the 1940's and 1950's of a danger in the release of atomic energy.

1929. Alexander Fleming (1881–1955) announced that the common mold *Penicillium* had an inhibitory effect on certain pathogenic bacteria. It was not until 1943 under the pressures of World War II, however, that the first antibiotic, penicillin, was successfully developed.

1930. Ronald A. Fisher (1890–1962) established in *The Genetical Theory of Natural Selection* that superior genes have a significant selective advantage, thus testifying that Darwinian evolution was compatible with genetics.

1941. George W. Beadle (1903–) and **Edward L. Tatum** (1909–) described an experimental assay which evaluated the exact relationships between specific mutant genes in mold and particular stages in the metabolic process.

1944. Ostwald T. Avery (1877–1955) and collaborators announced they had transmuted one type of pneumococcus bacteria into a second type by the transfer of DNA molecules.

1946. Willard F. Libby (1908–), and associates, developed *radiocarbon dating*, a method for ascertaining the absolute age of materials containing carbon.

1953. Francis H. C. Crick (1916–) and **James D. Watson** (1928–) offered a model for the structure of DNA which accounted for gene replication and conceived a biochemical code that could transmit a great variety of genetic information.

3. *Technological Achievements*

(From p. 507)

The Industrial Revolution, begun in the latter half of the 18th century, expanded into new geographical areas, revolutionized older technologies, created new ones, and continued to transform society and human life during the 19th and 20th centuries. Although historians might debate as to whether several industrial revolutions occurred during this two-century span, whether there were different phases of the same revolution, or whether industrialization had reached the point of a "continuing revolution," there was no doubt that technological advances from the mid-18th century to the present had given man greatly increased mastery over his environment, while at the same time posing problems and even threats to man's continued existence.

The culmination of Britain's leadership in the Industrial Revolution was reached at the **Great Exhibition of 1851** in London; after that Britain's position declined relatively while new industrial giants, America and Germany near the close of the 19th century, and Russia in the 20th century, gained in technological strength and capabilities. More recently, the "underdeveloped nations" (so-called because they are not so advanced technologically as some of the Western nations) have sought their own industrial development.

a. ENERGY AND POWER SOURCES

1800. The **galvanic cell,** or Voltaic pile, of **Alessandro Volta** (1745–1827) was the first electric battery (converting chemical energy into electrical energy).

1802. Richard Trevithick (1771–1833) built the first **high-pressure steam engine,** although the American **Oliver Evans** (1755–1819) had patented one in the United States in 1797. Other advances in steam-engine technology included the compound engine (adding a high pressure cylinder to the original Watt engine) by **William McNaught** (1813–1881) in 1845.

1806. First gas-lighting of cotton mills. Improvements made in production and distribution of gas as heat source (**Bunsen burner,** 1855) and for illumination (**Welsbach gas-mantle,** 1885).

1827. Benoit Fourneyron (1802–1867) developed the **water-turbine.**

1832. The first mechanical generation of electricity by **Hippolyte Pixii.** Major improve-

The locomotive (1804) of Richard Trevithick, 1771–1833

Oil well drilled by Edwin L. Drake (1819–1880) at Titusville, Pa.

Thomas A. Edison (1847–1931) photographed in 1915 with his Edison Effect lamps

ments in **electric generators** followed: the improved armature (1856) designed by **Werner von Siemens** (1816–1892); and the ring-armature (1870) of **Zénobe T. Gramme** (1826–1901), which represented the first practical dynamo.

1854. **Abraham Gesner** (1797–1864) manufactured kerosene.

1859. **William M. J. Rankine** (1820–1872) published the first comprehensive manual of the steam engine. The steam engine stimulated theoretical studies in thermodynamics by Clapeyron, Clausius, Joule, Lord Kelvin, and Gibbs.

1859. **Edwin L. Drake** (1819–1880) drilled the **first oil well** in Titusville, Pennsylvania, opening up the Pennsylvania oil field and starting the large-scale commercial exploitation of petroleum. **First oil pipeline** (two-inch diameter, six miles long) constructed 1865 in Pennsylvania.

1876. **Nicholas August Otto** (1832–1892) built the first practical gas engine, working upon the so-called **Otto cycle,** which is now almost universally employed for all internal combustion engines. Otto's work was based upon previous engines of **Étienne Lenoir** (1822–1900) and **Alphonse Beau de Rochas** (1815–1891). The Otto cycle was employed in the gasoline engine patented (1885) by **Gottlieb Daimler** (1834–1900).

1882. The Pearl Street (New York City) electric generating station, a pioneer central power station designed by **Thomas A. Edison** (1847–1931), commenced operations a few months after Edison dynamos had been installed at Holborn Viaduct Station in England.

1884. **Charles A. Parsons** (1854–1931) patented the **steam turbine.** The steam turbine (1887) of the Swede **Gustav de Laval** (1845–1913) proved successful for engines of smaller power.

1886. Beginning of the first great **hydro-electric installation** at Niagara Falls.

1888. **Nikola Tesla** (1856–1943) invented the **alternating current electric motor:** he also made possible the polyphase transmission of power over long distances and pioneered the invention of radio.

1892. **Rudolf Diesel** (1858–1913) patented his heavy oil engine, first manufactured successfully in 1897.

1921. **Tetraethyl lead,** gasoline anti-knock additive, produced by **Thomas Midgley** (1889–1944).

1930–1937. Development of gas turbine unit for jet propulsion in aircraft by **Frank Whittle.**

1930–1935. Development of first commercially practicable **catalytic cracking system** for petroleum by **Eugene J. Houdry** (1892–1962).

1942. **DAWN OF THE NUCLEAR AGE.** The first self-sustaining **nuclear chain reaction** achieved at Stagg Field, Chicago, by **Enrico Fermi** (1901–1954). The first full-scale use of nuclear fuel to produce electricity occurred at Calder Hall (England) in 1956.

1954. The **solar battery** developed by Bell Telephone Laboratories, making it possible to convert sunlight directly to electric power.

b. MATERIALS AND CONSTRUCTION

1800. Pioneer **suspension bridge,** hung by iron chains, built by **James Finley** (c. 1762–1828)

A view of the Erie Canal, 1825

in Pennsylvania; wire suspension employed by **Marc Seguin** (1786–1875) in bridge near Lyons (1825). The American, **Ithiel Town** (1784–1844), patented his truss bridge (1820).

1817–1825. Building of the **Erie Canal,** the first great American civil engineering work.

1818. The **Institute of Civil Engineers** (London), the first professional engineering society, founded.

Marc Isambard Brunel (1769–1849) patented the cast-iron **tunnel shield; Thomas Cochrane** (1830) used this shield to construct foundations on marshy ground.

1824. **Joseph Aspdin** (1779–1855) patented **Portland cement,** a hydraulic cement (impervious to water) as durable as that employed by the Romans.

1827. **Gay-Lussac tower** introduced in manufacture of sulphuric acid, largely replacing John Roebuck's lead-chamber process (1746). **Herman Frasch** (1851–1914) developed process (1891) for mining sulphur (by superheated water and pumping to the surface).

1836. **Galvanized iron** introduced by Sorel in France. Galvanized fencing and barbed wire (c. 1880) helped to fence off large tracts of

cattle land in American west during latter part of 19th century.

Rudolph Diesel, 1858–1913

1839. **Charles Goodyear** (1800–1860) **vulcanized rubber.** Although introduced into Europe

Charles Goodyear, 1800–1860

the manufacture of **tungsten steel.** Other steel alloys also developed: chromium steel (France, 1877); manganese steel (Robert Hadfield, England, 1882); nickel steel (France, 1888); stainless steel (many inventors, 1911–1920).

1872. **John W. Hyatt** (1837–1920) began commercial production of celluloid, discovered by Alexander Parkes (1855).

1877. **Joseph Monier** (1823–1906) patented a **reinforced concrete** beam. In the 1890's two other Frenchmen, Edmond Coignet and Francois Hennibique, utilized reinforced concrete for pipes, aqueducts, bridges, tunnels; E. L. Ransome employed it extensively in building construction.

1879. **Percy Gilchrist** (1851–1935) and **Sidney G. Thomas** (1850–1885) developed a method for making steel from phosphoric iron ores, thereby doubling in effect the world's potential steel production.

1886. **Charles M. Hall** (1863–1914) developed the electrolytic method of obtaining aluminum from its oxide (bauxite).

1889. Completion of the **Eiffel Tower;** wrought-iron superstructure on reinforced concrete base. Cast iron used for building construction earlier in the century by James Bogardus (1800–1874) for office buildings in New York and by Joseph Paxton (1801–1865) for Crystal Palace at Great Exhibition of 1851 (also employing wrought iron and glass, and prefabricated units). The first complete steel-frame structure was built in Chicago in 1890; steel made possible skyscrapers, as did the earlier invention (1854) of the elevator by **Elisha G. Otis** (1811–1861).

1902. **Arthur D. Little** (1863–1935) patented

The Eiffel Tower, Paris, France

Brooklyn Bridge, Manhattan Tower (1893), designed by John A. Roebling, 1806–1869

in 1615, rubber had not been commercially successful until a solvent for the latex was found (1765); bonding of rubber to cloth to produce raincoats (macintoshes) had been developed (1824) by **Charles Macintosh** (1766–1843).

1855. **John A. Roebling** (1806–1869) completed **wire cable bridge** at Niagara; Roebling utilized this same method for the **Brooklyn Bridge** (completed by his son, W. A. Roebling, in 1883), and it became standard construction technique for all great suspension bridges.

1856. **Henry Bessemer** (1813–1898) perfected the technique (*Bessemer process*) for converting pig iron into steel by directing an air blast upon the molten metal.

1856. *Mauve,* first of the **aniline** (coal-tar) **dyes,** discovered by **William H. Perkin** (1838–1907). Beginning of the synthetic dye industry, which was to develop greatly in Germany.

1861. **Ernest Solvay** (1838–1922) patented the

Solvay ammonia process for the manufacture of soda.

1863. The **open-hearth process** for the manufacture of steel developed by the Martin brothers in France using the regenerative furnace devised (1856) by **Frederick Siemens** (1826–1904) (also known as the Siemens-Martin process).

1867. **Alfred Nobel** (1833–1896) manufactured **dynamite.** Guncotton and nitroglycerine both discovered in 1846, had previously been used for blasting purposes. In 1875 Nobel discovered blasting gelatine, from which arose the gelignite industry. Cordite, another explosive, patented 1889 by Frederick Abel and James Dewar.

1863. **Henry Clifton Sorby** (1826–1908) of Sheffield discovered the microstructure of steel, marking the beginning of **modern metallurgical science.**

1868. **Robert F. Mushet** (1811–1891) began

rayon, the **first cellulose fiber,** and also artificial silk. Earlier (1884) Louis, Count of Chardonnet (1839–1924), had produced an artificial thread which was woven into a silk-like material. Cellophane developed by J. E. Brandenberger (1912); further developed by W. H. Church and K. E. Prindle (1926).

1909. The first polymer, **Bakelite,** discovered by **Leo H. Baekeland** (1863–1944). Subsequent development of polymers include neoprene, arising from work of Father Julius A. Nieuwland beginning in 1906; nylon, developed by Wallace H. Carothers and first manufactured in 1938; acrilan; orlon; dynel; and dacron (called terylene by its British inventors, J. R. Whinfield and J. T. Dickson, 1941). Synthetic polymers include elastomers, fibers, plastics. Silicon polymers developed c. 1945.

1928. The first steel-frame, glass-curtain-wall building completed. By 1960 this technique was practically universal for high buildings; developed particularly by **L. Mies van der Rohe** (1886–1969).

1941. **Shell molding,** a revolutionary process producing more accurate castings cheaply, invented by **Johannes Croning.** Powder metallurgy, although known since Wollaston's work at the beginning of the 19th century, achieved extensive application in mid-20th century.

1945. Industrial development of silicones proceeded apace for a wide variety of applications, including lubricants for exceedingly high and low temperatures; binding of fiberglass; water-repellent agents; etc.

1947. **Frank Lloyd Wright** (1869–1959) extended pure cantilever technique (earlier employed with iron and steel construction in bridges) by using concrete slab cantilevers for S. C. Johnson Research Building (Racine, Wisconsin).

1950 ff. Basic-oxygen process for manufacture of steel developed in Austria.

c. MACHINES AND INDUSTRIAL TECHNIQUES

1800. **Eli Whitney** (1765–1825) credited with introduction of **interchangeable parts** for manufacturing muskets. Although it had European precedents, the system of interchangeable parts became known as "the American system" because it was most fully exploited in the United States and became the foundation of the mass production characteristic of American industry at a later date.

1801. **Joseph M. Jacquard** (1752–1834) invented a loom for figured silk fabrics, later introduced into the making of worsteds. **William Horrocks** (1776–1849) developed the power loom (1813), improved (1822) by **Richard Roberts** (1789–1864). Machine combing of wool developed (1845); ring spinning frame (1830); the Brussels power loom invented by Erastus B. Bigelow (1814–1879) of Massachusetts for the weaving of carpets (1845); and the loom of J. H. Northrop of Massachusetts (1892), which was almost completely automatic.

1810. **Friedrich Koenig's** (1774–1833) **power-driven press** in use, followed by the flat bed press (1811). Other developments leading to mass production of printed matter, especially newspapers, were the rotary press of Robert Hoe (1846) and the web printing press, allowing for printing on a continuous roll (web) of

Johnson Research Building, Racine, Wis., designed by Frank Lloyd Wright, 1869–1959

paper by a rotary press, invented (1865) by William A. Bullock. In 1885 the linotype of **Otto Mergenthaler** (1854–1899) replaced monotype.

1823–1843. **Charles Babbage** (1792–1871) attempted to build calculating machines (following the lead of Thomas de Colmar, who built the first practical calculating machine in 1820); Babbage's machines were never completed, being too advanced for the technology of the time, but his theories formed a basis for later work in this field.

1830. **Joseph Whitworth** (1803–1887) developed the **standard screw gauge** and a machine to measure one-millionth of an inch, for standards. Made possible more precise machine tools for planing, gear-cutting, and milling.

1837 ff. Rapid **development of armament,** keeping pace with improvements in metallurgy, machines, and explosives: **Henri J. Paixhans'** (1783–1854) shell-gun, adopted by France,

1837; rifled, breech-loading artillery used by Piedmont, 1845; the French '75, the first quick-firing artillery piece, firing both shrapnel and high explosive, 1898; the cast steel breech-loading Prussian artillery manufactured by the Krupps from 1849 on. In small arms, there was the Colt revolver (1835), the Dreyse needle-gun (1841), the Minié bullet (1849), Winchester repeating rifle (1860), Gatling machine gun (1861), French chassepot (1866), and the Maxim gun (1884). The self-propelled torpedo was invented by Robert Whitehead (1823–1905) in 1864; smokeless powder appeared in 1884.

1839. **Steam hammer** invented by **James Nasmyth** (1808–1890). Also developments in drop-forging and die-stamping at this time.

1846. **Elias Howe** (1819–1867) invented the lock-stitch **sewing machine;** in 1851 **Isaac M. Singer** (1811–1875) invented the first practical domestic sewing machine. This became the

Isaac M. Singer's first sewing machine, 1851

William S. Burroughs' adding machine, 1888

first major consumer appliance, soon followed by the **carpet sweeper** of M. R. Bissell (1876), and the **vacuum cleaner** (I. W. McGaffey, 1869; J. Thurman, 1899).

1849–1854. Exploiting the increasing accuracy of machine tools, **Samuel Colt** (1814–1862) and **Elisha Root** (1808–1865) developed a practical system for manufacturing interchangeable parts, especially in connection with Colt's revolver.

1855. Development of **turret lathe** by American machine-tool makers. First true **universal milling machine** designed (1862) by **Joseph R. Brown** (1810–1876). Other machine-tool improvements included Mushet's tool steel, increasing the cutting speed (high speed tool steel, 1898, by Taylor and White), gear-box mechanisms for better control, multiple-spindle lathes (1890), and tungsten carbide tools (1926).

1873. First **use of electricity to drive machinery,** Vienna. Quickly adopted, usually with the motor incorporated into the machine rather than separate.

1877. **Elihu Thomson** invented a **resistance welder.** N. V. Bernardos of Russia patented carbon-arc welding, although arc welding (most popularly employed process today) did not come into its own until invention of the coated electrode in the 1920's. Oxyacetylene torch (invented in 1900 by Edmund Fouche) and gas welding was the dominant process until recently. Development of inert-gas-shielded arc welding after 1942.

1882 ff. Invention and use of electric appliances for consumer market: electric fan (S. S. Wheeler); flatiron (H. W. Seely, 1882); stove (W. S. Hadaway, 1896); separate attachable plug (H. Hubbell, 1904); sewing machine (Singer Co., 1889); washing machine (Hurling Co., 1907).

1884. **Dorr E. Felt** (1862–1930) made first accurate **comptometer.** **William S. Burroughs** (1857–1898) developed first successful recording **adding machine** (1888); Brunsviga calculating machine (1892).

1895. **Carl Linde** established **liquid air** plant. He had previously (1876) introduced the ammonia compressor machine (the first vapor compression machine invented by Jacob Perkins, 1834). Other refrigerating machines were: ammonia absorption machine (Carré, 1860), air refrigerator (Gorrie, 1845; improved by Kirk, 1862), open-cycle air machine (Giffard, 1873, and later by Bell and Coleman).

1895. **King C. Gillette** (1855–1932) invented **safety razor** with throwaway blades. **J. Schick** invented **electric razor** (1928). Stainless steel throwaway blades invented in Sweden (1962).

1898. **M. J. Owens** (1859–1923) invented automatic **bottle-making machine.**

1905–1910. Electric precipitation equipment, for prevention of atmospheric pollution by industry, developed by Frederick G. Cottrell (1877–1948).

1913. **G. Sundback** invented a slide fastener **(zipper);** earlier version patented by W. L. Judson (1891).

1914. **Conveyer-belt mass production** employed in the United States most dramatically in Henry Ford's assembly line for Model T Ford automobile, which became the symbol for American industrial technique.

1915. Development of **tank in warfare** by British (Sir Ernest Swinton).

1920 ff. Managerial techniques improved through development of "Scientific Management," whose principles were first enunciated by **Frederick W. Taylor** (1856–1915) in the first decade of the century. Taylor concentrated on time-motion studies. Other proponents of "rationalized" production were Frank Gilbreth and Charles Bedaux. Quality control developed 1926 ff.

1920. J. C. Shaw developed a **sensing device,** controlled by a servomechanism, for a milling machine. Hydraulic trace of J. W. Anderson (1927) allowed the reproduction of complex shapes. Machine tools further supplemented by electrolytic and ultrasonic machines, and cutting machines guided by an electron beam. **Development of laser** (light amplification by simulated emission of radiation) by Theodore N. Maiman (1960), also used for precision cutting.

1923. First mill for hot continuous wide strip rolling of steel, based on work of John B. Tytus.

1938. Ladislao J. and George Biro patented the **ball-point pen.**

1941–1945. Development of **rockets and missiles** during World War II.

1944. Harvard IBM Automatic Sequence Controlled Calculator, the first automatic general-purpose **digital computer,** completed. ENIAC (electronic numerical integrator and calculator), the first electronic digital computer, built in 1946. Development of special purpose computers and data processors (1950 ff.), including programmed **teaching machines.**

1947. Word *Automation* coined by John Diebold and D. S. Harder, to define "self-powered, self-guiding and correcting mechanism," and later extended to include all elements of "automated factory" and extension to office and clerical procedures.

1953. Electronic computers with feedback mechanism (servomechanisms), made possible new field of **Cybernetics,** defined by **Norbert Wiener** (1953) as "the study of control and communication in the animal and the machine."

d. AGRICULTURAL PRODUCTION AND FOOD TECHNOLOGY

1801. Franz K. Achard (1753–1821) built the first **sugar-beet factory** (Silesia). Sugar-beet cultivation and beet-sugar industry developed primarily in France and Germany.

1810. Nicolas Appert (c. 1750–1840) described system for food preservation by canning, using glass jars. Tin cans introduced 1811.

1834. Cyrus H. McCormick (1809–1884) patented his **reaper,** and began commercial manufacture c. 1840. Obed Hussey (1792–1860) invented a similar reaper simultaneously and independently.

1837. John Deere (1804–1886) introduced the **steel plow.** In 1819 Jethro Wood (1774–1834) had developed a cast iron plow; and John Lane had introduced a steel-blade plowshare in 1833. James Oliver's (1823–1908) chilled plow of 1855 was improved by the Marsh brothers (1857). Mechanical power applied to plowing with the introduction of **cable plowing** (1850); by 1858 John Fowler had introduced the **steam plow.**

1850–1880. Improvements in farm implements included the revolving disc harrow (1847),

Revolving disc harrow

IBM electronic data processing machine

Mechanical cotton picker

binder (1850), corn planter (1853), two-horse straddle-row cultivator (1856), combine harvester (1860), combine seed drill (1867), and sheaf-binding harvester (1878).

1860. **Gail Borden** (1801–1874) opened the first factory for the production of **evaporated milk.**

1861. After Louis Pasteur's work on microorganisms, **pasteurization** was introduced as a preservative for beer, wine, and milk.

1865 ff. Development of **mechanical refrigeration** for preservation of food products, especially Thaddeus Lowe's (1832–1913) compression ice machine (1865) and Linde's ammonia compression refrigerator (1873).

1869 ff. Transcontinental railway aided development of **meat-packing industry** in Chicago.

1877. **Gustav de Laval** (1845–1913) invented the centrifugal **cream separator.**

1880 ff. Application of **chemical fertilizers** increased food production. J. B. Lawes manufactured superphosphates (1842); Chilean sodium nitrate beds exploited from c. 1870 until methods of fixing atmospheric nitrogen were developed after 1900 by Fritz Haber (1868–1934); use of potash as an inorganic fertilizer from Strassfurt deposits.

1889. **Angus Campbell** tested the first spindle type **cotton picker;** this type of machine was not fully developed and marketed successfully until the 1940's, competing with the machine devised by John and Mack Rust in 1924 and also commercially produced in the 1940's.

1892. **Gasoline tractor** came into use for farming. **Caterpillar tractor** developed 1931.

1902. W. Normann patented a process for hardening liquid fats by hydrogenation, making available an ample supply of solid fats for soap and food.

1917. **Clarence Birdseye** (1886–1956) began development of method for quick **freezing of foods** in small containers; placed on market in 1929.

1939. Paul Muller synthesized DDT for use as an insecticide. Othmar Zeidler had prepared DDT in 1874, but its insecticidal qualities had not been suspected.

1940 ff. Development of **artificial insemination** to improve livestock breeding.

1945 ff. Unit **packaging of foodstuffs** improved by development of plastic packaging films. Trend toward prepared "convenience" foods for household use.

1950 ff. Mass-production, battery-raising of poultry increased production, lowered prices, and converted chicken and turkey from a holiday and Sunday luxury to an everyday food item.

e. TRANSPORTATION AND COMMUNICATION

1802. **Richard Trevithick** (1771–1833) patented a **steam carriage;** earlier attempts to use steam power for transport purposes had been made by Nicolas Cugnot in France (1769), William Murdock in England (1785), and Oliver Evans in the United States. In 1804 Trevithick designed and built a locomotive to run on rails.

1807. **Robert Fulton** (1765–1815) sailed the *Clermont* from New York to Albany. This was by no means the first steamboat: the Marquis Claude de Jouffroy d'Abbans (1751–1832) had built a paddle-wheel steamer in France (1783); John Fitch (1743–1798) had launched a steamboat on the Delaware (1787); James Rumsey (1743–1792) on the Potomac (1787); and John Stevens (1749–1838) had designed a successful screw-propeller steamboat (1802). However, Fulton's boat was the first steamboat to represent a commercial success. By 1819 steam augmented sail on the first transatlantic steamship crossing of the *Savannah*.

1814. **George Stephenson** (1781–1848) built his **first locomotive,** and in 1829 his *Rocket,* designed with the aid of his son Robert (1803–1859), won out in a competition with locomotives of other design and thereby set the pattern for future locomotive developments.

1825. Opening of the **Stockton-Darlington Railway,** the first successful railroad system, using a steam engine built by Stephenson. In 1829 the first railroads were opened in the United States (Pennsylvania) and France

(Lyon–St. Étienne), both employing English-built locomotives. The first American locomotive was built (1830) by Peter Cooper (1791–1883).

1837. **Charles Wheatstone** (1802–1875) and **William F. Cooke** (1806–1879) patented the **telegraph,** which was also independently invented by the American **Samuel F. B. Morse** (1791–1872), whose **telegraphic code** was universally adopted. By 1866, **Cyrus W. Field** (1819–1892) succeeded in laying a **transatlantic cable,** after two previous failures and after overcoming tremendous financial and technical difficulties.

1839. **Louis J. M. Daguerre** (1787–1851) evolved the **daguerreotype photographic process,** based on the work of Joseph Nicéphore Niepce (1765–1833). Although **William H. F. Talbot** (1800–1877) produced paper positives (1841), the first fully practical medium for photography was the wet collodion plate process (1851) of Frederick S. Archer (1813–1857).

1860. Construction began on the **London underground railway** system, which was electrified in 1905. Construction began on the Paris *metro* in 1898, on New York City subway in 1900.

1864. **George M. Pullman** (1831–1897) built the first **sleeping car** specially constructed for that purpose.

1867. **Ernest Michaux** invented the **velocipede,** the first bicycle to put cranks and pedals directly on the front wheel; the "safety" bicycle with the geared chain-drive to rear wheel was introduced in 1885.

1869. Union Pacific and Central Pacific Railroads met to complete the **first transcontinental line** in America. The **Trans-Siberian Railway** was begun in 1891.

1869. Opening of the Suez Canal, the work of the French engineer, **Ferdinand de Lesseps** (1805–1894).

1873. The Remington Company began manufacture of the **typewriter** patented by **Christopher L. Sholes** (1819–1890); shift-key system, with capital and small letters on same type bar, introduced in 1878.

Robert Fulton's Clermont *on the Hudson River, c. 1813*

Samuel F. B. Morse, 1791–1872

Daguerreotype of Louis J. M. Daguerre, 1787–1851

The first transcontinental railroad is completed, 1869

Trial exhibition of Bell's telephone, 1877

Henry and Edsel Ford in a 1905 Model F Ford

Flight of the Wright brothers in 1903, Orville at the controls, Wilbur on the ground (right)

1874. **Stephen D. Field's** (1846–1913) electrically powered **streetcar** began operation in New York City, replacing the horsecars introduced in 1832. The cable streetcar, invented by Andrew S. Hallidie (1836–1900), was put into use in San Francisco (1873). The first streetcars with overhead trolley lines were in use in Germany by 1884 and first installed in the United States at Richmond, Virginia in 1888.

1876. **Alexander Graham Bell** (1847–1922) patented the **telephone.** The first telephone exchange installed in New Haven (1877) and an automatic switching system introduced in 1879. Much previous experimentation had been done on telephones, including that of Philip Reis of Germany (1861), Antonio Meucci of Italy (1857), and Elisha Gray (simultaneously with Bell). The periodic insertion of loading coils (inductors), originated by M. I. Pupin (1899), made possible long distance transmission of telephone calls.

1878–1879. **Joseph W. Swan** (1828–1914) of England made the first successful carbon filament **electric lamp** in 1878; working independently Thomas A. Edison patented his **incandescent bulb** in 1879. Improved vacuum in the lamp bulb made possible by the high vacuum mercury pump developed by Hermann Sprengel (1865). At the same time successful experiments in public lighting were carried on with the use of arc lamps, the most successful systems being those of P. Jablochkoff (Paris, 1876)

and Charles F. Brush (Cleveland, 1879). Tungsten filament lamp introduced in 1913.

1885 ff. **Karl Benz** (1844–1929) produced the prototype of the **automobile** using an internal combustion motor operating on the Otto four-stroke cycle principle; the same year **Gottlieb Daimler** (1834–1900) also patented his **gasoline engine,** trying it first on a motorcycle, then on a four-wheeled vehicle. These may be said to have been the first automobiles, although there had been experiments with battery-powered electric automobiles from 1851 on and some previous internal combustion vehicles had been attempted by the Frenchman Étienne Lenoir (1859) and the Austrian Siegfried Marcus (1864). Other automobile pioneers included the Frenchmen Peugeot and Panhard. The first automobile patent in the United States was taken out by George B. Selden (1879), but the Duryea (1895) was the

first auto made for sale in the United States. **Henry Ford** (1863–1947) made his first car in 1896 and founded the Ford Motor Co. in 1903. Important in the development of the automobile was the invention (1888) of the **pneumatic tire** by **John B. Dunlop** (1840–1921).

1889–1890. **Thomas Edison** improved his first **phonograph** (patented 1878) by substituting wax for the tinfoil-coated cylinders and by adding a loudspeaker to amplify the sounds produced by the diaphragm. Emile Berliner (1851–1929) improved the quality of sound reproduction (1890) by utilizing disk-records and better cutting technique.

1888. **George Eastman** (1854–1932) perfected the **hand camera** (*Kodak*); he had previously invented the first successful roll film (1880). Leo Baekeland perfected (1893) a photographic paper (*Velox*) sufficiently sensitive to be printed by artificial light. Work of Rudolph

Early Daimler, 1889

Thomas A. Edison with his phonograph, 1878

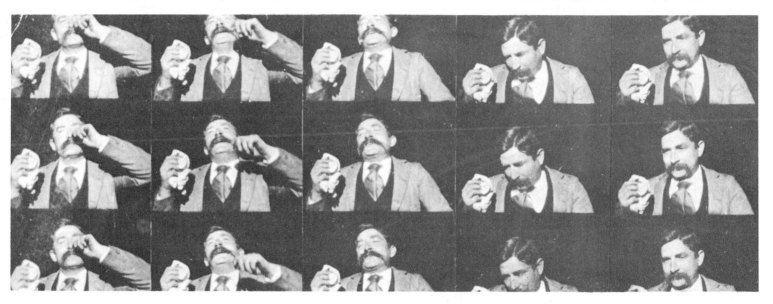

Kinetoscopic record of a sneeze (detail), made at Edison studio in 1894

Fischer and Siegrist in dye-coupler color processes (1910–1914) provided the basis for the development of a commercially practicable color film (*Kodachrome*) by Leo Godowsky, Jr., and Leopold Mannes (1935).

1895. The first public **motion picture** showing in Paris, by **Louis** (1864–1948) and **Auguste** (1862–1954) **Lumière,** inventors of the **cinématographe.** This followed by a year the opening of Edison's Kinetoscope Parlor (New York City) where the motion picture (peepshow) could be viewed by but one person at a time. Both these successful attempts at motion pictures had been preceded by earlier devices: the "thaumatrope" of J. A. Paris (1826); the magic lantern, devised by A. Kircher (1645) and improved by Pieter van Musschenbroek (1736); the multi-camera apparatus of Edward Muybridge (1872); the "photographic gun" of E. J. Marey (1882); the celluloid motion-pic-

ture film of William Friese-Green (1889). Prototype of the modern **film projector** was the Vitascope (1896), devised by **Charles Francis Jenkins** (1867–1934) and Thomas Armat on the basis of Edison's kinetoscope.

1895. **Guglielmo Marconi** (1874–1937) invented the **wireless telegraph,** based on the discovery (1887) of radio waves by Heinrich Hertz (1857–1894) (existence of these waves had been deduced by James Clerk Maxwell in 1873). Other contributors to wireless development were E. Branly, Thomas Edison, Alexander Popov (who contributed the aerial), Reginald E. Fessenden (improved transmitter, 1901). In 1901 Marconi succeeded in sending a wireless signal across the Atlantic.

1898. **Valdemar Poulsen** of Denmark invented the **magnetic recording of sound** (1898). F. Pfleumer of Germany replaced steel wire by plastic tape coated with magnetic material

(1930's), and Marvin Camras of the United States made further developments in magnetic recording (1940's).

1900. Count **Ferdinand von Zeppelin** launched the first of the **rigid airships** which were to be called by his name.

1903. **Orville** (1871–1948) and **Wilbur** (1867–1912) **Wright** made the first flight in a **heavier-than-air plane** on December 17 at Kittyhawk, North Carolina. This flight was the culmination of a long series of developments: George Cayley's glider (1804) and studies in aerodynamic theory; the glider flights (1895) of Otto Lilienthal and Octave Chanute; Samuel P. Langley's (1834–1906) steam-powered model plane (1896); Alberto Santos-Dumont's (1873–1932) model airplane with an internal combustion engine (1898); and others.

1904. **John Ambrose Fleming** (1849–1945) devised the diode thermionic valve **(radio tube);**

Lee de Forest (1873–1961) invented the Audion (1906), a three-electrode vacuum tube (triode amplifier), thereby providing the basis for the development of **electronics.**

1909–1927. The "heroic age" of **aviation,** commencing with **Louis Bleriot's** (1872–1936) flight (1909) across the English Channel, and including the exploits of the aerial "aces" of World War I, the flight (1919) of John W. Alcock (1892–1919) and Arthur W. Brown (1886–1958) across the Atlantic (Newfoundland to Galway), Richard E. Byrd's (1888–1957) flight (1926) across the North Pole, and culminating in **Charles A. Lindbergh's** (1902–   ) solo non-stop flight New York to Paris in *The Spirit of St. Louis* (1927). Many technical improvements made, including the first engine specifically intended for aircraft by Glenn Curtiss (1904), and the **gyroscope stabilizer** of Elmer A. Sperry (1913).

1911. Charles F. Kettering (1876–1958), who had previously invented lighting and ignition systems for the automobile, perfected the **electric self-starter.** The first fully **automatic transmission,** perfected by Earl A. Thompson, was introduced commercially in 1939. Harry Vickers and Francis W. Davis began work on hydraulic **power-assisted steering** systems in 1925 and 1926 respectively, and in 1951 power steering was introduced for passenger cars.

1913. Diesel-electric railway engines first used in Sweden. Coming into use in the United States during the later 1930's, they have largely replaced steam-locomotives.

1920. Frank Conrad (1874–1941) of the Westinghouse Co. began broadcasting radio programs in Pittsburgh, marking the **beginning of radio** as a mass communication medium.

1922. Herbert T. Kalmus developed **Technicolor,** first commercially successful color process for motion pictures.

1926. Sound Motion Pictures. Although Edison had attempted to put together his phonograph and motion picture inventions for sound movies as early as 1904, it was 1923 before de Forest successfully demonstrated his phonofilm system for recording sound on the motion picture film. The first motion picture with sound accompaniment was publicly shown in 1926, the first talking picture in 1927.

1926 ff. John L. Baird (1888–1946) successfully demonstrated **television** in England. His mechanical system of television, similar to that of C. F. Jenkins in the United States, was based on Paul von Nipkov's rotating disk (1886), but had technical limitations; modern electronic television developed from the cathode-ray tube (1897) of Ferdinand Braun and A. A. Campbell-Swinton's proposals (1911) for use of a cathode ray to scan an image. The crucial invention was the Iconoscope of the Russian-American **Vladimir Zworykin** (1889–   ), the device which transmits television images quickly and effectively. Philo Farnsworth of the United States contributed the image dissector tube (1927). General broadcasting of television began in England in 1936, in the United States in 1941, but languished until after World War II. Peter C. Goldmark of Columbia Broadcasting System demonstrated (1940) sequential method of color television which gave way to compatible electronic system developed by R. C. A. in the 1950's.

1932. Edwin H. Land (1909–   ) invented the first practical synthetic light-polarizing material **(polaroid glass),** found useful in sunglasses, cameras, and scientific optical instruments. In 1947 he invented the **Polaroid Land camera,** which developed the film inside the camera and produced a photograph print within one minute; in 1962 he introduced color film for his camera.

1933. Fluorescent lamps introduced for floodlighting and advertising. Developments leading up to this included experiments by George Stokes (1852) and Alexandre Becquerel (1859) to excite fluorescent materials by ultraviolet rays or in a discharge tube; Peter Cooper-Hewitt's invention of the mercury vapor lamp (1901); the introduction of the **Neon lamp** by Georges Claude and the work on cathodes by D. M. Moore and Wehnelt in the 1900's; and J. Risler's application of powder to the outside of tubular discharge lamps (1923). Subsequent developments have included increased cathode life and improved fluorescent powders.

1933. Edwin H. Armstrong (1890–1954), pioneer radio inventor (regenerative, i.e., feedback, circuit, 1912, and superheterodyne circuit, 1918), perfected **frequency modulation (FM)** providing static-free radio reception.

1937. Chester Carlson patented a new dry photographic process (*Xerography*) based upon principles of photoconductivity and electrostatics.

1939. Igor Sikorsky (1889–   ) flew the first **helicopter** of his design. The first helicopter capable of flight was the work of Ellehammer of Denmark (1912), based on C. Renard's articulated rotor blade (1904) and G. A. Crocco's cyclic pitch control (1906). Juan de la Cierva invented the autogiro (1922), differing from the helicopter in that its rotor auto-rotated and the engine drove a normal propeller. Further development work was done (1934–1936) by Louis Breguet and Heinrich Focke.

1939. First test flight of a **turbo-jet airplane** (Heinkel) with an engine designed by Hans von Ohain. Simultaneous and parallel work on jet airplanes in Britian, based on turbo-jet engine designed by Frank Whittle (1930). In 1958 **jet-powered transatlantic airline** service was inaugurated by BOAC and Pan-American Airways. In 1962 the British and French governments announced plans to co-operate on the production of a jet-propelled supersonic transport plane (the Concorde), and the U.S. government proposed American production of a supersonic commercial plane the following year. The first plane to exceed the speed of sound in level flight was the American rocket-

Charles A. Lindbergh arriving in France, 1927

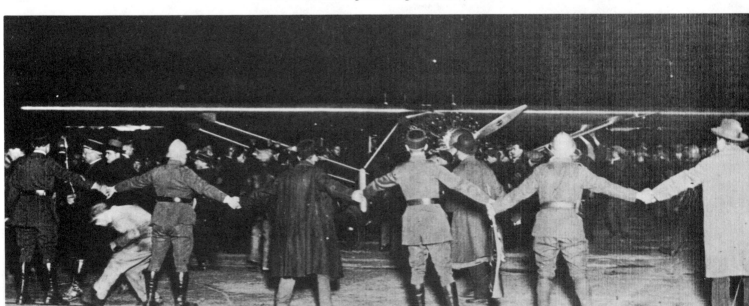

The nuclear-powered Soviet icebreaker Lenin

propelled Bell X-1, which reached Mach 1.06 (approximately 750 m.p.h.) on October 14, 1947.

1940-1945. Development of radar ("radio-detection-and-ranging") stimulated by World War II, for detection of aircraft, blind-bombing techniques, and naval search equipment. Based on Heinrich Hertz's demonstration (1887) that radio waves are reflected similarly to light rays, the technique was first applied by Edward Appleton in Britain (1924) and G. Breit and M. A. Tuve in the United States (1925) for investigating ionization in the upper atmosphere. Robert A. Watson-Watt showed the possibilities of employing radio waves to detect aircraft (1935); J. T. Randall and H. A. H. Boot developed the cavity magnetron for high-power microwave transmission. Simultaneously, radar development had been going on in Germany and the United States, including the development of equipment by Robert H. Page of the Naval Laboratory. After 1940 Britain and the United States co-operated in radar development, much of the work being done at the Radiation Laboratory in Cambridge, Mass.

1941-1945. Construction of 2500 miles of large diameter (20-inch-24-inch) **pipelines** to deliver petroleum from oil-producing regions in Southwest United States to East Coast depots. Development of welding of steelpipe sections (1913-1914) cut leakage and made possible large-scale pipeline construction.

1948. Long-playing phonograph record introduced, based on Peter Goldmark's development of the narrow-groove vinyl plastic record, a light-weight pickup, and a slow-speed (33⅓ r.p.m.), silent turntable.

1948. Basic research in semi-conductors at the Bell Telephone Laboratories resulted in the invention of the **transistor** by a group which included William Shockley, John Bardeen, and Walter H. Brattain. This tiny, rugged, amplifying device was increasingly used to replace vacuum tubes in electronic instruments. In 1954 the silicon transistor was developed.

1950 ff. Development of **nuclear propulsion** for submarines and surface ships. The United States submarine *Nautilus* (1955), built under the stimulus exerted by Admiral Hyman Rickover, was the first submarine to pass under the North Polar ice cap. The Soviet icebreaker *Lenin* was the first nuclear-powered surface vessel.

1953 ff. "Cinerama" system (invented and developed by Fred Waller) to produce three-dimensional films, released for commercial exhibition. At about the same time Cinemascope, employing a single large concave screen, and stereophonic sound were introduced for motion picture exhibition.

1954. Charles H. Townes (1915–   ) invented the **maser** (microwave amplification by the simulated emission of radiation), making it possible to transmit signals over great distances.

1957. Launching of first **man-made satellite,** *Sputnik I,* by Russia (Oct. 4) marked the beginning of the **Space Age.** This was the product of millennia of human dreams but, more materially, of the rocket researches of **Robert H. Goddard** (1882-1945) of the United States (first liquid-fuel rocket launched, 1926), the theoretical studies of the Russian **Konstantin Tsiolkovsky** (1903), and the German **Herman Oberth** (1923). Practical rocket development, for military purposes, took place in Germany during World War II, largely under Oberth, Walter Dornberger, and Wernher von Braun,

Konstantin Tsiolkovsky (1903)

who produced the V-2. Rocket development after the war was largely concentrated on missiles (in the United States: the *Redstone, Thor, Jupiter, Titan, Polaris*), but rocket launching of satellites was an outgrowth of the **International Geophysical Year** (IGY), a coordinated study of the earth's atmosphere, shape, magnetic field, etc. by the world's scientists.

1961. First controlled, individual free flight by Harold Graham (April 20), using rocket-belt designed by Wendell Moore of Bell Aerosystems.

4. *Arctic Exploration, 870–1940*

a. EARLIEST EXPLORATIONS

The first known civilization within the Arctic regions appears to have been that of the **Norsemen,** who, before the birth of Christ, seem to have superseded the Finns in Scandinavia. For a thousand years the Norsemen developed a rude form of political democracy and, from their own rocky coasts, ranged the coasts of western Europe.

c. 870. The Norseman, **Ottar** (Othere), claimed to have sailed around northern Norway, along the Murman Coast, and into the White Sea as far as the Kola Peninsula, in search of the walrus. Thereupon King Harald of Norway declared annexed all territory as far as the White Sea. His successors made various expeditions to that region, both for trade and conquest.

875–900. COLONIZATION OF ICELAND (previously discovered by Irish anchorites, *see p. 382)*

Sir Martin Frobisher, 1535–1594

877. Günnbjorn Ulfsson, driven westward from Iceland, sighted Greenland.

982–985. Eric the Red, outlawed from Iceland, founded a colony in **western Greenland** (c. 61° N.L.). The Norsemen seem to have carried on sealing and whaling expeditions as far north as Disco Bay. The settlement lasted until the 14th or 15th century.

1000–1006. LEIF ERICSSON and **THOR-FINN KARLSEFNI,** from Greenland, explored and tried to settle the **North American coast** *(p. 382)*.

1194. Iceland annals record the discovery of modern **Spitsbergen** (*Svalbard*). In the course of hunting, the Norsemen reached Novaya Zemlya. But after 1300 Norse enterprise seems to have fallen off (loss of Norwegian independence [1349] and domination of the Hanseatic League).

b. THE 16th CENTURY

During this period the initiative in Arctic discoveries was taken by England. **Bristol** had long carried on trade with Iceland and the Bristolers were therefore well acquainted with the northern routes. After the Portuguese discovery of the route to India, the English hoped to find an alternative passage to Cathay either by the northwest, around North America (rediscovered by the Cabots, 1497, *see p. 385),* or to the northeast, around Siberia. The Cabots, intent on finding a **northwest passage,** having failed in their quest, attention became focused on the Siberian route.

1553–1554. Expedition of **SIR HUGH WIL-LOUGHBY** and **RICHARD CHANCELLOR.** Two of their three ships reached the Russian coast near the mouth of the Pechora River and some new land which may have been Novaya Zemlya or Kolguev Island. They turned back to winter on the Kola Peninsula, where Willoughby and all his men died. The third ship, under Chancellor, reached the site of modern Archangel, whence Chancellor made a trip to Moscow. In 1554 he reached England with a letter from the tsar. One result of the expedition was the

1555. Foundation of the **Association of Merchant Adventurers** (the *Muscovy Company*), to trade with Russia. The company at once took the lead in northern exploration. Chancellor left on a mission to Moscow in 1555, but was lost on the return voyage (1556).

1565. The **Dutch,** under Olivier Brunel and Philip Winterkönig (a Norwegian) made a trade settlement on the Kola Peninsula, followed by another (1578) near present-day Archangel. Brunel traveled overland as far as the Ob and visited Novaya Zemlya.

1576. Expedition of **SIR MARTIN FRO-BISHER** to find a northwest passage. Frobisher had the support of Queen Elizabeth I as well as the London merchants. He discovered Frobisher Bay in southern **Baffin Land,** which he was sure was the desired passage. Rumors of gold in some earth that he took back led to further expeditions in the succeeding years. On the last of these Frobisher penetrated **Hudson Strait,** but was deterred from "sailing through to China" by orders to bring back loads of "gold ore."

Willem Barents wintering at Ice Haven, 1596

1585-1587. Voyages of **JOHN DAVIS,** sent out to follow up the work of Frobisher. Davis landed on the west coast of Greenland at Gilbert's Sound and thence crossed the strait named for him. He cruised along the Baffin coast south to Cumberland Sound, convinced that he had found the passage. In 1587 he explored the Greenland side of **Davis Strait** as far as 72° 41′. On his return voyage he followed up Cumberland Sound and passed Hudson Strait without realizing its importance.

1594-1597. The three voyages of **WILLEM BARENTS** and **CORNELIS NAY.** Barents and his Dutchmen explored much of the western coast of Novaya Zemlya, while Nay sailed into the Kara Sea and reached the west coast of the **Yalmal Peninsula.** Finding the sea open beyond, he was convinced that he had found the northeast passage. In 1595 he and Barents tried to get through, but in vain. In 1596 Barents struck north through the sea that bears his name, discovered **Bear Island** and sighted and named **Spitsbergen,** which he supposed to be part of Greenland. He rounded the north end of Novaya Zemlya and wintered at Ice Haven (the first expedition to weather an Arctic winter successfully). Barents died on the return voyage (1597), having laid the foundation for the lucrative Dutch whale and seal fisheries of the 17th and 18th centuries.

c. THE 17th AND 18th CENTURIES

During the 17th century the English and the Dutch continued their efforts to find a passage to China not under Spanish or Portuguese control. The Muscovy Company and individual members of it promoted most of the British expeditions (notably **William Sanderson,** who supported Davis, and **Sir Thomas Smith,** first governor of the East India Company). **Richard Hakluyt's** *Voyages* (1582) and *Principal Navigations* (1598-1600) as well as the collections of his successor, **Samuel Purchas,** were intended to preserve the records of English achievement and actually provided a great stimulus to exploration and colonization.

1607-1611. Voyages of **HENRY HUDSON,** commissioned by the Muscovy Company. In 1607 he set out in the *Hopewell* for China by way of the North Pole. He discovered the East Greenland coast at 73°, passed thence to Spitsbergen. On the return he discovered **Jan Mayen Island.** In 1608 he examined the edge of the ice pack between Spitsbergen and Novaya Zemlya in the vain search for a through passage. In 1609 he made yet another attempt, this time in behalf of the Dutch East India Company. Finding his way barred in the Barents Sea, he turned west to North America, where he discovered the Hudson River. In 1610, with English support, he sailed through Hudson Strait and explored the eastern coast of Hudson Bay. On the return voyage the crew mutinied and set out Hudson and the sick to perish in a small boat. Hudson's Spitsbergen explorations had much to do with the development of the Spitsbergen fisheries. In 1612 the Muscovy Company was given a monopoly over fishing in those waters. In 1613 it fitted out a large fleet under Benjamin Joseph. But the English were never able to exclude the Dutch and the Danes, who finally secured the best fishing grounds on the northern shore of Spitsbergen.

Last Voyage of Henry Hudson, *painting by John Collier*

1610-1648. The **Russian Cossacks,** in the course of the conquest of Siberia, reached the Siberian north coast at the mouths of the great rivers (Yenisei, 1610; Lena and Yana, 1636; Kolyma, 1644). In 1648 a Cossack named **Simon Dezhnev** led an expedition from the Kolyma through Bering Strait into the Gulf of Anadyr.

1612-1613. **Sir Thomas Button** reached the western coast of Hudson Bay and spent the winter at the mouth of the Nelson River. In the following summer he explored the shore of Southampton Island.

1615-1616. **Robert Bylot** (a former member of Hudson's crew) and **William Baffin** explored the coasts of Hudson Strait. On their second voyage they penetrated Baffin Bay and explored the coast far beyond the point reached by Davis. Baffin's fine scientific observations enabled Prof. Hansteen of Christiania to draw up his **first magnetic chart.**

1664. **Willem de Vlamingh,** in search of new whaling grounds, rounded the northern end of Novaya Zemlya and sailed east as far as 82° 10′.

1670. Royal charter granted to **Hudson's Bay Company,** under the auspices of Prince Rupert, for the purpose of trading with the Indians. The company sent out a reconnoitering expedition under **Zachariah Gillan** (Gillam), who wintered on Rupert's River and established a station at Fort Charles. Trading stations multiplied rapidly, but exploration was badly neglected for nearly a century, the only fruitful expeditions being those sent out by the admiralty to look for a northwest passage.

1721. **Hans Egede,** a Norwegian pastor, began the modern colonization of Greenland. He founded Gotthaab and began to convert the Eskimos. Other colonists, including missionaries, spread along the west coast. Trade (skins of seal, reindeer, fox, and bear, eiderdown, whale-bone, walrus tusks, and dried cod) was organized as a monopoly in private hands from 1750 to 1774, and, after it became less profitable, passed into government hands.

1725. Vitus Bering, a Dane in Russian service, was dispatched by Peter the Great to explore the waters off northeastern Siberia. In a series of voyages (1728–1741) he discovered **Bering Strait,** explored the Aleutian Islands, and discovered and named Mt. St. Elias on the American side.

1732–1743. Great survey of the whole Siberian coast, sponsored by the Russian government. Two Russian officers in 1738 made the voyage from Archangel to the mouths of the Ob and the Yenisei. In an effort to effect a passage from the Yenisei to the Lena, a journey was made (1738–1739) eastward past Taimyr Bay to Cape Sterlegov, and repeated attempts were made to round the northernmost point of Siberia by boat. These efforts were blocked by the ice. But in 1743 **S. Chelyuskin** succeeded in making the trip by sledge. **Dmitṛi Laptiev** in a series of voyages (1737, 1742) completed the delineation of the coast east from the mouth of the Lena to Cape Baranov.

1750–1820. Height of the British whaling industry in the Spitsbergen and Greenland Seas. Outstanding among the whaling captains for exploration and scientific work were the **William Scoresbys,** father and son.

1770–1773. Liakhov, a Russian fur merchant, discovered three of the New Siberian Islands.

1778. Capt. James Cook, sent by the admiralty to Bering Strait to find a passage northeast or northwest from the Pacific to the Atlantic, sailed north from Kamchatka in the *Resolution* and the *Discovery.* He rounded Cape Prince of Wales, cleared Bering Strait and penetrated eastward to Icy Cape before turning west again to discover and name Cape North on the Asiatic side.

d. THE 19th CENTURY

1806. William Scoresby reached a record north in the Spitsbergen region (81° 30′). In 1820 William Scoresby, Jr., published his *Account of the Arctic Regions,* which at once became the standard work.

1818. The British government, at the instigation of **Sir John Barrow,** renewed the offer of £20,000 for making the northwest passage and £5000 for reaching 89° N.L.

1818. Capt. John Ross and **Lieut. Edward Parry** set out on a twin expedition to Baffin Bay and pointed the way to the subsequent lucrative whale fishery in that region.

1819–1820. Parry penetrated Lancaster Sound and Barrow Strait, discovered Wellington Channel, Prince Regent Inlet, and the island of North Somerset, and finally advanced westward to **Melville Sound** and Melville Island, where the expedition wintered.

1819–1826. Exploration by land, carried on by the Hudson's Bay Company to fill in the "missing" coastline of northern Canada. The work was entrusted to Lieut. (later Sir) **John Franklin.** In 1820–1821, with Dr. John Richardson, George Back, and Robert Hood, he made a trip from Great Slave Lake to the Coppermine River and down the river to the polar sea. They explored 550 miles of coast east to Cape Turnagain.

1820–1823. Baron Wrangel explored the Siberian coast from Cape Chelagskoi to the mouth of the Kolyma.

1821–1823. Parry's second expedition, in quest of a passage at a lower latitude. During the summer of 1821 he verified the dead end of Repulse Bay. In 1822 he turned north to Fox Channel and discovered the ice-choked Fury and Hecla Strait.

1822. William Scoresby, Jr., in the specially constructed *Baffin,* forced his way through the ice and reached the east coast of Greenland, which he surveyed for 400 miles (75° to 69°).

1823. Capt. Douglas Clavering continued Scoresby's work and charted the East Greenland coast from 72° to 76°, while his associate, **Capt. Edward Sabine,** established for the admiralty a magnetic observatory on Pendulum Island.

1824. Parry's third expedition, on which he hoped to follow the Fury and Hecla Strait west to Prince Regent Inlet. He had to abandon the attempt when one of his ships was badly damaged.

1825–1826. Franklin's second expedition by land. He descended the Mackenzie River to the sea and advanced westward to Cape Beechey. A party under Dr. Richardson reached the shore between the Mackenzie and Coppermine Rivers, discovered and named Union and Dolphin Strait and Wollaston Land.

1826. Capt. F. W. Beechey led an expedition to the Arctic by way of Bering Strait, to connect with Franklin's explorations. He traced the coastline as far east as Point Barrow, and narrowly missed connection with Franklin's party.

1827. Parry tried to reach the North Pole from northern Spitsbergen, using sledge-boats, but the party did not get beyond 82° 45′ N.L. This remained the record north for fifty years.

1829–1833. Capt. John Ross and his nephew, **James Clark Ross,** embarked on a private quest for the northwest passage through Prince Regent Inlet. They found their way into the Gulf of Boothia, where they wintered. In 1830 James Ross crossed the Isthmus of Boothia by sledge, discovering to the west King William Land. In

1831, June 1. JAMES ROSS located and planted the British flag on the **north magnetic pole.** The expedition remained in the Arctic until 1833 and was rescued in Lancaster Sound by a whaler.

1833. Sir George Back and **Dr. Richard King** made an effort to reach the Rosses overland from Great Slave Lake and Great Fish River, which they descended to the mouth. Failure of supplies forced them to turn back.

1837. Thomas Simpson and **P. W. Dease,** of the Hudson's Bay Company, descended the Mackenzie and explored the remainder of the coast westward from Cape Beechey to Point Barrow. In 1839 Simpson explored east from the mouth of the Coppermine to Simpson Strait and the mouth of the Great Fish River. From there he went on to Montreal Island and as far as Castor and Pollux River. On the return trip he explored the southern coasts of King William Land and of Victoria Land.

1845–1848. The **EXPEDITION OF SIR JOHN FRANKLIN,** in the *Erebus* and *Terror,* to seek a northwest passage by way of Lancaster Sound. In 1846 he sailed south down Peel Sound and Franklin Strait and in the winter 1846–1847 was beset by heavy polar ice

drifting on the northwest coast of King William Land. In the spring a party went south as far as Cape Herschel, thus completing the **discovery of the northwest passage,** although unable to navigate its full length. Sir John died in June, as did twenty-three others in the course of the following winter. The rest abandoned ship (Apr. 22, 1848) and started for Great Fish River. According to later reports by Eskimos "they fell down and died as they walked." Not one member of the expedition survived.

1847. Dr. John Rae closed the gap remaining in the Canadian coastline between Boothia and Fury and Hecla Strait. He and his men of the Hudson's Bay Company explored 655 miles of new coast, on foot, and established the fact that Boothia is the northernmost extremity of the American continent.

1848–1859. THE FRANKLIN RELIEF EXPEDITIONS:

1848–1849. Sir James Ross followed Franklin's route by way of Lancaster Sound and explored the northern and western coasts of North Somerset, never realizing, when he turned back, how near he had come to solution of the Franklin mystery.

1848–1851. Dr. Rae and **Sir John Richardson** searched the American coast between the mouth of the Mackenzie and the mouth of the Coppermine.

1850–1851. A great relief expedition was organized in various sections and dispatched by the admiralty: **Capt. Horatio Austin** led a renewal of the search from Barrow Strait. He found Franklin's Beechey Island camp but found no further trace of Franklin.

1850–1854. Capt. Richard Collinson and **Capt. Robert M'Clure** were sent out by the admiralty to attack the problem from Bering Strait. M'Clure wintered in Prince of Wales Strait, whence he could see Banks Strait, blocked by ice. Once again the northwest passage was found, but could not be navigated. Collinson traced the shore of Prince Albert Land and reached Melville Island, thus connecting with previous explorations from the east.

1852. Capt. Edward A. Inglefield advanced north in Baffin Bay to Smith Sound, which he correctly surmised to be a channel to the Arctic Ocean. He named Ellesmere Land and explored 600 miles of new coast.

1852–1854. Sir Edward Belcher was sent out by the admiralty on a last effort to solve the Franklin mystery from the east. He and Sherard Osborn completed the exploration of Melville Island and Prince Patrick Island.

1853–1855. An American relief expedition under **Dr. E. K. Kane** advanced up Smith Sound and in 1854 discovered the great Humboldt Glacier.

1854. Dr. Rae, exploring in the region of King William Land, secured from the Eskimos the first information and relics of the Franklin expedition, thus winning the £10,000 admiralty award.

1857. Lady Franklin sent out **Capt. Leopold M'Clintock,** to complete the search. His party went over the Boothia and King William Land regions, and at Point Victory and Point Felix found the records and many relics of Franklin's party. In the last analysis the Franklin catastrophe resulted in the exploration of more than 7000 miles of coastline.

1860–1871. Expeditions of **Charles Hall,** an

James Ross's expedition is rescued (1833) in Lancaster Sound

Expedition of Sir George Back trying to reach the Rosses overland in 1833

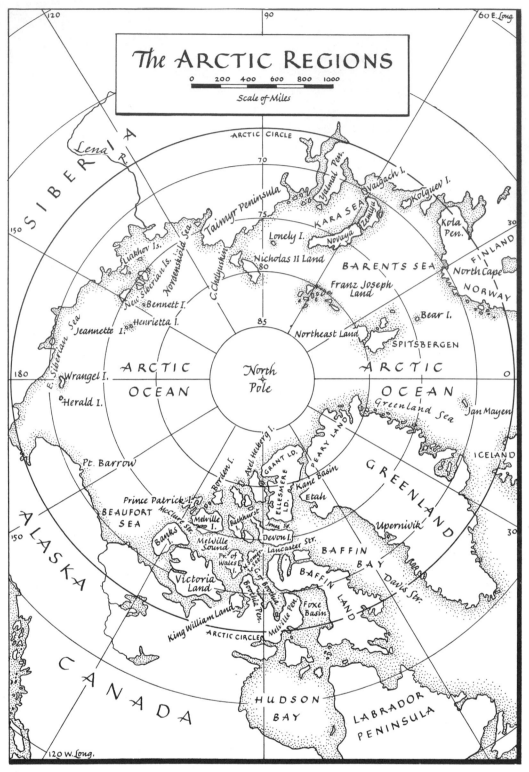

The ARCTIC REGIONS

0 200 400 600 800 1000

Scale of Miles

---

northwest passage. In 1876 **Albert H. Markham,** of the expedition, reached a new record north (83° 20′ on May 11). Another member, Lieut. Aldrich, explored the north coast of Ellesmere Land to Cape Columbia, while Lieut. Beaumont followed the north coast of Greenland to Cape Britannia.

1876. Foundation of the Danish committee for the geographical and geological investigation of Greenland. This committee stimulated popular interest and sent out many expeditions.

1878. The **Dutch,** under **Koolemans Beynen,** began sending out annual expeditions in the specially constructed *Willem Barents* to make scientific observations in the Spitsbergen area.

1878-1879. NORDENSKIÖLD for the first time made the **northeast passage** in the *Vega.* Rounding the northernmost point of Siberia (Cape Chelyuskin) on August 19, 1878, he was frozen in and obliged to winter on shore. The voyage was completed in the next year, Bering Strait being reached on July 20, 1879.

1879-1881. The American expedition of **Lieut. G. W. de Long** in the *Jeannette.* The purpose was to explore the northern coast of Siberia from Bering Strait. The ship was crushed in the ice and sank (June 13, 1881). De Long and most of the party perished, but a few reached the coast by way of the New Siberian Islands.

1880. **Leigh Smith,** an Englishman, reached Franz Joseph Land from Spitsbergen and explored the southern coast, naming it Alexandra Land.

1882. Establishment of **international polar stations,** an idea put forward in 1875 by Weyprecht and promoted at the polar conferences of 1879-1880. Norwegians, Swedes, Danes, Russians, Dutch, British, Germans, Austrians, and Americans agreed to co-operate. The Dutch were unsuccessful in establishing a station at the mouth of the Yenisei, but the other expeditions carried out their assignments. An American mission, under **Lieut. Adolphus W. Greely,** carried on observations in Lady Franklin Bay for two years (1881-1883). Greely explored the north coast of Greenland and reached a **new record north** (83° 24′) at Lockwood Island. In 1882 Greely penetrated Grinnell Land. In 1883 **Lieut. James Lockwood** crossed Grinnell Land to Greely Fjord. Relief ships having failed to arrive, the party had to winter in Smith Sound. All but six of the party of 24 were dead of starvation when the relief ships arrived in June 1884.

1883. **Nordenskiöld** penetrated 84 miles into the interior of Greenland, reaching an altitude of 5000 feet.

1886. **Lieut. Robert E. Peary** advanced 50 miles inland from Disco Bay and reached an altitude of 7500 feet.

1888. FIRST CROSSING OF GREENLAND, by **Dr. Fridtjof Nansen, Otto Sverdrup,** and five others. From near Kjoge Bay on the east coast they covered 260 miles of glacier on skis, reaching an altitude of nearly 9000 feet and striking the west coast near Gotthaab.

1892. **Peary** made a 1200-mile dog-sledge journey from Inglefield Gulf in northwest Greenland, north and east over the inland ice to Independence Fjord and back again.

1893-1896. EXPEDITION OF NANSEN in the *Fram.* Surmising that there was a drift across the polar basin, Nansen decided to be frozen in and travel with it. With Sverdrup

---

American. He explored Countess of Warwick Land and came across the ruins of a house built by Frobisher in 1578.

1863. Capt. E. Carlsen first circumnavigated Spitsbergen.

1869-1870. The Germans, inspired by Dr. A. Petermann, organized a great Greenland expedition under **Capt. Karl Koldewey.** He and his lieutenant, **Julius Payer** (an Austrian), explored the east coast of Greenland by sledge to Cape Bismarck in Germania Land. One of the ships, the *Hansa,* was crushed by the ice and for nearly a year her crew drifted 1100

miles south on a floe, eventually landing near Cape Farewell.

1870. Prof. A. E. Nordenskiöld and Dr. Berggren explored the interior of Greenland, advancing 35 miles from Auleitsivikfjord on the west coast and reaching an altitude of 2200 feet.

1871-1874. DISCOVERY OF FRANZ JOSEPH LAND by the Austrians Julius Payer and Carl Weyprecht. In 1872 they sought a northeast passage around Novaya Zemlya.

1875-1876. The British, under **Sir George S. Nares,** resumed the effort to penetrate the

---

he entered the pack off the New Siberian Islands in September 1893, drifted northwest until November 15, 1895. Thence the ship moved southward until it broke free off northern Spitsbergen (Aug. 1896). The ship reached 85° 55′ N.L. in the summer of 1895, but Nansen and Hjalmar Johansen in March left the ship and traveled north with skis and dog-sledges, reaching a **record north** of 86° 14′ on April 7. They wintered on Frederick Jackson Island and in the spring started for Spitsbergen, and were picked up by the relief ship *Windward.*

1894–1897. The **Jackson-Harmsworth expedition** to Franz Joseph Land reached 81° 19′ N.L. and surveyed a number of islands. Jackson covered about 600 miles of new coastline and demonstrated the complexity of the archipelago.

1897. **S. A. Andrée,** a Swedish flyer, undertook a balloon flight northeastward from Spitsbergen. His decapitated body was found on White Island in Barents Sea in 1930, with a diary which revealed that the balloon had come down on the ice pack after 65 hours and that the party had reached White Island, where all had perished.

1898–1902. **Capt. Otto Sverdrup** in the *Fram,* blocked by ice in his effort to circumnavigate Greenland, made several journeys over Ellesmere Land, discovering its western coast.

1899. The Russian admiral, **Makarov,** arranged a trial trip into the ice off Spitsbergen, using the great icebreaker *Yermak.* Though unsuccessful, he paved the way for later development of the icebreaker.

1899–1900. Expedition of the **DUKE OF THE ABRUZZI** to Franz Joseph Land. From Rudolf Land his lieutenant, **Capt. Umberto Cagni,** led a dog-sledge party on a 753-mile trip and reached a **new northern record** of 86° 34′ N.L. (200 miles from the pole).

1900. **Peary,** from his base in Lady Franklin Bay, made a journey along the northern coast of Greenland, rounding the northernmost point and reaching Cape Wyckoff, where he built a cairn (82° 57′ N.L.).

e. THE 20th CENTURY

(1) Conquest of the North Pole

1905–1906. Peary, with **Capt. Robert Bartlett,** went by ship to northern Grant Land and thence westward by sledge to Cape Hecla. From there he claimed to have reached 87° 6′ early in 1906. The claim is questioned by some geographers, since Peary was the only white man in the final party and because the record is unsatisfactory in certain respects.

1907–1908. **Expedition of Dr. F. A. Cook.** He followed a route discovered by Sverdrup (from Cape Sabine across Ellesmere Land and north along the coast to the northern tip of Axel Heiberg Island).

1908, Apr. 20. **Cook** claimed that he reached the pole on this date. Experts regard the claim as improbable, though not impossible. His observations were fuller than Peary's, but not very good. His chronological table of distances was entirely reasonable. The claim has not yet been accepted by authoritative opinion.

1909. Apr. 6. **Peary** claimed to have reached the pole on this date, from Cape Columbia, the northernmost extremity of Grant Land. Though generally accepted, the claim is questioned by some experts because of the inadequacy of the observations and the incredible time-table submitted. Possibly neither Cook nor Peary actually reached the pole.

No further progress in polar exploration was made until the airplane began to open up new possibilities.

1925, May. Roald Amundsen (Lieut. Riiser-Larsen as pilot) and **Lincoln Ellsworth,** in two flying-boats, flew from King Bay, West Spitsbergen, to 87° 43′ N.L., where they landed. They finally got one of their craft into the air again and managed to return.

1926, May. COMM. RICHARD BYRD and **FLOYD BENNETT** flew from King Bay and **reached the pole** (May 9). Using the Fokker monoplane *Josephine Ford,* they covered the 750 miles and return in 15 hours.

1926, May. ROALD AMUNDSEN, GEN. UMBERTO NOBILE, and **LINCOLN ELLSWORTH,** forestalled by Byrd in their effort to reach the pole first, took off in the dirigible *Norge* to fly from King Bay across the pole to Alaska. They landed safely near Nome, having sighted no land in the Beaufort Sea area.

1928, May. Nobile, in the dirigible *Italia,* made a number of flights from King Bay, one of which covered almost 20,000 square miles of unexplored regions. No new land was seen. The last flight was made (May 24) over northeastern Greenland to the pole. On the return flight the ship encountered a storm and crashed on the ice. Among many relief expeditions, Amundsen's ended disastrously in Barents Sea. Amundsen was lost. The *Italia* survivors were rescued by other planes and by the Russian icebreaker *Krassin.*

1937. May 26–1938, February 19. A SOVIET POLAR STATION organized by Prof. Schmidt, and consisting of four members, led by Ivan Papanin, was transported by plane to a floe near the pole (89° 26′ N.). Oceanographical and meteorological observations were taken over a period of nine months. The drift ultimately carried the party to the east coast of Greenland.

1937, June. Three Russian aviators (V. P. Chkalov, G. P. Baidukov, and A. V. Beliakov) flew non-stop from Moscow over the North Pole to Vancouver.

1937, July 14. Mikhail Gromov and two companions, all Russians, flew non-stop over the pole from Moscow to Riverside, California (6262 miles in 62 hours 17 minutes, a non-stop distance record).

(2) The Canadian Arctic

1903–1906. Capt. Roald Amundsen navigated the northwest passage by way of the east coast of King William Land, spending two winters at Petersen Bay and charting the coast of Victoria Land. In August 1906, he finally reached Bering Strait. This was the **first time a ship passed from sea to sea.**

1908–1910. The **CANADIAN GOVERNMENT** took formal possession of all islands to the north of the continent. **Capt. J. E. Bernier,** sent out by the government, formally annexed Banks and Victoria Islands.

Capt. J. E. Bernier (front) *with Eskimos on Victoria Island*

1913-1917. **Donald B. MacMillan** led the Borup Memorial Expedition to Ellesmere Land. From a base at Etah observations were made over a period of four years and a permanent meteorological station was established.

1913-1918. **Stefansson** led the **Canadian Arctic Expedition,** one section of which made observations for three years in the Coronation Gulf district, while the other, in command of Stefansson, was beset off northern Alaska. Stefansson himself remained in the field for four years and continued his investigations in a series of remarkable sledge journeys in the vicinity of Banks Island and Melville Island.

1921-1924. **Knud Rasmussen,** with two companions, carried out a 20,000-mile expedition across Arctic America by way of Fox Channel, Hudson Bay, King William Land, Coronation Gulf, and the Mackenzie Delta to Alaska.

1922- The Canadian government established an **annual police patrol** of the islands and opened a large number of government stations designed for observation, exploration, and the development of the Eskimos.

1934-1935. The **Oxford University Ellesmere Land Expedition** organized by **Edward Shackleton,** son of the famous antarctic explorer, and led by **Noel Humphreys,** made a sledge journey from Etah to northern Grant Land where the British Empire Mountains were discovered.

1936- The **British-Canadian Arctic Expedition,** under **T. H. Manning,** carried out scientific surveys around Southampton Island, Repulse Bay, and Melville Peninsula.

During and after the Second World War the Arctic became increasingly important as providing the most direct air-route from the United States to Europe and thereby acquired great strategic as well as commercial significance. Northern Canada was equipped with a great system of radar stations for early warning of attack by way of the Arctic and the Canadian Arctic has been intensively explored for raw materials such as coal and iron. In

1954. Scandinavian Airlines System initiated commercial flights from Copenhagen to Los Angeles by way of the Arctic.

1958, Aug. **Commander W. R. Anderson** (American) navigated the nuclear-powered submarine *Nautilus* under the North Pole, covering 1830 miles in 96 hours, from Point Barrow to a point between Greenland and Spitsbergen.

1959, Mar. The United States nuclear submarine *Skate* surfaced at the North Pole.

(3) Greenland

1905. The **duke of Orléans** in the *Belgica* traced the northeastern coast from Cape Bismarck to a new northern point (78° 30′, Duc d'Orléans Land).

1906-1908. **L. Mylius-Erichsen** led a Danish expedition from near Cape Bismarck to Northeast Foreland. A party under **Lieut. J. P. Koch** advanced to the northwest and connected with Peary's earlier explorations, thus completing the discovery of the entire Greenland coast.

1909-1912. **Einar Mikkelsen** led an American expedition to settle the question whether Peary Channel was really a channel or a fjord.

1912. **Knud Rasmussen** made two crossings of interior Greenland, the first eastward from Inglefield Gulf to Danmark Fjord, whence he explored Peary Land and Independence Fjord.

Finding that Peary Channel did not exist, he was obliged to make a second crossing from Navy Cliff to Inglefield Gulf.

1912. **Dr. de Quervain,** a Swiss scientist, crossed Greenland from Disco Bay to Angmagssalik, discovering the lofty mountain chain that contains Mt. Forel.

1912-1913. **J. P. Koch** and **Dr. Alfred Wegener,** a German, led a party on the long 700-mile crossing over the unknown middle part of Greenland.

1917. Denmark strengthened her claim on Greenland by treaty with the United States, ceding the Virgin Islands in settlement of American claims to areas discovered by Peary.

1919. Foundation of the **Danish East Greenland Company.** This led to the establishment of trapping stations at Danmark Harbor and Germania Harbor and later at other places.

1920-1923. **Lauge Koch** led a Danish expedition to northern Greenland to complete the survey of Peary Land.

1921. **Denmark proclaimed sole sovereignty** over the whole country and closed the coasts to foreigners. The Norwegians, however, continued to press a long-standing claim based on original discovery and settlement by the Norsemen.

1924. **Greenland Agreement** between Denmark and Norway, providing that, until 1944, Norwegian hunters and landing parties should suffer no restrictions on the east coast between 60° 27′ and 81°, except at Angmagssalik and the new Eskimo colonies around Scoresby Sound. Similar concessions made to the British. **Greenland became a crown colony of Denmark,** which exercises a trade monopoly and has undertaken a paternalistic program to preserve Eskimo culture.

1926, 1929. **J. M. Wordie** led two Cambridge University expeditions to East Greenland, mapping in detail a large area of mountains and glaciers around Clavering Island. On the second expedition Petermann Peak (9600 feet) was ascended.

1926-1927, and 1931-1934. **Lauge Koch** continued the Danish government surveys from Scoresby Sound northward. Four winter stations were established with radios, and various air surveys were carried out.

1930. **Capt. Ahrenberg** made an airplane flight from Sweden to Angmagssalik. In the same year **Wolfgang von Gronau** flew over the southern end of Greenland and landed at Ivigtut on his way from Iceland to the United States.

1930-1931. The **German Inland Ice expedition** under Dr. Alfred Wegener established parties at Scoresby Sound and at Kamarujuk Bay (West Greenland) and set up meteorological stations for winter observation.

1930-1932. The **British Arctic Air-Route Expedition,** led by twenty-three-year-old **H. G. Watkins,** established a base west of Angmagssalik and set up a weather station at an altitude of 8000 feet. Much of the coast was photographed from the air, and the lofty Watkins Mountains were discovered. In 1931 a party climbed Mt. Forel (11,100 feet). Another party crossed the icecap to Ivigtut, while yet another section crossed by a more northern route to Holsteinsborg.

1931, July 10. **Norway formally annexed the coastal region** north of Scoresby Sound, calling it *Eric the Red's Land*. After protests by Denmark the matter was referred to the Hague

Court which decided in favor of Danish sovereignty (Apr. 5, 1933).

1932-1933. The **Danish Scoresby Sound Committee** undertook large-scale aerial photography.

1934. **Martin Lindsay** led the **British Trans-Greenland Expedition** from Disco Bay to the west slope of the Watkins Mountains, following the range southward for 350 miles. The expedition traversed one of the largest "blank spots" and reached an icecap altitude of 10,400 feet.

1935-1936. The **Oxford University Greenland Expedition,** under **H. Hayward,** continued extensive investigations in West Greenland.

1935. **A. Courtauld,** a former companion of Watkins, scaled the highest known peak in the Arctic (about 12,200 feet) in the Watkins Range.

During the Second World War Greenland became important for the staging of aircraft flying from the United States to Britain. Various bases were built on the southwest coast and eventually, in 1951, a great radar-protected base was constructed at Thule in northwest Greenland. During the entire post-war period there have been many expeditions, mostly air-supported, studying weather conditions and exploring the Greenland ice-sheet. Among the most important were

1948-1957. The French **Expéditions polaires,** led by **Paul-Émile Victor.**

1952-1954. The British North Greenland Expedition, led by **C. J. W. Simpson,** and

1959-1961. The **International Expedition** to Greenland, led by Victor.

(4) The Spitsbergen Area

1907-1920. **Dr. W. S. Bruce** in a series of six expeditions made a complete cartographical, geological, and zoological survey of Prince Charles Foreland. In addition he staked a mining claim on which the Scotch Spitsbergen Syndicate was founded (1909), and took an active part in developing the mineral resources of the country.

1911. **Count Zeppelin** in the *Mainz* set up a German meteorological station at Ice Fjord.

1921-1924. A series of three **Oxford University expeditions,** largely promoted by **George Binney,** initiated the University School of Explorers, composed largely of undergraduates and professional scientists. In Spitsbergen these expeditions carried out extensive scientific investigations, as they did in Greenland.

1923. **Lieut. Mittelholzer,** a Swiss aviator, made a successful 500-mile flight over Spitsbergen and Northeast Land.

1925. **Norway acquired sovereignty** over the Spitsbergen Archipelago and Bear Island, the whole area becoming officially known by the old Norse name *Svalbard*. Since 1906 the government has supported annual surveying cruises, mostly under the leadership of **Prof. Adolf Hoel.** Since 1911 meteorological and other stations have been established and in 1936 aerial mapping was begun.

1925. **Beginning of the polar flights** of Amundsen, Byrd, Nobile, etc., which all started from King Bay *(p. 601)*.

1931. The **Norwegian-Swedish expedition** to Northeast Land, under **Prof. H. Ahlmann,** carried out a sledge tour over the inland ice and made many valuable scientific contributions.

1933-1936. Two Oxford University expeditions, led by **A. R. Glen,** concentrated on the little known New Friesland icecap in West Spitsbergen, explored and mapped the greater part of the interior, and carried on extensive biological researches. The second expedition (1935-1936) went to Northeast Land and carried out the most comprehensive scientific program of any British Arctic expedition.

(5) The Russian Arctic

The development of Siberia and the need for better communications with the Far East served as an important stimulus to Arctic work.

1910. The government inaugurated annual hydrographic cruises along the Siberian coast by the icebreakers *Taimyr* and *Vaigach,* and between 1912 and 1914 established five meteorological stations in the Arctic.

1913. Capt. B. Vilkitski, in an attempt to navigate the northeast passage from east to west, discovered the new and extensive Severnaya Zemlya (North Land), about 50 miles north of Cape Chelyuskin.

1914-1915. Capt. Otto Sverdrup first used radio successfully in the Arctic, communicating with the icebreakers off Cape Chelyuskin.

1915. Vilkitski arrived at Archangel, having completed the east-west passage.

1916. The **Russian government annexed Franz Joseph Land** (claimed by Austria after the discovery in 1873). At the same time the government claimed Wrangel Island, Henrietta Island, and Herald Island, all discovered by Americans in the late 19th century.

1918-1925. Capt. Roald Amundsen, with **Dr. H. Sverdrup,** in the specially built *Maud,* navigated the northeast passage and spent two winters (1918-1920) in the ice preparatory to his projected drift over the pole. The drift was carried out in 1922-1925, nearly duplicating that of the *Fram,* but without important geographical results.

1921. Stefansson attempted to plant a British colony on Wrangel Island, which he regarded as a possible future air base. Most of the colonists died before they could be relieved in 1923.

1921. Prof. R. Samoilovich, of the new Institute for the Exploration of the North (founded 1921), initiated the annual exploration cruises into the Barents Sea, Kara Sea, and Russian Arctic.

1924. The **Soviet government** founded a col-

Capt. Roald Amundsen, 1921

ony on Wrangel Island, which has been maintained ever since.

1924. The government created the **Islands Administration of the U.S.S.R.** and placed Novaya Zemlya, Kolguev, and Vaigach under its jurisdiction.

1925-1928. Prof. S. V. Obruchev explored the practically unknown territory between the Kolima and Indigirka Rivers, discovering some very high mountain ranges.

1926. The **Soviet government** hoisted the flag over Herald Island, and, after Amundsen's flight in the *Norge,* claimed all lands and islands that might be discovered north of Russia and Siberia by flight across the Arctic.

1927. The Soviet established a permanent station on the New Siberian Islands. **First Russian hydroplane flight** from Cape North to Wrangel Island.

1931. The German dirigible, *Graf Zeppelin,* commanded by **Dr. Hugo Eckener,** cruised

over the Franz Joseph Archipelago, Severnaya Zemlya, the Taimyr Peninsula, and unexplored parts of northern Novaya Zemlya.

1932. The **Soviet government** claimed Victoria Island, though this is generally regarded as part of the Spitsbergen group.

1932. Prof. Schmidt, in the icebreaker *Sibiriakov,* made a record passage by the northeast route from Archangel (July 28) to Yokohama (Nov. 5), that is, 3000 miles in nine weeks. It was the first time the passage had been made in one season. Since then at least one ship has gotten through each year. In 1936 fourteen ships made the passage.

1932. The government established a **polar radio station** on Prince Rudolf Land, in the Franz Joseph group.

1932. Prof. N. N. Zubow first circumnavigated the Franz Joseph Archipelago.

1935. Foundation of the **CENTRAL ADMINISTRATION OF THE NORTHERN SEA ROUTE** by the Soviet government. This was a chartered company entrusted with the exploration and development of all Soviet territory north of 62°. Under Prof. Schmidt it employed about 40,000 people. The extensive new program included: navigation of the great Siberian rivers and building of ports at their mouths (to be kept open by icebreakers); establishment on the coast of permanent stations (there were 57 in 1936) with radio and other scientific equipment; maintenance of planes for reconnaissance of ice conditions, etc.; charting of coasts and currents (warm currents discovered along the edge of the continental shelf in 1935); construction of a railway from the Yenisei to the Dudinka and Norilsk mining regions (coal, nickel, platinum, and copper); agricultural stations to develop a food supply for colonists (work on rapidly maturing wheat, etc.); education and development of the natives, and protection of reindeer herds, etc.

The Second World War saw the development of the Northern Sea Route as a regular part of the Soviet communications system. The Soviet government has supported intensive exploration of its entire Arctic coast and has, in the post-war period, organized several expeditions to study the Arctic drift.

1948. A Russian expedition discovered the **Lomonosov Ridge,** a great chain of submerged mountains running from Ellesmere Land to the New Siberian Islands and thus dividing the great polar basin.

5. *Antarctic Exploration, 1738–1940*

A legend dating from Greek antiquity and supported by Ptolemy related to the existence of an enormous continent in the southern hemisphere. This land-mass was shown by medieval cartographers, and even on maps as late as the end of the 16th century, on many of which it is extended to tropical latitudes in each of the three oceans. A series of voyages in southern latitudes during the 15th, 16th, and 17th centuries (Da Gama, 1497; Magellan, 1520; Drake, 1579; Tasman, 1642; and others, who were blown southward from their courses) progressively reduced the possible area of this legendary continent by pushing its limits farther and farther southward.

1738-1739. Pierre Bouvet, a French naval officer, deliberately set out to prove or disprove the existence of the southern continent, and

1400 miles south of Capetown he sighted land (Bouvet Island, 54° S.L.).

1756. The Spanish ship *Leon* discovered South Georgia (54°-55° S.) in the Atlantic.

1768. Capt. James Cook, on his first voyage, circumnavigated New Zealand, hitherto supposedly part of the Antarctic continent.

1771-1772. Capt. Yves Kerguélen sent out by France to look for "a very large continent."

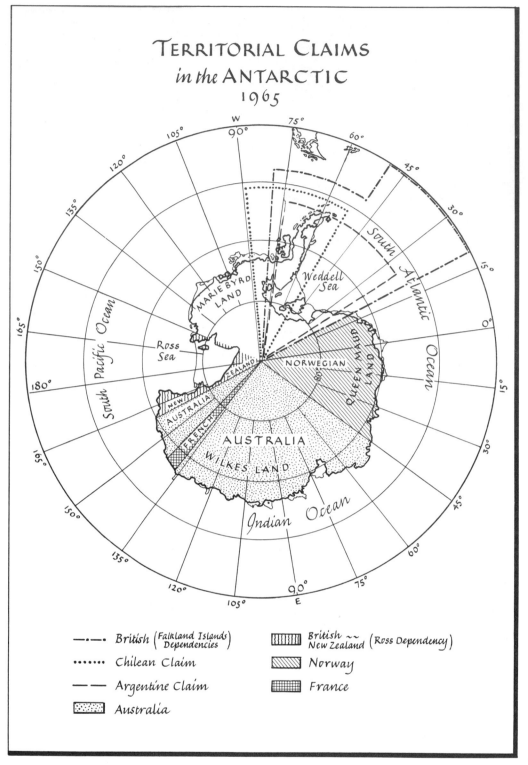

TERRITORIAL CLAIMS
in the ANTARCTIC
1965

Legend:
- —·—· *British* (Falkland Islands) *Dependencies*
- ········ *Chilean Claim*
- — — — *Argentine Claim*
- (stippled) *Australia*
- (vertical lines) *British ~~ New Zealand* (Ross Dependency)
- (diagonal lines) *Norway*
- (crosshatch) *France*

circumnavigated Antarctica, and discovered Alexander I Land and Peter Island (68° S.), the first land sighted within the Antarctic Circle.

1821.   George Powell, a British sealer, and Nathaniel B. Palmer, an American sealer, discovered the South Orkney Islands, and Powell annexed them for the British. Palmer and other American sealers further explored Palmer Archipelago, which skirts Graham Land.

1823.   Capt. James Weddell, an Englishman, discovered and penetrated Weddell Sea, establishing on February 20, 1823, the **record south** of his day (74° 15′, 945 miles from the pole).

1831–1832.   John Biscoe, an English sealer, circumnavigated Antarctica, named and annexed Graham Land, discovered the Biscoe Islands, Queen Adelaide Island, and sighted Enderby Land.

1837–1840.   Capt. J. S. C. Dumont d'Urville of the French navy, in the *Astrolabe* and *Zelée*, sighted Joinville Island, Louis Philippe Land (in Graham Land), and Adélie Land on the mainland due south of Tasmania.

1839–1840.   Capt. Charles Wilkes of the U.S. Navy cruised westward along the coast of Antarctica from 148° E. to 108° E., where he found his way blocked by Termination Barrier (Shackleton Ice Shelf).

1841–1843.   CAPT. JAMES CLARK ROSS (sent out by the British admiralty) in the *Erebus* and the *Terror* hoping to plant the Union Jack on the south magnetic pole and reach as high a latitude as possible. He got through the ice pack, but, finding his way barred by the lofty Admiralty Range, cruised southward for 430 miles into Ross Sea, along the scarped eastern coast of South Victoria Land. There he sighted and named, besides the Admiralty Range, the Prince Albert Range, and the volcanic mountains Erebus and Terror on Ross Island.   Finding further passage southward barred at the latter point by the **Great** (Ross) **Ice Barrier,** he cruised eastward along it for 350 miles, before returning to Hobart, Tasmania (Apr. 1, 1841). The following summer he returned to the head of Ross Sea near King Edward VII Land and made a **record south** (78° 9′, 710 miles from the pole) which held for 60 years. Altogether Ross charted about 1000 miles of coastline. He also took possession for Great Britain of all the continental land and islands that he discovered in 1841.

After the voyages of Ross there was a lull of 30 years in systematic exploration of the Antarctic, attention having shifted to the North Pole.

1872–1874.   H.M.S. *Challenger* (Capt. George S. Nares), the first steam-propelled vessel to cross the Antarctic Circle, renewed the study of oceanography in the Antarctic.

1873–1875.   Capt. Eduard Dallmann (German) established that Palmer Land was an archipelago by sailing behind it, and, beyond, discovered Bismarck Strait and the Kaiser Wilhelm Archipelago to the south off Graham Land.

1893.   Capt. C. A. Larsen (Norwegian) explored Weddell seacoast, discovering and naming Foyn Coast in Graham Land, King Oscar Land, Mt. Jason, and Robertson Island.

1894–1895.   Capt. Leonard Kristensen (Norwegian) discovered Ridley Beach at Cape

He discovered Kerguelen Island in the Indian Ocean (50° S.), which he named *New France.*
1772–1775.   SECOND VOYAGE OF CAPT. COOK. He was the first to cross the Antarctic Circle (Jan. 17, 1773). He circumnavigated Antarctica, and made extensive exploratory cruises in the surrounding waters, pushing to 71° 10′ S. on January 30, 1774 (1130 miles from the pole and the **record south** for the 18th century). He discovered the South Sandwich Islands, annexed South Georgia, and reported the presence there of enormous herds of seals.

1778–1839.   Explorations by the sealers. The discoveries made in this period were in the main incidental to the operations of British and American whalers and sealers drawn south by Cook's reports.

1819.   Capt. William Smith discovered and took possession of the South Shetland Islands for the British.

1820.   Edward Bransfield charted 500 miles of the southern coast of the South Shetlands, discovered his strait, and sighted Graham Land.

1820–1821.   Capt. Fabian Gottlieb von Bellingshausen, sent out by Alexander I of Russia,

Adare, where the **first landing on the continent** was made in January by Carsten Borchgrevink. He found the first vegetation—a lichen at Possession Island.

1895. The Sixth International Geographical Congress in London described Antarctic exploration as the most pressing geographical requirement of the time.

1897-1899. Lieut. Adrien de Gerlache (Belgian) with **Roald Amundsen** as mate, coasted Graham Land, discovered and made several landings in Belgica Strait (subsequently Gerlache Channel), discovered and named Danco Land to the east, and passed south of Peter Island. Here on March 3, 1898, they were beset and remained, the first prisoners through an Antarctic night, drifting with the pack ice until February 14, 1899.

1898-1900. Carsten Borchgrevink led the first party (British and Scandinavian) to winter on the continent, at Cape Adare, where meteorological observations were taken, penguin life studied, and geological collections made. Picked up by their ship in January 1900, they made several landings on the eastern shore of Victoria Land, discovered the Emperor Penguin rookery at Cape Crozier, and cruised along the Ross Barrier. February 19 they made a sledge journey on its surface to 78° 45′, a new **record south.**

1901-1903. The **German National Expedition,** led by **Prof. Erich von Drygalski,** discovered and named the Gaussberg and Kaiser Wilhelm II Land, where they sent out the first sledge parties on the Antarctic ice coast.

1901-1903. The **Swedish Expedition,** led by **Dr. Otto Nordenskiöld** and Capt. Larsen in the *Antarctic,* made exploratory cruises around Graham Land and in Weddell Sea, and discovered and charted the Crown Prince Gustav Channel and James Ross Island as well as the northern archipelago lying around it. The *Antarctic* was crushed and sunk by the pack ice and the expedition was obliged to spend two winters at Snow Hill Island, where it was finally rescued by an Argentine ship.

1902-1904. CAPT. ROBERT F. SCOTT (British), commanding a large expedition, including **Lieut. Ernest H. Shackleton** and **Dr. E. A. Wilson,** in the *Discovery,* reached Cape Adare, January 1902. Cruising southward along Ross's course in 1842, he discovered and named the Drygalski and Nordenskiöld ice tongues, Granite Harbor, and the Royal Society Mountains. He succeeded in surpassing his predecessor's record, reached the eastern end of Ross Barrier, sighted and named King Edward VII Land. Upon the return to winter at Ross Island in McMurdo Sound, Mt. Erebus was found to be an active volcano.

1903, Nov.-1904, Feb. Scott, Wilson, and Shackleton made a southern trip of 930 miles over the Ross Barrier in an effort to ascertain its limits. They discovered that its western boundary was formed by 350 miles of scarped coastline, backed by the lofty Britannia and Queen Alexandra Ranges, the latter containing 15,000-foot Mt. Markham. Their **record south** was 82° 17′ (500 miles from the pole), near Shackleton Inlet, where they were obliged to turn back. At the same time a reconnaissance party under **Lieut. Albert Armitage** made a western trip on to the continental ice-sheet of South Victoria Land's 9000-foot inland plateau, discovering and naming the Ferrar,

Taylor, and Blue Glaciers. The following season (1903-1904) a party under Scott pushed 200 miles farther over the plateau and on the return trip discovered and explored Dry Valley.

1903-1905. The **Scottish National Expedition,** led by **Dr. W. S. Bruce,** carried on oceanographical explorations in Weddell Sea, and wintered on Laurie Island.

1903-1905. Jean B. Charcot (French) operated off the west coast of Graham Land, charted the western side of Palmer Archipelago, sighted Alexander I Land, and discovered Loubet Land.

1907-1909. SIR ERNEST SHACKLETON (British), privately financed in the *Nimrod,* led an expedition including Douglas Mawson and Prof. T. W. E. David to the Ross Sea sector. **First ascent of Mt. Erebus** and discovery of the live crater (Mar. 5-10, 1908). From a base at Cape Royds on Ross Island, Shackleton and three others started on a journey to the pole (Oct. 29, 1908). Surpassing Scott's record, they discovered and passed the southern end of Ross Barrier, and struggled (Dec. 7-27) more than a hundred miles up to the head of Beardmore Glacier, where they discovered a seam of low-grade coal. At its head (9820 feet) they emerged upon the South Polar Plateau, across which they traveled to 88° 23′ S., on January 9, 1909, where a desperate food shortage obliged them to turn back, only 97 miles short of their goal.

1908, Oct. 5-1909, Feb. 4. David, Mawson, and Mackay on a 1260-mile sledge trip, explored 200 miles northward along the coast of Victoria Land, crossed Drygalski Glacier, and turning inland climbed up the 7000-foot Northern Plateau to plant the British flag on

the **south magnetic pole** (1200 miles from the true South Pole) on January 16, 1909. Altogether Shackleton's expedition discovered about 1000 miles, and explored 300 miles more of territory previously discovered. All the new land explored was formally declared to be British.

1908. Great Britain issued letters patent constituting the *Falkland Dependency* (South Georgia, the South Shetlands, the Sandwich Group, and Graham Land) under the jurisdiction of the governor of the Falkland Islands. The Dependency established a sector between 80° and 20° W. Long. running from 50° S. Lat. to the pole.

1908-1910. Second expedition of Jean Charcot. Advancing southward Charcot first reached Alexander I Land, but could not determine whether it was an island or mainland. In 1910 he discovered Charcot Land, farther to the southwest, and verified Bellingshausen's discovery of Peter Island.

1910-1912. DISCOVERY OF THE SOUTH POLE BY CAPT. ROALD AMUNDSEN. Beaten by Peary at the North Pole, Amundsen hoped to anticipate Scott at the South Pole. He chose a base on the Bay of Whales and with four others made the trip with dog-sledges (1911, Oct. 19-Dec. 14). The Norwegian flag was hoisted at the pole on December 16, 1911. On the trip Amundsen discovered the 15,000-foot Queen Maud Range which bounds Ross Barrier. He ascended this range to the Polar Plateau by way of Axel Heiberg Glacier, and discovered the Devil's Glacier beyond.

1910-1913. SCOTT'S LAST EXPEDITION. He aimed for the pole, but was interested mainly in scientific research. From a base at Cape Evans in McMurdo Sound, he and four

At the South Pole in 1912: (left to right) *Capt. Oakes, Lt. Bowers, Capt. R. F. Scott, Dr. E. A. Wilson, and Petty Officer Evans*

others started (Nov. 3, 1911) and followed Shackleton's route up Beardmore Glacier. Failure of transport and insufficient food resulted in ever slower progress. **The pole was reached January 16, 1912,** but the party was so exhausted that before getting back it was overtaken by bad weather. Halfway across Ross Barrier they all died in a blizzard (about March 29).

1911-1912. Dr. Wilhelm Filchner (German) discovered Leopold Land, delimited the southern boundary of Weddell Sea, and discovered the Wilhelm Ice Barrier, which fills its head.

1911-1913. Dr. Douglas Mawson (British) led a large-scale, well-equipped expedition to explore the 2000 miles of practically unknown coast between Cape Adare and the Gaussberg. He was the first Antarctic explorer to use wireless. The larger section of the expedition broke through the pack ice and discovered Mertz Glacier. Here the party made its base on Commonwealth Bay and (Nov. 1911-Jan. 1912) Mawson, Mertz, and Ninnis sledged 280 miles over the great ice plateau into King George V Land, crossing the Mertz and the still larger Ninnis Glacier, but Mawson was the only one who got through alive. Another party explored the coast to the east for 275 miles, and a third contingent was taken 1200 miles westward in the *Aurora* past the great ice barrier which they named Shackleton Ice Shelf, discovered Davis Sea, and named the land on its shores Queen Mary Land. The party camped on Shackleton Ice Shelf, on which Denman and Scott Glaciers were discovered.

Sir Hubert Wilkins in 1921

covered. From here also a party made a 215-mile trip to Gaussberg in Kaiser Wilhelm Land and back.

Mawson discovered that the greater part of Antarctica is bordered by ice coasts. Altogether his expedition discovered and explored 1320 miles of land, mapped 800 miles of coastline, and made more geographical and scientific discoveries than any previous expedition, although it worked under far worse weather conditions in the most desolate, blizzard-ridden part of the continent.

1914-1917. SIR ERNEST SHACKLETON, in the *Endurance,* proposed to cross Antarctica from Weddell to Ross Sea via the pole (1800 miles, half over unknown territory) to meet the complementary party under **Mackintosh** in the *Aurora.* This aim was defeated, Shackleton's way south to the destined landing-place being barred by heavy pack ice in Weddell Sea, but he discovered Caird Coast, which contains the Dawson Lampton Glacier—probably the world's largest. February 22, 1915, the *Endurance* was fast beset and drifted 570 miles northwest with the pack until November 21, 1915, when she was crushed and sunk by the pressure ice. The party drifted on the disintegrating floe until April 9, 1916, when they took to small boats. On April 14 they reached Elephant Island, where they were obliged to winter. Shackleton and five others made the 800-mile trip to South Georgia for help in a 20-foot open boat in 16 days, arriving May 10, 1916. A fourth relief expedition to Elephant Island was finally successful in removing the marooned party on August 30, 1916.

The Ross Sea party in the *Aurora* was left stranded with insufficient equipment at its base at Cape Evans when the ship was carried away by the pack in May 1915. Scantily-clad, half-starved, and suffering from scurvy, the land party nevertheless fulfilled its part of the plan, laying depots all the way to Beardmore Glacier for Shackleton to use on the last lap of his polar journey. This party was rescued by the *Aurora* in January 1917.

1921-1922. J. L. Cope and **G. H.** (now **Sir Hubert**) **Wilkins** (British), landed by Norwegian whalers on the west coast of Graham Land, were foiled in their plan to cross it to Weddell Sea, because the country was too rugged for sledging.

1923, July 30. A **British order in council** constituted the Ross Sea sector a British dependency, known as the *Ross Dependency,* under the governor-general of New Zealand, and fixed as its boundaries the meridians of 150° W., 160° E., and the 60th parallel S., a delimitation which included a large part of Amundsen's discoveries and excluded part of Scott's route to the pole across King Edward Plateau, part of Oates Land, and all of the extensive lands discovered by Mawson, including the south magnetic pole area, which had been claimed for the British by David in 1908.

1924. The **French government** put **Adélie Land** (between 136° 20′ and 142° 20′ E. Long.) under the governor of Madagascar.

1928-1930. FIRST ANTARCTIC FLIGHTS, BY SIR HUBERT WILKINS. The expedition was sponsored by the American Geographical Society and largely financed by W. R. Hearst. From Deception Bay, Wilkins, piloted by C. B. Eielson, made a 1200-mile flight (Dec. 20, 1928) southwest over Graham Land, discover-

ing Crane Channel, the Lockheed Mountains, and Stefansson Strait, which separates Graham Land from the mainland (named Hearst Land). On December 31, 1929, Wilkins, piloted by A. Cheesman, flew over Charcot Land, discovered that it was an island and dropped a flag claiming it for Britain. Altogether Wilkins mapped about 80,000 square miles, discovered a new portion of the continent, and determined the insularity of Graham Land.

1928-1930. COMM. RICHARD E. BYRD (American) led a large, scientifically equipped expedition with three airplanes. In January 1929 they built the base *Little America* on Ross Barrier. A flight on January 27 revealed the new Rockefeller Mountains and neighboring Scott Land. Another on November 18 discovered the Charles V. Bob Mountain Range east of the Queen Maud Range.

1929, Nov. 28-29. Byrd, Balchen, June, and McKinley, in the plane *Floyd Bennett,* flew to the pole and back (1700 miles) by way of the 10,000-foot pass over Liv's Glacier. In a further flight on December 5 Byrd went beyond the Rockefeller Mountains and discovered the huge Edsel Ford Range in a new territory which he named *Marie Byrd Land* and claimed for the United States (between 150° and 120° W.).

1929-1931. SIR DOUGLAS MAWSON led the co-operative British, Australian, and New Zealand Antarctic Research Expedition, in the *Discovery* (Capt. Davis), to explore the 2500-mile uncharted coastline between King Wilhelm II Land and Coats Land, including Kemp and Enderby Lands. Planes were carried along, to be used where pack ice prevented approach to the mainland coasts. December 29, 1929: Discovery of MacRobertson Land near Kemp Land by flight from the *Discovery.* January 13, 1930: Landing in Enderby Land, of which formal possession was taken for the crown. January 14, 1930: The *Discovery* met the *Norvegia* (Capt. Riiser-Larsen), which was also exploring. It was decided that the British should keep to the east and the Norwegians to the west of 40° E. (later changed to 45° E. by the two governments). The following (1930-1931) season a landing was made on Commonwealth Bay and all land from there eastward to Oates Land was claimed for the British crown under the name *King George V Land.* The coast west of Cape Denison was explored by plane and additional surveys of Adélie Land were made. Further discoveries were: Banzare Land (west of 127° E.), Sabrina Land (between 115° and 116° E.), Princess Elizabeth Land (between the Gaussberg and MacRobertson Land), and Mackenzie Sea, a huge bay in MacRobertson Land. These two cruises resulted in the discovery of new coasts covering 29° of longitude, about 1000 miles of which was charted. Mawson's major achievement on his two expeditions (1911-1914 and 1929-1931) was the demonstration that the coastline is continuous from Cape Freshfield in King George V Land to Enderby Land—more than 2500 miles.

1933. The British government accepted the **Australian claim** to the huge sector between 45° and 160° E. Long., exclusive of French Adélie Land.

1929-1931. Capt. Hj. Riiser-Larsen (Norwegian) led an expedition in the *Norvegia* to look for new whaling grounds and new land. He carried two planes and on December 22, 1929 flew to the coast of Enderby Land. January 15, 1930, he discovered Queen Maud Land (southwest of Enderby Land) and (Feb. 18) Crown Princess Martha Land (by flight), to which 150 miles of coastline was added by a flight on February 20. The following (1930–1931) season he extended his explorations of Queen Maud Land 200 miles farther to the west, the new land (between 24° and 30° E.) being called *Princess Ragnhild Land.*

1934–1935. THE SECOND EXPEDITION OF COMMANDER BYRD.
The equipment included four planes, four tractors, and an autogyro, and from January 17, 1934 to February 6, 1935 a comprehensive set of observations was taken in the fields of meteorology, biology, geophysics, botany, and cosmic rays. Byrd himself undertook to man single-handed a weather observation station 100 miles inland through the Antarctic winter, but fell ill and injured himself after three months, so that a relief expedition had to be sent in one of the tractors. Dr. Poulter's investigations of Ross Barrier bore out the Japanese contention that much of it was aground. One tractor party explored a new plateau discovered to the southeast of Little America, and another, aiming south, pushed up the glaciers bordering the Barrier, explored mountains only two hundred miles from the pole, where they found plant-fossils, coal, fossilized wood, and other indications that the climate had once been subtropical, and discovered a huge plateau to the east of Thorne Glacier.

Explorations were also carried on by flight, the main achievement being the demonstration that no strait connects Ross and Weddell Seas and that Antarctica is thus one continent. A new range called the *Horlick Mountains* was discovered east of Thorne Glacier.

1934–1937.
The **British Graham Land Expedition,** under **John Rymill** (Australian). In 1935–1936 it operated from a base at the Argentine Islands, exploring the Graham Land coast to Cape Evensen and discovering that it consists of an 8000-foot plateau, rising abruptly from the sea. In July 1936 two parties surveyed the coastline north from a base at Barry Island (Fallières Coast). On August 15 a flight was made westward along the shore of Alexander I Land, which was photographed. A flight on September 15 revealed to the south a long, ice-covered strait (King George VI Channel), which the expedition attempted to penetrate with sledges. At 72° S.L. the channel appeared to open into a large bay, which proved that Alexander I Land is larger and extends farther south than previously supposed. Meanwhile another sledge party penetrated the interior of Graham Land, discovered and scaled a 7500-foot pass and reached a point overlooking the east coast, which was mapped for 140 miles, south to 70° 40'. The expedition revealed that what looked like straits to Wilkins were in reality glaciers several thousand feet high and that Stefansson Strait, Casey Channel, and probably Crane Channel are fjords. Graham Land may, after all, be part of the Antarctic continent.

1935–1936. LINCOLN ELLSWORTH
(American) in the *Wyatt Earp,* commanded by Sir Hubert Wilkins, succeeded in his third attempt at a **transcontinental Antarctic flight.** On November 23, 1935, with Herbert Hollick-Kenyon

Commander Richard E. Byrd, 1888–1957

(Canadian), he took off in the *Polar Star* from Dundee Island in the northern part of the Antarctic Archipelago for the Bay of Whales, 2300 miles away. The trip was made in six stages, the last one by sledge after the exhaustion of their fuel. They reached Little America December 15 and were picked up January 15, 1936 by the *Discovery II,* an Antarctic research ship. The new territory between Hearst Land and Marie Byrd Land (80° to 120° W.) was named *James W. Ellsworth Land* and claimed for the United States, and a high mid-continental plateau was named after Hollick-Kenyon. Ellsworth also discovered the 12,000-foot Eternity Range in Hearst Land and the Sentinel Range in James W. Ellsworth Land.

1936.
Australia proclaimed her control over all Antarctic territory south of the 60th parallel between 160° and 45° E. Long. (except Adélie Land), this being the territory explored by Mawson on his two expeditions. It constitutes an area almost as large as that of Australia.

1938–1939.
Ellsworth, on another expedition, surveyed a large part of eastern Antarctica by air, claiming some 430,000 square miles for the United States. The Australian government at once protested against this claim.

1939, Jan. 14.
The **Norwegian government** laid claim to Queen Maud Land, Princess Ragnhild Land, and Crown Princess Martha Land and the sector running inward to the Pole, about 1,000,000 square miles covering roughly one-fifth of the Antarctic continent.

In the Antarctic scientific and political considerations together led to ever increasing activity in exploration, charting, and settlement.

1939–1941.
An American expedition under Admiral Byrd attempted to establish permanent bases in the sector of American interest, but failed for lack of financial support.

1940.
Chile claimed a sector running from 53° to 90° W. L., thus overlapping the Argentine claim. Competing Argentine, Chilean, and British expeditions were sent to the area.

1943.
The British government established more than a dozen meteorological stations throughout its Falkland Islands Dependencies.

1946–1947.
The United States government announced that it would make no specific territorial claim but would not, at the same time, recognize the claims of other nations to Antarctic territory.

1946–1947.
A huge American expedition under Byrd explored in the region of Ross Bay. In February 1947 Byrd made a **second flight to the South Pole.**

1949.
A **Norwegian-Swedish-British expedition** (the first international one) initiated a series of annual expeditions in Queen Maud Land.

1954.
The first permanent **Australian base** was established in MacRobertson Land.

1956–1957.
The American **Amundsen-Scott station** was set up at the South Pole.

1957–1958.
The **International Geophysical Year** devoted major attention to scientific work in the Antarctic.

1957, Nov. 24–1958, Mar. 2.
First crossing of Antarctica by land by a party under leadership of **Sir Vivian Fuchs.** The hugh area between the Pole and Weddell Sea explored for the first time.

1959, Dec. 1.
International **ANTARCTIC TREATY** signed in Washington. The signatories undertook, for a period of thirty years, to make use of the Antarctic continent for peaceful purposes only, and to ensure freedom for scientific research. Existing territorial claims remained unaffected, but new claims and the enlargement of existing claims were prohibited.

B. The Revolutionary and Napoleonic Period, 1789–1815

(From p. 471)

The period of the Revolution and Empire may be divided into these subperiods, distinguished by changes in the form of government:

(1) **Estates-General** and **Constituent Assembly** (*Constituante*) from May 5 (June 17), 1789, to September 30, 1791. Government a limited, constitutional monarchy. Dominance of the upper middle classes.

(2) The **Legislative Assembly** (*Législatif*), from October 1, 1791, to September 21, 1792. The monarchy continued as before, until suspended. Rising power of the lower classes.

(3) The **National Convention** (*Convention Nationale*), from September 21, 1792, to October 25, 1795. Height of the revolution. The convention, called to frame a new constitution, first abolished the monarchy and condemned the king to death; it supported the Reign of Terror, and then overthrew it. It led the resistance to foreign foes.

[N.B. In modern party terms the *Left* of the Constituent was the *Right* of the Legislative (though the actual *personnel* was by law different), and the *Left* of the Legislative was (at first) the *Right* of the Convention.]

(4) The **Directory** (*Directoire*), from October 26, 1795, to November 9, 1799 (18 Brumaire, An. VIII). The middle classes recovered their influence. Party divisions. The army. General Bonaparte's *coup d'état.* Form republican.

(5) The **Consulate** (*Consulat*), at first provisional, then definitive, from December 25, 1799, to May 20, 1804; civil and military rule, virtually of one man; progress of French arms. Form still nominally republican.

(6) The (first) **Empire**, from May 20, 1804, to (April 1814) June 22, 1815. **Napoleon I** made France the controlling power on the Continent, but was finally overthrown.

1. *Background of the Revolution*

The spirit of the 18th century—a spirit devoted to the destruction or reformation of existing institutions. Attacks of French writers upon church and state.

Agrarian conditions. The peasantry was almost wholly free (300,000 out of some 20,000,000 still subject to certain servile restrictions), and in many regions owned land. Often its holdings were too small for adequate support. It was subject to certain surviving feudal dues, not in the aggregate large, but annoying, and in 1789 no longer paid for protection. There is evidence that in the last half of the 18th century nobles and other owners of these dues were attempting to collect them to the full, and revive those that had lapsed (the so-called *feudal reaction*). Taxation bore heavily on the peasantry, especially the *taille*, a land-tax from which nobles and clergy were exempt. Yet as a whole French peasants were certainly better off than most European peasants, and they took part in the revolution, not because they were hopelessly downtrodden, but because they were well enough off to wish to better themselves.

The **rise of a middle class**, generally excluded from politics, and particularly from local politics (access to the royal bureaucracy was open to able and ambitious bourgeois), but which had been growing richer with the expansion of French trade, and which read and listened to the *philosophes.*

An **unwieldy and inefficient machinery of government**, not so much tyrannical as irresponsible and unsuited to the needs of a large commercial and agricultural state. Taxation was inequitable, neither clergy nor nobility paying their full share (the clergy did pay a not inconsiderable *don gratuit*, and nobles paid the *vingtième* and *capitation*). Moreover, the indirect taxes were farmed out, and the *fermiers généraux* most unpopular. The *gabelle*, or salt-tax, was particularly irregular in its incidence. There was no true representative assembly, though the parlements, and especially the parlement of Paris, sometimes took upon themselves in the 18th century the rôle of such an assembly. Justice was by no means arbitrary, and the judges (*noblesse de robe*), though they owned their offices, were generally competent and conscientious. The famous *lettres de cachet*, royal orders imprisoning without benefit of *habeas corpus* or similar proceedings, were less important in fact than in anti-governmental propaganda. Sometimes used against political offenders, their chief use was to back up the family discipline of the upper classes by providing a means of shutting up wayward sons and otherwise keeping the power of the *pater familias* intact.

An **ever-growing deficit**, which proved impossible of reduction. The estates-general were called to remedy practical bankruptcy. Once called, they took upon themselves the wholesale reform of the state. France in 1789 was a fairly prosperous society with a bankrupt government.

2. *The National Assembly*

1789, May 5. MEETING OF THE ESTATES-GENERAL at Versailles, with a **double representation** of the middle classes as the third estate (*tiers état*): nobles 300, clergy 300, commons 600. Dispute about the manner of debating and voting (whether votes should be cast by the orders as such, or by each member individually) which broke out during the verification of the powers of the members. The nobles and the clergy demanded a separate verification, the third estate wished that it should take place in common. The true question was whether the legislative body should consist of a lower house of commons, and an upper house (or two houses) of nobles and clergy which would check the lower, or of **one house** in which the commons equaled in number the nobles and clergy together. Upon the motion

Storming and destruction of the Bastille, July 14, 1789

of the **Abbé Siéyès** (author of the remarkable pamphlet asking, *What is the Third Estate?*) the representatives of the third estate assumed the title of the

1789, June 17–1791. NATIONAL ASSEMBLY (*Constituante*) and invited the other orders to join them.

June 20. Suspension of the meetings for three days; the hall closed to the members, who at last resorted to a neighboring **tennis court** (*jeu de paume*) and took an **oath** not to separate until they had given the realm a constitution. President Bailly. Many of the clergy and some nobles joined the assembly.

June 23. Fruitless royal sitting; the king ordered the assembly to meet in three houses. Principal orator of the assembly: **Count Honoré de Mirabeau** (1749–1791), a Provençal nobleman elected by the third estate. The representatives of the clergy and the nobility joined the third estate by request of the king. Concentration of troops near Paris. Rumors of the king's intention to dissolve the national assembly, and the **dismissal of Necker** (July 11) caused the

July 14. STORM AND DESTRUCTION OF THE BASTILLE in Paris (murder of its governor, Jordan de Launay). Paris in the hands of the mob scarcely controlled by the electors who had chosen the deputies from Paris and who now sat at the Hôtel de Ville as a provisional government. **Necker recalled. Lafayette** commander of the newly established **National Guard.** Bailly mayor of Paris. Adoption of the tricolor: blue, red (colors of Paris), white (color of France).

Beginning of the emigration of the nobles, headed by the **count of Artois,** second brother of the king, **prince of Condé, duke of Polignac.**

Rising of the peasants against the feudal lords in Dauphiné, Provence, Burgundy, and throughout France. This *grande peur* was not systematically spread from Paris but occurred sporadically as a series of mass movements with numerous centers. Riots, provisional governments, guards in the provincial cities.

Aug. 4. Voluntary surrender by the representatives of the nobles (Vicomte de Noailles) of all feudal rights and privileges, but only gradually over a period of years, and with compensation to the owners (this compensation was in most cases never paid; under the

convention these provisions were repealed); abolition of titles, prohibition of the sale of offices, dissolution of the guilds, etc.

Aug. 27. Declaration of the rights of man, a bill of rights compounded from English and American precedents and from the political theories current with the *philosophes.* Discussion of the veto power.

Oct. 5, 6. Outbreak of the mob of Paris, caused by hunger and rumors of an intended reaction. March of a band, consisting principally of women, to Versailles. The royal family, rescued by Lafayette, was obliged to go to Paris, whither the national assembly followed them. Two hundred members resigned.

Liberal monarchical constitution: one chamber with legislative power and the sole right of initiation. The royal veto was suspensive only, delaying the adoption of a measure for two legislative terms. The king could not declare war and conclude peace without the consent of the chamber, ratification by which was necessary for the validity of all foreign treaties.

In order to relieve the financial distress the ecclesiastical estates were declared public property. *Assignats,* notes of the government, having for security the public lands, the value of which was not to be exceeded by the issue of notes (a check which was inoperative). The state assumed the support of the clergy.

1790, July 14. **National federation in Paris; the constitution accepted by the king.** Abolition of the old provinces and governments; France divided into 83 *départements,* named after rivers and mountains; these departments being subdivided into 374 *districts* and *cantons.* The *communes* were left unchanged (44,000); tax qualifications for the exercise of *active* suffrage in the primary assemblies, which chose electors, who then elected the representatives (745) for a legislature with a term of two years. The administrative officers of the departments and districts were selected from the electors; the municipal officers and the judges were taken from the great body of voters, the *active* citizens. Active citizens, who voted, paid direct taxes equal to three days' wages of common labor in their locality: *passive* citizens, who did not vote, paid no direct taxes, or less than the above minimum. Each

department and each district had a local assembly. Abolition of the parlements and the old judicial constitution. Juries. Abolition of hereditary nobility, titles, and coats-of-arms. Dissolution of all ecclesiastical orders, excepting those having education and the care of the sick for their objects. Civil organization of the clergy; the priests to be chosen by the voters of the districts, the bishops by the voters of the departments. Somewhat less than half of the clerics submitted to the new constitution by taking the required oath, creating a distinction between the *prêtres assermentés* and the *prêtres réfractaires.*

Growing power of the clubs, which had existed since 1789. The *Jacobins* (meeting in a monastery formerly occupied by Dominicans in the Rue St. Jacques), under the leadership of **Maximilien Robespierre** soon became the greatest power in the state, making use of a network of daughter societies in the provinces. The *Cordeliers,* who met in a Franciscan monastery (leaders **Georges Jacques Danton, Jean Paul Marat, Camille Desmoulins, Jacques Hébert**). The *Feuillants,* moderate monarchists

who had separated from the Jacobins (**Lafayctte, Bailly** belonged to this group).

Reorganization of the municipality (*commune*) **of Paris:** 48 sections, with 84,000 voters in a population of 800,000; general council; executive board (44). Each section had a primary assembly.

Sept. **Fall of Necker.** Alliance between the court and Mirabeau, who endeavored to stem the revolution and prevent the overthrow of the throne.

1791, Apr. 2. **Death of Mirabeau.**

June 20–25. **FLIGHT OF THE KING** and his family to the northeast frontier, where loyal troops were to protect them. The party was recognized and stopped at Varennes, then brought back to Paris. At first suspended, then reinstated by the moderate party (Sept.), **Louis accepted the constitution** (Sept. 14) as revised and completed.

Sept. Annexation of Avignon and Venaissin to France.

Sept. 30. **Dissolution of the assembly,** after it had voted that none of its members should be eligible for election to the next assembly.

3. *The Legislative Assembly*

1791, Oct. 1–1792, Sept. The **LEGISLATIVE ASSEMBLY,** composed of 745 members, elected by the active citizens, still represented primarily the middle class. **Parties:** The *Right* (constitutionalists, royalists, Feuillants, etc.) became weaker almost day by day. The *Left,* comprising the majority, was divided into (1) the *Plain,* an unorganized group of moderate republicans or timid monarchists, swayed in turn by the next two groups; (2) the *Girondists,* so called because the leading members came from Bordeaux (department of the Gironde), had in **Elie Guadet, Pierre Vergniaud,** and **Jacques Brissot** a group of brilliant orators, advocating the establishment of a form of federal republic; (3) the *Mountain* (la Montagne, Montagnards), so called from their seats, which were the highest on the left side of the hall, was composed of the radicals, champions of a united, indivisible republic. The Mountain drew its strength from the Jacobin and Cordelier clubs. The division between Girondists and the Mountain did not attain its clearest form until the meeting of the convention (below), but its beginnings were evident in the legislative assembly. **Jérome Pétion,** the mayor of Paris, was a Girondist.

Aug. 27. Meeting at Pillnitz of **Frederick William II** of Prussia (1786–1797) and **Leopold II** (1790–1792), the emperor. The two sovereigns and their ministers reached a preliminary understanding regarding Near Eastern affairs *(p. 501)* and above all regarding the French situation. The **declaration of Pillnitz** was a carefully worded statement that the two rulers would intervene in French affairs only with the unanimous consent of the powers, in-

cluding Great Britain. But the French interpreted it as a bald threat of interference.

1792, Feb. 7. **Alliance of Austria and Prussia** against France.

1792–1806. **FRANCIS II,** emperor in succession to Leopold.

1792–1797. **WAR OF THE FIRST COALITION** against France. A Girondist ministry (Roland, Dumouriez) took the place of the constitutionalist ministry, whose fall was caused by the Pillnitz declaration. The Girondists actually sought the war, while on the Austrian side Francis fell completely under the influence of the war party. The French *émigrés* had long been trying to provoke intervention, while certain German princes with feudal rights in Alsace (*princes possessionés*) were demanding compensation for losses under the decrees of August 4, 1789. Many Prussian and Austrian leaders thought that France, weakened by the revolutionary dissension, would be easily beaten. Exact responsibility for the war is hard to allocate. In April 1792 both sides wanted it.

Apr. 20. The **French declared war against Austria** and put three armies in the field: Rochambeau (48,000) between Dunkirk and Philippeville; Lafayette (52,000) between Philippeville and Lauterburg; Luckner (42,000) between Lauterburg and Basel. The French suffered reverses, which increased the revolutionary exictement in Paris.

June 13. **Fall of the Roland ministry.**

June 20. **Attack of the mob on the Tuileries;** calm behavior of the king.

July 11. The assembly pronounced the country in danger. Formation of a voluntary

Georges Jacques Danton, 1759–1794

army throughout the country. Threatening **manifesto of the duke of Brunswick,** Prussian commander-in-chief. The Paris council was broken up and its place usurped by commissioners from the sections (new commune of 288 members).

Aug. 10. **STORMING OF THE TUILERIES** by the mob, in consequence of a command of the king ordering the Swiss guard to cease firing. Massacre of the Swiss guards. The king took refuge in the hall of the assembly, was suspended from his functions, and confined in the Temple (old house of the Knights Templar). Arrests of suspected persons. **Provisional government: Danton** (1759–1794), minister of justice; Lebrun, Roland, Servan, Monge, Clavière. The assembly virtually abdicated its powers, which passed to the Paris commune and the Jacobin clubs. Convocation of a national convention, to be elected by manhood suffrage, to draw up a new constitution.

Aug. 20. **Lafayette,** having been impeached and proscribed, fled from his army, was captured by the Austrians and imprisoned at Olmütz (till 1796). Verdun taken by the Prussians.

Sept. 2–7. The **SEPTEMBER MASSACRES** at Paris. Suspects were taken from the prisons and, after hasty trials by improvised tribunals, were summarily done away with by the mob. Blame seems to lie chiefly with Sergent, Panis, and other Paris ward politicians. **Danton,** if he cannot be proved to have instigated the massacres, certainly allowed them to run their course. Similar scenes were enacted at Versailles, Lyons, Rheims, Meaux, and Orléans.

Sept. 20. BATTLE OF VALMY. The French, under **Generals Charles Dumouriez** and **François Kellermann,** defeated the Prussians in an artillery duel fought in a heavy fog. The engagement, far from important in the military sense, was yet a crucial test. It gave heart to the revolutionary armies and was to prove a turning-point.

4. *The National Convention*

1792, Sept. 21–1795, Oct. The **NATIONAL CONVENTION,** longest-lived of the revolutionary assemblies. It was elected by manhood suffrage and was composed entirely of republicans (749 members, of whom 486 were new men). **Parties:** The **Girondists** now formed the Right, while the **Mountain,** under Robespierre, the duke of Orléans (Philippe Egalité), Danton, Collot d'Herbois, etc., formed the Left. The **Plain** (scornfully called the *Marsh* and the *Belly*) appeared as in the preceding assembly. Numerically it had the majority, but it was dominated first by the Girondists, then by the Mountain.

1792, Sept. 21. ABOLITION OF THE MONARCHY. France declared a republic.

Sept. 22 was the **first day of the year one** of the French republic. *Citoyen et citoyenne;* decree of perpetual banishment against emigrants; *tu et toi.* Inglorious retreat of the Prussians through Champagne to Luxemburg and across the Rhine. The French general, **Adam de Custine,** took Speier, Mainz, and Frankfurt-on-the-Main. Occupation of Nice and Savoy (Sept.).

Nov. 6. Victory of the French general Dumouriez at **Jemappes.** He took Brussels and conquered the Austrian Netherlands. The Prussians retook Frankfurt.

Nov. 19. Proclamation of the convention offering French assistance to all peoples who wished to throw off their government.

Nov. 27. Savoy and Nice annexed; the Scheldt opened to commerce.

1792, Dec.–1793, Jan. **Trial of Louis XVI** before the convention. Barère prosecutor; Malesherbes, Desèze, Tronchet, for the defense. Proposed appeal to the nation rejected. January 15, 683 votes out of 721 declared the king guilty. January 16, 361 votes, exactly a majority (among them that of the duke of Orléans) were cast unconditionally for death, 360 being cast for imprisonment, banishment, or death with respite.

1793, Jan. 21. EXECUTION OF LOUIS XVI.

Feb. 1. War declared against Great Britain, Holland, Spain. Britain, Holland, Spain, and the Empire joined the alliance against France, Sardinia having been at war with the latter power since July 1792. **Annexation of Bel-gium.** The *émigrés,* under the prince of Condé, proclaimed the young son of the dead king as **Louis XVII,** who was a prisoner in the Temple.

Mar. Royalist revolt in the **Vendée,** upon occasion of a levy of recruits. (Charette, Stofflet, Cathelineau, La Rochejaquelein.)

Mar. 18. The Austrians under the duke of Coburg defeated Dumouriez at **Neerwinden,** and recaptured Brussels. Dumouriez went over to the Austrians with the duke of Chartres, **Louis Philippe,** son of Egalité.

At Paris, in the convention, struggle for life and death, between the **Girondists** and the **Mountain.** After the failure of the plan of the Orléanists, belonging to the Mountain, to make the duke of Orléans protector, all power centered in the **Committee of General Security** and the

Apr. 6. Committee of Public Safety (*Comité du salut public*). Composed of nine (afterward 12) members, who exercised dictatorial power. **Leaders: Danton** (from the very start); **Robespierre, St. Just, Couthon** (these three in July); **Carnot,** who concerned himself exclusively with military matters; **Collot d'Herbois** (Sept.). The

Execution of Louis XVI, January 21, 1793

Marie Antoinette goes to the guillotine, sketched October 16, 1793, by Jacques L. David

third power in the state was the **commune of Paris,** now reorganized on the basis of manhood suffrage and acting through its committee (reduced to 20) at the Hôtel de Ville. **Leaders: Chaumette** and **Hébert** (editor of *Le Père Duchesne*).

Financial difficulties: New issues of *assignats,* based on the lands of the emigrant nobles, the sale of which was ordered. Attempts to check depreciation of the *assignats* by severe penalties.

June 2. Arrest of 31 Girondist deputies, forced on the convention by an uprising engineered by the commune and the Jacobin "machine," with the national guard, commanded by Henriot. Brissot, Vergniaud, Pétion were among the victims. Complete domination of the Mountain, itself the organ of the Paris commune.

June 22. The **Constitution of 1793,** an out-and-out democratic system, was sent to the primary assemblies for ratification, but was never actually put into effect.

July 13. Assassination of Marat by **Charlotte Corday,** an ardently patriotic girl from the provinces.

1793–1794. THE REIGN OF TERROR. Robespierre gradually came to dominate the whole government. He was never "dictator" in the modern sense, being checked by his colleagues in the committee of public safety, by the opposing Hébertist faction in the commune and convention, and by the commissioners of the convention sent into the provinces (*représentants en mission*). These commissioners, sent out to suppress counterrevolutionary movements, were often responsible for extreme terrorism in their districts. They collaborated with the local Jacobin clubs and revolutionary committees (*comités de surveillance, comités révolutionnaires*). Horrors perpetrated by Tallien at Bordeaux, Lebon at Arras, Carrier at Nantes, Couthon, Fouché, Collot d'Herbois at Lyons. Some commissioners, however, were fairly

clement and spared their regions (the younger Robespierre in the east and south, Lakanal in the southwest).

1793, July. Mainz recovered by the Prussians after a three-months' siege. The Allies also took Condé and Valenciennes. Custine executed by the French for negligence. British **siege of Toulon.** The troops of the republic were driven back on almost all fronts, with the result that revolts multiplied in the interior, frequently inspired by Girondists who had escaped the purge and had fled Paris. Energetic counter-measures of the committee of public safety.

Aug. 23. Levy of the entire male popula- tion capable of bearing arms. Fourteen armies hastily organized and put in the field. Caen, Bordeaux, Marseilles conquered by the republicans.

Sept. 29. Establishment of the maximum price for a large number of commodities; fixation of wages. The system was never fully worked out and the *maximum* was frequently violated. It did, however, prevent a catastrophic fall of the *assignats* and insured the provisioning of the armies. The whole experiment was less a socialistic measure than a way to ration goods during an emergency.

Oct. Lyons captured after a two-months' siege. The city was partially destroyed and

Execution of the 21 Girondists, October 31, 1793

Assassination of Jean Paul Marat, July 13, 1793

large numbers of the inhabitants were massacred.

Oct. 16. Execution of Marie Antoinette.

Oct. 20. Defeat of the Vendéans at Chollet, and at **Le Mans** (Dec. 12). Revolutionary tribunal at Nantes (15,000 put to death in three months by Carrier: *noyades, fusillades, mariages républicains*).

Oct. 31. Execution of the Girondists (21). Reign of the revolutionary tribunals and the guillotine (Place de la Révolution, now Place de la Concorde). **Fouquier-Tinville,** public prosecutor. Neglect of legal forms; sixty executions a month (including Bailly, Philippe Egalité, Madame Roland, etc.).

Nov. 10. Abolition of the worship of God. Cult of Reason (Hébert, Chaumette, Cloots). Profanation of the royal sepulcher at St. Denis.

Revolutionary calendar, dating from the year one of the revolution (Sept. 22, 1792). The months: Vendémiaire, Brumaire, Frimaire; Nivose, Pluviose, Ventose; Germinal, Floréal, Prairial; Messidor, Thermidor, Fructidor. Each month had 30 days, leaving five intercalary days (*sans culottides*) in the year. Every tenth day a holiday.

Creation of the new army, really an amalgamation of recruits with loyal elements of the old army. Successes of the new forces throughout the autumn, under Jourdan, Hoche, and Pichegru.

Dec. Retreat of the Allies across the Rhine. The French captured Worms and Speier, and took Toulon from the British (first appearance of **Napoleon Bonaparte,** a young artillery officer, closely connected with Robespierre and Jacobins).

1794. Robespierre (representing the committee of public safety) finally succeeded in crushing the rival powers represented by Hébert and Danton. Playing off Danton against the Hébertists, he engineered

Mar. 24. The **execution of the leaders** (Hébert, Chaumette, Cloots, etc.). Thereupon he turned on the Dantonists, whose past gave ample opening for accusation.

Apr. 6. Execution of Danton, Desmoulins, Hérault de Sechelles, etc.

Apr. 19. Treaty of The Hague between Britain and Prussia, Britain paying subsidies for 60,000 men.

May 18. Victory of Pichegru's army at Turcoing.

June 8. Festival of the Supreme Being, a cult of which Robespierre was the high-priest, having abolished the cult of reason.

June 10. Law of 22 Prairial, bestowing great power on the revolutionary tribunal: juries to convict without hearing evidence or argument. Tremendous increase of executions (up to 354 a month).

June 25. Capture of Charleroi by the French.

June 26. BATTLE OF FLEURUS, a French victory which obliged the duke of Coburg to evacuate Belgium.

July. Conspiracy against Robespierre, by members of the Mountain and by the more moderate elements (Tallien, Fréron, Fouché, Collot d'Herbois, Billaud-Varenne). This was due to jealousy of Robespierre within the committee of public safety, and to rivalry between the two "great committees."

July 27 (9 Thermidor). **FALL OF ROBESPIERRE.** He and his brother, as well as **Couthon** and **St. Just,** were arrested. Being released by friends, they were outlawed, surprised at the Hôtel de Ville, and executed, with 18 others. On the following days over 80 of the party met the same fate. The Paris commune was nearly extinct. This *coup d'état* was carried through by disparate elements, personal enemies of Robespierre, who were opposed to his effort to make France a "republic of virtue." The objective was to remove Robespierre, not to end the Terror. Public opinion, however, forced his successors to adopt more moderate policies.

1794–1795. End of the Terror. The convention dominated by the moderates (*Thermidoreans*), who gradually broke the power not only of the commune, but of the Jacobin clubs (the Paris club closed November 12).

Dec. 8. The **Girondists** who·had escaped with their lives were readmitted to the convention.

Dec. 24. Repeal of the maximum. New issues of *assignats;* increased depreciation.

1795, Apr. 1 (Germinal 12). **Bread riots in Paris;** attack on the convention suppressed; transportation of Billaud, Collot, Barère, Vadier, and other radicals. Growing reaction in the capital and throughout the country. *Jeunesse dorée;* revival of monarchist agitation; return of some of the *émigré* nobility; the **White Terror.**

May 20 (Prairial 1). Further riots and outbreaks. Fierce attack on the convention. Firmness of the president, Boissy d'Anglas. The movement was finally gotten in hand and resulted only in the extermination of the remnants of the Mountain.

Meanwhile the armies had been uniformly successful. Having overrun Belgium, Pichegru invaded Holland in the winter of 1794–1795, the prince of Orange-Nassau fleeing to England *(p. 464).*

1795–1806. The **BATAVIAN REPUBLIC** founded by the French. Flanders was surrendered to France.

1795, Mar. 5. TREATY OF BASEL between France and Prussia. Prussia, financially exhausted and at odds with Austria, withdrew from the war. Saxony, Hanover, and Hesse-Cassel followed suit. France was to retain the left bank of the Rhine until peace should be concluded with the Empire, but was to evacuate the right bank. Northern Germany was to be neutralized. Secret articles: Prussia consented to the absolute cession of the left bank to France and was given assurance of compensation through secularization of ecclesiastical territory on the right bank. On June 22 Spain and France concluded peace at Basel, Spain ceding St. Domingo but recovering other lost territories.

June 8. Death of the dauphin (Louis XVII, ten years old) in the Temple. Later numerous pretending dauphins appeared, even in the United States. The death of the dauphin is, however, as certain as such matters can ever be.

June 27. Landing of the British and *émi-* . *grés* at Quiberon (Brittany) to aid the royalists of the region (*Chouans*).

July 16–21. Victories of Hoche over the invaders. Over 700 *émigrés* executed. Retalia-

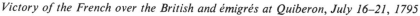

Victory of the French over the British and émigrés at Quiberon, July 16–21, 1795

tory massacre of 1000 republican prisoners by Charette.

Aug. 22. The **Constitution of 1795** (third of the revolution): the executive power vested in a directory of five; legislature of two chambers (*Council of Elders,* or Ancients, 250; *Council of Five Hundred*); for the first term, two-thirds of the members of both houses were to be taken from the rolls of the convention. This self-protective proviso led to opposition in Paris and the provinces. The Paris royalists instigated an outbreak of the sections. On the motion of Barras, the convention placed Gen. Bonaparte in charge of its troops.

Oct. 5. (Vendemiaire 13). **The Day of the Sections.** Bonaparte's "whiff of grape-shot." Cannonade from the Church of St. Roch. Complete victory of the convention.

Oct. 26. The **convention dissolved,** after voting that relatives of *émigrés* should not be permitted to hold office.

5. *The Directory*

1795-1799. THE DIRECTORY. The new government, much maligned by historians and frequently accused of dishonesty and corruption, was faced by an acute financial crisis, the *assignats* having fallen to a fraction of 1 per cent of their face value. Substitution of *mandats territoriaux,* convertible into a specified amount of land, for the *assignats.* The *mandats* in turn depreciated almost at once.

1796, Mar. 5. Final suppression of the insurrection in the Vendée and in Brittany, by Hoche.

In the **war against the Empire,** the directory, on advice of Carnot, arranged for a triple attack: (1) the army of the Sambre and Meuse, under **Jourdan,** was to advance from the lower Rhine to Franconia; (2) the army of the Rhine and the Moselle, under **Moreau,** was to penetrate from the upper Rhine into Swabia and Bavaria; (3) the army of Italy, under **Bonaparte,** was to drive the Austrians out of Italy and unite with the other armies by way of the Tyrol.

1796. The campaign in Germany. Jourdan and Moreau invaded South Germany, and Baden, Württemberg, and Bavaria were obliged to

Josephine de Beauharnais

conclude truces (Aug.), but suddenly the **Archduke Charles** (brother of Emperor Francis II) took the offensive against Jourdan and defeated him at **Amberg** (Aug.) and **Würzburg** (Sept. 3). Jourdan resigned his command. The archduke then turned on Moreau, who retreated through the Black Forest to the upper Rhine.

Mar. 9. Marriage of Bonaparte with Josephine de Beauharnais, former friend of Barras and one of the lights of Paris society.

1796-1797. BONAPARTE'S ITALIAN CAMPAIGN. Following the coast from Nice, he defeated the Austrians at **Millesimo** (Apr. 13) and the Piedmontese at **Mondovi** (Apr. 22), compelling Victor Amadeus to conclude a separate peace with France: Savoy and Nice ceded to the French Republic, and the French given the right to garrison Piedmontese fortresses. Napoleon then pursued the Austrians, whom he defeated in

1796, May 10. The **battle of Lodi** (storming of the bridge over the Adda).

May 15. Napoleon entered Milan, and then conquered all Lombardy as far as Mantua. The dukes of Parma and Modena, the pope, and the king of Naples purchased truces at the price of large payments in money and art treasures.

May 16. Napoleon set up the **Lombard Republic.**

July-1797, Feb. Siege of Mantua by the French. Four attempts by the Austrians to relieve the fortress. They were defeated in the **battles of Castiglione** (Aug. 15), **Roveredo, Bassano,** and in

Nov. 15-19. The **battle of Arcola,** and **1797, Jan. 14.** The **battle of Rivoli.**

Feb. 2. Mantua surrendered, and Napoleon started on an advance to Rome. The pope thereupon hastily concluded with him

Feb. 19. The **treaty of Tolentino,** ceding the Romagna, Bologna, and Ferrara.

Mar.-Apr. Bonaparte crossed the Alps to meet the Archduke Charles, advancing from Germany. The inhabitants of Venetia rose against the French, and in the Tyrol too the population was called to arms. In danger of being cut off, Bonaparte opened negotiations which led to

Apr. 18. The **PRELIMINARY PEACE OF LEOBEN: Austria** ceded the Belgian provinces to France; a congress was to arrange peace between France and the Empire on the basis of the integrity of imperial territory;

Austria ceded the region beyond the Oglio, receiving in return the Venetian territory between the Oglio, Po, and Adriatic (which she was to conquer for herself), Venetian Dalmatia and Istria, and the fortresses of Mantua, Peschiera, and Palma Nova. **Venice** was to be indemnified with the Romagna, Bologna, and Ferrara. Austria recognized the **Cisalpine Republic,** which was to be formed in northern Italy.

May. The French declared **war upon Venice,** under pretext of an outbreak at Verona. Abolition of the aristocracy and establishment of popular government. Occupation of the republic by French troops; also of the Venetian islands of Greece (Ionian).

July 9. Proclamation of the **Cisalpine Republic** (Milan, Modena, Ferrara, Bologna, Romagna). Transformation of the Republic of Genoa into the **Ligurian Republic** under French control.

Sept. 4 (18th Fructidor). **COUP D'ÉTAT AT PARIS.** Victory of the republican party over the party of reaction, which was represented in the council of five hundred, in the council of ancients, and in the directory. The three republican directors, Barras, Rewbell, and La Révellière, defeated their colleagues, Barthélemy and Carnot. The latter escaped by flight; Barthélemy and many of his adherents, including Pichegru, were transported to Cayenne.

Oct. 17. TREATY OF CAMPO FORMIO. (1) Austria ceded the Belgian provinces to France. (2) A congress was convened at **Rastatt** to discuss peace with the Empire. (3) Austria received the territory of Venice as far as the Adige, with the city of Venice, Istria, and Dalmatia. (4) France retained the **Ionian Islands.** (5) Austria recognized the Cisalpine Republic and indemnified the duke of Modena with the Breisgau. Secret articles: (1) Austria agreed to the cession of the **left bank of the Rhine** from Basel to Andernach, including Mainz, to France; the navigation of the Rhine was left open to France and Germany in common; those princes who lost by the cession were to receive indemnification in Germany. (2) France was to use her influence to secure to Austria, **Salzburg,** and that portion of Bavaria which lay between Salzburg, the Tyrol, the Inn, and the Salza. (3) Reciprocal guaranty that Prussia should not receive any new acquisition of territory in return for her cession on the left bank of the Rhine.

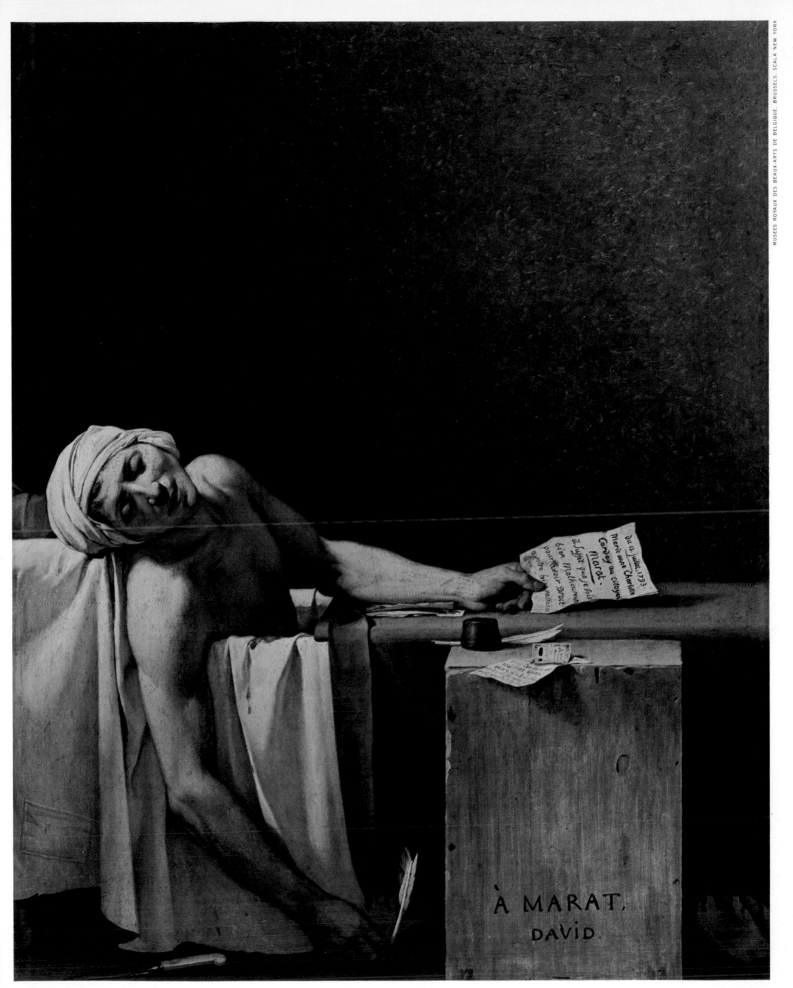

The Assassination of Marat (p.612) by Jacques Louis David

The Second of May, 1808 (p.622) by Francisco Goya

The French Campaign of 1814 (pp.627-628) by Jean Louis Meissonier

Napoleon Crossing the Alps, *by Jacques Louis David*

1796-1801. PAUL I, emperor of Russia, succeeded his mother Catherine II *(p. 499)*.

1797-1840. FREDERICK WILLIAM III, king of Prussia.

1797, Dec.-1799, Apr. Congress of Rastatt. No agreement.

1798, Feb. The French occupied Rome. Proclamation of the **Roman Republic. Captivity of the pope, Pius VI** *(p. 478)*.

    Apr. French invasion of Switzerland. Organization of the **Helvetic Republic** *(p. 481)*. Geneva annexed to France.

1798-1799. **BONAPARTE'S EGYPTIAN EXPEDITION,** prepared under the mask of an invasion of England (*Army of England* concentrated at Boulogne). Napoleon, having convinced himself of the impracticability of crossing the Channel, persuaded the directory to deliver a blow at Britain's Indian empire, by way of Egypt, a country that had long attracted the interest of French political writers. Napoleon sailed from Toulon with 35,000 men and a corps of scientists (May 19, 1798), surprised and took **Malta** (June 12), and landed in Egypt (July 1). **Capture of Alexandria** (July 2).

    July 21. BATTLE OF THE PYRAMIDS, outside Cairo. The French easily defeated the medieval Mamluk cavalry, and took Cairo (July 22).

    Aug. 1. BATTLE OF THE NILE. The British admiral, **Horatio Nelson,** having sought the French in vain throughout the eastern Mediterranean, finally located the French fleet in the harbor of **Abukir,** east of Alexandria. Without much difficulty he managed to destroy the fleet, which, being crowded in the anchorage, was unable to maneuver. Thus Nelson cut Napoleon and his force off from France.

1799, Feb. **The Syrian campaign.** The Ottoman government having declared war on France, Napoleon invaded Syria, stormed **Jaffa** (massacre of 1200 prisoners), but was frustrated in his efforts to take **Acre.** Outbreak of plague in the French army; hasty retreat to Egypt.

    July 25. **Battle of Abukir.** The Turks, supported by the British, had landed at Abukir, but were completely defeated by Napoleon and Murat.

    Napoleon left Egypt (Aug. 24) to return to France. **Kléber** in command. After long negotiations, he concluded with the Turks the **convention of El Arish** (Jan. 24, 1800), providing for evacuation of the French forces. This was opposed by the British. Kléber was assassinated (June) and succeeded by Menou, whom the British defeated at Alexandria (Mar. 21, 1801). The French force was repatriated and, by the **treaty of Amiens** *(p. 618),* Egypt was restored to the sultan.

Battle of the Pyramids, July 21, 1798

The French occupy Rome, February 1798

6. *The War of the Second Coalition*

1798, Dec. 24. Alliance between Russia and Great Britain, to which Austria, Naples, Portugal, and the Ottoman Empire adhered. This **Second Coalition** against France was the work primarily of Paul I of Russia, whom the Knights of Malta had elected as grand master.

Plan of campaign: An Anglo-Russian army under the duke of York was to drive the French from the Netherlands; an Austrian army under Archduke Charles was to expel them from Germany and Switzerland; a Russo-Austrian army was to force the French out of Italy.

A Neapolitan army, commanded by the Austrian general, Mack, had attacked the Roman Republic and occupied the city of Rome (Nov. 29), thus beginning hostilities. The French, under Championnet, recaptured the city (Dec. 15) and then overran the entire kingdom of Naples; Ferdinand was obliged to flee to Sicily, while the French proclaimed
1799, Jan. 23. The Parthenopean Republic, a client state of France. Even before this (Nov.-Dec. 1798) Gen. Joubert had conquered Piedmont and forced the king to flee to Sardinia (Dec. 9). On March 25, 1799 the grand duke of Tuscany was driven from his dominions and the French occupied Florence.

Mar. 25. The Archduke Charles defeated Jourdan and the army of the upper Rhine, at **Stockach.** Jourdan retreated across the Rhine and laid down his command. His army and that of the middle Rhine (Bernadotte) were united under command of **Masséna.**

Apr. 5. Battle of Magnano, in which the French army of Italy, under Schérer, was defeated by the Austrians under Kray. **Moreau** succeeded to the command, but was in turn defeated in the

Apr. 27. Battle of Cassano, by the Austrian general Melas and the Russian army under Suvorov. The Allies entered Milan and extinguished the Cisalpine Republic. Meanwhile,
Apr. 8. The congress of Rastatt had been dissolved. Mysterious murder of the French delegates, Roberjot, and Bonnier, on their way home, by Austrian hussars (Apr. 28).
May 27. Suvorov occupied Turin, and shut up remnants of Moreau's army in Genoa.
June 4-7. BATTLE OF ZÜRICH. The Archduke Charles defeated Masséna.
June 17-19. BATTLE OF THE TREBBIA. Suvorov defeated the French army under MacDonald, which had hurried north from Naples. In the interval the king of Naples returned from Sicily and overthrew the Parthenopean Republic (ruthless vengeance, with massacres). The Roman Republic met with the same fate. The directory now sent to Italy Gen. Joubert with a new army.
Aug. 15. BATTLE OF NOVI. Suvorov and Melas completely defeated Joubert as he attempted to advance from Genoa. Joubert himself was killed.
Suvorov then crossed the Alps by the St. Gothard Pass in order to unite with the second Russian army under Korsakov, who had taken the place of the Archduke Charles in Switzerland.
Sept. 26. Korsakov was defeated and driven out of Zürich by Masséna. Suvorov was unable to recover the position in Switzerland and was obliged to fall back to the Grisons with an army decimated by starvation and want. Masséna took Constance and threatened the flank of the Archduke Charles, who was preparing the invasion of France from the Rhine.
Oct. 18. Convention of Alkmar, by which

Lucien Bonaparte, 1745–1840

the British surrendered all prisoners taken in Holland, in return for unobstructed evacuation. The campaign in Holland had been an unqualified failure. The British and Russians had not co-operated effectively and the French, under Brune, had more than held their own in the fighting around Bergen (Sept. 19).

Oct. 22. The Russians withdrew from the coalition, disgusted with the conduct of their allies, especially the Austrians. In the interval (May 1799) a Russian-Turkish fleet had wrested the Ionian Isles from French control. The islands were organized as a republic **(Septinsular Republic)** under Turkish protection and under Russian guaranty. The Russians occupied them until 1807.

Nov. 9 (18 Brumaire). **THE COUP D'ÉTAT OF BRUMAIRE. Napoleon** had landed at Fréjus unannounced from Egypt (Oct. 8) and had effected an alliance with the directors Siéyès and Roger-Ducos. With the aid of his brother Lucien (president of the council of five hundred), he overthrew the directory and broke up the council on the following day.

7. *The Consulate*

1799-1804. The CONSULATE, representing a new system worked out by Siéyès in conjunction with Napoleon. **Napoleon was first consul** (term ten years) and was assisted by two other consuls appointed by him (Cambacérès and Lebrun), who had only consultative powers.
1799, Dec. 24. Constitution of the Year VIII, which was submitted to popular vote (3,011,107 in favor; 1567 opposed). It preserved the appearance of the republic, but in reality established the **dictatorship of Napoleon.** Below the consuls were the following institutions. the *senate* (80), appointed for life from lists of names sent in by the departments, legislative bodies, higher officials; the *tribunate* (100),

which discussed measures submitted by the government, but without voting on them; the *legislative chamber* (300), which accepted or rejected these measures, but without debate; the *council of state,* appointed by the first consul, and his chief support in the work of legislation.

The people voted for notables of the communes, who then elected one-tenth of their own number as notables of the departments, of whom one-tenth again became notables of France. From this final sifting were chosen, by the senate, the members of the legislative bodies.

Establishment of prefectures (administration

of the departments) and **subprefectures** (for the districts or *arrondissements*). The administration was gradually centralized. **New system of tax-collection:** a *receveur-général* for each department, and a *receveur particulier* for each *arrondissement.*

The new system, which proved to be highly efficient and which has, to a large extent, been retained to the present day, owed much to experiments and experience of the revolutionary assemblies and the directory. The civil service was recruited largely from former Jacobins. In his policy Napoleon, as first consul, followed closely the course marked out by his predecessors.

Napoleon's offers of peace. These were rejected by the Allies, though Russia had left the coalition. Defensive alliance between Russia and Sweden (1799); drawing together of Russia and Prussia. Friction between Russia and Britain over Malta. Renewal of the **armed neutrality** of 1780. Northern convention (1800).

1800. RENEWAL OF THE CAMPAIGN AGAINST AUSTRIA. In Italy the Austrians, having defeated Masséna at **Voltri,** advanced to Nice (Apr.). Obstinate **defense of Genoa** by Masséna and Soult. Capitulation of the city (June 4) after a horrible famine.

May. Napoleon crossed the St. Bernard Pass with 40,000 men, to attack the flank of the Austrians.

June 2. The French took Milan and restored the Cisalpine Republic.

June 14. BATTLE OF MARENGO, a great victory won by Napoleon, but by an extremely narrow margin. Truce between Napoleon and Melas: all fortresses west of the Mincio and south of the Po were surrendered to the French.

In Germany, Moreau was in command. He had crossed the Rhine in April and had advanced into southern Germany.

July. Moreau took Munich, after which operations were suspended for some months, causing dissatisfaction on both sides.

Dec. 3. BATTLE OF HOHENLINDEN. Moreau completely defeated the Archduke John, who had been appointed to take the place of his brother Charles. The French then advanced to Linz. Another army, under MacDonald, advanced into Tyrol, and in January 1801 Brune, with the army of Italy, crossed the Adige and began the invasion of Austria from the south. This decided the emperor to make peace.

1801, Feb. 9. TREATY OF LUNÉVILLE, which practically involved the destruction of the Holy Roman Empire. **Conditions:** (1) Ratification of the cessions made by and to Austria in the treaty of Campo Formio *(p. 614).* (2) Cession of the grand duchy of Tuscany (Austrian *secundogeniture*) to Parma, to be indemnified in Germany. (3) The emperor and Empire consented to the cession of the left bank of the Rhine to France, the valley of the Rhine (i.e. the middle of the river) to be the boundary. The princes who lost by this operation received indemnification in Germany. (4) Recognition of the Batavian, Helvetian, Cisalpine, and Ligurian Republics. Germany lost by this peace, taking the Belgic territory into account, 25,180 square miles with almost 3,500,000 inhabitants. The German princes received an increase of territory. The negotiations over the indemnifications lasted more than two years *(p. 619),* during which time the ambassadors of German princes haunted the antechambers of the first consul to beg for better terms, and bribed French ambassadors, secretaries, and their mistresses.

Tuscany was transformed into the **kingdom of Etruria,** for the satisfaction of Parma. Besides losing Parma (a Spanish *secundogeniture*), Spain ceded **Louisiana** to France, which afterward sold it to the United States (1803). The treaty of Lunéville was succeeded, after conclusion of a truce, by the

Mar. 18. Treaty of Florence with Naples. **Conditions:** (1) Closure of the harbors to British and Turkish vessels. (2) Cession of the Neapolitan possessions in central Italy and the island of Elba. (3) Reception of French garrisons in several Italian towns.

Prussia joined the Northern convention against Britain. **Occupation of Hanover.**

1801–1825. ALEXANDER I, tsar of Russia. Reconciliation between Russia and Britain (in 1801 Britain had attacked Denmark, the ally of Russia, and forced her to withdraw from the Northern convention). The Northern convention was now dissolved.

1801. CONCORDAT BETWEEN FRANCE AND THE PAPACY, concluded after long and trying negotiations. This was part of Napoleon's policy of pacification. The concordat provided that French archbishops and bishops should be appointed by the government, but confirmed by the pope. Clergy paid by the government. The pope agreed to accept as valid the titles of those who had bought former church property confiscated by the revolutionary government. **Pius VII** (elected 1800) was given possession of the Papal States, but without Ferrara, Bologna, and the Romagna. The liberties of the Gallican Church were strongly asserted. By the new organization of the **Université,** an incorporated body of teachers who had passed a state examination, the entire system of higher education was made dependent upon the government. The **Institut National** was reorganized and divided into four (later five) academies: (1) *Académie Française* (1635); (2) *A. des Inscriptions et Belles-Lettres* (1663, 1701); (3) *A. des Sciences* (1666); (4) *A. des Beaux Arts* (1648); (5) *A. des Sciences Morales et Politiques* (1832).

After the withdrawal of the younger Pitt from the British cabinet, and after long negotiations, the

1802, Mar. 27. TREATY OF AMIENS was concluded between Great Britain and France, thus achieving a complete pacification of Europe. (1) Surrender of all conquests made by Britain to France and her allies, excepting Trinidad, which was ceded by Spain, and Ceylon, which was ceded by the Batavian Republic. (2) France recognized the Republic of the Seven Ionian Islands. Malta must be restored to the Order of the Knights of Malta. In consequence of this treaty, peace was concluded also between France and the Porte.

Creation of the **Order of the Legion of Honor** (May 19, 1802). Assumption of regal state and authority. By a popular vote (plebiscite, 3½ millions),

Aug. 2. Napoleon became consul for life, with the right of appointing his successor.

New (fifth) constitution. The powers of the senate, which was ruled by the first consul, were enlarged; the importance of the legislative bodies and the tribunate was very decidedly reduced.

Napoleon had already become president of the **Italian Republic,** as the Cisalpine Republic was henceforward called. Elba and Piedmont were annexed to France. Military interference of the French in Switzerland, which was torn with civil dissensions. The **act of mediation** restored the independence of the separate cantons, but the country remained still so far a single state that it was represented by a land-amman and a diet.

As regards the internal relations of Germany, the treaty of Lunéville was executed according to a plan of indemnification established by France and Russia by the

1803, Feb. Enactment of the delegates of the Empire (*Reichsdeputationshauptschluss*): Of the ecclesiastical estates there were left only:

Battle of Marengo, June 14, 1800

Napoleon and Pius VII concluding the concordat in 1801

to indemnifications. The electoral bishoprics of Trier and Köln were abolished. Four new electorates: Hesse-Cassel, Baden, Württemberg, Salzburg.

Principal indemnifications: (1) To the **grand duke of Tuscany:** Salzburg, and Berchtesgaden. (2) To the **duke of Modena:** Breisgau (in exchange for which Austria received the ecclesiastical foundations of Trent and Brixen). (3) To **Bavaria:** bishoprics of Würzburg, Bamberg, Freising, Augsburg, the majority of the prelacies and imperial cities in Franconia and eastern Swabia, in return for which, (4) **Baden** received that portion of the Palatinate lying on the right bank of the Rhine (Heidelberg, Mannheim). Baden also received: the portion of the bishoprics of Constance, Basel, Strassburg, Speier, on the right bank of the Rhine, and many ecclesiastical foundations and imperial cities. (5) **Württemberg:** many abbeys, monasteries, and imperial cities, especially Reutlingen, Esslingen, Heilbronn, etc. (6) **Prussia:** the bishoprics of Paderborn, Hildesheim, the part of Thuringia which had belonged to Mainz (Eichfeld and Erfurt), a part of Münster, many abbeys, particularly Quedlinburg, and the imperial cities, Mühlhausen, Nordhausen, Goslar. (7) **Oldenburg:** bishopric of Lübeck. (8) **Hanover:** bishopric of Osnabrück. (9) **Hesse** (Darmstadt and Cassel) and **Nassau** divided the portions of the archbishoprics of Mainz, Trier, and Köln which remained upon the right bank of the Rhine. (10) **Nassau-Orange:** bishopric of Fulda, and abbey of Corvey. As a rule the indemnified princes gained considerably in territory and subjects.

New dissensions between France and England, caused by the refusal to surrender Malta and the quarrels of the journalists. The French occupied Hanover, where they nearly exhausted the resources of the state. The encampment at **Boulogne** threatened England with an invasion.

1804, Feb. Conspiracy against the life of the first consul discovered. Pichegru met a mysterious death in prison, **Georges Cadoudal** was executed. **Moreau** fled to America. The **duke of Enghien,** a Bourbon prince of the branch line of Condé, was taken by violence from the territory of Baden, condemned by a commission acting in accordance with the wishes and under the order of Napoleon, without observation of the ordinary forms of law, and shot at Vincennes on the night of March 20–21.

(1) The former elector of Mainz, now electoral archchancellor, with a territory formed out of the remains of the archbishopric of Mainz on the right bank of the Rhine, the bishopric of Regensburg, and the cities of Regensburg and Wezlar. (2) The masters of the Order of St. John and the Teutonic Order. (3) Of the 48 free imperial cities which still existed, only six were left, (the three Hanseatic cities: Lübeck, Hamburg, Bremen, and Frankfurt, Augsburg, Nürnberg). All other ecclesiastical estates and imperial cities were devoted

8. *The First Empire*

1804–1814 (1815). **NAPOLEON I,** emperor of the French. He was proclaimed by the senate and tribunate on May 18, and consecrated at Paris by Pope Pius VII on December 2. Napoleon placed the crown on his own head (in imitation of Pepin and Charlemagne). His elevation was ratified by a plebiscite (3,572,329 in favor, 2569 opposed). The imperial office was made hereditary, succession to be in the male line and the emperor having the right to adopt the children of his brothers; in default of such children, the crown was to pass to Napoleon's brothers, Joseph and Louis.

Napoleon at once established a brilliant court: grand dignitaries of the Empire; the eighteen marshals of France; development of a new nobility, with many of the privileges of the old, but based on achievement rather than on birth. Napoleon really revived the absolute monarchy, but on a more modern and efficient basis.

1805. **Napoleon** made himself king of Italy. His stepson, Eugène Beauharnais, became viceroy of Italy. The **Ligurian Republic** was incorporated with France.

The Coronation of Napoleon, *December 2, 1804, by Jacques Louis David*

9. *The War of the Third Coalition*

1805. Formation of the Third Coalition against France. Great Britain had been at war with France since May 16, 1803, and was now joined by Austria, Russia, and Sweden. Spain was allied with France.

Napoleon hastily broke up the camp of Boulogne and shelved his plans (genuine or pretended) for an invasion of England. The French armies, under Davout, Soult, Lannes, and Ney, marched quickly to the Rhine to meet the Austrian armies under Archduke Ferdinand and Gen. Mack. In Italy, Masséna commanded the French against the main Austrian army under Archduke Charles. Napoleon then took over the chief command in Germany, crossed the Rhine, and marched toward Bavaria, which had been invaded by the Austrians. Bavaria, Württemberg, Baden, Hesse, and Nassau supported the French.

Oct. 17. Mack was obliged to surrender at **Ulm**, with an army of 30,000 men, whom the French had surrounded.

Oct. 21. BATTLE OF TRAFALGAR, a great victory of **Nelson** (who died of wounds) over the combined French and Spanish fleets. This victory broke the naval power of France and established Britain as the mistress of the seas throughout the 19th century.

The French, after Ulm, marched down the course of the Danube and took **Vienna** without meeting much resistance. In Italy the Archduke Charles was driven back by Masséna, and returned to Germany. Meanwhile, however, a Russian army under Kutuzov and a second under **Tsar Alexander I** came to the aid of the Austrians in Moravia.

Dec. 2. BATTLE OF AUSTERLITZ (*battle of the three emperors*), one of the greatest victories of Napoleon. The combined Austrian and Russian armies were defeated, the Austrians hastily agreed to a truce, and the Russians retreated.

Dec. 15. Treaty between Prussia and France. The Prussians had been on the point of joining the coalition, but after Austerlitz agreed to cede to France the remaining part of Cleve on the left bank of the Rhine, and also Ansbach and Neuchâtel, in return for Hanover.

Dec. 26. TREATY OF PRESSBURG, between France and Austria. (1) **France** received Piedmont, Parma, and Piacenza. (2) **Austria** ceded to the kingdom of Italy all that she had received of Venetian territory by the treaty of Campo Formio, as well as Venetian Istria and Dalmatia; Austria also recog-

nized Napoleon as king of Italy. (3) **Austria** ceded to Bavaria the Tyrol, Vorarlberg, the bishoprics of Brixen and Trent, Burgau, Eichstädt, Passau, Lindau; Bavaria also received the free city of Augsburg. (4) **Austria** ceded to Württemberg and Baden what remained of the western lands of the Hapsburgs. (5) **Württemberg** and **Baden** were recognized as kingdoms. (6) **Austria** was indemnified by being given Salzburg, Berchtesgaden, and the estates of the Teutonic Order, which were secularized. The elector of Salzburg received from Bavaria Würzburg as compensation.

Dec. The **Bourbons** in Naples were dethroned by a proclamation of Napoleon from Schönbrunn.

1806. Joseph Bonaparte, elder brother of Napoleon, became king of Naples. The Bourbons withdrew to Sicily, where they enjoyed the protection of the British fleet.

Joachim Murat, brother-in-law of Napoleon, was created grand duke of Berg; Marshal Bertheir became prince of Neuchâtel; **Louis,** third brother of Napoleon, became king of Holland (the former Batavian Republic).

July 12. The **CONFEDERATION OF THE RHINE,** organized under French auspices. Napoleon was protector. **Members:** the prince primate, formerly electoral archchancellor; the kings of Bavaria and Württemberg; the grand dukes of Baden, Hesse, Darmstadt, Berg; the duke of Nassau, etc. Afterward all German princes joined the confederation except Austria, Prussia, Brunswick, and the elector of Hesse. Thus a large part of Germany came under French domination. Territorial changes were constantly made: many princes who held immediately of the empire were mediatized; Bavaria was given the free city of Nürnberg; Frankfurt passed to the prince primate (grand duke of Frankfurt).

Aug. 6. END OF THE OLD HOLY ROMAN EMPIRE. The Austrian emperor, Francis II, had already assumed the title of *Francis I, Emperor of Austria* (1804). He now laid down the old imperial crown.

1806–1807. WAR AGAINST PRUSSIA AND RUSSIA. Reasons for Prussia's entry into the war: establishment of the Confederation of the Rhine; annexation of Wesel; seizure of Verden and Essen; garrisoning of French troops throughout half of Germany; Napoleon's offer to Britain to take Hanover away from Prussia (on whom he had forced it a short time before). The Prussians were also embittered by the high-handed execution of Johann Palm, a book-seller of Nürnberg, who had published some strictures on Napoleon.

Dangerous **position of Prussia** at the outbreak of the conflict: the complete separation of the military and civil administration had resulted in the safety of the state resting on a half-trained army composed in part of foreigners, on a superannuated general, and on subordinate commanders who, overconfident in the military fame of Prussia since the time of Frederick II, regarded the French with contempt. Prussia had no allies, excepting Saxony and far-off Russia. Relations with Britain were filled with dissension.

The Prussian army was commanded by the duke of Brunswick, and was concentrated in Thuringia. As it advanced, it was defeated by the French at **Saalfeld** (Oct. 10) and in the

Oct. 14. BATTLES OF JENA AND AUERSTÄDT. The main Prussian armies were completely routed and quickly fell to pieces. A reserve force under the prince of Württemberg was defeated and scattered at **Halle** (Oct. 17).

Oct. 27. Napoleon occupied Berlin. The prince of Hohenlohe and 12,000 men were forced to surrender at **Prenzlau** (Oct. 28). Blücher, after a valiant defense of Lübeck, was also obliged to surrender at Ratkau (Nov. 7). Hasty surrender of the fortresses of Erfurt, Spandau, Stettin, Küstrin, Magdeburg, Hameln; only Kolberg (Gneisenau, Schill, Nettelbeck) and Graudenz (Courbière) defended themselves resolutely.

Nov. 21. BERLIN DECREE: Napoleon proclaimed a (paper) **blockade of Great Britain** and closure of the Continent to British trade, thus inaugurating the *Continental System.*

The French, supported by the Bavarians and Württembergers, invaded Silesia and called on the Poles to revolt.

Dec. 11. Separate peace between France and Saxony. The elector became *king,* allied himself with France, and joined the Confederation of the Rhine.

The war also became extended to the Near East. The French emissary, **Gen. Horace Sebastiani,** induced the Turks to abandon the alliance with Britain and Russia. Deposition of the Russophile governors (*hospodars*) of Moldavia and Wallachia (Aug. 1806) resulted in

1806–1812. WAR BETWEEN RUSSIA AND TURKEY.

1807. The French captured most of the Hanseatic towns and took Breslau and most other fortresses of Silesia. Meanwhile the Russians advanced to the aid of the Prussians. The combined armies fought against the French in the

Feb. 7–8. Battle of Eylau, a bloody but indecisive engagement. The armies then went into winter quarters. King Frederick William withdrew to Memel.

Feb. 17. A British squadron, under Admi-

Napoleon at the Battle of Eylau, *February 7–8, 1807, by Antoine Jean Gros*

ral Sir John Duckworth, forced the **passage of the Dardanelles** and appeared before Constantinople. Duckworth was, however, obliged to retire with a loss of two ships (Mar. 3), because of the threatening preparations of the Turks, inspired by Sebastiani.

Mar. 18. The **British occupied Alexandria,** but, meeting with vigorous opposition from the Turkish forces, evacuated again on September 25.

May 26. The **French captured Danzig** and, advancing eastward, fought

June 14. The **BATTLE OF FRIEDLAND** against the Russians. The French were victorious and the Russians fell back. Napoleon then occupied Königsberg and all the country as far as the Niemen River. After the conclusion of a truce, Napoleon met Alexander I and Frederick William III on a raft in the Niemen and concluded

July 7-9. The **TREATIES OF TILSIT,** between (A) France and Russia, and (B) France and Prussia.

A. (1) **Russia** recognized the grand duchy of Warsaw, which was formed from Polish territory acquired by Prussia through the partitions, under the king of Saxony. (2) Danzig restored to the condition of a free city. (3) A part of New East Prussia (Bialystock) ceded to Russia. (4) Russia recognized Joseph Bonaparte as king of Naples, Louis Bonaparte as king of Holland, Jerome Bonaparte as king of Westphalia, a new kingdom yet to be created; Russia, moreover, recognized the Con-

federation of the Rhine, and accepted the mediation of Napoleon in concluding peace with the Turks, while Napoleon accepted the like good offices from Alexander in regard to Britain. In a secret article, Alexander agreed to an alliance with France against Britain, in case the latter refused to accept the proffered peace.

B. (1) **Prussia** ceded: (a) to Napoleon for free disposal, all lands between the Rhine and Elbe; (b) to Saxony, the circle of Cottbus; (c) all lands taken from Poland since 1772 for the creation of a duchy of Warsaw, also the city and territory of Danzig. (2) Prussia recognized the sovereignty of the three brothers of Napoleon. (3) All Prussian harbors and lands were closed to British ships and British trade until the conclusion of a peace with Great Britain. (4) Prussia was to maintain a standing army of not more than 42,000 men. In regard to the restoration and evacuation of the Prussian provinces and fortresses, it was settled by the **treaty of Königsberg** (July 12), that Prussia should first pay all arrears of war indemnities.

These indemnities, fixed at 19 million francs by the Prussian calculations, were set at 120 millions by the French, which sum was raised to 140 millions in 1808. After 120 millions had been paid the fortresses were evacuated, excepting Stettin, Küstrin, and Glogau. Until this occurred the Prussian state, reduced as it was from 89,120 to 46,032 square miles, was obliged to support 150,000 French troops.

Aug. Foundation of the **kingdom of Westphalia** (capital, Cassel) by a decree of Napoleon, who reserved for himself half of the domains.

Sept. High-handed proceeding of the British against Denmark, which had been summoned to join the Continental system. A British fleet bombarded Copenhagen, and carried off the Danish fleet. Alliance of Denmark with France. Russia declared war upon Britain. Stralsund and Rügen occupied by the French.

Nov. **Portugal,** which refused to join the Continental system, occupied by a French army under **Junot** (duke of Abrantès). The royal family fled to Brazil.

Dec. 17. **Milan Decree,** reiterating the blockade against British trade. On paper, Napoleon had closed the entire European coastline to the British.

1808, Mar. **Spain invaded** by 100,000 Frenchmen under the pretext of guarding the coasts against the British. Charles IV *(p. 474)* abdicated in favor of his son Ferdinand, in consequence of an outbreak which had occurred against his favorite, Godoy. Father and son, with Godoy, were enticed by Napoleon to Bayonne and compelled to renounce the throne (May). Napoleon's brother **Joseph** became king of Spain, Murat taking the throne of Naples instead of Joseph. General uprising of the Spaniards.

10. *The Peninsular War*

1808-1814. **War of the British against the French in Portugal and Spain.** The British landed in Portugal, under command of **Sir Arthur Wellesley** (later the duke of Wellington) and defeated the French under Junot at **Vimeiro** (Aug. 21, 1808). Nevertheless, Wellesley's successor, Gen. Dalrymple, instead of continuing the campaign, agreed to

Aug. 30. The **convention of Cintra,** by which Junot agreed to evacuate Portugal.

The **popular insurrection in Spain** (May 1808) led to retirement of the French, under Murat, behind the Ebro. But on July 20 the French managed to recover Madrid. On the same day another French force, advancing toward Cadiz, was defeated by the insurgents and forced to capitulate at **Baylen.**

Sept. The **congress of Erfurt,** a conference between Napoleon and Alexander I of Russia, attended also by four kings and thirty-four princes, mostly obsequious German satellites. Ostensible reinforcement of the Franco-Russian alliance. Napoleon at the height of his power and splendor. But in secret the French statesman, **Charles de Talleyrand,** was negotiating with Alexander behind Napoleon's back, to frustrate further measures against

Austria. Immediately after the Erfurt meeting Napoleon proceeded to Spain in person, with an army of 150,000. He advanced at once upon Madrid (which the French had again abandoned), while his marshals defeated the Spaniards at **Burgos** (Nov. 10) and **Espinosa** (Nov. 11).

Dec. 13. **Madrid capitulated** to Napoleon. To distract the French from invasion of the south, the British, under **Sir John Moore,** invaded northwestern Spain from Portugal. Napoleon turned against him, forcing his retreat.

1809, Jan. 16. **Battle of Corunna.** Marshal **Soult,** succeeding Napoleon in the command, defeated and killed Moore. The British were forced to evacuate Spain. But in Spain guerrilla warfare continued: heroic **defense of Saragossa** (Palafox), which, however, was obliged to capitulate (Feb. 21). The French, meanwhile, invaded Portugal and took **Oporto.** To protect Lisbon, the British sent out Wellesley with reinforcements. Soult was driven out of Oporto, and the British again invaded northwestern Spain.

July 28. **Battle of Talavera,** an indecisive engagement, which, however, protected Portu-

Charles de Talleyrand, 1754–1838

gal against further invasion. Meanwhile the French pushed on with the conquest of the south.

Nov. 12. **Battle of Ocaña,** in which the Spaniards were defeated. The French thereupon overran all Andalusia, excepting Cadiz.

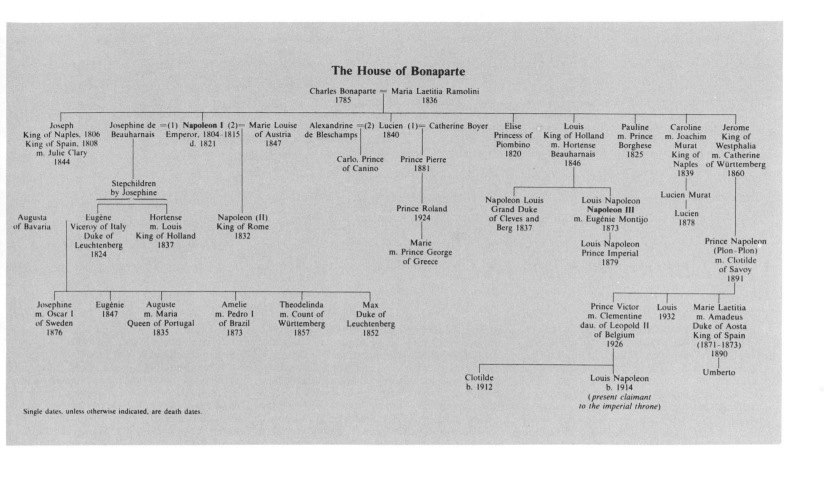

The House of Bonaparte

Charles Bonaparte = Maria Laetitia Ramolini
1785 — 1836

Joseph
King of Naples, 1806
King of Spain, 1808
m. Julie Clary
1844

Josephine de =(1) **Napoleon I** (2)= Marie Louise
Beauharnais — Emperor, 1804–1815 — of Austria
d. 1821 — 1847

Alexandrine =(2) Lucien (1)= Catherine Boyer
de Bleschamps — 1840

Carlo, Prince
of Canino

Prince Pierre
1881

Elise
Princess of
Piombino
1820

Louis
King of Holland
m. Hortense
Beauharnais
1846

Pauline
m. Prince
Borghese
1825

Caroline
m. Joachim
Murat
King of
Naples
1839

Jerome
King of
Westphalia
m. Catherine
of Württemberg
1860

Augusta
of Bavaria

Stepchildren
by Josephine

Eugène
Viceroy of Italy
Duke of
Leuchtenberg
1824

Hortense
m. Louis
King of Holland
1837

Napoleon (II)
King of Rome
1832

Prince Roland
1924

Marie
m. Prince George
of Greece

Napoleon Louis
Grand Duke
of Cleves and
Berg 1837

Louis Napoleon
Napoleon III
m. Eugénie Montijo
1873

Lucien Murat

Lucien
1878

Louis Napoleon
Prince Imperial
1879

Prince Napoleon
(Plon–Plon)
m. Clotilde
of Savoy
1891

Josephine
m. Oscar I
of Sweden
1876

Eugénie
1847

Auguste
m. Maria
Queen of Portugal
1835

Amelie
m. Pedro I
of Brazil
1873

Theodelinda
m. Count of
Württemberg
1857

Max
Duke of
Leuchtenberg
1852

Prince Victor
m. Clementine
dau. of Leopold II
of Belgium
1926

Louis
1932

Marie Laetitia
m. Amadeus
Duke of Aosta
King of Spain
(1871–1873)
1890

Umberto

Clotilde
b. 1912

Louis Napoleon
b. 1914
(*present claimant
to the imperial throne*)

Single dates, unless otherwise indicated, are death dates.

II. *The War against Austria*

After the disasters of 1805–1806, both Prussia and Austria undertook far-reaching political and social reforms, designed to modernize the state and develop greater strength for the further contest with Napoleon. In Prussia the greatest reformer was **Karl, Freiherr vom Stein** (1757–1831), assisted by **Prince Karl von Hardenberg.** Reorganization of town government, liberation of industry from burdensome restrictions, abolition of hereditary serfdom, reform of taxation and the whole financial system. Reorganization of the army, on the basis of universal military service, by **Gneisenau, Grolmann, Boyen, Clausewitz, Scharnhorst.** Foundation of the **University of Berlin** (1810), by **Humboldt, Altenstein, Niebuhr,** and **Schleiermacher.** **Fichte's** famous *Addresses to the German Nation* (1807–1808), a tremendous stimulus to national feeling; foundation of the *Tugendbund,* a patriotic organization; development of gymnastics by **Friedrich Jahn;** patriotic poems of **E. M. Arndt,** etc.

Similar, though less extensive, reforms were introduced in Austria, where **Count Johann von Stadion** became the leading figure. Reorganization of the army by **Archduke Charles.** The Austrians, impressed by the difficulties Napoleon was meeting with in Spain, and encouraged by the British, who promised subsidies, decided to take advantage of the situation.

1809, Apr. The **Archduke Charles** appealed to the whole German people to embark on a war of liberation, and with an army of 170,000 began the invasion of Bavaria. Only Tyrol heeded the appeal, and rose in revolt, under **Andreas Hofer.** Napoleon, having hurried back from Spain, engaged the Austrians in Bavaria (using German troops), drove the archduke across the Danube into Bohemia (**battles of Abensberg, Landshut, Eckmühl, Regensburg,** Apr. 19–23) and

May 13. **The French took Vienna.** Napoleon then crossed the island of Lobau, in the Danube, and fought the

May 21–22. BATTLE OF ASPERN AND ESSLING. Napoleon was defeated and forced to recross the Danube, where he united his forces with those of the Italian viceroy, **Eugene,** who had driven the Austrians, under Archduke John, from Italy into Hungary. With the combined forces Napoleon recrossed the river and defeated Archduke Charles in the

July 5–6. BATTLE OF WAGRAM. The Austrians, completely exhausted, agreed to the

Eugene Beauharnais, viceroy of Italy

Oct. 14. TREATY OF SCHÖNBRUNN: Austria lost 32,000 square miles of territory, with 3,500,000 inhabitants, as follows: (1) to **Bavaria:** Salzburg and Berchtesgaden, the Innviertel and half of the Hausrückviertel; (2) to the **grand duchy of Warsaw:** West

Galicia; (3) to **Russia:** the Tarnopol section of East Galicia; (4) to **France:** all the lands beyond the Save River (circle of Villach, Istria, Hungarian Dalmatia, and Ragusa). These territories were, together with the Ionian Islands (ceded to France by Russia in 1807), organized by Napoleon as a new state, the **Illyrian Provinces,** under **Auguste Marmont** as duke of Ragusa. Austria further joined the Continental system and agreed to break off all connections with Britain.

The **Tyrolese,** left to themselves, continued the war against the Bavarians and French with heroic courage, but in the end were subdued. In November 1809, **Hofer was captured and shot** by the French at Mantua. Southern Tyrol was annexed to the kingdom of Italy.

Similar **outbreaks in Germany** ended likewise in disaster: The bold attempt of Major Schill, a Prussian, to precipitate a war of liberation in April 1809 was frustrated by news of Napoleon's victories on the Danube. Schill fell while fighting at Stralsund (May 31). Eleven of his officers were court-martialed and shot at Wesel, while the captured soldiers were condemned by Napoleon to hard labor; after serving for six months in the French galleys, they were enrolled in the coast guard. Another effort was made in 1809 by the duke of Brunswick, who, with a force of volunteers from Bohemia and Silesia, made his way across Germany to Brunswick (July 31). Forced by superior numbers to withdraw, he managed to reach Bremen and transported his men to England.

12. *Europe, 1810–1812*

1810, Apr. MARRIAGE OF NAPOLEON WITH ARCHDUCHESS MARIE LOUISE, daughter of Emperor Francis I of Austria. Napoleon had divorced Josephine and was eager for an heir to his great empire. The marriage was arranged by **Count** (later Prince) **Klemens von Metternich,** the Austrian foreign minister after 1809, whose policy was that of alliance with France as the only protection for Austria during the period of recuperation. Birth of an heir to the throne, the king of Rome (Mar. 1811).

July 1. Abdication and flight of **Louis, king of Holland,** who had refused to ruin his country by joining the Continental system. Thereupon **Holland was annexed to France** (July 9), followed by the annexation also of the canton of Wallis, of Oldenburg, of a large part of the kingdom of Westphalia, of the grand duchy of Berg, of East Friesland, and of the Hanseatic cities. The French Empire thenceforth comprised 130 departments and extended along the entire Channel and North Sea coast. These annexations were provoked chiefly by the desire to stop smuggling of British goods, but as such they proved rather ineffectual.

THE REVOLUTION IN SWEDEN. By the **treaty of Tilsit,** Alexander of Russia had been given a free hand to conquer Finland, which he did in 1808, meeting with but feeble opposition from the Swedes. In the course of the war the Russians, under Gen. Barclay de Tolly, crossed the Gulf of Bothnia on the ice, captured the Aaland Islands, and threatened Stockholm. This situation, complicated by an unfortunate war between Sweden and Denmark, resulted in a military overturn. On March 13, 1809, **King Gustavus IV** was arrested by Generals Klingspor and Adlerkreutz, and forced to abdicate (Mar. 29). His uncle became king as **Charles XIII** (1809–1818) and a new constitution was promulgated, restoring the power of the aristocracy. The new king concluded with Russia the **treaty of Fredrikshamm** (Sept. 17) by which the Swedes abandoned Finland as far as the Tornea River, and also the Aaland Islands. Through the mediation of Russia, the Swedes secured also the **treaty of Paris,** with France. By this Sweden joined the Continental system, and received in return Swedish Pomerania. In January 1810, the Swedish estates elected as heir to the throne Prince Christian of Holstein-Augustenburg, and on his sudden death (May) they chose **Marshal Jean Baptiste Bernadotte** (prince of Ponte Corvo) as crown prince. Napoleon was unable to resist this compliment and Bernadotte accepted the position (Nov. 5). Thenceforth he controlled the Swedish army and foreign affairs.

ROME AND THE PAPACY. Growing friction between Napoleon and Pius VII after 1805, when the pope returned to Rome. Difficulties about the working of the concordat of 1801, high-handed action of Napoleon in depriving the pope of some of his territories. Pius steadfastly refused to join in the Continental system, as directed, so that on February 2, 1808, the French, under Gen. Miollis, occupied Rome. On May 17, 1809, the **Papal States were declared incorporated with France.** To this act Pius replied by excommunicating Napoleon (June 10), whereupon the emperor had him arrested (July 6) and taken to Savona, near Genoa, where he was held prisoner. Pius continued his attitude of opposition and in 1812 was removed to Fontainebleau.

PORTUGAL AND SPAIN. The British force in Portugal, under Wellesley, was in 1810 threatened by a twofold attack by the French, under Masséna in the north, and under Soult in the south. The French took **Ciudad Rodrigo** (July 10) and the British fell back toward Lisbon, where they held the lines of **Torres Vedras** (Oct.). All through the winter the two armies confronted each other, until finally Masséna fell back into Spain. The British pursued and besieged **Almeida** and **Badajoz.**

Pope Pius VII is arrested, July 6, 1809

In the **battle of Fuentes de Onoro** (May 5) Masséna was defeated, while another British force, under Gen. William Beresford, defeated Soult in the south (**battle of Albuera,** May 16). In 1812 (Jan. 19) the British took **Ciudad Rodrigo,** and somewhat later (Apr. 6) captured **Badajoz.** On July 22 Wellesley (Wellington) completely defeated the French under Marshal Marmont at **Salamanca.** Joseph Bonaparte had to abandon Madrid (Aug. 12) and fall back to the Ebro River. Meanwhile, a national assembly (cortes) elected in 1810 in the only part of the country then free, viz. Cadiz and vicinity, promulgated a famous **constitution** (May 8, 1812) of an advanced, democratic type (one-chamber parliament, universal suffrage, popular sovereignty, etc.).

THE OTTOMAN EMPIRE. War against Great Britain and Russia (1806–1812). This was conducted in desultory fashion by both sides. 1807: **Revolutions in Constantinople** *(p. 722)*. 1809, Jan. 5: The British concluded the **treaty of the Dardanelles** with the Turks and withdrew from the war. In the same year the Russians won a victory at **Silistria,** which was followed, in 1810, by the occupation of **Bessarabia, Moldavia,** and **Wallachia.** In 1811 the Russians crossed the Danube and began the advance through Bulgaria. These operations had to be broken off in view of the impending invasion of Russia by Napoleon. Despite French efforts to induce them to continue the war, the Turks were glad to accept the **treaty of Bucharest** (May 28, 1812), by which they gave up to Russia the province of Bessarabia.

13. *The French Invasion of Russia*

Causes: Latent rivalry between Napoleon and Alexander, both eager for leadership in Europe. Dissatisfaction of Alexander, aroused by Napoleon's marriage and alliance with Austria. Unwillingness of the Russians to carry through fully the Continental system. Irritation of the tsar over Napoleon's unwillingness to grant him free hand in the matter of Constantinople. Addition of West Galicia to the grand duchy of Warsaw (by the **treaty of Schönbrunn,** 1809) aroused Alexander's fear that Napoleon was planning the restoration of Poland. Deposition of the duke of Oldenburg and annexation of his territory to France offended Alexander, who was a near relative of the duke.

Preparations: Alliance of Napoleon with Austria (which agreed to furnish 30,000 men) and **Prussia** (20,000). **Denmark,** however, maintained neutrality throughout the war. **Sweden,** which had been forced by Napoleon to declare war on Britain (1810), now, under Bernadotte's guidance, shook off the French yoke and secured compensation for the loss of Finland. The French having reoccupied Swedish Pomerania and Rügen (Jan. 1812), the Swedes concluded with Russia

1812, Apr. The **treaty of St. Petersburg:** Russia promised Sweden the annexation of Norway, which belonged to Denmark, the latter to be indemnified elsewhere; Sweden agreed to make a diversion against the French in northern Germany.

May 28. **Russia made peace with the Turks** at Bucharest (above).

June. **Great Britain made peace with Russia and Sweden.**

Military preparations: the Grand Army of Napoleon, originally about 420,000 men, ultimately, with reinforcements, about 600,000, probably the greatest army ever assembled up to that time. It was only in part French, for there were large contingents of Italians, Poles, Swiss, Dutch, and German (from the Confederation of the Rhine members, as well as Austria and Prussia). The **Austrians,** under Prince Karl von Schwarzenberg, formed a separate army on the right wing, the **Prussians,** under Count Hans York von Wartenburg, held the left wing.

1812, June. **Passage of the Niemen River** and occupation of Vilna. The Russians, under Barclay de Tolly, retreated, allowing the French main army to reach Smolensk without offering battle. The Prussians meanwhile besieged **Riga** and the Austrians penetrated into **Volhynia.**

Aug. 17–18. **Destruction of Smolensk** by the French. Barclay de Tolly, criticized for his failure to resist the invasion, was replaced by **General Michael Kutuzov,** who fought the French in the bloody

Sept. 7. **BATTLE OF BORODINO,** on the Moskova River (terrific losses on both sides). The Russians were obliged to retreat farther, and abandoned Moscow.

Sept. 14. The **French occupied Moscow,** which had been deserted by most of the inhabitants. Napoleon established himself in the Kremlin.

Sept. 15–19. **BURNING OF MOSCOW,** evidently a disaster planned and executed by the Russians **(Count Fedor Rostopchin)** to make the place untenable. Napoleon offered Alexander a truce, which Alexander rejected. After waiting for five weeks in Moscow, Napoleon, frustrated in his hope of bringing the Russians to terms and unable to maintain himself so far from his bases, began the

Oct. 19. **RETREAT FROM MOSCOW** toward Smolensk. Attacks on the invaders by Kutuzov's army and by swarms of Cossacks and irregulars. Separate corps of the Grand Army fought at **Jaroslavetz** (Oct. 24) and at **Viazma** (Nov. 3). By the beginning of November very severe weather began to set in. Suffering of the troops from hunger and frost, combined with constant attacks by the enemy (e.g. at **Krasnoi** and **Borissov**).

Retreat of the French army from Russia, November 1812

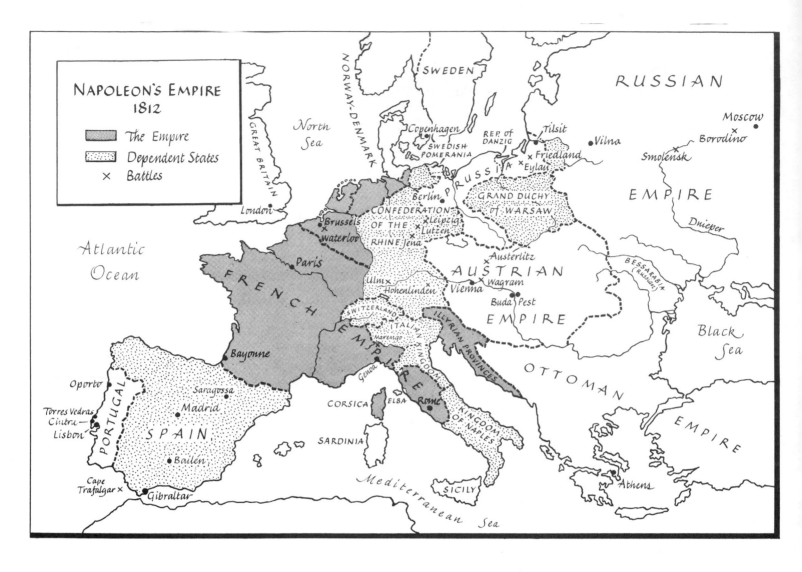

NAPOLEON'S EMPIRE 1812

The Empire
Dependent States
× Battles

Nov. 26–28. **CROSSING OF THE BERE-SINA,** one of the most horrible episodes in the retreat. Ney and Oudinot, with 8500 men, forced the passage against 25,000 Russians.

From this point on, the remaining fragments of the army became completely disorganized and the retreat became a wild flight. Napoleon left the army and hastened to Paris, where he arrived on December 18. At about the same time the remnants of the army (not more than 100,000 men) straggled across the Niemen.

14. *The Wars of Liberation*

Soon after the catastrophic invasion of Russia, the Prussians deserted the French and joined the tsar in a campaign in Germany. On December 30 General York concluded the **convention of Tauroggen** (an agreement of neutrality) with the Russian general, Count Ivan Diebitsch. Great pressure was brought to bear upon Frederick William III by his generals and advisers.

1813, Feb. 3. Appeal of Frederick William III, issued from Breslau and calling upon his people to form volunteer corps. Enthusiastic response, especially among the younger men and students.

Feb. 28. Treaty of Kalisch, between Prussia and Russia: (1) offensive and defensive alliance, enumeration of auxiliary armies to be furnished by either side; (2) in the event of victory Prussia to be given as much territory as she possessed in 1806; (3) invitation extended to Austria and Britain to join the alliance.

Mar. 3. Treaty between Great Britain and Sweden: Britain paid one million rix dollars in subsidies and promised not to oppose the union of Norway with Sweden. Sweden furnished the allies an army of 30,000 men under command of **Crown Prince Bernadotte.**

Mar. 17. Appeal of Frederick William III "to my people," and "to my army." Establishment of the **Landwehr** and the **Landsturm.** Iron Cross.

Mar. 18. Outbreak in Hamburg. A force of Russians occupied the city. The dukes of Mecklenburg withdrew from the Confederation of the Rhine.

Great preparations on both sides. The Elbe was the boundary between the combatants; Danzig, Stettin, Küstrin, Glogau, Modlin, and Zamosc, being, however, in the hands of the French.

Mar. 27. Occupation of Dresden by Russians and Prussians under Prince Ludwig Wittgenstein and General Gebhard von Blücher, after the withdrawal of Marshal Davout. Flight of the king of Saxony.

The French army and the contingents of the Confederation of the Rhine concentrated in Franconia, Thuringia, and on the Elbe. Napoleon, after the end of April, was at the head of 180,000 men in Germany. He was unexpectedly attacked by the armies of the allies, numbering 85,000 men.

May 2. Battle of Gross-Görschen or Lützen. Victory remained with the French, in spite of their losses. The Allies withdrew through Dresden to Lusatia. Napoleon in Dresden, in close alliance with the king of Saxony, who had returned from Prague.

May 20 and 21. Battles of Bautzen and Wurschen. Napoleon attacked the Allies at Bautzen, forced them to retreat across the Spree, and completed the victory at Wurschen, with great loss to himself. Duroc killed. The Allies retreated to Silesia.

May 30. Hamburg occupied by Davout, after the withdrawal of the Russians. The combatants, exhausted, waited for reinforcements and strove to secure the alliance of Austria.

June 4–July 26. Armistice of Poischwitz, afterward prolonged until August 10 (16).

June 15. Great Britain concluded a subsidy treaty with Prussia and Russia at Reichenbach.

July 5 (28)–Aug. 11. Congress at Prague. Austria played the part of mediator. After futile negotiations (Metternich, Caulaincourt, William von Humboldt), the congress was dissolved.

Aug. 12. AUSTRIA DECLARED WAR ON FRANCE.

The Allies, all supported by British subsidies, put three armies into the field: (1) **the Bohemian army,** under **Schwarzenberg** (with Kleist and Wittgenstein), was accompanied by the three monarchs; (2) **the Silesian army,** under **Blücher** (with York, Sacken, and Langeron); (3) **the Northern army,** under **Bernadotte** (with Bülow, Tauenzien, and Winzingerode).

Napoleon began operations by attacking Blücher, who retired behind the Katzbach. Meanwhile Schwarzenberg advanced from Bohemia upon Dresden. Napoleon left MacDonald to oppose Blücher and hurried to Saxony. Oudinot and Reynier were to march on Berlin, with the support of Davout, coming from Hamburg.

Aug. 23. Battle of Grossbeeren. Oudinot and Reynier were defeated by Bülow, the crown prince of Saxony having looked on inactive. Berlin was saved by this victory.

Aug. 26. Battle of the Katzbach. MacDonald's army was defeated by Blücher, who was made prince of Wahlstatt.

Aug. 26–27. BATTLE OF DRESDEN. Napoleon defeated the Allied army under Schwarzenberg. It was his last major victory on German soil.

Aug. 30. Battle of Kulm and Nollendorf. Vandamme, with a French force that tried to intercept the retreating Bohemian army, was defeated by Ostermann and Kleist.

Sept. 6. Battle of Dennewitz, in which Marshal Ney, attempting to take Berlin, was defeated by Bülow and Tauentzien.

Sept. 9. TREATY OF TEPLITZ, between Russia, Prussia, and Austria: (1) firm union and mutual guaranty for their respective territories; (2) each party to assist the others with at least 60,000 men; (3) no separate peace or armistice to be concluded with France. **Secret articles** provided for the restoration of the Austrian and Prussian monarchies to their territorial status of 1805.

Oct. 3. Battle of Wartenburg. York forced a passage across the Elbe for the army of Silesia. The Northern army also crossed the Elbe.

Oct. 8. Treaty of Ried, between Austria and Bavaria. Bavaria withdrew from the Confederation of the Rhine and joined the alliance against Napoleon. In return, the king was guaranteed his possessions as of the time of the treaty.

Oct. 16–19. BATTLE OF LEIPZIG (*Battle of the Nations*). Napoleon had left Dresden in order to avoid being cut off from France by the three allied armies, which were attempting to unite in his rear. The decisive battle was fought around Leipzig. **Oct. 16:** inconclusive engagement between Napoleon and the army of Bohemia at **Wachau** (south of Leipzig); victory of Blücher over Marmont at **Möckern,** north of Leipzig. **Oct. 17:** the main armies were not engaged; Napoleon sent peace offers to the emperor, who rejected them as too extravagant; toward evening the Allies united, being reinforced with a Russian reserve under Bennigsen (100,000); formed in a huge semicircle, they greatly outnumbered the forces of Napoleon. **Oct. 18:** general attack of the Allies, ending in complete victory after nine hours. The French army was driven back to the gates of Leipzig. The Saxon and Württemberg corps went over to the Allies. **Oct. 19: storming of Leipzig** by the Allies; capture of the king of Saxony. The army of Napoleon, having lost 30,000 men, began the retreat, harried by the Allied forces (**battle of the Unstrut,** and of **Hanau**).

As a result of the French defeat at Leipzig, King Jerome fled from Cassel and the **kingdom of Westphalia came to an end.** The same was true of the **grand duchies of Frankfurt and of Berg.** The old rulers were restored in Cassel, Brunswick, Hanover, and Oldenburg. The central administrative bureau, which had been created under Freiherr vom Stein at the beginning of the war to govern recovered territories, had only Saxony to concern itself with.

THE CAMPAIGN IN SPAIN. The British, unable to take Burgos, had been obliged to fall back again, and King Joseph was able to recover Madrid. But in February 1813, Soult and a large part of the French army had to be recalled to Germany. Once more Wellington advanced to the northeast, to cut off the communications of King Joseph with France.

June 21. Battle of Vittoria. Wellington completely defeated Marshal Jourdan. Joseph fled to France and the French abandoned most of the country. The British stormed **San Sebastian** (Aug. 21) and besieged **Pampeluna.** In the east, Marshal Suchet was driven out of Valencia into Barcelona. Pampeluna fell to the British and Spaniards (Oct. 31). **Wellington crossed the French frontier,** defeated Soult (Nov. 10), and invested **Bayonne** (Dec.).

Nov. Napoleon crossed the Rhine at Mainz. Württemberg, Hesse-Darmstadt, Baden, and the remaining members of the Confederation of the Rhine joined the alliance. One city after another surrendered to the Allied forces: Dresden (Nov. 11), Stettin (Nov. 21), Lübeck (Dec. 5), Zamosc, Modlin, Torgau (Dec. 26), Danzig (Dec. 30), Wittenberg (Jan. 12, 1814), Küstrin (Mar. 7). But Hamburg (Davout), Glogau, Magdeburg, Erfurt, Würzburg, Wesel, and Mainz remained in French hands until the conclusion of peace.

Nov. 8. The **Allies offered Napoleon peace,** leaving France the boundaries of the Alps and the Rhine. When Napoleon failed to accept, the Allies (Dec. 1) adopted a resolution to prosecute the war vigorously and to pass the Rhine and invade France.

Nov. 15. Revolt of the Dutch, who expelled the French officials. The allied army of Bülow entered Holland, while Bernadotte, with the northern army, invaded Holstein, and in a short winter campaign forced Denmark to accept the

1814, Jan. 14. TREATY OF KIEL: (1) **Denmark** ceded Norway to Sweden, with a guaranty to the Norwegians of the maintenance of their rights; (2) **Sweden** ceded to Denmark Western Pomerania and Rügen. At the same time peace was made between **Great Britain and Denmark,** Britain restoring all conquests except Heligoland.

Meanwhile the **Allied armies had crossed the Rhine** (Dec. 21–25). The army of Schwarzenberg crossed through Switzerland, whose treaty of neutrality was disregarded. On January 1, 1814, Blücher crossed the river at Mannheim and Coblenz. Altogether about 200,000 men invaded France. The main army proceeded through Burgundy, while Blücher advanced through Lorraine. Napoleon attempted to prevent their junction by attacking Blücher at Brienne and driving him back (Jan. 29). But Blücher united with part of the main army and defeated the emperor in the

Feb. 1. Battle of La Rothière. Napoleon retired behind the Aube River. Difficulties of supply forced the Allied forces to divide again. The main army was to advance on Paris by the Seine River, while Blücher was to follow the course of the Marne. Hearing of the division, Napoleon suddenly hurled himself on the various corps of Blücher's army and defeated them in four battles: **Champaubert, Montmirail, Château-Thierry, Vauchamps** (Feb. 10–15). Then, turning on the main army, he defeated it in engagements at **Nangis** and **Montereau** (Feb. 17–18). Blücher was obliged to fall back to Etoges, and Schwarzenberg to Troyes. Meanwhile the Allies met with Napoleon's envoy, **Marquis Armand de Caulaincourt,** in the

Feb. 5–Mar. 19. Congress of Châtillon (sur-Seine). Napoleon was offered the French frontier of 1792, but, elated by his recent successes, he overplayed his hand and the negotiations failed.

Feb. 27. Battle of Bar-sur-Aube. Schwarzenberg defeated Oudinot and MacDonald. Blücher, forced to retire across the Marne and Oise, joined the army of the north under Bülow and Winzingerode.

Mar. 9. TREATIES OF CHAUMONT, between the Allies. These were arranged by **Lord Castlereagh,** the British foreign minister, who had hurried to the Continent to forestall any breakup of the coalition. The treaties provided for continuance of the struggle and guarded against a separate peace. The alliance to continue for twenty years.

Mar. 9-10. Battle of Laon. The allied armies, combined, defeated Napoleon.

Mar. 12. The British, under Wellington, captured **Bordeaux.** The campaign in the south came to an end with Soult's final defeat in the **battle of Toulouse** (Apr. 10).

Mar. 20-21. Battle of Arcis-sur-Aube. Napoleon suffered another reverse. He then formed the desperate plan of throwing himself on the rear of the Allies in Lorraine, summoning the garrisons of the fortresses to his aid, and calling the population to arms. The Allies, with equal boldness, advanced on Paris, and, in

Mar. 25. The **battle of La Fère-Champenoise** defeated Marshals Marmont and Mortier. The French generals threw themselves upon the capital, which was valiantly defended, but which, after

Mar. 30. The **storming of the Montmartre** by the Allies, was obliged to capitulate.

Mar. 31. VICTORIOUS ENTRY OF THE ALLIES INTO PARIS. The senate, under Talleyrand's influence, declared that Napoleon and his family had forfeited the throne. The emperor, hastening to the defense of the capital, arrived a few hours too late. His marshals refused to join him in a foolhardy assault on the city, so in the end he was obliged to abdicate in favor of his son (Fontainebleau, Apr. 6). The Allies rejected this solution, and on

Apr. 11. Napoleon abdicated unconditionally. The Allies granted him the **island of Elba** as a sovereign principality, with an annual income of 2,000,000 francs, to be paid by France. His wife, **Marie Louise,** received the duchies of Parma, Piacenza, and Guastalla, with sovereign power. Both Napoleon and Marie Louise retained the imperial title. On May 4 the emperor arrived at Elba.

15. *The Peace Settlements*

1814-1824. LOUIS XVIII, king of France. He was the elder of the two surviving brothers of Louis XVI. His restoration to the throne was due in part to the failure of other candidacies (notably that of Bernadotte), in part to the clever managing and maneuvering of Talleyrand. The British were sympathetic and Alexander I of Russia was easily persuaded. Louis was induced by Talleyrand and his other advisers to issue a **constitution,** modeled on that of the British, but with many limitations. This was the charter (*Charte constitutionelle*), for which *see p. 649.*

May 30. THE FIRST TREATY OF PARIS. Leniency of the Allies, due to their desire to strengthen the Bourbon régime: (1) **France** retained the boundaries of 1792, which included Avignon, Venaissin, parts of Savoy, and parts of the German Empire and Belgium, all of which had not belonged to France in 1789; (2) **France** recognized the independence of the Netherlands, of the German states, the Italian states, and of Switzerland; (3) **Britain** restored the French colonies, excepting Tobago, Ste. Lucia and Mauritius (Isle de France); Britain also retained Malta; (4) the Allies abandoned all claims for indemnity, etc.; (5) **France** promised to abolish the slave trade.

Discussion of the general settlement of the reconquered territories among the Allies at Paris, and during the visit of Alexander I and Frederick William to England (June). In view of the complexity of the problem, it was decided to hold a congress at Vienna.

1814, Sept.-1815, June. The **CONGRESS OF VIENNA,** one of the most brilliant international assemblies of modern times. Lavish entertainment offered by Emperor Francis. Most of the rulers of Europe attended the congress, to say nothing of the host of lesser potentates, ministers, claimants, etc. The chief negotiators were: for Austria, **Prince Metternich;** for Prussia, **Hardenberg** and **William von Humboldt;** for Great Britain, **Castlereagh** and Wellington; for Russia, the tsar himself and his many advisers (**Czartoryski, Stein, Razumovsky, Capo d'Istrias, Nesselrode**); for France, **Talleyrand;** for the Papacy, **Cardinal Consalvi.**

The main decisions were made by the chief representatives of the four major Allied powers, the other members of the grand alliance (Spain, Portugal, Sweden) being allowed to participate only in the treatment of fairly obvious or unobjectionable subjects. The full congress never met officially. Talleyrand, in order to gain admission to the inner councils, tried to raise the **principle of legitimacy** to support his claim, but he was taken into the inner group only when the dispute between the Allies as to the fate of Poland and Saxony led them (Jan. 1815) to the verge of war and the deadlock between the two opposing groups (Russia and Prussia against Austria and Britain) had to be broken by enlisting the support of France on the anti-Russian side.

The work of the congress of Vienna was interrupted by the **return of Napoleon from Elba** and the reopening of the war (*p. 629*), but the various settlements were brought together and signed as

1815, June 8. THE ACT OF THE CONGRESS OF VIENNA. Chief provisions:

(1) **Restoration of the Austrian and Prussian monarchies:** (*a*) **Austria** received, besides her former domain, the Italian provinces of Lombardy and Venetia (to be called the *Lombardo-Venetian Kingdom*); the Illyrian provinces (French kingdoms of Illyria and Dalmatia); Salzburg and the Tyrol (from Bavaria); Galicia. (*b*) **Prussia** received part of the grand duchy of Warsaw (Posen) and Danzig; Swedish Pomerania and Rügen, in return for which Denmark was given Lauenburg; the former Prussian possessions in Westphalia, somewhat enlarged, as well as Neuchâtel; the greater part of Saxony, as compensation for the loss of former possessions, like Ansbach and Baireuth (ceded to Bavaria), East Friesland (to Hanover), and part of the Polish territory (to Russia).

The Congress of Vienna, September 1814–June 1815

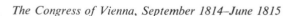

(2) Formation of the kingdom of the Netherlands, comprising the former Republic of Holland and the Austrian Netherlands (Belgium), under the former hereditary stadholder as King William I. Britain returned the former Dutch colonies, but not Ceylon or the Cape of Good Hope.

(3) Creation of the Germanic Confederation, to take the place of the old Holy Roman Empire. Schemes for a unified German state, advanced by the so-called "patriots," were put aside, and the federal bond was hardly more than a mutual defensive alliance. The confederation comprised 39 states, including four free cities. All other princes remained mediatized. The **Act of Confederation** was signed on June 8, 1815 and was later supplemented by the **Final Act of Vienna** (May 15, 1820).

(4) The kingdom of Poland: Most of the former grand duchy of Warsaw was handed over to Russia, and became a Polish kingdom, with the Russian tsar as king. Poland received from Alexander a liberal constitution; Polish was the official language and Poland had her own institutions, including a separate army. **Cracow** became a free state under the protection of Russia, Austria, and Prussia.

(5) Great Britain retained Malta, Heligoland, some of the French and Dutch colonies (see above), and assumed a protectorate over the Ionian Islands **(treaty of November 5, 1815).**

(6) Sweden retained Norway, which had been acquired by the treaty of Kiel (p. 649). **Norway** was given a separate constitution. **Denmark** was indemnified with Lauenburg.

(7) Switzerland was re-established as an independent confederation of 22 cantons. Geneva, Wallis, and Neuchâtel (a principality belonging to the king of Prussia) were now included in the federation.

(8) Restoration of the legitimate dynasties in Spain, Sardinia (which received Genoa), Tuscany, Modena, and the Papal States. The Bourbons were not reinstated in Naples until 1815, since Murat had secured possession of Naples for the time being through his desertion of Napoleon.

16. *The Hundred Days*

News of the discontent in France with the government of the Bourbons, and knowledge of the discord at the congress of Vienna, to say nothing of the encouragement of his adherents, induced Napoleon to make another effort to recover his throne.

1815, Mar. 1. Landing of Napoleon at Cannes, with 1500 men. He marched at once upon Paris. Troops sent to oppose him (even Ney's corps) espoused his cause.

Mar. 13. Ban against Napoleon, issued by the Allied monarchs from Vienna. **Flight of Louis XVIII** to Ghent.

Mar. 20. Napoleon entered Paris and began the short rule generally called the *Hundred Days* (Mar. 20–June 29).

Mar. 25. Austria, Britain, Prussia, and **Russia** concluded a new alliance against Napoleon: each engaged to supply 180,000 men. All European nations were invited to join the coalition, and most of them did, but not Sweden, which was engaged in the conquest of Norway. The contingents furnished against Napoleon amounted to over a million men. The **duke of Wellington** in command.

May 3. Murat, who had declared for Napoleon again, was defeated by an Austrian force at **Tolentino.** Naples was captured (May 22); Murat fled to France. The Bourbon king, **Ferdinand,** restored to the Neapolitan throne.

June 14. Napoleon, forced to fight, crossed the frontier into Belgium. Engagement at **Charleroi;** the advanced guard of the Prussians, under Ziethen, forced back.

June 16. Battle of Ligny. Napoleon obliged Blücher to fall back. The Prussians marched to Wavre. On the same day the prince of Orange defeated Marshal Ney in battle of **Quatre Bras.**

Meanwhile the army of Wellington had been concentrating. This consisted of British, Hanoverians, Dutch, and Germans from Brunswick and Nassau.

June 18. BATTLE OF WATERLOO (Belle Alliance). Napoleon hurled himself upon Wellington's army, believing that he had insured against the junction of Blücher and Wellington by ordering **Grouchy** to engage the Prussians. But Grouchy had allowed Blücher to get away. At Waterloo Wellington's army held its lines all day under terrific assaults from the French. The arrival of Blücher toward evening probably saved the day. The French were completely defeated, and the army, pursued by Gneisenau, was soon scattered.

June 22. SECOND ABDICATION OF NAPOLEON. The emperor was soon obliged to flee before the victorious Allies. He reached Rochefort where, after futile attempts to escape to America, he surrendered himself to the British admiral, **Hotham.** He was conveyed to England on the warship *Bellerophon.* By unanimous resolution of the Allies, he was taken, as a prisoner of war, to the island of **St. Helena,** in the South Atlantic Ocean. There he arrived in October. The remainder of his life he spent under close supervision. He died May 5, 1821.

July 7. Second capture of Paris by the Allies. Return of Louis XVIII ("in the baggage of the Allies"). Arrival of the Allied monarchs.

1815, Sept. 26. The **HOLY ALLIANCE,** a document drawn up by the Tsar Alexander I, signed by the Emperor Francis I and by Frederick William III and ultimately by all European rulers, excepting the prince regent of Britain, the pope, and the sultan of Turkey. It was an innocuous declaration of Christian principles, which were to guide the rulers in their relations with their subjects and with each other. These vague and unexceptionable principles were probably meant by the tsar merely as a preface to some form of international organization, along the lines recommended by the Abbé de St. Pierre a century earlier. The importance of the document lay not in its terms, but in its later confusion

Blücher at Waterloo

in the public mind with the **Quadruple Alliance** and more particularly with the reactionary policy of the three eastern powers, which were regarded as bound by a pact directed against the liberties of the people, camouflaged by religion.

Oct. 13. Murat, who had made a reckless attempt to recover his kingdom by landing in Calabria, was captured, court-martialed, and shot.

Nov. 20. SECOND PEACE OF PARIS. Terms: (1) France was obliged to give up the fortresses of Philippeville and Marienburg to the Netherlands, and Saarlouis and Saarbrücken to Prussia; Landau became a fortress of the Germanic Confederation; the surrounding region, as far as the Lauter River, was ceded to Bavaria. To Sardinia, France was obliged to cede that part of Savoy which she had retained in the first treaty of Paris. In general she was restricted to the boundary of 1790. (2) Seventeen fortresses on the north and east frontiers were to be garrisoned for not more than five years by troops of the Allies (at French expense). (3) France was to pay 700,000,000 francs for the expense of the war. In addition, art treasures which the French had taken from all over Europe were now to be returned to their original owners.

Nov. 20. RENEWAL OF THE QUADRUPLE ALLIANCE, between Great Britain, Austria, Prussia, and Russia. The members promised to supply each 60,000 men in the event that a violation of the treaty of Paris should be attempted.

(Cont. p. 649.)

C. Western and Central Europe, 1815–1914

1. *The Congress System, 1815–1822*

DURING THE **congress of Vienna** there was general agreement between the powers that some measures should be taken to maintain the peace settlements and to guard against the recurrence of war. But efforts to establish a guaranty of the peace terms came to nothing.

1815, Sept. 26. THE SIGNING OF THE HOLY ALLIANCE *p. 629.*

Nov. 20. The **QUADRUPLE ALLIANCE,** signed by the four victorious powers after the battle of Waterloo and the **second treaty of Paris** *(above)*. It developed the principles laid down in the **treaties of Chaumont** *(p. 627)* and was concluded for 20 years. It aimed at preventing the return of Napoleon or his dynasty; at preservation of the territorial settlement with France; at the protection of Europe against French aggression through co-operative action by the signatories. It was further provided, at the urgent request of Lord Castlereagh, that representatives of the signatory powers should meet periodically to discuss common interests and problems **(government by conference).**

1818, Sept. Congress of Aix-la-Chapelle, the first of the meetings. This settled the question of the French indemnity payments and arranged the withdrawal of Allied troops from France. France was admitted to the newly constituted **Quintuple Alliance** (the old Quadruple Alliance being retained, however). Questions of the slave trade, the status of Jews, etc., were also raised and there was indication that the congress system would develop into an effective international machine.

1820–1821. Congresses of Troppau and Laibach, called to consider the revolutions in Spain and Italy. Metternich induced the three eastern powers to accept the **Troppau protocol,** directed against revolutions which might disturb the peace. Castlereagh was prevented by English liberal opinion and by British tradition from accepting a policy of interference in the affairs of other states (cf. British state paper of May 5, 1820). This difference of view marked the first serious weakening of the congress system.

1822, Oct. Congress of Verona, last of the congresses, summoned to consider the Spanish and Greek situations. Castlereagh had committed suicide on the eve of the meeting. His successor, **George Canning** (1770–1827), was unsympathetic to the "European Areopagus," tended to stress the divergence between the "liberal" and the "conservative" powers, and was, above all, determined to prevent intervention in Spain for fear that the effort might be made to extend it to Spanish colonies in the New World. He refused to co-operate with the other powers and, though unable to prevent intervention in Spain, succeeded in destroying the congress system.

2. *The British Isles*

[For a complete list of the kings of England see Appendix VI.]

(From p. 461)

a. THE END OF THE TORY RÉGIME, 1815–1830

1815–1820. The cessation of the Napoleonic wars brought, not the anticipated prosperity, but widespread distress. A long and severe **economic depression** followed. Continental markets failed to absorb the overstocked supplies of British manufacturers; governmental demands for military supplies ceased; prices fell; thousands were thrown out of work. The ranks of the unemployed were swelled by more than 400,000 demobilized men. A complete dislocation of the country's war-time economic organization took place.

Remedial legislation took the form of: (1) further protection for agriculture (primarily in the interest of the landlords) by the **Corn Law of 1815,** which virtually excluded foreign grain from England until home-grown corn should reach the "famine price" of 80 shillings per quarter, after which it was to be admitted duty free (this measure was in part a blow at the working classes in the form of higher prices for bread); (2) **abolition of the 10 per cent**

income tax (1816, Mar.), but with the concomitant enactment of duties on many articles (raising prices); (3) **deflation of the currency** (1821, May) by the resumption of specie payments by the Bank of England. But the meager and unsatisfactory character of these "remedies" gave rise to widespread dissatisfaction.

Radical agitation turned particularly to **demands for parliamentary reform,** viewed as a panacea for social and economic ills by such leaders as the journalist, **William Cobbett.** Clubs were formed, petitions presented to parliament. As distress became more general, the radical movement revealed more extreme elements, violence was resorted to, middle-class moderates were driven more and more into the arms of the reactionary Tory ministry.

1816, Dec. 2. Acts of violence by a crowd gathered in **Spa Fields,** London, to hear an address on parliamentary reform precipitated the

1817, Mar. Coercion Acts: (1) temporarily suspending *habeas corpus;* (2) extending the act of 1798 against seditious meetings; (3) renewing the act for the prevention and punishment of attempts to seduce soldiers and sailors from their allegiance; (4) extending to the prince regent all the safeguards against treasonable attempts which secured the king himself. The government's repressive policy stimulated the activity of extremists in the radical movement, which reached a climax in the

1819, Aug. 16. Peterloo Massacre: a crowd gathered at St. Peter's Fields, Manchester, to hear a speech on parliamentary reform and the repeal of the corn laws was charged by soldiers ordered to arrest the speaker; several were killed and hundreds injured. The result was the passage of the repressive code known as the

Dec. Six Acts: (1) provided for the speedy trial of "cases of misdemeanor"; (2) increased the penalties for seditious libel; (3) imposed the newspaper stamp duty on all periodical publications containing news (a blow at the radical journalists); (4) once more greatly curtailed public meetings; (5) forbade the training of persons in the use of arms; (6) empowered magistrates to search for and seize arms dangerous to the public peace. The Six Acts rendered the cabinet unpopular, but its prestige was again momentarily revived when a band of twenty extremists plotted the assassination of the whole cabinet (they were to be blown up as they dined together), and the seizure of enough cannon to overawe the populace, occupy the Bank of England, and establish a provisional government. This was the famous

1820, Feb. 23. Cato Street conspiracy. The plot was discovered in time; the conspirators were arrested at their rendezvous. This conspiracy stimulated anew fears of radicalism, and the cause of moderate reform was dealt a serious blow.

Jan. 29. George III, declared insane and represented by the prince of Wales as regent since 1811, died. The regent became king as

1820–1830. GEORGE IV, promptly had his cabinet institute **divorce proceedings** against the queen, Caroline of Brunswick, whom he had married (Apr. 8, 1795) in accordance with an arrangement of his father, but from whom he had separated shortly after the marriage. With the accession of George IV she returned

from the Continent to claim her position as queen, was received with tumultuous demonstrations by the public, which viewed her as wronged by a prince whom it had learned to know as debauched and treacherous. The ministry brought in

July 5. A **Bill of Pains and Penalties,** depriving the queen of her royal title and dissolving the marriage. The bill passed the house of lords by a margin of nine votes, but was dropped by the government (Nov. 10) in face of certain defeat in the commons. The result of the fiasco was a serious decline in the cabinet's prestige.

1822–1830. Following the **death of Castlereagh** (1822, Aug. 12), the cabinet received a series of liberal accessions: **George Canning** as foreign minister; **Robert Peel** as secretary for home affairs—son of a self-made factory owner, Oxford-trained, independent, with a mind open to arguments for reform; **William Huskisson,** liberal financier of wide talent, as president of the board of trade. Between 1822 and 1830 the liberal wing of the Tory cabinet was responsible for a number of moderate but important reforms: (1) Peel secured passage of **legislation revising the antiquated criminal code** by which more than 200 offenses had become punishable by death. The reforms reduced the number of offenses so punishable by about 100, thus making conviction for many misdemeanors more certain, making the punishment more nearly approximate the offense (reflecting the growing humanitarian sentiment of the 19th century). (2) The **first breach in the protectionist mercantile system** was made by Huskisson in the budget of 1823–1825, which reduced duties on certain imports (silk, wool, iron, wines, coffee, sugar, cottons, woolens, etc.), and lifted the secular prohibition on the exportation of wool. Huskisson's reform was a foretaste of the sweeping movement toward free trade which began in the mid-forties. (3) The **repeal of the Combination Acts** was largely the work of **Francis Place,** master tailor who had retained his interest in the worker's cause from less fortunate days. Place collected a mass of evidence on the hardships occasioned for labor by the Combination Acts, and interested **Joseph Hume,** radical member of parliament, in the cause. Hume secured appointment of a select committee to investigate conditions, and the evidence produced convinced Peel and Huskisson. The acts were repealed (1824, June 21). Phenomenal, though short-lived, **development of trade-unionism.** Many strikes followed, accompanied by violence. A new law (1825, July 6) allowed workers to combine to secure regulation of wages and hours of employment, but, in effect, forbade them to strike by prohibiting the use of violence or threats, and introducing summary methods of conviction.

The sharp divergences in the cabinet between liberal and right-wing Tories had been smoothed over by the conciliatory **Lord Liverpool,** continuously prime minister from 1812 till 1827, when a stroke of apoplexy obliged him to resign.

1827, Apr. 30. Canning succeeded as prime minister with a cabinet of liberal Tories and moderate Whigs, but died soon after (Aug. 8).

1827, Aug.–1828, Jan. Cabinet of the conciliatory but incapable **Lord Goderich.**

1828, Jan.–1830, Nov. Cabinet of the **duke of**

Wellington, from whose great distinction and wide popularity much was hoped. But Wellington was sympathetic with the reactionary group in his cabinet and alienated the liberal Tories, who resigned. The complete failure of Wellington's policy in the Near Eastern crisis *(p. 724)* seriously discredited the cabinet.

1828, July 15. The corn law. The patent hardships (for consumers) of the corn law of 1815 obliged Wellington to introduce a measure permitting grain to be imported at any time and fixing duties on a sliding scale (high when the price of English corn was low and reducing the duty as the English price advanced). The act alienated the landlords, yet won Wellington no credit with the liberals, who remembered that the duke had earlier defeated the law when it was introduced by Canning.

1829. The Wellington cabinet again alienated its own supporters by its **Catholic emancipation policy.** When **Daniel O'Connell,** leader of the Catholic emancipation movement, was elected to parliament in 1828 from the county of Clare in Ireland, the Wellington cabinet was faced by a crisis. Under the provisions of the **Test Act** *(p. 451),* no Catholic (or Protestant Nonconformist) could hold public office. Wellington and Peel were bitterly opposed to emancipation, but feared that failure to relieve the Catholics of their disabilities would precipitate civil war in Ireland (the Catholic movement had been gathering strength steadily since the turn of the century).

1828, May 9. The **Test Act was repealed,** and
1829, Mar.–Apr. The **Catholic Emancipation Bill** was driven through parliament by Wellington in the face of vigorous opposition from the reactionary Tories. It granted the Catholics the right of suffrage and the right to sit in parliament, and declared their eligibility for any public office, save those of lord chancellor of England and lord lieutenant of Ireland—all this in return for an oath denying the pope any power to interfere in the domestic affairs of the realm, recognizing the Protestant succession, and repudiating every intention to upset the established church.

The radical and violent **agitation for parliamentary reform** which followed the Napoleonic wars yielded in the twenties to more moderate demands advocated by individual Whigs, notably **Lord John Russell.** The **July Revolution** in France, a triumph for the middle class *(p. 649),* stimulated the movement.

1830, June 26. George IV died, and was succeeded by his brother
1830–1837. WILLIAM IV. The accession necessitated a general election (a requirement abolished by the Reform Bill of 1867), and the reform of the house of commons became a campaign issue. There was a turnover of some 50 seats, almost all of them going to proponents of reform. In caucus the Whigs adopted reform as their program. Wellington maintained an intransigent attitude, but was forced to resign (Nov. 16), ending a continuous Tory rule (with one brief interval) of nearly half a century.

CULTURAL DEVELOPMENTS

(1) Literature

The early decades of the 19th century were characterized by the Romantic movement in

England as on the Continent. Lyric poetry flourished. **William Wordsworth** (1770–1850) and **Samuel Taylor Coleridge** (1772–1834) together published *Lyrical Ballads* (1798). The major poets were George Gordon, **Lord Byron** (1788–1824); **Percy Bysshe Shelley** (1792–1822); and **John Keats** (1795–1821).

Essays: In this period, subjective criticism received recognition; the new reviews which began to appear monthly and quarterly gave opportunity for expression of individual opinion on a variety of subjects (*Edinburgh Review*, 1802; William Cobbett's *Weekly Political Register*, 1802; *Quarterly Review*, 1809; *Blackwood's Magazine*, 1817; *London Magazine*, 1820; *Manchester Guardian*, 1821). **Charles Lamb** (*Essays of Elia*, 1823–1833) and **William Hazlitt** (*Table Talk*, 1821–1822) wrote outstanding critical essays; also **Walter Savage Landor** (1775–1864) and **Leigh Hunt** (*The Examiner*, 1808–1821).

Novels: The popular historical novels of the Scotsman **Sir Walter Scott** (1771–1832) overshadowed the earlier Gothic novels (*Waverly*, 1814; *Ivanhoe*, 1819; *Kenilworth*, 1821; *Talisman*, 1825). In England the domestic novel of **Jane Austen** (1775–1817) proved the local contemporary scene worthy of portrayal (*Sense and Sensibility*, 1811; *Pride and Prejudice*, 1813; *Emma*, 1816).

(2) Painting

Landscapes of **Joseph Mallord William Turner** (1775–1851) and **John Constable** (1776–1837); **Thomas Lawrence** (1769–1830) painted a series of official portraits at the congress of Vienna.

(3) Music

In music there was little of interest except for the church and organ music of **Samuel Wesley** (1766–1836).

b. AN ERA OF REFORM, 1830–1846

1830–1834. The Tory cabinet of Wellington was succeeded by the Whig cabinet of **Earl Grey** (1764–1845), including a membership of distinguished talents, widely representative of liberal opinion and determined on **parliamentary reform.** The existing system of representation reflected gross inequalities, the result of ancient provisions whose effect was greatly exaggerated by the growth and migration of population under the impact of the industrial revolution. In *pocket boroughs* the patron enjoyed the absolute right of returning candidates. In *rotten boroughs* the elections were controlled by bribery and influence. On the eve of the reform not more than one-third of the house of commons was freely chosen. Electoral inequalities constituted a second serious abuse: in various boroughs the right to vote rested on the possession of a forty-shilling freehold or some other financial basis, certain residence qualifications, membership in the governing body of the municipality (*close boroughs*). Even in boroughs of democratic electoral qualification the number of electors was usually small enough to be effectively bribed. Electoral conditions in the counties were better, but abuses were many. Grey's ministry undertook to reform this situation by redistributing parliamentary seats and extending the franchise.

Lord Byron, 1788–1824

Percy Bysshe Shelley, 1792–1822

1831, Mar. 22. The **First Reform Bill,** the work of Lord John George Durham and Lord John Russell, was passed on second reading by a majority of one, but defeated by amendment in the committee stage.

Apr. 19. Grey secured a **dissolution of parliament,** followed by a bitterly fought election, with public opinion warmly supporting "The Bill, the whole Bill, and nothing but the Bill." The election was a Whig triumph.

Sept. 21. The **Second Reform Bill** passed the new house of commons with a majority of 109, but the house of lords threw the measure out on second reading (Oct. 8). The ministry prorogued parliament and prepared a new bill. Extraparliamentary agitation now became violent, riots broke out, the mob held Bristol for two days.

1832. The **THIRD REFORM BILL** was passed by the commons with a larger majority (Mar. 23). But the lords in committee demanded amendments unacceptable to the ministry. They were greeted by a new blast of popular agitation. With the country on the verge of civil war, Grey advised the king to create enough new peers to pass the measure. The king refused, the cabinet resigned, Wellington was unable to form a ministry. The king recalled Grey, promised to appoint the new peers, but instead induced the recalcitrant Tories to withdraw during the final vote in the lords (June 4).

The act disfranchised 56 *pocket* and *rotten* boroughs (returning 111 members); 32 small boroughs were deprived of one member each. The available 143 seats were redistributed: 22 large towns received two each, 21 towns a single member each; county membership was increased from 94 to 159; 13 remaining members went to Scotland and Ireland. Extension of the franchise took the form of eliminating antiquated forms in the boroughs and giving the vote to all householders paying £10 annual rental. In the counties the area of enfranchisement was enlarged by retaining the 40-shilling freehold qualification for those owning their own land; other cases were covered by a £10 qualification for freeholders, copyholders, leaseholders for 60 years; and a qualification of £50 was fixed for leaseholders of shorter terms and tenants-at-will.

July–Aug. **Scotland and Ireland** were subjects of separate bills, in which the franchise was remodeled upon lines similar to those adopted in England.

The Reform Bill shifted the balance of power to the industrial and commercial class, revealed that the house of lords could not defy popular will, opened an era of reform. It failed to concede the secret ballot and left the bulk of the population still disfranchised.

1831. Tithe War in Ireland. The Irish, overwhelmingly Catholic, resented the enforced payment of **tithes** to support the established Episcopal Church and resorted to violence.

1833, Apr. A **Coercion Bill** gave the lord lieutenant unlimited powers of suppressing public meetings, of subjecting disturbed districts to martial law.

Aug. 2. The **Irish Church Temporalities Bill** introduced by the government as a counterpoise to coercion. The bill established a graduated tax on clerical incomes to relieve ratepayers from the burden of parish expenses, and provided for the reduction of the Irish episcopate. The bill failed to provide for the application to secular purposes of the savings effected and so outraged O'Connell and his following.

Aug. 23. Abolition of slavery in the colonies. **Edward Stanley,** secretary for Ireland, had incurred such unpopularity that he was transferred to the colonial secretaryship, where he carried the bill emancipating the slaves in the British colonies. The law was the crowning act in the long campaign of the abolitionists, led by **William Wilberforce,** agitation dating particularly from the abolition of the slave trade *(p. 808)*. The act provided for the immediate emancipation of children under six, a period of apprenticeship for those over six (eliminated four years later), and compensation of £20,000,000 to slaveowners.

Aug. 29. Factory Act. Investigations had

John Keats, 1795–1821

Sir Walter Scott, 1771–1832

Joseph Mallord William Turner, 1775–1851

revealed the frightful working conditions to which children were often subjected and against which the factory acts of 1802 and 1816 gave quite inadequate protection. The result was the factory act of 1833, carried in the face of opposition from the Tories and many Whigs (imbued with *laissez-faire* doctrine). It forbade employment of children under nine years, restricted labor of those between nine and 13 to 48 hours a week or nine in a single day, and of those from 13 to 18 years to 69 hours a week or 12 in a day. Children under 13 were to have two hours' schooling per day. A system of paid inspectors was set up. The law applied only to factories in the textile industries and was in itself inadequate, but it was the forerunner of further remedial legislation.

1834. Growth of trade-unionism. The movement had taken a phenomenal but short-lived spurt after the repeal of the Combination Laws in 1825, and was given momentum by the general dissatisfaction of the workers with the Reform Act of 1832. The pioneer was **John Doherty,** at whose instigation the **National Association for the Protection of Labor** (a federation of about 150 unions) had been formed in 1830. As the movement spread after 1832, Doherty and **Robert Owen** decided to attempt to form a general union of skilled and unskilled laborers.

Jan. The **Grand National Consolidated Trades Union** was organized. Within a few weeks it had over 500,000 members. The avowed policy was to promote a **general strike** for an eight-hour day. But the organization suffered from the confusion of trade-union aims with the co-operative and socialist aspirations of Owen and his disciple, **William Thompson.** The Grand National made one or two small and futile experiments in co-operative production, but spent most of its energies in a series of aggressive and unsuccessful strikes. The government became seriously alarmed and resorted to drastic measures.

Mar. Six Dorchester laborers, who had formed a lodge of the Grand National, were sentenced to seven years' imprisonment. The

Grand National dissolved in October, Owen quit the field, and a period of general apathy followed in the labor movement.

Apr. 22. Quadruple Alliance with France, Spain, and Portugal *(p. 630).*

July 9. Grey resigned.

July–Nov. First cabinet of **Lord Melbourne,** a right wing Liberal (the terms *Liberals* and *Conservatives* were beginning to replace the older *Whigs* and *Tories*). The king had hoped for a coalition government (with Peel), was disappointed at the reconstitution of the Whig ministry, and welcomed an early opportunity to accept the **resignation of Melbourne** (Nov. 15), who felt the strength of his party shaken by the loss of the leader in the house of commons, **Lord John Althrop,** who became Earl Spencer on the death of his father.

Aug. 14. The new poor law. Earlier relief legislation was fundamentally altered and given coherent form by the new law, which limited payment of charitable doles to sick and aged paupers and established workhouses where ablebodied paupers were put to work. The law ended the vicious system of giving the dole to laborers as a supplement to low wages. It supplanted the great poor law of 1601 and its amendments of 1722, 1782, and 1795.

Nov.–1835, Apr. The short-lived **first Peel ministry.** In the general election of January 1835 Peel set forth his conceptions of a new **liberal Conservatism** (*Tamworth Manifesto*): acceptance of the Reform Act of 1832, readiness to proceed further with "judicious reforms." He won wide support from the moderates of both parties, actively undertook the cause of reform, but was defeated shortly thereafter on the Irish question.

1835–1839. Second Melbourne cabinet. Melbourne promptly undertook the reform of the internal organization and administration of municipal government—untouched by the Reform Act, generally in the hands of self-elected, irresponsible, and corrupt councils.

1835, Sept. 9. The **Municipal Corporations Bill** provided a uniform plan of government for all boroughs and cities (London and 67 small

towns excepted): a town council was to consist of mayor, aldermen, and councilors, the last-named elected for three years by the rate-payers, together with the freemen who had survived the Reform Act (the freemen were a limited number of privileged persons who had formerly chosen the corporations). The mayor was to be chosen annually, the aldermen every six years by the councilors from among their own number.

Further reforms followed in 1836, notably legislation permitting civil marriages, some equalizations of episcopal and clerical incomes, permission to prisoners charged with felony to have full benefit of counsel, etc.

William IV died (1837, June 20) and was succeeded by his youthful niece,

1837–1901. VICTORIA (1819–1901), then eighteen. Victoria was the daughter of the duke of Kent (d. 1820) and the duchess, a princess of Saxe-Coburg (for the Hanoverian dynasty *see p. 456),* who had brought up Victoria in England, but surrounded her by German influences, notably that of her brother Leopold (king of the Belgians, 1831, *p. 646).* Victoria's education had been solid and sensible, and she brought to her heavy duties graciousness and poise rarely associated with one of her age. She was self-willed on occasion, "rebuked" her ministers, but made no serious attempt to invade their rights under the parliamentary system despite the influence of her German adviser, **Baron Christian von Stockmar,** who urged her to take a stand of greater independence.

The Melbourne government favored a conciliatory Irish policy (opposed by the Conservatives); it was faced by three Irish problems—poor relief, municipal reform, and the settlement of tithes.

1838, July 31. The **poor law bill** extended provisions similar to those in the **new poor law** to Ireland. It was opposed by the Irish members of the house of commons on the ground that the poor were too numerous to be provided for in workhouses. A second bill **converted the tithes** into a fixed rent charge, 75 per cent of their nominal value and payable by the landlord. The municipal corporations in Ireland were controlled by self-appointed Protestant councils. A **new municipal act** (1840) conferred the right to vote on all persons paying £10 rent a year.

Weakened by attack on its policy in England, Ireland, and Canada *(p. 782)* the Melbourne government was in no position to survive the disaffection occasioned by the settlement of the

1839, Apr. 9. Jamaica problem. Following emancipation of the slaves, economic conditions had grown rapidly worse for the planters, who were guilty of great brutality toward their former slaves. The upshot was the suspension for five years of the **Jamaica constitution,** a drastic measure carried by only five votes in the commons. Melbourne felt his position seriously shaken, resigned soon after (May 7).

May. Cabinet crisis. The queen turned regretfully to Wellington, then to Peel. The latter refused to form a ministry unless certain that the queen's lady attendants (all members of Whig families) were changed (the **Bedchamber Question**). The queen was indignant and turned again to Melbourne, who formed

1839, May–1841, Aug. The third Melbourne ministry.

1839. CHARTIST AGITATION. The Chartist movement was a direct outcome of dissatisfaction with the reforms of the Whigs among the laboring classes and of the failure of the

The "Penny Black," the world's first adhesive postage stamp, issued 1840, with a portrait of Queen Victoria

trade-union movement. It had its origin when (1836) a **Workingmen's Association** in London set forth its program in a petition or **charter** to parliament. This demanded: (1) manhood suffrage; (2) vote by ballot; (3) abolition of property qualification for members of parliament; (4) payment of members; (5) equal electoral districts; (6) annual parliaments. The working public was rapidly converted to this program by missionaries who toured the country, held huge meetings, and organized torchlight processions. Gradually more radical elements emerged, notably **Feargus O'Connor,** who headed a **party of physical force** opposed by **William Lovett's party of moral force,** both within the larger movement.

Feb. The first **National Convention of Chartists** met in London.

May 13. The **charter was presented to parliament,** which rejected it. The convention adjourned to Birmingham, issued a radical manifesto appealing to members to defend liberty by use of arms.

July. Serious riots in Birmingham and elsewhere.

Nov. 4. In a **riot at Newport** (Wales) the crowd was fired on by the constables and 20 were killed. **John Frost,** the leader, and others were sentenced to death, but ultimately transported to the penal colonies. The movement then turned back to more moderate channels.

Nov. 3. Outbreak of the Opium War with China *(p. 847)*.

1840, Jan. 10. A pamphlet by **Rowland Hill** on postal reform led to the institution of **uniform penny postage** (for letters under half an ounce to any point in the United Kingdom),

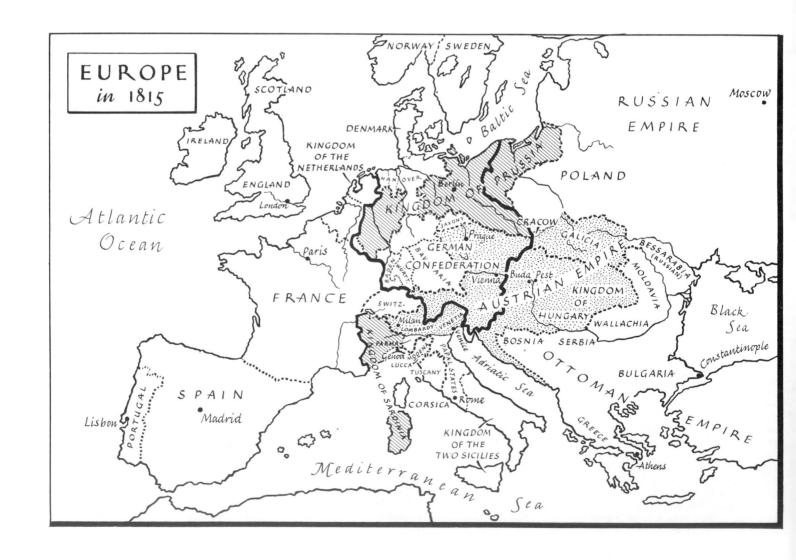

a substitute for the previous exorbitant rates and the cumbersome system of charges varying with size, weight, and shape of letters—a revolution in communication.

Feb. 10. The **queen married** her first cousin, **Albert of Saxe-Coburg-Gotha,** a sober and sensible prince, to whom she became profoundly devoted. The marriage was generally condemned by Conservative leaders, and Albert suffered from rumors that he was a "papist" (although all his family were Lutheran), from the demands of the queen that he be named *king consort* (he was made *prince consort* by royal letters patent only in 1857), and that he be voted a civil list of £50,000 (reduced to £30,000), etc. Albert succeeded Melbourne as royal private secretary, and in time became, with the queen, joint ruler of the nation, in fact if not in name.

In the spring of 1841 Melbourne's government was twice defeated on a tariff measure in the commons, appealed to the country, and was again defeated by the Conservatives.

1841, Aug. 28. Melbourne finally resigned following a vote of censure, and was succeeded by

1841, Sept.–1846, June. The **second Peel cabinet,** which included a number of men of distinction and young men of promise, notably **William Ewart Gladstone** as vice-president of the board of trade. Peel turned first to the deficit, the most pressing problem. He **modi-**fied the sliding scale of 1828 on corn imports (1842, Apr. 29) to encourage importation; **removed prohibitory duties** and drastically reduced duties on a vast number of imports, especially raw materials and prime foodstuffs; **revived the income tax** to provide against possible losses from lower tariffs; **abolished import and export duties on wool.** Peel, a protectionist, was already moving in the direction of free trade.

1842, Apr. 12–May 12. **Second National Convention of Chartists** in London. A second petition to parliament was again rejected (May 3) and a "turn-out" followed in August. In Lancashire the strike spread rapidly and the moderates were again outmaneuvered by the radicals. Nevertheless the movement gradually collapsed. It remained in eclipse until 1848, when a last national convention was held, a huge demonstration arranged, and the charter once more presented to parliament.

Aug. 9. **Webster-Ashburton treaty** with the United States *(p. 758).*

1844. The **Bank Charter Act,** designed to meet the problem presented by the rapid growth of joint-stock banks. These issued great quantities of paper money at a time when British gold reserves were being depleted by shipments abroad, largely to the United States. The Bank Charter Act separated the banking department from the note-issuing department of the Bank of England; required that note issues of the bank should be covered by coin or bullion, except for £14,000,000 covered by government securities; prohibited new banks from issuing notes and limited old banks to the existing amount. The tendency of the act was to eliminate by degrees all notes except those of the Bank of England.

1845. **Peel's second free-trade budget** eliminated export duties entirely, and also duties on cotton, glass, etc.

1845. Formation of the **National Association of the United Traders for the Protection of Labor,** marking the revival of the trade-union movement. The new organization undertook to deal with disputes between master and men, and to look after the interests of labor in parliament. The program showed that the movement had discarded the aggressive policy and ambitious aims of the years 1830–1834. Strikes were deprecated and the idea of the general strike abandoned in favor of conciliation and arbitration.

1845–1846. **Anti-corn law agitation.** This gradually absorbed much of the interest of the working classes. It centered in Manchester and was fostered by the political leaders of the **Manchester School,** notably **Richard Cobden** and **John Bright,** both manufacturers of middle-class origin. Their interests extended not only to free corn (i.e. grain import), but to **free trade** in general, in which they saw a boon both for the workers (cheap food and higher

Queen Victoria and Her Family, *painted in 1848 by Franz Xaver Winterhalter*

wages) and factory owners (cheap raw materials and the expansion of markets). The **Manchester Anti-Corn Law Association** (1838) was launched in the midst of the economic depression which began in 1837. Similar organizations rapidly appeared elsewhere, and all joined to form the **Anti-Corn Law League** (1839). The widespread propaganda of the league was met by the bitter opposition of Conservative landlords, but was carried to the farmers as well as the workers. The farmers were attracted by the argument that free trade meant low prices for means of subsistence, and cheap food meant low wages, by which Britain would be able to meet successfully foreign competition. The argument that appealed to the workers was as follows: the abolition of the corn duties would reduce the price of food, which would enable the people to spend more on manufactured goods and so increase the demand for them. This in turn would lead to more employment and higher wages in industry.

Peel's support for corn law reform finally came as a result of the ruin of the Irish potato crop and the consequent threat of famine in the island unless prompt relief measures were taken.

1845, Nov. 22. The Whig leader, **Lord John Russell,** announced his conversion to free trade. Unable to forestall a Whig success by the enactment of a repeal measure, **Peel resigned** (Dec. 5), but returned to office (Dec. 20) when Russell was unable to form a government.

1846, Jan. ff. **New free-trade proposals** met with stiff resistance from a block of Conservatives led by **Benjamin Disraeli,** who denounced Peel for betraying the protectionist principles

of his party. A struggle of two months was followed by the

1846, June 6. REPEAL OF THE CORN LAWS. After passage of both the corn and customs bills by the commons (May 15), Wellington again induced the lords to yield. The **corn law** provided for the immediate repeal of earlier legislation and fixed the duty on corn at a shilling a quarter from 1849, preserving a small protective duty in the intervening years. The **customs law** abolished the duties on all live animals and nearly every kind of meat, and reduced the duties on cheese, butter, and other foods. Many duties on manufactured goods were abolished and others greatly reduced.

June 15. Oregon Boundary Treaty with the United States (*p. 758*).

June 29. Peel's government was overthrown by a revolt led by **Benjamin Disraeli,** who objected to a new coercion bill for Ireland.

c. PALMERSTON AND RUSSELL, 1846–1868

1846, July–1852, Feb. Cabinet of Lord John Russell.

1847–1848. Young Ireland. The Irish famine of the forties resulted in the growth of a revolutionary movement in the island. Even before the **death of Daniel O'Connell** (1847), the leadership of the Irish nationalists had passed to the **Young Ireland Party** (founded 1840), under **William Smith O'Brien.** This radical group rejected O'Connell's peaceful methods to secure repeal of the union. A series of agrarian crimes in the autumn of 1847 was followed by the suspension of the *Habeas Corpus* Act for Ireland. This measure, together

with news of the revolutions on the Continent, precipitated an **insurrection in Tipperary** (1848, July 29), O'Brien hoping that the peasantry would support it. The rising proved abortive, as the rebels were unequal to the forces of the constabulary.

1850. The Don Pacifico affair. Don Pacifico was a Moorish Jew, but a British subject. He held large claims against the Greek government which he pressed with vigor until an anti-Semitic mob burned his house in Athens (1849, Dec.). Palmerston ordered a British squadron to the Piraeus to force a settlement of this and other claims on the Greek government. The Greeks proving obstinate, the British laid an **embargo on all Greek vessels** in the Piraeus and finally seized them (1850, Jan.). After abortive mediation by the French, the Greeks were eventually forced to comply (Apr. 26). Palmerston defended his action in his greatest parliamentary speech (June 29), in which he appealed to British pride and nationalism (*civis Romanus sum*).

1850–1851. Formation of the **Amalgamated Society of Engineers,** a new type of labor organization based on high contributions and provision of benefits as well as direct action and collective bargaining. A number of further "amalgamated societies" were organized and their leaders gradually assumed control of the trade-union movement.

The **Oxford Movement** centered at Oxford, and had as its chief **John H. (later Cardinal) Newman.** It endeavored to prove that the doctrines of the Anglican Church were identical with those of the Roman Catholic Church, therefore that every Catholic doctrine might be held by Anglicans. In 1845 Newman and many of his associates seceded to the Church

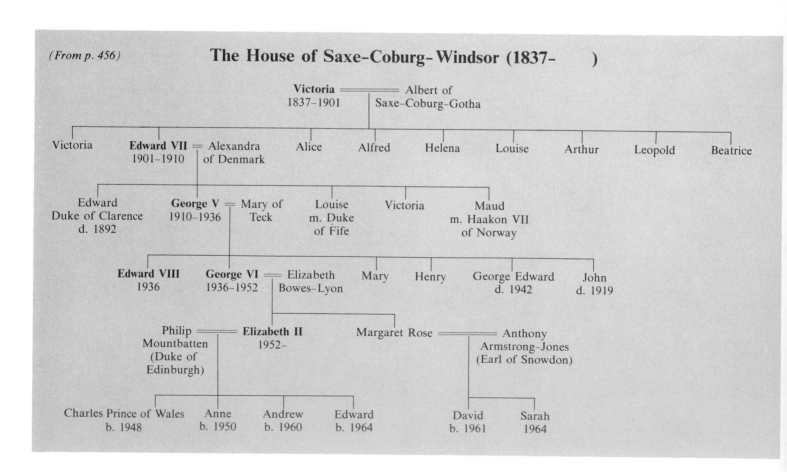

(From p. 456) **The House of Saxe-Coburg-Windsor (1837–   )**

The main avenue of the Great Exhibition of 1851

of Rome, whereupon the English people, thoroughly Protestant, became alarmed, fearing that the real object of the *Tractarians* (so called from the tracts they published) was to reconcile England with Rome. Popular apprehension of "papal aggression" was stirred by a papal bull (1850, Sept. 30) setting up a hierarchy of bishops in England who were to derive their titles from English sees created by the bull. The sympathies of the Whig ministry, and especially of Lord John Russell, the prime minister, were with the people.

1851, Feb. The **Ecclesiastical Titles Bill,** which forbade the assumption by priests and bishops of the Roman Catholic Church of titles taken from any territory or place within the United Kingdom, and declared null and void all acts of possessors of such titles. The law remained a dead letter and was repealed in 1871.

May 1-Oct. 15. The **Great Exhibition of 1851** (Crystal Palace) in Hyde Park, for which Prince Albert was largely responsible, included exhibits from all nations, and was the first of its kind. *Prosperity* was the note it sounded, and it was confidently expected that the exhibition would inaugurate an era of international peace.

Dec. Conflict between the queen and Lord Palmerston. Victoria had long been dissatis-

Lord Palmerston, 1784–1865

fied by the foreign minister's indiscretions and boisterous nationalistic policy, to say nothing of his tendency to ignore royal suggestions and advice. After the Don Pacifico incident, the queen, assisted by Prince Albert and Baron Stockmar, drew up a memorandum demanding that the queen be kept informed and that, once she had approved a measure, it should not be arbitrarily altered. Palmerston promised to mend his ways, but in the following months a new crisis occurred. Palmerston at once approved of the *coup d'état* of Louis Napoleon in France (Dec. 2), but the cabinet, adopting the queen's attitude, on December 5 instructed the ambassador at Paris to carry on as though nothing had occurred, passing no judgment. The resulting embarrassment enabled the queen to force **Palmerston's dismissal** (Dec. 19).

1852, Feb. 20. Lord John Russell's cabinet was defeated on a militia bill.

Feb. 27–Dec. 17. Cabinet of Lord Derby (Conservative).

1852, Dec. 28–1855, Jan. 20. Lord Aberdeen's ministry, with a coalition of Whigs and Peelites.

1854, Mar. 28. Outbreak of the Crimean War (p. 726).

Benjamin Disraeli, 1804–1881

1855, Feb. 5–1858, Feb. 22. First Palmerston cabinet, resulting from popular dissatisfaction with Aberdeen's policy in the war.

1857. The Indian Mutiny *(p. 841).*

1857–1858. War with China *(p. 847).*

1858, Feb. 25–1859, June 11. Second Derby ministry, after Palmerston's government was defeated on a bill to increase the penalty for conspiracy to murder (following French representations after the **Orsini bomb affair,** *p. 671).*

1858, June. An act brought to an end the property qualifications for members of parliament.

July 23. Removal of disabilities on Jews.

Aug. 2. India Bill, by which the British East India Company's political powers were brought to an end and the government of India was assumed by the crown *(p. 841).*

1859, June 18–1865, Nov. 6. Second Palmerston ministry, after the defeat of Lord Derby's reform bill.

1860, Jan. 23. The important **commercial treaty signed with France** (Cobden-Chevalier Treaty) marking a great advance toward free trade on the part of France.

1861, Nov.–Dec. The *Trent* affair. Crisis in Anglo-American relations resulting from the Civil War *(p. 764).*

Dec. 14. Death of the Prince Consort. For a period of many years Queen Victoria withdrew from all public functions and thereby suffered a period of marked unpopularity.

1864, June 5. Great Britain abandoned the protectorate over the **Ionian Islands** (assumed in 1815) and made over the islands to Greece, in order to stabilize the new Danish dynasty *(p. 714).*

1865, Oct. 18. Death of Lord Palmerston.

1865, Nov. 6–1866, June. Second ministry of Lord John Russell. On the death of Palmerston, Russell succeeded as prime minister. He was faced by urgent demands for further electoral reform, which he had previously sponsored in a perfunctory way. Only one man in six possessed the vote, and workers were virtually excluded. Repeated measures for

franchise extension had been defeated in the commons, while industrial growth had exaggerated electoral anomalies left by the act of 1832.

1866, Mar. Russell introduced an anodyne measure which was defeated as the result of the defection of a section of the Liberals. Russell resigned in June.

1866, July 6–1868, Feb. 25. The **third Derby ministry,** in which the dominant figure was to be **Benjamin Disraeli,** once more leader of the house of commons. Workers' demands for suffrage reform spread rapidly, and Disraeli was literally obliged to adopt the Liberal program of electoral reform, which in the end he had to extend radically, despite the opposition of many Conservatives.

1867, Aug. 15. The **SECOND REFORM BILL** extended the suffrage: in *boroughs* to all householders paying the poor rates and all lodgers of one year's residence paying an annual rent of £10; in the *counties,* to owners of land of £5 annual value, to occupying tenants paying £12 annual rental. All boroughs of fewer than 10,000 population lost the right of sending two members to the commons; Manchester, Birmingham, Liverpool, Leeds were given each a third member; two other large towns, Salford and Merthyr, received a second member; nine *new boroughs* were created; 25 additional members were allotted to the counties. The **Scottish Reform Bill** of 1868 (July 13) founded generally upon the same principles as the English bill, gave Scotland seven new seats. The **Irish Reform Bill** of 1868 (July 13) reduced the borough franchise requirement, left the county franchise unaltered, and left the Irish representation unchanged. A radically democratic step had been taken: the electorate was increased from roughly 1,000,000 to 2,000,000. Disraeli had "dished the Whigs," but had violated his party pledges and had taken a step bitterly opposed by many Conservatives and described even by Derby as a "leap in the dark."

1867–1868. Abyssinian expedition *(p. 814).*

d. DISRAELI AND GLADSTONE, 1868–1894

1868, Feb. 29–Dec. 2. First Disraeli ministry, which came to an end after the sweeping Liberal victory in the elections of November 1868.

1868, Dec. 9–1874, Feb. 17. First Gladstone ministry. Gladstone was the son of a Liverpool merchant, a product of the aristocratic influences of Eton and Christ Church, Oxford. He was learned, profoundly devout, possessed of typical Scottish industry. He had entered politics as a Tory, seceded with the Peelites, ended as a Liberal. He possessed a vast knowledge of internal problems, especially of financial questions. In the field of foreign relations he was hampered in an age of imperialist expansion by humanitarian principles and sympathies with minorities abroad.

1868–1869. The Irish Question. Prior to taking office Gladstone had declared: "My mission is to pacify Ireland." The **Fenian Brotherhood,** formed in 1858 in New York, collected funds among the American Irish, aimed to overthrow British rule in Ireland. **O'Donovan Rossa** and **James Stephens** were arrested (Sept., Nov. 1865) and supplies of arms were taken. A Fenian invasion of Canada (1866)

failed *(p. 783).* A general rising in Ireland miscarried (1867, Mar.). Further "outrages" followed, notably the attempt to deliver two prisoners from Clerkenwell, London (Dec. 13), when a blast in the wall caused the death of 12, the injury of 120 more. Gladstone attacked what he considered the causes of the discontent—disestablishment and land tenure (neither of which had figured among Fenian aims).

1869, July 26. The **Disestablishment Act** provided that the Irish (Episcopal) Church should cease to exist as of January 1, 1871. The Church's endowments were to be taken away with compensation for interests affected; church buildings, etc., were to be reserved to a new voluntary organization; the tithe rent-charge on estates, the Church's chief source of revenue, was to be purchased by the landlords for some £8,212,500; provision was made for the care of Episcopal clergymen during their lifetime. Irish Catholics were no longer to be obliged to support a state church of which they were not communicants. Despite the opposition of the Episcopal clergy, the Conservatives in general and the house of lords in particular (again threatened with the creation of new peers), the bill passed.

1870, Aug. 1. Irish Land Act. The sufferings of the Irish were in considerable measure due to the prevalent system of **land tenure.** There was a vast difference between the rural landlord in England and his Irish counterpart—the former putting money into the land and making improvements for the tenants; the latter merely drawing rack-rent which he often spent in England, leaving the tenants to do everything for themselves, and often evicting them wholesale without compensation for improvements. In 1850 a **Tenant-Right League** was founded to obtain for the tenant the "three F's"—a **fair rent, fixity of tenure,** and **free sale.** The movement spread rapidly. In 1870 Gladstone introduced an Irish land bill. It contained no recognition of the "three F's," but gave the tenant the right to compensa-

William E. Gladstone, 1809–1898

tion for disturbance (that is, eviction) and for improvements (if, without fault on his side, he was evicted, but not where the ejection was for non-payment of rent). The **Bright clauses** of the bill facilitated the creation of a peasant proprietorship by allowing government loans to be granted to tenants who wished to buy their holdings from their landlords. The act did not extinguish the evils with which it was designed to deal. It interfered with the landlord's right of disposing of his land on the absolute basis of free contract, but it did not protect the tenant against increased rent, nor did it give him security of tenure. The act of 1870 was important chiefly as the first of a great series of Irish agrarian laws. It did not allay Irish agitation. Even while the bill was in progress, in the spring of 1870, agrarian outrages occurred in County Mayo. By the **Peace Preservation Act** (Apr. 4), the government increased its powers of repression.

1870, Aug. 9. An important **Education Bill** aimed to remedy the existing chaotic situation: nearly half of the 4,000,000 children of school age were unprovided for; about 1,000,000 attended schools attached to the Church of England, government inspected and supported by voluntary subscriptions supplemented by government grants; another million attended schools unsupported by the government and uninspected. On the whole English education was far inferior to that in Prussia, Switzerland, the United States. The Education Bill, brought in by **W. E. Forster,** provided for two types of schools: (1) those voluntary schools doing good work were to be retained, government grants were to be increased, but they were to receive no aid from local rates; (2) elsewhere *board schools* (under the control of locally elected boards) were to be set up and maintained by government grants, parents' fees, local rates (the question of compulsory attendance was to be passed on by each local board). The question of religious education was crucial: the voluntary schools were permitted to continue religious instruction; all denominational religious instruction was prohibited in the board schools—a compromise satisfying neither of the extreme groups.

1870, June 4. **Order in council reforming the civil service,** by providing that candidates for ordinary posts should, in the discretion of department heads, be given competitive examinations. The new order was speedily adopted by almost all the chief departments, the foreign office remaining a notable exception.

1871, June. The **University Tests Act** conferred on Cambridge and Oxford students the right to obtain university degrees and to hold lay offices in colleges and universities without subscribing to any religious tests.

The **Army Regulation Bill** virtually reorganized the British army, a reform associated with the name of **Edward Cardwell,** the secretary of war. The system of purchasing commissions was abolished; short service was introduced, which made possible a well-trained reserve (six years with the colors and six in the reserves, instead of twelve years' service); etc.

1872. The **Ballot Act** made voting secret for the first time.

Sept. 14. Settlement of the *Alabama* claims *(p. 770).*

The prestige of the Gladstone ministry

rapidly declined: the education act alienated nonconformists and high churchmen alike; reduction in the number of dockyard workers caused dissatisfaction; the elimination of the purchase of army commissions irritated the upper classes. When Gladstone introduced a bill to unite Irish colleges in a single university open to Catholics and Protestants alike, he was defeated and resigned (1873, Feb.). Disraeli was reluctant to take office as yet, Gladstone returned, sponsored a notable reform of the law courts in

1873. The **Judicature Act,** which, along with supplementary acts, consolidated the three common law courts, chancery, and various other tribunals into one **supreme court of judicature,** to consist of two principal divisons: (1) The *high court of justice*—(*a*) queen's bench, (*b*) chancery, (*c*) probate, divorce, and admiralty; (2) the *court of appeal,* from which appellate jurisdiction lay to the house of lords, strengthened in 1876 by the addition of three (later four) law lords of life tenure.

1874, Feb. Gladstone appealed to the country in a **general election,** was overwhelmed by the Conservatives, who succeeded to power with Disraeli as prime minister.

1874, Feb. 21–1880, Apr. 22. The **second Disraeli ministry** came to power with the expressed purpose of "giving the country a rest" at home and pursuing a foreign policy more in accord with the demands of British prestige and interests. Certain measures of a domestic character were passed, notably a

1875. Public Health Act, a codification of earlier legislation which remains even today the backbone of English sanitary law; an

1875. Artisans' Dwelling Act, the first serious attempt by the government to grapple with the problem of the housing of the poor;

1876. The **Merchant Shipping Act,** aimed to prevent overloading ships or permitting use of unseaworthy vessels (the act a result of persistent efforts of **Samuel Plimsoll,** the "sailors' friend").

But the country's attention was riveted on foreign and colonial affairs.

1875, Nov. 25. Purchase of the Suez Canal shares. The completion of the Suez Canal under the direction of a Frenchman, Ferdinand de Lesseps, and under the auspices of an international company, greatly shortened the distance to India and the east and heightened British interest in Egypt. **Khedive Ismail** of Egypt, who held 44 per cent of the shares, was in perennial financial difficulties, and finally considered mortgaging his shares in Paris. This information came to Disraeli's attention; he sprang a *coup* by negotiating purchase of the shares on his own responsibility. A grateful parliament subsequently ratified the act. This marked the beginning of British penetration and presently occupation of Egypt *(p. 811).*

1876, Apr. The **Royal Titles Bill** declared the queen *Empress of India,* deeply flattered Her Majesty, was the occasion of great enthusiasm in India, caused considerable opposition among educated Englishmen—the title was "un-English" and in disrepute through the fall of Emperor Napoleon III and the tragedy of Emperor Maximilian of Mexico (the opposition was allayed by the promise that she would not use it in England).

Aug. Disraeli was elevated to the peerage as the **earl of Beaconsfield.** During the

remainder of its term of office the government was absorbed by the crisis of 1875–1876 in the Near East, culminating in the **Russo-Turkish War** and the **congress of Berlin** *(p. 732),* by the **Afghan War** of 1878–1879 *(p. 732),* and by the war with the **Zulus** in South Africa *(p. 829),* Beaconsfield's popularity had reached its zenith when he returned from the congress of Berlin.

1879. A severe **agricultural depression** with the worst harvest of the century accompanied by a decline in trade, strikes, the unpopular Afghan and Zulu wars, obstruction by the new **Irish Home Rule Party** in the house of commons.

Nov. **Gladstone** roundly denounced the government, alike for its imperialism and its domestic policy, in a series of speeches to his **Midlothian** constituents.

1880, Mar. 8. Beaconsfield appealed to the country in a general election, his party was defeated, and he resigned (Apr. 18), to be succeeded by Gladstone.

1880, Apr. 28–1885, June 8. Second Gladstone ministry. Much of the session of 1880 was occupied by the case of **Charles Bradlaugh,** newly elected to the commons, who as an atheist refused to take the oath (including the words "So help me God") and insisted on an affirmation instead. An **Affirmation Bill** was twice defeated (1881, 1883); Bradlaugh changed his mind, offered to take the oath, was refused the right (as a freethinker). Subsequently he was involved in eight lawsuits, was unseated and re-elected repeatedly, was finally permitted to take the oath (1886, Jan.). Bradlaugh secured passage of a bill (1888) legalizing affirmation both in the commons and the courts, removing the last religious disability for membership in the house.

1880, Sept. 13. First Employers' Liability Act, granting compensation to workers for injuries not their own fault.

1881–1882. The Irish Question. Foundation (1871) of the parliamentary **Home Rule for Ireland Party** by **Isaac Butt,** who aimed at securing by peaceful means a separate legislature for Ireland. The dominant figure soon became **Charles Stewart Parnell,** descendant of English Protestant settlers in Ireland, but consumed by hatred for England; brilliant orator, elected to parliament in 1875. Parnell hoped to unite all elements of Irish opposition and to force the grant of home rule by the use of obstruction in parliament. The Peace Preservation Act of 1875 expired in 1880 and the government, unable to maintain order under ordinary law, was obliged to resort to new **coercive measures.**

1881, Aug. Gladstone then passed the **Land Act,** which aimed to correct the defects in his Act of 1870 and to meet the Irish demand for the three "F's." The act recognized a dual ownership of land and provided for the creation of a court to mediate between landlord and tenant and fix a "fair" rent for a period of 15 years; it gave increased fixity of tenure to tenants who paid those rents, with the right to sell their interest in the holdings to the highest bidder. While it established a land court, with authority to cut down excessive rents, the act made no provision for dealing with accumulated arrears. It pleased neither landlords nor tenants.

Oct. 13. Parnell and others were sent to

Kilmainham Prison for inciting Irishmen to intimidate tenants taking advantage of the act. They were released (1882, May 2) when they agreed in the "Kilmainham treaty" to cease "boycotting" and co-operate with the Liberal party.

1882, May 6. **Lord Frederick Cavendish,** new chief secretary for Ireland, and **Thomas Burke,** permanent undersecretary, were murdered in broad daylight by Fenians in **Phoenix Park,** Dublin. Parnell repudiated all connection with the crime and offered to resign his leadership of the Home Rule party.

July. The government put through the draconian **Prevention of Crimes Bill** (limited to three years) suspending trial by jury and giving the police unlimited power to search and arrest on suspicion. Irish extremists, with whom Parnell denied all connection, resorted to a **campaign of terrorism,** punctuated by dynamiting of public buildings in England.

1883, Aug. The **Corrupt and Illegal Practices Act** in effect limited the total amounts that might be spent (all parties) in a general election to £800,000 (£2,500,000 had been spent in the general election of 1880); no candidate might spend more than a fixed sum for election purposes; penalties for corrupt practices were greatly increased.

1884. Gladstone's **Franchise Bill** aimed to extend the rights enjoyed by the borough voters to the rural classes and to unify substantially the franchise throughout the United Kingdom. The measure virtually provided manhood suffrage—only domestic servants, bachelors living with their families, and those of no fixed abode being excluded. Some 2,000,000 voters were to be added, nearly four times the number added in 1832, nearly twice that added in 1867. The bill passed the commons, was rejected by the lords, the Conservatives insisting on the importance of a concomitant redistribution of seats. Negotiations followed; Gladstone yielded in the matter of redistribution; the Franchise Bill itself passed easily (Dec.).

George Bernard Shaw, 1856–1950

1885, June. A **Redistribution Bill** followed—London received 37 additional members, Liverpool six, Birmingham four, Glasgow four, Yorkshire 16, Lancashire 15; single-member constituencies became the rule, except in the city of London and in cities and boroughs with a population between 50,000 and 165,000; boroughs of fewer than 15,000 population were merged with their counties. By this legislation the historic counties and boroughs ceased to be, as such, the basis of the house of commons. The individual for the first time became the unit, and numerical equality ("one vote, one value") the master principle.

Despite his resistance to the imperialist policy of Disraeli, his withdrawal from Afghanistan *(p. 839),* his concessions to the Boers in South Africa *(p. 829),* Gladstone was fated to play an active rôle in the field of **colonial expansion.**

1882. **Britain was obliged to intervene in Egypt** *(p. 812),* and the prestige of the cabinet was seriously damaged when it failed to rescue General Charles G. Gordon, isolated in the Sudan *(p. 813).*

1884–1885. Russian encroachments in Afghanistan nearly led to war, and the pacific policy of the foreign minister, Lord Granville, led to Conservative accusations of truckling to the Russians *(pp. 734, 839).*

1885, June 9. A hostile amendment to his budget led to **Gladstone's resignation.**

1885, June 24–1886, Jan. 27. First Salisbury ministry. Salisbury had become head of the Conservative Party on the death of Beaconsfield (1881, Apr. 19).

1885, Aug. Ashbourne Act. The Conservatives had previously been the party of Irish coercion, but Salisbury reached an understanding with Parnell that this policy should be reversed in return for Irish Nationalist support. A fund of £5,000,000 was provided by the Ashbourne Act for loans with which Irish tenants could purchase their holdings on an easy-interest, long-term basis (extending a feature of the Liberal land act of 1881). **Further land purchase acts** were adopted in 1887, 1891, 1896, and 1903 (the last named providing an eventual sum of £100,000,000).

1886, Feb. 12–July 20. Third Gladstone ministry. Gladstone's support for home rule had been secured (1885, Dec.), and during his third ministry he introduced his

1886, Apr. 8. First Home Rule Bill, providing for a separate Irish legislature of two orders (one of 28 representative peers, with 75 other members elected by and from the propertied classes, the other of 204 elected members). The Irish legislature was to have important powers, but legislation relating to the crown, the army and navy, trade and navigation, etc., were still to be dealt with by the British parliament, in which Irish members were no longer to sit. The measure was bitterly attacked by the Conservatives, caused a secession from the Liberal party of the **"Liberal Unionists"** (Marquis of Hartington, Joseph Chamberlain), and was finally defeated (July). A general election was called and produced a new defeat for the Liberals.

1886, July 26–1892, Aug. 13. Second Salisbury ministry. Arthur J. Balfour, the prime minister's nephew, was made chief secretary for Ireland and carried a new **Crimes Bill** (1887) whose passage was facilitated by the

publication of a notorious series of articles by the *Times* on "Parnellism and Crime," including an alleged letter of Parnell's declaring he had condemned the Phoenix Park murders only as a matter of policy. Parnell denied authorship of this and other letters, was cleared (1890) by a governmental commission (the author was Richard Piggott, broken-down Irish journalist and subsequent suicide). Soon thereafter Parnell's position was ruined when he was named co-respondent in a divorce suit brought by Captain O'Shea, one of his followers. Gladstone dropped him, a schism followed among the Nationalists, **Justin McCarthy** became leader of the majority. When Parnell died (1891, Oct. 6), **John E. Redmond** succeeded him as leader of the minority.

1889, May 31. Naval Defense Act, designed to meet growing sea power of France and Russia. It provided that the British fleet should always be as strong as the fleets of the two next strongest powers combined (**two-power standard**).

1889, Aug. 15–Sept. 16. Great **London dock strike,** in which almost all riverside workers joined. This great strike and the formation of the **Miners' Federation of Great Britain** (1888) marked the extension of trade-unionism from the skilled classes (represented in the Amalgamated Societies) to the less skilled.

1892. In the **general election** Gladstone made home rule the principal issue of the campaign, advocating also a series of additional reforms (**Newcastle program**): disestablishment of the Church of England in Wales, and of the Church of Scotland; local veto on liquor sales; abolition of plural voting; extension of the Employers' Liability Act; restriction of hours of labor. The election gave Gladstone sufficient votes, with the aid of 81 Irish Nationalists, to carry his home rule plank.

1892, Aug. 18–1894, Mar. 3. Fourth Gladstone cabinet.

1893, Feb. 13. Second Home Rule Bill. Its principal difference from the first bill was the provision that 80 Irish representatives should sit at Westminster. It passed the commons (Sept. 1), but was overwhelmed by the lords (Sept. 8). A period of comparative peace followed in Ireland and home rule sank in importance, to be revived only two decades later. **John Morley,** secretary for Ireland (1892–1895), ruled with sympathy and wisdom. The Conservative régime (1895–1905) continued its traditional tactics of killing home rule by kindness (new land purchase acts, 1896, 1903).

1893, Jan. Foundation of the Independent Labor party, a frankly socialist party. Socialism, which had declined in the forties, had revived in the eighties under the influence of the American Henry George's *Progress and Poverty* (1879). In 1884 **Henry M. Hyndman** founded the **Social Democratic Federation,** a Marxist organization. In 1883 was founded the **Fabian Society,** which became prominent with the publication (1889) of the *Fabian Essays.* Prominent among the Fabians were **Sidney** and **Beatrice Webb** and **George Bernard Shaw.** They preached practical possibilities—municipal socialism and state control of the conditions of labor—and expected socialism to come as a sequel to the full application of universal suffrage and representative government. In 1892 the first two avowed socialists were elected to parliament. One of them, **James Keir Hardie,** was mainly responsible for the foundation of the Labour party.

1894, Mar. Gladstone had lost his fight for home rule, had shattered the Liberal party. He resigned the premiership and was succeeded by the Liberal imperialist Lord Rosebery.

1894, Mar. 5-1895, June 21. **Cabinet of Lord Rosebery.** **Sir William Harcourt,** now leader of the house of commons, brought in a bill adding £4,000,000 to the budget by equalizing death duties on real and personal property and providing a graduated tax of 1 to 8 per cent—an attempt further to shift the burden of taxation to the wealthy. The cabinet was defeated on a matter of minor importance, and resigned.

e. A DECADE OF UNIONISM, 1895-1905

1895, June 25-1902, July 11. **Third Salisbury ministry,** with Salisbury himself as foreign minister, Balfour as first lord of the treasury and leader of the commons. The cabinet included some of the principal Liberal Unionists, notably Hartington (duke of Devonshire since 1891) and **Joseph Chamberlain.** The latter's political beginnings had been as a radical; as colonial secretary he now devoted his great energy and ability to the cause of enhancing British imperial prestige. The new government's attention was almost entirely absorbed by events abroad—the **Venezuela boundary dispute** with the United States *(p. 776)*, the **Armenian massacres** and the **Greco-Turkish war** *(pp. 737, 738)*, the struggle for power in the **Far East** *(pp. 738, 739)*, the **Hague conference of 1899** *(p. 739)*, the **South African problem** which culminated in the **Boer war** *(p. 831)*.

1900, Feb. Formation of the **Labor Representation Committee,** with **J. Ramsay MacDonald** as secretary. The committee represented the Independent Labour party, Trade-Union congress, and various socialist organizations. Its

Queen Victoria, photographed at her Diamond Jubilee, 1897

Edward VII, 1841-1910

aim was to establish a distinct labor group in parliament, but it had a hard struggle for existence. Only about 5 per cent of the unions affiliated themselves with it, the Social Democratic Federation soon withdrew, the attitude of the Fabians was cool, and the miners were hostile. At the general election of 1900 the committee ran 15 candidates, of whom only two were returned. But the decision of the lords in the **Taff Vale case** (1901, July), which declared unions legal entities capable of being sued, consolidated the ranks of labor and created the **Labour party,** which returned 29 members in the election of 1906.

1901. Jan 22. Death of Queen Victoria after one of the longest reigns in European history. She was widely mourned, reflecting the respect for her courage, strength of character, and the tact with which she had recognized the constitutional limitations of the crown and yielded to the steadily enlarging powers of her ministries. In the last decades Victoria had come to be regarded above all as the symbol of imperial unity, an aspect of the monarchy upon which attention had been brilliantly and effectively focused by the **Jubilee of 1887** (celebrating the fiftieth anniversary of the queen's accession) and by the **Diamond Jubilee of 1897.** The reign had witnessed a period of incredible industrial expansion and increasing material prosperity. The population of the United Kingdom had increased from 16,261,183 in 1831 to 37,518,052 in 1901.

1901-1910. EDWARD VII (b. 1841). Edward was nearly sixty, and Victoria had deprived him until recently of serious participation in matters political. He was possessed of great social charm and tact, read little, cared nothing for routine, gathered information largely from personal contact. He was gay and fond of pleasure, a yachting and racing enthusiast, supporter of philanthropic causes, widely popular with all classes before his accession.

1902, July 11-1905, Dec. 4. Cabinet of Arthur Balfour, following the retirement of Lord Salisbury.

1902, Dec. The **education act** was the most important legislative achievement of the Balfour government. For some time it had been felt that the school boards of the education act of 1870, although they had worked well in the towns, were on the whole too parochial in personnel and policy. The act of 1902 abolished the boards, placed elementary and secondary education in the hands of statutory committees of the borough and county councils. The denominational schools, hitherto belonging to and maintained by the Anglicans and Catholics, were brought into the reorganization *pari passu* with the undenominational board schools. For the first time in England the provision of secondary education was recognized as the duty of the state and was brought under public control. Educational progress under the act was rapid; in five years the number of secondary schools doubled.

1903, May. Joseph Chamberlain and the **Tariff Reform League** advocated a sweeping tariff reform, with moderate duties on corn, flour, meats, dairy produce, and foreign manufactures. The new system was to give Britain a basis for bargaining with the colonies, of preventing foreign dumping in Britain, of increasing the revenue. Balfour was unwilling to go so far, and Chamberlain resigned (Sept. 18).

1904. **Committee of Imperial Defense.** The South African war had revealed serious defects in the army. The report of the commission of inquiry was an "unsparing condemnation of war office methods." The upshot was the organization of the Defense Committee with the prime minister as its head; the commander-in-chief was replaced by an army council which included the war secretary, four military members, one civil and one finance member; a board of selection (duke of Connaught, president) was to control appointments.

Foreign relations bulked large in a period when Britain settled her differences with France in the **Entente cordiale** of 1904 *(p. 741)*, European peace was threatened in the **Moroccan crisis of 1905** *(p. 742)*, and the naval rivalry of Britain and Germany became increasingly embittered *(p. 738 ff.)*.

Balfour's cabinet steadily lost prestige because of its dilatory tactics regarding the tariff question; opposition to its Education Act of 1902, which roused the ire of Nonconformists because it left in existence state-supported denominational schools largely controlled by Anglicans; etc. Balfour resigned, expecting to be recalled, but was succeeded by

f. THE LIBERAL RÉGIME, 1905–1914

1905, Dec. 5–1908, Apr. 5. **Cabinet of Sir Henry Campbell-Bannerman,** leader of the Liberals. It included **Herbert Asquith,** chancellor of the exchequer, and **Sir Edward Grey,** foreign secretary. The **Liberal program of 1906** included exclusion of Chinese labor from the Transvaal; change of the Education Act of 1902 in favor of the Nonconformists; reduction in the number of liquor licenses and national control of the liquor trade; sweeping measures aimed at social amelioration.

1906, Jan. The Liberals won an overwhelming victory in the elections.

Dec. A **Trade Disputes Bill** met the demands of the trade-unionists by providing that a union could not be made liable for damage on account of illegal acts committed by its members; legalized peaceful picketing, etc.

At the same time a **Workingman's Compensation Act** developed the principle of employers' liability laid down in acts going back to 1880; the employer was now made liable for compensation for accidents to practically all employees receiving less than £250 annually except in case of "serious and willful misconduct."

1908, Apr. 5–1916, May 15. **Cabinet of Herbert Asquith,** following the resignation of Campbell-Bannerman on account of ill health (d. Apr. 22, 1908).

1909, Jan. The **Old-Age Pension Law,** outcome of thirty years of agitation, provided a pension for every British subject over 70 with an income of less than £31 10s.

1909. The **Peoples Budget,** brought in by David

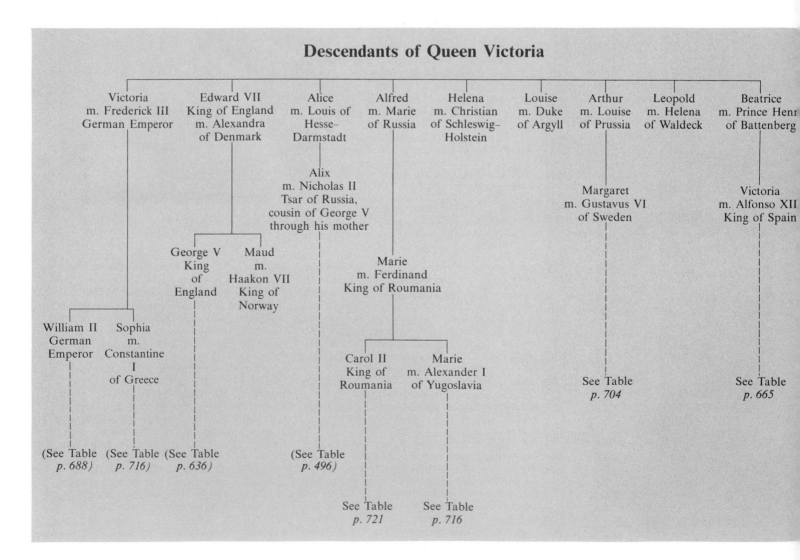

Descendants of Queen Victoria

Lloyd George, chancellor of the exchequer, leading spirit of liberal reform. Facing a large deficit (chiefly the result of naval expenditure and social legislation), Lloyd George devised a budget aiming to shift the tax burden from producers to possessors of wealth, in the form of income and inheritance taxes, levies on unearned income, heavy rates on monopolies (such as liquor licenses) and on unearned increments of land. The budget passed the commons after a hot fight (Nov. 5), but was rejected by the lords (Nov. 30) until the judgment of the country should have been expressed. The house of lords was the stronghold of opposition to the program of the Liberal majority in the commons, and had twice thrown out an education bill (1906, 1908) and a licensing bill (1908).

Dec. 2. Asquith denounced the action of the lords as a breach of the constitution.

1910, Jan. General election, fought out on the issues of the budget, the veto power of the lords, and home rule for Ireland (the Irish Nationalists having offered their support on condition that the power of the house of lords should be so far reduced that it could no longer defeat home rule). The Liberals lost considerable strength in the election, but determined to go on with their program.

May 6. Death of Edward VII.

1910–1936. GEORGE V (b. 1865), a sound but unimaginative ruler, filled with a sense of responsibility and rigid respect for the constitution.

1910, May 10. Three resolutions passed in the house of commons: (1) that the lords should have no right to veto a money bill; (2) that any other measure should become law after being passed in three successive sessions of the commons, even if vetoed by the lords, providing that two years had elapsed since its first introduction; (3) that the maximum life of parliament should be five instead of seven years. In the lords, **Lord Lansdowne** offered an alternative measure for the reconstruction of that body.

Nov. 28. Parliament was dissolved and a second general election held (Dec.). The Liberals gained only two seats.

1911, May 15. The **Parliament Bill** was again passed in the commons and ultimately passed the lords (July 20) with amendments unacceptable to Asquith, who threatened to have enough peers created to carry the bill. Thereupon the lords capitulated (Aug. 10).

Aug. 10. The commons for the first time voted salaries for their members (£400 per year).

Dec. The **National Insurance Act** provided: (1) insurance for the whole working population against loss of health and for the prevention and cure of sickness; (2) insurance against unemployment. Wage-earners 16 to 65 years old having less than £26 annual income from property were obliged to take health insurance. The second part of the act applied only to 2,250,000 workers engaged in trades specially liable to fluctuations—large building and engineering trades—and gave a maximum benefit of 15 weeks. Both health and unemployment insurance were supported by contributions from employers, employees, and the state.

1911–1912. Epidemic of strikes, of which the transport workers' and railwaymen's strikes

King George V and Queen Mary in coronation robes

(1911) and the miners' strike (1912) were outstanding. The strikes were the reflection of stationary wages and rising prices, and showed the influence of syndicalist ideas imported from the United States and the Continent. The **coal strike** (1912), involving 1,500,000 men, brought government action and

1912, Mar. 29. A **Minimum Wage Law,** which, however, did little to relieve unrest.

Apr. 11. The government introduced a bill for **home rule in Ireland.** It provided for a bicameral parliament for Ireland, but with continued representation in the house of commons. The bill was attacked for its injustice to Protestant Ulster, which would be submerged

in a united Catholic Ireland. Opposition brilliantly led by **Sir Edward Carson.**

1913. The **Home Rule Bill** was twice passed by the commons (Jan. 16, July 7) and twice rejected by the lords (Jan. 30, July 15). Meanwhile Ulster opposition grew steadily hotter. **A covenant** was signed at Belfast (1912, Sept. 28) pledging resistance to home rule and refusal to accept it if it were voted.

July 12. A resolution was adopted by a meeting of 150,000 Ulstermen at Craigavon to resist home rule by force of arms if necessary. By December 100,000 **Ulster volunteers** had been raised. Civil war appeared imminent if the government persisted in its home rule program, which it had pledged to the Irish Nationalists.

1914, Feb. 10. When parliament met, Unionist opposition had reached its peak. Asquith offered a compromise (Mar. 9): electors in each of the nine Ulster counties might determine whether their county should be excluded from the new arrangement for six years. The Home Rule Bill was passed for a third time by the commons (May 26). Under the Parliament Act of 1911 no further action by the lords was necessary: Ireland had now been given a unitary parliamentary system, with no separate position for Ulster.

June 23. **Asquith introduced his compromise** of March 9 on Ulster into the house of lords, which changed the bill to exclude the whole of Ulster without time limit. A three-cornered struggle of lords, commons, and Irish Nationalist leaders was overtaken by the World War.

Charles Dickens, 1812–1870

Thomas Carlyle (1795–1881), by Whistler

Illustration, 1850, for Charles Dickens' David Copperfield

Sept. 18. The **Home Rule Bill** received the royal assent and became law; but by a simultaneous act it was not to come into force until after the war, and the government pledged that, before it was put into force, an amending bill dealing with the question of Ulster would be introduced. The third Home Rule Bill, which never came into operation, was subsequently replaced by the Home Rule Bill of December 1920 *(p. 917).*

Sept. 18. Welsh disestablishment. The parliamentary course of the Welsh Disestablishment Bill was almost exactly parallel with that of the Home Rule Bill. A bill for the disestablishment of the Anglican Church in Wales had failed in 1894–1895, again in 1909. Introduced in 1912 (Apr. 12), it passed the commons twice, but was rejected by the lords (1913, Feb. 13, July 22). The bill was finally passed by the commons in 1914 (May 19)

and received the royal assent (Sept. 18); but along with it was passed a **Suspensory Bill,** postponing its action until the end of the war. The bill provided that the four Welsh dioceses should no longer form part of the province of Canterbury, that the Welsh bishops should no longer sit in the house of lords, that all ecclesiastical jurisdiction should be abolished, and the Welsh Anglicans should be free to set up their own church government.

(Cont. p. 914.)

CULTURAL DEVELOPMENTS

(1) Literature

In the Victorian era the novel was a favorite form, both as re-creation of history and as social commentary. In the former category: **Edward George Bulwer-Lytton** (1803–1873), *Last Days of*

William Morris, 1834–1896

Elizabeth Barrett Browning, 1806–1861

Sir Arthur Sullivan, 1842–1900

Pompeii (1834); **Charles Dickens** (1812–1870), *Tale of Two Cities.* The two foremost novelists of the period were **William Makepeace Thackeray** (1811–1863), who drew true pictures of a period in *Vanity Fair* (1847) and *Henry Esmond* (1852), and **Charles Dickens**, equally skilled in his portrayal of a lower stratum of society (*David Copperfield,* 1850; *Oliver Twist,* 1838). Also concerned with problems of their day; **Anthony Trollope** (1815–1882), **Charlotte Brontë** (1816–1855, *Jane Eyre,* 1847); George Eliot (1819–1880); George Meredith (1828–1909). The implications of *Alice in Wonderland* (1865) and *Through the Looking Glass* by Lewis Carroll (Charles L. Dodgson) continue to occupy students. The Scot Robert Louis Stevenson (1850–1894) is remembered chiefly for his adventure stories *Treasure Island* (1883), *Kidnapped* (1886), and his verses for children.

Thomas Carlyle (1795–1881) and **Thomas Babington Macaulay** (1800–1859) were essayists and historians: Carlyle's *French Revolution* (1837) and his lectures *On Heroes* (1841); Macaulay's *History of England* (1848–1861). Other critics and essayists: **John Ruskin** (1819–1900); **Matthew Arnold** (1822–1888); **Thomas Huxley**, the scientist (1825–1895); **Walter Pater** (1839–1894).

Poetry: **Alfred Lord Tennyson** (1809–1892; *Idylls of the King,* 1859–1885); **Robert** (1812–1889) and **Elizabeth Barrett Browning** (1806–1861; *Sonnets from the Portuguese,* 1850); the Pre-Raphaelite Brotherhood of **Dante Gabriel Rossetti** (1828–1882), **Christina Rossetti** (1830–1894), **Algernon Charles Swinburne** (1837–1909), **Edward Fitzgerald** (1809–1883), the translator of the *Rubaiyat* of Omar Khayyam, and **William Morris** (1834–1896).

(2) Music

William Sterndale Bennett (1816–1875); **John Stainer** (1840–1901); **Sir Arthur Sullivan** (1842–1900), best known for his "operas" written in collaboration with W. S. Gilbert.

(3) Painting

A group of Pre-Raphaelite painters followed the philosophy of the Brotherhood of poets, stressing faithfulness to nature, which resulted in a mystical quality in their art: **Edward Burne-Jones** (1833–1898); **Sir John Millais** (1829–1896); the poet and journalist **Dante Gabriel Rossetti** (see above). **Aubrey Beardsley** (1872–1898) illustrated Malory's *Morte d'Arthur*, Oscar Wilde's *Salomé,* Pope's *Rape of the Lock.*

3. *The Low Countries*

(From p. 464)

a. THE KINGDOM OF THE NETHERLANDS, 1814–1830

1814, June 21. Protocol of the Eight Articles, concluded between the prince of Orange and the representatives of the allied powers after the defeat of Napoleon. In order to create a bulwark against France, it was agreed to unite Belgium (the Austrian Netherlands) and Holland to form the **Kingdom of the Netherlands.** This arrangement was confirmed by the congress of Vienna (1815, June 9).

1815–1840. WILLIAM I, the former prince of Orange, a well-meaning but rather arbitrary and obstinate ruler. He granted a moderately **liberal constitution** (1815, Aug. 24), but failed to make the union of Belgium and Holland work. Traditions, customs, religion, and interests were different and the Belgians felt throughout that they were put in an inferior position. The seat of the government was in Holland, the king a Dutchman and a Calvinist; despite her larger population, Belgium had only equal representation in the lower chamber of the states-general or assembly; the majority of officers and officials were Dutch; the public establishments (banks, schools) were predominantly Dutch; Dutch was made the official

language in all except the Walloon districts of Belgium; the public debt was equally divided, though in 1814 that of Holland was many times greater than that of Belgium; the Catholic Church in Belgium resented the equality of religious denominations; the Belgians disliked the Dutch tariff system, which, being liberal, gave inadequate protection to Belgian industry.

1828, July. The two Belgian parties (Clericals and Liberals) united after the king had estranged the Clericals by concluding a **concordat with the pope** (1827) giving the king the right to veto the election of bishops, and had estranged the Liberals by a harsh press law. The program of the two parties called for free-

William I, 1815–1840

dom of press, instruction, and worship, and for ministerial responsibility. Increased agitation for the redress of grievances, accompanied by much economic distress.

1830, Aug. 25. The **BELGIAN REVOLUTION,** stimulated by the **July Revolution in Paris** and by unrest among the lower classes. The moderate liberal elements asked only an autonomous administration and were willing to accept the king's son as viceroy.

Sept. 23–26. Violent fighting in Brussels between the workers and the troops, who were obliged to evacuate the city. A provisional government was set up with **Charles Rogier** as leader.

Oct. 4. Proclamation of independence. A national congress was summoned to draw up a constitution.

Oct. 27. Bombardment of Antwerp by the Dutch made the Belgians irreconcilable.

Nov. 4. At the suggestion of Great Britain, a **conference of the powers** met at London and ordered an armistice.

Nov. 10. The Belgian national congress declared the house of Orange deposed, but voted for constitutional hereditary monarchy.

Nov. 15. Advent of **Lord Palmerston** to the British foreign office, following the downfall of the Wellington ministry. Palmerston was not unsympathetic to the Belgian claims, but was above all eager to check the spread of French influence in Belgium and to prevent war. Louis Philippe, confronted with a serious domestic situation in France, followed Britain and the two powers induced Russia (paralyzed by the Polish insurrection, *p. 706*), Austria, and Prussia to abandon the principle of legitimacy.

Dec. 20. The conference practically recognized the independence of Belgium by declaring the **dissolution of the Kingdom of the Netherlands.**

1831, Jan. 20, Jan 27. Two protocols set forth the bases of separation. The Dutch accepted the terms, but the Belgians refused.

Feb. 3. The Belgian national congress

elected as king the **duke of Nemours,** second son of Louis Philippe. Energetic warnings and threats of Palmerston induced Louis Philippe to reject the election.

Feb. 7. The Belgians set up a regency under **Surlet de Chokier,** and the congress drew up a constitution on the British pattern, one of the most liberal in Europe.

June 4. The Belgians elected as king **Prince Leopold of Saxe-Coburg,** widower of Princess Charlotte of England and uncle of the future Queen Victoria, a cultured and shrewd prince.

June 26. The London conference, having approved of Leopold, drew up the **Eighteen Articles,** regulating the separation and more favorable to the Belgians. It was accepted by the Belgians, but rejected by King William of Holland.

Aug. 2. Breaking off the armistice, William sent a large army over the frontier, which quickly defeated an improvised Belgian force. A French army thereupon invaded the country and forced the Dutch to retire.

Oct. 14. The **Twenty-Four Articles,** drawn up by the London conference and more favorable to Holland. Still King William refused to agree or to evacuate Antwerp.

1832, Nov.–Dec. A French army and a Franco-British and French to conclude an armistice

1833, May 21. The Dutch were obliged by the British and French to conclude an armistice of indefinite length on the basis of the *status quo.*

1839, Apr. 19. King William finally accepted a settlement much like that of the Twenty-Four Articles. He recognized Belgium and accepted substantially the frontier of 1790, except for Luxemburg and Limburg. The Belgians had claimed the whole of **Luxemburg,** but only the western part was given them; the rest, including the capital, remained a grand duchy with the king of Holland as grand duke. **Limburg** was also divided, the Belgians receiving about one-half. The **Scheldt** was declared open to the commerce of both countries and the national debt was divided. Article VII recognized Belgium as an **"independent and perpetually neutral state"** under the collective guaranty of the powers.

b. THE KINGDOM OF BELGIUM, 1830–1914

1831–1865. LEOPOLD I. During the early part of his reign the Clerical-Liberal coalition continued to rule the country, devoting itself to the consolidation of the kingdom, ably guided by the king.

1847. The coalition gave way to a party system and ministerial responsibility. Until 1884 the Liberals were generally in control of the government, first under the leadership of **Charles Rogier,** then of **Walther Frère-Orban.**

1848. A **new electoral law** lowered the franchise and doubled the number of voters. The success of the régime was attested by the fact that Belgium was almost alone among the Continental powers in escaping revolution.

1850. The **national bank** was founded as part of a general policy devoted to economic development.

1861–1862. Commercial treaties with France and Britain ushered in a period of free-trade policy.

1863. The **navigation of the Scheldt** was made free.

1865–1909. LEOPOLD II, like his father an able, energetic, strong-willed ruler and a man of vision.

1867–1870. A period of international uncertainty, arising from the **designs of Napoleon III** upon Belgium *(p. 655)* and culminating in the effort (1869) to secure control of the Belgian railways.

1870, Aug. 9, 11. Under British auspices, treaties were concluded between Great Britain, Prussia, and France guaranteeing **Belgian neutrality** during the Franco-Prussian War.

1879, July 1. Education act secularizing primary education. The public or "neutral" schools were to be supported by the communes with subventions from the government; no public support was to be given to the "free" or Catholic schools. This measure, passed by the Liberals, estranged the Clericals.

1880, June. The **Clericals won a majority** in the elections. They now replaced the Liberals and remained in power until the time of the First World War.

Leopold I, 1831–1865

Leopold II, 1865–1909

The Execution of Emperor Maximilian (p.655) by Edouard Manet

Victor Emmanuel (right) Meets Garibaldi (p.670) by Aldi

The Battle of Calatafimi (p.673) by R. Legat

Belgium: The House of Saxe-Coburg (1831–   )

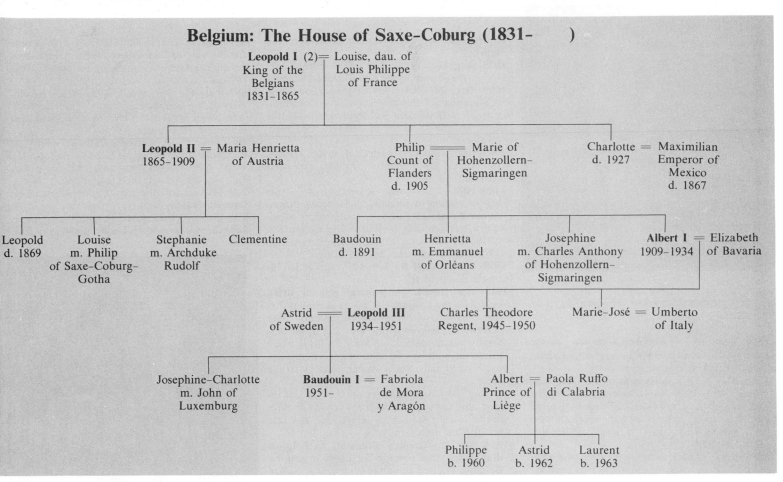

Leopold I (2) = Louise, dau. of
King of the   Louis Philippe
Belgians   of France
1831–1865

Leopold II = Maria Henrietta   Philip ═══ Marie of   Charlotte = Maximilian
1865–1909   of Austria   Count of   Hohenzollern–   d. 1927   Emperor of
                                     Flanders   Sigmaringen   Mexico
                                     d. 1905   d. 1867

Leopold   Louise   Stephanie   Clementine   Baudouin   Henrietta   Josephine   **Albert I** = Elizabeth
d. 1869   m. Philip   m. Archduke   d. 1891   m. Emmanuel   m. Charles Anthony 1909–1934   of Bavaria
           of Saxe-Coburg- Rudolf   of Orléans   of Hohenzollern–
           Gotha   Sigmaringen

                          Astrid ═══ **Leopold III**   Charles Theodore   Marie-José = Umberto
                          of Sweden   1934–1951   Regent, 1945–1950   of Italy

          Josephine-Charlotte   **Baudouin I** = Fabriola   Albert ═══ Paola Ruffo
          m. John of   1951–   de Mora   Prince of   di Calabria
          Luxemburg   y Aragón   Liège

                                                         Philippe   Astrid   Laurent
                                                         b. 1960   b. 1962   b. 1963

The House of Saxe-Coburg–Gotha (1800–   )

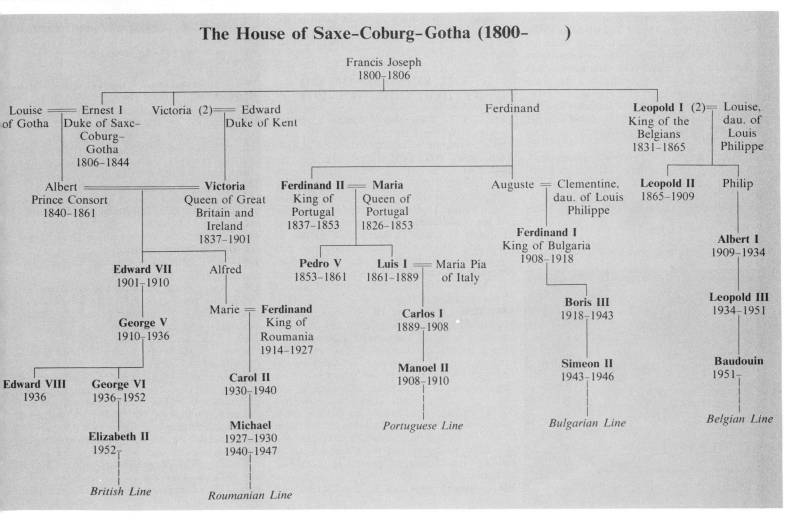

Francis Joseph
1800–1806

Louise ═══ Ernest I   Victoria (2) ═══ Edward   Ferdinand   Leopold I (2) ═ Louise,
of Gotha   Duke of Saxe-   Duke of Kent   King of the   dau. of
           Coburg–   Belgians   Louis
           Gotha   1831–1865   Philippe
           1806–1844

Albert ═══════════════ **Victoria**   **Ferdinand II** ═ **Maria**   Auguste ═ Clementine,   **Leopold II**   Philip
Prince Consort   Queen of Great King of   Queen of   dau. of Louis   1865–1909
1840–1861   Britain and   Portugal   Portugal   Philippe
                        Ireland   1837–1853   1826–1853
                        1837–1901   **Ferdinand I**
                                                                          King of Bulgaria   **Albert I**
       Edward VII   Alfred   **Pedro V**   **Luis I** ═ Maria Pia   1908–1918   1909–1934
       1901–1910   1853–1861   1861–1889   of Italy

                        Marie ═ **Ferdinand**   **Leopold III**
       George V   King of   **Carlos I**   **Boris III**   1934–1951
       1910–1936   Roumania   1889–1908   1918–1943
                                 1914–1927

Edward VIII **George VI**   **Carol II**   **Manoel II**   **Simeon II**   **Baudouin**
1936   1936–1952   1930–1940   1908–1910   1943–1946   1951–

                Elizabeth II **Michael**
                1952–   1927–1930
                                 1940–1947

British Line   *Roumanian Line*   *Portuguese Line*   *Bulgarian Line*   *Belgian Line*

Johan Thorbecke, 1798–1872

1884, Sept. 10. A **new education law** reversed that of 1879 and gave public support for church schools in Catholic districts.

1885, May 2. **Establishment of the Congo Free State,** with Leopold II as ruler. This great African empire had been built up by Leopold as a personal enterprise. Its recognition by the powers was a most unusual achievement *(pp. 734, 822).*

1886–1894. **Labor unrest,** with a series of major strikes. Economic development had been very rapid, with the result that social problems emerged in an acute form. With extensive coal mines, Belgium was able to industrialize to the point where it was the fourth manufacturing power in Europe. Under the circumstances socialism made great strides. The **Labor Party** was founded in 1885 and soon took the place of the declining Liberal Party as the chief organ of opposition to the Clericals. The Socialists demanded universal manhood suffrage and organized strikes as a method of bringing pressure.

1893, Apr. A general strike was proclaimed.

Apr. 27. The government introduced **universal suffrage,** but with a system of **plural voting** which gave two or three votes to about two-fifths of the voters who fulfilled certain re-

Albert I, 1909–1934

quirements as to age, income, education, and family.

1895, Aug. 30. Instruction in the Catholic religion made compulsory in all public schools.

1899, Dec. 24. Adoption of **proportional representation** for the protection of political minorities. An alliance was formed between the Liberals and Socialists to demand "one man, one vote."

1901–1905. Another period of **strike activity,** punctuated by anarchist outrages, especially dynamitings.

1903–1904. The **Congo scandal,** arising from the revelation in England of labor conditions under Leopold's rule. A commission of inquiry was sent out in 1905. The Congo was ceded by the king to the Belgian nation in 1908 and became the Belgian Congo.

1909–1934. **ALBERT I** (b. 1875) succeeded his uncle, Leopold II.

1913, Apr. 14–24. A **political general strike** ended on the assurance of the government that the electoral system would be revised. The reform was delayed by the World War, but was finally accomplished on May 6, 1919, when universal suffrage without plural voting was established and certain women were given the vote.

Aug. 30. **Army Law** enacted, with the introduction of universal military service in place of the earlier system by which one son was taken from each family.

1914, Aug. 2. **German ultimatum to Belgium** demanding free passage for German armies. Belgium rejected the ultimatum and appealed to Britain and France.

Aug. 4. Beginning of the **invasion of Belgium** and German declaration of war *(p. 749).*
(Cont. p. 919.)

c. THE KINGDOM OF THE NETHERLANDS, 1830–1914

1840, Oct. 7. **Abdication of William I,** who had become very unpopular because of his obstinate opposition to reform. He died in 1844.

1840–1849. **WILLIAM II** (b. 1792).

1848, Oct. The king, moved by the European revolutions of 1848 and pressed by the Liberals, under the distinguished jurist and statesman **Johan Thorbecke,** conceded a **revision of the constitution:** the power of the king was reduced and that of parliament greatly increased. Ministerial responsibility was provided and the upper house (thus far appointed by the king) was to be elected by the provincial assemblies. The lower house was still elected by a restricted suffrage.

1849–1890. **WILLIAM III** (b. 1817), an enlightened and benevolent ruler. His reign was marked by great **commercial expansion** and much internal development (canals, etc.). The political life of the country centered on the struggle of parties over the questions of religious education and the extension of the suffrage. The Liberals, largely representative of the trading classes and the towns, demanded a system of free secular schools. They were opposed by the Protestant Conservatives, the Calvinist peasantry and the Catholics, all of whom favored religious control of the public schools.

1862. **Slavery abolished** in the Dutch West Indies.

1867, Mar. The king made a treaty with France for the **sale of Luxemburg.** This gave rise to an international crisis and the dropping of the project. *(p. 692).*

1887, June 17. Introduction of **suffrage reform,** after a long period of agitation. The electorate was about doubled. The first Socialist was elected to parliament.

1889, Dec. 6. A **Calvinist-Catholic coalition,** following on a period of Liberal rule (1871–1888), passed a law providing financial assistance for all private denominational schools. Non-sectarian public schools continued to be state-supported.

1890–1948. **WILHELMINA** (b. 1880). Until 1898 the queen-mother, **Emma,** acted as regent.

Wilhelmina, 1890–1948

1894. A **serious revolt** broke out in the **Dutch East Indies.** Another rising, in 1896, was put down only with considerable difficulty.

1896, June 29. A **new electoral law,** carried by a Liberal cabinet, again doubled the electorate (from 300,000 to 700,000), but the system was still far removed from universal suffrage and drew fire from the working classes.

1897–1901. The **Borgesius ministry** (Liberal), which passed much **social legislation,** such as accident insurance, improvement of housing, compulsory education for children, etc.

1901, Feb. 7. **The queen married Duke Henry of Mecklenburg-Schwerin.**

1901–1905. **Ministry of Abraham Kuyper** (Clerical).

1903, Apr. **Great railway and dock strikes,** which the government broke up by the use of the military, thus arousing the forces of trade-unionism and socialism.

1905. The elections restored the Liberals to power, but the party, never very disciplined, continued to disintegrate.

1913, Aug. 25. An **extra-parliamentary cabinet** was formed by Cort van der Linden (Moderate Liberal) and set out to settle the suffrage and education questions. In 1917 (Nov.) **universal suffrage** and proportional representation were introduced. At the same time the Clericals were satisfied by the concession in full of the principle of absolute equality with regard to financial support for public nondenominational schools and private sectarian instruction.
(Cont. p. 919.)

4. *France*

[*For a complete list of the kings of France see Appendix VII.*]

(From p. 630)

a. THE RESTORATION MONARCHY, 1814-1830

1814-1824. LOUIS XVIII (b. 1755), brother of Louis XVI, easy-going, disillusioned, reasonable. He was permitted by the allies to return after the defeat of Napoleon, mainly through the influence of Tsar Alexander of Russia.

1814, June 14. The king granted the *charte constitutionnelle,* or **constitution,** a reflection of the tsar's liberalism and of Louis's desire to meet the demands of the middle classes. It created a system akin to that of the British, with an hereditary monarch, a chamber of peers nominated by the king, a chamber of deputies elected by a limited suffrage, and various guaranties of civil and religious liberty.

1815, Mar. 13. The sudden **return of Napoleon** from Elba obliged Louis to flee from Paris and remain in exile during the **Hundred Days** *(p. 629).* After Waterloo he made an undignified return to the capital "in the baggage of the allies" (July 7), whereupon the **second restoration** was accomplished. The king's influence was much reduced and he was unable to prevent a so-called **White Terror,** carried on by fanatical royalists, especially in the south, against revolutionaries and Bonapartists.

Aug. 22. The first parliamentary elections yielded a large majority for the **Ultra-royalist** group (*chambre introuvable*), whose reactionary policy was opposed by the ministry headed by the duke of Richelieu. The reaction went to such extremes that the king, under pressure from the allied representatives,

1816, Sept. Dissolved the chamber and called new elections. In the new chamber a majority of moderates supported the policy of Richelieu and that of his immediate successors, Dessolles (1818–1819), Decazes (1819–1820).

1816-1820. Moderate measures characterized the period of these ministries, among others laws freeing the press (1819, May 1).

1818. The **payment of the French indemnity** and the consequent evacuation of French soil by allied troops, the most notable achievement of Richelieu.

1820, Feb. 13. The **murder of the duke of Berri,** presumed to be the last of the Bourbon line, by an obscure fanatic, Louvel, was providential for the Ultras. The ministry of the duke of Decazes, favorite of the king, was overthrown and succeeded by a second Richelieu ministry (1820–1821).

1820. To preserve the country from the increasing danger from the Left, a **new electoral law** was passed (the *Law of the Double Vote*), which established a complicated system of election of two degrees, increased the electoral weight of voters in the upper tax brackets, and aimed to increase the influence of landed proprietors (source of Ultra support) at the expense of the middle class. This law, together with legislation on the press, personal liberty, etc., marked the beginning of the "reaction," which was to end only in the revolution of 1830.

1823, Apr. Invasion of Spain by French troops, in behalf of Ferdinand VII *(p. 664).*

1824-1830. CHARLES X (b. 1757).

1821-1827. Under the **Villèle ministry,** a resolute attempt was made to restore, in as large a measure as possible, the position which the monarchy had occupied under the old régime.

1825, Apr. A **Law of Indemnity** compensated the nobles for the losses of their lands during the revolution, at the expense of the holders of government bonds, largely the upper *bourgeoisie.* The Church was favored in various ways, notably by the adoption of the notorious

1826. Law of Sacrilege, imposing a death sentence for certain offenses of a "sacrilegious" character. The *bourgeoisie* was further alienated by the king's

1827, Apr. 30. Dissolution of the national guard, a preserve of the middle class. Secret societies sprang up, notably the Liberal electoral society, *Aide-toi, le ciel t'aidera.* Confident of his position, Charles X called a general election to strengthen his majority in the chamber.

1827, Nov. 17, 24. The election returned a Liberal majority, and the king was obliged to part with his Ultra minister, Villèle, and replace him with

1828, Jan. 3. Count Gay de Martignac, a moderate who, the king hoped, would please neither the Liberals nor the Ultras.

1829, Aug. 6. The **dismissal of Martignac** was followed by a revolutionary step, when the king appointed

Aug. 8. A ministry dominated by the **prince of Polignac,** "Ultra of the Ultras," which for the first time since 1816 did not possess the confidence of the chamber, a departure from the principle of ministerial responsibility, not stated in the constitution of 1814, but now generally accepted.

1830, Mar. 18. The king's act was censured in the answer to the address from the throne, signed by 221 Liberal deputies. Charles X dissolved the chamber.

May 16. New elections returned a majority unfavorable to the king, who, relying on the effect of the conquest of Algiers (June–July, *p. 815*), replied with the

July 26. FIVE "JULY" ORDINANCES, establishing a rigid governmental control of the press, dissolving the chamber, changing the electoral system in an attempt to insure an Ultra majority.

July 26. Adolphe Thiers, journalist and Liberal, drew up a protest against the ordinances on behalf of the Parisian journalists. The Liberal majority of the chamber also prepared a protest. But the dynamo of the **revolution of 1830** was radical Paris, in whose ranks a republican movement had been for some years forming.

July 28. The insurgents raised barricades, took the Hotel de Ville, and were masters of Paris (July 29.) The **marquis de Lafayette,** patriarch of the republican cause, headed the radical movement, which aimed to make him president of a French republic. The Liberal deputies hastily turned to **Louis Philippe,** duke of Orléans and representative of the younger Bourbon line, as the savior of the cause of constitutional monarchy.

July 30. Orléans was offered the lieutenant-generalship of the realm, was accepted by Lafayette on behalf of radical Paris, and was proclaimed *King of the French* by the Liberals

Coronation of Charles X, 1824

sitting as a rump chamber (Aug. 7) under the charter of 1814, revised to insure the perpetuation of the new constitutional régime.

b. THE JULY MONARCHY, 1830–1848

1830–1848. REIGN OF LOUIS PHILIPPE (b. 1773).

1830–1836. Agitation of Republicans and other radicals, who had accepted Louis Philippe as a revolutionary monarch only to discover their mistake too late. The radicals were disillusioned by the cautious policy of the

1830, Nov. 2–1831, Mar. 13. Laffitte ministry with respect to the revolutions in Italy and Poland and by the government's opposition to the demands of the workers.

1831, Mar. 13–1832, May 16. Ministry of Auguste Casimir-Périer, a strong man who managed to restore order, but died in the great cholera epidemic of 1831–1832. Radical agitation and violence continued.

1831, Nov. A large-scale **insurrection of workers at Lyons** was put down with difficulty. Rapid spread of secret societies. Under a régime of press freedom the king was unsparingly attacked in the radical newspapers and mercilessly caricatured (notably by **Honoré Daumier).**

1832, Oct. 11–1834, July 15. Ministry of Marshal Soult, which included the duke of Broglie, Thiers, and Guizot, and represented the more conservative wing of liberalism.

1833, June 28. The **Primary Education Law,** brought in by Guizot. In the interests of safe doctrine it gave the Church (formerly attacked by the Liberals) extensive control of the primary schools.

1834, Apr. Climax of the radical movement in the **great revolts in Paris and Lyons,** repressed with great severity.

1835, Mar.–1836, Feb. Ministries of the duke of Broglie.

1835, July 28. Sanguinary attempt on the life of Louis Philippe by the Corsican radical, **Fieschi.**

1835, Sept. The **September Laws,** including a severe press law and other acts to accelerate the trials of insurgents and assure their conviction. These repressive laws brought the radical movement under control.

1836, Feb.–Sept. First Ministry of Adolphe Thiers.

1836–1839. Ministries of Count Louis Molé, the king's personal friend. Louis Philippe managed to establish something like personal rule by playing off the strong men in the Liberal movement and by appointing weak men to office. But the two groups of the opposition (Right Center: *party of resistance,* led by Guizot; Left Center: *party of movement,* led by Thiers) united and overthrew Molé, who was followed by a short-lived Soult ministry (1839, May–1840, Feb.).

1840, Mar.–Oct. Ministry of Thiers, who led France to the brink of war during the acute Near Eastern crisis *(p. 725).*

1840–1847. Ministry of Soult, in which **François Guizot** was the commanding figure. Guizot became premier in 1847 and remained in power until February 1848. He dominated the political scene through political and electoral manipulation and followed the direction of the king in a conservative policy.

1840–1848. Revival of radicalism and emergence of "utopian" socialism. The period was one of rapid industrial development (600 steam engines in France in 1830, 4853 in 1847;

consumption of coal increased fivefold) and extension of communications (**Railway Act** of 1842: provided for government construction of roadbeds, bridges, tunnels, etc.). All this tended to raise a social question, which was treated by such eminent writers as **Henri de Saint-Simon, Charles Fourier, Étienne Cabet, Louis Blanc** *(p. 571).* The radical movement had been driven underground by the **September Laws,** but continued behind the façade of innocent **friendly societies** and in secret organizations of many kinds. Gradual merging of radical, republican, and socialist movements.

1846–1847. A severe **agricultural and industrial depression** caused widespread unemployment and suffering among the workers and predisposed them to revolutionary action when opportunity offered.

1847–1848. The **parliamentary opposition** to Guizot, led by Thiers and Odilon Barrot, demanding electoral reform (extension of suffrage) and an end of parliamentary corruption (office-holding by members, bribery, etc.), embarked upon an extra-parliamentary **campaign of banquets,** culminating in a great banquet in Paris, arranged for February 22, 1848, but prohibited by the government. The unrest engendered by this demonstration led to street disorders and to the revolution of February.

CULTURAL DEVELOPMENTS

The Romantic period of French literature flourished after the fall of Napoleon. Lyric poetry was revived by **Alphonse Louis-Marie de Lamartine** (1790–1869). The first novels of the Romantic period came from the pens of **Madame de Staël** (1766–1817), **François-René de Chateaubriand** (1768–1848), and **George Sand** (1804–1876); Alfred Victor, Comte **de Vigny** (1797–1863), wrote the first French historical novel (*Cinq-Mars,* 1826), in addition to poems and plays. **Victor-Marie Hugo** (1802–1885) was poet, novelist (*Notre Dame de Paris,* 1831; *Les Misérables,* 1862), and dramatist (*Hernani,* 1830; *Ruy Blas,* 1838). The poet **Alfred de Musset** (1810–1857) also wrote some prose and a few plays. **Alexandre Dumas** the Elder (1802–1870) wrote plays and historical novels of action and suspense (*The Three Musketeers,* 1844; *The Count of Monte Cristo,* 1844–1845; *The Black Tulip,* 1845). **Théophile Gautier** (1811–1872) was the author of short tales as well as novels. Charles Augustin de **Saint-Beuve** (1804–1869) gave up romantic poetry in favor of a *History of Port-Royal* (1840–1860) and numerous critical writings. An interest in historical studies was evident following the Revolution in the work of **Augustin Thierry** (1795–1856), **François Guizot** (1787–1874), **Jules Michelet** (1798–1874).

The novels of **Honoré de Balzac** (1799–1850) provide detailed realistic descriptions of people and places; the novels of both **Prosper Mérimée** (1803–1870) and **Stendhal** (Henri Beyle, 1783–1842) remain partly in the Romantic tradition.

In the field of painting, **Eugène Delacroix** (1798–1863) and **Jean Auguste Ingres** (1780–1867) led the field; **Honoré Daumier** (1808–1879) was acclaimed for his lithographed caricatures. **François Rude** (1784–1855) was the creator of the powerful "Marseillaise" sculpture of the Arc de Triomphe, Paris.

Arrival of Louis Philippe in Paris

George Sand, 1804–1876

Victor-Marie Hugo, 1802–1885

Alexandre Dumas, 1802–1870

Hector Berlioz (1803–1869) composed symphonic music and opera; **Frédéric Chopin** (1810–1849) composed for the piano.

c. THE SECOND REPUBLIC, 1848–1852

1848, Feb. 22. Workers, students, and others gathered to demonstrate in Paris. Barricades went up, and fighting began.

Feb. 23. The king replaced Guizot with Molé, satisfying the middle class but not the workers, who continued the struggle, and by the morning of February 24 had become masters of Paris.

Feb. 24. LOUIS PHILIPPE ABDICATED in favor of his grandson, the count of Paris, but the latter was ignored by a rump meeting of the chamber of deputies into which the Paris mob had filtered; the latter chose a provisional government, dominated by moderate republicans, which fused in turn at the Hôtel de Ville that evening with a more radical slate. The same evening the **republic was proclaimed** at the insistent demand of the mob (for the second time in France). The right wing of the government, dominated by the poet, **Alphonse de Lamartine,** was composed of members of the parliamentary opposition, willing to accept a republic and universal suffrage so long as the republic's program were moderate. The left wing, dominated by **Louis Blanc,** viewed the republic as the vestibule to far-reaching economic and social reforms, along the general lines sketched in Blanc's *Organisation du travail* (1839). The right wing had perforce to make concessions to the radicals, who had armed control of Paris during the days following the revolution.

Feb. 25. The government recognized the **right to work** (government guaranty of work relief) and implemented this promise with the

Feb. 26. Establishment of the national workshops, a large-scale but inefficient work-relief scheme in Paris. It also permitted Louis Blanc to set up

Feb. 28. The **Commission of the Luxem-bourg,** a kind of parliament of workers and employers to discuss questions of common interest, soon, however, deserted by the employers and accomplishing little. Meanwhile the right wing prepared to regain control of the situation by arranging for elections, by bringing troops to Paris, taking steps to render the national guard loyal to the "cause of order," etc. The workers became alarmed, organized

Mar. 17. A **monster radical demonstration** which might have overturned the government but for Louis Blanc, who guided it into moderate channels. Conservatives everywhere now became alarmed by the "specter of communism" which was raising its head.

Apr. 16. A **second demonstration** of workers in Paris completely miscarried.

Apr. 23. The **elections to the national or constituent assembly,** which was to give France a new constitution, were a victory for the moderate Republicans **(Lamartine)** with some 500 seats; the left wing **(Louis Blanc)** had fewer than a hundred; the Legitimists (seeking the return of the Bourbon line) had about a hundred; the Orléanists (supporters of the fallen dynasty of Louis Philippe), about 200.

May 15. In the face of the unfriendly national assembly, the workers prepared a new protest, organized a huge procession, which marched to the hall of the assembly, invaded it during a sitting, overturned the government, set up a new provisional government. The movement quickly collapsed. But the forces of order were by now terrified. They determined to dissolve the national workshops, whose membership had grown to more than a hundred thousand, denounced as "pretorians of revolt." The reply of the Parisian workers was

June 23–26. The **INSURRECTION OF JUNE,** which witnessed the bloodiest street-fighting Europe had seen. The executive commission, vacillating successor of the provisional government, was swept away; **General Louis Cavaignac** was made dictator *pro tempore* and suppressed the movement.

Stendhal, 1783–1842

July–Aug. A **reaction** followed, punctuated by severe press legislation (aiming to eliminate radical newspapers), the suppression of secret societies, and laws for the rigid control of clubs and political associations.

Nov. 4. The assembly completed the **new constitution,** providing for a single chamber and a strong president (with a separation of powers and direct election under universal suffrage). The moderate Republicans' candidate, Cavaignac, was opposed by **Prince Louis Napoleon Bonaparte** (1808–1873), nephew of Napoleon I and pretender to the Napoleonic succession. Louis Napoleon had profited by the flowering of the "Napoleonic legend"; by the publicity attending two personal attempts at a *coup d'état* in France (Strasbourg, 1836; Boulogne, 1840); and by the demand after the June Days for a "strong man" to govern France.

Dec. 10. The **presidential elections** gave Louis Napoleon 5,327,345 votes; his opponents, 1,879,298.

Dec. 20. PRINCE LOUIS NAPOLEON took the oath as **president of the French Republic,** and promptly gave evidence of his "republicanism" by appointing a ministry dominated by Orléanists, headed by **Odilon Barrot,** despite the fact that the majority of the national assembly was Republican. The president had the support of five million electors, the constituent assembly was already obsolete.

1849, Jan. 29. Under the menace of troops quartered in Paris for that purpose, the assembly was obliged to vote its own dissolution, after the budget and certain organic laws completing the constitution should have been passed.

The conservative forces in society—such diverse elements as Legitimists, Orléanists, Bonapartists, some moderate Republicans—were united by means of a central committee (*Union électorale*) to win the elections to the new chamber on a program of "saving society" ("threatened" by the radical elements of 1848) through revival of the influence of the Catholic Church.

Apr.–June. The **French intervention against the Roman Republic** *(p. 670)* was part of this program, connived at by the president. After **Oudinot's** first defeat (Apr. 30), "the honor of the country and of the army" was turned to account as a slogan by the Conservatives, who won a large majority of the seats in the election. Actually the Radical Republicans (the "Mountain") fared much better in the elections than they had anticipated. Their leader, **Alexandre Ledru-Rollin,** was returned in five departments by two million votes.

June 13. He engineered an **abortive revolt in Paris,** which played into the hands of the Conservatives: severe measures were taken against the Radical Republicans—arrests were made in Paris and the provinces, banquets forbidden, mutual benefit societies dissolved. The severity of these measures overshot the mark, stimulated Republican propaganda in turn. The history of the new legislative assembly (*Corps législatif*) now became that of the struggle between the royalist Catholic majority and the Liberal and radical, Republican opposition groups. Louis Napoleon was determined to be captured by neither, to use the struggle for his own ends.

Oct. 31. Although French troops had restored Rome to Pius IX, Louis Napoleon opposed reintroduction of an absolutist régime.

In this he was supported neither by his Catholic majority, nor by his own ministry. He accordingly dismissed Odilon Barrot and summoned **General d'Hautpoul** as premier, with a cabinet "devoted to his own person," in which the dominating figure was **Eugène Rouher,** minister of justice. With a ministry of his own men, the president had in fact established a thinly veiled dictatorship.

1850, Jan. 9. The president extended his control through a government bill, placing school teachers under the control of prefects.

Mar. 15. A **second education bill,** the so-called *Falloux Law* (prepared by the Catholic Legitimist, Vicomte Frédéric de Falloux), was grudgingly acquiesced in by the government, a concession to the Catholic majority. Its effect was to extend greatly Catholic influence in education, providing lower standards for Catholic than for state teachers, giving the clergy participation in school inspection, permitting the substitution of Catholic for lay schools by communes and departments (seeking to avoid the expense of maintaining state schools).

May 31. A further attack on radicalism was made in an **electoral law** requiring three years' residence in one place for all voters, to be attested by a tax receipt or employer's affidavit (affecting above all industrial workers, at once migratory and radical.)

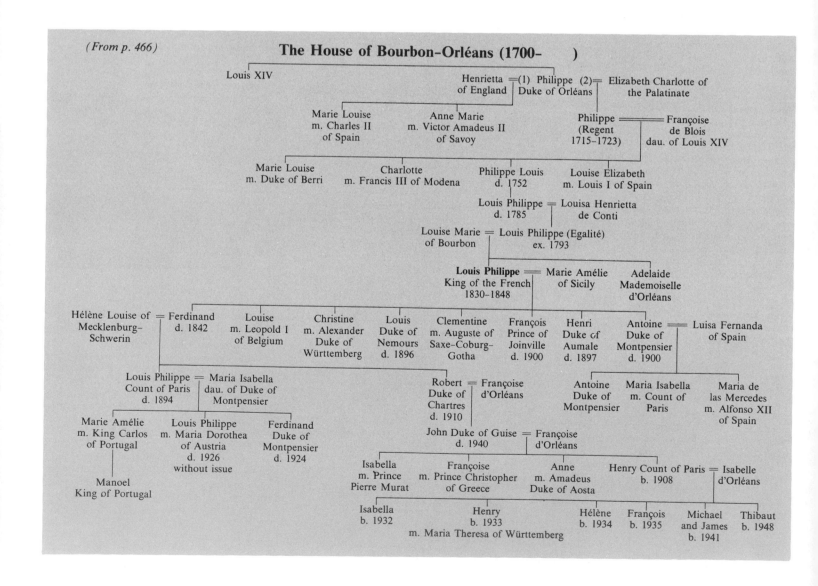

(From p. 466)

The House of Bourbon-Orléans (1700-   )

June 9. Another act **forbade clubs and public meetings,** even for election purposes. Republican propaganda was paralyzed by various other means: newspapers overwhelmed with lawsuits and fines, houses of Republicans searched, Republican civil servants dismissed on the slightest suspicion, etc.

By now, the empire was on the horizon. Was it to be accomplished legitimately or by force? Louis Napoleon turned first to legal methods, the **revision of Article 45 of the constitution,** which forbade two consecutive four-year terms for a president. The president had a clear majority in the assembly, but a vote of three-quarters was essential to revision.

1851, July 15. The proposal to revise was defeated by nearly 100 votes more than were needed. Not without considerable vacillation the president now decided to resort to force to accomplish his objects.

Dec. 2. THE COUP D'ÉTAT. Plans were laid in great secrecy late in November. During the night of December 1–2 (December 2 was the anniversary of the victory of Napoleon I at Austerlitz) **Count Auguste de Morny,** the president's half-brother, had a proclamation printed, informing the people of the dissolution of the assembly, the restoration of universal suffrage (Louis Napoleon was here posing as the friend of the people tricked by an unfriendly legislature), convening the electors for a plebiscite concerning fundamental revision of the constitution. The people of Paris found themselves confronted by the army which occupied the Palais Bourbon, seat of the assembly. Leading deputies, Republican and Royalist (notably generals), prominent journalists, *et al.* were arrested in their beds. Two hundred deputies who met and proclaimed the fall of Louis Napoleon were arrested.

Dec. 3. A group of Republican deputies organized a **popular rising** (Faubourg St. Antoine); barricades went up.

Dec. 4. Troops were hurled against the workers by General **Jacques de Saint-Arnaud,** minister of war; the movement promptly collapsed, but not before many insurgents had been killed and unarmed crowds of pedestrians had been fired upon (Massacre of the Boulevards). Large numbers of arrests followed in Paris and the provinces, where numerous risings were summarily repressed.

Dec. 21. The **plebiscite,** feverishly "prepared" by Morny (now minister of the interior), gave to the president (7,500,000 votes to 640,000) the right to draw up a constitution: the great majority of Frenchmen was weary of parliamentary struggles, alarmed by popular risings, and ready to seek security beneath the authority of a second Napoleonic dictatorship. Repressive measures continued: nearly 20,000 persons were sentenced—10,000 of them to transportation to Algeria.

1852, Jan. 14. The **new constitution** declared the chief of the state "responsible to the nation," but gave him "free and unfettered authority"; he commanded the forces on land and sea, could make war and peace, alone could initiate laws, promulgate laws, and issue decrees and regulations necessary to carry them into effect, etc. The constitution set up a **council of state,** chosen by the president, to formulate laws in secret sessions; a **senate,** with members appointed by the president, sitting in secret, empowered to reject

Arrest of the deputies, December 2, 1851

Barricades go up, December 3, 1851

laws judged unconstitutional, and to modify the constitution through its *consulta,* subject to the consent of the president; a **legislative assembly** (*Corps législatif*), which could accept or reject legislation, but which had no power to introduce or amend bills. Hence effective power rested in the hands of the president, who appointed the members of the council of state and the senate, and who exercised wide influence over the election of members of the legislative assembly through presentation of "official candidates," openly supported by the prefects. The constitution expressly stated: "The emperor governs *by means of* the ministers, the council of state, the senate, and the legislative assembly."

Sept. The president made a **provincial tour.** Under the influence of handpicked prefects, there were frequent cries of **Vive l'Empire!** The empire was the logical and obvious next step.

Nov. 2. The *senatus consultum* ratified by plebiscite (Nov. 21) and promulgated by decree (Dec. 2), declared the empire re-established.

d. THE SECOND EMPIRE: THE AUTHORITARIAN PERIOD, 1852–1860

1852–1870. NAPOLEON III, emperor.
1852, Feb. 17. Repressive measures. The **press** was kept under strict supervision by the police; newspapers could be established only with government permission and were obliged to deposit a large sum (50,000 francs in Paris) as guaranty of good behavior. The minister of the interior discharged and appointed editors, on nomination of the owners; he had power to suspend publication at any time.

Feb. 28. Promotion of material prosperity. The government authorized formation of joint-stock banks issuing long-term credit. The government-subsidized *Crédit foncier* (1852) was obliged to make loans at 5 per cent and later (1854) became a state institution. The *Crédit mobilier* (founded 1852 by the Pereire brothers) was a joint-stock bank whose function it was to initiate and support large companies, participate in public loans, etc. It played a large rôle in the development of railroads, shipping companies, public utilities. Napoleon embarked also upon an active **social policy:** improvement of workers' dwellings, donations to charitable institutions, formation of friendly societies. A huge program of **public works** was initiated, especially the rebuilding of Paris by **Baron Georges Haussmann,** made prefect of the Seine. Streets were widened and new boulevards opened. Paris

Napoleon III, 1852–1870

soon became a new city, enlarged from 12 to 20 arrondissements by the annexation of the suburbs (1860). Its population grew from 1,297,064 in 1851 to 1,825,274 in 1866.

Dec. 25. The **powers of the emperor** were further extended by a *senatus consultum.* He was given authority to conclude treaties of commerce; the budget of every ministry was voted by the legislative assembly, but the subdivision of sums granted was to be settled by imperial decree.

1853, Jan. 30. Marriage of the emperor to Eugénie de Montijo, countess of Téba, daughter of a Spanish grandee. Beautiful and charming, the empress was simple and dignified in manner, but she was impulsive and ignorant, incapable of grasping affairs of state. Her rigorous religious training made her an enemy of liberalism and a leader of the Clerical party at the palace.

Napoleon III continued the policy of **concessions to the Church** initiated by the Falloux law: Catholic missions were developed, government grants were made to churches and religious bodies of a charitable or educational character, Catholic schools were favored and offered increased competition to state schools. Catholics as a whole welcomed and supported the empire as a "heaven-sent blessing," although the Liberal Catholic wing, notably **Count Charles de Montalembert,** urged the importance of a liberal political régime as the only type under which Catholicism could flourish.

1854, Mar. 28. FRANCE DECLARED WAR ON RUSSIA (Crimean War, *p. 726*). The war grew out of a dispute between France and Russia regarding the custody of holy places in Palestine (1850–1853). In part to please the Clericals, in part to assert French claims and maintain French prestige, Napoleon III, mindful of the poor impression made by Louis Philippe's cautious foreign policy, took a strong line and carried Britain with him.

1855, May–Nov. The **Paris International Exposition** bore witness to the technological and economic progress of France. Wages were rising rapidly, though costs of living rose even more. General prosperity. Height of Napoleon's popularity.

1856, Feb.–Apr. Peace congress at Paris *(p. 728)*. France once again the leading power in Europe, enjoying great military prestige.

Mar. 16. Birth of the Prince Imperial, assuring the succession to the throne.

1857. A **railway law** encouraged railway companies through an elaborate system of state guaranties of bonded interest. Railways developed rapidly from 3627 kilometers in 1851 to 16,207 in 1858.

1858, Jan. 14. Attempt of Felice Orsini to assassinate Napoleon and the empress. Two persons were killed and a hundred wounded. This unfortunate episode initiated Napoleon's active participation in the problem of Italy, resting on his interest in oppressed nationalities and national self-determination, as well as the desire to acquire for France her "natural frontiers."

1859, May 12–July 12. WAR OF FRANCE AND PIEDMONT against Austria *(p. 672)*. The war, which took a turn not intended by Napoleon, estranged the Clerical elements in France, but brought France

1860, Mar. 24. The **annexation of** the Piedmontese provinces of **Savoy** and **Nice.**
1860, Jan. 23. Commercial treaty with Great Britain, marking the initiation of a free-trade policy.

e. THE LIBERAL EMPIRE, 1860–1870

1860, Nov. 24. Extension of the powers of the legislature. Napoleon, his popularity shaken by the Italian war and the commercial treaty with Britain, decided to revive parliamentary life, create parties, and exercise his power more indirectly by acting as mediator. The decrees of 1860 empowered the senate and legislative assembly to move and discuss freely a reply to the address from the throne; parliamentary debates were to be fully reported (thus saving governmental prestige in cases of failure by emphasizing the approval of a measure by a parliamentary majority). Both parties seized upon these concessions as an opening wedge to demand wider powers, the eventual revival of parliamentary institutions.

1861, Nov. 4. The **financial powers of the legislature** were next extended. A grandiose program of public works, an extravagant foreign policy had entailed rapidly mounting expenses. The annual deficit was about 100 million francs; by the end of 1861 the floating debt had reached nearly a billion francs. Financial policy was unsettled by the emperor's power to redistribute the estimates for the various departments after the budget had been voted *en bloc* and by his power to authorize supplementary loans on his own responsibility. To restore the confidence of the business world and to oblige the legislature to share imperial responsibility, Napoleon renounced the right to borrow money while the legislature was not in session and agreed that the budget should be voted by sections. But the emperor retained the right to alter the estimates, section by section. This defeated parliamentary control, gave rise to constant demands for an enlargement of the chamber's financial powers.

An opposition coalition rapidly grew up in the country, composed of such diverse elements as Catholics (outraged by the papal policy of Napoleon), Legitimists, Orléanists, Protectionists, and even Republicans—republican opposition had been reborn in the legislature when "the Five" (Emile Ollivier, Louis Darimon, Jacques Hénon, Louis Picard, Jules Favre) were returned in the elections of 1857 and by-elections of 1858.

Napoleon's position was rapidly undermined during the sixties by a series of failures in foreign policy.

1861–1867. THE MEXICAN EXPEDITION (*p. 803*). Owing to the refusal of the revolutionary Juarez government to meet its obligations, France, Britain, and Spain decided (**convention of London,** Oct. 13, 1861) to force fulfillment of these obligations. They all landed troops at Vera Cruz (Dec. 1861), but the British and Spanish soon withdrew when they recognized Napoleon's more far-reaching plans, viz. to establish a Catholic Latin empire in Mexico while the United States was engaged in the Civil War. French troops took Mexico City (June 1863) and proclaimed Archduke Maximilian (brother of Francis Joseph I

French troops take Mexico City, June 1863

of Austria) as emperor. Maximilian was unable to maintain himself without French support. By 1866 the United States was vigorously demanding the withdrawal of the French and Napoleon was in dire need of his troops because of European complications. He therefore deserted Maximilian, who refused to abdicate (1866, Dec.). He was captured and executed by the Mexicans (June 19, 1867).

1862, Sept. 25. An attempt to conciliate the Papacy by warning the Italian government against a march on Rome succeeded only in estranging the Italian government.

1863. Napoleon's efforts to intervene against Russia in the **Polish Insurrection** *(p. 708)* broke down through the lukewarm attitude of the British and Austrians and through Prussia's support of Russia. The effect of the policy was to estrange Russia, with which power France had been on close terms of friendship since 1857.

1864. The September Convention. Reversing his attitude on the Roman question, Napoleon agreed to withdraw his troops from Rome within two years in return for a promise from the Italian government not to attack papal territory. This move outraged French Catholic opinion. The pope issued the encyclical *Quanta cura* and the *Syllabus of Errors(p. 676)* which were in part an attack on the French government (e.g. condemnation of the supremacy of the nation and of universal suffrage). Napoleon at once forbade publication of the *Syllabus* in France, and thereby further aroused the ire of the clergy.

These failures led to a more outspoken attitude on the part of the parliamentary opposition, which, in the elections of 1863, had polled a vote of almost two million and had returned 35 deputies to the chamber, of whom 17 were Republicans. Thiers denounced the extravagance in Mexico (Jan. 11, 1864) and demanded "the indispensable liberties" which became the slogan of his group.

1866, Mar. More than 40 members of the government majority in the chamber broke away and formed a **Third Party** which asked the emperor "to further the natural development of the great Act of 1860."

July 3. Prussian victory over Austria at Sadowa *(p. 690)*. The French, who had expected a long war ending with French mediation and compensation, regarded the victory as a national humiliation. But the army was not ready and Napoleon's will was crippled by physical suffering occasioned by bladder stones. He failed to mobilize and acquiesced in the formation of the North German Confederation. His belated attempts to secure compensation from Prussia in the Rhineland, Luxemburg, or Belgium (1866-1867) failed completely and left him badly discredited.

1867, Jan. 19. The **right of interpellation** was granted the chamber, but every interpellation required the previous approval of four committees, so that the majority could forestall undesired questions.

Mar. 12. The senate demanded and was accorded the **right to examine the projected laws** in detail (instead of merely passing on their constitutionality) and to return them to the legislative assembly for further action. Thus the senate became a collaborator in legislation, though a reactionary one.

Nov. 3. Napoleon again alienated the Liberals and Republicans by sending troops to crush the Garibaldians before they could attack Rome (Mentana, *p. 673)*.

1867-1870. ALLIANCE NEGOTIATIONS WITH AUSTRIA AND ITALY. These were part of the preparation for ultimate conflict with Prussia (regarded as inevitable after the Luxemburg affair of 1867, *p. 692)*. **Napoleon** met Francis Joseph at Salzburg (1867, Aug. 18-21) and Francis Joseph paid a visit to Paris (Oct.). After the reorganization of the French army had begun (**army law of January 1868** adding 100,000 men and providing for complete rearmament), negotiations were initiated first with Austria, then with Italy, leading in 1869 to a draft treaty and to an exchange of letters between the sovereigns. The main obstacles to a firm agreement were the unwillingness of the Austrians to commit themselves to immediate action in a dispute between France and Prussia on a purely German issue, and the insistence of the Italians on the evacuation of Rome by the French. Nevertheless the French government mistakenly proceeded on the supposition that in case of war with Prussia, Austria and Italy could be relied upon to participate.

By 1868 there had been a marked **revival of republicanism** and **radicalism.** Strikes had been permitted by an act of May 1864 and trade unions, though still illegal, were connived at after an act of March 25, 1868. The result was a growing epidemic of strikes and a wide spread of trade-unionism, with a corresponding strengthening of the republican sentiment. By 1868 the enemies of the imperial régime could be silenced only by candid concessions.

1868, May 11. A **liberal press law** made possible establishment of a newspaper by simple declaration; eliminated administrative interference in the form of warning, suspension, and suppression.

June 11. Limited right of public meeting was granted, each meeting to be held, however, in a closed building subject to supervision by a police officer empowered to dissolve it. Republican newspapers promptly multiplied; workers met to discuss economic problems, to end in attacking the political régime.

1869, May 23, 24. Parliamentary elections gave the government 4,438,000 votes to 3,355,000 for the opposition; the new chamber included 30 Republicans.

June 28. The Third Party interpellated the

Maximilian (1832–1867), emperor of Mexico

government, demanded the creation of a responsible ministry. With the co-operation of 40 deputies of the Left, the "116" of the Third Party had a majority. The emperor had to yield or embark on a struggle with at least one-half of his subjects.

July 12. He adopted the program of the 116. By decree of the senate (Sept. 6), the **new régime** was initiated: the legislative assembly was given the right to propose laws, criticize and vote the budget, choose its own officers; the senate became a deliberative body with public sessions, had the right to discuss laws voted by the assembly and send them back for consideration; ministers were declared responsible but were to "depend on the emperor alone"—an equivocal position casting doubt on how far the new régime could be considered "parliamentary."

Dec. 28. The Third Party pressed Napoleon for clarification of this situation, and he entrusted their chief, **Emile Ollivier,** with the formation of a "homogeneous cabinet, representative of the majority of the legislative assembly." Ollivier was faced by divisions within his own party, by growing revolutionary agitation in the country. **Leon Gambetta's** Republican **program of Belleville** demanded universal suffrage, freedom of the press, right of meeting, of combination, trial by jury for all political offenses, separation of Church and State, suppression of the standing army. Labor was rapidly organizing in trade unions, on one hand, and its more radical elements in the Marxist **First International.** This was twice dissolved in France by official action (Mar. 1868; June 1870). France was swept by an epidemic of strikes.

1870, Jan. 10. When the Republican journalist, **Victor Noir,** was shot by Prince Pierre Bonaparte, cousin of the emperor, his funeral was the occasion for a demonstration against the empire of some hundred thousand people. Ollivier's problem was no longer that of converting a liberal into a constitutional monarchy, but of saving the empire by concessions. Sweeping constitutional reforms followed:

Apr. 20. The senate was made an **upper house,** sharing legislative power with the assembly; constituent authority was taken from the senate and given to the people (no constitutional change was to be made without a plebiscite). The Bonapartists then sought a plebiscite (to strengthen the hand of the emperor): the nation was asked "whether it approved the liberal reforms effected in the constitution since 1860 . . . whether it ratified the *senatus consultum* of April 20, 1870." Battle was joined between empire and republic (Right Republicans, however, as the *Gauche ouverte,* supporting the government).

May 8. The **plebiscite** gave 7,358,786 "ayes," 1,571,939 "noes"; the Napoleonic empire seemed to have won new strength by this sweeping triumph. Within four months it was to be swept away by the war of 1870 (*p. 694*).

f. THE THIRD REPUBLIC, 1870–1914

1870, Sept. 2. The **capitulation of Napoleon III at Sedan** (*p. 695*) was a blow the empire was unable to survive.

Sept. 4. When the news became general in Paris, the mob invaded the Palais Bourbon and obliged the reluctant members of the rump of the legislative assembly to join in proclaiming the fall of the empire. In accordance with accepted revolutionary ritual, the **republic was proclaimed** at the Hôtel de Ville after a provisional **government of national defense** had been set up, of which **Gambetta** was the outstanding member, **General Louis Trochu** (who had recently sworn to die defending the Napoleonic dynasty) the president. The new government seemed faced by a hopeless task—winning a war already lost.

Sept. 19. After Sedan two German armies swept on and invested Paris. The government devoted itself to a desperate defense of the country, sent a delegation to Tours to organize resistance in the provinces, which was pres-

The republic is proclaimed at the Hôtel de Ville, Sept. 4, 1870

ently joined by Gambetta, who escaped from besieged Paris in a balloon and virtually governed France (beyond Paris) in the succeeding months.

The populace of Paris was disgusted by the inactivity of Trochu, who possessed a force superior in size to the investing army; was further outraged by the "treasonable"

Oct. 27. Surrender of General Achille Bazaine at Metz, with 173,000 men.

Oct. 31. This discontent crystallized in a Paris *putsch* of **socialists and radicals,** aiming to establish a commune in the tradition of 1792 and carry on the war to the finish. The movement collapsed. By January the Parisian populace was reduced to a miserable state. With only eight days' supply of food remaining, **1871, Jan. 28. Paris capitulated.** The armistice agreement yielded the forts to the Germans, provided for an indemnity of 200,000,000 francs, and disarmed the troops of the line in the city. By the armistice Bismarck also agreed to permit election of a representative assembly to determine whether the war should be continued or on what terms peace should be made.

Feb. 8. Elections were held.

Feb. 13. The national assembly met at Bordeaux. From Tours Gambetta had organized armed resistance in the provinces, with the aid of a young mining engineer, **Charles de Freycinet;** the obstinate fighting of these

hastily improvised forces amazed the German command. But by mid-January this resistance had been substantially crushed, the country was exhausted, the majority of Frenchmen wanted peace. Under these conditions only the **Radical Republicans** and **Socialists** wanted to continue the war "to the last ditch." Hence the country elected an assembly two-thirds of whom were conservatives.

Feb. 16. The assembly elected **Adolphe Thiers,** who had won a reputation as the Cassandra of imperial collapse, **chief of the executive power.**

Feb. 28. Thiers introduced the **terms of a peace treaty** negotiated with Bismarck by **Jules Favre** and himself providing for the **cession of Alsace and a part of Lorraine,** an indemnity of five billion francs, an army of occupation to remain until the indemnity should have been paid. The terms were hotly opposed by the representatives of Alsace and Lorraine, by Louis Blanc, Gambetta, Georges Clemenceau, and others; but accepted, 546 to 107 (Mar. 1).

May 10. The definitive **treaty of peace was signed at Frankfurt,** embodying the terms accepted March 1, but with certain territorial rectifications, etc. Thiers proclaimed his own neutrality in the face of party division within the assembly and urged the necessity of the co-operation of all in the task of national recovery (**pact of Bordeaux,** Feb. 19). The

assembly adjourned (Mar. 11) to meet again at Versailles (Mar. 20).

Mar.-May. THE PARIS COMMUNE. Mar. 1-3. Radical Paris, which had undergone the fruitless suffering of four months' siege, felt itself further humiliated by the entry of German troops into the capital and by the peace terms accepted by the national assembly; it was alarmed by the composition of the assembly, whose majority was obviously unfriendly to the republic. Discontent spread rapidly. The national guard, which the Germans had failed to disarm by the armistice of January 28, appointed a central committee, seized cannon belonging to the regular army, prepared for the eventualities of conflict.

Mar. 18. Thiers sent troops of the line to seize the cannon; they fraternized with the crowd, refused to fire; the mob seized and executed Generals **Lecomte** and **Thomas;** the troops retired, leaving Paris in the hands of the radicals. Election of a municipal council (the **Commune of 1871**) was called by the central committee of the national guard for March 26. The **Commune** included Moderate Republicans, Radical Republicans (of the 1793 Jacobin tradition), followers of Proudhon, followers of Blanqui, members of the **First International.** A body of such diverse tendencies had no clear-cut program, "socialist" or otherwise. It sought to decentralize France by

Fighting on the Place Pigalle during the Paris Commune (*Bloody Week, May 21–28, 1871*)

enlarging the powers of municipalities; to substitute the national guard for the standing army; to separate Church and State **(law of April 2)**. But opportunity for carrying through a legislative program was cut short by the armed struggle with the government of the national assembly at Versailles.

Apr. 2. The Versailles troops took the offensive, defeated the troops of the Commune repeatedly, entered Paris, reduced the city in the face of desperate but unorganized resistance behind barricades in the **Bloody Week** (May 21–28). Hostages taken by the Communards, including **Archbishop Darboy** of Paris, had been executed. The victors replied by visiting summary and sanguinary punishment through courts-martial on a large but indeterminate number of prisoners; others in large numbers were deported or imprisoned.

1871–1873. THE MONARCHIST OFFENSIVE. The Monarchist majority of the national assembly, summoned to answer the question of war or peace, was determined to settle the question of a new régime for France before separating. The Monarchists were divided: of those originally elected, some 200 were **Legitimists** (supporters of the "legitimate" Bourbon line and of its pretender, the **count of Chambord**), the same number **Orléanists** (supporters of the **count of Paris,** grandson of Louis Philippe), some thirty **Bonapartists.** Legitimists and Orléanists would hear nothing of a restoration of the "parvenu" Napoleonic dynasty.

1871, July 6. The **count of Chambord** alienated both the Orléanists and the country by declaring categorically that he must rule under the white flag of the Bourbons. Meanwhile Republicans gained ground in by-elections to the national assembly.

Aug. 31. Thiers's title became *President of the Republic* by the **Law Rivet-Vitet,** which, however, also declared that the assembly possessed constituent powers. Thiers, originally a staunch Orléanist, was rallying to the *conservative republic* as a *pis aller* ("the government which divides us least"). The Monarchist majority permitted him to accomplish the patriotic task of paying the German indemnity (through two government loans, June 21, 1871, July 15, 1872), bringing with it **evacuation of French territory** (the last German soldier crossed the frontier September 16, 1873). They then condemned the government of Thiers as insufficiently "conservative" (vote of 360 to 344).

1873, May 24. Thiers promptly resigned, and **Marshal Marie Edmé MacMahon** was elected president at the same session. MacMahon, soldier by profession, monarchist by predilection, neophyte in politics, was to prepare the way for the restoration.

Aug. 5. The count of Chambord and the count of Paris became reconciled, and it was agreed that the latter should succeed the former, who was childless.

Oct. 27. The plan foundered when the count of Chambord insisted once again on the white flag.

Nov. 20. To give itself time to reform its forces, the Monarchist majority conferred the powers of president on MacMahon for seven years **(Law of the Septennate).**

1875. THE CONSTITUTION OF 1875. After prolonged discussion of various constitutional projects, a **Law on the Organization of the Public Powers** was introduced.

Jan. 21. Henri Wallon proposed an amendment: "The president of the republic is elected by an absolute majority of the votes of the senate and the chamber of deputies sitting together as the national assembly. He is chosen for seven years. He is eligible for re-election." The term *republic* was crucial: acceptance of the amendment meant acceptance of the republic. The *impasse* caused by the failure of the Monarchists had resulted in some disintegration in their ranks.

Jan. 30. The **Wallon amendment was adopted** by one vote—353 to 352. The **Law on the Organization of the Public Powers** was accepted as a whole (Feb. 25); the **Law on the Organization of the Senate** had been accepted (Feb. 24). A **Law on the Relation of the Public Powers** (passed July 16) completed the so-called **Constitution of 1875.** The executive was a president (who was not to be a member of the legislative body) elected according to the Wallon amendment, possessed of the usual executive powers (command of the army and navy, right to choose civil officials and military officers, etc.), but requiring a counter-signature for each of his acts by the relevant minister. The ministers were declared responsible, each for his own acts, together for the general policy of the government. The senate was to have 300 members, 225 chosen for nine years, on the basis of a complicated and indirect system of election, 75 named by the national assembly (later by the senate) for life (senators for life were discontinued in 1884). The senate shared the right to initiate legislation (except finance laws) with the chamber of deputies, whose members were elected by universal, direct, manhood suffrage. The chamber could be dissolved only by the president, with the consent of the senate. The seat of the government was fixed at Versailles, reflecting fear of Republican Paris.

Apr.–May. The famous **war scare** during which the duke of Decazes, French foreign minister, secured the intervention of Britain and Russia at Berlin *(p. 731).*

President MacMahon, 1873–1879

1877, May 16. CRISIS OF *SEIZE MAI.* The national assembly came to an end and the new senate and chamber met for the first time (1876, Mar. 8). The senate had a Conservative majority, the chamber was overwhelmingly Republican. In the next quarter-century the new republican institutions were to be repeatedly attacked by their enemies of the Right. The first test came in the affair of the *Seize Mai* when MacMahon, irritated by what he considered inadequate opposition of the premier, **Jules Simon,** to the anti-clerical attitude of the Left, forced Simon to resign. Had the power of dismissal of ministries been conceded to the president, the chamber's control of ministries would have disappeared, and the president would have been given the powers held by Louis Napoleon, 1848–1851 *(pp. 652, 653).*

June 19. A new cabinet, headed by the Orléanist **duke of Broglie,** was given a vote of "no confidence" by the chamber, 363 to 158; MacMahon dissolved the chamber with the consent of the senate (the only dissolution in the history of the Third Republic).

Oct. 14, 28. In the elections, despite vigorous governmental pressure, the Republicans lost only 36 seats.

Nov. 19. The Broglie ministry was forced to retire by an adverse majority (312 to 205); its successor, the presidential **Rochebouët ministry** (Nov. 24) fared the same.

Dec. 13. MacMahon was forced to retreat, named **Jules Dufaure** to head a ministry with the confidence of the chamber. The principle of ministerial responsibility had won over that of the personal power of the president.

1879, Jan. 5. In the **senatorial election** the Republicans gained 58 seats; faced by a hostile majority in the senate and chamber.

Jan. 30. MacMahon resigned (although his term of office had more than a year to run), and was succeeded by a Conservative Republican, **Jules Grévy.**

1879–1887. PRESIDENCY OF JULES GRÉVY. The Conservative Republicans **(Opportunists),** in power from 1879 to 1885, proceeded to a series of **anti-clerical laws:**

1880, Mar. 29, 30. Two decrees (1) enjoining all non-authorized **religious associations** to regularize their position within three months; (2) ordering dissolution and **dispersion of the Jesuits** within three months and dissolution of all religious teaching associations within six months (giving effect to the decree of 1762 and later legislation).

July 11. A law providing virtually **full amnesty to the Communards** of 1871.

1881, Mar.–May. French occupation of Tunis (treaty of Bardo, May 12), largely the work of Jules Ferry (1832–1893); important as marking the emergence of French imperialism and the expansion of the second French Empire (pp. *733, 817).*

1882, Mar. 29. Primary education law, making education from six to thirteen free, obligatory, and "neutral" (i.e. public schools were to give no religious education).

1884, July 27. Law re-establishing divorce substantially as it had been permitted under the civil code (divorce had been abolished by the law of May 8, 1816).

Further important legislation included

1884, Mar. 21. The **Trade-Union Act** legalizing unions forbidden by the *Loi Chapelier* (of

1791) and subsequent legislation, but tolerated since 1868. By this time the **labor movement,** temporarily in eclipse after the Commune, had begun to revive and to veer in a Marxian direction. In 1876 **Jules Guesde** had returned from exile and had begun to propagate Marxian ideas. At the **third congress of French workers** (Marseilles) in October 1879 the Guesdists had won the day over the more idealistic co-operative socialists and steps were taken to organize a socialist political party, the *Fédération du Parti des Travailleurs Socialistes de France.* In the party the more moderate group **(Possibilists)** were at first dominant. In 1882 the Guesdists withdrew and formed the *Parti Ouvrier Français,* while the Possibilists reorganized the majority as the *Parti Ouvrier Socialiste Révolutionnaire Français.*

1884–1885. French advance in Tonkin, resulting in war with China *(p. 848)* and downfall of the second Ferry ministry (1883–1885).

1886–1889. THE BOULANGER CRISIS. This arose from widespread discontent with the Conservative Republican régime. The Radical Republicans wished to democratize further the constitution and to separate the Church and State; the workers were suffering from depression and demanding state action in their behalf; the Monarchists continued to hope for an eventual restoration. The **elections of 1885** were a victory for the Right (202 seats as against 80 in 1881), although the various Republican groups still had 372 seats.

1886, Jan. 4. General Georges Boulanger became minister of war in the Freycinet cabinet. He was the friend and protégé of **Georges Clemenceau,** dominant figure among the Radical Republicans, who had imposed Boulanger on Freycinet. Boulanger won popularity in the army through various reforms (improvement of soldiers' food and living conditions, etc.); among the people by frequent and impressive appearances in public, notably on July 14, 1886. He was celebrated in poem and song, became a national figure with the **Schnaebelé incident** *(p. 735)* and the attacks of the German press, and was greeted as the incarnation of the *révanche.*

1887, May 18. When **Boulanger** left office (fall of the Goblet cabinet), his popularity only increased. The government became alarmed, exiled Boulanger to Clermont-Ferrand as commandant of the 13th Army Corps. The **Wilson scandal** shook the prestige of the republic and offered Boulanger an opportunity to widen his contacts. Daniel Wilson, son-in-law of President Grévy, was discovered to have been trafficking in medals of the Legion of Honor: Grévy, although not guilty of complicity, was forced to resign the presidency (Dec. 2). He was succeeded by **Marie François Sadi-Carnot.**

1887–1894. Presidency of Sadi-Carnot, an honest but undistinguished politician, grandson of Lazare Carnot, "organizer of victory" in 1793.

During the Wilson crisis, Boulanger maintained relations with the Radical Republicans and made contact with the Orléanist leaders (*Nuits historiques,* Nov. 28–30, 1887)—apparently ready to satisfy his ambitions by whatever path offered. Boulanger, although ineligible for the chamber, permitted his candidacy to be posed repeatedly as a test of his popularity.

1888, Mar. 27. The government, alarmed, put him on the retired list; he was now eligible for the chamber, to which he was promptly elected (Apr. 15). He initiated a vigorous **campaign for revision of the constitution** (in what sense was not specified); demanded dissolution of the chamber as an essential preliminary; resigned from the chamber (July 12) and was returned in three constituencies simultaneously (Aug. 19).

1889, Jan. 27. Boulanger won a striking victory in Paris. It was believed he would march on the Elysée Palace that night and make himself master of France. But he failed to seize the opportunity to make himself dictator and his popularity rapidly declined. The government prepared to have him tried for treason by the senate; and he fled into exile (Apr. 8), where he eventually committed suicide on his mistress' grave in Brussels (1891, Sept. 30).

July 17. Meanwhile a law was adopted forbidding **multiple candidacies.** The general elections of 1889 were a triumph for the Republicans, a crushing defeat for the Boulangists.

1890 ff. The Ralliement. The Boulangist fiasco was a blow to the monarchists and their ally, the Church. **Pope Leo XIII,** discouraged by the failures of the monarchists, turned to a policy of conciliation of the republic.

1890, Nov. 12. Charles Cardinal Lavigerie, primate of Africa, in a famous toast at a banquet to French naval officers at Algiers **(Algiers Toast),** declared it the duty of all citizens to "rally" to the support of the existing form of government, once that form of government had been accepted by the people. This so-called *ralliement* to the republic was vigorously combated by Monarchists and Clericals on the one-hand, and by Radical Republicans and Socialists on the other. But the pope was influenced, notably by the international situation *(p. 677),* to espouse Lavigerie's policy.

1891, May 15. The encyclical *Rerum novarum* (on the condition of the workers) attempted to win the support of both Radical and Conservative Republicans through a more liberal (though by no means radical) statement of papal views on the social question; more spe-

Ferdinand de Lesseps, 1805–1894

cific support to the movement came in the encyclical *Inter innumeras* (Feb. 16, 1892), which declared that a government once established was legitimate. Despite opposition, the *ralliement* introduced a new spirit into the relations of Church and State in France: the period of the **Méline ministry** (1896–1898) has been termed "the Golden Age of Clericalism." Eventually the *ralliement* foundered in the struggle over Dreyfus *(p. 660).*

July. Visit of a French squadron to Cronstadt. Beginning of the **Franco-Russian Alliance** negotiations *(p. 736).*

1892–1893. THE PANAMA SCANDAL. Attracted by the name of **Ferdinand de Lesseps,** builder of the Suez Canal, and president of the Panama Company (*Compagnie du Canal Interocéanique*), French investors, from peasant to capitalist, had contributed to the Panama Canal project to the extent of 1,500,000,000 francs. The company collapsed (1889, Feb.) as a result of corruption and mismanagement, but despite the uproar, it was nearly four years before legal action was taken against Lesseps and his associates (1892, Nov. 19). In the course of a parliamentary investigation and two trials, it was revealed that the company had made lavish distributions to the press and to a certain number of deputies and senators (in the interest of securing their support for parliamentary authorization of a stock lottery). The company's intermediary was **Baron Jacques Reinach,** Jewish banker of German origin, who was found dead the day after he was summoned for trial. The revelations caused widespread consternation, increased by knowledge that the government had attempted to silence the whole affair.

1893, Feb. 9. Ferdinand de Lesseps and some of his associates were condemned by the court

President Grévy, 1879–1887

of appeal to pay large fines and serve prison sentences, but the decree of the court was set aside by the *cour de cassation* (June 15) on the grounds that the three years under the criminal statute of limitations had expired. Of the numerous senators, deputies, and others tried before the court of assizes, only three were found guilty, one (Baïhaut) on his own confession that he had received 375,000 francs.

Further development of **socialism** and the **labor movement.** In 1890 a further split in the ranks of the Possibilists had taken place, precipitated by **Jean Allemane,** who criticized the majority for accepting public office and co-operating with the bourgeoisie. The new faction took the name *Parti Ouvrier Socialiste Révolutionnaire.* With the progress of the industrial revolution and the consequent growth of the proletariat, the social question became ever more acute. Collisions between workers and the forces of "order" became more and more frequent. In the **Massacre of Fourmies** (1891, May 1) the troops fired on a crowd of demonstrating workers and killed women and children, causing a great sensation. The government of the Conservative Republicans continued lukewarm in the matter of social reform, with the result that extremist elements in the labor movement became more and more active. The **anarchists** (disciples of **Michael Bakunin** and **Prince Peter Kropotkin**) began a long series of outrages (dynamiting and assassination). In March 1892 a number of bombings were carried out by **François Ravachol,** an anarchist.

Oct. Visit of a Russian squadron to Toulon, followed by the conclusion (1893, Dec.–1894, Jan.) of the **Franco-Russian Alliance** *(p. 736).*

Dec. 9. Auguste Vaillant, another anarchist, exploded a bomb in the chamber of deputies.

1894, June 24. President Carnot was stabbed at Lyons by an Italian anarchist, **Santo Caserio.**

Meanwhile, the various socialist parties had begun to concert action. In 1893 they had elected some 50 deputies. The trade unions, which had developed rapidly after the law of 1884, organized nationally in the *Fédération des Syndicats* (by trades) and in the *Fédération des Bourses du Travail* (each representing the different trades in one locality). Under the influence of anarchism

1894. The **Trade-Union Congress at Nantes** adopted the principle of the **general strike.**

1894, June 27–1895, Jan. 17. Presidency of Jean Casimir-Perier, who resigned in disgust.

1895. The **Trade-Union Congress** at Limoges organized the *Confédération Générale du Travail* (C.G.T.) with a program of direct action, seeking to destroy the capitalist régime and the state by means of the general strike and to prepare for this eventual cataclysm through local strikes, boycotts, and sabotage (a theory later given classic formulation by **Georges Sorel** in his *Reflections on Violence,* 1908). By the end of the century the workers' organizations—radical revolutionaries harking back to Auguste Blanqui; socialists of various stamps; anarchists; syndicalists—constituted a real power in the country, which was, however, dissipated by divergences of view and mutual antagonism.

1895–1899. Presidency of Félix Faure (1841–1899), prosperous and conservatively minded

business man and politician. During his presidency the **ministry of Félix Méline** marked the last flowering of conservative, protectionist, clerical republicanism.

1894–1906. THE DREYFUS AFFAIR. Captain Alfred Dreyfus, probationer (*stagiaire*) of the general staff of the army, was arrested (1894, Oct. 15) charged with treason. He was tried by a court-martial *in camera,* condemned (Dec. 22), degraded, deported to Devil's Island in French Guiana. The evidence was a list of military documents (the *bordereau*), apparently submitted by a treasonable member of the general staff to the German military attaché, later purloined from the latter's mail by a French spy and submitted to the French intelligence service. The latter's handwriting experts disagreed as to whether the writing was that of Dreyfus; further "secret" evidence, subsequently shown to be irrelevant or forged, was also introduced and was said to have been considered conclusive. The presence of treason in the general staff had been aired in the press and had excited public opinion; the honor of the army seemed to be engaged; a victim was needed, and Dreyfus was the only one to whom the evidence pointed at all. Moreover, the real culprit was a friend of a member of the general staff, **Major Hubert Henry,** who sought to protect him. Dreyfus was a Jew, intensely disliked by most of his conservative colleagues of the general staff, who were Catholic, royalist, anti-Semitic. Dreyfus, wealthy and ambitious, son of an Alsatian patriot who had opted for France after the cession of 1871, apparently had no motive for treason.

1896, Mar. Colonel Georges Picquart, new chief of the intelligence service, had delivered to him a second document (the *petit bleu*), a card of the type used in the Paris pneumatic postal service. The card was addressed to a former member of the general staff, **Major Count Walsin-Esterhazy,** then stationed at Rouen, French by birth, former officer in the Austrian army, in the papal zouaves, in the foreign legion; *débauché,* gambler, *arriviste.*

Aristide Briand, 1862–1932

Picquart compared a specimen of Esterhazy's writing with that of the *bordereau,* concluded they were identical, submitted his evidence to General Gonse (second in command of the general staff), was told to say nothing of the matter—that the affair could not be reopened. Picquart was transferred to a frontier post in Tunis.

1897, Nov. 15. Mathieu Dreyfus, brother of Alfred, discovered independently that the *bordereau* was in Esterhazy's writing, and demanded the latter's trial.

1898, Jan. 11. Esterhazy was tried by a military tribunal, and triumphantly acquitted.

Jan. 13. The novelist **Émile Zola** promptly published an open letter (*J'accuse*) to the president of the republic, denouncing by name the members of the general staff associated with the condemnation of Dreyfus.

Feb. 23. Zola was tried and condemned to one year imprisonment.

It was presently discovered that a decisive document in the secret Dreyfus *dossier* had been forged by **Colonel** (formerly Major) **Henry,** now chief of the intelligence service.

Aug. 30. When Henry admitted the forgery (only the first of a series to be discovered), **General de Boisdeffre,** chief of the general staff, resigned. Henry was imprisoned and committed suicide the next day. A rehearing for Dreyfus was promptly sought by his wife (Sept. 3).

Sept.–Nov. The **Fashoda crisis** *(p. 739)* brought France and England to the brink of war.

By this time France was divided into two camps, and the *Affair* had taken on a profound political complexion: **Dreyfusards** (those interested in preserving the republic) ranged themselves against **anti-Dreyfusards** (the army and a large body of Royalists and Catholics—forces interested in a restoration of the monarchy). A violent campaign in the press, both Nationalist and Republican followed. Street clashes were frequent. The various socialist parties, who had at first considered the *Affair* a mere "bourgeois" quarrel," now saw the republic threatened.

Oct. 16. In a mass meeting in Paris the socialists concerted forces to defend the republic against its "attackers."

1899, Feb. 16. The sudden **death of President Faure,** opponent of a retrial for Dreyfus, was followed by the election of the colorless **Émile Loubet,** considered a friend of revision.

1899–1906. Presidency of Émile Loubet.

1899, June 3. The *cour de cassation* (highest court of appeal) set aside the condemnation of Dreyfus, and summoned a court-martial at Rennes.

Sept. 9. Dreyfus was again found guilty, this time with "extenuating circumstances"; he was condemned to ten years' imprisonment.

Sept. 19. By presidential decree, he was pardoned—first act of pacification of the **ministry of René Waldeck-Rousseau,** formed June 22, 1899, to bring internal peace to the country. The Dreyfusards painfully accumulated new evidence, and Dreyfus finally asked a rehearing. On July 12, 1906 the *cour de cassation* set aside the judgment of the court-martial at Rennes, declaring it "wrongful" and "erroneous." The government decorated Dreyfus (July 13) and raised him to the rank of major.

1901-1905. SEPARATION OF CHURCH AND STATE. The outcome of the Dreyfus affair was a victory for the republic, a defeat for its enemies (monarchists, the clergy, the army). In matters affecting the Church, Waldeck-Rousseau wished to remain faithful to the Napoleonic **concordat** *(p. 618)*, but was a proponent of stringent regulation (not suppression) of religious associations, many of whose members had intervened on the side of the anti-Dreyfusards.

1901, July 1. The result was the **Associations Law,** whose terms relative to religious "congregations" were most important: (1) no congregation could be formed without a law defining its scope and activity; (2) all congregations lacking authorization, or which parliament failed subsequently to authorize, were to be dissolved. Since the treatment of congregations was to depend on the will of the legislature, the general elections were all-important. The elections were a victory for the Radical Republicans and Socialists.

The **Republican bloc** (formed in 1900 to defend the republic against its anti-Dreyfusard opponents) was determined to proceed with vigor against the Church, viewing the Associations Laws as a *pis aller.*

1902, June 2. **Waldeck-Rousseau,** unsympathetic with extreme measures, **resigned,** an unprecedented act for a premier who possessed the confidence of the majority of the chamber. His successor was **Émile Combes,** known for his probity and anti-clerical convictions. His ministry proceeded to enforce the Associations Law with vigor: closing some 3000 unauthorized schools until they should apply for, and receive, authorization; preparing 54 bills refusing the applications for authorization of as many male congregations (all 54 bills were passed by parliament, 1903, Mar.); etc.

1904, July 7. All teaching by congregations was forbidden by a further law, such congregations to be suppressed within ten years.

Relations of the French government with the Papacy were rapidly embittered.

1904, Mar. **President Loubet's visit to the king of Italy,** the pope's enemy, irritated the papal government, which sent to the Catholic powers an official protest against this offense to papal dignity.

May 21. The French ambassador to the Vatican was recalled.

Nov. Combes, who thus far had wished to preserve the concordat of 1801, introduced a bill for the **separation of Church and State.** It was not Combes's bill (his ministry came to an end, January 19, 1905), but that ably defended by **Aristide Briand,** reporter of the chamber's committee on the separation of Church and State, that was carried, the law being promulgated December 9, 1905: (1) it guaranteed complete liberty of conscience; (2) it suppressed all connection of the Church with the state—henceforth the state would have no connection with the appointment of Catholic ecclesiastics or with the payment of their salaries; (3) the property of the Church was to be taken over by private corporations formed for that specific purpose. Thus ended the relationship of the state to the Catholic Church as established by the concordat of 1801, as well as the separate régimes establishing the relation of the state to the Protestant and the Jewish faiths (the Protestant Church had been

state-supported and controlled since 1802, under the Organic Articles of April 8; the Jews had been under state control since 1808 and had been given state support in 1831).

Apr. 8. **Conclusion of the Entente Cordiale** with Great Britain *(p. 741).*

1905. An acute **crisis in Franco-German relations,** arising from the Moroccan question *(p. 742).* Dramatic downfall of **Théophile Delcassé** (June 6), foreign minister since June 1898.

1906-1913. **Presidency of Clément Armand Fallières.**

1906-1911. Striking **revival of French nationalism and royalism.** This was an outcome of the conflict over Dreyfus and particularly of the international tension resulting from the Moroccan crisis. The new "integral nationalism" assumed a sophisticated form in the writing of **Charles Maurras** and **Léon Daudet** in the newspaper *Action Française* (founded 1899). They sought the restoration of the monarchy, the aggressive development of French power at home and of French prestige abroad. **Maurice Barrès,** the eminent novelist, though unsympathetic to the restoration of the monarchy, also sought the promotion of national unity in terms of French "traditional development," with decentralization and harmonizing of the forces of nationalism and socialism, an ideology in some respects foreshadowing National Socialism.

1906-1911. **Epidemic of strikes and labor troubles.** Decline in wine prices caused a crisis in that industry and the organization of vineyard workers in the *Confédération Générale des Vignerons* (1907). There were manifestations on a grand scale in the south, and considerable violence.

1909, Apr.-May. **Strike of the Paris postal workers.** Civil servants had demanded the right to unionize and affiliate with the *Confédération Générale du Travail.* The former demand had been granted, the latter refused. The government of **Georges Clemenceau** (1906-1909) met the strikers with severe measures: more than 200 employees were discharged and the right of civil servants to strike was denied. Labor agitation was accompanied by violent passages between radicals and socialists, notably between Clemenceau and **Jean Jaurès,** the outstanding figure of French socialism.

1909-1910. **The first ministry of Aristide Briand.**

1910, Oct. 10. **A strike of railway workers** on the Northeastern Railway was answered by Briand (long a socialist) by calling out the troops. The National Union of Railway Workers and Employees thereupon called a **general strike,** but when it became clear that the movement was collapsing, the strike committee ordered the resumption of work (Oct. 18). Briand defended the use of force to maintain the functioning of the railroads as essential to the life of the nation and its defense.

1911. New strikes of vineyard workers in Champagne, similar to those in the south in 1907.

1911, June-Nov. **The second Moroccan** (Agadir) **crisis** *(p. 745).* The ministries of **Joseph Caillaux** (1911, June 27–1912, Jan. 10) and **Raymond Poincaré** (1912, Jan. 14–1913, Jan. 18) were taken up largely with the Moroccan problem and other questions of international

Émile Zola, 1840–1902

Anatole France, 1844–1924

import, notably those arising from the Tripolitan War *(p. 745)* and from the Balkan Wars *(pp. 746, 747).*

1913, July-Aug. The government of **Louis Barthou** (1862–1934) carried a **law increasing the military service** from two to three years. This measure was vigorously opposed by the Radical Socialists and Socialists and its revocation was hotly debated until the very eve of the First World War.

1913-1920. **Presidency of Raymond Poincaré,** ardent patriot, one of the most eminent French statesmen in modern times.

(Cont. pp. 875, 920.)

CULTURAL DEVELOPMENTS

Realism was the means and the end for prose writers after mid-century. The greatest of these were **Gustave Flaubert** (1821–1880; *Madame*

Pierre Proudhon with His Children, *by Gustave Courbet, 1819–1877*

Don Quixote in His Library, *by Gustave Doré, 1833-1883*

Bovary, 1857), **Alphonse Daudet** (1840–1897), **Émile Zola** (1840–1902), and **Guy de Maupassant** (1850–1893), master of the short story. **Anatole France** (1844–1924) appears as a satirist in his novels (*Penguin Island,* 1908). The Belgian-born dramatist **Maurice Maeterlinck** (1862–1949) is recognized for his contributions to French literature as one of the foremost of the symbolists (see under Low Countries). **Edmond Rostand** (1868–1918) was the poet-dramatist who created *Cyrano de Bergerac* (1897) from the 17th-century figure. The poet **Frédéric Mistral** (1830–1914) wrote in Provençal.

In painting a parallel movement is apparent: the romantic-realist qualities of paintings of **Jean-Baptiste Camille Corot** (1796–1875) and **Jean François Millet** (1815–1875); the realism of **Gustave Courbet** (1819–1877); the horror of **Gustave Doré's** illustrations (*Gargantua, Don Quixote, La Bible*); the impressionist influence in the works of **Edouard Manet** (1832–1883), **Henri de Toulouse-Lautrec** (1864–1901); the neo-impressionism of **Georges Seurat** (1859–1891) and **Paul Signac** (1863–1935); the post-impressionism of **Paul Cézanne** (1839–1906), from whom "modern art" is said to date; and the expressionism of **Paul Gauguin** (1848–1903), **Henri Rousseau** (1844–1910), and **Henri Matisse** (1869–1954).

Composers **Giacomo Meyerbeer** (1791–1864; *Les Huguenots,* 1836) and **Charles Gounod** (1818–1893; *Faust,* 1859) were best known for their operas; organ music was the medium of **César Franck** (1822–1890), while **Camille Saint-Saëns** (1835–1921), **Claude Debussy** (1862–1918), and **Maurice Ravel** (1875–1937) composed orchestral works; **Gabriel Fauré** (1845–1924) composed songs, piano music, and a *Requiem.*

For the **Paris Exposition of 1889,** Alexandre Gustave Eiffel designed the **Eiffel tower.**

Antoine Baryé (1796–1875) was the foremost sculptor of animals in his era, but the sculptor whose influence was greatest was **Auguste Rodin** (1840–1917).

Claude Debussy, 1862–1918

The Thought, *by Auguste Rodin, 1840–1917*

5. *The Iberian Peninsula*

a. SPAIN, 1814–1914

(From p. 622)

1814–1833. FERDINAND VII, restored to the throne (1814, Mar.) after the conquest of Spain by Wellington in the Peninsula War *(p. 622)*. The king had promised to maintain the liberal **constitution of 1812** *(p. 625)*, but refused to keep his promise, knowing the absolutist temper of the country and relying on the support of the Church and the army. Ferocious persecution of the liberals and the king's capricious and incapable rule caused widespread dissatisfaction, notably in the army. The loss of the colonies in America *(p. 788)* deprived the government of one of the chief sources of income and determined Ferdinand (who was encouraged by Russia and France) to undertake their reconquest. Forces were concentrated at Cadiz, one of the chief centers of disaffection, where the troops became demoralized.

1820, Jan. Mutiny of the troops under Colonel Rafael Riego. They began to march to Madrid. Other revolutionary movements broke out in the north and ultimately the garrison in Madrid mutinied. Ferdinand yielded and restored the constitution. The revolutionaries held him practically a prisoner until 1823.

1822. The **congress of Verona** *(p. 630)*, after much previous debate among the powers, gave France a mandate to suppress the movement. Great Britain, under Canning, did its utmost to prevent intervention, but in vain. A French army crossed the Pyrenees in the spring of 1823, marched to Madrid to the cheers of the unenlightened peasantry, and drove the revolutionaries south to Cadiz, taking the king with them.

1823, Aug. 31. The **battle of the Trocadero** brought the revolution to an end. Ferdinand was restored. He ignored the advice of the French to introduce a moderate constitutional régime and delivered the country over to an orgy of repression which lasted until his death.

    Dec. 2. Monroe's message to Congress (**Monroe Doctrine,** *p. 756*). This warned European countries against intervention in South America, and was the outcome of Canning's approaches to the American minister, Richard Rush, for joint action to oppose reconquest of the colonies. The danger of such action was almost nil on account of the attitude and sea power of Britain.

1833, June 30. To assure the succession of his infant daughter **Isabella,** Ferdinand, under the influence of his energetic queen, **Maria Cristina,** set aside the Salic Law, thus depriving his brother, **Don Carlos,** of the throne. The king died September 29.

1833–1868. ISABELLA II. She was represented by her mother, Maria Cristina, as regent. Realizing that she must depend on the Liberals for support, the latter granted

1834. The **Estatuto Real** (royal constitution): Spain was divided into 49 administrative provinces, on the model of the French *départements;* a bicameral legislature (*cortes*) was given financial powers, but the government retained the right of dissolution and control of the ministry. The constitution was less advanced than that of 1812, and led to a split in the ranks of the Liberals: the *Moderados* accepted the statute; the *Progresistas* demanded restoration of the constitution of 1812.

1834–1839. THE CARLIST WAR. Don Carlos, claiming the throne, was supported by the conservative elements, the Church, and much of the north of the country (Basques, Navarre, Aragon, Catalonia) where regional and autonomous feeling revolted against the centralizing tendencies of the Liberals.

1834, Apr. 22. Quadruple Alliance between Great Britain, France, Spain, and Portugal, aimed at the support of the constitutionalists against the pretenders. The British government went so far as to suspend the Foreign Enlistment Act and allow the formation of a foreign legion, under **Sir De Lacy Evans.** In 1836–1837 the Carlists were defeated, and the war was concluded by the **convention of Vergara** (1839, Aug. 31). Don Carlos left the country for France.

1836, Aug. 10. Progressist insurrection in Andalusia, Aragon, Catalonia, and Madrid. Cristina, who had become very unpopular through her secret marriage to **Ferdinand Muñoz** (1833), was obliged to restore the constitution of 1812 and summon a Progressist ministry, which had the cortes adopt the **constitution of 1837,** a compromise between the constitution of 1812 and the statute of 1834.

1840, Oct. Revolt of General Baldomero Espartero, "Duke of the Victory," who had embraced the Progressist cause. Cristina was forced to leave the country and Espartero became practically dictator, acting as regent.

1841, Oct. Espartero defeated a Cristina insurrection at Pampeluna.

1842, Nov. Rising in Barcelona, accompanied with much bloodshed. A republic was proclaimed, but was suppressed by Espartero (Dec.).

1843, June. A coalition of *Moderados, Progresistas,* and republicans declared against Espartero. **General Ramón Narvaez took Madrid** (July 15) and Espartero fled the country (Aug.). Isabella, though only 13 years old, was declared of age, with Narvaez as lieutenant-general of the kingdom. Cristina returned (1844, Mar.), but Narvaez remained practically dictator until 1851.

1845. A **new constitution** virtually re-established the statute of 1834.

1846, Oct. 10. Isabella married her cousin, Francisco, duke of Cadiz, while her sister, **Luisa Fernanda,** married the duke of Montpensier, youngest son of Louis Philippe of France. The **affair of the Spanish marriages** caused the breakdown of the *entente* between Britain and France which originated in their

Ferdinand VII, 1814–1833

collaboration in the Belgian question (1830–1831) and in the Quadruple Alliance of 1834. In 1843 and 1845 Aberdeen and Guizot had made **agreements at Eu,** according to which the choice of Isabella's husband should be confined to the Spanish and Neapolitan branches of the Bourbon house (i.e. the descendants of Philip V). This eliminated the two most desirable candidates, the duke of Montpensier and Prince Leopold of Saxe-Coburg. It was further provided that the Infanta Luisa should not be married to a French prince unless her sister, the queen, should have first been married and borne children. Ignoring the Eu pacts, Palmerston sent a dispatch to Sir Henry Bulwer, the British ambassador at Madrid (July 19, 1846), mentioning three candidates for Isabella's hand, and Prince Leopold first. The second part of the dispatch discussed the Spanish domestic situation and condemned the French-supported *Moderados* for their violence and arbitrary methods. The French and Spanish governments, united in distrust of Palmerston and fearing British support of the *Progresistas,* precipitated the engagement of Isabella to the duke of Cadiz and of Luisa to Montpensier. When the double marriage had taken place Palmerston was furious and invoked the treaty of Utrecht with its precautions against the union of France and Spain. This was of no effect, but Franco-British relations were seriously compromised.

1851, Mar. 16. Concordat with the Papacy. It recognized the Catholic religion as the sole authorized faith, gave the Church sweeping control of education and censorship; in return the Papacy recognized abolition of ecclesiastical jurisdictions and the sale of confiscated church lands.

1852, Dec. A **constitutional reform** virtually eliminated the powers of the cortes and established the dictatorship in law. A **camarilla** had complete power in its hands.

1854, July. A revolution led by **General Leopoldo O'Donnell** (a Moderate) and Espartero (Progressive) overthrew the government and forced Cristina to leave the country. O'Donnell then formed a new party, the **Liberal Union,** espousing a program between that of the moderates and progressives. When the cortes adopted a law confiscating church lands, Isabella threatened to abdicate.

1856, July 15. Espartero resigned in favor of O'Donnell, who re-established the constitution of 1845 with an amendment guaranteeing annual assembly of the cortes and presentation of the budget at the beginning of each session.

    Oct. O'Donnell was dismissed and two years of reaction followed, punctuated by numerous insurrections.

1858–1863. O'Donnell back in power, governing with the support of the Liberal Union and avoiding thorny questions of domestic policy.

1859–1860. Successful **campaign against the Moors** in Morocco.

1861. Annexation of Santo Domingo followed by insurrection in the island. Relinquishment of the island (1865).

    Spain also joined France and Britain in intervention in Mexico.

1864, Sept. Narvaez made premier, supported by the *Moderados* and many of the absolutists. Reversion to a Catholic and reactionary policy.

The Liberal parties united in opposition to the régime, the *Progresistas* boycotting the elections.

1864–1865. Dispute with Peru over the Chincha Islands *(p. 798).*

1865–1866. War with Chile *(p. 796).*

1865. A severe **press law** was accompanied by the dissolution of political clubs.

1866, Jan.–June. An insurrection organized by General Juan Prim failed, but was followed by many executions.

1868, Apr. 23. Death of Narvaez, which had been preceded by O'Donnell's (d. 1867, Nov. 5). Gonzalez Bravo attempted to continue the absolutist régime, but the army escaped from his control. The Liberal parties united on a revolutionary program. Scandals which gathered about the queen's name were ruthlessly exposed in the newspapers and undermined her position. Her latest favorite, **Carlos Marfori,** a cook's son and an actor by profession, was made minister of state.

    Sept. 18. Admiral Juan Topete issued a revolutionary proclamation at Cadiz, followed by a manifesto by the Liberal generals. By the end of September the movement had spread to all Spain.

    Sept. 28. Royal forces defeated at **Alcolea** by Marshal Francisco Serrano. The queen fled to France (Sept. 29) and was declared deposed.

    Oct. 5. A **provisional government** was formed, with **Serrano** at the lead and with **Prim** as the moving spirit. Reactionary laws were annulled, the Jesuit and other religious orders abolished. The government established universal suffrage and a free press.

1869, Feb. A **constituent cortes** met.

    May 21. The cortes voted for the continuance of monarchical government.

    June 6. The new constitution promulgated.

    June 15. Marshal Serrano made regent. Prim head of the ministry. The new régime was bothered by Carlist and republican uprisings and other disturbances, but its chief concern was to find a ruler. The duke of Montpensier was passed over out of consideration for Napoleon III; the duke of Aosta; Prince Ferdinand of Saxe-Coburg; the duke of Genoa; General Espartero, all these declined the throne when offered. Finally the offer was made to **Prince Leopold of Hohenzollern-Sigmaringen,** who accepted, but then withdrew. This candidacy became the occasion for the war between Germany and France *(p. 692).*

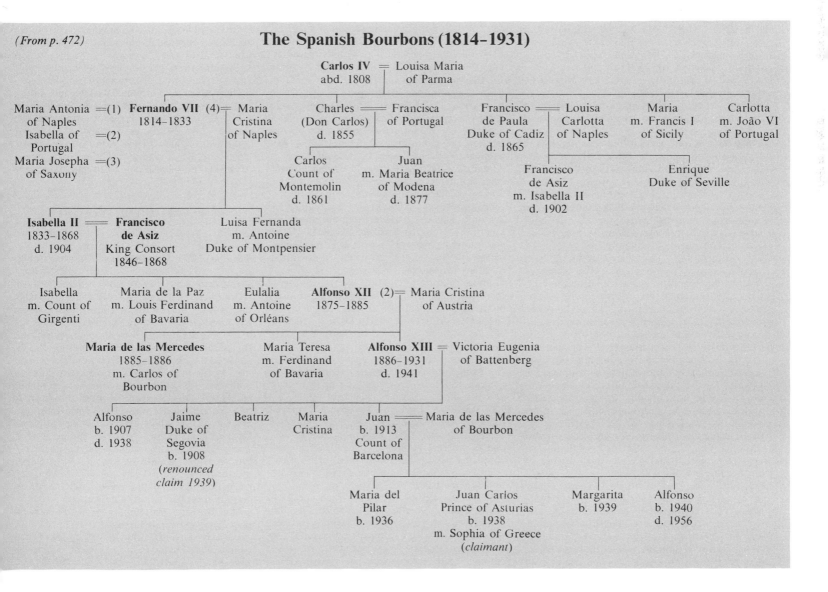

The Spanish Bourbons (1814–1931)

(From p. 472)

THE IBERIAN PENINSULA   **665**

1870, Dec. 30. The **duke of Aosta,** son of Victor Emmanuel II of Piedmont, was prevailed upon to accept. Death of Prim, victim of an assassin.

1871–1873. AMADEO I, the duke of Aosta (b. 1845). Amadeo ruled for two years—isolated, opposed on every side, greeted as a "foreigner"—and then abdicated (1873, Feb. 12).

1873–1874. The **FIRST SPANISH REPUBLIC,** proclaimed (Feb. 12) by the radical majority in the cortes elected in August 1872 (the Carlists having abstained).

1873, May 10. A **constituent cortes,** now elected, was divided among partisans of different types of federal republic.

Sept. 8. In the midst of Carlist risings, **Emilio Castelar,** partisan of a centralized republic, was made head of the government, with the mission of restoring order.

1874, Jan. 2. Castelar retired. A military *coup* promptly followed, with Marshal Serrano as head of a provisional government. The Carlist war continued, marked by exceptional brutality.

Nov. 24. Alfonso, son of Isabella, came of age and declared for a constitutional monarchy. A party of Liberal Unionists and Moderates supported him.

Dec. 29–31. A **group of generals,** disgusted with the republic, **rallied to Alfonso,** who was proclaimed king.

1875–1885. ALFONSO XII. Continuation of the Carlist War, until February 1876, when Don Carlos again fled. The pope, who had recognized Carlos as **Carlos VII,** king of Spain, was won over to recognition of the new régime by a governmental increase of the ecclesiastical budget, closing of Protestant schools and churches, abolition of civil marriages, and other concessions.

1876, July. A **new constitution** accepted by the cortes elected in January was a compromise between the constitutions of 1845 and 1869 and established a system midway between Carlist "absolutism" and republican "anarchy." It provided for a bicameral legislature and a responsible ministry, but with a limited suffrage—a parliamentary régime in appearance only. The cortes, as before the revolution, was "ministerial" (i.e. elected under government auspices and obedient to the ministry). The ministry, in turn, was selected by the king, who thus remained the effective ruler of the state. Constitutional forms were, however, observed, and during the succeeding decades there was neither *camarilla* nor insurrection. The ministerial power alternated between two parties, both supporting the régime: the **Conservatives** (led by **Canovas del Castillo**) and the **Liberals** (under **Práxedes Sagasta**). The country prospered, but the king, though courageous and humane, was indulgent and lost much popularity through scandals at court. In foreign policy he followed the lead of the central powers. From 1887 to 1895 Spain was associated with Britain, Italy, and Austria in the **Mediterranean Agreements** *(p. 735).*

1885–1902. Regency of Maria Cristina, widow of Alfonso, who ruled for her son, born 1886, May 17, after the death of his father. The Conservatives and Liberals continued to alternate in power.

1890. Universal suffrage was again introduced. The economic development of the country led

Alfonso XIII, 1902–1931

to increasing labor unrest, especially in centers like Barcelona. **Anarchist outrages** became frequent and resulted in many executions and in much repressive legislation.

1895. The **Cuban Revolution** *(p. 775).* It continued for three years and ended in the loss of both Cuba and the Philippines.

1898. THE SPANISH-AMERICAN WAR *(p. 775).* It left Spain weak and discredited, and resulted in further disintegration of the parliamentary régime. The **Conservatives** divided into an authoritarian wing (led by **Juan La Cierva,** allied to the clergy), and the **Liberal Conservatives** (followers of **Augustino Silvela**). The **Liberals** (Progressives) were led by **Sigismondo Moret** after the death of Sagasta. A small **Carlist Party** continued to exist in the mountains of the north. A **Republican Party** had headquarters in Madrid, Andalusia, and Catalonia. A **Socialist Party** was rapidly winning recruits among the laborers of Catalonia and the miners of the Basque region. Anarchists continued their activities and even made attempts upon the king's life. The centralized character of the government system gave rise to a **regionalist movement** in Catalonia, where the **United Catalans** (*Soldiarios*) demanded an autonomous administration and a separate budget. In its literary and linguistic aspects this movement took the form of a cultural revival.

1902–1931. ALFONSO XIII. Though declared of age, he at first allowed his mother to continue the government.

1904. Agreement between Spain and France regarding Morocco *(p. 741).* This marked the veering of Spanish policy to the side of France and Britain.

1906, May 31. Marriage of Alfonso to Princess Eugenia of Battenberg, granddaughter of Queen Victoria. The succeeding period was one of internal conflict. Army influence secured the passage of a law (1906) to try press offenses "against the fatherland and the army" by court-martial.

1909. When troops were embarked for Morocco, protests of extremists followed, directed against the inequality of the military service régime, under which obligatory service fell on the poorer classes. A **general strike** was proclaimed at Barcelona and extended to other

Catalonian cities under the direction of a revolutionary committee.

July. At Barcelona the insurgents burned convents and massacred priests and monks. Vigorous repression followed, and **Francisco Ferrer,** propagandist of the anti-clerical opposition, was executed (Oct. 13), with resulting criticism throughout Europe and many repercussions in Spain.

Oct. 21. The king called a Liberal ministry. In the succeeding years he even consulted with the Republican leader, **Gumersindo Azcarate,** and declared himself accessible to all parties, even those of anti-dynastic complexion.

1910–1913. The **Liberals were in power,** supported by the king.

1912, Nov. 12. Assassination of the advanced Liberal premier, **José Canalejas,** pledged to an anti-clerical program. He had passed (1910, Dec. 23) the **Padlock Law,** forbidding the establishment of more religious houses without the consent of the government. The industrial enterprises of the religious orders were taxed, and public worship of non-Catholic bodies was expressly permitted.

Nov. 27. Treaty with France, defining their respective spheres in Morocco *(p. 818).*

1913, Oct. 27. The **Conservatives returned to power** after the king's unsuccessful attempts to reconcile the Liberals, who had split up after Canalejas' death.

1914, Aug. 7. Spain declared neutrality in the First World War, the king having given France assurances that she might denude her Pyrenees frontier of troops. *(Cont. p. 925.)*

Spanish literature in the 20th century was characterized first by romanticism, later by realism (**José de Espronceda y Delgado,** 1808–1842), a romantic poet; **Ramón de Campoamor** (1817–1901), writer of epigrams and narrative poems; **José María de Pereda** (1833–1906), realistic novelist. Turn-of-the-century composers in the romantic tradition were **Isaac Albéniz** (1860–1909) and **Enrique Granados** (1867–1916).

b. PORTUGAL, 1820–1912

(From p. 622)

1820, Aug. 29. Revolution at Oporto, stimulated by the revolution in Spain. The insurgents drove out the regency, established in November 1807 under British auspices to rule the country during the sojourn of **King John VI** (ruled 1792–1826) in Brazil.

1822. A **constitution** was adopted similar to the democratic Spanish constitution. Brazil declared independence. King John accepted the invitation to return as constitutional monarch and left the government of Brazil to his eldest son, **Dom Pedro.**

1823, June 5. John revised the constitution in the interest of absolutism. His second son, **Dom Miguel,** in the meantime started a civil war (1823–1824) supported by the reactionaries.

1826, Mar. 10. Death of King John. He left the throne to Dom Pedro of Brazil, who became **Peter IV.** Peter drew up a charter providing for moderate parliamentary government of the British type. But he refused to leave Brazil and eventually handed over the Portuguese throne to his infant daughter, **Maria da Gloria,** with Dom Miguel as regent.

1826–1853. MARIA II. Miguel united the reactionaries and clericals in a movement against constitutional government.

1827, Jan.-1828, Apr. 28. A **British force landed at Lisbon** to support the constitutionalists. They withdrew when Miguel promised to respect the constitution.

1828, May. *Coup d'état* **by Miguel,** who abolished the constitution and had himself proclaimed king (July 4). Maria da Gloria fled to England.

1828-1834. **The Miguelite Wars.**

1831, Apr. 7. **Dom Pedro abdicated the Brazilian throne** and returned to Europe (England), to fight for the restoration of Maria.

1832, July 8. **Pedro,** with the connivance of Britain and France, organized an expedition and **took Oporto.** The Miguelists were defeated and

1833, Sept. Maria was restored.

1834, Apr. 22. **Quadruple Alliance** between Great Britain, France, Spain, and Portugal, aimed at the expulsion of Miguel.

May 26. **Final defeat of Miguel,** who left the country.

1834-1853. A period of ministerial instability and chronic insurrection, reflecting the conflict between those championing the radical constitution of 1822 and those supporting the charter of 1826.

1836, Apr. 9. The queen married Duke Ferdinand of Saxe-Coburg.

1853-1861. **PETER (PEDRO) V.**

1861-1889. **LOUIS (LUIS) I.** Under these two reigns Portugal had some respite from civil strife, and the country was ruled by two opposing factions of professional politicians, the **Regenerators** (or Conservatives) and the **Progressives** (or Liberals), who adopted the system of *rotavism:* skillful manipulation of the electorate, enabling the two parties to hold office in rotation. This sterile, pseudo-parliamentary system resulted in the formation of a **Republican Party** (1881).

1889-1908. **CARLOS I,** who gained notoriety by his extragavance and licentiousness. Discontent grew, especially in the cities, and there were sporadic revolts, strikes, and conspiracies.

1906, May 19. The king appointed **João Franco** as prime minister, with dictatorial powers. Parliamentary government was suppressed, the press gagged, and all opposition to the government sternly punished.

1908, Feb. 1. **Assassination of King Carlos** and the crown prince in the streets of Lisbon.

1908-1910. **MANUEL (MANOEL) II.** He put an end to Franco's régime and restored constitutional government, but, like his father, was scandalously extravagant.

1910, Oct. 3-5. **Insurrection in Lisbon.** The king was forced to flee to England.

Oct. 5. **PROCLAMATION OF THE PORTUGUESE REPUBLIC.** A provisional government was organized under **Dr. Theophilo Braga.** It proceeded to a frontal attack upon the Catholic Church, which was regarded as the backbone of royalism. Religious orders were expelled, their establishments closed and their property confiscated. Religious teaching in primary schools was forbidden.

1911, Apr. 20. **Separation of Church and State,** along the lines followed in France.

Aug. 20. A constituent assembly adopted a very **liberal constitution.**

Aug. 24. **Dr. Manoel de Arriaga** elected first president. He was confronted with royalist plots and with growing unrest among the workers, who were disappointed when the revolution failed to bring them relief.

1912, Jan. A serious **general strike** broke out in Lisbon. The city was put under military rule and hundreds of syndicalists were arrested. But radical outbreaks continued throughout the rest of the period. *(Cont. p. 928.)*

Proclamation of the Portuguese republic, Oct. 5, 1910

Louis I, 1861–1889

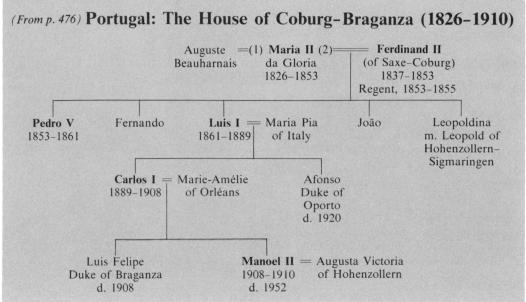

(From p. 476) **Portugal: The House of Coburg-Braganza (1826-1910)**

Auguste =(1) **Maria II** (2)==== **Ferdinand II**
Beauharnais   da Gloria   (of Saxe-Coburg)
           1826–1853   1837–1853
                      Regent, 1853–1855

Pedro V   Fernando   **Luis I** = Maria Pia   João   Leopoldina
1853–1861   1861–1889   of Italy   m. Leopold of
                                         Hohenzollern-
                                         Sigmaringen

Carlos I = Marie-Amélie   Afonso
1889–1908   of Orléans   Duke of
                          Oporto
                          d. 1920

Luis Felipe   **Manoel II** = Augusta Victoria
Duke of Braganza   1908–1910   of Hohenzollern
d. 1908   d. 1952

6. *Italy*

(From p. 479)

a. THE ITALIAN STATES, 1815–1848

With the collapse of the Napoleonic Empire in 1814, the states of the Italian peninsula were reconstituted under the effective domination of Austria, which attempted a thoroughgoing restoration of the old régime. The new states were nine in number: kingdom of Sardinia (Piedmont), Modena, Parma, Lucca, Tuscany, Papal States, kingdom of Naples, the republic of San Marino, and Monaco. Lombardy and Venetia were annexed by Austria. The only important territorial changes, as compared with the pre-Napoleonic situation, were the annexation of the former Venetian Republic by Austria, of the former Genoese Republic by Piedmont.

In cultural matters the early part of the century was marked by the writings of **Alessandro Manzoni** and **Giacomo Leopardi** *(p. 477)* while Italy's traditionally dominant position in opera was maintained by **Giacomo Rossini** (1792–1868, *Barber of Seville,* 1816), **Vincenzo Bellini** (1802–1835, *La Sonnambula,* 1813) and **Gaetano Donizetti** (1797–1848, *Lucia di' Lammermoor,* 1835).
1815, May. The Bourbon **Ferdinand I** (1751–1825), restored to the throne of Naples by Austrian arms, despite his promises of political liberty and the maintenance of French reforms (**decrees from Messina,** May 20–24, 1815), quickly descended to a rule of almost unrelieved despotism. In the **Papal States, Pope Pius VII** returned from his long exile to reestablish the obscurantist and semi-feudal ecclesiastical rule of the 18th century and to restore the Company of Jesus (suppressed in 1773). In **Modena, Duke Francis IV** entered upon a policy of candid reaction, rigorously concentrating power in his own hands, turning the universities over to the Jesuits. In **Parma** and **Lucca** the return to the old régime was rapid but less violent than in Modena and the south. **Maria Louisa of Parma** (former empress of the French) and the infanta **Maria Louisa of Bourbon-Parma,** duchess of Lucca, owed their thrones to Austria and heeded the wishes of Metternich. In **Lombardy** and **Venetia,** with separate governments, Metternich organized a thoroughly Austrian administration. Despite the arbitrary features of the government, Lombardy was in most respects (education, communications, administrative efficiency) the most advanced part of Italy. **Victor Emmanuel I of Piedmont** returned in 1814 hoping to restore the old régime intact, even to the return of officials who were holding office in 1798. The Jesuits were cordially welcomed, religious toleration denied, the French code swept away, old and brutal punishments restored.

The Italian conquests of Napoleon and the reorganization of Italy (1) had revealed to Italians the advantages of enlightened laws and administration; (2) had awakened a desire to free themselves from foreign rule. The restorations of 1815 lost for the Italians in large measure the advantages of French rule and substituted the foreign domination of Austria. Hence revolutionary sentiment grew, aiming at first to overthrow existing governments and gradually embracing the idea of unity for all of "Italy." Secret societies multiplied, most famous being the **Carbonari** (*Charcoal-Burners*), inspired by Christian and humanitarian principles, organized on republican lines, borrowing Masonic ritual. The Carbonari prepared to combat "tyranny," to overthrow existing governments. They grew rapidly in numbers in the kingdom of Naples, and spread to other Italian states.
1820, July 2. The Neapolitan Revolution. Encouraged by news of the success of the revolution in Spain *(p. 664),* the Carbonari in the army, led by **General Guglielmo Pepe,** precipitated a revolt.

July 13. Ferdinand I granted a constitution similar to that introduced in Sicily under British auspices in 1812. The representatives of the powers, meeting in congress at Troppau and Laibach to consider the Spanish situation, were persuaded by Metternich (Britain dissenting because of British public opinion, but not opposing) to adopt the principle of intervention (**Troppau protocol**) against revolutions that might endanger the European peace. Austria was given a mandate to restore order in Italy. An army was marched to Naples, overthrew the revolutionary government (1821, Mar.) with little difficulty, and restored Ferdinand I to his former position.

1821, Mar. 10. Rising in Piedmont, engineered by the Carbonari, who hoped that **Charles Albert,** prince of Carignan, would place himself at the head of a constitutional government.

Mar. 12. Victor Emmanuel I abdicated in favor of his brother, Charles Felix, then absent from Turin. Charles Albert was made regent and granted a constitution like that of Spain.

Mar. 22. Charles Felix arrived, ordered Charles Albert to flee, which he did.

Apr. 8. The **Piedmontese revolution col-**

Alessandro Manzoni, 1785–1873

Giacomo Rossini, 1792–1868

Pope Pius VII, 1742–1823

lapsed with the defeat of the constitutionalists near **Novara** by a combined force of royalists and Austrians.

1831, Feb. **Risings in Modena and Parma** inspired by the July Revolution in Paris *(p. 649)* and connected with a general movement aiming to free all northern Italy; they were accompanied by widespread revolts in the Papal States.

Mar. With the aid of Austrian troops the insurrections were put down.

May 21. The ambassadors of the powers demanded certain reforms in the Papal States, but the pope contented himself with an amnesty and a few concessions in the administration and the judiciary. Fresh revolts broke out in the Papal States at the end of 1831. Order was again restored by Austria (Jan. 1832), which led to the **occupation of Ancona** by the French (Mar. 1832). It was not until 1838 that the foreign troops were withdrawn.

The failure of insurrections indicated the ineffectiveness of secret societies, notably of the Carbonari, and of small-scale, sporadic risings which they promoted. The importance of unified effort by Italians everywhere and of careful preparation through propaganda and organization was recognized by **Giuseppe Mazzini** (1805–1872), former Carbonaro, who launched a

Mar. **New revolutionary society** (*Young Italy*). From early youth Mazzini had dreamt of freeing Italy from her present rulers and giving her a republican constitution—as a prelude to a free confederation of all Europe dominated by a spirit of Christian brotherhood. Through the widely ramifying channels of Young Italy, Mazzini launched his propaganda from exile in Marseilles. Before a general rising in Italy (planned for June 1832) could take place,

1832, Mar. Piedmontese authorities discovered existence of the plans; arrests followed, the rising collapsed.

1834, Feb. Another Mazzinian **attack on Savoy** ended in ludicrous failure. Mazzini now extended the scope of his activity by organizing the **Young Europe movement,** composed of Young Italy, Young Germany, Young Poland, and kindred organizations. From London he carried on his work of direction and propaganda. Abortive risings followed with almost monotonous regularity, but accomplished nothing but the creation of martyrs to the cause.

1843. Publication of **Vincenzo Gioberti's** *On the Moral and Civil Primacy of the Italians,* and of **Count Cesare Balbo's** *The Hopes of Italy.* These two books represented the views of the Italian moderate Liberals, especially in northern Italy. They found Mazzini's republicanism offensive and his methods dangerous and impractical. The moderates distrusted universal suffrage and advocated constitutional reform and some type of unification for the peninsula. Some favored a federation of states under the presidency of the pope. These were the **Neo-Guelphs,** led by Gioberti. Balbo and his followers were intent chiefly on the extrusion of Austria (by peaceful means if possible) and the organization of Italy under Piedmontese leadership.

1846, June 15. **ELECTION OF PIUS IX** (Cardinal Mastai-Ferretti) as pope led to an outburst of liberal enthusiasm and to boundless hopes. In contrast to his predecessor,

Giuseppe Mazzini, 1805–1872

Gregory XVI, Pius was democratic in his attitude. He proclaimed an amnesty for political prisoners and refugees, relaxed the censorship laws, organized an advisory council composed of laymen, replaced the mercenary army by a civil guard, and established a municipal council for Rome. These reforms were opposed by the reactionaries (Gregorians) at every step, but the pope's popularity grew throughout Italy.

1847, July 17. **Occupation of Ferrara** by Austrian troops (actually exercising a right conferred by the treaty of Vienna). This step called forth a storm of indignation among Liberals in all Italy and did much to fan the anti-Austrian sentiment.

Oct. Charles Albert of Piedmont (succeeded Charles Felix in 1831), though conservatively inclined, dismissed his reactionary minister, **Solaro della Margarita,** and began to yield to the liberal agitation (*King Wobble, Re Tentenna*). He consented to the revision of the criminal code, mitigation of the censorship, amendment of the law on public meeting.

1848, Jan. 12. A **revolutionary movement** broke out in **Sicily** and stimulated the Neapolitan liberals to action.

Feb. 10. **Ferdinand II** (*Bomba,* 1830–1859), unable to secure Austrian aid in the face of the pope's opposition to the crossing of his territory, promulgated a liberal constitution modeled on the French charter of 1830.

Feb. 17. **Grand Duke Leopold** of Tuscany was obliged to grant a constitution.

Mar. 4. **Charles Albert promulgated a constitution** for Piedmont (the *Statuto,* the basis for the later constitution of the kingdom of Italy).

Mar. 14. The pope followed suit, introducing a constitution establishing an elective council of deputies, but reserving a veto power to the pope and college of cardinals.

b. THE ITALIAN WAR OF INDEPENDENCE, 1848–1849

1848, Mar. 18–22. The **FIVE DAYS OF MILAN,** marking the culmination of dissatisfaction with Austrian rule and the influence of the

Coronation of Pius IX, 1846

news of the revolution in Vienna (Mar. 13). Barricades were thrown up in the narrow streets. The Austrian general, **Josef Radetzky,** held the entire circle of fortifications, preventing the insurgents from communicating with the outside world. The rebels, fighting without plan or organization, but greatly outnumbering the Austrian forces, gradually reduced the garrisons inside the town and, after repeated assaults, took **Porta Tosa** (Mar. 22). Radetzky was obliged to order a general retreat to the famous **Quadrilateral** (four fortresses: Mantua, Peschiera, Legnano, Verona, between Lombardy and Venetia).

Mar. 22. **Proclamation of the Venetian Republic,** following agitation and some violence after the arrival of the news from Vienna. A provisional government was established, with **Daniele Manin** as president.

Mar. 22. **PIEDMONT DECLARED WAR ON AUSTRIA,** in response to an appeal from the Milanese. Charles Albert was very hesitant about allying with the revolution and very suspicious of possible action by the radical French Republic, but finally yielded for fear of radicalism in his own territory.

Apr. 25. Papal forces under **General Giacomo Durando** joined the Piedmontese. Contingents also arrived from Naples and other parts of Italy. Wild enthusiasm, but little discipline.

Apr. 29. A **papal encyclical,** the result of Austrian protests, disclaimed all intention of making war on the Catholic Austrians. This paralyzed all action by the papal troops.

May 15. **Collapse of the revolution in Naples,** after a counter-offensive by the king's Swiss mercenaries. Neapolitan troops withdrawn from the north.

May 30. The Piedmontese won the **battle of Goito,** but failed to follow up their advantage. Acute danger of intervention by the French Republic, which had concentrated 30,000 troops on the Alps. Austrian efforts to secure British support **(Hummelauer mission).** Palmerston urged the abandonment of both Lombardy and Venetia.

June 15. The Austrian government ordered Radetzky to seek an armistice to permit an offer of independence to Lombardy. Radetzky sent **Prince Felix Schwarzenberg** to Vienna and induced the government to continue the war.

July 24. BATTLE OF CUSTOZZA. Radetzky overwhelmingly defeated the Piedmontese and (Aug. 4) drove them out of Lombardy. Charles Albert finally appealed to the French for mediation, but after the **June Days** *(p. 651)* the French government was too deeply engrossed in domestic affairs to be willing to embroil itself with Austria and Britain.

Aug. 9. Armistice of Salasco (the general who negotiated it). The Piedmontese gave up Lombardy. Charles Albert accepted joint Anglo-French mediation, on the understanding that he would get Lombardy later. The Austrians accepted mediation after much resistance (Sept. 3), but nothing came of it, especially after the formation of the Schwarzenberg ministry (Nov. 21), which refused to entertain the suggestion of territorial cessions.

Sept. 16. The pope appointed **Count Pellegrino Rossi** prime minister, after several ephemeral cabinets and a steady growth of radicalism at Rome. Rossi was a disciple of Guizot, a moderate, clear-headed administrator, whose aim was to restore order. His efforts at reform earned him the hatred of all factions.

Nov. 15. Rossi was murdered by a fanatical democrat.

Nov. 16. Popular insurrection in Rome. The pope was forced to appoint a democratic ministry under Monsignor **Carlo Muzzarelli.**

Nov. 25. Pius, alarmed by radical agitation (clubs), fled from Rome to Gaeta where he enjoyed Neapolitan protection. He attempted unsuccessfully to maintain his power in Rome through a commission of regency.

1849, Feb. 9. Proclamation of the Roman Republic, after the meeting of a constituent assembly (Feb. 5).

Mar. 12. Piedmont denounced the armistice with Austria, the king yielding to radical pressure.

Mar. 23. BATTLE OF NOVARA. Radetzky again decisively defeated the Piedmontese. Charles Albert abdicated in favor of his son, **Victor Emmanuel II.** Peace negotiations dragged on through the spring and summer, the size of the indemnity being the chief point in dispute. Peace was finally signed August 9, Piedmont agreeing to an indemnity of 65,000,000 francs.

Mar. 29. On news of the Piedmontese defeat at Novara, the leaders at **Rome set up a triumvirate** (Mazzini, Saffi, Armellini) which introduced a moderate, conciliatory régime and restored order. But since January there had

been discussion of intervention by France or Austria, or both, to restore the pope.

Apr. 14. The French assembly voted funds for an expedition, being led by the government to suppose that the purpose was to forestall the Austrians. In reality the aim of Louis Napoleon was to win the approval of the Catholics.

Apr. 24. The **French expedition,** under **General Nicolas Oudinot,** landed at Cività Vecchia.

Apr. 29–30. Oudinot, supposing that Mazzini's followers were a minority in Rome, attacked the city, but was repulsed by improvised forces led by **Giuseppe Garibaldi,** republican patriot and guerrilla leader.

May 29. Ferdinand de Lesseps, later builder of the Suez Canal, having been sent by the French government to negotiate, signed a treaty with the Roman Republic by which the city gates were to be opened to the French in return for a promise to respect the rights of the republic and to guarantee it against foreign aggression.

June 1. Lesseps was abruptly recalled and later disavowed. Oudinot was reinforced and ordered to take the city.

June 3. He attacked without warning, but Garibaldi and his men fought so valiantly that the French had to settle down to a siege.

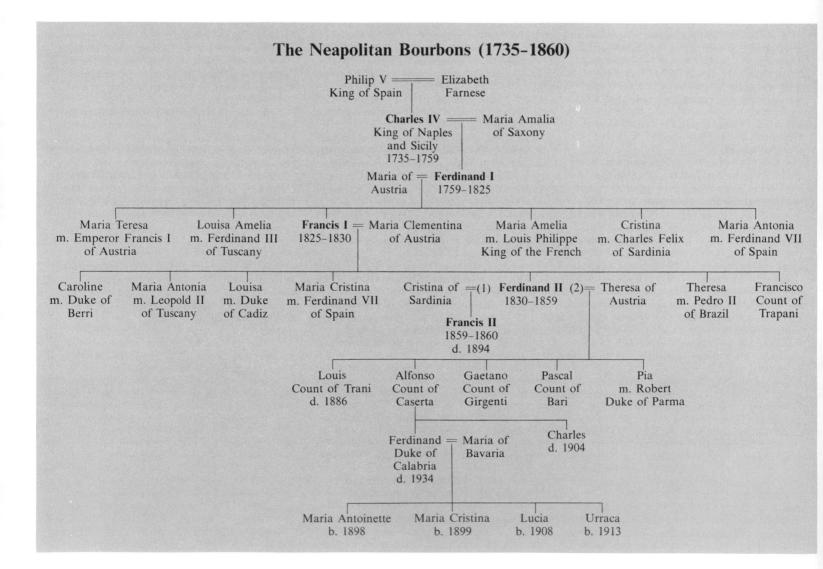

The Neapolitan Bourbons (1735–1860)

Philip V (King of Spain) == Elizabeth Farnese

Charles IV (King of Naples and Sicily, 1735–1759) == Maria Amalia of Saxony

Maria of Austria == **Ferdinand I** 1759–1825

- Maria Teresa m. Emperor Francis I of Austria
- Louisa Amelia m. Ferdinand III of Tuscany
- **Francis I** 1825–1830 == Maria Clementina of Austria
- Maria Amelia m. Louis Philippe King of the French
- Cristina m. Charles Felix of Sardinia
- Maria Antonia m. Ferdinand VII of Spain

Children of Francis I:
- Caroline m. Duke of Berri
- Maria Antonia m. Leopold II of Tuscany
- Louisa m. Duke of Cadiz
- Maria Cristina m. Ferdinand VII of Spain
- Cristina of Sardinia ==(1) **Ferdinand II** 1830–1859 (2)== Theresa of Austria
- Theresa m. Pedro II of Brazil
- Francisco Count of Trapani

Francis II 1859–1860 d. 1894

- Louis Count of Trani d. 1886
- Alfonso Count of Caserta
- Gaetano Count of Girgenti
- Pascal Count of Bari
- Pia m. Robert Duke of Parma

Ferdinand Duke of Calabria d. 1934 == Maria of Bavaria

Charles d. 1904

- Maria Antoinette b. 1898
- Maria Cristina b. 1899
- Lucia b. 1908
- Urraca b. 1913

Count Camillo Benso di Cavour, 1851–1861

French troops enter Turin, 1848

June 30. Garibaldi, regarding the situation as hopeless, made terms with the French.

July 2. After reviewing his troops, Garibaldi marched forth with some 5000 men on his famous retreat. All were presently killed, captured, or dispersed, Garibaldi himself escaping after dramatic adventures.

July 20–Aug. 28. Austrian siege and bombardment of Venice. The city surrendered, ravaged by cholera and faced with starvation.

By this time the revolutionary movement had been everywhere suppressed. Neapolitan troops had reconquered Sicily and entered Palermo (May 15) and the Austrians had entered Florence to support the restored Grand Duke Leopold (May 25).

c. THE UNIFICATION OF ITALY, 1849–1870

The abysmal failure of the revolutionary movements of 1848–1849 revealed the military weakness of the Italian states (hence the need of foreign aid for the extrusion of Austria); demonstrated the unsuitability of the pope as a leader of the unity movement; undermined the prestige of the Mazzinians and republicanism in general; pointed to the steadfastness of Piedmont, only state to retain its liberal constitution. Piedmont was henceforth recognized as the hope of liberal Italy. In the parliamentary life of Piedmont there rapidly came to the fore a new man,

1851–1861. Count Camillo Benso di Cavour, a liberal who had drawn his ideas from French and especially English sources; believer in the *juste milieu,* profound admirer of British parliamentarism, convinced of the importance of reforms (commercial, industrial, agricultural, political) if Piedmont were to take its place as the leader of the movement for Italian independence. Scientific farming on western lines he introduced on his father's estates, and then made it the subject of wider propaganda through the medium of the **Agrarian Society**

(founded 1842). He was active in the promotion of banking, railroads; welcomed the repeal of the Corn Laws in England. He entered actively into the necessarily veiled political activity of the fortics; founded the first **Whist Club** at Turin, innocuous façade for political discussions. When Charles Albert reformed the censorship (1847), Cavour promptly founded, with Cesare Balbo, *Il Risorgimento,* a newspaper urging the independence of Italy, a league of Italian princes, and moderate reforms. Cavour assumed a leading rôle in the demand for a constitution during January 1848. The king yielded (Feb. 8); published the new constitution (Mar. 4) providing for a system modeled principally after that of Great Britain, with a senate, whose life-members were to be appointed by the king; a chamber of deputies, with members elected on the basis of a limited suffrage (leaving electoral influence in the hands of the nobility and middle class); a ministry responsible to parliament. Parliament met for the first time, May 8, 1848. Despite vigorous opposition of democratic elements, suspicious of Cavour as an aristocrat, he played an increasingly important rôle in the period following the disasters of 1848–1849.

1850, Mar. On the advice of Cavour, **Giuseppe Siccardi** was made keeper of the seals by Premier Massimo d'Azeglio. Siccardi brought in a bill (of which Cavour was the author) seriously curbing the powers of the Catholic Church—abolishing ecclesiastical courts, and all their special jurisdictions; eliminating the right of asylum; limiting the number of holidays; restricting the right of religious bodies to acquire real property. Elsewhere these questions had been settled by concordat with the pope; in Piedmont they were settled by unilateral action (Oct. 10).

1850–1851. Cavour entered d'Azeglio's government as minister of agriculture and commerce, the portfolio of the navy being shortly added, and later that of finance.

1852, Nov. 4. After a short period out of

office, **Cavour became premier,** a post he was to hold uninterruptedly for seven years. Cavour by now had deserted the Right and governed with the aid of a coalition of the Liberals of the Right Center and Left Center (the *connubio*). His government reorganized finances; negotiated commercial treaties and revised tariffs (first approach to free trade); fostered legislation on co-operative societies, agrarian credit, banks; accelerated railroad construction; reorganized the army.

1855, Jan. 26. Cavour managed to insinuate his country into the **Crimean War** on the side of France and Britain. The Piedmontese troops took part in the victory of the **Chernaia** (Aug. 16) and thereby regained morale and prestige. Though Piedmont received no reward as a result of its participation (unwillingness of Britain to estrange Austria), Cavour was given an opportunity at the **congress of Paris** *(p. 728)* to expound the grievances of Italy. His moderation made a most favorable impression on the British and French.

1856. Foundation of the National Society by Giuseppe Farina, Daniele Manin, and Giorgio Pallavicino. The organization, aiming at the unification of Italy under the king of Piedmont, enjoyed the secret encouragement of Cavour, and at the same time was backed by many Mazzinian republicans, like Garibaldi.

1858, Jan. 14. The attempt of **Felice Orsini** to assassinate Napoleon III and the empress. From prison Orsini appealed to Napoleon to help free Italy. The effect of the episode was to prick Napoleon (himself originally an Italian conspirator) into action.

July 20. SECRET MEETING OF NAPOLEON III AND CAVOUR AT PLOMBIÈRES. Agreement: Napoleon to join Piedmont in war on Austria provided it could be provoked in a manner to justify it in the eyes of French and European opinion; after expulsion of the Austrians, Italy to be organized as a federation of four states, under presidency

The UNIFICATION of ITALY

▨	Kingdom of Sardinia (Piedmont)
▨	Area added 1860
▨	" " 1866
▨	" " 1870

of the pope—(*a*) an **upper Italian kingdom** of Piedmont, Lombardy, Venetia, Parma, Modena, and the Papal Legations; (*b*) a **kingdom of Central Italy,** Tuscany with Umbria and the Marches; (*c*) **Rome** and the surrounding territory, to which the temporal power of the pope was to be restricted; (*d*) the **kingdom of Naples;** France was to be compensated by Savoy and Nice; Princess Clotilde, 15-year-old daughter of Victor Emmanuel, was to marry Prince Joseph Charles Bonaparte, cousin of the emperor.

Dec. 10. The **formal treaty signed** by France and Piedmont, after Napoleon had assured himself of the good-will of Russia (mission of Prince Jerome to Warsaw, September).

1859, Jan. 1. Napoleon's warning remarks to the Austrian ambassador let the secret out. Strong protests of Napoleon's ministers and of some sections of French opinion. Desperate efforts (Jan.–Apr.) of the British to prevent a clash. These proved abortive, since there was no will to peace on the French and Italian side.

Mar. 9. Piedmontese reserves called to the

colors including volunteers, chiefly fugitives eluding conscription in Lombardy (a direct provocation to Austria).

Apr. 7. Austria mobilized.

Apr. 23. Austrian ultimatum to Piedmont, directing her to demobilize in three days. This was a blunder, since it supplied Cavour with the provocation he needed. The ultimatum was rejected.

Apr. 29. The **Austrians,** under General Franz Gyulai, **invaded Piedmont,** but Gyulai delayed action so long that the French had ample opportunity to arrive on the scene.

May. Peaceful revolutions in Tuscany, Modena, and Parma, engineered by the National Society. The rulers fled the country.

May 30. Piedmontese victory at Palestro. The allies crossed the Ticino into Lombardy.

June 4. BATTLE OF MAGENTA, a disorganized fight ending in the retirement of the Austrians.

June 13–15. Insurrection in the Papal Legations (Ravenna, Ferrara, Bologna).

June 24. BATTLE OF SOLFERINO and San Martino, sanguinary but indecisive. The Austrians began to withdraw to the Quadrilateral.

Napoleon III had been depressed by the sight of bloodshed on the fields of Magenta and Solferino; was alarmed by the risings in Tuscany and the Papal States with the threat of rapid spread of the unification movement; was faced by the possibility of a Prussian attack on the Rhine and the reality of a prolonged siege of the Quadrilateral fortresses, into which the Austrian army had retired. Without preliminary understanding with Victor Emmanuel, Napoleon proposed an armistice to Emperor Francis Joseph, concluded July 8, followed by the

July 11. Meeting of the two emperors at **Villafranca,** with agreement that Lombardy (except Mantua and Peschiera) should be ceded to France and might then be ceded by France to Piedmont; Venetia was to remain Austrian; Italian princes should be restored to their thrones subject to amnesty of their revolting subjects. These terms were accepted as preliminaries of peace by Victor Emmanuel who reserved his liberty, however, respecting the risings in central Italy. **Cavour resigned** in a rage. The final **treaty of Zürich** (Nov. 10) embodied substantially the provisions of the preliminaries of Villafranca.

Aug.–Sept. In Parma, Modena, Tuscany, and Romagna, representative assemblies decreed the downfall of their late rulers and union with constitutional Piedmont. The Piedmontese government dared not accept without the consent of Napoleon.

1860, Jan. 20. Cavour returned to power as premier, negotiated the annexations with Napoleon, whose price was the cession of Nice and Savoy.

Mar. 13–15. Plebiscites in Parma, Modena, Romagna, and Tuscany resulted in vote for annexation to Piedmont.

Mar. 24. Treaty of Turin, by which Piedmont ceded Savoy and Nice to France, after plebiscite.

Apr. 4. Abortive rising in Sicily against the Bourbons.

May 5. Garibaldi and his Thousand Redshirts sailed from Genoa for Sicily. They had been preparing an expedition to Nice, Gari-

Landing of Garibaldi and his force at Marsala, May 11, 1860

baldi's natal city, which he meant to hold against the French. He was diverted to Sicily by Cavour, who secretly supported this filibustering expedition.

May 11. Garibaldi and his force landed at **Marsala,** in western Sicily. He marched inland, gathering recruits as he went.

May 15. He defeated the Neapolitans at **Calatafimi** and marched on Palermo.

May 27. Garibaldi took Palermo and set up a provisional government.

July 20. He defeated the Neapolitans at **Milazzo,** whereupon they evacuated Sicily, except Messina.

Aug. 22. Garibaldi crossed the straits, with the connivance of the British government (Lord Palmerston).

Sept. 7. He took **Naples** after a triumphal march, during which the Neapolitan army faded before him. **Francis II** (succeeded Ferdinand II in May 1859) fled to Gaeta. He had made desperate attempts to ward off the danger by forming a Liberal ministry (June 28) and re-establishing the constitution of 1848 (July 2), but was faced by defection on all sides.

Garibaldi's plan was to defeat the remnants of the Neapolitan army, march on Rome, and then proceed to the conquest of Venetia. Despite Garibaldi's loyalty to Victor Emmanuel, Cavour became alarmed, fearing French intervention on behalf of the pope and possible action by the Austrians. He therefore decided to take a hand and march Piedmontese troops to the scene, a course favored by the British to thwart supposed French schemes for a Muratist restoration in Naples.

Sept. 8. An **uprising in the Papal States** gave Cavour an excuse to intervene. He called upon **Cardinal Antonelli,** papal secretary of state, to disband his "adventurers" (the *Zouaves,* an international force of ardent Catholics). The demand was rejected.

Sept. 10. The Piedmontese crossed the papal frontier.

Sept. 18. They virtually annihilated the papal forces at **Castelfidaro** and advanced into Neapolitan territory, joining forces with Garibaldi.

Oct. 21-22. Naples and Sicily voted by plebiscite for union with the north. Similar votes were taken in the **Marches** (Nov. 4) and in **Umbria** (Nov. 5).

Oct. 26. Garibaldi defeated the Neapolitans on the **Volturno.**

Nov. 3-1861, Feb. 13. Siege of Gaeta. The operations were much hampered by the French fleet, which made attack by sea impossible until it was withdrawn (Jan. 19).

1861, Mar. 17. The **KINGDOM OF ITALY** proclaimed by the first Italian parliament, with Victor Emmanuel as first king and a government based on the Piedmontese constitution of 1848.

June 6. Cavour died at the age of 51.

1861-1862. Ministry of Baron Bettino Ricasoli, ardent Tuscan patriot, who embarked upon a vast national **agitation for the annexation of Rome,** still garrisoned by French troops. Garibaldi left his place of retirement, the island of Caprera, and organized the

1862, Mar. 9. Society for the Emancipation of Italy. He organized an abortive conspiracy against Austria, then made a triumphant visit to the scenes of his victories in Sicily. Defying the government, he raised the cry *Rome or Death,* crossed to the mainland (Aug. 24) and advanced north.

Aug. 29. Battle of Aspromonte, a skirmish in which Garibaldi and his volunteers were

defeated by government troops. Garibaldi wounded and captured. He and his men were amnestied soon after (Oct. 5).

1864, Sept. 15. The **September convention,** by which Napoleon finally agreed to evacuate Rome within two years (beginning February 5, 1865), in return for an Italian promise to move the capital from Turin to Florence. Napoleon regarded this as the renunciation of Rome. The agreement raised a storm of protest in Piedmont and was denounced by Garibaldi, but was approved by the parliament.

1866, May 12. Alliance of Italy and Prussia, encouraged by Napoleon *(p. 690).*

June 20. Italy declared war on Austria.

June 24. Italians defeated at **second battle of Custozza,** by Archduke Albert.

July 3. VENETIA CEDED TO ITALY after its cession to France by Austria.

July 20. Resounding **defeat of the Italian fleet** by the Austrians under Admiral Wilhelm von Tegetthoff, near **Lissa.**

Oct. 12. Treaty of Vienna, ending the war.

Dec. Last **French troops withdrawn from Rome.** Garibaldi again placed himself at the head of volunteers and began the invasion of the papal territory, despite disavowals of the government. He was twice captured, but escaped (1867, Sept.).

1867, Oct. 27. A plan for an insurrection in Rome failed, but Garibaldi defeated a papal force.

Oct. 28. A French force landed at Cività Vecchia and marched to Rome.

Nov. 3. BATTLE OF MENTANA. Garibaldi defeated by papal troops supported by French, who mowed down the enemy with the new breech-loading *chassepots.* Garibaldi was captured and sent to Caprera. Napoleon tried at first to summon an international congress to discuss the Roman question, but accomplished nothing. The Roman question continued to be an open sore in Franco-Italian relations, and did much to prevent the formation of an alliance *(p. 655).*

1870, Aug. 19. Final withdrawal of French

Victor Emmanuel II, 1820–1878

troops from Rome, in view of the **Franco-German War** *(p. 694)*.

Sept. 20. After a short bombardment the **Italians**, capitalizing the defeat of France at Sedan, **entered Rome** after making a breach at the Porta Pia.

Oct. 2. After a plebiscite, **Rome was annexed** to Italy and became the capital.

d. THE KINGDOM OF ITALY, 1870–1914

1871, May 13. The **LAW OF GUARANTIES**, defining the relations between the government and the Papacy: the person of the pope was to be inviolable; he was granted royal honors and prerogatives and full liberty in the exercise of his religious functions (free intercourse with Catholics throughout the world, liberty to hold conclaves, control of papal seminaries, etc.); representatives of foreign powers at the Vatican were conceded diplomatic rights and immunities; the pope was to have an annual income of 3,250,000 lire from the Italian treasury (the equivalent of his previous income from his territories); he was left in full enjoyment of the Vatican and other palaces, with rights of extraterritoriality. This law was not accepted by the pope, who henceforth posed as *the prisoner of the Vatican.* Relations between the Papacy and the Italian government were not regularized until the **Lateran treaty** of 1929 *(p. 933).*

1873–1876, Ministry of Marco Minghetti following that of Giovanni Lanza. The outstanding statesman was **Quintino Sella**, minister of finance, whose great aim was to balance the budget and organize the economic life of the new kingdom. He exercised "economy to the bone" (cutting down the civil list, salaries of ministers, etc.) and imposed taxes on cereals, incomes, land, etc. The government **reorganized the army** (350,000 men in peacetime) and re-created the navy (Italy the third sea-power by 1885). **Railroads** were pushed to the south (mileage 1758 kilometers in 1860; 7438 in 1876) and the **merchant marine** developed (10,000 tons in 1862; 1,000,000 in 1877, next to Britain and France).

1876, Mar. 18. **FALL OF THE MINGHETTI CABINET** and of the party of the Right (the party of enlightened conservatism following the teaching of Cavour, which had ruled the country since 1849).

Mar. 28. **First ministry of the Left**, under **Agostino Depretis.** Depretis was an early disciple of Mazzini, but had been converted to monarchism. Cold, cynical, disillusioned, he relied for maintenance of his power upon adroit parliamentary tactics, upon corruption and upon political alliances (*trasformismo*). By generous use of government pressure the Right was overwhelmingly defeated in the elections and returned to parliament a mere rump. Depretis remained premier, with two short interruptions, until his death in 1887. The unpopular taxes, against which the Left had protested, were restored and free rein was given to agitation against Austria (*irredentism*), aiming to acquire the **Trentino** and **Trieste** (*Italia Irredenta*), Italian-speaking districts still under Austrian rule. Italian stock in international affairs reached a low point.

1878, Jan. 9. **Death of King Victor Emmanuel.**
1878–1900. **UMBERTO I,** king.

1878, Feb. 7. **Death of Pius IX.**
1878–1903. **LEO XIII** (Cardinal Pecci), pope. Various attempts were made to reach an agreement on the Roman question (notably in 1886) but they all foundered on the pope's demand for at least some part of Rome.

1881. **Extension of the franchise,** by reduction of the age limit from 25 to 21 and lowering the tax-paying requirement from 40 to 19 lire. The result was an increase of the electorate from about 600,000 to about 2,000,000.

1882, May 20. **Triple Alliance** of Italy, Austria, and Germany *(p. 734).*

1885. An act of parliament farmed out the **state railways** to three private companies for 60 years, with possible termination at the end of 20 or 40 years.

Another act introduced **employers' liability for accidents,** but was so poorly administered as to be ineffective, like the act (1877) making elementary education compulsory for children from six to nine years.

1885. **Italian occupation of Assab and Massowa** on the Red Sea, after the French (1881) had frustrated Italian hopes for Tunis *(pp. 733, 816).*

1887, July 29. **Death of Depretis.**
1887–1891. **First ministry of Francesco Crispi,** minister of interior under Depretis, former republican and member of Garibaldi's "Thousand," a proud, self-centered, vigorous individual. After abortive negotiations with the Papacy he turned to a violently **anti-clerical policy:** abolition of ecclesiastical tithes and of compulsory religious instruction in elementary schools. The erection of the **statue of Giordano Bruno** confronting the Vatican (1889) brought relations to such a pitch of tension that the pope seriously considered leaving Rome.

In **foreign policy** Crispi took his stand unwaveringly by the alliance with Austria and Germany *(p. 735).* He suppressed radical and irredentist organizations. Relations with France became so strained that they almost resulted in a rupture.

1887–1889. **The Ethiopian venture.** Crispi was a convinced imperialist and was determined to expand the Italian footing on the Red Sea. This led to war with Ethiopia and to a serious setback at **Dogali** (Jan. 25, 1887). Nevertheless the Italians were able to strengthen their position by backing **Menelek,** king of Shoa, against the Ethiopian king of kings, Johannes.

1889, May 2. The **treaty of Uccialli** by which, according to the Italian version, Menelek accepted an Italian **protectorate over Ethiopia.** Menelek became king of kings (Nov.) on the death of Johannes.

1891, Jan. 31. **Fall of Crispi,** after a gratuitous outburst against the Right.

1891–1892. **Ministry of Marquis Antonio di Rudini,** member of the Right, who governed with a coalition cabinet and support from the Left. He attempted to balance the budget, notably by reducing the expenditures for army and navy.

1892–1893. **First ministry of Giovanni Giolitti.** In the midst of a banking crisis, Giolitti made the managing director of the *Banca Romana,* Signor Tanlongo, a senator. The senate refused to confirm the appointment; an interpellation resulted in the arrest of Tanlongo and other prominent persons. A parliamentary investigation revealed that he had issued large sums

in duplicate bank notes, that two preceding cabinets had been aware of his irregularities, that loans had been made by him to deputies, etc. Giolitti was overthrown and left the country for a time.

1893, Dec. 10–1896, Mar. 5. **Second Crispi ministry.** The cabinet was faced with serious peasant troubles in Sicily (*fasci*), which were ruthlessly put down by the military. In similar manner Crispi dealt with anarchist outrages. Laws of July 11 and October 22, 1894, suppressed anarchist and socialist organizations.

The desperate financial situation was attacked by **Baron Sidney Sonnino,** the minister of finance. The Bank of Italy had been established by a law of August 10, 1893, to liquidate the insolvent Banca Romana. The law forbade state banks to make loans on real estate, limited their powers of discount, and reduced the paper money maximum. Other measures sought to increase economy and produce larger income. By 1896 Sonnino had practically balanced the budget despite the added expenses of the war in Africa.

1895–1896. **THE ETHIOPIAN WAR.** Menelek had, in 1891, rejected the Italian interpretation of the **treaty of Uccialli** and all efforts at compromise had failed. By 1895, after Menelek had secured the necessary munitions, he was ready to take up the Italian challenge.

1895, Dec. 7. The Italians, having advanced into northern Ethiopia, were badly defeated at **Amba Alagi** by Ras Makonen, who then besieged the key fortress of **Makallé,** which fell January 20, 1896. Crispi now felt that Italian honor and his own position were at stake. He insisted that **General Oreste Baratieri** make an advance and secure a victory. The general, against his better judgment, obeyed orders.

1896, Mar. 1. **BATTLE OF ADUA** (Adowa). The Italians (25,000) were completely defeated by some 100,000 Ethiopians under Menelek. Those who were not killed were for the most part captured and held for ransom. One of the worst colonial disasters in modern history. The Italians were obliged to sue for peace and signed the **treaty of Addis Ababa** (Oct. 26), in which they recognized the independence of Ethiopia and restricted themselves to the colony of Eritrea.

Mar. 5. **Downfall of Crispi,** resulting from a storm of public indignation and unrest.

1896–1898. **Second Rudini ministry,** based on an understanding with **Felice Cavalotti,** the radical leader. There followed a period of acute unrest.

1896, Sept. 30. **Agreement between France and Italy** with respect to Tunis. The Italians gave up many of their claims. First step in the policy of assuaging French hostility.

1898, May 3–8. **THE "FATTI DI MAGGIO."** Serious bread riots in various parts of the country culminated in open conflict with the troops in Milan. Martial law was proclaimed, but order was restored only after considerable loss of life. Heavy sentences by courts-martial, especially against socialists, ensued. Rudini was obliged to resign.

1898, June 28–1900, June 18. **Ministry of General Luigi Pelloux.** He presented to parliament a drastic **Public Safety Law,** which was violently opposed by all radical groups. An attempt was made to change the chamber's standing orders, but this was again opposed. Pelloux appealed to the country (1900), but the elections only strengthened the radical elements. Having already granted an amnesty (Dec. 30, 1899), Pelloux was forced to resign.

1898, Nov. 21. A commercial treaty signed with France, bringing to an end the tariff war that had been raging since 1886, much to the detriment of Italy.

1900, July 29. King Umberto assassinated by an anarchist at Monza.

1900–1946. VICTOR EMMANUEL III, king. He was regarded as more liberal than his father and the government's policy gradually turned more and more to the Left for support.

1900, Dec. 14. Franco-Italian agreement exchanging a free hand in Morocco (for France) for a free hand in Tripoli (for Italy). An important stage in the Franco-Italian rapprochement *(p. 740)*.

1901. Development of a large-scale **strike epidemic,** reflecting the growth of socialism, the organization of labor, and the more active spread of radicalism.

1902, Jan.–Feb. Strike of the employees of the Mediterranean Railway, demanding, among other things, recognition of their union. In February there was real danger of a general strike, following a strike of gas employees in Turin. The government met the situation by calling up all railway workers who were reservists. By mediation a settlement was finally reached in June.

1903, Oct.–1905, Mar. 4. Giolitti prime minister. Strikes and disorders continued unabated.

1904, Sept. General strike proclaimed. Much violence in Milan and other large cities.

Oct. In the **general elections** the socialists and radicals lost considerably, evidently a popular protest against the excesses of the labor organizations, but probably influenced also by the attitude of the pope (Piux X since 1903), who gave permission to Catholics to take part in political struggles involving the safety of the social order.

1906, May 30–1909, Dec. 2. Ministry of Giolitti, following the short-lived cabinets of Fortis and Sonnino.

1908. Giolitti continued his policy of **concession to the Church** by sponsoring a measure of facilitate religious education, such education to be optional with the communal councils, which were, however, obliged to supply such education if parents desired it.

Dec. 28. An **earthquake** of appalling severity shook southern Calabria and eastern Sicily, completely destroyed **Reggio** and **Messina** and many villages, with loss of life estimated at 150,000. At Messina a "tidal wave" added to the destruction.

1909, Dec. 2. Giolitti's government was overturned and was followed by the **cabinets of Sonnino** (1909, Dec.–1910, Mar.) and **Luzzatti** (1910, Mar.–1911, Mar.).

1911, Mar. 29–1914, Mar. 10. Giolitti prime minister again.

1911, Sept. 29–1912, Oct. 15. The **TRIPOLITAN WAR,** with Turkey. By various agreements (with Germany and Austria, 1887; with Britain, 1890; with France, 1900; with Russia, 1909) Italy had secured approval for eventual action to acquire Tripoli. The second Moroccan crisis *(p. 745)* and the prospects of a French protectorate in Morocco induced the Italian government to act before it was too late. Its decision may have been influenced by the pressure exerted by the **revived nationalist movement** (writings of **Gabriele d'Annunzio, Enrico Corradini,** *et al.*) after 1908. The pretext used was Turkish obstruction of Italian peaceful penetration. An ultimatum was sent (Sept. 28), but was rejected by the Turks.

1911, Oct. 5. The **Italians landed a force at Tripoli** and occupied the town. The other coastal towns were taken in rapid succession.

Nov. 5. The Italian government proclaimed the **annexation of Tripoli,** though the country was far from being conquered (valiant opposition of a small Turkish force under **Enver Bey,** supported by the Arabs).

1912, Jan.–Feb. Naval operations in the Red Sea and on the Syrian coast. The Italians bombarded several coastal cities, but the general operations were much hampered by Austrian refusal to permit war on the Balkan or Aegean coasts (forbidden by the Triple Alliance and other agreements). All efforts at mediation by the powers were frustrated by the refusal of the Turks to abandon Tripoli.

Apr. 16–19. Italian naval demonstration at the Dardanelles. The Turks closed the Straits (till May 4) causing much loss to Russian commerce.

May 4–16. The **Italians occupied Rhodes** and the other Dodecanese Islands. Peace negotiations were finally opened in July, but neither side was ready to yield an iota of its claims and only the threatening Balkan War finally induced the Turks to give in. The preliminary **treaty of Ouchy** (definitive **treaty of Lausanne,** October 18) ended the war: the Turks abandoned sovereignty of Tripoli, but the Italians were to recognize a representative of the sultan as caliph (i.e. Turkish religious authority); the Italians were to restore the Dodecanese Islands as soon as the Turks evacuated Tripoli.

June 29. Extension of the franchise, increasing the number of voters from about three to about eight and a half million. This amounted to practically universal suffrage. The same bill provided for salaries for members of parliament.

1913, Oct. The **general election** gave the Liberals a majority, but showed a marked increase of various socialist groups (78 seats together in place of the previous 41) and the Catholics (35 instead of 14).

1914, Mar. 9. General strike proclaimed at Rome, largely the outcome of popular resistance to taxation made necessary by the war.

Mar. 10. Cabinet of Antonio Salandra, following the resignation of Giolitti. The revolutionary railway union demanded an increase in wages, but the question was finally compromised.

June 7. On the national holiday of the *Statuto,* **riots broke out in Ancona,** where an anti-militarist demonstration had been prohibited. A general strike followed in the town and spread to other parts of the Marches, Romagna, etc. The leader was **Enrico Malatesta. Benito Mussolini** *(p. 929),* then editor of the socialist newspaper *Avanti,* took a prominent part. Mobs held a number of towns for a week until nationalists and troops restored order.

Aug. 3. Italy proclaimed neutrality in the World War. *(Cont. pp. 884 ff., 929.)*

Giuseppe Verdi (1813–1901) was the greatest composer of Italian opera. He adapted Shakespearean plots (*Macbeth,* 1847; *Otello,* 1887; *Falstaff,* 1893) as well as episodes from his country's history and heritage (*Rigoletto* 1851; *Il Trovatore,* 1853; *La Traviata,* 1853; *Simon Boccanegra,* 1857; *La Forza del Destino,* 1862; *Aïda,* 1871). The operas of **Giacomo Puccini** (1858–1924) have remained popular (*La Bohème,* 1896; *Madama Butterfly; La Tosca,* 1900).

The poet **Giosuè Carducci** (1835–1907) was an outstanding exponent of neo-classicism.

7. *The Papacy*

[For a complete list of the Roman popes, see Appendix IV.]

(From p. 478)

In the period of the restoration the Papacy recaptured much of the ground lost during the chaos of the revolutionary era. Throughout Europe there was a revival of Catholicism, and even in Protestant states sympathy had grown for the Catholic Church as the mainstay of the throne and the most effective force for holding the revolutionary spirit in check. The governing classes regarded as axiomatic this "union of throne and altar" against the disruptive tendencies of liberalism and nationalism. The Papacy was also assisted by the Romantic movement, with its idealization of the past, and by the influential writings of men like **René de Chateaubriand, Félicité de Lamennais,** and **Joseph de Maistre** (*Du Pape,* 1819), which glorified the Catholic Church and the authority of the pope.

1814, May 24. Ultramontanism reigned in Rome upon the return of the gentle and cour-

Pius IX, 1846–1878

The Vatican Council, 1869–1870

ageous **Pius VII.** The **Jesuit Order** and the **Inquisition** were re-established in Rome (Aug. 7), and the **Index** was reconstituted.

1815. Through the efforts of his able secretary of state, **Cardinal Consalvi,** the pope obtained from the congress of Vienna the **restitution of the States of the Church.** The temporal administration was reorganized, a bureaucracy established on the French model. Considerable opposition developed against this highly centralized administration, which excluded laymen from all high offices. Discontent against the "rule of the priests" centered in the **Carbonari,** a Liberal secret society *(p. 668).*

1821, Sept. 13. After the **rising in Naples** *(p. 668),* Consalvi had their leaders prosecuted, and the pope condemned their principles.

The chief activity of the Papacy in the reign of Pius VII was concerned with efforts to recover its international influence in Europe. Toward the accomplishment of this program, Consalvi negotiated a series of valuable **concordats** with all the Roman Catholic powers save Austria.

1823–1829. **LEO XII** (Annibale della Genga) continued the policy of Pius VII and secured further advantageous concordats, extending the policy to the South American republics. His extreme **reactionary policy** in domestic affairs strengthened the underlying current of liberalism. He persecuted the Jews, harshly supervised morals, condemned the Protestant Bible societies and all dissenters (1824, 1826), and made vigorous efforts to root out the Carbonari. On the constructive side, Leo promoted missions, encouraged scholars, improved the educational system in Rome, reduced taxes, made justice less costly, and found money for public improvements. Of noble character, Leo lacked insight into, and sympathy with, the temporal developments of his period.

1829–1830. **PIUS VIII** (Francesco Castiglione) —a short, reactionary reign noteworthy for the **Catholic Emancipation Act in England** *(p. 631).*

1831–1846. **GREGORY XVI** (Bartolomeo Al-

berto Cappellari). Apogee of the reaction. The new pope was greeted by revolts which had broken out under his predecessor and which were promptly suppressed *(p. 669).*

1832, Aug. 15. The encyclical *Mirari vos* condemned complete and unrestrained liberty of conscience, liberty of the press, and revolt for any reason against an established government. Though Gregory did much to promote **public welfare** (establishment of a decimal coinage and a bureau of statistics, and of a steamship service at Ostia; foundation of public baths, hospitals, and orphanages; lightening of various imposts), he would not concede the demand for separation of the ecclesiastical and the civil administration. The secretary of state, **Cardinal Lambruschini,** suppressed all aspirations for political liberty with extreme severity. The last three years were again occupied with rebellions in the Papal States. The embarrassing financial condition in which Gregory left his dominions was due to his lavish expenditure on architectural and engineering works, and to his liberal patronage of learning.

1846–1878. **PIUS IX** (Giovanni Mastai-Ferretti), wildly greeted in Italy as the "pope of progress" *(p. 669).*

1848, Apr. 29. Placing the universal significance of the Papacy above national aspirations, Pius proclaimed his neutrality in the national war against Austria. For this he was denounced as a traitor, and forced to flee (for details on Pius IX and the Revolution of 1848, see *(p. 669).*

1850, Apr. 12. **Pius returned to Rome,** embittered, and henceforth stubbornly hostile to liberalism in all its forms. The constitution of 1848 was not restored, though half-hearted efforts were made to modernize the state through the grant of self-government, with participation of laymen. In the reactionary policy which prevailed, **Cardinal Antonelli,** secretary of state, with medieval views and

Machiavellian temperament, exerted a paramount influence. In the achievement of Italian unity (1859–1860) the Papal States were lost, to be followed by the taking of Rome in 1870 *(p. 674).* Pius and his successors persistently refused the offer of the Italian government to accord the pope the rights and honors of a sovereign, and an annual endowment *(p. 674).* Faced by the loss of his temporal sovereignty, Pius sought compensation by strengthening the machinery of the Church and the spiritual influence of the Papacy. The political reaction following the stormy years 1848–1849 offered promising soil for the pope's efforts to conclude advantageous concordats, and in several countries, notably Spain (1851) and Austria (1855), he was able to regulate church-state relations to the advantage of the curia. Pius also re-established Roman Catholic hierarchies in England (1850) and Holland (1853). Seeking popularity, the pope, unaided by an ecumenical council, promulgated a new dogma, the first since the council of Trent.

1854, Dec. 8. **Dogma of the Immaculate Conception** of the Virgin, which made a belief long widely held in the Church an article of faith. The "infallibility" of the pope implied in this act was openly acknowledged in 1870 by the Vatican council.

1864, Dec. 8. When the temporal power of the Papacy was tottering to its fall, Pius flung down the gauntlet of defiance to the new social and political order in the encyclical *Quanta cura,* with the appended *Syllabus errorum.* The pope censured the "errors" of pantheism, naturalism, nationalism, indifferentism, socialism, communism, freemasonry, and various other 19th-century views. He claimed for the Church the control of all culture and science, and of the whole educational system; denounced the enjoyment of liberty of conscience and worship, and the idea of tolerance; claimed the complete independence of the Church from state control; upheld the necessity of a continuance of the temporal power of the Roman See, and declared that "It is an error to believe that the Roman Pontiff can and ought to reconcile himself to, and agree with, progress, liberalism, and contemporary civilization." The Ultramontane party was loud in its praise of the *Syllabus,* but the Liberals were amazed, and treated it as a declaration of war by the Church on modern civilization. It was also a blow aimed at the **Liberal Catholics,** who were reconciled to religious liberty and democratic government.

1869, Dec. 8–1870, Oct. 20. THE VATICAN COUNCIL. The zenith of Pius' pontificate was attained when the Vatican council (the first general council since that of Trent, three centuries earlier) proclaimed (1870, July 18) the **dogma of papal infallibility**—the dogma that the pope, when speaking *ex cathedra,* possesses infallibility in decisions regarding faith or morals, in virtue of his supreme apostolic power. The new dogma was attended by important results. It marked the final triumph of the Papacy over the episcopal and conciliar tendencies of the Church. It attempted to exalt the Papacy above all secular states and to extend "faith and morals" to the political domain.

1870, July 30. Austria immediately annulled the **concordat of 1855.** In Prussia the *Kulturkampf* broke out *(p. 695),* and in France the council so accentuated the power of ultramontanism that the state took steps to curb it. At his death in 1878, Pius left the Church shaken to its foundations and in feud with almost every secular government.

1878–1903. LEO XIII (Gioacchino Pecci), a gifted diplomat, marked a change. Leo possessed a more liberal and tolerant spirit than his predecessor. He narrowed the intellectual gulf between the Church and modern society: by encouraging a renewed study of St. Thomas Aquinas in all Catholic seminaries (the result of which was to spread the doctrine that between true science and true religion there was no conflict); by fostering the study of Church history (on the theory that it would augment the prestige of the Church by showing its contributions to the progress of civilization); by supporting experimental science among eminent Catholics.

1885. Leo was appointed arbitrator in a dispute between **Germany and Spain** over the possession of the Caroline Islands. He also acted as arbitrator in a number of other cases. As his reign wore on, Leo perceived that democracy might prove fully as useful as monarchy for preserving and strengthening Catholic principles. He therefore encouraged Catholic political parties, with distinctly liberal tendencies, in Germany and Belgium, and adopted a friendly attitude toward the government of the French Republic. Instructions were given to French Catholics to break with monarchical principles, and to support the republic.

1890. However, the policy of the *Ralliement* in France *(p. 659)* was also motivated by the pope's desire to secure French aid for the **solution of the Roman question,** the mainspring of his whole policy. Relations with the Italian government had grown steadily worse, and in an encyclical addressed to the Italian clergy (1898, Aug. 5) Leo insisted on the duty of Italian Catholics to abstain from political

life while the pope remained in his "intolerable position."

1891, May 15. The encyclical on labor questions, *Rerum novarum,* aimed to apply Christian principles to the relations between capital and labor, and won for Leo the title of "the workingman's pope." It pointed out that the possessing classes, including the employers, have important moral duties to fulfill; that it is one of the first duties of society (state and church collaborating) to improve the position of the workers.

Of the political principles of Pius IX, Leo altered little. He expressed in his encyclicals the same condemnation of many phases of liberalism and nationalism, and reiterated the view that the Church should superintend and direct every form of secular life. But, unlike his predecessor, Leo never appeared as a violent partisan of any particular form of government. It was his object to bring about harmonious collaboration between church and state. In the *Kulturkampf* he adopted a moderate and conciliatory attitude, and succeeded in obtaining the repeal of the legislation against the Church.

1903–1914. PIUS X (Giuseppe Sarto), known as the "pope of the poor and the humble," applied himself with determination to the task of fortifying the inner life of the Church. He carried out (1908) an extensive reorganization of the curia in order to modernize its machinery. Another important reform, the codification of canon law (1904), was undertaken (com-

pleted under Benedict XV, promulgated June 28, 1917).

Encouraged by the liberal tendencies in Leo's reign, a group of Catholics known as **Modernists** (notably **Father George Tyrrell** in England, the **Abbé Loisy** in France, and **Antonio Fogazzaro** in Italy) had begun to agitate for a revision of the dogmas and policies of the Church to bring them in line with the findings of scientific scholarship and the modern spirit. Pius had only bitter scorn for the Modernists.

1907, Sept. 8. The encyclical *Pascendi gregis* expounded and condemned the Modernist system, and set up a new and effective censorship to combat it.

Pius was not greatly interested in political affairs. Relations with the Italian government improved, and the pope qualified the absolute prohibition imposed by his predecessors of the participation of Catholics in political elections *(p. 675).* But the pope experienced great bitterness in his relations with France, which adopted legislation for the separation of church and state *(p. 661).*

1914, Aug. 2. Pius' last circular was an appeal for peace addressed to the Catholics of the world on the eve of the World War.

1914–1922. BENEDICT XV (Giacomo della Chiesa), whose reign was taken up by efforts to maintain an even balance between the warring nations, many of them essentially Catholic. The pope twice (1915, July 30; 1917, Aug. 1) appealed to the belligerents to make

Coronation of Leo XIII, 1878–1903

peace, but these appeals earned him nothing but a reputation for pro-Germanism.

With the victory of the Allies and Italy, the pope began to give up opposition to the Italian government. He definitely revoked (1919) the decree forbidding Catholics to participate in politics, and authorized (1920) Catholic sovereigns to visit the king in Rome. Negotiations were opened which led ultimately to the Lateran treaty of 1929 *(p. 933)*.

(Cont. p. 929.)

8. *Switzerland*

(From p. 481)

1815, Mar. 20, 29. Two acts of the **congress of Vienna** regulated the Swiss problem. They laid down the principle of the **perpetual neutrality** of Switzerland, restored the old frontiers, with two exceptions, and smoothed over the internal difficulties of the country. A constitutional convention drew up a new **federal pact** which restored the old institutions, and gave wide autonomy to the 22 cantons. The diet had very restricted powers, being little more than a congress of ambassadors representing the cantons. Racial and religious differences, and differences in political ideals, still existed among the cantons, which made for division and disunion.

1815-1828. The early part of the restoration period was characterized by a serious economic crisis, due to the war. Swiss industry, no longer protected by the Continental blockade, found itself unable to compete with English industry, especially in the textile trade. The cantons were unable to agree upon a common customs policy. In the political sphere most of the cantons followed reactionary policies. Under the pressure of the Holy Alliance, Switzerland was obliged to persecute the liberal refugees from neighboring countries, and in 1823 was compelled to restrict the freedom of the press.

1828-1848. The so-called **"Era of Regeneration,"** in which revision of the constitutions of several cantons was undertaken.

1828-1829. The cantonal governments were wise enough to grant the concessions demanded, such as universal suffrage, freedom of the press, and equality before the law. The movement was strengthened by the July Revolution in Paris. Between 1830 and 1833 some ten cantons liberalized their constitutions.

1832, Mar. 17. The Siebener Concordat. The liberal cantons joined together to guarantee their new liberal constitutions.

July 17. The question of revising the federal pact in the direction of a stronger central government was brought before the diet by a large majority of the cantons, whereupon the conservative cantons concluded an alliance **(league of Sarnen)** to maintain the pact of 1815.

1834, Jan. 20. The struggle for the revision of the constitution was transformed into a **religious quarrel** when the liberal cantons adopted the *Articles of Baden,* which contained a program of ecclesiastical reform. The Liberal party stood for freedom of worship, secular education, a lay state, and was especially irritated by the paramount position in the Catholic cantons of the **Jesuits,** who had returned after 1814. By increasing the power of the central government, the Liberals hoped to be able to impose their views upon the whole confederation. Religious and political passions gradually rose to fever pitch.

1845, Dec. 11. THE *SONDERBUND*. The seven Catholic cantons—Lucerne, Uri, Schwyz, Unterwalden, Zug, Freiburg, and Valais—replied to the organized armed bands of the Liberal cantons by concluding a league (the *Sonderbund*) for the purpose of protecting their interests.

1847, July 20. The Liberals were able to get a vote through the diet ordering the **dissolution of the *Sonderbund*** as being contrary to the constitution. The seven cantons refused, and war resulted.

Nov. 10-29. The federal general **Guillaume Dufour** quickly defeated the forces of the *Sonderbund.* Lord Palmerston's policy of masterly inactivity and Dufour's rapid victory averted an intervention being planned by Metternich and Guizot. The *Sonderbund* was dissolved, the Jesuits were expelled, and the victors proceeded to strengthen the federal government.

1848, Sept. 12. The **NEW CONSTITUTION,** replacing the **pact of 1815.** It organized Switzerland as a federal union closely modeled on that of the United States. While preserving the historic local government of the cantons, it established a strong central government. Legislative authority resided in two chambers: The **council of state** (*Ständerat*) consisting of two members from each canton; the **national council** (*Nationalrat*), members of which were elected by universal suffrage in numbers proportional to the population of each canton. The executive was a **federal council** (*Bundesrat*) of seven members, elected by the two chambers. Its annual chairman was given the title *President of the Confederation,* but he enjoyed no wider powers than his colleagues.

1848-1857. The Neuchâtel problem. The canton of Neuchâtel (part of the confederation, but under the sovereignty of the king of Prussia) had proclaimed a republic (Mar. 1848), the constitution of which was guaranteed by the federal diet. In 1856 a conservative revolution aimed at the restoration of the king. War with Prussia was narrowly averted by the mediation of Napoleon III. In May 1857 the king renounced his rights, in return for a money payment, which he later renounced. He kept his title, but this was discontinued by William I.

Swiss internal history in the ensuing period was dominated by economic problems and by a general trend toward **government centralization.** The public services (telegraph and postal systems, customs, currency, weights and measures) had been brought under federal control, and were reorganized.

1874, Apr. 19. A **revision of the constitution** further enlarged the powers of the federal government, especially in military affairs. Free elementary schools under federal supervision were authorized and the principle of referendum was introduced for national legislation. Thereafter, by means of the initiative and referendum, federal authority was extended to many fields.

Oct. The **International Postal Congress** met at Berne. Switzerland became a favorite meeting-place for international conventions and headquarters for many international organizations.

1882, May 20. Opening of the St. Gothard Railway; first of the great railroad tunnels through the Alps.

1887, May. The federal government was given a **monopoly of sale of spirits.**

1889. Acute tension in relations with Germany, resulting from the expulsion of a police officer on the trail of political offenders. Switzerland had long been a haven for political refugees and for radicals and conspirators of all hues. The asylum extended to them caused constant friction with neighboring powers.

1890, June. The federal government was empowered to enact measures of **social insurance.**

1898, Feb. The federal government was authorized to **purchase privately owned railways.**

Nov. The federal government was empowered to unify and enforce the **civil and penal codes.**

1907, Apr. 12. A **new army bill** reorganized the forces. Although Swiss neutrality was guaranteed by the powers in 1815, growing international tension necessitated precautions. A unique military system was built up (1847, revised 1907): the army was a type of standing militia, with short periods of required training biennially.

Switzerland made steady progress in the economic sphere, but despite growing prosperity and the expansion of federal power, democracy remained. In six of the smallest cantons the people continued to exercise their local powers through mass meetings (*Landesgemeinden*) without the intervention of any assembly. In the larger cantons representative systems were used, but they were based on universal suffrage and in most of them the initiative and referendum were employed. *(Cont. p. 933.)*

German-Swiss literature in the 19th century: novels of **Jeremias Gotthelf** (1797-1854); stories and verses of **Gottfried Keller** (1819-1890) and **Conrad Ferdinand Meyer** (1825-1898); historical writings of **Jakob Burckhardt** (1818-1897); poetry of **Carl Spitteler** (1845-1924).

Artists: Arnold Boecklin (1827-1901) and **Ferdinand Hodler** (1853-1918).

(CONTINUED IN VOLUME TWO)